The fun, fast, and easy way to get productive online

Internet Yellow Pages

2007 EDITION

Mikal E. Belicove

Joe Kraynak

INTERNET YELLOW PAGES, 2007 EDITION

International Standard Book Number: 0-7897-3629-2

Library of Congress Cataloging-in-Publication Number: 2006934771

Printed in the United States of America

First Printing: October 2006

09 08 07 06 4 3 2 1

WARNING AND DISCLAIMER

Every effort has been made to make this book as complete and as accurate as possible, but no warranty or fitness is implied. The information provided is on an "as is" basis. The author and the publisher shall have neither liability nor responsibility to any person or entity with respect to any loss or damages arising from the information contained in this book.

TRADEMARKS

All terms mentioned in this book that are known to be trademarks or service marks have been appropriately capitalized. Que Publishing cannot attest to the accuracy of this information. Use of a term in this book should not be regarded as affecting the validity of any trademark or service mark.

BULK SALES

Que Publishing offers excellent discounts on this book when ordered in quantity for bulk purchases or special sales. For more information, please contact

U.S. Corporate and Government Sales

1-800-382-3419

corpsales@pearsontechgroup.com

For sales outside of the U.S., please contact

International Sales

international@pearsoned.com

Publisher
Paul Boger

Associate Publisher
Greg Wiegand

Acquisitions Editor
Stephanie J. McComb

Development Editor
Mark Cierzniak

Managing Editor
Patrick Kanouse

Senior Project Editor
San Dee Phillips

Indexer
Ken Johnson

Publishing Coordinator
Cindy Teeters

Interior Designer
Anne Jones

Cover Designer
Anne Jones

Page Layout
Tolman Creek Design

TABLE OF CONTENTS

ACCOUNTING 1
ACTIVISM 2
ADDICTIONS/RECOVERY 4
Alcoholism 4
Drugs 5
Gambling 6
Sex Addiction 6
Stop Smoking 6
Substance Abuse and Recovery 7
ADOPTION 10
ADVENTURE TRAVEL/ECOTOURISM .13
ADVICE 15
AGRICULTURE 18
AIRLINES 22
ALLERGIES 24
ALTERNATIVE MEDICINE 26
Acupuncture 27
Aromatherapy 28
Cleansing/Detox 29
Herbs 30
Homeopathy 31
Magnet Therapy 32
Massage 32
ALZHEIMER'S 34
AMUSEMENT & THEME PARKS 36
ANATOMY 39
ANIMATION 40
ANIME 41
ANTIQUES 42
ARCHITECTURE 44
ART (SEE ALSO MUSEUMS—ART) ...46
Instruction Reference 46
Graphic Design 47
ASTROLOGY 48
ASTRONOMY 49
AUCTIONS 53
AUTO RACING 55
Champ Cars 55
Formula One 56
IRL 56
NASCAR 57
AUTOMOBILE CLUBS AND ORGANIZATIONS 58
AUTOMOBILES 60
Buying Online 60
Classic Cars 62
Information 62
Manufacturers 62
Repair 66
AVIATION 68
BABIES 71
BACKGROUND CHECKS 74
BALLOONING 75
BARGAINS 77
Coupons 78
Freebies 80
BASEBALL 81
College 82
Fantasy (See Fantasy Sports) 83
Professional 83
BASKETBALL 85
College 86
Professional 87
BEER 89
BICYCLES 92
Maintenance & Repair 94
Mountain Biking 95
BILLIARDS 97
BINGO 99
BIOGRAPHY 101
BIRDS 102
BLOGS & BLOGGING 105
Directories & Search Engines 105
Blog Hosting & Tools 106
BOATS & SAILING 108
BOOKS 111
Audio Books 112
Book Reviews 112
Bookstores 114
Books Online 116
Publishers 117
BOWLING 119

BOXING **121**
BUSINESS **123**
Franchising 126
Home-Based Business 128
International Business 130
Patent Information 132
Small Business-Products & Services 134
Small Business–Webstorefront Support 136
CAMPING **137**
Backpacking 139
Hiking 139
CAMPS (SUMMER) **142**
CANADA **143**
CANCER **145**
CANDY **148**
CANOEING/KAYAKING **150**
CAR RENTAL **151**
CASINOS **152**
CATS **154**
CELIAC DISEASE **156**
CENSORSHIP **157**
CHEERLEADING **158**
CHESS **159**
CHILD ABUSE AND MISSING CHILDREN **160**
CHILDCARE **162**
CHIROPRACTORS **164**
CIGARS **166**
CIVIL RIGHTS **167**
CLASSIFIEDS **169**
COACHING SPORTS **170**
COLLECTING **172**
Beanie Babies 173
Coins 173
Dolls 174
Hot Wheels and Matchbox Cars and Trucks 175
Posters 176
Stamps 177
COLLEGES & UNIVERSITIES **179**
Financial Aid & Scholarships 180
Graduate Schools 182
COMICS **184**
COMPUTERS **188**
Computer Companies: Hardware & Software 189
Macintosh 190
PCs 191
Programming Language 193
Software–Antivirus 196
Software–Downloads 196
Software–Miscellaneous 197
Troubleshooting 198
CONSUMER ISSUES **200**
COOKING & RECIPES **203**
CRAFTS **206**
Cross Stitch (see Needlecrafts) 207
Jewelry (see JEWELRY) 207
Needlecrafts (see Needlecrafts) 207
Origami (see Origami) 209
Sewing (see SEWING) 208
CROCHETING **208**
DANCE **209**
Ballet 210
Ballroom Dancing 211
DARTS **213**
DATING **214**
Personals/Services 214
Tips 215
DEAFNESS **217**
DEATH & DYING **220**
DEBT MANAGEMENT **222**
Bankruptcy 224
Credit Cards 224
Foreclosure 225
DENTISTRY **226**
DIABETES **228**
DIET & NUTRITION **230**
DINOSAURS **233**
DIVORCE & CUSTODY **235**
Child Support 236

DOGS **237**
DOMESTIC VIOLENCE **239**
DREAM INTERPRETATION **240**
E-COMMERCE **241**
EDUCATION **244**
Distance Learning 245
Experiential (see EXPERIENTIAL/ OUTDOOR EDUCATION) 246
Foreign Languages 247
Homeschooling 247
International Education 249
K–12 250
K–12-Educational Television 253
K–12-Homework Help 255
K–12-Montessori Education 257
K–12-Private Education 258
K–12 -Public Education 259
Preschool 259
Resources 260
ELDERCARE **264**
ELECTRONICS **266**
EMERGENCY SERVICES **269**
EMPLOYMENT (SEE JOBS/ EMPLOYMENT) **271**
ENVIRONMENTAL & GLOBAL ISSUES **271**
Conservation 271
Ecology 274
Preservation 275
Recycling 276
ETIQUETTE **278**
EXERCISE & FITNESS **279**
Cross-Country Running 280
Fitness 280
Pilates 282
Running 282
Walking 284
Weightlifting & Body Building 284
EXPERIENTIAL/OUTDOOR EDUCATION **286**
Associations 286
Outdoor Education 288
Ropes/Challenge Courses 290
EXTREME SPORTS **292**
Hang Gliding & Paragliding 293
Skateboarding 294
Skydiving 294
Snowboarding 295
EYECARE **297**
FANTASY SPORTS **299**
FASHION **300**
FENG SHUI **302**
FINANCE & INVESTMENT **303**
Banking 304
Bonds 305
Investment Clubs 306
Investment Information 306
IPOs (Initial Public Offerings) 309
Mutual Funds 310
Online Trading 311
Stocks 313
FISH/AQUARIUMS **314**
FISHING **315**
FOOD & DRINK **317**
Alcohol 318
Coffees & Teas 319
Gluten-Free (See Celiac Disease) 320
GROCERIES **321**
Organic Foods 322
Wines (see WINES) 323
FOOD ALLERGIES **324**
FOOTBALL **325**
College 325
Fantasy (see FANTASY SPORTS) 325
Professional 326
FOREIGN POLICY **328**
FRUGAL SPENDING **330**
FUN SITES **331**

GAMBLING **333**
Online 333
Tips 333
GAMES & PUZZLES **334**
Board Games 338
Card Games (nonpoker) 339
Cheat Codes 339
Kakuro 340
Mah Jongg 340
Multi-User Games 341
Poker (see POKER) 341
Sudoku 341
Trivia 342
GARDENING **343**
Flowers 345
GAYS/LESBIAN/BISEXUAL/ TRANSGENDER **346**
Colleges & Universities 346
Crisis Intervention & Counseling 347
Home & Family 347
Media & Culture 348
Political & Legal Issues 349
Publications 349
Religion 350
Travel 350
GENEALOGY **351**
GEOGRAPHY **353**
GIFTS **355**
GOLF **358**
GOVERNMENT INFORMATION/ SERVICES **360**
GRAPHIC NOVELS **362**
HEALTH **363**
AIDS/HIV Treatment & Prevention 365
CPR 367
Children 367
Disabilities 369
Disease & Conditions 370
Healthcare Administration & Management 371
Health Insurance 372
Institutes 373
Medical History 374
Travel Resources 374
HISTORY **375**
Africa 376
Americas 377
Ancient 377
Arctic & Antarctica 378
Asia 378
Australia & Oceania 380
Canada 381
Current Affairs 382
Documents & Landmarks 382
Europe 384
Mexico 385
Middle East 386
Russia 387
United States 388
World 389
HOBBIES **391**
Radio Operation 391
RC Cars 392
RC Planes 392
Models 393
Model Trains 394
HOCKEY **395**
HOLIDAYS & CELEBRATIONS **397**
HOME **399**
Construction 399
Decks & Patios 401
Decorating/Painting 401
Electrical 404
Flooring 405
Heating & Air Conditioning 406
Home Automation 406
Home Design 407
Home Improvements & Repair 408
Inspection 410
Interior Design 410
Plumbing 411
HORROR **412**
Dark Fantasy 413
Ghosts 413
Occult 414
Vampires 414

HORSES **415**
HUMOR **418**
Cartoons 420
Jokes 421
HUNTING **423**
HYPNOSIS **426**
INSECTS **427**
INSURANCE **429**
Automobile 431
Companies 431
Homeowners/Renters 432
INTERNET **433**
Antispam 434
Chats & Social Groups 435
Connecting 436
Connection Speed 437
Email 438
Instant Messaging & Internet Phone 439
Online Telephone Directories 441
Opt-In Email 441
Privacy 442
Search Engines 444
Security/Virus Hoaxes 446
Web Page Development 447
Web Page Software & Resources 450
INVENTIONS AND INVENTORS **452**
JAILS **455**
JANITORIAL **457**
Services 457
Supplies 458
JETSKI **459**
JEWELRY **461**
Appraisal 462
Designer & Designers 462
Repair 463
JOBS/EMPLOYMENT **464**
Company Information 465
Employee Incentives 466
Humor Resource Assistant 466
Job-Hunting Tips 467
Job Search 468
Job-Sharing Tips 471
JOURNALISM **473**
JUNK **475**
KIDS **477**
Kids' Internet Games 487
Safe Surfing 489
Sites by Kids 491
KNITTING **492**
LANDSCAPE **495**
Lawn Care 495
Planning 496
Shrubs 496
Trees 497
LANGUAGES/LINGUISTICS **498**
Chinese 499
English 500
Farsi 501
French 501
General Language and Linguistics 501
German 502
Greek 502
Italian 503
Japanese 503
Learning Languages 504
Russian 505
Sign Language 505
Spanish 506
LAW **507**
Cyber Law & Cyberspace Issues 509
Law Schools 509
Legal Organizations 511
Legal Publications 512
LITERATURE **514**
MAGIC **517**
MAPS **519**
MANGA (SEE GRAPHIC NOVELS) **519**
MARKETING **521**
MARRIAGE **524**
MARTIAL ARTS **525**
Capoeira 526
Judo 526
Jujitsu 527
Kung Fu 527
Shotokan 527

Tae Kwon Do .527
Tai Chi .528
MATHEMATICS .529
Algebra .530
Calculus .531
Chaos .531
Fractals .532
Geometry .532
Mathematicians .532
Numeric Analysis .533
Statistics .533
Trigonometry .533
MEDIATION .534
MEDICINE .535
Drug Information .536
First-Aid Information .536
Medical Resources .537
Nursing (see NURSING) .539
Pain Management .539
MEMORY .541
MEN & MEN'S ISSUES .542
MEN'S HEALTH .544
MENTAL HEALTH DISORDERS .545
Agoraphobia .546
Anorexia Nervosa (see Mental Health Disorders–Eating Disorders) .546
Anxiety & Panic Disorders .546
Attention Deficit Hyperactivity Disorder .547
Autism & Asperger's Sundrome .548
Bipolar Disorder (see Mental Health Disorders–Deprsssion) .550
Conduct Disorder .549
Cyclothymic Disorder (see Mental Disorder–Depression) .550
Delirium .550
Dementia .550
Depression .550
Eating Disorders .551
Obsessive-Compulsive Disorder .553
Oppositional Defiant Disorder (see Mental Health Disorder–Bipolar Disorder .550
Panic Disorder (see Mental Health Disorders–Anxiety & Panic Disorders .553
Paranoia .553
Personality Disorder .553
Post-Traumatic Stress Disorder .554
Psychosis .555
Schizophrenia .555
Tourette's Sundrome .556
MEXICO .557
MOTIVATIONAL & SELF-IMPROVEMENT INFORMATION .558
MOTORCYCLES/CHOPPERS .560
MOVIES/FILMS .562
Festivals .562
Independent Films .563
Reviews .564
Studios .564
Theaters .565
MUSEUMS .567
Architecture .567
Art .568
History & Culture .571
Natural History .572
Photography & Film .573
Organizations .574
Science & Technology .574
MUSIC .576
Buying CDs .576
Buying MP3s .577
Information, News, & Reviews .580
Lyrics .582
MP3 Sharing/Search Engines .583
Music Events .584
Music Genres–Alternative .585
Music Genres–Bluegrass .586
Music Genres–Christian Music .588
Music Genres–Classical .588
Music Genres–Country .590
Music Genres–Ethnic .591
Music Genres–Jazz .594
Music Genres–Opera .595
Music Genres–Pop Music .597
Music Genres–MP3 PLayers, Rippers, and Burners .597
Music: Instruments .599
Organizations and Clubs .601
Radio Sites .603

MYSTERY 607
MYTHOLOGY 609
NATURE 611
NEEDLECRAFTS 614
NETWORKING 616
NEW AGE 622
NEWS 624
Resources 627
Services 629
U.S. News Media 631
Webzines 633
NONPROFIT & CHARITABLE ORGANIZATIONS–RESOURCES 635
Associations 637
Charitable Contributions 637
Fundraising 639
Organizations 639
Volunteering 641
NURSING 643
NUTRITION (SEE DIET & NUTRITION) 646
OCEANS 647
OFFICE MANAGEMENT 650
Office Supply Stores 651
Resources & Tips 653
ORIGAMI 655
OSTEOPOROSIS 656
PAINTING 657
PARENTING 659
Adolescents 661
Babies and Toddlers (see Babies) 663
K–6 664
Single Parenting 666
Special Needs 668
Stay-at-Home Parents 670
Stepparenting 671
PARKS 673
PEDIATRICS 677
PETS 680
Cats (see CATS) 681
Dogs (see DOGS) 681
Fish (see Fish/Aquariums) 681
Exotic 681
Pet Care 681
Pet Supplies 684
PHILOSOPHY 686
PHOTOGRAPHY 688
Cameras 688
Digital Photography 690
Online Sharing 691
Resources 692
PODCASTS 695
POETRY 698
POKER 701
POLITICS 703
Political Campaigns 705
Political Parties 708
PREGNANCY & BIRTH 710
Birth & Babies 712
Contraception & Abortion Clinic Directory 713
Infertility 714
Midwifery 715
Miscarriage 716
PRESIDENTS & RULERS 718
PSYCHIATRY(SEE ALSO MENTAL HEALTH DISORDERS) 720
PSYCHOLOGY 722
PUBLICATIONS 724
Journals & Ezines 724
Magazines 725
QUILTING 733
QUOTATIONS 736
RAILROADS 739
REAL ESTATE 742
Buying/Selling 742
Financing/Mortgages 745
Flipping 749
Fraud 750
Relocation Services 750
Timeshares 752
REFERENCE 754
Dictionaries and Thesauri 754
Encyclopedias 755

Libraries 757
Phone Books 760
Research Help 761
REIKI 765
RELATIONSHIPS 766
RELIGION 767
Ancient 768
Atheism 768
Buddhism 769
Christianity 770
Cults 774
Hinduism 774
Islam 775
Judaism 776
Prayer 778
RETIREMENT 780
ROCK CLIMBING 783
RODEO 786
ROMANCE 788
SCI-FI & FANTASY 789
SCRAPBOOKING 795
SELF-HELP (SEE MOTIVATIONAL & SELF-IMPROVEMENT) 797
SENIORS 797
SEWING 802
Machines 803
Patterns 805
SEXUALITY 807
SHOPPING 810
Clothing 811
Comparison Bots 812
Discount Stores 814
Jewelry (see Jewelry) 814
Perfume 814
Search Engines 815
Specialty 816
SKATING 817
Figure Skating 817
Inline Skating 818
Roller Skating 819
Speed Skating 819
SKIN CARE/COSMETICS 821
SNOW SKIING 824
SNOWMOBILING 827
SOCCER 829
SOCIAL WORK/SERVICES 832
SOFTBALL 835
SUICIDE PREVENTION 837
TABLE TENNIS 839
TATTOOS/BODY ART 841
TAXES 843
TEACHING 846
TEENS 851
TELEVISION 854
TENNIS 857
THEATER & MUSICAL 860
TOYS 864
TRACK & FIELD 868
TRAVEL & VACATION 871
Adventure (see ADVENTURE TRAVEL/ECOTOURISM) 871
Air Travel 871
Airlines (see AIRLINES) 872
Budget Travel 872
Car Rental (see CAR RENTAL) 874
Car Travel 874
Cruises 875
Information/Travel Tips 876
International Travel 880
Island Travel 883
Lodging 884
Train Travel 886
U.S. Travel 887
Weekend Getaways 891
UFOS 893
U.S. GOVERNMENT INFORMATION/SERVICES 895
VEGETARIAN (SEE COOKING & RECIPE–VEGETARIAN) 900
VETERAN & MILITARY ORGANIZATIONS 900

VETERINARY MEDICINE 904
VIDEO & MULTIMEDIA 906
DVD 906
Multimedia Search Engines 907
Video 907
VITAMINS & SUPPLEMENTS 909
VOLLEYBALL 911
WAR 913
American Civil War 914
Cold War 915
Korean War 916
Vietnam War 916
War on Terrorism 917
World War I 918
World War II 919
WATCHES 920
WATER SPORTS 921
Rafting 921
Rowing 922
Scuba Diving 924
Snorkeling 926
Surfing 927
Swimming 928
Water-Skiing 930
WEATHER & METEOROLOGY 932
WEBCASTING 935
WEDDING PLANNING 937
WEIGHT LOSS 940
WINE 943
WOMEN/WOMEN'S ISSUES 948
WOMEN'S HEALTH 956
WOODWORKING 957
WRESTLING 958
WRITING 960
YOGA 963
YOUTH ORGANIZATIONS 966
ZOOS 968

About the Authors

Mikal Belicove is a seasoned blogger and information-age visionary who's hotwired to the Internet and the Internet community. Mikal maintains his own blog at Belicove.com, where he encourages the exploration and exchange of ideas in the online community. His enthusiasm over electronic publishing and information sharing and his drive to steer others to the highest-quality web resources boost this version of Que's *Internet Yellow Pages* to the next level. Mikal currently freelances as a business blogging strategist, brand positioning and marketing consultant, and publicist. His work involves consulting with his clients on the most effective ways to establish authentic "thought-leader" status through their blogs and websites.

Joe Kraynak has taught hundreds of thousands of novice computer users how to master their computers and their software. His long list of computer books includes *Easy Internet, The Complete Idiot's Guide to Computer Basics, Using and Upgrading PCs,* and *Absolute Beginner's Guide to Excel.* Joe's wide range of computer and training experience has helped him develop a strong commitment to making computers, software, and the Internet more easily accessible to users of all levels of experience.

WE WANT TO HEAR FROM YOU!

As the reader of this book, *you* are our most important critic and commentator. We value your opinion and want to know what we're doing right, what we could do better, what areas you'd like to see us publish in, and any other words of wisdom you're willing to pass our way.

As an associate publisher for Que Publishing, I welcome your comments. You can email or write me directly to let me know what you did or didn't like about this book—as well as what we can do to make our books better.

Please note that I cannot help you with technical problems related to the topic of this book. We do have a User Services group, however, where I will forward specific technical questions related to the book.

When you write, please be sure to include this book's title and author as well as your name, email address, and phone number. I will carefully review your comments and share them with the authors and editors who worked on the book.

Email: feedback@quepublishing.com

Mail: Greg Wiegand
Associate Publisher
Que Publishing
800 East 96th Street
Indianapolis, IN 46240 USA

For more information about this book or another Que title, visit our website at www.quepublishing.com. Type the ISBN (excluding hyphens) or the title of a book in the Search field to find the page you're looking for.

THE SECRETS OF SUCCESSFUL SEARCHING

by Michael Miller

The most common activity for web users isn't online shopping or auctions, and it isn't downloading MP3 files, and it isn't even playing online games or viewing dirty pictures. No, the most common web-based activity is *searching*. That's because the Web is big and disorganized, so you have to actively search for just about anything you want to find. The reality is that most users spend at least part of every Internet session searching for some type of information—and hating every minute of it!

There are a number of perfectly valid reasons people hate searching the Web. First, searching isn't easy—or, at least, it's not always intuitive. Second, it isn't immediately gratifying because you seldom find what you're looking for (on the first try, anyway). And third, it isn't fun—unless you're one of those odd birds who thinks thumbing back and forth through the cross-references in an encyclopedia is a blast.

Those objections aside, you're still forced to search the Web for the information you want. Fortunately, the more you know about *how* and *where* to search, the more likely it is you'll find what you're looking for, fast.

THE NEEDLE-IN-THE-HAYSTACK PROBLEM

Here's something you need to know: Web searching is more an art than a science. You need to develop a *feel* for how and where to search; following a set of hard-and-fast rules won't always deliver the best results. That's because every search site not only operates differently, but also contains a different set of data; entering the same identical query at different sites more often than not produces wildly different results.

So, even though the act of searching is deceptively easy (just enter a query in a Search box and click a button), finding useful information is hard. Of course, it doesn't help that the Internet is big—really, *really* big—more than 80 billion documents and growing! With these numbers, your odds of finding a single page of information on the Web are in the neighborhood of 80 billion to 1.

The size problem is compounded by the fact that information online is not stored or organized in any logical fashion. You have to realize that the Internet itself is not run or managed by any central organization; the Web is nothing more than a collection of millions of individual computers, all connected by a bunch of wires and wireless signals crisscrossing the globe. Nobody is in charge; therefore, everybody has to manage his or her own computers and servers with no rules or regulations for guidance.

In addition, no standards or guidelines require laying out web pages so that certain types of information always display the same way, using the same words, positioned in the same place. There is no guarantee that the topic described in a web page's title is even mentioned in the text of the page. There is no assurance that a page that was on the Web yesterday will still be there tomorrow.

In short, the Web is a mess.

THE ART OF SEARCHING

Not surprisingly, over the years several attempts have been made to organize this mess we call the Internet. This book, Que's *Internet Yellow Pages*, is one such attempt. However, as helpful as this book is, all attempts to organize the Internet ultimately fall short, simply because the Internet is *so* big and *so* disorganized and growing *so* fast. Even the best attempts (and I view this book as one of the best) can document only a small part of the Internet; literally billions of other web pages go undocumented.

So, when you're looking for something on the Internet, you should first go to a good printed directory, such as this book. If you can't find what you're looking for there—or if you're looking for even more current information—where do you turn?

You are now faced with the prospect of *searching the Internet*. But if there are no rules for *storing* information on the Internet, what procedures can you follow when you're *searching* for information?

To get good results—results that zero in precisely on the information you want, without throwing in pages and pages of irrelevant data—you need to know the right way to search. And the right way to search is all about asking the right questions.

Imagine you're a detective questioning a suspect, and you have only a limited number of questions you can ask. Do you waste a question by asking, "Where were you on the night of the crime?" The suspect can answer that question many different ways, most of them vague: "California." "Home." "Out." "Someplace better than here."

A better question is one that is more precise, and allows less latitude in the way it is answered. "Were you at 1234 Berrywood Lane on the night of the crime?" This question has only two acceptable answers: "Yes" or "No." Either of these answers will give you the information you're looking for, with no chance for evasion or misinterpretation.

Searching the Web is like playing detective. Ask the right questions, and you get useful answers. Ask vague questions, and you get useless answers.

Effective searching requires a combination of innate ability, productive habits, and specific skills. It also helps to have a kind of "sixth sense" about where to look for information, and a lot of patience to make it through those long stretches when you can't seem to find anything useful, no matter how hard you try.

In other words, successful searching is a blend of art and science, of intuition and expertise—something some are born with and others have to learn.

THE DIFFERENCE BETWEEN SEARCH ENGINES AND DIRECTORIES–AND WHY YOU SHOULD CARE

Hundreds of websites enable you to search the Internet for various types of information. The best of these sites are among the most popular sites on the Web, period—even though each of these sites approaches the search problem in its own unique fashion.

Directories: Manually Cataloging Web Pages

One approach to organizing the Web is to physically look at each web page and stick each one into a handpicked category. After you collect enough web pages, you have something called a *directory*. Directories can be appealing because they enable you to browse for a website by category, often finding what you didn't know you were really looking for. Most directories also provide a Search box for searching for specific sites in the directory.

A directory doesn't search the Web; in fact, a directory catalogs only a small part of the Web. However, a directory is organized and easy to use, and lots and lots of people use web directories every day.

Many directories are specialized—designed to be used by people sharing a common interest or having a special need. For example, Education Planet (www.educationplanet.com) catalogs information and websites specifically for teachers.

Search Engines: Scouring the Web, Automatically

It's important to note that a directory is *not* a search engine. A *search engine* is not powered by human hands; instead, a search engine uses a special type of software program (called a *spider* or *crawler*) to roam the Web automatically, feeding what it finds back to a massive bank of computers. These computers hold *indexes* of the Web. In some cases, entire web pages are indexed; in other cases, only the titles and important words on a page are indexed. (Different search engines operate differently, you see.)

In any case, as the spiders and crawlers operate like little robot web surfers, the computers back at home base create a huge index (or database) of what was found. The largest search engine index (Google) contains more than eight billion entries—which still leaves the vast majority of the Web untouched and unavailable to searchers.

When you go to a search engine, you enter a *query* into a Search box on the home page. This query represents, to the best of your descriptive ability, the specific information you're looking for. When you click the Search button, your query is sent to the search engine's index—*not* out to the Internet itself. (You never actually search the Web itself; you search only the index that was created by the spiders crawling the Web.) The search engine then creates a list of pages *in its index* that match, to one degree or another, the query you entered.

And that's how you get results from a search engine.

Directories or Search Engines: Which Is Better?

So, which is better, a directory or a search engine? What is better for you depends on what you want:

- If you want the *most* results, use a search engine. (A search engine's automatic index is *much* bigger than a manually constructed directory.)
- If you want the *best handpicked* results, use a directory. (People generally make better decisions than machines.)
- If you want the most *current* results, use a search engine. (Search engine bots crawl the Web daily; it takes time for human beings to manually enter and delete directory entries.)
- If you want the *best-organized* results, use a directory. (Human editors are best at sorting the results into the proper categories.)

It's tempting to say that search engines deliver quantity, and directories deliver quality, but that isn't always the case. Some of the best and most powerful search engines—such as Google—can deliver quality results matching or besting those from the top directories. And, to complicate matters even further, many search engine sites include web directories as part of their services—and the major directories often include search engine add-ons. It's all very confusing.

WHERE TO SEARCH

There are, by several counts, more than 200 separate search engines and directories on the Internet. With that many options available, you almost need a search engine to search for a search engine!

If you go by usage trends, however, you end up with a couple of big search sites and then a long list of "other" sites. The Big Two are a search engine and a directory: Google and Yahoo! The "other" category includes all the other sites.

Google

The most popular search engine today is Google (www.google.com). Google offers a huge search index (more than eight billion entries), highly relevant search results, extremely fast searches, and a variety of specialty searches.

The basic Google search page is extremely simple; you get a Search box and a Google Search button. You also get an I'm Feeling Lucky button, which will take you directly to the first listing on the Google results page. (I don't recommend feeling lucky; it's better to view a variety of result listings, just to get a feel for what else is available.)

In addition to its main web search, Google also offers the following specialty searches, all available from links near the top of the main page:

- **Images**—This option lets you search for pictures and graphics. Because a normal text-based search typically ignores pictures in its results, you can use this search when you're looking for specific types of images.
- **Groups**—This option enables you to search the Internet's Usenet newsgroup archives. You can search the entire archive, or narrow your search by date or newsgroup.
- **News**—This page gathers the top news stories from more than 4,500 news sources on the Web and presents you with a front page, headline "newspaper." Here, you can keep yourself informed about U.S. and world news, sports, business, entertainment, and health.
- **Froogle**—A search engine specifically for online shopping. Froogle lets you search thousands of online stores for the lowest prices on items you want to buy.
- **Local**—To find local businesses, services, or organizations, click Local and enter the search term along with a city and state or ZIP code. Google displays a list of businesses or services that match your search term and are located in the specified geographical area.

You can perform either simple or advanced searches from Google's main page, using the wildcards, modifiers, and Boolean operators discussed later in this introductory material. Even easier, you can click the Advanced Search link and use the form-based features on Google's Advanced Search page. Here, you can fine-tune your search by language, date, file format, domain, or keyword. (If your search turns up pages from foreign-language sources, Google often provides a link for translating the page!)

Google also offers filtered searches via its SafeSearch feature. SafeSearch is a great way for kids to search the Web; when it's activated, inappropriate content is filtered from Google's normal search results. (You activate SafeSearch from the Advanced Search page or by clicking the Preferences link on Google's home page.) And, Google has its own search toolbar that you can add to your browser! Click the More link on Google's opening page to access links to the toolbar and learn more about other features and tools.

Google features some advanced search operators that can really optimize the results it returns:

- **cache:** shows the version of the web page that Google has in its cache. For example, **cache:www.foxnews.com** shows the snapshot of the Fox News web page that Google took when it indexed the site. (Note that there is no space between cache: and the site's address.)
- **link:** shows all sites that link to the specified site. Type **link:** immediately followed by the site's address—no spaces.
- **related:** shows all pages that have similar data to the specified page. You can find related pages two ways. The first way is to type **related:** followed by the address of the website or page; for example, **related: www.google.com/help.html**. Another way is to perform a search as you normally do, and then in the list of search results, click Similar Pages next to the description of the page for which you want to view related pages.
- **info:** displays any information that Google has about the specified web page.

- **define:** displays a definition for the specified word.
- **stocks:** displays the current price of a stock for the specified ticker symbol.
- **site:** limits the search to a specific domain. For example, if you search for **caribbean cruise site:www.carnival.com**, Google searches only the www.carnival.com sites for "caribbean cruise."
- **allintitle:** shows only those pages that have in their title all the search words you entered. For example, **allintitle: stand up comedy** looks only for pages that have the words *stand, up*, and *comedy* in their titles. Without this, Google searches for pages that have the specified words anywhere in their title or text.
- **intitle:** shows only those pages that have the word directly following intitle: in their title. For example, **intitle:holistic medicine** finds only pages that have *holistic* in their title and *medicine* in their title or anywhere else on the page. Note that no space can be between intitle: and the key word.
- **allinurl:** shows only those pages that have in their URL (page address) all the search words you entered. For example, **allinurl: jazz club** looks only for pages that have *jazz* and *club* in their URL.
- **inurl:** shows only those pages that have the word directly following inurl: in their URL. For example, **inurl:coaching soccer** finds only pages that have *coaching* in their URL and *soccer* in their URL, title, or anywhere else on the page. Note that no space can be between inurl: and the keyword.

For additional details on how to properly enter these operators and limitations to them, go to www.google.com/help/operators.html.

Yahoo!

Over the years, Yahoo! (www.yahoo.com) has been transformed from a search directory into more of a standard search engine. Search bots are responsible for 99 percent of the pages in the databases. However, Yahoo! also features a searchable directory of hand-picked sites reviewed by its editors. When you first arrive at Yahoo!, it displays the Search the Web box, where you can type your search terms to search all the web pages Yahoo! has indexed. To search only the directory, click the Directory link. Yahoo! also features special searches for images (photos and illustrations) and video, local businesses and services, news, and products. If you would like to browse the Yahoo! directory, as you could in the good old days, scroll down the page and click the More Yahoo! Web Directory link. You can then follow the trail of links to the desired content.

Everybody Else

When it comes to the "other" search sites, the best of the rest tend to be defined by their convenience rather than their results. That's because most of these other sites (such as Yahoo!, actually) are really full-service *portals* that offer search features, rather than dedicated search engines. (Of course, Yahoo! is a portal, too, so being a portal isn't necessarily a negative.)

That doesn't mean that these sites don't give good results; some are almost as good as Google, and most are better than Yahoo!. But most of these sites probably wouldn't get much traffic at all if it weren't for all the other information and services they offer, so searching is definitely an auxiliary function.

Just what are these "other" sites? Here's an alphabetic list of the most popular of these second-level search options:

- **About.com (www.about.com)**—In the recent past, About.com has become less of a general search site and more of a collection of articles and links. The site is organized into thousands of major categories managed by human "guides"; the site has a strong editorial voice and covers more than 50,000 topics.
- **AllTheWeb (www.alltheweb.com)**—AllTheWeb is the official site for the FAST search engine, which rivals Google in terms of size and speed. It also offers separate news, pictures, video, and audio searches.
- **AltaVista (www.altavista.com)**—AltaVista is a powerful, no-frills search engine that indexes a huge number of sites. In addition to normal text searches, AltaVista also offers audio, video, image, and news searches; and it includes a directory listing. You can limit your search to the United States, expand it to a worldwide search, or specify language preferences—all languages or only English and Spanish.
- **AOL Search (search.aol.com)**—AOL Search is a streamlined search tool that sports some "smart" features that give the search process a more human feel. As you type your search term, AOL Search "guesses" ahead and completes the entry for you. The search results page includes a navigation bar on the left that breaks the search results down into categories, including web matches, images, video, audio, news, and local.

- **Ask (www.ask.com)**—Ask got its start as a "natural-language" search engine that enables you to ask questions in plain English. That didn't work too well, so today Ask offers more traditional search index results, as well as picture, product, and news searches.
- **HotBot (www.hotbot.com)**—HotBot used to be a major contender in the search engine wars, but in recent years has been eclipsed by Google's strength and power. It's still a relatively big and relatively fast search engine, and also offers buttons for searching Google and Ask Jeeves.
- **LookSmart (search.looksmart.com)**—LookSmart is a combination directory/search engine, sort of like Yahoo!. You can type a search phrase to search all listings or scroll down the page to browse by category.
- **MSN Search (search.msn.com)**—This is the default search engine for Microsoft's MSN online service and the search feature of the Internet Explorer web browser. Your search options are the Web, News, Images, Desktop (your own Windows desktop), Encarta (encyclopedia), or Near Me (local businesses and services). You can also choose to search in Spanish or English.
- **Open Directory (www.dmoz.org)**—The Open Directory is the largest directory on the Web, with millions of human-edited listings. The Open Directory is unique in that it's a public project. Through the collective efforts of thousands of users, the Open Directory can catalog many more sites than can be cataloged by a small staff of paid workers, such as the staff at Yahoo!. In fact, Open Directory powers the directory services of several search engines and portals, including Netscape Search, AOL Search, Google, Lycos, and HotBot.
- **Gigablast (www.gigablast.com)**—Gigablast is a relative newcomer to the search engine party, offering some interesting options that you might not find elsewhere. Like Google, Gigablast opens with a Spartan screen. From this screen, you can search for web pages, browse the directory by category, search for blogs, or search for travel information or government sites. Most of the search tools, when we visited the site, were still in development.

You'll also find a number of search engines that enable you to search multiple search engines and directories from a single page—which is called a *metasearch.* The top metasearchers include Beaucoup (www.beaucoup.com), CNET's Search.com (www.search.com), Dogpile (www.dogpile.com), Mamma (www.mamma.com), MetaCrawler (www.metacrawler.com), and WebCrawler (www.webcrawler.com).

Other Types of Search

While we're on the topic of professional search sites, you should make note of three other paid search sites. Dialog (www.dialogweb.com), Lexis-Nexis (www.lexisnexis.com/), and ProQuest Direct (www.proquest.com) are all well known and well regarded in the professional research world, and worth your attention if you want results beyond what you can achieve with Google or Yahoo!

If you'd rather not spend any cash, consider searching one of the Internet's many library-related websites. These sites include both the online arms of traditional libraries and the new generation of completely digital web-based libraries, such as Argus Clearinghouse (www.clearinghouse.net), Berkeley Digital Library SunSITE (sunsite.berkeley.edu), Internet Public Library (www.ipl.org), Library of Congress (www.loc.gov), the New York Public Library Digital Library Collections (www.nypl.org/digital/), and Refdesk.com (www.refdesk.com).

For that matter, several online encyclopedias are good sources for a variety of information. These sites include versions of traditional encyclopedias in addition to completely new web-based encyclopedias, such as Encarta Online (encarta.msn.com), Encyclopaedia Britannica Online (www.britannica.com/), Encyclopedia.com (www.encyclopedia.com), and Wikipedia (www.wikipedia.org). Some of these sites require paid subscriptions to access all available content.

If you're looking for people or places, consider using a dedicated online people finder site. These sites feature directories of phone numbers, street addresses, and email addresses, and include AnyWho (www.anywho.com), Bigfoot (www.bigfoot.com), InfoSpace (www.infospace.com), Switchboard (www.switchboard.com), The Ultimates (www.theultimates.com), WhoWhere (www.whowhere.lycos.com), and Yahoo! People Search (people.yahoo.com).

HOW TO SEARCH

Every search site you visit works in a slightly different way, using a slightly different logic (and technological infrastructure) to perform its search operations. To master the intricacies of every single search site would appear to be an insurmountable task.

Fortunately, some common logic is used in almost all the major search sites. This logic is represented by a series of commands, modifiers, and operators that work in similar fashion across most search engines and directories. If you can master these basic skills, you'll be 80 percent of the way there in mastering each individual site.

Just follow these general steps wherever you choose to search:

1. Start by thinking about what you want to find. What words best describe the information or concept you're looking for? What alternative words might some use? Can you exclude any words from your search to better define your query?
2. Determine *where* you should perform your search. Do you need the power of a Google or the better-qualified results of a Yahoo!? Should you use topic-specific sites rather than these general sites?
3. Construct your query. If at all possible, try to use modifiers and Boolean expressions to better qualify your search. Use as many keywords as you need—the more, the better. If appropriate (and available), use the site's advanced search page or mode.
4. Click the Search button to perform the search.
5. Evaluate the matches on the search results page. If the initial results are not to your liking, refine your query and search again—or switch to a more appropriate search site.
6. Select the matching pages that you want to view and begin clicking through to those pages.
7. Save the information that best meets your needs.

The bottom line? Think more *before* you search and spend more time learning from your results afterward.

FIVE TIPS FOR MORE-EFFECTIVE SEARCHING

Savvy searchers approach their task quite seriously. Smart searching involves more than just entering a few keywords in a Search box; thought needs to be given as to how to construct the query, what words to use, and what operators and modifiers can be used to help narrow the search results.

If you want to improve your search results—both in terms of effectiveness and efficiency—learn from these tips, garnered from search professionals across the Internet.

Tip 1: Think Like the Creators

Websites are created by human beings. That isn't necessarily a good thing because human beings are less than logical—and less than perfect.

To look for information created and managed by a human being, you have to *think* like that human being. Did the person writing about Internet Explorer call it *Internet Explorer* or *Microsoft Internet Explorer* or just *Explorer* or *IE* or *IE6* (including the version number), or was it simply called a *browser* or a *web browser* or even (somewhat incorrectly) a *navigator*? You see, any or all of those words and phrases could have been used to refer to the single thing you thought you were looking for. If all you do is look for *one* of these words or phrases, you could skip right over important information that happened to use a slightly different word or phrase.

The best search engines in the world can't anticipate human beings who use alternative words or (heaven forbid!) use the wrong words by mistake, or even misspell the right words. But you must somehow learn to overcome these human shortcomings if you're to find all the information you want to find.

You have to learn how to think like the people who created and organized the information you're looking for. If you're looking for old plastic model kits, you have to realize that some people call them *kits* and some call them *model kits* and some call them *plastic model kits* and some call them *models* and some call them by name (*Aurora model kits*) and some call them *ready-to-assemble kits* and some even have poor spelling skills and call them *modal kits.*

When you construct your queries, think through all the different ways people refer to the topic you're looking for. Think like the people who put the information together, like the people who create the web pages. *Visualize* the results you'd like to find and what they might look like on a web page. Then, and only then, should you construct your query, using the keywords and operators and modifiers you need to return the results you visualized. Master this skill, and you'll almost always find what you want.

Tip 2: Use the Right Words

When you construct your query, you do so by using one or more *keywords.* Keywords are what search engines look for when they process your query. Your keywords are compared to the index or directory of web pages accessible to the search engine; the more keywords found on a web page, the better the match.

Choose keywords that best describe the information you're looking for—using as many keywords as you need. Don't be afraid of using too many keywords; in fact, using too *few* keywords is a common fault of many novice searchers. The more words you use, the better idea the search engine has of what you're looking for. Think of it as describing something to a friend—the more descriptive you are (that is, the more words you use), the better picture your friend has of what you're talking about.

It's exactly the same way when you "talk" to a search engine.

If you're looking for a thing or place, choose keywords that describe that thing or place, in as much detail as possible. For example, if you're looking for a car, one of your first keywords would, of course, be *car*. But you probably know what general type of car you're looking for—let's say it's a sports car—so you might enhance your query to read **sports car**. You might even know that you want to find a foreign sports car, so you change your query to read **foreign sports car**. And if you're looking for a classic model, your query could be expanded to **classic foreign sports car**. As you can see, the better your description (using more keywords), the better the search engine can "understand" what you're searching for.

If you're looking for a concept or idea, choose keywords that best help people understand that concept or idea. This often means using additional keywords that help to impart the meaning of the concept. Suppose you want to search for information about senior citizens, so your initial query would be **senior citizens**. What other words could you use to describe the concept of senior citizens? How about words such as *elderly*, *old*, or *retired*? If these words help describe your concept, add them to your search, like this: **senior citizens elderly old retired**. Trust me—adding keywords such as these will result in more targeted searches and higher-quality results.

One other point to keep in mind: Think about alternative ways to say what it is that you're looking for. (In other words, think about *synonyms*!) If you're looking for a *car*, you also could be looking for a *vehicle* or an *automobile* or an *auto* or *transportation*. It doesn't take a search guru to realize that searching for **car vehicle automobile auto transportation** will generate more targeted results than simply searching for *car*.

Tip 3: When You Don't Know the Right Words, Use Wildcards

What if you're not quite sure of which word form to use? For example, would the best results come from looking for *auto*, *automobile*, or *automotive*? Many search sites let you use *wildcards* to "stand in" for parts of a word that you're not quite sure about. In most instances, the asterisk character (*) is used as a wildcard to match any character or group of characters, from its particular position in the word to the end of that word. So, in our preceding example, entering **auto*** would return all three words—*auto*, *automobile*, and *automotive*.

Wildcards are powerful tools to use in your Internet searches. I like to use them when searching for people and I'm not totally sure of their names. For example, if I'm searching for someone whose name might be Sherry or Sheryl or Sherylyn, I just enter **sher*** and I'll get all three names back in my results. To take it even further, if all I know is that the person's name starts with an *s*, I **s***—and get back Sherry and Susan and Samantha as matches.

Wildcards also can return unpredictable results. Suppose you're looking for Monty Python, but you're not sure whether Monty is spelled *Monty* or *Montey*, so you search for **mon***. Unfortunately, this wildcard matches a large number of *mon* words, including *Monty*—and money, monsters, and Mongolia. In other words, if you go too broad on your wildcards, you'll find a lot more than what you were initially looking for.

Tip 4: Modify Your Words with +, –, and " "

A *modifier* is a symbol that causes a search engine to do something special with the word directly following the symbol. Three modifiers are used almost universally in the search engine community:

- \+ (always include the following keyword). Use the + modifier when a keyword *must* be included for a match. For example, searching for **+monty +python** will return Monty Python pages or pages about pythons owned by guys named Monty—because any matching page must include both the words, but not necessarily in any order.
- – (always *exclude* the following keyword). Use the – modifier when a keyword must *never* be part of a match. For example, searching for **+monty –python** will return pages about guys named Monty but will *not* return pages about Monty Python—because you're *excluding* "python" pages from your results.
- " " (always search for the exact phrase within the quotation marks). Use the " " modifier to search for the precise keywords in the prescribed order. For example, searching for **"monty python"** will return pages only about the British comedy troupe Monty Python—you're searching for both the words, in order, right next to each other.

Of these three modifiers, I find quotation marks to be the most useful. Whenever you're searching for an exact phrase, just put it between quotation marks. You'll get more accurate results than if you listed the words individually.

Tip 5: Use OR, AND, and NOT in a Boolean Search

Modifiers are nice, but they're not always the most *flexible* way to modify your query. The preferred parameters for serious online searching are called *Boolean operators.*

Here are the most common Boolean operators you can use at most search sites:

- **OR** (A match must contain *either* of the words to be *true.*)—Searching for **monty OR python** will return pages about guys named Monty or pythons or Monty Python. With an OR search, you're searching for *either* monty *or* python, so both words don't have to appear on the same page together to make a match. The more words connected by OR operators, the less precise your search, but the more matches you'll receive.
- **AND** (A match must contain *both* words to be *true.*)—Searching for **monty AND python** will return Monty Python pages or pages about pythons owned by guys named Monty, but *not* pages that include only one of the two words. The more words connected by AND operators, the more precise your search, and the fewer matches you'll receive. (Remember, however, that in an AND search, you're searching for both the words, but *not necessarily in order.* If you want to search for both words in order, next to each other, search for the exact phrase by putting the phrase inside quotation marks, like this: **"monty python"**.
- **NOT** (A match must exclude the next word to be *true.*)—Searching for **monty NOT python** will return pages about guys named Monty but will not return pages about Monty Python—because you're excluding *python* pages from your results. (Note that at some search engines, this operator must be used in the form AND NOT.)

True Boolean searching also lets you use parentheses, much like you would in a mathematical equation, to group portions of queries together to create more-complicated searches. For example, let's say you want to search for all pages about balls that are red or blue but not large. The search would look like this:

balls AND (red OR blue) NOT large

There are a handful of other Boolean operators, such as ADJ or NEAR or FAR, that have to do with *adjacency*—how close words are to each other. However, very, *very* few search engines use these adjacency operators, so you probably won't have much of an opportunity to use them.

Note that not all search sites allow Boolean searching, and even those that do might limit Boolean searching to their advanced search page. For example, Google lets you use the OR operator, but not AND or NOT. (With Google, AND is assumed, and you use – rather than NOT. If you want to force Google to include a common word, such as *the* or *how,* you can precede it with the + sign.)

In addition, not every search site implements Boolean searching in exactly the same way. For example, some sites use AND NOT rather than the more common NOT operator. Because of these differences, it's a good idea to read the Help files at a search site before you attempt Boolean searching.

A Bonus Tip—Search for Other Places to Search

Here's a sixth tip, at no extra charge. Given that even the biggest search engines index only a fraction of the total Internet, sometimes you have to turn to proprietary sites to find specific data. For example, if you're looking for a recent news story, you're better off searching a newspaper or magazine's online archives than you are trying to find that information at Google or Yahoo!. Or, if you're looking for medical information, you can probably find the information you want faster and easier at one of the many online health sites.

Here's a real-world example. My brother was thinking about buying a new home and wanted to know the original selling price of a particular home in a nearby neighborhood. In the offline world, this information is typically recorded by some county government office and sometimes listed in the local newspaper. It made sense, then, to search these entities online.

The problem is, we didn't know where to search. So, we turned to Google, and searched for **broward county property values**. (My brother lives in Broward County, Florida.) One of the first results was the Broward County Property Appraiser's Network, which enabled my brother to search for properties by street address, owner name, or subdivision. Using this topic-specific site, my brother quickly found the information he was looking for—which he couldn't have found at Google or any of the other generalist search sites.

So, it pays to use your normal search engines to search for more specific directories of information. And the more specific the information you're looking for, the more likely it is you'll have to perform a "double search" in this fashion.

SAFE SEARCHING FOR CHILDREN

If you have children, be sure to monitor their activity on the Internet. Even when kids are not looking for adult content, it can pop up on screen and either upset them or encourage them to explore further. In either case, you, as a parent or guardian, need to be aware of what's going on. You should also encourage your children, especially young children, to use child-safe search directories. These directories enable you to search, but the search returns links to only those sites that are appropriate for kids. Here are some of the better web directories for kids:

- **Yahooligans!** at www.yahooligans.com is the child-friendly version of Yahoo!. Parents and teachers can find useful tips at this site for ensuring their children and students explore the Internet safely.
- **Google Safe Search** at www.google.com/preferences.html enables parents and guardians to set options that filter out most of the undesirable content.
- **Ask Kids** at www.askforkids.com provides a kid-friendly version of Ask, enabling children to type in their questions and find safe answers. This site also features a reference library to help kids with their homework and some safe games to play when they need a break.
- **Education World** at www.education-world.com provides a directory of more than 500,000 resources that are safe for kids to explore. This site is more focused on teachers, but kids can find plenty of good information here.
- **Kids Click** at sunsite.berkeley.edu/KidsClick! is a simple web directory that organizes sites by categories, including Facts & Reference, Health & Family, and Popular Entertainments.

A FINAL WORD ABOUT SEARCHING

You hold in your hands one of the best available guides to the Internet. Que's *Internet Yellow Pages, 2007 Edition* catalogs thousands of the best sites on the Web and is a great first place to look when you're searching for information. I especially like the fact that you can use this book to find the *best* sites in any given category; it's more than a simple site listing. There's a good chance you'll find exactly what you want listed in this book and never have to use a web search engine or directory.

If you do need to use a search site, however, be smart about it. Construct an intelligent and sophisticated query and use the same query on multiple search sites. Examine your results and learn from them to fine-tune your query. Don't limit yourself in where you search or how you search; try new sites and new methods with regularity.

Above all, maintain a sense of curiosity. Don't stop looking with the first page you visit. When you visit a web page, look for links on that page to other pages. Follow those links, and then follow the next set of links. Always be on the lookout for good sources of information, no matter where they might come from. You'll be surprised just how much information you can find, if you're only open to finding it!

Michael Miller is the author of Que's *Absolute Beginner's Guide to eBay, Tricks of the eBay Masters, Absolute Beginner's Guide to Computer Basics, The Complete Idiot's Guide to Online Search Secrets, Bargain Hunter's Secrets to Online Shopping,* and more than 50 other bestselling how-to books. Mr. Miller is known for his ability to explain complicated subjects to the average consumer; he has established a reputation for practical advice, accuracy, and an unerring empathy for the needs of his readers.

A publishing industry professional since 1987, Mr. Miller is currently president of The Molehill Group, offering writing and consulting services on a variety of topics. You can find more information about Mr. Miller and The Molehill Group at www.molehillgroup.com.

BLOGS, POP-UPS, PODCASTS, AND WEBCASTS

by Joe Kraynak and Mikal Belicove

The Web is constantly evolving, presenting users with new tools, new forms of expression, and new annoyances. Since the first edition of the *Internet Yellow Pages*, the Web has seen the introduction and explosive growth of blogs, easier mobile access via cell phones, and the escalation of unsolicited advertising via pop-up ads. The following sections provide the information you need to keep abreast of the latest, most-significant developments and enhance your web browsing experience by reducing the number of ads that pop up on your screen.

BLOGS ARE WEBSITES, TOO

Short for *web log*, *blogs* are personal and business-related journals that enable individuals to voice their opinions and insights, keep an online journal of their lives or activities, or enable families and other groups and communities to stay in touch. Blogging hosts provide all the tools and instructions a user needs to create a blog and update it in a matter of minutes. This enables even the least tech-savvy web users to establish a presence on the Web.

In section B, look for the Blogging category. We have included a list of blogging hosts that can help you create and manage your own blog, along with a list of blog directories that can help you sift through the thousands of excellent blogs already on the Web.

BLOCKING POP-UPS

The commercialization of the Web has enhanced it a great deal by providing a profit motive that has generated the investment and innovation required to seed its growth. However, it has also inspired some companies to attempt to force-feed unsolicited advertisements to web users. Many of the most annoying ads are in the form of *pop-ups*, ads that automatically appear in separate windows or boxes on your computer screen.

Pop-ups come from two sources:

- Pop-up software and/or spyware that is installed on your computer with or without your knowledge. Some sites automatically install software on your computer that can track your web browsing habits, or they automatically call for pop-ups as you browse. Web users often unwittingly install adware on their own computers when they install a "free" game or other software from a website on their computers.
- Websites themselves often are programmed to generate pop-ups. You just open the site or click a particular link, and the pop-up appears.

If pop-ups are driving you crazy, you need to attack the problem using two utilities: a spyware remover and a pop-up blocker. You can download two freeware programs on the Web at Tucows (www.tucows.com) that, together, can prevent at least 90 percent of the pop-ups on your computer:

- **Spybot Search and Destroy** removes spyware. Install the software and run it every week or so to remove any spyware installed on your computer. (Ad-aware is another excellent utility, which you can download from www.lavasoft-usa.com.) Research any companies that offer heavily advertised adware or spyware removal utilities before purchasing any of them. They are often scams.
- **12Ghosts Popup Killer** blocks most pop-ups that websites try to automatically display on your screen. The only mild inconvenience this adds is that if you click a link for a site and the link is set up to open in a separate window, 12Ghosts prevents it from opening; to get the window to open, you simply hold down the Ctrl key while clicking. The Google and MSN toolbars and other specialized browser add-on toolbars also offer pop-up blocking.

Many of the newer antivirus programs and Internet security packages, such as Norton Internet Security, have finally begun to treat adware as they have traditionally treated viruses; so if you have an old antivirus program, consider updating it.

TUNING IN TO PODCASTS AND WEBCASTS

With the proliferation of portable audio players, including iPods and MP3 players, has come a proliferation of audio and video broadcasts on the Web. Commonly referred to as *podcasts* or *webcasts*, this content gives users on-demand access to audio or video broadcasts via their portable players. A small utility on the user's computer typically transfers content from the Web to the player. Users can even subscribe to their favorite sites to be notified of the latest podcasts or webcasts. In Que's *Internet Yellow Pages, 2007 Edition*, we point out sites that offer podcasts and webcasts by marking these sites with special icons.

Refer to the Podcast category in section P and the Webcast category in section W for sites that feature tools and instructions for creating podcasts and webcasts.

HOW THIS BOOK IS DESIGNED

Here's a quick look at a few structural features designed to help you get the most out of the book.

Best This icon identifies *the* best website in any given category. If you have time to visit only one site in a category, look for the Best of the Best!

1 2 3 4 5 ▲ Our quality indicator rates sites on a scale of 1 to 5 based on content, appearance, and ease of use. Top sites earn our highest rating of 5, but 3 is the lowest score—our book omits sites that we would consider to be below average.

Blog When you're looking for sites that encourage users to interact and contribute, keep an eye out for the Blog icon. Blogs can function as personal diaries, corporate kiosks, and even political platforms; but to qualify as a blog, they must enable users to provide input.

With more and more sites broadcasting their content or at least a portion of it with streaming video, we decided to spotlight those sites with a special Webcast icon. Look for the Webcast icon for dynamic audio-visual content.

iPods and other audio players have revolutionized the way web developers distribute their content. With an iPod or another audio player, you can download audio broadcasts from the Web and carry them with you wherever you go. Look for Podcast icons to locate sites that provide audio-on-the-go content.

RSS RSS stands for Rich Site Summary or Really Simple Syndication. It's a technology that enables web masters and bloggers to include live feeds from their sites that make it easy for readers to stay on top of the site's latest blog or text entries. Many sites now offer RSS feeds, and we highlight those sites with our RSS icon.

Some websites might not provide a lot of quality information on their own but do, instead, point you in the direction of some of the best sites that deal with a particular topic. We draw your attention to these sites with our Directory icon.

Tip: This icon alerts you to valuable insider site-specific tips that can enhance your experience at a particular site.

We also provide several cross-references throughout the book to help you locate websites that might not appear in the category where you first think of looking.

The child-rating icon is designed to help you weed out sites that are inappropriate for children. Look for

Not for kids for sites that include content inappropriate for children (violence, drugs, racism, or adult content).

WARNING:

Although we made every attempt possible to identify sites that children should not visit, ratings are not always reliable. Sometimes, a site will lose the right to use a particular address, and a company will purchase the address and use it for a site that contains content inappropriate for children. In addition, some sites might include links that point to other sites that have unsuitable content. Every parent should monitor his or her child's activity on the Internet and consider using monitoring or censoring software, such as CyberPatrol, to filter out inappropriate content. However, even censoring software is not foolproof.

ACCOUNTING

Accounting Terminology Guide

1 2 3 4 5

www.nysscpa.org/prof_library/guide.htm

If you need to know what a specific accounting term means, no matter how obscure, this is the site for you. Hosted and maintained by the New York State Society of CPAs, nearly 500 different accounting terms are defined on this page, all sorted in an easy to use alphabetic list.

Best American Institute of Certified Public Accountants

1 2 3 4 5

www.aicpa.org

The American Institute of Certified Public Accountants is the national, professional organization for all Certified Public Accountants in the United States. Its mission is "to provide members with the resources, information, and leadership that enable them to provide valuable services in the highest professional manner to benefit the public as well as employers and clients." Site features an Accounting Education Center, Accounting Standards, Anti-Fraud Resource Center, information about the CPA Exam, a directory of links, and much more. This site is packed with valuable information in an easily accessible format, making it an easy choice for Best of the Best in the Accounting category.

CPA Directory

www.cpadirectory.com

When April rolls around and you find yourself scrambling to find a Certified Public Accountant, this site will help. Search for a CPA by ZIP code, name, industry, or area of specialty. This site even has details on the differences between a CPA and an accountant, along with articles to help you prepare for meeting with a CPA.

The CPA Journal Online

1 2 3 4 5

www.cpaj.com

Read what the accounting industry reads, for free. Although it's published by the New York State Society of CPAs, the CPA Journal Online is a great resource for anyone interested in going in-depth, especially public practitioners, management, educators, and other accounting professionals.

SmartPros

1 2 3 4 5

accounting.smartpros.com

SmartPros Ltd. offers "products and services primarily focused in the accredited professional areas of corporate accounting, financial management, public accounting, governmental and not-for-profit accounting, banking, engineering, and ethics and compliance." Site opens with a couple feature articles on accounting and offers a Resource Library, Career Center, and Professional Education Center.

B C D E F G H I J K L M N O P Q R S T U V W X Y Z

ACTIVISM

Activism.net

1 2 3 4 5

www.activism.net

When you want to get involved in a cause, but you're not sure where to start, check out Activism.net. Here, you can find information and links to additional resources on everything from cyber-rights to drugs, e-voting, and war. This site provides a comprehensive directory of activist organizations.

AlterNet

www.alternet.org

Online magazine dedicated to strengthening and supporting independent, alternative journalism. Site features news, investigative articles, and opinions on a range of topics covering everything from environmental and political issues to cultural trends, technology, and sexuality.

CorpWatch.org

1 2 3 4 5 Blog RSS

www.corpwatch.org

Home of the CorpWatch.org corporation watchdog group, dedicated to ensuring that large corporations follow ethical business, political, and environmental practices. Visit this site to learn more about CorpWatch.org's campaigns, activities, issues, and research; and be sure to check out the CorpWatch blog.

Digital Freedom Network

1 2 3 4 5

www.dfn.org

Digital Freedom Network (DFN) is "a non-profit group that seeks to promote human rights as an attainable goal for all countries." DFN believes that "free enterprise, limited government, rule of law, and individual freedom are the most effective means to ensure the rights of men and women across the world." Site features current events, biographies and stories about activists who are fighting to make a difference, a freedom handbook for activists, reading lists, banned reading lists, and much more. Some excellent articles.

Idealist.org

1 2 3 4 5

www.idealist.org

Home of Action Without Borders, a worldwide network of individuals and organizations devoted to promoting freedom and human dignity throughout the world. Features an excellent directory of activist organizations, lists of jobs and volunteer opportunities, available services and resources, Kids & Teens section, and much more. If you're looking for ways to make the world a better place to live, check out this site.

Indybay.org

www.indybay.org

This independent media center strives to provide independent media makers with an infrastructure for distributing their ideas, visions, and creations in whatever form of media they choose to express themselves. This group is also dedicated to helping fight against exploitation and oppression. Site features information and support for a wide variety of issues, including the environment, arts, poverty, globalization, and war, and also allows visitors to post their own articles.

PETA.org

www.peta.org

Home of People for the Ethical Treatment of Animals (PETA), this site provides a list of action alerts—specific causes for which PETA needs your immediate support. Also features a list of PETA campaigns, information on how to live in greater harmony with animals, and a PETA mall where you can shop for books, clothing, and other items online.

Protest.Net

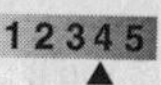

protest.net

Protest.Net features a calendar of protests scheduled in major cities around the world. The opening page presents a list of upcoming protests along with a list of International Days of Action and an extensive listing of protests by city. You can click the regional map to browse for protests in a particular area of the world. Site also offers an Activists Handbook, newsletter, news and action alerts, and other valuable information and resources.

They Rule

www.theyrule.net

If you suspect that a handful of powerful corporate leaders control most of the world's resources, this site will confirm your suspicions. They Rule provides a virtual map of the most powerful corporate leaders in the world and shows how they are all interconnected in a mass conspiracy to control the world's economies and resources.

Tolerance.org

12345

www.tolerance.org

Dedicated to promoting greater understanding and tolerance of diverse groups of people, this site provides information on how to combat hate and intolerance in our daily lives. Includes articles on hate and hate crimes, studies on hate and racial bias, information on gay rights, and advice on how to track hate groups.

VoiceOfThePeople.com

http://www.globalseeker.com/voxpop

This site gives you a voice in government. Here, you can cast your vote on any of several hot issues and find contact information for various leaders at the White House.

A World Connected

www.aworldconnected.com

A World Connected is dedicated to fostering an environment that encourages open discussion about the need for true globalization of the world economy to help citizens of underdeveloped countries achieve some degree of prosperity. Site features articles, stories, and discussions. Visitors can also choose to get involved to make a difference.

B C D E F G H I J K L M N O P Q R S T U V W X Y Z

ADDICTIONS/RECOVERY

Addiction Intervention Resources

12345

www.addictionintervention.com

When someone you love is on the road to self-destruction, you don't have to simply stand by and watch. You can stage an intervention in the hopes of convincing your loved one to get help. Addiction Intervention Resources is "a national organization of professional intervention specialists, counselors, and consultants that provide fast and effective crisis management services through a proven protocol of education, action, and healing." Here, you can find out more about the organization and learn how it can help you stage an effective intervention.

The Addiction Recovery Guide

12345

www.addictionrecoveryguide.org

The Addiction Recovery Guide "assists individuals struggling with drug addiction and alcoholism find help that best suits their needs." Here, you can learn about the company's recovery programs and discover an excellent collection of information and resources. Site features several menus: Treatment Options, Addiction Medication (including heroin, cocaine, methamphetamine, and alcohol), Holistic Approaches, Message Boards, and Beyond Recovery. Many articles on this site contain links to other valuable resources on the Web.

ALCOHOLISM

Al-Anon

12345

www.al-anon.org

Al-Anon is a self-help recovery program for family and friends of alcoholics. Included here is a program overview and a list of contacts and events. Subscribe to *The Forum*, Al-Anon's monthly magazine, at this site.

Alateen

12345

www.al-anon.org/alateen.html

Alateen provides support and information for young people whose lives have been affected by someone else's alcoholism. This site includes information on meetings, a list of literature, and facts about Alateen.

Alcoholics Anonymous

12345

www.alcoholics-anonymous.org

From the home page, choose the English, Spanish, or French version of the text, and continue. You'll find 12 questions you can answer to help determine whether A.A. might be helpful. You'll also find local contact information, a calendar of events, information on A.A. meetings, and a special section for professionals.

College Drinking Prevention Website

12345

www.collegedrinkingprevention.gov

The National Institute on Alcohol Abuse and Alcoholism (NIAAA) created this site to give high school and college students, parents, teachers, and school administrators comprehensive research-based information on issues related to alcohol abuse and binge drinking among college students. Site features College Alcohol Policies, Alcohol Myths, Calculators, a guide for getting help, and free educational materials for distribution. You can access content at the site that's most relevant to you by clicking one of the buttons in the navigation bar: College Presidents, College Parents, College Students, H.S. Administrators, or H.S. Parents & Students.

The Cool Spot

12345

www.thecoolspot.gov

The Cool Spot is a hangout for kids 11–13 years old created by the National Institute on Alcohol Abuse and Alcoholism (NIAAA). This engaging, interactive site is designed to give kids the straight facts about alcohol consumption among their peers and provide them with the guidance and tools they need to resist the peer pressure to start drinking. Site features Reality Check quizzes, Deep Digging advice on why alcohol is not a solution to problems, a Peer Pressure Bag of Tricks, and a Know Your No's activity to help kids develop an arsenal of ways to deflect peer pressure.

Drinking: A Student's Guide

12345

www.mcneese.edu/community/alcohol/help.html

This is a fun site about a serious topic. Aimed at high school and college students, the site presents the facts about binge drinking, alcohol and health, and alcohol and drugs. After reading all the facts, you can do the self-assessment to determine whether you're at risk. If so, the site offers an extensive list of resources to contact.

DrinkWise

12345

www.med.umich.edu/drinkwise

An educational program that helps people reduce alcohol consumption. Includes a self-evaluation form and phone number to contact DrinkWise for more information.

Best National Institute on Alcohol Abuse and Alcoholism

12345

www.niaaa.nih.gov

NIAAA provides leadership in the national effort to reduce alcohol-related problems. This site provides a huge collection of resources that can help alcoholics, their loved ones, and the people who counsel them. The opening page presents dozens of links grouped into several categories, including Publications, Research Information, News and Events, Frequently Asked Questions, and Resources. Under Resources, click Related Websites for a directory of links to other alcoholism-related sites.

Sobriety and Recovery Resources

12345

www.recoveryresources.org

A great Alcoholics Anonymous (A.A.)–related site with many personal stories from individuals struggling with addiction and recovery, as well as treatment information and encouragement. Links to online recovery resources are helpful, as is the listing of local addiction treatment organizations.

DRUGS

CrystalRecovery.com

12345

www.crystalrecovery.com

If you're recovering from an addiction to crystal meth, visit this site to get help from others who are dealing with the addiction. Here, you can find a question and answer forum, recovery tips, and personal stories to help you get through the most challenging times.

Related Site

www.kci.org

Drugnet

12345

www.drugnet.net

Dedicated to treating and preventing drug abuse, this site offers prototype assessment tools, online training, help in preparing research grants related to drug abuse, and access to databases with prevention and treatment guidelines and tools.

Narcotics Anonymous

12345

www.na.org

Serving as a resource primarily for health professionals, Narcotics Anonymous provides plenty of resource material, including reports, periodicals, and access to a database of past publications and news.

B C D E F G H I J K L M N O P Q R S T U V W X Y Z

B C D E F G H I J K L M N O P Q R S T U V W X Y Z

Substance Abuse Treatment Facility Locator

12345

dasis3.samhsa.gov

Clickable map of the United States that enables you to search for a substance abuse treatment facility by specifying the state and city in which you reside. Site also offers a list of state treatment facilities and a FAQ.

GAMBLING

Help Guide: Gambling Addiction

12345

www.helpguide.org/mental/gambling_addiction.htm

Excellent guide defines "gambling addiction," points out the signs and symptoms, explores the three phases that gambling addicts commonly experience, explains the negative effects of compulsive gambling, and reveals various treatment strategies that can help.

Illinois Institute for Addiction Recovery

12345

www.addictionrecov.org/addicgam.htm

This site offers a wide range of information, tools, and resources to help you understand and overcome a gambling addiction. Find out what a gambling addiction really is, whom it commonly affects, and which programs are most effective in dealing with it. The site also provides a useful questionnaire to determine whether you are suffering from a gambling addiction, along with a description of various types of gamblers.

National Council on Problem Gambling

12345

www.ncpgambling.org

The National Council on Problem Gambling is dedicated to "increasing public awareness of pathological gambling, ensuring the widespread availability of treatment for problem gamblers and their families, and encouraging research and programs for prevention and education." Best of all, this site gives you a 24-hour, toll-free number to call when you're ready to do something about your gambling addiction.

SEX ADDICTION

Internet Sex Screening Test (ISST)

www.sexhelp.com/internet_screening_test.cfm

Are you addicted to Internet sex? Take the ISST to find out.

Sexual Addiction Recovery Resources

12345

www.sarr.org

Sexual Addiction Recovery Resources offers a collection of articles, information, and resources that can help sex addicts, their partners, and sex addiction counselors. Content is grouped by category, including For Addicts, For Partners, For Counselors, For Couples, and Support Groups.

STOP SMOKING

Action on Smoking and Health (ASH)

12345

www.ash.org

ASH is the nation's oldest and largest antismoking organization, providing visitors to its site with information on nonsmokers' rights, the health risks of smoking—to smokers and nonsmokers—and legislative updates. The tone is definitely antismoking, with a slant toward lawsuits to protect nonsmokers' rights. This is a membership-based site.

Campaign for Tobacco-Free Kids

tobaccofreekids.org

Information on antitobacco campaigns, including up-to-date special reports on the dangers associated with teen smoking. The site also presents press releases and news items, fact sheets, and information on each state's efforts in the fight against tobacco.

CDC's Tobacco Info-Quit Site

12345

www.cdc.gov/tobacco/quit/quittip.htm

Available in English or Spanish, this site provides five tips on quitting, plus plenty of links to related information, including Surgeon General's reports, educational resources, smoking-cessation tools, and health databases.

Definition of Nicotine Dependence

12345

www.mayoclinic.org/ndc-rst

This page, part of the Mayo Clinic's site, provides a clear explanation of nicotine dependence and provides several options to help you quit.

Nicorette

12345

www.nicorette.com

From the makers of Nicorette gum, this site offers a dependency quiz, hints on how to quit, and FAQs. You can purchase Nicorette online here.

Nicotine Anonymous

12345

www.nicotine-anonymous.org

Nicotine Anonymous provides support for people wanting to quit smoking and live free of nicotine. The site also includes a state-by-state list of Nicotine Anonymous meetings and information about meetings in 40 different countries.

Quit Smoking Support.com

12345 RSS

www.quitsmokingsupport.com

This site lists more than 40 sites that offer tips and articles to help quit smoking. Recommended stop-smoking products are advertised on this page.

The QuitNet

12345

www.quitnet.com

QuitNet provides a collection of online resources, news, and guides for individuals who want to quit smoking. You can buy T-shirts and sweatshirts with the QuitNet logo. Links to your favorite retail for prescription drugs to help you quit smoking are also provided.

Tip: Click the Enter as a Guest link at the top of the page for access to free resources.

QuitSmoking.com

12345

www.quitsmoking.com

Billed as "The Quit Smoking Company," QuitSmoking.com is the place to go for smoking-cessation products. Here, you will find the largest collection of nicotine substitutes, vitamins, books, tapes, and even T-shirts. This site also features stop-smoking methods, articles, a free email newsletter, and FAQs.

Smoke-Free Families

12345

www.smokefreefamilies.org

Smoke-Free Families is dedicated to encouraging and helping pregnant women to stop smoking. This site provides a link for emailing a supportive card to a pregnant smoker and access to a free Medicaid Tool Kit for "educating decision-makers about the importance of comprehensive tobacco treatment under Medicaid for pregnant women."

SUBSTANCE ABUSE AND RECOVERY

12 Step Cyber Café

12345 Blog

www.12steps.org

Find recovery resources for addictions of all kinds. This site focuses on the 12 Step program made famous by Alcoholics Anonymous and features a blog, chat room, and e-cards that you can send to your friends.

Addiction Resource Guide

www.addictionresourceguide.com

The primary purpose of this site is to provide a comprehensive listing of addiction treatment facilities, but the online guide to treatment options and alternatives is a useful resource, too.

Betty Ford Center

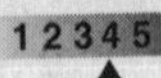

www.bettyfordcenter.org

Betty Ford Center is the first and most famous of addiction treatment centers. Here, you'll find information about the inpatient and outpatient programs at the Betty Ford Center. You can also find information on a codependency treatment plan, along with news of upcoming events.

D.A.R.E.

12345

www.dare.org

This is the home page of the Drug Abuse Resistance Education (D.A.R.E.) organization. It offers information for kids, parents, and educators. Find out how law enforcement is cooperating in your community and elsewhere to stop drug use. This is a family-friendly site.

Get It Straight: The Facts About Drugs

www.usdoj.gov/dea/pubs/straight/cover.htm

A drug-prevention book targeted at kids, put out by the Drug Enforcement Administration. Provides serious resources and information about the laws related to drugs and drug abuse.

Indiana Prevention Resource Center

www.drugs.indiana.edu

Indiana University's Prevention Resource Center is a clearinghouse for prevention-oriented technical assistance and information about alcohol, tobacco, and other drugs. The site has statistics, publications, a search engine, and a library.

Join Together Online

www.jointogether.org

Join Together is a national resource center for communities working to reduce substance abuse and gun violence. The site includes policy alerts, news updates, discussion boards, fact sheets, and a calendar of events, a directory of national organizations, and more.

The Marijuana Anonymous World Services

www.marijuana-anonymous.org

Learn the facts about marijuana addiction. Take the quiz to find out whether you need help. Learn the 12 steps for recovery. Benefit from the shared experiences of others. Find out how to join Marijuana Anonymous.

National Institute on Drug Abuse

12345

www.nida.nih.gov

The National Institute on Drug Abuse, established in 1974, works on research and programs to prevent and treat drug addiction. The site features information on the organization including its programs and publications on drug abuse.

Partnership for a Drug-Free America

12345

www.drugfreeamerica.org

A searchable database of drug information makes this site one of the best places to start researching addictions to specific drugs. It also includes answers to frequently asked questions about drugs, a section of advice for parents, and a page specifically directed at teens.

Prevention Online

www.health.org

Provides information for those people battling substance abuse or who know someone battling substance abuse. Press releases, publications, forums, and calendars of upcoming events are all available, including several publications for kids age 8 and older.

Substance Abuse & Mental Health Services Administration

www.samhsa.gov

A division of the United States Department of Health and Human Services, SAMHSA offers help for those who are struggling with an addiction or a mental health problem. Upon reaching the opening page, click the Get Help for Substance Abuse Problems link. This opens a page with links to several tools and resources, including a Treatment Facility Locator, self-tests to determine whether you have a problem, and SAMHSA's National Clearinghouse for Alcohol and Drug Information.

ADOPTION

Adopting.org

1 2 3 4 5

www.adopting.org

Billed as a community adoption site, it allows visitors to gain access to information on the adoption process, resources, discussion forums, and available children and families interested in adoption.

Adoption Benefits: Employers as Partners in Family Building

1 2 3 4 5

www.adopting.org/employer.html

Provides information about company-sponsored adoption benefit plans, including who is eligible for benefits, how company-sponsored benefit plans actually work, what expenses are covered and when they are paid, what types of adoption benefit plans cover, and whether adoption leaves of absence are available from the workplace. Also provides a list of companies that offer adoption benefits, as well as other adoption-assistance programs. If you are considering adopting a child, this is a great place to go to learn about company-sponsored benefits.

Adoption.com

www.adoption.com

Offers information about alternatives to abortion, such as adoption and single parenting, and provides chat rooms and information on localized counseling. You can buy books about adoption and child rearing, as well as toys and other items for your adopted child.

The Adoption Guide

1 2 3 4 5

www.theadoptionguide.com

Published and distributed by the creators of *Adoptive Families* magazine, The Adoption Guide is a comprehensive and up-to-date introduction to the world of adoption. Here, you can learn more about the publication and find links to several additional online resources and a hefty collection of articles on various adoption topics.

Adoption Search

www.adoptionsearch.com

This adoption-focused search engine enables users to quickly locate information on adoption resources, as well as parenting, birth registries, health, infertility, and pregnancy.

Adoption Travel

1 2 3 4 5

www.adoptiontravel.com

Potential adoptive parents intending to adopt internationally will find this site's links to country-specific travel and adoption sites helpful. Advice from parents who have already adopted on what to bring, what to expect, and so on is especially useful.

Adoption Shop

1 2 3 4 5

www.adoptionshop.com

Billed as the world's largest adoption store, this site specializes in books, videos, and tapes about the adoption experience and carries essential kids stuff, such as baby clothes, games, and toys.

Adoption Today Magazine

1 2 3 4 5

www.adoptinfo.net

Adoption magazine that offers a wide variety of articles covering everything from adopting a child to building a multicultural atmosphere in your home where children from all countries will feel welcome. This site gives nothing away for free, but it does enable you to sign up for a subscription to the magazine and order back issues online.

AdoptUsKids

1 2 3 4 5

www.adoptuskids.org

AdoptUsKids is a project dedicated to devising and implementing a national adoptive family recruitment and retention strategy, operating the AdoptUsKids.org website, encouraging and enhancing adoptive family support organizations, and conducting a variety of adoption research projects. Click Meet the Children to search for a child who needs a home or visit the Resource Center for information on how to adopt a child. Information is offered both for prospective parents and for adoption professionals.

Best Child Welfare Information Gateway

1 2 3 4 5

www.childwelfare.gov/adoption

Managed by the U.S. Department of Health and Human Services Administration for Children & Families, this site features a collection of information and resources for all aspects of the adoption process. Here, you can find a national adoption directory, a list of adoption professionals, information on tracking down birth parents, information on how to prepare to become an adoptive parent, and much more. This site's basic design makes it easy to access its vast store of information, earning it our choice as Best of the Best.

Dave Thomas Foundation for Adoption

1 2 3 4 5

www.davethomasfoundationforadoption.org

Dave Thomas, founder of Wendy's restaurants, was dedicated to finding good homes for children in need. Here, you can learn more about the foundation and gather some useful information on adopting a child. Site also offers some professional resources.

Holt International Children's Services

1 2 3 4 5

www.holtintl.org

Provides information and support for birth parents and adoptive parents, information and resources for professionals in the adoption field, and links to other websites that provide information about adoption. The site is current thanks to weekly updates. You can buy books, T-shirts, and calendars through the online store.

Independent Adoption Center: Open Adoptions for Birth Mothers and Parents

1 2 3 4 5

www.adoptionhelp.org

The site boasts that the Independent Adoption Center is the largest nonprofit open-adoption program in the United States, with offices on the West Coast, the East Coast, and the Midwest, and almost two decades of experience with open adoption. The site is inviting and offers a wealth of information and resources about open adoption.

National Adoption Center

1 2 3 4 5

www.adopt.org

A national program, in the United States, that pairs up homeless children with parents who are looking to adopt. Also includes information on legislation, the adoption process, lists of adoption agencies and organizations, conferences and seminars, and other material pertinent to all aspects of adoption. The Waiting Children link displays pictures and biographies of children currently waiting for a family to adopt them.

A
B
C
D
E
F
G
H
I
J
K
L
M
N
O
P
Q
R
S
T
U
V
W
X
Y
Z

National Council for Adoption

12345

www.ncfa-usa.org

The National Council for Adoption is an activist organization that promotes adoption internationally and works domestically to push for improvements in federal and state adoption legislation. At this site, you can download the NCFA Adoption Factbook, learn more about the organization, become a member, and find out how you can become a more active member in the adoption community.

Our Chinese Daughters

12345

www.ocdf.org

This site is dedicated to supporting any and all efforts (travel grants, scholarships, and so on) that encourage single mothers to adopt from China and that benefit the children they adopt.

Precious in HIS Sight (Internet Adoption Photo Listing)

12345

www.precious.org

This site contains a photo listing of more than 500 children from 15 countries available for international adoption, as well as lots of adoption-related information (including a FAQ) and links to other adoption sites . You can sort the children in the listings by multiple criteria. In addition, you can select to view a list of agencies with accounts and email all of them at once.

ADVENTURE TRAVEL/ECOTOURISM

Adventure Center

www.adventurecenter.com

Adventure Center provides safaris, treks, expeditions, and active vacations worldwide in Antarctica, South America, Europe, Africa, Asia, and the South Pacific. Tribal encounters are common, and you can see images of past trips at this site, where you can find out more about upcoming travel opportunities.

Adventure Travel Tips

www.adventuretraveltips.com

This site provides links to more than 1,000 adventure travel outfitters grouped by category, including animal treks, bicycling, bird watching, sailing, hunting, scuba diving, and much more.

Alpine Ascents International

12345

www.alpineascents.com

For the extreme vacation adventure, check out Alpine Ascents's expeditions, treks, and tours. You can learn about the school, its various expeditions and guides, the gear required and provided, and much more. Be sure to read the FAQ before signing up for your first expedition.

Backroads

12345

www.backroads.com

Backroads bills itself as the World's #1 Active Travel Company. It features trips that require you to use your body to get around, either walking or biking your way around the countryside. Trips are organized by type, including walking, biking, multisport, family, camping, classic, easy, epic, private, and solo.

EarthRiver Expeditions

12345

www.earthriver.com

EarthRiver Expeditions can lead you on an adventure in North or South America, the South Pacific, or Asia by raft, kayak, and on foot. Check out this site's interactive map for more details. From this point of departure, you can check out the available expeditions, check the calendar for a time that fits your schedule, learn about the guides, view expedition maps, take a virtual tour, and much more. Nicely designed site with beautiful graphics and excellent content.

GORPtravel.com

12345

www.gorptravel.com

From rock-climbing trips and fly-fishing expeditions to nature cruises and snowmobiling trips, this site has access to it all, including hot deals on last-minutes packages and in-depth articles to help you prepare for nearly any type of adventure.

Great Pacific Adventures

12345

www.greatpacificadventures.com

Learn more about whale-watching tours in the Pacific Northwest with this company and view pictures from past trips.

iExplore

12345

www.iexplore.com

This site is packed with interesting trips to the world's hidden treasure destinations. Click the Trip Finder link to check out some of the more intriguing trips or scroll down the page to view the top destinations or explore trips by country. Online trip finders, destinations guides, and expert advice help you pick the trip that's right for you. You can also check out exclusive trips, great deals, and membership benefits. If you're looking for a journey that's off the beaten track, you'll find it here.

Mountain Travel Sobek

1 2 3 4 5

www.mtsobek.com

You'll find a huge number of different types of adventure travel trips described at this company's site—from hiking adventures to river rafting, biking, small boat cruises, and many more. Look at photos from past trips and learn about the gear you'll need to make your adventure a comfy one.

> **Tip:** Click on the Request a Catalog link, and within a few weeks you'll be amazed at the stunning photography and trip descriptions that fill this company's catalog!

Best Outside Online

1 2 3 4 5 Blog RSS

outside.away.com

Outside Online is a tremendous resource and travel guide for the outdoor adventurer. At this site, you can find gobs of stories about the greatest adventures and adventurers, travel guides to the most exhilarating outdoor adventures and destinations, daily briefings on wildlife and tourism, special reports, buyers guides for travel gear, and everything else you need to plan and prepare for your next adventure trip.

Recreation.gov

1 2 3 4 5

www.recreation.gov

This site from the U.S. federal government can help you explore a huge selection of adventure treks and outdoor activities in the United States. You can click the map to browse by location or select the desired activity from the list on the left.

Rod and Gun

1 2 3 4 5

rodgunresources.com

An international adventure travel company offering hunting and fishing trips around the world. See the site for information about destinations and to see comments from past travelers.

Silver Lining Tours

1 2 3 4 5

www.silverliningtours.com

Ever wanted to see a storm up close? Then check out this site for information on storm-chasing adventures. Learn about what you might see and how you can sign up for these increasingly popular tours. This site has a lot of information about tornadoes and severe storms. If you don't want to pay for a tour, just move to the Midwest—if you don't already live there. The site has contact information for reserving space on an upcoming trip, along with lots of photos and client testimonials.

Smithsonian Journeys

1 2 3 4 5

www.smithsonianjourneys.org

Some people travel to relax. Other people like to learn something. Smithsonian Journeys, although they do provide plenty of relaxation, are more for those who like to return home from vacation a little more knowledgeable than when they left. At this site, you pick a departure date, an interest (such as archeology or philosophy), a tour type (such as countryside, private jet, hiking, or cruise), or a destination (say, France or China), and Smithsonian Journeys suggests several journeys that you might find appealing.

Storm Chasing Adventure Tours

1 2 3 4 5

www.stormchasing.com

Another storm-chasing travel operator that will tell you about upcoming trips and accommodations. Trips vary in length, but most are 6 days/7 nights. The site also has contact information for helping you plan your tour online.

Walking Adventures International

1 2 3 4 5

www.walkingadventures.com

Consider taking a walking tour of interesting places all around the world with this outfitter, which travels through the United States, Europe, the Mediterranean, and many more places. Check the calendar to see when and where you might like to go. You'll find information to help you conveniently sign up for the tour.

A B C D E F G H I J K L M N O P Q R S T U V W X Y Z

ADVICE

All Experts

12345

www.allexperts.com

Ask a question of a volunteer expert on virtually any topic, from arts and entertainment to relationships to business and more, for free. This site is organized by category, so you can quickly browse for the desired topic and then submit your question. The site covers virtually every topic—from automobiles to television shows. If you can't find your answer here, you may not be able to find it anywhere!

Answer Bag

12345 RSS

www.answerbag.com

When you're looking for an answer and you need it quick, check the answer bag. Here, you can type your question and get an immediate answer or scroll through a collection of answers to questions that others have posted.

Ask a Chef

12345

www.askachef.com

When you need some professional cooking advice, turn to Ask a Chef, where you can read through recent questions and answers or post a question to have it answered via email. This site also features plenty of original recipes.

Best Daily Candy

12345

www.dailycandy.com

For advice on fashion, food, and fun, turn to Daily Candy, where you can find cutting-edge information on the current social scene. Here, you can learn which jeans are the hottest on the market, where to score a pair of the hippest shoes that haven't yet hit the market, what to read, which movies are must-sees, and which concerts to attend. Read about the latest beauty tips and hairstyles. Sign up for the newsletter to get the latest advice via email or visit this site to explore some of the slightly older recommendations. This well-designed site is packed with good, solid advice that makes it our pick for Best of the Best.

Dear Abby

12345

www.uexpress.com/dearabby

Write to Dear Abby, read her latest column, or search past columns in the archive at this site, where you also can buy books by Abigail Van Buren.

Dr. Laura

12345

www.drlaura.com

When you're having trouble with a relationship, see what Dr. Laura has to say about it, and don't expect a sugar-coated answer! This popular radio and TV personality shoots straight from the hip to tell you just what *you* need to do to fix your relationship. Here, you can learn more about Dr. Laura, read her advice, listen to her show, get tips for working at home, shop online for Dr. Laura's books and other merchandise, and much more.

Dr. Ruth Online!

12345

www.drruth.com

Ask Dr. Ruth your own questions about sex or take a look at recent questions posed by others. You can also find a sex tips section and the results of sex polls.

drDrew

12345

www.drdrew.com

Learn more about sex, health, and relationships, from the co-host of MTV's *Loveline*, Dr. Drew. Submit questions, and participate in online communities with concerns about a wide range of personal health issues.

Elder Wisdom Circle

12345

www.elderwisdomcircle.org

Elder Wisdom Circle is a group of senior volunteers who offer advice and know-how from their many years of learning. Their goal is to "elevate the perceived value and worth of our senior community." Click the Browse Advice tab to find answers to recently asked questions or click Seek Advice to submit your own question.

Everything2

www.everything2.com

At Everything2, you can find discussions on every topic imaginable—some light and funny, some deep and intriguing, and some just plain pointless.

Experts Exchange

12345

www.experts-exchange.com

Computer experts who want to barter their expertise for the knowledge of others in the field should check out this site. Here, you can offer advice to earn points that enable you to "buy" advice from other experts.

Femina

12345

femina.cybergrrl.com

This women-only site features information, resources, and advice dealing exclusively with female issues. The site is a web directory of women-friendly sites that contain information primarily targeting the female crowd. Here, you can check out Femina's site of the month, read the latest women's news, submit an article, check the calendar, or add an event.

Go Ask Alice!

www.goaskalice.columbia.edu

Alice! is the Columbia University Health Service's online nurse, essentially. Designed to provide health information, Ask Alice can field questions for most health-related topics. You can Ask Alice! a health question, search past Q&As, or search Alice!'s database for health information on your own. Most areas of this site are strictly off limits for children.

Kasamba

12345

www.kasamba.com

Kasamba is a commercial referral service that connects people who have questions to experts who can answer them, for a fee. Fees vary, of course, on the difficulty of the question and the expertise needed to provide the answer.

KnowledgeHound

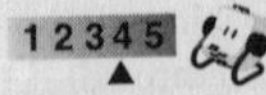

www.knowledgehound.com

This searchable directory of how-to sites is the ultimate guide for the do-it-yourselfer. Here, you can learn everything from how to care for a baby to how to cook with solar energy. Categories include Animals, Cooking, Environment, Arts & Humanities, Money & Law, and much more.

Relationship-Talk.com

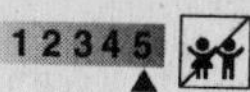

www.relationship-talk.com

Is your relationship on the rocks? Then check out this site where you can obtain relationship guides, counseling, and community support. You can post a question, participate in online polls, and even get a few chuckles on the humor page. This site is still planning a LoveMinders feature to keep you informed of important dates, such as birthdays and anniversaries.

Teen Advice Online

www.teenadviceonline.org

Teen Advice Online (TAO for short) has been providing advice and support for teenagers since 1996. Here, you can read questions that teens commonly have along with answers posted by the volunteer counselors. Most of the topics deal with dating, but a number deal with other issues. Parents can also benefit by reading through the warning signs of a troubled teen.

A B C D E F G H I J K L M N O P Q R S T U V W X Y Z

AGRICULTURE

Agricultural Network Information Center (AgNIC)

12345

www.agnic.org

Listing of resources and activities for the agricultural community. The site provides links to universities and institutions providing online reference assistance, including listservs, newsgroups, products and services, and frequently asked questions.

Agriculture in the Classroom

12345

www.agclassroom.org

A fun website designed to help kids and teachers learn more about the critical role of agriculture in our economy and society. A great place for teachers to learn about hands-on projects for teaching students about agricultural topics.

Best Agriculture Online

12345

www.agriculture.com

Read legislative news, market news, news from around the world, technology news, weather forecasts, and more. Clearly organized and visually attractive, this site is packed with all the most current information available for farmers and others who are devoted to agriculture and agribusiness. If you're a farmer or in the farming industry, be sure to bookmark this Best of the Best site, and visit it daily.

AgWeb

12345

www.agweb.com

Information on farming industry topics, headline news (updated twice daily), lists of upcoming industry events, and a variety of farm-related links, including a list of handy links to weather forecast sites. Includes industry financial information such as investment news and the latest agriculture market statistics.

American Dairy Science Association (ADSA)

12345

www.adsa.org

This site posts information about association meetings and articles from the *Journal of Dairy Science* (including an index that is searchable by author or content) and instructions on submitting manuscript for publication. Also includes links to other dairy- and agriculture-related sites.

American Egg Board

12345

www.aeb.org

Devoted to egg lovers, this site offers recipes, FAQs about eggs, nutrition information, and industry facts and statistics. Excellent site for both kids and adults.

American Farm Bureau: Voice of Agriculture

12345

www.fb.com

Provides links to agricultural, ranching, and farm-related sites, as well as state and county farm bureaus. Also offers links to national and rural news, educational materials, agricultural legislation, and bulletin boards where members of the agricultural community share information and ideas.

American Farmland Trust

12345 RSS

www.farmland.org

The American Farmland Trust is concerned with preserving farmland and wildlife habitats. The trust's site includes statistics on the loss of farmland to urban sprawl and details on what users can do, as well as links to related resources and other organizations. The site is kept current.

Beef Home Page

www.beef.org

This is the home page of the National Cattlemen's Beef Association. The site is inviting and oriented primarily toward consumers interested in beef information, although the site contains information that might interest people in the industry. Categories of information include Nutrition, Kitchen (cooking), Food Safety, Shopping, Beef Production, Research, New Products, and News.

Ceres Online

www.ceresgroup.com/col

Ceres Online specializes in providing information for agriculture professionals. The site's search functions enable users to connect to other professionals in the agriculture industry. Other site features include a calendar database that lists hundreds of upcoming events and weather maps that include world, national, and hot-spot information.

Economic Research Service (USDA)

www.ers.usda.gov

Provides economic and social science information and analysis for public and private decisions on agriculture, food, natural resources, and rural America. It features reports, catalogs, publications, USDA data statistics, and employment opportunities. Also offers other agriculture-related links. This site is updated every weekday.

Farm Safety 4 Just Kids

www.fs4jk.org

This site advocates farm safety and the prevention of farm-related injuries. Here, you'll find information on membership and becoming a sponsor, chapter listings, Dr. Danger's safety tips, and a catalog of items to help teach kids about farm safety. The kids' section is graphical and fun.

FarmCredit

12345

www.farmcredit.com

Home of Farm Credit Services—a national network of providers of interactive financial solutions for the agricultural community. If you're looking for a farm loan, this site helps you locate companies that service your part of the country.

Farmland Information Center

www.farmlandinfo.org

This site is devoted to individuals interested in agriculture, and contains information about upcoming events and legislation, literature, Internet resources, farm statistics (United States, by state), and an agricultural library.

Food and Agriculture Organization of the United Nations

12345

www.fao.org

The Food and Agriculture Organization of the United Nations is dedicated to leading "international efforts to defeat hunger." This site provides a neutral area, where all countries can share knowledge, information, and expertise and openly negotiate agreements and debate policies that affect all nations. FAO also works toward ensuring the preservation of resources, such as ocean fish and fresh water that may be shared among multiple countries.

Gempler's

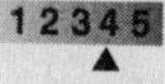

www.gemplers.com

At Gemplers.com, you can search the secure online store for thousands of hard-to-find products for agriculture, horticulture, and grounds maintenance.

GrainGenes

wheat.pw.usda.gov/GG2/index.shtml

This database, sponsored by the USDA, provides molecular and phenotypic information on wheat, barley, rye, oats, and sugarcane.

House Committee on Agriculture

12345

agriculture.house.gov

This site from the House Committee on Agriculture provides information on legislation and government policies regarding agriculture, including the schedule of upcoming hearings, current and past press releases, pending legislation, committee history, and much more.

Related Site

agriculture.senate.gov

John Deere–Agricultural Equipment

12345

www.deere.com

Offers product information on the entire John Deere farm machinery line and other Deere products. Includes lists of dealers in the United States and Canada.

Kansas City Board of Trade (Kansas City, Missouri)

12345

www.kcbt.com

Provides detailed articles about wheat and natural gas futures, historical and trading information, membership information, and links to other exchange centers. This site is also packed with futures trading charts, calendars, and quotes.

National Agricultural Library (NAL)

12345

www.nalusda.gov

Part of the USDA, this site is a resource for ag research, education, and applied agriculture. It contains a huge collection of downloadable agricultural images, as well as government documents, access to assistance from special research sites, and links to other Internet agriculture sites. In addition, its AGRICOLA database provides millions of agriculture-related citations from publications.

National Corn Growers Association (NCGA)

12345

www.ncga.com

This site contains interesting statistics on corn crops, news and headlines for corn growers, a searchable archive of past news articles, and announcements of upcoming industry trade shows.

National Pork Producers Council

12345

www.nppc.org

Includes current news, articles of interest, market summaries, and information on such topics as government regulation and swine care. The Producers link enables you to connect to discussion forums, weather reports, and information about pork markets.

Small Farm Today Magazine

12345

www.smallfarmtoday.com

Small Farm Today is dedicated to the preservation and promotion of small farming, rural living, community, and agricultural entrepreneurship. This site focuses on issues relating to small farms (179 acres or less in size, or earning $50,000 or less in gross income per year). Here, you can find articles on alternative farming, such as growing high-value crops, raising unusual livestock, and direct marketing.

Sunkist

12345

www.sunkist.com

Visit the Sunkist Growers site for historical information about citrus growing and corporate goings-on, such as job openings and the most recent annual report. You can purchase food service equipment such as juicers from the business-to-business online store. Features recipes and a Sunkist Kids area, where kids can play and learn at the same time.

Today's Market Prices

1 2 3 4 5

www.todaymarket.com

Listing of worldwide wholesale market prices on fruits and vegetables (going as far back as 1996). Product prices reported by product and location of origin; the site features an extensive searchable index. You'll also find links to university and government agriculture, horticulture, agronomy, biology, and other related departments.

USDA (United States Department of Agriculture)

1 2 3 4 5

www.usda.gov

Contains information about USDA programs, news releases, current events, and legislation dealing with the agricultural industry. Also contains employment lists and links.

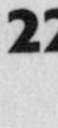

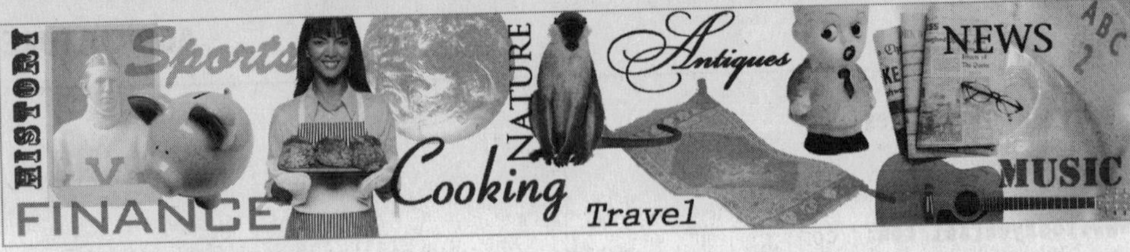

AIRLINES

Aer Lingus

1 2 3 4 5

www.aerlingus.ie

Air Canada

1 2 3 4 5

www.aircanada.ca

Alaska Airlines

1 2 3 4 5

www.alaska-air.com

Aloha Airlines

1 2 3 4 5

www.alohaairlines.com

American Airlines

1 2 3 4 5

www.aa.com

ATA

1 2 3 4 5

www.ata.com

Austrian Airlines

1 2 3 4 5

www.aua.com

British Airways

1 2 3 4 5

www.ba.com

Cathay Pacific

1 2 3 4 5

www.cathaypacific.com

China Airlines

1 2 3 4 5

www.china-airlines.com

Continental

1 2 3 4 5

www.continental.com

Delta

1 2 3 4 5

www.delta.com

Frontier

1 2 3 4 5

www.frontierairlines.com

Hawaiian Airlines

1 2 3 4 5

www.hawaiianair.com

JetBlue Airways

1 2 3 4 5

www.jetblue.com

Lufthansa

1 2 3 4 5

www.lufthansa.com

Malaysia Airlines

1 2 3 4 5

www.malaysiaairlines.com

Mexicana Airlines

1 2 3 4 5

https://www.mexicana.com

Midwest Airlines

1 2 3 4 5

www.midwestairlines.com

New England Airlines

1 2 3 4 5

users.ids.net/flybi/nea

Northwest

1 2 3 4 5

www.nwa.com

Qantas Airlines

1 2 3 4 5

www.qantas.com

Singapore Airlines

1 2 3 4 5

www.singaporeair.com

SkyWest Airlines

1 2 3 4 5

www.skywest.com

Southwest

1 2 3 4 5

www.southwest.com

Spirit Airlines

1 2 3 4 5

www.spiritair.com

Turkish Airlines

1 2 3 4 5

www.turkishairlines.com

United

1 2 3 4 5

www.united.com

US Airways

1 2 3 4 5

www.usairways.com

ALLERGIES

Allegra: Allergy Answer Site

1 2 3 4 5

www.allegra.com

Devoted to allergy sufferers everywhere, this site offers tips for relief from allergy discomfort, Allegra product information, and an allergy tip of the day. Sponsored by Sanofi-aventis.

Allergy, Asthma, and Allerpet

1 2 3 4 5

www.allerpet.com

Allerpet markets products designed to substantially reduce the level of pet-related allergens in the home. The company offers a lot of useful information covering nearly everything related to allergies. Site categories include Allergy Questions/Answers, Allergy Facts and Fiction, Allergy Supply Sources, Allerpet Products, Allerpet Literature, Allerpet vs. Washing, Allerpet Clinical Studies, Pet Related Allergy Sites, Allergy and Asthma Sites, and Allergy and Asthma Articles.

Allergy Info

1 2 3 4 5

www.allergy-info.com

Sponsored by the manufacturers of ZYRTEC, this site promises to provide helpful tips for managing indoor and outdoor allergy suffering. Learn how to manage your allergies with a combination of allergy medication, environmental changes, and other treatments. The site provides excellent general information about allergies, as well as a list of questions to ask your doctor.

The Allergy Store

1 2 3 4 5

www.foryourallergy.com

This site provides useful information on allergies, asthma, and sinus problems, as well as products for people who are allergic to pollen, pets, mold, house dust, and dust mites.

Best American Academy of Allergy, Asthma, and Immunology Online

1 2 3 4 5

www.aaaai.org

The AAAAI is the definitive medical organization for allergy, asthma, and immunology information. The academy's website allows you to search the National Allergy Bureau—the AAAAI's up-to-date count of pollen and mold spore levels broken down on a state-by-state level for the United States, refer to its Physician Referral Directory, and consult its Patient/Public Resource Center and Media Information Hub. Parents should feel comfortable sharing the Just for Kids section with their children. The content and structure of this site also makes it a great resource for physicians.

Dust Free

1 2 3 4 5

www.dustfree.com

A resource for purchasing electrostatic air filters, antimicrobial UV light systems, room air cleaners, and other allergy products.

Food Allergy & Anaphylaxis Network

12345

www.foodallergy.org

This site aims to further the understanding of food allergies, offering FAQs, updates, a searchable database, access to recipes and research reports, a daily allergy alert, and two sections devoted to kids and teens. If you're looking for timely, accurate, and complete information on food allergies, this should be your first stop.

Food Allergy Initiative

12345

www.foodallergyinitiative.org

FAI is dedicated to "a strategic, comprehensive, multi-disciplinary approach to food allergies" to "help the millions of children and adults who live in fear of eating the wrong food with every bite they take." Site features some excellent, timely information on food allergies along with links to other excellent resources.

HealingWell's Allergy Resource Center

12345

www.healingwell.com/allergies

HealingWell's Allergy Resource Center features articles, discussion forums, and other current resources on causes and treatments of allergies. Also provides a link to New Books on Allergies, enabling you to shop for publications online, and a link to additional online resources pertaining to allergies.

HowStuffWorks: Allergies

12345

health.howstuffworks.com/allergy.htm

Ever wonder why you have allergies or how your body reacts to certain allergens? Turn to HowStuffWorks for the answer. Click on the Table of Contents links for illustrated guides that take you step by step through the process of an allergic reaction, so you can see and understand what's really going on when you break out in hives or are consumed by a sneezing fit.

National Institute of Allergy and Infectious Diseases

12345

www.niaid.nih.gov/default.htm

NIAID's mission is to support research aimed at developing better ways to diagnose, treat, and prevent the many infectious, immunologic, and allergic diseases that afflict people worldwide. NIAID's site enables users to search for information about any related topic and to access information about current research activities.

Pollen

12345

www.pollen.com

Anyone who is plagued by airborne allergies will love being able to access Pollen.com's up-to-the-minute allergy forecasts for cities across the United States. Check out the pollen count for virtually any U.S. city at this site. You can also sign up to have allergy alerts emailed to you every morning.

Priorities

12345

store.priorities.com/index.html

This site offers a complete line of medically tested allergy control products, all proven effective in protecting you from allergens, asthma triggers, and airborne irritants. Includes a "How to Create an Allergen-Free Home" guide.

ALTERNATIVE MEDICINE

AlternativeDr.com

1 2 3 4 5 Blog

alternativedr.com

This site features links for Conditions and Treatments, Drug Interactions, Alternative Therapies, Herbs, Drugs, Supplements, a Practitioners' Directory, a list of Medical Terms, and alternative medicine Forums (discussion groups). You can choose to browse conditions listed alphabetically or research them by symptoms or by the affected body part. Also provides reviews of books.

Alternative Health News

1 2 3 4 5

www.altmedicine.com

Offering updated news and information about alternative medicine, this site covers a variety of approaches, counseling visitors to be cautious when reading about untried or unproven methods.

Alternative Medicine Magazine Online

1 2 3 4 5

www.alternativemedicine.com

Check out alternative health products, find alternative treatments for various conditions, catch up on the latest news about alternative therapies, find local providers through the Find a Practitioner link, or locate an alternative health clinic near you. The Buyer's Guide tab contains links to various alternative health products.

American Holistic Health Association

1 2 3 4 5

ahha.org

Dedicated to promoting holistic health (health of the mind, body, and spirit), this site features self-help articles, a searchable index of holistic health practitioners, and tips on living a healthful lifestyle.

Ayurveda Yoga Ultra-Nutrition

1 2 3 4 5

www.ayurvedaonline.com

Ayurveda means "science of life." It is a natural medicine tradition that has helped millions of people feel healthier and more alive for the past 50 centuries. Mentioned in Dr. Deepak Chopra's book *Perfect Health*, Ayurveda considers that each of us is a unique individual with a unique mind-body type. Visit this site to learn more about the Ayurvedic therapeutic health plan and to order products online.

Chi-Lel Qigong

1 2 3 4 5

www.chilel-qigong.com

Visitors can subscribe or read excerpts from the current and past issues of the *Chi-Lel QiGong News!* magazine. Other selection options include World's Largest Medicineless Hospital, Miracles of Natural Healing, Certification Program, Workshops and Retreats, Books and Tapes, Chi-Lel Methods, and more.

Best HealthWorld Online

1 2 3 4 5

www.healthy.net

HealthWorld contains links to a wide variety of healthcare topics covering everything from mainstream medicine to alternative therapies. Turn to the experts at this site for answers to your alternative medicine questions, or rely on the resource center for information. You can also participate in online discussions and sign up for the free newsletter. The opening page displays a virtual HealthWorld that makes navigating to the desired area fun and easy.

Life Matters

12345

www.lifematters.com/index.html

These pages are designed for easy access and reading with many interactive features on such topics as counseling, biofeedback, physical education, Tai Chi, and Pilates. Excellent information on managing and relieving stress.

Mayo Clinic: Complementary and Alternative Medicine

12345 RSS

www.mayoclinic.com/health/alternative-medicine/CM99999

Excellent site from the Mayo Clinic offers competent medical advice on complementary and alternative medical treatments. Here, you can read an overview to learn the basics, explore alternative and complementary treatments by disease, discover the potential benefits of massage and other manipulation and touch therapies, and get the straight story on herbs.

National Center for Complementary and Alternative Medicine

12345

nccam.nih.gov

Get information on the NCCAM, which identifies and evaluates unconventional healthcare practices. You'll find the latest information on research, training, education, and development for complementary and alternative medicine. Investigate areas such as alternative therapies, bioelectromagnetics applications, diet/nutrition/lifestyle changes, herbal medicine, manual healing methods, mind/body interventions, and pharmacological/biological treatments. Also includes a FAQ.

Natural Health and Longevity Resource Center

12345

www.all-natural.com/index.html

Provides information on alternative and holistic approaches to healing and the exposure of health hazards in modern society. You'll get information on articles, health news updates, nutrition, recommended books, and links to other health sites. Includes a guide to nutritional and herbal remedies.

Qi: The Journal of Traditional Eastern Health & Fitness

12345

www.qi-journal.com

Browse through articles on acupuncture, meditation, Qigong, Tai Chi, yoga, TCM, herbs, and health exercises or shop for herbs, books, and other alternative health products at the online store.

WholeHealthMD.com

12345

www.wholehealthmd.com

WholeHealthMD.com takes a holistic, preventive approach to healthcare by focusing on all aspects of human health. Here, you can find information on proper nutrition, nutritional supplements and vitamins, WholeHealth complementary treatments for specific conditions, expert opinions, a reference library, and the latest health news. This site offers a comprehensive list of supplements and herbs, explaining what each of them does, any interactions they might cause, and precautions.

ACUPUNCTURE

Acupuncture/Acupressure Internet Resources

12345

www.holisticmed.com/www/acupuncture.html

Huge collection of links to various acupuncture and acupressure websites.

Best Acupuncture.com

12345

www.acupuncture.com

This site features information for the practitioner, student, and patient in different areas of traditional Chinese medicine. Also provides current events and news concerning laws that affect the practice of traditional Chinese medicine. Here, you can research various Chinese medical practices, including acupuncture, Chinese herbal medicine, Qi Gong, Tui Na, dietetics, and more. Excellent sources for research and a comprehensive FAQ.

B C D E F G H I J K L M N O P Q R S T U V W X Y Z

American Academy of Medical Acupuncture

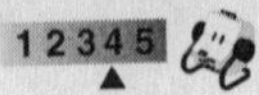

www.medicalacupuncture.org

Approaching acupuncture from a Western perspective, this site provides information on the role of acupuncture in traditional Western medicine and serves as a resource for both professionals and those who seek help from them. The site features a directory of acupuncturists, up-to-date news, and information about the academy's membership and licensure.

American College of Acupuncture & Oriental Medicine

www.acaom.edu

ACAOM's vision is to strengthen the role of acupuncture and Oriental medicine in providing complementary healthcare delivery in the United States. Using this site, you can find out how to become a trained, nationally certified health practitioner in the diagnosis and treatment of health problems based on theories and principles of acupuncture and Oriental medicine.

Blue Poppy Press

www.bluepoppy.com

Established in 1982, Blue Poppy is a publisher of books about acupuncture and Chinese medicine. Here, you can purchase books, oils, herbs, and other products; conduct research using the Free Articles section; and read a list of FAQs. By registering, you can gain access to the Practitioner's Store.

National Certification Commission for Acupuncture and Oriental Medicine

www.nccaom.org

If you want to become an acupuncture practitioner or administer Chinese medicine legally, visit this site to learn how to become certified. Here, you can learn about state regulations and requirements, certification programs, exam dates and deadlines, and other information you need to become a qualified, certified practitioner. Patients can visit this site to find a certified acupuncturist.

AROMATHERAPY

Amateur Aromatherapy

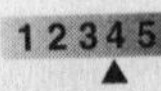

www.smellyonline.com

Click on Essential Oils to get started. The site is designed as an introduction to aromatherapy for the inexperienced. Here, you can learn the properties and uses of various oils, the chemistry behind them, and various massage techniques. The site also features dozens of recipes for therapeutic scents.

AromaWeb

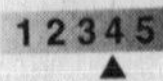

www.aromaweb.com

Read articles about aromatherapy, scan product information and suppliers online, and find aromatherapy books through this resourceful and attractive site. This site also features an excellent collection of recipes.

Canadian Association of Aromatherapists

www.cfacanada.com

The Canadian Federation of Aromatherapists "fosters continuing growth, quality and high standards of education and practice within the aromatherapy profession, and provides on-going information about quality of aromatherapy products and services to the public." Here, you can find a good article on what aromatherapy is, find CFA schools and members, and learn more about the organization and what it does.

National Association for Holistic Aromatherapy

www.naha.org

The National Association for Holistic Aromatherapy is dedicated to "enhancing public awareness of the benefits of true aromatherapy." This organization also promotes the study and attempts to raise the academic standards in aromatherapy education and practice. Here, you can learn more about the medicinal qualities of aromatherapy; search an online directory of schools, products, publications, and speakers and consultants; and read up on aromatherapy safety.

Precious Aromatherapy

12345

www.aromatherapy.com

This commercial site doesn't look like much from the opening page, but it contains an excellent primer on aromatherapy, explaining the essential oils and how to care for your oils, your olfactory response, how the oils are extracted and their various properties, and methods of application. The site also provides secure web pages where you can order oils and related products online.

Best A World of Aromatherapy

12345

www.aworldofaromatherapy.com

At this site, beginners as well as experts will find everything they need to get started with aromatherapy and master the oils and techniques that are most effective. Learn about the 10 essential oils, explore the comprehensive directory of oils, or check out which oils are most effective at treating body and mind. This site also provides aromatherapy recipes and links to shops where you can purchase books, oils, and other related items online. Packed with excellent information that's easily accessible, this site wins our Best of the Best site award for aromatherapy.

CLEANSING/DETOX

Arise & Shine Herbal Products

12345

www.ariseandshine.com

In addition to selling its own line of cleansing and detoxification products, Arise & Shine's website features a detailed library covering such topics as benefits and guidelines for colon cleansing, proper nutrition before and after detoxification, super foods and their role in cleansing, as well as topics specific to both women and men. Be sure to visit the site's Herbal Library, where you can lean about "today's most talked about and researched herbs."

Cleanse.Net

12345

www.cleanse.net

Cleanse.net is home to Dr. Richard Anderson, author of the *Cleanse and Purify Thyself* series of books. This site is packed with resources, including a detailed FAQ and free access to nearly 35 in-depth articles about cleansing and detoxing.

Energise For Life Detox and Cleanse Guide

12345

www.energiseforlife.com/detox-guide.php

This U.K. site has a tremendous amount of information on detoxing and cleansing. From recipes and detailed FAQ to products and advice on why exercise is a critical component of any successful detox, this site has it all.

HSP-Online.com

12345

www.hps-online.com

HSP-Online.com bills itself as the ultimate online resource for cleansing. Here, you will find information on cleansing theories, colon cleansing, dieting, therapeutic foods and juices, organic farming, and HSP's own line of cleaning tools and products.

WebMD.com: Detox Diets and Cleaning the Body

12345 Blog

www.webmd.com/content/article/11/1671_52826.htm

Lots of sites on the Web claim to have a detox or cleaning cure-all for what ails you, but few sites provide as much unbiased information as WebMD.com. If you're looking for detailed information on the pros and cons associated with detox and cleaning programs, visit this site, which contains a great MD-reviewed and approved article by medical writer Jeanie Lerche Davis.

A B C D E F G H I J K L M N O P Q R S T U V W X Y Z

HERBS

American Botanical Council

1 2 3 4 5 ▲

www.herbalgram.org

At this site, the American Botanical Council offers herbal news and information for herbalists as well as the general public. Here, you can sample articles from *Herbgram*, the American Botanical Council's journal, search for articles (Herbclips) on specific topics, research a wide variety of herbs (by clicking Healthy Ingredients), and much more. Site offers excellent information and a lot of it.

Digestive System

1 2 3 4 5 ▲

www.healthy.net/scr/article.asp?ID=1497

This site offers a varied and comprehensive look at alternative medicines and herbal therapies for treating and curing digestive ailments. Shop for everything here, from teas to eye drops.

Henriette's Herbal Home Page

1 2 3 4 5 ▲

www.henriettesherbal.com

Henriette has the best FAQs for medicinal herbs on the Net. This site is absolutely huge and very informative. Check out the culinary herb FAQ while you are here.

Herb Research Foundation: Herbs and Herbal Medicine for Health

1 2 3 4 5 ▲

www.herbs.org

This nonprofit foundation studies the use of herbs in health, environmental conservation, and international development. Provides frequently updated links to the latest herb-related news, features, information, and other related sites. You can also join and subscribe to the foundation's magazine.

Herb.org

1 2 3 4 5 ▲

www.herbnet.com

For anything herb-related, stop here. Read the herb magazine that is posted the first Monday of each month and learn more about the healing properties of various herbs. Comprehensive Herbalpedia has information on just about every herb you might encounter.

Herbal Encyclopedia

1 2 3 4 5 ▲

www.naturalark.com/herbenc.html

Search for information on a particular type of medicinal herb by clicking on the appropriate letter, or start by reading short articles on how to use herbs, how to collect and store them, and more. A complete herb site with an appropriate cautionary warning up front about the proper use of herbs.

Herbs First

1 2 3 4 5 ▲

www.herbsfirst.com

This site strives to educate people on the proper use of herbs. Also offers high-quality, affordable herbal health food products, books, videos, and tapes.

Related Site

pregnancytoday.com/reference/articles/herbspreg.htm

Medline Plus on Herbal Medicines

1 2 3 4 5 ▲

www.nlm.nih.gov/medlineplus/herbalmedicine.html

Before you take any medicinal herbs, you should do some research to discern between fact and fiction. Medline Plus features this site to reveal the potential risks and benefits of herbal treatments. Use the Go Local link to find herbal medicine-related services and providers in your area.

National Center for Complementary and Alternative Medicine

1 2 3 4 5

`nccam.nih.gov/health/supplements.htm`

Just how safe and effective are those herbal supplements you're taking? Check this site to find out. The NCCAM, from the National Institutes of Health, reports on the effectiveness and potential risks of alternative medicines and therapies that flow outside mainstream medicine. Here, you can get the lowdown on those "all-natural" substances you might consider taking.

PlanetHerbs

1 2 3 4 5

`www.planetherbs.com`

Dr. Michael Tierra combines the best of Eastern with Western herbalism and more. You can learn about herbal therapies here and keep updated on workshops and seminars. Purchase items from magnets to herbal compounds.

Related Sites

`nature.webshed.com`

`www.richters.com`

`world.std.com/~krahe`

Rocky Mountain Herbal Institute

1 2 3 4 5 RSS

`www.rmhiherbal.org`

A wealth of information and education on herbs based around traditional Chinese medicine.

The Whole Herb Company

1 2 3 4 5

`www.wholeherbcompany.com`

The Whole Herb Company prides itself on superior quality botanical herbs. Check out the company and its products at this site.

HOMEOPATHY

abc Homeopathy

1 2 3 4 5

`www.abchomeopathy.com`

This site consists of three basic elements—an introduction to homeopathy and homeopathics, a remedy finder, and links to online stores where you can purchase homeopathic products. Near the bottom of the opening page is a list of the most common homeopathic remedies.

Finding Professional Homeopathic Care

1 2 3 4 5

`www.homeopathic.com`

Dana Ullman, one of the leading spokespeople for homeopathy, has put together this excellent FAQ page on finding a homeopathic practitioner. Go to this site and click the Finding Care link.

Homeopathic FAQs

1 2 3 4 5

`www.elixirs.com/faq.htm`

A complete guide to homeopathic remedies. This site provides answers to FAQs about homeopathic remedies.

Homeopathy Internet Resources

1 2 3 4 5

`www.holisticmed.com/www/homeopathy.html`

A lengthy list of homeopathic links organized by the type of site they lead to. This site includes addresses for online mailing lists and discussion groups, too.

Homeopathy Online

1 2 3 4 5

`www.lyghtforce.com/HomeopathyOnline`

An international journal of homeopathic medicine for laypersons, students, and practitioners alike. Begins with a foreword and cover story, proceeds through the basic philosophy of homeopathy, provides a background on how some homeopathic treatments are discovered, and provides some case reviews.

National Center for Homeopathy (NCH)

1 2 3 4 5

www.homeopathic.org

At the NCH site, visitors can learn about membership and catch up on recent research results, as well as look at a copy of the center's media kit, which features articles about homeopathy in the news. You can also search the NCH directory for a certified homeopathic practitioner.

MAGNET THERAPY

Health and Magnets

1 2 3 4 5

www.healthandmagnets.com

This online store features a wide selection of magnet therapy products, including health magnets, car seats, insoles, jewelry, and mattresses. Also includes links to other alternative health-related sites.

Quackwatch: Magnet Therapy

1 2 3 4 5

www.quackwatch.com/04ConsumerEducation/QA/magnet.html

Skeptical about magnet therapy? Then check out this article by Stephen Barrett, M.D. Here, Dr. Barrett questions the effectiveness of magnet therapy.

MASSAGE

American Massage Therapy Association

1 2 3 4 5

www.amtamassage.org

This site gives you the opportunity to learn more about the AMTA, an association that represents more than 46,000 massage therapists in 30 countries. Includes information for consumers on how to find a qualified massage therapist, what to expect when receiving a massage, and a glossary of massage terms.

Associated Bodywork and Massage Professionals

1 2 3 4 5

www.abmp.com

ABMP has 15 years of experience serving the massage therapy profession and more than 40,000 active members. Find out about becoming a member and learn about bodywork, massage, and somatic therapies. Read the current issue of *Bodywork & Massage* magazine or browse through the archive of hundreds of articles on massage or click on the Find a Massage Therapist link at the bottom of the page.

Body Therapy Associates

1 2 3 4 5

www.gotyourback.com

Massage tables, ergonomic chairs, natural bedding products, treatment chairs, inversion systems, and more.

Bodywork and Massage Information

1 2 3 4 5

www.gems4friends.com/massage.html

Learn about the various types of massages, tips for getting the most out of a massage, and links to other massage websites. You can also register for a free newsletter.

Boulder School of Massage Therapy

1 2 3 4 5

www.bcmt.org

The Boulder School of Massage Therapy is a nationally recognized, accredited program that combines "advanced coursework in anatomy and physiology with progressive bodywork techniques allowing for a more field-focused approach to massage therapy." If you're serious about becoming a licensed massage therapist, visit this site.

Living Earth Crafts

12345

www.livingearthcrafts.com

Providing massage and spa tables and bodywork supplies for more than two decades.

Massage Magazine

12345

www.massagemag.com

Home of *Massage Magazine,* the self-proclaimed "definitive massage and touch-therapy resource for practitioners, instructors, students and consumers." Here, you can read articles from the current and past issues, find schools that teach various massage and touch therapy techniques, and find links to dozens of additional massage resources.

Massage Network

12345 

massagenetwork.com

Find a massage therapist near you through a searchable database at this site and link to other sites where you can purchase retail massage-related merchandise.

Massage Therapy

12345

www.massagetherapy.com

Excellent site for learning more about massage therapy and careers in massage therapy. If you are looking for a massage therapist near you, the search tool at this site enables you to search not only by location but also by type of massage—for example, reflexology, hydrotherapy, or healing touch.

Best Massage Therapy 101

12345

www.massagetherapy101.com

Massage Therapy 101 is "an independent information guide, written, edited and maintained by Geosign Technologies Inc., a leading publisher of online consumer information guides." This site is packed with information about massage therapy, including what it is, its benefits, various massage therapy techniques, links to massage schools, a massage FAQ, and more.

Massage Today

12345

www.massagetoday.com

This site features news stories and articles about massage and enables you to search for a massage therapist near you, learn more about the benefits of massage therapy, and even submit a question to have it answered by a qualified massage therapist. You can join discussion forums to learn even more.

Massage Warehouse

12345

www.massagewarehouse.com

Owned and operated by massage therapists, Massage Warehouse features thousands of massage supplies. Whether you're shopping for a new massage table or massage chair or looking for massage creams, oils, lotions, sheets, anatomical charts, books, tapes, or virtually anything related to massage, you've come to the right place.

Utah College of Massage Therapy

12345

www.ucmt.com

Provides training in massage therapy, acupressure, shiatsu, reflexology, rolfing, and much more.

ALZHEIMER'S

Ageless Design, Inc.

12345

www.agelessdesign.com

An education, information, and consultation service company founded to help seniors have what they really want—a home that is easy to live in and that accommodates the difficulties associated with growing older. Using the Ageless Designs site, you can learn how to modify a home to care for a loved one with Alzheimer's, and access unique ideas and products that embrace the special needs of people as they age.

Alzheimer Research Forum

12345

www.alzforum.org

The Alzheimer's Research Forum is a nonprofit organization that promotes collaboration of Alzheimer's researchers worldwide to hasten development of new ways to prevent and treat the disease. Well-known science writer June Kinoshita, a consulting editor of the journal *Science*, manages the site.

Alzheimer Society of Canada

12345 

www.alzheimer.ca

Provides information about care, research, and programs to help those affected by the disease. This site also features a creative area, where Alzheimer's patients and their friends and family members have posted short stories, poems, and artwork. Discussion forums are available to exchange information with others who are dealing with Alzheimer's disease in their lives.

Best Alzheimer's Association

12345

www.alz.org

Superb site. Attractive, well designed, and comprehensive, including FAQs, resources on medical issues relating to Alzheimer's (such as steps for proper diagnosis and current/future treatment options), updates on advances and legislation, and information about finding a local chapter. This site is designed for Alzheimer's patients, family caregivers, professional caregivers, and researchers.

Alzheimer's Disease Education and Referral Center

12345

www.nia.nih.gov/alzheimers

Sponsored by the National Institute on Aging, this site answers questions about Alzheimer's, offers research reports and publications on the disease, and responds to email queries. You will find a list of government resources and services, too.

Alzheimer's Disease International

12345 

www.alz.co.uk

Internet home of Alzheimer's Disease International provides information about the possible causes of Alzheimer's disease, ways it is diagnosed, and common treatments. It also provides a list of frequently asked questions, information for caregivers, and a directory of Alzheimer's associations around the world.

Alzheimer's Foundation of America

12345

www.alzfdn.org

The Alzheimer's Foundation of America's goal is to "provide optimal care and services to individuals confronting dementia, and to their caregivers and families, through member organizations dedicated to improving quality of life." This site provides an extensive collection of resources to help visitors understand Alzheimer's and dementia, find support, find local memory screenings, obtain information on legal and financial planning, and much more. One of the best offerings at this site is the guide for caregivers; click the Education and Care link.

Alzheimer's Watch

12345

www.go60.com/go60alzheimers.htm

Part of the Go60.com seniors site, this section offers information about Alzheimer's as well as the latest medical breakthroughs and developments and up-to-date news links.

Healthy Aging, Geriatrics, and Elderly Care

12345

www.healthandage.com

The Health and Age Foundation supports education and innovation in healthful aging, geriatrics, and the care of elderly people. This site includes a Reuters Health Information news feed that provides both healthcare professionals and patients with late-breaking health news. When you don't know where to turn for the latest information on aging and healthcare for the elderly, this is the place to start.

National Library of Medicine (NLM)

www.ncbi.nlm.nih.gov/entrez/query.fcgi

NLM's search service enables users to access the nine million citations in MedLine and Pre-MedLine (with links to participating online journals) and other related databases. By entering "Alzheimer's," you will access virtually anything published on the topic.

AMUSEMENT & THEME PARKS

Adventure City

1 2 3 4 5

www.adventurecity.com

This affordable California theme park is built especially for younger kids. The site contains information about the available rides, petting farm, shows, and so on. You can also print coupons from this site.

Amusement Park Physics

1 2 3 4 5

www.learner.org/exhibits/parkphysics

You might be surprised at how safe roller coasters and other amusement park rides really are. This site demonstrates how roller coaster designers use the laws of physics to create the illusion of danger. This site covers roller coasters, bumper cars, carousels, free-fall rides, and pendulums. You also get the opportunity to design your own ride online.

Anheuser-Busch Theme Parks

1 2 3 4 5

www.4adventure.com

Contains links to all Anheuser-Busch adventure parks across America, including Sea World, Busch Gardens, Water Country USA, Adventure Island, Discovery Cove, and Sesame Place. They're all over the country; one surely is located near you. Buy your tickets online, too!

Canobie Lake Park

1 2 3 4 5

www.canobie.com

Canobie Lake Park is a family-oriented amusement park located in Salem, New Hampshire. This site offers a detailed description of the park's rides, shows, hours, and rates. Canobie Lake Park offers more than 45 rides, including four coasters.

Cedar Point

1 2 3 4 5

www.cedarpoint.com

This 364-acre amusement park/resort located in Ohio claims to host the largest collection of rides (69) and roller coasters (15) in the world. You gotta see it to believe it. This site gives you a bird's-eye view of all the attractions along with the opportunity to buy tickets online, get information on resorts, and lots more.

Best Disney.com—The Website for Families

1 2 3 4 5

disney.go.com

Contains links to all things Disney, which by now is more than just a cute little mouse. Includes information about its theme parks as well as movies, the TV channel, videos, books, its cruise line, and much more. This site also features a games area where kids can play online video games and a music area for playing audio clips. If you have a credit card, you can even shop online for Disney trinkets and apparel. If you're looking for the best theme parks in the world and are leaning toward taking your family on a Disney adventure, introduce your entire family to this site. You can plan your trip and figure out the best places to go, and your kids can find plenty to keep them busily entertained.

Great Escape and Splashwater Kingdom

1 2 3 4 5

www.sixflags.com/greatescape

This Lake George, New York, theme park contains more than 125 rides, shows, and attractions. For roller coaster enthusiasts, the site boasts of the Comet, which was rated the best wooden coaster by readers of *Inside Track* magazine.

A B C D E F G H I J K L M N O P Q R S T U V W X Y Z

Hershey Park

12345

www.hersheypa.com/attractions/hersheypark

Celebrating its 100th anniversary in 2007, Hershey Park has more than 60 rides, including 9 roller coasters, 7 water rides, and 20 kiddie rides, plus professional shows, concerts, talent shows, and other entertainment. Here, you can find information about the park and its features, along with driving directions, merchandise, and information about food and lodging, and admission prices.

LEGOLAND California

12345

www.legoland.com/california.htm

LEGOLAND California is LEGO's 128-acre theme park located in Carlsbad, a seaside community 30 miles north of San Diego and one hour south of Anaheim. Visit the site to get a park tour, plan your visit, learn about upcoming special events, find out what's new, and link to other LEGO parks or to LEGO's toy site.

Paramount's Great America

12345

www.pgathrills.com

This official site provides a virtual tour of this Santa Clara, California, theme park and its attractions. Also contains employment and season ticket information and a section about what's new.

Paramount's Kings Island

12345

www.pki.com

Visit the amusement park choice of the Brady Bunch! (Remember the infamous tube mix-up?) Take an online tour of the Mason, Ohio park and discover the latest live stage shows and more.

Sea World

12345

www.seaworld.com

Get park information for one of several Sea World locations, order tickets online, and investigate new attractions.

Six Flags Theme Parks

12345

www.sixflags.com

The largest regional theme park company in the world, with 30 parks in the United States, one in Mexico, and nine in Europe. According to the site, "85% of all Americans live within just a day's drive from a Six Flags Theme Park." Click Pick a Park and then click any of the dots on the globe to view detailed information about that particular Six Flags park or property.

Theme Park Review

12345

www.themeparkreview.com

Contains a photo gallery, video clips, and trip reports from some of the world's best theme parks and roller coasters. You can order full-length videos of Robb Alvey's latest coaster season.

Universal Studios

12345

themeparks.universalstudios.com

Click the link for one of four Universal Studio Theme Parks: Orlando, Hollywood, or Japan. Check out park hours and new rides and attractions, buy merchandise, and order tickets online. This site also features a game area, where kids can play video games online.

Walt Disney World

1 2 3 4 5

disneyworld.disney.go.com

Everything you need to plan your magical Walt Disney World Resort vacation is right here. Point to Parks to review a list of Disney Theme Parks and then click the park you want to tour. Use the navigation bar to find what you want. Order admission tickets online, check out FAQs and special events, review resort and spa options, and lots, lots more!

Related Sites

- www.adventurelanding.com
- www.napavalley.com/napavalley/outdoor/marinewo/marinewo.html
- www.holidayworld.com
- www.knotts.com
- www.kingsdominion.com
- www.santasvillage.com

A B C D E F G H I J K L M N O P Q R S T U V W X Y Z

ANATOMY

Gray's Anatomy of the Human Body

1 2 3 4 5 ▲

www.bartleby.com/107

Presented by Bartleby.com, this site contains nearly 1,250 engravings from the 1918 book, complete with a subject index that has over 13,000 entries. Use the site's handy search feature to exactly what you're looking for or scroll down the front page to access an outline of illustrations.

Human Anatomy at EnchantedLearning.com

1 2 3 4 5 ▲

www.enchantedlearning.com/subjects/anatomy

This site, offered by Enchanted Learning—which produces children's-oriented websites designed to capture the imagination while maximizing creativity, learning, and enjoyment—provides a children and school teachers alike with the basis for understanding and teaching human anatomy. Great for home schoolers because of the free printouts, Human Anatomy at EnchantedLearning.com offers classroom exercises and an easy to access site index.

Human Anatomy Online

1 2 3 4 5 ▲

www.innerbody.com

This site features an interactive breakdown of almost every body part imaginable. Want to know more about the inner workings of the digestive, nervous, or skeletal systems? It's as easy as clicking on the proper icon, followed by mousing over the appropriate body parts on the ensuing page. Great site for anyone studying or interested in human anatomy.

Instant Anatomy

1 2 3 4 5 ▲

www.instantanatomy.net

Based on Robert Whitaker and Neil Borley's book by the same title, this site contains a number of compelling features, including a detailed site map that provides easy access to all the body parts, podcasts linked to specific sections of the site's content, and a nice questions and answers section to help learners brush up on their anatomy.

Best WebAnatomy

1 2 3 4 5 ▲

www.msjensen.gen.umn.edu/webanatomy

If you need to practice for an upcoming anatomy or physiology test or if you're just the type of person who enjoys a fun anatomy-related challenge, this site's for you. Click on Race Against the Clock for an interactively timed test complete with audio cheers and jeers. Or test your own knowledge in the multiple-choice Self Test section. There's even a multiplayer section where you can test your knowledge against your friends in a Jeopardy-style Flash-enabled game show. Truly a one-of-a-kind site that's worthy of this section's Best designation.

ANIMATION

American Royal Arts

1 2 3 4 5

www.ara-animation.com/misc.htm

Billed as the "leading publisher of Animation and Entertainment Fine Art," American Royal Arts features an enormous collection of still shots and animations. Search by artist, animated series, or company (Warner Bros., Disney, and so on). Or just flip through the many tabbed pages: Cartoon Network, Peanuts, Talking Art, Fine Art & Photography, Vintage, and so on. You can purchase images and learn about licensing at this site.

Animation Library

1 2 3 4 5 

www.animationlibrary.com

Collection of more than 13,000 animated clips you can download for use on your web pages, organized by category to make them easy to find.

Animation World Network

1 2 3 4 5 RSS

www.awn.com

Anyone interested in animation should check out this site! It includes links to *Animation World Magazine*; a career connection; and an animation village, gallery, and vault. Links to all kinds of animation-related products.

Chuck Jones Website

1 2 3 4 5

www.chuckjones.com

Check out the official site of the late Chuck Jones, the famous Warner Brothers/Loony Tunes animator and animation director. At this site, you can read about Mr. Jones and his many famous cartoon characters. This is an exceptionally well-constructed site, both visually and content-wise.

Best Computer Graphics World

1 2 3 4 5

cgw.pennnet.com/home.cfm

Home of *Computer Graphics World* magazine, a good source for industry news and product information. Don't miss the Gallery (accessible from the home page navigation bar).

International Animated Film Society

www.asifa-hollywood.org

ASIFA is a "membership organization devoted to the encouragement and dissemination of film animation as an art and communication form." It has more than 1,700 members in more than 50 countries, providing links to various chapters and events around the world. Here, you can find announcements for screenings, festivals, and other events, as well as information about the organization.

B C D E F G H I J K L M N O P Q R S T U V W X Y Z

ANIME

Anime 100

12345

www.anime100.com

Anime 100 presents the top 100 anime websites as voted on by users.

Animé Café

12345

www.abcb.com

The Animé Café might not be much to look at—especially when compared to other anime websites—but it sure does pack a punch, even if it hasn't been updated since 2004. Parents should use this site to learn more about different types of anime and what is and is not appropriate for children. There's also an anime encyclopedia and a deep list of reviews.

Anime News Network

12345

www.animenewsnetwork.com

The Anime News Network presents news and information related to Japanese animation (anime) and Japanese comics (manga). The site is updated on a daily basis with news stories from the anime industry and features editorials, columns, reviews, and news releases from all the major players in the industry.

Best Anime

12345

www.bestanime.com

Search this site for the best in anime by title, director, genre, year, production, or certification. Site covers 1,400 anime titles and includes 120,000 images, 3,500 movie clips, 9,000 songs, and lots of information.

theOtaku.com

12345 Blog RSS

www.theotaku.com

theOtaku.com bills itself as the most comprehensive "one-stop Japanese anime resource online." Run entirely by fans of the anime genre, this site features thousands of anime characters, hundreds of articles, and lots of downloadable files.

Best VIZ Media

12345

www.viz.com

Viz is a major player in the world of anime. They publish books and magazines and distribute anime all over the world. Use this site to learn about the company's releases, order products, and download trailers of upcoming shows.

ANTIQUES

Antiqnet.com

12345

www.antiqnet.com

This site's simple design makes it easy to navigate this company's extensive collection of fine antiques. Here, you can find antique advertisements, architecture, books, clocks, furniture, glass, jewelry, pottery, silverware, textiles, watches, and much more. If you have a specific item in mind, use the Search box to track it down. Crystal-clear graphics make it easy to see just what you're getting.

The Antiques and Collectibles Guide

12345

www.acguide.com

The Antiques and Collectibles Guide offers a searchable index of more than 3,000 quality antique and collectible dealers in the United States and other countries. Search by state or country.

The Antiques Council

12345

www.antiquescouncil.com

The Antiques Council is an association of professional antique dealers, formed to educate the public about antiques, promote high standards, and provide show management services for charities. Use this site to locate council members by name and area of specialty.

Best Antiques Roadshow

12345

www.pbs.org/wgbh/pages/roadshow

Even if you're an inexperienced antiquer, PBS's *Antiques Roadshow* is a great show and website to visit to learn from the experts. The show comes to cities around the country to meet with the locals and appraise their items. The show's experts not only spot the real antiques but also make a point to appraise fake items so that you, the viewer, learn what to look for in your antiquing jaunts. Check out the appraisal contest. You can buy books and videos about antiques through the online store.

Artnet.com

12345

www.artnet.com

Artnet has an extensive listing of art galleries and artists, in addition to offering online auctions of fine artwork. This site also offers research tools and *Artnet* magazine information.

Early American History Auctions, Inc.

12345

www.earlyamerican.com

The online site for the EAHA specializes in antique Americana, such as maps, Civil War memorabilia, newspapers, coins, and so on. Check out the price list of current items and submit a bid, either by email, fax, or snail mail. You can submit payments online using PayPal.

Eureka, I Found It!

12345

www.eureka-i-found-it.com

This site offers unusual items for sale, such as signed vintage costume jewelry, toy sewing machines, toy steam engines, and vintage fans. You can submit payments online using PayPal.

Finer Times

12345

www.finertimes.com

Finer Times features an incredible selection of vintage timepieces—more than 400 personally selected wrist and pocket watches, as well as accessories that can enhance your collection. Discussion boards helps you get in touch with others who collect vintage timepieces.

GoAntiques

12345

www.goantiques.com

GoAntiques offers an impressive collection of antiques from more than 1,800 dealers in 29 different countries. Collection includes antiques, collectibles, estate merchandise, and antique reproductions. You can browse the aisles by category or search for specific products, shop online, or bid at live auctions.

ICollector.com

www.icollector.com

Bid on items from more than 350 auction houses and dealers worldwide or search auction house catalogs for upcoming sales around the world. Search a selection of archived catalogs from auction house sales since 1994 and find out about dealers and galleries, related associations, and publications. Go to the Community section to meet other collectors, participate in live chats with industry experts and celebrities, or check out the selection of exhibitions.

Maine Antique Digest

12345

www.maineantiquedigest.com

The web supplement to the print publication, this site offers articles, up-to-date news, a dealer directory, price database, directory of appraisers, and antique discussion forum. Auction and show ads on the site will alert you to upcoming events.

Newel

12345

www.newel.com

Search the entire inventory of Newel antiques or study along with the tutorial to get started. Click on the Glossary link if you're new to antiquing and learn how to talk like a pro.

Tias

12345

www.tias.com

Tias is an online mall where collectors can advertise their shops. Think of it as a directory of online antique dealers.

ARCHITECTURE

The American Institute of Architects

1 2 3 4 5 Blog

www.aia.org

The collective voice of America's architects, this organization has advanced the profession since 1857. The website serves 58,000 members and provides information on their mission statement, history, events, chapter offices, and member services. The information for consumers includes help in finding a local architectural firm for a particular project.

Arch Inform

1 2 3 4 5

www.archinform.net

An international architectural database consisting of 11,000 plus projects, some built and some unrealized.

Best Architectural Record

1 2 3 4 5 RSS

archrecord.construction.com

Architectural Record provides "a compelling editorial mix of design ideas and trends, building science, business and professional strategies, exploration of key issues, news products, and computer-aided practice" for architects and builders. Site features a navigation bar that provides quick access to News, Features, Projects, Products, People & Firms, Opinion, and Resources. Excellent information with excellent graphics to match.

Architects USA

1 2 3 4 5

www.architectsusa.com

A directory listing more than 20,000 architectural firms in the United States.

Architecture.com

1 2 3 4 5

www.architecture.com

Internet home of the Royal Institute of British Architects (RIBA), this site is dedicated to further the cause of architecture in Britain and internationally. Here, you will find abundant resources relating to architecture, including articles, reference libraries, links to great buildings, information on what an architect does and how to become an architect, a searchable directory of architects, and links to architectural museums. Architects and students can also learn how to submit an entry for the RIBA Award. Excellent site and easy to navigate.

Architecture Magazine

1 2 3 4 5 RSS

www.architecturemag.com

Review back issues of this monthly magazine for the architecture industry, subscribe to the magazine, enroll for online courses, search for building services, or read one of several current articles on design and culture issues.

Association of Collegiate Schools of Architecture

1 2 3 4 5

www.acsa-arch.org

Prospective architectural students will want to visit this site to learn about architecture programs and the application process and to obtain information about and deadlines for upcoming design competitions.

Design Basics Home Online Planbook

1 2 3 4 5

www.designbasics.com

Design Basics, Inc. provides single-family home plans with available technical support and custom design options. Build your dream home with plans that are also marketed through catalogs, newsstand magazines, and home building industry trade publications. Decorative home accessories are available in the Web Store, making this a one-stop, comprehensive site for people seeking to build and decorate their own homes.

First Source Exchange

1 2 3 4 5 ▲

www.cmdfirstsource.com

A comprehensive architectural site designed to help architects develop accurate construction documents, including plans and estimates. First Source Exchange provides a collection of tools and resources to deliver essential product information, early-planning project leads, reliable cost data, an online library of state and local building codes, and industry news from respected industry sources.

GreatBuildings.com

1 2 3 4 5 ▲

www.greatbuildings.com

This site presents pictures and background information concerning nearly 1,000 of the world's greatest buildings. GreatBuildings.com also features biographies of hundreds of famous architects and a searchable, browsable index of architectural wonders from all around the world. Browse the collection of 3D models, research various architectural styles, and even download free CAD software. This is an excellent site for architecture students, teachers, and interested members of the general public.

Metropolis Magazine

1 2 3 4 5 ▲

www.metropolismag.com

A look at architectural, furniture, clothing, and other design disciplines in a changing world. Check out events and exhibitions, read articles, and subscribe. Also features a great collection of photos showcasing some cool home and office furniture and accessories.

The Pritzker Architecture Prize

1 2 3 4 5 ▲

www.pritzkerprize.com

The Pritzker Architecture Prize, sponsored by the Hyatt Foundation, is the world's most prestigious architecture award. Learn about its laureates and about its international traveling exhibition, "The Art of Architecture."

ART (SEE ALSO MUSEUMS–ART)

Absolutearts.com

12345 Blog RSS

blog.absolutearts.com

Absolutearts.com is a blog that where you can find criticism and discussions related to contemporary art and philosophy.

Artcyclopedia

12345

www.artcyclopedia.com

Artcyclopedia is an online encyclopedia of art that features a list of the Top 30 Artists (as determined by the frequency their names are searched on the Web), articles, art news, links to art museum websites, an art glossary, and more.

Art History Resources on the Web

12345

witcombe.sbc.edu/ARTHLinks.html

Find out all you need to know about prehistoric, ancient, middle ages, baroque, renaissance, eighteenth-, nineteenth-, and twentieth-century art at this site, which also features information on museums and galleries and links to other art history sites. A well-designed site for anyone researching art history.

Art on the Net

12345

www.art.net

Art on the Net is "a collective of artists helping each other to come up on the Internet and share their works on the World Wide Web. Artists create and maintain studios and rooms in the gallery where they show their works and share about themselves." You can sample the work of more than 450 artists from around the world, including poets, musicians, painters, sculptors, digital artists, performance artists, and animators. If you're an artist, you can use this site to showcase your work. Site also features links to other worthwhile art sites.

INSTRUCTION/ REFERENCE

Academy of Art University

12345

www.academyart.edu

Based in San Francisco, California, the Academy of Art University offers instruction, certification, and degrees in advertising, animation, computer arts, fine art, fashion, graphic design, illustration, industrial design, and more. With nearly 8,000 students, this school is one of the largest private art and design schools in the United States. Use this site to learn more about admission requirements, online class offerings, and campus news.

Artista Creative Safaris for Women

12345

www.artistacreative.com

Artista believes that women were born to paint, and when you choose to participate in one of their stress-free courses, called Safaris, you learn how. Visit this site for information about three- and five-night safaris, accommodations, rates, and classes.

Creative Spotlite

12345

www.creativespotlite.com

This site bills itself as an "online resource for free art and craft lessons and instruction, discount art supplies, instructional art books, videos and more." Use this site to learn more about oil painting and drawing and sketching, to purchase art instruction aids such as books and DVDs, and to connect with other artists through the site's online forums.

Developing Art Skills

12345

www.artgraphica.net

Click on the Free Art Lessons link and walk yourself through tutorials on how to draw like the pros. This site also features an online shop where you can purchase CDs that provide detailed and step-by-step instructions on drawing and sketching.

GRAPHIC DESIGN

Best American Institute of Graphic Arts (AIGA)

12345

www.aiga.org

AIGA is a professional membership association for graphic designers. With chapters in nearly every state, AIGA offers its members and the public access to a wealth of resources, including an online forum, publications, conferences, and job listings. If you're looking for a graphic designer, click on the Need a Designer link, and be sure click on the Gallery link for information on the organization's latest exhibitions.

Freelance Designers Directory

12345

graphicdesign.freelancedesigners.com

If you're looking for a freelance graphic designer, this site is for you. Here, you'll find a state-by-state list of graphic designers who are ready, willing, and able to help with your next project, as well as articles and resources geared toward hiring the right person for the job.

Graphic Artists Guild

12345

www.gag.org

The Graphic Artists Guild (GAG) represents illustrators, designers, and other artist types who are interested in furthering their graphic art-related skills while improving "the ability of visual creators to achieve satisfying and rewarding careers." GAG publishes the *Graphic Artists Guild Handbook: Pricing & Ethical Guidelines*, which most graphic artists use as a guide in setting their prices and contractual terms. Visit this site to learn more about the guild or graphic design as a career.

How Magazine's HowDesign.com

12345

www.howdesign.com

This website is the graphic design industry's "trusted source for creative inspiration, business advice, and tools of the trade." Designed with the graphic artist in mind, it is visually appealing and offers a wide range of content, including feature articles and information on design conferences and competitions. There's even an online forum for connecting with other graphic artists, a job bank, and a store where you can subscribe to the magazine.

ASTROLOGY

Astrology Online

12345

www.astrology-online.com

Astrology Online provides an in-depth look at astrology, covering everything from your daily horoscope to basic concepts that you need to understand to effectively read the cosmos. You can order custom horoscopes and birth charts online.

Astrology on the Web

12345

www.astrologycom.com

Astrology on the Web is the result of a collaboration of some of the top astrologists. Here, you can find your daily horoscope and check your love compatibility with other signs, read about the sign of the month, obtain an annual forecast, and sample an excellent collection of feature articles.

> **Tip:** In the center of the page is a Click to Find It Quick! menu that presents a complete site index; click the menu, and then click the desired topic area.

Best MSN Astrology

12345

astrocenter.astrology.msn.com/msn

MSN Astrology is packed with horoscopes, love advice, automated Tarot readings and numerology forecasts, charts and reports, and much more. By entering your name and birthday, you can configure this site to automatically display your horoscope for today, this week, and this month. Your horoscope offers information on your career, family, and health. Site also features a cool Tarot reading; you simply enter your name and click three cards to obtain your reading. Here, you can also get numerology readings and check your sign on the Chinese calendar.

Yahoo! Astrology

12345

astrology.yahoo.com/astrology

Excellent site for pop astrology features three tabs: Home, Astrology, and Chinese Astrology. The Home page presents a Daily Cosmic Calendar that gives you an overview of the movements of the planets and their influence along with zodiac symbols you click to obtain your horoscope for the day and a menu of Chinese animals from which you can select to obtain your Chinese horoscope. The Astrology and Chinese Astrology pages enable you to focus on your preferred approach.

ASTRONOMY

Adler Planetarium and Astronomy Museum

1 2 3 4 5

www.adlerplanetarium.org

Located in Chicago, on the shores of Lake Michigan, the Adler Planetarium and Astronomy Museum is one of the premier astronomy museums in the United States. Here, you can find the latest astronomy news and information, a skywatcher's guide, ideas for family fun, a visitor's guide, and much more. You can even shop the museum store online.

Amazing Space

1 2 3 4 5

amazing-space.stsci.edu

Designed for classroom use, Amazing Space provides a collection of interactive web-based activities to teach students various topics, such as understanding light and how black holes function. Some cool features, such as Planet Impact, where you can smash a comet into the planet Jupiter, make this site well worth a visit.

American Astronomical Society

www.aas.org

Provides general astronomy information of interest to professionals and amateur enthusiasts, including job listings and information on grants and prizes. Maintains links to other astronomy resources on the Net.

Astronomy for Kids

1 2 3 4 5

www.dustbunny.com/afk

Astronomy for Kids is designed for kids and supervised by adults to foster and feed kids' enthusiasm for our solar system and the rest of the universe. Kids can learn about planets and constellations, view current sky maps to learn what to watch for each month, pick up the basics of beginning-level astronomy, and even send their friends electronic postcards of astronomical photos.

Astronomy Magazine

1 2 3 4 5

www.astronomy.com

This site contains an almanac of current sky happenings, a calendar of star parties, directories of planetariums and clubs, a well-stocked photo library, as well as product reviews on telescopes and binoculars. Well designed, this site is a pleasure to explore. Although not much at this site is designed specifically to appeal to kids, amateur astronomers will find many of the articles fascinating and comprehensible.

Astronomy Now On-Line

1 2 3 4 5

www.astronomynow.com

Check out late-breaking stories about the most significant astronomical events and space missions. The News area is the site's main feature, providing current stories on astronomical events and space exploration. You can click the Store link to shop for calendars, books, T-shirts, patches, and other items.

Astronomy Picture of the Day

1 2 3 4 5

antwrp.gsfc.nasa.gov/apod/astropix.html

An up-to-date picture of a particular celestial body or scene, complete with a brief description of the photo or explanation of the phenomenon it represents. You can also search through the archive for past pictures of the day by clicking the Calendar, Search, or Index link.

Bad Astronomy

www.badastronomy.com

The advice not to believe everything you hear or read applies to the sciences as well, including astronomy. Here, you can read about common misconceptions and claims about space and find out the truth. For example, few people realize that there is no "dark side of the moon."

Chandra X-Ray Observatory

chandra.harvard.edu

This is the home of NASA's Chandra X-Ray Observatory, where you can learn everything from the basics of x-ray astronomy to the intricacies of how Chandra functions. View digital images of Chandra's discoveries, learn about galactic navigation, track Chandra's progress, submit a question to one of NASA's experts, and play interactive games online.

Constellation X

constellation.gsfc.nasa.gov

This site offers information on studies of black holes and the life cycles of matter throughout the universe using a network of powerful x-ray telescopes. A cool welcome screen, excellent graphics and video clips, and clear descriptions of various astronomical phenomena combine to make this one of the most intriguing astronomy sites in the group.

Earth & Sky

Blog RSS

www.earthsky.com

Internet home of the popular *Earth & Sky* radio program, a science program created by Deborah Byrd and Joel Block for kids. Each program is one and a half minutes long and provides a brief explanation of a particular science topic. Here, you can replay the radio shows and/or read along with the scripts. Teachers can visit this site to obtain lesson plans and other resources, and anyone can shop online for calendars, books, and software. Kids should check out the Activities area for games and quizzes.

The Event Inventor: Web Sites for Space Mission Projects

kyes-world.com/spacesites.htm

Consider this site a launch pad for online space exploration. This site provides several links to interesting astronomy and space travel sites around the Web, especially sites that appeal to younger space enthusiasts.

Griffith Observatory

www.griffithobs.org

Griffith Observatory is located in Los Angeles, California. This site offers useful information along with an informal but comprehensive listing of excellent astronomy sites; click the Star Awards button to view a list of Star Award recipients on the Web, and the Sky Information link for lots of great information about the phases of the moon and more.

High Energy Astrophysics Science Archive Research Center

heasarc.gsfc.nasa.gov/docs/HEASARC_HOME_PAGE.html

Contains general information on supernovae, x-ray binaries, and black holes. This site is definitely for the more advanced astronomers and scientists.

Best HubbleSite

www.hubblesite.org

This is the home of NASA's Hubble telescope, where you can explore the heavens through the incredible photos that Hubble has sent back to Earth. View digital images of Hubble's discoveries, read expert analysis of those discoveries, learn about the technology that powers the Hubble telescope and its digital imaging and transmission capabilities, play games, check out the reference desk, and explore Hubble's future. Site is easy to navigate, packed with great information and dazzling graphics, and even includes a Fun & Games section for kids and teenagers, making this our universal pick for Best of the Best in Astronomy!

International Astronomical Union

www.iau.org

Contains access to current and past bulletins and reports posted by association members. Information is also available on grants, union meetings, and more.

Lunar and Planetary Sciences at NSSDC

nssdc.gsfc.nasa.gov/planetary

NSSDC provides online information about NASA and non-NASA data and information about spacecraft and experiments that generate NASA space science data. Here, you can find details about specific space exploration missions plus links to planetary events and other astronomy sites. Excellent site for researching the various planetary bodies in our solar system.

Mount Wilson Observatory

www.mtwilson.edu

Located in the San Gabriel Mountains of Southern California, the Mount Wilson Observatory features a historic 100-inch telescope and a small astronomical museum. This site overviews several ongoing astronomy projects using innovative techniques and modern detectors and provides information for professionals, amateurs, tourists, and educators alike.

NASA Earth Observatory

earthobservatory.nasa.gov

This public access site is designed to provide visitors with current satellite images and information about Earth—mainly its environment and how environmental changes are affecting the landscape. The Breaking News section is especially relevant and up-to-date.

NASA History Office

www.hq.nasa.gov/office/pao/History/index.html

The NASA History Program was launched one year after NASA itself was formed, in 1959, and to this day continues to "document and preserve the agency's remarkable history through a variety of products," including this site. Visit this site to trace documents related to U.S. space exploration, and be sure to check out the Topical Index, which covers everything from human spacecraft to space policy.

NASA Human Space Flight

spaceflight.nasa.gov/home/index.html

Study the history of NASA's space missions from Mercury to the present, get real-time data on sighting opportunities, track the orbit of NASA spacecraft, obtain detailed information about the space station and space shuttle programs, check out NASA's photo gallery, and much more.

NASAKIDS

kids.msfc.nasa.gov

This site from NASA is designed specifically to appeal to kids. Here, children can view NASA cartoons, learn about rockets and airplanes, explore the Milky Way and other celestial frontiers, tour the astronaut's living space, play games and animations, and much more. For kids who are interested in space, there's no better site on the Web.

National Geographic Star Journey

www.nationalgeographic.com/stars

View the nighttime sky using the online sky chart, complete with images from the Hubble telescope. You can also set your own course to investigate the heavens. Although you cannot shop directly at this site, it displays a link to *National Geographic*'s online store. Older children who are interested in astronomy will find some of the information here interesting and clearly presented.

SEDS Internet Space Warehouse

1 2 3 4 5 ▲ (4)

www.seds.org

The home of Students for the Exploration and Development of Space (SEDS), this site is dedicated to building enthusiasm for space exploration in younger generations. Contains many links to space resources on the Internet, a few multimedia documents, and information about the organization. It's a good place to share enthusiasm for model rocketry, too.

Sky and Telescope

1 2 3 4 5 ▲ (5)

www.skypub.com

This site offers information from current and back issues of *Sky and Telescope* magazine and links to information that can help you set up your own observatory, including news reports about up and coming astronomical events and information on how to take pictures through your telescope.

Star Stuff: A Guide to the Night Sky

1 2 3 4 5 ▲ (3)

www.starstuff.com

"For astronomy students of all ages," Star Stuff is an excellent resource for learning about the universe and solar system, complete with images located in the Planets for Kids section.

Views of the Solar System

1 2 3 4 5 ▲ (4)

www.solarviews.com/eng/homepage.htm

Features a vivid tour of the solar system, and includes images and information about the sun, planets, moons, asteroids, comets, and meteoroids. You can purchase books and equipment with which to view the planets here.

AUCTIONS

Amazon Auctions

12345

auctions.amazon.com

Visit Amazon's auction area, where you can scout for deals on everything from antiques to jewelry to clothing, and even automotive parts and accessories. For those users looking to simplify their life, Amazon Auctions also accepts items for sale. For an additional fee, Amazon will cross-sell your item on the Amazon website, which puts your products in front of millions of potential buyers.

Andalé

12345

www.andale.com

This auction management site is designed for auction sellers who want to save time and money in listing their products and services at online auction sites. In other words, Andalé acts as a middleman between auctioneers and online auctions, such as eBay, Amazon, and Yahoo! Auctions.

AuctionAddict.com

12345

www.auctionaddict.net

AuctionAddict.com is designed as a meeting place for buyers and sellers. Sellers can put individual items up for sale, create their own storefronts and market items at a fixed price, or designate them for an online auction where prospective buyers can bid.

eBay

www.ebay.com

It's the world's largest online trading community. Bid on millions of items from books, to computer products, to antiques, and everything else in between. Join millions of registered users who frequent this site, and test your expertise at finding the best deals on the Internet. By some counts, eBay is the busiest site on the Internet, possibly the largest free market in the world. Because of its incredible popularity and its ease of use, this is truly the Best of the Best.

InetAuction

12345

www.softglobe.com

Auctioneers and auction managers should check out this site. For a 3 percent cut of the proceeds, you can use InetAuction software to host a traditional auction online. This site allows you to interact with bidders just as you would at a live auction.

Internet Auction List

12345

www.internetauctionlist.com

Click a category (art, military memorabilia, horses and livestock, and many more) and choose from dozens of online auctions. Go to the calendar and see which auctions are being held on a particular date. Check for links to other auction sites or subscribe to the free newsletter. This is the most complete list of auctions available on the Web.

MastroNet, Inc.

12345

www.mastronet.com

This site specializes in niche auctions—one-of-a-kind collectibles, such as the football that Emmitt Smith carried when he surpassed Walter Payton as the all-time leading rusher in NFL history. This auction site deals mostly in sports collectibles, but you can find other rare items here, too.

A B C D E F G H I J K L M N O P Q R S T U V W X Y Z

Overstock.com Auctions

12345

auctions.overstock.com

Overstock.com Auctions is a branch of the Overstock.com website. This site combines the Internet auction model with personal networks to offer visitors a robust auction experience. Anything you could possibly want, including collectibles, jewelry and watches, cameras, real estate, and sporting goods can be found on this site.

Priceline.com

12345

www.priceline.com

Name your price for airline tickets, hotel rooms, cars, and cruises on this site. Priceline then approaches potential sellers who might be willing to fulfill your request. Many users have reported saving hundreds of dollars on plane tickets using this site.

Sotheby's

12345

www.sothebys.com

This, as you might expect, is a classy web page. Read about upcoming auctions or results of recent auctions, browse or order catalogs, or browse the categories of collections currently being auctioned. Sotheby's online auction is managed by eBay.

uBid

12345

www.ubid.com

A huge auction site featuring many products. The opening page displays thumbnail photos of products, and the navigation bar on the left side of the page makes it easy to browse available items by category. uBid now allows you to sell your own items on the site, making it even more useful for everyone.

U.S. Department of Treasury Auctions

12345

www.ustreas.gov/auctions

The United States government acquires a lot of stuff through criminal seizures, repossessed homes, lost mail items, and other government activities and inactivity. Using this site, you can find out how to bid on those items and where the government holds its various auctions.

Vendio Productions

12345

www.vendio.com

If you're looking to sell products on the Web, either through fixed pricing or auctions, Vendio can help you set up an automated system for promoting, selling, and distributing your products online.

Yahoo! Auctions

12345 RSS

auctions.yahoo.com

Yahoo! has a fairly decent auction site, where you can sell or bid on items in dozens of categories ranging from Art to Automobiles to Video Games. You can easily navigate the site and find items you want to bid on.

AUTO RACING

Andretti Home Page

12345

www.andretti.com

View photos of the drivers in action and read personal profiles of Mario, Michael, Jeff, John, and Marco. If you enjoy that, join the fan club or purchase gear worn by the drivers in IRL races!

Best Auto Racing Daily

12345 Blog RSS

www.autoracingdaily.com

A comprehensive auto-racing site designed primarily for fans who like to follow all racing events around the world, including NASCAR, Formula One, Indy Racing League, stock cars, Champ Cars, and motorcycles. This site gathers the latest news and information from other sources, so you can obtain all your racing news from a single location. The site also features some active message boards.

CATCHFENCE.com

12345

www.catchfence.com

From headline racing news to race information and explanations, this site is a one-stop racing library. Also includes chat rooms and a message board, so you can share your racing enthusiasm with fellow fans.

Honda Racing

12345

www.hondaracing.com

Find out what's going on this week at the track and enjoy racing images here, where you can also learn more about drivers and their cars, current standings, and all the latest racing news.

Motorsports Hall of Fame

12345

www.mshf.com

Dedicated to preserving the legacy of the "Heroes of Horsepower," the Motorsports Hall of Fame of America houses more than 40 racing and high-performance vehicles, including various types of cars, trucks, boats, motorcycles, air racers, and even racing snowmobiles. Click the Museum link to explore a small selection of the museum's offerings. Check out the list of Hall of Fame Inductees to read biographies of your favorite drivers.

NHRA Online

www.nhra.com

Follow the progress of your favorite racers in the National Hot Rod Association, or get up-to-date news and information on upcoming races.

Racecar

12345

www.racecar.co.uk

Racecar creates websites for a number of companies in the specialty auto field. This site features stories from around the world related to various car races and racing leagues, including F1 and Le Mans.

CHAMP CARS

Champcar World Series

www.champcarworldseries.com

Formerly run by CART, the Champcar World Series is an open-wheel racing series. At this comprehensive site, visitors can find out just about anything about racing teams, drivers, past and future events, and results. An online gallery, discussion forums, and a shopping area round out the site.

Newman/Hass Racing

www.newman-haas.com

Home of the Newman/Hass Champ Car racing team, this site features interactive overviews of all the tracks they race on, along with news and information about the team's drivers and sponsors.

FORMULA ONE

Atlas F1

12345 RSS

www.atlasf1.com

For in-depth coverage of events, racing enthusiasts will want to visit this online magazine, which also provides daily news updates. With stats and commentary, this is one of the richest sites for Formula One content. Buy T-shirts and posters and other photo memorabilia through the online store.

Formula1.com

12345

www.formula1.com

This "unofficial" site is packed with information about F1 drivers, teams, history, stats, schedules, and news. True racing fans will enjoy the results archive, gallery, and technical analysis provided on this site.

ITV Formula 1

12345 RSS

www.itv-f1.com

ITV is the largest commercial television network in the United Kingdom. ITV's F1 site provides in-depth coverage and lots of photos related to F1 racing, including coverage of teams, drivers, and pit crews.

News on F1

12345

www.newsonf1.com

Detailed racing information and driver updates are featured here, as are current standings and team information.

Shell and Ferrari Motorsports

12345

www.shell.com/home/Framework?siteId=ferrari-en

If you want a history of Formula One, pre- and post-race reports, and car statistics, come to this site sponsored by Shell and Ferrari Motorsports. Very cool, well-designed site. Check out the Flash animation of the Shell Track Lab, among other high-tech offerings, in the Interactive Zone.

IRL

ESPN's IndyCar Page

12345

sports.espn.go.com/rpm/seriesIndex?seriesId=1

ESPN, the "World Wide Leader in Sports," hosts this up-to-date and feature-rich site dedicated to the Indy Racing League. Here, you will find the latest news, standings, and schedules, along with access to an IRL-specific message board and information about the drivers. For a small fee, you can even sign up for IRL RaceCast, an online service that provides live leader boards and views from driver's cockpits during actual races.

Indy Racing League

12345

www.indycar.com

Dedicated to Indy Racing League (IRL) fans, this site provides a schedule of events, complete with information about how to tune in to races on TV or radio. You can also check the point totals to find out where your driver is in the standings and check out the latest headlines.

A B C D E F G H I J K L M N O P Q R S T U V W X Y Z

NASCAR

Fox Sports NASCAR Site

1 2 3 4 5

msn.foxsports.com/nascar

Visit this site for the latest news, information, driver profiles, gear, standings, and results from the fast-paced world of NASCAR. This site, which is updated on a daily basis—and hourly during races—is sure to please NASCAR fans, both old and new. If you're into fantasy sports, sign up for Fox's Fantasy Auto Racing challenge, or vote and view the latest NASCAR-related poll.

My Brickyard: Brickyard 400

1 2 3 4 5

www.brickyard400.com

Get the latest news and information about NASCAR and one of its premier events: the Brickyard 400. Check out the schedule of events, history of the race, and photos.

NASCAR.com

www.nascar.com

There's no better place to learn about NASCAR and stay on top of the sport's latest news and information than NASCAR.com. This site features everything—and we mean *everything*—you could ever possibly want to know about America's fastest-growing motor sport, including news and information on the drivers, their cars, race results and series standings, and a lot more. There are even live web cams of race garages and weather reports for the tracks where the races take place.

> **Tip:** Click on the TrackPass link to gain access to live updates during races. A small fee applies; but if you're really into NASCAR, it's well worth the price of admission.

AUTOMOBILE CLUBS AND ORGANIZATIONS

Best AAA Online

1 2 3 4 5

www.aaa.com

Go directly to your state's "Triple A" office by entering your ZIP or Postal code in the AAA website. In addition to information about AAA's famous Triptiks and the 24/365 road service that offers car lockout help, jump-starts, and fixed flats, find out about travel reservations and discounts, domestic and international tours, and national gas prices. If there's one auto club site you should visit, this is it.

The Antique Automobile Club of America

1 2 3 4 5

www.aaca.org

The AACA is not just for people who like old cars. Actually, this club wants to preserve and celebrate all modes of "self-propelled vehicle," which is any vehicle meant to carry people and that runs on gasoline, diesel, steam, or electricity. Founded in 1935, the AACA has more than 400 chapters all over the world, and its website is exhaustive in its coverage of history, legislation, film and video, museums, links, and much more.

Classic Car Club of America

1 2 3 4 5

www.classiccarclub.org

Headquartered in Des Plaines, Illinois, near Chicago, the Classic Car Club of America promotes "the development, publication, and interchange of technical, historical and, other information for...motorcars built between and including the years 1925 and 1948." Here, you can learn more about the organization and its history and events, as well as participate in online forums and learn about which vehicles are recognized as CCCA Classics.

The Electric Auto Association

1 2 3 4 5

www.eaaev.org

The EAA is a nonprofit organization dedicated to the advancement and adoption of the electricity-powered car. The principle of the EAA is that electric vehicles (EVs) are more efficient and better for the planet than those that run on standard fossil fuel. A long list of links to other EV-related sites is provided.

The National Motorists Association

1 2 3 4 5

www.motorists.com

The NMA exists to protect your rights as a driving citizen. Among its many services, the NMA lobbies for sensible road traffic laws and engineering, argues for your right to drive whatever you want, helps you fight tickets, and opposes camera-based enforcement (as well as speed traps designed to generate revenue). Don't leave without clicking the Fight Your Traffic Ticket button and reading through the tips on how to avoid getting a ticket.

The Sports Car Club of America

1 2 3 4 5

www.scca.org

If you've ever driven down the street and made car racing noises to yourself, the SCCA is the club for you. You are encouraged not only to love sports cars and racing, but also to enter racing school and go racing yourself. This site provides a huge list of pro and amateur races and other events.

Women's Auto Help Center

1 2 3 4 5

www.mpilla.com/images/ford/wac_home/wac_home.html

At Women's Auto Help Center, you will find more articles and help than you can shake a stick shift at. Excellent information on car care for both men and women, including an auto affordability calculator and a carpooling organizer.

AUTOMOBILES

BUYING ONLINE

Auto World

12345

www.autoworld.com

Unlike the Kelley Blue Book (a competitor of Auto World), Auto World updates its Vehicle Information and Pricing Service on a daily basis and takes into account variations in regional pricing. In addition to dynamic pricing reports, you can get a quote on a car or read tips on buying a car.

AutoBuyingTips

12345

autobuyingtips.com

Consult this resource when buying your next car or extended warranty. Includes resources on loans, warranties, insurance, dealer costs, and even a place to get quotes. An excellent site to consult.

Autobytel.com

12345

www.autobytel.com

Buy or sell your car here, in addition to researching dealers, models, invoice pricing, Blue Book value, warranties, and dealer incentives. You can also apply for financing and insurance online.

AutoTrader.com

12345

www.autotrader.com

If you're looking for a used car, you'll want to search this database of more than two million used cars being sold by private individuals and dealers across the country. You can also limit your search geographically.

Carprice.com

12345

www.carprice.com

Carprice.com is a search engine designed specifically to find vehicles (new and used) over the Internet. You simply specify the car you want and the desired options and enter your ZIP code. For new cars, the search turns up the manufacturer's suggested retail price and the invoice price; you can then fill out a form to have a local dealer contact you. For used cars, the search displays the asking price and a link for contacting the seller.

Cars.com

www.cars.com

Get the background information on used cars for sale at the site, or research new car performance and pricing and then get an online quote.

CarsDirect.com

12345

www.carsdirect.com

Search and compare new car alternatives that meet your needs, then get an online price quote, and arrange for delivery. For $25, you can list your car for sale online.

CarSmart.com

12345

www.carsmart.com

Check Consumers Guide reports on cars of interest and then search the database of available used cars or get a quote on a new one. You can locate specific cars and dealers from the site. You can also do a lemon-check, using a vehicle's vehicle identification number (VIN), to ensure you don't get stuck with a defective vehicle. When you find a new car, you can sell your old car here, too.

ConsumerGuide.com

12345

auto.consumerguide.com

Consumer Guide has been providing sage advice to consumers for nearly 40 years and provides this advice online at this site. Here, you can obtain quotes on new car prices from dealers in your area, determine the trade-in value of your old vehicle, and even check the history of a used vehicle via its vehicle identification number (VIN). Site features some informative articles, too.

DealerNet

12345

www.dealernet.com

A very comprehensive guide to buying a car via the Internet. Enter your specific search criteria on the make, model, year, price range, and dealership location of your desired vehicle, and DealerNet gives you a list of options. You can also use this site to read up on reviews of new cars.

eBay Motors

www.motors.ebay.com

eBay Motors—a part of eBay.com, the world's largest online marketplace—is one of the Internet's largest marketplace for buying and selling all things automotive. This site offers everyday cars for everyday drivers, as well as collector cars, motorcycles, auto parts, and accessories.

Edmunds.com

12345 RSS

www.edmunds.com

The place to go when thinking of buying a new or used car. A multitude of information is available, including price guides, dealer cost information, buyer advice and recommendations, recall information, and much, much more. Click on the Inside Line link for more detailed information on up-and-coming makes and models.

Best Kelley Blue Book

12345

www.kbb.com

Before you sell a car or purchase a used car, you should check its "Blue Book" value, and Kelley Blue Book is the standard nearly all auto dealers use to determine the value of a used car. At this site, you can plug in a few details—including the make, model, year of the car, and its condition—to see the Blue Book value for yourself. This site is packed with information and tips about buying new and used cars and provides all the tools you need to finance and purchase a car online.

LeaseGuide.com

12345

www.leaseguide.com

If you're debating whether to purchase or lease your next car, this site provides all the information you need to make a good decision. You can even plug numbers into the lease calculator to take a quick look at the bottom line.

Newspaper Advertising

12345

www.newspapers.com/npcom1.htm

If you are interested in selling rather than buying a vehicle, you could try listing your vehicle in your local newspaper online. This site provides entry into numerous newspaper sites throughout the United States and elsewhere.

Vehix.com

12345

www.vehix.com

Vehix.com is the self-proclaimed "Roadmap to the Automotive World." Through this single portal, you can find quality new and used cars, locate a dealer, finance and insure your new car, and sell your old car. Research tools enable you to do quick side-by-side comparisons, look up vehicle reviews, check trade-in values, look up safety ratings and vehicle histories, download DMV forms, and more.

A B C D E F G H I J K L M N O P Q R S T U V W X Y Z

CLASSIC CARS

Auto Restorer On-Line

1 2 3 4 5

www.autorestorer.com

Get inspired by stories and photos of successful restoration projects, and then investigate how to do it yourself through Q&As and message boards from those who've done it.

Best Classic Car Source

1 2 3 4 5 Blog RSS

www.classicar.com

For car lovers interested in bonding with fellow classic car buffs, this site has a community spirit combined with articles, photographs, chat, auctions, message boards, and restoration help.

Hemmings Motor News

1 2 3 4 5 Blog RSS

www.hmn.com

Hemmings Motor News is the authority on classic collector cars. Check out this site for classifieds, upcoming events, and links to museums, dealers, parts locators, and much more.

Model T Ford Club

1 2 3 4 5

www.modelt.org

Learn more about Model Ts at this site, where you can also find out about the Model T club and search the database for information on the car's history and manufacture.

INFORMATION

AutoAdvice.com

1 2 3 4 5

www.autoadvice.com

This site walks you through the whole process of researching a new car, selling your old one, and negotiating with dealers.

Car Buying Tips

1 2 3 4 5

www.carbuyingtips.com

With information provided at this site, you should be able to negotiate a car purchase without falling victim to common scams. Be sure to scroll down the home page and read some of the angry email messages this site's owner receives from car dealers.

Carfax Lemon Check

1 2 3 4 5

www.carfax.com

An essential resource for anyone thinking of buying a used car. Click on Find a Car; enter your desired car's make, model, and year; and find out whether any cars are available in your area. If so, you can find out for free whether any have been labeled a lemon (or one with repeated problems). If you like the service, you can look up specific VINs for a small fee.

CarInfo.com

1 2 3 4 5

www.carinfo.com

Learn the secrets of a successful lease or purchase from consumer advocate Mark Eskeldson. Mark also provides information on how to avoid being ripped off by inscrutable auto mechanics.

MANUFACTURERS

Acura

1 2 3 4 5

www.acura.com

The classy Acura has become an urban status symbol, and you can find out why on this page. It provides information about the newest models, searching for Acuras online, plus service and benefit information for current owners.

Audi

12345

www.audiusa.com

The sleek home page highlights the design, performance, technology, and safety features that go into making Audi vehicles premium products. Search online for a new or used Audi, locate a dealer, and even check out Audi's contribution to motorsports.

Austin Healey

12345

www.healey.org

Home of the Austin Healey club. Here, you can locate other Austin Healey owners worldwide, learn about planned excursions and trips, and view car images and links to other Healey-related sites.

BMW of North America

12345

www.bmwusa.com

Whether you're a current BMW owner or a wannabe, you'll find plenty of information at this site. Learn about the new models by clicking Vehicles, or visit the pre-owned area to find out how you can acquire a gently used BMW.

Buick

12345

www.buick.com

Request a brochure, find a dealer nearby, purchase Buick merchandise, learn about Buick's involvement with charity events and golf tournaments, or buy a car online. Lots of information is available in a neatly laid-out site.

Cadillac

12345

www.cadillac.com

Check out the Interactive Module on this site and experience videos that will make you feel like you're in a Cadillac. You can also learn more about available models and order yours online.

Chevrolet

12345

www.chevrolet.com

Gather information on Chevy cars and trucks on this site, learn about special offers, view brochures, and find a local dealer.

Daihatsu

12345

www.daihatsu.com

Daihatsu specializes in designing and manufacturing compact, energy-efficient vehicles. To enter the showroom, click the On-Line Catalogues link. You can also use this site to read Daihatsu's environmental reports and information about its industrial engines.

DaimlerChrysler

12345

www.daimlerchrysler.com

Your one-stop shopping spot for all the models made by DaimlerChrysler Corporation, including Dodge, Chrysler, Jeep, and Mercedes-Benz. Click the Brands & Products link and then click the logo for the desired model to browse available vehicles. Some of the manufacturer sites that are part of DaimlerChrysler enable you to shop online for accessories.

Ford Motor Company

12345

www.ford.com

Here's the master page from which you can access all the model-specific pages for vehicles made by the Ford Motor Company. They include Aston Martin, Ford, Lincoln, Land Rover, Mazda, Mercury, Volvo, Aston Martin, and Jaguar. Click the Services link for information on caring for and servicing your vehicle.

General Motors

1 2 3 4 5

www.gm.com

This page is the jumping-off point for individual websites for the various models made by General Motors, including Chevrolet, GMC, Buick, Holden, Isuzu, Opel, Pontiac, Saab, Saturn, Chevy Trucks, Cadillac, Vauxhall, and Oldsmobile. This site also features links for pages on safety issues, innovations, parts and service, and other GM products and services.

Honda

1 2 3 4 5

www.honda.com

Check out all the latest Honda and Acura models here, locate nearby dealers, and visit the Honda corporate headquarters, all in one trip. This site also features links to other Honda products, including motorcycles, power equipment, personal watercraft, and boat engines. Click Honda Automobiles and then click the Build Your Honda link to start shopping for a Honda vehicle online, or simply click the desired model to get started.

Hummer

1 2 3 4 5

www.hummer.com

This militaristic site stresses durability and strength just by its design, which fits the product well. Look at the photo gallery, check out current models, and learn the history of the Hummer. A cool interactive tool enables you to build your dream Hummer online and immediately experience the sensation of sticker shock.

Hyundai Motor Company

1 2 3 4 5

www.hyundaiusa.com

This easy-to-navigate site offers profiles on the new Hyundai models, a company profile, and current company news. A great place to check out the various Hyundai models and get a ballpark figure on the price.

Isuzu

1 2 3 4 5

www.isuzu.com

Comparatively speaking, this site is fairly basic. Click the desired model for a brief description of it and links for checking out the vehicle's features, specifications, and comparisons to other vehicles in its class. You can also build a custom Isuzu online, request a brochure, or view 360-degree images of the various models.

Lexus

1 2 3 4 5

www.lexus.com

With a focus on its newest models, Lexus offers information on all its vehicles, providing stunning photography and information. As with other manufacturer sites, you can tour the showroom, locate a dealer near you, search a database of preowned Lexuses, and build a custom Lexus online.

Mazda

1 2 3 4 5

www.mazdausa.com

Learn all about the latest Mazda models in this online showroom . If you own a Mazda, you can enter the Owners area, which offers news about your vehicle, plus driving, safety, and maintenance tips. Zoom zoom!

Mercedes-Benz

1 2 3 4 5

www.mbusa.com

Learn all about the various models of Mercedes-Benz vehicles, locate a dealer, and take advantage of special offers.

Mercury

1 2 3 4 5

www.mercuryvehicles.com

View current Mercury models, get a glimpse of next year's models, and arrange for a test drive at this site.

Mini Cooper

1 2 3 4 5

www.mini.co.uk

If you own a Mini Cooper or are one of many drivers who dream of owning one, visit the official Mini Cooper home page. Here, you can check out the latest models, learn how to find a good used Mini Cooper, and shop for some nifty accessories.

Mitsubishi Motors

1 2 3 4 5

www.mitsubishi-motors.com

Mitsubishi Motors presents dealer listings, financing information, model specifications, and motorsports information. Click the link for the desired model to research its design and features, and build a custom vehicle online to estimate its full cost.

Nissan

1 2 3 4 5

www.nissanusa.com

Learn about special offers available to potential Nissan owners and fully research all Nissan models at this sleek website. Financing information is also available online, making your shopping experience more convenient.

Porsche

1 2 3 4 5

www.porsche.com

In addition to scoping out luscious models of Porsche engineering, you can also learn about the company's involvement with international motorsports. Catch up on race news and plan for upcoming events with the help of the Race Activities link. Current Porsche owners will want to check out the local Porsche clubs and visit the online shopping pages. Beautiful photography throughout the site.

Rolls-Royce

1 2 3 4 5

www.rolls-roycemotorcars.com

Unlike most other car websites, the Rolls-Royce Motor Cars site provides much more information about the Rolls-Royce Phantom, its history, and production process. However, you can also locate worldwide dealers here, too.

Saab

1 2 3 4 5

www.saabusa.com

Explore Saab's current models, learn about current offers, and read about Saab services.

Saturn

1 2 3 4 5

www.saturn.com

Home of the no-haggle policy, this Saturn site allows you to research various models and build a custom package online. And, because the price is nonnegotiable, you can be sure that the price you see online is the price the dealer is going to quote you. To find a Saturn dealer near you, click Find Retailer and enter your ZIP code.

Subaru

1 2 3 4 5

www.subaru.com

Learn about Subaru's newest vehicles, locate a dealer near you, and take a look at manufacture suggested retail price (MSRP). You'll also find in-depth information on the company's all-wheel driving system plus an archive of industry reviews.

Toyota

1 2 3 4 5

www.toyota.com

Configure a new Toyota, locate a used one, or just browse the news and corporate information at Toyota's website. Owners can access a special area of the site by entering their Toyota VIN. Information about future Toyota vehicles is also available, for those visitors just starting to consider a new purchase.

Best Volkswagen

1 2 3 4 5

www.vw.com

This Volkswagen site is fun and active, geared to the young and hip web audience. The specs are detailed with more than enough information to help you make an informed decision or point you toward your local dealer for more information.

Volvo

1 2 3 4 5

www.volvocars.us

Visit the official Volvo site to browse the online showroom, build a custom Volvo, check out certified pre-owned Volvos, and find a dealer near you. Volvo owners can visit the site to obtain additional information about caring for and servicing their vehicles.

REPAIR

ALLDATA Auto Repair Site

1 2 3 4 5

www.alldata.com

Publisher of electronic automotive diagnostic and repair information for professional mechanics and consumers.

Bob Hewitt's (Misterfixit's) Autorepair Page

1 2 3 4 5

www.MisterFixit.com/autorepr.htm

In addition to auto repair links provided at this site, you'll find helpful and humorous stories about mysterious auto problems encountered by fellow car owners. It's obvious that Bob Hewitt has spent a few hours under the hood of his own vehicles.

The Body Shop, Inc.

1 2 3 4 5

www.thebodyshopinc.com

If you live in the Chicagoland area and you have a fender bender that you want fixed right, check out The Body Shop, Inc., a body shop that not only offers free estimates, expert collision and paint workmanship, and paintless dent removal, but also professional detailing, to make your car, van, or SUV look like new.

Car Care Council

1 2 3 4 5

www.carcarecouncil.org

Perhaps the most complete list of preventive maintenance tips on and off the Web. Just don't anticipate the opportunity to ask questions; the site is dedicated to keeping you out of trouble in the first place. This site provides some excellent information in an easily accessible format.

Car Talk

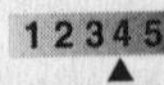

RSS

cartalk.cars.com

The online version of NPR's radio show provides advice and information on cars, mechanics, and repairs. The site also features *Car Talk* trivia, a puzzler, virtual postcards, online classifieds, and *Car Talk* hate mail.

Chilton's Online

1 2 3 4 5

www.chiltonsonline.com

If you're looking for the authoritative book on repairing your own vehicle, visit this site to find the book you need. Chilton's is the largest publisher of automobile repair manuals and has earned a stellar reputation for its consistent quality and accuracy.

Discount Auto Repair Manuals

1 2 3 4 5

www.discountautorepairmanuals.com

Order the Haynes Auto Repair Manual for your vehicle from this site. These manuals are written with the do-it-yourselfer in mind.

DoItYourself.com: Auto Repair and Care Tips

1 2 3 4 5

www.doityourself.com/scat/carstrucksandboats

Designed specifically for do-it-yourselfers, this site provides basic instructions on a wide range of auto-care topics covering everything from purchasing a new car to dealing with roadside emergencies.

Factory Auto Manuals

12345

www.factoryautomanuals.com

If you're trying to work on a vintage vehicle but can't find a service manual to refer to, check out this site.

Family Car Web Magazine

12345

www.familycar.com

Now in it's 10th year, this site is dedicated to the proper selection and care of the family vehicle, this site also provides driving tips and news. You can even learn how to become a better driver.

Yahoo! Autos

12345 

autos.yahoo.com/maintain/repairqa

Yahoo!'s auto repair site is unique, in that it leads you step by step through the process of troubleshooting and diagnosing your car's problem. If your car has a problem you can see, hear, feel, or smell, you can find the cause right here.

B C D E F G H I J K L M N O P Q R S T U V W X Y Z

AVIATION

ACES HIGH: The Finest in Aviation Photography

1 2 3 4 5

www.aviationphoto.com

Whether for personal enjoyment or to spice up a presentation, look at this site for downloading aviation photography. This site also offers tips for taking your own photographs.

Air Affair

1 2 3 4 5

www.airaffair.com

Focuses on different types of flying machines. Includes a calendar of flying shows, a listing of aviation fuel prices, and an aviation library.

Air Combat USA

1 2 3 4 5

www.aircombatusa.com

Find out how you can fly actual air-to-air combat in a real, state-of-the-art military aircraft! You don't even need a pilot's license. If you've been a student of aerial warfare for years and have only dreamed of taking a seat behind the wheel of a real warplane, check out this site!

Air Force Link

1 2 3 4 5 RSS

www.af.mil

The official U.S. Air Force site offers timely news, information on career opportunities, and exciting aviation images.

Air Safe

1 2 3 4 5 RSS

www.airsafe.com

A treasure trove of information for fearful flyers about flying safely—whether that means identifying the safest airline, aircraft, or airport—and tips for having a safe, comfortable flight.

Aircraft Images Archive

1 2 3 4 5

www.cs.ruu.nl/pub/AIRCRAFT-IMAGES

Collection of pictures of mainly military aircraft. All photos are in JPEG format.

Amelia Earhart

1 2 3 4 5

www.ellensplace.net/ae_eyrs.html

Interested in Amelia Earhart? This site provides a nice biography detailing her life from her youth until her last flight.

Aviation Museum Locator

1 2 3 4 5

www.aero-web.org/museums/museums.htm

If you're looking for an aviation museum in Canada or the United States, visit this site to pinpoint their locations. The site lists Canadian provinces and U.S. states that you can click to find nearby aviation museums. (You can't click the points on the map.) For each museum, the site displays its address, a map showing its location, and a visitor ranking.

AVWeb

1 2 3 4 5 RSS

www.avweb.com

An Internet aviation magazine featuring up-to-the-minute aviation news, articles by top aviation writers, links to online shopping, and a searchable aviation database.

Basics of Space Flight Learners' Workbook

12345

www.jpl.nasa.gov/basics

Maintained by NASA's Jet Propulsion Laboratory, this site provides orientation to space flight and related topics, including the solar system, gravity and mechanics, interplanetary trajectories, orbits, electromagnetic phenomena, spacecraft types, telecommunications, onboard subsystems, navigation, and phases of flight.

The Boeing Company

12345

www.boeing.com

Home page for the world's largest producer of commercial jetliners. Provides information on employment opportunities and company news as well as background information and facts about the company's families of airplanes. Contains interesting, downloadable pictures of its airplanes.

Delta SkyLinks Home Page

12345

www.delta.com

Loads of useful information for those interested in flying with Delta. You can check flight schedules, reserve tickets, or just read news about the company.

Embry-Riddle Aeronautical University

12345

www.db.erau.edu

Learn about the world's largest aeronautical university. This site contains admission information, research opportunities, and a tour of the campus.

Embry-Riddle Aeronautical University Virtual Library

12345

www.embryriddle.edu/libraries/virtual

This site covers practically every imaginable aspect of aviation. It is a library containing links to hundreds of other related sites. This would be an excellent place to begin a search into the area of aviation.

FAA

12345

www.faa.gov

The home of the Federal Aviation Administration (FAA), this site is an excellent resource for both pilots and passengers. Here, you can check on flight safety, advisories, and airport status. You can also determine the steps you need to take to become a pilot, air traffic controller, security screener, or other airline professional.

Fear of Flying

12345 

www.fearofflying.com/fear.htm

If you are among the 50 million Americans who have given up flying, fly with anxiety, or have never flown, Seminars On Aeroanxiety Relief (SOAR) is here to help you overcome your fear of flying. You must pay for the course, but success is 100 percent guaranteed.

Flight Safety Foundation

12345

www.flightsafety.org

Read about aviation safety, stay updated on safety statistics and reports, and search for scheduled upcoming events.

Helicopter Adventures, Inc.

12345

www.heli.com

Learn about this helicopter flight-training school and how you can learn to fly helicopters. This site also contains several links to other helicopter-related sites.

Jesse Davidson Aviation Archives

12345

www.aviationhistoryphotos.com

This site features photographs of various aircraft and famous aviators throughout history. Most of the photos are small, low-resolution versions, but they do provide a taste of what it was like to fly back in the old days.

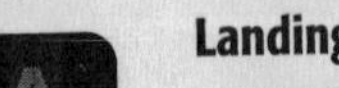

A B C D E F G H I J K L M N O P Q R S T U V W X Y Z

Landings

12345

www.landings.com/aviation.html

Excellent and informative text-based site that provides a wide variety of aviation information for all levels, including recent news items and editorials.

Lockheed Martin

12345

www.lockheedmartin.com/aeronautics

Lockheed Martin's public site provides information about the Lockheed Martin company, its airplanes, press releases, and more.

NASA Home Page

12345

www.nasa.gov

Acts as the starting point for all of NASA's Internet-based information. Offers links to resources, including space shuttle information, home pages for the NASA centers around the country, space images, and educational resources.

NASA Television

12345 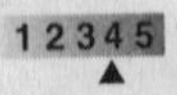 

www.nasa.gov/multimedia/nasatv

Helps visitors learn how to access live images and audio from NASA using RealPlayer, QuickTime, or Windows Media Player software. Provides links for obtaining the required software.

National Aeronautic Association

12345

www.naa-usa.org/website

The NAA's home page states that "by promoting safety, rights of access, and better public understanding of aviation and air sports, the NAA is not only for the experienced pilot, but for aviation enthusiasts of all kinds." See the NAA home page to learn about the association and how to become a member.

National Museum of the U.S. Air Force

12345

www.wpafb.af.mil/museum

Excellent museum of the U.S. Air Force covers the history of the U.S. Air Force from its early days (prior to World War I) to the present. Site features content on airplanes, missiles, and space flight, plenty of well-stocked photo galleries, and information that can help you plan a visit to the museum.

Pilot Shop

12345

www.aipilotshop.com

Offers a wide range of pilot supplies from several manufacturers. Pictures and descriptions of goods are available as well as an online order form.

Best Smithsonian National Air and Space Museum

12345

www.nasm.si.edu

This site features a robust collection of online versions of the museum's most popular exhibits. There's no replacement for visiting the museum in person, but this is pretty close. An excellent tool for parents and teachers to introduce kids to the wonderful world of flight.

Student Pilot Network

12345

www.ufly.com

Learn about flight schools, read interviews with pilots, and purchase instructional books on piloting and flying from this instructional and inspirational site. You can also purchase navigational and safety equipment through the online store.

X Prize

12345

www.xprize.com

The X Prize dared competitors to design and build a spacecraft that could carry three people safely to an altitude of 70 miles (100 kilometers), return to Earth, and complete the same trip within two weeks. The winner would receive $10 million for this space taxi, plus bragging rights in the world of aviation. The X Prize project was designed to encourage inventors to develop technology that would build a future space tourism industry. In 2004, someone actually won, and you can learn all about it and the future of space tourism at this site.

BABIES

American Academy of Pediatrics

12345

www.aap.org

Offers information relating to the mental, physical, and social health of infants through young adults. A searchable, easy-to-navigate site filled with valuable information for parents and pediatric professionals.

Babies Online

12345 RSS

www.babiesonline.com

Excellent links for finding baby freebies, preparing for your baby's arrival, and obtaining printable baby product coupons. You can even enter your baby in a cute-baby contest! Message boards provide a way to communicate with other parents and expectant mothers and fathers.

Babies "R" Us

12345

www.babiesrus.com

Possibly the biggest baby store in the world, Babies "R" Us carries just about every baby product imaginable, from pacifiers and rattles to baby backpacks and cribs. You can also register online to make it easier for friends and family to buy what you need for the new addition to your family. This site also features some useful articles on baby care, including a tutorial on how to clip your baby's nails and care for your baby's belly button. Amazon.com handles the orders, so you can sure of receiving quality service.

Babies Today Online

12345 Blog

babiestoday.com

Part of the iParenting network, this site provides a community for parents with babies. Full of information to guide you through the first year of your child's life, the site has extensive message boards, expert Q&A, articles, and news. You can research baby names, enter your baby's birthday to find out his or her exact age, and flip through a series of daily facts and information for each day of the first year of your baby's life.

Baby Bag Online

12345

www.babybag.com

Catch up on product recalls and warnings, download baby food recipes, and check baby product reviews. You also can access a wealth of information in just about any baby-related category imaginable. Lots of good information on nutrition plus quizzes and informative articles.

Baby Beechnut

12345

www.beechnut.com

Beechnut Baby Foods features this site as an information service for parents or parents-to-be on how to properly feed and care for their babies and toddlers. Site features a guide for how to feed your baby at different stages of his or her development, Caring for Baby (tips about feeding, nutrition, and general care), information on the importance of DHR and ARA in nutrition, and product descriptions.

Baby Center

12345

www.babycenter.com

A shopping site owned by Johnson & Johnson dedicated to providing all you'll need for your baby, including clothing, nursery furniture, car seats, strollers, and toys. Plus numerous bulletin boards categorized by topics and child development stages. Personalize the site by entering your baby's birthday and your email address, to have the site display information specifically related to your child's current developmental stage. You can go directly to the shopping area by visiting store.babycenter.com.

A B C D E F G H I J K L M N O P Q R S T U V W X Y Z

Baby Names

12345 Blog

www.babynames.com

Check out the results of recent polls regarding baby names before searching the Names database. Learn which names visitors love and hate, as well as the most popular ones this year. An excellent site to browse when you have no idea what to name your baby.

Baby Place

12345 Blog

www.baby-place.com

Offers baby and parenting information including pregnancy and birth FAQs, parenting FAQs, baby care, and even some baby jokes. Also gives links to baby-related newsgroups, sites offering services to new and expectant parents, and coupons for baby products and the Baby Place Store. Though you cannot purchase products directly from Baby Place, it offers plenty of links that take you to other online baby supply stores. A good jumping-off point for additional baby information.

Best Baby Zone

12345

babyzone.com

You can personalize this site to best suit your needs by your body, baby, location and even if you are adopting a child. The 12 different zones allow you to get specific information based on the age of your child. The Regions area provides pertinent information based on where you live or where you plan to travel. The Community Zone provides chat rooms and message boards where you can keep in touch with other parents. This site is packed with links to other useful pregnancy and parenting sites and features links to money-saving coupons and product offers, too. Parents will soon realize why we picked this site as the Best of the Best.

Crying Babies

12345

www.crying-babies.com

This site is devoted to helping parents resolve their newborn's colic by learning what causes it and what can be done about it. You can purchase Tummy Calm, a natural product that reportedly works quickly to relieve newborn colic, and other natural products for your baby.

Gerber

12345

www.gerber.com

Gerber, one of the most trusted names in baby foods, has created and maintains this site to provide expectant and new parents with a wealth of information to help them properly care for their baby's health, nutrition, and well-being. Here, you can learn about the various phases a baby passes through from prenatal to toddler, get free tips and tools, get an online feeding plan for your baby to ensure proper nutrition, check out some Gerber products, and learn more about the benefits of breastfeeding.

Huggies Baby Network

12345

www.huggiesbabynetwork.com

Excellent site for expectant and new mothers. Site content is presented in two sections: Happy & Healthy Pregnancy and Happy Baby. It features news, interviews, and advice from the experts, along with fun activities, including a Keepsake Story Book, Virtual Room Creator, and Activity Playhouse.

National Healthy Mothers, Healthy Babies Coalition

12345

www.hmhb.org

The National Healthy Mothers, Healthy Babies Coalition is dedicated to distributing the latest information on mother and baby health to consumers, doctors, and businesses to improve healthcare for mothers and their babies. Although this website is relatively new, this organization has been working for many years to support families and the child healthcare industry. If you're a parent or parent-to-be, check out this site for late-breaking healthcare issues and announcements.

Pampers Parenting Institute

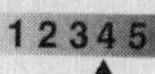

`us.pampers.com`

Get parenting help from experts and learn more about taking care of children up to age 4. Don't miss the Playing Center, where you can learn ways to stimulate your child's mind through creative games and activities. Procter & Gamble sponsors this site.

Parents of Premature Babies

`www.preemie-l.org`

If you're a parent of a premature baby looking for information, advice, or support, turn to this site for help. This site functions as an online support group, offering a useful FAQ plus links to online discussion groups and other resources of helpful information.

Related Site

`www.nlm.nih.gov/medlineplus/prematurebabies.html`

Pregnancy & Parenting

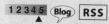

`parenting.ivillage.com`

Learn everything from how to improve your conception odds to how to baby-proof your home. Find information about the development of your baby from birth to preteen and tips for caring for and interacting with your child. Weekly newsletters are posted at this site, and message boards and chats are available. You can even test your baby knowledge by taking an online quiz.

Sesame Workshop

`www.sesameworkshop.org/sesamebeginnings/index.php`

This site comes to you from the creators of Sesame Street. Here, you will find games and activities for children and advice and articles for parents. In addition, you can order any Sesame Street product from the Sesame Store.

BACKGROUND CHECKS

Background Check Gateway

12345

www.backgroundcheckgateway.com

Entering into a personal or business relationship with someone is always risky, but you can feel more comfortable if you know that the person you're dealing with has a clean background. The Background Check Gateway provides the services you need to track down friends, classmates, or relatives; research the background of a prospective mate, employee, business associate, or tenant; and protect your identity.

Choice Point

12345

www.choicepointinc.com

Choice Point is dedicated to helping businesses and the government screen out applicants by verifying credentials and providing background checks of prospective employees. Visit this site to learn more about the service and what it has to offer plus articles and videos about the latest news concerning security.

Discreet Research

12345

www.discreetresearch.com

At Discreet Research, you become your own public records researcher. Simply sign up and log on to gain access to the databases and tools you need, and then start searching for your long-lost relative, an old classmate, or a prospective employee. Read all the fine print and find out current rates before you sign anything.

Best Docusearch

12345

www.docusearch.com

Docusearch is an investigative service that can check the identity, reputation, conduct, affiliations, associations, movements, and whereabouts of potential business partners, suspicious employees, prospective spouses, and relatives-to-be. You specify the purpose of the investigation, the person(s) you want investigated, and the types of services you want. When the investigation is complete, the results are posted on a secure server for you to view. Docusearch is Forbes Favorite Web Site for 2005 and our Best of the Best.

Employment Background Checks

12345

www.privacyrights.org/fs/fs16-bck.htm

Wondering what your employer can find out by doing a background check? This site provides the answers and advice on how to prepare for a background check. A list of frequently asked questions appears at the top of the opening page with links to the answers.

KnowX

12345

www.knowx.com

KnowX.com is a searchable public records database that can help users track down old friends and classmates; verify credentials; and perform background checks on prospective employees, mates, and others. System is easy to navigate and offers several levels of access depending on the required depth of the search. Of course, if you want the goods, you need to pay the price—about $7 for a standard background report or $20 for an all-day pass.

National Association of Professional Background Screeners (NAPBS)

12345

www.napbs.com

The NAPBS is a not-for-profit trade association that represents the business-related needs of employment and background screening companies. Visit this site for a list of NAPBS members, along with information about consumer rights under the Fair Credit Reporting Act.

BALLOONING

The Balloon Federation of America

www.bfa.net

This American ballooning organization's site includes membership information, events, competition standings, and products for sale—all geared to the experienced balloonist and junior balloonist. Basic site layout places all resources right at your fingertips.

Balloon Life Magazine

www.balloonlife.com/bl.htm

This site doesn't provide much in the way of free information; you must subscribe to the magazine to access most of the content. However, subscribers will find a wealth of information about ballooning, including articles on insurance, photography, special events, and contests. Be aware that you cannot subscribe from the website but must email the subscription department.

Balloon Pages on the World Wide Web

www.euronet.nl/users/jdewilde

A comprehensive list of World Wide Web addresses for all things related to ballooning. From here, you can jump to sites for various "Around the World" attempts, as well as to several pages of ballooning history, advice, and photography. Excellent site to start your exploration of ballooning.

Blast Valve

www.blastvalve.com

This most excellent directory contains dozens of links to a wide variety of ballooning sites. Links are grouped by category, including Balloon Festivals, Balloon Systems, Merchandise, Regulations, Balloon Rides, Learn to Fly, Organizations, and Weather.

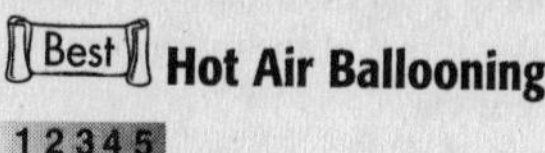

Best Hot Air Ballooning

www.launch.net

Locate a ride or festival, learn how to become a pilot, place a classified ad for balloon parts and accessories, or just sign up for the online newsletter at the site. This is a great site to learn more about ballooning as a recreational activity and a sport. At the top of the page is a navigation bar containing links to balloon rides, festivals, news, and weather reports. Along the left side of the page are several buttons that lead to discussions of balloon basics, balloon questions and answers, balloon-ride promotional deals, a pilot's corner, and a pilot's shop. If you have time to visit only one balloon site, this is where you should land.

Hot Air Balloons USA

www.hot-airballoons.com

A colorful, complete, and thoroughly enjoyable site. Features an interactive Take a Cyber-Ride balloon ride expedition, a mall area for shopping for balloon-related items, and a map showing balloon ride vendors all over the United States. Though the site has a link for the Balloon Store, the trails of links that lead to the various stores are dead ends.

Jet Stream Information

virga.sfsu.edu/crws/jetstream.html

View images of the jet stream over the eastern Pacific, northern hemisphere, or North America, and track the latest jet stream analysis prepared by the San Francisco State University Meteorology department. Excellent site for balloonists who are planning a flight.

National Scientific Balloon Facility

12345

www.nsbf.nasa.gov

The NSBF is a NASA facility managed by the Physical Science Lab of New Mexico State University. It launches, tracks, and recovers scientific balloon experiments all over the world, and this page shows some of its PR materials and photographs. This site offers great information, photos and a layout that makes it one of the more attractive of the ballooning sites.

Nova's Online Balloon Race Around the World

12345

www.pbs.org/wgbh/nova/balloon

On March 20, 1999, Bertran Piccard of Switzerland and Brian Jones of Britain finally achieved one of aviation's last great challenges, which was to fly nonstop around the world in a balloon. You can delve into the history of science and ballooning, follow the attempts of earlier balloonists to make the round-the-world flight, and more on this site.

BARGAINS

Airfare.com

1 2 3 4 5

www.airfare.com

Get up to 60 percent off on published ticket prices for major airlines, car rental agencies, and hotels. Just plug in your departure and destination points and specify your dates to have Airfare.com track down the best prices. You can even speak to a live agent if you prefer.

Amazing-Bargains

1 2 3 4 5

www.amazing-bargains.com

View bargains by category or by store. You'll find everything from books to jewelry to office supplies, all reduced in price. You cannot order products from this site; the links carry you to any of several online stores where you can purchase the products listed.

Ben's Bargains

1 2 3 4 5

www.bensbargains.net

This is the place "where ghetto dogs come for the lowdown on deals." Visit Ben's to find the latest on freebies, coupons, rebates, and other hot deals. The top of the page displays the most recent headlines. Scroll down the page for more lowdown deals.

Birkenstock Express

1 2 3 4 5

www.birkenstockexpress.com/Discounts/sale.cfm

Birkenstock Express Online has two types of bargains to offer: regular stock items at reduced prices and lists of discontinued or "as is" items at even better prices.

Bridal Bargains

1 2 3 4 5

www.windsorpeak.com/bridalbargains/default.html

Order the Bridal Bargains book or just browse through the overview, tips, or articles at this site. Message boards are divided into Gowns, Other Wedding Topics, and Local Talk.

ConsumerWorld Bargains

1 2 3 4 5

www.consumerworld.org/pages/bargains.htm

ConsumerWorld features four bargain categories: Stores/Outlets, Discount Computers, Discount Travel, and Deals/Coupons/Tips. Simply click the link for the desired category and then scroll down the list of current bargains, coupons, tips, and advice. Navigation bars that run along the left and right side of the page provide links to other useful consumer resources. You can also register for their newsletter.

CurrentCodes.com

1 2 3 4 5

www.currentcodes.com

Visit this site for the latest deals and discounts codes for online businesses that sell books, flowers, toys, clothing, and even ink cartridges. Search alphabetically or by category or company.

DealCatcher.com

1 2 3 4 5

www.dealcatcher.com

DealCatcher.com provides a searchable directory of the greatest deals at hundreds of popular stores along with coupons and rebates for a host of products and services. Join in the discussion forums for additional leads, check the Sunday ads, or do a price comparison.

A B C D E F G H I J K L M N O P Q R S T U V W X Y Z

ItsRainingBargains

12345

www.itsrainingbargains.com

Opening page features today's top bargains and provides a list of categories you can browse for additional deals, including Art, Baby, Computers, Electronics, Furniture, and Sporting Goods. On the right side of the page is a long list of retailers that display products on this site.

LowerMyBills.com

12345

www.lowermybills.com

Dedicated to providing a single site where you can lower your unavoidable bills in several budget categories, LowerMyBills.com is a free service that helps you find the best prices for long-distance telephone service, automobile and homeowner's insurance, loan rates, cell phone rates, credit card rates, and much more.

Best Overstock.com

12345

www.overstock.com

Save as much as 70 percent by buying manufacturers' overstock and discontinued items at this site. Products in inventory change daily, so visitors are encouraged to check back often or to sign up for the overstock newsletter. With its huge collection of overstock items updated daily and its easy-to-use format, this site is the hands-down winner as the Best of the Best.

Priceline.com

12345

www.priceline.com

Almost anything travel related you can get through Priceline. Name the price you want to pay for airline tickets, hotels, rental cars, vacation packages, cruises, city tours, and attractions. Priceline negotiates on your behalf to get a bargain from the service provider. They won't always accept your bid for their products or services, but it's worth a shot! If they do, you can save tens or even thousands of dollars.

SalesCircular.com

12345

www.salescircular.com

Instead of sifting through tons of sales circulars each week to track down a bargain locally, visit this website, click on your state, and find out which department stores have the best deals on items you need. You can also download and print valuable coupons from this site.

SecondSpin

12345

www.secondspin.com

Buy or sell used CDs. Rummage through the just-in bin for the latest available CDs, search for a specific artist or album, or browse for music by genre. You can even join the Spin Dealer program and make some extra cash on the side. Named Best of the Web by *US News & World Report* and Editor's Pick by AOL.

techbargains.com

12345

www.techbargains.com

Features a search tool that tracks down the best deals on computers, hardware, digital cameras, CD and DVD players and recorders, and other electronic equipment and gadgets. Links to other sites where you can place your order. If you're an electronics gadget guy or gal, bookmark this site!

COUPONS

car-pons.com

12345

www.car-pons.com

Dedicated to distributing coupons for automobile services, this site features coupons for oil changes, tune-ups, tires, and other auto-maintenance and repair jobs. You can also find a car shop and make an appointment online.

Best Cool Savings

12345

www.coolsavings.com

Register to be notified of major retailers' sales. Plus the Cool Savings site offers lots of inside scoops on rebates and coupons to print out, all for free. If you're tired of flipping through the Sunday paper in search of coupons and special deals, register here to gain access to coupons you know you can use. This site is well designed, making it easy to locate the best deals around.

Coupon Pages

12345

www.couponpages.com

The focus of this site is on coupons for local businesses, supermarkets, car rental agencies, fast food restaurants, retail stores, casinos, and much more!

CouponSurfer

12345 RSS

www.couponsurfer.com

Visit this site for personalized coupons at national stores or for major brands. Browse categories such as baby items, books, health and beauty, or sports, and then look at coupons available toward a purchase.

Daily e-Deals

12345 RSS

www.dailyedeals.com

A great site to find online shopping bargains, online coupons, and free stuff available on the Internet. You'll save a lot of time and effort with deals you wouldn't find anywhere else. To keep up to date on the latest and greatest bargains, join the mailing list.

Fat Wallet

12345 RSS

www.fatwallet.com

Fat Wallet offers three ways to save: its Cash Back program, coupons and rebates, and forums where you can obtain leads from other online bargain hunters. This site is accessible, easy to navigate, and packed with great opportunities to get cash back on the products you purchase.

MyCoupons

12345

www.mycoupons.com

The purpose of MyCoupons/DirectCoupons is to save you the time of surfing the Net for hours looking for savings. You can register for a free 30-day trial or upgrade your membership to receive special products and services. Lots of great coupons delivered right to your email inbox.

RedTagDeals.com

www.redtagdeals.com

Huge, searchable, and browsable collection of coupons, specials, rebates, and other money-saving deals for dozens of categories including automobiles, entertainment, apparel, books, long-distance telephone service, and much more.

RoomSaver.com

12345

www.roomsaver.com

Before you head out the door on your next vacation or business trip, check out RoomSaver.com for hotel and motel coupons and bargains. This site acts mainly as a referral service to send you to the websites of hotels and motels that are offering the deals.

TouristFlorida.com

12345

www.touristflorida.com

Planning a trip to Florida? Then visit this site for information, maps, and to pick up coupons for some of the major attractions including Sea World, Busch Gardens, and Universal Studios Theme Park.

A C D E F G H I J K L M N O P Q R S T U V W X Y Z

U-pons

12345

www.upons.com

U-pons specializes in grocery store coupons for some of the major supermarkets including Kroger, Giant Eagle, and Dillons. If you like to grocery shop at these stores, you can find a good collection of coupons to save you money, right here.

ValPak

12345 RSS

www.valpak.com

The ValPak folks send you that blue envelope of savings every month. They now offer coupons online, too.

FREEBIES

#1 Free Stuff

12345

www.1freestuff.com

This site is an index of free and trial offers available on the Internet. Select a category or check out the most popular free items to start your search.

100 Hot Free Stuff

12345

www.100hotfreestuff.com

Sign up for the Free Stuff newsletter to get regular notice of new freebies on the Internet. When you subscribe, you check a box next to each type of freebie you want to be notified about in several categories, including Beauty, Computers, Health, Sports, Entertainment, and so on. When freebies are available, you receive a newsletter via email letting you know about them.

Freaky Freddies Free Funhouse

12345

www.freakyfreddies.com

With the motto "If it ain't free, it's not for me," Freaky Freddy greets you with a stack of freebies, coupons, and special offers from hundreds of leading manufacturers and dealers. Free stuff for everyone, including free chocolate! This site is updated daily and features more than 70 categories of freebies. Sign up for Freaky Freddy's daily or weekly newsletter to keep up on the latest deals.

The Free Site

12345

www.thefreesite.com

Huge resource for finding freebies, especially those relating to computers and the Internet, including products and services, graphics, samples, games, email accounts, technical support, and much more.

Free Site X

12345

www.freesitex.com

Offers an incredible array of free stuff and looks to be well maintained. You can find free stuff ranging from free clothing to free software. More than 100 free offers!

FreeShop.com

12345

www.freeshop.com

Check out hundreds of offers of free stuff and free trials, organized by categories such as apparel, computers, health and beauty, food, and gourmet. Lots of links to free catalogs, but the free product offering is a little light.

Best Refundsweepers.com

12345

www.refundsweepers.com

Search the site for freebies on clothing, food, and jewelry. You can also sign up for coupons, rebates, and sweepstakes. You can find information about good deals on low-interest credit cards. Many links kick you out to other sites where you can obtain freebies. Site features hundreds of links to some of the best deals on the Web. If that's not enough, you can sign up for the newsletter to receive the inside scoop on deals as soon as their available.

Seasonal and Holiday Freebies

12345

www.thefreesite.com/Seasonal_Freebies

A unique collection of freebies organized by holiday. You can find freebies for Christmas, Valentine's Day, Halloween, April Fool's day, and more.

A B C D E F G H I J K L M N O P Q R S T U V W X Y Z

BASEBALL

Babe Ruth League Official Website

12345

www.baberuthleague.org

Play Babe Ruth Home Run Derby or learn all about the Babe Ruth League's history, divisions, and camps.

Baseball Almanac

12345

baseball-almanac.com

"Sharing Baseball, Sharing History." Students of the game will want to visit this site, providing a veritable encyclopedia of baseball facts and figures. Here, you can read about baseball legends, get the scores of every All-Star Game, view hitting and pitching charts, and play games.

Baseball America

12345 RSS

www.baseballamerica.com

This online version of Baseball America magazine covers all levels of baseball from high school to the major league. Check out scoreboards and stats, read the latest news and features, follow the draft, or do a little online shopping at Baseball America's electronic store.

Baseball Archive

12345

www.baseball1.com

The Baseball Archive features the largest collection of baseball statistics available, covering the history of baseball from 1871 to the end of the previously completed season. If you're into baseball trivia, this is the site to test your knowledge and expand it. If you're not into baseball, this is a good place to start becoming more interested as you explore its history.

Baseball Links

12345

www.baseball-links.com

Skilton's Baseball Links is a comprehensive collection of links to baseball-related resources, containing more than 10,000 unique links. Check out baseball equipment, read daily analyses of player performance, participate in reader polls, and much more on this site for baseball fanatics.

Baseball-Reference

12345 Blog

baseball-reference.com

If you want to know something about baseball, past or present, and you're not really sure where to turn, turn here. This site features player and team statistics, records, league leaders, awards, Hall of Fame information, manager bios, team schedules, and much more. You will find some links to other great baseball sites, too.

Best Baseball Think Factory

12345 Blog

www.baseballthinkfactory.com

Founded by Jim Furtado and Sean Forman, the Baseball Think Factory addresses a wide range of baseball interests and information through four distinct areas: Baseball-Reference.com, BaseballPrimer.com, BaseballNewstand.com, and BaseballStuff.com. Baseball-Reference.com includes statistics from 1871 to the present for players, teams, and leagues and includes a Baseball Travel Guide to help you track down events near you. BaseballPrimer.com offers inside information and commentary from the authors of this site to keep the thinking fan thinking. BaseballNewstand.com collects all the latest news and information about each team from various sources across the country to place all the information available for your favorite team in one location. And BaseballStuff.com provides links and additional information that you might find useful, or at least interesting.

Little League Online

1 2 3 4 5

www.littleleague.org

Provides lists of past state champions and a Little League World Series link that details the happenings of that event. Information on summer camps is provided, along with an online shop where you can purchase gifts and equipment. A great place for parents and coaches to learn the rules and pick up coaching tips. Information is also available on the Little League Child Protection Program.

Negro Baseball League

1 2 3 4 5

www.blackbaseball.com

This site introduces visitors to the history of the Negro Baseball League. It covers the history, players, and teams and explores the reasons why the league no longer exists. Memorabilia, collectibles, and books are also available.

COLLEGE

Baseball America

www.baseballamerica.com/today/college

If college baseball is your thing, this site is for you. Brought to you by the same people who publish *Baseball America* magazine, this site provides in-depth coverage of college baseball in America. From the first pitch of the season to the final crack of the bat at the College World Series, this site has it all, including player stats and profiles, feature articles, team scores and standings, and much more.

CollegeBaseballInsider.com

1 2 3 4 5

collegebaseballinsider.com

Although this site might not be much to look at, it does contain a wealth of up-to-date college baseball-related information, including scores and schedules, polls, player profiles, NCAA statistics, player journals, and information about college players drafted by Major League Baseball teams.

Collegiate Baseball News

1 2 3 4 5

www.baseballnews.com

Collegiate Baseball Newspaper is published twice a month from January to June and once in September and October. This site offers little from the newspaper, but it does provide information on how to subscribe and contact people at the newspaper. Site also features links to other college baseball sites.

NCAA Baseball

www.ncaasports.com/baseball/mens

Visit this site for the official word on all things college baseball. Brought to you by the National Collegiate Athletic Association (NCAA), here you will find standings, scores, and headline news for all three NCAA divisions. You can also purchase tickets to games and logo'd gear on this site.

Sports Illustrated: College Baseball

1 2 3 4 5

sportsillustrated.cnn.com/baseball/college

Sports Illustrated, the top sports magazine in the country, offers this site specifically for college baseball fans. We visited the site in the off season, making it a little tough to rate, but when season the season is in full swing, this site promises to offer schedules, scores, polls, and more.

FANTASY *(SEE FANTASY SPORTS)*

ESPN Fantasy Baseball

1 2 3 4 5

games.espn.go.com/cgi/flb/front

ESPN—the World Wide Leader in Sports—lives up to its moniker with this site, which is packed with games, news, analysis, player ratings, and statistics. Join an existing league or create one of your own.

Fantasy Index

1 2 3 4 5

www.fantasyindex.com/baseball

Fantasy Index offers subscribers inside information and analysis to give them an edge going into the season. Not much on this site for nonsubscribers, but subscribers can find plenty of news and commentary along with a toolbox that's packed with stuff you won't get in the magazine.

Major League Baseball Fantasy and Challenge Games

mlb.mlb.com/NASApp/mlb/mlb/fantasy/index.jsp

Available in English, Japanese, and Spanish, Major League Baseball's official fantasy sports site offers up-to-the-minute stats and breaking news stories that help you manage your team or an entire league. This feature-rich site also provides in-depth analysis of players, updates on starting lineups, and injury reports. Some areas of the site require that you pay a fee, but if you're a diehard fantasy baseballer, you probably won't mind.

Sports Illustrated

1 2 3 4 5

sportsillustrated.cnn.com/fantasy

Sports Illustrated hosts its own fantasy baseball league where you can assemble your team of all stars and see how they stack up to other all-star teams around the league. And because *Sports Illustrated* is packed with the latest information on teams, players, and stats, you have everything you need to make the right trades.

PROFESSIONAL

American League Websites

1 2 3 4 5

Baltimore Orioles
baltimore.orioles.mlb.com

Boston Red Sox
boston.redsox.mlb.com

Chicago White Sox
chicago.whitesox.mlb.com

Cleveland Indians
cleveland.indians.mlb.com

Detroit Tigers
detroit.tigers.mlb.com

Kansas City Royals
kansascity.royals.mlb.com

Los Angeles Angels of Anaheim
losangeles.angels.mlb.com

Minnesota Twins
minnesota.twins.mlb.com

New York Yankees
newyork.yankees.mlb.com

Oakland Athletics
oakland.athletics.mlb.com

Seattle Mariners
seattle.mariners.mlb.com

Tampa Bay Devil Rays
tampabay.devilrays.mlb.com

Texas Rangers
texas.rangers.mlb.com

Toronto Blue Jays
toronto.bluejays.mlb.com

Major League Baseball

mlb.com

Official site of Major League Baseball contains an up-to-date scoreboard, daily video of an amazing play, and a section for kids. Also included are links to individual player stats and career highlights, as well as links to each team's home page. Perhaps best of all, when the players or umpires strike, the site still works!

A B C D E F G H I J K L M N O P Q R S T U V W X Y Z

Minor League Baseball

www.minorleaguebaseball.com/app/index.jsp

Whether you prefer Minor League Baseball over Major League Baseball, you live in a town without a Major League Baseball team, or you like to follow young players as they try to make it into the big leagues, the Minor League Baseball site can help you follow your favorite players and teams. Site features news, a scoreboard, team standings, a schedule, a history of the league, and more.

National Baseball Hall of Fame

www.baseballhalloffame.org

The Hall of Fame site provides admission prices and hours of operation. You can link to directions on how to get to Cooperstown, access the Hall of Fame newsletter "Around the Horn," and view online special exhibits.

National League Websites

Arizona Diamondbacks
arizona.diamondbacks.mlb.com

Atlanta Braves
atlanta.braves.mlb.com

Chicago Cubs
chicago.cubs.mlb.com

Cincinnati Reds
cincinnati.reds.mlb.com

Colorado Rockies
colorado.rockies.mlb.com

Florida Marlins
florida.marlins.mlb.com

Houston Astros
houston.astros.mlb.com

Los Angeles Dodgers
losangeles.dodgers.mlb.com

Milwaukee Brewers
milwaukee.brewers.mlb.com

New York Mets
newyork.mets.mlb.com

Philadelphia Phillies
philadelphia.phillies.mlb.com

Pittsburgh Pirates
pittsburgh.pirates.mlb.com

San Diego Padres
sandiego.padres.mlb.com

San Francisco Giants
sanfrancisco.giants.mlb.com

St. Louis Cardinals
stlouis.cardinals.mlb.com

Washington Nationals
washington.nationals.mlb.com

USA Today: Baseball Weekly

www.usatoday.com/sports/baseball/front.htm

This site features just about everything a Major League Baseball fan could ever want: the latest scores and game highlights, league standings, statistics, schedules, rosters, trades, fantasy baseball games, and much more. Check this site frequently for updates on game scores, stats, team match-ups, and baseball news.

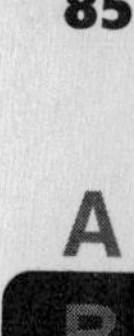

BASKETBALL

Coaching Well Basketball Journal

12345

www.havenport.com/hosa/cjournal.html

If your kid just volunteered you to coach the neighborhood basketball team, this site should be your first stop on your journey to becoming coach of the year. Here, you can find strategies, drills, skills lessons, practice plans, and other information you need to become a successful coach.

FIBA: Fédération International de Basketball Amateur

12345 RSS

www.fiba.com

FIBA (*Fédération International de Basketball Amateur*), the world governing body for basketball, is an independent association formed by 212 national federations of basketball throughout the world. At this site, you can get news, information about upcoming events and competitions, game rules and a glossary of terms, instructor guides for players and coaches, and much more. Whether you're a fan, a player, a coach, a referee, or a doctor who's interested in international basketball competition, you can find plenty of information of interest at this site.

Five Star Hoops

12345

www.bbhighway.com

This is the site for coaches, players, parents, and fans. Use this site to keep up on basketball–related news, tournaments, and more.

Full Court Press

12345

www.fullcourt.com

Full Court Press covers women's basketball at the high school, college, professional, and international levels. The site is full of articles about players, teams, conferences, and coaches.

Harlem Globetrotters Online

12345

www.harlemglobetrotters.com

The Globetrotters have been beating the Washington Generals (and entertaining us along the way) for decades, and now you can find them on the Web. This site covers the history, current schedule, information about the team members, and all things Globetrotter. Special kids area includes puzzles and games and information on how to sign up for the Globetrotters' basketball camp.

National Wheelchair Basketball Association

12345 RSS

www.nwba.org

The NWBA consists of 185 teams with more than 2,000 athletes, which adds up to a lot of wheels! The association has teams for men, women, students, and children of all ages. The website has a team directory, the official rules, the history of wheelchair basketball, and more.

Power Basketball

12345

www.powerbasketball.com

Power Basketball is dedicated to helping coaches improve their players' skills and their own coaching strategies. Here, you can find an online coachs' clinic, coaching tips, instructions on fundamentals, books, videos, and other resources. This site offers an excellent collection of articles on all aspects of coaching basketball.

Sports Illustrated Basketball

1 2 3 4 5

sportsillustrated.cnn.com/basketball/nba

Sports Illustrated is one of the top names in sports news and information. At this site, *Sports Illustrated* focuses its expertise on college and professional basketball, providing articles, statistics, standings, player biographies, injury lists, and much more.

USBasket

1 2 3 4 5

www.usbasket.com

USBasket is part of Eurobasket, a group devoted to providing the most in-depth coverage of basketball-related news and information from around the world. This site covers all aspects of U.S. basketball—the NCAA and NBA, plus U.S. players who play professionally and semi-professionally in other countries. Great site for fans, players, and agents.

COLLEGE

ESPN's Men's College Basketball Site

1 2 3 4 5

sports.espn.go.com/ncb/index

For everything you could ever possibly want to know about men's college basketball—including scores, player stats and profiles, and in-depth analysis and coverage of the games—visit this site, where you'll also find schedules, rankings, and the latest news on all the players and coaches.

Related Women's Site

sports.espn.go.com/sports/womenbb/index

NCAA Sports: Home of the Final Four

1 2 3 4 5

www.ncaasports.com/basketball/mens

Watch video from your favorite NCAA team's participation in the Final Four Championship. If your team didn't make it, keep up on men's and women's team news. You can also buy Final Four merchandise on this site to show your spirit.

Related Kids Site

www.ncaa.org/bbp/basketball_marketing/kids_club

Sports Illustrated College Basketball

1 2 3 4 5

sportsillustrated.cnn.com/basketball/ncaa

Sports Illustrated hosts this college basketball site where you can get the latest scores and team standings, statistics, and schedules. In the off season, visit this site to learn more about the college draft and learn about your team's prospects for the coming season. Excellent reporting and analysis.

USA Basketball

1 2 3 4 5

www.usabasketball.com

USA Basketball is the governing body of men's and women's basketball in the United States and is recognized by the International Basketball Federation and the U.S. Olympic Committee. The organization selects and trains USA teams for national and international play. Its website offers a FAQ, news releases, photos, links, schedules, athlete bios, and much more. If you like to keep abreast of the top up-and-coming basketball players in the nation, bookmark this site and visit it often.

yocohoops

1 2 3 4 5 Blog RSS

www.yocohoops.com

yocohoops, created and maintained by self-proclaimed college basketball junkie Yoni Chohen, is "a forum for educated, informed, and passionate commentary on college basketball." Visit this site to get involved in the lively banter and discover links to other basketball blogs that you might find engaging.

PROFESSIONAL

Basketball Daily

1 2 3 4 5

www.basketballdaily.com

Check out the daily basketball scores and game summaries at this site. On weekends and during the playoffs, this site is packed with information. On off days, you'll find little to keep you going.

Naismith Memorial Basketball Hall of Fame

1 2 3 4 5

www.hoophall.com

This is the official online site for the Naismith Memorial Basketball Hall of Fame in Springfield, Massachusetts. You can find museum information and a detailed biography on the game's creator, James Naismith. Be sure to check out all the items that you can buy from the Hall of Fame gift store, from books to gift items.

Best National Basketball Association

1 2 3 4 5 Blog RSS

www.nba.com

This Internet home of the National Basketball Association features the latest scores and reports about your favorite professional basketball teams and players. Here, you find links to the NBA, Jr. NBA, the WNBA (Women's National Basketball Association), and the Jr. WNBA. Each of these links takes you to a page devoted to the selected league, and each page contains links for the teams, players, news, statistics, standings, scores, schedules, transactions, and more. If you're a professional basketball fan, you'll find that this site or one it links to has everything you want.

NBA Development League

1 2 3 4 5

www.nba.com/dleague

The NBA Development League is the minor league for the NBA, where players compete for a shot to play in the NBA. Here, you can learn more about the players, teams, standings, and statistics.

NBA Eastern Conference Websites

1 2 3 4 5

Atlanta Hawks
www.nba.com/hawks

Boston Celtics
www.nba.com/celtics

Charlotte Bobcats
www.nba.com/bobcats

Chicago Bulls
www.nba.com/bulls

Cleveland Cavaliers
www.nba.com/cavaliers

Detroit Pistons
www.nba.com/pistons

Indiana Pacers
www.nba.com/pacers

New Jersey Nets
www.nba.com/nets

New Orleans Hornets
www.nba.com/hornets

New York Knicks
www.nba.com/knicks

Miami Heat
www.nba.com/heat

Milwaukee Bucks
www.nba.com/bucks

Orlando Magic
www.nba.com/magic

Philadelphia 76ers
www.nba.com/sixers

Toronto Raptors
www.nba.com/raptors

Washington Wizards
www.nba.com/wizards

NBA Western Conference Websites

1 2 3 4 5

Dallas Mavericks
www.nba.com/mavericks

Denver Nuggets
www.nba.com/nuggets

Golden State Warriors
www.nba.com/warriors

Houston Rockets
www.nba.com/rockets

Los Angeles Clippers
www.nba.com/clippers

Los Angeles Lakers
www.nba.com/lakers

Minnesota Timberwolves
www.nba.com/timberwolves

Phoenix Suns
www.nba.com/suns

Portland Trail Blazers
www.nba.com/blazers

Sacramento Kings
www.nba.com/kings

San Antonio Spurs
www.nba.com/spurs

Seattle SuperSonics
www.nba.com/sonics

Utah Jazz
www.nba.com/jazz

Memphis Grizzlies
www.nba.com/grizzlies

WNBA Eastern Conference Websites

12345

Charlotte Sting
www.wnba.com/sting

Chicago Sky
www.wnba.com/sky

Connecticut Sun
www.wnba.com/sun

Detroit Shock
www.wnba.com/shock

Indiana Fever
www.wnba.com/fever

New York Liberty
www.wnba.com/lynx

Washington Mystics
www.wnba.com/mystics

WNBA Western Conference Websites

12345

Houston Comets
www.wnba.com/comets

Los Angeles Sparks
www.wnba.com/sparks

Minnesota Lynx
www.wnba.com/lynx

Phoenix Mercury
www.wnba.com/mercury

Sacramento Monarchs
www.wnba.com/monarchs

San Antonio Silverstars
www.wnba.com/silverstars

Seattle Storm
www.wnba.com/storm

Women's National Basketball Association

12345

www.wnba.com

Check out the scoreboard for the latest results of WNBA play at the official site. You also can chat with players during frequent online chat sessions, get the latest WNBA news, review the upcoming season's schedule, and buy tickets.

BEER

Ale Street News

1 2 3 4 5 ▲ (4)

www.alestreetnews.com

Find out about upcoming brew events "Hoppenings" and stay current on beer-related news at this site, which also features links to Pubcrawler, a database that allows you to search for breweries, pubs, and bars in the United States.

All About Beer

1 2 3 4 5 ▲ (5)

www.allaboutbeer.com

This is the Internet home of All About Beer magazine, which is packed with beer news, opinions, ratings, home-brew secrets, international beers, and much more. Plenty of articles are available in this site.

Related Sites

www.beerparadise.ltd.uk

www.hogshead.com

www.alaskanbeer.com

Badger Brewery

1 2 3 4 5 ▲ (3)

www.badgerbrewery.com

This site reveals the English Badger Brewery and its beers. You can view the brewing process, learn about the ingredients Badger uses in its beers, and even go on a virtual pub walk. Click the Ecard link to send a friend a custom greeting card from Badger Brewery. A very quaint site.

Beamish & Crawford Brewery

1 2 3 4 5 ▲ (4)

www.beamish.ie

The Beamish & Crawford Brewery has been brewing Beamish Genuine Irish Stout in Cork, Ireland, for more than 200 years. The site contains, among other things, a movie file about the brewery plus wallpaper and a screensaver to "Beamish" your computer.

BeerAdvocate.com

1 2 3 4 5 ▲ (5)

www.beeradvocate.com

BeerAdvocate.com has been advocating for the craft of brewing beer since 1996 and now boasts more than two million visitors every month. That's a lot of beer drinkers cruising the Web! Here, you can learn more about beer and how to appreciate it, review beers and train your palate, and hook up with other beer lovers in the discussion forums.

Beer, Beer, and More Beer Home Brewing Supplies

1 2 3 4 5 ▲ (5)

www.morebeer.com

Pick up everything you need to turn your home into the neighborhood brewery. Here, you'll find home brewing kits, ingredients, dispensing equipment, and other home brewing essentials.

BeerBooks.com

1 2 3 4 5 ▲ (5)

www.beerbooks.com

Tired of drinking beer brewed by others? Then brew your own with the help of BeerBooks.com's hefty collection of beer books and videos. Here, you can purchase almost any book published on the topic of beer, from tasting and cooking with beer to brewing your own concoctions. Pick from a wide selection of recipe books, too.

Beer Hunter

1 2 3 4 5 ▲ (4)

www.beerhunter.com

Learn how to taste beer, learn about beer from around the world, and get updates on the Michael

Jackson (the beer hunter) World Beer Tour. Michael Jackson himself answers questions with his beer FAQ.

Beer Institute Online

www.beerinstitute.org

The Beer Institute is dedicated to promoting sound public policy concerning the distribution and consumption of beer in the United States. Here you can learn more about the Beer Institute, check out a few interesting beer facts, perform research on various topics related to beer, and learn about the Beer Institute's public educational initiatives.

Beer Me!

www.beerme.com

Meet The Good Soldier Svejk on this website (formerly called Beer Is My Life) and learn all about home brewing as well as the fine art of pub crawling. Offerings here are humorous and informative at the same time. Features links for Regional Brewery Guides, Beer List, Beer Styles, a Beer Library, and much more.

Brewers Association

www.beertown.org

The Brewers Association was "established in 2005 by a merger of the Association of Brewers and the Brewers' Association of America." The association is dedicated to promoting and protecting the interests of the beer brewing industry. At this site, you can find general information about beer, advice on home brewing, event calendars, an online shopping area, and much more.

Bud Online

www.budweiser.com

A colorful, innovative site from Budweiser, the King of Beers. Features information on the history of beer and how Budweiser is improving the quality of beer. Order Budweiser paraphernalia, check out the latest Budweiser-sponsored/endorsed events, and download Budweiser screensavers or wallpaper. This site even "cards" you before allowing you to enter.

Guinness

www.guinness.com

This high-tech site invites you to visit St. James' Gate, the home of Guinness beer. Learn about the beer, the can, and much more. You can even download a Guinness screensaver. Don't miss the Pearls of Wisdom link, where you can learn some beer trivia and read up on some bizarre facts.

Heineken

www.heineken.com

Provides history of the Heineken brewery and offers a virtual tour. Send customized email postcards and e-invitations and participate in Heineken's online game to win prizes.

Leinenkugel's Leinie Lodge

www.leinie.com

Learn all about this Wisconsin brew and other specialties in the Leinenkugel family of beers. Purchase T-shirts, sweatshirts, hats, and other promotional items from the online gift shop.

Pabst Brewing Company

12345

www.pabst.com

Provides a history of beer in general as well as of this brewing company, one of the oldest in America, and currently one of the most popular "retro" beers. Also under the Pabst umbrella are Olympia, Hamm's, Pearl, and other labels. Click the Beer 101 link to learn about the brewing process. You can check out the gift store for promotional items sporting the names and logos of several popular brands of beer, including Old Milwaukee, Old Style, Schlitz, and Rainier

The Pub Brewing Company

12345

www.pubbrewing.com

Thinking about opening your own brewpub? This is the company to show you the ropes. It provides layouts, equipment, installation, training, inspections, and more. Your comprehensive guide to getting into the brew business.

RealBeer.com: The Beer Portal

12345

www.realbeer.com

The quintessential site for home brewers and microbreweries alike. Host to three beer-of-the-month clubs, message boards, and more than 150,000 pages about beer, this site appeals to the most enthusiastic beer lovers on the Web. With a huge cache of links to other related websites and places where you can purchase special brews, this site is truly the Best of the Best when it comes to breweries.

Redhook Ale Brewery

12345

www.redhook.com

Provides information on the Washington-based microbrewery that has begun to make its existence known nationwide for its diversity and excellence. Take a virtual tour of the brewery and evaluate the stock value of this up-and-coming brewery. Purchase T-shirts, hats, glasses, mugs, and more from the online gift store.

Sam Adams

12345

www.samadams.com

The definitive guide to the different styles of Samuel Adams Beers; learn the history, brewing, and flavor characteristics of Sam Adams's handcrafted beers. Order items including mugs, steins, hats, T-shirts, and more from the online store or download the Sam Adams animated screensaver!

Siebel Institute of Technology

12345

www.siebelinstitute.com

The classes many college students dream about are offered at this brewing training establishment. Take courses such as Sensory Evaluation of Beer, Advanced Brewery Technology, or Yeast Management Workshop. Lab services also are offered, and you can consult the institute's newsletter.

Related Sites

www.shenandoahbrewing.com

www.sierranevada.com/index1.asp

A B C D E F G H I J K L M N O P Q R S T U V W X Y Z

BICYCLES

Adventure Cycling Association

12345

adv-cycling.org

This site features a touring map, a list of events, online catalogs, articles on biking, a list of bargains, a guide to cross-country adventures, and details on how to become a member of Adventure Cycling Association. You can even use the online version of the Cyclist's Yellow Pages to find bicycle stores and resources near you.

Aegis Bicycles

12345

www.aegisbicycles.com

Technical details about the carbon fiber bicycle frames and forks created by Aegis, plus tips on bicycle fit and details on Aegis dealers throughout the United States.

Analytic Cycling

12345

www.analyticcycling.com

Cyclists can chart speed, equipment performance, and more with this service, which allows riders to enter their data into predetermined formulas. Excellent site for competitive cyclists—very techie.

Bianchi

12345

www.bianchi.it

Get information about the Bianchi line of bikes and accessories, championship biking event results, magazines, and advice from expert bikers.

Best Bicycling.com

12345 RSS

www.bicycling.com

This full-featured bicycling site from *Bicycling* magazine features everything from beginning bicycling to the Tour de France. The tabbed navigation system provides quick access to Gear, Rides, Training, Skills, Fix-It, Community, Shop, and Subscriptions. Scroll down the home page for summaries and links to current articles and to sign up for your own automated personal trainer. Site also offers links to deals on biking gear and search tools for quickly tracking down bikes, events, components, and discussion forums. Excellent information and tools combined with easy navigation make this an easy choice for our Best of the Best award.

Bike Lane

12345

www.bikelane.com

Great links to manufacturer sites, custom frame builders, magazines, and the latest news in competitive biking.

Bike Ride Online

12345

www.bikeride.com

An exceptional bicycling web directory that features links to hundreds of resources, including regional clubs, manufacturers, retailers, racing events, mountain biking, training, coaching, and more. If you run out of links to click, you can check out the newsgroups to find messages posted by other bicycling enthusiasts.

Cambria Bicycle Outfitters

12345

www.cambriabike.com

Cambria stocks everything imaginable for the avid bicyclist, including parts, tires, tools, bags, carriers, apparel, and even food. Before your next tour, check out this site to make sure you're properly equipped.

Cannondale

12345

www.cannondale.com

Check out Cannondale's listing of awesome mountain bikes as well as other Cannondale products. Site also features owner's manuals, kit lists, tech notes, bicycle safety information, and much more.

Competitive Cyclist

12345

www.competitivecyclist.com

A complete inventory of cycling products for the serious competitor, including bicycles, frames, components, clothing, and more. If you're looking to build your own custom bike or have it built for you, this is the site for you. Excellent selections combined with superior service make this a great place to shop.

Cycling Web

12345

www.cyclingweb.com

Cycling fans will want to check out this site for the latest news about races, teams, and cyclists.

Cyclingnews.com

12345

www.cyclingnews.com

If you like to follow bicycle races, this is the place for it. Cyclingnews.com is packed with the latest news and information about bicycle races from around the world. Read about the latest races and racers, check the racing calendar, browse the photo index, and much more.

Lowrider Bicycles

12345 RSS

www.lowriderbike.com

If you're looking for bicycles that have a little more character, check out these lowrider models. They're basically pedal-power choppers—not your average racing bike or mountain bike, but definitely more stylish. This site offers feature articles, a message board, a tech area, a showroom, a calendar of upcoming lowrider events, and more

Marin

12345

www.marinbikes.com

Marin provides technical specifications of its product line at this site. Information on the design and construction of Marin bikes is included.

Merlin Bicycles

12345

www.merlinbike.com

Merlin Bicycles builds mountain bikes as well as road bicycles. Check out this site to see the latest models and current apparel available. Very high-tech, cutting-edge bikes and equipment.

Performance Bicycles

12345

www.performancebike.com

In the 1980s, Garry and Sharon Snook began Performance, Inc. in the basement of their home in Chapel Hill, North Carolina. It has since grown into the nation's leading bicycle mail-order and retail company.

Schwinn

12345

www.schwinn.com

Anyone considering buying a Schwinn bike or exercise equipment will want to stop by here to research each model, locate a dealer, and hear about how the Schwinn racing team is doing this year. If you already own a Schwinn bike, you can register for your warranty online, download a replacement owner's manual, or find a dealer near you.

Shimano

1 2 3 4 5 ▲

bike.shimano.com

Learn more about the ins and outs of Shimano racing technology at this site, where you'll learn why so many professional racers choose to ride Shimano bicycles. This site also helps you locate a local dealer and contact customer support. Very well-designed site.

Specialized

1 2 3 4 5 ▲

www.specialized.com

This site is packed with racing news and cycling tips. You can shop for bikes and accessories online or access owner's manuals and obtain tech support. Features a useful and thorough glossary of many of the more technical terms you will encounter in the world of bicycling.

Tour de France

1 2 3 4 5 ▲

www.letour.fr

Search the archives to learn more about past winners of the Tour de France at this bilingual official site, which will also track the progress of this year's racers online. Click the link for your preferred language: English or French.

Trails from Rails

1 2 3 4 5 ▲

www.trailsfromrails.com

Find the best bike trails across the United States. This site provides a list of trails that are paved with asphalt, concrete, or crushed limestone/gravel—trails that are suitable for touring or cross-bikes. Many of the trails are also open to hikers, cross-country skiers, snowmobilers, and roller bladers. Most trails pass through small towns, giving riders a bit of the local flavor and some outdoor adventure.

Trek Bicycle Corporation

1 2 3 4 5 ▲

www.trekbikes.com

Trek offers information about its bicycles and accessories here. You can also find your local Trek dealer or read the latest Trek news. Kids area has safety tips, instructions on how to select a bike, and tips for riding together as a family.

VBT

1 2 3 4 5 ▲

www.vbt.com

You'll consider a cycling tour through Europe, New Zealand, Vietnam, Canada, or even the United States after visiting this site, which will tell you about upcoming tours, equipment, and tour leaders.

VeloNews Interactive

1 2 3 4 5 ▲

www.velonews.com

A journal of competitive cycling. Offers news, Tour de France information, and links to other pages. Stay current on racing news or get training tips at this site.

Virtual Bike Barn

1 2 3 4 5 ▲

www.bikebarn.com

A great starting point for information about everything from bike repair and safety to bicycle magazines, newsgroups, and clubs. Includes a good collection of links to other premier bicycling sites and includes information about kids' bikes. Use this site to shop for virtually any type of bicycle product, too.

MAINTENANCE & REPAIR

Harris Cyclery with Sheldon Brown

1 2 3 4 5 ▲

sheldonbrown.com/repair

A great site for learning how to repair your bicycle. Merchandise also available by ordering via email, fax, phone, or standard mail. Be sure to read the articles written by Sheldon Brown while you're at this site.

Wrench

12345

www.jimlangley.net/wrench/wrench.html

This site, created and maintained by bicycle enthusiast Jim Langley, features free bicycle repair and maintenance tutorials, including basic bike care, fixing flats, rebuilding wheels, adjusting brakes, washing your bike, and much more. Langley also provides information on useful tools you might want to add to your toolbox.

MOUNTAIN BIKING

Big Island Mountain Biking Trail Guide

12345

www.interpac.net/~mtbike/bigmap.html

A clickable map of Hawaii's big island allows users to access information on bike trail distances, difficulty levels, elevations, and estimated riding times.

Diamondback Bikes

12345

www.diamondback.com

Since 1977, Diamondback has been producing quality mountain and BMX bicycles. You can get detailed descriptions of all models, read tech specs, and see available accessories. A special section just for kids lets them shop for a new bike online, too!

Dictionary of Mountain Bike Slang

12345

www.frostbytes.com/~jimf/biking/slang.html

If you're going to ride like a mountain biker, you should learn to talk like one, too. Check out this site to view a list of mountain biking slang terms and their definitions.

Best Dirt World

www.dirtworld.com

DirtWorld.com is a favorite of mountain bike enthusiasts from beginners to racers, offering product reviews, event listings, trail guides, feature stories, and much more. Using the navigation bar that runs down the left side of the page, you can access several content areas, including Rider Pics, Vids, Athlete Blogs, Feature Stories, Gear Reviews, Trail Guides, and Tips & Tricks. Click Resources to find bike stores, manufacturers, lodging, and links to other engaging mountain bike sites.

International Mountain Bicycling Association

12345 RSS

www.imba.com

The International Mountain Bicycling Association (IMBA) is dedicated to "enhancing and improving trail opportunities for mountain bikers worldwide." This group claims a membership of more than 32,000 riders worldwide and 450 bicycling clubs. Here, you can learn about the organization and its projects, read the rules of the trails, learn what you can do to help, and search for trails.

Mountain Bike Action

12345

www.mbaction.com

Mountain Bike Action is a magazine that contains information, articles, and advice on all aspects of mountain biking. Use the navigation bar on the left to jump to the desired area, including Flat Tire Topics, Photo Gallery, Tech Garage, Racing News, Bike Tests, Riding Tips, and Tech Tips.

Mountain Bike Hall of Fame

12345

www.mtnbikehalloffame.com/home.cfm

Located in Crested Butte, Colorado, the funky Mountain Bike Hall of Fame covers the history of mountain biking, the background of the Crested Butte mountain biking scene, a list of inductees and nominees, a calendar of events, and a shopping area.

Mountain Bike Magazine

12345

www.mountainbike.com

A trail finder, details on bike gear, updates on racing news, and product reviews are listed here. If you're a mountain biking enthusiast, you'll want to bookmark this site for return visits.

A C D E F G H I J K L M N O P Q R S T U V W X Y Z

Mountain Bike Trailsource

www.trailsource.com/biking/index.asp

Adventure travel guide to 3,000 biking single tracks in more than 100 countries around the globe. Just click on the map to find mountain bike trails where you want to go.

Mountain Cycle

www.mountaincycle.com

Great site for browsing through a collection of high-end mountain bikes or communicating with other mountain bikers on the message board. Choose a bike type, make, and model, and then customize by selecting the desired options. You can even purchase your bike online and have it delivered to your home.

Mountain Workshop Dirt Camp

www.dirtcamp.com

This is the site for America's only national, award-winning mountain biking instructional and guide program. With more than 10,000 guests to date from nearly 50 states and overseas, Dirt Camp is for enthusiasts of all ages and abilities. This is a great source for mountain biking adventures.

MTBR.com: The Ultimate Mountain Biking Resource

www.mtbr.com

A guide developed by mountain bikers for mountain bikers, delivering user-provided reviews of mountain bike products, news, and tips. This site has 50,000 product reviews and brings together 30,000 riders daily (or so MTBR.com claims). Excellent directory of Internet resources on biking.

Road Bike Review

www.roadbikereview.com

If you're in the market for a new road bike, check out this site's reviews and rankings first. Site also features road cycling news and a review of the day.

Rocky Mountain Bicycles

www.bikes.com

Overviews of the mountain bikes created by Rocky Mountain Bicycles, plus team profiles, photos, and action video clips. Create your own custom bike using this site.

Santa Cruz Bicycles

www.santacruzmtb.com

Technical details and reviews of Santa Cruz mountain bikes, plus a color picker that allows potential buyers to envision the bike of their dreams. You can shop online for T-shirts, shorts, and other apparel.

Trails.com

www.trails.com

Chosen as Forbes Best of the Web, this site offers locations and ideas for mountain biking trips, as well as hiking, paddling, and skiing excursions. If you have a bike and think there's no place to ride it, check out this site. It features biking trails throughout the United States and Canada and is easy to search. Free 14-day trial was available when we checked.

Western Spirit Cycling

www.westernspirit.com

Operates mountain bike (and road) tours in Utah, Colorado, Idaho, and Arizona. Includes photos and tour information. Learn about the various bike tours available and then sign up for a trip online.

A B C D E F G H I J K L M N O P Q R S T U V W X Y Z

BILLIARDS

American Poolplayers Association

12345

www.poolplayers.com

Geared primarily toward the competition-minded player, this site offers complete rules for the games of 8-ball and 9-ball, plus an opportunity to join the APA or start up an APA tournament franchise. Also includes a link to *American Poolplayer* magazine articles.

Billiard Congress of America

12345

www.bca-pool.com

The Billiard Congress of America is the governing body for the sport of pocket billiards in North America. Its site is primarily educational, providing official rules and guidelines for equipment, but you can also join the organization and read about its publications.

Billiards Digest Interactive

12345

www.billiardsdigest.com

The online complement to the most comprehensive magazine in billiards. Rather than replacing the magazine, the site offers features that supplement the paper copy, such as coverage of upcoming tournaments, chat rooms, and opinion polls. Several links to billiard-supply retailers. Order your subscription online.

Best Brunswick

12345

www.brunswickbilliards.com

Product information and dealer locations can be found at this manufacturer site, as well as information about what makes a Brunswick table different. Great place to learn the basic rules that govern the most common games, including 8-ball, 9-ball, and straight pool. For the best information about billiards presented in the most easily accessible format, visit this site.

Illustrated Principles of Pool and Billiards

12345

www.engr.colostate.edu/~dga/pool

Created and maintained by David G. Alciatore, Ph.D. ("Dr. Dave"), this site provides a video library of lessons on the basics of pool and billiards. Each mini-lesson exposes a key concept or technique that can help you hone your skills and improve your game.

McDermott Handcrafted Cues

12345

www.mcdermottcue.com

When you're ready for a real pool cue, check out McDermott's handcrafted models. Site features cues, shafts, accessories, services (repair, maintenance, and warranty), retired pool cues, and limited-edition cues. Site offers some free maintenance tips, and you can take a video tour of the company.

Pool Hall

12345

www.poolhall.com

Find a pool hall in your area by searching the state listings of pool halls here, shop at the pro shop, or check up on pool tournaments. Also offers some useful instructions and tips on how to play.

U.S. Billiard Association

www.usbilliardassn.org

Find a billiard hall near you, read past issues of the organization newsletter, hear about upcoming tournaments, or join the chat room. Click the Instruction link to brush up on the rules of the game, get tips from the pros, and learn the do's and don'ts of practicing. Clicking the Room Directory calls up a list of pool halls organized by state. Not the most intuitive site to navigate, but lots of good information.

Women's Professional Billiard Association

www.wpba.com

Read the biographies of leading players, check up on their current rankings, and find out when the next competition is being held. A good history of the game along with a bullet list of rules for 9-ball and classic billiards. Attractive site.

BINGO

Bingo Bugle Online Newspaper

12345

www.bingobugle.com

The definitive resource for the Bingo enthusiast. Here, you'll find plenty of links to articles about online gaming, plus links to the best gaming sites on the Web. Play bingo, slot machines, Keno, and other gambling games. Bingo Bugle also offers its own (no-wager) games, just in case you want to play for fun.

Bingo.com

12345

www.bingo.com

Billed as "The World's Largest Bingo Hall," Bingo.com features dozens of free bingo games, including several five-in-a-row, pattern, and speed games. Next to each game is a number showing the number of games of each type that are currently in progress. Sign up for your free account and start playing.

Bingo Gala

12345

www.bingogala.com

Bingo Gala is one of the premier bingo sites on the Web. New games start every 3 to 5 minutes. Just register online, deposit at least $10 into your account (via credit card), pick your card, and join in the next game. Play at your own risk.

Bingo Novelty World

12345

www.bingonoveltyworld.com/shopping

If you're running your own Bingo night, look to this site as a resource for all your bingo needs: ink daubers, cards, waiters, cups, mugs, and can coolers, all for the bingo enthusiast.

Bingo Online

12345

www.bingoonline.com

Play free bingo games for fun, or for cash and prizes, 24 hours a day, 7 days a week. To play for cash, click the Sign Up link on the opening page and follow the onscreen instructions to register.

Bingo Zone

12345

www.bingozone.com

The Lycos Bingo Zone is one of the most popular bingo sites on the Web. This site also features a brief introduction to bingo history and trivia. Play free for the chance to win thousands in prize money.

Best CyberBingo

12345 Blog

www.cyberbingo.net

Billed as America's first and largest bingo network, CyberBingo has been named Top Bingo Site by Gambling Online Magazine. Join thousands of other players in the largest bingo hall on the Internet.

Dot-Bingo.com

12345

www.dot-bingo.com

Dot-Bingo.com is a port that provides access to online bingo games. Site offers reviews of the most popular bingo sites along with bonuses. One of the largest and most colorful portals of its kind.

A B C D E F G H I J K L M N O P Q R S T U V W X Y Z

Instant Bingo

1 2 3 4 5

www.instantbingo.com

Play for fun, points, or cash at this online gaming site. Players can enter weekly drawings and win merchandise, prizes, and special offers.

Which Bingo

1 2 3 4 5

www.whichbingo.com

Games, newsletters, and bingo news are all available here. This site features links to both land-based and online games. Merchandise and equipment can be found, as well as links to other bingo sites. An incredible directory of bingo games and resources.

BIOGRAPHY

Biographical Dictionary

12345

www.s9.com

The Biographical Dictionary introduces visitors to the lives and legacies of more than "28,000 notable men and women who have shaped our world from ancient times to the present day." You can search the dictionary by birth year, death year, positions held, professions, literary and artistic works, achievements, and other keywords. Site also features a Master Challenge and a Spelling Wizard that can help you out if you can't think of the right spelling for someone's name.

Best Biography

12345

www.biography.com

Learn more about the backgrounds of your favorite historical figures or celebrities; they're all profiled here on the Biography Channel's site, which also includes information on the TV show and magazine of the same name. Many of the Biography television shows are available on videotape and are for sale at this site.

Biography Center

12345

www.biography-center.com

Boasting access to over 11,000 different biographies, Biography-Center.com seems to have it all. From German painter Hans von Aachen's bio to Russian inventor Vladimir Kosma Zworykin's, if you can't find their bio here, it may not have ever been written. You can even suggest a biography for the site to include in its next update.

The Biography Maker

12345

www.bham.wednet.edu/bio/biomaker.htm

The Bellingham, Washington, public schools brings us this site, which takes you step by step through the process of writing a biography. Especially useful for junior high and high school students writing their first biography, as well as for adults interested in penning their own.

The Pulitzer Prize

12345

www.pulitzer.org

Using the Category Search feature on the Archive page, you can find a list of all of the Pulitzer Prize winners for Biography (and Autobiography) going as far back as 1917. The list of winners from 1995 to the present includes details such as a book citation, author biography, the jurors who selected the book as the winner, and additional details from the winning book itself.

A
B
C
D
E
F
G
H
I
J
K
L
M
N
O
P
Q
R
S
T
U
V
W
X
Y
Z

BIRDS

About Birding and Wild Birds

12345 RSS

birding.about.com/library/blcard.htm?once=true&pid=2804&cob=home

An array of information about bird sites, articles, and bird products. Plus you can send a free Internet postcard of a wild bird to your favorite person.

All About Birds

12345

www.birds.cornell.edu/AllAboutBirds

This site, from the Cornell Lab of Ornithology, is an excellent guide for anyone interested in bird watching. Site features Birding123 for beginners, a Bird Guide, a Gear Guide, a how-to on Attracting Birds, Conservation, Birding News, an online Quiz of the Week, a photo gallery, and more.

Related Site

www.ebird.org/content

American Birding Association

12345

www.americanbirding.org

Dedicated to increasing the knowledge, skills, and enjoyment of birding and to contributing to bird conservation, the American Birding Association's home page features links to publications, programs, tours, conventions, and other birding resources.

Bird Art

12345

www.chartingnature.com

Definitely will appeal to bird lovers, but also to fish and botanical enthusiasts. Sells Audubon prints, bird posters, and note cards.

Bird Song Matcher

12345

www.virtualbirder.com/vbirder/matcher/matcherDirs/SONG

Test your bird knowledge with this site's bird-identification game. The game gets tricky when you are dealing with multiple habitats and multiple bird species indigenous to any one habitat. To hear and see all the birds, you'll have to play several games.

BIRDTALK.com Magazine

12345

www.birdtalkmagazine.com

A monthly online magazine devoted to the care of exotic birds, providing helpful hints from fellow bird lovers and a vet. Buy bird products online. Species descriptions, an online photo gallery, and behavior and training areas make this site a must-visit for bird owners.

Best Bird Watchers Digest

12345

www.birdwatchersdigest.com

For bird watchers everywhere, this site provides advice on bird watching from the experts, whether you're watching birds from exotic locations or just out your back window. You can also learn about bird gardening, identification, and new birding products. Purchase binoculars, paintings, CDs, books, and other items online. Packed with useful information about bird watching in an easy-to-access format, this site is an easy pick as the Best of the Best.

Birder

12345

www.birder.com

Enjoy virtual birding if you don't have access to local birds or make plans for a bird watching vacation from this site, which emphasizes the sale of bird-watching equipment, books, and other products.

Birding.com

12345

www.birding.com

A site that has a section specifically for beginning birders, Birding.com also lists bird records, birding hot spots, organizations, and links to other resources of potential interest. You can shop online for binoculars, bird feeders, birdhouses, books, and just about anything an avid birder could ever want.

Birding in British Columbia

12345

www.birding.bc.ca

Very current site devoted to birding and ecological sites in British Columbia, Canada. Read birding articles, check out field reports from other birders, get visitor and weather information, and try some links to other birding sites in British Columbia.

Birds n Ways

12345

www.birdsnway.com

Look to Birds n Ways for pet parrots, exotic birds, bird supplies, and pet bird information; it's a complete guide to pet parrots and exotic birds on the Net! You'll find information on dozens of varieties of birds, as well as information on e-zines, chats, forums, bird shows, and more!

Cockatiel Society

12345

www.acstiels.com

The official site of the American Cockatiel Society, which features information for other clubs, upcoming shows, articles, and photos. Dedicated to both cockatiel owners and professional breeders, this site offers a small selection of articles from the A.C.S. Magazine.

The Fabulous Kakapo (Strigops Habroptilus)

12345

www.kakapo.net

Focuses on the kakapo bird, a rare nocturnal, flightless parrot native to New Zealand. Once prevalent throughout the area, the kakapo population is slowly diminishing; there are only about 62 left. This site details how New Zealanders are working to help the population recover.

Field Guides

12345

www.fieldguides.com

Look into birding tours around the world or in your area at this site, which provides information on upcoming tours and guides to help you make your decision.

Finch World

12345

www.finchworld.com

A finch search engine complete with directories of bird lovers and breeders, as well as articles on various finch species. Links to Amazon.com for books and videos on finches.

Hot Spots for Birders

12345

www.birder.com/birding/hotspots/index.html

This site is exactly what its title suggests: a list of the best sites around the world for viewing birds in their natural habitats.

Hotspot for Birds

12345

www.multiscope.com/hotspot

If you keep pet birds, bookmark this site for quick reference; it's packed with expert articles on cleaning, feeding, and caring for your birds. This site also functions as a mega mall for bird-care products.

Life of Birds

1 2 3 4 5

www.pbs.org/lifeofbirds

The *Life of Birds* is a PBS series hosted by Sir David Attenborough. Easy navigational links lead you through several sections on Bird Brains, Evolution, Champion Birds, Parenthood, and Bird Songs. This site provides links to additional PBS specials on birds.

Majestic Macaws

1 2 3 4 5

www.exoticbird.com

Excellent site for macaw owners and admirers. Learn all about the health, behavior, and care for the exotic macaw. The help desk provides excellent information on treating injuries and illnesses, and the Parrot Humor link provides a nice touch. The site also has links for macaw food recipes, supplies, books, breeders, and more.

National Audubon Society

1 2 3 4 5

www.audubon.org

This site, the home page of the National Audubon Society, provides information on the conservation issues and programs the society is currently working on. Those campaigns currently target the marine ecosystems of the world and bird sanctuaries that protect wildlife habitats, including legislation affecting wetlands. Some excellent information on how to increase biodiversity in your own backyard.

Optics for Birding

1 2 3 4 5

www.optics4birding.com

This site is designed to educate those who want to buy optics such as binoculars, night vision, and telescopes. Although the target audience is those who enjoy watching birds, much of the information is generally applicable. This site contains reviews of optical equipment, FAQs, and manufacturer contacts, and allows you to search for a topic.

PETBird

1 2 3 4 5

www.upatsix.com

Introduces aviary practices; provides FAQs; and offers links to numerous breeders, vendors, artists, and avian associations. Check out the Fun and Games section to rate your bird addiction, share your favorite bird names, or check out a colorful photo album.

Peterson Guide for Birds Online

1 2 3 4 5

www.houghtonmifflinbooks.com/peterson

Where do you begin when you want to identify a new bird? To narrow down the possibilities quickly, first put the bird into one of Peterson's eight visual categories. This site also offers birding links and resources, a skill-builder section, a calendar of bird-related events and spectacles, a bird watcher's digest, a bird identification area, and more. Easy-to-navigate site.

Wild Birds Unlimited

1 2 3 4 5

www.wbu.com

Wild Birds Unlimited is the first and largest franchise system of retail stores catering to the backyard bird-feeding hobbyist. Find all kinds of seed, bird feeders, birdhouses, nesting boxes, books, and more at this one-stop shopping site. Email questions directly to the experts.

A B C D E F G H I J K L M N O P Q R S T U V W X Y Z

BLOGS & BLOGGING

DIRECTORIES & SEARCH ENGINES

Blog Catalogue

www.blogcatalog.com

Blog Catalogue bills itself as the ultimate blog directory. Although it might not quite live up to that self-proclaimed label, it does feature hundreds of blogs in dozens of categories, making them easy to browse. The directory relies on users to submit blogs for consideration.

BlogHub

www.bloghub.com

This site catalogs more than 20,000 blogs from over 200 countries. Although this directory provides access to a good collection of blogs, it concentrates on the most popular blogs or the ones that it has most recently registered, making it difficult to track down a specific blog or browse blog categories.

BlogSearchEngine

12345

www.blogsearchengine.com

At BlogSearchEngine, you can search thousands of blogs or scroll down the page and browse through the collection by category.

BlogWise

www.blogwise.com

Here, you will find an extensive directory of more than 16,000 blogs sorted by popularity and browsable by keyword. If you have your own blog, you can register it here.

Digg

www.digg.com

Digg is a "user driven social content site," which is another way of saying that everything you see on the site was submitted by visitors just like you. Use this site to discover the hottest blog postings and videos from tech–related sites and bloggers, as well as to see how bloggers rate each other's blog postings.

Globe of Blogs

www.globeofblogs.com

This site functions as a directory of blogs that you can browse by topic, title, or author. If you have a blog, you can visit this site to register it and have it included in the directory.

LA Blogs

www.lablogs.com

If you live in Los Angeles or are just curious as to what the LA crowd has to say, visit LA Blogs. This self-proclaimed "blog of blogs" provides a loosely organized directory of blogs that relate to life in Los Angeles.

Longhorn Blogs

www.longhornblogs.com

Are you interested in learning and discussing the latest news and information about Microsoft's new version of Windows, code-named Longhorn? Then check out this site, which provides links to 50 of the best Longhorn blogs.

A B C D E F G H I J K L M N O P Q R S T U V W X Y Z

Best Technorati

12345

www.technorati.com

Technorti.com actively tracks what's happening on over 45 million blogs. Using this real-time blog-specific search engine, you can track who is blogging about what and who else is blogging about the same thing. Basically, Technorati.com "makes it possible for you to find out what people on the Internet are saying about you, your company, your products, your competitors, your politics, or other areas of interest."

BLOG HOSTING & TOOLS

Blog-City.com

12345

www.blog-city.com

At Blog-City.com, you can sign up for free blog hosting, so you can create and maintain your own blog. Blog-City.com also features access to several blogs, so you can see how they work. For about $2.50 per month, you can upgrade to premium service for advanced features such as taking online polls, password-protecting your blog entries, and keeping an online photo album.

Blogger

12345 Blog

www.blogger.com

Publish your thoughts and insights on the Web for the general public to read or ponder. At Blogger, you can create your own blog (short for web log) and publish messages simply by completing a form. Blogger also offers a feature that enables you to use a web-based cell phone to record and post your messages when you're on the go; visitors to your blog can then listen to your recorded messages.

BlogIt.com

12345 Blog

www.blogit.com

If the general public finds your words of wisdom valuable, people will be willing to pay you for sharing your opinions and insights. At Blogging Network, you can publish your thoughts online and get paid every time someone clicks a link to read one of your articles. The service charges visitors $2.99 per month for access to all blogs and then divvies up the money among all writers based on each writer's popularity. The more people read your writing, the more you earn.

Bloglines

12345 Blog

www.bloglines.com

Bloglines is a blog service that enables you to search for blogs, subscribe to blog that interest you, and publish and share news feeds, blogs, and web content. Site is divided into four sections: Search, Subscribe, Publish, and Share.

ebloggy

12345

www.ebloggy.com

ebloggy is a no-frills blog host that provides simple, easy-to-use blog templates and free hosting.

Facebook

12345

www.facebook.com

Facebook is designed as a blogging tool as well as a social networking tool to place people in touch with one another. With more than 7.5 million people networking with one another, Facebook has become one of the most frequently visited sites on the Web.

Friendster

12345

www.friendster.com

Friendster is more of a social blogging site, where friends can share photos, stories, insights, ideas, art, and anything else that can be digitized and placed on the Web.

LiveJournal

12345 Blog RSS

www.livejournal.com

LiveJournal is a blog hosting service that enables you to create and update your own blog, check out other blogs in the community, and share your interests with other bloggers. Visit this site to take a free tour of the service and find out what it has to offer.

Movable Type

www.sixapart.com/movabletype

Movable Type is a program that installs on your web server and provides you with the tools you need to create and manage your blog. To use Movable Type, you need to know how to install and configure the software on your web server. At the Movable Type site, you can learn how to access the TypePad service, which provides an easier way for most users to create and manage their blogs.

MySpace

www.myspace.com

MySpace is a social hangout/blogging area, where you can create your own blog for free, create your own community of friends, post photos, share your ideas and insights, and much more. This is one of the more popular blogging sites on the Web.

tBLOG

www.tblog.com

tBLOG offers free blog hosting along with a fine collection of templates that simplify the process of designing and creating a blog. In a matter of minutes, you can have your very own blog up and running on the Web.

TypePad

www.typepad.com

TypePad is a powerful blogging host that gives users a comprehensive set of features and tools to publish and update their blogs right on the Web. You don't need to install or configure a separate program on you computer. Service costs about $5 per month, and when we checked, a free trial was available.

Best WordPress

www.wordpress.org

WordPress is a "state-of-the-art semantic personal publishing platform with a focus on aesthetics, web standards, and usability." Now that's a mouthful! Really, all you need to know is that WordPress is one of the best content management systems that can run your blog, and that it's free and priceless at the same time. Easy to install, manage, and update. WordPress is quickly becoming the standard by which all blog management systems strive to achieve.

Xanga

www.xanga.com

Xanga offers a free blogging service that's pretty basic. For as low as $2 per month (if you pay upfront for a two-year subscription), you can upgrade to the premium service and get powerful tools for creating and updating your site online, so you don't need to install any special software or learn complicated website management software.

BOATS & SAILING

1001 Boats for Sale

1 2 3 4 5

www.1001boats.com

Search a large photo database of powerboats and sailboats by price, size, and location from across the United States to find the boat of your dreams. There is no commission to sellers, although there is a minimal listing fee.

American Sail Training Association

1 2 3 4 5

tallships.sailtraining.org

ASTA's site outlines all that the association offers in the way of Tall Ships sail training, sea education, and sailing travel adventures. It promotes the association's book, newsletter, and benefits of membership, too. You'll find detailed information about vessels, scholarships, ship events, and much more.

American Sailing Association

1 2 3 4 5

www.american-sailing.com

Aspiring sailors will likely find a school near them—no matter where they live—that is staffed by instructors who have earned ASA certification through rigorous training and studies. This site includes a nice forum and information for prospective members.

Boat Owner's World

1 2 3 4 5

www.boatownersworld.com

If you have a boat but need stuff for it, this is the place for you. This site specializes in supplies and accessories, including boat covers, mooring, trailers, and camping gear.

Boating 4 Kids

1 2 3 4 5

www.gomilpitas.com/homeschooling/explore/boating.htm

For kids who are interested in learning about building, navigating, and controlling a boat, this is where you should start. Site features a directory of other sites where kids can learn how to build a milk carton boat, paddle a canoe, practice water safety, sail a boat, and much more.

Boating Magazine

1 2 3 4 5 Blog

www.boatingmag.com

Boating Magazine provides this website for its subscribers and visitors who are looking for the latest reliable information and advice on purchasing, repairing, and getting the most out of their boats. Site features several sections, including Tests, Boat Doctor, Gear Head, Web Exclusives, and Ultimate Angler. Site also features discussion forums and sweepstakes.

BoatSafeKids

1 2 3 4 5

boatsafe.com/kids

An extremely informative site for kids about boats and boating that features their questions and then answers from experts. The site also offers a boat safety checklist for adults.

Boats.com

1 2 3 4 5

www.boats.com

Looking to buy or sell a boat? Then this is the place for you. Boats.com features tabbed navigation to provide quick access to buying and selling boats, both new and used. You can even apply for financing and insurance online and locate a marina to dock and store your boat. But Boats.com is much more than an online boat store. It also provides news articles, features, reviews, and boating tips, so you can fully enjoy your boating experience.

Best Discover Boating

1 2 3 4 5

www.discoverboating.com

Discover Boating programs "focus on increasing participation and creating interest in recreational boating by demonstrating the benefits, affordability, and accessibility of the boating lifestyle while helping to educate potential boaters and offering opportunities to experience the fun and togetherness of being on the water on a boat." Content is presented in six sections: Getting Started, Why Boating, Buying a Boat, Activities and Locations, Owning and Operating, and Resources. This site introduces visitors to safe boating practices while at the same time showing how to get the most out of your boating adventures. You can also order a free DVD online that introduces you to boating and provides video footage that you can't get at the site.

Good Old Boat Magazine

1 2 3 4 5

www.goodoldboat.com

Good Old Boat Magazine is devoted to fostering and supporting a community of sailors who are dedicated to keeping their older model sailboats afloat. Here, you can find articles, tips, and suppliers to help keep your sailboat in tip-top condition—or at least ensure that it remains seaworthy.

Mark Rosenstein's Sailing Page

1 2 3 4 5

www.apparent-wind.com/sailing-page.html

An extensive sailing directory where you can get the latest sailing news, information about maritime museums and magazines, individual stories from around the world, and much more.

Sailboats Inc.

1 2 3 4 5

www.sailboats-inc.com

Anyone considering purchasing a big boat might want to investigate a three-day cruise and seminar from Sailboats Direct. This site will tell you all about the course and what you can expect. And, when you complete the course, be sure to come back here to shop for a yacht and learn about available marina services.

SailNet

1 2 3 4 5 Blog RSS

www.sailnet.com/sailing

The online version of the magazine. Read back issues, as well as the current one. Leave messages on the Message Center and surf through the many sailing links.

Sea-Doo

1 2 3 4 5

www.seadoo.com

In the market for a boat? Sea-Doo has a wide selection of unique designs to tempt your pocketbook, from the 5-person to the 12-person Islandia. The online showroom has a sleek design to match the beauty of Sea-Doo's watercraft.

United States Power Squadrons Web Page

1 2 3 4 5

www.usps.org

Presents USPS, a private boating organization. Focuses on USPS's Basic Boating Course and the purpose of the club. Provides a FAQ, link, and tells how to locate a squadron near you.

U.S. Coast Guard Office of Boating Safety

1 2 3 4 5

www.uscgboating.org

The U.S. Coast Guard's Office of Boating Safety is "dedicated to reducing loss of life, injuries, and property damage that occur on U.S. waterways by improving the knowledge, skills, and abilities of recreational boaters." Use this site to learn about boating regulations, product recalls and safety alerts, boat safety statistics, and more.

U.S. Sailing

1 2 3 4 5

www.ussailing.org

The home page of the official governing body of the sport of sailing in America. The United States Sailing Association features information on sailing publications, racing events and schedules, educational courses, Olympic sailing, and more. Includes excellent information for aspiring young sailors and offers links to other youth-related boating sites.

Yachtingnet

1 2 3 4 5

www.yachtingnet.com

A complete online boating guide that provides marine forecasts for your ZIP code, as well as information on new boats, helpful gear and apparel, a database of available boats, and a community of fellow boaters.

Related Sites

www.sailing.org

BOOKS

American Booksellers Association

1 2 3 4 5 (rating: 5)

www.bookweb.org

American Booksellers Association is "a not-for-profit organization devoted to meeting the needs of its core members of independently owned bookstores with retail storefront locations through advocacy, education, research, and information dissemination." Site features information about the association, the latest Booksense Bestseller Lists, and online discussion forums.

Banned Books Online

1 2 3 4 5 (rating: 3)

digital.library.upenn.edu/books/banned-books.html

Banned Books Online celebrates the freedom to read. You'll find links to e-texts on the Web featuring authors who have at one time been banned in America and elsewhere. The books range from *Candide* to *Huckleberry Finn*. Also present is some censorship history of the books featured on the page and commentary on banning and censorship attempts currently underway.

BookCrossing

1 2 3 4 5 (rating: 4)

www.bookcrossing.com

Do you like to share books with others and meet people who love the same books? Then check out BookCrossing, where you can review your favorite books, tag them, release them into the wild, and track their journeys to readers in your community or around the world. When someone finds a book you released, by leaving it somewhere or donating it to a library or other organization, the person can sign on to BookCrossing and report finding the book. If the person enters a journal entry about the book, BookCrossing notifies you by email so that you can read the entry. BookCrossing's goal is to turn the whole world into a great big library.

BookWire

1 2 3 4 5 (rating: 4)

www.bookwire.com

BookWire is the book industry's most comprehensive and thorough online information source. BookWire's content includes timely book industry news, features, reviews, original fiction, guides to literary events, author interviews, thousands of annotated links to book-related sites, and more.

Best Children's Literature Web Guide (CLWG)

1 2 3 4 5 (rating: 4)

www.acs.ucalgary.ca/~dkbrown

Must-visit site for anyone interested in great books for kids. The Children's Literature Web Guide is an attempt to gather and categorize the growing number of Internet resources related to books for children and young adults. The ideal audience for this site is teachers, librarians, parents, book professionals, and *kids*!

Conservation OnLine

1 2 3 4 5 (rating: 2)

palimpsest.stanford.edu

A guide to preserving books, articles, pictures, and other media for professionals and amateurs alike. This site is dedicated to the preservation of information of many media.

Great Books Foundation

1 2 3 4 5 (rating: 4)

www.greatbooks.org

Interested in starting a reading discussion group? Visit this site for information about this nonprofit organization's approach. Headquartered in Chicago, Great Books publishes reading series for children and adults and conducts training in the Shared Inquiry method. Includes link to Junior Great Books, for K–12 readers.

A B C D E F G H I J K L M N O P Q R S T U V W X Y Z

Harry Potter (Scholastic Books)

1 2 3 4 5

www.scholastic.com/harrypotter/home.asp

Harry Potter fans should check out this site for information about the books, a reference guide, a discussion forum, games, a portrait gallery, a downloadable screensaver, and much more. Near the top of the page is a navigation bar that enables visitors to view other features of the Scholastic Books site. This site is beautifully designed, easy to navigate, and engaging for all ages.

Related Site

www.fictionalley.org

Henry Miller Library

1 2 3 4 5

www.henrymiller.org

Peruse rare Miller books, literature, an online bookstore, a gallery, interactive forums, and more at the online home of the Henry Miller Library, located in Big Sur, California.

A Hundred Highlights from the Koninklijke Bibliotheek

1 2 3 4 5

www.kb.nl/kb/100hoogte/menu-tours-en.html

This large Dutch library has a searchable index of resources. It also contains many pictures that were either created specifically for the library or archived at the library. This library mainly houses older books, and its site enables the library to bring them to the public in a way that makes them less vulnerable to battery and the caustic effects of being in the open.

AUDIO BOOKS

Audible

1 2 3 4 5

www.audible.com

If you like to listen to books being read to you as you travel, exercise, or relax, but you don't like to mess with tapes or CDs, check out Audible's collection of downloadable audio books. You can download the audio file to your computer and then burn it to a CD, transfer it to an MP3 player or Pocket PC, and then carry the book with you wherever you go. If you become a member, you can download a set number of books every month for a monthly fee. You have 18,000 books to choose from.

Audio Books on Compact Disc

1 2 3 4 5

www.abcdinc.com

Browse the large selection of books on CD, which are available at a 20 percent discount.

Audiobooks.com

1 2 3 4 5

www.audiobooks.com

Search the database of a wide variety of audiobooks and place your order online.

AudioBooks Online

1 2 3 4 5

www.audiobooksonline.com

Another audiobook site that features books on tapes and CDs and downloadable MP3 files.

Best Books on Tape

1 2 3 4 5

www.booksontape.com

One of the very few audiobook sites that let you rent rather than buy tapes. You can also listen to audio clips of certain selections at the site. With its huge collection of audio samples, audio books for purchase, and easy navigation, this site is an easy pick for Best of the Best.

BOOK REVIEWS

Atlantic Online

1 2 3 4 5

www.theatlantic.com/index/books

Visit Atlantic Online for book reviews, author interviews, information about new releases, and more. Excellent resource for learning about the latest in the literary world.

BookHive

12345

www.bookhive.org

BookHive is designed to help teachers, parents, and kids from reading age to about 12 years old to find quality books and literature. This site is attractive, especially for kids, and includes several valuable features, such as a recommended book list, Zinger Tales (audio books), Find a Book (which helps you search for books by category), and Fun Activities (where you can play games online).

Booklist

12345

www.ala.org/ala/booklist/booklist.htm

The online counterpart to the American Library Association's publication, Booklist, this website offers new reviews every two weeks on adult, children's, and reference books. Visitors will also find feature articles, author interviews, bibliographies, book-related essays by well-known writers, and several columns.

BookPage

12345

www.bookpage.com

This site offers monthly book reviews of the latest in new fiction, nonfiction, business, children's, spoken audio, and how-to books. Reviews are available online, and the print version is purchased by booksellers and libraries to distribute to their patrons. The site also conducts interviews with authors.

Bookspot

12345

www.bookspot.com

Get recommendations on good books by looking at recent award-winning titles, reviewed works, and popular selections. Links to many online bookstores.

Boston Book Review

12345

www.bookwire.com/bookwire/bbr/bbr-home.html

Providing scholarly commentary on contemporary literary works, the Boston Book Review site is the online companion to the print edition. Well-respected experts and educators evaluate fiction, poetry, interviews, and essays.

Related Site

www.bookwire.com/bookwire/bbr/children/children.html

Oprah's Picks

12345

www2.oprah.com/books/favorite/books_favorite_main.jhtml

Oprah likes Steinbeck and Toni Morrison, so she has verifiably good taste in literature. Here, you can find Oprah's complete list of favorite books and even join Oprah's book club to receive recommendations via email.

New York Review of Books

12345 RSS

www.nybooks.com

The online version of the popular print publication that seeks to discuss important contemporary literary works and issues.

New York Times Book Review

12345 RSS

www.nytimes.com/pages/books/index.html

Extensive book reviews from the *New York Times* book reviewers. Forums, reading groups, and first chapters are offered.

The Scoop

12345

www.friend.ly.net/scoop

Provides reviews of popular activities and adventure books for children. Site includes biographies of authors and illustrators, author interviews, and links to other sites. You can shop for books through links to Amazon.com.

BOOKSTORES

Abe Books

1 2 3 4 5

www.abebooks.com

If you're looking for hard-to-find books or collectible books, visit Abe Books online. This site is designed to make it easy to browse or to search for specific titles and authors. Abe Books also provides tools for those who have rare books that they want to sell.

Adler's Foreign Books

1 2 3 4 5

www.afb-adlers.com

Adler's Foreign Books imports and distributes French, Spanish, German, Italian, and Portuguese language books in the United States. It also supplies books in Chinese and Russian. Adler's has an estimated 18,000 foreign titles in its inventory, making it one of the largest foreign book distributors in the United States. Its inventory consists primarily of novels, anthologies of both prose and poetry, literature, history, philosophy, language-learning resources, dictionaries, and other reference materials.

Alibris

1 2 3 4 5

www.alibris.com

Browse titles from a wide variety of categories and then rely on Alibris to find them for you. The company specializes in tracking down those hard-to-find books.

Antiquarian Booksellers' Association of America (ABAA)

1 2 3 4 5

abaa.org

Specializes in rare and antiquarian books, maps, and prints. Provides a search service by specialty and location, catalogs and links to other services for more than 330 dealers online, current information on book fairs nationwide, links to online public access catalogs at libraries worldwide, and articles of interest to booksellers and book collectors from the ABAA Newsletter.

Astrology et al Bookstore

1 2 3 4 5

www.astrologyetal.com

Features online catalog of astrology, occult, pagan, UFO, metaphysical, and other related titles. Includes a listing of out-of-print and hard-to-find books the bookstore has in stock.

Barnes & Noble.com

1 2 3 4 5

www.barnesandnoble.com

Visit the online version of the popular Barnes & Noble bookstore and search its inventory for new and out-of-print titles. Order online and have the book you want delivered right to your door. Barnes & Noble also carries audio CDs, VHS and DVD videos, and software.

BookCloseOuts.com

1 2 3 4 5

www.bookcloseouts.com

The online division of one of the largest closeout/remainder bookstores in North America. The parent company (Book Depot) has been in business for years; the company offers more than five million books at blowout prices. Because it features closeouts exclusively, you might not find today's bestsellers, but you will find books on your favorite subjects and by your favorite authors—at super cheap prices!

BookFinder.com

1 2 3 4 5

www.bookfinder.com

Anyone looking for a new, used, out-of-print, or first-edition copy of a particular title might want to start with Book Finder. The option to request a first edition is unique to this site and might be of interest to book collectors.

Books for Cooks

1 2 3 4 5

www.books-for-cooks.com

The Internet extension of a family-run cookbook store. This site features thousands of cookbooks, organized into more than 140 cooking categories.

From Pacific Rim cooking to chocolate desserts to diabetic meals to garnishing ideas, this site has something for everyone. Each title includes a picture of the cover and a brief description. A recipe symbol tells you that a sample recipe is attached for you to try. New recipes are added to the site every week.

Borders.com

1 2 3 4 5

www.borders.com

Connects you to the Amazon/Borders team site, where you can search the largest collection of books and magazines online and order them right from the comfort of your own computer. Also provides a list of Borders bookstore locations and events.

City Lights Bookstore

1 2 3 4 5

www.citylights.com

Creative and innovative site representing the historic City Lights Bookstore, founded by poet Lawrence Ferlinghetti, in San Francisco's North Beach area. This site offers cutting-edge literature and books on compelling social and political issues. Whether you're interested in the Beat generation or the latest cutting-edge literary works, this is the place to track down copies of your favorite books.

East Bay Book Search

1 2 3 4 5

www.eastbaybooks.com

Billed as the "World's Premier Book Search Service," East Bay Book Search can track down rare and out-of-print books. Call the toll-free number or fill out the online search form; a representative will contact you with search results.

Guidon Books

1 2 3 4 5

www.guidon.com

Online site for Guidon Books, a 35-year-old bookseller located in Scottsdale, Arizona. The store's claim to fame is an extensive collection of new and out-of-print books on the American Civil War, Western Americana, Lincoln, Custer, and American Indian history and arts and crafts, too. You can place your order by phone, email, fax, or regular mail, but no online sales are currently available.

Juilliard Bookstore

1 2 3 4 5

www.bookstore.Juilliard.edu

The Juilliard Bookstore features an inventory of more than 30,000 titles, including sheet music, scores, and classical music books. It also carries CDs and DVDs, videos, apparel, and gifts. When you're having a tough time tracking down items for a play or musical, check this site.

LawCatalog.com

1 2 3 4 5

www.lawcatalog.com

A one-stop legal resource service for lawyers and law students. You can find casebooks and supplements, legal references, study guides, and tools for managing your legal practice. Fifty years of experience helping lawyers and law students excel.

Loganberry Books

1 2 3 4 5

www.logan.com/loganberry

This bookstore features a diverse collection of used books and offers book-of-the-month clubs specializing in women's, children's, arts, and out-of-print books. Choose the club that is right for you. The store will also do book searches.

NHBS Environmental Bookstore

1 2 3 4 5

www.nhbs.com

Catering wildlife enthusiasts, scientists, and conservationists, you can browse books by category: botany, zoology, biology, biodiversity, conservation, Earth, environment, and so on. Or, you can search for specific publications by title. The bookstore is located in England, so all prices are in British pounds.

Powell's Books

12345 RSS

www.powells.com

Powell's Bookstore has a long history, from its humble beginnings in Chicago to its expansion in Portland, Oregon. Although shopping online cannot replace the experience of browsing the aisles of Powell's outstanding collection of new and used books, this site provides a little of the flavor along with some powerful tools for tracking down rare, out-of-print books or even the more popular fare. Within two years of the origin of this website, Powell's entire inventory was online! Check it out here.

Publisher Direct Online Bookstore

12345

www.pdbookstore.com

Find deals on a wide assortment of titles, including biographies, novels, computer books, religious writings, and more. Not a huge selection of books but great prices.

Words Worth Books

12345

www.wordsworthbooks.com

Besides offering a wonderful selection of books at a discounted price, Words Worth Books is a book lover's dream, with its book selection of the day; interviews with authors; great selection of children's books; contests for adults and children; autographed copies of books; the independent bestseller list; and all literary award winners, for fiction, nonfiction, and children's literature.

Zanadu Comics

12345

www.zanaducomics.com

Specializes in alternative and mainstream comics, graphic novels, and more. Features reviews by staff and customers, promotions, and a virtual catalog.

BOOKS ONLINE

Best Amazon.com

12345

www.amazon.com

Touted as the "Earth's Biggest Bookstore" and one of the largest online shopping centers, Amazon.com offers millions of books, CDs, audiobooks, DVDs, computer games, and more. If you want a book and can't find it anywhere else, check out Amazon.com.

Visit www.currentcodes.com to see whether any discount codes are available before placing your Amazon.com order.

Best Book Buys

12345

www.bestwebbuys.com/books

Find the lowest prices for any book imaginable. Search for the book you want. Best Book Buys locates the book at several online bookstores and displays a list, showing which bookstore offers the best deal. Simply click the link for the desired store and order the book. Search includes new and used copies.

Bigwords.com

12345

www.bigwords.com

Specializing in college textbooks, Bigwords buys and sells used textbooks for less.

Books A Million

12345

www.booksamillion.com

This online bookstore advertises discounts of 20 percent to 55 percent off retail book prices, which can be found at its brick-and-mortar locations, too. Search the database to find the title you're looking for.

BookSelecta

1 2 3 4 5

www.bookselecta.com

Download electronic versions of books to read on your computer. With text-to-speech software, you can even have your computer "read" the book to you. Some free books, including *The Red Badge of Courage* and *Aesop's Fables*. Most e-books for purchase cost less than half the price of the printed versions.

The eBook Directory

1 2 3 4 5 

www.ebookdirectory.com

Links to thousands of electronic books, many of which are self-published. Learn how to publish your own e-books online, too.

NetLibrary

1 2 3 4 5

www.netlibrary.com

NetLibrary is a collection of electronic versions of books, some of which are available to read free and others available for purchase. After locating an e-book at NetLibrary, visitors have the option of either purchasing or borrowing the e-book. By borrowing an e-book, users have exclusive access to the book during the checkout period. (No one else can borrow the same book unless there are multiple copies.) E-books are automatically checked back in to the NetLibrary collection when the checkout period expires. Some free e-books are available in the Reading Room.

Online Books

1 2 3 4 5

digital.library.upenn.edu/books

Here is a remarkable collection of books on the Web: 18,000+ listings with an index searchable by author or title. For just browsing, try the subject listing and view the scores of timeless and copyright-free great works, with an especially strong showing in philosophy, religion, and history.

Project Gutenberg

1 2 3 4 5

www.gutenberg.net

Search the archives of Project Gutenberg to find the 18,000 e-texts in the public domain that are available free for download. Great collection of classic literature and reference books for free!

PUBLISHERS

Association of American Publishers

1 2 3 4 5

www.publishers.org

The Association of American Publishers (AAP), with some 310 members located throughout the United States, is the principal trade association of the book publishing industry. AAP members publish hardcover and paperback books in every field: fiction, general nonfiction, poetry, children's literature, textbooks, reference works, Bibles, and other religious books and scientific, medical, technical, professional, and scholarly books and journals.

Books AtoZ

1 2 3 4 5

www.booksatoz.com

Books AtoZ brings together in one place all the vendors needed to publish a book. Its specialty is helping self and small publishers with layout, printing, marketing, and fulfillment. In addition, this site provides award-winning information and links on publishing.

Books @ Random

1 2 3 4 5

www.randomhouse.com

Home of Random House, Inc. Use this site to access its library, bookseller, and teacher services, or browse for books by the subject that interests you. Includes links to other Random House pages that feature titles for kids of every age group.

A B C D E F G H I J K L M N O P Q R S T U V W X Y Z

Canadian Publishers' Council

1 2 3 4 5

www.pubcouncil.ca

Association representing book publishers in Canada since 1910. This site includes links to publishing-related sites, FAQs, industry studies, statistics, and information on copyright.

Houghton Mifflin Company

1 2 3 4 5

www.hmco.com/indexf.html

Houghton Mifflin Company online. Houghton Mifflin publishes educational books and materials for elementary through college levels; its site includes links to subsidiaries.

John Wiley & Sons

1 2 3 4 5

www.wiley.com

Once known for publishing the works of Washington Irving, Edgar Allan Poe, and Herman Melville, this nearly 200-year-old publishing company is now known for publishing the popular For Dummies, CliffsNotes, Frommer's, and Betty Crocker series. Use this site to search and purchase the latest Wiley titles.

McGraw-Hill Bookstore

1 2 3 4 5

books.mcgraw-hill.com

This bookstore offers a huge selection of science and technical, reference, professional, business, and computer books from all publishers—not just McGraw-Hill.

Best Pearson Technology Group

1 2 3 4 5

www.pearsoned.com/professional/technical.htm

Search Pearson Technology Group's vast collection of professional, technology, and computer books. Searchable collections of reference content, books and software for sale, links to valuable third-party sites, and related resources covering the topics business and technology professionals are looking for. Here, you can find books on business, computers, engineering, science, and vocational skills. The top imprints in the business call this site home, including Addison-Wesley Professional, Que, New Riders, Sams, Cisco Press, and more.

Perseus Books Group

1 2 3 4 5

www.perseusbooksgroup.com

Specializing in nonfiction books on topics ranging from psychology and sociology to politics and public policy, this site provides links to the various imprints that make up Perseus Books Group: Basic Books, Civitas, Counterpoint, Da Capo Press, PublicAffairs, Running Press, and Westview Press.

Publishers Marketing Association (PMA) Online

1 2 3 4 5

www.pma-online.org

This trade association represents independent publishers of books, audio, video, and CDs. Find member directories, information, discussion forums, and more.

Publishers Weekly

1 2 3 4 5

www.publishersweekly.com

International news source for book publishers and sellers features reviews of the latest books, bestseller lists, trade information, and much more. If you're in the publishing business, bookmark this site and visit often.

Time Life

1 2 3 4 5

www.timelife.com

Explore the many products Time Life offers in books, music, and videos. The Kids area includes books and recordings for kids from birth up to age 12.

BOWLING

Amateur Bowling Tournaments

www.bowling300.com

If you're a bowler and want to find a tournament to participate in, check out this Official Page of Amateur Bowling.

AMF Bowling Worldwide

www.amf.com

AMF is the largest company in the world focused solely on bowling. Check out AMF's site for more information on the company, its bowling centers, and its products; tips from the pros; fun and games; product reviews; and more.

Bowl.com: Official Site of the United States Bowling Congress

12345

www.bowl.com

Industry news, feature stories, events, tournaments and results, games, trivia, newsletter, tips, links to shopping sites, and more. Check out the tabs near the top of the page for links to various bowling associations. Links to some junior bowling sites for the younger crowd.

Bowling.com

12345

www.bowling.com

Complete line of bowling equipment, including balls, bags, shoes, and shirts from all the major manufacturers. Includes a special area for kids.

BowlingIndex

www.bowlingindex.com

BowlingIndex is an extensive directory of bowling-related content on the Web. Links are organized by category, which include Products, Centers, Instruction, Who's Who (the stars and leaders), Bowling Links (links to other bowling websites), and Industry Pages. Excellent place to start your search.

Bowlers Journal International

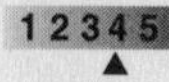

www.bowlersjournal.com

Launched in February 1998, the Bowlers Journal International website has set out to complement its print counterpart by making many of its monthly columns, instructional articles, and tournament insights available to the online reader.

Bowler's Paradise

12345

www.bowlersparadise.com

Bowler's Paradise is the official online retailer of the Professional Bowlers Association. Here you can find bowling balls, bags, shoes, books, videos, PBA apparel, articles, and bowling tips. If you're serious about bowling, bookmark this page.

Bowling This Month Magazine

12345

www.bowlingthismonth.com

Bowling This Month magazine is for serious bowlers who want to improve their scores. It provides the most up-to-date technical information available on subjects ranging from advanced technique through lane play to balls and ball motion. Topics include comprehensive new equipment reviews, lane play, ball motion and reaction, tips to improve mechanics, mental conditioning, physical conditioning, and an updated ball comparison chart.

Bowling World

1 2 3 4 5

www.bowlingworld.com

Bowling World's website contains a reproduction of the printed version of the Bowling World Newspaper, which has been covering the world of bowling for 36 years.

Bowling Zone

1 2 3 4 5

www.bowlingzone.com

With more than 1,300 linked sites, you can find directions to lanes, scores and stats, PBA players' home pages, clinics and instruction, and international organizations and associations.

Brunswick Online

1 2 3 4 5

www.brunswickbowling.com

Whether you're interested in building a bowling alley or just building your average, this site points the way. Find out about the Brunswick products that can help. You can also play a Blockbuster Bowling online game (if your browser supports Shockwave).

Dick Ritger Bowling Camps

1 2 3 4 5

www.ritgerbowlingcamp.com

Information about a training camp that bowlers can attend to help improve their game. Summer and winter sessions are offered, plus instructor certification.

Duckpin Bowling

1 2 3 4 5

www.fountainsquareindy.com/action.html

Looking for a bowling alley off the beaten track? Then head to Indianapolis, just a little south of downtown, and try your hand at duckpin bowling. Here, you can bowl with a ball that fits in the palm of your hand on lanes that are more than 70 years old.

Related Site

www.robinsweb.com/duckpin

International Bowling Museum and Hall of Fame

1 2 3 4 5

www.bowlingmuseum.com

The International Bowling Museum and Hall of Fame is a facility located in downtown St. Louis. This site includes information about the history of the sport (starting in ancient Egyptian times), weekly trivia, and a museum shop where you can purchase clothing and novelty items online.

LeagueSecretary.com

1 2 3 4 5

www.leaguesecretary.com

LeagueSecretary.com is the only site that can generate Interactive Standing sheets and provide bowlers with a graphical image of the bowlers' historical records. This is the only site that provides total integration between a leading software product, CDE Software BLS, and the Internet.

Best PBA Tour

1 2 3 4 5

www.pba.com

The official site of the Professional Bowlers Association tour, this site profiles the key competitors, provides updated scores and standings, and lets you know when various bowling tournaments will be broadcast on television.

Related Sites

www.igbo.org

dir.yahoo.com/Recreation/sports/bowling

Youth Bowling

1 2 3 4 5

www.bowl.com/youth

The website for young bowlers, this site is maintained by Bowl.com and is the top bowling site for young bowlers. It features news, tournaments and results, coaching tips, bowling tips and rules, and a fun and games section. Several links to online stores that carry bowling equipment, apparel, and novelty items.

BOXING

Boxing: CBS SportsLine

12345 RSS

cbs.sportsline.com/boxing

A well-designed online newspaper from CBS Sports that focuses on professional boxing. Includes articles, a message board and current scores as well as photos from major competitions.

Boxing Game

12345

www.boxinggame.com

Do you yearn to be a boxing manager but question your ability to make a living at it? If so, this site might be for you. Join the site and create your own stable of fighters. Then follow their careers as they punch their way through a season of fights. The site informs you five days prior to each bout, so you have a chance to check out your fighter's opponent and come up with a fight strategy. After each fight (you need not be present), you receive a blow-by-blow description of how your fighter fared.

Boxing Monthly

12345

www.boxing-monthly.co.uk

Sample articles from the current print issue of this popular boxing magazine, plus information about subscribing.

Boxing Talk

12345 RSS

www.boxingtalk.net

This site, for the serious boxing fan, feature articles, short video clips, and a great collection of announcements about upcoming fights. Online chats are always active. To get the good stuff, you need to become a member.

The Boxing Times

12345 RSS

www.boxingtimes.com

Excellent source for fight previews, fight analyses, columns, and world rankings. You can also visit the archives for reports from past fights. Though you cannot purchase products directly from this site, it provides a link to Amazon.com, which makes the transition from browsing to shopping nearly transparent.

Cyber Boxing Zone

12345

cyberboxingzone.com/boxing/cyber.htm

The Cyber Boxing Zone offers late-breaking boxing news, bout previews, and a lineage of past to present champions in classes ranging from the strawweights to heavyweights. You will also find the CBZ Boxing Encyclopedia, a book and video store, message board, and Cyber Boxing Journal.

Best Doghouse Boxing

12345

www.doghouseboxing.com

Updated daily, this site is the source of the freshest boxing news on the Internet. Packed with boxing articles, fight schedules, and a good dose of humor, this site promises to keep boxing fans entertained for hours. This site's clean design, unpretentious presentation of the information, and informative, engaging (and free) articles made it a hands-down pick for Best of the Best!

ESPN.com Boxing

12345

sports.espn.go.com/sports/boxing/index

The latest boxing news stories from ESPN. Updated daily, this is your best source for up-to-the-minute coverage. Home of *Friday Night Fights.*

A B C D E F G H I J K L M N O P Q R S T U V W X Y Z

HBO Boxing

1 2 3 4 5 ▲

www.hbo.com/boxing

All the latest HBO boxing news, updated fight schedules, announcements, and more. Includes free video clips and an HBO store where you can purchase sports videos and other items.

International Boxing Hall of Fame

1 2 3 4 5 ▲

www.ibhof.com

An attractive tribute to the great fighters in boxing history, this site spotlights many boxing legends and provides information about the newest inductees.

International Female Boxers Association

1 2 3 4 5 ▲

www.ifba.com

Dedicated to promoting the sport of female boxing, this site provides a list of boxing champions, rankings, and fight results, plus a schedule of upcoming events. Check out the photo library for pictures of your favorite female fighters in action.

Max Boxing

1 2 3 4 5 ▲

www.maxboxing.com

This site has almost everything a boxing fan could ever dream of: up-to-the-minute-news, fight schedules, video coverage, fight picks, profiles, message boards, a trivia quiz, and much more. This site even contains a link you can click to place a bet on your favorite fighter...or at least the one you think will win the fight. Some good stuff for free, but to access the good stuff, it'll cost you—about $5 a month.

Showtime Championship Boxing

1 2 3 4 5 ▲

www.sho.com/site/boxing/home.do

Showtime's pay-per-view boxing matches are some of the best spectacles in boxing. Check this site for Showtime's fight schedule, biographies of Showtime boxers, and descriptions of past fights. You can even submit a question to Showtime's boxing expert and view video clips of great knockouts.

USA Boxing

1 2 3 4 5 ▲

www.usaboxing.org

Home of the U.S. national governing body for Olympic-style boxing, which is a member of the International Amateur Boxing Association (AIBA). This site provides news, information about the boxers representing the United States, event announcements, rankings, and more.

World Boxing Association

1 2 3 4 5 ▲

www.wbaonline.com

The World Boxing Association is one of the main boxing organizations in the United States that governs the sport, makes the rules, and decides who gets the title. This site features a history of the association, rankings, results, records, schedules, statistics, and more.

World Boxing Council

1 2 3 4 5 ▲

www.wbcboxing.com

The WBC has "161 affiliated countries and 9 Continental Boxing Federations, becoming the leading institution in the World of Boxing for its size, safety, opportunities for all and human equality." Here, you can learn more about the WBC, get the latest result, check out the rankings, visit the photo gallery and the Hall of Fame, and more.

BUSINESS

411.com

12345

www.411.com

Get the 411 and find anyone, locate a business, find a ZIP code, perform a trademark search, compare phone rates, and more at this convenient and informative site. Easy to navigate.

All Business Network

12345

www.all-biz.com

The All Business Network has links to hundreds of online publications, business directories, job banks, accounting resources, professional reference materials, economic reports, and other websites relating to business.

BigBook

12345

www.bigbook.com

This site allows you to conduct a quick search on virtually any U.S. company. It provides addresses, phone numbers, profile information, and maps indicating where the businesses are located.

Bigfoot

12345

bigfoot.com

Fast telephone, address, email, and home page finder. Accepts queries in several languages.

Brint.com

12345

www.brint.com

This business research site specializes in management and technology concerns. The searchable database provides access to hundreds of full-text articles and research papers on topics such as outsourcing, virtual corporations, online commerce, and more.

BusinessTown

12345

www.businesstown.com

BusinessTown is a bare-bones directory of information, resources, and business-to-business contacts for small-business owners. Here you can learn everything from accounting to valuing a business, hiring and firing employees, managing time and people, and even selling your business when you're ready to retire.

Businesstravelnet.com

12345

www.businesstravelnet.com

A first-class website for people accustomed to flying first class. If your business means travel, Businesstravelnet.com has lots of useful resources.

The BizWiz

12345

www.clickit.com/touch/bizwiz.htm

With 300,000+ members, BizWiz is one of the largest business-to-business service companies on the Web. Designed to put businesses in contact with one another, the site is searchable by category and keyword.

Business 2.0

12345 RSS

www.business2.com

Business magazine that highlights the most innovative and successful businesses and reveals the secrets of their success. Also provides useful insights and shows how to put the best business strategies into action.

Business.com

12345 RSS

www.business.com

Comprehensive, browsable, or searchable business directory that helps you or your company find the products and services you need. The opening page acts as the directory, but don't miss the other two tabs: News and Jobs. Together, the three pages provide a very comprehensive collection of links for all areas of business.

BusinessWeek.com

12345 RSS

www.businessweek.com

Home of *BusinessWeek* magazine, this site features a daily briefing, investment information, small business tips, career information, and industry news. Also features some pay services, including investment services, databases, and reprints.

Business Wire

12345

www.businesswire.com

Business Wire has the latest international press releases related to business and marketing, updated hourly. Visitors can also search for more information by name or state.

CorporateInformation

12345

www.corporateinformation.com

An online directory of corporate information resources organized by country. Searches more than 350,000 company profiles, 20,000 of which are analyzed at this site.

Dun & Bradstreet

12345

www.dnb.com

Home of the leading provider of business information, this site is essentially a marketing service for Dun & Bradstreet's business advice. Database tracks more than 70 million companies worldwide.

Fast Company

12345 RSS

www.fastcompany.com

Online magazine focusing on business innovation, creativity, and productive practices in the workplace. This site features a wide range of articles on how to find a job, keep a job, and climb the corporate ladder. Also provides information on how to establish a business on the Web, how to become an effective manager, and much more. Excellent content presented in an easily accessible format.

Best Forbes Online

12345 RSS

www.forbes.co

Technology, investing, media, and politics—all are covered in this site from Forbes publications. You'll also find articles on companies, entrepreneurs, the economy, and the world's wealthiest people. The site features easy navigation, the latest financial news, and a good collection of personal finance tools, making it the Best of the Best business site on the Web.

Fortune.com

12345 RSS

www.fortune.com

The online version of *Fortune* magazine offers feature articles, personal computing and finance sections, and other business and finance-related information and news.

Harvard Business Online

12345

harvardbusinessonline.hbsp.harvard.edu

Harvard Business Online focuses on the issues confronting top managers in today's business environment. The site offers ideas, research, and subscription information. Shop for publications online that have to do with important business topics, such as communication, finances, leadership, innovation, sales, and management.

Hoover's Online

12345

www.hoovers.com

Free access to business directories with operations and products, financials, officers, and competitors. Links for investing, sales prospecting, jobs, marketing, competitive research, and more. Links to other sites where you can purchase company reports online.

The Industry Standard

www.thestandard.com

The Industry Standard aims to be the single source for critical, timely information about the Internet economy. When you need to know the latest, most significant information about what's happening in the world of technology and the Internet, this is the place to go.

InfoSpace.com

12345

www.infospace.com

One of the best people-finder directories, including a global telephone and address search, email lookup, and reverse lookup.

Infobel: Telephone Directories

12345

www.infobel.com/teldir/default.asp

Links to online phone books worldwide, including white pages, yellow pages, business directories, email addresses, and fax numbers.

LEXIS-NEXIS Communication Center

12345

www.lexis-nexis.com

LexisNexis online is a legal research system, launched in 1973, that many law firms and businesses have found to be indispensable in helping them resolve any corporate legal issue.

OneSource

12345

www.onesource.com

Dedicated to delivering corporate, industry, financial, and market information to professionals who need to keep abreast of the latest business data. Compiles data from more than 25 information providers, drawing from more than 2,500 sources. For a fixed annual subscription price, you can access the OneSource database over the Internet using a standard web browser.

STAT-USA

12345

www.stat-usa.gov

Provides statistical releases, export and trade databases and information, and domestic economic databases and information. Some free information; but for the good stuff, you must pay an annual $175 subscription fee.

Related Sites

dir.yahoo.com/Business_and_Economy/Trade

ibc.katz.pitt.edu

Switchboard: The Internet Directory

12345

www.switchboard.com

Offers all kinds of lookup features. You can find a person, a business listing, an email address, maps and directions, or you can search the Web.

Web100: Big Business on the Web

12345

www.metamoney.com/w100

This site contains a list of the 100 largest U.S. companies that have a presence on the Internet. It also has links to each company and a list of the 100 largest companies in the world.

A B C D E F G H I J K L M N O P Q R S T U V W X Y Z

Related Sites

American International Group, Inc.
www.aig.com

AT&T Corporation
www.att.com

Bank of America Corporation
www.bankofamerica.com

Boeing
www.boeing.com

Chase Manhattan Corporation
www.chase.com

Citigroup
www.citi.com

Coca-Cola Company
www.cocacola.com

DuPont www.dupont.com

Federal Express Corporation
www.federalexpress.com

Ford Motor Company
www.ford.com

General Electric Company
www.ge.com

General Motors
www.gm.com

Goodyear Tire and Rubber Company
www.goodyear.com

Hewlett-Packard Company
www.hp.com

IBM Corporation
www.ibm.com

Intel Corporation
www.intel.com

Kmart Corporation
www.kmart.com

Lucent Technologies
www.lucent.com

Merck & Co.
www.merck.com

Merrill Lynch
www.ml.com

Microsoft Corporation
www.microsoft.com

Mobil
www.mobil.com

Motorola
www.motorola.com

The Procter & Gamble Company
www.pg.com

Prudential Insurance Company of America
www.prudential.com

Sears, Roebuck & Company
www.sears.com

State Farm Insurance Companies
www.statefarm.com

SBC Communications
www.sbc.com

Texaco
www.texaco.com

TIAA-CREF
www.tiaa-cref.org

United Parcel Service of America, Inc. (UPS)
www.ups.com

Verizon
www22.verizon.com

Wal-Mart Stores, Inc.
www.walmart.com

The Walt Disney Company
disney.go.com

FRANCHISING

American Association of Franchisees & Dealers

1 2 3 4 5

www.aafd.org

This organization represents the rights of both franchisees and dealers. Here you can learn about upcoming events, read some free publications online, order other publications from the bookstore, and become a member.

Be the Boss

1 2 3 4 5

www.betheboss.com

Visit this site to post a franchise opportunity or to investigate an opportunity. Lots of information, including alphabetic and category listings, and features with detailed information on specific franchises.

BizBuySell

1 2 3 4 5

www.bizbuysell.com

Looking to buy a business? Good chance you'll find one here at BizBuySell. From restaurants in

California to auto shops in Florida, you can search more than 25,000 businesses currently for sale. New businesses are added every weekday. Get notified about new listings by email. It's free! Selling your biz? Visit the Sell area. Post a free ad. New to franchising? Read the Buyer's Guide section.

Canadian Business Franchise Magazine

12345

www.cgb.ca

Latest news, tips, and features on franchising in Canada. You can subscribe to the magazine and order other publications online.

Centercourt USA

12345

www.centercourt.com

Covers franchises in the United States and information on the latest trends; check out their business showcase section, and search their database for details on franchises that interest you. You'll also find a section devoted to classifieds; another offering products and services to purchase; and one offering marketing, legal, and operational tips.

Federal Trade Commission: Franchises and Business Opportunities

12345

www.ftc.gov/bcp/franchise/netfran.htm

This site has lots of information, including a FAQ section, Guide to the FTC Franchise Rule, consumer alerts, Before You Buy pamphlets, state disclosure requirements, and more.

Franchise.com

12345

www.franchise.com

Learn more about available franchise opportunities or advertise your franchise to potential buyers at this site, which aims to connect franchise buyers and sellers, as well as anyone thinking of starting one.

The Franchise Handbook On-Line

12345

www.franchise1.com

Features various franchises and offers a directory of franchise opportunities, industry news, and articles. Order a subscription online.

The Franchise Registry

12345

www.franchiseregistry.com

Hosted for the U.S. Small Business Administration by FRANdata. The registry lists names of franchise companies whose franchisees enjoy the benefits of a streamlined review process for SBA loan applications.

Franchise Solutions

12345

www.franchisesolutions.com

Franchise Solutions has been featured in *Entrepreneur* magazine, *USA Today*, *Nation's Business*, and on CNBC. Find franchise and business opportunities at this site. Good collection of articles, tips, and advice from franchise experts, along with a FAQ, glossary, and suggested reading list.

Franchise Update

12345 RSS

www.franchise-update.com

Check out detailed articles about franchising, find experienced franchise attorneys, and learn more about available franchises at the site.

Best Franchise Zone by Entrepreneur.com

12345

www.entrepreneur.com/Franchise_Zone

Dedicated to linking enthusiastic entrepreneurs with the top franchises, this site provides all the information you need to find the best franchises and become a successful franchisee. How-to articles, advice from experts, and lists of the top franchises in various categories make this the first site to turn for those considering the purchase of a franchise. Don't miss the article on How to Buy a Franchise.

Franchising.com

www.franchising.com

Franchising.com features a collection of top franchising opportunities, along with the information and tools you need to successfully operate your own franchise. The extensive Franchise Opportunity directory can help you find the right business opportunity.

FRANInfo

12345

www.franinfo.com

Information about franchising and whether you're suited for it, lists of available franchises, and existing franchise operations for sale. Some excellent resources on the history of franchising and what it's all about, plus a guide to selecting the right franchise for you. Great place for when you're just starting to consider becoming a franchise owner.

International Franchise Association

12345

www.franchise.org

Membership organization of franchisers, franchisees, and suppliers. Provides a franchise directory, information on how to build your franchise, a resource center, and bookstore.

USA Today Franchise Solutions

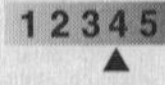

usatoday.franchisesolutions.com

USA Today, a reliable resource for news and information, also offers reliable information on franchise solutions. Here you can find hundreds of franchise opportunities presented in several categories, including Popular, Unique, Home-Based, Automotive, and Children's, to name only a few. To search for a specific franchise, you can specify the price range you can afford and select a category.

HOME-BASED BUSINESS

At-Home Based Business Online

www.ahbbo.com

Attorney Elena Fawkner created and maintains this site for independent souls who want to open their own businesses or work out of their homes. This site has a sleek, clean design that makes finding the information you're looking for quite easy. Links are organized by category, including Online Business, Home Business, Trafficking in Information, and Legal. The navigation bar that runs down the left side of the page provides quick access to Business Ideas and Tools of the Trade.

Bizy Moms

www.bizymoms.com

Business ideas, recommended books and resources, and work-at-home scams and how to avoid them. Be sure to sign up for the free newsletter that's sent once a week. And don't forget to check out the message board for more ideas on a variety of topics! If you weren't busy before you visited this site, this place can keep you busy for days.

Business Owners' Idea Cafe

12345

businessownersideacafe.com

Business Owners' Idea Cafe takes a "fun approach to serious business," as you can tell from the design of its opening page. Categories of help include Biz Grant Center, Cyberschmooz, Starting Your Biz, Running Your Biz, and Take Out Info. This site provides excellent information for the small-business owner in a format that makes it accessible and entertaining.

Getting New Business Ideas

12345

www.planware.org/ideas.htm

A seven-step process for developing ideas for a business. These seven simple steps take you through the initial search for business ideas through copyrighting and legal stuff. Links to free business planning and financing software.

Jim Blasingame: The Small-Business Advocate

www.jbsba.com

Jim Blasingame is a renowned small-business advocate and syndicated talk-show host who has assembled one of the largest communities of small-business experts in the world. He refers to this group as the Brain Trust, and he interviews one of them every 30 minutes on his show. This site contains a wealth of information and advice for small-business owners and entrepreneurs.

PowerHomeBiz.com

www.powerhomebiz.com

PowerHomeBiz.com is a great website both for those who are just considering the opportunity of starting their own home-based business and for those who already have a business in place. This site features "how I did it" success stories, step-by-step instructions on getting started, tips and hints for gaining an edge in the competitive marketplace, motivational articles, and advice from the pros. You can also find plenty of ideas for home-based businesses.

Pros and Cons of Working at Home

12345

www.homebasedwork.com/advantages.html

This article presents a clear discussion of the good sides and bad sides of working at home.

Quatloos

12345

www.quatloos.com

Thinking of buying into a franchise or investing in a promising business opportunity? Check out Quatloos before you lay out any cash. Here you can learn about and avoid some of the most sinister scams—tax scams, general fraud, investment fraud, and more.

Small & Home-Based Business Links

www.bizoffice.com

Directory to references, news, services, opportunities, and work-at-home programs.

Women's Work

www.wwork.com

Women's Work is dedicated to helping women move from standard 9-to-5 jobs to flex careers—telecommuting, small business, and other options. This site is packed with articles, advice, how-to guides, flexible career choices, and success stories to inspire, motivate, and ease the transition. Site also features a discussion forum.

WorkAtHomeindex.net

www.work-at-home-index.net

A human-edited directory of home business opportunities designed to help entrepreneurs find quality opportunities and the tools and resources they need to build a successful home-based business.

WorkingFromHome.com

12345

www.workingfromhome.com/homeworks.htm

This website, created and maintained by Paul and Sarah Edwards, authors of *Finding Your Perfect Work*, includes articles, advice, a forum, a detailed FAQ, and links to other resources for people who work out of their homes or are planning to start a home-based business.

INTERNATIONAL BUSINESS

Australian Department of Foreign Affairs and Trade

1 2 3 4 5

www.dfat.gov.au

Australian business information site managed by the Australian government. Here, you can brush up on Australian foreign policy, obtain travel advice, and research global issues that affect Australia and its businesses.

BISNIS

1 2 3 4 5

www.bisnis.doc.gov

BISNIS is "the U.S. Government's primary market information center for U.S. companies exploring business opportunities in Russia and other newly independent states." U.S. companies use BISNIS to access the latest market reports, news, and developments; gather export and investment leads; and learn strategies for doing business in the former U.S.S.R.'s Newly Independent States (NIS).

Export-Import Bank of the United States

1 2 3 4 5

www.exim.gov

An independent U.S. government agency that helps finance the overseas sales of U.S. goods and services. In more than 65 years, Export-Import Bank has supported more than $400 billion in U.S. exports, primarily to emerging markets worldwide.

Federation of International Trade Associations

1 2 3 4 5

www.fita.org

The Federation of International Trade Associations (FITA), founded in 1984, "fosters international trade by strengthening the role of local, regional, and national associations throughout the United States, Mexico, and Canada that have an international mission." FITA is made up of a membership of more than 450 independent international associations.

FinFacts

1 2 3 4 5 RSS

www.finfacts.ie

Extensive information on Irish finance and business.

Best Gateway to the European Union

1 2 3 4 5

europa.eu.int

The Gateway to the European Union opens with a list of languages—20 in all. Simply click your language of preference to get started. This informative site opens with a page that makes it easy to navigate. You can begin by checking out the feature articles or daily European Union (EU) news; use the navigational bar on the left to discover the EU, learn about living in the EU, or interact with the EU; or use the navigation bar on the right for quick access to the most popular content. If you're planning on doing business with the European Union, there's no better place to start.

globalEDGE

1 2 3 4 5

globaledge.msu.edu/ibrd/ibrd.asp

Maintained by the Michigan State University Center for International Business Education and Research (CIBER), this site serves as an index of business, economics, trade, marketing, and government sites with an international focus. If you're thinking of expanding or moving your business to another country, you will find the information at this site most valuable.

Infonation

1 2 3 4 5

cyberschoolbus.un.org/infonation3//menu/advanced.asp

Interested in statistics? This is the site for you. Compare data within the countries of the United Nations, including urban growth, top exports, and threatened species. A great resource for adults and kids.

Related Site

www.cia.gov/cia/publications/factbook

International Business Ethics Institute

12345

www.business-ethics.org

The IBEI is dedicated to promoting "business ethics and corporate responsibility" through roundtable discussions, educational resources, its own website, and by working individually with companies. At this website, IBEI offers educational materials, information about its professional services (including a list of the top 10 mistakes businesses make when developing global ethics programs), a list of resources (including a Business Ethics Primer), and the IBEI's own publications. Visit this site to learn more about the institute and how you can help ensure that your business follows the proper international code of ethics.

International Business Forum

www.ibf.com

Provides links to information about international business opportunities, resources, advertisement agencies, and much more.

International Monetary Fund

12345

www.imf.org

A cooperative institution that 184 countries have voluntarily joined to maintain a stable system of buying and selling their currencies so that payments in foreign money can take place between countries smoothly and without delay. This site features up-to-date news and information about the IMF's events, publications, and agenda. The student section is great for kids of all ages but especially teenagers doing research.

International Trade Center

12345

www.intracen.org

Home of the ITC, a group dedicated to supporting developing countries and transition economies achieve a goal of sustainable growth. ITC provides information, maps, and services designed specifically to help developing economies better expedite exports and imports.

The Internationalist

12345

www.internationalist.com

The source for books, directories, publications, reports, maps on international business, import/export, and more. Easy-to-navigate site and loaded with choices. Provides links to Amazon.com and other retailers.

JETRO (Japan External Trade Organizations)

12345

www.jetro.go.jp

A nonprofit, Japanese government-related organization dedicated to promoting mutually beneficial trade and economic relations between Japan and other nations.

Latin Trade

www.latintrade.com

Business source for Latin America. Excellent, up-to-date articles, a business-to-business directory, and other resources make this site a must-visit for anyone doing business or planning to do business in Latin America.

Newsweek International Edition

12345 Blog RSS

www.msnbc.msn.com/id/3037881/site/newsweek

Newsweek's international news site, where you can read the latest news from around the world.

OverseasJobs.com

12345

www.overseasjobs.com

Does the prospect of international travel appeal to you? Then consider looking for a job in a foreign country. Here, you can search for jobs by keyword or browse openings in a particular location. You can even post your resumé to advertise your qualifications to prospective employers.

Tilburg University Marketing Journals

www.tilburguniversity.nl/faculties/few/marketing/links/journal1.html

Long list of links that point to various marketing journals on the Web, including many noteworthy international journals.

United Nations Economic Social Commission for Asia and the Pacific

www.unescap.org

Home of the United Nations Economic and Social Commission for Asia and the Pacific (ESCAP), this site is dedicated to promoting economic and social development in Asia and the Pacific. Here, you can learn about the commission and read various reports.

United Nations and Business

www.un.org/partners/business/index.asp

Procurement information, statistics, and publications in a number of different business categories. See the role that the United Nations plays in helping developing countries and improving economic globalization.

U.S. International Trade Commission

www.usitc.gov

An independent, quasi-judicial federal agency that provides objective trade expertise to both the legislative and executive branches of government; determines the impact of imports on U.S. industries; and directs actions against certain unfair trade practices, such as patent, trademark, and copyright infringement.

United States Council for International Business

www.uscib.org

The United States Council for International Business encourages and assists companies to succeed abroad by joining "together with like-minded firms to influence laws, rules and policies that may undermine U.S. competitiveness, wherever they may be." In other words, this organization helps U.S. companies break down trade barriers in other countries.

United States Trade Representative

www.ustr.gov

Responsible for developing and coordinating U.S. international trade, commodity, and direct investment policy, and leading or directing negotiations with other countries on such matters.

World Bank Group

www.worldbank.org

Offers loans, advice, and an array of customized resources to more than 100 developing countries and countries in transition. Also helps finance disease-control and -eradication efforts in underdeveloped countries.

World Trade Organization

www.wto.org

The only international organization dealing with the global rules of trade between nations. Its main function is to ensure that trade flows as smoothly, predictably, and freely as possible. Here, you will find information on the WTO's agenda, events, and publications.

PATENT INFORMATION

All About Trademarks

www.ggmark.com

A detailed online directory offering an overview of trademarks and their use, along with hundreds of links to federal and international laws, journals, and organizations. An excellent resource for anyone just starting to learn about trademarks.

A B C D E F G H I J K L M N O P Q R S T U V W X Y Z

American Intellectual Property Law Association (AIPLA)

12345

www.aipla.org

The American Intellectual Property Law Association guide to patent harmonization, committee reports, and congressional testimony.

American Patent and Trademark Law Center

12345

www.patentpending.com

Some useful information about patents and how to obtain a patent using the expertise of a certified patent attorney.

The British Library: Patents

12345

www.bl.uk/collections/patents.html

Excellent site maintained by the British Library to help users fully exploit the world's greatest patent resources. Explains what a patent is and how to go about getting something patented. Also provides information on how to search for trademarks and registered designs.

By KIDDS For KIDDS

12345

kids.patentcafe.com/index.asp

One of the best invention/patent sites on the Web for novice innovators of all ages, this site is specifically designed for kids. Provides information on how to invent, famous inventors, and discoveries. Also provides an inspiring list of products invented by some of the site's kid members.

Community of Science: U.S. Patent Search

12345

patents.cos.com

This site enables you to search through a database of more than 2.5 million U.S. patents issued since 1975. The Main Search provides you with a form to fill out, where you can supply the date, full-text description, title, patent number, and other information to narrow the search. More basic searches enable you to search by state, country, and classification.

Delphion Intellectual Property Network

12345

www.delphion.com

Subscription service that provides a comprehensive database of U.S. patent descriptions dating back to 1971. Subscribers can search for patent information that can help them generate new ideas and gain a competitive edge in the marketplace.

General Information Concerning Patents

12345

www.uspto.gov/web/offices/pac/doc/general

Provides general information about applying for and granting patents in non-technical language. Great for inventors, students, and prospective patent applicants.

Intellectual Property Mall

12345 Blog

www.ipmall.fplc.edu

This comprehensive directory includes a guide to intellectual property sites and links to more than 2,700 related resources. The site also features valuable information on copyright laws, and tools for conducting IP-related searches.

KuesterLaw Resource

12345

www.kuesterlaw.com

Directory to intellectual property law, with links to statutes, journals, organizations, government agencies, and case law. Covers patent, copyright, and trademark law. Excellent information for beginners, plus some interesting descriptions of actual court cases.

Patent Act

12345

assembler.law.cornell.edu/uscode/html/uscode35/usc_sup_01_35.html

Text of the Patent Act, covering patentability of inventions, grants of patents, protection, and rights.

Patent and Trademark Office

1 2 3 4 5

www.uspto.gov

Official site for searching the U.S. patent database. Includes international treaties, statutes, and patent news. Young inventors should check out www.uspto.gov/go/kids for access to a special kids area where they can learn about inventions, inventors, and patents and play some cool games online.

Patent Law Links

1 2 3 4 5

www.patentlawlinks.com

Great place to learn about patent law. An impressive collection of links grouped in categories including Case Law, Statutes & Limitations, Journals, Patent Offices, Patent Law Firms, and more.

U.K. Patent Office

1 2 3 4 5

www.patent.gov.uk

The U.K. Patent Office has a well-designed site that makes it easy to navigate to the main sections: Trade Marks, Copyright, Designs, and Patents. The Patents page covers everything from the definition of a patent and instructions on how to apply to detailed patent information that might appeal to lawyers more than the average citizen.

SMALL BUSINESS—PRODUCTS & SERVICES

AllBusiness.com

1 2 3 4 5 Blog RSS

www.allbusiness.com

AllBusiness wants to be the resource for small business owners and has compiled a wide range of online services to make it easier for business owners to focus on their companies. Although there is a range of services available, from developing a human resource manual to designing an e-commerce venture, there are costs involved.

CenterBeam

1 2 3 4 5

www.centerbeam.com

Small businesses in need of sophisticated computing systems might want to check out CenterBeam for subscription computing services. Rather than invest in equipment, companies can pay a monthly fee to CenterBeam to provide what is needed.

Doba

www.doba.com

If you operate a retail business, you may be wondering what to sell. Doba streamlines product sourcing (which is product selling) for small business owners. Doba's web-based platform allows entrepreneurs and retailers to find and sell products either online or in a bricks and mortar storefront. While an annual fee is involved, for business owners looking to get a leg up on their competitors, this site offers a valuable service.

eFax.com

1 2 3 4 5

www.efax.com

People who are away from their faxes and telephones frequently might want to sign up for free efax service that accepts incoming faxes and then converts them to an email message. Be able to pick up your faxes from your computer wherever you are.

Entrepreneur.com

1 2 3 4 5 Blog

www.entrepreneur.com

Published by the same folks who bring you *Entrepreneur* magazine, this is an excellent site for small-business owners, featuring a solid collection of articles and tips from experts, plus hundreds of links to other small-business resources on the Web.

Microsoft Small Business Center

1 2 3 4 5 RSS

www.microsoft.com/smallbusiness/bc/default.mspx

Microsoft's Small Business Center is a vehicle for selling various Microsoft small-business products, including software, accounting services, customer-management tools, online business hosting, and so on. That's not a bad thing, though, and this site provides plenty of excellent information and advice entirely for free. If you're starting or running your own small business, Microsoft's Small Business Center is an excellent place to learn from the experts.

NASE (National Association for the Self-Employed)

12345 (rating: 5)

`www.nase.org`

NASE is an association of small-business owners and self-employed individuals. Its website provides access to excellent information and advice. NASE supports self-employed workers by offering its own health insurance and providing referrals to other companies that can help you save money and manage your business. Explore this site by clicking on the Women's Resource Center, Legislative Action Center, Health Resource Center, or any of the other up-to-date and robust sections.

Onvia

12345 (rating: 4)

`www.onvia.com`

Subscribe to Onvia's customized daily report filled with projects and new business opportunities for entities interested in doing business with the United States government. This site's newsletter goes out to thousands of consultants, contractors, suppliers, and service providers every day. If you're new to the world of government contracting, click on the Government 101 link for an overview.

Best Small Business Administration

12345 (rating: 5)

`www.sba.gov`

Before you decide to quit your day job and start your own business, visit this site from the U.S. government's Small Business Administration. Here, you can learn how to start your own business and finance it. The site also provides information on business opportunities, local SBA offices, laws and regulations, and much more.

Stamps.com

12345 (rating: 4)

`www.stamps.com`

Tired of standing in line at the post office? Then download Stamps.com's free software and print postage right from your printer. The amount of your postage will be deducted from your prepaid account, and there are no hidden charges—just the cost of postage.

Quicken Small-Business Center

12345 (rating: 3)

`www.quicken.com/small_business`

If you use or plan to use Quicken to manage your financial accounts, and even if you don't, the Quick Small-Business Center is a great place to pick up advice on starting and running a small business. Learn how to get started, know your customers, benefit your employees, and protect your assets. Click the Quicken Business Solutions link for information on various products and services that can help you manage both your business and personal finances and other aspects of running your business.

United States Postal Service

12345 (rating: 4)

`www.usps.com`

Use the United States Postal Service's online ordering system and have postage stamps delivered to your door. No more waiting in line at the post office for all your stamp and postal needs. You can also use this site to track packages, change your mailing address, and find ZIP codes for any town in the United States.

Visa Small-Business Center

12345 (rating: 3)

`usa.visa.com/business`

Visa provides several useful tools that enable the small-business owner to manage business finances, especially when it comes to tracking expenses and inventory. At this site, you can apply for a Visa business credit card and learn about the many services that Visa has available for small businesses. Visa also offers online workshops that can help you start and manage your own business.

A B C D E F G H I J K L M N O P Q R S T U V W X Y Z

SMALL BUSINESS—WEBSTOREFRONT SUPPORT

aplus.net

12345

hosting.aplus.net/ecommerce.html

aplus.net is one of the top-rated e-commerce website hosting services around. Features 99.99 percent uptime, free domain registration, free payment gateway, and free marketing tools, as well as a 30-day money-back guarantee. Through aplus.net, you can connect your store with Amazon.com, eBay, Froogle, and Shopping.com.

Bigstep.com

12345

go.bigstep.com

Bigstep is a great way to build a website yourself (with help from Bigstep) and then host and manage it for an affordable price. You can add e-commerce capabilities at any time, and make use of follow-up tools, such as newsletters. An excellent, low-cost way to get your business on the Web!

EarthLink Business

12345

start.earthlink.net/channel/BUSINESS

Rely on EarthLink for a variety of business/e-commerce services, such as setting up an intranet, providing web hosting, or holding an online meeting. You can also stay abreast of Internet news with regular online updates at the site. Plenty of services, but it's hard to know where to start.

HostMySite.com

12345

hostmysite.com

HostMySite.com features personal, developer, e-commerce, and dedicated server Web hosting for prices starting around $10 per month. HostMySite.com offers three levels of e-commerce hosting, depending on your budget and the desired features. All levels offer an unlimited number of secure transactions, excellent technical support, and a 30-day money back guarantee if you are not satisfied.

PayPal

12345

www.paypal.com

If you're planning on opening your own store on the Web but you're not sure how to take orders and collect payments, go to PayPal. PayPal can add a payment option to your site that allows users to pay you via PayPal. It costs you about 30 cents plus 1.9 percent to 2.9 percent of each transaction. PayPal has more than 105 million accounts and is available to users in 55 countries around the world.

ProStores

12345

www.prostores.com

ProStores is an eBay company that provides all the tools you need to open and manage a store on the Web. Here, you can choose from several plans starting at about $30 per month up to about $250 a month for the tools you need to manage your web store and track your suppliers' inventory. Here you can learn the benefits of opening a ProStore and take a short course in E-commerce 101.

TopHosts.com

12345 RSS

www.tophosts.com

Great place to shop for web hosting services. For a list of companies, click on the Top 25 Web Hosts link.

ValueWeb

12345

www.valueweb.com

When you're looking for a quick, easy, and affordable way to place your business online, check out ValueWeb. You can quickly build your online store and promote up to 100,000 products and services. ValueWeb manages the credit card transactions for you, helps you draw more traffic to your site, and provides easy checkout tools for your customers.

CAMPING

Adventure Network

www.adventurenetwork.com

Planning a camping trip? Then you'll want to visit this site, which offers camping FAQs, product recommendations, and a Fabrics and Fibers glossary of terms. Who knew fabrics could be so important? But to a camper faced with rain, wind, and snow, they make all the difference in the world.

Best Altrec.com

www.altrec.com

Shop here for hiking, camping, climbing, cycling, paddling, fly-fishing, snow skiing, and running gear. Whichever outdoor activity interests you, you can find all the gear you need at this site. Attractive and well-organized layout makes this site easy to find outdoor camping equipment and supplies.

American Park Network–Camping

www.americanparknetwork.com

Planning a camping trip to a national park? Check here first for site availability, park activities, fees, and much more. Camping in some national parks requires reservations, and you'll find contact information here. Some park campgrounds are available on a first-come, first-served basis, and this site provides information on how to make sure you get a spot.

Camp-A-Roo

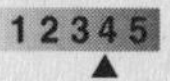

www.camp-a-roo.com

Maintained by outdoor recreation enthusiast Mary Bould, this site features information about camping and hiking with an emphasis for parents who want to camp with their children.

Campfire Cooking

www.eartheasy.com/play_campfire_cooking.htm

Before you head out on your next camping adventure, stop by this site for some great campfire cooking recipes. This site also features instructions on how to build a safe campfire that's conducive to cooking.

Campground Directory

www.gocampingamerica.com

Find a campground or RV park quickly and easily using the searchable directory or pull-down menus. Special kids area is full of activities to keep kids busy on long trips, and includes safety tips, state information, and campfire recipes.

Camping World Online

www.campingworld.com

Camping World is a leading supplier of products for RVs in particular and camping in general. Use this site to request a free catalog, check out products, get special online bargains, or find a Camping World store closest to you. You'll also find links to some other great camping websites.

Coleman.com

www.coleman.com

Besides descriptions of Coleman products you can buy online, here you'll find advice on how to prepare for a camping trip, how to set up camp, where to go, how to cook meals in the great outdoors, and more.

Get Knotted

12345

www.42brghtn.mistral.co.uk/knots/42ktmenu.html

Animated knots for scouts, plus the do's and don'ts of knot tying. Not the glitziest site of the lot; but if you need to tie something, this site can show you 15 ways to do it.

KOA Home Page

12345

www.koakampgrounds.com

If you like plenty of luxury while you're camping—hot showers, recreation rooms, convenience stores—KOA is the way to go. Check here for a list of the KOA campgrounds across North America, an explanation of the different ways to camp at a KOA, a list of services available, and, if you're looking for an enjoyable and profitable way to earn your living, ways to open a KOA of your very own.

L.L. Bean Welcome Page

12345

www.llbean.com

Keeping warm is a primary concern when you're camping, and L.L. Bean is the place to go for warm (and stylish) clothes, snowshoes, camping accessories, and more. Request a free catalog, check out the online product guide, and use the park search page (located in the Explore the Outdoors section). With hundreds of national and state parks, forests, and wildlife refuges, it's a handy tool.

Minnesota State Parks

12345

www.dnr.state.mn.us/state_parks/index.html

If we had to pick only one state to highlight in the camping section, Minnesota would be the one. Whether on the prairie, in a hardwood forest, or near the Great Lakes, Minnesota state parks offer every possible camping experience, from canoeing and portaging the Boundary Waters, to just sitting outside your RV listening to the wolves howl. Find the park you'd like to visit and make your reservations—all at this site. Click on Newsroom to sign up to receive enewsletter updates on boating regulations, safety tips, and more.

Ocean City, MD's Frontier Town Campground

12345

www.frontiertown.com

Afun site to visit, brought to you by a unique family camping experience. This campground features more than 500 campsites, a pizza parlor, and access to many area attractions, including golf courses and harness racing.

Outdoor Action Program

12345

www.princeton.edu/~oa/index.shtml

Maintained by Rick Curtis, Princeton University hosts this site, which you should check before undertaking any kind of wilderness trip. Loaded with places to go and things to do, the site is equally jam-packed with safety and health facts. A comprehensive site for outdoors folk to visit.

U.S. Scouting Project

12345

usscouts.org/usscouts/start.asp

The U.S. Scouting service is a not-for-profit organization that's dedicated to supporting and promoting the scouting movement. This site acts as a comprehensive directory, or portal, to a vast collection of online resources dealing with the scouting movement.

Visit Your National Parks

12345

www.nps.gov/parks.html

This is an official National Park Service page. Learn about U.S. national parks, pick one that is right for your camping needs, find out what the fees are, and make reservations. This site features a Park Spotlight and a guide to lesser-known parks, along with lots of useful and up-to-date information.

A B C D E F G H I J K L M N O P Q R S T U V W X Y Z

BACKPACKING

 Backpacker Magazine

12345

www.backpacker.com

This is the home of *Backpacker* magazine, where you can learn about every aspect of backpacking, including gear you need to pack, interesting destinations, and skills and techniques. You can connect with other backpacking enthusiasts in the Community area, shop online, or even subscribe to *Backpacker* magazine online.

Eastern Mountain Sports

www.ems.com

Great place to shop for camping gear and equipment for hiking, climbing, kayaking, and other outdoor adventure activities. Click the EMS Adventure Treks link to plan an outdoor vacation.

Leave No Trace

12345

www.lnt.org

The Leave No Trace Center for Outdoor Ethics is a "nonprofit organization dedicated to promoting and inspiring responsible outdoor recreation through education, research, and partnerships." This site provides tips on how to interact with nature without leaving your human footprint behind in the form of litter, noise, erosion, or anything else that can damage the pristine outdoor environments you visit.

The Backpacker.com

www.thebackpacker.com

TheBackpacker.com caters to all levels of backpackers, from those just thinking about it to seasoned veterans. Here, you can find reviews of the latest gear, search for trail reviews by state, learn basic backpacking techniques, find out what you need to pack, and hook up with other backpackers in your area.

The Lightweight Backpacker

www.backpacking.net

Find useful information on researching and purchasing lightweight backpacking gear here. You can also read contributions from visitors dedicated to making backpacking safer and more fun.

HIKING

America's Roof

www.americasroof.com

View a map of the United States or the world to identify the highest points in the world that you might want to hike. In addition to helping you find places to hike, this site helps you catch up on hiking news and register online for upcoming events.

American Hiking Society

www.americanhiking.org

News and information from an organization dedicated to promoting hiking and establishing, protecting, and maintaining foot trails throughout North America. Sign up to volunteer to help maintain trails, and learn how to take "kid-friendly" hikes and adventures. All of this and more can be found on this site, which boasts thousands of members nationwide.

American Long Distance Hiking Association-West

www.aldhawest.org

This site supports hikers by providing information about trails, hiking equipment , and recipes divided by meal type. Also provided are tips on how to avoid common hiking problems, such as giardia. You'll even find a listing of the Triple Crown members—those who have completed the Pacific Crest Trail, Continental Divide Trail, and Appalachian Trail.

A B C D E F G H I J K L M N O P Q R S T U V W X Y Z

American Volkssports Association

www.ava.org

The American Volkssport Association is a nonprofit group that encourages people to "walk scenic trails at your own pace for health, fitness, and fun." AVA has a network of 350 walking clubs that collectively organize more than 3,000 annual walking events in all 50 states. They occasionally organize biking, skiing, and swimming events, too.

Appalachian National Scenic Trail

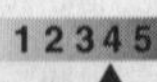

www.nps.gov/appa

This is the National Park's Service website for the famous Appalachian Trail, which is 2,167 miles long and traverses 14 states. This site offers basic information about hiking the trail and provides addresses you can write to for more information. Link to information about Shenandoah and Great Smoky Mountains National Park hiking, too. You can buy books, posters, decals, and other merchandise through the online store.

Barefoot Hikers

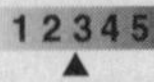

www.barefooters.org/hikers

Home of the barefoot hikers, where you can kick off your shoes and hike the way Mother Nature intended you to. If you're new to the world of barefoot hiking, or to learn more about this sensational trend, click on the Beginner's Guide link halfway down the home page.

Best GORP–Great Outdoor Recreation Pages

www.gorp.com

Find trails, vacations, books, and more at this comprehensive site. Online discussions about hiking-related topics, news, and equipment-selection tips help to keep you informed about hiking and the great outdoors. Links to retail merchants where you can buy equipment, books, and maps. Pop-up ads can become a little annoying, but except for that slight drawback, this is an excellent site. On your first visit to this site, you'll quickly realize why it's the Best of the Best.

Great Outdoor Emporium Mall

www.tgoemall.com/ecamping.htm

Index of camping and hiking supply websites organized by category (Tents, Sleeping Bags, Apparel, Binoculars, Flashlights, Shoes, and Food).

LightBackpacker.com

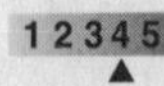

www.backpacking.net/gearshop.html

The key to any successful backpacking trip is the packing, and the secret is to pack light. At this lightweight gear shop, you can find specialized products that lighten your load, including backpacks, tents, sleeping bags, and hiking poles.

Newfoundland Backcountry

www.cdli.ca/~cpelley

Opens with beautiful, full-color photos of the mountains in Newfoundland, Canada. You can select from a panel of trails and places to hike to get more information.

Superior Hiking Trail Association

www.shta.org

The Superior Hiking Trail is a long-distance footpath modeled after the Appalachian Trail that follows the shore of Lake Superior in northeastern Minnesota. The association itself was conceived by a group of visionaries in the mid-1980s who banded together to form the Superior Hiking Trail Association. Click on the Buddy link to find other hikers in search of hiking partners.

Trails.com

12345

www.trails.com

Founded in 1999, Trails.com is a comprehensive "online planning resource for self-guided outdoor and adventure travel throughout North America." As a result of its partnerships with leading guidebook publishers, this site gives you access—for a small fee—to more than 30,000 trail descriptions covering more than 20 outdoor activities. Additional website features include USGS topographical maps, GPS tools, aerial photos, and much more.

Trailplace

12345

www.trailplace.com/portal/index.php

Find out what an Appalachian Trail "thru-hiker" is and learn about the amazing Appalachian Trail at this site.

Washington Trails Association

12345

www.wta.org

This site provides hiking guides, photos, trip reports, and more. You can see recent trail reports with up-to-date conditions, and buy memberships, books, and maps through the online store. If you live or are traveling to the state of Washington, and hiking's your think, then this site is for you.

Yosemite Trails Pack Station

12345

www.sierranet.net/web/highsierrapackers/ yth.htm

A nice site if you want to learn about trips through the Yosemite Trails on horseback. A variety of rides are available, and large groups are welcome. Wagon rides and horsemanship camps are also offered.

Related Sites

www.webwalking.com/hiking.html

www.moonshadowadventures.com

www.traildatabase.org

www.worldwidequest.com

A B C D E F G H I J K L M N O P Q R S T U V W X Y Z

CAMPS (SUMMER)

Best American Camp Association

12345

www.acacamps.org

Families can find a summer camp for their child by searching the camp directory, and camp directors can find tips and suggestions for improving the quality of a camp here. The site also offers product suggestions and information about joining the association, which is about to celebrate its 100th anniversary.

Camp Channel

12345

www.campchannel.com

Looking for a summer camp for your child? Then tune in to the Camp Channel. Here, you can search through a huge database of summer camps by theme and location. Covers camps in the United States and all over the world. Visit the Camp Store for links to other sites that sell camping gear. Easy-to-navigate site.

Christian Camping International

12345

cci.gospelcom.net/ccihome

This nonprofit organization provides information on more than 1,000 Christian summer camps, campgrounds, retreats, and conference centers nationwide. Information about all these services can be obtained free via CCI's website. Whether you are an outdoor enthusiast or someone who is interested in sending a child to a religiously-affiliated summer camp, you ought to check out this detailed site.

Kids Camps

12345

www.kidscamps.com

If you're looking for a camp for your child this summer, you're sure to find one here. Using topics broken down by interest, such as sports, arts, academics, and special needs, families can locate day and residential camps nationwide.

Summer Camps

12345

www.summercamps.com

Search a national database of kids' summer camps to find the setting that fits your child's interests and needs and your pocketbook.

CANADA

Air Canada

www.aircanada.ca

Home of Canada's official airline, this site enables you to plan a trip, book a flight, and find out about special rates that are available.

Canada

canada.gc.ca

The government of Canada's official site, available in both English and French, covering information about the country and providing access to government agencies, publications, weather reports, and much more.

Best Canada.com

www.canada.com

The premier site for Canada and everything Canadian, this site provides information about all of Canada's major cities, including Calgary, Edmonton, Winnipeg, Toronto, Montreal, and Ottawa. Here, you can find the latest local, national, and international news; obtain weather reports; check out the latest sports scores; and keep abreast of the latest news in business and finance. Whether you live in Canada or just plan a visit to this great country, bookmark this Best of the Best site and visit it daily!

Citizenship and Immigration to Canada

www.cic.gc.ca

After visiting the other sites in this section and reading about everything that Canada has to offer, you might decide to move there...permanently. If you do, make sure this site is the next stop on your journey. Here, you can learn everything you need to know to move to Canada and get a job!

Montreal Official Tourist Info

www.tourisme-montreal.org

Visit more than 80 Montreal sites and locations via QuickTime videos on the site and learn more about visiting and staying in Montreal at this friendly site.

moreMontreal.com

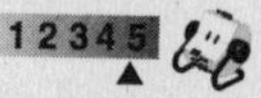

www.moremontreal.com

This exhaustive list of how to get to Montreal and what to do after you're there contains information on what to see and where to eat and sleep. Details are divided by district and category of activity.

Ontario Science Centre

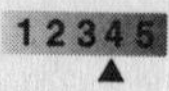

www.ontariosciencecentre.ca

Get the details regarding more than 800 exhibits at this child-oriented museum and directions, pricing, and facility rental information. Explore the robot zoo, take nature walks, test your knowledge with online trivia games, and check out some of the museum's other exhibits at this site. Online games, travel exhibits, ideas for science projects, and more designed especially for kids.

Paramount Canada's Wonderland

www.canadas-wonderland.com/visit.jsp

Find out how to get to this theme park and where to stay after you're there. The park offers more than 60 rides and shows on its 330-acre grounds. Twenty acres are devoted to its water park. You can buy a season pass through the online store.

Toronto.com

12345

www.toronto.com

Learn more about this city to the north, including upcoming theater performances and concerts, restaurant suggestions, shopping and fashion guidance, and news.

Yahoo! Canada

12345

ca.yahoo.com

The Canadian version of the Yahoo! search engine, which provides results from Canadian businesses and news organizations.

CANCER

ACOR.org

12345

www.acor.org

ACOR (the Association of Cancer Online Resources) provides a unique and current collection of online information and resources on various types of cancer. This site features a comprehensive list of cancer types and treatment options, announcements concerning clinical trials, discussion groups and mailing lists, and much more.

American Cancer Society

12345 RSS

www.cancer.org

Online support resources include information on a wide variety of programs such as the Great American Smokeout, the Breast Cancer Network, and Man-to-Man prostate cancer information. You can buy books about cancer and coping with it through the online bookstore.

Avon: The Crusade

12345

www.avoncompany.com/women/avoncrusade

Avon touts itself as the largest corporate supporter of breast health programs in America. This site gives information about Avon's Breast Cancer Awareness Crusade, which is targeted at providing women—particularly low-income, minority, and older women—direct access to breast cancer education and early-detection screening services, at little or no cost. Find out how much has been raised to date and what grants have been awarded as a result.

Breast Cancer Action

12345

www.bcaction.org

Available in both English and Spanish, this site is home to one of the most popular and powerful breast cancer action groups in the world. Designed to inform and empower breast cancer patients and others concerned about breast cancer, here you will learn about the latest preventions and treatments as well as political issues that should concern all citizens.

Cancer Detection and Prevention

12345

www.cancerprev.org

Established by the International Society for Preventive Oncology, this site provides information on the activities of *The Cancer Detection and Prevention Journal*, including the biannual symposia, a searchable database of abstracts published in the *Journal*, and links to other research sources. Primarily for health professionals.

Cancer Directory

www.welcomefunds.com/cancer-links.htm

Alphabetic list of dozens of the top websites focusing on cancer risks, treatments, drugs, and support.

Cancer Facts

12345

www.cancerfacts.com

This site provides information on various types of cancer and the latest treatments. It features the NexProfiler Tools for Cancer to help those with cancer and their family members and caregivers find the best treatment plans available. Site also features news, profiles, and links to support groups.

Cancer Group Institute

12345

www.cancergroup.com

Read about the causes and treatments of virtually every type of known cancer here. Excellent

A B C D E F G H I J K L M N O P Q R S T U V W X Y Z

collection of articles on the latest breakthroughs in cancer research and treatments, for both women and men.

Best Cancer411.com

12345

www.cancer411.com

The Mission of the Rory Foundation and the Joyce Foundation is to "increase public awareness of and access to alternative and conventional choices available for the treatment of cancer." Take advantage of this tremendous library of cancer information and resources, collected and made available by these two foundations. Learn about the latest treatment options, even if they're not promoted by the mainstream medical community. This is *the* site to go for the latest information in cancer research and treatments, and easily earns out Best nod for this category.

Cancerbackup

12345

www.cancerbacup.org.uk/Home

Maintained by Europe's leading cancer information charity, this site features information on cancer and its treatment. Designed for people facing cancer, their families, friends, and health professionals, here you can learn whether there are local cancer centers in your area, especially if you live in or near the United Kingdom.

CancerCare.org

12345

www.cancercare.org

CancerCare.org is a not-for-profit organization dedicated to dispersing information and providing support services for all those that cancer affects, including patients and their caregivers, relatives, children, and friends. Learn where to go for financial assistance, drug assistance programs, home care and hospice alternatives, and much more. Discussion forums help you connect with others who are dealing with similar issues and concerns.

CancerKids

12345

www.cancerkids.org

Exceptional electronic support for kids with cancer and their families through personal websites and mailing lists. Provides a place where kids who have cancer can post their own web pages.

CancerNews on the Net

12345

www.cancernews.com

This site provides patients and their families the latest news on cancer diagnosis, treatment, and prevention. Features include a calendar of upcoming events and a newsletter distributed via email.

CanTeen

12345

www.canteen.org.nz

A peer support organization run by teenage cancer patients in New Zealand. A shining example of how online support should work. Many corporations have come together to sponsor this site, including Pam's and BP.

Community Breast Health Project

12345

www.cbhp.org

Nonprofit project aimed at offering information and support. In addition to learning more about the organization, visitors can access a variety of breast cancer-specific links as well as general cancer links. The site categorizes links, making it easy for you to find exactly what you're looking for.

Faces of Hope

12345

www.facesofhope.org

First of its kind site in that it offers private one-on-one Internet mentoring and support to newly diagnosed breast cancer patients through its mentor-matching program. Visitors can read the stories of breast cancer survivors and access a message board offering breast cancer information resources. Designed to give hope to women with breast cancer.

National Cancer Institute

1 2 3 4 5 (rating: 5)

`www.cancer.gov`

The National Cancer Institute (NCI) coordinates the U.S. government's cancer research program. NCI's website is for cancer patients, the public, and the mass media; on it, you will find news and information on many of its programs and resources, general cancer information, and news about clinical trials.

OncoLink: University of Pennsylvania Cancer Center Resources

1 2 3 4 5 (rating: 5)

`oncolink.upenn.edu`

A comprehensive site for cancer patients and professionals that provides information on many types of cancer, treatments, new drug treatments, clinical trials, the social and emotional aspects of coping with the disease, and FAQs.

Prostate.com

1 2 3 4 5 (rating: 5)

`www.prostate.com`

Sponsored by a drug manufacturer, here you will find a thorough explanation of the functions of the prostate and information on how to keep the prostate healthy, and alternative treatments for people diagnosed with prostate diseases.

Steve Dunn's Cancer Guide

1 2 3 4 5 (rating: 5)

`cancerguide.org`

When you or a loved one is first diagnosed as having cancer, you want answers, but at this point, you don't even know the questions. Steve Dunn, a veteran cancer survivor does know, and at this site, he shares the questions he had throughout the process of dealing with his own diagnosis and answers he discovered. When you're looking for solid cancer care advice from the trenches, turn here.

Susan G. Komen Breast Cancer Foundation

1 2 3 4 5 (rating: 5)

`www.komen.org`

A site from the Susan G. Komen Foundation dedicated to detailing research, community projects, and news about breast cancer prevention and control. Find out more about the Foundation's popular Race for the Cure running event at this user-friendly site.

Testicular Cancer Resource Center

1 2 3 4 5 (rating: 5)

`tcrc.acor.org`

A wealth of information about testicular cancer—diagnosing, treating, and recovering from it.

A B C D E F G H I J K L M N O P Q R S T U V W X Y Z

CANDY

Abbott's Caramels

www.abbottscandy.com

One of the best caramel candies you will ever have! These buttery treats are available with or without nuts, so be sure to try both.

Altoids

12345 RSS

www.altoids.com

A fun site for this strongly flavored peppermint candy. Play interactive games, enter contests, listen to music, or check out results of the Altoids survey.

Bubblegum

12345

www.bubblegum.com

At this site geared squarely at kids and preteens, you can learn more than you ever wanted to know about various Armurol bubblegum products and entertain yourself. One of the coolest areas is the Your Room section where after registering you can build your own room, complete with games, activities, homework helpers, and a personal journal.

Best Candy Critic

12345 RSS

www.candycritic.org

For a more humorous look at candy, check out this site, where various candy critics discuss their preferences, bust candy myths, and play around with their favorite candies. A great way to kill even the highest of sugar highs.

Candy Direct: World's Largest

12345

www.candydirect.com

Search for past candy favorites deeply missed or make new discoveries. Thousands of selections available. Great place for schools or sports concessions stands to order candy in bulk. Also features candy bouquets.

Candy's Apples

12345

www.candysapples.com

Gourmet caramel-coated Granny Smith apples with cashews, peanut butter, almonds, pistachios, walnuts, Heath bars, macadamias, pecans, and drizzled with chocolates.

Candy USA

12345

www.candyusa.org

Home page of the largest organization of candy producers, this site features candy history, statistics, information about health and nutrition, candy FAQs, information about chocolate, candy trivia, a special kids area, recipes for using candy in your cooking, and more. The kids area is designed for a younger crowd.

Candy Wrapper Museum

12345

www.candywrappermuseum.com

True candy fans will love this site, where you can travel back in time to check out and appreciate the art of candy wrappers. This huge collection of digitized candy wrapper photos is broken down into categories, including Big Eats, Celebrities, Classics, Classy, Don't Eat, and Vices, making it easy and fun to browse.

Godiva Chocolatier

www.godiva.com/godiva

Offering some of the best chocolate in the world, this site enables you to order online or to locate the Godiva retailer nearest you. Even the graphics make your mouth water. Definitely a stop for chocoholics with discriminating taste.

Hershey Chocolate North America

www.hersheys.com

Hershey chocolate might not be the best milk chocolate on the planet, but this website is unmatched for design, ease of use, and fun. The opening page presents an automated slide show of Hershey products and sites and displays links you can click to access various sections of the site, including Hershey's Brands and Promotions, Hershey's Gifts, and Hershey's Kitchens. Check out Hershey's Kitchens for recipes, baking hints and tips, and product information. If you're looking to have a little fun online, click Discover Hershey and then click the Fun Stuff link for access to games, facts, craft ideas, activities, downloads, and lots of freebies.

Hometown Favorites

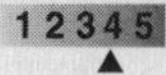

www.hometownfavorites.com

If you're longing for candies and food from the 1940s, 1950s, or 1960s, chances are good that this online store carries it and can ship it to you. Search by brand name or type of food to find your old favorites.

Kailua Candy Company

12345

www.kailua-candy.com

The Kailua Candy Company has been handcrafting fine chocolate candies in its Kona, Hawaii, kitchen since 1977. Use the secure order form to order candies online!

Name That Candybar

www.smm.org/sln/tf/c/crosssection/namethatbar.html

Shows cross-sections of various candy bars, prompting you to guess the name of each bar.

PEZ Candy

www.pez.com

Home of PEZ Candy, this site dispenses a good collection of information about this famous candy and its dispensers. Learn the history of PEZ, shop at the online store, play games, or register for the PEZ Collectors newsletter.

The Ultimate Bad Candy Website

www.bad-candy.com

Dedicated to the eradication of bad candy products, such as Circus Peanuts, this site is the funniest of the candy sites. The humor is directed more at adults and older kids who have had memorable experiences of eating bad candy.

CANOEING/KAYAKING

A B C D E F G H I J K L M N O P Q R S T U V W X Y Z

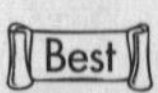 American Canoe Association

1 2 3 4 5

www.acanet.org

The American Canoe Association (ACA) is a nationwide, not-for-profit organization dedicated to "providing education on matters related to paddling, supporting stewardship of the paddling environment, and enabling programs and events to support paddlesport recreation." The ACA website is packed with resources and information related to boating safety, training and instruction, certification, insurance, water trails, access and navigability, and boating regulations.

Canoe & Kayak

1 2 3 4 5 RSS

www.canoekayak.com

Brought to you by the folks who publish *Canoe & Kayak* magazine, this site features gear reviews, paddling news, feature articles, tips, photos, message boards, polls, and information on paddling destinations located throughout North America and elsewhere.

Paddling.net

1 2 3 4 5

www.paddling.net

One of the Internet's leading sources of information on canoeing and kayaking. Includes buyers' guides, articles, classifieds, photos, links to outfitters and dealers, and message boards for connecting with other paddling enthusiasts.

WetDawg.com

www.wetdawg.com

This site was built by padding enthusiasts for paddling enthusiasts, and includes gear reviews, photos, forums, blogs, and information about paddling clubs and vacations. Click on the Tide Finder link for updated information on tide levels in 23 states, or the River Flows link for information on rivers in all 50 states and the District of Columbia.

HISTORY Sports FINANCE Cooking NATURE Travel Antiques NEWS MUSIC

CAR RENTAL

Advantage Rent-A-Car

1 2 3 4 5

www.arac.com

Alamo Rent-A-Car

1 2 3 4 5

www.alamo.com

Avis

1 2 3 4 5

www.avis.com

Budget Rent-a-Car

1 2 3 4 5

www.budget.com

Dollar Rent-A-Car

1 2 3 4 5

www.dollar.com

Economy Car Rental Aruba

1 2 3 4 5

www.economyaruba.com

Enterprise Rent-A-Car

1 2 3 4 5

www.enterprise.com

Europcar

1 2 3 4 5

www.europcar.com

Fox Rent-A-Car

1 2 3 4 5

www.foxrentacar.com

Hertz

1 2 3 4 5

www.hertz.com

Best **National Car**

1 2 3 4 5

www.nationalcar.com

Payless Car Rental

1 2 3 4 5

www.paylesscarrental.com

Rent-A-Wreck

1 2 3 4 5

rent-a-wreck.com

Thrifty Car Rental

1 2 3 4 5

www.thrifty.com

CASINOS

Best Caesar's Resorts

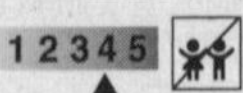

www.caesars.com

Caesars Entertainment, Inc. is one of the world's leading gambling and gaming companies , claiming billions of dollars in annual net revenue. It has "21 properties in three countries, 25,000 hotel rooms, two million square feet of casino space and 52,000 employees." If you like to gamble or simply find the aura of the casino exhilarating, you'll find this to be the web equivalent. It contains links to all of the Caesar's Resorts, plus information on responsible gaming.

Casino Center

www.casinocenter.com

If you're a gaming enthusiast, you need to bookmark this comprehensive site. Brush up on your gaming strategies with the online gaming magazine, find information on hundreds of casinos across the country from an extensive database, and learn the rules of all the casino games from keno to blackjack. Also, you can check out current stock prices and company news from the industry's publicly owned companies. You can buy merchandise from the online gift store or indulge in a magazine subscription.

Casino City

www.casinocity.com

This glitzy site makes you feel like you're on the Strip in Vegas. Browse the bookstore and order online, search the casino database, try your hand at the Virtual Casino, or go to Wall Street and take a gamble on gaming stocks. And for the diehard enthusiast, the site lists a who's who of casino executives.

Cliff Castle Casino

www.cliffcastlecasino.net

Arizona casino designed to appeal not only to gamblers but to families too. The site features information about the casino and a Family Fun link where kids can learn more about what the casino has to offer them.

Golden Nugget

www.goldennugget.com

Find out all you wanted to know about this Las Vegas landmark and casino. Make reservations online and link to affiliated establishments.

Mississippi Casinos

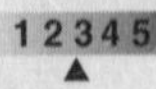

www.mississippicasinos.com

Thirteen casinos populate the Mississippi Gulf Coast. Discount gaming vacation packages and free stuff are for the taking, and this is the place to cash in. Also, check out the area weather, maps, entertainment, and golf opportunities. You'll also find links to Mississippi's Memphis-area casinos and some gambling games you can play for fun or for real.

Peppermill Reno Hotel Casino

www.peppermillreno.com

Peppermill is one of the top, if not *the* top, casino hotel and destination resort in Reno, Nevada. Here, you can check it out online, take a virtual tour, learn about rates and promotions, find free games and screensavers, check out a map of Reno, send postcards, and much more.

Sands Hotel and Casino

www.acsands.com

One of Atlantic City's best casinos comes to your desktop. This resort offers the latest games, world-class performers, and high-quality dining. Reservations are just a mouse click away.

Spirit Mountain Casino

www.spirit-mountain.com

This casino, offering the best in casino games and entertainment, is operated by the Confederated Tribes of the Grand Ronde Community of Oregon and is located well away from the bustle of the city. Check out the complimentary shuttle bus service from Portland and Salem. There's also an interesting page covering where and how casino revenues are being invested by the casino's Spirit Mountain Community Fund in the local community.

Venetian

www.venetian.com

The Venetian—a luxurious all-suite resort, hotel, and casino—sits in the heart of Las Vegas. It features 17 restaurants, the Guggenheim Hermitage Museum, the Canyon Ranch SpaClub, Grand Canal Shoppes, and gondola rides. Check out promotions online, book a room, or just enjoy the view.

CATS

American Cat Fanciers Association

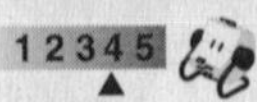

www.acfacat.com

This site showcases ACFA, a national cat registry that sponsors shows and annually ranks the top-scoring cats. The site guides you to local cat shows and breeders and includes photos and forms to register and join this ever-growing organization.

Beware of Cat!

1 2 3 4 5

www.geocities.com/Heartland/Meadows/6485

Surfing all these cat sites may make you a cat lover. If you decide to add cat pages to your own site, come here to find a wide array of feline graphics, animation, backgrounds, and icons.

Big Cats Online

1 2 3 4 5

dialspace.dial.pipex.com/agarman

This site offers information regarding all aspects of nondomestic cats, including their conservation. Many links to other sites are provided.

Cat Fanciers

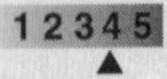

www.fanciers.com

Provides cat-related information. This site offers numerous FAQs on different cat breeds, feline health, and care issues. It also offers links to show schedules, cat organizations, FTP and gopher sites, as well as links to commercial sites, picture sites, and cat owners' home pages.

Cat Fanciers Association

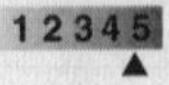

www.cfainc.org

The world's largest purebred cat registry features its top award-winning felines and information on each recognized breed. This site encourages responsible cat ownership and advises how you can show purebred and household pet felines and participate in local CFA cat clubs and shows throughout the world.

Cat House (EFBC/FCC)

1 2 3 4 5

www.cathouse-fcc.org

Contains pictures and some audio clips straight from the cat's mouth. The Cat House (a.k.a. the Feline Conservation Center) is a desert zoo that contains a variety of wild cat species. More than 50 cats, representing 13 species, live at the compound. Photos of recent births are included.

Cats Protection League

www.cats.org.uk

Learn more about caring for cats through online guides at this nonprofit organization's site that is dedicated to providing new homes for cats throughout the UK. At this site you can track down an adoption location and find out how to care for a kitten or cat that's been rescued. You can also sign up for a free enewsletter and download kitty-cat wallpaper for your computer.

Catsbuzz Bookstore

12345 

members.aol.com/catsbuzz

Books, books, and more books about cats. On this site, you'll find books about specific breeds, books with general information, books for kids, and even cat-related books for Christmas time. Link over to Catsbuzz Central and check out cats in the news, great cat links, and cat poetry.

Best CatToys.com

12345

www.cattoys.com

Check the list of recommended toys for your particular breed of cat and then purchase it online here. You'll want to visit frequently to see what the featured products are each week. One of the most fun things you can do with cats is to watch them play with that new toy you just bought them, and this site will allow you to order many types of toys for them as your heart and wallet can stand. If you're a cat lover, you must visit this Best of the Best site.

How to Toilet-Train Your Cat

12345

www.karawynn.net/mishacat/toilet.shtml

If you're tired of buying cat litter and emptying it, it may be time to consider toilet training. No, really, according to this site, you can toilet train your cat! This site offers its own advice and techniques. Karawynn explains the basics, while Misha demonstrates the techniques and positions.

Taking Care of Your Cat

12345

www.nutroproducts.com/takingcarecat.asp

Nutro Products features this guide to cat care that covers everything from meeting other household members and setting up a litter box to caring for your cat's health and playing cat games. Excellent site for anyone new to owning or taking care of a cat.

Virtual Kitty!

12345

www.virtualkitty.com

Very much like the popular Tamagotchi pets, Virtual Kitty lets you adopt your own online cat (or dog). You can read the Owners Manual to get some tips for caring for your kitty, and you can mail a kitty to a friend as a gift.

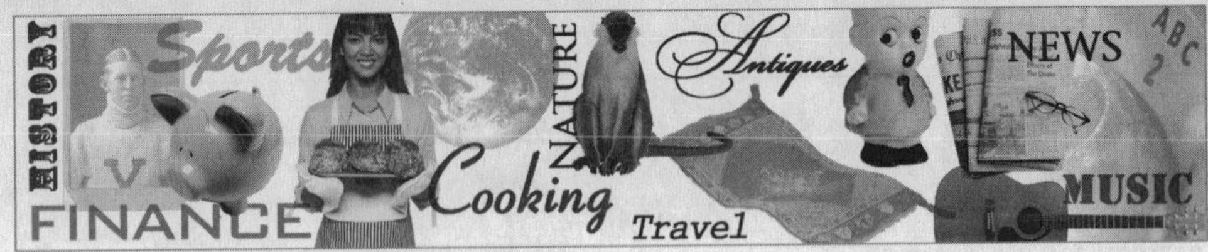

CELIAC DISEASE

Best Celiac Disease Foundation

1 2 3 4 5

www.celiac.org

The Celiac Disease Foundation "provides support, information and assistance to people affected by Celiac Disease/Dermatitis Herpetiformis." This easy-to-use site includes a wealth of information, including access to information about Celiac Disease, Foundation events, news items, lifestyle tips, books, and more. There's even a Kids Korner where parents can find information about summer camps that cater to children with Celiac disease.

Celiac Disease and Gluten-Free Diet Support Center

1 2 3 4 5

www.celiac.com

This site provides "important resources and information for people on gluten-free diets due to celiac disease, gluten intolerance, dermatitis herpetiformis, wheat allergy, or other health reasons." Here, you will find lots of great gluten-free and wheat-free resources, including message boards, FAQs, an electronic newsletter, information on gluten-free foods, and an e-commerce-enabled store where you can buy books and gluten-free restaurant cards.

Celiac Sprue Association

1 2 3 4 5

www.csaceliacs.org

This group bills itself as "the largest nonprofit celiac support group in America, with over 95 chapters and 55 resource units across the country, and over 10,000 members worldwide." CSA hosts annual gatherings on both the national and local levels, provides guidance on self-managing a gluten-free diet, publishes guides and gluten-free menus, and provides a wealth of free information to anyone interested in learning more about the gluten-free lifestyle.

GlutenFreedom.net

1 2 3 4 5

www.glutenfreedom.net

GlutenFreedom.net is maintained by noted Celiac expert and author Danna Korn. Visit this site to learn more about Celiac disease, and read about why even if you do not have wheat or gluten sensitivities, you should consider the gluten-free diet and lifestyle. This site, which includes information about Danna's award-winning books, also touches on the gluten sensitivity spectrum, testing for gluten intolerance, and the symptoms of gluten allergies.

CENSORSHIP

Center for Democracy and Technology

www.cdt.org/speech

The Center for Democracy and Technology works to "promote democratic values and constitutional liberties in the digital age." Visit this site to learn the basic issues revolving around free speech and the Internet, including pending legislation, combating spam, and more.

Related Site

cctr.umkc.edu/~bhugh/indecent.html

 Electronic Frontier Foundation

www.eff.org

One of the premier sites dealing with electronically relayed free speech and press, it contains extensive material and global links covering this issue and is the origin of the Blue Ribbon icon of support for the cause. This site, which was started to promote free speech on the Internet, continues to address the most current threats to free speech, including antiterrorism, bloggers' rights, and privacy issues that arose as a result of the 9-11 tragedy.

Freedom of Expression Links

www.efc.ca/pages/chronicle/censor.html

A big list of interesting sites that deal with freedom of ideas and expression, including organizations, documents, legal cases, and newsgroups. Focuses mostly on the issue of censorship.

Index on Censorship

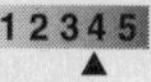

www.indexonline.org

The most recent and back issues of this magazine are available in their entirety online. Look here for well-written articles on the ramifications of freedom of speech in our everyday lives.

National Coalition Against Censorship

12345

www.ncac.org

National Coalition Against Censorship is a group that fights for freedom of speech in the United States. Here, you can learn more about the coalition, read articles about cases and issues, subscribe to email alerts, and check up on action items.

Project Censored

12345

www.projectcensored.org

A research group that reviews hundreds of stories each year that appear in independent journals and newsletters but that do not appear or are underreported in the mainstream press. The group then picks the top 25 stories from the batch and publishes them in a yearbook titled *Censored: The News That Didn't Make the News.* Here, you can learn more about Project Censored, find out how to submit articles for review, and find links to an archive of the top 25 news stories that didn't make the news.

CHEERLEADING

About: Cheerleading

12345

cheerleading.about.com

About's cheerleading site contains dozens of links to articles and resources focused on cheerleading. Learn cheers and chants, jumps, pyramid formations, stunts, and more. Information for coaches and fundraising ideas are also available here, as are fun cheer quizzes.

American Cheerleader Junior Magazine

12345

www.americancheerleader.com/jrzone/index.html

Cheerleading site for younger cheerleaders—between the ages of 7 and 12. Provides a spirit shop, message boards, articles from the magazine, and other features.

American Cheerleader Magazine

12345

www.americancheerleader.com

Excellent articles about cheerleading, covering both novice and advanced techniques. Links to other cheerleading and dance resources. Younger cheerleaders should check out the sister site, American Cheerleader Junior, by clicking on the Junior Zone link.

Cheerleading.net

12345

www.cheerleading.net

Cheerleading.net is a comprehensive directory of cheerleading links to other cheerleading resources on the Web. Links are organized into categories including College, Cheerleaders and Coaches, High School and Earlier, Independent, Suppliers, and Events.

RAMGraphics: Spiritwear

12345

www.ramgraphics.com

Spiritwear offers a wide range of cheerleading apparel that you can order online. Choose from special camp packs and cheer accessories, or have products custom-made for your squad. Inventory reduction items are available through the Closeouts page, and 101 Fundraising Tips for cheer squads can be found on the Resources page.

Team Cheer Online

12345

www.teamcheer.com

Whether you want pom-poms, jackets, team bags, or cheer shoes, Team Cheer Online offers competitive pricing based on volume. (The more you buy, the better price you get.) Browse the online catalog and call (toll free), fax, or mail in your order.

U.S. Open: Cheerleading Competition

12345

www.uscheerleading.com

Learn about and register for the U.S. Open Cheerleading and Dance competitions. Questions about rates, regulations, registration, and accommodations are all answered here.

Best Varsity.com

12345

www.varsity.com

Top site for cheerleaders, offering links for coaches, cheerleaders, parents, and anyone else who is involved or interested in cheerleading. Find out about school traditions, learn tips and techniques, find out about fundraising and scholarships, check out camps and clinics, and much more. Special area for cheerleading coaches. Connect with other cheerleaders from around the country in the site's interactive forums/discussion boards. Fun and games area provides a little extra diversion online. Clothing, books, videos, and other items are all available at the online store.

CHESS

Caissa's Web Home Page

12345

caissa.com

Provides a page where Caissa members can play chess live over the Internet. Includes membership rules and information.

Internet Chess Club

12345

www.chessclub.com

Register to play chess against other players at this site, where you can also search for game strategies and learn from grandmasters and international masters. Parents may want to supervise the registration for younger players.

This Week in Chess

12345

www.chesscenter.com/twic/twic.html

This Week in Chess is Mark Crowther's news and information site for true chess enthusiasts. This site features original news items from the world of tournament chess, player rankings and match results, a calendar of upcoming events, and much more.

Best United States Chess Federation (USCF)

12345

www.uschess.org

The USCF is the governing body for competitive chess in the United States. Here, you will find information on chess tournaments, rules, USCF membership, chess-related news, player rankings, and books and products for purchase.

A
B
D
E
F
G
H
I
J
K
L
M
N
O
P
Q
R
S
T
U
V
W
X
Y
Z

CHILD ABUSE AND MISSING CHILDREN

Abuse-Excuse.com

1 2 3 4 5 Blog

www.abuse-excuse.com

If you have been falsely accused of abusing a child, visit this site for help. Dean Tong, internationally known family rights and forensic consultant on child abuse, domestic violence, and child custody cases, manages this site, where he provides useful resources and tips for those who have been falsely accused.

AmberAlertNow.org

1 2 3 4 5

www.amberalertnow.org

In association with the Polly Klaas Foundation, AmberAlertNow.org works toward ensuring that the Amber Alert system stays in place and functioning optimally in all 50 U.S. states. Congress passed a National Amber Alert Plan, and here you can learn what you can do to improve the execution of the plan in your state.

childabuse.org

1 2 3 4 5

www.childabuse.org

Dedicated to ending child neglect and abuse, this site is focused on increasing awareness of the problems associated with neglect and abuse, informing parents of their responsibilities, and keeping children aware of their rights. Click on Recognizing Abuse for telltale signs of abuse and what you can do about it.

Child Crisis Network

1 2 3 4 5

www.childcybersearch.com

Canadian site that provides a database of missing children; a list of Canada's missing children agencies; and a library that contains helpful tips, pamphlets, and special-interest articles about missing children, childcare, and parenting. Mostly geared toward Canadians, but some information is universal.

Best ChildHelp

1 2 3 4 5

www.childhelpusa.org

ChildHelp is dedicated to meeting the physical, emotional, educational, and spiritual needs of abused and neglected children, focusing efforts and resources upon treatment, prevention, and research. Childhelp operates the Childhelp National Child Abuse Hotline, 1-800-4-A-CHILD; residential treatment villages and group homes for severely abused children; foster family agencies; advocacy centers to reduce the intake-processing trauma for severely abused children; community outreach; and education programs. At least 85 cents of every dollar spent goes directly to its programs benefiting children. Now donations can be made online using a Visa or MasterCard. Special area just for kids.

CodeAmber.org

1 2 3 4 5

codeamber.org

The AMBER alert is a system that coordinates the efforts of law enforcement and the media to broadcast and track down children who are suspected of being abducted. This site is the web extension of the AMBER system.

National Center for Missing and Exploited Children

1 2 3 4 5

www.missingkids.com

Site of a private, nonprofit organization working in cooperation with the U.S. Department of Justice dedicated to the search for missing children and the pursuit of child protection laws. Offers training for those involved in child protection and recovery, search assistance to those looking for missing children, and publications and resources pertinent to the safety of children. Also provides access to a missing children database, and answers to FAQs.

Child Welfare Information Gateway

1 2 3 4 5

nccanch.acf.hhs.gov

Formerly the National Clearinghouse on Child Abuse and Neglect Information and the National Adoption Information Clearinghouse. The Child Welfare Information Gateway is a national resource for professionals seeking information on the prevention, identification, and treatment of child abuse and neglect and related child-welfare issues.

Pandora's Box: The Secrecy of Child Sexual Abuse

1 2 3 4 5

www.prevent-abuse-now.com

Extremely comprehensive and current site offering information about preventing the sexual abuse of children, lists of other resources, statistics, news, publications, newsletters, legal information, guides for getting involved in the fight against abuse, recovery information, and more.

The Polly Klaas Foundation

1 2 3 4 5

www.pollyklaas.org

Named after an abducted and murdered child, this site has pictures of and information about missing children. It also has relevant information on how to keep your children safe, how to educate the public, and how to report missing children.

Prevent Child Abuse America

1 2 3 4 5

www.preventchildabuse.org

Home of Prevent Child Abuse America, working since 1972 toward "building awareness, providing education and inspiring hope to everyone involved in the effort to prevent the abuse and neglect of our nation's children." Here, you can learn more about the organization and its programs and 40 statewide chapters.

SOC-UM: Safeguarding Our Children-United Mothers Organization

1 2 3 4 5

www.healthyplace.com/Communities/Abuse/socum/index.html

Dedicated to safeguarding children both online and off, this site is an excellent resource for the prevention of child sexual abuse and violence. Provides links for education, prevention, and pedophile information and a collection of links to state sex-offender registries.

YesICAN (International Child Abuse Network)

1 2 3 4 5

www.yesican.org

You can help prevent child abuse, and YesICAN can help you learn how. YesICAN is dedicated to working worldwide to break the cycle of child abuse. This site delivers on its promise by providing some excellent information, including a definition of child abuse and domestic violence, statistics, instructions on what to do if you suspect a case of child abuse, and articles on child abuse. The chat areas and online discussion forums act as a support network that can place you in touch with others who are fighting child abuse in their own homes and around the world.

CHILDCARE

Best Administration for Children and Families

1 2 3 4 5

www.acf.hhs.gov

The U.S. Department of Health and Human Services is in charge of the Administration for Children and Families, which is "responsible for federal programs that promote the economic and social well-being of families, children, individuals, and communities." This site provides information on adoption, childcare, child abuse and neglect, disabilities, the Head Start program, and more. Click on Child Care under Services for Families, and you'll find an easy to navigate page for individuals, families, and organizations in search of detailed information on childcare-related issues.

Related Site

www.acf.hhs.gov/programs/ccb

AFDS, Inc.

1 2 3 4 5

www.afds.com

The American Federation of Daycare Services, Inc. provides liability insurance for in-home daycare providers. If you're interested in starting your own daycare facility, you can research insurance plans and get an online price quote on this site.

Bright Beginnings Family Child Care

1 2 3 4 5

www.juliefcc.com

Originally created by someone to promote her daycare business, this site now offers information that's useful for any parent who's shopping for daycare and for daycare providers. This site stands as an excellent model of a website for small businesses: attractive and easy to navigate.

Child Care PPIN (Parent Provider Information Network)

1 2 3 4 5

childcare-ppin.com

Includes information and articles from *Child Care Provider* magazine on various health issues as well as a discussion forum to share childcare-related ideas and problems. You can buy children's books, posters, and reproductions of paintings featured on the site through the online outlet. Kids can click the Fun Stuff link to access a list of more than a dozen links to fun sites on the Web.

ChildCareAware

1 2 3 4 5

www.childcareaware.org

This site is dedicated to helping parents locate quality childcare facilities. Features articles on how to evaluate a childcare provider, types of care, and five steps to choosing a provider. Also features a search tool to help locate providers or childcare referral services in or near your ZIP code area.

DaycareUniverse.com

1 2 3 4 5

www.daycareuniverse.com

Dedicated to providing daycare centers with connections to the products, resources, and information needed to provide quality daycare, this site features articles, product reviews, and a robust collection of links to additional resources.

drSpock.com

1 2 3 4 5

www.drspock.com

Staying in the spirit of the late world-renowned pediatrician, Dr. Benjamin Spock, this site is dedicated to providing parents with the expert information they need to raise healthy, happy children.

Search this site for medical information, product alerts, and parenting advice from some of the world's top experts in childcare.

Individual States' Childcare Licensure Regulations

1 2 3 4 5

nrc.uchsc.edu/STATES/states.htm

Just what the title suggests. Click your state to access the childcare licensure regulations that apply. The site lists each regulation and provides a full-text document so you can read the actual regulation. As indicated, the information is specific to each state. Use this site to set up your own childcare facility or to see what your state does to ensure the safety and well-being of your child.

Kiddie Campus U

1 2 3 4 5

www.kiddiecampus.com

Kiddie Campus U owns and operates daycare centers in the New York area. In addition to the KCU program and consulting options, this site serves as a primer for daycare considerations and includes a number of kiddie links and resources for the care provider. Parents of preschool kids should click the Kids Links link to view a list of fun places on the Web.

Monday Morning Moms

1 2 3 4 5

www.mondayam.com

Monday Morning Moms provides paperwork and management support for childcare providers and their employers. This company helps working parents find quality care, complete the tax paperwork in support of the care provider, and monitor provider activities to ensure quality. This site explains services of Monday Morning Moms in detail.

NAEYC Accredited Centers

1 2 3 4 5

www.naeyc.org/accreditation

The National Academy of Early Childhood Programs, a division of the National Association for the Education of Young Children (NAEYC), administers a national, voluntary, professionally sponsored accreditation system for all types of preschools, kindergartens, childcare centers, and school-age childcare programs. To date, more than 10,000 programs serving more than 700,000 children have achieved NAEYC accreditation. NAEYC-accredited programs have demonstrated a commitment to providing high-quality programs for young children and their families. Find the accredited centers closest to you by selecting Search for an NAEYC accredited program.

National Association of Child Care Resource & Referral Agencies (NACCRRA)

1 2 3 4 5

www.naccrra.org

NACCRRA is a "network of more than 800 childcare resource and referral centers (CCR&Rs) located in every state and most communities across the United States" with a mission "to help families, childcare providers, and communities find, provide, and plan for affordable, quality childcare." You can find information about programs, public policy, conferences, and careers. Click the Resource Exchange tab for access to the NACCRRA library of childcare and early learning resources.

National Network for Child Care (NNCC)

1 2 3 4 5

www.nncc.org

This site is packed with quality resources that all have been chosen and reviewed by knowledgeable NNCC staff members. You can also sign up at the site to receive a newsletter or be included on a listserv mailing list.

CHIROPRACTORS

American Chiropractic Association

1 2 3 4 5

www.amerchiro.org

The official site of the largest professional organization in the world representing the interests of chiropractors, this site provides information for chiropractors, patients, and insurers; access to its publications; educational materials for consumers; updates concerning legislation; and products for chiropractic doctors to purchase. The site also features a searchable directory of chiropractors.

CHIROdirectory.com

1 2 3 4 5

www.chirodirectory.com

This site offers a free search to find a chiropractor in your area by city, first or last name, or county.

Chiropractic in Canada

1 2 3 4 5

www.ccachiro.org

This site is the official home page of the Canadian Chiropractic Association. It provides the general public with valuable information about chiropractic healthcare.

Chiropractic Internet Resources

1 2 3 4 5 

www.holisticmed.com/www/chiropractic.html

While not the most visually appealing of sites, here you will find a detailed list of chiropractic links that can help you find a local practitioner, read about chiropractic care, contact related healthcare organizations, and participate in discussion forums.

The Chiropractic Resource Organization

1 2 3 4 5

www.chiro.org

This site is maintained by and for chiropractors and provides dozens of links to useful resources. Also provides information on nutrition, acupuncture, and pediatrics.

ChiroStore Online

1 2 3 4 5

www.chirostore.com

ChiroStore provides chiropractic and health products for chiropractors and the general public.

ChiroWeb

1 2 3 4 5 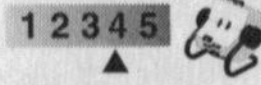

www.chiroweb.com

Of potential interest to chiropractors, chiropractic students, and consumers, this site provides discussion forums, news and information, a database of chiropractic colleges, and links to other resources.

International Chiropractors Association

1 2 3 4 5

www.chiropractic.org

If you are a chiropractic doctor or student, you will find this site useful. It contains news and information relating to chiropractic topics, details about continuing education programs, and the latest developments in legislation. Consumers can click the Chiropractic Information link for more general information about chiropractic services, or the Find a Doctor link to locate a chiropractor.

Best MyBackStore.com

12345

www.backworld.ca/mbs.asp

Back World specializes in selling products specifically for people suffering from back or neck pain. This includes home seating and office seating solutions and all those products to help deal with back problems. This site offers sales in Canadian dollars as well as American dollars. If you're looking for products to help your back—at home, in the office, or on the road—this is your one-stop shop.

Spine-Health.com

www.spine-health.com

Read about back pain symptoms, causes, and treatments at this well-organized site.

SpineUniverse.com

www.spineuniverse.com

Excellent site for both patients and professionals who must deal with back pain. This site provides everything you need to know about diagnoses, treatment options, new technologies, and preventive care.

A
B
C
D
E
F
G
H
I
J
K
L
M
N
O
P
Q
R
S
T
U
V
W
X
Y
Z

CIGARS

Cigar Aficionado

www.cigaraficionado.com

If you love cigars, you'll love this site. Features of cigar ratings, searchable directory of local retailers, restaurants that are cigar-friendly, people highlighted on the covers of *Cigar Aficionado* magazine, a *Cigar Aficionado* magazine archive, a list of drinks that go well with a good cigar, online forums, and much more.

Cigar.com

www.cigar.com

Excellent online store that carries a diverse collection of cigars, humidors, and accessories. To sample cigars, consider joining the Cigar of the Month Club. Site also features some great gift ideas and an online forum to connect with other cigar enthusiasts.

Cigar Friendly.com

www.cigarfriendly.com

Locate cigar-friendly restaurants, resorts and lounges in your city by searching the online directory, and then order your favorite brand there.

Cigar Nexus

www.cigarnexus.com

Read unbiased cigar reviews before you buy your next set of cigars, enjoy cigar-related articles, and enter contests to win free cigars here. You'll find more information about cigars than you ever thought possible.

Cigar World

www.cigarworld.com

The General Cigar Company has created this site to serve its customers, share its enthusiasm for cigars, and foster an online community of cigar aficionados. Here, you can read the history of the General Cigar Company, check out the events calendar, locate the best tobacconists near you, read and post messages in the discussions area, check out reviews of various brands, view headline videos, and more.

Internet Cigar Group

www.cigargroup.com

The self-proclaimed "largest organization of cybersmokers" provides smokers with a place to congregate and share their enthusiasm for smoking in a world that is fast becoming smoke-free. The site centers around its message boards but also functions as a directory of cigar websites and other Internet resources.

Top 25 Cigars

www.top25cigar.com

Top 25 Cigars is an online club for cigar aficionados. It provides feature articles, staff reviews and recommendations, member reviews and recommendations, news, an online store where you can shop for gifts and apparel, and more.

CIVIL RIGHTS

Best The American Civil Liberties Union

12345 Blog RSS

www.aclu.org

Lots of information about this powerful organization, which champions the rights of individuals. Read about the issues that the ACLU says threaten our freedoms and rights, and get on an email alert list that warns of events that threaten our liberties. Learn about the latest legal cases in areas ranging from racial preferences to the separation of church and state. You can buy "liberty" items such as tote bags and T-shirts through the online store. For information on current civil rights issues and cases, no site is better than this!

Amnesty International

www.amnesty.org

Amnesty International is a worldwide campaigning movement that works to promote all the human rights enshrined in the Universal Declaration of Human Rights and other international standards. In particular, Amnesty International campaigns to free all prisoners of conscience; ensure fair and prompt trials for political prisoners; abolish the death penalty, torture, and other cruel treatment of prisoners; end political killings and "disappearances"; and oppose human rights abuses by opposition groups.

Birmingham Civil Rights Institute

12345

bcri.bham.al.us

Birmingham is the capital of the civil rights movement in the United States, so it's fitting that Birmingham have its own Civil Rights Institute and accompanying website. This site is visually stunning and provides general information about the institute and specific information about events, activities, and exhibitions. This is also a great place to go when you want or need to do research on the civil rights movement.

Cato Institute

www.cato.org

Dedicated to promoting the "traditional American principles of limited government, individual liberty, free markets and peace," the Cato Institute seeks to inspire intelligent citizens to take a more active role in improving the United States government. This site provides information about the Cato Institute and its programs, events, experts, and publications.

Civil Rights Division (of the Department of Justice)

12345

www.usdoj.gov/crt/crt-home.html

This site provides an overview of the U.S. Department of Justice's Civil Rights Division, along with a list of section sites within the division, a reading room, press releases, speeches, case briefings, and more concerning the division's work on civil rights issues. Updated regularly.

civilrights.org

12345 RSS

www.civilrights.org

Home to both the Leadership Conference on Civil Rights and the Leadership Conference Educational Fund, this site explains both organizations and provides a wealth of information and links. The home page features news articles plus a navigation bar that provides quick access to Campaigns, Issues, the Action Center, the Press Room, the Research Center, the Calendar, and more. Content covers everything from affirmative action to religious freedom, voting rights, and hate crimes.

Law Research: The United States Department of Justice

www.lawresearch.com/v2/cusdoj.htm

A huge collection of links to every imaginable division of the Department of Justice.

Related Sites

www.cccr.org

www.freedomhouse.org

www.acrc1.org

www1.law.ucla.edu/~volokh/ccri.htm

www.ceousa.org

Minority Rights Group International

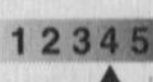

www.minorityrights.org

An international nongovernmental organization that promotes the rights of ethnic, linguistic, and religious minorities.

National Civil Rights Museum

www.civilrightsmuseum.org

A collection of civil rights artifacts, including Dr. Martin Luther King Jr.'s speeches and replicas of civil rights monuments. No specific areas for children, but kids will find some good educational information at this site.

Office for Civil Rights: U.S. Department of Education

12345

www.ed.gov/about/offices/list/ocr/index.html

Do you know your civil rights? You should, and with this site, there's no excuse for any citizen not to know his or her civil rights. This U.S. Department of Education site keeps you informed. Very easy to navigate. Click on the Know Your Rights link for information on sex, race, national origin, age, and disability discrimination.

United States Commission on Civil Rights

12345

www.usccr.gov

The United States Commission on Civil Rights (USCCR) is an independent, bipartisan, fact-finding agency of the executive branch. Check out its publications, upcoming commission briefings, regional office locations, and information about filing a complaint.

CLASSIFIEDS

Bargain Trader Online

1 2 3 4 5 (rating: 4)

www.bargaintraderonline.com

A division of Trader Online, this very reliable and up to date site features tens of thousands of classified ads for everything from household trinkets to motor homes and yachts. Browse the many categories, search for specific items, place an ad, or personalize Bargain Trader Online to keep you informed of the type of items you like to keep your eye on.

BuySellBid

1 2 3 4 5 (rating: 4)

www.buysellbid.com

Place online classified ads for virtually anything that you want to sell, from car parts to timeshares in Bermuda. Or search the database to find bargains up for sale or bid.

Best craigslist.org

1 2 3 4 5 (rating: 4) Blog RSS

www.craigslist.org

Craigslist.org is the leading online classifieds and community forum on the Net today. Here, you will find advertisements for jobs, housing, goods & services, social activities, a girlfriend or boyfriend, advice, community information, and just about anything else, all for free, and in a relatively noncommercial environment. Search the more than 10,000,000 classified advertisements spread out over 300 craigslist sites in all 50 U.S. states and more than 50 countries. Hands down, the Best of the Best for this category.

sell.com

1 2 3 4 5 (rating: 3)

www.sell.com

sell.com is an online classifieds service where you can shop for items or list items you want to sell, just like the classifieds in your local newspaper. You can browse for items by category or search for specific items by clicking the Search tab and entering one or more keywords to describe the item. This site's basic design and use of tabbed navigation makes it easy to find the item you're looking for.

Trader Online

1 2 3 4 5 (rating: 3)

www.traderonline.com

TraderOnline.com is a collection of more than 20 high-traffic websites receiving millions of visitors each month, and is a division of Trader Publishing Company, publisher of classifieds and editorial magazines with an emphasis on bringing buyers and sellers together efficiently. The publications cover a diverse mix of categories such as automobiles, trucks, heavy equipment, boats, motorcycles, aircraft and general merchandise, jobs, homes, and apartments. TraderOnline.com collects fresh data from each of Trader's more than 750 weekly and 14 monthly classifieds publications and posts this data to the Internet every day.

Yahoo! Classifieds

1 2 3 4 5 (rating: 4)

classifieds.yahoo.com

Post a full-page ad on the Internet complete with graphics for less than you might typically pay for a newspaper ad. Your free ad remains online one week, while paid ads remain active for around four weeks (30 days).

COACHING SPORTS

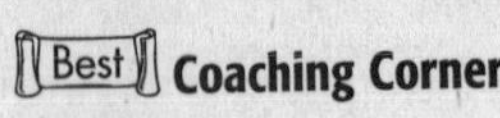

Coaching Corner

12345

www.thecoachingcorner.com

When you're called on to coach your kid's team, whether it's baseball, basketball, football, or soccer, this is the first place you need to visit for basic coaching techniques, information, tips, and suggestions on how to do it right. The goal of this service is "to enable youth sport coaches to be better informed, more organized and more professional in their communications and interactions with their players, parents and association," and they do a great job of meeting this goal.

eTeamz

12345 Blog

eteamz.active.com

Giving your team a presence on the Web helps you keep in touch with both players and parents and gives your team a sense of pride. This site is home to more than 1.5 million teams. If you're not interested in building a website for your team, you can visit this site to see what it has to offer for more than 80 sports. For example, the soccer area contains coaching tips, drills, and a whiteboard. Tips are not available for every sport listed.

Football Drills

12345 Blog

www.footballdrills.com

Football coaches will love this site, where they can find football drills for every position from linebacker to quarterback. Drills are free for registered users (free registration). You can also purchase Teamanizer software for additional drills and tips.

MyCoachOnline

12345

www.mycoachonline.com

Drill, plays, and fundamentals for baseball, basketball, football, softball, tennis, and volleyball...you'll find it all here in streaming video. Just click the tab for the desired sport and be prepared to receive the enlightening sports instruction you need to become a competent coach. MyCoachOnline features a free area; but if you want the good stuff, you need to subscribe.

National Alliance for Youth Sports

12345

www.nays.org

The National Alliance for Youth Sports is a not-for-profit group that promotes positive and safe sports and activities for children. This visually enhanced site features areas for parents, coaches, and administrators and provides a National Standards for Youth Sports guide that can help communities plan and structure their youth programs.

SoccerROM

12345

www.soccerrom.com

Although soccer coaching requires some attention to strategy, skills and techniques are what really matter on the playing field, and this site provides the suggestions and tips that coaches at all levels need to help their players hone their skills. If you're coaching soccer and need some drills, this is the place to go. With over 600 training exercises and plenty of free features , this site is worth a visit, or two or three. For the really good stuff, you need to subscribe ($34.95 per year). Site also features some team management tools.

Sports Coach

www.brianmac.demon.co.uk

Sports Coach provides a wealth of information and resources on becoming an effective coach and conditioning your athletes. This site provides dozens of links to articles dealing with sports science, coaching, fitness training, sports and events, and sports products. If you're a serious coach or athlete and find yourself looking for ways to improve performance, the Sports Coach can whip you into shape.

WebBall

1 2 3 4 5

www.webball.com

Coaching baseball has never been easier with WebBall at your side. Site opens with page that displays several tabs for coaching, hitting, pitching, catching, infield, outfield, and youth. Drills, conditioning exercises, strategies, and tips are all discussed here. If you're coaching younger kids, you'll find plenty of tips for helping them keep their heads in the game.

A B D E F G H I J K L M N O P Q R S T U V W X Y Z

COLLECTING

Beckett Collectibles Online

1 2 3 4 5

www.beckett.com/estore

Specializing in sports cards and memorabilia, this site claims more than 10 million items for sale through a network of dealers. In addition to making purchases and trades, you can also learn more about the value of cards and purchase related products, such as binders and books. This site also features a wiki called Beckettpedia, which serves as a free collaborative encyclopedia featuring sports and non-sports collectibles information, created and maintained by site visitors from around the world.

Collectics

1 2 3 4 5

www.collectics.com

Collectics is "one of the Internet's largest and most diverse online shopping and resource destinations for finer antiques and collectibles." It's basically an online consignment shop that also features books, an online museum, a gourmet food shop, and other offerings. While you're here, take the Collectics Quiz to have your name and email address entered into a drawing for a free $50 gift certificate.

CollectingChannel.com

1 2 3 4 5

www.collectingchannel.com

Have a passion for artwork? Or maybe bridal cake figurines? No matter what you're into collecting, you'll have fun chatting with fellow collectors and learning more about your hobby at CollectingChannel, which links dealers and collectors of a vast array of items, including antiques, glass & pottery, stamps & coins, toys & dolls, and much more.

Collector Online

1 2 3 4 5 RSS

www.collectoronline.com

Collector Online covers collectibles from art to World's Fair items and everything in between. You can browse for items by category or price or search for specific items, sell items you own, and find contact information for hundreds and hundreds of collector clubs. Click the Community tab to access discussion forums where you can obtain additional information and support from site visitors with similar interests.

Collectors.org

www.collectors.org

This is the official website for the National Association of Collectors and the Association of Collecting Clubs. Site features a good directory of collecting sites along with calendars for upcoming events.

Collectors Universe

1 2 3 4 5

www.collectors.com

If you collect autographs, coins, currency, sports memorabilia, or stamps, you'll want to check out Collectors Universe for more information and authentication services. Using the searchable price guide, you can determine what your high-end item is worth, too.

Curioscape

1 2 3 4 5

www.curioscape.com

Unlike other online auction sites, Curioscape is a directory of more than 13,000 independently owned shops that carry antiques and collectibles. The sites have all been checked by the staff to make sure they are reputable and are within the right category. You can also advertise your wares at the site for a minimal investment.

BEANIE BABIES

Beanie Babies Official Club

12345

www.beaniebabiesofficialclub.com

Ty Corporation's official Beanie Babies club featuring members-only special offers, newsletter, "Pin-Demonian" trading, a message board, FAQs, and access to the BBOC online store.

Beanie Babies: Wholesale and Retail

12345

www.barrysbeanies.com

Barry Stein has been selling Beanie Babies on the Internet since 1997 and features a huge collection of Beanie Babies at this site. When he's not selling Beanie Babies on eBay, Barry is selling Beanie Babies here.

Beanie History

12345

www.aboutbeanies.com

This site provides an excellent collection of Beanie news, history, and facts. Here, you can view Beanie Baby art and history, brush up on your knowledge of Beanie tags and Beanieology, buy and sell Beanies, learn how to spot counterfeit Beanies, and much more.

Best Ty's Beanie Site

12345

www.ty.com

The official home of Beanie Babies, this site is offered in six languages (English, Spanish, Italian, French, German, and Japanese) and is organized into several sections, including Boppers, Beanie Kids, Beanie Buddies, Attic Treasures, and Baby Ty. Includes a Funorama where kids can play games, create Beanie Greetings that can be emailed to friends and family, and a Tyfolio that helps you catalogue your Beanie collection. Shop online at the Ty store. Lots more here, too.

COINS

American Numismatic Association

12345

www.money.org

The ANA, a nonprofit, educational organization chartered by Congress, is dedicated to the collection and study of coins, paper money, tokens, and medals, and was created for the benefit of its members and the numismatic community. The association provides this comprehensive site with links, articles, online exhibits, educational programs, and much more. Special area for young collectors is available, too.

Coin Shows

12345

www.coinshows.com

More than 500 worldwide coin shows are listed here. Since 1996, users from 95 countries have accessed this site. Find the region you're interested in (United States, Canada, or international) and click on the state or country that interests you.

Best Coin Site

12345

www.coinsite.com

View images of coins for sale, ask the Coin Doctor a question that's been perplexing you, search the database of coins for sale, and track down up-to-date information on what your coins are worth. Some fun stuff is available, such as the coin quizzes, that will appeal to young coin collectors. This site is operated by a couple of nationally renowned numismatists who have a thorough knowledge of the hobby. This site is packed with useful information and is one of the easiest sites in this group to navigate.

Coin World

12345

www.coinworld.com

Here's the online version of the print publication, providing a searchable database of thousands of coins for sale. Catch current news and information about the world of numismatics. Get a preview of upcoming state quarter designs being considered.

A B C D E F G H I J K L M N O P Q R S T U V W X Y Z

Links to online stores where you can shop for coins and coin collecting supplies.

CoinCollector.org

12345 Blog RSS

coincollector.org

This site features a compilation of interesting and current news stories about coin collecting, a gallery of U.S. coins, coin collecting FAQs, a message board, book recommendations, and links to other coin collecting sites.

CoinLink Numismatic and Rare Coins Index

12345

www.coinlink.com

Large rare coin index with links to more than 800 numismatic sites. Piles of links to sites dealing with currency exchange, gold prices, ancient coins, statehood quarters, and exonumia (coinlike objects, such as tokens and medals). Sites are rated, providing links to only the best resources.

Forum Ancient Coins

12345

www.forumancientcoins.com

This site not only sells coins, but also provides coin collectors, history buffs, and students a fun and informative place to explore and learn about the history of coins and coin collecting itself. All sales are guaranteed.

Heritage Rare Coin Gallery

12345

www.heritagecoin.com

A site that claims to be the world's largest numismatic dealer and auctioneer. This site is full of inventory and information and neat coin stuff to see and learn about. Participate in online auctions and maintain a wish list of coins you want. The site will notify you when items on your want list become available.

NumisMedia–Numismatic Interactive Network

12345

www.numismedia.com

Register to bid for NumisMedia online auctions, offering rare coins supplied by the member dealers of NumisMedia. Featured coin auctions close every Monday through Friday between 6 p.m. and 7 p.m. Eastern time (or 5 minutes after the last bid), and coins in all categories are available 24 hours a day, 7 days a week.

The United States Mint

12345

www.usmint.gov

View all U.S. Mint products, see coin production, find fun facts about the mint, and lots more. Click on the 50 States Quarters Program, which describes how a series of five quarters with new reverses will be issued each year from 1999 through 2008, celebrating each of the 50 states of the Union (the coins are being issued in the sequence in which the states became part of the United States of America). You can see the current year's five quarters, learn about each state and when it joined the Union, and view the 10-year Schedule of Quarters.

DOLLS

Alexander Doll Company

12345

www.alexanderdoll.com

This manufacturer of Madame Alexander dolls since 1923 has established a presence on the Internet with this website. Here, you can flip through doll catalogs, check out the new chic collection, purchase new releases of the latest dolls, visit the doll hospital, and locate other places to purchase these classic dolls.

American Girl

12345

www.americangirl.com

American Girls dolls and clothing allow young ladies to select a doll that matches their personalities. Girls can even order clothing if they would like to dress up like their dolls! Young girls and their mothers often plan special trips to the American Girl stores to bond through shopping. Visit this site to browse a large selection of dolls, subscribe to *American Girl* magazine, or plan a visit to one of the American Girl stores (currently located in Los Angeles, Chicago, and New York).

Best Barbie.com

12345

barbie.everythinggirl.com

Barbie isn't just in toy stores anymore. You can now find her on the Web, where you can even go shopping with her. This site is beautifully designed and offers tons of fun stuff and freebies. Kids can play games online, keep a calendar, and even register to tell friends and relatives which Barbie dolls and accessories they want. Kids can even download Barbie wallpaper and screensavers for their computers. Special area for parents, too.

Barbie Sites
www.joeslist.com
www.dollhabit.com
www.katyskollectibles.com
www.dollhotline.com

Blythe Dolls

12345

www.blythedoll.com

This wide-eyed doll from Japan has developed a strong international following. This innovative site features an interactive forum that introduces you to the Blythe doll and its following. There's also shopping info, news, and galleries featuring images of these popular dolls.

collectiblestoday.com

12345

www.collectiblestoday.com

Great site for finding all sorts of collectibles, including dolls. Special categories for angel figurines, Ashton Tate dolls, Barbies, Madame Alexander dolls, porcelain dolls, and more.

Corolle Dolls

12345

www.liveandlearn.com/corolle

Home of dolls by Corolle of France. The babies are fabulous. The heads, hands, and feet are vinyl, and the bodies are soft and weighted so that you think you're holding a little baby. They are sized for little mommies and come in adorable outfits. The best part about this site is the discounted prices! Corolle dolls can be hard to find in stores, so why not get them via the Internet at discounted prices?

minishop.com

12345

www.mottsminis.com

A good source for dolls, dollhouses, miniature furniture, building components, landscaping accessories, porcelain doll china, and other miniature accessories. One-stop shop for building, decorating, and furnishing miniature dollhouses. From miniature banisters and handrails to tiny restaurant and home electronic equipment, this site has it all.

Raggedy Ann & Andy Museum

12345

www.raggedyann-museum.org

This is the official website of the Johnny Gruelle Raggedy Ann & Andy Museum in Arcola, Illinois. Here, you can obtain information about the museum, learn the history of Raggedy Ann and Andy, read up on Johnny Gruelle, and even check out what's offered at the museum's gift shop.

The United Federation of Doll Clubs, Inc.

12345

www.ufdc.org

UFDC is a nonprofit corporation aimed at creating, stimulating, and maintaining a national interest in all matters pertaining to doll collecting, and promoting and assisting in the preservation of historical documents pertaining to dolls. Visit this site to learn about UFDC membership, news, seminars, and online forums.

HOT WHEELS AND MATCHBOX CARS AND TRUCKS

Hot Wheels

12345

www.hotwheels.com

This official home of Hot Wheels cars and trucks enables visitors to browse through a huge collection of cars and trucks, tracks, helicopters, airplanes, games, and accessories. Links to Target.com for shopping. An innovative navigation system allows you to browse by toy or by age group. Links to other cool Hot Wheels sites can be found here, too.

Hotwheels Collectibles

1 2 3 4 5

www.hotwheelscollectors.com

This official site for novice and seasoned Hot Wheels collectors features several tabbed sections, including News and Events, Showroom, Collecting, Message Board, and Shop. If you're collecting a particular series and want to make sure you have all the Hot Wheel makes and models in that series, click Showroom and then Collection Checklist. The Message Boards provide online areas where you can connect with other collectors and possibly work out some trades.

Matchbox

1 2 3 4 5

www.matchbox.com

This is the official Internet home of Matchbox cars and trucks, enabling visitors to browse through a huge collection of cars, trucks, and other Matchbox toys. Links to other cool Matchbox sites can be found here too. Separate sites are accessible from the home page—a site for kids and a site for collectors.

POSTERS

AllPosters.com

1 2 3 4 5

www.allposters.com

Billing itself as the "World's Largest Poster and Print Store," AllPosters.com features a hefty collection of posters. If you're looking for a poster or print of your favorite movie, movie star, musician, band, athlete, fine art painting or drawing, or a photo, go to AllPosters.com and track it down...or just tour the gallery. It really is an amazing collection of posters!

Best Art.com

1 2 3 4 5

www.art.com

Art.com is one of the best places on the Web to shop for posters and prints. The vast collection spans more than 10,000 categories, including Abstract, Motivational, Sports, Cultural, and Movies. You can browse by subject, artist, collections, and best sellers, locate original art and photographs, and even have your poster or print mounted and framed for delivery. Great place to purchase gifts and gift certificates and to furnish your own home or apartment with beautiful artwork at reasonable prices.

Chisholm-Larsson Vintage Posters

1 2 3 4 5

www.chisholm-poster.com

Search this collection of more than 30,000 vintage posters, and purchase them online. This site is more for collectors who know what they're looking for. You can browse new acquisitions by category.

PosterGroup.com

1 2 3 4 5

www.postergroup.com

This site features an incredible collection of vintage posters that is both searchable and browsable. Browse by size, price, artist, or category, including Liquor, Food & Beverages, Entertainment, Travel, Transportation, War & Military, Sports, and Original Art. Crystal-clear digital images show you just what each of these beautiful posters looks like.

Posters, Inc. Historical Posters

1 2 3 4 5

www.postersinc.com

This site specializes in historical posters, prints, and postcards—especially items with a patriotic, military, and/or political theme. If you're looking for posters or other graphics from World War I, World War II, the Korean War, the Civil War, and the 1960s, this is the place to go.

Rick's Movie Graphics and Posters

1 2 3 4 5

www.ricksmovie.com

Have you ever gone to a movie and wondered whether you could get one of those cool posters they have hanging at the theater? Well, wonder no more. At Rick's Movie Graphics and Posters, you can order the poster you want and have it delivered to your door. This site has a vast collection of posters and other graphics for new and old movies alike.

STAMPS

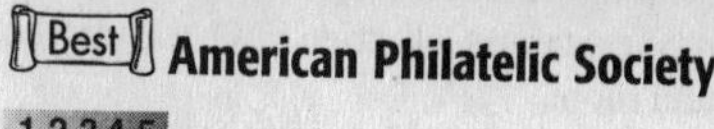

American Philatelic Society

12345

www.stamps.org

This well-designed site features the American Philatelic Society's journal, a dealer locator, a searchable library catalog, a printable membership application, extensive information on the basics of stamp collecting, and details on its expert service. If you're interested in stamp collecting, whether you are a novice or an expert, bookmark this site and visit it often. This site is packed with the most useful information you'll find on the subject of stamp collecting, making it a sure winner of the Best of the Best designation. There's even a special area where kids can learn the basics of stamp collecting.

Antarctic Philately

12345

www.south-pole.com/homepage.html

This site is dedicated to the stamps, postal history, and heroic explorers of the great white continent and its surrounding islands. Click on Arctic or Antarctic Philately for a chronological overview of postal history from both poles.

AskPhil

12345 Blog

www.askphil.org

Sponsored by the Collectors Club of Chicago, AskPhil (short for AskPhilatelic) provides an excellent resource for stamp collectors. Here, you can learn stamp collecting from the experts. This site offers a tremendous collection of resources for novice stamp collectors, a Q&A list, and the AskPhil Academy, where you can take online courses.

British Library Philatelic Collections

12345

www.bl.uk/collections/philatelic

Details on United Kingdom's National Philatelic Collections are featured here, including the Crown Agents Collection, Board of Inland Revenue, and Foreign Office Collection. Click on the Images link to view stunning images of stamps in a number of categories, including Buildings, Entertainment, Exploration, Historical Events, Industry & Agriculture, Law & Politics, Maps & Landscapes, Medicine, Military and Combat, the Natural World, Religion, Science & Technology, Trade and Commerce, and Travel & Transportation.

British North America Philatelic Society Stamp Collecting for Kids

12345

www.bnaps.org/stamps4kids

This stamp collecting site for kids is great for all ages of stamp collectors. Covers teens, preteens, and parents, and provides instructions on how to get started, what to collect, and how to judge the condition of a stamp. Also features a list of multiple-choice questions and an area where you can submit a question via email.

Joseph Luft's Philatelic Resources on the Web

12345

www.josephluft.com/joeluft

Extensive inventory of links to stamp collecting resources: supplies, shows, dealers, image collections, software, auctions, and individual collectors. Frequently updated.

Open Source Directory of Philatelic Sites

12345

dmoz.org/Recreation/Collecting/Stamps

The Open Source directory has a category devoted to stamp collecting. You can find hundreds of listings here for stamp collecting sites.

philbasner.com

12345

www.philbansner.com

This site for serious stamp collectors provides a wealth of information plus an excellent search tool for tracking down and ordering rare stamps.

S.C. Virtes Stamps

12345

www.scvs.com/stamp

Catering to novice and advanced collectors, this site includes classifieds, a beginners' corner, and an extensive list of stamp inscriptions. Click the link to shop the Scott Virtes Stamps store at eBay.com.

Stamp Finder.com

12345

www.stampfinder.com

Find stamps and supplies, buy entire stamp collections, check out the calendar of events, browse the classifieds, and much more on this comprehensive site. In addition to searching for particular stamps of interest, you can also register your own "want list," to alert other collectors to your needs. You can even download stamp collecting software and review news about upcoming events. Affiliate programs are also available.

Stamp Shows

12345

www.stampshows.com

Locate stamp shows anywhere in the world from this directory. Stamp shows are grouped by country and state. Also the home of the Stamp Yellow Pages Directory, where you can find hundreds of links to postal authorities, stamp stores, kids sites, restoration services, publications, and much more.

Stamps.net

12345

www.stamps.net

When you're looking for the latest news and information about the world of stamp collecting, turn to Stamps.net. The opening page has headline news, and you can use the navigation bar off to the left to access stamp collecting basics, show dates and locations, information for clubs, and links to other sites. A solid site for stamp collectors, especially the seasoned veteran.

United States Postal Service

12345

shop.usps.com

Buy stamps online and have them delivered to your door. The For Education section keeps you informed with information on Forthcoming Issues, Release Archive, Stamp Collecting FAQ, a Philatelic Glossary, and more.

Virtual Stamp Club

12345

www.virtualstampclub.com

News, message boards, and chat rooms to keep stamp collectors in touch with one another and informed about the latest stamps being issued around the world. Some excellent and current articles on stamp collecting–related issues can be found here, too.

COLLEGES & UNIVERSITIES

ACT

www.act.org

Learn more about the ACT, buy products to help you prepare for it, and register for upcoming tests online. In addition to providing information for students, the site also provides information for educators and parents on helping students prepare.

Campus Tours

www.campustours.com

Campus Tours is a unique college directory that links to college and university websites where you can take virtual tours of their campuses and obtain additional information.

Chronicle of Higher Education

RSS

chronicle.com

The *Chronicle of Higher Education* is "the number one source of news, information, and jobs for college and university faculty members and administrators." Here, you can access the latest news and information from colleges across the United States. This site opens with the headline news of the day, but also enables you to browse previous articles on college athletics, faculty, information technology, government and politics, and other subjects. This site also features opinion pieces, discussion forums, and a well-designed job-search tool.

College Answer

www.collegeanswer.com

College Answer is a full-featured college selection and financial aid site for students, parents, and guidance counselors. A tabbed navigation system leads you step by step through the college selection financing process: preparing, selecting, applying, paying, deciding, and financing.

College Board

www.collegeboard.com

Students planning to apply to college and teachers who want to help them do well on the SAT should visit this site to learn more about the test, take practice tests, find out about upcoming test dates and locations, and register for the SAT.

College View College Search

www.collegeview.com

Check out hundreds of colleges using College View's virtual tours or just search for a college using its database. You can also collect financial aid information here and find plenty of college-related articles.

Community Colleges

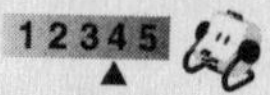

www.50states.com/cc

This site features a thorough index of community colleges listed by state. If you're interested in starting you college career at the community college level, or if you need to finish up a few classes to earn your degree, visit this site for links to schools that can help.

Mapping Your Future

www.mapping-your-future.org

Having trouble narrowing down your choice of potential colleges? Mapping Your Future, with its 10-step approach, might be able to help. Here, you can access counseling on financial aid packages, too. Great place for parents and students to start planning for the college years.

mtvU

12345

www.mtvu.com

Former home of the College Television Network, this site is dedicated to covering lifestyle-oriented programming and experiences that tap into the fabric of the college audience, the trends, the culture, and the issues relevant to their lives. mtvU is the largest television network just for college students; it broadcasts to more than 730 colleges across the country, with a combined enrollment of 7 million.

Music Schools

12345

www.music.ua.edu/resources/addressesall2.html

If you're considering an education in music, then take a look at this database of more than 900 colleges and universities with music schools and majors.

Petersons.com: The College Channel

12345

www.petersons.com

A resource of online course offerings from colleges and universities across the United States. Find out what courses and degrees are available online, or search by institution. Then request scholarship information online, too. Educators can find out more about distance learning, how to develop an online curriculum, and how to market such offerings to students.

Best Princeton Review Rankings

12345

www.princetonreview.com/college

This complete ranking of colleges provides feedback on various colleges' overall educational program. You enter the college name and receive a ranking report that includes information on enrollment, average GPA, average SAT scores, most popular majors, application deadlines, and student faculty ratios. An excellent place to start your search for a two- or four-year college or university, and easily one of this category's Best of the Best winners.

Ulinks

12345

www.ulinks.com

Considering colleges only in a particular state or area? This directory will make your search much easier. Click on Enter Database to get started.

Xap

12345 

www.xap.com

Xap is a full-featured college-selection and financial aid center that assists high school student and their parents and counselors weave their way through the college selection and financial assistance process, and even through career planning. Xap gets its edge by partnering directly with associations and institutions of higher learning to develop regional, university-approved *mentor* websites. Mentor sites use the Internet to guide students through the comparison, selection, admission, and financial aid stages of preparing for college. The site is attractive, easy to navigate, and packed with useful tools.

FINANCIAL AID & SCHOLARSHIPS

Citibank StudentLoan.com

12345

www.studentloan.com

Information for high school students on selecting a college and estimating financial aid need, for college students on repaying their student loans, and for parents on how much their child might qualify for. A student loan application can be completed online here, too. Special offers are also listed for graduate students.

College Is Possible

12345

www.collegeispossible.org

You'll find basic facts about college prices and student aid at this site, which is full of statistics regarding what typical students receive in the way of financial aid at state and private schools. Students can learn some general guidelines regarding what to expect in the way of assistance by visiting this site.

eStudentLoan.com

12345

www.estudentloan.com

Compare student loans online to find the best deal for you. After completing the online application, you will be provided with loan options that meet your criteria. After you've selected one, you can complete the loan application online, too.

Best FAFSA (Free Application for Federal Student Aid)

12345

www.fafsa.ed.gov

Almost every college you apply to requires that anyone seeking any form of financial aid first complete and submit a FAFSA. The federal government and most colleges use the data you supply to estimate your family's annual contribution toward your higher education. Even if you think you don't need to complete the FAFSA, fill it out anyway, just in case. If the deadline passes, you're out of luck. Because this site provides the easiest way possible to complete one of the most essential steps required in the financial aid process, it receives our Best of the Best award in the category of financial aid and scholarships.

fastWEB! (Financial Aid Search Through the Web)

12345

fastweb.monster.com

At this site, you'll gain access to fastWEB's database of more than 1.3 million scholarships worth more than $3 billion. By registering, you get regular updates on scholarships of interest. Come back regularly for information on hot new awards and updates on current scholarships.

FinAid!

12345

www.finaid.org

A huge site with information about applying to college and financing it. You can locate scholarships; calculate what you'll need to attend; learn about other ways to finance your studies, such as military service; and download financial aid application forms.

Financial Aid Resource Center

12345

www.theoldschool.org

At this site, you can learn about basic forms of financial aid, loans and lenders, and general sources of financial aid. You'll also find free financial aid databases to search for potential scholarships and grants for college.

The Princeton Review

12345

www.princetonreview.com/college/finance/

One-stop information and resource center for helping students understand and apply for financial aid. High school counselors of college-bound students will want to check out this site, too.

Student Financial Assistance

12345

studentaid.ed.gov

SFA is one of the largest sources of student aid in America, providing more than $40 billion a year in grants, loans, and work-study assistance. Here, you'll find help for every stage of the financial aid process, whether you're in school or out of school. If you or your child is planning on attending college, this should be one of your first stops.

United Negro College Fund

12345

www.uncf.org/scholarships/index.asp

Read about program and scholarship information to learn more about money available through the United Negro College Fund. You'll find information about qualifying for a scholarship and background facts about the organization itself.

Welcome to the Harry Truman Scholarship Foundation

12345

www.truman.gov

The Truman Scholarship is a highly competitive, merit-based award offered to U.S. citizens and U.S. nationals who want to go to graduate school in preparation for a career in public service. The scholarship offers recognition of outstanding

A B C D E F G H I J K L M N O P Q R S T U V W X Y Z

potential as a leader in public service and membership in a community of persons devoted to helping others and to improving the environment.

Yahoo! Education: Financial Aid: College Aid Offices

12345

dir.yahoo.com/Education/Financial_Aid/College_and_University_Aid_Offices

This page offers links to the college aid office for nearly 150 major colleges and universities in the United States. By clicking on a school's link, you'll gain access to information on all the financial aid opportunities available at the school.

Related Sites

www.scholarships4college.com

www.college-scholarships.com

www.universitysports.com

GRADUATE SCHOOLS

Accepted.com

12345 Blog RSS

www.accepted.com

On this website, you will find comprehensive advice on the writing tasks associated with applying to graduate and professional schools and general information on the admissions process. You can read articles on the writing tasks specific to your specialty or review sample essays. Also find out which books will really help you through the admissions derby. To keep abreast of admissions news, the latest tips, and developments at Accepted.com, sign up for the free monthly electronic newsletter, Accepted.com Odds 'N Ends.

Advice for Undergraduates Considering Graduate School

12345

www.acm.org/crossroads/xrds3-4/gradschool.html

A nice overview of the process of evaluating whether attending grad school is a smart move for undergraduates to make. Takes into account interests, ambitions, and career goals.

All About Grad School

12345

www.allaboutgradschool.com

Provides a comprehensive geographic directory of graduate schools in the United States. Click one of four categories (Business Schools, Engineering Schools, Law Schools, Medical Schools, or Online Graduate Degree Programs), and you'll be linked to an alphabetic list of states. Click on your state, and you'll find an alphabetic list of graduate schools with links to all of them (and email addresses, too).

ETS Net

12345

www.ets.org

Educational Testing Service Network provides information about college and graduate school admissions and placement tests, with links to AP, GRE, GMAT, SAT, The Praxis Series, and TOEFL sites and other educational resources. ETS Net provides sample test questions, test preparation, and test registration. This site also contains information on ETS research initiatives, teacher certification, college planning, financial aid, and links to college and university sites.

Gradschools.com

12345

www.gradschools.com

With more than 50,000 free program listings, this site claims it is the "#1 online resource for graduate school and grad program information." Click the Search function, select a program category, and see a list of not only U.S. programs, but international programs, too.

GradView

12345

www.gradview.com

A site devoted to helping students get into and successfully completing a graduate school program, with help for taking graduate entrance exams, studying, and securing financial aid. Comprehensive and easy to navigate.

GRE Online

12345

www.gre.org

Learn about registering and taking the Graduate Record Examination (GRE) in your area, and take practice tests to boost your confidence and point out your weak spots.

Kaplan Online

12345

www.kaptest.com

As far as testing goes, this site holds the top online spot for information and service. Good site if you are in admissions counseling, student services, advising, or if you're trying to find information on graduate school testing for yourself. You can shop for and order test preparation books and software from this site.

Lawschool.com

12345

www.lawschool.com

One-stop resource center for current and prospective law school students. Features everything from law school rankings to bar exam information, plus links to a law book library and law fiction.

U.S. News and World Report Best Graduate Schools Rankings

12345

www.usnews.com/usnews/edu/grad/rankings/rankindex_brief.php

U.S. News & World Report's annual ranking of graduate programs can help you evaluate academic quality. Start by selecting a field of study, or choose to review one of the many Top 50 lists available on this site. Paid registration is required to view many parts of this site.

COMICS

Animation Art

1 2 3 4 5

www.ara-animation.com/misc.htm

Billed as "The Best Animation Art Gallery on the Web," Animation Art features an enormous collection of still shots and animations. Search by artist, animated series, or company (Marvel, Disney, and so on). Or just flip through the many tabbed pages: Cartoon Network, Disney, Talking Art, Fine Art & Photography, Vintage Animation, and so on. You can purchase images and learn about licensing online.

Animation World Network

1 2 3 4 5

www.awn.com

Anyone interested in animation should check out this site! It includes links to *Animation World Magazine*; a career connection; and an animation village, gallery, and vault. Links to all kinds of animation-related products.

Archie

1 2 3 4 5

www.archiecomics.com

Archie and the gang from Riverdale High School are featured prominently at this Archie Comics site. You'll find Jughead, Betty, and Veronica here in the Today's Features section with Archie. And you'll also find games, the latest comics, puzzles, and contests.

Batman Superman Adventures

1 2 3 4 5

www.batman-superman.com

Warner Brothers brings you this site, which provides information about the New Batman Adventures and Superman Adventures cartoons. Here, you can learn more about the heroes and villains who do battle on the shows, check out the multimedia libraries, and play some games online. Fans of all ages will love this site.

Big Cartoon Database

1 2 3 4 5

www.bcdb.com

Cartoon fans will love this site, which features in-depth coverage of the most popular, high-quality cartoons and animated films. Here, you can find a searchable database of cartoon information and browse cartoons by animation studio. Each entry provides information about the cartoon, episode guides, and crew lists.

Calvin and Hobbes

1 2 3 4 5

www.ucomics.com/calvinandhobbes

If you like the comic strip, you'll be in heaven when you hit this site. Initially, you're greeted by today's strip, but a calendar below the strip lets you flip through an entire gallery of Calvin and Hobbes episodes. Peruse the book list and then examine the latest Calvin and Hobbes picture books. This site also includes icons and desktop patterns, a popularity poll, a random picture generator, links to newsgroups, and interviews with the creator, Bill Watterson.

Best Cartoon Brew

1 2 3 4 5 Blog RSS

cartoonbrew.com

Cartoon Brew is actually a blog where you can view news and articles about a wide range of topics dealing with cartoons and animation. The main page features today's news, but you can also access the Brew archives and check out Brew favorites—other blogs and websites that appeal to the Brew crew.

Cartoon Network.com

12345

www.cartoonnetwork.com

The official website of *Krypto the Superdog, Teen Titans*, the *Totally Spies, Atomic Betty*, and other favorites. Here, you can find loads of games to play online, visit your favorite cartoon character, and check on program times. Includes an online store where you can shop for books, videos, apparel, toys, games, collectibles, and other items. A fun site!

Cartoonster

12345

www.kidzdom.com/tutorials

Eventually, anyone who loves cartoons begins to wonder, "How do they do that?" At Cartoonster, you can find out not only how cartoons work but also how to start creating your own cartoons. This site, created by a teenager in 2001 for fellow teenagers and kids, features free tutorials on how to create animated cartoons.

Chuck Jones Website

12345

www.chuckjones.com

Check out the official site of the late Chuck Jones, the famous Warner Brothers/Loony Tunes animator and animation director. At this site, you can read about Mr. Jones and his many famous cartoon characters. This is an exceptionally well-constructed site, both visually and content-wise.

Comic Book Movies

12345

www.efavata.com/CBM

For those who follow movies based on comic books, this site is a must-visit. Here, you find the latest information and gossip about comic book movies, including who's slated to play your favorite heroes, heroines, and villains; how successful or unsuccessful a particular movie is; where you can find trailers; and more.

Comic Book Resources

12345 RSS

www.comicbookresources.com

Nice site that includes special sections with hundreds of links regarding Marvel, DC, Dark Horse, miscellaneous, independent, and self-published comics.

Comics.com

12345

www.unitedmedia.com/comics

United Media's Comics.com is the "Home of Comics on the Web." If you're looking for newspaper comics, including *For Better or for Worse* and *Frank and Earnest*, you'll find many of them right here.

Computer Graphics World

12345

cgw.pennnet.com/home.cfm

Home of *Computer Graphics World* magazine, a good source for industry news and product information.

Dark Horse Comics Home Page

12345 RSS

www.dhorse.com

Provides news, information, artwork, and upcoming release information for Dark Horse Comics, publisher of *Star Wars, Aliens*, and many more titles. Includes many different articles about Dark Horse titles and artists.

DC Comics

12345

www.dccomics.com

Download the latest cover images from DC comic books, watch QuickTime movies of some of your favorite characters, follow links to other sites where you can buy comic merchandise, and join a chat to discuss your love of comic books.

A B D E F G H I J K L M N O P Q R S T U V W X Y Z

Diamond Comic Distributor, Inc.

12345

www.diamondcomics.com

This comic distributor's online page has comic news, previews, and a catalog. Find out many interesting facts at this businesslike site! Click on the Previews link for a look at what's about to be published.

Digital Webbing

12345

www.digitalwebbing.com

Great source for finding comic book-related websites and information. Includes an extensive database of comic book websites, news, interviews, previews, and talent search area.

Disney.com

12345

disney.go.com/characters/today

A nice website for families to explore together! Has links to some of Disney's best known cartoons, along with activities for kids and families. Also has a Disney shop online.

EX: The Online World of Anime and Manga

12345

www.ex.org

Provides an online magazine dedicated to Japanese anime and manga. Includes back issue and subscription information. EX features many different articles, pictures, and much more dealing with anime.

International Animated Film Society

12345 Blog

www.asifa-hollywood.org

ASIFA is a "membership organization devoted to the encouragement and dissemination of film animation as an art and communication form." It has more than 1,700 members in more than 50 countries, providing links to various chapters and events around the world. Here, you can find announcements for screenings, festivals, and other events, as well as information about the organization.

International Museum of Cartoon Art

12345

www.cartoon.org

Internet home of the International Museum of Cartoon Art represents the work of artists from more than 50 countries and has a huge collection of original drawings, books, videos, interviews, and other items related to comic book illustrations and animations. Here, you can check out some select items and learn more about your favorite cartoonist.

Marvel Comics

www.marvel.com

The home of Spiderman, the Hulk, Captain America, and other famous heroes, this site is marvelous! Here, you can learn about your favorite Marvel comic books, preview upcoming issues, and shop online.

MTNCartoons

12345

www.mtncartoons.com

See the work of cartoonist Marc Tyler Nobleman at his site, where you can also purchase rights to feature his work.

Official Peanuts Website

12345

www.snoopy.com

Kids can play the Peanuts trivia game and color in the coloring book, while adults might want to read more about Peanuts' creator, the late Charles Schulz. There is also a comic archive to find past strips. Shopping link to SnoopyStore.com.

Shark Tale

12345

www.sharktale.com

If you're a fan of the animated film *Shark Tale*, you can visit Lenny and the rest of the gang at this site. Tour the Gallery, find out more about the making of the film, play games, watch video clips, download freebies, or just...fuggetaboutit.

A B C D E F G H I J K L M N O P Q R S T U V W X Y Z

The Simpsons

12345

www.thesimpsons.com

Explore Springfield using the virtual map and view the latest antics of Homer and Bart. Meet the voice actors, guest stars, and show's creator. Get character bios, view episode descriptions, and share your enthusiasm for the show with other fans. Mmm, excellent site!

South Park

www.southparkstudios.com

Home of Comedy Central's *South Park* cartoon. View a trailer of the latest *South Park* production, submit your vote in this week's poll, or buy *South Park* memorabilia online. This site is packed with free games and downloads, a BBS, a FAQ, behind-the-scenes footage, and a host of other goodies. Kids like this animated cartoon, but it's not really suitable for kids.

Spongebob Squarepants

12345

www.nick.com/all_nick/tv_supersites/spongebob

Follow the antics of Spongebob Squarepants and his fellow silly sea creatures online at Nickelodeon's official Spongebob website. Here, you can play a boating game, feed the anchovies, download a screensaver, view a talking cast picture, and more. Excellent site for young kids, but older fans will like it, too.

WebComics

www.webcomics.com

Huge collection of links to comics on the Web. Features include WebComic of the Day, WebComic of the Week, Top 30 Toons, and a discussion area.

Related Site

www.cartoonsforum.com

A B C D E F G H I J K L M N O P Q R S T U V W X Y Z

COMPUTERS

Chumbo.com

12345

www.chumbo.com

Chumbo is a great place to shop for hardware, software, electronics gizmos and gadgets, DVDs, and video games. It provides product ratings and features some excellent bargains.

Computer History Museum

12345

www.computerhistory.org

Learn about the history of computers from 1945 to 1990. Check the historical timeline, learn about its collections and exhibits, and find out about upcoming events.

CNET

www.cnet.com

Get hardware and software reviews here before you buy, compare prices from various suppliers, and catch up on tech news. You can also download freeware, learn more about website building, and lots more at this popular site.

Related Site

shopper.cnet.com

CompUSA.com

12345

www.compusa.com

Get information and details about which computer products to buy and then buy them online from CompUSA. You can also download software here.

egghead

12345

www.egghead.com

At Amazon.com-powered egghead.com, you can check out a wide selection of Egghead products. Browse by category and check out some great deals. Egghead has always been a great place to find bargains on cutting-edge electronics and software. Now it has Amazon's service to ensure that you receive great deals and service, too.

MSN Tech

12345

tech.msn.com

MSN's tech site is packed with excellent information and resources for PC/Windows users of all levels of experience. Includes product reviews, downloads, how-to instructions, news, trends, virus and security information, and much more.

Old-Computers.com

12345

www.old-computers.com/news

If you're growing nostalgic about your old Commodore computer, visit Old-Computers.com to reminisce about the good old days when you actually understood (somewhat) about how your computer worked. This site features tabbed navigation to provide quick access to several areas, including news, museum, history, magazine, forums, collectors, and fun. Online shopping is provided through cafepress.com, where you can find Old-Computers apparel and gifts.

PC Connection

12345

www.pcconnection.com

Scout hot deals and bargains before placing your order online at PC Connection, where a nice perk of shopping here is that your order will be shipped overnight.

Related site

www.macconnection.com

Smart Computing

www.smartcomputing.com

Home page of *Smart Computing* magazine, one of the most popular computer magazines for beginning-level PC users, features articles, techniques, and tricks for using and optimizing PCs. Subscribers can log on for additional features.

Related site

www.macworld.com

ZDNet

www.zdnet.com

Read industry news, download useful software, scan product reviews, and go shopping for hardware and software at affiliate sites.

ZDNet Shopper

shopper-zdnet.com.com

Browse dozens of hardware and software categories for the items you need, read product reviews and recommendations, and learn how to shop for various computer products.

COMPUTER COMPANIES: HARDWARE & SOFTWARE

AMD

1 2 3 4 5

www.amd.com

Are you wondering whether an AMD-powered PC can hold its own against an Intel-powered PC? Then turn to this site to see what AMD has to say about it. Here, you can find product information, support, downloads, press releases, and investor information.

Apache Digital Corporation

1 2 3 4 5

www.apache.com

Provides information on ALPHA-based, NeXTSTEP, Linux/BSD UNIX, Windows NT, SPARC-based, and other custom-design systems sold by Apache.

Best Apple Computer Home Page

1 2 3 4 5

www.apple.com

Apple provides an online storefront where you can purchase customized hardware configurations of your favorite Macintosh models. Provides information on Apple's latest products and supplies software updates. Check out this site for the latest on Apple technology.

Dell.com

www.dell.com

This site provides secure online shopping for Dell personal computer products. You can custom configure a system and buy it online. The site also lets you search for information by type of user and provides the standard corporate information. And, if you own a Dell computer, this site features excellent online technical support that can help you solve most of the problems you might encounter with it.

Gateway

1 2 3 4 5

www.gateway.com

Gateway's site is designed for easy navigation. If you're looking for a computer for your home or home-based business, click the Home & Home Office link and start shopping. Business users should click the Small Business or hr the Mid & Large Business link to shop for computers and other products designed for business applications. You can configure and purchase a computer online from this site. The site also provides access to technical support and corporate information.

A B C D E F G H I J K L M N O P Q R S T U V W X Y Z

A B D E F G H I J K L M N O P Q R S T U V W X Y Z

Hewlett-Packard

www.hp.com

A leader in desktop hardware and network servers provides this website to learn about HP's newest systems, including technical information on HP printers and notebooks.

IBM Corporation

www.ibm.com

Here, you can reach all of IBM's myriad divisions from the home page. You can also read about IBM systems solutions via articles. Take online training courses, attend real-time seminars, or chat with people with similar interests. An extensive search engine is also provided for navigating this large corporate site.

Intel

12345

www.intel.com

This site provides all the information you ever wanted to know about Intel's integrated circuits and latest processor. The site showcases software running on Intel-based hardware and hardware implementations, and it offers business opportunities as well as the standard technical support and news briefs.

MPC

12345

www.buympc.com

Less popular than Apple, Gateway, and Dell, this online computer store (formerly Micron PC) has been providing quality products and service to its customers for just as long. Shop online or obtain technical support and downloads for a Micron or MPC PC you already own.

Sony Style

12345

www.sonystyle.com

Sony has always been stylin' with its desktop and laptop PCs. If you're looking for a PC that not only performs well but looks good, too, turn to this site for a look at the complete line of Sony PCs and accessories. A cool site that makes it almost too easy to buy a new PC.

Sun

12345 Blog RSS

www.sun.com

At Sun Microsystems, "The network is the computer." Visit this site to find out why and to obtain product information, technical support, downloads, and documentation.

Toshiba

www.toshiba.com

Toshiba is one of the top manufacturers of quality laptop PCs. Here, you can find out about the latest products on the market, obtain technical support and documentation, and download updated software drivers.

MACINTOSH

Apple Insider

12345 RSS

www.appleinsider.com

AppleInsider covers all the latest news and rumors swirling around Apple and its products. You can find headline news and forums, participate in polls, submit a story, and even chat with other interested Mac users.

Apple Links

www.applelinks.com

News, reviews, buyers' guides, and Mac information all in one place. Many links to retail sites, too.

iLounge

www.ilounge.com

You have an iPod, but are you getting the most you can out of it? Hang out in the iPod lounge to find out. Here, you can find an iPod 101 tutorial and other useful articles, product reviews, help, tips and tricks, discussion forums, free downloads, and more.

Related Sites

www.apple.com/ipod

www.apple.com/support/ipod/index.html

iPod Hacks

www.ipodhacks.com

You've mastered your iPod...or so you think. Can you hack it? Can you make it do things that even its engineers hadn't imagined? Well, this site can let you in on a few secrets for customizing your iPod to personalize it and enhance its performance.

Mac Addict

www.macaddict.com

Sign up for the Mac Addict newsletter, jump into some discussions to share and gather Mac information, and stay tuned for up-to-date news and rumors.

Mac Design Online

www.macdesignonline.com

Involved in the graphics industry? Mac Design is devoted to covering Macintosh graphics, multimedia, and web issues specifically for Macs.

MacGamer.com

RSS

www.macgamer.com

Game reviews, previews, interviews, editorials, and downloads for Macintosh games. Join an online discussion of your favorite Mac games and find deals and freebies.

Mac Home

www.machome.com

Looking for a Mac product review? You'll find more than 1,000 from the pages of *MacHome* magazine here and downloadable software, updates, and tips. Subscribe to the magazine online.

Macintosh News Network

www.macnn.com

Excellent source for Macintosh news, reviews, discussion, tips, troubleshooting, links, and reviews. Tracks and reports on the latest developments in the industry. Great site, especially for IT professionals.

Mac Update

www.macupdate.com

Download Macintosh software and games here. Links to additional Mac-related resources can be found here, too.

Macworld

www.macworld.com

Macintosh industry news, product reviews, newsletters, and forums. Search for the best deals on Mac hardware and software with Macworld's Pricefinder. If you're a Mac enthusiast, this is *the* place to learn what's going on in the world of Apple Macintosh. Macworld also serves up a fair share of information on the Apple iPod. This site features a menu bar that makes it easy to navigate to the various sections: News, Product Info, Mac Help, Magazine, and Forums. Simplified navigation coupled with a vast collection of informative articles and useful resources makes this a no-brainer pick as Best of the Best Mac sites.

PCs

Annoyances.org

annoyances.org

This site shines the spotlight on the most annoying computer and software features you might encounter, including Microsoft Office's Clippit. This site lists the top Windows annoyances and provides instructions on how to avoid them. Additional information is available for tweaking the Windows Registry, customizing the desktop, improving performance, and much more.

GoToMyPC

www.gotomypc.com

Online service that enables you to connect to and use your desktop computer from any Internet-connected computer in the world via a secure connection. If you frequently find yourself on the road without access to the programs and documents you need to survive, connect to this site to sign up for a free trial.

> **Tip:** Since GoToMyPC is not available for Apple computers, visit www.apple.com/remotedesktop for the Apple equivalent, Apple Remote Desktop.

Microsoft Product Support Services

support.microsoft.com

If you have a PC that runs any version of Windows and any other Microsoft product, such as Microsoft Office, bookmark this site. Here, you'll find a searchable knowledgebase where you can find answers to most of your technical support questions. Simply click the Search the Knowledgebase link, select the product that's giving you trouble, type a few key words that describe the problem, and click Go.

PC Guide

www.pcguide.com

Everything you always wanted to know about PCs, from how a PC works to troubleshooting common problems, can be found here. This site provides a useful PC buyer's guide and information on how to care for and optimize your computer's systems. Plain presentation, but excellent content and easy to navigate.

PC World

www.pcworld.com

Get PC help, downloads, news about the most popular software, as well as reviews of the best PCs, accessories, and software from this site, which is the online companion to *PC World* magazine.

PCs for Everyone

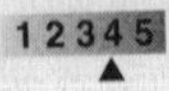

www.pcsforeveryone.com

PCs for Everyone designs and builds custom PCs and sells PC cases and components for users to build their own PCs. Instructions and technical support are provided online, and you can order products online or over the phone.

Windows

www.microsoft.com/windows

Windows product downloads, tips, and support are all available here.

Best WinPlanet

www.winplanet.com

Premium site for all topics related to Microsoft Windows and Windows applications. Take an online tutorial to learn a new skill, pick up some tips and tricks, and learn how to customize Windows with some tech-savvy tweaks. Excellent collection of downloadable shareware and updated drivers. When you want to learn more about your computer's operating system, this is the place to go.

Woody's Watch

office-watch.com

Woody Leonhard, Microsoft Office expert, features Office advice, troubleshooting, and tips via his newsletter, which you can subscribe to at this site. Newsletter features no-nonsense, unbiased advice from the world's leading experts on Microsoft Office products.

PROGRAMMING LANGUAGES

Active State

12345 RSS

www.activestate.com

Produces Perl scripting software for web developers. The site provides software purchases and support to Perl programmers.

Amzi! Prolog+ Logic Server

12345

www.amzi.com

Produces Amzi! Prolog+ Logic Server, a software add-on you embed in C++ and other programming languages to create logic-based intelligent agents and intelligent components, which are used in software that relies on artificial intelligence. Amzi!'s products assist programmers who need to create software that configures, schedules, diagnoses, advises, recognizes, lays out, plans, understands, or teaches. Downloadable demos and tutorials are provided to show how this Prolog-based programming language works.

Applescript

12345

www.apple.com/applescript

Macintosh users who want to create customized programs to automate and schedule time-consuming tasks can do so using Applescript. This site, hosted by Apple, introduces you to Applescript and teaches you the basics. It includes a partial list of existing applications, an Applescript Studio where you can obtain the required tools, a page for developers, and links to an extensive collection of additional resources.

ASP 101

12345 RSS

www.asp101.com

Whether you've just started learning Active Server Pages programming or consider yourself a pro, you can find something that's new and informative at this site. Includes lessons and tutorials, sample code, news, resources, and links to other ASP-related sites.

ASP Alliance

12345 RSS

www.aspalliance.com

Founded in 1997, the ASP Alliance has grown to include more than one hundred contributors and more than 1,000 articles related to ASP programming. This site supports forums and has spawned several related sites. Visit to obtain free tutorials, articles, resources, and code snippets or to connect with other ASP enthusiasts through this site's online communities and email lists.

ASP Free

www.aspfree.com

This site, presented in any of six languages, is packed with articles, news, and development updates relating to ASP programming. Includes ASP code and examples.

Borland C++

12345

info.borland.com/devsupport/borlandcpp

Borland C++ 5 is one of the top-selling C++ programs on the market. This website includes press releases about Borland C++, the latest patches for various versions of C++, technical support information, and bug information. It also includes a link to other sites devoted to Borland C++.

Builder.com

12345 RSS

builder.com

TechRepublic maintains this site as a resource dedicated to helping computer users build better websites. Topics include web authoring and scripting, graphics, and design. User can download tools and participate in user forums.

CGI Extremes

www.cgiextremes.com

This site provides an accurate and up-to-date database of more than 2,100 CGI scripts for web programmers. Descriptions, ratings, and user feedback are provided for each script to help programmers make an informed choice.

CGI Resource Index

cgi.resourceindex.com

Dedicated to the CGI programmer, this site contains thousands of links to CGI scripts, documentation, books, programmers, and even jobs.

Code Guru

www.codeguru.com

Get the latest information and tips for .NET, C++, Java, Visual Basic, JavaScript, and XML as well as access to discussion forums where you can connect with other programmers who can answer your questions. Links to Fatbrain where you can purchase book titles.

developers.net: Jobs for Technical Professionals

12345

www.developers.net/tech-jobs

Put your programming skills to work and earn a pretty good living. This site provides a long and up-to-date list of openings for programmers and other technical professionals.

EarthWeb

www.earthweb.com

Comprehensive collection of the latest information and resources for IT professionals, programmers, webmasters, and others interested in computer technology.

eXtreme Programming

12345

www.extremeprogramming.org

Learn the basics of Extreme Programming (XP)—the "deliberate and disciplined approach to software development." Learn when to use this approach, how to get started, and where to find out more information about it.

Related Site

www.xprogramming.com

Hotscripts.com

www.hotscripts.com

With links to thousands of web programming resources in more than 1,000 categories, Hotscripts.com is one of the best places for webmasters and programmers to find what they need to enhance their sites. Hotscripts.com evaluates resources and presents a collection of the best resources on the Web.

HTML Center

www.htmlcenter.com

Learn about HTML, Java, JavaScript, Flash, and more. Online tutorials teach the basics, product reviews evaluate the best HTML authoring software, help forums answer your questions.

HTML Goodies

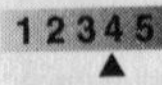

htmlgoodies.earthweb.com

Programmers will find the tutorials and primers a great start to learning more about various programming tools, including HTML, JavaScript, ASP, Perl, and CGI. Visitors can also ask questions of experts and search the site for more information.

HTML Guru

www.htmlguru.com

An unusual site that demonstrates what is possible with dynamic HTML programming through reference material and tutorials.

A B D E F G H I J K L M N O P Q R S T U V W X Y Z

HTML Help

12345

www.htmlhelp.com

Great tools and guidelines available for programmers and designers here and FAQs and informative articles.

JavaScripts

12345

webdeveloper.earthweb.com/webjs

In addition to FAQs and free newsletters, visitors to this site can access and download more than 5,000 JavaScripts.

java.sun.com

12345 RSS

java.sun.com

Maintained by Sun Microsystems, this site is the official home of Java. Here, you will find the latest news and information about Java, downloads, tutorials, code samples, support, and much more. If you program in Java, you will definitely want to bookmark this site.

Linux Advisor

12345 RSS

linuxadvisor.net

Linux Advisor is the online version of *Linux Advisor* magazine, which provides news, information, technical advice, business solutions, and other resources concerning the Linux operating system. If you develop programs for Linux, Linux Advisor can provide support and information you might need.

Linux Planet

12345

www.linuxplanet.com

Huge collection of information and resources about the Linux operating system. Here, you will find discussion groups , opinions, reports, reviews, and tutorials. If you're planning on ditching Windows and using Linux instead, or if you are programming for Linux, check out this site before you proceed.

MSDN Online

12345 RSS

msdn.microsoft.com

Resources, downloads, magazines, and more are available at this comprehensive site For Microsoft Developers Network (MSDN) programmers and developers. Links to additional information about .NET technology can also be found here.

Related Sites

www.acm.org/sigplan

www.math.uio.no/doc/gnu/emacs/program_modes.html

Perl: CPAN Comprehensive Perl Archive Network

www.cpan.org

Comprehensive collection of links to the best Perl resources on the Web. Locate Perl source code, modules, and scripts; research documentation; and find answers to the most frequently asked questions.

Perl.com

www.perl.com

O'Reilly and Associates Perl site is a premier site for learning about Perl. Here, you can find blogs and links for documentation, training, downloads, books, FAQs, and other resources focusing on Perl.

Programmers' Heaven

12345 RSS

www.programmersheaven.com

Online resource for beginner to expert programmers. Download source code and files for various programming languages or order them on CD-ROM. You'll also find thousands of links to programming-related sites. Subscribe to the mailing list to receive email updates.

VBWire

12345

www.vbwire.com

VBWire features the latest news and about Visual Basic, plus developer forums where you can exchange information with other Visual Basic developers.

Visual Basic: Microsoft Visual Basic

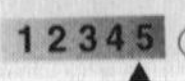 Blog RSS

msdn.microsoft.com/vbasic

When you're looking for information on Microsoft Visual Basic, go to the source itself: Microsoft. This site features an introduction to Microsoft Visual Basic along with developer forums, tools, articles, downloads, tutorials, and support.

Webmonkey

hotwired.lycos.com/webmonkey

A great list of how-to libraries for topics ranging from e-commerce to authoring, design, multimedia, programming, and more. Excellent resource for web developers.

SOFTWARE—ANTIVIRUS

AVG AntiVirus

12345 RSS

www.grisoft.com

This is the home of one of the better antivirus utilities around! Here, you can check out its features and decide whether you want to stick with the old standards (McAfee AntiVirus or Norton AntiVirus) or try something that some tests have proven to be even more effective...and maybe even more affordable.

McAfee.com

12345

www.mcafee.com

Get new virus alerts at McAfee and help buying, installing, and running its VirusScan software and instruction in eliminating existing viruses on your computer system. This site also features a searchable database of viruses, to help you determine whether a virus warning is a hoax and to learn more about a particular virus and how to eliminate it from your computer.

Symantec

12345

www.norton.com

Buy Norton AntiVirus here, learn about protecting your system from viruses and other threats, and download virus definition updates (if you own the program).

SOFTWARE—DOWNLOADS

5 Star

www.5star-shareware.com

Check the laundry list of types of shareware available for download, or read the expert recommendations before making your selection. Coverage available for both the PC and Apple platforms. Categories include home, business, desktop, games, graphics, hobbies, music, utilities, and web development.

BlackICE Update Center

12345

blackice.iss.net/update_center/index.php

Protect your computer and files from potential hack attacks by downloading Black Ice Defender, a personal firewall. Tech support and customer service are available on this site, as are a variety of solutions for protecting your computer.

Download.com

 RSS

www.download.com

Download software for virtually any application—virus protection, productivity, multimedia, and more.

freshmeat.net

freshmeat.net

freshmeat maintains one of the Web's largest index of open-source UNIX and cross-platform software and Palm OS software. Each entry contains a description of the software, a link for finding out more about it and downloading it, and a brief history of the product's development. If you're looking for Linux software, this should be your first stop.

Happy Puppy

www.happypuppy.com

This gaming site provides shareware games and reviews for a wide variety of games for Mac and PC. Subscribe to the newsletter to keep abreast of the latest news and reviews.

Jumbo!

www.jumbo.com

Huge collection of freeware and shareware for download organized by categories, including Internet, MP3 Players, Utilities, Wallpaper, Business, Drivers, and more. Excellent descriptions and reviews of each available program.

Qwerks

www.qwerks.com

This site helps smaller software manufacturers get their products into the hands of users like you. To get started, you can go to See Who's Hot, View All Software, or Do A Search. Read a description, order it online, and download it immediately.

softpedia.com

www.softpedia.com

This "encyclopedia of free software downloads" offers a wide selection of freeware and shareware for Windows PCs, Macs, and mobile devices.

Navigation buttons provide quick access to the desired categories, including Windows, games, drivers, Mac, mobile, and news. After selecting a general category, you can click the drop-down list for the Sections in This Category to pick a more selective grouping. You can select the desired viewing mode, as well—Normal, Freeware, or Shareware—to screen out any versions you don't want to consider. Automated updating enables this site to remain current up to the minute.

Best Tucows

www.tucows.com

One of the largest, most popular shareware/freeware sites, Tucows features more than 40,000 software titles for the Macintosh operating system, Windows, Linux, OS/2, and others. Ranks, describes, and reviews each program in its collection. Here, you can find Internet programs, computer utilities, games, themes, multimedia players, and more.

SnapFiles

www.snapfiles.com

Formerly WebAttack.com, this site features one of the "world's largest Internet-related software collection." It also features a good collection of software that is not related to the Internet. SnapFiles is unique in that it reviews and rates all shareware that is submitted before making it available to users. This site is nicely designed, easy to use, and provides excellent descriptions of the available software.

SOFTWARE—MISCELLANEOUS

Adobe

www.adobe.com/products

Product feature information for Adobe software products, including PageMaker, Acrobat, and Photoshop. Great place to find shareware versions of Adobe products, order products online, and obtain technical support.

Family Tree Maker Online

12345

www.familytreemaker.com

An online genealogy library with lessons, columns featuring researching techniques, and tips on how to trace immigrant origins. Buy the genealogy software and family archive CDs online.

International Data Group

12345

www.idg.com

Publisher of magazines such as *Computer World/ InfoWorld, PC World, Network World, MacWorld, Channel World,* and *Specialty.* Find links to each of these publications. Many feature software previews, reviews, and recommendations.

Laurie McCanna's Photoshop, Corel, Painter, and Paintshop Pro Tips

12345

www.mccannas.com/pshop/menu.htm

This site features tips and tutorials for Photoshop, Corel, Painter, and Paintshop Pro users. A multitude of examples for the applications that are offered.

Web Copier

12345

www.maximumsoft.com

Web Copier is a powerful offline browser that records websites and stores them on your hard drive until you are ready to view them. Save time by storing records locally before referencing them.

ZDNet

12345 Blog

downloads-zdnet.com.com

Demos and downloads site for *ZD Internet* magazine, providing Internet applets, demos, product reviews, and free software for all platforms. Updated weekly.

TROUBLESHOOTING

5 Star Support

12345

www.5starsupport.com

At this site, volunteer technical support personnel help users resolve computer and software issues for free. Get free technical support, meet the techs, visit the security center, or sign up for the free newsletter. You can also donate your time or money to keep the service running.

ActiveWindows

12345 Blog RSS

www.activewin.com

ActiveWindows is packed with up-to-date news regarding most aspects of the computer industry, including Macintosh and PC hardware, Mac OS and Windows, DVD technology, and DirectX. Includes interviews, downloads, reviews, tech tips, and more.

Answers That Work

12345

www.answersthatwork.com

Answers That Work is an online help desk that can assist you in solving both hardware and software issues. Registered users can submit a query. Unregistered users must browse through the task list directory to find a topic that matches their specific problems. This site also provides a nifty utility called TUT: The Ultimate Troubleshooter. TUT focuses on identifying background operations suspected of causing about 65 percent of the most common computer problems.

Apple Technical Support

12345

www.apple.com/support

Apple Computer's technical support site, featuring free downloads and patches and answers to common questions. Check out products and services, search the knowledgebase, download files, participate in the discussion groups, or find online user manuals.

A B D E F G H I J K L M N O P Q R S T U V W X Y Z

AskDrTech

12345

www.askdrtech.com

For about 45cents a day, you can get expert technical support over the phone for all of your computer questions and problems 24 hours a day, 7 days a week. At this site, you can learn more about the service and sign up. Both Mac and PC tech support is available.

Help2go

12345

www.help2go.com

Get free computer advice in the form of helpful articles at this site, which also offers to answer your first live question free if the articles don't do it—through Expertcity.

MacFixIt

12345

www.macfixit.com

Mac owners who have encountered a problem they can't solve should head to MacFixIt, where they can participate in forums, read archived articles that might answer questions, look at a troubleshooting report, or download shareware and freeware designed to correct bugs.

Best PCMechanic

12345 RSS

www.pcmech.com

If you like to tinker with your own PC rather than calling in a technician every time something goes wrong, check out PCMechanic. Here, you can find tutorials on everything from upgrading and repairing PCs to building your own PC from scratch. PCMechanic provides four complementary forms of assistance—the website itself, offline publications and CD content, online discussion forums, and a newsletter. Tabs provide easy navigation to sections that deal with specific PC components and additional sections on how a PC works, PC optimization and troubleshooting, and more. An excellent site for the PC weekend mechanic.

PC Pitstop

12345

www.pcpitstop.com

Have an automated technician check your PC for problems and help you optimize your system. PC Pitstop checks to see whether your computer is vulnerable to attacks from viruses or hackers, determines if the hard drive has enough space and is fast enough, checks the memory, reports on the speed of your Internet connection, and much more. Very cool tool for tuning up a PC.

SoftwareLifeTips.com

12345 RSS

software.lifetips.com

Provides tips for using several software applications, including Excel, PowerPoint, AutoCAD, Word, Outlook, and Windows. Site enables users to submit questions to online "gurus" to have those questions answered.

VirtualDr

12345

www.virtualdr.com

Dedicated to providing computer users the tools and information they need to maintain their computers and troubleshoot problems. Tutorials on how to keep your computer running correctly and forums where you might be able to find the answer to your problem.

CONSUMER ISSUES

Better Business Bureau

12345

www.bbb.org

The Better Business Bureau allows visitors to access a database of business and consumer alerts. Visitors can also file a complaint with the BBB, find an office, and learn about membership and various BBB programs. You can also check the BBB's database to determine whether a particular online store is a safe place to shop.

Bicycle Helmet Safety Institute Home Page

12345

www.bhsi.org

The helmet advocacy program for the Washington Area Bicyclist Association. You'll find a consumer pamphlet, information on helmet laws, a toolkit for organizing bicycle helmet programs, plus the latest issue of The Helmet Update, a newsletter devoted to discussing helmet news.

The Consumer Law Page

12345

consumerlawpage.com

Provides information related to consumer law. Offers articles on topics such as insurance fraud and product liability; brochures on topics such as automobiles, funerals, and banking and corporate fraud; and useful links to other resources related to consumer law.

Related Site

www.epic.org

Consumer World

12345 Blog

www.consumerworld.org

Find 2,000 Internet consumer resources from reporting fraud to looking for the best airfare. Search the database for your specific consumer issue, and read the latest public service–related consumer news.

ConsumerLine

12345

www.ftc.gov/ftc/consumer.htm

The Office of Consumer and Business Education of the Bureau of Consumer Protection operates this online service. Find published articles on various consumer issues (in English or Spanish), read about current consumer problems, report a consumer complaint, or check out educational campaigns.

ConsumerWebWatch

12345 RSS

www.consumerwebwatch.org

ConsumerWebWatch, from Consumer Reports, keeps an eye on the Web to ensure that companies are providing accurate information and making legitimate claims about their products, services, and prices. By keeping consumers informed and telling them what to watch for, ConsumerWebWatch makes sure the entire consumer base remains populated with savvy users and shoppers.

Corporate Watch

12345 RSS

www.corpwatch.org

Website designed for investigating corporate activity. Get the hottest consumer news, learn about the organization's latest campaigns, and learn the research techniques needed to dig up dirt on your favorite company.

FDA Consumer Magazine

12345

www.fda.gov/fdac

Publication of the U.S. Food and Drug Administration; includes reports of unsafe or worthless products. Electronic copies are available through this website, or you can subscribe to the magazine for $14 for six issues by sending in the online form. Archives can be searched at this site, too.

Federal Citizen Information Center

12345

www.pueblo.gsa.gov

Access over 200 federal publications regarding consumer issues. A catalog offers information on a wide range of areas, such as cars, healthcare, food, travel, and children. You can also order the entire catalog of publications.

Best FirstGov for Consumers

12345

www.consumer.gov

FirstGov for Consumers functions as an all-inclusive kiosk for online federal information resources. Links are organized by easily recognizable categories, including Food, Health, Public Safety, Transportation, Children, Careers and Education, and Technology. Because this site features an easy way to obtain almost all the more useful government information for the average consumer, we've chosen to award it the Best of the Best award for this category.

Foundation for Taxpayer and Consumer Rights

12345

www.consumerwatchdog.org

Run by the nonprofit, nonpartisan Foundation for Taxpayer and Consumer Rights, Consumer Watchdog.org is dedicated to protecting the rights of the consumer, taxpayer, and medical patient. Find out the latest in consumer news and events, or search for your area of interest. You can even donate funds or volunteer to help out the cause. Sign up for a alerts that addresses the corporate and governmental crises of today and that call attention to the problems of tomorrow.

Internet ScamBusters

12345 RSS

www.scambusters.com

Free online newsletter dedicated to exposing Internet fraud and protecting consumers from misinformation and hype. Subscribe to the newsletter, share your own Internet scam experience, or enter the Internet ScamBusting Contest.

National Consumer Protection Week

12345

www.consumer.gov/ncpw

Find out when National Consumer Protection Week will be celebrated this year and pick up tips on securing your personal information and safety. Site also includes links for young people and is available in Spanish.

National Consumers League

12345

www.natlconsumersleague.org

Founded in 1899, this advocacy group represents consumers on workplace and marketplace issues. Find out the latest on consumer scams. Learn how to become an NCL member and when and where the NCL's next event is scheduled.

The National Fraud Information Center

12345

www.fraud.org

Originally formed in 1992 to battle telemarketing fraud, the NFIC now has a toll-free hotline for reporting telemarketing fraud, asking for advice about telemarketing calls, and investigating Internet fraud. The website also offers a section on fraud targeting the elderly.

U.S. Consumer Product Safety Commission

12345

www.cpsc.gov

Protects Americans against possible injury and death caused by consumer products. If you have had an experience with an unsafe product, report it on the Report Unsafe Products page. Check out the latest recalled products. You'll find an Especially For Kids page that addresses issues such as the risks of scooters, the importance of wearing bike helmets, and tips for playing on the playground safely.

Related Sites

www.sec.gov/investor/pubs/cyberfraud.htm

www.nhtsa.dot.gov/cars/problems

COOKING & RECIPES

Betty Crocker

12345 RSS

www.bettycrocker.com

Betty Crocker is almost synonymous with cooking, and here you'll find a collection of her favorite recipes organized by appetizers, breakfast/brunch, lunch, dinner, and desserts. Betty Crocker also provides some meal ideas grouped by Appetizers, Breakfasts & Brunches, Lunch, Dinner, and Desserts. This online kitchen offers some other sections, as well, including Baking Ideas, Products, and Coupons.

Bread

12345

www.cs.cmu.edu/~mjw/recipes/bread/bread.html

Provides an index of bread recipes, including recipes for bagels, biscuits, scones, and pretzels.

Chef Talk

12345

www.cheftalk.com

Turn to this site to learn all about cooking from the professionals. Culinary 101 offers lessons from the experts themselves, who also offer some of the best new recipes around. You can also participate in online forums and sign up to receive free Chef Talk updates via email.

Chile Pepper Magazine

12345

www.chilepepper.com

One hot little site! Chile pepper culture, recipes, restaurants, botany, and chat.

Cookbooks Online Recipe Database

12345

www.cook-books.com/reg.htm

Cookbooks Online recipe database is one of the largest recipe database on the Web. If you're looking for recipes, this is the place to start!

The Cooking Couple Clubhouse

12345

www.cookingcouple.com

Jump out of the frying pan and into the fire with the bestselling cooking couple on a website dedicated to food, romance, love, and lust.

Cooking Light

12345

www.cookinglight.com

Learn how to cook and eat lighter meals. Includes a Cooking 101 tutorial, recipes for some tasty dishes, menu and meal planning guides, bulletin boards, surveys, and more. This is an excellent site that also includes fantastic pictures showing how a dish *should* look when it's ready to be served.

Cooks Online

12345

www.cooksillustrated.com

Calling itself the "Consumer Reports of Cooking," this site does a great job of evaluating cookware and testing recipes for its readers, who can also find cookbook reviews and helpful cooking tips.

Creole and Cajun Recipe Page

www.gumbopages.com

Mark Twain once said, "New Orleans food is as delicious as the less criminal forms of sin." He'd love this site. It features a comprehensive guide with recipes that distinguish the fine art of New Orleans Cajun and Creole cuisine. Also contains links to several online cookbooks and food-related sites.

Culinary Schools

www.starchefs.com/community/html/schools.shtml

Lists culinary schools in the United States that describes the programs and what sorts of courses and degrees are offered.

Culinary World Tour

gumbopages.com/world-food.html

Impressive text-based site that includes a nice representation of international recipes ranging from African *bobotie*, a curried bread custard with lamb, to *kloi buad chi*, a dessert from Thailand.

Dinner Co-Op

12345

dinnercoop.cs.cmu.edu/dinnercoop

This site offers more than your run-of-the mill food-related site. More than 750 recipes plus 3,000 links to sites concentrating on recipes, culinary education, restaurant reviews, and gourmet food stores. Not pretty but well organized and useful—definitely worth a bookmark!

Best Epicurious

www.epicurious.com

Boasting a 40,000 plus collection of recipes for meals and cocktails from *Bon Appetit* and *Gourmet* magazines, this site acts as your electronic cookbook. Search for a specific recipe or search by food, such as asparagus or chicken. Site also features a restaurant guide, travel guide, and online shopping. Advertises food, wine, cooking, and travel products. And if that's not enough, the site's design and tantalizing photos will almost make your mouth water!

Fabulous Foods

12345

www.fabulousfoods.com

Looking for low-carb recipes to help you lose some weight? This site has several sets of recipes for people watching what they eat, even around the holidays. It also offers primers on types of food, describing how to prepare it and providing recipes to follow. Meet celebrity chefs and pick up some special-occasion menus.

FatFree Vegetarian Mailing List Archive

www.fatfree.com

Contains 4,667 fat-free and low-fat vegetarian recipes that can be accessed from a searchable archive. Also contains links to other low-fat/vegetarian-oriented Internet resources.

Food Network

12345

www.foodnetwork.com

Home of Iron Chef America, Boy Meets Grill, Molto Mario, and dozens of other gourmet cooking, food, and drink shows, the Food Network provides culinary information and resources for those who truly enjoy and appreciate fine cuisine.

Kosher Express

12345

www.koshercooking.com

A generous collection of kosher recipes for all times of the year, including Passover, the High Holidays, and Chanukah. Also contains links to Usenet kosher recipe archives.

Mushroom Recipes

12345

www.mushroominfo.com

Excellent collection of mushroom facts and recipes. Find out how mushrooms grow and how to handle mushrooms properly. Explains mushroom varieties and basic preparation of mushrooms. Includes recipes for mushroom appetizers and lots of nutritional information.

National Pork Producer's Council

1 2 3 4 5

www.nppc.org

Find out all there is to know about "the other white meat," including industry facts, health statistics, and pig facts.

New England Lobster

1 2 3 4 5

www.877givelobster.com

This site offers fresh lobster, guaranteed for overnight delivery right to your doorstep. Provides online ordering through a secure server. Be sure to check out the extensive indexed collection of seafood recipes, too.

Pasta Home Page

1 2 3 4 5

www.ilovepasta.org

A little out of date, but this site still does a fairly nice job of providing answers to frequently asked questions about pasta, information about the National Pasta Association and its brands, pasta nutritional information, information about various pasta shapes and which sauces to use them with, and several pasta recipes.

Prevention.com

1 2 3 4 5

www.prevention.com

From *Prevention*'s Healthy Ideas; includes nutrition news and a "healthy" collection of recipes. When you get to Prevention.com's home page, click the Food & Nutrition tab.

Stuart's Chinese Recipes

1 2 3 4 5

www.dcs.gla.ac.uk/~blairsa/Chinese_Recipes.html

A short collection of Chinese food recipes gathered from submissions by visitors of the site. Visitors are encouraged to add their Chinese culinary wisdom to the present collection.

TexMex

1 2 3 4 5

www.texmex.net/Rotel/main.htm

Provides a collection of traditional TexMex recipes. A good foundation of dishes sure to please the palate suited for spicy food.

Top Secret Recipes

1 2 3 4 5

www.topsecretrecipes.com

Top Secret Recipes on the Web is the world's only website that brings you original custom recipes that have been created from scratch in the test kitchen of the guy who has devoted the past decade to kitchen cloning. Links to online shopping.

WeightWatchers Recipes

1 2 3 4 5

www.weightwatchers.com/food/index.aspx

If you're following the WeightWatcher's diet and you need a little help planning your meals, turn to the WeightWatchers recipe page. This site offers a few freebies; but if you want more, you'll need to subscribe.

CRAFTS

Art Glass World

1 2 3 4 5

www.artglassworld.com

A searchablesite specializing in stained art and art glass. See visitors' glass artwork or display your own at the Visitors Gallery. Grab some free patterns, order stained-glass books, find a list of suppliers, join a live chat, locate retail stores, discover what's new in glass art, peruse glass art magazines, and dig into the Q&A section.

Arts and Crafts Society

1 2 3 4 5

www.arts-crafts.com

In the spirit of the societies created during the early twentieth century in response to the arts & crafts movement, this site has been created to provide an online "home" for the present-day arts & crafts movement community. If you aren't sure what the arts & crafts movement is/was, check out the Archives for more information. Links to artisans and publications.

Aunt Annie's Crafts

1 2 3 4 5

www.auntannie.com

Takes the craft how-to book one step further by putting it on the Web and taking advantage of the flexibility that the Internet offers. New craft projects are offered up every week.

Craft Fairs Online

1 2 3 4 5

www.craftsfaironline.com

Craft-y people will be delighted to see so many links—to artists, fairs, supplies, publications, newsgroups, software, and more.

Crafts Etc!

1 2 3 4 5

www.craftsetc.com

Find the kits and supplies you need for your arts and crafts projects and order them online at this site.

Craftster.org

1 2 3 4 5

www.craftster.org

If you're creative but paint-by-numbers doesn't do anything for you, check out Craftster.org. Here, you can pick up ideas from other craft outlaws who like to think up projects on their own. Most of the projects are accompanied by photographs, so you can get a good look at the finished product. A robust online forum allows you to connect with others who are not inspired by cross-stitched home sweet home plaques and wooden boxes with ducks in bonnets painted on them.

Do-It-Yourself Network

www.diynet.com

Huge collection of projects complete with step-by-step instructions for the do-it-yourselfer. Projects include everything from creating your own party favors to weatherproofing your home. If you're handy around the house or you just enjoy doing creative projects on your own, you'll find plenty to keep you busy. Click on the Crafts or Hobbies link for more information.

Get Crafty

1 2 3 4 5 Blog RSS

www.getcrafty.com

This "home of the craftistas" doesn't look like much from the opening page, but it offers some pretty cool crafts, such as how to make a Skull and Crossbones quilt and more, It also features step-by-step instructions for throwing a kick-ass party. As you can see, this isn't your average craft-show stuff.

Best Hands-on Crafts

12345

www.handsoncrafts.org

This is a cool interactive site directed toward the younger audience but certainly suitable and interesting for older artists and crafts people, too. The opening page provides access to two studios: Studio 1 is all about clay; and Studio 2 deals with string, cloth, and fiber. Click the link for the desired studio and start exploring. Here, you can find excellent illustrated primers on various popular craft media along with some interesting sidebars. The interactivity and multimedia features of this site are what really bring it to life. Well worth a visit!

Michael's: The Arts and Crafts Store

12345

www.michaels.com

At this site, you can get craft tips and new project ideas, find out about upcoming store activities, have fun on the Kids pages, join in the online activities and interactive crafts, find the Michael's store nearest you, or even find investor information. Kids tab features activities, crafts, events, and games that appeal to younger kids.

ReadyMade

12345 Blog RSS

www.readymademag.com

This site is "for people who like to make stuff." Here, you can find articles from *Ready Made* magazine, along with a store where you can buy plans and kits for many of the projects. ReadyMade can show you how to make everything from posters to your own modular dwelling! Subscribe online, sample the current issue, dig through the archives, read and post messages in the forums, and much more. When you're ready make something with your own two hands, visit ReadyMade.

CROSS STITCH *(SEE NEEDLECRAFTS)*

JEWELRY *(SEE JEWELRY)*

NEEDLECRAFTS *(SEE NEEDLECRAFTS)*

ORIGAMI *(SEE ORIGAMI)*

SEWING *(SEE SEWING)*

CROCHETING

Crochet Pattern Central

www.crochetpatterncentral.com

Crochet Pattern Central is "an online directory featuring thousands of links to free crochet patterns, with over 90 categories from which to choose, including afghans, hats, doilies, ponchos, kitchen, clothing, holiday and baby crochet." You can search for a pattern by keyword or browse by category. Site also features tips and tricks and links to other useful crocheting sites.

Hip Vintage Crochet

1 2 3 4 5

www.hipvintagecrochet.com

Hip Vintage Crochet claims that "crochet is the new yoga," enabling crocheters to relax, have fun, and create their own hip clothing that you can't find in your average store. This site features a collection of vintage crochet and knit books that offer hippie, retro, and mod fashions from the 1960s and 1970s. Most of the books come complete with CDs that contain cleaned-up, printable scans of the original patterns in PDF format. You can simply print your pattern and start crocheting.

Best Learn to Crochet Easily

1 2 3 4 5

www.learncrocheteasily.com

If you'd like to learn to crochet but you're not sure where to start, start here. The author of this site has spent years tweaking these instructions on how to crochet and presents them on this site for free. Here, you can learn yarn and needle basics, how to hold your yarn and needle, and how to stitch and create knots and master basic stitches and pattern stitches. Site also features a directory of pictures, a printer-friendly index, and a link you can click to order the author's crochet book at Amazon.com.

NextStitch

www.nextstitch.com

NextStitch is an online crochet pattern company that carries a wide selection of patterns for ponchos, shawls, scarves, handbags, and bikinis. Each pattern includes step-by-step instructions, and you can instantly download the patterns you order. Site also features some free crochet videos to help you learn stitches.

Smart Crochet

www.smartcrochet.com

Smart Crochet offers everything you need to get started with crocheting and hone your skills. At this site, you'll find hundreds of free patterns in dozens of categories, including Afghans, Borders, Purses, Wall Hangings, and Women's Clothing. Site also features a Filet Crocheting Tutorial, a Q&A area, discussion forums, online polls, and links to other crocheting sites.

DANCE

ANYTOWN: Stories of America

1 2 3 4 5

shapiroandsmithdance.org

Hi-tech dance site set up to promote the ANYTOWN: Stories in America performance—"a unique artistic collaboration pairing the choreography of Danial Shapiro & Joanie Smith with the legendary music of Bruce Springsteen, Patti Scialfa, and Soozie Tyrell (the E Street Band)." The show combines dance and music to tell American stories in a way that transcends the music and lyrics alone. At this site, you can learn more about the show, view short video clips, check tour dates, and find out more about the dance company.

BornToSalsa.com

1 2 3 4 5

www.borntosalsa.com

Whether you were born to salsa or simply want to learn why the salsa is so exciting and erotic, visit BornToSalsa.com. This site features a calendar of events, a photo gallery, featured dancers, an online store, and videos. You must join to access many of the more alluring areas.

C.L.O.G.

1 2 3 4 5

www.clog.org

Home of the National Clogging Association, this site features information about the Association and its conventions, national competitions, lists of certified instructors, and more. Not much for the general public about clogging, but cloggers and clogging instructors will find plenty.

Dance Magazine

1 2 3 4 5

www.dancemagazine.com

Highlights of the current print issue of *Dance* magazine, plus links, reviews, and editorials.

Dance Spirit

1 2 3 4 5

www.dancespirit.com

Find out "what's up in dance," use the dance directory by clicking Resources, learn about fundraising, and pick up some dance pointers. Developed by the publishers of *Dance Spirit* magazine.

Dance Teacher Magazine

1 2 3 4 5

www.dance-teacher.com

Samples from the current issue, plus a library of back issues to peruse and writers' guidelines for article submissions. A great resource for any dance instructor, although some of the material is dated.

Dancer Online

1 2 3 4 5

www.danceronline.com

Internet home of *Dancer* magazine, this site provides access for subscribers to articles and archives covering everything from fashion to yoga. Sign up for a free subscription to check out what this site has to offer. Shop at the Dancer Mall, where you can find links to several online dance stores. Links to other dance sites are also available here.

La Musica

1 2 3 4 5 

www.lamusica.com

Learn about Latin dancing and music, including club, concert, and tour guides for the United States and Europe. Includes resources to find dance classes, books, radio, and TV shows. Covers Latin music and dancing in the news and provides live chat areas and online quizzes.

Luna Kids Dance Programs

www.lunakidsdance.com

Luna Kids Dance offers programs to teach young children how to express themselves through dance. Visit this site to learn more about the programs available for kids. This site is designed more for teachers and parents, but kids can check out what the programs have to offer for them.

Pow Wow Dancing

www.powwows.com

Learn about this Native American form of dancing in all its various forms. Learn about the etiquette, the instruments (drums), and the songs used in Pow Wow dancing, too. Includes a calendar of events.

So You Think You Can Dance

www.fox.com/dance

So You Think You Can Dance, a dance competition hosted by FOX, has set up this website for fans of the show to find out more about it, view photos and short video clips, check out the contestants, connect with other fans on the message boards, and more. Much of the site was under construction when we visited, but the site looks promising.

Voice of Dance

www.voiceofdance.com

Providing "the latest on news, events, and just plain fun stuff," this site has it all. From learning a new dance step to finding out about upcoming performances of virtually any major dance organization, staying current with dance news, reading reviews and commentary, and purchasing dance products, you'll find it here. Site features a huge directory of dance classes for just about every type of dance imaginable and enables you to search the directory by location to find classes near you.

BALLET

American Ballet Theatre

www.abt.org

An information site for this touring classical dance company. Includes performance schedules, photos, and information about the ballets performed and the dancers in the company. Special area for ABT kids.

Ballerina Gallery

www.ballerinagallery.com

The Ballerina Gallery provides photos and brief biographies of the most famous and accomplished ballerinas, past and present, around the world.

ballet.co

www.ballet.co.uk

The most comprehensive ballet website, this site features information and resources on all things related to ballet and dance in the United Kingdom and throughout the world. The Magazine section is updated monthly and features the latest reviews, interviews, articles on the history of ballet, and regular columns by choreographers Christopher Hampson and Cathy Marston. You can also access articles from past issues of the magazine. The Updates area keeps you abreast of the latest happenings in the world of ballet, and the Postings page lets you communicate with other ballet enthusiasts. You can also register for a free weekly newsletter.

Boston Ballet

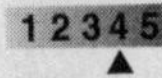

www.bostonballet.org

At the Boston Ballet site, visitors can learn about the current season's schedule of performances, check ticket prices, shop online (except for tickets), bone up on the basics of the Boston Ballet, find out about educational opportunities, and obtain contact information.

CyberDance: Ballet on the Web

1 2 3 4 5

www.cyberdance.org

A collection of more than 3,500 links to dance-related websites (classical ballet and modern dance). Also features links to stores on the Web that carry dancewear, jewelry, and other accessories.

International Dance Directory

1 2 3 4 5

www.dancedirectory.com

Impressive international directory features more than 15,000 links to dancers, teachers, merchants, competitions, and places to dance. Includes links to more than 1,500 dance-related websites worldwide. You can search the directory by name, category, state/province, and country.

New York City Ballet

1 2 3 4 5

www.nycballet.com

This NYC Ballet site features the standard information on getting tickets, planning trips to performances, and buying NYC Ballet merchandise, along with some fun features including trivia questions and games. You can also read about the history of the organization and catch up on troupe members.

Russian Classical Ballet

1 2 3 4 5

www.aha.ru/~vladmo

For those who are interested in Russian ballet, this site provides a one-way ticket to Moscow, where you can visit the photo gallery for some wonderful images of great performances. This site presents a great collection of information organized by categories including theatres, soloists, ballet companies, and ballet education.

San Francisco Ballet

1 2 3 4 5

www.sfballet.org

Find out about the upcoming repertory season of the San Francisco Ballet. Also discover opportunities to study dance with the dancers, learn how to support the organization, and get tickets to performances.

BALLROOM DANCING

Arthur Murray

1 2 3 4 5

www.ballroomdancing.com

Home of the oldest and largest dance school on the planet, this site features a description of available dance programs along with a history of the franchise and a fairly comprehensive dictionary of dance terms. Site also features a calendar of special events and news stories.

Ballroom Dancers.com

www.ballroomdancers.com

Learn dances from the waltz to the rumba at this site. You can purchase videos and CDs here and can also "try before you buy" by listening to the music before ordering it. Some useful, though a bit brief, how-to videos, along with instruction and tips. Many of the most popular ballroom dance styles are featured at this site.

Dance Directory–Ballroom

1 2 3 4 5

www.sapphireswan.com/dance/ballroom.htm

Search links organized by type of dance on this large site devoted to all kinds of dance. Leans toward ballroom dance.

Best Take the Lead

12345

www.takeltheleadmovie.com

Official home page of *Take the Lead*, the Antonio Banderas movie that melds classical ballroom dancing with break dancing. Here you can view trailers, additional short video clips, and photos. You can create your own music mixes and use the animated virtual dancer to create your own dance and then e-mail the animated sequence to a friend. This hi-tech site is one of the most interactive movie sites available and does a tremendous job of going way beyond what the movie has to offer.

United States Amateur Ballroom Dancers Association

12345

www.usabda.org

The USABDA is a not-for-profit group dedicated to promoting and supporting ballroom dancing throughout the United States. Much of its work centers on educating the public and fostering a climate in which ballroom dancing is appreciated as much as an Olympic sport as it is an art. Visit this site to learn more about the USABDA, its mission, its history, and its activities.

DARTS

Crow's Dart Page

12345

www.crowsdarts.com

Tremendous site! Covers the basics, equipment, strategy, tips and articles, links, stuff for your league, tournament information, dart stuff, dart chat rooms, dart graphics and cartoons, and more. The site might be a bit out of date when you visit because the creator is moving to Belgium, but he promises to update the site after he gets settled in.

Dart Bars

12345

www.dartbars.com

Looking for a local bar where you can hang out, drink, and throw pointed objects across a crowded room? Then check out Dart Bars, a directory of more than 4,000 bars that support drinking and throwing darts. Of course, some bars only allow the soft-tip variety.

Darts World Magazine

12345

www.dartsworld.com

This online home of *Darts World* magazine features some teasers, but for the meaty information from the world of darts, you'll need to subscribe to the printed version.

Sewa-Darts

12345

sewa-darts.com

Currently, Sewa-Darts is more of a darts discussion forum, where dart players from around the world can connect to swap stories and post announcements. Site also features a directory of links to other dart websites, free downloads, reviews, and additional offerings that are available only if you choose to register at the site.

Smilie Darts

12345

www.smiliegames.com/darts

Pick a single or multi-player game and enjoy an online game of darts. You can get help on how to play and see who are the best players.

Best Top 100 Darts Sites

12345

www.darts100.com

This isn't the fanciest site in the darts world, but it does provide an excellent directory of the top 100 dart websites ranked by popularity. Site displays a link for each dart site along with the number of hits it received today and the number of unique hits, so you can see where the real dart players and fans are hanging out. Great place to start your search for great dart sites, bars, and stores.

World Darts Federation

12345

www.dartswdf.com

Fifty-five countries are represented on this site, which is the home of the World Darts Federation. Learn the rules and regulations of the game, check out the various tournaments, check out the history pages, and access dozens of links to various dart organizations from around the world.

DATING

Dating Sites

www.datingsitesguide.com

To increase your odds of finding someone to date, search here for a well-populated directory of dating sites arranged by category. You can browse the directory by location or by classifications, including Divorced, Religion, Mature, and Plus Sizes.

PERSONALS/SERVICES

2ofaKind Online

www.2ofakind.com

Soul mates and perfect pen pals connect by using more than 150 match options, match analysis reports, anonymous email, and free registration. This is not your typical personals service!

Christian Matchmaker

www.christian.matchmaker.com

Christian Matchmaker provides a place for Christians to find friends, mates, love, romance, and personals. Give yourself a half hour to fill out the registration/profile form. It is extensive.

eCRUSH

www.ecrush.com

eCRUSH will send whomever you choose a confidential email telling them that someone has listed them and inviting them to register their own eCRUSHes. When they do, eCRUSH will see whether there's a match. If there is, you'll both be invited to the match lounge. If not...they'll never know who eCRUSHed them! Lots of fun stuff at this site!

eHarmony.com

www.eharmony.com

Because of its TV commercials, eHarmony.com is one of the most popular matchmaking services on the Internet. And, as you can guess, when a service is more popular, it's stocked with more prospective fish, making it much more likely that you'll hook a potential mate. Visit this site to find out what eHarmony is all about and complete the free personality profile to determine your prospects of matching up with someone who's at least somewhat compatible with your temperament and interests. Site now features an area to help married couples deepen their relationships through online tools.

LoveCity

www.lovecity.com

This dating site has been online since 1996 and has been accessed more than 100 *million* times. Basic design makes it easy to search for potential dates by state.

Match.com

www.match.com

Millions of singles worldwide have used the services of Match.com. Match.com strives to provide a safe and easy way for members to meet other quality singles on the Web. After you create your own unique profile, Match.com's superior matching technology provides you with instantaneous matches based on your preselected dating criteria. It's fast, convenient, and simple to use. Whether you're looking for an activity partner, a casual date, or a lifelong companion, Match.com just might have the person for you. You can search for free, but if you want to contact members, you must register and pay a monthly subscription fee; rates vary depending on the total number of months you choose to subscribe. Match.com boasts that it has twice as many marriages as any other online matchmaking service.

www.okcupid.com

From the creators of SparkNotes comes this free dating service that promises not only to hook you up with the right person for you but also to keep you amused along the way. At this site, you can check out who's online and get in touch with that person, find free advice, and take various tests to help others evaluate their prospects. Excellent site, although your choices may be a bit more limited than you might find on the glitzier commercial sites.

> **Tip:** OkCupid! is free, so even if you post your profile on another, pay, site, consider posting it here for free to see who does a better job of hooking you up with the right person.

Related Sites

www.syl.com

www.americansingles.com

www.dating.com

www.drdating.com

www.lovecompass.com

TIPS

Dating Advice for Geeks

www.geekcheck.com

If all your friends and family have labeled you a geek, and you're single, check out this site for some specialized dating advice mixed in with a good dose of humor. Guide Brenda provides tips on giving yourself a makeover, carrying on a conversation (using a flow chart), composing a winning personal (what not to say), a list of dates from hell, and much more. If this site were just a tad bit more up to date and a little more functional (some links don't work), we'd name it our choice for Best of the Best in the Dating category. We didn't, but the site still deserves a mention for being original.

Dating Fast

www.datingfast.com

Dating Fast offers short articles primarily about communicating effectively in a dating relationships. Articles are grouped by category, including Men's Communication Guide, Women's Communication Guide, Flirting & Courting, and Singles Chatter. Site features links to several e-books on dating, courting, and maintaining a relationship.

Dating Tips

www.datingtips.ws

Site features dating tips, articles, quizzes, information about online dating, and separate sections for guys and girls. You can also post your own dating tip.

Girl Dating Tips

www.girldatingtips.com

With a focus on the female side of dating, this site offers tips that cover everything from the first date to seduction secrets. As with any of the dating tip sites, this one offers some excellent advice along with a good collection of questionable guidance, but that's what dating is all about. Site features a good collection of articles along with a robust directory of links to additional sites.

Links2Love Dating Tips

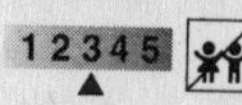

www.links2love.com/dating_tips_3.htm

The Links2Love Dating Tips page opens with a long list of tips on what to do on your first date. Site offers additional links to Love Quotes and Love Poetry, Body Language, Gift Ideas, and Quizzes. Definitely directed to those in puppy love.

Top Dating Tips

www.lovecompass.com

Top Dating Tips offers free articles, advice, and tips for all the singles out there looking for Mr. or Ms. Right. Articles cover topics in highest demand, including places to date, dating at work, dating online, dating and sex, and how to survive the single life. Separate sections keep the information you need most easily accessible; just click the desired section: Articles, Tips, Advice, Men, or Women to begin your search.

DEAFNESS

Alexander Graham Bell Association for Deaf and Hard of Hearing

12345

www.agbell.org

Learn more about membership benefits of this international organization, which was established to serve parents of deaf and hard-of-hearing children. You'll find information on local chapters, publications, and financial assistance here.

ASL Access

12345

www.aslaccess.org

Information about American Sign Language videos and how to order them is available here, as well as information about supporting the group's efforts to get more ASL videos into public libraries.

Captioned Media Program

12345

www.cfv.org

CMP lends open captioned videos to members who complete an application form, enabling them to borrow videos on a wide variety of topics, for school, entertainment, or information. You can access some of the offerings with your Web browser via streaming video.

Deaf Chat

12345

www.deafchat.com

A chat community that brings together deaf, hard of hearing, and hearing individuals to discuss issues, share information, trade jokes, or talk about whatever's on their mind without fear of harassment. The Deaf Chat monitor makes sure of that.

Deaf Resources

12345 Blog

www.deafresources.com

This site offers a variety of home décor items and gifts using ASL as the theme. Baby blankets, for example, are embroidered with the ASL sign for "I love you." You'll find jewelry, jackets, videos, tote bags, and many other interesting items.

DeafandHH.com

12345

www.deafandhh.com

Extensive information and resource kiosk for health professionals, patients, and families dealing with hearing loss. Site features discussion forums, a FAQ, and job listings.

Deaf.com

12345

www.deaf.com

Deaf.com acts as a gateway for the deaf community, providing links to several websites that provide useful information and resources, including DeafChat, DeafVote, and DeafSports.com. You can also find links to several sites that are dedicated to helping those who can hear understand those who can't.

deafkids.com

12345

www.deafkids.com

Designed as a fun place for deaf and hard-of-hearing children, 17 years old and younger, to meet and chat.

DeafNation

www.deafnation.com

For those who want to remain informed concerning the latest news and events in the deaf and hard of hearing community, check out DeafNation. DeafNation Expo is the top exhibition and celebration of, by, and for the deaf and hard-of-hearing community. To get involved, stay informed; this site can help.

Best DeafZONE

www.deafzone.com

Chat rooms, links, current events, and information on a wide variety of topics ranging from ADA laws to a workshop calendar. Find relay services and interpreters on this site. It even has a page with some hilarious jokes contributed by members. If you're deaf and you feel all alone, visit this site to tap the vast resources for the deaf and to make some friends along the way. This very comprehensive directory is an excellent place to start your search.

Gallaudet University, Washington, D.C.

www.gallaudet.edu

The world's only four-year university for deaf and hard-of-hearing undergraduate students.

GG Wiz's FingerSpeller

12345

wowway.com/~ggwiz/asl

This is a must-see site. Type a phrase and see it finger spelled, and test your reading skills with hidden phrases.

HandSpeak

12345

www.handspeak.com

HandSpeak is the largest, fast-growing visual language dictionary online. Check out the baby and international signs as well as ways to use sign language with animals. This is a cool site with lots of good information and ideas.

Helen Keller National Center for Deaf-Blind Youth

12345

www.helenkeller.org/national

The Helen Keller Center provides evaluation and training in vocational skills, adaptive technology and computer skills, orientation and mobility, independent living, communication, speech-language skills, creative arts, and fitness and leisure activities for deaf-blind youth. Learn more about the center and its work here.

National Association of the Deaf (NAD)

12345

www.nad.org

This national nonprofit organization provides grassroots advocacy and empowerment for deaf individuals, captioned media, certification of American Sign Language professionals and interpreters, deafness-related information and publications, legal assistance, and policy development and research. The group also works to improve awareness of issues specific to deaf individuals.

National Institute on Deafness and Other Communication Disorders

12345

www.nidcd.nih.gov

Robust collection of information and resources for those suffering from hearing loss and for physicians and other health professionals. Includes links for information directed toward parents, children, and teachers. Plus Spanish translations of much of the material.

Oral Deaf Education

12345

www.oraldeafed.org

Home to the Oral Deaf Education website. ODF's position is that deaf children can learn to talk by using the hearing technology options available today and the instruction provided at ODF schools. You will find specific information about these schools and their programs and services, and other information on oral deaf education in its library. Use the Search or the What's New page to find a specific topic.

SignWritingSite

1 2 3 4 5

www.signwriting.org

Learn more about SignWriting, which enables people to read and learn using sign language, including taking lessons and joining in discussion forums about its use. There is a search engine and online library for further research and learning.

Zoos Software

1 2 3 4 5

www.zoosware.com

Learning American Sign Language (ASL) is now easier with this software package for Palm devices. The software enables you to study the sign language alphabets and numbers at your own pace. After you're more familiar, you can type in the words, and PalmASL will show them to you using American Sign Language.

DEATH & DYING

Beyond Indigo

1 2 3 4 5

www.beyondindigo.com

Beyond Indigo is a company in Minnesota that provides "grief support, products, and services to individuals and companies who assist people who are grieving." Site features "channels" on Children & Grief, Grief Support, Death & the Spirit, Funerals & Customs, Healing from All Losses, Sudden & Violent Death, and Caregiving & Illness. You can share your grief and hardships with others and obtain valuable advice on the message boards, take online quizzes, submit your story of loss, and even post a memorial to your loved one. Excellent content at a site that's easy to navigate.

Euthanasia World Directory

1 2 3 4 5 Blog

www.finalexit.org

Includes pages on the Euthanasia Research and Guidance Organization; the World Federation of Right to Die Societies; and acts, laws, and news about euthanasia.

GriefNet

1 2 3 4 5

griefnet.org

GriefNet is an Internet community of persons dealing with grief, death, and major loss providing an integrated approach to online grief support. GriefNet is supervised by Cendra (ken'dra) Lynn, Ph.D., a clinical grief psychologist, death educator, and traumatologist. Special area for kids who are dealing with the death of a loved one.

Hospice Foundation of America

1 2 3 4 5

www.hospicefoundation.org

Learn all about hospice and how it works, as well as read articles on grieving and loss. News archives contain information on death, and events such as teleconferences enable individuals to deal with the prospect of someone close to them dying. Click Links to access a directory of other useful sites.

Best Hospice Net

1 2 3 4 5

www.hospicenet.org

Find a hospice location near you and learn more about the hospice concept at Hospice Net. Also learn more about the role of caregiver, the bereavement process, and what patients can do to control how they die. A comprehensive site with information for just about everyone who faces losing a loved one. Though this site does not contain an area specifically for children, it does contain a Children area, where parents can learn how to communicate with their children about death and dying. Nothing fancy here, just high-quality content.

Hospice Web

1 2 3 4 5

www.hospiceweb.com

Find answers to your questions about hospice here and find a hospice near you through the hospice search engine. For questions not answered in the FAQ section, you can get an email response.

Medline Plus: On Death and Dying

12345

www.nlm.nih.gov/medlineplus/deathanddying.html

Medline Plus is a medical website that provides information on healthcare. This particular section, though, acts as a directory to some of the best articles on death and dying from various resources on the Web. Medline Plus categorizes the articles to make them easy to locate. Categories cover almost every aspect of death and dying, including overviews, coping, specific conditions, financial issues, law and policy, and children.

National Hospice and Palliative Care Organization

12345

www.nhpco.org

Gain an understanding of hospice and palliative care at this nonprofit organization's site, which provides a central contact point for end-of-life organizations nationwide. You can search for a hospice near you and stay current on end-of-life issues at this site.

Related Site

summum.kids.us

A B C D E F G H I J K L M N O P Q R S T U V W X Y Z

DEBT MANAGEMENT

123Debt.com

12345

www.123debt.com

Buried in debt? Then visit this site for the information and tools you need to dig yourself out and strengthen your financial position. This site features a host of credit and debt calculators, along with articles on credit cards, credit reports, credit scoring, debt consolidation, and refinancing.

American Consumer Credit Counseling

12345

www.consumercredit.com

A nonprofit organization dedicated to helping people who are having money trouble or considering bankruptcy regain control of their financial lives. Site offers some valuable advice on how to steer clear of debt management services that charge fees up front.

American Debt Management Services

12345

www.americandebt.com

The world's largest nonprofit debt management organization can help you become debt free! American Debt Management Services, Inc., debt consolidation is supported mainly by voluntary donations, contributions, and community grants. ADMS has "met the stringent licensing requirements of the NYS Banking Commission, the State of Maryland Department of Labor, Licensing, and Regulations, we are ISO-9000 certified, and our credit counselors are fully certified by the NIFCE, and required to complete additional continuing education credits annually."

AnnualCreditReport.com

12345

www.annualcreditreport.com

The U.S. Congress passed the Fair Credit Reporting Act and has provided each consumer the right to one free credit report each year. Here's where you go to get your free report. The report can help in at least two ways. First, it provides you with a number that represents your credit rating, so you can see how eligible you are to receive loans. Second, it can help you identify any incidents of potential identity theft; for example, if your credit report shows accounts you never opened, you should be a little suspicious. For more information, visit the FTC Credit website at www.ftc.gov/credit.

Bankrate.com

12345

www.bankrate.com

Bankrate.com is "the Web's leading aggregator of financial rate information," serving both financial institutions and consumers, but this goes far beyond simply supplying loan rates. Here, you can click the Debt Management tab to access dozens of insightful, informative articles on managing your debt. Site also features a collection of useful tools, including a pay-down advisor, a mortgage calculator, a loan vs. credit line calculator, and a home-equity loan calculator. Site features a list of five Do's along with a series of articles that help visitors distinguish good debt from bad debt and develop a general understanding of how debt works.

Consumer Credit Counseling by Springboard

12345

www.credit.org

A helpful resource for people struggling to stay afloat financially. Individuals can get budget counseling and debt management assistance online, as well as access several tools for analyzing mortgage, car loan, and credit card debt.

Department of Veterans Affairs Debt Management

12345

www.va.gov/debtman

Information for people who owe debts to the Department of Veterans Affairs. If you took out a VA loan and you're having trouble making your payments on it, this is the place to go to seek assistance.

Best Federal Trade Commission Credit Section

12345

www.ftc.gov/credit

When you're looking for a credit manager you can trust, there's no better place to look than the FTC. Congress passed a Fair Credit Reporting Act that has made it possible for each individual to obtain one free credit report every 12 months. You can learn how to obtain your free credit report through this site. You can also learn all about your other rights and obligations as a consumer and pick up some tips and techniques for managing your credit. This site also provides instructions on how to prevent identity theft, scams, and credit card fraud. If you're wondering what your government has done for you lately, check out this Best of the Best Site for at least one concrete example of how your government works for you.

InfoHQ Online CPA

12345

www.infohq.com/CPA/OnlineCPA.htm

Original articles and advice on mortgages and refinancing, income taxes, and debt management. Personal financial questions are answered for a small fee. If you're considering debt consolidation, this site offers some sage warnings on debt consolidation services that work against you rather than for you.

Money Management International

12345

www.moneymanagement.org

When you're in debt and don't know where to turn, look to this site for help. Money Management International is a "nonprofit, community service organization that provides professional financial guidance, counseling, community-wide educational programs, debt management assistance, and debt consolidated loans to consumers." At this site, you will find money management advice, calculators, and other tools to help you manage your money and reduce your debt.

MSN Money: Savings and Debt Management

12345

moneycentral.msn.com/smartbuy/home.asp

MSN Money features several tools to help you analyze your credit, manage your debts, and reign in your expenses. The Debt Evaluation calculator can help you determine if your ratio of debt to income is manageable or too high. You can also take a credit quiz to determine just how credit savvy you are.

National Foundation for Credit Counseling

12345

www.nfcc.org

National organization that sets debt-reduction and credit counseling training standards and guidelines for companies that provide credit counseling to consumers. Consumers can find some information about reducing debt and managing their credit. Site features a link to CNN's budget calculator, where you can establish a budget in comparison with others who have annual earnings in your same bracket.

Smart Money

12345

www.smartmoney.com/debt

Smart Money magazine has a long history of offering solid financial advice to subscribers. At its website, you can peruse many of its archived articles on debt management along with a mortgage calculator, a Rates Center, and a list of commonly asked questions (and their answers) relating to debt and home ownership.

Ten Strategies to Reduce Your Debt

12345

moneycentral.msn.com/content/Savinganddebt/Managedebt/P36233.asp

The average American pays more than $1,000 a year in interest fees to carry a balance of $8,500 on two to three bank credit cards, according to recent estimates. And credit card companies are tacking on new fees and raising interest rates that make it even more expensive. Learn 10 winning strategies for paying down your credit card debt.

U.S. National Debt Clock

12345

www.brillig.com/debt_clock

The National Debt Clock keeps a running total of outstanding public debt and provides an explanation of the problem and links to sites that discuss the subject and propose solutions.

BANKRUPTCY

American Bankruptcy Institute

www.abiworld.org

ABI World offers up-to-date bankruptcy news, statistics, legislative updates, and information on how to file for bankruptcy. Most of the content at this site is directed toward bankruptcy attorneys and other professionals. Click the Consumer Education Center link for consumer content, including an answer to the most pressing question—Should I file for bankruptcy?

Bankruptcy Action

12345

www.bankruptcyaction.com

The Bankruptcy Action site opens with a clickable map of the United States, which you can use to post a question to a local bankruptcy lawyer. Site also features current articles on bankruptcy, a Flash presentation, several audio recordings of answers to commonly asked questions, a FAQ, and a list of the site's most popular pages.

Bankruptcy: An Overview

12345

www.law.cornell.edu/topics/bankruptcy.html

This introduction to bankruptcy is provided by Cornell Law School. Includes links to sources mentioned in the introduction and to other helpful bankruptcy sites on the Web.

InterNet Bankruptcy Law Library

12345

bankrupt.com

Provides information about various large companies in the United States that are facing bankruptcy or are currently having serious financial problems. Includes a library of books and periodicals related to struggling businesses and features a list of local bankruptcy rules organized by state.

Personal Bankruptcy Information

12345

www.bankruptcyinformation.com

This excellent resource on personal bankruptcy provides information on state and federal exemptions, a credit card debt calculator, a primer on Chapter 7 and Chapter 13 bankruptcy, a brief introduction on the process of filing for bankruptcy, and other useful information and advice.

CREDIT CARDS

American Express

12345

www.americanexpress.com

Apply online for an American Express card, find out how the card can save you money, and learn about other financial services. This site provides features for individuals, small businesses, corporations, and merchants.

CardWeb

12345

www.cardweb.com/cardtrak

Get the latest news on credit card deals and usage from this site, which has areas for consumers and business professionals in the credit industry.

Credit Card Goodies

12345

www.creditcardgoodies.com

If you like to reap rewards from using credit cards but you pay your balance in full when you receive your bill, visit this site to learn which credit cards can deliver you the greatest benefits. If you carry a

A B C D E F G H I J K L M N O P Q R S T U V W X Y Z

balance, the best card for you is the card that delivers the lowest interest rate, which you can find through other debt management sites, such as 123Debt.com.

Discover Card

12345

www.discovercard.com

You can apply for a Discover card online at this site, pay your Discover bills, learn about cash-back bonuses, shop for deals, and obtain customer service.

MasterCard

12345

www.mastercard.com

MasterCard's home page offers help in finding a card, emergency services for information on reporting a lost or stolen card, an ATM finder, a list of special offers, a consumer education area, and more. You can apply online at this site for a MasterCard credit card.

Visa

12345

www.visa.com

Home of the International Visa site, where you can click a country to jump to the Visa site in that locale. Here, you can apply for a Visa credit card, obtain information about special deals, and even pick up a few tips on managing your credit. Designed for individuals, small businesses, corporations, and merchants. If you lose your card, you can also visit this site to obtain a toll-free number to call to report it missing.

FORECLOSURE

Foreclosure.com

12345

www.foreclosure.com

This site is directed toward real estate investors who want to purchase foreclosure and pre-foreclosure and REO (Real Estate Owned or repossessed) properties. Subscribers to the site can search for listings by state and city or town. However, most of the information provided at this site can be obtained for free by visiting your local Register of Deeds office and networking in your neighborhood.

How to Avoid Foreclosure

12345

www.ehow.com/how_7235_avoid-foreclosure.html

Excellent article on how to avoid foreclosure and avoid falling victim to mortgage broker lies.

HUD (Housing and Urban Development)

12345

www.hud.gov/foreclosure/index.cfm

Homeowners who are facing foreclosure often fall victim to con artists and other opportunists who use the homeowner's ignorance and shame against them. This site provides a reliable and trustworthy resource for accurate information on foreclosure and offers free advice on the steps you should take if you're facing foreclosure. In most cases, selling your home to get out from under it is your best option, so don't listen to anyone who tells you otherwise. Get the facts at this site, and then get in touch with your mortgage company to learn your options.

Related Site (PDF Booklet)

www.pueblo.gsa.gov/cic_text/housing/foreclosure/avoid.pdf

National Consumer Law Center

12345

www.consumerlaw.org

The National Consumer Law Center offers plenty of advice to consumers on how to best manage debt, avoid scams, and protect their rights. Scroll down to the bottom of the navigation bar and click For Consumers to start your search. You may have to poke around a little to find the foreclosure information you need, but you'll likely find additional helpful information that you didn't realize you needed.

A B C D E F G H I J K L M N O P Q R S T U V W X Y Z

DENTISTRY

Academy of General Dentistry

12345

www.agd.org

This site is primarily for the dental practitioner, but it also offers some solid advice and a referral service for consumers. Site features over 50 articles on various oral health topics along with a message board on which you can post your most pressing dental question. Dental practitioners can access the online library and learn about continuing education and other programs to further their knowledge and careers.

American Academy of Cosmetic Dentistry

12345

www.aacd.com

This site features three separate areas for dental professionals, patients, and the media. Patients can visit this site to locate a cosmetic dentist, learn the basics of cosmetic dentistry, obtain patient information, and submit a before and after image of their smile in the photo gallery. Professionals can learn more about the organization and why they should join it, peruse the directory of members, research credentialing information, and check out the Cosmetic Dentistry Blog. If you're a member of the media, you can find all the information you need to write your next feature article on cosmetic dentistry.

American Dental Association

12345

www.ada.org

If you've ever shopped for toothpaste or floss, you know at least a little about the ADA. It's the organization that recommends Crest and a host of other dental-care products. Site features a host of resources for dental professionals, including information on DAT (Dental Admissions Testing), a discussion forum, and a calendar of events and meetings. Patients will find a search tool for tracking down an ADA member dentist, games and animations for kids, oral health education videos, and more.

American Dental Hygienists' Association

12345

www.adha.org

ADHA is "the largest professional organization representing the interests of dental hygienists," and most of the content at this site is specifically for hygienists, including information about education, careers, continuing education, and membership. Consumers can click the Oral Health Information link in the navigation bar to access articles on oral health. Special area is featured just for kids.

Best Dentistry.com

12345

www.dentistry.com

Dentistry.com is a "privately operated organization that provides information-based resources, catering to dental professionals and consumers." Dentists and other dental practitioners can visit this site to include themselves in the directory and to subscribe to newsletters and articles. Consumers can visit the site to find a dentist, orthodontist, or other dental professional or consult with featured specialists online. Patients should check out the Patient's Corner for featured articles on dental care. Site also features a game room for kids, a list of specialty centers, case studies, and an area just for parents. Site is easy to navigate and packed with all the dental information you need, making it an easy selection for our Best of the Best site in the Dentistry category.

HealthWeb

12345

www.healthweb.org/dentistry

HealthWeb provides this directory of dentistry-related resources on the Web. Here you can find links to dental libraries, continuing-education seminars and workshops, information on practice management, and sites on specialties such as implantology. Great site for dental professionals to visit when they're not sure where to look for information on the Web.

Sports Dentistry Online

12345

www.sportsdentistry.com

This site invites dentists, athletes, and coaches to learn more about dental issues relating to sports, including lost teeth, smokeless tobacco, and concussions. This site offers an overview of sports dentistry for the uninitiated, explains the importance of dental health in athletic performance, provides statistics on sports dentistry, promotes custom-made mouth guards, and explains the health risks of smokeless tobacco.

DIABETES

Best ADA: American Diabetes Association

1 2 3 4 5

www.diabetes.org

The American Diabetes Association website offers the latest information on diabetes and living with the disease. The American Diabetes Association is the nation's leading voluntary health organization supporting diabetes research, information, and advocacy. The association supports an affiliated office in every region of the country, providing services to more than 800 communities. If you or a loved one suffers from diabetes, make this Best of the Best site your first stop to learning more about the disease and available treatments. Also features an online bookstore.

ADA Recipe of the Day

1 2 3 4 5

www.diabetes.org/recipeoftheday.jsp

A recipe every day from the American Diabetes Association.

Center for Disease Control Diabetes FAQ

1 2 3 4 5

www.cdc.gov/diabetes/faq/basics.htm

The Center for Disease Control presents this diabetes question and answer area, where you can learn what diabetes is, types of diabetes, common causes, successful treatments, and more. Site also features links to other diabetes pages at CDC and other websites.

Children with Diabetes Online Community

1 2 3 4 5

www.childrenwithdiabetes.com

An online community for kids, families, and adults with diabetes, featuring message boards, chat rooms, and questions and answers from medical professionals. This site has a vast collection of information and resources, as you can tell just by scrolling down the navigation bar on the left. Site features a family support network, an area for parents that includes parental humor, a separate section for grandparents, an online booklet on how to deal with diabetes at school, information on scholarships and financial aid, and much more.

Children with Diabetes Recipes

1 2 3 4 5

www.childrenwithdiabetes.com/d_08_200.htm

Readers' favorite recipes with a special emphasis on recipes for children with diabetes. Each is on its own page so that you can easily print a copy.

Diabetes Health Magazine

1 2 3 4 5

www.diabeteshealth.com

Home for *Diabetes Health*, this site features a great primer for kids with type 1 or type 2 diabetes, nutritional advice and recipes, reviews of meters and pumps, products, resources, and stories about celebrities who have diabetes. Excellent content at a site that's easy to navigate.

Diabetes Insight

12345

`www.diabetes-insight.info`

A wonderful site for those recently diagnosed with diabetes and those who have been living with the disease. An email support group and online forum are just a couple of notable features. Excellent guide for those who are living with diabetes.

Diabetes Mall

12345

`www.diabetesnet.com`

Find out about clinical trials in your area as well as diabetes news, delicious recipes, and books on the topic of managing your diabetes. Lots of links to other diabetes sites, too.

Diabetic Gourmet Magazine

12345

`diabeticgourmet.com`

Search the recipe archives of *Diabetic Gourmet* magazine for all diabetic recipes. The site also provides a great resource for additional information on diabetes, including the Diabetes 101 tutorial, tips on healthful living and exercise, and forums where you can communicate with others who suffer from diabetes and related conditions.

Gourmet Connection Network

12345

`gourmetconnection.com`

Learn how to cook healthful meals, whether you suffer from diabetes or not. Diabetes headlines, cooking tips, and recipes.

Joslin Diabetes Center

12345

`www.joslin.harvard.edu`

Joslin is the only U.S. medical center dedicated solely to diabetes treatment, research, cure, and education. On its site, you'll find news, lifestyle and nutrition information, discussion groups, a directory of nationwide affiliates, and more.

Kids Learn About Diabetes

12345

`www.kidslearnaboutdiabetes.org`

This site, designed specifically for kids, begins with an explanation of diabetes and provides links to topics that address Complications, Testing, Shots, Diet, Balance, Activities, Feelings, and The Future. Also provides a place where kids can chat. Nicely designed and packed with excellent information.

Medical Alert Charms for Children

12345

`www.missbrooke.com`

One of the few sources of medical IDs for children and teens.

National Diabetes Education Program

12345

`ndep.nih.gov=`

The NDEP is "a partnership of the National Institutes of Health, the Centers for Disease Control and Prevention, and more than 200 public and private organizations" dedicated to providing the most current information and resources on diabetes prevention, diagnosis, and treatment. Here, you can learn about NDEP's awareness campaigns and access electronic versions of NDEP's brochures, booklets, and other publications, including *Four Steps to Control Your Diabetes for Life, 7 Principles for Controlling Your Diabetes for Life,* and *Tips for Helping a Person with Diabetes.*

National Institute of Diabetes & Digestive & Kidney Disorders

12345

`www.niddk.nih.gov`

A component of the U.S. National Institutes of Health, this site is packed with information about diabetes and other major health issues. Under Health Information, click Diabetes to access diabetes topics, research, publications, and additional resources.

DIET & NUTRITION

American Heart Association

www.americanheart.org

Better food habits can help you reduce your risk for heart attack. This comprehensive site offers a healthful eating plan as a means for choosing the right foods to eat and preparing foods in a healthful way. One of the better sites for nutrition information. After opening the home page, click the Healthy Lifestyle link to access the nutrition page.

Ask the Dietitian

12345

www.dietitian.com

Ask the Dietitian is an advice column hosted by registered dietitian Joanne Larsen. Topics discussed range from nutrition and vitamin-related issues to eating disorders such as anorexia. Check out the Healthy Body Calculator to determine your target weight and nutritional and exercise needs. Covers diet and vitamin topics from A to Z, alcohol to zinc.

Blonz Guide to Nutrition, Food, and Health Resources

12345

blonz.com

Dr. Ed Blonz, a nutritionist and syndicated newspaper columnist, offers this collection of websites about food, nutrition, and health. Provides link to Amazon.com to purchase Dr. Blonz's books.

Center for Science in the Public Interest

12345

www.cspinet.org

The CSPI website features health-related newsletters, nutrition quizzes, updates on health news, and an archive of its reports and press releases. The page also includes links to other health-related sites. Kids should click the Kids Stuff link to go to an area designed specifically for the younger crowd.

Consumer Information Center: Food

12345

www.pueblo.gsa.gov/food.htm

This consumer information catalog presents a series of free or low-cost publications. Topics include buying fresh produce and roasting a turkey.

DietSite.com

12345

www.dietsite.com

Excellent site provides general information on healthful diets. Nutrition topics for disease prevention, performance improvements in sports, nutrition facts, diet news, and alternative diets. Also features free diet and recipe analysis and tools for tracking your weight and exercise.

Dole 5 a Day

12345

www.dole5aday.com

A graphics-rich site devoted to the health and nutrition benefits of fruits and vegetables. A fantastic educational tool for teachers and parents and a fun place for kids to learn about nutrition. Sponsored by the Dole Food Company.

A B C D E F G H I J K L M N O P Q R S T U V W X Y Z

Best eDiets

12345

www.ediets.com

eDiets has a goal of "building a global online diet, fitness, and motivation destination to provide consumers with solutions that help them realize life's full potential." This is an excellent site for learning the basics of popular diets, including the Glycemic Diet, the Eating for Life Plan, and the Mediterranean Diet. Site features a tabbed navigation bar that provides quick access to News, Diet, Fitness, a Recipe Club, Community (support groups, mentors, experts, chat rooms, and success stories), View Plans (meal, health & fitness, and healthy living plans), and more.

Pick a diet at this site, learn about it, and then use the Community features to build a plan and support network that's more likely to lead to your diet success.

Feingold Association of the United States

12345

www.feingold.org

This site offers information about the connection between diet and behavior. Get details on the Feingold nutrition program and take advantage of all the resources and links, too. Definitely worth investigating if you are dealing with a diagnosis of ADD, ADHD, or asthma.

Food and Nutrition Information Center

12345

www.nal.usda.gov/fnic

The National Agricultural Library runs this Food and Nutrition Information Center. This site features sections on dietary supplements, food composition, dietary guidelines, a Consumer Corner, and a searchable directory of topics from A to Z. The site also provides access to printable documents for your own use or for distributing to classes and groups.

Food Pyramid

12345

schoolmeals.nal.usda.gov

Click the pyramid and find out what to eat daily. Provides a nutritional breakdown of food groups and a guide to servings. Great place for kids to learn about nutrition.

Healthfinder

12345 RSS

www.healthfinder.gov

Browse this vast archive of health and nutrition information or search for a specific topic. If you have time for only one site, start here! Also features a site just for kids—click the Kids link.

LifeClinic

12345

www.lifeclinic.com/focus/nutrition

Devoted to empowering individuals to manage their own health through nutrition, preventive care, and fitness, this site offers a wealth of information on healthful living. Visit the nutrition center to research vitamins, minerals, nutrients, and other diet-related topics. You can also track your exercise and nutrition online. Excellent site.

Mayo Clinic Food & Nutrition Center

12345 RSS

www.mayoclinic.com/health/HealthyLivingIndex/HealthyLivingIndex

When you reach the Mayo Clinic's Healthy Living Index, click Foods & Nutrition link to go to the Food & Nutrition Center. Here you'll find a primer on Healthy Diet Basics that explains the pros and cons of the various stuff you consume and, in many cases, overconsume, along with a healthy cooking guide that's packed with plenty of tips. Well worth the visit. Site also offers a useful calorie counter.

Meals for You

12345

www.mealsforyou.com

Fabulous recipe site. Calculator enables you to customize recipes based on the number of servings. Nutrition-conscious visitors will especially like the fact that each recipe is accompanied by complete nutritional information. The site also contains special sections devoted to dietary exchange information and recipes grouped by nutrition content and popularity.

Nutrition Café

12345

www.exhibits.pacsci.org/nutrition/nutrition_cafe.html

The Nutrition Café provides a fun place for kids to learn about foods and nutrition. The site provides several interactive games, including Nutrition Sleuth, Grab a Grape, and Have-a-Bite Café, that help inspire and foster kids' curiosity about the foods they consume.

Nutrition Explorations

12345

www.nutritionexplorations.org

Maintained by the National Dairy Council, this fun site helps kids, teachers, parents, and families learn more about nutrition. Family Food Guide presents the food guide pyramid, recipes for families on the go, kids recipes, an ask-the-expert feature, and much more. Some excellent teaching tools for educators and a link to a special site just for kids.

Nutrition.gov

12345

www.nutrition.gov

A new federal resource, this site provides easy access to all online federal government information on nutrition. Obtain government information on nutrition, healthful eating, physical activity, and food safety. Provides accurate scientific information on nutrition and dietary guidance.

Prevention's Healthy Ideas

www.prevention.com

Contains news and information about nutrition, natural healing, weight loss, fitness techniques, tips on healthful cooking, and lifestyle-related articles from *Prevention* magazine.

Self Magazine

www.self.com

Home of *Self* magazine. Visitors to this site can calculate their body fat percentage, ideal weight, and daily nutritional requirements. Users can also create their own personalized diet plan and take a health-risk assessment quiz. Tips on health and nutrition are also included, plus dozens of health-related articles and a food fact finder that displays the bad news on the fat content of thousands of popular foods.

DINOSAURS

Best BBC Walking with Dinosaurs

1 2 3 4 5

www.bbc.co.uk/dinosaurs

Excellent site features dinosaur chronology, fact files, articles and reports from the experts, dinosaur games and quizzes, and much more. Great place to learn about life on our planet during prehistoric times. Excellent graphics combined with comprehensive information make this an easy Best of the Best pick.

Dinosaur National Monument

1 2 3 4 5

dinosaur.areaparks.com

The Dinosaur National Monument is located in northwest Colorado and northeast Utah, straddling the border of these states. About two thirds of the park is in Colorado. Dinosaur Park spans 210,000 acres, offering plenty of room for you to find solitude, view magnificent scenery, hike a wild landscape, and renew your relationship with nature. The Dinosaur Quarry Visitor Center is the area of the park where dinosaur bones can be seen.

Dinosaurs: Facts and Fiction

1 2 3 4 5

pubs.usgs.gov/gip/dinosaurs

Plain and simple site that offers plain and simple information about dinosaurs, separating facts from fiction.

Discovering Dinosaurs

1 2 3 4 5

www.britannica.com/dinosaurs/dinosaurs/index2.html

Discovering Dinosaurs explores our evolving conceptions of these extraordinary creatures. Trace the great dinosaur debate through time by traveling down through each color-coded theme. The historical exploration of not only the scientific discoveries and the dinosaurs themselves but also the interpretation of those discoveries put in chronological order teaches us about the evolution of the current scientific theories as well as the steps in the evolution of life on Earth.

Discovery Channel: When Dinosaurs Roamed America

1 2 3 4 5

dsc.discovery.com/convergence/dinos/dinos.html

The Discovery Channel has a strong reputation for developing high-quality educational programming, and when you visit this site, you'll immediately know why. Here, Discovery Channel provides an interactive, multimedia presentation on dinosaurs. The Zip Code Finder is a cool idea, but we entered several ZIP codes only to find that we didn't have any dinosaur neighbors, which was a little disappointing.

Extinctions.com

1 2 3 4 5 Blog

www.extinctions.com

Huge collection of the most popular fossils for sale and show. Shop the web store for related merchandise. Secure online ordering.

Field Museum of Natural History

1 2 3 4 5

www.fieldmuseum.org

Internet home of the Field Museum of Natural History in Chicago, Illinois, this site features online versions of many of the exhibits along with information about the museum. While you're here, be sure to say hello to Sue, "the world's largest, most complete, and best preserved Tyrannosaurus rex." Special area for kids, plus e-cards are available for most of the main attractions.

Sue's Site

www.fieldmuseum.org/sue

Smithsonian NMNH Dinosaur Home Page

12345

www.nmnh.si.edu/paleo/dino

The Smithsonian National Museum of Natural History dinosaurs is a fantastic site to discover our planet's early inhabitants. Learn about a dinosaur bone injury, view some "mummified" dinosaur skin impressions, learn about herbivore versus carnivore teeth, examine the brain cavity of a Triceratops, and much more.

DIVORCE & CUSTODY

Children's Rights Council

1 2 3 4 5

www.gocrc.com

Site of Children's Rights Council (CRC), a national, nonprofit, tax-exempt children's rights organization based in Washington, D.C. Provides information about children's rights, legislation regarding children's rights, and data on the state and national levels.

Divorce Magazine

1 2 3 4 5

www.divorcemag.com

This is the online home of *Divorce* magazine, a publication dedicated to serving "generation ex." The magazine, along with this site, provides information to help those who are dealing with the difficult transitions of separation and divorce. Articles deal primarily with the emotional, physical, financial, and legal aspects of divorce, but also take some time out for divorce humor.

DivorceCare Home Page

1 2 3 4 5

www.divorcecare.com

Site of the DivorceCare support group. Provides a list of DivorceCare support groups in your area; resources for self-help; and information on children and divorce, financial survival, and more. Links to the HelpCenter bookstore, where you can shop for books about divorce. Parents can go to DivorceCare for Kids at www.divorcecare.com/dc4k/ to find a support group for their children.

Best DivorceNet

www.divorcenet.com

Contains FAQs with the most common questions pertaining to divorce and family law, an online newsletter and index, a state-by-state resource center, an interactive bulletin board, international and national laws pertaining to child abduction along with a link to the U.S. State Department, and more. Also contains helpful information regarding child custody and child support. Whether you're divorced, going through divorce proceedings, or are considering divorce, this site has the information you need in an easy-to-find format.

DivorceWizards

1 2 3 4 5

www.divorcewizards.com

Getting divorced has never been easier. At DivorceWizards, you can get divorced online, as long as it's an uncontested divorce. Just pick a desired divorce package and follow the onscreen instructions. The site also provides useful information on choosing the right type of divorce for you: paralegal, mediation, or litigation. Also features articles on how to protect yourself financially.

FamilyLaw.org

1 2 3 4 5

www.familylaw.org

Comprehensive list of links to other sites that primarily cover child-custody issues. Features family law code by state, a directory of lawyers, and thousands of articles relating to child custody cases.

A B C D E F G H I J K L M N O P Q R S T U V W X Y Z

SmartDivorce.com

1 2 3 4 5

www.smartdivorce.com

Home of Wolf Hollow Publishing, which specializes in books on divorce, relationships, and marriage-enhancement topics. Before, during, or after a divorce, visit this site to gather the information you need to make wise decisions and cope with situations over which you have no control. Scroll down the page to check out the Free Articles list, where you can find great articles such as Dirty Divorce Tricks.

CHILD SUPPORT

American Coalition for Fathers and Children

1 2 3 4 5

www.acfc.org

The aim of this site is to educate fathers about their rights, help them avoid becoming deadbeat dads, and make sure all parties in a dispute are treated fairly. ACFC believes that "children need both parents."

Child Support Calculators

1 2 3 4 5

www.divorcehq.com/calculators.html

Divorce HQ provides child support calculators for every state in the union. If you suspect your ex and your ex's lawyer are quoting you the wrong figures, do your own calculations. Of course, you might want to visit this site before you get a divorce to see just how much it's going to cost you. Calculator figures your weekly obligation.

Child Support Enforcement (CSE)

1 2 3 4 5

www.supportkids.com

The nation's largest and most experienced private company helping parents collect court-ordered child support. Claims a 90 percent success rate.

Child Support Law at freeadvice.com

1 2 3 4 5

family-law.freeadvice.com/child_custody

Find answers from top lawyers about child support, attorneys, and lawyers who can help you with a legal claim or problem in family law.

Federal Office of Child Support Enforcement

1 2 3 4 5

www.acf.dhhs.gov/programs/cse

Provides helpful information about the child support system, including basic child support program facts, newsletters and announcements, recent policy documents, and the opportunity to offer feedback. Click the Links to States link for information about child support guidelines specific to your state.

NCSEA: National Child Support Enforcement Association

1 2 3 4 5

www.ncsea.org

Brings together professionals from all aspects of the nation's child support program, including public and private sectors, state and local agencies, judges and court administrators, prosecutors, and private attorneys. The goal is to protect the well-being of children through effective child support enforcement.

U.S. State Child Support Agencies

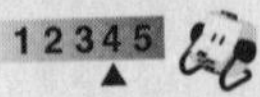

www.acf.dhhs.gov/programs/cse/extinf.htm

Child support enforcement is typically a state responsibility, so you should turn to your state agency first whenever you run into problems with child support. Does your state have its own website? The Federal Office of Child Support Enforcement website has a clickable map of the United States that provides quick access to state agencies all across the nation.

DOGS

Adopt a Greyhound

1 2 3 4 5

www.adopt-a-greyhound.org

Greyhounds may have been famous for their speed and grace on the track, but recently, people have begun to adopt them upon retirement from the races—saving them from euthanasia or worse. This site provides a huge amount of information as well as links to other sites. Check out the many adoption agencies specializing in greyhounds.

Best American Kennel Club (AKC)

1 2 3 4 5

www.akc.org/index.cfm

Find out more about this organization, read about different breeds, and locate an AKC near you. You'll also enjoy the informational brochures covering everything from boarding your dog to showing your dog. This site is packed with information! Besides the great graphics layout, ease of use, and all the information, the site enables you to purchase everything concerning dogs from books, videos, and apparel to artwork.

Dog Breed Info Center

1 2 3 4 5

www.dogbreedinfo.com

Before investing in a new pet, visit this site to select the best breed for your family situation, temperament, living space, or whatever criteria you want to use. It's a good place to assess whether you're ready for the responsibilities of being a dog owner. This site is well organized and offers the information you need to have before taking that big step of owning a dog. The site has great graphics, is easy to navigate, and will help you in the selection process, which is important because you want to make sure you select an animal you will be happy with.

Dog.com

1 2 3 4 5

www.dog.com

Well-stocked online doggy store offers just about everything a dog owner needs and plenty of extras, from beds and bones to pet ramps and training aids. The only thing this store doesn't carry is food. Shop online and have your order shipped to your home so that you can spend more time with your dog.

Dog-Play

1 2 3 4 5

www.dog-play.com

Literally an A–W (no X, Y, or Z) of fun things to do with your dog, this site also gives pet owners something different to think about: animal-assisted therapy. The author of this site details the experience of using dogs to help reach out to the elderly and confined individuals. The site includes links to organizations involved in animal-assisted therapy, books and publications on therapy dogs, and links to other dog-related sites.

Dogs in Review

1 2 3 4 5

www.dogsinreview.com

Whether you show dogs or just like to watch dog shows, *Dogs in Review* magazine can provide you with the information you need—articles written by some of the top dog experts in the country. Site features a huge collection of articles covering everything from choosing the right breed and adopting a dog to caring for your canine companion and enhancing your enjoyment of your pet with fun activities. Special articles just for kids.

GORP: Great Outdoor Recreation Pages

12345

www.gorp.com/gorp/eclectic/pets.htm

Tired of walking the dog just around the block or to the local park? These pages detail countless destinations that will cater to you and your canine. Complete lists by activity, region, interest, and lodging are provided. Includes information about emergency care for your dog.

Guide Dogs for the Blind

12345

www.guidedogs.com

Guide Dogs for the Blind is a "nonprofit, charitable organization with a mission to provide Guide Dogs and training in their use to visually impaired people throughout the United States and Canada." Here, you can find out more about the organization and what it has to offer. Links include Campus Locations, Puppy Raising, and Guide Dog Training. Learn how to apply for student training.

iLoveDogs.com

12345

www.i-love-dogs.com

Exhaustive directory of dog sites listed in categories that include All About Dogs, Dog Award Sites, Dog Breeders, Dog Shopping, and Dog Humor.

Next Day Pets

12345

www.nextdaypets.com

Excellent website designed to help people find and adopt pets and help those who can no longer keep their pets track down good homes for their pets. Here, you can find ads for dogs for sale, rescued animals, and breeders; read dog care instructions and guides; gather some ideas for naming your new dog; shop for supplies; or swap dog stories in the discussion forum. You have to register to use most of the features on this site, but that's just to keep out the riffraff.

Taking Care of Your Dog

12345

www.nutroproducts.com/takingcaredog.asp

Nutro Products features this guide to dog care that covers everything from dog-proofing your home and preliminary housebreaking to emergency care, training, and traveling with your canine companion. Excellent primer on caring for your canine, especially if you're a first-time dog owner.

Terrific Pets

12345

www.terrificpets.com

Terrific Pets is a terrific place to visit to share your enthusiasm of pet ownership with others of your breed. Site focuses on dogs, cats, and horses, and provides discussion forums, chat rooms, pet games, and links to other useful websites. Breeders, animal rescuers, and pet owners who can no longer keep their pets post ads on the site, making it a great place for tracking down the right pet at the right price.

Three Dog Bakery

12345

www.threedog.com

After stocking up on your own sticky buns and cake, remember to stop by this website to order some treats for Spot. The bakery's doggie treats were a knee-jerk reaction to commercial biscuits that had up to 50 ingredients, and pups all over the world love them, including Oprah's Fresh baked and all-natural ingredients.

DOMESTIC VIOLENCE

A Safe Place

12345

www.asafeplacedvs.org

Supportive services for battered women and their children in the Northern California East Bay region. The agency works to decrease the number of women and children returning to violent relationships and educate the community on issues surrounding domestic violence. Hotline number is also available.

End Abuse

12345

endabuse.org

This site is devoted to fighting all forms of family violence. Here, you can learn more about various programs that are available, read news stories relating to family violence issues, check out celebrities in the Hall of Fame and Hall of Shame, and access additional information and resources.

National Coalition Against Domestic Violence

12345

www.ncadv.org

The National Coalition Against Domestic Violence offers public education and advocates for social change.

Tip: Click the Learn link for links to additional pages that'll get you up to speed, and then look to the Resources link for additional information.

National Network to End Domestic Violence

12345

www.nnedv.org

Offers up-to-date facts about domestic violence and training and education for advocates.

Best Office on Violence Against Women

12345

www.usdoj.gov/ovw

Since its inception in 1995, the Office on Violence Against Women has "handled the Department of Justice's legal and policy issues regarding violence against women, coordinated departmental efforts, provided national and international leadership, received international visitors interested in learning about the federal government's role in addressing violence against women, and responded to requests for information regarding violence against women." Visit this site to learn more, and to get law enforcement help, if you need it.

Related Site

www.now.org/issues/violence

Safe Horizon

12345

www.safehorizon.org

An outstanding resource for referrals to local help for victims of domestic violence from all over the world. If you or someone you know is a victim of domestic violence, and you don't know where to turn, turn here. Site also features an online quiz to test your knowledge of domestic violence and information on what to do when you're a victim of a particular type of violence, such as Domestic Violence, Stalking, Child Abuse, or Torture.

DREAM INTERPRETATION

Dream Doctor

1 2 3 4 5

www.dreamdoctor.com

Dream Doctor is the home of Charles Lambert McPhee, the former director of the Sleep Apnea Patient Treatment Program at the Sleep Disorders Center of Santa Barbara, California. He is also the author of *Stop Sleeping Through Your Dreams* and founder and president of Dream Doctor, Inc. His radio program, *The Dream Doctor Show*, airs nightly in Santa Barbara, Ventura, and San Luis Obispo counties, in central coast California. Here, you can find the phone number to call in to the Dream Doctor and have him interpret your dream on his show. Site also features some tips on how to remember your dreams along with links to other useful dream interpretation sites. Perhaps the most valuable free resource on this site is the Dream Dictionary, where the Dream Doctor explores common dream themes.

Best Dream Moods

1 2 3 4 5

www.dreammoods.com

Dream Moods is an online guide designed to help visitors interpret and come to terms with their dreams. Here, you can find basic information about dreams, descriptions of common dreams and symbols, and a discussion forum where you can share your dreams and insights with others. Site also features a dream dictionary and an online exam.

Dreams Foundation

1 2 3 4 5

www.dreams.ca

The Dreams Foundation provides some useful information on dream interpretation along with tips on how to improve your dream recall, end nightmare reruns, learn how to incubate your dreams, and explore the science of sleep and dreams.

International Association for the Study of Dreams

1 2 3 4 5

www.asdreams.org

The International Association for the Study of Dreams is dedicated to promoting "an awareness and appreciation of dreams in both professional and public arenas; to encourage research into the nature, function, and significance of dreaming; to advance the application of the study of dreams; and to provide a forum for the eclectic and interdisciplinary exchange of ideas and information." Site offers information about its journal and upcoming conferences along with a discussion forum and a bookstore. Some excellent articles on dreams, but you have to poke around a little to find them—navigating the site is a nightmare.

Swoon@Glamour

1 2 3 4 5

www.glamour.com/swoon

Swoon@Glamour is *Glamour* magazine's astrology and dream interpretation site. You can search for your dream by typing a brief description of it or choosing a common theme from the list. Site also features a list of the top 20 symbols that commonly recur in dreams.

A B C D E F G H I J K L M N O P Q R S T U V W X Y Z

E-COMMERCE

Beginner's Guide to E-Commerce

12345

www.nightcats.com/sales/free.html

E-commerce and all its jargon can be confusing. This site offers a little help sorting it all out, including information in the following categories: Definition of Terms, Facts About Accepting Credit Cards Online, and E-Commerce Solutions Compared.

CommerceNet

12345 Blog RSS

www.commerce.net

The site for members of this Internet industry association provides research reports, some of which are free; a searchable database of articles; and information about upcoming conferences.

Best Doba.com

12345

www.Doba.com

Doba helps entrepreneurs and small businesses find products to resell by connecting them to wholesale suppliers and arranging for drop shipping to consumers. To complement Doba's web-based platform, the company provides retailers and suppliers with premium services such as advanced tools, resources, and education to enable maximum growth and profitability. If you want to sell stuff on the Internet, but you're not sure what to sell, where to get it, or how to go about setting up an e-commerce site, visit Doba.

eBay

12345

www.ebay.com

We cover eBay under the Auctions category, but it belongs here, too. eBay has revolutionized the e-commerce industry by enabling and empowering the average person to set up an electronic storefront and start selling merchandise online without having to carry a lot of overhead.

TIP: Combining the power of eBay with a product sourcing company, such as Doba, also covered in this section, any mom and pop operation can do quite well on the Internet.

E-Commerce Guide

12345

www.ecommerce-guide.com

Provides instructions, tips, and advice relating to various e-commerce topics, including how to build an e-commerce site, how to attract and keep customers, and how to get paid. Additional tabs at this site enable you to read e-commerce news and book reviews, research companies, and join discussion groups.

E-Commerce Times

12345 RSS

www.ecommercetimes.com

Lots of e-commerce news and discussions, as well as a free newsletter, offered either on a daily or weekly basis, to keep you updated. The information is categorized into current events or news, marketing, opinions, special reports, industry reports, and emerging technology, to name a few. Even includes a cartoon. You can readily access stock quotes and watch the tech market from this site.

eMarketer.com

12345

www.emarketer.com

eMarketer supplies "market research information related to the Internet, e-business, online marketing, and emerging technologies. eMarketer aggregates and analyzes e-business research from more than 2,000 sources, and brings it together in analyst reports, daily research articles and the "eStat Database"—the most comprehensive database of e-business and online marketing statistics in the world." Visit this site to subscribe and order reports online.

The Emerging Enterprise

12345

www.theemergingenterprise.com

Devoted to giving small businesses an edge on the Internet, this site features a collection of articles addressing the concerns of small-business owners. Includes a vendor directory and marketing resources.

Federal Trade Commission's E-Commerce Publications

12345

www.ftc.gov/bcp/menu-internet.htm

Complete list of publications from the Federal Trade Commission that apply to transactions on the Internet and other issues regarding privacy, security, and protecting children on the Internet. Includes information on scams, spam, pyramid schemes, and online investments, to name only a few. Separate areas available for businesses and consumers.

FreeMerchant.com

12345

www.freemerchant.com

One of the largest e-commerce providers in the world, FreeMerchant.com is home to a mega-mall of online stores. At FreeMerchant.com, you can set up your own store, locate vendors to stock your "shelves," and have a FreeMerchant design specialist build your store for you.

Google AdSense

12345

www.google.com/adsense

Millions of Internet users habitually search Google for information, resources, and products every day. With Google AdSense, you can place an ad for your website front and center whenever someone happens to search a keyword that applies to your site. When you need to sell your products on the Web, Google AdSense can be a great marketing tool.

Guide to E-Commerce

12345

www.ilr.cornell.edu/library/subjectGuides/ecommerce.html

Directory of e-commerce resources on the Web that are arranged in a way to provide an overview of e-commerce. Provides a brief introduction to e-commerce and links to other sites in the following categories: General Sites, Industry Associations and Organizations, International, Legal Resources, Online News and Journal Sources, and U.S. Government Sites.

Internet.com

www.internet.com

Internet.com is a hi-tech website for e-commerce professionals, Internet developers, vendors, and IT professionals. When you want to know the technology side of e-commerce, this is the place to go for information on the latest developer software and techniques, Internet news and resources, and Windows technology.

Internet Marketing Center

12345

www.marketingtips.com

The Internet Marketing Center offers an eight-step process to starting and growing your Internet business. The first four steps help you get your business up and running, and the final four steps show you how to boost sales and expand your business. This site features how-to courses, software, and plenty of success stories to inspire you to get off your duff and start making your first million.

Jupiter Direct Research

12345

www.jupiterdirect.com

JupiterResearch "provides unbiased research, analysis and advice, backed by proprietary data, to help companies profit from the impact of the Internet and emerging consumer technologies on their business." Service caters to investors and others who need reliable information about what's happening in the industry overall and what's happening inside specific companies.

Marketing Tips

www.canadaone.com/technology/smallbizstrat060898.html

Maps out a strategy for small business online marketing efforts and campaigns. From CanadaOne.

PayPal

www.paypal.com

One of the fastest growing e-commerce sites on the Web, PayPal is a service that handles credit card transactions for small businesses. If you have a mom-and-pop operation and you want a simple way to enable your customers to order and pay for products on the Web, check out PayPal.

SellItOnTheWeb

www.sellitontheweb.com

SellItOnTheWeb is an online magazine that provides practical information and resources you can use to start and manage your own successful online business. Simply click the link that best describes your goal, such as I Would Like an Introduction to e-Commerce or I Would Like to Start a Web Business. The site provides a brief tutorial addressing the selected topic.

Sloan Center for Internet Retailing

elab.vanderbilt.edu

Vanderbilt University's Owen Graduate School of Management runs the Sloan Center to research and study various aspects of e-commerce. The Sloan Center's purpose is to explain the challenges of online marketing, target online business opportunities, and determine viable business models for e-commerce. You can navigate the site using its tabs to access sections, including the Research and eLab Panel. By joining the eLab panel, you can qualify to win a cash prize.

TechWeb

www.techweb.com

TechWeb caters to IT professionals, but it also provides plenty for business professionals who are seeking to expand their businesses and make them run more efficiently via the Internet and other technologies. Before you decide to implement a cutting edge technology in your business, check out this site to learn the facts about it.

Wilson: Web Marketing and E-Commerce

www.wilsonweb.com

Excellent resource for information on how to market products and services on the Web. Obtain marketing advice from one of the top Web marketers, Dr. Ralph Wilson. Site includes tools for searching Dr. Wilson's articles and for searching an archive of thousands of Web marketing articles. You can find plenty of useful information at this site.

Wired.com

www.wired.com

Find the latest Internet news here, as well as international news, along with information on e-commerce court decisions and timely issues.

EDUCATION

Education World

12345

www.education-world.com

Education World's stated goal is "to make it easy for educators to integrate the Internet into the classroom." The site offers articles, lesson plans, school information, employment listings, links, and other resources for educators of preschoolers through older children. Offers a search engine that searches 500,000 education-specific sites that are safe for kids.

GreatSchools.net

12345

www.greatschools.net

GreatSchools.net is a great place for parents to go school shopping. If you're a parent planning to relocate your family, GreatSchools.net can help you track down the best performing schools in town.

JASON

12345

www.jasonproject.org

Brainchild of Dr. Robert Ballard, who discovered the wreck of the RMS *Titanic* in 1986, this site is dedicated to providing an avenue for students to perform field work online through various expeditions. Also provides continuing education opportunities for teachers.

MarcoPolo

12345

www.marcopolo-education.org

MarcoPolo is an excellent resource for K–12 teachers. This program provides teachers with lesson plans, classroom activities and materials, links to valuable content, and powerful search tools. MarcoPolo even provides teacher guides for elementary and secondary schoolteachers that give additional instructions on how to use MarcoPolo effectively in their classrooms. Visit this site for more information.

National Education Association

12345

www.nea.org

The National Education Association is an organization representing the interests of the public school system. This site contains information about the organization, its publications, and legislative activities. Offers education resources, links to grant information, teacher-specific resources, parenting resources, and lots more.

U.S. Department of Education

12345

www.ed.gov

The U.S. Department of Education is responsible for setting the standards for education in the United States, gathering and reporting statistics related to educational performance, assessing the quality of schools, and ensuring that public schools receive the federal funding they're entitled to. This site provides useful information for students, parents, teachers, and school administrators. In addition to providing information for students concerning financial aid, the site features an area with educational activities for students of all ages.

Best Yahoo! Education Directory

12345

education.yahoo.com

You can go to Yahoo!'s home page and search for various education topics, but you'll have much more luck by starting a more directed search at this site. Yahoo! provides an excellent portal to a wide range of education resources on the Web, including K–12 Schools, College and Grad Schools, Courses and Degrees, and Study Guides. You can access several reference resources, including a dictionary, world fact book, and encyclopedia; check out standardized tests, including the SAT and GRE; and read up on some informative and current articles.

Young Investor

12345

www.younginvestor.com

Tomorrow's moguls can learn money fundamentals and investing at this clever, colorful financial education site from Liberty Financial of Boston (which offers mutual funds geared to young people).

DISTANCE LEARNING

American Institute for Paralegal Studies

12345

www.americanparalegal.edu

Paralegal students at the American Institute can attend its nationally accredited program via computer-mediated distance learning, the institute's unique interactive learning environment.

ConferenceCalltraining

12345

www.conferencecalltraining.com

ConferenceCalltraining is a place where instructors, coaches, authors, and experts from many fields teach the skills, provide the education and training, and answer your questions—over the phone.

Distance Education Clearinghouse

12345

www.uwex.edu/disted

This University of Wisconsin site offers distance education news, highlights, resources, course descriptions, information on technologies, and more. Also features definitions, a glossary, and overviews of distance learning so that you will know what to expect.

Distance Education at a Glance

12345

www.uidaho.edu/eo/distglan

What's this distance learning thing all about? Barry Willis, the associate dean for Outreach at the University of Idaho, has developed this guide to lead students and teacher through the basics. The guide is organized by topic, covering overview, teaching, development, evaluation, television, computers, print, and several additional topics. If you would like to be involved with distance learning, this is a great primer.

Distance Learning and Online Education

12345

www.distancelearningonlineeducation.com

Distance Learning and Online Education is a directory of distance learning and online education providers and programs. Whether you are looking for a college degree, certification in a particular field or area, or continuing education opportunities, you can find them all on this site.

Distance Learning on the Net

12345

www.hoyle.com

Glenn Hoyle is the creator and manager of this excellent directory of distance-learning programs offered on the Internet. Browse the directory by category to find a list of the best distance-learning providers in that category along with a brief description of each provider and a link to its site.

H. Wayne Huizenga School of Business and Entrepreneurship

12345

www.huizenga.nova.edu

Internationally accredited, online MBA combining convenient Internet-based learning technologies, doctoral faculty, and years of experience in distance education.

Mindedge: Online Education

1 2 3 4 5

www.mindedge.com

Provides a listing of online courses, degrees, and certificates offered by accredited colleges and universities. Pick from Find A Course, Get A Degree, or Get A Certificate. Search thousands of courses offered by dozens of fully accredited schools.

Petersons.com: The Lifelong Learning Channel

1 2 3 4 5

www.petersons.com/distancelearning

Comprehensive distance-learning resource brought to you by Peterson's—the world's largest education information and services provider. What's cool about this site is that it gets right down to business. The opening page prompts you to select a course of study and the desired degree, so you can embark on your lifelong learning immediately.

TEAMS Distance Learning

1 2 3 4 5

teams.lacoe.edu

TEAMS Distance Learning provides interactive distance-learning programs for K–12 classes. A studio teacher runs the class from a remote location, while the classroom teacher and the students watch, listen, and ask questions. Visit this site to learn more about the available programs and how TEAMS works. Special area for students includes a directory of links to educational sites.

Technology Enhanced Learning and Research (TELR) at Ohio State University

1 2 3 4 5

telr.ohio-state.edu

Distance-learning courses, seminars, videotapes, and other resources developed and created by faculty at Ohio State and other institutions.

United States Distance Learning Association

1 2 3 4 5

www.usdla.org

The USDLA advocates distance learning and supports the distance learning community by providing information, networking, and opportunities for it to develop. Here, you can find the USDLA definition of distance learning, become a member, find state chapters, check out career opportunities, and explore the many distance learning programs provided by members.

University of Phoenix Online

1 2 3 4 5

www.uopxonline.com

If you've spent much time on the Web, you've probably seen a pop-up ad for the University of Phoenix. Here, you can enroll in distance learning classes and earn your degree online. University of Phoenix is the leader in providing distance learning courses for college and graduate students along with continuing education options for professionals.

Best WorldWideLearn

www.worldwidelearn.com

WorldWideLearn is an extensive directory of online distance learning websites and resources. Search for online degrees, MBA programs, business skills, online training, career and vocational courses, personal development classes, continuing education certification, or language courses. Online evaluations help you determine the right course of study and career path for you. This site even provides links to financial aid resources that can help you finance your online education.

EXPERIENTIAL *(SEE EXPERIENTIAL/ OUTDOOR EDUCATION)*

FOREIGN LANGUAGES

Best American Council on the Teaching of Foreign Languages

12345

www.actfl.org

If you're a foreign language teacher, you probably belong to ACTFL already. If you're not a member, you should be. ACTFL is "the only national organization dedicated to the improvement and expansion of the teaching and learning of all languages at all levels of instruction throughout the U.S." Here, you can find job opportunities, continuing education workshops, information on conventions, ACTFL publications, and much more.

Discovery Foreign Language Programs

www.discovery-language.com

Discovery Language Programs develops and markets foreign language programs for kindergarten through eighth grade. Here, you can check out the curriculum, the language offerings, the programs, and teacher training opportunities. You can also order teaching materials online.

don Quijote

12345

www.donquijote.org

Why learn Spanish at home, when you can travel to places where it's the native language? At don Quijote, you can explore various study-abroad programs in Spain and Mexico and find out if one of them is right for you. Site provides information on accommodations, destinations, activities, and prices and allows you to book your educational trip online.

Learn Spanish Online

12345

www.studyspanish.com

Take Spanish lessons online, complete tests, and keep track of your own report card. Plenty of tools and information for free. Premium services (for about $15 per month or $40 for six months) provide you with additional tests, resources, and study guides.

Lingolex

12345

www.lingolex.com/spanish.htm

Lingolex is packed with interesting and useful content for students of the Spanish language, including a Spanish Word of the Month, Christmas Vocabulary, a 61-word Hangman game, a Spanish verb conjugator, and plenty of online tutorials. Site design could use some work, but the content is stellar. Site also features an excellent directory of links to other Spanish learning sites.

Spanish Language Exercises

12345

mld.ursinus.edu/~jarana/Ejercicios

You can brush up on your Spanish and test your skills at this site, which provides several exercises, some of which you can grade yourself.

World Language Resources

12345

www.worldlanguage.com

More than 725 languages are supported through products available at this site, from dictionaries to spell checkers to videos and other teaching tools.

HOMESCHOOLING

A to Z Home's Cool Homeschooling Website

12345

homeschooling.gomilpitas.com

Created and maintained by Ann Zeise, an enthusiastic homeschooling advocate, this site is a huge directory of articles and resources on homeschooling. This site offers something for everyone, from those considering the homeschooling option to those in the trenches. Learn the basics, the laws, places to find study materials and lessons, methods to homeschool gifted children, and much, r

A B C D F G H I J K L M N O P Q R S T U V

California Homeschool Network

12345

www.californiahomeschool.net

A California-based organization devoted to protecting the rights of families to educate their children without government interference and to provide support for parents who choose to homeschool their children. Although the CHN is dedicated to families in California, this site offers some valuable resources for all homeschoolers, including articles on how to develop social skills and how to deal with irate relatives.

Eclectic Homeschool Online

12345 

www.eho.org

This site promotes creative homeschooling through "unique resources, teaching methods, and online helps." Shows how to teach important skills through daily activities and other innovative approaches.

Homeschool Central

12345

homeschoolcentral.com

This directory of resources for homeschoolers features an excellent article for new homeschoolers that lays out an overall education plan. Also includes a link to the Homeschool Central Mall (at homeschoolcentralmall.com), where you can shop online for curriculum, software, and supplies. Message boards, online chat, and pen pal links help you keep in touch with other homeschoolers and help your child keep in touch with other children.

Homeschool Legal Defense Association

12345 RSS

www.hslda.org

The HSLDA promotes and defends the rights of parents who desire to homeschool their children, but this site provides much more information than you might expect. In addition to featuring articles on legislation and how to defend your rights when they are challenged, this site offers articles on how to start homeschooling and where to find the information and other resources you need to homeschool effectively. Excellent site!

Home School Foundation

12345

www.homeschoolfoundation.org

The Home School Foundation is dedicated to providing assistance to needy homeschool families. Visit this site to learn how you can help the foundation and how the foundation can help you.

Related Site

www.youcanhomeschool.org

Best Home School World

12345

www.home-school.com

This award-winning site features a Home Life catalog, a listing of homeschool support groups, directories of courses and lesson plans, and a mammoth homeschool mall where shoppers can find hundreds of items. This site also offers online book purchases from its secured server. If you're a parent who's home schooling your children or considering home schooling, bookmark this Best of the Best site and return to it whenever you need assistance.

Homeschool.com

12345

www.homeschool.com

Homeschool store that carries a wide selection of products for homeschoolers, including a Getting Started kit, books, CDs, videos, software, and online courses. If you want to homeschool your child but you don't know where to start, start here. Also features adult learning materials.

HomeSchoolZone.com

12345

www.homeschoolzone.com

A community for homeschoolers (parents and kids), providing libraries of activities and events, as well as information and advice. Great place for homeschooled students to share their work with others.

Oregon Home Education Network

12345

www.ohen.org

A nonprofit organization established to support Oregon's homeschooling families, the Oregon Home Education Network (OHEN) acts as a clearinghouse for homeschooling activities and resources at the local, state, and national level. The website includes FAQS about homeschooling, Oregon administrative rules, and a number of homeschooling resources.

INTERNATIONAL EDUCATION

AFS Intercultural Programs

12345

www.afs.org

This nonprofit organization offers intercultural learning opportunities through its international student exchange programs. The site offers information on AFS programs, current AFS news, links, and more.

American Councils for International Education

12345

www.americancouncils.org

The American Council is devoted to improving education, professional training, and research within and about the Russian-speaking world, including both the Russian Federation and the many non-Russian cultures of Central and Eastern Europe.

Council on International Education Exchange

12345

www.ciee.org

CIEE is an organization that's dedicated to globalizing communities, campuses, and corporations through its foreign exchange programs. Here, you can learn about opportunities to work or teach in foreign countries or to bring foreigners to your country for educational or work opportunities.

The Digital Education Network's EduFind

12345

www.edufind.com

This site provides a wide range of resources for students and professionals interested in international education. Many schools offering courses to international students are featured on the site, and information can be found on language schools, universities, business schools, colleges, and vocational schools all over the world. The site also hosts a number of award-winning learning resources, such as the Online English Grammar and the ELT/TEFL Centre.

GoAbroad.com

12345 RSS

www.goabroad.com

GoAbroad.com is "the leading international education and experiential travel resource. Our directories contain more than 25,000 opportunities abroad updated daily including study abroad, internships, volunteer opportunities, teach abroad, language schools and much more." Site features travel guides, a list of embassies and language schools, job leads in foreign countries, detailed descriptions of available programs, information on international health insurance and global phone services, and much more.

The International Education Site

12345

www.intstudy.com

Students interested in studying abroad should visit this site. Find details on colleges and universities, course options, chat with other students worldwide, and take advantage of the free application service.

NAFSA: Association of International Educators

12345

www.nafsa.org

This site offers information about this association and its activities promoting international educational opportunities.

A B C D E F G H I J K L M N O P Q R S T U V W X Y Z

TIP: Click the Yellow Pages link in the upper-right corner of the opening page to access a Rolodex packed with contact information for everything you need to plan and finance your international education.

Rotary International Eastern States Student EXchange Program, Inc. (ESSEX)

12345

`www.exchangestudent.org`

Find out about Rotary International's student-year-abroad youth study programs.

Study Abroad Directory

12345 Blog

`www.studyabroad.com`

Listing of more than 1,000 study abroad programs. The site offers links to a marketplace of related products and services. It also offers recommended reading and several sections that provide information on every aspect of choosing a study abroad program.

K–12

ALA Resources for Parents and Kids

12345

`www.ala.org/parentspage/greatsites`

This educational site, which is maintained by the American Library Association, includes Internet guides for kids and teens, book lists, and links to hundreds of recommended sites for kids.

ArtsEdge Network

12345

`artsedge.kennedy-center.org`

The National Arts and Education Information Network focuses on using technology to increase access to arts resources and increase arts education in the K–12 school environment. Features an online newsletter, an information gallery, curriculum guides, and links to other arts-related online information.

Awesome Library

12345

`www.awesomelibrary.org`

Contains 30,000 carefully reviewed resources, including the top 5 percent in education. Pick the category that applies to you (Teacher, Parent, Kid, Teen, Librarian, or Community) and see an "Awesome Library" designed for your needs.

ClassroomConnectDirect.com

12345

`www.classroomdirect.com`

Offering a wide selection of classroom activities, software, and supplies at reasonable prices, this is a one-stop shopping site for classroom teachers.

Discovery Channel School

12345

`school.discovery.com`

From The Discovery Channel, resources for teachers of science, humanities, and social studies. Includes lesson plans, email lists, and a schedule of upcoming science specials. You can buy educational and stimulating toys and gifts for children, including telescopes, dinosaurs, videos, and books through the online store. Students area provides homework and study help and tips, a weekly brain booster quiz, a clip art gallery, puzzles, and science fair project ideas. Special area for parents and homeschoolers provides additional teaching resources.

EducationJobs.com

12345

`www.educationjobs.com`

An employment resource for jobs in the education field providing services to school systems, teachers, and administrators. Service provides access to more than 10,000 jobs, contact information for more than 15,000 schools, and resources to help educators land the job they want. For about $15, you get three months access to the site.

A B C D E F G H I J K L M N O P Q R S T U V W X Y Z

Education Week News

1 2 3 4 5 Blog RSS

www.edweek.org

Featuring the latest news relating to education in America, this site keeps teachers, administrators, and parents informed of legislation and other happenings in the world of education. Links to *Teacher Magazine*, special reports, and state education numbers and statistics.

EduHound

1 2 3 4 5

www.eduhound.com

Huge searchable directory of educational resources for K–12. Sites are organized into dozens of categories, including Administration, Animals, Back to School, Culture, Marine Life, and World & Countries. Special areas include Clip Art for Kids, Schools on the Web, Classrooms on the Web, Weekly Spotlight, and EduHound Weekly (a newsletter for educators). Teachers, parents, homeschoolers, and students will all want to bookmark this site.

Family Education Network

1 2 3 4 5

fen.com

The Family Education Network offers something for everyone: teachers, parents, kids, teens, and homeschoolers. It functions as a leading source of information and resources for all those involved in the K–12 education process. Site offers free trials of most of its premier educational tools.

FunBrain

1 2 3 4 5 Blog

www.funbrain.com

FunBrain is a fun, educational site developed by Pearson Education that organizes its content into three distinct areas: one for kids, one for parents, and one for teachers. In the kids' area, you can click a link to visit any of the three main arcades, browse games by grade level, check out the entertainment areas, or play any of the classic games. The teachers' area features a quizlab, gradebook, curriculum guide, standards finder, and additional tools. Parents can check out the homework relief center. Offering something for everyone in an easily accessible format, FunBrain earns its selection as our Best of the Best site for K–12 education.

Global Online Adventure Learning Site

1 2 3 4 5

www.goals.com/classrm/classfrm.htm

Tune in to learn more about adventures in progress or already completed by people around the world. Learn about actual ocean-crossings, bike trips, and hiking treks being undertaken and transmitted to this site, which aims to teach kids about science, nature, and technology.

KidsBank.com

1 2 3 4 5

www.kidsbank.com

KidsBank.Com is a tutorial website developed by Sovereign Bank that explains the fundamentals of money and banking to children. The site provides parents with information and a place to share with kids to aid their understanding of the benefits of saving.

Kindergarten Connection

1 2 3 4 5

www.kconnect.com

Provides resources for the primary school educator. Offers teacher tips, lesson plans, book reviews, and links to other related sites.

Microsoft Education

1 2 3 4 5

www.microsoft.com/education

The Microsoft Education website is an online resource for school technology coordinators and educators. Offers articles, solutions, ideas, and resources for schools building connected learning communities and integrating technology in the classroom. Site could use some content specifically for parents, who are the ones who dole out the money for the products that make their children more computer savvy.

Mr. Dowling's Virtual Classroom

12345

www.mrdowling.com

This site was created by Mr. Dowling, a sixth-grade geography teacher. He presents a variety of historical and geographical topics that students, educators, and parents can utilize. Homework assignments are also included here.

NASA John C. Stennis Space Center Education and University Affairs

12345

wwwedu.ssc.nasa.gov

A broad-spectrum collection of K–12 and other educational WWW resources, with special focus toward space and aerospace studies. Includes teacher resources, lesson plans, and links to many other education-related topics.

Newbery Medal

12345

www.ala.org/ala/alsc/awardsscholarships/literaryawds/newberymedal/newberymedal.htm

This annual award is given for excellence in American children's literature. Find information about the award, a printable list of past winners, and detailed information on award-winning and honor books. You can purchase books, jewelry, posters, and cards through the online store.

On2

www.pbs.org/newshour/extra

The Public Broadcasting Service provides this bimonthly magazine aimed at elementary and junior high students. It features world news, science and technology updates, and real-life accounts from people in the news. You can buy books and videos from the online store.

Questacon: The National Science and Technology Center

12345

www.questacon.edu.au

This site is a scientific learning show for kids. It includes online games that teach scientific concepts and theories, a virtual tour of the center in Australia, and features that focus on international science events. You can purchase T-shirts and thought-provoking gifts for children from the online store. Very engaging.

Questia: World's Largest Online Library

12345

www.questia.com

Subscribe to this library to place a huge collection of books, magazines, journals, newspapers, and encyclopedias right at your fingertips. Some good free samples, too. If a window pops up asking you to subscribe to the newsletter, don't think you have to subscribe to connect to the site; just click the button to close the window. You do, however, have to subscribe to the site to access the full content of more than 65,000 books from more than 250 publishers. Also features an excellent tutorial on how to write a research paper.

Scholastic.com

12345

www.scholastic.com

The home of the largest publisher of children's books in the world, including the *Harry Potter* series, Scholastic.com provides an excellent learning kiosk for parents, teachers, and children. Scholastic's goal is to instill the love of reading and learning for lifelong pleasure in all children. This site is well designed and packed with high-quality content.

The Science Source

12345

thesciencesource.com

Manufactures and sells more than 300 items for teaching physics, physical science, chemistry, biology, environmental science, and design technology. High-quality innovative science and technology teaching materials.

USA Today Education

12345

`education.usatoday.com`

This site features a new cross-curriculum lesson plan every day that covers the core subjects and reaches a little beyond the basics. Content at this site is intended to make students more aware of and knowledgeable about the world and the various cultures around them. Site does a great job of using current events to make learning more engaging and applicable to real life.

> **Tip:** College students can click the Collegiate link in the upper-right corner of the opening page to access an edition of *USA Today* that contains articles related to college studies, careers, and interests.

World Almanac for Kids

12345

`www.worldalmanacforkids.com`

World Almanac for Kids is an excellent site for kids to visit to learn more about the world, including its animals, its history, human inventions, religions, populations, and much more. Plenty of games to help kids learn while having fun.

Yahoo! Education: K-12 Directory

`dir.yahoo.com/Education/K_12`

Excellent directory includes dozens of subdirectories covering everything from Arts and Humanities to Social Studies, Math, and Science. Additional subcategories include Academic Competitions, Distance Learning, Student Resources, and Homeschooling. Great place to start a search.

K-12—EDUCATIONAL TELEVISION

Bill Nye the Science Guy's Nye Labs Online

12345

`www.billnye.com`

The website for one of the hippest geeks on television, Bill Nye. Entertaining as well as educational, Bill Nye the Science Guy's website has listings, a search mechanism, and other goodies. The Home Demos can keep you busy for hours experimenting with common household items.

Biography

`www.biography.com`

A website based on the A&E program of the same name. The Biography website has a 25,000-person search engine, quizzes and games, and chapters from published biographies of important people. You can also get video clips and a calendar of upcoming programs. You can buy books, videos, and posters from the online store.

Cable in the Classroom

`www.ciconline.com`

Can television be educational? Find out what the cable industry thinks and see what it has to offer in the way of educational programming. Teachers are especially welcome at this site, where they can find details about various educational shows available through the Cable in the Classroom initiative.

ChannelOne.com

`channelone.com`

Home of the Channel One Network, a cable television network that broadcasts news stories and current events to middle school, junior high, and high school students from around the world. Here, you can find some of the top stories along with quizzes and other resources. Also features message boards and polls.

Children's Television Workshop

12345

`www.sesameworkshop.org`

Offers many features for kids and parents alike, including a lineup of *Sesame Street*'s new season, ratings of various children's television shows for parents, information about the *Ghost Writer* series (among others), and online games galore for children. The parents' section includes discussions on child development, education, product reviews, behavior and discipline, and others. Parents of young children should not miss this site.

Related Site

www.greentv.org

The Discovery Channel

www.discovery.com

Cable channel covering history, technology, nature, exploration, and science-related issues. The site has special feature sections and "did you know" facts that make it a unique experience. Includes the standard programming schedules and sections on kid-related programming. The opening page provides information about current shows on the Discovery Channel, but you can access other related networks for additional information, including TLC (The Learning Channel), Discovery Health, Travel Channel, Discovery Times, Discovery Kids, the Science Channel, and FitTV. The Discovery Education link provides access to even more information.

KET: Kentucky Educational Television

www.ket.org

KET embraces the philosophy of no child left behind and no adult left behind through this PBS-related site. Here, parents, teachers, and students can find a well-stocked library of audio and video content designed to engage and educate. Site features a complete programming guide along with webcasts and podcasts of most shows. Special areas for kids and tools for teachers are also readily available.

Merrow Report

www.pbs.org/merrow

The Merrow Report is a TV series that focuses on youth and learning in an attempt to reveal some of the shortcomings of the U.S. educational system and improve standards.

MyETV: South Carolina Educational TV and Radio

www.scetv.org

MyETV is the Internet home of South Carolina Educational TV and Radio, which is closely linked with PBS. At this site, you can check program listings, learn a bit about featured shows, download Podcasts, view streaming video of many past shows, and find classroom resources to help teachers integrate show content into their curriculum.

Noggin

www.noggin.com

Noggin is a commercial-free educational channel for preschoolers that's available via digital cable and satellite TV. It broadcasts shows that most preschoolers love, including *Blue's Clues*, *Sesame Street*, and *Oobi and Tweenies*. This site provides some cool interactive computer games that are both fun and educational...for the younger crowd, of course.

PBS Teacher Source

www.pbs.org/teachersource

If you're a teacher looking for ways to integrate PBS educational television into your classroom, visit this site for lesson plans and other materials that can make your job much easier and help optimize the learning experience for your students. Content is organized by subject, including Arts & Literature, Health & Fitness, Math, Science, Social Studies, and Library Media. After selecting a show, you can choose the desired grade level to obtain lesson plans specifically for your level of students. Register to personalize your Teacher Source.

Stephen Hawking's Universe

www.pbs.org/wnet/hawking/html/home.html

This PBS show addresses the big bang theories, why the universe is the way it is, where we come from, and other cosmic questions in an entertaining way accessible to all adult audiences. The site includes a schedule of programs, teacher's guide, and a Strange Stuff Explained section, which discusses black holes and antimatter, among other topics.

Street Cents Online

cbc.ca/streetcents

Tied to the Canadian television show *Street Cents*, which teaches young people how to be informed consumers. Covers all the highlights of the week's program and also offers an essay contest.

K–12—HOMEWORK HELP

About Schools

www.aboutschool.com

Extensive directory of resources for K–12 students, parents, and teachers. Resources are broken down by grade level: Preschool, Kindergarten, Grades 1–3, Grades 4–6, Grades 7–8, and High School. Within each category are subcategories for each subject, including reading, writing, arithmetic, chemistry, and so on.

Atlapedia Online

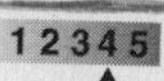

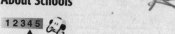

www.atlapedia.com

A virtual world almanac of planetary proportions. Atlapedia Online provides facts and vital statistics for every country on the globe.

B.J. Pinchbeck's Homework Helper

school.discovery.com/homeworkhelp/bjpinchbeck

B.J. "Beege" Pinchbeck is a Pennsylvania teenager who, with Dad's help, maintains this rich and handy K–12 educational reference directory.

California State Science Fair

1 2 3 4 5

www.usc.edu/CSSF/Resources/GettingStarted.html

A great supporting resource for any student considering entering a science fair, and for any parent who's been requested to help. You can find ideas for getting started, information about judging, and plenty of other science links to look through. Some of the links are a little dated and don't work, but this site still provides you with some good leads.

Dictionary.com

1 2 3 4 5

www.dictionary.com

A complete resource library on the Web, this site features a searchable dictionary, thesaurus, medical dictionary, translator, grammar and style guide, and foreign language dictionaries. Toss those tomes in a tomb, and look stuff up online!

Fact Monster

1 2 3 4 5

www.factmonster.com

Fact Monster, from infoplease, features a searchable index of facts on everything from geographical locations to people of interest. If you're doing a research project and need to verify information or check up on some background details, turn to the Fact Monster for assistance. This site also offers games and quizzes to help you hone your trivia knowledge and test-taking skills.

Grolier's Online: The American Presidency

1 2 3 4 5

ap.grolier.com

The American Presidency at Grolier Online Encyclopedia presents a history of presidents, the presidency, politics, and related subjects. Some audio and video of past presidents are available.

Homework Help for Parents

12345

`www.nea.org/parents/homework.html`

If you're a parent, you might wonder how to handle issues that deal with your kids' homework, such as how much help you should provide. This page, from the National Education Association, provides an excellent overview of the topic.

Homework Helper Page

12345

`www.geocities.com/Athens/Parthenon/7726`

This page was created for all students on the Web by a Collingwood, West Vancouver, parent. This site is a great place to research K–12 materials. Also be sure to investigate the "enrichment" websites, which are continually updated.

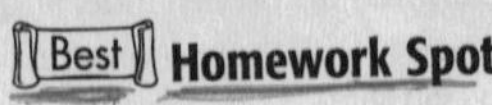

Best Homework Spot

12345

`www.homeworkspot.com`

Excellent directory of homework help sites provides links to homework sites in nearly every subject area grouped by class level: Elementary, Middle, and High School. Also provides links to reference materials and sites for parents and teachers. If you need help with your homework, this is the best place to start looking.

infoplease: Homework Center

12345

`www.infoplease.com/homework`

The infoplease Homework Center is open 24 hours a day, 7 days a week to help students with homework in just about every subject, including geography, history, math, science, language arts, and social science. This site is packed with reference materials, calculators, and other tools that place everything you need in a single, easily accessible location.

Jiskha Homework Help

12345

`www.jiskha.com`

Find answers to your questions about nearly every school-related topic here. This site offers help for Art, Computers, English, Foreign Languages, Math, Science, and more. Most answers are in the form of essays written by experts. You can submit a question or join a discussion group to find your answer or browse through the topics in a particular subject area. Some annoying ads, but to keep this excellent site free, you have to put up with them.

Merriam-Webster Online

12345

`www.m-w.com/home.htm`

You can look up words in the Merriam-Webster Dictionary and build your vocabulary in other ways via this generous English language reference site.

ProQuest K–12

12345

`www.proquestk12.com`

ProQuest K–12 provides education materials to librarians, students, and teachers in more than 43,000 schools across the country. At the top of the ProQuest home page is a Homework Central search tool for obtaining homework help in nearly every subject based on grade: K–5, 6–8, and 9–12. You can also browse for homework help by clicking the link for the desired grade level near the top of the page.

Refdesk.com

12345

`www.refdesk.com`

This site provides daily tidbits of information, from historical trivia to astronomical facts. You'll also find a crossword and quote of the day.

Time for Kids

12345

`www.timeforkids.com/TFK`

Time magazine's edition for kids online. Students can browse articles on current events or search past issues for specific topics. Links for teachers and parents, too.

K-12—MONTESSORI EDUCATION

American Montessori Society

12345

www.amshq.org

The official AMS site has everything you need to know about Montessori education. Learn what Montessori education is all about, how effective it is, what goes on in the Montessori classroom, and how Montessori programs work in public schools.

Best Association Montessori Internationale

12345

www.montessori-ami.org

Dr. Maria founded the Association Montessori Internationale in 1929, and this remains the official association for Montessori schools worldwide. The Association coordinates teacher training programs, encourages the creation of Montessori schools, oversees the development and production of Montessori training materials, and much more. Here, you can learn about the Montessori pedagogy and the key people who started and developed the Montessori system, check out job opportunities, locate books and teaching materials, and learn about the training of teachers.

The Center for Contemporary Montessori Programs

12345

minerva.stkate.edu/offices/academic/montessori.nsf

This site offers information about The Center for Contemporary Montessori Programs' teacher education programs, which are American Montessori Society affiliated. You can get course descriptions and check out links to other Montessori sites.

International Montessori Index of Schools

12345

www.montessori.edu

Site opens with an explanation that anyone can open a school and call it "Montessori." To help parents choose a school that's more in line with the original tenets and philosophy of Dr. Maria Montessori, this site offers an annotated index of schools and teacher-training centers.

International Montessori Society

12345

imsmontessori.org

Learn what Montessori education is all about. Request Montessori publications and get information on the society's Montessori teacher education program. Find out which schools are recognized by the International Montessori Accreditation Council (IMAC). If you'd like to, you can even join the society by filling out a simple form; when you join, you receive valuable information and materials about Montessori education.

The Materials Company of Boston

12345

www.thematerialscompany.com

This site offers Montessori teaching materials at low prices. It has a Montessori consultant on staff to answer any of your questions. You can buy everything from math beads to furniture.

The Montessori Foundation

12345

www.montessori.org

Read about the Montessori Foundation and its purpose, learn about the variety of Montessori schools in America, and subscribe to *Tomorrow's Child*, a magazine for Montessori parents and educators. Check out the Montessori school directory, where you can search for Montessori schools around the world. You can add your school to the directory, too. Visit the Montessori Foundation Bookstore, where you can order original works of Maria Montessori translated into English.

Nienhuis: Montessori Teaching Materials

12345

www.nienhuis.com/USA/html/home.html

Nienhuis Montessori is a Dutch company that has a headquarters in Mountain View, California. Here, you can order Montessori books, curriculum support materials (for printed labels, control charts, control maps, and language material), and toys. This site also provides news and promotional deals.

A B C D E F G H I J K L M N O P Q R S T U V W X Y Z

K-12—PRIVATE EDUCATION

Council for American Private Education

1 2 3 4 5

www.capenet.org

CAPE is a "coalition of national organizations and state affiliates serving private elementary and secondary schools." The United States has more than 29,000 private schools, which represent about one quarter of all schools with more than 6 million students in attendance. Members of CAPE represent about 80 percent of that 6 million. Here, you can learn about private schools and public policy on private schools. You can also check the job boards.

Eschoolsearch.com

1 2 3 4 5

www.eschoolsearch.com

Search this directory of more than 30,000 private schools (elementary through high school) by city, state, school type, and/or grade. Schools can register here to be added to the directory. Great for tracking down schools, but this site provides little help in gauging a school's quality.

Independent Schools Association of the Central States

1 2 3 4 5

www.isacs.org

This site is designed to provide administrators, teachers, trustees, parents, and students with answers to all their independent school questions. Includes a searchable database of private schools, market research services, a career center, a recommended reading list, and more.

New York State Association of Independent Schools

1 2 3 4 5

www.nysais.org

This site should be a first stop for parents beginning the school-selection process in the State of New York. Includes information on how to select schools, how to narrow the choices, and how the schools choose the students. Also provides information on what to do if your child is not admitted. If you're a parent, click the For Families link next to Resources at the top of the page.

Best Peterson's Education Center

1 2 3 4 5

www.petersons.com/pschools

Find private secondary schools by name, location, or type of program. Or identify schools to meet your child's special needs. A rich database of information, including help on financing a private education. You can purchase books about colleges, find out how to apply, and locate information to help you prepare for college through the online store.

Private School Review

1 2 3 4 5

www.privateschoolreview.com

If you're searching for a private school for your child and don't have a clue where to start, this is *the* place to look. Private School Review provides several flexible tools that enable you to search for private schools. You can browse by state, plug in your ZIP code, and even view the economic ratings for the top 20 towns or counties in a particular state. The only drawback at this site is that its ratings are based more on the socio-economic makeup of a community than on student performance at a particular school.

Student Loans and Education Financing

1 2 3 4 5

www.gateloan.com

This site provides information about student loans and financing education. Even offers a place to apply online.

TABS—The Association of Boarding Schools

1 2 3 4 5

www.schools.com

This site provides answers to questions you may have about boarding schools. It also provides the means to find a boarding school and a common application form to start the process. International opportunities are also presented.

K–12—PUBLIC EDUCATION

Center on Re-Inventing Public Education

12345

www.crpe.org

Founded by the University of Washington's Daniel J. Evans School of Public Affairs, the Center on Re-Inventing Public Education seeks to discover a way for urban school systems to provide "strong, coherent schools that create equal opportunity for all children." Here, you can check out the Center's work and publications and access news reports about the Center.

Parents for Public Schools

12345

www.parents4publicschools.com

With more and more parents clamoring for a voucher system that enables them to send their children to the school of their choice, Parents for Public Schools is "working to strengthen public schools through broad-based enrollment." If you believe that all schools, public and private, should provide equal education for all students, check out this site and learn how to advocate for legislation that supports public schools.

Public Education Network

12345

www.publiceducation.org

The goal of this organization is to marshal support for improving the quality of education in public schools. Find out how to join, how you can support its efforts, and what can be done in your area.

The Story of Public Education

12345

www.pbs.org/kcet/publicschool

PBS special that examines the history of public education in the United States and the innovators who changed the course of public education.

PRESCHOOL

Chateau Meddybemps

12345

www.meddybemps.com

A whimsical site for parents and young children. The offerings for preschoolers include a list of the best books for preschoolers and young readers and fun learning activities designed to develop math, observation, memory, and reasoning skills.

Everything Preschool

12345

www.everythingpreschool.com

If you're a preschool teacher or are homeschooling your child, you will want to visit this site often. It features a vast collection of resources for teaching preschool children, including lesson plans, alphabet ideas, bulletin boards, recipes, songs, games, coloring pages, and holiday calendars.

Best FamilyEducation

12345

www.familyeducation.com

A resource for families to find out more about encouraging children to learn. You can find child development Q&As, links to other educational sites, ideas to get your child to read, and many other useful ideas for helping your child get ready for and succeed at school. You can buy books, videos, software, toys, and games through various vendors who advertise at this site. The site provides links categorized by age group—Young Kids (0–8), Kids (9–13), and Teens (14–18).

First-School

12345

www.first-school.ws

First-School is a great place for preschool teachers to find activity and project ideas for their classes.

KinderCare

1 2 3 4 5

www.kindercare.com

The largest preschool and childcare company in the United States. You can learn about KinderCare and its programs, tour a center online, or find a facility near you.

The Perpetual Preschool

1 2 3 4 5

www.perpetualpreschool.com

More than 12,000 free resources and ideas for preschool teachers. This site offers an incredible array of themes for nearly every occasion, learning center ideas, teacher tips, playtime ideas, and even a directory of stores where you can purchase equipment and supplies.

PreschoolEducation.com

1 2 3 4 5

www.preschooleducation.com

This site provides a collection of resources for preschool teachers, including art and craft ideas, software and book reviews, calendars, snack ideas, plays, and much more. The pop-up ads can be annoying, but the site does provide some excellent resources for preschool teachers.

Preschool Express

1 2 3 4 5

www.preschoolexpress.com

If you're a parent, grandparent, or teacher looking for engaging, educational activities for your preschooler, check out this site for some ideas. Content is organized by stations, including Calendar Station, Art Station, Discovery Station, and Story Station.

Preschool Page

1 2 3 4 5

www.kidsource.com/kidsource/pages/Preschoolers.html

The Preschool area of KidsSource Online offers articles that provide information, tips, and suggested activities for children ages 3 to 6. Although part of the site's focus is on education, it also covers safety, recalls, new product information, health, and nutrition.

ReadyWeb Home Page

1 2 3 4 5

readyweb.crc.uiuc.edu

Information and resources sponsored by the ERIC Clearinghouse on Elementary and Early Childhood Education. Look into getting your child ready for school by turning to these U.S. Department of Education publications.

SuperKids Software Review

1 2 3 4 5

www.superkids.com/aweb/pages/reviews/early/3/elmopre/merge.shtml

Provides full reviews of educational software for early learners and older students. The reviews are written by teams of parents, teachers, and kids. Summary ratings of the titles include educational value, kid appeal, and ease of use.

RESOURCES

AskTheBrain

1 2 3 4 5

www.askthebrain.com

AskTheBrain is an online encyclopedia/directory that serves up answers about more than 200,000 interesting topics. When you can't find whatever you are looking for using one of the main search engines on the Web, Ask The Brain!

Benjamin Franklin: Glimpses of the Man

1 2 3 4 5

sln.fi.edu/franklin/rotten.html

Provides multimedia information about Ben Franklin by using pictures, documents, and movies. Covers his family, inventions, diplomacy, philosophy, and leadership. Provides a bibliography for further study of Franklin, his accomplishments, and the time period.

CliffsNotes

12345

www.cliffsnotes.com

Generations of slackers and procrastinators have relied on the printed versions of CliffsNotes to catch up on their reading before a major exam or essay was due. Now, you can access these valuable "study guides" online for free.

Community Learning Network

12345

www.cln.org

Shares information about educationally relevant Internet resources. Click the Subject Areas link to explore resources by subject or click Teachers & Tech to improve your computer skills. The Kids Stuff area provides some fun online activities for students.

Council for Exceptional Children

12345

www.cec.sped.org

Parents of exceptional children, whether they are physically challenged or gifted, might want to learn more about the work of this organization, which aims to improve the quality of services provided to these students. The site contains legislative information, a clearinghouse of information on the subject, and discussion forums to link parents and educators on this issue.

Education Index

12345

www.educationindex.com

Huge collection of links to the best education-based websites. Browse by subject or life stage, hang out in the Coffee Shop with your pals, or play around with Web Weasel.

Educause

12345 Blog

www.educause.edu

Offers searchable archives of *EDUCOM Review*, archives of the LISTSERV EDUPAGE, and other online documents. Supports EDUCOM's focus on educational technology in higher education. Also offers links to several other telecom/educational technology–related sites and programs. You can subscribe to various periodicals online.

Encarta

12345

encarta.msn.com

Encarta online places a reference library right at your fingertips. Here, you can find the award-winning Encarta encyclopedia, a dictionary, a world atlas, quizzes, homework help, and areas for aspiring college students, college students, grad students, and more.

Best FREE: Federal Resources for Education Excellence

12345 RSS

www.ed.gov/free/index.html

The Federal Department of Education provides free resources from more than 30 different federal departments and agencies for use in education. Subjects covered include arts, educational technology, foreign languages, health and safety, language arts, mathematics, physical education, science, and social studies. Click the Searches & Subjects link to look for specific materials or click More for Students for additional materials directed more toward students than teachers. If you're a teacher looking for some valuable free activities and materials, bookmark this site.

A B C D E F G H I J K L M N O P Q R S T U V W X Y Z

infoplease.com

12345

www.infoplease.com

A huge library of reference material, including biographies, history, government facts, atlases, almanacs, encyclopedias, dictionaries, current events, and more.

Kid Info

12345

www.kidinfo.com

A great resource for young students, this site features a Student Index, where you can find homework help, a comprehensive list of reference resources, educational search engines, and some fun links to keep from frying your brain cells. Also includes resource centers for parents, teachers, and younger students. Most links take you to other sites.

The Math Forum @ Drexel

12345

mathforum.org

Focuses on math education. Offers links to resources such as the Coalition of Essential Schools, a web-based lesson on vectors, a geometry LISTSERV, and more. Also offers a section on projects for students, such as "Ask Dr. Math."

NASA Education Sites

12345

quest.arc.nasa.gov

Offers a collection of servers specifically geared for teachers, students, and administrators, as well as a selection of math and science education resources, connectivity to numerous education servers, journals, and grant and project participation information.

Peterson's Education Center

12345

www.petersons.com

Seeks to catalog all U.S. K–12 schools, colleges, and universities, both public and private, as well as community and technical colleges. Links to study guides for passing standardized tests, plus some free tips, strategies, and sample questions. Some excellent information on career and college planning.

PinkMonkey

12345

www.pinkmonkey.com

Students can access more than 400 free study guides, book notes, and chapter summaries at this site. Everything offered on the site is rated G, so parents don't have to worry.

scifair.org

12345

www.scifair.org

Are you having trouble coming up with an idea for a science fair project? Then scifair.org can help. Step-by-step instructions explain how to think of a unique idea on your own. If you're really stuck, you can find dozens of ideas in the Idea Bank or see what other budding scientists are up to on the Idea Board. Tips on using the scientific method, writing your report, and putting together a killer display.

Best SparkNotes

12345 Blog RSS

www.sparknotes.com

SparkNotes quickly unseated CliffsNotes as the most popular publisher of study guides by offering free access to many of its study guides online. Barnes & Noble now owns the imprint but continues to provide the free stuff. Here, you can find study guides for most of the classical works you need to read in high school and your early years in college, along with test prep tools, guides for entering college, and fun stuff such as movies, music, and television.

Tutor.com

12345

tutor.com

Tutor.com provides products and services for library systems, schools, and communities to help deliver information, resources, and assistance to students. It also provides a subscription service that features individual tutoring for students (but not for free).

United Nations Cyberschool Bus

cyberschoolbus.un.org

The next time you or your child needs to do a report on a specific country, this is the first site you should visit. Compare data within the countries of the United Nations, including urban growth, top exports, and threatened species. A great resource for adults and kids.

YourDictionary.com

www.yourdictionary.com

This website lists free and subscription online dictionaries and thesauri containing words and phrases to help students locate the best word to use. You can search YDC (Your Dictionary.Com) for dictionaries, courses, glossaries, and 'Nyms & Stuff (abbreviations, acronyms, style guides, and so forth).

ELDERCARE

AgeNet Eldercare Network

12345

www.agenet.com

AgeNet Eldercare Network features a list of current articles on elderly health and caregiving. Here, you can find helpful information on a host of common ailments that affect the elderly, checklists and tools for improved caregiving, a list of medications for common illnesses, legal and financial guidance, insurance information, and assistance in evaluating housing options.

CareGuide@Home

12345

www.eldercare.com

This well-designed and well-organized site acts as a resource guide that covers the main topics of eldercare, including Health & Well Being, Mind & Memory, Care at Home, Living Alternatives, Legal & Financial, Care for Caregivers, and Childcare. At CareGuide you can learn more about various telephone consultation options they offer, read a host of excellent, free articles, and check out the featured links.

ElderCare Advocates

12345

www.eldercareadvocates.com

ElderCare Advocates is "a team of geriatric care managers and other social work and health care professionals dedicated to keeping seniors healthy and independent and living in their homes as long as possible." Site features an excellent article on eldercare issues that connects with caregivers and eases them into the difficult task of assessing long-term healthcare options for their elderly relative. Here, you can also find an ElderCare Resource Center with dozens of informative articles.

Eldercare at Home: A Comprehensive Guide

12345

www.healthinaging.org/public_education/eldercare

From the Foundation for Health in Aging comes this comprehensive online guide for elderly care, a 28-chapter book that covers everything from physical problems to mental and emotional issues and practical advice on care management. Nothing fancy here, just high-quality information.

Eldercare Locator

12345

www.eldercare.gov

Eldercare Locator is a searchable directory designed to help the elderly and their caregivers track down sources of information on senior services. The service "links those who need assistance with state and local area agencies on aging and community-based organizations that serve older adults and their caregivers." Site also features some useful articles.

Best ElderWeb

12345 Blog

www.elderweb.com

ElderWeb is an award-winning resource, directory, and community center for the elderly and their caretakers. This site was created and is maintained by Karen Stevenson, who has spent 20 years focusing on the intersection of technology and eldercare. Site features topics on aging, college programs for professional caregivers, common diseases of the elderly, legal issues, finances, Medicare and prescription medications, and just about every other topic that applies to aging and the elderly. Excellent site to begin your research. When we visited ElderWeb, Karen was transitioning it from a website to a blog, so this site promises to get even better and more interactive over time.

FCA: Family Caregiver Alliance

1 2 3 4 5

www.caregiver.org

Family Caregiver Alliance was "the first community-based nonprofit organization in the country to address the needs of families and friends providing long-term care at home. FCA now offers programs at national, state and local levels to support and sustain caregivers." At this site, caregivers can find plenty of information, tips, and advice; read and post messages in the discussion forums; and read a good collection of fact sheets and publications. You can also learn about workshops, conferences, and classes.

Health and Age

1 2 3 4 5 Blog RSS

www.healthandage.com

Sponsored by the HealthandAge Foundation (HAF), an independent nonprofit organization, this site offers "interactive health information for people as they move towards their senior years, and for those who take care of them." Content is provided by medical professionals, so it promises to be accurate, credible, and reliable. Health and Age is dedicated to empowering "people of all ages to identify, understand, prevent, treat, and communicate effectively with their health professionals about a wide variety of medical conditions." Excellent articles plus a primer on aging to get you up to speed in a hurry.

ELECTRONICS

Alpine of America

12345

www.alpine-usa.com

Known for its high-end car stereos and speakers, Alpine also has a full product line of CD changers, head units (components that combine CD and cassette players, receivers, equalizers, and more), and auto security systems. Get full product features, links to Alpine sites in other countries, and technical support at this attractive site.

Audio Ideas Guide

12345

www.audio-ideas.com

Read audio and video product reviews by category or brand, and search the archives for back issues of this print magazine. You can subscribe online.

Audio Video News

12345

www.audiovideonews.com

For a look at audio, video, and home electronics news, new products, and upcoming electronics events, this site is a quick read.

Best Buy

12345

www.bestbuy.com

The number-one specialty retailer of consumer electronics, personal computers, entertainment software, and appliances in the United States. Compare products, get coupons and rebate forms, shop, and rent DVDs online.

Bose Corporation

12345

www.bose.com

One of the leaders in high-end consumer audio, Bose prides itself on using unconventional thinking and products to solve conventional problems. Here, you can find company history, current news and contests, and a secure site where you can purchase popular Bose products.

Cambridge SoundWorks

12345

www.cambridgesoundworks.com

Get help choosing the best audio or home theater product, or go straight to the special deals and find out how much you can save.

Circuit City

12345

www.circuitcity.com

This consumer electronics retailer offers products in a number of categories, including home video and audio, car audio, digital cameras, phones, games, computers, and movie and music titles. Before buying, however, you'll want to read purchasing tips, check out product comparisons, and scan online reviews.

> **TIP:** Scroll to the bottom of the page to check out the Deals links before you go shopping.

Consumer Electronics Show

12345

www.cesweb.org

CES is the electronic industry's equivalent of the Cannes Film Festival. Every year, electronics developers and manufacturers parade their cutting-edge technology to distributors, retailers, and the press at this magnificent show. Here, you can obtain news about the most recent show and any upcoming shows and events. This site serves attendees, exhibitors, the press, and international visitors.

Crutchfield

1 2 3 4 5

www.crutchfield.com

This well-known home and car electronics catalog has gone online, offering products for sale via the Internet. A huge selection of products is available at competitive prices. Crutchfield has a solid reputation for quality and service, offering free shipping, 30-day money-back guarantee, free shipping on returns, free technical support, free car stereo installation kits, expert advice on what to buy, and more.

Dynamism.com

1 2 3 4 5 RSS

www.dynamism.com

If you're looking for the latest, greatest, coolest, cutting-edge electronics gizmos on the market, Dynamism can help you find (and purchase) them online.

eCoustics.com

1 2 3 4 5 RSS

ecoustics.com

eCoustics.com specializes in home theater and hi-fi systems and provides everything you need to know in terms of instructions, product reviews to help you determine what you need, and how to assemble a killer home-entertainment center. This site also features other consumer electronic equipment, including digital cameras, MP3 players, car audio equipment, notebook computers, and much more. This site features an excellent collection of articles from some of the top consumer electronics magazines.

Home Theater Magazine

1 2 3 4 5 Blog

www.hometheatermag.com

Devoted to keeping home theater enthusiasts informed of the latest technology, this magazine serves a huge selection of articles and product reviews. If you're a home theater novice, click the Home Theater 101 link to learn the basics. You can even subscribe to the magazine online. Site contains a few too many pop-up ads, but other than that, you can find some excellent information here.

IEEE Home Page

1 2 3 4 5 Blog

www.ieee.org

Home of the Institute of Electrical and Electronics Engineers, this site holds a great deal of information about the institute itself, its publications, the events it sponsors, and the ever-growing list of standards that it develops and supports. Find regional chapters and learn about training and career development programs through the organization. Site also features an editor's blog.

Internet Mall

1 2 3 4 5

www.internetmall.com

Huge online mall where you can shop for just about anything at hundreds of stores. When you reach the mall, click the Electronics link to view links for various electronics shops in the mall.

Jerry Raskin's Needle Doctor

1 2 3 4 5

www.needledoctor.com

Just because digital is the latest thing doesn't mean that analog is dead. The Needle Doctor specializes in keeping the vinyl sound alive with catalogs of new turntables, needles, cartridges, and belts. You're not the only one out there still listening to records.

Mega Hertz

1 2 3 4 5

www.megahz.com

Mega Hertz specializes in the broadcasting and receiving end of the electronics spectrum. Products include amps, antennas, demodulators, satellite receivers, and TVs and monitors.

Nextag

1 2 3 4 5

www.nextag.com

When you know which electronic gadget you want, visit Nextag and search for the best price. Nextag does the comparison shopping for you, quoting you the best price on a particular product, including tax and shipping. Now that's quality service!

Phone Scoop

12345 Blog RSS

www.phonescoop.com

Finding the right cell phone and carrier can be a nightmare, but Phone Scoop can help. This site helps shoppers track down the perfect cell phone and comparison-shop for carriers. Expert reviews plus online forums can help you find the right phone/carrier combination for your needs.

Radio Shack

12345

www.radioshack.com

Radio Shack is still one of the leaders in consumer electronics. Find out about its many products, including mini satellite TVs, toys, cellular services, and home security. Also get the details on the international franchise program and employment opportunities.

Best Reviews at cnet.com

12345 RSS

reviews.cnet.com

Get gift ideas, read product reviews, find out which are editors' choices, and select from a long list of product categories—from TVs to DVD players to MP3 players, digital cameras, handheld devices, and much more. Current and helpful information presented in an easily accessible format makes this an easy pick for the Best of the Best award.

Sony

12345 RSS

www.sony.com

Sony is one of the most recognizable names in electronics, and its site doesn't disappoint. Here, you can shop online for Sony equipment, including TVs, computers, stereos, and DVD players; track down your favorite Sony music CDs and DVD movies; and obtain customer support and service. Site is attractive and easy to navigate.

SoundStage

12345

www.sstage.com

The online magazine for high-end music and audio fans provides product and album reviews to guide you to your purchases. Plenty of links to manufacturers and retailers.

TWICE: This Week In Consumer Electronics

12345

www.twice.com

When you need to stay on top of what's going on in the world of consumer electronics, turn to *TWICE*, the magazine that rides the waves. This site covers all aspects of consumer electronics, from accessories to major appliances, home audio, video, and computer technology. A product finder can help you track down the gizmos and gadgets that catch your eye.

Unbeatable.com

12345 RSS

www.unbeatable.com

Unbeatable.com boasts more than 10,000 products ready to ship. Find an extensive catalog of consumer electronics, from palmtop computers to karaoke machines to leisure wear. Subscribe to the RSS feed for the latest bargains.

EMERGENCY SERVICES

911: National Emergency Number Association

12345

www.nena.org

This site is packed with information for those who are responsible for implementing 911 programs in their communities, but it also features an area for the average person to learn more about the 911 program. This site addresses common concerns such as dialing 911 on your cell phone and using 911 with VoIP (Voice over IP) connections. Site also features links to other sites that offer education packets that can be useful for classroom teachers.

AfterDisaster

12345

www.afterdisaster.com

If your home or business has been damaged by fire, flood, or other natural disaster (or vandalism), this group promises to get you back on your feet as soon as possible while minimizing your loss and downtime. Specializing in responding to fire and water damage, the company has skills in drying documents, deodorizing, treating mold/mildew, getting clean water to your site, and much more.

American College of Emergency Physicians

12345

www.acep.org

This site holds a warehouse of information about the ACEP, its policies and guidelines, and current news. Features a large "members-only" section, but much of it is focused on nonmembers, too. Find out about ACEP's views on managed care and other current concerns, as well as membership and dues information for doctors, residents, and medical school students. Site also features some excellent guidance for patients and consumers on what to do in the event of an emergency.

Best American Red Cross

12345 RSS

www.redcross.org

The jewel in the emergency services crown, the Red Cross exists to aid disaster victims and help people prevent and prepare for emergencies. Find out about the organization's current interests, locations in which it is currently helping disaster victims, and volunteer opportunities. Whether you're a victim of a terrible tragedy or are looking for a way to contribute to your community and lessen someone else's suffering, this site is a must-visit.

Computer Emergency Response Team

12345 RSS

www.cert.org

A site that tracks and reports on threats to computer security, such as viruses and worms.

FEMA: Federal Emergency Management Agency

12345

www.fema.gov

Whenever a major disaster strikes—hurricane, tornado, flood, or earthquake—FEMA is there to pick up the pieces and help rebuild the area. This site provides the latest news and information about FEMA and helps you access its services when you need them most. FEMA also features a special area just for kids.

FireFighting.Com

www.firefighting.com

This jam-packed, energized site is like a giant recreation room for emergency-service workers of all flavors. Featuring news, articles, links, a chat area, and even poetry and other writing, FireFighting.Com caters mostly to firefighters, but it will also interest law enforcement workers, EMTs, and other public safety professionals.

Lifesaving Resources

12345

www.lifesaving.com

Dedicated to the prevention of drowning and aquatic injuries, this site is a resource for lifeguards and other safety and rescue professionals. Articles on aquatic safety and rescue, information about upcoming seminars and training courses, case studies, online shopping, and much more. Very comprehensive site.

Related Sites

www.americancpr.com

www.worldwideaquatics.com/lifeguards.htm

Lifesaving Society (for Lifeguards)

12345

www.lifesaving.org

If you're a lifeguard or would like to become a lifeguard, this is an excellent resource to help you obtain the proper training and continuing education required to be the best. Site features information about its training programs, public education (lifesaving procedures that everyone should know), competitive lifesaving links, lifesaving management resources, and a store where you can shop online for the latest gear.

Mountain Rescue Association

12345

www.mra.org

A volunteer organization that provides mountain safety education and volunteers for search-and-rescue operations.

Paramedic

12345 

www.paramedic.com

This site's goal is to be a resource to paramedics and those interested in paramedicine. Includes articles, news, research tools, educational links, list of top EMS sites, access to 24/7 Paramedic TV, and online forums. Shop online for books and emergency equipment. Site also features a huge directory of links to paramedic, firefighter, and EMT sites organized by category.

Rock-N-Rescue

12345

www.rocknrescue.com

This company specializes in equipment for the narrow field of rock climbing and rope rescue. Browse the large catalog of ascending and rappelling devices, ropes and pulleys, and media resources. Whether your need is industrial, sports-based, or for a rescue squad, this site has what you need.

Related Sites

www.aaa.com

www.hurstjaws.com

www.land-shark.com

EMPLOYMENT (SEE JOBS/ EMPLOYMENT)

(SEE JOBS/ EMPLOYMENT)

ENVIRONMENTAL & GLOBAL ISSUES

CONSERVATION

Arbor Day Foundation

12345

`www.arborday.com`

Learn how you can help the environment by planting a tree in your community. Learn about the many Arbor Day programs for supplying trees to communities and educating the population about the importance of trees. You can find out what kinds of trees will do well in your area just by entering your ZIP code. You can order a wide variety of trees from this site at discount prices, with proceeds going to the foundation. Make a difference in your community by checking out this site and placing an order. Special area just for kids teaches them the importance of trees in a fun and engaging format. This site is well designed, making it nearly impossible to get lost in its forest of information.

Atlantic Salmon Federation

`www.asf.ca`

As if the salmon of North America didn't have enough trouble swimming upstream, now they have to contend with the possibility of extinction. The ASF's goal is to find solutions to all issues that could possibly affect the salmon's survival.

Bat Conservation

12345

`www.batconservation.org`

This site has information about bats and a section for kids to visit. You can adopt a bat and provide for its care. The Organization for Bat Conservation cares for orphaned and injured bats, including those on the endangered species list. You can find an online gift store where you can purchase shirts and even a bat detector.

The Butterfly Web Site: Conservation and Ecology

12345

`butterflywebsite.com`

Provides articles calling for the conservation of butterflies, lists of butterfly gardens around the world, tips for attracting various types of butterflies, a well-stocked photo gallery, and much more. Plenty of links to related sites, plus online shopping through The Nature Store.

Conservation Breeding Specialist Group

12345

`www.cbsg.org`

A conservation group whose mission is "to assist conservation of threatened animal and plant species through scientific management of small populations in wild habitats, with linkage to captive populations where needed." Check out this site to learn more about the group's programs and publications, read the current issue of its newsletter, or find out how you can assist. Global Zoo Directory lists zoos throughout the world.

Conservation International

12345

`www.conservation.org`

Learn all about the company that works in rainforests, coastal and coral reef systems, dry forests,

A B C D F G H I J K L M N O P Q R S T U V W X Y Z

deserts, and wastelands in more than 40 countries on four continents. Site also features an online quiz about amphibians that's pretty challenging.

Earth Island

12345

www.earthisland.org

Earth Island is an organization dedicated to conserving, preserving, and restoring Earth's environment and biodiversity by encouraging people around the world to play an active role. Earth Island also educates visitors on the various threats to our environment and potential ways to reverse the degradation of our natural habitats. Here, you can find a wide range of activities and projects to get involved in. If you don't see a conservation or preservation program that you are interested in, this site provides the information, resources, and contacts you need to start your own.

Environmental Education Resources

12345

eelink.net

The goal of the EE-Link is to contribute to the protection and conservation of endangered flora and fauna. Site features areas for teachers, students, and professionals, environmental news, leads on jobs and grants, mailing lists, publications, and a directory of links to other environmental sites.

green home

12345

www.greenhome.com

Are you trying to live a more environmentally conscious lifestyle? Then look no further. At green home, you can find all the information and products you need to live a life that's environment-friendly. Products include items for conserving energy and water, composting waste, and recycling materials. You can also shop for organic pesticides and herbicides, environmentally friendly cleaning solutions, products made from recycled materials, and much more.

International Rivers Network

12345

www.irn.org

International Rivers Network works to halt the construction of destructive river development projects and to promote sound river management options worldwide.

MrSolar.com

12345

www.mrsolar.com

MrSolar.com was started by a man in Utah who, along with his wife, has been living on solar energy for more than 20 years. His goal is to help everyone become as self-sufficient as he and his wife have been. Now the site acts as an information center and online store, where you can learn how to harness energy from the sun, wind, and water for yourself.

National Audubon Society

12345

www.audubon.org

Get background information on the society, its namesake John James Audubon, and his natural art. Find your local chapter and get membership information. You can even join online.

National Oceanic and Atmospheric Administration

www.noaa.gov

Get the full story, complete with pictures, of some of the nation's natural disasters, from tornadoes in the Midwest to forest fires burning out of control on the West Coast. The NOAA has pictures and information on what's going on. An educational site with great photos and a small collection of videos. Site also features an extensive collection of links for job leads at NOAA, grants, and other useful websites.

National Wildlife Federation

12345

www.nwf.org

Remember *Ranger Rick* magazine? Well, it's still being published by the NWF, which works to protect and teach people about nature and wildlife. At the site, you can learn about the work of this organization and ways to support it. You can also order publications such as *Ranger Rick* and introduce kids to the KidZone, where they can learn more about the wild.

The Nature Conservancy

nature.org

The Nature Conservancy puts an emphasis on saving entire habitats, including both plants and animals. Learn about its activities and programs and how you can join the organization in its conservation efforts. A colorfully designed page.

> **TIP:** Click the Activities link to gather ideas for fun activities, including free eCards, quizzes, videos, slide shows, and nature story podcasts.

The Ocean Alliance

www.oceanalliance.org

Concerned with protecting and conserving whales through research and international education initiatives. Though not designed for young children, some kids who are interested in whales and conservation issues will find this site fascinating.

RAINFORESTWEB.ORG

www.rainforestweb.org

Works to protect Earth's rainforests by providing a comprehensive resource bank for concerned citizens, companies, and institutions. This is a great place for students to learn more about rainforests, why they are important, and what they can do to help preserve them.

Surfrider Foundation USA

www.surfrider.org

This grassroots eco-surf organization is dedicated to the preservation of biological diversity on our coasts. It emphasizes low-impact "surfaris" and environmental education among surfers and others to maintain a synergy between man and beach.

USDA–Natural Resources Conservation Service

12345

www.nrcs.usda.gov

The NRCS helps private landowners develop conservation systems suited to their land. It also works with rural and urban communities alike to reduce erosion, conserve water, and solve other resource problems. A few offerings for teachers and students.

Wildlife Conservation Society/Bronx Zoo

12345

wcs.org

The Wildlife Conservation Society, headquartered at the Bronx Zoo, is dedicated to the conservation of wildlife around the world. Nicely designed site features an excellent collection of information on wildlife issues and conservation efforts around the world.

Best World Wildlife Fund

12345

www.wwf.org

Dedicated to protecting the world's threatened wildlife and the biological resources they depend on. The opening page isn't all that impressive; but if you click on a country link, the site reveals a huge offering of information and resources on wildlife issues and conservation efforts in various parts of the world. Here, you can learn about endangered species, global challenges that must be met to ensure the long-term health of the planet, and WWF programs and activities designed to address specific problems. The Explore links provide engaging educational opportunities for the younger crowd, where they can learn the importance of establishing a healthy balance between humans and the rest of the living world.

ECOLOGY

Coastal America Partnership National Web Site

12345

www.coastalamerica.gov

The Coastal America program is a collaborative effort between organizations to protect the ecological systems and wildlife of America's coastal regions. This site provides general information on the program itself, publications, information centers, and success stories.

Earthwatch

12345

www.earthwatch.org

A nonprofit membership organization that sponsors scientific field research projects. Read about the planned field research projects or participate online via expedition photos, reports, and online lessons. Membership information is also available at the site.

Ecologia

12345

www.ecologia.org

ECOlogists Linked for Organizing Grassroots Initiatives and Action is a group "replacing cold war competition with environmental cooperation." Headquartered in the United States, this group's mission is to provide assistance to environmental groups in the former Soviet Union, Eurasia, and the United States.

Ecology.com

12345

www.ecology.com

Home of Ecology Communications, Incorporated (ECI), a broadcasting company specializing in programs about ecology. Here, you will find the latest news, featured stories, quotes, links, and other resources dealing with ecological issues.

Best Ecology Fund

12345

www.ecologyfund.com

The Hunger Site Network set up the EcologyFund as a fundraiser for various conservation projects around the world. All you have to do to donate is click one of the sponsor's links. Register, and the Hunger Site Network donates 500 square feet of wilderness in your name and keeps "a running tally for you of all the land you have preserved." Best of all, you don't have to donate any money. The site simply requests that you visit the sponsor pages to check out what they have to offer as a way of saying thanks. Because this site offers such a painless way to take action, we've bestowed upon it our Best of the Best ranking in the Ecology category. While you're here, click the Resources tab to access special content for kids and educational materials for teachers.

Ecology and Society

12345

www.ecologyandsociety.org

Journal that explores the interaction between human societies and their ecosystems. Articles investigate various socio-ecological systems in an attempt to discover what works and what doesn't and how politicians and cultures can develop a healthy, sustainable balance between their societies and the ecosystems in which they exist.

The Environment Directory

12345

www.webdirectory.com

Extensive directory of links to environmental websites is organized by category including Agriculture, Energy, Land Conservation, Pollution, Sustainable Development, Water, and Wildlife. Excellent place to launch research into the many facets of ecology.

Greenpeace

12345

www.greenpeace.org

Promoter of biodiversity and enemy of ecological and environmental pollution, Greenpeace and its links are accessible through this site. Links include the biodiversity campaign, the North Sea oil rig tour, a hot page, and more.

Home Energy Saver

hes.lbl.gov

Visit this site to learn how you can cut down on energy consumption in your home. Simply enter your ZIP Code and complete a brief survey to obtain a list of ideas on how you can trim your home heating bill and conserve electrical consumption.

International Ecotourism Society

www.ecotourism.org

Provides resources for travelers who want to be environmentally responsible. Learn how to tour intriguing ecological areas without destroying natural habitats. Site also features a fairly extensive directory of other ecotourism sites.

Kids Do Ecology

www.nceas.ucsb.edu/nceas-web/kids

At Kids Do Ecology, kids learn why ecology is so important and what they can do on a daily basis to protect and preserve their environment. Sections include Learn About Ecology, World Biomes, Marine Mammals, and Conservation Projects. This site is bilingual and offers educational materials that teachers can use in their classrooms.

Sierra Club

www.sierraclub.org

Home page for the nonprofit public interest conservation organization. The site focuses on activist news, current critical "ecoregions," and the Sierra Club National Outings Program, as well as an internal Sierra Club search engine. Site also links to an occasional feature blog.

U.S. Fish and Wildlife Service–National Wetlands Inventory

www.fws.gov

Provides a list of the national wetlands and news related to them. Nineteen files are available for downloading, including a list of plant species found in wetlands. Also contains links to product information, ecology, and educator information.

PRESERVATION

American Shore and Beach Preservation Association

www.asbpa.org

The United States beaches are one of its most valuable assets, not only for their beauty and recreational use but also because they support much of the marine life. The ASBPA is dedicated to preserving the beaches neighboring ecological areas. Visit this site to learn what you can do to help.

Environmental Defense Fund

www.environmentaldefense.org

The group that formed in 1967 to fight the use of DDT is still going, and is more than 400,000 strong. The group needs your help in addressing what it feels are critical environmental issues; check out this site to find out what those issues are and what you can do. Site features an online quiz to test how much you know about environmental issues and provides practical advice on what you can do now to reduce pollution in your car, at home, and on vacation.

Environmental Explorers Club

www.epa.gov/kids

The United States Environmental Protection Agency's kids site provides information for students, teachers, and parents; a place where kids can submit questions; an art room; a science room; a game room; an area with information on trash and recycling; and much more. Great place for kids to learn about our environment and what they can do to help keep it clean.

Environmental Protection Agency's Office of Water

12345

www.epa.gov/ow

This beautifully produced site explores American water resources with an emphasis on the quality of our nation's water, and features powerful searching, imagery, animation, kids' pages, valuable publications, and informative hot links. See also the following entry for the "Environmental Protection Agency."

Environmental Protection Agency

12345

www.epa.gov

At the EPA home page, you can access documents such as official EPA press releases, the *EPA Journal*, and more. All EPA programs are documented online, from Acid Rain to Wetlands. Through this page, you can send your comments directly to the EPA, as well as apply for employment.

Environmental Protection Agency's Office of Water

12345

www.epa.gov/ow

This beautifully produced site explores American water resources with an emphasis on the quality of our nation's water, and features powerful searching, imagery, animation, kids' pages, valuable publications, and informative hot links. See also the previous entry for the "Environmental Protection Agency."

NEI: Nuclear Energy Institute

12345

www.nei.org

This Nuclear Energy Institute website is designed to promote the benefits of nuclear energy in respect to its impact on the environment. Site features basic information about nuclear energy production and waste disposal along with public policy information, statistics, and a science club with resources for both students and teachers.

The Whale Museum's Orca Adoption Program

12345

whale-museum.org

What better way to "save the whales" than to adopt one? By adopting Ralph, Saratoga, Missy, Princess Angeline, Deadhead, Raven, or any of the number of orcas that swim the waters of Puget Sound and southern British Columbia, you'll be supporting orca research and education.

RECYCLING

BioCycle: Journal of Composting and Organics Recycling

12345

www.jgpress.com/biocycle.htm

You might be surprised to hear this, but *BioCycle* is the only journal of composting and organics recycling. This site gives you the opportunity to check out some sample articles, check out the Reader Q & A section, and do a little extra research on equipment and recycling systems.

Computer Recycling

12345

www.usedcomputer.com/nonprof.html

Computers are packed with hazardous materials, so don't dump your old computer in the trash. This site shows you where to take your old PC to have it recycled. You might even get a tax credit!

Best Earth 911

12345

www.earth911.org

Earth 911 is the Yellow Pages of recycling. It consists of a comprehensive directory of recycling centers, hazardous waste disposal programs, and cell phone and computer recycling services. The opening page instructs you to enter your ZIP code first. When you do that, you work your way through a couple screens of options to specify the type of material you need to recycle or dispose of, and the site provides a list of the closest recycling centers or disposal services that accept those materials for processing. Site also features excellent guides on how to shop to produce less waste, how to reduce air pollution, how to recycle batteries, how to conserve energy, and so on. Special area where kids can learn more about recycling.

Freecycle

1 2 3 4 5 ▲

www.freecycle.org

If you want to get rid of something but don't want to go through the hassle of trying to sell it or dump it, consider *freecycling* it. At Freecycle, you can give and receive, but you cannot buy or sell. This site places you in contact with the Freecycle organization in your area, where you can post your goods to give to charity organizations or anyone who's willing to take it off your hands.

Recycle City

1 2 3 4 5 ▲

www.epa.gov/recyclecity

United States Environmental Protection Agency's site teaches kids about recycling to conserve resources and keep our environment clean. Visit Recycle Town to see how its citizens reduce use, reuse wastes, and recycle. Play the Dumptown game. Find out where trash ends up.

Recycle This!

1 2 3 4 5 ▲

www.recyclethis.org

The Erie County Recycling Program has put together this site to help educate consumers about the three R's: Reduce, Reuse, and Recycle. Find out who's recycling and learn specific ways to reduce, reuse, and recycle. You can also find out more about the program and check out additional resources. A special area is available just for kids. When we clicked links at this site, the content appeared way down on the page, making it difficult to navigate, but the content is good.

Recycler's World

1 2 3 4 5 ▲

www.recycle.net

This trading site offers links to recycling associations, publications, traders and recyclers, equipment, brokerage group services, and more. You'll find pages for every possible recyclable material, from automotive parts to wood and plastics. The site even has a section for organic and food waste recycling.

Shred-It Mobile Paper Shredding and Recycling

1 2 3 4 5 ▲

www.shredit.com

Provides onsite shredding and recycling services to businesses and individuals nationwide. Information request form provided.

A B C D E F G H I J K L M N O P Q R S T U V W X Y Z

ETIQUETTE

Best Emily Post Institute

1 2 3 4 5

www.emilypost.com

Emily Post has become an etiquette icon, deferred to on matters of etiquette and manners for more than 60 years. The Emily Post Institute, "created by Emily in 1946 and run today by third generation family members, serves as a 'civility barometer' for American society and continues Emily's work." Here, you can find answers to your etiquette questions, read answers to previously submitted questions, learn proper etiquette in a variety of social situations, and book a speaker for your next event. Very classy website without a lot of bells and whistles—just excellent advice.

Etiquette Hell

1 2 3 4 5

www.etiquettehell.com

This entertaining site features etiquette horror stories in various categories, including wedding, business, everyday, and money etiquette. While laughing, half in shock, you unconsciously develop your etiquette skills by learning from other people's misfortunes and mistakes. Site also provides a Mail Bag area where you can read letters from other visitors and a discussion forum. If we were giving out awards for humor, this site would certainly qualify.

Golf Etiquette from the PGA

1 2 3 4 5

www.pga.com/play/golf-etiquette.cfm

Before you tee off and get others tee'd off on your next golf outing, visit the PGA's Golf Etiquette page to learn the basics of being a considerate golfer. Site provides a basic guide to golf etiquette that's clear and to the point.

Miss Manners

1 2 3 4 5

www.washingtonpost.com/wp-dyn/style/columns/missmanners

Miss Manners has been teaching us how to behave for years, and continues to keep us updated on what's considered rude and distasteful as our culture changes. Here, you can search the archive or Miss Manners's latest recommendations to readers.

Netiquette Home Page

1 2 3 4 5

www.albion.com/netiquette/index.html

This site features excerpts from Virginia Shea's book *Netiquette*. Read the 10 core rules of the Internet, take a Netiquette quiz, and even join a mailing list to stay current on the newest ways to be polite online.

Related Site

www.phish.net/discussion/netiquette.html

The Original Tipping Page

1 2 3 4 5

www.tipping.org/TopPage.shtml

How much do you tip a skycap at the airport? This site gives recommended tipping standards for 10 different service categories, covering dozens of different service workers and situations. Includes ushers at sports arenas, manicurists, cruise ship cabin boys, and much more. New software for Palm computers is equipped with a tip calculator.

EXERCISE & FITNESS

24HourFitness

12345

www.24hourfitness.com

You can find a wealth of information that changes daily on fitness, sport, nutrition, and health with worldwide links. A community of persons committed to active and healthy living.

Aerobics and Fitness Association

12345

www.afaa.com

Starting a healthy exercise program is the focus of this site, which covers proper nutrition, equipment, goal setting, and safety. You'll also learn how to select the best instructor for yourself.

Best American Council on Exercise

12345

www.acefitness.org

The American Council on Exercise is "the largest nonprofit fitness certification and education provider in the world. Widely recognized as 'America's Authority on Fitness,' ACE continually sets standards and protects the public against unqualified fitness professionals and unsafe or ineffective fitness products, programs and trends." You can visit this site knowing that you're going to get accurate, reliable, and timely information on exercise and fitness. Site features a Get Fit menu with Fit Facts, Fitness Tips, a Fitness Q&A, a Fitness Library, Recipes for nutritious meals and snacks, and much more. You can also track down local trainers who are ACE certified and shop for ACE apparel, videos, and other merchandise online. Although the site provides little that may attract kids, it does offer information on its Operation FitKids, which can be useful to parents and teachers.

American Heart Association: Exercise & Fitness

12345

www.americanheart.org

The American Heart Association focuses not only on curing heart disease but also on preventing it and helping everyone maintain a healthy ticker. At this site, you can learn how moderate exercise can keep your heart pumping well into your later years. To get to the Exercise & Fitness page, point to the Healthy Living link in the navigation bar on the opening page and click Exercise & Fitness. Other links on the main page are useful, too.

Calories Per Hour

12345

www.caloriesperhour.com

When you want to get in shape and lose some weight, the formula is simple: burn more calories than you consume. This site features calculators that can help you do the math: a weight-loss calculator; food calories and nutrition calculator; and a BMI, BMR, and RMR calculator. Here, you can also find a fitness FAQ, fitness tutorial, and diet and weight loss tips.

Medline Plus Exercise & Fitness

12345

www.nlm.nih.gov/medlineplus/exerciseandphysicalfitness.html

Medline Plus features an excellent collection of articles on exercise and fitness broken down into categories that include News, From the National Institutes of Health, Overviews, Pictures/Diagrams, Health Check Tools, and Nutrition. Site features separate sections for children and seniors, an interactive tutorial, and links to related areas of Medline Plus that might interest you.

Why Exercise Is Cool

1 2 3 4 5

kidshealth.org/kid/stay_healthy/fit/work_it_out.html

Article for kids on why it's cool to exercise. The home of this page, kidshealth.org/kid/, provides additional information for kids about health issues that relate directly to them. Offered in both English and Spanish.

CROSS-COUNTRY RUNNING

Cool Running

1 2 3 4 5

www.coolrunning.com

Comprehensive site showing the latest running news, calendar of running events, and race results. You'll find a Runner's Voice page, where a successful runner is interviewed each month (you can listen with RealAudio). You can also find out about racing locations and events around the world. Site also features discussion forums.

KidsRunning.com

1 2 3 4 5

www.kidsrunning.com

Site that encourages kids of all ages to start running for their health and well-being. Presented by *Runner's World* magazine.

USATF on the Web

1 2 3 4 5

www.usatf.org

Chosen for the LycosTop 5% of the Web award, this site is home of USA Track and Field, the national governing body for track and field, long-distance running, race walking, and cross country. USATF's 100,000+ members are from clubs, colleges and universities, schools, and other organizations across the country. You can search the site for just about anything related to running.

FITNESS

Bally Total Fitness

1 2 3 4 5

www.ballyfitness.com

From the largest commercial fitness center in the world comes this site, where you can read articles on various fitness-related topics, see what Bally has to offer, find a Bally fitness center near you, and create an online fitness log. Links to Bally Total Fitness store, where you can purchase exercise equipment, clothing, and other items.

The Diet Detective

1 2 3 4 5

www.dietdetective.com

DietDetective.com is "a nutrition, fitness and health resource with thousands of original articles on subjects ranging from beginner athletics to in-depth analyses of exercise equipment and from popular low-calorie food choices to informative break downs on nutrients, disease prevention and the importance of a balanced diet." Most of the content on the site is supplied by none other than the Diet Detective himself, Charles Stuart Platkin, author of more than 250 syndicated columns.

Fitness.com

1 2 3 4 5

www.fitness.com

Fitness.com is "a highly targeted Fitness & Health Search Engine, built to provide you, the Internet users, with the best Fitness & Health results possible." Here, you can find links to the top exercise and fitness websites and discussion forums.

Fitness Jumpsite

1 2 3 4 5

primusweb.com/fitnesspartner

Two certified personal trainers provide quality fitness, health, and nutrition information for anyone interested in getting in shape. The online fitness library offers effective training ideas, proper techniques, books, and fitness news. You'll also find discussion areas, bulletin boards, and a handy calorie calculator.

Fitness Magazine

12345

www.fitnessmagazine.com

Home of *Fitness* magazine, this site features articles from the magazine along with a daily fitness tip, suggested fitness workouts, calorie charts, a BMI calculator, shopping lists, weekly polls, and more.

Best Fitness Online

12345

www.fitnessonline.com

The online home of Weider Productions, Inc., publisher of *Flex, Men's Fitness, Natural Health,* and other magazines, this site features an incredible wealth of information organized in an easy-to-navigate format. Links to exercise, nutrition, and health lead to articles on each subject. An online trainer, fitness calculators, and forums make this the best fitness site on the Web.

Fitness Zone

12345

www.fitnesszone.com

The Fitness Zone offers weekly fitness articles, chat areas, discussions, a library, and FAQs. Visitors can also shop online for fitness equipment, from weights to treadmills and everything in between. And for those of you looking to upgrade your equipment or get into a new sport, the classified ads can help you sell off what you don't want.

Melpomene

12345

www.melpomene.org

Melpomene is dedicated to helping women and girls of all ages get in shape and stay in shape by becoming more physically active and involved. A creative use of menus encourage visitors to Get Informed, Get In Touch, Get In Shape, Get Involved, Get Inspired, and Get In Style. Young women might want to go directly to the Girls Health page by clicking Get Informed and then About Girl's Health.

Men's Fitness.com

12345

www.mensfitness.com

A little soft porn mixed in with a respectable collection of articles on exercise, fitness, nutrition, fashion, and entertainment.

Mirkin Report

www.drmirkin.com

Breakthroughs in health, fitness, nutrition, and sexuality are covered at this site. Dr. Mirkin's radio broadcasts are also available for listening each day, and you can also purchase Dr. Mirkin's books, CDs, and videos through the secure server.

NetSweat

www.netsweat.com

Termed a "goldmine" for gathering useful information on exercise and nutrition through a plethora of links. You can also find a fitness instructor, create a fitness plan, place classified ads, and review a site of the month.

President's Council on Physical Fitness and Exercise

12345

www.fitness.gov

Learn about the President's Challenge to all Americans, especially children, to get fit and stay fit. This site includes quick references for parents, teachers, coaches, and kids, along with a well-stocked reference library of the council's publications.

Walking for Fitness

12345

walking.about.com

This site is a jam-packed resource of recreational walking tips and hints. You can find information about the correct type of walking shoes, the importance of staying hydrated, and walking/diet plans.

PILATES

Balanced Body Pilates

1 2 3 4 5

www.pilates.com

If you're looking for quality Pilates equipment, gear, videos, books, and other Pilates-related merchandise, this should be your first stop. Site features an introduction to the Pilates method, links for Pilates equipment and instruction, a description of the benefits of Pilates, and a calendar of upcoming Pilates events. Plenty here for both novice and professional. You can order a free printed catalog online.

The Pilates Center

1 2 3 4 5

www.thepilatescenter.com

This online home of The Pilates Center, in Boulder, Colorado, provides information about the center and its classes and instructions. It also offers some general information about the history of Joseph Hubertus Pilates and links to other useful sites.

Pilates Method Alliance

1 2 3 4 5

www.pilatesmethodalliance.org

The Pilates Method Alliance is a not-for-profit organization that's dedicated to preserving and promoting classic Pilates method as developed and taught by Joseph Pilates. Here, you can learn what Pilates is all about, check out the background and history of its founder, learn more about the PMA, find a qualified Pilates teacher near you, find out about training programs to become a Pilates teacher, and download useful documents and forms.

Pilates Studio

1 2 3 4 5

www.pilates-studio.com

Pilates Studio is the official website of the New York Pilates Studio. Here, you can learn "the history of the Pilates method of body conditioning and its benefits, locate a certified teacher or studio in your area, discover the value of teacher certification, chat in the forum or shop online to purchase videos, books, clothing and equipment." You can also search for certified Pilates instructors online.

Best Power Pilates

1 2 3 4 5

www.powerpilates.com

Founded by Dr. Howard S. Sichel, Power Pilates is committed to preserving and promoting classical Pilates as taught through the methods of its founder, Joseph Pilates. This site features an introduction to Power Pilates, a brief history of Pilates, myths and truths, a 15-minute foundation workout, and tools for finding studios and instructors. The site itself has a solid foundation, is easy to navigate, and provides excellent information about Pilates, making this our choice as Best of the Best site in the Pilates category.

Winsor Pilates: Official Site

1 2 3 4 5

www.winsorpilates.com

Millions have benefited from low-impact Pilates routines, and now you can visit the official birthplace of Pilates online at the Winsor Pilates site. Here, you can read a handful of success stories, research the background and philosophy behind this innovative fitness approach, and learn more about the trainer behind the movement: Mari Winsor.

RUNNING

American Running Association

1 2 3 4 5

www.americanrunning.org

Good site to visit for exercise information. You'll find sections devoted to nutrition information, injury prevention, rehabilitation, healthcare, strength training, weight management, equipment, and more. A free monthly newsletter is also available.

American Track & Field

1 2 3 4 5

www.american-trackandfield.com

This racing magazine provides an event calendar, race results, training tips, regional and national racing news, and links to related resources.

Best Marathon Training

www.marathontraining.com

If you're planning on becoming a serious marathon runner, this site provides the information you need to train yourself from start to finish. Site features a complete guide on how to begin your training, build up your mileage, prevent common injuries, stretching, weight training, cross training, choosing the right shoes, nutrition, and much more. Site also provides a FAQ, an excellent directory of links to other valuable sites, a discussion forum, a newsletter, and a featured article.

New York City Marathon

www.nyrrc.org/nyrrc/marathon/index.html

New York Road Runners Club maintains this site with information on the New York City Marathon. It includes application information, a course description, advice on how to train for a marathon, and more.

Portland Marathon

1 2 3 4 5

www.portlandmarathon.org

Details about the Portland Marathon, including online registration, a calendar of related events, souvenirs, and results.

Road Running Information Center

1 2 3 4 5

www.runningusa.org

Sponsored by the USA Track & Field organization, this site provides running news, records, rankings, and statistics.

The Runner's Schedule

1 2 3 4 5

www.theschedule.com

This running and racing magazine lets visitors search for event locations, dates, and results. Find subscription information and several running resources.

Runner's Web

1 2 3 4 5

www.runnersweb.com/running.html

Resource for runners. Links to magazines, downloadable software, race results, sports medicine sites, and more. Geared mostly for triathlon competitors.

Runner's World Online

www.runnersworld.com

Runners will turn to this site for calendars of road races and marathons, as well as hyperlinks to other running sites to assist in training for such events. You'll also find nutrition advice, daily running news, a bookstore, recent road and track results, and home remedies for common running conditions.

Running Network

www.runningnetwork.com

Provides a national event calendar, editorials, current news, shoe reviews, results, and links to related pages.

Running Times

1 2 3 4 5

www.runningtimes.com

Home of *Running Times* magazine, this site features articles about runners, running, running races, training tools, shoe reviews, city guides, marathon directories, women's races, coaching tips, and more.

Venue Sports Inc.

www.venuesports.com

Browse or order from the comprehensive catalog of running and track shoes and gear for serious track and field athletes.

WomenRunners.com

www.womenrunners.com

Special running site for women runners who run not only for the fitness aspect of it, but also for the

A B C D E F G H I J K L M N O P Q R S T U V W X Y Z

power it instills in them. Here, women can find special training tips, stretches, and other information that deals specifically with issues relating to women runners. Site also provides areas where you can learn about upcoming races, check race results, follow the progress of your favorite women runners, and learn about new products. Good directory of links to other valuable sites.

WALKING

American Volkssport Association

12345

www.ava.org

Association of pedestrian activist groups in the United States. Great place to track down walking clubs in your area and learn about upcoming events.

Hiking and Walking Home Page

12345

www.webwalking.com/hiking.html

News, hiking and walking clubs, places to go, boots and shoes to wear, walking tips, and more.

Kids Walk to School

12345

www.cdc.gov/nccdphp/dnpa/kidswalk

This site, created by the United States Centers for Disease Control, encourages kids to walk to school and ride their bikes as part of an exercise program to keep our kids fit. In a time when kids are becoming more and more sedentary, this is just the approach we need.

Pedestrian and Bicycle Information Center

12345

www.walkinginfo.org

The PBIC (Pedestrian and Bicycle Information Center) is "a clearinghouse for information about health and safety, engineering, advocacy, education, enforcement and access, and mobility. The PBIC serves anyone interested in pedestrian and bicycle issues, including planners, engineers, private citizens, advocates, educators, police enforcement and the health community." Here, community leaders and interested citizens can learn specific steps to take to make their communities safe places to walk and bicycle.

Racewalk.com

12345

www.racewalk.com

Official race walking home page of USATF provides information to start and improve your walking program, walking events, and products.

The Walking Connection

12345

www.walkingconnection.com

Home of *Walking Connection* magazine, which features articles about walking for exercise and pleasure. Includes articles on walking, training regimens, walking tips, suggested places to walk, walking vacations, treatments for walking injuries, and much more.

Best The Walking Site

12345

www.thewalkingsite.com

This site provides a list of resources for walkers of all fitness levels, especially beginners, and is maintained by an active, enthusiastic walker and marathon walking coach. The site features sections on power walking, race walking, marathon walking, injuries, stretching, nutrition, treadmill walking, and much more. Also includes information about various walking clubs. Although the site doesn't provide an area that will appeal to kids, parents may want to check out the Fit Kids tab to learn the benefits of walking as a family.

WEIGHTLIFTING & BODYBUILDING

Gold's Gym

12345

www.goldsgym.com

Official site of Gold's Gym, this site features articles on fitness and nutrition, a newsletter, discussion areas, and a tool for finding a Gold's Gym near you.

International Powerlifting Federation

12345

www.powerlifting-ipf.com

Everything a powerlifter needs to know about training, competition, and classification. A great site with tons of links! This site includes a link to the technical rulebook in PDF format, as well as information on refereeing. You can also find information on the federation, including the constitution and the bylaws.

Best International Weightlifting Federation

12345

www.iwf.net

The International Weightlifting Federation website is the heavyweight of the Weightlifting category. This well-designed site is packed with great information for weightlifters, coaches, and fans. Links are organized by category including Sport & Organization, Events, News & Media, World Weightlifting, Fan Zone, Shop, and Links. (When we visited the site, the Links option led us only to commercial sites.)

USA Weightlifting

www.msbn.tv/usavision

Home of the National Governing Body (NGB) for Olympic weightlifting in the United States, USAW is a member of the United States Olympic Committee (USOC) and a member of the International Weightlifting Federation (IWF). Here, you can learn more about the organization and the weightlifting competitions it sponsors. Also features information about USAW weightlifters, weightlifting basics, and links to other resources.

Related Site

www.qwa.org

Weight Training & Weightlifting Exercises

12345

weight-training.realsolutionsmag.com

Excellent collection of exercises that focuses on different muscle groups—chest, abs, back, arms, legs, and so on. Each recommended exercise is accompanied by a collection of high-quality photos that shows you in addition to telling you how to perform the exercise.

Weights.net

www.weightsnet.com

Online directory of links to more than 1,700 weightlifting-related sites.

EXPERIENTIAL/OUTDOOR EDUCATION

EnviroEducation.com

12345

www.enviroeducation.com

Site features an extensive, searchable directory of links to environmental schools and programs, along with information on applying to a school, careers and jobs you might qualify for, financial aid to pay for your experiential education, and an excellent introduction to what experiential education is all about.

Outdoor Ed

12345 RSS

www.outdoored.com

Outdoor Ed is "an ever-expanding resource for professionals in the outdoor and experiential education community." Here, you can find articles, conference dates and locations, information on the latest gear, jobs, news, and more.

Outdoor Education Research & Evaluation Center

12345

www.wilderdom.com/research.html

This site revolves around a collection of feature articles that run down the middle of the page, but the links off to the sides open the doors to a host of additional features. Here, you can find an excellent introduction to experiential education (history, philosophy, theory, and research), lesson plans, journals, books, a discussion forum, announcements of upcoming conferences, and more.

Outdoor, Experiential, and Environmental Education

12345

www.ericdigests.org/2003-2/outdoor.html

Good article defining the three closely related educational approaches tries to differentiate the three and explores the question of whether these three disciplines are divergent or convergent.

ASSOCIATIONS

ACCT: Association for Challenge Course Technology

12345

www.acctinfo.org

This site opens with a brief description of the organization and its purpose, but it provides several links to pages that provide additional information. A good place to start is the What Is a Challenge Course? link. The Challenge Course Service Providers link leads you to a list of accredited service providers who are certified to install and inspect challenge courses, train students on them, and provided other related services. Most of the other content at this site is directed toward professional challenge course designers, inspectors, and trainers.

AEE: Association for Experiential Education

12345

www.aee.org

The AEE is "a nonprofit, professional membership association dedicated to experiential education and the students, educators and practitioners that utilize its philosophy." The organization has several goals, including increasing the awareness and recognition of experiential education, offering convenient access to the latest information on experiential education, raising the quality of programs through its accreditation program, and helping educators in the discipline communicate more effectively with one another. Site features publications and other resources, membership information, an online store, a job list, a calendar of conferences, and an excellent introduction to experiential education.

AO: America Outdoors

www.americaoutdoors.org

America Outdoors is an international company whose members are travel outfitters, tour companies, and outdoor educators. These members offer services that include whitewater rafting, canoeing, kayak touring, guest ranch vacations, bicycle touring, fishing trips, teambuilding, climbing, jeep tours, winter sports, and hunting. You can search the directory by state or activity to find fun, educational trips and programs that suit your tastes and interests.

AORE: Association of Outdoor Recreation & Education

12345

www.aore.org

AORE is "a grass roots organization dedicated to advancing the field of outdoor recreation and education." At this site, you can discover more about the organization and how to become a member, check on upcoming conferences, learn about the various awards the association bestows upon those who excel in the field, and visit the career center to receive assistance in producing a resume that gives you the best chance of landing a job in the growing field of experiential education.

CEO: Coalition for Education in the Outdoors

12345

www.outdooredcoalition.org

The Coalition for Education in the Outdoors is "a nonprofit network of environmental education centers, conservation and recreation organizations, schools, fish and wildlife agencies, and businesses to support outdoor education." This site features access to the current and past editions of the *Taproot Journal*, a CEO publication for experiential educators. You can also visit this site to learn more about the organization and how to become a member.

NAAEE: North America Association for Environmental Education

www.naaee.org

The North American Association for Environmental Education (NAAEE) is a network of professionals, students, and volunteers who "promote environmental education and support the work of environmental educators." Site features membership information, notices of upcoming conferences and reports from past conferences, NAAEE publications, an annotated directory of additional resources, NAAEE guidelines for developing effective environmental education programs, and more. The offerings at this site are directed more toward educators and administrators.

NAI: National Association for Interpretation

www.interpnet.com

The first task this site accomplishes is to define *interpretation*: "on-site, informal education programs at parks, zoos, nature centers, historic sites, museums, and aquaria." Now that you know what "interpretation" means, feel free to explore the site for additional information and resources. Site features an association store, a calendar of events, dates and locations of certification programs and training workshops, a list of international programs, a job board, a directory of green pages, and a list of leadership resources.

NRPA: National Parks and Recreation Association

12345

www.nrpa.org

For more than 100 years, the NRPA has been advocating for the significance of making parks, open spaces, and recreational opportunities available to all Americans, so get involved and do your share to help. At this site, you can find out more about the NRPA, its work, and its vision; research the various branches of the NRPA; learn how to become an active advocate in your community; and find out the latest news and information about our national parks. You can shop online for publications, multimedia, apparel, and accessories.

NYSOEA: New York State Outdoor Education Association

1 2 3 4 5 ▲

www.nysoea.org

The New York State Outdoor Education Association is "the leading professional group supporting outdoor education, environmental education, and interpretive services in New York State." Site features a mission statement and a list of the association's goals along with membership information, conference dates and locations, and notices of upcoming events. Not much here for the average student.

PPA: Professional Paddlesports Association

1 2 3 4 5 ▲

www.propaddle.com

If you find yourself upstream without a paddle—or a canoe or a raft or a kayak—check out this site to track down outfitters and retailers by state, city, country, or name. Site also features some good, brief guides on choosing a type of watercraft to paddle and the proper techniques for paddling your craft.

WEA: Wilderness Education Association

1 2 3 4 5 ▲

www.weainfo.org

When we visited this site, it was under construction. We didn't want to omit it, and we certainly couldn't, with clear conscience, pan it by giving it a 1 or a 2, so we gave it a pity score of 3 and recommend that you visit the site as one of your many adventures in your experiential education.

OUTDOOR EDUCATION CENTERS

Adventure Associates

1 2 3 4 5 ▲

www.adventureassoc.com

Companies looking for imaginative team building and corporate training workshops will want to visit this site to see what Adventure Associates has to offer. Company offers ropes courses, team sailing adventures, rock-climbing expeditions, rural and urban search and find missions, and much more. Participants engage in exciting, often fun, activities that hone communication skills, strengthen bonds, and improve leadership skills.

Colorado State Outdoor Adventure Programs

1 2 3 4 5 ▲

campusrec.colostate.edu

Colorado State has a recreation program that reaches far beyond what most colleges and universities have to offer. Here, you can learn about some of its top outdoor adventure programs, including mountaineering expeditions, trips to Ecuador, and introduction to rock climbing, the peak ascent in the Colorado State Forest, and the whitewater rafting expedition. Site features a slide show of Colorado State's challenge course, too.

Glenmore Lodge

1 2 3 4 5 ▲

www.glenmorelodge.org.uk

Glenmore Lodge is located in the heart of Cairngorm National Park, Scotland, and is the home of Scotland's National Outdoor Training Centre. At this site, visitors can learn about the various nature adventure programs that Glenmore Lodge has to offer in mountain biking, paddling, and mountain sport. After you decide on a program that appeals to you, you can learn about costs and dates, how to book your trip, and what to bring. Site also features an unimpressive photo gallery plus a list of tips from the instructors. You can request free brochures online.

Leave No Trace

12345

www.lnt.org

Although Leave No Trace isn't exactly an outdoor education center like NOLS or Outward Bound, it does educate wilderness adventurers and those who seek recreation in the wilderness on their ethical responsibility in leaving nature as they found it. This site introduces visitors to the Leave No Trace seven principles of outdoor ethics and provides additional information and resources for teaching and training others to follow these guidelines.

Best National Outdoor Leadership School

12345

www.nols.edu

After viewing a good sampling of experiential education sites, we were beginning to think that maybe some of these experiential educators needed to climb down from the trees and learn how to use the Internet. This site proves that a few of them have. The NOLS site is attractive, easy to navigate, and packed with useful information. Here, you learn why NOLS is the leader in experiential education. You can explore their various educational programs both for students and for educators. You can apply for a course online, shop at the store, and connect with the school's alumni. Site features an excellent course finder tool that you can use to search for courses by location, desired skill, student age, duration, and month.

North Carolina Outward Bound

12345

www.ncobs.org

This site is the Internet home of Outward Bound's North Carolina location. Here, you can learn about specific Outward Bound educational opportunities in North Carolina. Like the official Outward Bound site described next, this site is attractive and well organized, making it easy to find your way around.

Outward Bound USA

12345

www.obusa.org

Outward Bound single-handedly popularized the concept of experiential education by proving its method capable of turning around the lives of kids who were not excelling in the standard classroom. Outward Bound is continuing to build on its past success with five core programs that "change lives, build teams, and transform schools." The site is built around these five core programs: Wilderness Expeditions, Expeditionary Learning Schools, Professional Programs, Urban Centers, and Outreach/Discovery Programs. Here, you can learn more about these programs and search for a course that's appropriate for a particular age level or search by geographical location. Well-designed site makes it easy to find what you're looking for.

Project Adventure

www.pa.org

Project Adventure is an innovative, not-for-profit, teaching organization dedicated to providing leadership in the expansion of adventure-based experiential programming. Open page provides easy access for a variety of interested visitors. Simply click the link that best describes who you are: Info for Schools, Info for Youth at Risk, Info for Youth and College Programs, Info for Business, Info for Donors, Info for Credentialing, or Grants and Funding. Site features videos, a helpful glossary, a guide for selecting a workshop, and much more.

Shumla School

12345

www.shumla.org

Shumla (education through Studying Human Use of Materials, Land, and Art) promotes learning through hands-on course study. Students are encouraged and empowered to "take responsibility for their social and natural environment and begin to bridge the cultural, social, and economic gaps that mark our society today." At the top of the opening page is a navigation bar that invites visitors to Imagine, Experience, Discover, Participate, and Join. Click Participate to learn about the various programs Shumla has to offer.

A B C D F G H I J K L M N O P Q R S T U V W X Y Z

A B C D E F G H I J K L M N O P Q R S T U V W X Y Z

Wilderness Travel Course

12345

`angeles.sierraclub.org/wtc`

The Sierra Club offers its Wilderness Travel Course as a way of teaching city slickers and others who are less than comfortable in the wilderness how to prepare for their adventures, navigate the wilderness without road signs and clearly marked paths, and survive when your journey doesn't quite go as planned. These courses fill up early, so if you think you might want to enroll, visit this site early and book your trip well in advance.

ROPES/CHALLENGE COURSES

Adventure Experiences, Inc.

12345

`www.advexp.com`

If you're looking to build a challenge course, check out this site to learn what's involved in the design and construction of an effective course and to pick up some ideas of the possibilities. Adventure Experiences, Inc. designs, builds, and maintains challenge courses and trains people on how to use them. What we liked most about this site is that it reveals the many challenges in course design and construction and then provides brief descriptions and explanations of options for meeting those challenges and overcoming any limitations you might face. Each explanation has an accompanying photo, and the photos combine to give you a sense of the vast number of attractive features you can implement in your own challenge course.

Challenge Course Construction

12345

`www.challenge-course-construction.com`

Excellent primer on designing and building a challenge course, covers desired educational goals, costs, equipment, staff training and certification, and steps to building an effective, successful program. Some excellent illustrations on the various components you can build into your challenge course.

ChallengeCoursesWorldwide: A Frappr Map

12345 RSS

`www.frappr.com/challengecoursesworldwide`

A somewhat useful map for locating challenge courses all around the world, but mostly in the United States. Mouse over a marker on the map for the location of the course and instructions on how to obtain additional information.

> **Tip:** Frappr is short for Friend Mapper. It was created by Brian, Kun, and James at Rising Concepts, who wanted to see where all their high school and college friends went. Now it's used by hordes of people to find just about everything.

Northeast Adventure Challenge Courses

12345

`www.neadventure.com`

Northeast Adventure is a "full service challenge course company, offering standard and custom designed elements, installation, skills training, inspections, and repairs." Not much offered here for the average adventure seeker; but if you're in the adventure education business, this site shows you some of the options you have for building a ropes course and hooks you up with professionals who are well qualified to design, build, and maintain a custom course that fits your needs and train your instructors on how to safely use it.

Project Adventure: Challenge Courses

12345

`www.pa.org/chcourses/index.php`

In addition to its wide selection of experiential adventure education courses and workshops, Project Adventure has designed and installed thousands of challenge courses, in all 50 of states and in more than 20 countries around the world. Project Adventure promises to design a course that most effectively meets your educational objectives within the limitations of your grounds or facility.

Ropes Courses

1 2 3 4 5 (rating: 4)

wilderdom.com/ropes

This site offers an excellent introduction to ropes courses—what they are, the benefits they have to offer, and how they simulate some of the experiences we lost through modernization. Site also features discussions of low ropes, high ropes, the history of ropes courses, and the theory and research behind them. Ropes course designers and schools can post photos of their favorite ropes courses and join in the discussion forums.

Boardz

1 2 3 4 5 (rating: 5)

www.boardz.com

Boardz is an online board sports magazine providing entertainment and information for board riders of all kinds, including snowboarders, skateboarders, surfers, skiers, and wakeboarders. In addition to chat and sports-specific information, you can also find surf forecasts and snow reports.

EXTREME SPORTS

Best EXPN Extreme Sports

expn.go.com

ESPN's extreme sports site. Find continuously updated news about extreme sports here. Site features photos, videos, a community center complete with message boards, an event calendar, and plenty of reports from the top eXtreme sports events from around the world. Site links to additional partner sites where visitors can wander off for additional coverage and information. Very well-designed site packed with features to keep eXtreme enthusiasts engaged and entertained.

Extreme Sports Channel

www.extreme.com

Started in 1999 by three extreme sports enthusiasts, the Extreme Sports Channel is dedicated to broadcasting extreme sports videos to as many people it can reach all around the world, including skate, surf, snowboard, moto-x, and BMX videos. Here, you can get a little taste of the contents, check out the program schedule, learn about competitions, connect with other extreme sports fans, and much more. Plenty of photos, videos, and podcasts.

Extreme Sports Online

www.xtsports.com

If you're interested in biking or kayaking in Charlottesville, Virginia, check out this site. Here, you can find out where to go to rent kayaks or mountain bikes and take kayaking classes. Some good general information on choosing the right bike or kayak.

Outside Online

1 2 3 4 5

outside.away.com

Outside Online is the place to go when you're inside and have the urge to set out on an adventure in the great outdoors. Here, you can explore travel opportunities, pick up some great fitness facts, learn new extreme sport techniques and tips, and gear up for your next adventure. You can also check the profiles of your favorite extreme sport athletes.

Parachute Industry Association

1 2 3 4 5

www.pia.com

The objectives of the Parachute Industry Association are to advance and promote the growth, development, and safety of parachuting and to engage and serve participants in the parachute industry. The PIA consists of companies and individuals united by a common desire to improve business opportunities in this segment of aviation. Site contains PIA publications, parachuting Yellow Pages, a product listing, meeting schedule, and more.

PointXCamp

1 2 3 4 5

www.pointx.com

Looking for a summer camp where your kid can learn some new extreme sports moves? Then PointXCamp might be just the thing. Located in Southern California approximately one to two hours from San Diego, Orange County, and Los Angeles, PointXCamp offers sessions on skating, BMX freestyle, inline skating, motocross, and downhill mountain biking.

Sandboard Magazine

12345

www.sandboard.com

Hear all about the sport of riding snowboards over sand dunes, buy equipment, jump into a chat, get the latest sports news, and watch video clips of sandboarders in action.

HANG GLIDING & PARAGLIDING

A–Z of Paragliding

12345

www.paragliding.net

Sensibly categorized, this site contains a useful collection of links and an excellent general paragliding resource.

Adventure Productions

12345

www.adventurep.com

Do you want to learn how to fly an ultralight? Paraglide? Hang glide? Trike? Then this is the place to go for training materials. Based in Reno, Nevada, Adventure Productions offers a variety of videos, CDs, books, and pilot tools designed to help pilots and flight students to take off.

All About Hang Gliding

12345

www.all-about-hang-gliding.com

Comprehensive resource for learning everything you need to know to begin hang gliding and improve your technique and enjoyment of hang gliding. Great collection of books, CDs, and videos you can purchase online. Includes a Getting Started FAQ, photo and video galleries, a list of places to fly organized by state, lists of clubs and organizations, and much more.

BHPA

12345

www.bhpa.co.uk

The British Hang Gliding & Paragliding Association "oversees pilot and instructor training standards, provides technical support such as airworthiness standards, runs coaching courses for pilots...and a host of other services, providing the infrastructure within which U.K. hang gliding and paragliding thrive." Click the Hang Gliding link for a brief overview of hang gliding. Additional links enable you to track down flight schools in the United Kingdom, learn more about BHPA, and explore other hang gliding and flying alternatives you might have not yet considered.

How Hang Gliding Works

12345

www.howstuffworks.com/hang-gliding.htm

Ever wonder how a hang glider remains suspended in the air? Well, this site has the answers. Learn how a hang glider flies and the equipment that's required, and check out a description of a sample flight. Provides links to other related resources too.

Lookout Mountain Hang Gliding

12345

www.hanglide.com

Commercial hang gliding company based in Georgia hosts this site to introduce prospective customers to their various products and services. If you live in Georgia or you're planning a visit and you want to go hang gliding or paragliding, check out this site to see what Lookout Mountain Hang Gliding has to offer. Nicely designed site with excellent photos.

Sydney Hang Gliding Centre

12345

www.hanggliding.com.au

Home of Sydney, Australia's first and only full-time hang gliding centre, where you can learn about tandem hang gliding training, the various courses available, and the equipment you need. Also features a Stories area and a Photograph Gallery, where you can get a small taste of the experience.

United States Hang Gliding Association

12345

www.ushga.org

The association's web page provides plenty of useful information for the hang gliding professional, including the latest in regulations and details on pilot ratings (how to earn your rating, available endorsements, and so on), as well as information on membership benefits, local USHGA chapters, and upcoming competitions and other events.

Related Sites

www.hang-gliding.com

www.birdsinparadise.com

www.wallaby.com

SKATEBOARDING

AKA: GIRL SKATER

12345

www.girlskater.com

Do you think that skateboarding is just for boys? Then visit this site to have your misconception shattered. These girls can ride, and they have the photos and video footage to prove it.

Skateboard.com

12345

www.skateboard.com

Skateboard.com is a hip skateboard store where you can shop online for shoes, decks, trucks, wheels, parts, safety gear, and other skateboard-related merchandise.

Skatepark.org

12345

www.skatepark.org

Not just another skate page, Skatepark.org actually has a cause! If you are working to ensure the legalization of skateboarding in your town or want to build a skate park, come here first to get the latest tips, success stories, and other useful links.

Transworld Skateboarding Magazine

12345 

www.skateboarding.com

Transworld Skateboarding magazine features an excellent collection of videos, photos, trick tips, message boards, online chat rooms, and a searchable directory of skate parks in the United States.

Tum Yeto

12345

www.tumyeto.com

Tum Yeto is a commercial skateboarding site that is mentioned in a several of the top skatingboarding websites. Site features rider profiles, recommended gear, news, a calendar of upcoming events, photos, and links to various companies that market approved skateboarding merchandise. You can sign up online to add your name to the mailing list.

Related Site

www.rollercycle.com

SKYDIVING

Best DropZone

12345 RSS

www.dropzone.com

When looking for skydiving information on the Web, this is the first site you should drop in on. Here, you can find an incredible collection of articles and interviews on skydiving, profiles of skydivers, a list of drop zones, photo and video galleries, discussion forums, a calendar of events and upcoming competitions, and even an auction site where you can buy and sell equipment.

National Skydiving League

12345

www.skyleague.com

Various teams from around the country have websites you can access through this site. You can also access the latest news, information, and products offered by the NSL. Some video footage is also available.

Skydive!

12345

www.afn.org/skydive

This excellent resource for skydiving enthusiasts is full of photos, FAQs, recommended places to skydive, skydiving humor, the sport's history and culture, the latest safety and equipment, training, links to other skydivers, and more. Also includes specific skydiving disciplines such as base jumping, paraskiing, relative work and canopy relative work, freestyle, VRW, and sit-flying. It is one of the most extensive websites available on skydiving and definitely a "don't miss" for any serious skydiver.

Skydiving Fatalities

12345

www.dropzone.com/fatalities

This skydiving fatalities page, created and maintained by DropZone, provides statistics of skydiving fatalities from around the world. It reports fatality statistics in several categories, including collisions, landings, malfunctions, and no pulls. Site also provides links to safety education resources on the Web.

SkyPeople

12345

www.parachutehistory.com/sp/index.php

A directory of skydivers across the country and a huge list of other skydiving links. An exhaustive resource for a variety of skydiving information. Visit this site and cruise the links.

United States Parachute Association

12345

www.uspa.org

Another great resource for skydivers. This national organization's site promotes parachuting issues in government and legal matters. The site contains safety information, training advisories, details of competitions around the world, and USPA membership information.

Related Sites

www.cspa.ca

www.skydiveu.com

www.skydive.ie

SNOWBOARDING

Board the World

12345

www.boardtheworld.com

A complete snowboarding site, offering techniques and tips to improve your form, resort reviews, weather reports, and clothing shopping all in one place.

Burton Snowboards

12345

www.burton.com

Need gear or clothing for your next snowboarding run? Backhill has one of the most extensive selections of technical gear. You can request a catalog if you prefer to order by phone, or have fun participating in a backhill online contest.

Ski Central

12345

skicentral.com

See the views at 220 mountains via snowcams and catch up on ski and snowboarding news, techniques, tips, and trip-planning advice. Links to stores where you can shop for ski and snowboarding equipment online.

Snowboarding2.com

www.snowboarding2.com

Post pictures of yourself in action and check snowcams in place at resorts across the country, including images of competitors at recent competitions. Excellent collection of photos, videos, tips, and snowboard games. Product reviews, gear shopping, and news and weather reports are available here.

Transworld Snowboarding

www.transworldsnowboarding.com/snow

Online magazine only for the most serious snowboarders. Check out the feature articles, buyers' guides, instructions and tips, resort and travel guides, and announcements about the various snowboarding competitions. Site features photos, video clips, message boards, and online chat. You can also check out some cool snowboarding video games and shop online.

HISTORY Sports FINANCE Cooking NATURE Antiques Travel NEWS MUSIC

EYECARE

American Academy of Ophthalmology

12345

www.aao.org

This site provides all the information you will need in the field of eye care—from finding an ophthalmologist near you, to keeping up with recent news stories pertaining to your eyesight, to career options for students interested in the field. You can also purchase educational modules for ophthalmologists as well as other doctors and allied healthcare workers on CD-ROM or in print through the online store. Other items available for purchase include kits to start your own practice.

Eye Care America

12345

www.eyecareamerica.org

EyeCare America's mission is "to reduce avoidable blindness and severe visual impairment by raising awareness about eye disease and care, providing free eye health educational materials and facilitating access to medical eye care." Site features several sections on Seniors Eye Care, Glaucoma Eye Care, Diabetes Eye Care, and Children's Eye Care. If you're currently concerned about the condition of your eyes and you don't know where to turn, check out the Helpline Information for a toll-free number to call. Plenty of helpful resources, including free downloadable brochures, are available at this site.

Best Eye Care Source

12345

www.eyecaresource.com

Eye Care Source is packed with information for eye care professionals, patients, and interested visitors. It covers almost every topic related to vision correction and eye care, including Lasik surgery, macular degeneration, and contact lenses. The Optometrist Directory is a little limited, providing lists of optometrists primarily in big cities. However, the site is well designed and offers an excellent variety of information for both patients and doctors, making it our choice as the Best of the Best in the Eye Care category.

Eyeglasses.com

12345

www.eyeglasses.com

Learn how to choose eyewear that complements your face here, where you can find many frames and lenses to choose from, including many by well-known designers. You can buy glasses including prescription lenses here.

Eye Injury First Aid

12345

eyeinjury.com/firstaid.html

Brief list of emergency procedures for treating traumatized eyes. Covers everything from specks in the eye to chemical burns.

Financial Aid for Eye Care

12345

www.nei.nih.gov/health/financialaid.asp

Information on organizations that fund eye care treatments is available at this site, so if your vision is suffering or you've been diagnosed with a condition that you can't afford to treat, check out this site for financing options.

Finding an Eye Care Professional

12345

www.nei.nih.gov/health/findprofessional.asp

General strategies and information resources suggested for identifying a qualified eye care professional appropriate for your particular vision situation are provided at this site.

Macular Degeneration Foundation

12345

www.eyesight.org

Learn about what macular degeneration is, what causes it, and what research is being conducted to find out about it.

National Eye Institute

12345

www.nei.nih.gov

Visitors will find comprehensive information about eye diseases, including diagrams of healthy and diseased eyes and videos. Suitable for consumers and professionals, this site is objective and helpful. Additional links to other eye care organizations are available.

Prevent Blindness America

www.preventblindness.org

Preventing blindness often starts by recognizing when there is a problem with your eyes. So, one of the best tools available at this site is an eye test you can take. You'll also find information about eye health and safety for adults and children.

FANTASY SPORTS

ESPN.com Fantasy Sports

1 2 3 4 5 ▲ Blog

games.espn.go.com/frontpage

ESPN.com provides dozens of online fantasy sports from football and baseball, to basketball, hockey, tennis, and more. Here, you will find indexes with information and tools, current games, and teams. Join the message forum to discuss your favorite teams, games, and athletes. You can also set up or join a league for the current season of fantasy football.

Fantasy Sports Central

1 2 3 4 5 ▲

www.fantasysportscentral.com

Calling itself "the best-kept secret in fantasy sports," this site provides the latest information on fantasy football, baseball, and basketball. See what's new, read the updates, and find out about current rankings, projections, and mock drafts. Apply online to become an FSC member. This site also provides a link to purchase tickets to your favorite sporting events.

Sandbox: Fantasy Sports

1 2 3 4 5 ▲

www.sandbox.com

With more than 25 fantasy sports games and a host of powerful features, Sandbox is *the* place to go to engage in fantasy sports. Draft your players, build your team, and go head to head with other players to compete for the championship and win big cash prizes. Membership is available; sign up online.

SportsLine.com's Fantasy Page

1 2 3 4 5 ▲

www.sportsline.com/fantasy

Find information on fantasy football, baseball, golf, soccer, and racing here. Read about fantasy news and purchase your own fantasy league. Get scores and draft information about your favorite teams and players.

FASHION

Dior

1 2 3 4 5

www.dior.com

Christian Dior calls this site home, and you can now obtain information about the latest Dior designs, fragrances, jewelry, makeup, and other products. Site is bilingual—English and French. Interesting images, but site is not user friendly.

Donna Karan

1 2 3 4 5

www.dkny.com

Home of the popular DKNY line, this site provides an online newspaper with information about the goings on at Donna Karan, plus a link that takes you to the Donna Karan Fragrances page. The design and graphics are pretty cool, but some of the links were nonfunctional. Click on the FAQs for order information. You can also search the store locator to find a DKNY store near you. Looking for a job? Click on the Career button at the bottom.

ELLE.com

1 2 3 4 5 RSS

www.elle.com

Self-described as a "complement and counterpart to the magazine," this French fashion site provides a more intellectual, sophisticated approach to fashion, beauty, and style. In addition to being packed with beauty and fashion tips, ELLE.com goes behind the scenes in the fashion industry to provide readers with hands-on techniques and the best fashion secrets. The Shop link provides links to other sites where you can purchase items online. Provides information on your favorite designers and runway shows.

Givenchy

1 2 3 4 5

www.givenchy.com

Check out the Givenchy fashions and products. This site provides one-click access to women's and men's fashion, accessories, sunglasses, perfumes & cosmetics, boutiques, news, and history.

Hint Fashion Magazine

1 2 3 4 5 

www.hintmag.com

This cutting-edge fashion magazine features interviews with the top fashion designers, articles about various fashion shows, photos by top fashion photographers, columns, message boards, classified ads, and more. There's even a Hit Shop where you can purchase cool T-shirts. This site requires online registration for access to most of the good stuff.

Issey Miyake

1 2 3 4 5

www.isseymiyake.com

This Flash-enabled site features a virtual fashion show that might not be the most intuitive to navigate, but features impressive graphics. Connect to this home page, click the desired season, and then point and click to move through the fashion show. Don't expect any buttons or onscreen clues—just point and click. Choose from women's and men's collections.

Polo.com

www.polo.com

You can browse Ralph Lauren's Polo line at this site, which provides quick links to fashions for men, women, and children; shoes; home products; fragrances; and gifts. You can shop online, search for stores, or scan the Polo ads. Check out the Style Guide for answers to fashion and decorating tips. There's also a video to watch the latest RL fashion shows.

STYLE.com

www.style.com

Home of *Vogue* and *W* magazines. This site features fashion advice for the chic, online fashion shows, shopping, and more. Includes information on the latest styles, model and celebrity profiles, and fashion tips. Visit this site to keep up on the latest fashion and lifestyle trends.

Tommy Hilfiger

www.tommy.com

This site provides information and online shopping for Tommy Hilfiger fashion and products. By registering, you can receive the Tommy Hilfiger newsletter via email, become eligible for contests and sweepstakes, download wallpaper and screensavers, play games, obtain free chat icons, and more.

Vogue

www.style.com/vogue

Home of *Vogue* magazine, one of the top style magazines in the world. Here, you can find the current feature article, the latest fashion news and talk, and the editor's picks. The site also offers links to nutrition, fitness, and weight loss information. You can subscribe to *Vogue*, and use the forum to chat about fashion, shopping, and beauty.

Yves Saint Laurent

www.ysl.com

This official site of Yves Saint Laurent introduces you to the latest men's and women's fashions, accessories, and beauty aids of one of the premier designers. Not the most exciting site; Flash pages can load a bit slowly.

Best ZOOZOOM.com Magazine

www.zoozoom.com

The "original online glossy," this intriguing, refreshing online fashion magazine goes beyond fashion to explore the interconnectedness of art, culture, society, and other human factors in the evolution of fashion. Very cutting edge, this site presents various fashion concepts and designs in slide-show format. Also features profiles of some of the top fashion designers. Small videos for viewing available here. Easy pick for the Best of the Best award.

FENG SHUI

American Feng Shui Institute

12345 RSS

www.amfengshui.com

"The mission of the institute is to teach the art of Feng Shui as a scientific discipline developed by Master Sang." Here, you can get information about learning Feng Shui online or in person; visit the bookstore; view the calendar of classes and events; meet instructors; and read answers to frequently asked questions.

Cyber Feng Shui Club

12345

www.cyberfengshui.com

Feng Shui is the ancient Chinese art of the proper and auspicious arranging and placement of furnishings and accessories. This site helps you apply the concepts of Feng Shui to your own interior designs and room arrangements. Provides free Feng Shui information including a list of benefits, daily four pillars, and horoscope. You can ask a question and shop for Feng Shui items. There is also a message board and a chatroom. However, you must be a registered member to gain access to most pages.

Best Fast Feng Shui

12345 Blog RSS

www.fastfengshui.com

This site provides a wealth of information about Feng Shui to help energize your home and all aspects of life. Purchase books, products and gifts; and find Feng Shui tips and articles. You can also learn about the nine principles of Feng Shui and read through the FAQs and newsletter for more insight.

Feng Shui Times

12345

www.fengshuitimes.com

Here, you will find featured articles about classical and general Feng Shui, and tutorials for beginners, intermediate, or advanced students. Read about the featured book of the month, find out what's new, and join in a discussion on the news forums. Find a Feng Shui practitioner in your area; just click on the country where you live, and a list of names will come up.

FINANCE & INVESTMENT

About Credit

12345 RSS

credit.about.com

Learn how high-interest loans can torpedo your personal finances. Reduce and eliminate your personal debt by budgeting and consolidation. Huge collection of articles dealing not only with credit management but also with personal and family finances, living a frugal lifestyle, investing, and planning for retirement. Log into the forum to join discussions about credit/debt management.

Related Sites

- financialplan.about.com/mbody.htm
- retireplan.about.com/mbody.htm
- economics.about.com/mbody.htm
- beginnersinvest.about.com/mbody.htm
- mutualfunds.about.com/mbody.htm

CreditReport.com

12345

www.creditreport.com

Want to know what your bank and mortgage company already know about your finances? Then order a credit report with information from the big three credit agencies—Experian, Equifax, and Trans-Union. For about $30, you can order a report online and view the report right on your computer or receive it through the mail. Credit reports can reveal discrepancies between your records and the records of credit card companies and other credit institutions. They might even show if someone else is charging purchases using your name and Social Security number! Be sure to read the FAQs for answers to general credit report questions.

ManagingMyMoney.com

12345

www.managingmymoney.com

This site features an excellent grouping of articles on how to stabilize your finances by practicing fiscal restraint. Here, you learn how to live within your means, manage debt, develop a spending plan, pay your taxes, shop for insurance, turn your dreams into goals, and more. Tips and worksheets provide the tools you need to begin evaluating your current finances and planning for the future.

Microsoft Money Central's Planning Section

moneycentral.msn.com/planning/home.asp

Learn how to budget, plan for retirement, stash away some cash for junior's college tuition, and shop for homeowner's and car insurance.

Best Money Magazine's Money 101 Tutorial

12345 RSS

money.cnn.com/pf/101

Money magazine's step-by-step tutorial on how to take control of your personal finances consists of 23 lessons covering everything from drawing up a budget, and controlling debt, to estate planning, and investing in stocks. Learn how to plan for retirement, save for a child's education, finance a new home, reduce your tax burden, and much more. When you decide to start taking control of your finances, be sure to bookmark this site, and return to it often for advice and ideas.

Quicken.com

12345

www.quicken.com

Home of Intuit's Quicken, the most popular personal finance management program on the market. Here, you'll find articles on buying a new home, refinancing, planning for retirement, preparing your taxes, and tips and resources for using Quicken. Advanced features enable you to create an investment portfolio so that you can constantly monitor how your investments are doing. You can also research specific investment vehicles, get up-to-date alerts and news, and update personal files created using Quicken to monitor your investments.

BANKING

Best Bank of America

12345

www.bankofamerica.com

Bank of America is a full-service bank that provides its customers with online savings and checking accounts, credit cards, loans and mortgages, investment information and opportunities, and much more, plus educational information and resources to help them manage their finances more intelligently. Includes other helpful information about buying a home, moving, and purchasing a car. This site is attractive, well organized, and packed with useful information, products, and services, making it our choice as Best of the Best banking website.

Citibank

12345

www.citibank.com

Tired of calling your bank every time you need information about your account, or want to make a transfer? Then consider banking online at Citibank. From the home page, you can see what types of products and services Citibank has to offer: savings and checking accounts, online bill payment, credit cards, loans and mortgages, investment opportunities, paperless bank statements, email and wireless alerts, wire transfers, and more.

EH.net

12345 RSS

eh.net

Excellent site featuring information about economics and finance. The How Much Is That? feature is particularly interesting, providing statistics on the history of inflation, the fluctuating value of the dollar, changes in the price of gold, and much more. This site is managed by Economic History Services, which supports the study and teaching of economic history. Download information from the databases, read course syllabi and abstracts, and review links to related sights.

E*TRADE Banking

12345

https://bankus.etrade.com

E*TRADE provides all the banking services normally available—checking and savings accounts, online transfers, money market accounts, CDs, and credit cards. And, if you can keep a minimum balance of $5,000, most of the services are free. In addition, E*TRADE will refund any ATM charges you pay when getting cash from any ATM! Online bill payment is available through Bill Pay. Find information on mutual funds, ETFs and bonds, retirement & advice, and mortgages & home equity.

EverBank

12345

www.everbank.co

EverBank is one of the fastest growing banks in the nation, due in part to its customer bill of rights. Here, you will find all the products and services you expect, along with higher than average investment returns on savings, checking, and money market accounts. View and compare banking rates, and get credit card and home loan information. You can also search employment opportunities, just click on the careers link at the top. Visit this site to see what EverBank has to offer, and if you like what you see, open an account today.

NetBank

1 2 3 4 5

www.netbank.com

With the motto "No branches means better value," NetBank explains why it can offer such low fees and high interest rates on its customers' accounts. NetBank offers the usual banking services and accounts, but also offers loans, financial planning, investments, and insurance to provide for all of your financial needs. Interested in working with NetBank? Click on their careers link at the bottom of the page for more information. Site is attractive and easy to navigate.

Wells Fargo

www.wellsfargo.com

Wells Fargo offers a complete line of banking products and services, including online banking, bill pay, ATM withdrawals, check cards, savings accounts, and CDs. In addition, it features loans and credit, investment options, and insurance. Use the self-service option to view account balances, view check images, request a statement, set up direct deposit, and more. No matter what your financial needs, Wells Fargo has a product or service that can meet it.

Related Sites

- www.americanexpress.com/banking
- www.ascenciabank.com
- www.boh.com
- www.chase.com
- www.commerceonline.com
- www.53.com
- www.fleet.com
- www.huntington.com

BONDS

Best Bond Market Association

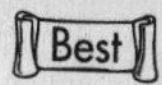

www.investinginbonds.com

Read about what percentage of your portfolio should be in bonds, run through the investors' checklist to determine whether you should invest in bonds, learn about the different types of bonds, and stay updated on current bond prices at this site. Read market headline news and recent commentary. If the stock market frightens you or you're just looking for investments that are a little less risky, this is the site for you.

Bonds Online

1 2 3 4 5

www.bonds-online.com

Extensive market information for tax-free municipal bonds, treasury/savings bonds, corporate, bond funds, and brokers. Bond investment information is available from the Bond Professor. Read about today's market, investor tools, and use the search/quote center for pricing and information on more than 3.5 million stocks and bonds. Link to Bondpage.com where members can trade bonds online.

CNNfn Bond Center

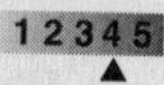

money.cnn.com/markets/bondcenter

Get the latest rates, short-term rates, and more information on municipal and corporate bonds. This page also has information on hot stocks and commodities.

TreasuryDirect

1 2 3 4 5

www.savingsbonds.gov

Whether you want to invest in United States savings bonds or have some that you want to cash in, this is the site for you. Here, you can learn more about a low-risk investment option and how much you can expect to earn in interest over the life of the bond. You can even purchase bonds online. Information for individual/personal, institutional, and government securities.

A B C D E F G H I J K L M N O P Q R S T U V W X Y Z

INVESTMENT CLUBS

Bivio

1 2 3 4 5

www.bivio.com

Bivio is a web-delivered application that enables groups of individual investors to create and manage their own investment clubs online, kind of like creating your own personal mutual fund. Browse club home pages, search the club café, and know your options. The name Bivio is derived from the Latin *bivium*, "where two roads meet."

Best Motley Fool's Guide to Investment Clubs

1 2 3 4 5 RSS

www.fool.com/InvestmentClub/InvestmentClubIntroduction.htm

Excellent tutorial on investment clubs by two savvy but motley fools. Explains what an investment club is, why such clubs are useful, how to join an existing club or create your own, and much more. Even discusses potential pitfalls. A must-read for anyone considering joining an investment club. Products & Services include a Blue Chip report, how-to guides, discussion boards, and more.

INVESTMENT INFORMATION

10K Wizard

1 2 3 4 5 Blog RSS

www.10kwizard.com

Online financial toolbox packed with utilities designed to gather data concerning various companies whose stock is traded publicly. 10K Wizard, originally designed to help users search the SEC database, provides additional search tools for grabbing data from a multitude of online databases. Other products include the Portfolio Wizard, for helping you track your stocks, and a free trial of Hoover's Online, for gaining additional insights from professional analysts. Become a subscriber to gain unlimited access, and view full-text searches and real-time alerts.

American Association of Individual Investors

1 2 3 4 5

www.aaii.com

AAII provides investment education, including investment basics, financial planning, retirement, and building an investment portfolio. Here, you can register for the newsletter, read articles, access tools and publications, and much more. Excellent site for beginning and intermediate investors. Become a member and enjoy such benefits as the monthly AAII Journal, AAII.com access, stock & fund portfolios, and much more. FAQs answer questions about technical/troubleshooting, investing basics, stocks, bonds, mutual funds, and personal finance.

Biospace

1 2 3 4 5

www.biospace.com

If you focus your investing on biotech companies, Biospace can help provide the information and analysis you need to make more educated decisions. Check out specific biotech companies by name, read late-breaking biotech news and results of clinical trials, and check out the investor newsletters. There is also a career center for job seekers and employers.

Financial Engines

1 2 3 4 5

www.financialengines.co

Co-founded and chaired by Bill Sharpe, Financial Engines is a financial service company devoted to helping financial institutions, employers, and financial advisers make sound investment decisions for their clients. Here, you can learn more about the company and its products, and by registering, you gain access to some valuable online tools. Go through the Financial Forecast to learn more about where you stand and what you can expect to need for your retirement, and then collect information on how you should be investing to meet your future needs. View the advisory services for a personal evaluation, personal online advisor, personal asset manager, and fiduciary FAQs.

Financial Times

12345 RSS

news.ft.com/home/us

This site is packed with late-breaking business news from around the world. Get the scoop on what OPEC is up to, how the dollar stacks up against the euro, and how business is doing in the Pacific Rim. Excellent reports, commentary, and analysis! Some articles require a subscription to view them, you can subscribe to the *Financial Times* on this site.

GreenMoneyJournal Online Guide

www.greenmoneyjournal.com

An information resource from the *GreenMoney Journal* for people interested in socially and environmentally responsible business, investing, and consumer resources. Information on companies' environmental track records is available, along with tips for socially responsible investing. Links to related information and subscriptions to the *GreenMoney Journal* are available here.

Hoover's Online

12345

www.hoovers.com

A great research tool for investors. Hoover's provides company profiles plus free access to records on public and private companies. Here, you can find out how well a company has done in the past. Take a free tour of Hoover's, which includes samples of subscriber content including research, prospecting, competitive analysis, public and private companies, and FAQs.

Investopedia

12345 RSS

www.investopedia.com

Are you thinking about investing? Have you started investing but you really don't feel comfortable yet? Then check out Investopedia, the online encyclopedia where you can take a tutorial on the basics, move up to more-advanced topics, peruse an assortment of investment information and tips, access free tools and calculators, play an investment game, test your knowledge with quizzes, and much more. Purchase exam prep materials for financial certification exams, professional education, and career resources.

Investor's Business Daily

12345

www.investors.com

Investor's Business Daily is a magazine focusing on issues important to today's investor. On this site, you can read today's issue. IBD also offers access to a free online IBD investment education course. You'll also find information on news, research, and analysis, IBD stock list, how to invest, and free membership.

Kiplinger

12345

kiplinger.com

Kiplinger puts financial events in perspective on a daily basis. Stock quotes, mutual fund rankings, financial FAQs, financial calculators, and interactive resources are available. You'll also find information on personal finance and business forecasts, newsletters, and subscriptions to *Kiplinger's* magazine.

Marketocracy

12345

www.marketocracy.com

Find out when and what the top investors are buying, and follow their lead by subscribing to Marketocracy. Here, you can obtain alerts about which stocks to buy that often goes against the current trend. Become a member and test your skills at running a fund. You will get a chance to try out investing strategies in a realistic trading environment. There is also information about the top-ranking funds.

Money Central

12345

moneycentral.msn.com/investor/home.asp

Geared for subscribers, this site provides helpful investing information to nonsubscribers as well, although not as detailed as the subscriber data. Use Microsoft Investor to get up-to-date company information, news, and stock market quotes. Here, you can research stocks and funds, get stock ratings, and view accounts. Read message boards for more investing information.

A B C D E G H I J K L M N O P Q R S T U V W X Y Z

A B C D E F G H I J K L M N O P Q R S T U V W X Y Z

Money Magazine

12345

money.cnn.com

From the editors of CNN and *Money* magazine, this site features an up-to-the-minute overview of the day's stock markets. Includes business news and events likely to affect the day's stock prices, plus some informative articles on personal finance, jobs and economy, and real estate.

Prophet.net

12345

www.prophet.net

Prophet.net has a reputation as one of the leading sites for providing technical analysis of stocks. Tim Knight, founder of Prophet.net, has based the system he created on his own investment approach to combine the power of software with the immediacy of streaming data and the availability of the Web to help investors achieve consistent profits in an inconsistent market. Sign up for a free seven-day trial to see what Prophet.net has to offer. Here, you can explore tools that will help you find new trading opportunities, analyze charts, and manage your money, and find answers to FAQs.

Red Herring

12345 RSS

www.redherring.com

Provides recent stock market information and in-depth analysis on the forces driving innovation, technology, entrepreneurship, and financial markets. Categories include daily stock charts, bimonthly mutual fund charts, and top stocks. Read articles and Q&A, and find out about upcoming events.

Reuters Investor

12345 RSS

www.investor.reuters.com

Excellent information and resource site for investors to check stock prices, check late-breaking news, ETFs, and commodities, track stock performance, and research potential investment opportunities. Reuters has a long history and a solid reputation for providing accurate, timely information, which is crucial to helping investors make the right decisions. Registration is free, but access to the better research data and analyses will cost you.

RiskGrades

12345

www.riskgrades.com

How risky are those investments you're making or thinking about making? Here, you can run your stock symbols through the system and have them graded from 0 (no risk) to 10,000 (roll-the-dice risky). Find out how your stocks would fare in a crisis. There is also information to guide you through starting your own RiskGrade Measure, a portfolio analysis, asset selection, and a course for understanding risk.

Silicon Investor

12345

www.siliconinvestor.com/index.gsp

Consists of five innovative areas for technology investors: Stocktalk, Market Tools, Market Insight, Customize, and Portfolio. These areas enable you to participate in discussion forums, create individual charts and comparison charts, view company profiles, get quotes and other financial information, and track your portfolio. As a member, you will be eligible for many features and privileges. Read the FAQs for answers to many questions about investing.

The Stock Market Game

12345

www.smgww.org

Stock market game created and maintained by the Securities Industry Foundation for Economic Education (SIFEE), an affiliate of the Securities Industry Association. This game is intended for use in schools, primarily for grades 4–12, to help teach children and teenagers about money and investments. Check out the FAQs for more information about the program, educational value, participant requirements, and technical questions.

Stock-Track Portfolio Simulations

12345

www.stocktrak.com

Put together your own investment portfolio and track its progress online. The portfolio simulator costs about $19 per account and is used primarily in high schools, colleges, and other schools to provide a relatively safe place for investors to get some hands-on trading without losing any real money. Information available to college professors and students, as well as individual investors. Use the Research Desk to get basic information, read newsletters, find investment sites, and read the glossary of finance and investment terms.

TheStreet.com

thestreet.com

Free services at The Street include market reports, commentary, news, and research access, but you'll have to pay a fee to get live market updates and stock analyses. Also find information for personal finance, markets, and view StreetWatch videos.

ValueEngine.com

12345

www.valuengine.com

ValueEngine.com provides the same stock valuation, risk management, and forecasting technology to individual investors that professional investors have been using for years. Here, you can check the valuations of stocks you own or plan on buying to evaluate potential risk, check breaking news, and obtain detailed analysis of various stocks. You can also access tools for tracking your portfolio. Visit the user forum to ask a question or read what members have to say. Read FAQs for more information.

Yahoo! Finance

12345

finance.yahoo.com

Provides financial data for investors, including current quotes on stocks, options, commodity futures, mutual funds, and bonds. Also provides business news, market analysis and commentary, financial data, and company profiles. Excellent place to check the latest market overview and see what other investors have to say about market trends. Also includes information on retirement & planning, banking & credit, loans, and taxes.

Yodlee

12345

corporate.yodlee.com

Yodlee is a company that specializes in account aggregation—providing consumers with single-site access to all their accounts, including bank accounts, investment accounts, insurance, and so on. Provides solutions for consumer banking, payments, and risk and wealth management. Yodlee is a third-party provider of account aggregation for banks, insurance companies, and financial institutions, so average users like you and me won't have much direct contact with Yodlee.

Young Investor.com

www.younginvestor.com/

This is a great site for kids and novice investors alike to learn the basics of investing and test their skills without the risk of losing money. Sign up to compete with other investors for bragging rights, or play one of the many online money games. Also features a lounge for parents and teachers that provides tips on teaching youngsters about money.

IPOS (INITIAL PUBLIC OFFERINGS)

IPO Controversy

12345

www.corante.com/reports/ipo

Are some IPOs a scam orchestrated by companies to rip off the public? Many might be. This report, from *CORANTE Daily*, takes an in-depth look at IPOs and the process that promotes them to reveal how ethical the process really is. Read through the special five-part report, and find book related to the topic. You can also subscribe to their newsletter, which is emailed to you every morning.

IPO Home

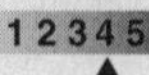

www.ipohome.com/default.asp

Like other IPO sites, this site provides a ton of information about upcoming IPOs, planned pricing, and rankings of past performers to give you a sense of how IPOs typically perform. Also includes tool and information for the IPO newcomer. Stay up-to-date with breaking IPO news, too. And research companies of interest.

MUTUAL FUNDS

Brill's Mutual Funds Interactive

www.brill.com/features.html

Features articles on what's happening in the mutual fund industry, including topics such as "Investing for Retirement" and "The Best Choices in Variable Annuities." Read insightful articles and browse the archives. Other features include The Clip Board, which gives helpful tips from fellow investors, and the Investor's Bookstore, which provides selected books for fund investors.

Dreyfus Corporation

www.dreyfus.com

The Dreyfus Online Information Center provides listings and descriptions of some of the mutual funds offered by Dreyfus, along with the Dreyfus services. The site provides information that can help investors get a clearer sense of the direction to take to meet their investment objectives. In addition to general information on investing, you'll also find current economic commentaries on the financial markets updated weekly by Dreyfus portfolio managers. Interested in working with Dreyfus? Check out their Career section for job postings.

Fidelity

www.fidelity.com

A comprehensive site full of investment information. Fidelity provides services to the personal and institutional investor. Fidelity is a well-known and trusted investment firm, and its site is worthwhile reading for anyone wanting to use Fidelity's services. Products include mutual funds, trading, 401(k) rollovers, IRAs, active trading, college planning, and annuities.

Janus Funds

ww4.janus.com

Janus Funds provides access to information on the funds the company manages. You can check your funds' latest share prices and account values 24 hours a day, 7 days a week. You can also find projected year-end dividends for each fund. All account information is accessed through security-enhanced web pages utilizing SSL. Janus can get you started with investing basics, helping establish your goals, and provides applications and forms.

Morningstar

www.morningstar.com

Start at Morningstar University to find answers to all your investing and mutual fund questions, and then check the Fund Quickranks for ideas of which stocks and mutual funds are performing the best. You can also do more in-depth research on funds, read up on previous Morningstar reports, and track your portfolio. For about $100 annually, you can subscribe to Morningstar to take advantage of premium services. Join forums to discuss topics on investment banking, mutual funds, and stock picks, among others.

Best Mutual Fund Investor

www.mfea.com

Find funds that cost less than $50 or the ones that have the lowest minimum investment with the help of the Mutual Fund Education Alliance. You can also use online calculators to estimate what you'll need for your retirement or other major purchases, such as your child's college education. With information on how to get started with little money down, this site is one of the better ones. Find information on how to buy mutual funds, and read news and commentary to learn about what's happening in the world of investing.

Personal Fund

12345

`personalfund.com`

Find the fund that best meets your needs—whether it's for a high-yield investment or no taxes. Find out how your funds compare cost-wise and sign up for Andrew Tobias's regular mutual fund newsletter. Read investing Q&A, and use the tools to find more information about the high cost of mutual funds.

ProFunds

12345

`www.profunds.com`

At this site, you can obtain ProFunds overviews, profiles, prices, and performance statistics for the various mutual funds. Read through the ProFunds Overview for FAQs, investment strategies, hot topics, and news. You can also open an account online.

Putnam Investments

12345

`www.putnam.com`

Get the latest news on new Putnam funds, decide whether a Roth IRA is for you, and find out how well your Putnam investment is doing. Provides information for individual investors including mutual funds, college savings 529 plans, annuities, rollover IRAs, and non-U.S. funds. A listing of career opportunities is also available.

T. Rowe Price

12345

`www.troweprice.com`

Use the T. Rowe Price investment service to track down the fund that's right for you and then track its performance at the site. Small business owners, investment advisors, and people planning for retirement might want to look into the specialized sections on the individual investing needs of these groups of people. Career information at T. Rowe Price is also available.

TCW Mutual Funds

12345

`www.tcw.com`

For more than 30 years, TCW has been providing investment management services. TCW specializes in U.S. Equities, U.S. Fixed Income, Alternatives, and International strategies. Their client services provides Institutional Investors, Consultants, Private Clients, Financial Advisors, Individual Investors, and Managed Account Services. Read through the FAQs for answers to questions about investing with TCW.

Vanguard

`www.vanguard.com`

Learn about investing, develop a personal financial plan, search for a mutual fund, and check pricing and performance here at Vanguard's site. You can also do more research and get news updates. Also includes information for financial advisors. Search the career page to find jobs and internships with Vanguard.

ONLINE TRADING

CyberTrader

12345 RSS

`www.cybertrader.com`

A full-featured investment program and service for cutting-edge trading on the NASDAQ and listed NYSE stocks. Supports real-time trading as low as $9.95 per trade (minimum of 20 trades). Open an account online, review information regarding margin & fees, platform, equities & derivatives, and education & resources.

A B C D E G H I J K L M N O P Q R S T U V W X Y Z

A B C D E F G H I J K L M N O P Q R S T U V W X Y Z

E*TRADE

1 2 3 4 5

www.etrade.com

E*TRADE is another online trading service geared toward the individual investor. With E*TRADE, you can buy and sell securities online for NYSE, AMEX, and NASDAQ. Stock performance information and company information are available. Find information on trading & portfolios, quotes & research, mutual funds, ETFs & bonds, retirement & advice, banking & credit cards, and mortgages & home equity. Open an account online. Pricing from $6.99 per trade.

Firstrade

1 2 3 4 5

www.firstrade.com

Offering trades for as low as $6.95, Firstrade is one of the least-expensive online investing services on the Internet. The purchase of each trade includes no inactivity or maintenance fees, no minimum to start investing, unlimited account protection, and online fixed income investing. Its research tools are a little sparse; but if you subscribe to an investment information newsletter already and just need a vehicle for placing trades, this might be the place for you. Includes information on commissions & fees, a broker comparison, products & services, and retirement.

FOLIOfn

1 2 3 4 5

www.foliofn.com

FOLIOfn is an online broker that uses a slightly different model for its investors, enabling investors to create a diversified portfolio for less in trading costs. Ready-to-go portfolios allow you to purchase a collection of securities (typically 30 to 50 different securities) for the price of a single trade. For a monthly fee of about $20, you get unlimited trading to create a custom portfolio, or you can trade for about $4 per transaction. Check out this site to learn more. Open a personal, business, or retirement account online.

Best Investing Online Resource Center

1 2 3 4 5

www.investingonline.org

Whether you're just thinking about investing online or you have already started, this site provides some revealing and useful information that can help you become a more savvy investor and avoid potential scams. If you haven't tried online investing, take the quiz to determine whether you're ready, and then move on to other sections to learn how to open an account, check online broker ratings, and check up on your broker or advisor. If you're somewhat of a veteran, you can learn more about your rights, determine the real cost of day trading, and check out some of the best investment resources on the Web. This site also features several simulators that enable you to practice online investing without getting burned. Read the eight things every online investor should know.

Merrill Lynch Direct

1 2 3 4 5

www.mldirect.ml.com

Receive stock opinions and recommendations from Merrill Lynch analysts, and then execute stock trades for $29.95, or do some more research on your own. Access free S&P reports; get free real-time stock quotes; and check into the performance of stocks, bonds, and mutual funds. Read a list of FAQs for answers to your questions about mutual funds and stock options with Merrill Lynch.

Morgan Stanley

1 2 3 4 5

www.morganstanley.com

A nice all-around solid site, with online trading available, as well as educational tools, mutual fund research, IPO information, market news, and the option to open a free, no-fee IRA. On this site, you can also track your checking and savings accounts as well as your credit cards. Information on careers available here, too.

Online Trading Academy

www.tradingacademy.com

Do you want to try your hand at day trading? Then check out this site, where you can find courses, books, and other training materials to bring you up to speed. Free Direct Access Training workshop, and free online classes and trading quiz.

Schwab Online Investing

www.schwab.com

This online trading service from Charles Schwab offers discount brokering services to individual investors. Trading online with Schwab offers convenience and control, at stock commissions of $29.95. You'll also find an extensive listing of mutual funds. Find products & services for mutual funds, active trading, margin loans, and investment advice. Read news & insights about the Schwab Security Guarantee, a daily market update, webcasts, and Chuck Speaks to Investors.

Scottrade

www.scottrade.com

Another online trading site, where you can place market orders for as low as $7 per trade. Products available include stocks, options, mutual funds, IRAs, bonds, CDs, and fixed-income investments.

Wachovia

www.wachovia.com

Do all your banking and investing from one central location at Wachovia. This site provides one-click access to its Banking Center, Investment Center, Lending Center, Insurance Center, Retirement Center, and Investing Center. And if you run into problems, you can find assistance at the Customer Service Center.

STOCKS

BusinessWeek Online Stocks

www.businessweek.com/investor/stocks.html

BusinessWeek online provides articles on Q&A, S&P stock picks and pans, investing, hot growth companies, and more. Also includes information on investing tools, and you can use the portfolio tracker to follow your investments, and get real-time quotes for a nominal monthly fee. Registration is required to access some pages.

Smartmoney.com

www.smartmoney.com/stocks

Here, you will find everything you need to know about stocks. You can set up a portfolio; use helpful tools to track stocks, use the stock screener to search out hidden stock from the database, and use the price check calculator to find a stock's value. Keep up-to-date through news stories and news alerts. Find cheap stock from the many stock trade sites advertised here.

Stocks.about.com

stocks.about.com

Do you need to learn more about stocks? This site provides the essentials with an introduction to stocks, how to pick stocks, a free Investing 101 mail course, FAQs, and the basics of trading. Learn about penny, blue chip, and micro cap stocks, and get stock tips.

A B C D E F G H I J K L M N O P Q R S T U V W X Y Z

A
B
C
D
E
F
G
H
I
J
K
L
M
N
O
P
Q
R
S
T
U
V
W
X
Y
Z

FISH/AQUARIUMS

AquariumFish.net

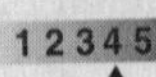

www.aquariumfish.net

AquariumFish.net offers pages of useful information for everything you need to know about buying fish to keep as pets, setting up an aquarium or a fish pond, and helpful tips about caring for many different kinds of fish. Learn which fish are better to keep in fish ponds, and which types of fish live best in saltwater. There is also an online store where you can purchase fish and fish equipment. Read about water quality, fish stress, breeding and feeding fish, and what you should do to keep fish and their environments healthy.

Freshwater Aquariums

freshaquarium.about.com

Want to learn more about keeping freshwater fish? This site provides a do-it-yourself guide to building your own aquarium. Read information about the different types of freshwater fish, and which ones lives best together. You'll also find plenty of topics about fish, fish supplies, fish profiles, Q&A, maintenance, and more. Also, check out the common mistakes people make when starting a new tank.

National Fish & Wildlife Foundation

12345

www.nfwf.org

The National Fish & Wildlife Foundation "conserves healthy populations of fish, wildlife and plants, on land and in the sea, through creative and respectful partnerships, sustainable solutions, and better education." Read about the More Fish Campaign, working to protect and conserve national fish populations and their habitats. Find out how you can donate to this organization and its programs. A career information site is also included and has a small list of job opportunities.

FISHING

eders.com

12345

www.eders.com

Choose to learn more about salt- or freshwater fishing through forums and tips at this site, which also has an extensive online catalog of fishing and hunting gear. Check out the huge online shopping area! Categories including Archery, Clothing, Camping, and Marine make it easy to browse the aisles and find what you need. After you've found the items you want, you can set up an account and purchase the items, or add them to your wish list.

Field & Stream Online

12345 Blog

www.fieldandstream.com

This popular magazine has set up an extensive site that features a Q&A section, RealAudio fishing tips, and current articles. Search the large reference section for a vast selection of books, tips, and charts to prepare yourself for a successful fishing trip. You can even search the fish database to get information specific to the type of fish you want to catch, including information about freshwater, saltwater, and fly-fishing. Read fishing Q&A, and view the photo gallery for fun fishing photos.

Fishing.com

12345

www.fishing.com

Fishing.com is one of the most all-inclusive fishing sites on the Web, covering the sport of fishing in North and South America, Europe, Africa, Asia, and Oceania. Here, you'll find a well-stocked sea of fishing tips, gear, boats, product reviews, guides, resorts, and everything else you could possibly imagine being related to fish and fishing. Shop for fishing equipment, books, clothing, and tools. Find information about associations and clubs, directories, and expos & shows. Before you head out to your favorite fishing hole, climb aboard Fishing.com and learn a few new tips and techniques.

FishingWorld.com

12345

www.fishingworld.com

Offers all types of fishing information, services, products, tournament information, and magazines, and serves as a place to visit other fishermen. Read featured articles and top news stories, upcoming events, and industry news. The Marketplace provides information on marine dealers, manufacturers, retailers, tournaments, lodging, guides, and other services.

Gulf Coast Angler's Association

12345

www.gcaa.com

This group exists to help you plan the perfect fishing vacation. The site contains links and information about marinas, guides, bait and tackle, weather, and tides and currents in the Gulf states. Special features include the Celebrity Pro Corner, Ask the Pros, Guide Trips of the Month, Game Fish Profiles, and more. Read fishing articles, view the photo gallery, and search the classifieds for jobs with the GCAA.

Nor'east Saltwater Online

12345 RSS

www.noreast.com

Avid fishers will want to sign up for the free fishing report to be emailed to them daily. Tune in to Nor'east Sportfishing Web Radio, send a friend a fishing postcard, read how-to articles, and check out the current issue of the *Nor'east Saltwater* magazine. You'll also find fishing reports, sport fishing news, new product information, boats for charter, party boat schedules, a weekly saltwater fly-fishing column, editorials, reader feedback, discussion board hot topics, classifieds, and more. Get information on tide charts and marine weather for the northeast area.

Saltwater Sportsman

12345

www.saltwatersportsman.com/saltwater

Tired of fishing for bluegills? Then hook up with the Saltwater Sportsman site to fish for saltwater trophy fish, including marlin and striped bass. Test your fishing IQ and view photos. Find information on weather & tides, traveling fisherman destinations, and fishing news & events.

Top Fishing Secrets

12345

www.topfishingsecrets.co

This site is full of fishing information to help you keep the fish on the hook. Get tips about different kinds of fish, the best types of bait, casting marksmanship, and more. There are also plenty of fishing stories and articles for you to enjoy, and information to help you identify different species of fish. Links to great fishing locations across the United States.

United States Fish and Wildlife Service

12345

www.fws.gov

The FWS, a division of the Department of the Interior, created this site to tell you a little about itself. Find out what the group does to protect endangered species and learn what the government—and you—can do to keep your old fishing hole clean and healthy. There are also links to hunting and fishing licenses statistics, where you can go fishing on a national wildlife refuge, and learn about the fish-hatchery system.

FOOD & DRINK

BevNet

1 2 3 4 5 Blog

www.bevnet.com

The Beverage Network is the premier beverage site. It has reviews of hundreds of different beverages, as well as industry news and classifieds. Join the Bevboard discussion forums, and see what's new on the BevBlog. Search the directory for services, suppliers, distributors, and industry resources.

Coca-Cola

1 2 3 4 5

www.coca-cola.co

Provides information about the most renowned soft drink company. Buy, sell, and trade Coca-Cola paraphernalia online. Check out Coca-Cola-sponsored sporting events. See how Coca-Cola is doing in the business world before you decide to buy some stock in soft drinks. Features some cool fun and games that kids of all ages will enjoy. Also has information about careers with Coca-Cola.

Global Gourmet

1 2 3 4 5

www.globalgourmet.com

Online food magazine with lots of links. Departments include information about wines, desserts, cookbooks, and shopping. View archives and cooking resources, and read or leave a messages on the message board.

Great Cookware

1 2 3 4 5

www.p4online.com

The finest cookware products for your kitchen. Featuring Calphalon, ScanPan, AllClad, Wustof, Essence of Emeril, and much more. You can also find fondues, bakeware, cutting boards and wine racks, pepper mills and salt shakers, smoothie machines, cutlery, and other cooking tools. Use the registry to purchase items for bridal gifts.

Instawares: Restaurant Supply Superstore

1 2 3 4 5

www.instawares.com

This restaurant supply superstore can equip your restaurant or kitchen with the cookware, cutlery, and other cooking products you need at affordable prices. This site uses tabs that enable you to quickly access sections on dining, kitchen, equipment, disposables, janitorial, and replacement parts. Also provides a list of top restaurant supplies. A link to InstaOffice takes you to a section where you can find and order office supplies, too.

Maine Lobsters and New England Clambakes

1 2 3 4 5

www.lobsterclambake.com

Live lobsters and clambakes shipped overnight. Read what their customers have to say. Includes tips on cooking lobsters, lobster recipes, gift certificates, and FAQs about ordering live lobsters.

Omaha Steaks

1 2 3 4 5

www.omahasteaks.com

Omaha Steaks has earned a reputation for offering first-rate steaks, meats, and other gourmet foods. Check out specials, purchase steaks, or enter to win some. You can also choose to learn more about the company, find and exchange recipes, and get all sorts of facts on preparing and storing Omaha steaks. Order food and gifts online; view job listings, too.

Smucker's

www.smuckers.com

"With a name like Smucker's, it has to be good." The famous tagline of one of the most recognized food brands. This site features Smucker's Products, which include jams, jellies, and preserves, peanut butter, sandwiches, and ice cream toppings. Check out the Smucker's Recipes section for yummy ideas for creating appetizers, entrees, desserts, and beverages. A Family Company gives you the history, news, investor relations, and career opportunities. Check out current promotions for trip give-aways, free products, and winning recipes. Go to Shop Smucker's for items you can buy online.

Snapple

www.snapple.com

Snapple's site offers information on its current and future flavored beverages—"Made from the best stuff on Earth." Enter the Snapple Dream-A-Drink contest online, shop for Snapple gear, play a fun online game, take the Snapple Aptitude test, visit the News Shack, check out the Job House for job listings at Snapple, or just drop in to experience a cool website design.

Best Wet Planet Beverages

www.wetplanet.com

One of the best "wet sites" on the Web. With the advantage of having a computer-oriented core audience of jacked-up geeks, Global Beverage presents a Java-powered site featuring information on its carbonated beverages: Jolt, Pirate's Keg, DNA, plus Martinelli's "the #1 selling apple juice in the USA." Its excellent product line, excellent site design, and incredible graphics combine to make this the best food and drink site on the Web.

ALCOHOL

Bombay Sapphire

www.bombaysapphire.com

Bombay Sapphire is the premier gin for the discerning palate. This site features content in three sections: Essence, Entertaining, and Inspired. The Essence section will educate your palate, provide tasting notes, and share information on the distillation process. Inspired has information on advertising, the Bombay Sapphire Foundation, the designer glass competition, and ways to get involved. The Entertaining section provides drink recipes and the mixologist with drink demos, tips & tricks, and videos. Must be 21 years of age to enter this site.

Intoximeters Inc. Drink Wheel Page

www.intox.com/wheel/drinkwheel.asp

Intoximeters Inc. hosts this site, which is designed to encourage the responsible use of alcohol. This company's specialty is in providing blood and breath alcohol testing. Click on the Drink Wheel option for an online simulated version. In addition to finding information on this company and its products, you'll also find a list of annotated links to lots of other drug or alcohol awareness and prevention resources. Information about training, class schedules, links, and FAQs.

Jack Daniels

www.jackdaniels.com

Visit the famous Tennessee distillery online and learn about the Jack Daniels distilling process. Read about legends & lore, find promotions, find recipes that use Jack Daniels, and take a virtual tour of the distillery. Online store for purchasing Jack Daniels merchandise. This site "cards" you.

Jim Beam

12345

www.jimbeam.com

Play the 10mm Barrel Jim Beam game. Try out some of the drink recipes, including the holiday drinks. Read the history of Jim Beam Bourbon. You can even buy Jim Beam–related merchandise online. Check out upcoming Jim Bean-sponsored events. Download some cool Jim Beam wallpaper or just hang out and play a game. This site "cards" you.

MixedDrink.com

12345 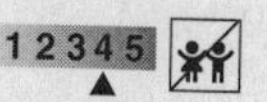

www.mixed-drink.com

Don't know how to mix your favorite drink? This site offers a comprehensive guide to making and serving mixed drinks. Go Behind the Bar for bar jokes, bar shots, nomenclature, and "bar shots"-fun pick-up lines. Also includes a section for party foods.

World's Best Bars

12345

www.worldsbestbars.com

Tour the world's best bars from Amsterdam to Zurich and read reviews from people who actually frequent these bars. Just pull up this site, click the name of a city on the list, click the name of a bar or club, and read the reviews. You can also read about the bar of the month, use the cocktail mixer to create drinks, and click on links for related resources.

COFFEES AND TEAS

Cafe Maison Coffee Roasters

12345

gourmetcoffeeroaster.com

What makes Cafe Maison gourmet coffees different from all other coffee roasters? They adhere to the 21-day rule, telling you the exact date of the roast and reminding you that coffee is fresh for only 21 days after roasting. Plus, Cafe Maison uses only authentic extracts and essences to flavor its coffee—never sugar syrups! Select the Coffee Roastery option, and you'll be guided through the process of ordering your own custom-roasted coffee. Shop for products online, including coffee and espresso makers, grinders, and other accessories.

China Mist Tea Company

12345

www.chinamist.com

Retail store over the Internet that offers many types of iced teas, especially green teas. You can also purchase black teas, caffeine-free herbal teas, and organic & fair-trade items. Choose from the teabag series, the sachet series, whole leaf teas, and steeping systems. Items can be purchase online through the e-shop.

CoffeeAM.com

12345

store.yahoo.com/cjgo

This company promotes itself as the Internet's largest coffee store. It will roast and ship your coffee when you order it, which guarantees you the freshest product available. CoffeeAM.com guarantees every purchase. In addition to coffees and teas, you will also find syrups and sauces, chai, coffee candies, biscotti, equipment, and accessories. Gift ideas and gift certificates also available. Interested in starting your own coffee shop or tea business? Submit your name to be contacted, or call directly for more information.

Java Coffee & Tea Co.

12345

www.javacoffee.com

Supplies "freshly roasted coffees, world class teas, and unique gifts." Select from dozens of flavored coffees, blends, straights & dark roasts, and rare & fancy assortments. There are also many teas to choose from, including green, black, semi-fermented, scented, blends, and naturally flavored. Custom blend your own flavors, and purchase gifts online.

Kona Coffee Times

12345

www.coffeetimes.com

Kona Coffee Times is Hawaii's purveyor of fresh-roasted 100 percent Kona coffee and Hawaiian mail order gifts. Publishing since 1993 and roasting mail-order coffee since 1994, Coffee Times is a proponent for the preservation of 100 percent Kona coffee and an advocate for truth in labeling for all 100 percent Hawaiian-made products. You also get a free gift for mentioning that you found this site on the Internet when making an order. Read about the Blair Estate organic coffee farm, articles, and a brewer's guide to the perfect cup of coffee.

Orleans Coffee Exchange

1 2 3 4 5

www.orleanscoffee.com

Gourmet coffee from the heart of the French Quarter. Orleans Coffee offers a free pound of java with every order of five pounds or more. Choose coffee by region, fair trade, monthly specials, and easy buy. Check out the Explore Coffee section to learn about the history of coffee, cultivating & roasting, how to brew coffee, and coffee terminology.

Peet's Coffee & Tea

1 2 3 4 5

www.peets.com

Order online for home delivery. Visitors to this site can browse through journal entries from travel writers as they search for fine coffees and teas. Also includes a page called Coffee Wisdom for tips on how to brew the best cup of java possible. Choose from a variety of coffees and teas, and essentials, including grinders, brewing equipment, mugs & tumblers, and gifts.

Best Starbucks

1 2 3 4 5

www.starbucks.com

Use this fun and funky site, which is for coffee lovers only, to find out the history of Starbucks, check out job opportunities, shop online, check out ice creams (and cool fruit-blended drinks and other "beyond the bean" products), locate a store near you, visit the FAQ spot, and more. Buy a Starbucks card and listen to music.

Related Sites

www.coffee-ent.com

www.coffeeadagio.com

www.coffeereview.com

GLUTEN-FREE *(SEE CELIAC DISEASE)*

A B C D E F G H I J K L M N O P Q R S T U V W X Y Z

GROCERIES

12345

www.albertsons.com

Online grocery store featuring more than 25,000 items including meat, produce, and bakery goods. Specially trained order selectors pick the freshest items for you and deliver them right to your door. Use the Plan guide to help you prepare and print a shopping list and get ideas for meals, then start shopping, and sign up for a preferred savings card. Available only in the following West Coast cities: Los Angeles, San Diego, San Francisco, Portland, Seattle, and Vancouver.

EthnicGrocer.com

12345

www.ethnicgrocer.com/eg/hm/eg.jsp

EthnicGrocer is an online source of ethnic food ingredients and consumer products from around the world, available for shipment overnight. Shop by country, by dish, by product, or by recipe—all available at the site. Click on the tab for The EthnicGrocer Cooking School, for a complete list of recipes. Purchase gifts and read the FAQs. You can also find Kosher and organic foods here, too.

Groceries-Express.com

12345

www.groceries-express.com

Groceries-Express is an online grocery store where you can shop for items and have them delivered to your door. To start shopping, you must enter your ZIP code. This enables Groceries-Express.com to determine whether it can ship highly perishable items to you. If it cannot, it automatically removes those items from the list of selections, so you won't be tempted to place them in your cart. Read the FAQs for more information about using Groceries-Express.

Best NetGrocer

12345

www.netgrocer.com

Thousands of food and general merchandise products to choose from. A great way to make sure your mother, grandmother, and child in college gets the food they need, no matter where you live. Just shop for food at NetGrocer and enter shipping information at the checkout page. You can even set up a recurring order that sends your shipment at an interval you choose. Kosher and organic food products available are available here, too. With this Best of the Best site, you may never need to go grocery shopping again!

Peapod

12345

www.peapod.com

This site bills itself as America's Internet grocer—and with one million orders delivered, that's easy to believe. Shop online any time of day or night. Delivery is available seven days a week; you pick the time convenient for you. Orders are packed so perishables stay fresh and frozen items stay frozen. Use the Quick Guide for answers to your questions about grocery shopping online. Browse the aisles, make your shopping list, view weekly specials, find recipes, and more. Available in Chicago, Boston, Long Island, D.C., and a few other select cities and states.

Price Chopper Supermarkets

12345

www.pricechopper.com

Price Chopper is a medium-size chain of supermarkets in the Northeast, with headquarters in Upstate New York. This site offers coupons and recipes, and helps you create a personalized shopping list. You can also send flowers, order deli platters, fruit baskets, and party cakes online. Search and apply for jobs, too.

A B C D E F G H I J K L M N O P Q R S T U V W X Y Z

Ralphs: First in Southern California

1 2 3 4 5

www.ralphs.com

Ralphs offers things you won't find at other stores, but it does not offer online shopping. Some of its perks include a Club Card, giving you discounts all over Southern California on everything from car rentals to fine dining. You'll also save on your favorite wines with Ralphs Wine Club. You can also send flowers and purchase gift cards online and have them sent anywhere. Ralphs was recently purchased by Kroger.

Safeway

1 2 3 4 5

www.safeway.com

If you live in Sacramento, California (or the San Francisco Bay Area; Portland, Oregon; or Vancouver, Washington), you can tack on an extra 10 bucks to your grocery bill and avoid the hassle of having to shop and carry your groceries yourself. Shop online with Safeway for all of your grocery store needs. Here, you can create a shopping list, create an express list of items for faster service, shop by aisle, and find weekly specials, and online savings and coupons.

ThaiGrocer

1 2 3 4 5

www.thaigrocer.com

Learn about and shop online for Thai foods. This site provides Thai and oriental groceries, recipes, food ingredients, cookware, and a cooking school, too. Search products by category.

Trader Joe's

1 2 3 4 5

www.traderjoes.com

With locations in 22 U.S. states, and more new stores constantly being added, this "unique" grocery store's mission is to bring the best food and beverage values and information to their customers. Trader Joe's is a fun place to shop with free sample tasting, low prices, and a friendly and helpful crew. Not satisfied with an item you bought? No problem, you can bring it back and get a full refund, no questions asked. Get a copy of the Trader Joe's Fearless Flyer for information about weekly and seasonal products, or one-time specials. Interested in working for Trader Joe's? Check out their employment opportunities and recruiting events. After you've finished shopping at Trader Joe's you'll leave with a bag full of quality products, and a balloon.

Best Wild Oats

1 2 3 4 5

www.wildoats.com/u/home

Shop Wild Oats for "better food. Pure and simple." Here, you will find fresh, quality fruits and vegetables, seafood, meats, and baked goods. There is also a salad bar, a deli, and a juice and java bar. This site also carries holistic health products, among other unique products. Wild Oats offers in-store events, such as cooking demonstrations and speaker topics on healthy living. There are many brands to choose from that you won't find in a conventional grocery store, including the Wild Oats brand. Do your shopping online, or find a store near you. Currently, there are 24 Wild Oats stores open throughout the United States.

ORGANIC FOODS

Campaign to Label Genetically Engineered Foods

1 2 3 4 5 Blog

www.thecampaign.org

If you are what you eat, you'd better know about what you're eating, including whether your food is genetically engineered. If this issue concerns you, consider joining the campaign to force the food industry to label any genetically engineered foods it chooses to bring to market. This site reveals what you can do to help. Read links about legislation, resolutions, and initiatives. Study the issues and literature, and join news forums to find out more about this campaign.

Eden Foods

1 2 3 4 5

www.edenfoods.com

Home of one of the most successful organic food suppliers in the United States. This site features more than 800 free organic and macrobiotic recipes for appetizers, main courses, healthy beverages, condiments, salads, soups, and desserts. Enter your ZIP code to find a health food store near you that carries Eden Foods products. Or shop at the Eden store online.

GAIAM.com Lifestyle Company

1 2 3 4 5

www.gaiam.com

This site sells natural and organic foods and beverages, as well as healthcare products, home & outdoor, mind-body fitness, and mind-spirit products, and books & media items, while offering information on the benefit of such purchases. You'll also find a database to research organic products and issues. A nicely designed site.

Organic Alliance

1 2 3 4 5

www.organic.org

The Organic Alliance is a nonprofit organization that promotes organic produce. Find organic farmers, farmers' markets, and stores, locate recipes, and read up-to-date organic news. Join the organic forum, find answers to FAQs, and more. A well-designed site and easy to navigate.

Organic Consumers Association

1 2 3 4 5 Blog RSS

www.organicconsumers.org

Learn all about the hazards of genetically engineered food, as well as diseases and food-related problems at this site, which aims to encourage consumption of organic foods. You can search the site for keywords and find vendors that sell pure food. Organic food activists will love this site. Read top stories, take action at the OCA action center; read about farm issues, politics, fair trade, and social justice; and search links to find organic products. A very informative site.

Organic Gardening Magazine

1 2 3 4 5

www.organicgardening.com

The online version of this print favorite. Get news on organic issues in the Watchdog section, learn the secrets of growing favorite plants and flowers organically, and search for organic solutions to age-old gardening problems. Read organic gardening discussion boards or you can log in and leave a message.

Organic Trade Association

1 2 3 4 5

www.ota.com

The Organic Trade Association (OTA) is a national association representing the organic industry in Canada and the United States. Growers, shippers, processors, and more will find the site useful in learning about organic trends, finding upcoming events, and staying on top of industry happenings. Become a member; sign up here. You can also search for featured projects and organic products online. Read about organic facts, peruse the bookstore, and research directories for additional links to online information about organic products and services.

WINES *(SEE WINES)*

Food Allergies/Intolerances

1 2 3 4 5 RSS

allergies.about.com/cs/foods/a/blfood.htm

This site provides essential information about food allergies, including allergy symptoms and treatment options, skin conditions, and a physician locator. Other topics include allergies in children, chemical reactions, skin conditions, seasonal allergies, and preventions tips, among others. There are plenty of articles covering all different types of food-related allergies, forums you can join to discuss allergies, and a buyers guide to allergy test kits, air purifiers, and books.

FOOD ALLERGIES

Food Allergy Initiative

12345 ▲ (4)

www.foodallergyinitiative.org

The Food Allergy Initiative is an organization that invests funds in the search for more-effective treatments and cures for food allergies. Here, you will find information about common food allergies to peanuts, eggs, milk, shellfish, wheat, tree nuts, soy, and fish. Read articles covering topics such as diagnosis, treatment of anaphylaxis, living with food allergies, tips for caregivers, and more. This site also offers links to other allergy resources, public policy, and research. You can make a contribution to this organization by using their secure online donation form.

The Food Allergy & Anaphylaxis Network

12345 ▲ (4)

www.foodallergy.org

Covers plenty of food allergy topics including anaphylaxis, schools and childcare, recipes, research, information about common food allergens, and a listing of FAQs. Join the FAAN and receive member benefits, make a donation, take action; find information about how you can contact Congress to support food allergy research funding. There is also a teen and kids website, travel tips, and news.

American Football Coaches Association

12345 ▲ (3)

www.afca.com

The American Football Coaches Association is dedicated to supporting the football coaching community, recognizing outstanding achievements and service, and promoting the profession of football coaching. Here, you can learn more about the association, obtain the latest news regarding football coaches and explore the association's various awards. This site also provides up-to-date rule changes and other information football coaches might find quite useful. Also includes information about the AFCA Convention, AFCA programs and events, and other football-related resources, including a job board.

FOOTBALL

Football.com

www.football.com

NFL, CFL, NCAA, the draft, fantasy football, cheerleaders, scores, predictions, statistics, schedules, and more...you'll find it all here at Football.com, in season and off. You'll also find discussion forums, information about football camps, NFL franchise history, and an online playbook. Read breaking news stories and commentary and search the list of teams and find their stats and standings. This is a serious site for serious football fans, but it's a lot of fun, too.

COLLEGE

College Football Hall of Fame

collegefootball.org

Located in South Bend, Indiana, the College Football Hall of Fame website provides information on events, facility rentals for special occasions, including the Press Box, Locker Room, Stadium Theater, and the Gridiron Plaza. Find out about group sales, take a quick tour of the Hall, and search the Hall of Famers for your favorite player. Become a member and find links to other college football-related sites.

CollegeFootballNews.com

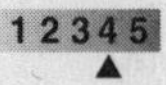

www.collegefootballnews.com

This site is loaded with college football information, including features, previews, top stories, and schedules. Lists all teams and conferences from the ACC to the WAC, predictions, polls, and a College Football News forum where you can post and read messages.

College Sports TV

www.cstv.com/sports/m-footbl

A comprehensive resource of men's and women's college sports television programs. Here, you can find program schedules, watch short videos, find team scores and rankings by division and sport. Watch live games, review highlights, read student blogs, and message boards. Purchase tickets, shop the Fan Store for team merchandise, bid on auctions, and read breaking news stories.

ESPN's College Football Page

sports.espn.go.com/ncf/index

ESPN provides current college football news. Here, you will find information about team standings, rankings, stats. You can also view the scoreboard, the Bowl results, and watch videos, and read the College Insider to learn about the latest rumors and breaking news. Find out who's being recruited and read the latest college football blogs.

NCAA Football

www.ncaafootball.net

This official collegiate football site provides access to college teams from Division III all the way up to Division 1-A. It features several sections where you can view polls, bowl games, records and rules, statistics, standings, scores, and award winners. View the week in pictures, listen to audio feeds, and watch videos feeds about the latest collegiate football news. You can also shop online for your favorite team merchandise.

Play Football: The Official NFL Site for Kids

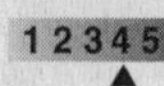

www.playfootball.com

The NFL is committed to its fans, young and old, and it hosts this site to keep young players and fans interested, connected, and informed. Young players can click the Be a Player link to get a brief description of the various positions, along with instructions and tips on how to play the position. Click Football Facts for a collection of football facts and trivia that can keep you entertained for hours. Site also features a collection of games, information on how to get involved, online polls, links to team sites for kids, and much more.

FANTASY *(SEE FANTASY SPORTS)* PROFESSIONAL

Canadian Football League

www.cfl.ca

Canada's answer to the NFL, the CFL has its own website where you can learn more about the league, its rules and regulations, its teams, its history, and, of course, its cheerleaders. During the season, this site can keep you abreast of injuries, trades, standings, and game results. It also features a poll where you can cast your vote on the topic of the day. Also includes a listing of events and a Fan Zone where you can join forums and purchase team merchandise from the CFL shop.

National Football League

www.nfl.com

Get the latest information on every team, every player, and every game from the official NFL site. You can find statistics and scores, play fantasy football online, and even sign up for the official NFL email newsletter. Ticket information is also available, although tickets to games are not available from this site. You can even get information about international NFL. There's also an official NFL site for kids, links to other football-related sites, and NFL job listings. For the best that football has to offer, this is the site for you.

AFC Websites

Baltimore Ravens	www.baltimoreravens.com
Buffalo Bills	www.buffalobills.com
Cincinnati Bengals	www.bengals.com
Cleveland Browns	www.clevelandbrowns.com
Denver Broncos	www.denverbroncos.com
Houston Texans	www.houstontexans.com
Indianapolis Colts	www.colts.com
Jacksonville Jaguars	www.jaguars.com
Kansas City Chiefs	www.kcchiefs.com
Miami Dolphins	www.miamidolphins.com
New England Patriots	www.patriots.com
New York Jets	www.newyorkjets.com
Oakland Raiders	www.raiders.com
Pittsburgh Steelers	www.steelers.com
San Diego Chargers	www.chargers.com
Tennessee Titans	www.titansonline.com

NFC Websites

Arizona Cardinals	www.azcardinals.com
Atlanta Falcons	www.atlantafalcons.com
Carolina Panthers	www.panthers.com
Chicago Bears	www.chicagobears.com
Dallas Cowboys	www.dallascowboys.com
Detroit Lions	www.detroitlions.com
Green Bay Packers	www.packers.com
Minnesota Vikings	www.vikings.com
New Orleans Saints	www.neworleanssaints.com
New York Giants	www.giants.com
Philadelphia Eagles	www.philadelphiaeagles.com
San Francisco 49ers	www.sf49ers.com
St. Louis Rams	www.stlouisrams.com
Seattle Seahawks	www.seahawks.com
Tampa Bay Buccaneers	www.buccaneers.com
Washington Redskins	www.redskins.com

NFLPlayers.com

12345 RSS

www.nflplayers.com

Check out the web page of your favorite players and contemplate who the unsung heroes have been this past season, as well as the draft favorites for the upcoming year. Read headline news, play fantasy sports, games, find out which players have retired, and watch the video clip of the week.

Pro Football Hall of Fame

12345

www.profootballhof.com

Find out more about hall of famers and learn about the annual Hall of Fame Game. You'll also find information about pro football history and a franchise history directory. The Hall of Fame store offers many interesting items for sale. Read the FAQs for more information about the Hall of Fame.

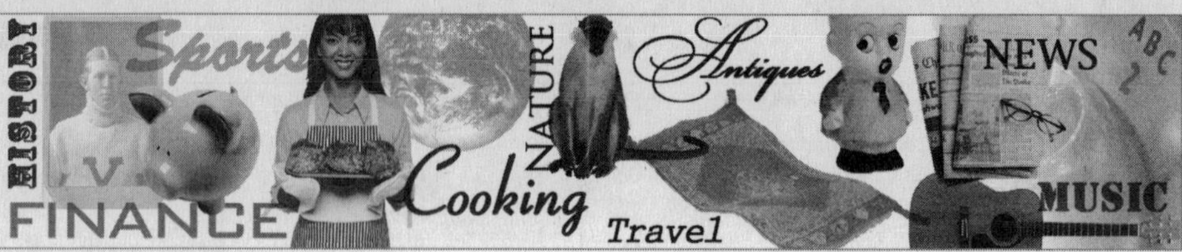

A B C D E F G H I J K L M N O P Q R S T U V W X Y Z

FOREIGN POLICY

Carnegie Council on Ethics and International Affairs

12345 RSS

www.cceia.org

Carnegie Council is an independent, nonpartisan, nonprofit organization dedicated to increasing the understanding of ethics and international affairs. Obtain edited transcripts and articles from the council's *Ethics & International Affairs* publication, access interviews and book reviews, check out the online forums, and much more. You can order past issues and other publications online. Become a member and support the Carnegie Council by making a donation online. This site's excellent design and top-notch information make it an easy choice as Best of the Best.

The Center for Security Policy

12345

www.centerforsecuritypolicy.org

The purpose of the nonprofit, nonpartisan Center for Security Policy is to stimulate and inform the national and international debate about all aspects of security policy—notably those policies bearing on the foreign, defense, economic, financial, and technological interests of the United States. Read articles about the latest news and commentary, and become a member or make a tax-deductible donation.

embassy.org

12345

www.embassy.org

embassy.org is a connection to most of the U.S.-based embassies and consulates. Features a searchable diplomacy database with more than 50,000 addresses, phone numbers, and email addresses of diplomatic posts worldwide. embassy.org focuses on websites maintained by foreign representations all over the world. Includes business directories for Americans traveling abroad, help & resources, and news.

Best Foreign Policy Association

12345

www.fpa.org

The Foreign Policy Association works to educate the public on significant world issues that affect and are affected by the United States. The opening page features current articles on foreign policy as it relates the headline news from around the world. A navigation bar on the left provides quick access to additional stories grouped by country, department, or issue. Special areas are available for teachers and for students. Join a global forum to discuss current issues with others around the world. Purchase books through the bookstore, and check out the job board for a list of job openings.

Foreign Policy in Focus

12345 RSS

www.fpif.org

Foreign Policy in Focus "seeks to make the U.S. a more responsible global leader and global partner." It bills itself as a "think tank without walls." More than 650 policy analysts and advocates contribute content and steer the think tank toward the most pressing foreign policy issues of the day. It seeks to make foreign policy a global activity driven by citizens rather than politicians. Here, you can purchase books and other FPIF items, read press releases and Op-Eds, or subscribe to the e-zine.

NATO: The North Atlantic Treaty Organization

www.nato.int

This site offers, in part, a short history of the alliance and a brief introduction to its main policies. A guide to NATO's structure, and its members and partners, as well as staff vacancies. A complete archive of all official documents and both general and specific NATO publications. Read stories, opinions and analysis, and the FAQs for more information about NATO.

The United Nations

www.un.org

Home page of the United Nations. Six languages to choose from and five categories of information to select from: Peace and Security, International Law, Humanitarian Affairs, Human Rights, and Economic and Social Development. Find out more about every facet of the UN. Read the Q&A section, find out about conferences and events, and more. Employment opportunities are also listed.

U.S. Agency for International Development

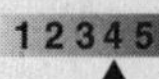

www.usaid.gov

Investigate U.S. Aid budget numbers, learn about countries currently being aided by the United States, and get background economic research on various countries and regions. Read about current news, search topic on policy, public affairs, and business. There is also a career page for employment opportunities at USAID.

A B C D E F G H I J K L M N O P Q R S T U V W X Y Z

FRUGAL SPENDING

About Frugality

12345 Blog RSS

frugalliving.about.com

Huge collection of resources on how to trim expenses and live on less income. Everything from saving on groceries to trimming the high costs of pet care. Many tips, topic, and resources to help you live a more frugal lifestyle. Includes plenty of links to related topics.

BetterBudgeting.com

12345 Blog

www.betterbudgeting.com

This site provides loads of tips and techniques for making a living on whatever you earn. Learn about debt consolidation, budgeting, cooking frugally, avoiding impulse buying, and much more. Lots of free information, but the subscription promises even more money-saving suggestions. Find books to help you save money, and read through dozens of money-saving topics.

Cheapskate Monthly

12345 Blog RSS

www.cheapskatemonthly.com

Get your daily tip for debt-free living at this site, which also features a radio interview with author Mary Hunt, the editor-in-cheap. By joining the site and buying a subscription to her debt-free living newsletter, you'll also gain access to discussion boards and get even more information about saving money. Read the Tip of the Day and helpful articles at News You Can Use Today. You can purchase books written by Hunt and other money experts that offer more creative ways to live a frugal life.

The Dollar Stretcher

12345 RSS

www.stretcher.com

A weekly online newsletter with tons of articles and information about frugal living. This site's motto is "living better...for less." Frugal-living hints are available in a vast number of categories, including coupons, food, medical care, debt, hobbies, pets, children, auto care, retirement, and many others. Visit the Dollar Saving Library for free money-saving articles.

The Frugal Shopper

12345

www.thefrugalshopper.com

Find articles on how to save money on your daily expenses. Provides information on freebies and special offers, coupons, rebates, and other money-saving stuff. Includes a shopping directory and other links & resources.

Best Frugal Village

12345

www.frugalvillage.co

The Frugal Village is a community where you can learn to appreciate the beauty of living on less. The village is populated by Frugal Forums, Sara's Column, Frugal Village Chat, a Community Cookbook, Dessert Cards, Frugal Tips and Tricks, and plenty of articles on how to trim expenses and become fiscally liberated. This site also features calculators and other tools and printables, including a meal planner and expense log. Read and join in the latest forum discussions. When you're ready to cut your expenses and live a simpler life, there's no better site for you.

FUN SITES

Al Lowe's Humor Site

www.allowe.com

Al Lowe, creator of Leisure Suit Larry, calls this site home. Here, you can find sight gags, audio and video humor, text jokes, Leisure Suit Larry and Freddy Phargas games, free game and screensaver downloads, information about Al Lowe, and much more. All funny and entertaining. Stop by the free message board and tell Al what you think.

Burning Man

www.burningman.com

Home of Burning Man, the famous and infamous annual personal-expression-art-fair-and-mayhem ritual, where more than 25,000 participants gather in the desert every summer to form an interactive community, in which participants do some pretty weird stuff. Visit this site to learn more about Burning Man and what it means to its various participants. Get the latest news, stay connected, find out how you can participate, view images from past events, and get more information about this unusual experience.

Caricature Zone

www.magixl.com

This site features a huge collection of caricatures of the rich and famous organized by categories, including political figures, actors and actresses, rock stars, and famous athletes. Check out the gallery, generate your own caricature online, email a greeting card, download clip art and wallpaper, or shop online. The whole site has a cartoony look and feel, but it's easy to get around and offers an extensive collection of valuable freebies. Includes links to other great caricature websites.

Comedy Central

www.comedycentral.com

Visit the home of Comedy Central, the irreverent TV network responsible for such shows as *South Park* and *The Man Show*. Here, you can check the TV listings for your favorite show, enter contests, play games, find jokes, movies, or just waste time. Call me a prude, but I don't recommend this site for kids.

Dane Cook

www.danecook.com

Dane Cook is a hilarious stand-up comedian well known to fans of Comedy Central. Here, you can listen to portions of Dane Cook's edgy stand-up routine, view short cartoons, chat online, follow his tour, shop online, view photos, get downloads, and other related links, and much more. Very cool design and plenty of material to keep you entertained.

Extreme Funny Humor

www.extremefunnyhumor.com

Extreme Funny Humor features a collection of hilarious Flash animations, audio and video clips, games, optical illusions, and text jokes that test the socially acceptable limits...well, they actually cross over. The site also features screensavers, funny e-cards, and other freebies and a collection of links to sites that offer similar types of humor. Also includes the newest funny movies and animations.

Fortean Times

12345

www.forteantimes.com

This site chronicles some of the strange phenomena occurring in the world today, combing various news sources to bring you the stranger stories of the day. The day we visited the site, we found a story on how to reduce dog flatulence (from a local ABC news station out of Toledo, Ohio), photos of camel spiders from Baghdad (at www.snopes.com), and a story from *The Union* about a murder suspect who claimed he was fleeing aliens. Read the latest additions and breaking news, view the picture of the week, and join the discussion forum. When the daily news no longer interests you, visit this site to get a different perspective on what's newsworthy.

Marshall Brain's How Stuff Works

RSS

www.howstuffworks.com

Ever wanted to know how a car engine works? Or how toilets work? Well, the articles on this site are sure to answer many of your "How does that work?" questions. Includes information on Home stuff, Money stuff, Health stuff, Electronics stuff, People stuff, and more.

Best SlashNOT

Blog

www.slashnot.com

Slashdot.org is the news site for nerds, dedicated to keeping geeks all around the world informed of the latest developments in Linux, Windows, Mac OS, and Bill Gates. This site is dedicated to undercutting the importance of everything related to computer technology. Here, you can learn about the new Microsoft .LIP server, the new religious sect formed by Linux users, and studies on the environmental impact of satire. Read and submit stories. If you're fed up with techno-hype, visit this site for a healthy dose of techno-humor.

Stupid.com

12345

stupid.com

Stupid candy, stupid games, stupid toys, and stupid gifts.... If you're looking for something stupid to buy for yourself, a friend, or a relative, look to Stupid.com. This site features the stupidest products imaginable, complete with product reviews. Find clearance items, the best and worst sellers, politically incorrect items, and weird Japanese stuff. Best of all, you can purchase them online, so you won't look stupid in public.

Uncle Roy All Around You

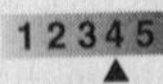

www.uncleroyallaroundyou.co.uk

Uncle Roy All Around You is a computer game that combines reality with virtual reality. Street players with handheld computers comb the streets of a real city looking for Uncle Roy. Online players assist in the search by following a virtual map of the same area. They provide instructions to their teammates on the street, working together to reach the secret destination in 60 minutes or less. Read the FAQs for more information about this game.

Worth1000

12345 RSS

www.worth1000.com

A picture used to be worth a hundred words, but here it's worth a thousand. This site features an online contest where photographers can submit phony photos to compete with others online. Each contest has a theme. For example, Supernatural Phenomena 2 calls for contestants to submit photographs that demonstrate a supernatural phenomenon, such as spoon bending, levitation, a religious miracle, or some other supernatural hoax. You can browse through submitted photos or enter your own photo in one of the many contests. Check out the contest, view the images gallery, join the discussion forum, and find photoshop tutorials. Want to know more? Read the FAQs.

GAMBLING

I Stopped Gambling.com

www.istoppedgambling.com

I Stopped Gambling is the site to go to if you want to stop your compulsive gambling addiction or you know someone who has a compulsive gambling problem. Resources available including books, articles, and chatrooms to move toward a solution to problem gambling.

Gambling Online Magazine

www.gamblingonlinemagazine.com

This online magazine provides information on online and sports betting. Includes gambling news, message boards, and tips.

National Council on Problem Gambling

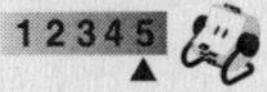

www.ncpgambling.org

The mission of the National Council on Problem Gambling is to "increase public awareness of pathological gambling, ensure the widespread availability of treatment for problem gamblers and their families, and to encourage research and programs for prevention and education." This site lists a variety of resources including literature, links, a Counselor Search, and a residential treatment facility directory.

ONLINE

Gambling.com

www.gambling.com

Search gambling.com to find a wide choice of online gambling sites including casinos, live Internet roulette, and sports gambling as well as bingo, lottery, and slots.

Gambling-Win.com

www.gambling-win.com

At Gambling-Win, you will find in-depth reviews of all major casinos and poker rooms so that you can decide which site is best for you. Read the poker and casino strategy articles before you gamble. They also provide the latest news in the areas of casinos and poker rooms.

Gone Gambling

www.gonegambling.com

Gone Gambling is an online casino and gambling portal. Several chat forums are available here.

Real Vegas Online

www.realvegasonline.biz/index2.html

Real Vegas Online Casino offers prominent casino games including Texas hold 'em, blackjack, baccarat, Caribbean stud poker, video poker, roulette, slots, and much more. Their mission is to provide you with exclusive casino entertainment.

TIPS

Gambling Times

12345

www.gamblingtimes.com

The self-proclaimed authority on gambling since 1977. The site has links to articles on every type of casino game, sports betting, and poker. Has a beginners guide to each form of gambling, tips, and reviews online casinos.

GAMES & PUZZLES

1MoreGame.com

12345

1moregame.com

This Austrian site features an arcade with more than 15 Java games, including Wuzzler (Foosball), Tiny Pinball, Cybercourt (Tennis), and Speedbiker. You can log in as GUEST using the password GUEST, or register to have your scores saved and compete with other players. Excellent graphics and responsive controls.

3D Realms

12345

www.3drealms.com

Download shareware games like Duke Nukem and Max Payne, as well as many, many others, and get daily updates on gaming industry news here.

Apple Corps

12345

apple-corps.westnet.com/apple_corps.2.html

The game you lost all the pieces to as a child is back. Mr./Mrs. Potato Head is here, under an online, no copyrighted form, except now s/he's an apple. You can place eyes, nose, teeth, mouth, whatever, onto the apple. A new twist is also available: Change the vegetable if you like.

Banja

12345

www.banja.com

In this intriguing online, role-playing game, you take on the identity of Banja the Rasta, a hip islander who makes his way around a semi-inhabited island looking for hidden passages, useful tools, and other things that might make his adventure more rewarding. Check out this site and join in the fun!

Best Big Fish Games

12345 RSS

www.bigfishgames.com

For free online games and downloads, Big Fish Games is unmatched in quality and selection, featuring puzzles, puzzle games, mahjong, action games, card games, jigsaw puzzles, arcade games, word challenges, and plenty of free downloads. This site features a new game every day, so you're always sure to see something fresh. The site, as well as its games, is well designed, easy to navigate, and sure to entertain. Visit the online store to purchase game packs, CDs, T-shirts, and other items.

Boxerjam.com

12345

www.boxerjam.com

Online game site where you can play against the computer or against other people at the site. Compete on virtual game shows, play solitaire, or try your hand at some puzzles. Some games are for kids, but gambling is definitely encouraged here.

BrettspielWelt

12345

www.brettspielwelt.de

This is one of the best sites on the Web for playing computer games. This German site also has an option for English speakers.

Chinook

www.cs.ualberta.ca/~chinook

If checkers is your game, Chinook is your website. Beat Chinook and you will have outmaneuvered the world man-made checkers champion. Good collection of links to other checkers sites as well.

ClueMaster

www.cluemaster.com

If you're a word puzzle fanatic, you'll want to visit this site for hundreds of free puzzles to solve as well as the ability to archive puzzles in progress.

CoffeeBreakArcade

www.coffeebreakarcade.com

CoffeeBreakArcade.com is a directory of free Internet games. You can search for specific games or browse games through various categories: classic, cool, sports, shooting, racing, and casino. Some games and pop-up ads might be unsuitable for young children, and some are just plain lame.

EA.com

www.ea.com/home/home.jsp

Home of Electronic Arts, producers of some of the most popular video games, this site provides information about EA's product line. Plus you'll find gobs of free games divided into categories that include everything from board games and bingo to online video games and trivia contests.

FreeArcade.com

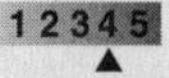

www.freearcade.com

Great place to play free Java-based arcade games, including Wickywoo, Pheasant Hunter Shapeshifter, Boulder Dash, and Tanx. Puzzle games and board games also featured. Some pop-up ads may not be suitable for young children.

The Fruit Game

www.2020tech.com/fruit

Offers the challenging fruit game. Players remove fruit from the screen; the last player to remove fruit wins. Try this mathematical adventure. Great for parents and kids, students and teachers.

G4 Media Network

www.g4tv.com

Television network devoted to computer games provides articles, tips, tricks, and reviews of some of the most popular computer games on the market.

Gamasutra

www.gamasutra.com

Catering to the game developer, this site is designed for serious video game players and creators. Here, you can learn about the latest trends in video games, find out more about what game players want, pick up some new design techniques, learn about the latest programs and technologies, and much more.

GameColony.com

www.gamecolony.com

GameColony.com features traditional games of skill, including chess, checkers, solitaire, poker, backgammon, FreeCell, and pool, in head-to-head and multiplayer tournaments. You can compete here just for fun or register to win cash prizes.

Games Domain

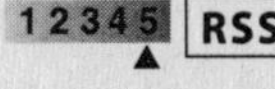

www.gamesdomain.com

Download demos, read news and interviews with leading game programmers as well as game reviews, and chat with fellow gamers here. You can also find cheats to a number of games, as well as find links to

A B C D E F G H I J K L M N O P Q R S T U V W X Y Z

official game pages. Many online games are available here, too. This is a jam-packed site for the avid gamer! Some content will appeal to younger players, but some of the games covered here can be a little suggestive/violent.

GamesIndustries.biz

www.gamesindustry.biz

Keep up on the latest developments in the video game industry at this site. Here, you can read game reviews, check out game charts and planned release dates, check stock prices for the top game companies, and even look for a job in the industry. This site features plenty of current articles to keep any game enthusiast well informed.

Gamespot

www.gamespot.com

For all-around gamers who aren't devoted to any particular system, Gamespot features a little of everything: news, reviews, previews, surveys, contests, downloads, and more. Links to online stores where you can compare prices for various games and game gear. Some material appeals to younger players, as well, but some suggestive and violent games are covered here. Parents should visit the site first.

GameSpy

www.gamespy.com

This site plays host to a huge collection of multiplayer arcade games and a popular gaming community. Join more than 4.4 million members worldwide playing nearly 300 of today's hottest games!

Gamesville

www.gamesville.lycos.com

Gamesville is a huge online gaming site, where visitors can play games against the computer or against each other. Play for cash prizes or play for fun. Plenty of links to online casinos, too. Some games will appeal to children; but because gambling is promoted at many of these sites, kids are best off not visiting.

GlobZ

www.globz.com

GlobZ offers free interactive web games, including Globulous, Trackwars Challenge, Keyball, and Little Rockettes. Most games you play online, but you can download others to play offline.

Homers

www.vicious-arrogance.com/Homers

This site is an online game that requires you to put Homer Simpson's head on straight, among other games. Includes rules and links to other online games. Some areas of this site may be suitable for younger children.

IGN

www.ign.com

News, codes, reviews, previews, features, releases, hardware, contests, a game store, affiliates, links to magazine subscriptions, and more. This site is geared for serious gamers and contains some material that is not suitable for younger children.

Kids Domain Online Games

12345

www.kidsdomain.com/games

Wide selection of games designed for fun and for educational purposes. Most games are for elementary-school kids. Plenty of trivia games that not only ask questions but present interesting facts in an engaging format. Excellent site for parents to introduce to their children.

MSN Game Zone

12345

zone.msn.com

Microsoft's gift to the gaming community, this high-tech site serves up a huge collection of free games broken down into categories, including Puzzle Games, Word & Trivia, Card & Board, Zone Casino, Racing & Sports, and Kids' Zone. Free downloads and chat area populated by an active community of gamers make this one of the best sites to play games on the Web.

Multi-Player Online Games Directory

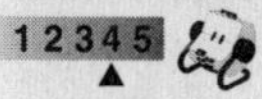

www.mpogd.com

A guide to the best multiplayer games. Game titles are broken down into categories ranging from action to sports. Game of the month poll helps you quickly identify the most popular games, and news headlines keep you abreast of the latest information in the online gaming world. Game reviews and other resources are also available.

NovaLogic

www.novalogic.com

Download war game demos such as Delta Force, Comanche, and Tachyon; and purchase the ones you like. You'll also find gaming news and announcements to keep you up-to-speed on up-and-coming games.

PopCap Games

12345

www.popcap.com

Online game room where you can play a collection of simple, yet deeply layered games that will challenge your coordination and your intellect. All games are Java-based, so you need not download any additional software to play them; they play right inside your Web browser. Also features downloadable games for Palm computers.

SegaNet

12345

www.sega.com

Sega's game site features articles about a variety of its games, plus some free mini-games you can play online, downloadable wallpaper and movie clips, and a discussion forum where you can trade secrets with other gamers and share your enthusiasm for playing.

Star Wars Galaxies

12345

starwarsgalaxies.station.sony.com

This site features Sony's Star Wars Galaxies multiplayer online role-playing game based on the *Star Wars* classics. At this site, you can find support and updates, connect with other players and fans, check for new releases, and much more.

There

12345

www.there.com

There is an online chat area and game room, where you can hook up with other players from around the world, chat, and play games all at the same time. You start by creating your own avatar to represent you online. You get to choose the avatar's facial features, body shape, clothing, hairstyle, and other features and accessories, and then explore the 3D world of There, where you are guaranteed to meet someone new every time you sign on.

A B C D E F H I J K L M N O P Q R S T U V W X Y Z

Velvet-Strike

www.opensorcery.net/velvet-strike

Velvet-Strike features a collection of virtual spray paints that you can use in the video game *Counter-Strike* to paint antiwar slogans and graffiti on the backgrounds. Here you can download spray paints, submit your own spray paints, and check out videos and screenshots of the spray paints in action.

Wizards of the Coast, Inc.

www.wizards.com

Provides information for Wizards of the Coast, producers of the popular card game Magic: The Gathering and a series of *Harry Potter* games. This site includes information about Magic and other games produced by the Wizards, as well as company background and news.

World Village Games

www.worldvillage.com/wvgames/index.html

A handful of online games designed to keep you entertained for hours. Great selection for young players.

Yahoo! Games

games.yahoo.com

Excellent collection of multiplayer games. A populous and active group of online gamers make this one of the best places to hang out and play checkers, chess, blackjack, poker, fantasy sports, and dozens of other games.

Yohoho! Puzzle Pirates

12345

www.puzzlepirates.com

Join an online community of Buccaneers to solve several puzzles in your quest for treasure. As you set sail and cruise the high seas, this site launches appropriate puzzle games to challenge you and the rest of the crew. Solve the puzzle, and the site bestows great riches upon you and your mates.

BOARD GAMES

Board Games at About.com

boardgames.about.com

Information on this site ranges from winning at Monopoly to the latest in fantasy board games. It is arranged by Essentials, Topics, Buying Games, Discussion Forums, and links to the latest Blogs. No matter what kind of board game you like to play, you can find helpful information here.

Board Game Central

boardgamecentral.com

This site is a central resource for board game information, rules, software, and links, focused on traditional and family board games as well as new games you might not yet be familiar with.

BoardGameGeek

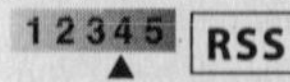

www.boardgamegeek.com/welcome.htm

BoardGameGeek is a board gaming resource and community. The site is updated on a real-time basis by its large and growing user base. There is no charge to become a registered member of BGG, although members are encouraged to help improve the site by adding their own reviews and thoughts on games to the existing database! There are reviews, articles, ratings, images, play-aids, and session reports from board game geeks across the world, as well as a live discussion forum.

Monopoly

12345

www.hasbro.com/monopoly

Pick up tips on winning at Monopoly, find out about upcoming Monopoly tournaments, learn about game news—such as a new token—and see the latest Monopoly merchandise at this site devoted to the famed board game.

Official Worldwide Scrabble Home Page

12345

www.mattelscrabble.com

Get help forming words with the anagram builder and double-check words in the online Scrabble dictionary. The site also offers tips for improving your score and for playing with kids. In need of your own Scrabble game? Check out all your Scrabble options and find your nearest retailer.

CARD GAMES (NONPOKER)

The Card Games Site

12345

www.pagat.com

This site brings you rules and information about card and tile games from all parts of the world, plus strategies for each. Links to sources of card games software, places to play cards online, other collections of card game rules, information about playing cards, sources of cards and equipment, card game books, discussion groups, tournaments and meetings, and more.

Cardboard Cognition

12345

edweb.sdsu.edu/courses/edtec670/cardboard/CardTOC.html

This site lists 132 games that were designed to be educational. You will find a short description of the game. They are not available for sale but you can write to the authors for permission to create your own version of the games and "They'll say yes!"

Download Free Games

12345

www.download-free-games.com/card_game_download

There are 200 game downloads on this site. The card games include several variations of solitaire, some classics like hearts and spades, puzzle type games using cards, and some poker card game variations. All the card games are free to try. The ones labeled freeware are completely free and have no time limits.

Freecell.com

12345

www.freecell.com

Are you a self-proclaimed FreeCell junkie? Then this is the site for you. Study the finer points of FreeCell, play FreeCell online, get FreeCell for your Palm Pilot, shop for FreeCell paraphernalia, or learn how to get the monkey off your back with the 12-step recovery plan.

The House of Cards

12345

thehouseofcards.com

This site features all your favorite traditional and family card games. You can learn the rules to new card games, download card game software, and play card games online. You can also learn a bit about playing cards themselves, from history to collecting.

CHEAT CODES

1UP.com

12345

www.1up.com

1UP.com is a Ziff-Davis site that features video game cheats along with game news, previews, reviews, techniques, and tips from some of the top gaming magazines, including *Computer Gaming World*, *Electronic Gaming Monthly*, *GMR*, *Official U.S. PlayStation Magazine*, and *Xbox Nation*.

A B C D E F G H I J K L M N O P Q R S T U V W X Y Z

GameCube Code Center

12345

www.gamecubecc.com

Cheats, codes, and FAQs for Nintendo's GameCube system. Online store links to Amazon.com for purchasing games.

GameWinners.com

12345

www.gamewinners.com

One of the most informative video game help sites on the Web, tips for more than 18,500 games played on nearly 50 different game systems. Features cheats, hints, FAQs, strategy guides, and gameshark codes. Links to game books and game stores for online shopping.

Go! Go! Cheat Codes!

12345

gogocheatcodes.com

This "destination for gamers on the go" features cheat codes for the most popular game systems, including Xbox, Playstation 2, GameCube, Game Boy, and Dreamcast. Also features cheat codes for PC games. Just click the desired game system, and then click a letter in the directory to browse the available games.

Thinks.com

12345

www.thinks.com

This U.K.-based site calls itself "The Fun and Games for Playful Brains" site, offering visitors daily crosswords of all kinds, word contests, and plenty of other puzzles and games to make you think. Links to some cash games where gambling is promoted.

KAKURO

DoKakuro.com

12345

www.dokakuro.com

This site provides an online player that is much easier than with pencil and paper. You can place both solution and pencil mark digits (working to help you decide which numbers go where), and you can resize it as big or small as you like. Plus you can even save your game—complete with pencil marks—and come back later.

Kakuro.com

12345

www.kakuro.com

This site introduces kakuro, the newest puzzle craze from Japan! Sometimes called "cross-sums" or "kakro," kakuro is sudoku's bigger (and harder) brother. There is a free daily kakuro puzzle or you can download puzzles for a fee.

MAH JONGG

The Mah Jongg Website

12345

www.mahjongg.com

This site aims to provide "comprehensive information on the classic Chinese game for four players." Here, you will find related software, beginner's guides, rules, history, symbolism, and club and tournament listings.

Mahjong Escape from Spin Top Games

12345

www.spintop-games.com/mahjong_game_download/mahjong_escape.html

Here, you can download Mahjong Escape for free, which includes two modes: Dynasty Adventure and Classic Mah Jong solitaire. Five special power-up tiles help you along your journey. Unlimited hints and shuffles are available, too.

Primary Games

12345

www.primarygames.com/holidays/chinese/games/mahjongg/start.htm

Great site that teaches kids how to play mahjong and other Chinese games. Great for adults just learning how to play, too.

MULTI-USER GAMES

MPOGD

12345

www.mpogd.com

This site is devoted to strictly multiplayer games. The directory allows you to search by name, genre, status, price, platform, interface, player rating, and updates. If you think online multiplayer games is your thing, you'll want to start at this site.

MultiPlayerGames.com

12345 RSS

www.multiplayergames.com

MultiPlayerGames.com is an online game community featuring downloads, reviews, patches, news, and forums.

Play Free Online Games

12345

play-free-online-games.com

To be eligible for inclusion in this multiplayer game directory, a game must be: free, multiplayer, online, and played in real time with a strong graphical interface. Players are invited to submit any multiplayer game they know of that are not already in the directory.

POKER *(SEE POKER)*

SUDOKU

Daily Sudoku

12345

www.dailysudoku.com/sudoku/index.shtml

Get your daily sudoku fix here. This site has a sudoku puzzles, puzzles for kids, FAQs, and discussion groups.

MiniClip.com

12345

www.miniclip.com/sudoku/sudoku.php

A Flash-enabled version of sudoku offering three levels of play. Birds chirping in the background make this a relaxing way to play this mind-bending game.

Sudoku.com

12345

www.sudoku.com

Use this site to learn how to solve sudoku puzzles, browse the forums for more tips, or check the solutions to sudokus you may have seen in print. Download a free 28-day trial or buy the program for $14.95.

Web Sudoku

12345

www.websudoku.com

An online version of the popular brain game. Know how you doing after each move by clicking on the How Am I Doing Link. Very fun site!

A B C D E F G H I J K L M N O P Q R S T U V W X Y Z

A B C D E F G H I J K L M N O P Q R S T U V W X Y Z

TRIVIA

Ariel's Simpsons Trivia Quiz

1 2 3 4 5

www.geocities.com/Athens/1530/simptriv.html

Provides an online trivia quiz about the popular television show *The Simpsons*. Includes many different questions and links to other related sites.

FunTrivia.com

1 2 3 4 5 Blog

www.funtrivia.com

Over 65,973 quizzes in 9,974 categories built by the site's community. Features forums, chatrooms, and tournaments. Interesting and entertaining!

The Daily 100

1 2 3 4 5

www.80s.com/Entertainment/Movies/Daily100

A fantastic site featuring 1980s movie trivia. The site provides the clip; you provide the actor, movie, and year it debuted. The site keeps track of players; that is, it's a contest. Closed on weekends.

Trivia Company's Trivia Wars

1 2 3 4 5

www.triviawars.com

Sharpen your wits, trivia junkies, for here is your site. Cruise through this site if you know everything about nothing important. Some questions here will stump all challengers with 100 different categories.

GARDENING

American Horticultural Society

www.ahs.org

This site, for the horticulture connoisseur, provides links to several articles from *The American Gardener*. Membership in the AHL and a subscription to *The American Gardener* permit you to order several varieties of seeds free in the month of January. Includes a gardening Q&A. Members are graced with many other privileges, too.

Better Homes and Gardens Online Garden Page

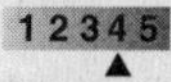

www.bhg.com/bhg/gardening

This site offers a garden forum with questions and answers, some great long articles, shorter handy tips, and even how-to videos. Plant Hardiness and First Frost maps allow you to click on your state and can be magnified right down to your county.

Botany.com

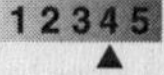

www.botany.com

An encyclopedia of plants. Each entry provides a description of the plant, instructions on how to grow the plant, and information on how to propagate the plant.

Best Burpee Seeds Home Page

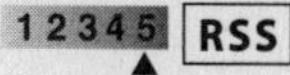

www.burpee.com

More than 12,000 products—plants, flowers, gardening supplies, accessories, and gifts. Gardening tips, an online magazine, and a 24-hour chat are also available. Membership and monthly newsletter are free. Burpee offers several advantages that your local nursery can't match; it features a wider selection of vegetables and other plants, all the tools and supplies to get the job done, and the information and advice you need to deal with plant diseases, unbalanced soils, and other problems you might run into. Whether you're a novice or expert gardener, you will find plenty to satisfy you at this Best of the Best site.

Container Garden Guide

www.gardenguides.com/TipsandTechniques/container.htm

Succinct guide to growing a flower or vegetable garden on your porch or patio.

Cortesia Sanctuary and Center

www.cortesia.org

This site is divided into five sections, including The Cortesia Sanctuary Project: everything you need to know about creating a sanctuary; The Sanctuary Garden: gardening, garden products/books, garden inspiration, flower essences, composting, and so on; Music; Inspiration; and Publications & Products.

Earthly Goods Online

www.earthlygoods.com

Earthly Goods is a supplier of wildflower seeds, wildflower seed mixtures, and grass seeds. Advice on growing from seeds, garden planning, and online ordering are a few of its features. Earthly Goods offers custom seed packets for advertising, fundraising, and special promotions.

Gardener's Supply Company

12345

www.gardeners.com

Huge mail-order gardening store now has a website where you can place your order online. Carries a wide variety of gardening tools and accessories designed to simplify your gardening experience, make it more enjoyable, and beautify your garden.

GardenGuides

12345

www.gardenguides.com

Guides to herbs, bulbs, perennials, and annuals cover both basic information and interesting tidbits to help you appreciate what you plant. Several discussion groups for all of your plant questions. An easy-to-use site that new gardeners especially will find invaluable.

Garden Humor

12345

home.golden.net/~dhobson

Dedicated to "boldly grow where no one has groan before," this site seeks to keep you laughing while you're recovering from working on your lawn and garden. Be sure to take the survey to determine whether you qualify as a member of the Mad Gardener Society.

GardenNet

www.gardennet.com

Comprehensive directory of websites that feature gardening information and products. Links are grouped by individual plant names, plant groups, equipment and products, gardening types such as Bonsai or Urban, general information, events, and services. Excellent place to start your search.

Gardenscape

12345

www.gardenscape.on.ca

At this site, you can find an excellent collection of innovative garden products and accessories, including tools from companies such as Felco, Fiskars, Haws, and Dramm, and a unique line of gifts for gardeners.

GardenWeb

www.gardenweb.com

GardenWeb is the largest gardening site on the Web, including forums, Q & A, events, directories, contests, and catalogs.

Kidsgardening.com

12345

www.kidsgardening.com

Created and maintained by the National Gardening Association, this site is dedicated to getting children involved in the wonderful world of gardening. Includes a Kidsgarden store, lesson plans for teachers, ideas for gardening activities, and a list of frequently asked questions and answers.

Missouri Botanical Garden

12345

www.mobot.org

The MBG's website contains beautiful photographs of some of the many rare plants grown at its greenhouse. Information is also available from the research division in the field of biodiversity. A collection of online books is also accessible.

National Gardening Association

12345

www.garden.org

Gardeners will find the FAQs, tips, and reminders a great help, although the NGA was originally established to help foster gardening as a pastime. At the site, you'll find information on gardening programs in schools, available gardening grants, and other ways that the organization can help.

New Jersey Weed Gallery

1 2 3 4 5

www.rce.rutgers.edu/weeds

From Aster to Yellow Rocket, an award-winning weed identification site from Rutgers University.

Secret Garden

1 2 3 4 5

www.pbs.org/wnet/nature/secretgarden/index.html

This site, derived from the PBS Nature series on the *Secret Garden*, presents information and tips on transforming your backyard into a haven for wildlife.

Smith & Hawken

1 2 3 4 5

www.smithandhawken.com

Smith & Hawken sells well-built gardening tools and products so as to encourage gardening and preserve natural resources. The products are beautiful, as is the site. A good place to start if you're looking for a new garden trowel or teak bench.

FLOWERS

1-888-Orchids.com

1 2 3 4 5

www.1888orchids.com

Buy orchids, orchid books, orchid supplies, orchid pots, orchid baskets, and anything else related to orchids at this site.

The American Orchid Society

1 2 3 4 5

www.orchidweb.org/aos

Anyone interested in trying to grow orchids will want to visit this site for guidance in creating conditions suitable for orchid growing. You'll also find information on upcoming orchid events, publications, research, and a discussion forum.

American Rose Society

1 2 3 4 5

www.ars.org

If you're a rose lover, you'll want to consider joining this nonprofit organization, which is dedicated to the enjoyment, enhancement, and promotion of this flower. In addition to providing plenty of information about the thousands of varieties of roses, the site also offers answers to your rose-related questions, information on upcoming floral competitions, and membership FAQs.

Butterfly Gardening

1 2 3 4 5

www.butterflyworld.com

Home of Butterfly World, the first and largest butterfly house in the United States. Take a virtual walk through the gardens, shop the online store, or learn how to help the campaign by creating butterfly-friendly environments.

Wildflower and Prairie Grass Seed

1 2 3 4 5

www.prairiefrontier.com

Purchase seeds and plants for the prairies here, and you'll also get all the information you need to help you to create your own. Helpful information from basic definitions to how-to articles, and a Q&A area. If you're interested in prairie plants or plantings, this is a great first stop.

Zen Gardens

1 2 3 4 5

academic.bowdoin.edu/zen

This site, from Bowdoin College, features a virtual tour of Japanese gardens consisting of both text descriptions and photos.

A B C D E F G H I J K L M N O P Q R S T U V W X Y Z

GAYS/LESBIAN/BISEXUAL/TRANSGENDER

Gay.com

www.gay.co

A news, information, and chat site for gay men. Links to stores where you can shop online.

Gay Men's Health Crisis

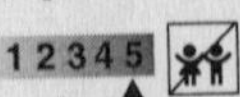

www.gmhc.org

Find out more about the nation's oldest and largest not-for-profit AIDS organization: Gay Men's Health Crisis (GMHC), founded in 1981. Learn how you can get involved, get resources for support, access its AIDS Library, read about GMHC's latest efforts, and more.

GayScape

www.gayscape.com

Specialized search tool for gay, lesbian, and bisexual sites on the Web. This search index lists more than 68,000 sites.

PlanetOut

www.planetout.com

Premier gay and lesbian website, features articles, photos, video clips, FAQ, and products for the gay and lesbian community. By joining PlanetOut, you can post messages in numerous forums, chat online, create a member profile (with or without a photo of yourself), and subscribe to free newsletters.

PrideLinks.com

www.pridelinks.com

Bills itself as "The Internet's premiere gay, lesbian, bi, and transsexual search engine." And with more than 8,000 links, this site lives up to its reputation. If you are looking for links, resources, information, support, or just fun, start here.

Best Queer Resources Directory (QRD)

www.qrd.org/qrd

Widely thought to be the biggest and best gay and lesbian information source on the Internet, the Queer Resources Directory breaks down all kinds of resource information into easy-to-understand categories. You can surf the categories or jump directly to the Resource Tree.

COLLEGES & UNIVERSITIES

Financial Aid for Lesbian, Gay, Bisexual, and Transgender Individuals

www.finaid.org/otheraid/gay.phtml

FinAid, a company that provides advice and information on college financial aid for all students seeking a college education, provides this section specifically for lesbian, gay, bisexual, and transgender individuals. Here you can find information about national scholarships, campus-specific s-cholarships, and federal and state programs.

Harvard Gay & Lesbian Caucus

www.hglc.org/index.html

Harvard Gay & Lesbian Caucus members include more than 2,200 gay, lesbian, bisexual, and transgender Harvard and Radcliff alums, faculty, and staff. This site, run primarily for caucus members, details the organization's goals and activities.

Related Sites

www.columbia.edu/cu/gables

www.gwu.edu/~lgba

www.northwestern.edu/gluu

CRISIS INTERVENTION & COUNSELING

Association for Gay, Lesbian, and Bisexual Issues in Counseling

www.aglbic.org

AGLBIC is dedicated to "educating mental health service providers about issues confronting gay, lesbian, bisexual, and transgender (GLBT) individuals." Here counselors, therapists, and social workers can find information on how gay, lesbian, and bisexual issues might affect their clients and how they can help their clients deal with emotional and psychological issues caused by society's treatment of them.

The GLBT National Help Center

www.glnh.org

A nonprofit organization dedicated to meeting the needs of the gay, lesbian, bisexual, and transgender community by offering free and totally anonymous information, referrals, and peer counseling. Offers a toll-free phone number that anyone can call for gay/lesbian support and information. You can also submit email from this website and get a confidential reply.

HOME & FAMILY

Family Diversity Projects Inc.

www.familydiv.org

Family Diversity Projects is a nonprofit organization founded in 1996 by photographer Gigi Kaeser and writer Peggy Gillespie. Since that time, they've toured with their four traveling photo-text exhibits around the country to great acclaim. In addition, the book *Of Many Colors: Portraits of Multiracial Families*, (UMass Press, 1997) has been published; along with *Love Makes a Family: Portraits of Lesbian, Gay, Bisexual, and Transgender Parents and Their Families*, (UMass Press, 1999). Family Diversity Projects also provides speakers and workshop leaders for conferences and exhibit venues.

Family Pride Coalition

www.familypride.org

Dedicated to advancing "the well-being of lesbian, gay, bisexual, and transgender parents and their families through mutual support, community collaboration, and public understanding." Here, you can find links to events, programs, libraries, and other sources for helping families succeed.

Gay Parent Magazine

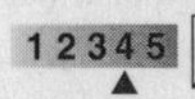 

www.gayparentmag.com

Gay Parent magazine is "the oldest nationally distributed publication dedicated to lesbian, gay, bisexual, and transgender parenting (LGBT)." Here you can subscribe to the magazine, sample its content, and access other information and resources that focus on gay parenting and families.

Best Parents, Families, and Friends of Lesbians and Gays (PFLAG)

www.pflag.org

PFLAG promotes the health and well-being of gay and lesbian persons, as well as their families and friends, through support, education, and advocacy. This organization provides counseling to help straight families and friends accept and support their gay and lesbian loved ones and organizes grassroots efforts to end discriminatory practices toward gays and lesbians. This site's excellent design and content combine to make it an easy Best of the Best pick.

Partners Task Force for Gay and Lesbian Couples

www.buddybuddy.com

Information and resources for gay and lesbian couples seeking ways to ensure their rights as a family. Includes discussion of marriage laws, surveys, legal information, and political news.

MEDIA & CULTURE

Gay Media Express

www.gaymediaexpress.com

Gay Media Express is a commercial service that helps businesses and organizations place ads in different media channels that broadcast to the gay and lesbian community. Here, you can learn more about the company and the advertising opportunities it offers.

In The Life TV.org

www.inthelifetv.org

A national television series in a news magazine format that reports on gay and lesbian issues and culture. Broadcasts on more than 130 public television stations nationwide, including all the top 20 viewer markets, reaching more than 1,000,000 viewers per episode.

International Association of Gay Square Dance Clubs

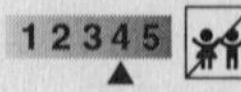

www.iagsdc.org

The IAGSDC is the International Association of Gay Square Dance Clubs, a lesbian and gay organization that is the umbrella organization for gay square dance clubs in the United States, Canada, and Australia, formed by and for lesbians and gay men in their community and for their friends.

International Gay Rodeo Association

www.igra.com

The gay rodeo association holds its own rodeos all over the country, including gay meccas such as Los Angeles and Washington, D.C., plus smaller cities such as Billings, Montana, and Omaha, Nebraska. Get the full touring schedule here and find out how to become a member.

The Isle of Lesbos

www.sappho.com

Well-designed pages of poetry, art, and links to other lesbian-related sites. Coverage of Sapphic poetry is extensive.

Lesbian and Gay Bands of America

www.gaybands.org

Lesbian and Gay Bands of America (LGBA) is the national musical organization composed of concert and marching bands from cities across America. Find out here about the 29 member bands and their parade and concert appearances.

Women in the Arts

wiaonline.org

WIA is the organization that produces the National Women's Music Festival, the oldest and largest all-indoor festival of women's music and culture each June. Find out what it has in store for this year's festival and learn more about this nonprofit organization.

POLITICAL & LEGAL ISSUES

American Civil Liberties Union–Lesbian and Gay Rights

www.aclu.org/LesbianGayRights/LesbianGayRightsMain.cfm

A whole branch of the ACLU is devoted to lesbian and gay rights, and this section of the ACLU website provides updates on recent court rulings and bills coming up in Congress. You'll also find information about joining the ACLU here.

Gay and Lesbian Alliance Against Defamation (GLAAD)

www.glaad.org

GLAAD bills itself as "your online resource for promoting fair, accurate, and inclusive representation as a means of challenging discrimination based on sexual orientation or identity." If you, a gay or lesbian person you know have been the victim of discrimination or abuse, this is the group to contact to find out what you can do.

Gay/Lesbian Politics and Law

www.indiana.edu/~glbtpol

From Indiana University, this site features links to information and other resources on various topics relating to gay rights, politics, and policy.

Human Rights Campaign

www.hrc.org

The Human Rights Campaign is the United States' largest lesbian, gay, bisexual, and transgender political organization. It works to end discrimination, secure equal rights, and protect the health and safety of all Americans. This good-looking site contains a lot of political news for anyone interested in these issues.

National Gay and Lesbian Task Force (NGLTF)

www.thetaskforce.org

NGLTF is a leading progressive civil rights organization that, since its inception in 1973, has been at the forefront of every major initiative for lesbian, gay, bisexual, and transgender rights. This organization is at work at national, state, and local levels, combating antigay violence, battling radical-right antigay legislative and ballot measures; advocating an end to job discrimination; working to repeal sodomy laws; demanding an effective governmental response to HIV; and reform of the healthcare system and much more.

PUBLICATIONS

365Gay

www.365gay.com

365Gay is an online news magazine that goes way beyond just presenting GLBT headline news. It also features movie and video reviews, gossip, gay and lesbian fitness and health information, style guides, financial advice, travel articles, games, and opinion columns.

The Advocate

www.advocate.com

One of the oldest and most respected gay magazines. You can browse article summaries for the current issue here (but you have to buy the print edition for the full text) and participate in the *Advocate*'s latest poll.

Girlfriends Magazine

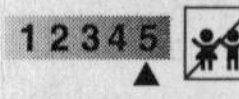

www.girlfriendsmag.com

A national lesbian magazine. Each issue is loaded with coverage of culture, politics, and sexuality from a lesbian perspective. You can sample all that analog stuff here, but take time to enjoy the web-only content, too. If you're missing a special *Girlfriends* back issue, you can get a copy at the online store. Ask Dr. Dyke your health questions or get advice in the Kiss and Tell area.

Whosoever

www.whosoever.org

A great magazine for gay, lesbian, bisexual, and transgender Christians, it includes theological articles, inspiration, and political-action alerts.

RELIGION

Affirmation: Gay and Lesbian Mormons

www.affirmation.org

With chapters around the world, Affirmation serves the needs of gays, lesbians, bisexuals, transgenders, and their supportive family and friends through social and educational activities. This site includes news, events, and support resources.

Dignity/USA

www.dignityusa.org

Dignity is an international organization for gay, lesbian, bisexual, and transgender Roman Catholics. There are chapters in most major cities. Visit Dignity's website to learn about ongoing projects, news, worship, and liturgy. Check the FAQ list to learn more.

Gay Religion and Spirituality

www.cbel.com/gay_religion_and_spirituality

This site features hundreds of handpicked links to sites that cover gay religion and spirituality, making it a great directory to available Web resources. Links are grouped by religion and denomination, including categories of Atheism, Christianity, Hinduism, Islam, and Judaism, among others.

Unitarian Universalist Association

www.uua.org

The Unitarian Universalist Church is a "big-tent" group that welcomes a wide variety of believers, including the LGBT community. Find out more about this organization at this page.

TRAVEL

The Guide Online

www.guidemag.com/travel/travelhome.cfm

The Guide is a travel magazine for gays that features news and politics. This travel section prompts you to type your destination (anywhere in the world) for help in finding gay sites and attractions at your desired destination.

QT Magazine

www.qtmagazine.com

QT is a gay and lesbian travel magazine that features articles about selected destinations. Some articles are generic, similar to what you might find in any travel magazine, but most articles provide information specifically for the gay and lesbian traveler.

Related Sites

www.abovebeyondtours.com

www.alysonadventures.com

www.journeysbysea.com

www.gay-travel.com

www.discoveryvallarta.com/guide.html

www.venture-out.com

A B C D E F G H I J K L M N O P Q R S T U V W X Y Z

GENEALOGY

Ancestry.com

1 2 3 4 5

www.ancestry.com/search/main.htm

Looking for someone? You have several options at Ancestry.com. Here, you can access a limited number of free search databases or pay a monthly subscription fee of $12.95 to $29.95 to gain access to all the databases. This site includes the Social Security Death Index, AIS Census Records Index, global searching, maps, books, and much more.

Beginner's Guide to Family History Research

1 2 3 4 5

www.arkansasresearch.com/guide.html

If you can't even spell the word g-e-n-e-a-l-o-g-y, this is the place for you to start. Everyone has ancestors, and if you're wondering who yours are, it's time to get involved in family history and genealogy research.

Cyndi's List of Genealogy Sites on the Web

1 2 3 4 5

www.cyndislist.com/howto.htm

Great index of genealogy sites on the Web, listing everything from beginner's guides and books to articles on using maps and microfiche. The links on this site comprise a veritable course on teaching people how to become genealogy experts.

Ellis Island

1 2 3 4 5

www.ellisisland.org

If one of your ancestors passed through Ellis Island or the Port of New York on his or her way to becoming a U.S. citizen, chances are this website can turn up a record of that person's arrival. At this site, you can search for and (optionally) purchase passenger documents that record a relation's arrival in the United States. You can even build a family scrapbook online to share with other visitors or check out some family scrapbooks that other people have already constructed.

Everton's Genealogical Helper

1 2 3 4 5

www.everton.com

Search the genealogical database for an ancestor, buy products to help you in your research efforts, check out thousands of links listed here, and get help from others who've been at their search longer than you have. This site is packed with information and resources for novice and expert genealogists alike.

Best Family Search

1 2 3 4 5

www.familysearch.org

This is the site to visit if you are looking for the largest collection of genealogical information in the world. The site was created by The Church of Jesus Christ of Latter-Day Saints and contains links to 400 million names of people dating back to the 1500s. In many cases, you'll find family pedigree charts. Because the Church's family history efforts are funded by charitable donations, it freely offers this website to anyone interested in finding their family's roots.

FamilyTreeMaker.com

1 2 3 4 5

familytreemaker.genealogy.com

In addition to searchable databases and family-finder information, you can also access how-to information to help in your search and buy genealogical products and reference material.

FamilyTreeMaker is one of the most popular programs around for researching family history and constructing family trees.

The Genealogy Home Page

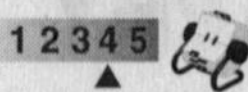

www.genhomepage.com

This extensive set of pages offers information about maps and geography, communication with other genealogists, a compendium of genealogy databases, a list of other genealogy home pages, and other genealogy resources both in North America and around the world.

German Genealogy Resources

www.germanroots.com

Do you have some German blood in your family? Then check out this site, where you can track down links to your Germanic ancestry.

JewishGen: The Home of Jewish Genealogy

www.jewishgen.org

For people researching their Jewish ancestry, this nonprofit site offers a family finder database of 250,000 names and towns, access to discussion groups, and infolinks.

National Archives and Records Administration: Genealogy Page

www.archives.gov/research_room/genealogy/index.html

NARA offers online microfilm catalogs, which are also available for purchase. The microfilms are available for census records, military service records, and immigrant and passenger arrival records. These records can be used for genealogical research.

Origins.net

www.origins.net

Are you descended from British royalty? Search the records at this site to find out. Here, you can search Scots, Irish, and English records, including census data, Griffith's valuations, ships' passenger lists, church records, convict records, and more. Click the How to Trace Your Family History link to learn the seven steps of an effective search, even if you're not Irish, Scottish, or English.

Vital Records Information: United States

vitalrec.com

This page contains information about where to obtain vital records from each state, territory, and county of the United States.

Related Sites

www.ctssar.org

www.geo.ed.ac.uk/home/scotland/genealogy.html

www.ngsgenealogy.org

GEOGRAPHY

CIA World Factbook

12345

www.cia.gov/cia/publications/factbook

One of the CIA's best-kept secrets is its World Factbook, which provides detailed information about various regions, countries, islands, and areas around the world. If you're planning a trip to a particular country or are doing a report about a country, check here for the latest information. Great site for kids to visit when they're doing their geography homework.

FirstGov for Kids: Geography

12345

www.kids.gov/k_geography.htm

The Federal Citizen Information Center provides this useful site to help kids find out about certain regions, countries, and cities; investigate volcanoes, rain forests, and other geographical features; view pictures of the earth from space; and much more. Provides links to additional resources.

GeoCommunity

12345

data.geocomm.com

Free access to the largest Geographical Information Systems database on the Internet.

Geography at the University of Buffalo

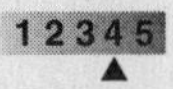

www.geog.buffalo.edu

Wondering what geography is and why geography could be a possible focus of undergraduate or graduate study? This site addresses both of these questions, as well as describes what the Geography department at UB has to offer in four different concentrations: Cartography and GIS, Urban and Regional Analysis, Physical Geography and Environmental Systems, and International Business and World Trade. Also find out what geographers do after they get their degree.

Geography World

12345

members.aol.com/bowermanb/101.html

Plenty of information for students studying geography—ranging from homework help to background information on cultures and history of countries around the world. You'll also find climate, conservation, and calendar information, as well as geography games to enjoy.

GPS Primer

12345

www.garmin.com/pressroom/gpsPrimer.html

Learn about global positioning systems (GPS) and how you can use them to navigate the globe.

Related Site

www.howstuffworks.com/gps.htm

Best National Geographic

12345

www.nationalgeographic.com

Learn geography from the experts. Home of *National Geographic*, the magazine that has traveled the world and taught children and adults to appreciate geography, nature, and various cultures for decades. Here, you will find online versions of *National Geographic*'s award-winning photographs, plus the latest articles from around the globe. Special areas for kids, parents, and teachers. Easy to navigate and packed with great information, *National Geographic* is an obvious Best of the Best selection.

Test Your Geography Knowledge

1 2 3 4 5 ▲ (rating: 4)

www.lizardpoint.com/fun/geoquiz

After you study all the information at all the sites in this category, come to this site to test your knowledge.

USGS Learning Web

1 2 3 4 5 ▲ (rating: 5)

www.usgs.gov/education

Map lesson plans and activities from the U.S. Geological Survey, geared toward grades K–12.

WorldAtlas.com

1 2 3 4 5 ▲ (rating: 5) RSS

www.worldatlas.com/aatlas/world.htm

Cool interactive globe. Click a continent and then a country to get a quick overview of its borders and geographical features plus a wealth of information about the country's economy, language, climate, currency, and more. Great resource for kids.

GIFTS

ArtisanGifts.com

12345

www.artisan-gifts.com

Choose distinctive, handcrafted gifts and have them wrapped and sent with just a few keystrokes. Pick by the occasion, or your budget, or select a category to get started.

Ashford.com

12345

www.ashford.com

Ashford offers fine personal accessories, such as watches, writing instruments, jewelry, and more, as well as information on what gifts are hot to help you make your selection.

Baby Shower Gifts

12345

www.adorablebabygifts.com

Thoughtful gifts for a new baby. Specializes in baby clothing, gift baskets, children's jewelry, christening gifts, baby shower games, and information on baby names.

Bath and Body Works

12345

www.bathandbodyworks.com

One of the best smelling places on the Web, Bath and Body Works offers a popular collection of face and body lotions, shampoos and conditioners, fragrances, candles, and special gift packages.

Blue Mountain Cards

12345

www.bluemountain.com

Blue Mountain is well known for its online greeting cards. Here you can find cards for every occasion and holiday, customize your cards, and email them to friends and family. Printable cards also are available.

Brookstone

12345

www.brookstone.com

When you need a gift for the person who has everything or if you just love cool gadgets, check out Brookstone's website, where you can find everything from foot massagers and CD players to robotic vacuum cleaners.

Computer Gear

12345

www.computergear.com

When you need gift ideas for a geek, this is the place to go. Here you can find gifts, gadgets, and apparel for computer geeks, engineering geeks, Einstein enthusiasts, and *Star Wars* devotees. How about a crystal mouse? A binary clock? A stuffed Linux doll? You can find all that and more things you could never imagine in existence at this store.

FragranceNet.com

12345

www.fragrancenet.com

Featuring more than 8,000 genuine, brand-name fragrances, skin-care, and hair-care products for both women and men, plus scented candles and other gifts. Discounts range from 20 percent to 70 percent off. Free shipping on orders over $60.

The Gift Collector

12345

www.giftcollector.com

With more than 8,000 items, this online store features figurines, crystal, china, and other collectibles from Waterford, Swarovsky, Department 56, Herend, Lladro, Harmony Kingdom, TY Beanie Babies, and more.

GiftCertificates.com

12345

www.giftcertificates.com

Gift certificates that are great as gifts, and corporate incentives or small business rewards can all be found here. Choose from more than 700 merchants, enter the value you want to purchase, and choose the gift-wrapping and card you want sent along with it. Your shopping is done, and an original gift certificate will arrive at the recipient's door in no time.

Best Gifts.com

12345

www.gifts.com

Find great gifts and great gift ideas here. Seasonal gifts and ideas for special holidays are featured. You can find a large number of special gift ideas for him, for her, even for pet owners, for any occasion. Gifts range from plants to jewelry to gift baskets filled with food, wine, bath items, golf-related items, and more. Just about anything a gift giver could want can be found on this Best of the Best site!

Gump's

12345

www.gumpsbymail.com

Shop the famous Gump's San Francisco department store online or request a catalog. Search by type of product or get ideas at the site for home furnishings, decorative accessories, and special occasion gifts.

Hammacher Schlemmer

12345

www.hammacherschlemmer.com

Search for unusual gifts for business and personal gift giving here.

Harry and David Gourmet Food Gifts

12345

www.harryanddavid.com

Order gourmet food items and have them shipped to you or a friend. Specializes in fresh fruit and gift baskets.

MarthaStewart.com

12345

www.marthastewart.com

Shop Martha By Mail for special gift ideas, as well as flowers, all from this site. She specializes in entertaining and keepsakes.

Perfect Present Picker

12345

presentpicker.com/ppp

This expert shopping program will select a gift that's just right, based on someone's profession, interest, life, age, sex, and personality. Links to a large variety of online retailers.

Perfumania.com

12345

www.perfumania.com

"America's largest online fragrance store," this site carries fragrances for women, men, and children, plus bath and body products and gift sets. Order online to have products shipped to your door.

RedEnvelope Gifts: The Right Gift, Right Away

1 2 3 4 5

www.redenvelope.com

Promotes the last-minute approach to gift giving. RedEnvelope offers an extensive collection of imaginative, original gifts for every occasion, recipient, and budget through its website and catalog. The company's merchants travel the world for unique products and often commission artists and vendors to create exclusive gifts just for RedEnvelope shoppers.

SeniorStore.com

1 2 3 4 5

www.seniorstore.com

Products, birthday gifts, and gift ideas for seniors, grandparents, and the elderly.

Sharper Image

1 2 3 4 5

www.sharperimage.com

Select gifts from this catalog site, known for its unusual, harder-to-find personal and home items. Great place for gadget shoppers or for those seeking the perfect gift for the person who has everything.

Spencer Gifts

www.spencergifts.com

Looking for a gift that's out of the ordinary? Then check out Spencer Gifts' huge line of odd and irreverent gifts. Living-dead dolls, bobblehead Spiderman figurines, dorm room accessories such as black lights and lava lamps, gag gifts, light-hearted birthday party accessories, erotic gifts, and more. Shop online, so you won't have to face the embarrassment of visiting the store in person.

Surprise.com

1 2 3 4 5

www.surprise.com

At Surprise.com, you get gift ideas from other users. You can shop for ideas by the person's relationship to you (brother, sister, friend, kid's coach), by occasion (birthday, Halloween, graduation), or by category (unusual sense of humor, dog owner, loves to cook). Follow the trail of links to the item you want and then purchase it online.

Target

1 2 3 4 5

www.target.com

Shop for gifts at Target without ever leaving your home. If you're engaged or expecting a baby, you can register online, making it easy for friends and family members to shop for gifts.

GOLF

BadGolfMonthly.com

1 2 3 4 5

www.badgolfer.com

The golf site "for the golfer who really sucks," this site is more of a serious vacationer's guide to golf courses from TravelGolf.com. Some humorous articles provide a little levity for an otherwise-frustrating sport.

Ben Hogan Golf Products

1 2 3 4 5

www.benhogan.com

Whether you're a Ben Hogan fan or you just like to swing his golf clubs, you'll love this site. Fans can find a complete timeline of Ben Hogan's career from 1938 to 1959 and view a few of his closest friends reminisce about their experiences with Ben Hogan. Customers and dealers can learn about the complete line of Ben Hogan golf clubs and accessories; Demo Days, when and where products will be demonstrated; and meet the staff pros. Very polished site.

FootJoy

1 2 3 4 5

www.footjoy.com

FootJoy is the #1 shoe and glove in golf, offering dozens of shoe styles and a wide selection of gloves. Check out FootJoy's products in its online catalog or enter your ZIP code to find the nearest golf shop that sells FootJoy products.

Golden Tee

1 2 3 4 5

www.goldentee.com

Golden Tee Golf is the most popular coin-operated video game on the planet. You're likely to find a game in many pubs and restaurants near you. At this site, you can learn more about the game and various tournaments its company sponsors, access news and discussion forums, find a game near you, and check your statistics if you choose to keep them online.

 Golf.com

1 2 3 4 5 RSS

www.golf.com

Golf.com, from GolfServ, provides the best in golf content, commerce, and services. This site covers every aspect of golf and caters to all those involved in golf—from fans to players, duffers to pros. The opening page displays a list of links to the latest news stories in professional golf along with tabs for other sections of the site, including tour central, courses and travel, USGA handicap, instruction, games and contests, and golf market. Plenty of content is offered for free; but if you want to access some of the more interactive areas, you need to subscribe.

Golfcourse.com

1 2 3 4 5

www.golfcourse.com

Golf magazine's directory of golf courses, this site provides information on thousands of golf courses throughout North America and the world. The site includes comprehensive course descriptions and a list of the world's best courses.

GolfGuideWeb.com

1 2 3 4 5

www.golfguideweb.com/golfcourses.html

Comprehensive list of golf courses across the nation listed by state and city. GolfGuideWeb.com provides stats for most golf courses and reviews for many. If you're planning on visiting a particular state or city and would like to know what's available in the way of golf courses, this is the site for you.

Golfsmith

www.golfsmith.com

Golfsmith International began more than 30 years ago and is now the largest direct marketer and superstore retailer of golf equipment in the world. The company makes and fits clubs and sells more than 20,000 different golf-related products. It even runs its own golf academy.

Golf Tips Magazine

www.golftipsmag.com

Excellent collection of golf tips from the experts. Tips for driving, using irons, working on your short game, and putting. Some helpful video clips that show you just what to do.

GolfWeb

www.golfweb.com

Here, you can access the regular golf stuff: tournament results, online pro shops, and so on. But you can also link to the Lesson Tee for golfing tips, go to a link for women in golf, and write a personal message to the winner of a current tournament. This site has an easily accessible design and is packed with useful information and golf tips.

LPGA.com

www.Lpga.com

Get complete LPGA (Ladies Professional Golf Association) tournament coverage at the site, as well as an animated online lesson. You'll find schedules, player bios, headline golf news, and lots more about the LPGA at this official site. Area for junior golfers, too.

The Masters

www.masters.org

Official site of the Masters, including everything you want to know about the history of the Masters tournament and this year's event.

The Open Championship

www.opengolf.com

The world's oldest championship, one of golf's four major annual events; played in Scotland, it is the only one outside of America. Find out all the details about this year's Open at this official Open Championship site.

PGA.com

www.pga.com

PGA.com is the Official website of the PGA. PGA works with IBM as an alliance partner for the website. In addition, through IBM's role as official scoring and information system of the PGA, PGA.com continues to provide the world's best real-time golf event scoring system. PGA.com is one of the most highly trafficked golf sites on the Web, delivering millions of page views surrounding PGA major championships including the PGA Championship, Ryder Cup, PGA Seniors' Championship, and the MasterCard PGA Grand Slam of Golf.

USGA

www.usga.org

The United States Golf Association (USGA) has served as the national governing body of golf since its formation in 1894. It is a nonprofit organization run by golfers for the benefit of golfers. The USGA consists of more than 9,100 golf facilities. The USGA's Members Program has grown to more than 800,000 golfers who help support the game and the association.

Related Sites
www.callawaygolf.com
www.cobragolf.com
www.macgregorgolf.com
www.maxfli.com
www.nevercompromise.com
www.orlimar.com
www.taylormadegolf.com
www.topflite.com

GOVERNMENT INFORMATION/SERVICES

Afghanistan
dir.yahoo.com/Regional/Countries/Afghanistan

Australia
www.gov.au

Belgium
www.belgium.be/eportal/application?pageid=aboutBelgium

Brazil
www.brazil.gov.br

Canada
canada.gc.ca/main_e.html

Chile
www.gobiernodechile.cl/index/index.asp

China
dir.yahoo.com/Regional/Countries/China

Costa Rica
www.casapres.go.cr

Ecuador
www.ec-gov.net

Egypt
www.shoura.gov.eg/shoura_en/index.asp

European Union
ec.europa.eu/index.htm

France
dir.yahoo.com/Regional/Countries/France

Germany
www.bundesregierung.de/Webs/Breg/DE/Homepage/home.html

Greece
dir.yahoo.com/Regional/Countries/Greece

Iceland
government.is

India
goidirectory.nic.in

Indonesia
www.indonesia.go.id

Iran
www.majlis.ir

Iraq
dir.yahoo.com/Regional/Countries/Iraq

Israel
www.mfa.gov.il/mfa

Italy
dir.yahoo.com/Regional/Countries/Italy

Japan
dir.yahoo.com/Regional/Countries/Japan

Kenya
www.kenya.go.ke

Kuwait
www.moc.kw/ar.htm

Lithuania
www.lrvk.lt/main_en.php

Mexico
dir.yahoo.com/Regional/Countries/Mexico

Netherlands
www.overheid.nl

New Zealand
www.govt.nz

Nigeria
www.nigeria.gov.ng

Pakistan
www.pakistan.gov.pk

Peru
www.peru.gob.pe

Russia
www.pravitelstvo.gov.ru/government/index.html?he_id=38

Saudi Arabia
dir.yahoo.com/Regional/Countries/Saudi_Arabia

South Africa
www.gov.za/index.html

South Korea
www.assembly.go.kr/index.jsp

Spain
www.la-moncloa.es/default.htm

Thailand
dir.yahoo.com/Regional/Countries/Thailand

Turkey
dir.yahoo.com/Regional/Countries/Turkey

United Kingdom
www.direct.gov.uk/Homepage/fs/en

United States of America
www.firstgov.gov

GRAPHIC NOVELS

Graphic Novel Review

1 2 3 4 5 (rating: 3) Blog

www.graphicnovelreview.com

The casual reader can look at book-length comics on this site. Usually there is a substantial review of one graphic novel at some point each weekend. Then, midweek, they post links to other people's reviews, along with creator interviews that have been done in support of the book, and so on. A great way to "read" more graphic novels.

Manga Graphic Novels

1 2 3 4 5 (rating: 4)

www.bargainanime.com/manga-graphic-novels.html

This site lists Manga graphic novels by title. You can save 25 to 30 percent off the list price by making your purchases here. Also offered are anime DVDs and merchandise.

NBM Publishing

1 2 3 4 5 (rating: 4)

www.nbmpub.com

NBM is a critically acclaimed graphic novel publisher that showcases works from North America and Europe. This site references more than 150 graphic novels including ComicsLit, Humor, Mystery, Fantasy, Horror, and Fairy Tales.

No Flying, No Tights

1 2 3 4 5 (rating: 5) Blog

www.noflyingnotights.com

The original No Flying, No Tights site reviews graphic novels for teens. They have also introduced Sidekicks, a site devoted to all those kids' graphic novels out there. On the other end of the spectrum is The Lair, featuring graphic novels for older teens and adults. Check them all out at this site.

HEALTH

Aetna InteliHealth

www.intelihealth.com

This is a comprehensive and easy-to-navigate site that covers all aspects of human health, including health for children, men, women, and seniors. Site is organized into four sections: Diseases & Conditions, Healthy Lifestyles, Your Health, and Look It Up. Special features include health commentaries, dental health, a drug resource center, ask the expert, and interactive tools. Great site to bookmark for all your health needs and concerns.

eCureMe Self Diagnosis

www.ecureme.com

Answer a few questions to obtain a diagnosis online. Site also features general health resources, including a medical encyclopedia, health charts, information about prescription medications and treatments, a calorie counter, a Health-O-Matic Meter, a list of specialty topics, online directories, and much more.

FamilyDoctor.org

familydoctor.org

Created and maintained by the American Academy of Family Physicians, this site has the basic information you and your doctor need to know about all aspects of adult and child health. The home page provides quick access to a database of nearly all illnesses; simply click a letter to view the names of illnesses that begin with that letter, and then click the link for the specific illness or condition. From the home page, you can also read the daily health tip, access a health dictionary and other tools, and check out the five most popular topics. This site features separate sections for men's and women's health, seniors, healthy living, and parents and kids. Much of the content is also available in Spanish.

HealthWeb

healthweb.org

HealthWeb features an extensive directory of links to hundreds of health topics in dozens of categories.

Healthy Ontario

www.healthyontario.com

This Canadian health site is a great resource for individuals, families, and healthcare professionals to research health concerns, medications, treatment options, and preventions. Special areas for children, men, women, and seniors. Also features a page for looking up various conditions and locating health services in Canada.

MayoClinic.com

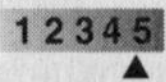

www.mayoclinic.com

This is the website of the famed Mayo Clinic in Rochester, Minnesota. Site opens with an index of health conditions, a symptom checker, and a first aid guide to place a virtual medical bag full of tools at your fingertips. Or, you can begin your search using the navigation bar at the top of the page, which contains links for Diseases & Conditions, Drugs & Supplements, Treatment Decisions, Healthy Living (articles and tips), Ask a Specialist (Q&A area), and Health Tools (BMI calculator, calorie calculator, self-assessments, and quizzes). Special area focuses on women's health, and the site offers content just for kids, although it has no separate kids section. Well-designed site enables you to quickly find answers to your questions and concerns, and the site is packed with useful health information, tips, and tools.

Medline Plus

1 2 3 4 5

www.nlm.nih.gov/medlineplus

Brought to you by the National Library of Medicine and National Institutes of Health, Medline Plus features articles on more than 700 health-related topics, information on prescription and over-the-counter medications, a health encyclopedia, a medical dictionary, current news stories, a searchable directory of doctors and dentists, interactive tutorials, information on clinical trials, and other information and resources. An excellent site!

Medscape

1 2 3 4 5

www.medscape.com

Targeted at healthcare professionals, this site offers journal articles, up-to-date research, and daily summaries, as well as access to articles, discussions, images, and self-assessment tools. Patients and consumers can also find plenty of current and reliable information at this site.

MSN Health

1 2 3 4 5

www.health.msn.com

Search for medical news and articles, find out the latest thinking in various treatments and preventive measures, and communicate with others via the message boards about issues on your mind, such as diabetes, hypertension, pregnancy, or mental health.

National Institutes of Health

1 2 3 4 5

www.nih.gov

The U.S. Department of Health and Human Services National Institutes of Health provides an often-overlooked goldmine of health information for healthcare providers and consumers alike. Here, you can find information on the latest proven treatments for a wide variety of conditions, learn about clinical trials and alternative treatment options, find health hotlines and prescription drug information, and much more. This site also features information about grants, the latest news and events, scientific resources, and visitor information.

National Safety Council

1 2 3 4 5

www.nsc.org

Information at this site is focused on preventing accidents, such as those involving cars and other machinery. You'll find a phone number you can call to report someone who routinely lets his or her children ride without a seat belt. And you can learn more about preventing injuries from everyday situations, such as using suntan lotion to reduce the chance of skin cancer.

NOAH: New York Online Access to Health

1 2 3 4 5

www.noah-health.org

NOAH, available in English and Spanish, provides a list of disorders and conditions indexed by body location, a list of local health resources (in and around New York City), information on common medical procedures and medicines, special areas for groups including seniors and children, and articles that address topics on health and wellness.

Prevention Magazine

1 2 3 4 5

www.prevention.com

Prevention's Healthy Ideas is stocked with herbal remedies, vitamin databases, alternative medicine news, advice from naturopathic doctors, and interactive forums. Check weekly for new features on women's health.

Quackwatch

1 2 3 4 5

www.quackwatch.org

Skeptical that the claims made by a product are untrue? Heard unbelievable information about a medical procedure or practice? Check out this site to learn more about medical frauds and to find out how to recognize one in the future. You can also report fraudulent activity here.

WebMD

www.webmd.com

You'll find articles, news, and tips for improving your health and well-being. Searchable database packed with information, including definitions of diseases, prescription information, and treatments. A comprehensive encyclopedia of health and medicine.

World Health Network

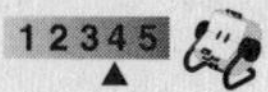

www.worldhealth.net

Dedicated to health, vitality, and longevity. Contains information on anti-aging, nutrition and exercise, and traditional and alternative healthcare.

AIDS/HIV TREATMENT & PREVENTION

AIDS Education and Research Trust

www.avert.org

This site contains HIV and AIDS statistics, information for young people, personal stories, a history section, information on becoming infected, a young and gay section, free resources, and lots more. This site can also be translated into several different languages.

AIDSinfo

www.aidsinfo.nih.gov

Sponsored by six Public Health Service agencies, this site provides information about federally approved treatment guidelines for HIV and AIDS. Check out the What's New page for updates on the latest news on antiretroviral agents, protease inhibitors, and other treatment possibilities. Check out the Treatment Information page for history, glossary, current treatment information, and more.

AIDS.ORG

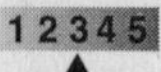

www.aids.org/index.html

Nonprofit organization that provides AIDS education and prevention programs and essential HIV resources. Here, you can find information about AIDS testing and treatments and join a community of people in supporting AIDS patients, preventing the spread of AIDS, and finding new treatments.

AIDS Outreach Center

www.aoc.org

This organization, based in Fort Worth, Texas, has one of the most complete resource listings available online for HIV/AIDS. Links are indexed by category and alphabetically for quick access. AOC also offers a variety of services; information on each is available from the website.

AEGiS

www.aegis.com

Until someone develops a cure for AIDS, the best weapons in the arsenal against it are information and education. That's what AEGiS (AIDS Education Global information System) is all about. AEGiS began and still functions as a BBS (bulletin board system) where people can read and post messages and share data, but it also functions as a central database of more than one million files that provide information on the history, prevention, and treatment of AIDS around the world. This is an excellent site for everyone interested in AIDS, limiting the spread of AIDS, and finding a cure.

The Body: A Multimedia AIDS and HIV Information Resource

www.thebody.com

In addition to selected coverage of AIDS, HIV, and related issues in the news, this site provides various forums with questions answered by a team of medical experts. Site features more than 550 topic areas and directs the presentation of a good portion of its contents toward those who have recently been diagnosed with AIDS or are concerned that they may have been infected with the virus. Click the All Topics link for a table of contents that makes it easy to navigate to the desired topic. The home page features quick access to information on the most pressing issues: HIV Testing Basics, Just Diagnosed,

HIV Medications, HIV Monitoring Tests, and Inspiring Stories, to name a few. Excellent content in a format that makes it easy to navigate.

Centers for Disease Control and Prevention: HIV

www.cdc.gov/hiv/dhap.htm

The CDC provides "national leadership in helping control the HIV epidemic by working with community, state, national, and international partners in surveillance, research, prevention and evaluation activities." This site acts as an information kiosk for a variety of topics on HIV and AIDS. You can check out the A-Z Index to find information on a specific issue or navigate by categories, which include African Americans, Basic Information, Statistics & Surveillance, Testing, Prevention Programs, Research, Funding, and Women. Site also features questions and answers, brochures, slide shows, software, journal articles, and reports. The home page lists links to the most current articles.

Children with AIDS Project

www.aidskids.org

Children with AIDS Project of America is a publicly supported 501(3) nonprofit organization, providing support, care, and adoption programs for children infected with HIV/AIDS. Find details on services and fees, register to become an adoptive parent, and learn how to help the cause.

HIV InSite: Gateway to AIDS Knowledge

hivinsite.ucsf.edu

InSite features one of the most comprehensive collections of medical information about AIDS on the web. Directed more toward healthcare professionals than the average person, this site is packed with the most current articles and research about AIDS, including testing and treatments. Healthcare professionals who deal with AIDS will want to bookmark this site for repeat visits. If you're an AIDS patient or your loved one has been diagnosed with AIDS and you want to learn as much about available testing and treatments as possible, you'll find just what you need to begin your in-depth research at this site.

Magic Johnson Foundation, Inc.

www.magicjohnson.org

The Magic Johnson Foundation is dedicated to raising money to support organizations that provide HIV/AIDS education, prevention, and care for young people. Information on educational resources, available grants, and ways you can help. Be sure to sign up for the newsletter.

Project Inform

www.projinf.org

Project Inform has maintained one primary focus: to remain dedicated to providing free, confidential, and empowering information about HIV/AIDS to anyone who asks, as well as speeding the search for a cure. Project Inform has earned an international reputation as a vocal, active, and effective advocate for the HIV/AIDS community it serves. Site features an article on treatment options and another article for those who have just been diagnosed complete with links for accessing related content on the site.

Stop AIDS Project

www.stopaids.org

Based in San Francisco, this organization's aim is to reduce the transmission of HIV and help the community of "self-identified gay and bisexual men." Educational materials and training manuals are free for downloading and adaptation (crediting the site, of course). Calendar of events and meetings, news updates, answers to common questions, an extensive list of resources, and more.

UNAIDS

www.unaids.org

UNAIDS is the United Nation's AIDS site, where you can learn about AIDS hotspots and find out what the UN is doing to combat the spread of AIDS and assist AIDS survivors. This site features valuable statistics about AIDS around the world.

CPR

CPR

12345

http://www.americanheart.org/presenter.jhtml?identifier=3011764

The American Heart Association guidelines and information booklets on CPR methods and technique. Check this site for any updates or corrections and to find out about CPR training programs.

CPR for AIDS Patients

www.americanheart.org/presenter.jhtml?identifier=4417

You must take some specific precautions when performing CPR on patients with AIDS. This site explains these precautions.

Learn CPR

depts.washington.edu/learncpr

The best way to learn CPR is to take a class that gives you hands-on training. The next best way is to turn to this site, which features animations and videos that show the basics. You can pull up CPR instructions to print and carry with you, check out some CPR facts, take a CPR quiz, watch a video demonstration, and learn variations for adults, children, and infants. Here, you can even learn CPR for dogs and cats!

Mayo Clinic First Aid Guide

www.mayoclinic.com/findinformation/firstaidandselfcare

Few organizations are more qualified to teach first aid and CPR than the Mayo Clinic. This site features links to an extensive list of first aid topics covering everything from anaphylaxis to toothaches. Near the top of the list is a link for cardiopulmonary resuscitation (CPR). Click the link to obtain instructions on how to perform CPR.

CHILDREN

American Academy of Pediatrics

12345

www.aap.org

Home of the American Academy of Pediatrics, this site is primarily designed for pediatricians, parents, and childcare workers to keep them informed of the latest healthcare issues related to children.

Child and Adolescent Health and Development

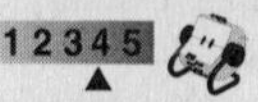

www.who.int/child-adolescent-health

Created and maintained by the World Health Organization, this site promotes the health and well-being of children and adolescents around the world. Here, you can browse three different areas: infant, child, and adolescent. You can also browse sections on prevention and care, nutrition, and development. Site includes a short directory of links to other child healthcare sites.

Child Health Research Project

www.childhealthresearch.org

Learn the latest about international child health issues and case management tools. This site is primarily for doctors and other healthcare providers and for ministries of health in countries all around the world.

Children's Hospital Boston

web1.tch.harvard.edu

According to a survey by *U.S. News and World Report*, Children's Hospital Boston is the top pediatric healthcare center in the nation, and has been for 13 years straight. This hospital offers "a complete range of healthcare services for children from 15 weeks gestation through 21 years of age (and older in special cases)." The site includes a searchable children's health encyclopedia, specialist locator, list of clinical resources, a map of the facility, and information for healthcare providers. Site also hosts patient websites, essentially blogs, that enable patients to keep in touch with family members during their stay at the hospital.

The Children's Hospital of Philadelphia

12345

www.chop.edu/consumer/index.jsp

Opened in 1855 as the first hospital devoted exclusively to administering to the healthcare needs of children, the Children's Hospital of Philadelphia continues to be one of the best pediatric healthcare facilities in the world. This site provides useful information for parents and childcare providers about common childhood medical conditions, along with information about the hospital itself. Special area to help prepare kids for a stay at the hospital.

Children's Hospital and Regional Medical Center, Seattle

12345

www.seattlechildrens.org

Since 1907, Children's Hospital and Regional Medical Center has provided healthcare for children in the Pacific Northwestern United States. Children's is "the only regional pediatric referral center devoted to the medical, surgical and developmental needs of children ages birth to 21 in the four-state area of Washington, Alaska, Montana, and Idaho." Visit this site to learn more about the hospital and its staff, programs, and research. You can also access general information about child healthcare issues and search for a physician.

drSpock.com

12345

www.drspock.com

Staying in the spirit of world-renowned pediatrician, Dr. Benjamin Spock, this site is dedicated to providing parents with the expert information they need to raise healthy, happy children. Search this site for medical information, product alerts, and parenting advice from some of the world's top experts in childcare. Site also features a message board.

KidsHealth

12345

www.kidshealth.org

Created by the medical experts at the Nemours Foundation, KidsHealth has trainloads of information on infections, behavior and emotions, food and fitness, and growing up healthy, as well as cool games and animations! This site is sectioned off into three areas for Parents, Kids, and Teens.

National Institute of Child Health and Human Development

12345

www.nichd.nih.gov

Primarily provides news and information about the National Institute of Child Health and Human Development, but also provides helpful information for parents on nutrition and care of their children. Features areas designed especially for children that include games and other activities.

Riley Hospital for Children

12345

www.rileyhospital.org

Located in Indianapolis, Indiana, Riley Hospital for Children is consistently ranked as one of the top children's healthcare facilities in the United States. At this site, you can learn more about the hospital and its pediatricians, find general information about childcare and common childhood diseases, email a patient, and take a virtual tour of the hospital.

St. Jude Children's Research Hospital

12345

www2.stjude.org

Located in Memphis, Tennessee, St. Jude Children's Research Hospital is "one of the world's premier centers for research and treatment of catastrophic diseases in children, primarily pediatric cancers." At this site, you can learn about the St. Jude Children's Research Hospital and staff, its research programs, various treatment options, and much more.

DISABILITIES

Disability.gov

1 2 3 4 5

www.disabilityinfo.gov

Disability.gov is the United States government site that functions as a gateway to all information and resources that the government provides on the subject of disabilities. Tabbed navigation provides quick access to the following sections: employment, education, housing, transportation, health, benefits, technology, community life, and civil rights. Each page has a navigation bar off to the left that features a list of topics. When you have a disability and are wondering where to find various types of government assistance, this is the place to go.

LD Online

1 2 3 4 5

www.ldonline.org

Leading website for parents, teachers, and others to obtain information and resources relating to learning disabilities. Learn the basics, go into more depth, or view Dr. Silver's Q&A list. Features a Kids Zone with some fun activities, as well as a discussion forum and a list of agencies and organizations where you can go for help. Links for books and videos point you to Amazon.com, where you can place your order.

National Association for Visually Handicapped

1 2 3 4 5

www.navh.org

People with vision impairment or their caregivers will want to visit this site for information on helpful products, events, and interesting articles. You can also purchase low-vision aids here, from writing aids to reading magnifiers. Site uses large type and offers an option you can click to make it even larger.

Paralyzed Veterans of America

www.pva.org

This nonprofit organization serves as an advocate for veterans with spinal cord injuries, working to ensure quality healthcare and benefits and to increase opportunities to this group of military heroes. Video clips show visitors how to send a veteran a note of thanks.

Social Security Administration: Disability Benefits

1 2 3 4 5

www.ssa.gov/disability

If you have a disability and are a U.S. citizen, you have rights to certain Social Security benefits, including potential disability pay, Medicare, and Medicaid. Here, you can find information on the various benefits and links to the forms you need to fill out. If you know someone who's scamming the Social Security Administration, you can visit this site to report them.

UCPnet

1 2 3 4 5

www.ucpa.org

United Cerebral Palsy's site provides information—after you type in your ZIP code—about your local chapter, its mission and activities, FAQs, and grant and research overviews.

World Association of Persons with Disabilities

1 2 3 4 5

www.wapd.org

WAPD is an activist organization devoted to "advancing the interests of people with disabilities at national, state, local and home levels." Features membership information, a newsletter, chatrooms, a well-stocked directory of resources broken down by disability, and more.

youreable.com

1 2 3 4 5

www.youreable.com

A nonpolitical service for people with disabilities, run by people with disabilities. Not only can you find information here on travel, money, health, and equipment, but you can also choose and correspond with a pen pal. Site also features a list of jobs and discussion forums.

DISEASES & CONDITIONS

American Cancer Society

www.cancer.org

American Cancer Society (ACS) is "a nationwide, community-based voluntary health organization. Headquartered in Atlanta, Georgia, the ACS has state divisions and more than 3,400 local offices." At the top of the opening page is a guide that helps you choose an entry point. You can choose a cancer type or topic, learn about treatment options, find help and support, access research information and other resources, or learn how to donate and volunteer. The opening page also features a list of the most frequently visited pages at the site and a news center.

American College of Gastroenterology

www.acg.gi.org

The American College of Gastroenterology "represents more than 8,500 digestive health specialists and is committed to providing accurate, unbiased and up-to-date health information to patients and the public." Content at this site is divided into four sections: members, physicians, patients, and media. Those suffering from gastroenterological conditions can click the patients link to access a comprehensive list of maladies. Clicking a disease in the list leads to an online booklet or PDF file that covers the main topics you need to know about.

Arthritis Resource Center

www.healingwell.com/arthritis

Excellent site for arthritis sufferers as well as those who are concerned about getting this often debilitating disease. Site provides feature articles on current breakthroughs and discoveries, discussion forums and chat, videos, and additional resources.

Association of Cancer Online Resources

www.acor.org

This site offers access to more than 130 electronic mailing lists as well as links to a variety of unique websites. The mailing lists are specifically designed to be public online support groups, providing information and community to more than 60,000 patients, caregivers, or anyone looking for answers about cancer and related disorders.

Down Syndrome WWW Pages

www.nas.com/downsyn

Excellent directory of links to sites focusing on Down Syndrome, including articles, healthcare guidelines, a worldwide list of organizations, and education resources. The site also features a brag book containing photos of a number of children with the syndrome.

Endometriosis

www.ivf.com/endohtml.html

A variety of information on the puzzling disease, endometriosis, a common cause of infertility. The site includes a lengthy FAQs area, case studies, and a number of articles on the subject.

Introduction to Skin Cancer

12345

www.maui.net/~southsky/introto.html

Intended as a general introduction to skin cancer, this page provides basic information such as determining what causes skin cancer, what it is, what your personal risks are, and how to reduce those risks.

MedicineNet.com

12345 RSS

www.medicinenet.com

MedicineNet.com is "an online, healthcare media publishing company. It provides easy-to-read, in-depth, authoritative medical information for consumers via its robust, user-friendly, interactive website." Tabbed navigation provides quick access to News & Views, Diseases & Conditions, Symptoms & Signs, Procedures & Tests, Medications, onhealth & living, and a MedTerms dictionary—everything you need to make a preliminary diagnosis, determine when it might be time to see your physician, and assess your treatment options and the medications your doctor may recommend. Very comprehensive site.

Muscular Dystrophy Association

`www.mdausa.org`

Learn all about the MDA and what it does to help combat neuromuscular diseases. Also learn what you can do to help besides just watching the Jerry Lewis telethon. Donate online using your credit card. Site also features online chat.

National Organization for Rare Diseases

`www.rarediseases.org`

NORD (National Organization for Rare Diseases) features a list of more than 1,150 rare diseases. If you've just been diagnosed as suffering from a rare disease or disorder and can find little information about it in other sources, check out the NORD site to see whether it's listed. This site also provides valuable information for doctors and others in the healthcare fields.

National Osteoporosis Foundation

`www.nof.org`

The NOF seeks to reduce the incidences of osteoporosis by making the public more informed about it. This site provides background information on the disease, information about who's at risk, and prevention and treatment ideas.

National Prostate Cancer Coalition

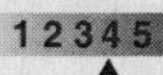

`www.fightprostatecancer.org`

Includes pages on screening for prostate cancer, understanding diagnoses and treatments, and finding support groups.

NewsRx

`www.newsrx.com`

The world's largest weekly database of news dedicated entirely to medical and health news. Headlines and glimpses of the stories are available for free, but to get the full articles, you must subscribe. Sample issues are available.

StopPain.org

`www.stoppain.org`

Excellent collection of articles and other resources dealing with pain management. Describes the various conditions that often require pain management, including chronic lower-back pain, fibromyalgia, headaches, and shingles and provides a list of general treatment options. The site also features a list of frequently asked questions and an area for caregivers and professionals.

Sudden Infant Death Syndrome (SIDS) Information Home Page

`sids-network.org`

Provides information about Sudden Infant Death Syndrome, recent research, and ongoing information sharing among parents who have been affected by the syndrome. You can also make a donation to the SIDS Network through PayPal.

HEALTHCARE ADMINISTRATION & MANAGEMENT

ACHE: American College of Healthcare Executives

`www.ache.org`

A professional membership society for healthcare executives. Offers publications, policy statements, and educational programs.

Agency for Health Care Administration

`www.fdhc.state.fl.us`

The Agency for Health Care Administration (AHCA) is a government agency dedicated to improving the quality of healthcare in the state of Florida and educating the state's healthcare providers and administrators, as well as helping consumers, especially the elderly, find quality care. Site features information on Medicaid, health facilities and providers, consumer information, publications and forms, licensing and certification, and much more. Click the 411 tab to find contact information for various agencies, schools, subjects, and other areas that you might find helpful.

American Association of Healthcare Administration Management

www.aaham.org

The American Association of Healthcare Administrative Management (AAHAM) is "the premier professional organization in healthcare administrative management," dedicated to the professional development of healthcare administrators. This site offers information about the association and its member benefits, certification programs, job openings, advocacy and networking, and local chapters. If you're in the field of healthcare administration and management, definitely check out this site.

American Physical Therapy Association

www.apta.org

A national professional organization representing more than 66,000 physical therapists across the nation, this group's goal is "to foster advancements in physical therapy practice, research, and education." Calendar of events, continuing education resources, information about practicing physical therapy, a list of FAQs, and much more make this a valuable site for any physical therapist. Also provides some job leads.

Health Economics

www.healtheconomics.com

Lists national and international links to biotech firms, medical libraries, journals, employment opportunities, and health databases.

Institute for Healthcare Improvement

www.ihi.org/ihi

IHI is dedicated to improving healthcare around the world. This site features information about IHI's programs, a collection of articles on the hot topics in the world of healthcare, discussion groups, tools for connecting with other healthcare professionals, and tools for helping you track improvement in your healthcare business or organization.

modernhealthcare.com

www.modernhealthcare.com

Modern Healthcare "is the industry's leading source of healthcare business news." This service works hard to keep healthcare professionals, especially hospital administrators, informed about the latest developments and trends in the healthcare industry, so they can stay ahead of the curve.

HEALTH INSURANCE

AFLAC

www.aflac.com

Provides guaranteed renewable supplemental health insurance. Get information on insurance options, locate an agent near you, and learn about the company at this site.

America's Health Insurance Plans

www.ahip.org

America's Health Insurance Plans is a trade organization that represents approximately 1,300 health insurance companies responsible for insuring more than 200 million Americans. Here, you can learn more about the organization and access information for members and consumers.

eHealthInsurance

www.ehealthinsurance.com

When you need to find affordable health insurance, this is a great place to start looking. Enter a few pieces of information about where you live and the number of people in your family that you want to insure, click a button, and immediately receive a long list of quotes from various health insurance companies. If you find a quote that looks like it's in the ballpark, you can enter additional details to apply.

HealthInsuranceFinders.com

12345

www.healthinsurancefinders.com

When you don't know where to look for health, dental, life, or travel insurance, go to HealthInsuranceFinders.com to get some suggestions. Here, you can obtain quotes from several top providers.

Related Sites

www.insure.com

www.health-medical-insurance-company.com

HealthInsuranceInfo.net

12345

www.healthinsuranceinfo.net

The Georgetown University Health Policy Institute has written a booklet for each state in the United States that summarizes your protections in each state. Here, you can obtain an electronic, printable version for your state that provides valuable information when you're shopping for health insurance.

Insurance Fraud

12345

www.insurancefraud.org

The Coalition Against Insurance Fraud maintains this site to help insurance companies, service providers, and consumers avoid getting ripped off. Content covers all types of insurance, but it provides a special area to inform consumers of health insurance scams and the warning signs they should watch out for. To access this area, point to Consumer Info, click Scam Alert, and click Health Insurance Schemes.

International Medical Group

12345

www.imglobal.com

Provides medical insurance to individuals, families, and groups who are living or traveling abroad.

Related Site

www.medibroker.com

PacifiCare

12345

www.pacificare.com

This site is geared to anyone who wants to assess his or her own health or learn more about HMOs.

INSTITUTES

Arkansas Children's Hospital

12345

www.ach.uams.edu

Private, nonprofit institution. Offers children comprehensive medical care from birth to age 21. Available to every county in Arkansas and many nearby states, regardless of a family's ability to pay. Special area for kids provides pre-admission orientation, games, and puzzles.

Catholic Health Association

12345

www.chausa.org

Nonprofit association that represents more than 2,000 Catholic health care sponsors, systems, facilities, and related organizations. CHA unites members to advance selected strategic issues that are best addressed together, rather than as individual organizations. The site provides information about the association's purpose, educational programming, newsletters, and ethical information.

OSHA (Occupational Safety and Health Administration)

12345

www.osha.gov

OSHA establishes and enforces prot
and offers technical assistance
American workplace. P
safety announc

www.phi.org

The Public Health Institute is a not-for-profit organization in California that works to "promote the health, well-being, and quality of life for people throughout California, across the nation, and around the world." Here, you can find an article called Public Health 101 that describes how the public health field improves people's lives, browse the latest news and events, check out the online resource materials, and learn more about the people and programs of PHI.

MEDICAL HISTORY

History of the Health Sciences Worldwide Links

www.mla-hhss.org/histlink.htm

This site contains an extensive directory of links to medical history sites and resources on the Web. At the top of the page are medical history categories, including organizations in the history of the health sciences, history of the health sciences libraries and archives, organizations and museums with history of the health sciences interests, and important figures in health sciences—their lives and works. Each category contains multiple links to different sites. If you're doing research on medical history, this should be your first stop.

History of Medicine

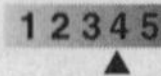

wwwihm.nlm.nih.gov

Nearly 60,000 images, including portraits, pictures of institutions, caricatures, genre scenes, and graphic art in a variety of media, illustrating the social and historical aspects of medicine.

[TRA]VEL RESOURCES

Cente[rs ...]: Travel Health

www.cdc.gov/travel

Are you planning a trip abroad? Then check this site before you go to determine whether you need to be aware of any diseases you might encounter on your trip and recommended vaccines or medicines you should obtain before you leave.

Visit the CDC travel site a few months before your planned departure. Some vaccinations require a series of shots over a long period of time to be effective.

Gimponthego.com

12345

www.gimponthego.com

Pick up travel tips for disabled individuals on the go and hear hotel/motel and restaurant feedback from people who've visited. Find out which chains are the best in terms of wheelchair accessibility. When we visited the site, it was undergoing a major restoration, so it promises to be even better when you get there.

Best MDTravelHealth

www.mdtravelhealth.com

MDtravelhealth.com, a travel health site created and maintained by David Goldberg, MD, features health advice for world travelers and the physicians who treat them. Information is updated daily and includes sections on Destinations, Infectious Diseases, Illness Prevention, Special Needs, Travel Health Clinics, Useful Links, and a FAQ. You can also sign up to have international health alerts emailed to you. The opening page features a clickable map of the world, which you can use to select your destination. When you choose a destination you're greeted with links to everything you need to know about preparing yourself for a disease-free trip.

Travel Health Online

www.tripprep.com

Shoreland, a trusted resource of travel medicine practitioners, created and maintains this site to help world travelers remain healthy as they skip around the globe. Content at this site is organized into three logical divisions: Destinations from A to Z ([Afg]hanistan to Zimbabwe), Traveler Information and Providers (... common diseases and conditions com... ...tion tips, vaccination information, ...), and Travel Medicine ...ry). You have to register to access this ... information ... of travel health

HISTORY

Best of History Sites

www.besthistorysites.net

The Best of History Sites is unmatched in breadth and depth of coverage, providing links to more than 1,000 of the best history sites on the Web, plus links to hundreds of quality sites for history teachers and students: lesson plans, teacher guides, activities, games, quizzes, and additional resources. References to other sites are annotated to help guide you in your selections. This site features a list of history categories to get you started, including prehistory, ancient/biblical, medieval, U.S. history, twentieth century, art history, and maps. Separate categories are available for teacher/classroom resources.

Conversations with History

globetrotter.berkeley.edu/conversations

Important figures in recent history, including politicians, diplomats, news professionals, authors, and more, are featured in unedited interviews conducted in past years. The home page for this site is rather unimpressive, but the content at the site is pretty cool. You can view webcasts of the conversations, download Podcasts, and visit Professor Harry Kreisler's blog, where he follows up on intriguing discussions. When you hit the home page, scroll down to the bottom to access links for searching the database of interviews by name or date.

EyeWitness to History

www.eyewitnesstohistory.com

Read eyewitness experiences of historical events, sorted by date, to get a better idea of what life was like during specific time periods. Covers everything from ancient history to World War II and features snapshots, audio recordings of voices from the past, an index, and the EyeWitness Store. Very cool site that's easy to navigate and packed with interesting, first-hand historical reports.

History Channel

www.historychannel.com

Select a decade back to 1800 and search for information on events during that time period at this site. Read articles about historical events, find out about upcoming TV reports on the History Channel, and chat with other history buffs. Don't miss the History Channel store; see what books and videotapes are available for purchase. Also features guides for history teachers.

History House

www.historyhouse.com

A history site devoted to digging up and reporting the dirt of historical events and characters, helping to make history come alive. Search the archives for past articles and stay tuned for more interesting historical trivia. Site now features a discussion forum.

History Matters

historymatters.gmu.edu

Developed by the American Social History Project/Center for Media & Learning, City University of New York, and the Center for History and New Media, George Mason University, this site provides resources for high school and college-level history teachers. Provides sample syllabi, reference texts, teaching materials, and links to dozens of other resources on the Web. Whether you teach history for a living or just enjoy studying it, this is a fantastic site.

A B C D E F G H I J K L M N O P Q R S T U V W X Y Z

History On-Line

1 2 3 4 5

www.history.ac.uk

Developed by the Institute of Historical Research (IHR), this site is devoted to "promoting high-quality resources for the teaching and learning of history in the UK." Here, you can learn about the Institute for Historical Research, search History On-Line, or check out a useful collection of links to resources on researching and teaching specific topics.

History Place

1 2 3 4 5

www.historyplace.com

Find images, documents, speeches, and more historical information compiled for students and educators, but available to anyone. Students can come here to get help with their history homework.

Irish History on the Web

1 2 3 4 5

larkspirit.com/history

Irish History on the Web provides a unique resource for anyone interested in learning about or researching a wide variety of Irish history topics. Like a sourcebook, most of the links found here will lead to primary documents, original essays, bibliographies, or specific informational sites.

National Women's History Project

1 2 3 4 5

www.nwhp.org

Committed to providing education, promotional materials, and informational services to recognize and celebrate women's contributions to society.

Smithsonian Natural History Museum

1 2 3 4 5

www.mnh.si.edu

The National Museum of Natural History is part of the Smithsonian Institution in Washington, D.C., and is dedicated to understanding the natural world and our place in it. This site provides an abundance of online resources about the natural sciences. Be sure to spend a few minutes browsing the online store at smithsonianstore.com!

AFRICA

Africa South of the Sahara

1 2 3 4 5 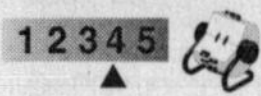

library.stanford.edu/africa/history.html

This site features a huge collection of links to other websites that offer information about a host of topics ranging from Afrocentrism and Archeology to Slavery and South Africa. Links are annotated, making this an excellent guide for beginning your exploration of African history, culture, economy, genealogy, and religion.

Internet African History Sourcebook

1 2 3 4 5 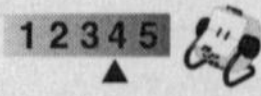

www.fordham.edu/halsall/africa/africasbook.html

Africa is a continent easy to delineate geographically, but diverse and complex historically, politically, and culturally, which are the areas that this website explores. This site is organized as a book on the history of Africa from ancient to modern times, providing links to content and resources scattered all over the Web.

South African History Online

1 2 3 4 5

www.sahistory.org.za

South African History Online (SAHO) is "a nonpartisan people's history project," dedicated to promoting research, popularizing South African history, and addressing the history and cultural heritage of Black South Africans in an unbiased way. Site features separate areas for People, Places, Arts & Culture, Chronology, and Resources and is packed with animations, photos, maps, biographies, and additional information about the fascinating history of South Africa.

AMERICAS

Ancestors in the Americas

1 2 3 4 5

www.cetel.org

The Center for Educational Telecommunications created and maintains this site to inform visitors of "the untold history and contemporary legacy of early Asian immigrants to the Americas, from the 1700s to the 1900s." Based on CET's three-part television series, this site features overviews of each part: *Part I: Coolies, Sailors, Settlers: Voyage to the New World*; *Part II: Chinese in the Frontier West: An American Story*; and *Part III: Crossing the Continent; Crossing the Pacific*. The series is intentionally left without an ending because the story is still in progress. This site features a companion book, study guide, sample movie clips, and areas where you can search for your Asian ancestors (if you have Asian ancestors) and post your story (if you're an immigrant from an Asian country).

Cultures & History of the Americas

1 2 3 4 5

www.loc.gov/exhibits/kislak

Presentation by the Library of Congress in celebration of the donation of the Jay I. Kislak Collection. This exhibition features "50 highlights from the more than 4,000 rare books, maps, documents, paintings, prints, and artifacts that make up the Jay I. Kislak Collection at the Library of Congress." The exhibition "focuses on the early Americas from the time of the indigenous people of Mexico, Central America, and the Caribbean through the period of European contact, exploration, and settlement." This site features photos of the many exhibits, each accompanied by a brief description of the item. A couple interactive presentations are also available.

Hispanic History in the Americas

1 2 3 4 5

teacher.scholastic.com/activities/hispanic/americas.htm

Interactive map that enables you to trace the history of Spanish influence on the Americas back 500 years. Click on a city, state, country, or continent and then use the resulting timeline to obtain information on critical eras events in the development of that city, state, country, or continent in respect to its Spanish heritage. The interactive nature of this site makes it a great place for students of all ages. Special content, including lesson plans, is available for teachers.

History of the Americas

vlib.iue.it/history/americas

This site is a virtual library of links to sites that cover the history, politics, culture, and other aspects of various South and Central American countries, including Argentina, Bolivia, Columbia, Cuba, and Peru, to name a few. The address provided here points to an FTP server, which displays a list of folders for each country, and when we visited the site, nobody was currently in charge of maintaining it, so the site's appearance isn't top notch. However, the site does offer an outstanding collection of links, many of which point to official country sites, where you can learn a great deal about the country and its history.

ANCIENT

Ancient Greece at the World History Compass

1 2 3 4 5

www.worldhistorycompass.com/greece.htm

Search for information about ancient Greek literature, art, and culture. Huge directory of links to other resources on Athens, Archimedes, medicine, art, architecture, astronomy, mathematics, and much more.

Ancient Worlds

1 2 3 4 5

www.ancientsites.com

This site features some excellent content on the popular hangouts in ancient history: Rome, Athens, Egypt, Babylon, Celtia, Germania, Machu Picchu, and the Orient. The site design leaves a lot to be desired, making it difficult to locate specific content, but that's because the content at this site comes primarily from a wide range of contributors making it difficult to give everything a consistent look and feel. Nonetheless, this site does feature excellent content and graphics.

BBC: Inside Ancient History

12345

www.bbc.co.uk/history/ancient

The BBC's site on ancient history is unmatched in both breadth and depth. The opening page provides links to the major players in the ancient world: Egyptians, Greeks, Romans, Vikings, British Prehistory, and Anglo Saxons. When you click a link, the site takes you to a page packed with additional content organized by subject. For example, click Egyptians pulls up a page with sections on Pyramids and Monuments, Mummification, Gods and Beliefs, Pharaohs and Dynasties, Daily Life, and Hieroglyphs. Site offers excellent content, plenty of photos and interactive activities, and other engaging features.

Jaguar: Icon of Power Through Mayan History

12345

www.oneworldjourneys.com/jaguar/history.html

Ancient Mayan civilizations were some of the most advanced civilizations on the planet. At this site, you can explore the timeline from 12,000 B.C. to the present, investigate highlights in Mayan history and view a map that shows the areas where they were most active. Nicely designed site.

ARCTIC & ANTARCTICA

Antarctica: History and Exploration

12345

www.factmonster.com/ce6/world/A0856635.html

Good introduction to Antarctic history covers early expeditions up to the Antarctic Treaty and current research. Great place for kids to do research projects on Antarctica.

Antarctic History

12345

www.antarcticaonline.com/antarctica/history/history.htm

Antarctica was discovered only a couple hundred years ago and began to be inhabited by humans only a hundred years or so after that, so its history is relatively brief, but people suspected its existence long before that. Visit this site to learn more about the intriguing history of Antarctica and how humans eventually happened upon it. Content covers prediscovery, the heroic age (of discovery), early seal hunting, whaling, the mechanized age (of discovery), territorial disputes, and more.

Arctic Studies Center

12345

www.mnh.si.edu/arctic

The Smithsonian Institute's Arctic Studies Center "explores the history of northern peoples, cultures, and environments, and the issues that matter to northern residents today." This site features an excellent collection of multimedia presentations on everything from the Ainu, an ancient people of northern Japan; the Vikings; Arctic wildlife; and the gateways to the north.

ASIA

Best AsianInfo.org

12345

www.asianinfo.org

"AsianInfo.org is devoted to introducing Asian culture, traditions and general information to the world," and this site delivers on that promise. Site is well-designed, easy to navigate, and packed with useful and reliable information about the many countries that comprise Asia. The opening page contains a few feature articles along with a list of links that run down the left side of the page for individual countries listed alphabetically from B to V—Bhurma to Vietnam. When you click a link for

A B C D E F G H I J K L M N O P Q R S T U V W X Y Z

a country, the resulting page presents a few more feature articles along with links for History, Politics, People, Transportation, Languages, Religion, and other aspects of that country. Site features plenty of maps and photos to keep visitors engaged and informed while they're touring this fantastic site.

East Asian History

rspas.anu.edu.au/eah

The International Journal East Asian History is "a compilation of articles on subjects of historical significance in the East Asian area, as well as on issues of contemporary concern or neglected aspects and subregions of Asia." Here, you can also find articles on "art and architecture, technology and the environment, and the history of ideas, emotions, and subjective experience." You can access online versions of past issues back to 1991.

East & Southeast Asia: An Annotated Directory

newton.uor.edu/Departments&programs/AsianStudiesDept

Robert Y. Eng at the University of Redlands assembled this annoted directory of links to the best websites that provide content on East and Southeast Asia history and politics. Links are organized by country, including the following: China, Japan, Korea, Hong Kong, Taiwan, Mongolia, Indonesia, Philippines, and Vietnam, to name a few. Very extensive and comprehensive, making this a great place to start your search on Asian history.

> **Tip:** Look for the thumbs-up icon to spot the most content-rich sites.

History of China

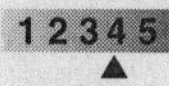

www-chaos.umd.edu/history/toc.html

Online book that covers the history of China from the dawn of history up to the reform periods (1980–1988). The opening page contains a clickable table of contents, making it easy to jump to the desired topic. Coverage of each topic is brief and to the point.

Indian History

www.indhistory.com

Excellent guide to the history of India and its people from ancient times to the present. The opening page provides a brief introduction. The navigation bar on the left enables you to explore various topics related to Indian history, including Hindu Gods and Temples, the Aryans, Hinduism, the Upanishads, and links to other websites. Scroll down to the bottom of the page for a timeline that's basically broken down into early, middle, and recent. The site doesn't look like much at first glance; but if you follow the trail of links, you'll find that the site contains some excellent content.

Japanese History

www.japan-guide.com/e/e641.html

The Japan Guide is a site primarily for those who plan on visiting Japan for a cultural experience. The History page helps tourists and other interested individuals learn the basics of Japanese history. Content covers Early Japan to the Postwar Period and includes links to plenty of other related content, including the Samurai, Emperors, Castles, Religion, Politics, and Atom Bombs. Site features photos, too.

Korean History Project

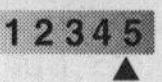

www.koreanhistoryproject.org

The Korean History Project began as "an educational effort to research, produce and publish Korean and East Asian history online, to promote history education and cultural understanding, and to make a valuable history resource easily accessible to a worldwide audience." This site features two main components—a full-length book called *Korea in the Eye of the Tiger*, which reveals "East Asian History and the complex relationships among Korea, China, Manchuria, Mongolia, Russia, Japan, Europe, and the United States in their quest for power and influence in Asia, and *Journey to Asia*, "a guide to learning about the geography, weather, languages, and governments of Korea, China, Japan, Mongolia, and Russia." When you open one of the books, you're greeted with a brief introduction. Point to the Table of Contents link to display a pop-up menu that enables you to jump to the desired chapter in the book.

The Most Comprehensive Reference on the Political History of Pakistan

12345

www.storyofpakistan.com

The title of this website says it all—this truly is the most comprehensive reference on the political history of Pakistan, leading visitors from the prehistory of Pakistan up to the present day. A clickable timeline that runs down the left side of the page enables you to head quickly to the period in which you're interested. Site also features links to the most significant people in the history of Pakistan and includes a discussion board where you can discuss history with those who share your interest. Outstanding site.

TravelChinaGuide: History

12345

www.travelchinaguide.com/intro/history

The TravelChinaGuide is designed to get tourists up to speed on all aspects of the country, including its history, geography, climate, and national identity. The History page opens with a clickable timeline of China history, from prehistoric times to the Quing Dynasty (1644–1911).

Related Site

www.historyforkids.org/learn/china/index.htm

AUSTRALIA & OCEANIA

Australia: Tertiary History

12345

www.teachers.ash.org.au/aussieed/terthistory.htm

Huge, annotated directory of links that cover all aspects of Australian history. Links are grouped in categories including Australian History, Convicts and Transportation, Explorers, Federation, World War I, and World War II.

Australian History: Selected Websites

12345

www.nla.gov.au/oz/histsite.html

The Australian government provides a small collection of links to websites that cover the history of Australia. Sites are grouped into several categories: General; Historical Texts Online; Manuscripts, Archives, and Registers; Museums; Libraries; Associations; and Overseas Sources. Good place to start your research.

Countries Quest: Oceania

12345

www.countriesquest.com/oceania.htm

Oceania is comprised of a large group of islands that includes Australia and New Zealand. Finding sites on the history of Australia and New Zealand is relatively easy, but finding sites that cover the history of the Cook Islands, Marshall Islands, Palau, and Tokelau can be quite a challenge. This site covers the history of those islands and island groups, along with many others.

Indigenous Australia

12345

www.dreamtime.net.au

The Australian Museum Online presents this site, which "explores Indigenous Australia through storytelling, cultures and histories. It includes Stories of the Dreaming, teachers' resources and content for students." Click the About Indigenous Australia link to access a timeline, and then click the timeline links to jump to the era in which you're interested. This site reaches beyond the basic history to provide background information on cultural heritage, religion, family, land, and social justice. Special area is included to provide students with fact sheets, an online dictionary that explains terminology, and tips for navigating the site. Teachers can find special content for their classes, too.

New Zealand History

12345

history-nz.org

Excellent introduction to New Zealand history covers the discovery of New Zealand by the Polynesians and Europeans, the colonization of the country, its wars, the Maori people, and New Zealand as it is today. The navigation bar on the left makes moving around the site and finding specific information easy.

Related Sites

www.nzhistory.net.nz

www.zealand.org.nz/history.htm

CANADA

Canada History

www.canadahistory.com

This site opens with a page of links to various areas of Canadian history, including News, Periods, Documents, Conflict, Political, and Geography. The site design is a little antiquated, but the articles provide an excellent introduction of Canada from early times to the present.

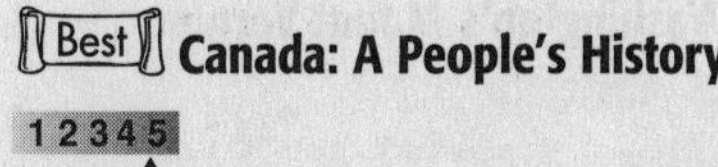

history.cbc.ca/histicons

This outstanding history site features a clickable timeline that runs across the top of the page. Click a century and then click a specific decade or quarter in that century to pull up the corresponding page. (You can rest the mouse pointer on the orange decade or quarter century links to display a brief overview of significant events.) The resulting page provides an illustrated article on the selected period along with links that enable you to navigate the article and pull up additional content. Or, you can click the Search This Site box to look for specific content. Site also provides biographies, bibliographies, special content for teachers, discussion forums, and games and puzzles.

Civilization.ca

www.civilization.ca

The Canadian Museum of Civilization features a great collection of online articles and exhibits, and a fair collection of resources on Canadian history. From the opening page, click the History link (in the navigation bar on the left), and follow the trail of links to specific exhibits related to Canadian history. Special exhibits include the A History of the Native People of Canada, Canadian Inuit History—A Thousand-Year Odyssey, and Immigration to Western Canada: The Early 20th Century. Links to dozens of other fascinating museum exhibits along with a directory of links to other sites.

The Halifax Explosion

www.cbc.ca/halifaxexplosion

On December 6, 1917, the world witnessed one of the largest and most devastating man-made explosions it had ever seen—the Halifax explosion, leaving nearly 2,000 people dead and 9,000 injured. Visit this site to experience some of the horror of that day and see what survivors have to say about it.

Historica: The Canadian Encyclopedia

www.histori.ca

This online encyclopedia of Canada opens with a page that provides you with links to access many of its special areas, including Youth Links, a program that encourages students to discuss and explore Canadian history online. The site features a History Resources link at the top of the page, but you may have better luck clicking the link for *The Canadian Encyclopedia* on the left and then clicking the link Timeline of Canadian History. Site also features links for the 100 Greatest Event in Canadian History, a Canucklehead Quiz, Interactive Resources (including games and interactive maps), and much more. Excellent site for students, teachers, and anyone else who's interested in Canadian history. This site also includes plenty of short audio and video presentations, primarily dramatizations of historical events.

The History of Canada

1 2 3 4 5

www.linksnorth.com/canada-history

This site provides an excellent overview of Canadian history starting with its discover and rediscovery and leading up to the current times. A clickable timeline runs down the right side of the page, enabling you to quickly jump to a specific period in the history of Canada. Articles are short, so don't expect any in-depth discussions.

A B C D E F G H I J K L M N O P Q R S T U V W X Y Z

CURRENT AFFAIRS

Current Affairs

1 2 3 4 5

www.currentaffairs.com

This site gathers news feeds from around the world and presents them on a single page, providing quick access to news from around the world.

Politics and Current Affairs Forum

1 2 3 4 5

www.politicsandcurrentaffairs.co.uk/Forum

Online discussion forum out of the United Kingdom that enables participants to discuss events and issues of the day. Site features discussions on world events, the U.S., the economy and the environment, and other special interest areas. One forum called Anything Goes, leaves the floor wide open. Online polls are often common.

DOCUMENTS AND LANDMARKS

American Memory

1 2 3 4 5

memory.loc.gov/ammem

This site is part of the National Digital Library Program, which is an effort to digitize and deliver electronically the distinctive, historical Americana holdings at the Library of Congress, including photographs, manuscripts, rare books, maps, recorded sound, and moving pictures. Here, you can view maps, images, and materials related to our country's history.

A Chronology of U.S. Historical Documents

1 2 3 4 5

www.law.ou.edu/hist

A huge list of historical documents in chronological order, with explanations of the significance of each.

England Landmarks and Historical Sites

1 2 3 4 5

www.england.worldweb.com/Photos/LandmarksandHistoricSites

From the WorldWeb travel guide comes this collection of landmarks and historical places in England, complete with photographs. If you're planning to visit England, check here first to scope out some of the more interesting attractions.

Frank Lloyd Wright Home and Studio

1 2 3 4 5

www.wrightplus.org

Take a tour of Frank Lloyd Wright's home and studio. He and his family lived there from 1898 to 1909. See where the Prairie School of Architecture was born. Check out where Wright experimented with designs in his home and studio before he shared them with clients. If you're in the Oak Park, Illinois, area, you can visit the house in person; the site lists the tour hours.

George Washington's Mount Vernon

1 2 3 4 5

www.mountvernon.org

Tour, archaeological, membership, and lesson-plan information about the home of the first president of the United States. Site also features an archeological concentration game for kids.

Guggenheim Museum

1 2 3 4 5

www.guggenheim.org

Read about the New York museum's history and architecture; its numerous programs, including tours; upcoming exhibitions; ways to become a member and all the benefits of membership; and the museum store, where you can buy art books, gifts, jewelry, children's books and toys, and signature Guggenheim products. Also available is information on the other four international museum locations.

Henry Ford Estate: Fair Lane

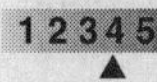

www.umd.umich.edu/fairlane

Visit the estate of automotive pioneer Henry Ford. You can take a virtual tour of the estate and visit the beautiful rooms. If you're in the Dearborn, Michigan, area, you can visit the estate in person; check out the list of tour times. Christmas is a special time at Fair Lane, with activities for the whole family, including Ginger Bread House making, breakfast with Santa, tea, a sumptuous traditional Christmas dinner, and a candlelight tour. Be sure to check out the new gift shop page for books, jewelry, and gifts.

Landmarks for Schools

www.landmark-project.com

The Landmarks Project was established to help teachers find valuable teaching resources on the Internet. This site provides links primarily to earth science and social studies sites. The section on Words of Humankind features the complete text of many historical documents.

League of Nations Statistical and Disarmament Documents

www.library.northwestern.edu/govinfo/collections/league

Northwestern University Library houses its digital collection "League of Nations Statistical and Disarmament Documents" at this website. It "contains the full text of 260 League of Nations documents. The documents in this digitized collection focus on three areas: the founding of the League, international statistics published by the League, and the League's work toward international disarmament." You can browse the directory of documents or search for a specific document. All documents are presented in PDF format.

Moscow Landmarks

www.moscow-landmarks.com

This site features information on the main three landmarks in Moscow: The Kremlin, Red Square, and Gorky Park, providing details on tourist attractions you might find interesting.

Mount Rushmore

www.nps.gov/moru/index.htm

History of the sculpture, current and historical pictures, and tourist information. Also provides information on the Junior Ranger Program for young visitors.

National Civil Rights Museum

www.civilrightsmuseum.org

Virtual tour of exhibits of the museum located on the site of Martin Luther King, Jr.'s assassination in Memphis.

National Parks and Monuments

1 2 3 4 5

www.nps.gov

Information on the United States national parks and monuments. Pick a park to learn about its main attractions and the history of the park, or print out a tour guide.

Best Our Documents

www.ourdocuments.gov

Top 100 documents in the history of the United States, including the Declaration of Independence, Articles of Confederation, the patent for the cotton gin, Thomas Edison's patent application for the light bulb, and 96 other documents that marked milestones. Site features a preview of the each document, the complete text of each document, and a PDF that shows each document in high resolution. You can cast your vote for the most significant document in U.S. history. Site also features special tools for educators, news and events, national competitions, and links to related resources.

A B C D E F G H I J K L M N O P Q R S T U V W X Y Z

Statue of Liberty–Ellis Island Foundation

12345

webcenter.ellisisland.netscape.com

The Statue of Liberty—Ellis Island Foundation was formed in 1982 to help with the restoration of the Statue of Liberty. This site provides a brief history and background of the foundation and of the restoration. It also features a passenger search area for genealogy buffs, and several pages that introduce visitors to the history of Ellis Island.

Susan B. Anthony House Museum and National Landmark

12345

www.susanbanthonyhouse.org

Take an online tour of the Susan B. Anthony house located in Rochester, New York. Learn about this great women's suffrage leader and antislavery activist. Be a part of history and donate to the capital campaign drive to help preserve and expand the house so that people might visit for years to come. Visit other historical links to learn more about famous women in history.

EUROPE

British Timeline

12345

www.bbc.co.uk/history/timelines/britain/o_neo_bronze.shtml

The BBC history pages are some of the best multimedia presentations of history. This particular site focuses on British history, from the Neolithic and Bronze ages, which began around 8300 B.C., through the Middle Ages, and on to modern times. Simply click the desired era in the list on the left and follow the trail of links to the year you want to research. Site features articles, a multimedia zone, and links to biographies of historical figures. Great place to bone up on your knowledge of kings and queens.

European History

12345

www.lib.washington.edu/subject/History/tm/europe.html

Annotated directory of websites broken down by category, including General European Sites, World War I, and Regional Sites (France, Germany, Italy, Netherlands, Nordic Countries, Spain & Portugal, and Switzerland & Austria). Also contains links to Ancient History, Medieval History, History of Science, British & Irish History, and World War II, which provide additional leads to topics related to European history. An excellent starting point for your research.

European NAvigator

www.ena.lu

This site provides an interactive, multimedia presentation of the history of post WWII Europe. The opening page features a navigation bar for accessing links to Historical Events, European Organizations, Special Files, Interviews (with historians and government officials), and ENA & Education (which offers plenty of tips on how to use ENA as an educational tool).

European Union History

12345

europa.eu/abc/history/index_en.htm

With all this recent talk of the European Union, it's hard to believe that the ball started rolling shortly after World War II with a speech from none other than Winston Churchill. This site opens with a list of links from 1946 to the current year. Each link points to a page that describes significant events and documents that fueled the establishment and growth of the European Union. Content doesn't go into much depth, but this provides an excellent overview.

France History

12345

www.justfrance.org/france/france-history.asp

This France Travel guide provides an excellent, though somewhat brief, overview of the history of France, beginning with Early Civilizations and leading up to Chirac's Presidency. Each period in France's history is followed by a short introduction. You can then click the period link for a more detailed article.

Germany History

1 2 3 4 5

www.germany.info/relaunch/culture/history/history.html

From the German Embassy in Washington, D.C. comes this synopsis of the history of Germany. Site organizes its content in five main areas: Milestones in History (a timeline from Charlemagne to the present), History Overview, History Features (including Prussia, the German revolution, the Berlin airlift, and the Marshall Plan), German Unification, and Links (under construction). Site also covers geography, economy, population, politics, culture, social system, and higher education.

The Holocaust Chronicle

1 2 3 4 5

www.holocaustchronicle.org

Free online edition of the book *The Holocaust Chronicle*, this site opens with a clickable timeline of the Holocaust so you can move from one year to the next—1933 to 1946, when the world finally began to seek justice for those persecuted by the Nazis.

Italy History

1 2 3 4 5

www.arcaini.com/ITALY/ItalyHistory/ItalyHistory.html

This site features an excellent introduction to the history of Italy. It begins with a brief history of where Italy got its name, proceeds to early Italy and the Bronze Age, and finishes with a discussion of postwar Italy—Italy after WWII.

Periodical Historical Atlas

1 2 3 4 5

www.euratlas.com/summary.htm

Here, you can view 21 maps of Europe to obtain a pictorial of how Europe has changed over the years politically and geographically.

Spanish History

1 2 3 4 5

www.donquijote.org/culture/spain/history

Don Quijote, a company that organizes Spanish language learning trips to Spanish-speaking countries, has an area on its site that provides an excellent overview of the history of Spain from before the Roman Conquest up to the point when Spain embraced democracy.

MEXICO

Ancient Mexico

1 2 3 4 5

www.ancientmexico.com

Ancient Mexico presents an interactive guide to the history of Mexico from prehistoric times to 1500 A.D. This site features a clickable map, where you can explore the main cities and settlements of ancient Mexico; a timeline for various areas in Mexico, including Central Mexico, Oaxaca, the Gulf Coast, Western Mexico, the Mayan Highlands-Pacific Coast, and the Mayan Lowlands; information on the gods and myths of ancient Mexico; and a small collection of historical documents.

History Channel: The History of Mexico

1 2 3 4 5

www.historychannel.com/exhibits/mexico

This site, from the History Channel, covers the history of Mexico from prehistoric times up to about the year 2003. The opening page displays a list of periods and additional topics you can click to jump to the desired content: Ancient Civilization, Colonial Mexico, Mexico at War, Cinco de Mayo, Political Upheaval, Mexico Facts, Maps, Resources, and an online store. Unlike other History Channel presentations, this one includes few photos or video clips. The maps are excellent, but don't expect a huge collection of graphics.

History, Myths, Arts, and Traditions of Mexico

1 2 3 4 5

www.mexconnect.com/mex_/cultureindex.html

Mexico Connect offers this page as an introduction to Mexican history, mythology, art, and culture. The opening page provides links for exploring Mexico's history by using a timeline, a list of the most influential people in Mexico's history, a chronological listing of leaders and presidents, or a month-by-month list of important events that happened in history for each of the 12 months of the year. Scroll down the opening page for gobs of links on ancient Mexico and its mythology, articles on its art, and information on cultures and traditions.

Mexexperience

1 2 3 4 5

www.mexperience.com/history

Mexexperience is a travel guide designed to help visitors plan and enhance their trip to Mexico. This history page presents a clickable timeline that enables you to explore Mexico's history from the Pre-Columbian period (1200 B.C. to 1500 A.D.) up to modern times.

Museum of the History of Mexico

1 2 3 4 5

www.museohistoriamexicana.org.mx

Located in Monterey, Mexico, this museum is dedicated to preserving and promoting the history of Mexico. Visitors to this site can explore the museums permanent and temporary exhibits, obtain information about the museum including hours and directions, and check out its well-stocked library.

> **Tip:** The content at this site is in Spanish. If you have the Google Toolbar installed, which you can access by going to Google and clicking More, you can right-click the page and click Translate Page into English. This won't translate the buttons, which are actually graphic objects.

Best U.S. Mexican War

1 2 3 4 5

www.pbs.org/kera/usmexicanwar/index.html

PBS presents this site to educate visitors about what happened leading up to, during, and after the U.S. Mexican war. Site features sections on the Prelude to War, the War Years (1846 to 1848), the Aftermath, and Bibliographies of the major players. You can also access an interactive timeline map and special resources to help teachers incorporate this site into their curriculum. The interactive timeline map enables you to explore the history in a geographical context, so you can learn not only what happened but where it happened. The timeline extends way beyond the war years, covering a period from 1519 to 2003. Excellent content accompanied by an outstanding collection of maps and photos. Site is presented in both English and Spanish.

MIDDLE EAST

eHistory: Middle East

1 2 3 4 5

ehistory.osu.edu/middleeast/index.cfm

The Middle East comprises 16 countries in northeast Africa and southwestern Asia. This site opens with a map of the region along with links to the 16 countries. Click a country link to learn more about a specific country and a timeline of important events in the history of that country. Not in-depth, but this provides a good overview and context for additional research:

History of Iran

1 2 3 4 5

www.iranchamber.com/history/historic_periods.php

Excellent collection of articles that collectively paint the picture of Iran history from 2500 B.C. to 1988 A.D. Site also features biographies of key historical figures and personalities. Most articles have accompanying photos that show some of the art, events, and people of the period.

History of Israel and Palestine in Map Form

12345

www.masada2000.org/historical.html

This site takes an original approach to describing the Israeli-Palestinian conflict. Instead of merely presenting a narrative of the political events, this site leads you through the timeline with a series of maps that show the various territories that Israel has claimed over the years. If you're looking for balanced coverage of events, this isn't the site for you—it's biased in favor of the Israelis.

History in the News: The Middle East

www.albany.edu/history/middle-east

This site takes you on a journey through various websites to explore Middle Eastern history, culture, society, religions, economics, politics, and geography. Links kick you out to other sites where you can investigate specific topics. All links are annotated, helping you decide whether or not a site contains what you need before you decide to visit.

The Middle East: A Century of Conflict

www.npr.org/news/specials/mideast/history

In 2002, NPR (National Public Radio) News presented "a special series on the roots of the Israeli-Palestinian conflict to bring context and perspective to the story, and to help listeners understand the complex situation in the Mideast, the history, and the consequences of the confrontation." Here, you can access the series online, listen to the actual radio broadcasts, view maps and a timeline of the conflict, access biographies of the most important people in the history of the conflict, read transcripts of the broadcasts, and learn about the strained relations between the Middle East and the West.

Middle East History & Resources

www.mideastweb.org/history.htm

If you're trying to unravel the mystery of Middle East politics and figure out what all the fighting is about, this site is an excellent place to start. Site features links you can click to begin exploring the history of the various countries that comprise the Middle East, including Israel and the Israeli-Palestinian conflict, Arabia, Egypt, Iran, and Iraq. Here, you can also find links to bibliographies of the most significant people in the history of the Middle East, a timeline that covers the Israeli-Palestinian conflict, discussion boards, and more. Site also offers a Middle East trivia quiz. The site isn't pretty, and it's tough to navigate and find what you're looking for, but it provides excellent content.

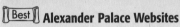

RUSSIA

Alexander Palace Websites

12345

www.alexanderpalace.org

This site functions as a starting point for explorations of museums, online books and exhibits, and other resources dealing with Russian history. Simply click a link and then follow the trail of links to the desired page. Site features a link to the Alexander Palace Time Machine, "the world's most popular website for Russian and Romanov history": Letters from Tsar Nicholas to His Wife During WWI, the Real Tsarista (an online book by Madame Lily Dehn); Thirteen Years at the Russian Court (a personal account of the last years and death of Tsar Nicholas II); and much more.

The Face of Russia

www.pbs.org/weta/faceofrussia

In 1998, PBS ran a three-part series called *The Face of Russia*, which attempted to find the answers to several questions: "Who are the Russian people? How have they expressed their character and inner conflicts in their art and culture? And, as Russia's long-awaited democracy develops, how will the Russian people redefine themselves culturally, spiritually, and politically?" At this site, you can still access some of the content presented in the series primarily through its interactive timeline. You can also learn more about the series and its creators and order the videos and the companion book online. A reference area is also available, where you can access a glossary, bibliography, media index, web links, and lesson plans.

A B C D E F G H I J K L M N O P Q R S T U V W X Y Z

History of Russia

12345

www.geographia.com/russia/rushis01.htm

This site provides an excellent overview of Russian history, beginning in ancient times and leading up to the Soviet era. When we visited the site, the navigation bar on the left side of the window didn't work. We had to click the links below each article to move on to the next or previous article in the collection.

U.S. Department of State: Russian History

12345

www.state.gov/r/pa/ei/bgn/3183.htm

The U.S. Department of State features this page where you can read a brief overview of Russian history and gather some additional information about Russia, including facts on its government, political conditions, economy, defense, and foreign relations (particularly with the United States).

UNITED STATES

American Memory

12345

memory.loc.gov

The Library of Congress' American Memory provides access to "primary source materials relating to the history and culture of the United States." One hundred collections feature more than seven million artifacts in digital format. You can explore the site by selecting one of the collections, searching for a specific item or topic, or choosing any of several guided lessons. The home page also features a link to learn a historical event that happened on this day. Another link gives you quick access to the site's FAQs list.

CIA History for Kids

12345

www.cia.gov/cia/ciakids

Maintained by the U.S. Central Intelligence Agency, this site provides a behind-the-scenes look at the history and development of the CIA. It also provides some fun stuff for kids, including a challenge to break a secret code and solve puzzles.

Eyes of Glory

12345

www.eyesofglory.com

This unique history of America focuses on the drive of our multiethnic citizenry to work toward a common goal of forming a great nation. The opening page contains links to family history, Jewish history, black history, and artifacts.

TheHistoryNet

12345

www.historynet.com

The Weider History Group, the world's largest publisher of history magazines, created and maintains this site, which offers a huge collection of informative articles on a broad range of historical topics. Site features content from all ten of the Weider History Group's magazines: America's Civil War, American History, Aviation History, British Heritage, Civil War Times, Military History, MHQ, Vietnam, Wild West, and World War II. Site also features a Daily Quiz, Picture of the Day, and a Today in History list of historical events. Discussion forums are also available.

Best Outline of U.S. History

12345

usinfo.state.gov/products/pubs/histryotln/index.htm

Online book from the federal government that covers U.S. history from the height of the Ice Age to the beginning of George W. Bush's second term. The navigation bar that runs down the left side of the page provides quick access to all 15 chapters of the book, a bibliography, and a picture profile. For students of U.S. history, this book provides an excellent overview and establishes a solid base for future research.

National Security Archive

12345

www.gwu.edu/~nsarchiv

For those interested in the history of U.S. foreign policy, this site provides a gold mine of declassified National Security documents—more than 2 million pages in more than 200 collections.

National Trust for Historic Preservation

1 2 3 4 5

www.nationaltrust.org

Opportunities to learn about the latest preservation issues. This site lists the 11 most endangered historical sites and offers you a way to help preserve these sites through your donation. Information is also available on how to make a positive impact by doing more than just providing a donation of money.

Smithsonian National Museum of American History

1 2 3 4 5

americanhistory.si.edu

The National Museum of American History is part of the Smithsonian Institution in Washington, D.C. Here, you can check out many of the museum's most popular exhibits online, including the history of the presidency and the *Star Spangled Banner*; visit the music room, to learn about musical performances at the museum; and check out the timeline of United States history.

USHistory.org

1 2 3 4 5

www.ushistory.org

Created and hosted by the Independence Hall Association in Philadelphia, this site presents U.S. history in the context of this former United States capitol. Here, you can learn about Philly's most beloved son, Benjamin Franklin, discover the history of the flag and read about Betsy Ross, explore the history of the Liberty Bell, visit Valley Forge online, and much more. If you can't quite make it to Philadelphia to see the sites up close, this is the next best thing to being there. And if you can make it to Philly, this site can help enhance your trip.

WORLD

Encyclopedia of World History

1 2 3 4 5

www.bartleby.com/67

Online version of the *Encyclopedia of World History*. The opening page displays a clickable table of contents you can use to navigate through the book. Site also features links to maps and genealogical tables included in the book.

History of the World Timeline

1 2 3 4 5

www.historychannel.com/timeline

The History Channel's timeline of world history covers the history of the world from 500 B.C. to the present. To begin your journey back in time, click Select a Century (you may have to click it twice), and then click the desired time period. The timeline displays a list of the most significant events or people in that period complete with a description of each event or person. Site also features a link for accessing an excellent collection of history maps.

Best HistoryWorld

www.historyworld.net

This database contains 400 interconnecting narratives and 6,000 selected events (amounting in all to more than a million words) and was created and written by Bamber Gascoigne. The opening page provides you with several options for navigating the content at this site. You can check out the 400 histories, which are arranged alphabetically; take a tour through time; select What Where When to search for content by specifying a person or event, a place, and a time; peruse a collection of timelines or create your own; or explore a collection of special articles by region, category, or contributor. Site also features a link to the OCEAN (One-Click Edited-Access Network) of additional historic sites on the Web and an online Whizzard Quiz.

HyperHistory

12345

www.hyperhistory.com/online_n2/History_n2/a.html

Comprehensive guide to the past 3,000 years of world history, this ever-growing tome attempts to provide a balanced view of history, covering not only wars and political events, but also scientific, cultural, and religious facets. A 116-chapter book by Frank A. Smitha provides a more cohesive view of world history. Timelines help you navigate the content at this site, but with so much time to cover, they feel a little cramped.

Related Site

www.hyperhistory.com

World History Archives

www.hartford-hwp.com/archives/index.html

The World History Archives is a huge collection of "documents to support the study of world history from a working-class and non-Eurocentric perspective." The opening page displays a collection of links grouped into the following categories: The World, The Americas, Asia and Oceania, Africa, and Europe. Click a link and then follow the trail of links to the desired article. The source of each link is cited, but links are not accompanied by any extensive annotations.

HOBBIES

A2Z Hobbies

12345

www.a2zhobbies.com

Find all the kits and supplies you need to fuel your enthusiasm for remote-controlled airplanes, model rocketry, pine cars, plastic models, and model trains. You won't find candles, lace, or floral arrangements at this shop.

eHobbies

12345 Blog RSS

www.ehobbies.com

Looking to develop a hobby? You'll find plenty of ideas, expert advice, and product information to get you in the right direction. There are also contests and products to order.

HOBBYLINC

12345

www.hobbylinc.com

A full resource of hobby supplies—more than 10,000 items available. View an extensive graphical catalog and take advantage of links, hints for hobbyists, biweekly specials, and educational information about various hobbies. Place or check the status of your order. Online gift certificates available for gift giving.

HobbyTown USA

12345

www.hobbytown.com

Except for its Art and Craft Town, HobbyTown is a shop that caters more to an engineer's taste in hobbies, providing separate areas for RC airplanes, cars, boats, and helicopters; model rockets; railroads; and plastic models.

RADIO OPERATION

Amateur Radio and DX Reference Guide

www.ac6v.com

Huge directory of links to more than 700 amateur radio topics, 6,000 websites, and 132 pages of high-quality content. One of the first links on the page leads you to sites where you can learn how to obtain a ham radio license. Scroll down the page for a clickable list of more than 30 topics, including Antenna Projects, Software, Manuals, Repeater Guides, Propagation, Licensing, DX Pages, and Product Reviews.

Related Site

www.dxzone.com

ARRL: National Association for Amateur Radio

12345 RSS

www.arrl.org

ARRL is a national association for amateur radio operators, representing more than 150,000 members. You can visit this site to learn more about the organization, access information about classes and exams, and find out about local clubs and hamfests. Site also features news and bulletins, a list of services provided by ARRL, licensing information, and an online store.

eHam.net

12345

www.eham.net

eHam.net is a dynamic community of ham radio operators on the Internet. This site provides ham radio operators with "a place to go for information, to exchange ideas, and be part of what's happening with ham radio on the Internet." If you're a novice, click the New to Ham Radio? link for a primer on what ham radio is, what ham radio operators do, instructions on how to become a ham radio operator, and other resources to get you started. For experienced operators, this site features all the information and resources you need, including articles, discussion forums, news and reviews, links to ham exams and other ham sites, a calendar of events, and more.

Ham Radio Outlet

12345

www.hamradio.com

Ham Radio Outlet is the world's largest supplier of ham radio equipment. Here, you can find a huge collection of high-quality HF transceivers, satellite transceivers, hand-held devices, marine and aviation radios, shortwave radios, base station receivers, and much more. HRO also has specials on used and opened-box equipment. You can search for products by manufacturer, description, product type, and manufacturer; find out about coupons, rebates, and special offers; access links to manufacturers' websites; and much more.

RC CARS

Hobby People

12345

www.hobbypeople.net

This is one of our favorite RC stores, because from the opening page, you can click the All Radio Control tab to focus in on RC cars, boats, and airplanes. This serves up a clean page from which you can choose the type of RC device in which you're interested: Cars & Trucks, Glow Planes, E-Flight Planes, Helicopters, or Boats. Online store carries a robust collection of RC toys complete with controls, chargers, accessories, and parts.

Radio Control Car Action Magazine

www.rccaraction.com

Self-billed as "The World's Best-Selling Radio Control Car Magazine," *Radio Control Car Action Magazine* features articles on the hobby and provides the latest results and reports on major races and competitions. Site features articles, videos, information on upcoming races, a track directory, spec sheets, classifieds, a discussion forum, and an online store.

Tower Hobbies

12345

www.towerhobbies.com

Huge online store that carries not only RC cars and trucks but also RC airplanes, helicopters, boats, model trains, and rockets. Store also carries accessories and parts. Site also features a guide on how to get started in radio control modeling that can help the novice get up and running. Company is BizRate certified, offers plenty of great deals, and guarantees your satisfaction.

RC PLANES

 Great Planes

12345

www.greatplanes.com

The Great Planes Model Manufacturing Company presents this outstanding site for RC airplane hobbyists. The opening page features a navigation bar that makes moving around the site a whole lot easier than flying an RC airplane. The navigation bar provides several drop-down menus for R/C Airplanes, Supplies, Adhesives, Tools, Field Equipment, Building Equipment, and Electrify Accessories. Simply point to a menu and then click the desired option. Site also features technical data, a glossary of terms, an airplane skill-level guide (for help in selecting a model that matches your skill level), and suggested engines and radio systems. Great Planes is a great place for RC airplane hobbyists of all levels.

Radio Control Zone

12345

www.radiocontrolzone.com/plane/index.asp

Brought to you by the publishers of *RC Microflight,*

Model Airplane News, and *Backyard Flyer*, this site is designed to support the RC airplane hobbyist community. Central to this site are a collection of bulletin boards where you can share your enthusiasm with like-minded RC airplane aficionados, post questions and obtain advice, and share your knowledge. Site also features an ever-growing glossary of RC airplane terms, links to the magazines (where you can read a selection of articles and subscribe online), classified ads, and RC videos. Great place to hang out when you're not flying.

RC Plane Talk

www.rcplanetalk.com

RC Plane Talk is an excellent guide to flying remote control airplanes, mini RC airplanes, RC helicopters, mini RC helicopters, and RC jets. Site features a beginner's guide, glossary, and guides that are specific to different types of RC aircraft. Here, you can also find links for other sites, hobby shops, discounts and coupons, RC plane reviews, gift ideas, and much more. If you're a novice, this should be your first stop on a long and enjoyable journey into RC airplane flying.

MODELS

FineScale Modeler Magazine

www.finescale.com

FineScale Modeler magazine features this online version of its magazine, where you can sample articles and order a subscription. Site features galleries, articles, workbench reviews, modeling products, and a discussion forum. Most of the good stuff is available only to subscribers.

Internet Hobbies

www.internethobbies.com

Excellent site for a wide selection of plastic model cars, plastic and wooden model boats and airplanes, die cast models, model rockets, sci-fi and space models, adhesives, paint, and accessories.

Model-Ships

www.model-ships.com

If you're interested in assembling your own model ships, this is the place to go. Model-Ships carries a robust collection of model kits for plastic sailing, military, and commercial ships; wooden ships (by Constructo, Dumas, Latina, and Woodcrafter); adhesives; building tools; paint and painting equipment; and ships in a bottle.

Related Site

www.plastic-models.com

Revell

www.revell.com

Revell is one of the most well-known and well-established model companies in the world and continues to serve the hobby industry with its model kits, diecast models, and modeling supplies and accessories. Here, you can check out the entire product line of Revell models, read feature articles, learn about programs and events, and obtain service and support. Separate sites are available for North America, Europe, and Asia Pacific. You can also search this site for local dealers.

Testors

www.testors.com

When you think of companies that are the foundation of the plastic modeling industry, Testor has to be one of the first names that pops into your head. Testor manufactures a wide selection of models, adhesives, paints, tools, and accessories for assembling and painting plastic models. Use the navigation bar on the left to track down the product you're looking for: Airbrushes & Accessories, Finishing Supplies, Tools, Model Kits, Games, or Paints. Site also features specials, a FAQ, a list of authorized dealers, hobby guides, replacement parts, and a gallery.

Related Site

www.scaleworkshop.com

A B C D E F G H I J K L M N O P Q R S T U V W X Y Z

MODEL TRAINS

Euro Rail Hobbies & More

www.eurorailhobbies.com

Huge online store that carries all the trains, supplies, tracks, and accessories you need to build and run your model trains. You can search the site for specific products, browse the product line, check out the gallery for hints and tips and a getting started guide, look at photos to stimulate your own creative thinking, and sample a few online videos.

Model Train Magazine Index

index.mrmag.com

The Model Train Magazine Index helps take some of the legwork out of finding specific articles about model trains. This site contains a complete index of more than 70,000 magazine articles and 329 books on the subject. You can search the index by keyword, title, category, road name, or trackplan, or select a general content category, pick a magazine in that category, and browse the table of contents of various issues.

National Model Railroad Association

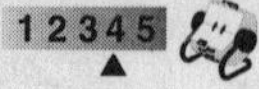

www.nmra.org

NMRA members built and maintain this site as a service to the model railroading community. Here, you can find a beginner's guide, a railroad track maintenance guide, a robust collection of photographs and illustrations, a scratch built showcase, NMRA news and calendar, a free screensaver, information about national and regional conventions, a directory of links to other model railroad sites, and much more. The directory of links is impressive and well-organized, helping you find just about anything a model railroad enthusiast might need, including manufacturers, layout tours, modeling clubs, and hobby shops.

San Diego Model Railroad Museum

www.sdmodelrailroadm.com

The San Diego Model Railroad Museum's mission is to preserve the heritage of railroading through a series of miniature representations of California railroads; research and preserve the history of model railroading; and educate the public in the many different aspects of railroading. Here, you can check out a few of the museum's many exhibits, learn about activities at the museum, peruse the online library, and find links to additional model railroad museums and sites.

Terrain for Trains

12345

www.terrainfortrains.com

Terrain for Trains specializes in manufacturing hard shell plastic layouts for model trains both in N-scale and HO-scale. Here, you can check prices and find a dealer.

Trains.com

www.trains.com

Trains.com is a one-stop resource to everything you need to fuel your enthusiasm for model trains. Content at this site is organized into six branches: Model Trains, Railroading, Rail Travel, Community, Kids Trains, and Train Shops are color coded for easy navigation. The navigation bar on the left presents links to the most popular features at this site: Downloadable Articles, Trains for the Young, Hobby Basics, World's Greatest Hobby, Resources, Glossary, Classified Ads, and Links. Site also features links to Trains.com train magazines, where you can obtain additional information and instructions on how to subscribe to the magazine of your choice. Excellent site for novice and expert alike.

HOCKEY

AHL: Official American Hockey League Website

www.theahl.com

Fans of the American Hockey League should visit this site, which provides team and player information, broken down by conference and division. Also provides minute-by-minute game updates and scores, information on future games, player profiles, AHL record book data, hockey forums, and all the other good stuff related to the AHL.

ESPN Hockey Site

sports.espn.go.com/nhl/index

ESPN's hockey page includes hockey headline news, the latest scores, team standings, statistics, trades, and much more.

HockeyBrain

www.hockeybrain.com

Catch all the latest scores, rankings, league headlines, and hockey news here. Covers the NHL, AHL, ECHL, UHL, WCHL, and CHL. Check out the ITC auction to find hockey memorabilia for sale. Photo gallery, message boards, and NHL rules are also featured. To leave comments on this blog, you must register.

Hockey Hall of Fame

www.hhof.com/index.htm

Play the Hockey Hall of Fame trivia game, track down statistics and rankings, and learn more about the best hockey players in history. This site features a cool, clickable map of the museum that you can tour to check out the many exhibits and attractions. Plenty of photos available.

The Hockey News Online

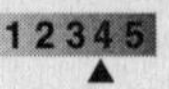

www.thn.com

The online version of *The Hockey News* magazine. Take a look at the latest issue, take part in this week's poll/drawing, and access all sorts of other timely and interesting online articles. Site also features online chat for fans and fantasy hockey leagues.

Hockey's Future

www.hockeysfuture.com

Want to know who's rumored to be the top draft pick? Keep up on trade tips and rumors, read columnist opinions, and stay current on the latest hockey news.

Internet Hockey Database

www.hockeydb.com

Huge browsable directory of hockey information, including player statistics, team standings, records, draft picks, trading cards, and more.

National Hockey League Players' Association

www.nhlpa.com

The official players' association page has links to past and present Player of the Day profiles, along with other NHL player information.

A B C D E F G H I J K L M N O P Q R S T U V W X Y Z

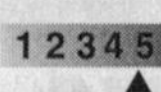 NHL: Official National Hockey League Website

www.nhl.com

This is the official NHL website where you can get all the news about NHL hockey you could want. Check out individual teams and NHL schedules, and take the most recent poll. The gift shop is also worth a look for items ranging from hats to official NHL jerseys of your favorite player. Although the Hockey category is packed with outstanding sites, we had to make this site our pick as Best of the Best due to its depth of coverage, up-to-the-minute information, and fan-based features, including fantasy leagues, blogs, and live chat area.

National Hockey League Eastern Conference Team Sites

Atlantic Division

New Jersey Devils	www.newjerseydevils.com
New York Islanders	www.newyorkislanders.com
New York Rangers	www.newyorkrangers.com
Philadelphia Flyers	www.philadelphiaflyers.com
Pittsburgh Penguins	www.pittsburghpenguins.com

Northeast Division

Boston Bruins	www.bostonbruins.com
Buffalo Sabres	www.sabres.com
Montreal Canadiens	www.canadiens.com
Ottawa Senators	www.ottawasenators.com
Toronto Maple Leafs	www.mapleleafs.com

Southeast Division

Atlanta Thrashers	www.atlantathrashers.com
Carolina Hurricanes	carolinahurricanes.com
Florida Panthers	www.floridapanthers.com
Tampa Bay Lightning	www.tampabaylightning.com
Washington Capitals	www.washingtoncaps.com

National Hockey League Western Conference Team Sites

Central Division

Chicago Blackhawks	www.chicagoblackhawks.com
Columbus Blue Jackets	www.bluejackets.com
Detroit Red Wings	www.detroitredwings.com
Nashville Predators	www.nashvillepredators.com
St. Louis Blues	www.stlouisblues.com

Northwest Division

Calgary Flames	www.calgaryflames.com
Colorado Avalanche	www.coloradoavalanche.com
Edmonton Oilers	www.edmontonoilers.com
Minnesota Wild	www.wild.com
Vancouver Canucks	www.canucks.com

Pacific Division

Mighty Ducks of Anaheim	www.mightyducks.com
Dallas Stars	www.dallasstars.com
Los Angeles Kings	www.lakings.com
Phoenix Coyotes	www.phoenixcoyotes.com
San Jose Sharks	www.sj-sharks.com

Science of Hockey

www.exploratorium.edu/hockey

The Science of Hockey takes you inside the game of hockey, utilizing RealAudio and video to bring you science bits from leading physicists and chemists. It also gives you insights from NHL players and coaches from the San Jose Sharks. Want to know why ice is slippery or how to shoot a puck 100 miles per hour? Check it out.

U.S. College Hockey Online

www.uscollegehockey.com

Men's and women's college ice hockey news, schedules, scores, recaps, polls, and players of the week are available here. You can also check out your favorite college team's players and rankings.

USA Hockey

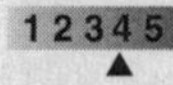

www.usahockey.com

The official site of USA Hockey. Site covers the Olympics, Adult Players, Youth Players, Alumni, Coaches, Disabled Hockey, and much more. Site also features a calendar of events, a special area for women's hockey, and online shopping. Come skate through this site for yourself.

HOLIDAYS & CELEBRATIONS

Christmas Around the World

1 2 3 4 5

christmas.com/worldview

Asia, Europe, Latin America, the Middle East, and the Netherlands are among the regions with Christmas traditions explained on this site. Here, you'll also learn how to say "Merry Christmas" in more than 30 languages, and you'll find a list of other holidays that fall around the Christmas season.

The Fourth of July

1 2 3 4 5

wilstar.com/holidays/july4.htm

This patriotic site is filled with links to historic documents such as the Magna Carta, Declaration of Independence, Constitution, Emancipation Proclamation, and more. Also contains flag-flying rules.

Hallmark.com

1 2 3 4 5

www.hallmark.com

The home page of the company known for spreading holiday cheer. Here, you can shop for cards and gifts, send flowers, and send eCards.

History of Hanukkah

1 2 3 4 5

www.historychannel.com/exhibits/holidays/hanukkah

The History Channel presents this site to educate visitors about the history and traditions associated with this major Jewish holiday. Site content is presented in three sections: History, Traditions, and Amazing Hanukkah Feats (record-breaking events in honor of Hanukkah).

Best Holidays on the Net

1 2 3 4 5

www.holidays.net

Collection of multimedia presentations for nearly every holiday of the year. Each presentation provides a brief history of the holiday, its meaning and significance, suggested activities, and a way to send an eCard to a friend or relative. Site includes holiday calendars, crafts, and recipes, a holiday store, and even ideas for holiday travel! Don't miss the fun and wacky daily holidays. If you're into celebrating holidays, bookmark this Best of the Best Holidays site and visit daily.

KidProJ's Multicultural Calendar

1 2 3 4 5

www.kidlink.org/KIDPROJ/MCC

You can search this holiday calendar by month, holiday, country, or author or submit a holiday to include in the calendar.

Kids Domain Holidays

1 2 3 4 5

www.kidsdomain.com/holiday

Link to sites that explain and explore the meaning of a whole list of annual holidays to kids, from Veterans Day to Fathers Day, Valentine's Day, and just about every other major day. Even Guy Fawkes Day is explained here! This site also features some cool gift-making ideas.

Martin Luther King, Jr. Day

1 2 3 4 5

www.holidays.net/mlk

This site is dedicated to the memory of slain civil rights leader Dr. Martin Luther King, Jr. and the national holiday that honors him. It features a biography, links to his famous "I Have a Dream" speech, and more.

Passover on the Net

www.holidays.net/passover

This easy-to-navigate site offers the story of Passover, information about the Seder meal (plus recipes), and a collection of downloadable Passover songs in MIDI format.

Ramadan

www.islamicity.com/ramadan

IslamiCity features this area of its website as an educational center where visitors can learn more about this major Islamic holiday. Site features articles and audio recordings that introduce a variety of topics, including information about the tradition of fasting and prayer and the importance of reading and following the teachings of the Quran. A navigation bar on the left provides quick access to other features on this site, including Islamic History, Prayer Times, a Q&A, Islamic Quiz, and a Quran search. Excellent site both for followers of the religion and those who wish to gain an understanding of it.

Related Site

www.ramadan.co.uk

HOME

Ask the Builder

www.askbuild.com

Search the archives of this syndicated columnist (Tim Carter) to learn the best way to tackle a problem around the house. Project archives will tell and show you (using streaming video) how to clean a deck, for example. Straightforward advice. You can also purchase books, CDs, and other related merchandise here.

Best DoItYourself.com

doityourself.com

If you know your way around a toolbox and prefer doing your home repairs and remodeling yourself, bookmark DoItYourself.com. Here, you can find all the information you need to deal with plumbing, electricity, home décor, exterior remodeling, and more. This site provides access to tutorials and discussion forums where you can learn from experienced professionals...or at least from people who know a little more than you might know. This site has an attractive design, plenty of tools to help you find the information you want, and an outstanding collection of instructions, tips, and advice, making it our choice as Best of the Best in the Home category.

Habitat for Humanity

www.habitat.org

Home of Habitat for Humanity International, a nonprofit, nondenominational, Christian housing organization devoted to "building simple, decent, affordable houses in partnership with those in need of adequate shelter." Learn more about Habitat for Humanity and find out how you can help.

Sound Home Resource Center

www.soundhome.com

Ask the Sound Home consultant a question about your home-building project, or check the articles and FAQs posted here on the topic. The glossary of terms will also help put you on par with your contractor.

CONSTRUCTION

B4UBUILD.com

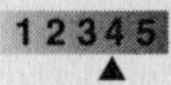

www.b4ubuild.com

For home builders, this site offers more than 11,000 home plans, home-building guides, a sample construction schedule, information about construction contracts, and a complete overview of the home-building process. It also offers links for kids, to get them involved in the process, too.

Bricsnet

www.aecinfo.com

World's largest and most active database for architecture, engineering, construction, and home building. Site features interactive discussion forums, products, firms, services, news, events, projects, articles, classifieds, specifications, and schools.

Build.com

www.build.com

Find suppliers and contractors through this site, broken down by categories relating to the type of project you want to undertake. You'll find flooring, paint and wall covering, decks, kitchens, baths, and just about every other potential home project.

Builder Online

www.builderonline.com

The online version of *Builder* magazine, the site offers trade and consumer information, such as building plans and projects, products, contractors, industry news, and links to other home improvement sites.

BuildingCost.net

www.building-cost.net

How much would it cost to build a replacement house on your lot? With the BuildingCost.net calculator, you can figure it out in about five minutes. Simply enter values for the variables—materials used, design features, quality, size, shape, heating, cooling, and geographic area—and the calculator spits out a printable estimate detailing labor and material costs for each of 34 construction cost categories.

Building Industry Exchange

www.building.org

Extensive directory of contractors, subcontractors, and suppliers for the building industry. Includes listings for architects, concrete workers, electricians, plumbers, and just about any other service required in the building industry. Also features discussion forums and job leads for construction professionals.

Construction-Resource.com

www.construction-resource.com

Construction-Resource.com provides construction and remodeling information for home owners and sellers, realtors, and builders. Here, you can find articles on construction and remodeling, discussion forums, construction calculators, and other information, tools, and resources to help you with your home construction and home improvement projects.

HomeBuilder.COM

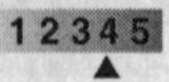

www.homebuilder.com

Shop for a new home in the area where you plan to settle. Just specify the state, area, ZIP code, and price range to view new home listings in the area. Here, you can also find custom builders, lots for sale, and everything you need for home improvement projects and home furnishings. Online shopping lets you compare prices at several stores.

Housing Zone

www.housingzone.com

Search more than 2,500 home building sites from this one location, as well as look at popular home designs, catch up on building industry news, and learn more about affording a home through HUD. Site also features plans and projects, cost estimators, news and articles, and discussion forums.

National Association of Home Builders

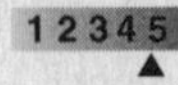

www.nahb.org

NAHB (National Association of Home Builders) is a trade-based association whose mission is "to enhance the climate for housing and the building industry." Home builders should definitely bookmark this site and perhaps even join the association for additional perks. But this site isn't only for professional builders. It also features useful information for homeowners and people who may be considering buying or building a home. To access content for homeowners, click the Resources link and point to Consumers. This displays a menu of options including Building a Custom Home, Floor Plans, Home Maintenance, and Remodeling Your Home. Under Education, you can find special resources on home building and homeownership for teachers and students.

> **Tip:** It's a little tough to figure out how to get to the site for teachers and students, so just go there directly: www.homesofourown.org.

DECKS & PATIOS

BestDeckSite

www.bestdecksite.com

Self-billed as "Best Deck Site," this site features illustrated instructions on how to build decks and gazebos. Online guides include Plan & Design, Footings, Legerboards, Support Beam, Floor Joists, Stairs & Rails, and Gazebo Roofs. Site also features a FAQ, links to other sites, and a few online calculators. When we visited the site, it offered a few gazebo plans for purchase, but the deck plans were still in the works. Excellent site if you're a do-it-yourselfer getting ready to build your first deck or gazebo.

ConcreteNetwork.com

www.concretenetwork.com/concrete/concrete_patio/index.html

The ConcreteNetwork presents this page to promote stamped concrete patios. They look like brick or stone, but they're concrete. Scroll down the page for a free design tool that enables you to check out various styles and patterns.

Deck Design

www.deckdesign.com

This site features some excellent photographs of a wide selection of deck designs to spark your imagination.

DecKorators

www.deckorators.com

DecKorators manufactures balusters for decks. Here, you can check out the complete line of products, view photos of completed projects, and check out an animated presentation of various styles. Illustrated installation instructions are also available at this site.

Hometime.com

www.hometime.com/Howto/projects/decks.htm

Excellent illustrated instructions on how to build a deck from scratch. This site presents an overview and a list of tools you'll need along with detailed instructions on installing a ledger board, laying footings, raising posts, installing beams and joists, laying floorboards, and building stairs and railings.

PatioPavers

www.pacificpavingstone.com/patio-design-menu.html

If you're planning on building a patio with pavers, check out this site for ideas. Site features three galleries of photos that demonstrate the possibilities: Driveway Gallery, Patio Gallery, and Walkway Gallery. Here, you can also find a list of ideas and common questions (and their answers). Not much how-to stuff here, but the site features a collection of short videos that show you what's involved and how to choose a quality contractor.

Treatedwood Home Page

www.treatedwood.com

If you're building a deck, chances are fairly good that you'll be using treated lumber. Check this site for the latest news and information about treated lumber along with some tips for maintaining it to keep it looking its best. Site features some useful illustrations of deck design and construction.

DECORATING/PAINTING

All-Home Decor

www.all-homedecor.com

All-Home Decor features articles about decorating and provides links to other sites where you can shop for home decorating products. Articles are grouped by category, including more articles, decorating basics, and rooms.

American Society of Interior Designers

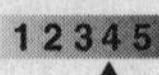

www.interiors.org

An online referral service for the largest organization of professional interior designers in the world. Find information about the organization that has more than 30,000 designers, educators, and media members; more than 7,000 student members; and 3,500 industry foundation members. Learn how designers work or find the right designer for your project.

Ballard Design

www.ballarddesigns.com/home.jsp

Mail-order source for fine home furnishings and accents. You can find everything here from beds and bedding to office furniture.

Bed Bath & Beyond

www.Bedbathandbeyond.com

Shop the online store for bed, bath, kitchen, and home accessories, and check the latest circular for the best deals.

Best Better Homes and Gardens

www.bhg.com

Better Homes and Gardens is much more than simply the online version of the magazine. This site features a huge collection of articles on decorating your home and establishing a beautiful garden, along with an entire box of free tools that can help you select colors and furnishings for a room, settle on a floor plan for your new house or renovation, and design your garden. You'll find slide shows, short video clips, and plenty of photos to spark your imagination and invigorate your enthusiasm for improving your home. Site also features blogs, message boards, and more tips than you can possibly pursue.

cMYVision

www.cmyvision.com

Interactive design software that allows users to experimentally make changes to any digital photograph of a home, room, or yard to create a new look. Home decorators can drag and drop different paints, doors, trim, plants, siding, flooring, and so on, into their chosen image.

CrateandBarrel.com

www.crateandbarrel.com

This retail store now provides online access to its furniture, bedding, kitchen and bar accessories, and home goods. The gift registry makes selecting purchases even easier.

Design Addict

www.designaddict.com

As this site proclaims, you can "discover the design world through Design Addict." More than 350 of the world's top designers are in the spotlight here, representing thousands of beautifully crafted home furnishings...and the collection grows daily as new designers visit the site and add their work to the gallery. When you're looking for a look, look here.

Designing Online

www.designingonline.com

Designing Online originated to provide advice on furniture placement and has expanded to address all areas of home design. Here, you can find plenty of articles, news, how-to's, photos, and discussion forums. Site also features an excellent collection of links to other home décor and decorating sites on the Web.

EZblinds.com

www.ihomedecor.com

Incredible selection of window coverings. You can order free swatch samples online, and if you like what you see, come back and order to your window dressings online.

FurnitureFind.com

www.furniturefind.com

Search for furniture for virtually every room in your house here and get free national delivery after placing your order. Lots of options from which to choose. You can shop for a particular type of furniture piece or a style.

FurnitureOnline.com

www.furnitureonline.com

An online catalog of office and limited home furnishings. Check out the weekly specials for discounted prices on individual pieces and accessories.

Home Fashion Information Network

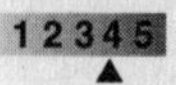

www.thehome.com

Find information on a variety of home furnishing topics under one roof, displayed in rooms for convenience. Topics include tips and tricks, information on how to select items, and assistance with your bridal registry.

Home and Garden Television (HGTV)

www.hgtv.com

Home and Garden Television's website features a huge collection of articles, advice, illustrated instructions, and how-to videos. Tabbed navigation gives you quick access to topic categories, including Decorating, Gardening, Kitchens, Baths, and Remodeling. Site features a good collection of before and after photos and videos, revealing the magic of home renovation and décor.

Longaberger Baskets

www.longaberger.com

Introduces you to the Longaberger company and all the Longaberger products, including baskets, pottery, fabrics, home décor, and home accessories. The site does not allow you to purchase products directly, but it does help you locate an independent sales consultant. Jump to the kitchen, dining room, library, and living room areas to see the goods available and get valuable information.

No Brainer Blinds and Shades

www.nobrainerblinds.com

If you're looking for a wide selection of blinds, shades, and shutters, this is the place to go. No Brainer opens with a page that makes finding what you want much easier than wandering the aisles at your local home improvement store. Simply select the desired style, pick a size, and check out.

Pier 1 Imports

www.pier1.com

Pier 1 Imports is well known for its line of exotic home décor, and now you can shop Pier 1 online, use its bridal registry feature, check out specials, and peruse its furniture guide.

Pottery Barn

www.potterybarn.com

The pottery barn has everything you need to fill those empty rooms with beautiful furniture and home décor. Products are grouped by furniture, bedding & bath, rugs, pillows & windows, accessories, lighting, tableware & entertaining, rooms, and sale items. You can shop online, set up a gift registry, or purchase items for a friend or relative who has set up a registry here.

Rental Decorating

www.rentaldecorating.com

This is one of the few sites that focuses on interior decorating for renters. Here, you can learn the basics of interior design, organization, color schemes, and styles. Site also features tips for specific rooms, decorating on a shoestring, decoration small spaces, and maintaining a garden in a rental unit. Excellent site for college students, whether they're living in a dorm or apartment.

A B C D E F G H I J K L M N O P Q R S T U V W X Y Z

Stencil Ease Home Décor and Craft Stencils

stencilease.com

Flip through the Stencil Ease catalog and order online. Stencils, paints, brushes, decorating stamps, and accessories are available. One page also gives detailed instructions on how to stencil. You can also order the Stencil Ease Decorator catalog.

Traditional Home Magazine

www.traditionalhome.com

Traditional Home magazine offers an outstanding collection of articles, advice, and photos for decorating and remodeling your home, entertaining guests, and creating and maintaining your garden. Site features tabbed navigation to areas that include Antiques & Collecting, Dream Homes, Entertaining, Gardening, Home Decorating, Home Furnishings, and Kitchen Remodeling.

unicaHOME

www.unicahome.com

This site features thousands of hard-to-find items that can give your home just the right touch. Very modern, cool, and well-designed for anyone who likes to browse the aisles looking for home décor. Shop by company, designer, or genre (barroom, bathroom, kitchen, bedroom, and so on).

Related Site

www.jamilin.com

UrbanScapes

www.widerview.com/urban.html

Great-looking modern furniture, lighting, kitchen tools, bath ware, and playful kitsch. These designs will add a touch of urban sophistication to your loft or city apartment.

ELECTRICAL

DoItYourself.com Electrical and Electronics

www.doityourself.com/scat/electricand-electron

DoItYourself.com provides useful information on all aspects of home ownership and maintenance. This particular page contains dozens of links to informative how-to articles on electrical wiring inside your home. Here, you can learn the basics, plus find specific instructions for wiring ceiling fans, dimmer switches, track lighting, computers, home automation systems, communication systems, and more. Learn how to use an electrical meter, and much more.

Electrical Safety Foundation

www.esfi.org

Electrical wiring is an integral part of any home, but it can be quite dangerous if the wiring is faulty or unsafe products appliances are used. To make sure your house is wired safely and that you are using appliances safely, check out the information provided here, or download your ESFI Electrical Safety brochure today.

Home & Family

www.homeandfamilynetwork.com/homeim-provement/electrical.html

Home & Family provides an excellent collection of how-to articles for all sorts of home repairs and improvements. This page focuses on installing, maintaining, and repairing the electrical circuitry and fixtures in the home. Here, you can learn the basics, explore the overall electrical wiring in a house, obtain step-by-step guides for various lighting projects, pick up some basic wiring techniques, and learn how to troubleshoot common problems.

Home and Garden Television: Electrical

www.hgtv.com/hgtv/rm_electric_appliances

This site provides some excellent articles, instructions, and tips on electrical home appliances and home wiring. Learn how to install or replace a light fixture, install a new light switch or outlet, install a phone jack, use a circuit tester, and more.

HomeTips

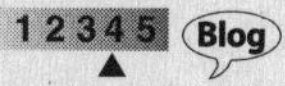

www.hometips.com/home_improvement/electrical_systems.html

HomeTips provides illustrated guides for common electrical and lighting tasks around the home, including ceiling fans, three-way switches, dimmers, GFCI (ground fault circuit interrupters), and more.

Saving Electricity

michaelbluejay.com/electricity

Michael Bluejay has put together this outstanding site to educate consumers on the best ways to conserve energy and trim their electrical bills. Site offers advice for conservationists at every level. If you're an average homeowner trying to figure out which appliance uses the most electricity, you can find out here. If you're a little more sophisticated and curious, you may want to dip into more advanced articles that show you how to use a meter to measure the electricity that a particular appliance uses or learn ways to generate and store your own electricity.

FLOORING

Armstrong Flooring

1 2 3 4 5

www.armstrong.com

The leader in vinyl and linoleum flooring provides products for residential and commercial use. Visit this site to explore your flooring options. Also features laminate "hardwood" flooring.

Flooring America

1 2 3 4 5

www.flooringamerica.com

Flooring America is the place to go not only to learn about your flooring options but also to obtain information and tips on floor care and cleaning. Here, you can learn the benefits of all types of flooring, including hardwood, carpet, laminate, ceramic, vinyl, and area rugs; apply for credit online; and find a Flooring America Store near you.

iFloor

1 2 3 4 5

www.ifloor.com

Online flooring store that carries a wide selection of hardwood, laminate, bamboo, and cork flooring, as well as rugs. Site features types of flooring you can't get at most local stores.

Pergo Laminate Flooring

1 2 3 4 5

www.pergo.com

Home of the fake wood floors that look like real hardwood floors. Consumers can check out the showroom, check out different products, and plan a project.

Woodfloors.org

1 2 3 4 5

www.woodfloors.org

National Wood Flooring Association maintains this site for consumers and professional installers. Consumers can visit this site to learn about the benefits of real hardwood floors and how to care for wood floors. Professionals can check out the NWFA site to learn more about membership and conferences. This site features an interactive Design a Room program that you can use for free to see how different flooring styles and finishes will look in a room. Select a room and a color for the walls, pick a type of wood, and select the direction of the floorboards—vertical or horizontal. The program automatically applies your selections to a digital photo, showing exactly how the room will look.

A B C D E F G H I J K L M N O P Q R S T U V W X Y Z

HEATING & AIR CONDITIONING

AC Doctor

www.acdoctor.com

AC Doctor is a referral service that can help you track down a qualified heating and air conditioning technician in your area. However, this site goes far beyond simply helping you find a qualified technician. It provides beginners guides that teach you how an air conditioning or heating system works, tips for keeping your heating and cooling system running most efficiently, and articles on how to improve your system's ventilation and filtering. Special area on Energy Savers can help you trim your heating and air conditioning bills.

American Society of Heating, Refrigerating, and Air-Conditioning Engineers, Inc.

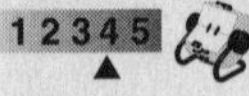

www.ashrae.org

ASHRAE (American Society of Heating, Refrigerating, and Air-Conditioning Engineers) presents this site as an educational kiosk for consumers and HVAC professionals alike. Here, you can learn about the history of air conditioning, check out ASHRAE seminars and other educational programs, visit the consumer area for tips on trimming your heating and air conditioning costs, check the latest standards, and locate HVAC&R supplies and services.

Bryant Heating and Cooling Systems

www.bryant.com

One of the big names in the heating and cooling industry, Bryant offers this site as a way of introducing its products on the Internet and providing customer service. Site features some excellent educational articles for consumers along with guidance on how to select a heating and cooling system that meets your needs. You can also find product guides and manuals at this site along with technical support and a troubleshooting guide.

Carrier

www.residential.carrier.com

Carrier is the world's leading manufacturer of heating, air conditioning, and refrigeration systems. Here, you can check out their products, search the knowledgebase for technical support, and read some general articles to develop a deeper understanding of home heating and cooling.

Lennox

www.lennox.com

Lennox is one of the top manufacturers of heating and air conditioning equipment for both residential and commercial use. Here, you can learn more about the current product line, customize a system to suite your needs, and find a local Lennox dealer. The Comfortsphere System Customizer leads you step by step through the process of selecting the right system for your needs and then customizing it.

Trane

www.trane.com

If you're shopping for a new air conditioning system, check out this site for a checklist on how to start shopping. Here, you can learn what Trane air conditioning systems have that the competitors' products don't have, customize your system online, and find out how to contact a local Trane dealer.

HOME AUTOMATION

EH (Electronic House) Publishing

www.ehpub.com

Which home automation products are to die for and which can you do without? The online reviews at this site will tell you, as well as give you ideas for new technology you might want to install. A bimonthly e-zine with information on the latest technology in home automation and home theater systems.

Home Automation

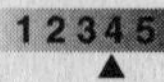

www.homeauto.com

Home Automation, Inc. provides this site to introduce customers to its line of home automation products; but if you want to purchase any of the products, you need to contact a dealer. This site helps you find a dealer near you. The product guide is a PDF file you can download and view or print. Separate sections of the site are available for builders, architects, training, and support.

Home Controls, Inc.

www.homecontrols.com

Home Controls, Inc. features a collection of more than 3,000 home automation gadgets ranging from simple automated lamp controls that cost about $12 up to complete home automation systems that run in the thousands of dollars. Here, you can shop online for these products and obtain technical support and installation information for products you already purchased.

SmartHome.com

www.smarthome.com

Take the guided tour of home automation products before viewing the catalog and considering products. You can also learn about the latest technology and why you need it. Incredible selection of home automation products.

X10

www.x10.com/homepage.htm

X10 is the home of one of the largest digital camera stores in the world. If you need a camera for surveillance or for telecommunicating over the Internet, this is the place to get it. Also sells a variety of home automation products.

HOME DESIGN

AARP: Universal Design

www.aarp.org/families/home_design

AARP (American Association of Retired Persons) maintains this page to educate its members and others on the benefits of building homes that can accommodate the needs of aging residents. Site offers plenty of tips for designing more-accessible stairways, safer countertops, improved lighting, and more. AARP promotes the Universal Design approach to home design so that homes are accessible and comfortable for people of all ages and abilities.

Consumer's Guide to Energy Efficiency and Renewable Energy

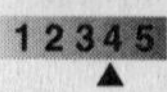

www.eere.energy.gov/consumer

The U.S. Department of Energy maintains this site to educate homeowners on how to conserve energy and take advantage of renewable energy resources to heat and cool their homes. Site includes a few articles on how to design a home that's more energy efficient. Good article on building a home that uses passive solar energy to heat it.

Design Community Forums

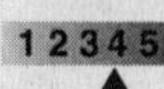

arch.designcommunity.com

If you're designing your own home or you're an architect who wants to share ideas with others in the community, check out the Design Community discussion forums. Here, you can read messages posted by other designers and post your own questions, insights, and replies.

Home Planners

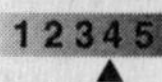

www.eplans.com

Design your dream home online using some of the most popular home plans, take a look at the design in 3D, and then price out the work and put together a construction calendar.

HomePlans.com

12345

www.homeplans.com

HomePlans.com carries a selection of more than 11,000 home plans. You can narrow your search by specifying a minimum and maximum square footage and the desired number of bedrooms and baths. Site also features a resource center where you can read free articles about home design and construction, search through a product directory, and post your question to have it answered by a qualified designer.

New Home Source

12345

www.newhomesource.com

Search more than 250,000 homes and house plans by the top builders in your area. Specify your state, area, and ZIP code; enter the desired price range; and receive a list of the top home builders in your area from the New Home Source. Click a button to view a snapshot of a home's exterior or the floor plans.

Punch Software

12345

www.punchsoftware.com

Punch Software develops home, landscape, and interior software for amateurs and professionals who want to preview their visions in 3D before they begin construction.

Sustainable House Design

12345

www.cidnetwork.com/sustainable-design.htm

Modern homes are becoming more like tiny ecosystems than simply buildings in which people live. At this site, you can explore the four main factors that contribute to making a house ecologically sustainable: vegetation management, solar orientation and design, water use and reuse, and energy efficiency. Site shows options for ecologically friendly design in new construction and retrofit options for existing homes.

HOME IMPROVEMENT & REPAIR

Ace Hardware

12345

www.acehardware.com

Find a hardware store close to you, get answers to frequently asked questions, and learn hardware hints and tips at this site. You can also participate in seasonal contests and find out about store specials.

Best BobVila.com

12345 Blog

www.bobvila.com

Bob Vila, host of the popular TV show *This Old House* and *Bob Vila's Home Again*, is almost synonymous with home restoration and improvement projects. Here, you can visit Bob and his crew online, check out the TV shows, peruse his how-to library, sample his software design tools, post a question, and even shop for home improvement tools and products. This Best of the Best home improvement and restoration site shows little room for any improvement—it's easy to navigate, offers plenty of useful information, and its graphics are crisp and clear.

diyfixit

12345

www.diyfixit.co.uk

Whether you need to fix squeaky floorboards, leaky faucets, or freaky electrical problems, this site can help you troubleshoot the cause and fix the problem. Several categories of fixes are available, including kitchen, bathroom, bedroom, loft, and outside. Site also features a link to a sister site, called motorfixit, where you can obtain tips for troubleshooting and repairing problems with your car.

Fiberglass Insulation by Owens Corning

12345 Blog

www.owenscorning.com

Get in the pink with information about the fiberglass insulation products this company has developed for homes, as well as other products, including roofing, vinyl siding, windows, and patio doors.

HandymanUSA

www.handymanusa.com

If you're pretty handy around the house but you need some advice, turn to HandymanUSA. This site covers every area of home maintenance and repair from appliances to wallpaper, and everything in between. Here, you can also find a list of frequently asked questions and expert discussion forums for additional information and advice.

Home Depot

www.homedepot.com

Get project help and information on Home Depot store locations and products. Check out store specials and also see whether you are in the Home Depot online ordering area. Hints, tips, tricks, and illustrated how-to instructions abound at this site.

Homedoctor.net

homedoctor.net

Homedoctor.net is a community of neighbors helping neighbors with information and advice about various home repair and restoration projects. Central to this site are its discussion forums, where you can post a question and read responses.

Hometime

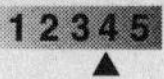

www.hometime.com

Home page of the popular PBS television series. Offers text and still-frame highlights from the show and step-by-step instruction on several home-improvement projects.

Ian Evans' World of Old Houses

1 2 3 4 5

www.oldhouses.com.au

If you're in the process of fixing up an old house, this site could become your best friend. Get advice on bringing a house back to its original form, track down old parts and accessories, and commiserate with fellow older-home owners from around the world.

Lowe's Home Improvement Warehouse

1 2 3 4 5

www.lowes.com

Lowe's Companies, Inc., is one of America's top 30 retailers serving home improvement, home décor, home electronics, and home construction markets. Lowe's website offers step-by-step guides for home improvement projects, featured products, and tips from Lowe's Home Safety Council. You'll also find a store locator, recent corporate financial data, and a list of employment opportunities. You can also order merchandise from this site through a secure server.

Natural Handyman

www.naturalhandyman.com

At this site, the Natural Handyman, Jerry Alonzy, offers free home repair and do-it-yourself tips. Content is organized in three sections: Articles, Q&A, and the Links Library. Use the brick-and-mortar navigation bar near the top of the screen to get around. This site also provides a tool that enables you to search for a handyman near you, but we found that the tool provided few references for the areas we searched.

The Old House

www.oldhouseweb.com

If you've purchased an older fixer-upper, the first step you should take is to visit The Old House website, where you can find products and suppliers, do-it-yourself guides, feature articles, online forums, and much more. If you're looking for something more in-depth, check out the store for books and how-to videos.

On the House with the Carey Brothers

www.onthehouse.com

On the House is a weekly syndicated radio talk show offering advice, hints, and solutions relating to all aspects of home maintenance, repair, and improvement.

Pella Windows and Doors

12345

www.pella.com

Research the world of windows and find the latest products this company has to offer. Terminology and energy efficiency are explained.

Remodeling Online

remodeling.hw.net

Home of *Remodeling* magazine, a publication devoted to remodeling experts. Check out the reputations of the 50 top remodelers, research building codes, apply for building permits online, learn about conferences and special events, and more.

This Old House

12345

www.thisoldhouse.com/toh

An interactive doorway into *This Old House*, featuring articles and columns from the magazine, as well as topics related to building, renovation, and restoration. Current news, information on personal appearances by the TV series crew, and project house updates are posted regularly.

Tools of the Trade

12345

www.toolsofthetrade.net

Online buyer's guide for construction and building tools. Find out about the newest tools and building materials on the market and see how they fare when run through a series of toughness tests.

Your New House with Michael Holigan

www.michaelholigan.com

One-stop resource center for building, buying, and remodeling homes, this site features advice from Michael Holigan, an expert in all things related to home improvement. Here, you can find project plans, step-by-step tutorials, online video demonstrations of popular products, floor plans, and more.

INSPECTION

American Society of Home Inspectors

www.ashi.org

This professional organization of home inspectors can help you find a certified inspector in your area, answer any questions you may have about home inspections, and take you on a tour of a virtual home inspection. Before you buy a home, you should have it inspected. Before you have it inspected, visit this site to learn how to hire someone with the right qualifications to inspect it.

Related Site

www.homeinspections-usa.com

Home Inspector Locator

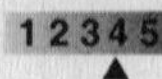

www.homeinspectorlocator.com

Enter your ZIP code, and the database of more than 3,000 inspectors will provide a list of professionals in your area. Site also features some excellent articles on home safety and repair.

National Association of Certified Home Inspectors

12345

www.nachi.org

The National Association of Certified Home Inspectors is a "nonprofit organization helping home inspectors achieve financial success and maintain inspection excellence." Site features a message board, code of ethics, standards of practice, continuing education resources and exams, and a collection of business success tips.

INTERIOR DESIGN

American Society of Interior Designers

www.asid.org

Whether you're an interior designer, you want to hire an interior designer, or you want to become an

A B C D E F G H I J K L M N O P Q R S T U V W X Y Z

interior designer, this is the place for you. Home and business owners can visit this site to track down a certified interior designer in their area. Professional designers can visit for support and resources. And interested students can visit to learn what it takes to become an interior designer. Site features a student center, a resource center, and a small collection of feature articles on assorted interior design topics.

DoItYourself Interior Design

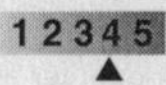

www.doityourself.com/scat/interiordesign

This site helps the do-it-yourselfer get up to speed on interior design by focusing on a room and offering ideas and tips. Site includes several areas including Decorating for Kids, Design by Room, Designers and Ideas, Holiday Decorating, and Home Accents.

Home Décor Advice

www.the-creative-home.com

This site features an excellent introduction to interior design. Includes step-by-step instructions, a guide on how to decorate with color, room ideas, an explanation of basic interior design concepts, and guest articles.

Home Decorating Digest

www.homedecoratingdigest.com

Home Decorating Digest is an "online digest of decorating tips and ideas for your home and garden." Content is divided into five areas: The Basics, Decorating Ideas, DIY-How To Guide, Outdoor & Garden, and Organizing. Site offers some excellent articles accompanied by full-color photos that illustrate basic design principles in action.

Interior Design

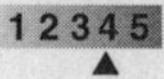

www.interiordesign.net

Interior Design is a magazine that caters to interior designers. Here, you'll find current industry news, product reviews, a buyer's guide, a GreenZone, the Interior Design Hall of Fame, industry catalogs, and more. For the latest information on interior designs and furnishings, check out this site.

PLUMBING

theplumber.com

12345

www.theplumber.com

This site is much more than your average how-to and plumbing advice site. Sure, it has a great plumbing FAQ and award-winning discussion forums where you can find answers to most of your plumbing questions, but it also features plumbing history, links to plumbing awards (such as the Thomas Crapper Memorial Plumbing Poll), and plumbing articles that appear in the mainstream media.

Plumbing 101

www.friendlyplumber.com/plumbing101.html

Good collection of articles for beginners and do-it-yourself-plumbers. Site features articles on care and cleaning, septic systems, garbage disposals, dishwasher, toilets, sinks and drains, and other common plumbing topics.

Plumbing Tips

12345

www.allabouthome.com/directories/dir_plumbing.html

Plumbing Tips can help you troubleshoot and repair most common plumbing problems. If you're wondering why your pipes make noise, how to thaw frozen pipes, or how to unclog drains and fix leaky faucets, visit this site for answers.

Toiletology 101

12345

www.toiletology.com/index.shtml

Everything you ever needed to know about fixing and maintaining your toilet. Helpful guidance and instruction.

A B C D E F G H I J K L M N O P Q R S T U V W X Y Z

HORROR

Dark Worlds

1 2 3 4 5

www.darkworlds.com

DARKWORLDS has been "designed and developed to serve as the primary portal for fans of dark fantasy, science fiction and horror." Here, you'll find plenty of news, reviews, movie trailers, and games to keep you horrified and amused. Site also features online shopping at the Shopping Maul.

HorrorChannel.com

1 2 3 4 5

www.horrorchannel.com

The Horror Channel is "the first 24/7 broadband, multiplatform, high definition TV, VOD and linear, rich media, programming network in the U.S. to be dedicated to the horror genre. Established in 2001, The Horror Channel has emerged as the leading broadband provider of horror content by leveraging emerging technologies to deliver full length feature films, documentaries and other horror, terror and suspense themed content directly over the Internet." Site features reviews, interviews, news, editorials, and retrospectives.

Horror.com

1 2 3 4 5 

www.horror.com

Horror.com is a good place on the Web to learn about horror movies past and present. Site features reviews, discussion forums, a couple photo galleries, and a directory of links to other horror websites. Most of the site is structured around its discussion forums, so if you're looking for a community of horror fans to share your enthusiasm for horror, this is a great place to hang out.

HorrorFind

1 2 3 4 5 

www.horrorfind.com

Searchable directory of all things related to horror fiction. You can browse the directory by category, including Dark Art, Ghosts, Gothic, Halloween, Monsters, Sci-Fi, and Vampires, to name a few. Or, you can search the directory by keyword. This site can point you to hundreds of websites in dozens of categories. Site also includes some freebies, such as horror fonts.

HorrorMovies.com

1 2 3 4 5

www.horrormovies.com

Horror movie fans will love this site where they can purchase their favorites and find out about the latest releases. You can search the site for a specific title or browse the collection by category, including B Movies, Classics, Cult, Erotic Horror, Sci-Fi, Slashers, and Zombie. This online horror store also carries collectibles, music, and posters.

Horror.net

1 2 3 4 5 

www.horror.net

Horror.net is a searchable directory of more than 3000 links to horror sites in about a dozen categories, including General Horror, Haunted Houses, Horror Collectibles, Horror Movies, Horror Television, and Science Fiction.

Horrorview.com

1 2 3 4 5

www.horrorview.com

Horrorview.comfeatures "up-to-date horror movie news, horror movie reviews, and more."

Horrorview.com stocks a total of more than 3,000 titles in its database, representing one of the largest and most comprehensive horror review archives anywhere.

Horror Writers Association

www.horror.org

Horror Writers Association is "a worldwide organization of writers and publishing professionals dedicated to promoting dark literature and the interests of those who write it." Visitors to this site can find free excerpts, a directory of links to other horror websites, links to author pages, a reading list, and writer's tips.

Upcoming Horror Movies

www.upcominghorrormovies.com

If you've seen all the old horror movies and can't wait for the new ones to come out, visit this site to find out about movies that have just been announced or are nearing release. You can even find descriptions of movies that were in the works but were never quite finished.

DARK FANTASY

Fantasy Book Clubs

www.fantasybookclubs.com

Online book club, complete with book reviews, news, and discussion forums, for fantasy fans. Each month, club members vote on a book for all of them to read and discuss. Site also features online games, such as a collective effort at writing a fantasy novel.

H. P. Lovecraft

www.hplovecraft.com

No writer's work exemplifies the dark fantasy category better than that of H. P. Lovecraft's. This site reveals Lovecraft's life, writings (including fiction, letters, and poetry), creations, study, and influence on modern culture.

GHOSTS

Halloween Ghost Stories

www.halloweenghoststories.com

If you're looking for a scary story to tell at Halloween or around the campfire, check out this site. Here, you'll find an excellent collection of scary stories grouped by categories: Spooky Halloween Tales, Classic Ghost Stories, Real Life Hauntings, Tales of Terror, Beyond Bizarre, Urban Legends, and Dark Poetry. Site also features a collection of Halloween eCards.

The Moonlit Road

www.themoonlitroad.com

This site features "ghost stories and strange folktales of the American South, told by the region's most celebrated storytellers." Site offers featured stories, a ghost story archive, a bookstore, and message boards. Most stories include audio recordings, enabling you to listen to the story being told by its author.

Obiwan's UFO-Free Paranormal Page

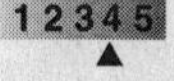

www.ghosts.org

Obiwan's UFO-Free Paranormal Page focuses on paranormal experiences not having to do with UFOs and aliens. Site features a ghosts and hauntings FAQ, true ghost stories, ghostly photos, a list of haunted sites, a message board, and some other offerings.

The Shadowlands: Ghosts & Hauntings

theshadowlands.net/ghost

Real stories about ghosts and haunted houses. Ghost experts Dave Juliano and Tina Carlson, co-hosts of this site, have helped thousands of people deal with their ethereal roommates in one way or another. Here, you can read thousands of true stories, check out an extensive list of haunted houses, read Ghost Hunting 101, access a list of frequently asked questions and their answers, research famous hauntings, listen to ghost sounds, check out a handful of photos and a small collection of videos, and much more. The video clips of the flying orbs look like the reflections I commonly see off of my watch, but then again, there may be something to this ghost thing.

OCCULT

Occult 100

www.occult100.com

This site features a directory of 100 top websites dealing with the occult. Categories include Celtic, Ceremonial, Magick, Chaos, Goth, Voodoo, and Wicca, to name a few. Links take you to sites where you can learn the witch's alphabet, learn how to read and write with Runes, brush up on your spell casting, explore chakra alignments, and much more.

VAMPIRES

Anne Rice, Official Site

www.annerice.com

Anne Rice, author of *Interview with the Vampire* and other novels on vampires, mummies, and historical and mythological characters, hosts this site, where you can learn more about her works, her visions, and her special causes. Site also includes a link you can click to email Anne Rice personally.

Bram Stoker's Dracula

www.literature.org/authors/stoker-bram/dracula

Literature.org provides the complete text of Bram Stoker's *Dracula* online.

Federal Vampire and Zombie Agency

www.fvza.org

Phony federal agency dedicated to keeping the nation's vampire and zombie populations in control. Content is organized into several areas including Vampires, Zombies, Famous Cases, Historical Tales, and a discussion forum.

Temple of the Vampire

www.vampiretemple.com

Temple of the Vampire is an organization of bona fide vampires and a recognized religion, legally registered with the U.S. federal government. Here, you can learn what vampires believe and how they choose to live during the day and at night. Site also explains the laws that govern the temple, offers the Vampire Bible for purchase, and presents a list of frequently asked questions and their answers. Temple of the Vampire forbids its members from drinking blood.

Vampire Church

www.vampire-church.com

The Vampire Church is a community of vampires and those interested in vampirism. Site features articles, interviews, art, poetry, questions and answers, comments, mailing lists, and more. If you're interested in dating a vampire, check out the vampire personals.

Vampire Rave

www.vampirerave.com

Vampire Rave was designed as "an online resource for the Vampire community," which attempts to catalog everything about vampires that appears on the Web. Site organizes links in several categories, including Accessories, Articles, Bands, Books, Clubs, Jewelry, Radio, and TV.

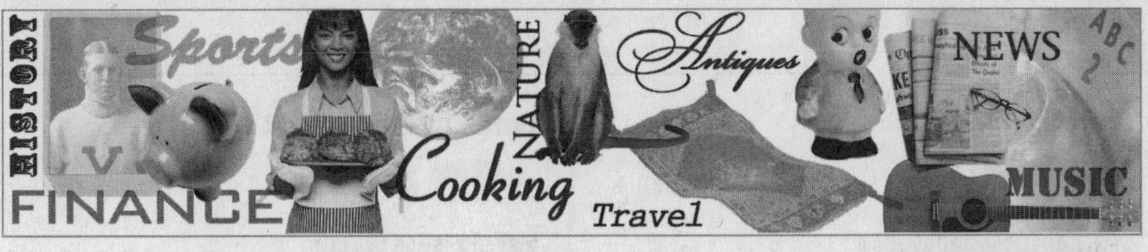

HORSES

American Paint Horse Association

www.apha.com

Official site of the American Paint Horse Association. Obtain information on APHA membership and products, and the history, breeding, training, racing, showing, sales, and enjoyment of American Paint Horses. Lots of equine links, too. Order merchandise from the secure server.

The American Saddlebred Horse

www.american-saddlebred.com

Anyone interested in horses—and show horses in particular—will enjoy viewing the video clips of the various gaits displayed during competitions. Detailed descriptions and diagrams of the horses' structure and history of the breed are also featured. The site includes a small photo gallery and links to saddlebred horse museums and national organizations. Be sure to submit your favorite saddlebred picture for consideration in the annual calendar. Anyone interested in horses and horseback riding should visit this and return to it often.

BarrelHorses.com

www.barrelhorses.com

For barrel horse racing information, no site is better than this. It is packed with informative articles, show results, organizations, events, and much more. The Ask a Vet section enables you to post an equine health question and have it answered by a veterinarian. You can also check out horses for sale, post and read messages on the bulletin boards, locate barrel trainers, and learn some of your own training tips.

Breeds

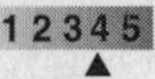

www.ansi.okstate.edu/breeds/horses

This site features a long list of horse breeds along with a description and photograph of each breed. Great place to learn about the various breeds of horses and other livestock, including cattle, goats, sheep, and swine.

Care for My Horse

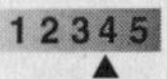

www.care-for-my-horse.com

Because horses cannot tell humans how to care for them, this site acts as a spokesman for horses, providing information on horse health, nutrition, and housing, and the equipment you need to properly care for your horse. When you've mastered basic care, you're ready to move on to understanding horse behavior. Click the Horse Behavior link to jump to that site, also covered in this section on horses.

Choosing a Horse

1 2 3 4 5

www.choosing-a-horse.com

Planning to buy your first horse? Then check out this site to learn what to look for and understand why you might want to look a gift horse in the mouth. After you've purchased your horse, check out the Care for Your Horse and Horse Behavior sites, also covered in this section on horses.

A B C D E F G H I J K L M N O P Q R S T U V W X Y Z

Churchill Downs

www.kentuckyderby.com

Official home of the Kentucky Derby, this site provides coverage of the derby, complete with a list of contenders, the latest news, the history of the derby, and online shopping. Even includes a recipe for mint juleps!

EquiSearch

www.equisearch.com

EquiSearch represents several horse magazines, including *EQUUS, Dressage Today, Practical Horseman, Horse & Rider, Arabian Horse World, Discover Horses at the Kentucky Horse Park, Everything for Horse & Rider,* and *Growing Up with Horses.* EquiSearch helps these magazines deliver content on the Web that is most useful and interesting to riders, trainers, owners, and others who are interested in the care and enjoyment of horses. Site features industry news, quizzes, active online forums, classified ads for horses for sale, buyers guides, and an Ask the Expert area where you can post a question and obtain tips on riding, training, and caring for your horse. Site offers free access to more than 2,500 articles. This site, together with the magazines it links you to, is our blue ribbon choice as the Best of the Best equine site on the Web!

Horse Behavior

www.horse-behavior.com

Horse Behavior examines the various factors that contribute to developing the ways horses behave. At this site, you can learn about horse communication, variations in behavior that are age or gender related, common origins of horse vices, and instincts that play a role in horse behavior. If you dream of becoming a horse whisperer, this is the site for you.

Horse Centric

www.horsecentric.com

Horse Centric covers just about every aspect of horse ownership and care. Topics cover nutrition, exercise, grooming, vets, routine checkups, checklists, and links to other websites and resources.

HorseCity.com

www.horsecity.com

HorseCity.com is a portal for equine information and resources. According to management, more than 6 million pages and 18 million ads are available and are accessed each month by more than 750,000 visitors! The opening page features a collection of informative articles, along with links to additional articles, bulletin boards, shopping opportunities, and entertainment.

> **Tip:** On the opening page, scroll down to the bottom of the Featured Content box and click View More Articles. This opens a page with dozens of topics you can click to access a vast collection of articles.

TheHorse.com

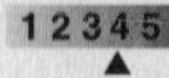

www.thehorse.com

Online magazine devoted to helping horse owners and healthcare providers stay informed. Articles cover general health issues, injuries, and preventive care. Check back regularly for any health alerts in your area.

The Horse Source

source.bloodhorse.com/thehorse

A directory of horse-related sites, organized by category. You'll find kids' sites, sites with classified ads, sites for mailing lists, and much more. Well-organized site makes it easy to navigate.

PBS Nature: Horses

www.pbs.org/wnet/nature/horses/main.html

The PBS Nature show on horses covers the definition and evolution of horses, the therapeutic bond between horses and humans, and the various ways the horse has contributed to world development. Features of this site include teacher's guides, feedback, videos, puzzles and fun, and contests. Like most PBS specials and websites, the design and content of this site are exceptional.

Related Site

www.pbs.org/wnet/nature/horseandrider/index.html

United States Dressage Federation

www.usdf.org

Learn more about the sport of dressage, locate upcoming competitions and instructors to help you prepare, and find the results of recent events. Merchandise available (some freebies), but you must print and mail the order form.

WesternHorseman.com

www.westernhorseman.com

This is the homepage of *Western Horseman* magazine, which provides articles and information on everything related to Western horsemanship. Here, you can find equine healthcare advice, training tips, and information about various events updated daily. Site also features a cartoon of the day, featured articles, a virtual vet, bulletin boards, and an online poll. Excellent site.

A B C D E F G H I J K L M N O P Q R S T U V W X Y Z

HUMOR

Aardvark Archie's Guide to Rude Humor

www.aardvarkarchie.com

If you're looking for low-brow humor, this site can get you there in a hurry. Site is packed with dirty jokes, bar jokes, blonde jokes, ethnic jokes, and tasteless photos and other pictures.

Break.com

www.break.com

At the core of this site is a collection of amateur video clips of amazing, shocking, stupid, and sometimes erotic human activities. Although most of the material is clean, some of it pushes the limits.

Chickenhead

www.chickenhead.com

Chickenhead is "a sickening repository of tasteless and self-congratulatory garbage, produced by a detestable clique of New York City losers, who toil needlessly in abject poverty and well-deserved obscurity." Need I say more? Kids should stay away, but college students and older folks looking for sick, stupid humor should definitely visit.

CollegeHumor.com

www.collegehumor.com

CollegeHumor.com is packed with funny pictures, movies, games, text files, and other humorous material that college students and recent graduates might find particularly hilarious and entertaining.

Comedy Central

www.comedycentral.com

Visit Comedy Central for the online version of *South Park, The Daily Show with Jon Stewart, Dog Bites Man*, and other humorous shows with lots of extras. Shop the online store for T-shirts and other Comedy Central show-related merchandise! Site also features games, jokes, free desktop wallpaper, and other stuff to keep you entertained and encourage you to waste time.

Comedy-Zone.net

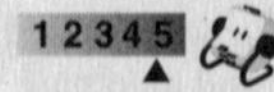

www.comedy-zone.net

Huge collection of funny stuff, including jokes, T-shirts, trivia, cartoons, games, TV comedy, stand-up comedy, and a humor directory with links to hundreds of additional funny sites. The Stand Up Comedian directory had no entry for Louis Black, so we can't give this site our Best of the Best ranking, but it's an excellent comedy site just the same.

Cruel Site of the Day

www.cruel.com

Tired of a Pollyanna outlook? This site offers a cynical look at the Web by awarding sites that are the most perturbing and cruel, yet entertaining. This site provides a great starting point for what's warped, obscure, and peevish on the Web.

Darwin Awards

www.darwinawards.com

The Darwin Awards honor "those who improve our gene pool by removing themselves from it in really stupid ways." When I last checked, winners of the Darwin Award included three Vietnamese men who tried to roll a 500-pound bomb down a hillside to salvage it as scrap metal and an electrician who used a piece of thin copper wire to add a little length to his kite string. Order your T-shirt online.

Despair, Inc.

www.despair.com

Ever get tired of seeing those posters and note cards with soaring eagles and sappy motivational sayings? Despair, Inc. has an answer to these annoying props. Check out the posters, calendars, and coffee mugs, and sign up for the newsletter. Learn the art of demotivation from the experts. This is one of the cleverest sites to come along in a long time.

Humor 100

www.humor100.com

List of the top 100 humor sites on the Web as voted on by web users.

JibJab

www.jibjab.com

This site features political parodies, eCards you can send to your friends via email, screensavers, and much more. The opening page offers several areas to explore, including classic JibJab (original movies), a personal joke box where you can store your favorite jokes and share them with friends, a list of most-linked picture jokes, and links to featured JibJabber sites.

LaughNet

www.laughnet.net

Directory of humor sites that organizes sites into categories, including Crude Humor, Workplace Humor, Computer Humor, Political Humor, and more than a dozen other categories. Some of the humor is fine for kids of all ages, other sites are acceptable for teenagers, and others are definitely for adults only.

Modern Humorist

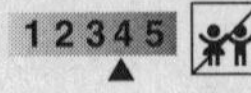

www.modernhumorist.com

Modern Humorist is an entertainment company founded by John Aboud and Michael Colton in 2000. In addition to creating comedy for radio, TV, and other media outlets, the company created this online magazine, which showcases the work of some of the top humorists in America. Although the site is no longer updated with new content, it still provides archived content that can keep you laughing for hours.

National Lampoon

www.nationallampoon.com

Home of *National Lampoon* magazine, the same folks who brought us the *Vacation* movies, *Animal House*, and other edgy comedies. Here, you can find a humorous look at the news, flashbacks, joke analysis, and true facts. Very funny site.

The Onion

www.theonion.com

An irreverent version of local, national, and international news, this site provides hilariously funny satirical reports that are both timely and acerbic. If you're easily offended, however, steer clear of this site.

The (un)Official Dave Barry Blog

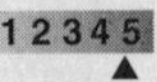

davebarry.com

Check out this site to get information about the latest books and articles written by humor columnist, Dave Barry. Brief biography of Dave Barry, plus a list of Barry's books with a brief synopsis of each. Links to Amazon.com, where you can purchase the books. Links to other fan sites too. Check out Dave's blog at blogs.herald.com/dave_barrys_blog.

Red Vs. Blue

rvb.roosterteeth.com

Red Vs. Blue is an animated tongue-in-cheek science fiction adventure consisting of 4- to 5-minute episodes. You can check out the archived episodes online, join discussions with fans in the forum, submit and see viewer-submitted art, and shop online for T-shirts, hats, and other stuff.

Un-Cabaret

www.uncabaret.com

This cyber-companion to L.A.'s *Un-Cabaret*, the "mother-show of the alternative comedy scene," where "writer-performers can experiment in long-form comedy storytelling and monologue," is rife with audio and video clips from the likes of Bobcat Goldthwaite, Julia Sweeney, Moon Zappa, Andy Dick, and Merrill Markoe, to name a few.

The Weird Site

www.theweirdsite.com

Weird is often funny, but this site makes a point of promoting the funniest weird stuff it can find. Categories of weird funny stuff include weird news, weird sites, weird pictures, funny cartoons, and awards. Some free stuff; but if you want full access, you need to subscribe for a meager $15 per year.

Whitehouse.org

1 2 3 4 5

www.whitehouse.org

Not to be confused with www.whitehouse.gov (the official Whitehouse site) or www.whitehouse.com (a porn site), this site is packed with satire directed at the national political scene. See your favorite and least favorite politicians lampooned. See national policies dragged through the mud. Take a tour of the White House, if you can afford it. And, if you have any time left, visit the Office of Fraternal Affairs.

Working Wounded

www.workingwounded.com

Brainchild of author and columnist Bob Rosner, this site is designed to provide no-nonsense advice to workers concerning issues they face at work. Real-life stories, office webcams, confessionals, gallery of cubicles, bad boss stories, and much more.

CARTOONS

Big Cartoon Database

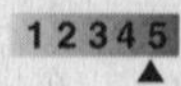

www.bcdb.com

Big Cartoon Database features a huge collection of cartoon information, episode guides, and crew lists for your favorite classic cartoons. Content is organized by studios, including Columbia Pictures, Walt Disney, Hanna-Barbera, and Warner Bros. Great place to do cartoon research and reminisce about the good old days, when animations were done by hand.

CartoonBank

www.cartoonbank.com

The *New Yorker* is known for its highbrow cartoons. At CartoonBank, you can order prints of some of the top cartoons and other *New Yorker* products, enter the weekly caption-the-cartoon contest, and check out the current edition of the *New Yorker*.

Cartoon Network

www.cartoonnetwork.com

Cartoon Network is the TV station that most kids gravitate toward when they need a cartoon fix. Here, you can find out about the programming on Cartoon Network, check on when you favorite cartoons are scheduled to air, learn more about the shows, play games and trade cards online, and much more.

Daryl Cagle's Pro Cartoonist Index

www.cagle.com

If you're looking for political cartoons and cartoonists, visit this site to get a glimpse of today's best political cartoons and a clickable index of the world's top political cartoonists.

The Frown.com

www.thefrown.com

This site features some hilarious cartoons by Brian Frisk & Company, including *We Are Robots, The Bad Life*, and *White Bread Blues.* Site also offers free downloads and online shopping for The Frown apparel and gifts.

Jerry Beck's Cartoon Research

www.cartoonresearch.com

World-renowned animated-cartoon historian Jerry Beck presents this site as a tool to help other animated-cartoon enthusiasts learn more about classic cartoons from the past, present, and future. You can browse animated features by year or check out some classic shorts. Site also features Cartoon Brew (Jerry's blog), an animated history discussion forum, an animated movie guide, a list of frequently asked questions and their answers, and occasionally some stuff that Jerry has for sale.

National Cartoon Museum

cartoon.org

The National Cartoon Museum is dedicated to collecting, preserving, and exhibiting animation and cartoon art to entertain the public, serve as an educational resource, and broadly promote public awareness of the art form. Here, you can learn about the museum's many exhibits, obtain visitor information, and read up on the latest happenings at the museum.

Todays Cartoon by Randy Glasbergen

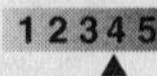

www.glasbergen.com

Randy Glasbergen, a freelance cartoonist, creates cartoons for newsletters, presentations, websites, intranets, advertising, blogs, and more. Here, you can check out today's cartoon or scroll down the page to browse through dozens of categories of cartoons from the past.

JOKES

A Joke a Day

www.ajokeaday.com

Get a clean, funny, politically correct joke every day by visiting this site or registering to receive your free daily joke via email. Site archives its jokes and organizes them by category, so you can read past jokes all day long until you get tired of laughing.

Jokeathon

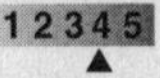

www.jokeathon.com

This site features a good collection of jokes, a random joke generator, funny (mostly doctored) images, cartoons, and fun downloads (games and animations).

Joke Frog

www.jokefrog.com

Joke Frog presents an eclectic collection of funny photos and cartoons, dirty jokes, and interesting observations.

JokeWallpaper.com

www.jokewallpaper.com

Download free joke wallpaper to liven up your computer screen. Choose from political statements, news and popular culture, celebrities, or a laundry list of others. Make your cursor do funny things, too.

A B C D E F G H I J K L M N O P Q R S T U V W X Y Z

Joke Yard

www.thejokeyard.com

Huge collection of hilarious jokes. Along the top of the opening page, you can select a joke category: dirty jokes, clean jokes, blonde jokes, funny insults, pickup lines, practical jokes, funny stories, and sexist jokes. The list on the left displays a couple dozen additional categories. Site also features a directory of links to additional joke sites.

Lots of Jokes

www.lotsofjokes.com

Nothing fancy at this site, just lots of jokes. You can find jokes in a wide range of categories, including bar jokes, blonde jokes, and redneck jokes. Site also features new jokes and funny photos.

Mefco's Random Joke Server

www.randomjoke.com

Choose the type of joke you want from a large list of categories, including Light Bulb Jokes, Murphy's Law, Jokes for Nerds, and so on. Read some funny stories, too, or submit your own joke, if you like.

Ray Owen's Joke a Day

www.jokeaday.com

Visit this site for a free laugh, updated daily, or subscribe (for a fee) to gain access to archives of letters, Dweeb Letters, last week's jokes, babes, hunks, Video Minutes, Twisted Tunes, Weird Pictures, and lots more! You can also sign up to have jokes delivered daily via email. On the discussion forums, you can swap one-liners about the day's headline stories.

HUNTING

Bowhunting.Net

1 2 3 4 5

www.bowhunting.net

Catch up on the latest news in bowhunting here, as well as pick up some tips for improving your form and for increasing your hunting domain. You'll also find competition information.

The Bowsite

1 2 3 4 5

www.bowsite.com

The opening page prompts you to select a state. Select the state in which you'll be hunting and click the Go button to enter the site that contains the primary content. Here, you'll find links to Big Game forums, State Bow Hunting forums, Feature Articles, News and Events, Ask the Experts, Live Nightly Chat, and more. Must register to access the Live Nightly Chat area.

Browning Home Page

1 2 3 4 5

www.browning.com

Shotguns, rifles, archery equipment, hunting wear, gun cases, knives—Browning makes it all, and you can find ready access to local dealers and price information on the company's home page. Order a catalog or check out job opportunities. You'll also find links to other hunting-related sites here.

Buckmasters Magazine Online

1 2 3 4 5

www.buckmasters.com

Whitetail deer hunters can get hunting season information, jump into a chatroom, check the message boards, view the trophy gallery, buy hunting gear, pick up hunting games, and read whitetail magazine articles at this rich site.

Clay Pigeon Shooting Association

1 2 3 4 5

www.cpsa.co.uk

Become a member of the CPSA; check out scores, news, and links; and learn where the next competitions will be held.

Ducks Unlimited

1 2 3 4 5

www.ducks.org

Home base for the world's leading organization for conserving wetlands and promoting duck hunting.

Easton Archery

1 2 3 4 5

www.eastonarchery.com

Investigate all of Easton's archery products and buy them online after you've made your selection.

> **Tip:** Click the Downloads tab to access a collection of free tools and cool stuff, including shaft selector software, a tuning guide, and product logos.

Eders.com

1 2 3 4 5

www.eders.com

This online hunting catalog has an amazing selection of equipment, from bows to calls to slingshots and scents. You can even find bobblehead turkeys, which make great gifts for all your hunting buddies.

Field & Stream Online

www.fieldandstream.com

The outdoorsman's bible has a site on the Internet. The current issue is here with features, articles, and editorials. You can even pick an area of the country and find out what's in season and where to hunt. Along the top of the page is a navigation bar that provides quick access to your outdoor adventure preference: Hunting, Fishing, Gear, Guns, or Outdoor Skills. Site also features blogs and some well-stocked photo galleries.

Hunting Information Systems: An Online Guide

www.huntinfo.com

Lots of products and outfitters listed here, and the site is updated often. Check out the recommended outfitters or suggest one of your own. You'll find the latest hunting news here, including alerts, state and regional information, news about swap hunts, and lots more.

Best HuntingNet.com

12345

www.HuntingNet.com

The ultimate hunting site on the Web covers everything from turkey hunting to Elk hunting, bowhunting, sporting dogs, hunting outfitters, and hunting gear. Chat areas, message boards, auctions, and swaps put you in touch with other hunters online. HuntingNet.com is actually a publisher with more than 2,000 domain names under the umbrella HuntingNet.com. When we visited the site, its developers were planning a major renovation to harness the power of all the sites resources and domains by placing them under one roof. No matter what type of game you hunt or how you hunt it, you'll find plenty of quality information at this site.

Hunting Trail WebRing

www.hunting-trail.com

A community of websites all relating to the topic of hunting. Find articles, newsletters, product reviews, chatrooms, message boards, and more.

Idaho Archery

www.idahoarchery.com

Idaho Archery opens with a page that displays a few announcements, the events calendar, and the daily poll. Along the top of the page runs a navigation bar that provides quick access to additional content, including archery and bow hunting clubs, and Features (custom designed arrows, online games and downloads, a trophy wall where members can post photos of their proudest kills, and hunting stories.

Maine Guides Online

www.maineguides.com

Considering a hunting trip to Maine? Check out this site and then go to either the Big Game Hunting, Small Game Hunting, or Bowhunting section. You'll find everything you need right here: places to stay, places to hunt, guides, hunting equipment retailers, and things to do when you're not hunting. A well-maintained site.

MyOAN (Outdoor Adventure Network)

www.myoan.net

An Outdoor adventure site that covers everything from backpacking to hunting and fishing. It features a tip of the day, information about various types of outdoor adventures, and links to other resources.

National Rifle Association

www.nra.org

Keep up-to-date with the latest in gun legislation at this site. The NRA is one of the strongest advocates of the Second Amendment to the Constitution, guaranteeing the right to bear arms in the United States. The NRA offers programs benefiting gun safety, marksmanship, personal safety, hunting, and more. Find out about its services, latest news, and legislative activities at this site. This site also has an online store where you can buy hats, shirts, and other NRA merchandise.

North American Hunting Club

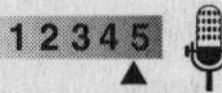

www.huntingclub.com

North America Hunting Club is America's largest club of hunting enthusiasts. This site presents a few sample articles and photos and invites you to become a member. By registering for free, you gain access to members-only content and features at the site, you receive a free issue of *North American Hunter* magazine, and you get a free 30-day membership to the club.

Pearson Archery

www.benpearson.com

Learn more about Ben Pearson bows and dealers at this site, and locate a dealer close to you. Site also features a Build Your Own Bow contest, a Trophy Room, a place where you can show off your bow (by posting a photo of it), a discussion forum, and plenty of tech tips.

Texas Parks and Wildlife

www.tpwd.state.tx.us/huntwild

The Texas Parks and Wildlife site is packed with information for hunters, including seasons and bag limits, hunter education, public hunting access, and Texas Big Game Awards. Site also includes an area specifically for kids that deals less with hunting and more with exploring wildlife at the many state parks.

Related Sites

myfwc.com

www.dnr.state.mn.us/hunting/index.html

www.state.tn.us/twra/huntmain.html

dnr.wi.gov/org/land/wildlife/hunt

dnr.state.il.us/admin/systems

www.huntingpa.com

www.dgif.state.va.us/hunting

U.S. Fish and Wildlife Service

1 2 3 4 5

www.fws.gov

Dedicated to conserving nature in the United States, this site helps hunters get appropriate permits and learn more about safe hunting. It also aims to teach kids what it means when a species is endangered. Click the Hunting link for a list of frequently asked questions about hunting and how hunters can benefit conservation efforts.

U.S. Sportsmen's Alliance

1 2 3 4 5

www.wlfa.org

This is the place to go if you want to get serious about wildlife management and the future of hunting, fishing, and trapping. This is the only organization whose sole mission is the conservation of natural resources. Learn about its mission and how to join.

HYPNOSIS

American Society of Clinical Hypnosis

www.asch.net

Most of the information at this site is either for members only or uninteresting to the general public, but the site does offer some content for the general public, including an introduction that explains how hypnosis works, its benefits, and how to choose a qualified hypnotist. This introduction attempts to dispel the many myths people commonly have regarding hypnosis. Site also features a directory of links to other sites that explore and promote the benefits of hypnosis directly or indirectly.

Hypnosis.com

www.hypnosis.com

If you're looking to become a properly trained and certified hypnotist, then check out this site for basic information on hypnosis and available courses of study. This site features various FAQs on hypnosis along with scripts for inductions, interventions, and stage hypnosis.

HypnosisDownloads.com

www.hypnosisdownloads.com

HypnosisDownloads.com features more than 200 professional hypnosis downloads from leading hypnotherapy educators that you can listen to and use for self-hypnosis. Downloads are available for self-improvement, personal development, overcoming fears and phobias, weight loss, stress management, relationships, and more. Site also offers complete audio courses that teach you the art of hypnosis, professional scripts designed to induce hypnotic states, and courses on CDs and tapes.

Hypnosis Motivation Seminar

www.hypnosis.edu

This is the web home of America's first nationally accredited college of hypnotherapy. Here, you can search for a certified hypnotherapist in your area, learn about various programs and courses of study, and check out some free, streaming videos.

Best Hypnosis Online

hypnosisonline.com

This site offers everything you could possibly want or need regarding hypnosis, whether you're looking to learn hypnosis or want to experience its benefits. Along the top of the opening page is a navigation bar that provides quick access to Services, Products, Scripts, Information, Online Services, Web Sites, and Customer Service. The online store carries a selection of products, including downloadable audio clips, materials on tapes and CDs, books, scripts, videos, and music. Read the FAQs to find the answers to the most common questions, find a hypnotherapist online, check out the blogs, and explore other hypnosis websites.

INSECTS

A B C D E F G H I J K L M N O P Q R S T U V W X Y Z

BugBios.com

12345

www.insects.org

Bug fans will consider this insect heaven. The colorful and information-packed site offers incredible pictures and descriptions of insects. The digest section offers information on how insects are present in every facet of our life. You'll also find an ordinal key to help you identify insects. Explore this site's links to other websites and resources. BugBios.com has even taken the time to categorize and review them.

Bugscope

12345

www.bugscope.beckman.uiuc.edu

Bugscope is "an educational outreach program for K–12 classrooms" that gives teachers and students remote control, over the Web, of a scanning electron microscope. The microscope provides high-magnification, high-resolution images that most schools would otherwise not be able to access. At this site, you can learn more about this innovative program, how you can become a participant, and how to set up your classroom computer.

Bugwood Network

12345

www.bugwood.org/entomology.html

The Bugwood Network is an organization that's dedicated to providing timely and accurate information to professionals in the fields of entomology, forestry, forest health, and natural resources. Most of the information at this site focuses on insects that damage trees, crops, lawns, and other plant life that's important for human survival and enjoyment.

The Butterfly Website

12345

butterflywebsite.com

Join a discussion group, learn how to attract butterflies with a butterfly garden, or become part of the effort to preserve butterfly habitats. The impressive photo gallery will help you identify the various species of moths and butterflies, and you can visit many butterfly gardens and zoos.

Best eNature.com

12345

www.enature.com

National Wildlife Federation's eNature.com is a comprehensive encyclopedia of animal life. At this site, you can access field guides for a variety of animals, including insects, spiders, butterflies, birds, mammals, reptiles, and amphibians. For each insect, eNature.com displays a picture, a physical description, and information about the insect's food, life cycle, habitat, and range. This is an excellent site to visit when you discover an insect and need to identify it in a hurry. Site also features ZipGuides, which enable you to search by ZIP code for all species in your area or for mammals, poisonous animals, or threatened species; a park finder; games; quizzes; screensavers; an ask the expert forum; and much more.

> **Tip:** When you reach the home page, click Wildlife Guides, Field Guides, and then click Insects.

Entomology Index of Internet Resources

12345

www.ent.iastate.edu/List

Iowa State has provided a searchable database of websites pertaining to insects and related organisms. Very extensive collection of links.

Forensic Entomology

12345

www.forensic-entomology.com

Insects are often the first and only witnesses of the crime, and for scientists who know what to look for, these insects can often provide clues as to what really occurred and when. At this site, you can find out what forensic entomology is all about. Crime scene investigators can visit this site to learn how to properly collect evidence at the scene and submit it to have it analyzed by an expert.

Insect Bites and Stings from Medline Plus

1 2 3 4 5

www.nlm.nih.gov/medlineplus/insectbitesandstings.html

Excellent guide on what to do when you're bitten or stung by a common insect. Site features first aid information for a variety of bites and stings from insects including stinging insects, spiders, mosquitoes, and bedbugs. Site also includes links to special areas where kids can learn about insects that bite and sting and what they can do when they encounter these pesky insects.

Insecta-Inspecta.com

1 2 3 4 5

www.insecta-inspecta.com

This site covers common insects that commonly bug us, including ants, bees, fleas, termites, and mosquitoes, and those that don't, such as butterflies. Scroll down the page for some interesting features, including bugs on coins, bugs in the news, and questions that bug us.

Insectlopedia

www.insectclopedia.com

Insectlopedia is a huge directory of insect websites and other resources on the Internet.

Insects Hotlist

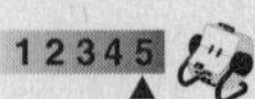

www.sln.fi.edu/tfi/hotlists/insects.html

More information than you probably ever thought you needed about insects—beetles, butterflies, ants, moths, roaches, and more—from the Franklin Institute.

Iowa State's Entomology Image Gallery

1 2 3 4 5

www.ent.iastate.edu/imagegallery

They might not win an Academy Award, but the tick and beetle movies that you can view at this website provide a fascinating look at the lives of these industrious creatures. The site also contains an entomology index and special features on mosquitoes, lice, and corn borers. To view the movies, look for an icon featuring a strip of film. Many still images, too.

Iowa State University's Tasty Insect Recipes

1 2 3 4 5

www.ent.iastate.edu/misc/insectsasfood.html

Most people don't want to see bugs anywhere near their kitchen, but Iowa State's entomology department is determined to change all that. Here, you can learn not only how to bring insects into your kitchen but also work them into your dinner menu. Site features a collection of recipes for bug blox, banana worm bread, rootworm beetle dip, chocolate chirpie chip cookies, and more. Site also presents nutritional information for common insects, links to cooking-with-insect books, information on where to purchase insects, and dates and times for the ISU Insect Horror Film Festival.

Spiders

1 2 3 4 5

www.spiderzrule.com

Check out this site to learn more than you ever wanted to know about our creepy friend, the spider. All information was written and pictures gathered by the fifth-grade class at Rochedale State School in Australia. And if you have some spider pictures you'd like to share, the kids will put them on their website!

The Yuckiest Site on the Internet

1 2 3 4 5

yucky.kids.discovery.com

"Yuckiest" is not a distinction many websites would want, but Wendell the Worm and Ralph the Roach take great pride in introducing you to their world. Read all the exciting facts about the creepy crawlers and then take the Roach Quiz. Let Ralph give you the lowdown on all his friends, including the earthworm and the bearded worm. This informative site is a lot of fun. When you're finished exploring bugs, branch out and explore your "gross and cool body." This site offers a tremendous Parent's Guide that will lead you to great resources for kids of all ages, especially young kids.

INSURANCE

A.M. Best Company

www.ambest.com

When you see ratings for various insurance companies and products, they probably came from this company. A.M. Best has a strong reputation for providing accurate company ratings and has been recognized as a Nationally Recognized Statistical Rating Organization (NRSRO) by the U.S. Securities and Exchange Commission. This site provides a form you can use to look up company ratings, but you must be a member to receive the results.

American Insurance Association

12345 RSS

www.aiadc.org

The leading property/casualty trade association for more than 125 years. Find out about AIA, access current workers' compensation laws online, read its publications, get membership information, and find lots of insurance resources and links.

Chubb Group of Insurance Companies

www.chubb.com

The Chubb group of insurance companies provides insurance for businesses and individuals to protect their assets. Here, you can learn more about the company and its products, services, and specialized solutions.

Claims

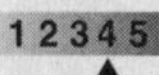

www.claimsmag.com

An insurance industry magazine that covers major news stories, articles on the "business of loss," and upcoming conference information. You can also check the editorial calendar for information on upcoming articles. Insurance professionals will find an excellent collection of timely and informative articles on this site dealing with insurance fraud, insurance forensics, terrorism, and a host of other topics of interest.

Independent Insurance Agents of America

www.independentagent.com

Pick up useful information on crash test results and general insurance tips, and locate an independent agent in your city through the site.

Insurance Information Institute

www.iii.org

This site provides a free resource open to the media, individuals, and organizations seeking insurance facts, figures, and general industry information.

> **Tip:** Near the bottom of the page, under Insurance Tools, click Life Stages for a tool that shows you the types of insurance you should consider based on your age group.

Insurance Institute for Highway Safety

www.hwysafety.org

Learn more about vehicle ratings, find out which cars are rated safest, and read the latest crash-test results online. You can also order videos and other materials online to help in driver education programs or for personal use.

Insure.com

12345

www.insure.com

If you're trying to decide which insurer to go with, visit this site first. Insure.com provides free ratings from Standard & Poor's and Duff & Phelps Credit

Rating Co. Their ratings will help you evaluate the quality and financial soundness of the insurers you are considering. You'll also find in-depth articles, and insurance tips on auto, homeowners, health, life, and business insurance. Perhaps best of all, this site does not sell insurance and is not owned or operated by an insurance company.

InsWeb

1 2 3 4 5 (rating: 5)

www.insweb.com

Online insurance shopping service. You provide input and receive quotes from a variety of insurers. Comparison shop and choose what suits your needs best. InsWeb compares quotes from more than 15,000 insurance companies to find the most affordable insurance options for you. Site also features a Learning Center that can help you become a more educated shopper.

IntelliQuote.com

1 2 3 4 5 (rating: 4)

www.intelliquote.com

Answer simple health and age questions to get term life insurance quotes or complete online forms for quotes on home and auto insurance. The glossary, FAQs, and How To information are also helpful.

National Association of Insurance and Financial Advisors

1 2 3 4 5 (rating: 4) RSS

www.naifa.org

Home to the National Association of Insurance and Financial Advisors, a federation of state and local associations representing 70,000 life and health insurance and financial services professionals. Learn about the part the NAIFA plays in encouraging legislation that safeguards policyholders and promoting a well-regulated insurance marketplace.

National Association of Insurance Commissioners (NAIC)

1 2 3 4 5 (rating: 3)

www.naic.org

Many sites are devoted to the interests of insurance professionals. This one is home to the National Association of Insurance Commissioners (NAIC), an organization of insurance regulators from the 50 states, the District of Columbia, and the four U.S. territories. The function of NAIC is to protect the interests of insurance consumers. Visit this site to learn more about the NAIC and what this organization does on your behalf.

National Safety Council

1 2 3 4 5 (rating: 4)

www.nsc.org

Learn how to reduce insurance claims by driving and living more safely. Interesting articles on understanding the hazards of radiation, fall-proofing your home, and creating an emergency plan for your home or business.

Nationwide Insurance

1 2 3 4 5 (rating: 5)

www.nationwide.com

For more than 75 years, Nationwide has provided quality insurance options for homes, cars, families, and the incomes of those who choose to retire. Features three core businesses: domestic property and casualty insurance, life insurance and retirement savings, and asset management. Learn more about the various products and services at this site.

QuickQuote

1 2 3 4 5 (rating: 4)

www.quickquote.com

Information on various forms of insurance, plus the ability to get quotes.

State Insurance Regulators

1 2 3 4 5 (rating: 5)

www.consumeraction.gov/insurance.shtml

Before you sign up for any insurance policy, check with your state insurance regulator to determine whether the company and the insurance broker are legitimate. But how can you find out? You contact your state insurance bureau. This site provides a list of contact information for the insurance bureau in every state.

AUTOMOBILE

AAA

www.aaa.com

Register at this national automotive organization and get access to maps, road condition reports, and discount travel arrangements. By joining, you also get discount insurance and other member benefits.

Allstate

www.auto-insurance.allstate.com

Learn more about auto insurance, common terms, and what they mean. Also, get information on Allstate's products and services here.

Comparison Market

www.comparisonmarket.com

Read Comparison Market's insurance tips for a car or motorcycle before making insurance decisions, and you'll probably save some money. Then get an online quote for your insurance needs.

eSurance

www.esurance.com

Determine what kind of coverage you need using the online planning tools and then get a quote from this online insurance company. Policyholders can also access customer service and their account from the Internet. Site features learning centers for auto, home/renter, and life/health insurance. Each learning center provides a frequently asked questions list and a glossary.

GEICO Direct

www.geico.com

Get a free quote from the gecko or report anything to do with your existing account, such as an accident, at this site. GEICO carries insurance for auto/motorcycle, homeowner/renter, life, and boat. Site also features a section on auto safety and an online store, where you can purchase GEICO apparel and other merchandise.

National Motor Club

www.nmca.com

Like AAA, the NMC provides automotive travel services such as discount accommodations, maps, travel planning assistance, and emergency service on the road.

Progressive

www.progressive.com

Request an insurance quote for your car, locate a local office, and make a claim online at Progressive's site. Special area for teen drivers. Site is also offered in Spanish.

State Farm

www.statefarm.com

Look at the financial management section of this site to help you save money in a number of areas of your life, such as deciding whether to refinance your mortgage right now, and then request an insurance quote or locate a local State Farm agent.

COMPANIES

AIG

www.aig.com

AIG agents write insurance for both consumer and business needs, from marine insurance to property, life, and financial. Learn more about the company here.

Farmers Insurance

www.farmers.com

Calculate your need for auto, flood, home, life, business, or healthcare professional liability insurance at the Farmers website. Excellent collection of

A B C D E F G H I J K L M N O P Q R S T U V W X Y Z

online calculators to help you determine your insurance needs and better manage your personal finances. Checklists for bicycle safety, home inventory, and emergencies. Lots of great information and tools. Plus, you can get an insurance quote or file a claim right online.

The Hartford

1 2 3 4 5

`www.thehartford.com`

Find an agent, request a quote, or report a claim at The Hartford's personal insurance area of the site. Hartford can also help you manage your investments and retirement. Scroll down the page and use the tools on the left to quickly find an agent, get a quote, look up a healthcare provider in your area, or find a local auto-repair shop.

MetLife

1 2 3 4 5

`www.metlife.com`

The MetLife website is an excellent place to learn about insurance, assess your insurance needs, and get quotes online. The opening page features a Dental Center, Products & Services for Individuals, a Life Advice Series (articles about various insurance topics), and a Tools box (with calculators and quizzes). Along the top of the page, you'll find a navigation bar that provides quick access to the major areas of the site, including Individuals, Employers, and Brokers & Consultants.

Prudential

1 2 3 4 5

`www.prudential.com`

Search for information on all of Prudential's products and services, from real estate to financial services, such as loans, to life, auto, and property insurance.

The Travelers

1 2 3 4 5

`www.travelers.com`

Get information about auto, property, life, and small business insurance at this site from Travelers.

HOMEOWNERS/ RENTERS

Consumer's Guide to Homeowner's Insurance

1 2 3 4 5

`www.oci.wi.gov/pub_list/pi-015.pdf`

A 30-page guide from Wisconsin's Office of the Commissioner covers everything from why you need homeowner's insurance to tips on loss prevention. Some of the information is specifically for residents of Wisconsin, but most of the information is useful no matter where you own your home.

Insure.com: Renters Insurance

1 2 3 4 5

`www.info.insure.com/home/renters.html`

Good article on renter's insurance that covers the basics: what standard policies cover, cash value versus replacement cost, the importance of taking inventory, and tips for keeping your premium low.

National Student Services, Inc.

1 2 3 4 5

`www.nssinc.com`

If you're a student living at home or in campus housing, your belongings are probably covered on your parents' homeowner's policy, but you should have them check to be sure. If your stuff isn't covered, and you have some valuable belongings, you may be able to obtain affordable coverage here. NSSI specializes in providing insurance for students.

Twelve Ways to Save Money on Homeowner's Insurance

1 2 3 4 5

`www.pueblo.gsa.gov/cic_text/housing/12ways/12ways.htm`

From the FCIC (Federal Citizen Information Center) comes this 12-step guide to trimming your homeowner's insurance costs.

INTERNET

European Telecommunications Standards Institute

1 2 3 4 5

www.etsi.org

This European group is dedicated to setting standards for the telecommunications industry to help ensure its stability and growth. ETSI has "699 members from 55 countries, and brings together manufacturers, network operators, and service providers, administrations, research bodies and users—providing a forum in which all key players can contribute."

Grid Café

1 2 3 4 5

www.gridcafe.web.cern.ch

Learn about the latest developments in distributed computing over the Internet. With distributed computing, users all over the world contribute their computer power (when they're not using the computer) to a collective pool that scientists, artists, and anyone else can tap into for additional computing power. Here, you can learn more about the potential for this technology and what experts in the field have to say about it.

Internet Architecture Board

1 2 3 4 5

www.iab.org

Internet Architecture Board is a committee of the Internet Engineering Task Force and an advisory body of the ISOC (Internet Society). In these roles, it seeks to steer the future development of the Internet and ensure its continued growth and stability by way of establishing standards.

Internet.com

www.internet.com

Internet.com is the definitive Internet resource for developers and IT professionals. Here, you can find a huge stock of timely and informative articles on all aspects of Internet development, security, and the latest tools and technology. Use the navigation bar on the left to skip around to the main content areas: Developer, International, Internet Lists, Internet News, Internet Resources, IT, Linux/OpenSource, Personal Technology, Windows Technology, Small Business, and xSP Resources.

Internet Storm Center

1 2 3 4 5 RSS

www.isc.sans.org

The Internet Storm Center tracks Internet activity and analyzes trends to help the Internet community and law enforcement agencies predict and prevent Internet attacks. Here, you can obtain information supplied from millions of sources daily.

InterNIC

1 2 3 4 5

www.internic.net

InterNIC provides public information regarding Internet domain name registration services. If you need information about domain-name registration or want to find out whether a particular company is licensed to sell domain names, this is the site to visit.

ISOC (Internet Society)

1 2 3 4 5

www.isoc.org

The Internet Society is an international organization of more than 20,000 individuals and 100 organizations representing more than 180 different countries. ISOC functions as a global clearinghouse of information about the Internet, past, present, and future, and helps guide the future development of the Internet.

Wi-Fi Planet

1 2 3 4 5 RSS

www.wi-fiplanet.com

If you are interested in wireless broadband technology, this is the place to learn about it. This site features news, reviews, insights, tutorials, a comprehensive glossary, forums, and many more resources devoted to wireless broadband.

World Wide Web Consortium

1 2 3 4 5

www.w3.org

World Wide Web Consortium is the agency in charge of governing the Web. Here, you can find information about the agency and the work it does, find out about the latest standards and web technologies, and obtain support for some of the latest technologies and development tools available.

ANTISPAM

ActivatorMail

1 2 3 4 5

www.activatormail.com

Antivirus and antispam email account that filters out spam and porn and can forward acceptable messages to your main email account. Unique filter system that relies on blacklists and user reports to identify unsolicited messages and prevent them from reaching your computer. ActivatorMail service is available for both corporate and personal use.

Antispam!

1 2 3 4 5

www.members.hostedscripts.com/antispam.html

Grassroots activist site that promotes submitting fake email addresses to known spammers to clutter their databases.

CAUCE

1 2 3 4 5

www.cauce.org

A site devoted to fighting unwanted email, the Coalition Against Unwanted Commercial Email (CAUCE) provides information about the problems of junk email, proposed solutions, and resources for the Net community to make informed choices about the issues surrounding junk email.

Fight Spam on the Internet

1 2 3 4 5

www.spam.abuse.net

Learn more about how to market without using spam and what to do about unwanted email (and what not to do). Also, read views on why spamming is so bad.

Best FTC Spam Page

www.ftc.gov/spam

The Federal Trade Commission has the job of enforcing the CAN-SPAM law—a law enacted by congress that prohibits the sending of unsolicited and deceptive commercial email. This site offers gobs of information for consumers, including scam alerts, instructions on how to limit spam, and tips on protecting your personal information. Site also features a link to OnGuard Online, a partner site that features tips and tools from technology experts to help you "be on guard against Internet fraud, secure your computer, and protect your personal information." Although the site doesn't have content specifically for kids, it does offer a great video for parents on how to protect their children on the Internet.

GetNetWise: Spam

www.spam.getnetwise.org

This site provides tips and tools to reduce or eliminate spam on your computer and information on how to become an antispam activist.

SpamCon Foundation

www.spamcon.org

The SpamCon Foundation works to mitigate the proliferation of spam and encourage users, administrators, marketers, antispam businesses, and activists to work together on establishing Internet marketing methods that are not so annoying and antiproductive.

SpamCop

www.spamcop.net

SpamCop helps you learn how to report spam and punish the sender by alerting the hosting ISP of what the spammer is doing. In many cases, the offending company will lose hosting privileges if too many people complain. Read the introduction first to learn how the process works.

Related Sites

www.chrishardie.com/tech/qmail/qmail-antispam.html

www.elsop.com/wrc/nospam.htm

CHATS AND SOCIAL GROUPS

Bold Chat

www.boldchat.com

Bold Chat is a product that enables online merchants to strike up live chat dialogues with customers or potential customers in the hope of strengthening the merchant's connection with the customer. Here, you can find out more about the product and how it might help boost your sales.

Chathouse

www.chathouse.com

Chathouse, created and maintained in coordination with Channel 1, is intended to be a safe, clean place to chat. Chat rules are posted, rooms are monitored, and supposedly the management can track down abusers, no matter how hard they try to maintain anonymity. When we visited the site, we saw no evidence of obscenity or other indecency, but most chat rooms have their fair share of abusers, so parents should still monitor chat room use.

Chat-Zone

www.chat-zone.com

Chat-Zone consists of Java-based chat rooms where hundreds of people from all over the world gather to chat throughout the day and night. Chat rooms are available for general audiences, adults, college students, and teen communities. Discussion boards are also available.

Cubic Space Main

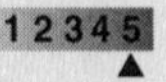

www.cube3.com

Cubic Space Main is a company that believes that the future of the Web will ultimately consist not of pages but of places—a 3D landscape where people can meet, play, and shop online. Here, you can check out some of the places the company has created and join a community of builders online.

CyberTown

www.cybertown.com

Cutting-edge, 3D virtual community where you can settle down online and become a citizen. Think of it as an online version of *The Sims*. You select a 3D character to represent you. You can then build a house, get a dog, find a job, create your own clubs, dance in the Black Sun nightclub, gamble at casinos, and much more. Very innovative online-community site. Not the easiest site to navigate if you have a standard modem connection.

mIRC

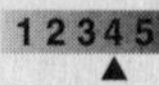

www.mirc.co.uk

This program enables you to connect to the Internet Relay Chat (IRC) network. Learn more about mIRC and IRC and download the latest version free.

MSN Groups

12345

www.groups.msn.com

Provides a place for family members, graduating classes, hobbyists, and any other group of people who share a common cause or common interests to gather. The group's leader must set up a community and then send email invitations asking others to join. Members can then post messages to the group, upload digital photos, post a calendar of events, and even chat online.

SpinChat

12345 Blog

www.spinchat.com

SpinChat features chat rooms, blogs, online games, and discussion boards. This isn't the most active online chat service around, but it's worth checking out if you're just curious to learn how this online chat thing works.

Talk City

12345

www.talkcity.com

Gain free access to chat rooms and start meeting thousands of other users at Talk City. Upgrade to Basic Service (for about $8 per year) or own your own room for about $50 per year.

Worlds 3D Ultimate Chat Plus

12345

www.worlds.net

Provides a 3D multiuser chatting system. Allows you to use images and sound while you chat with others, interacting through your computer instead of with it. Links to online shopping, too.

Yahoo! Chat

12345

www.messenger.yahoo.com

Yahoo! used to have a Java-based chat program at chat.yahoo.com, which enabled you to chat online right inside your web browser. Yahoo! has replaced the Java chat program with an instant messaging program that not only enables you to communicate with people you know but also hook up with strangers in chat rooms.

Yahoo! Groups

12345

www.groups.yahoo.com

Enables family members, graduating classes, organizations, and other groups of people to organize on the Web. Group moderator can broadcast messages, alerts, and newsletters to group members, and all members can post messages, digitized photos, and other information to the group.

CONNECTING

The Directory

12345

www.thedirectory.org

Claiming to be the largest directory of ISPs on the Web, the Directory provides thousands of listings of Internet providers as well as web hosting companies, telephone prefix locators, and mailing lists.

Earthlink

12345

www.earthlink.net

Earthlink provides dial-up Internet service for about $10 per month and high-speed Internet for about $30 to $40 per month in selected areas. (The $13 a month figure is good for only the first six months.) Check out this site for more information.

Free Internet Connections

12345

www.freeinternetconnection.com

This site offers an absolutely free dialup Internet connection. Here, you can obtain all the details and download the required software. What's the catch? Various companies support the free service in the hopes that users will sign up for their free offers, at least occasionally. The service provider asks that you voluntarily sign up for some free offers to encourage the companies to continue their financial support.

Free ISP Directory

12345

www.findanisp.com/free_isps.php?src=findwhatfree

Use this site to find free and low-cost Internet connection services.

The Free Site

12345

www.thefreesite.com/Free_Internet_Access

Lists a variety of free Internet connections and other free Internet services. Worth a look.

ISP Check

12345

www.ispcheck.com

Search this site for ISPs and web hosting companies or take a look at the Best Deal advertised here.

ISP Planet

12345

www.isp-planet.com

Industry information for Internet service providers. Articles address topics such as the cost of setting up a fixed wireless business, ways to fight spam, and ways to market your ISP.

Juno

12345

www.juno.com

Get free Internet access minus customer support, or pay a flat monthly rate for Juno Premium service and get 24-hour customer service and priority connections. NetZero and Juno were both acquired by United Online in 2001, and each ISP provides the same free service: receive 10 hours per month free or pay about $15 per month for unlimited connect time and fewer pop-up ads.

NoCharge.com

12345

www.nocharge.com

Western Washington's premier free Internet service provider offers free Internet access and email to users in selected communities in western Washington state. No limitations on connect time and no ads. Premium service offering more-reliable connections and support.

PeoplePC

12345

www.peoplepc.com

PeoplePC is one of the cheapest ways to get on the Internet. Dialup connections cost less than $6 a month for the first three months and about $11 per month after that. A 30-day free trial is available.

CONNECTION SPEED

Broadband Home Central

12345

www.broadbandhomecentral.com

Sandy Teger and Dave Waks host Broadband Home Central, where you can learn about the latest in broadband technology, its practical applications, and products and services that can help you tap the full potential of broadband. Site leans toward the more technical aspects of broadband, but all users can benefit from the more general articles.

Broadbandwidthplace Speed Test

12345

www.bandwidthplace.com/speedtest

Wondering how fast your Internet connection is? Then come here and test your connection speed. This site performs a test, displays the results, rates your connection speed, and provides links to products that can improve the speed.

DSL Reports Speed Test

12345

www.dslreports.com/stest

DSL Reports is a great place to pick up tips and utilities for increasing the speed of your Internet connection. Here, you can also test your connection speed to determine whether it needs fixing.

PC Pitstop Internet

12345

www.pcpitstop.com/internet/default.asp

PC Pitstop can test the speed, performance, and security of your computer to determine whether it is running at its peak performance. The site then makes recommendations concerning how you can address particular issues that might be slowing it down or making it less secure.

Toast.net Performance

12345

www.toast.net/performance

Toast.net Performance provides free bandwidth speed tests. You can perform the test with an image, text, or a combination of text and image.

EMAIL

Bigfoot

12345

www.bigfoot.com

Bigfoot provides a free web-based email account that blocks spam (junk mail) and enables you to manage your email account from a computer anywhere in the world that's connected to the Internet. 3MB of free storage is offered per account, and you receive a daily quota of 50 forwarded messages.

emailaddresses.com

12345

www.emailaddresses.com

This site features reviews of and links to hundreds of free and for-fee email services and offers guidance on how to search for email addresses of friends and family and get the most out of your email services.

Eudora

12345

www.eudora.com

One of the top email programs around, Eudora has its own website where you can learn more about its features and download the product. You can download the free version, which displays a few ads on its window, or buy the program to get additional features minus the ads.

Gmail

12345

www.mail.google.com

Google has its own web-based email, and, like Hotmail and other popular web-based email services, it's free! Check it out at this site and register to become a Gmail user. Gmail also supports online chat.

Harness Email

12345

www.learnthenet.com/english/section/email.html

Excellent tutorial on email, covering everything from learning how it works to managing your email account. Learn how to follow the rules of email etiquette, join mailing lists, work with file attachments, keep email private, and more.

Lycos Mail

12345

www.mail.lycos.com

Get free email with 5MB of space set aside for you, as well as a handy-dandy reminder service and a spam-blocking service to keep unwanted junk mail out of your mailbox.

MSN Hotmail

12345

www.hotmail.com

Start here to learn more about setting up a free email account through MSN's Hotmail, a web-based email service, which allows users to access their email from anywhere.

Netiquette

12345

www.albion.com/netiquette/corerules.html

The core and much more: business netiquette, social netiquette, philosophical issues, *everything*. This online version of a book (originally published in 1994) is a must-read.

A B C D E F G H I J K L M N O P Q R S T U V W X Y Z

Talking Email

www.4developers.com/talkmail

Have your email messages read to you by animated characters rather than reading them yourself. The ultimate multitasker tool. Features talking reminders that notify you of upcoming meetings and appointments, a talking clock, and a talking clipboard.

Thunderbird

www.mozilla.com/thunderbird

If you think you might prefer using an email program other than Microsoft Outlook Express, consider trying Thunderbird, from the creators of Netscape Mozilla. Thunderbird "supports IMAP and POP mail protocols, as well as HTML mail formatting. Easily import your existing email accounts and messages. Built-in RSS capabilities, powerful quick search, spell check as you type, global inbox, deleting attachments and advanced message filtering round out Thunderbird's modern feature set."

Yahoo! Mail

www.mail.yahoo.com

From the Yahoo! home page, you can sign up for free email. As an added bonus, you'll gain access to other Yahoo! services. You can also link your Yahoo! email address to a pager.

ZapZone Email

www.zzn.com

Gives businesses large or small a way to provide free email service to their customers and clients.

INSTANT MESSAGING & INTERNET PHONE

America Online Instant Messenger

www.aim.com

Get the most popular instant messaging program on the planet, register for a screen name, and start chatting online with all your friends and relatives who already use AOL's Instant Messenger. AIM supports text, voice, and video chat.

iChat AV

www.apple.com/ichat

Apple's entry into web-based chat is iChat AV, an instant messaging program that feature true audio-visual teleconferencing over broadband connections. iChat AV works with AOL Instant Messenger, so you can connect with both Mac and PC users. Learn more about iChat AV at this site.

ICQ.com

www.icq.com

Download the free trial ICQ (I Seek You) software so that you can immediately identify when a friend or family member logs on to the Internet. The software eliminates the need to regularly search for people you want to talk to. After you find someone you want to chat with, you can send text or voice messages in real time.

Instant Messaging Planet

www.instantmessagingplanet.com

Instant Messaging Planet provides an information kiosk for instant messaging developers and providers. Articles examine "how companies use instant messaging and associated technologies to conduct business, and the specific obstacles/problems they face with using IM technology in our connected world." Covers both wired and wireless forms of IM.

Jabber

www.jabber.com

Jabber is an XML-based open-source system and protocol for real-time messaging and presence notification. Jabber is also being applied in the realms of wireless communications, embedded systems, and Internet infrastructure to "transform the rules of business and streamlines business processes by enabling instant, context-driven connectivity anytime, anywhere."

MSN Messenger Service

1 2 3 4 5

www.messenger.msn.com

The free MSN instant messaging software allows you to see which of your friends are online and then send instant messages to them. You can also have group meetings or play a real-time game. MSN Messenger supports text, voice, and video chat; PC-to-PC calling with no long-distance charges; and online gaming.

Net2Phone

1 2 3 4 5

www.net2phone.com

Free PC-to-PC "phone calls" to anywhere in the world and free limited time PC-to-phone calls to any phone in the nation, plus low rates on PC-to-phone calls to other countries. With Net2Phone, users can talk to each other over Internet connections and phone lines using their PC's sound card equipped with a microphone.

Odigo.com

1 2 3 4 5

www.odigo.com

Odigo, Inc., is the leading provider of instant messaging (IM) and presence solutions. Odigo's services include IM clients, IM and Presence Servers, and hosting of IM and Presence services. The company is a founding member of IMUnified and the PAM Forum, two coalitions that are working to establish industry standards for IM and Presence interoperability.

PalTalk

1 2 3 4 5

www.paltalk.com

Using free PalTalk software, you can have voice conversations with other users around the world, send text-based instant messages, have group voice conversations, and leave voice messages for other PalTalk users. Download the software at this site. PalTalk is interoperable with America Online's Instant Messenger, ICQ, and Yahoo! Chat.

REBOL Internet Operating System

1 2 3 4 5

www.rebol.com/ios-intro.html

Home of REBOL, an innovative new Internet operating system that enables you to set up and maintain your own private network via the Internet. With REBOL, you can establish a communications network and share resources with hundreds of other users of your network. Great for businesses both large and small. Free trial is available.

Skype

1 2 3 4 5

www.skype.com

Skype is an Internet telephony program that enables you to call other people over the Internet for free, assuming they use Skype. You can also use the Skype program to call ordinary telephones within the United States and Canada for free. At this site, you can learn more about Skype and download the software. Skype is undergoing some changes, so the free call thing might disappear early in 2007.

Trillian

1 2 3 4 5

www.ceruleanstudios.com

Trillian is an instant messaging program that enables you to communicate with all your instant messaging friends using a single program. In Trillian, you can enter account information for AIM, MSN Messenger, Yahoo! Messenger, and ICQ. You can then use Trillian to send and receive messages to all of these services. You can also use Trillian to access IRC chat rooms

Yahoo! Messenger

1 2 3 4 5

www.messenger.yahoo.com

Using Yahoo!'s free instant messaging software, you can send instant messages to friends, make free PC-to-PC voice calls, video-chat with friends and family members, and access Yahoo! chat rooms. Yahoo! Messenger has a very attractive interface that makes the program easy to use and plenty of features to enhance your instant messaging experience.

ONLINE TELEPHONE DIRECTORIES

411.com

1 2 3 4 5

www.411.com

411.com features phone number lookups for individuals and businesses and reverse phone number and address lookups—you supply the phone number or address, and the site provides the name of the business or resident(s) at that address (if the information is available).

411 Locate

www.411locate.com

Find people through white page searches or email address searches and businesses through yellow page searches, or track down public information at this site.

AT&T AnyWho Info

1 2 3 4 5

www.anywho.com

Find a person or business that has a listing in the phone books by typing the name or category of business.

Infobel World

1 2 3 4 5

www.infobel.com

Telephone directories on the Web can help you track down the phone number for a person or business in virtually any country. You can search more than 400 directories from countries around the world at this one site.

Internet Address Finder

www.iaf.net

Find a person's email address by entering his or her name and other information, such as the company that person works for or the domain name of his or her ISP. Also features reverse phone number lookup, background checks (for a fee), and Yellow Pages lookup.

Switchboard.com

1 2 3 4 5

www.switchboard.com

This simple interface enables you to perform a variety of searches, some of which you can't perform at similar sites. Near the top of the page are six buttons: Find a Business (Yellow Pages), Find a Person (White Pages), Maps & Directions (a map of an area or directions from a departure point to a destination), Search by Phone (find a person's name by entering their phone number), Area & ZIP Codes (enter a city and state to find an area or ZIP code or enter an area or ZIP code to find a city and state), and Web Search (to search for websites and pages).

WorldPages

www.worldpages.com

Do a search for people or businesses and then pull up a map of how to get to where they are.

YellowPages.Com

1 2 3 4 5

www.yellowpages.com

The official place where you can let your fingers do the walking. This site goes far beyond what's offered in the typical Yellow Pages book. Here, you can search for businesses by name or category, access a White Pages directory to search for people, get maps and driving directions, peruse city guides and consumer guides, and create your own address book for storing the information you need most often.

OPT-IN EMAIL

HTMail

1 2 3 4 5

www.htmail.com

HTMail is a mom-and-pop opt-in email service that enables you to expand your customer base through direct email marketing. To advertisers, HTMail offers postal mailing lists, email lists, feedback reports, market research, tips on how to make the most of your mailings, and email list demographics.

Lyris.net

1 2 3 4 5

www.lyris.net

Lyris provides this email marketing resource guide to promote the benefits of direct marketing via email over traditional mass mailings to postal addresses. At this site, you can get all the information, tips, services, and software you need to create and manage your own successful direct marketing campaigns via email. Lyris offers a ListManager for handling the emailing yourself and ListHosting for outsourcing your promotional campaign.

PostMasterDirect.com

1 2 3 4 5

www.postmasterdirect.com

Direct mail companies looking to do email marketing will want to consider buying addresses of people who have agreed to receive those messages. PostMasterDirect.com manages those lists and sells them. Get more information here.

PRIVACY

Ad-Aware

1 2 3 4 5

www.lavasoftusa.com

One of the best, free anti-spyware, anti-popup programs on the market is Ad-Aware, developed by Lavasoft. At this site, you can download a free version of the program or purchase the professional version. You can also obtain additional information about adware and spyware.

AD Muncher

1 2 3 4 5

www.admuncher.com

AD Muncher significantly reduces banner ads and pop-up promotional messages that come through the Web. Download a free trial version here; $15 to purchase the program.

Anonymizer.com

1 2 3 4 5

www.anonymizer.com

If you're concerned about the amount of personal information you share every time you visit a website, come to this site first and type in the address you want to visit. Your identity will be protected at no cost. Or sign up for paid services to protect your identity and prevent cookies from being shared every time you visit a site.

Anti-Phishing Workgroup

1 2 3 4 5

www.antiphishing.org

Anti-Phishing Workgroup (APWG) is "the global pan-industrial and law enforcement association focused on eliminating the fraud and identity theft that result from phishing, pharming and email spoofing of all types." You can learn about two techniques that con artists use to steel personal information from users: *phishing* and *pharming*. Here, you can read the latest news about various Internet-based crimes, learn about new scams, and even submit a report if someone has tried to con you on the Internet.

> **Tip:** Click the Vendor Solutions button to access a directory of technology companies who develop products to discourage phishing and pharming.

BBBonline

1 2 3 4 5

www.bbbonline.org

Pick up tips for protecting your personal information at this site, sponsored by the Better Business Bureau. You can also search the database to find out which online companies subscribe to the organization's code of conduct.

Center for Democracy and Technology

www.cdt.org

Keep current on issues and legislation regarding Internet privacy issues through regular updates at this site. The opt-out forms available on the site are a godsend to consumers who want their names removed from corporate mailing lists.

A B C D E F G H J K L M N O P Q R S T U V W X Y Z

CookieCentral.com

12345

www.cookiecentral.com

Visit this site to better understand what cookies are, how they collect information, and what you can do to prevent or eliminate them.

CyberPatrol

12345

www.cyberpatrol.com

Download a free trial of this filtering system that pulls together lists of inappropriate sites and restricts access via your computer. Three variations of the software are available, for home, business, or school, with lists of good and bad sites customized depending on the application. Parents can also revise the lists, adding or subtracting sites children can view.

Electronic Frontier Foundation

www.eff.org

This site describes the mission and work of this nonprofit organization dedicated to protecting the rights of privacy and free expression on the Internet. Learn why these issues are so significant and what you can do to support the organization's work.

Fight Identity Theft

www.fightidentitytheft.co

This site provides information and tools to help you avoid becoming a victim of identity theft, determine whether you have been a victim, and repair any damage if you are a victim.

How Not to Get Hooked by a 'Phishing' Scam

12345

www.ftc.gov/bcp/conline/pubs/alerts/phishingalrt.htm

Good article from the FTC (Federal Trade Commission) on how to prevent Internet con artists from stealing your personal information or conning you into giving it to them.

ID Theft Affidavit

12345

www.ftc.gov/bcp/conline/pubs/credit/affidavit.pdf

If you are a victim of identity theft, contacting the banks and other companies where fraudulent debts and accounts have been set up in your name can be a nightmare. Visit this site to download and complete a single form that informs multiple companies that you have been a victim of identity theft.

Internet Watcher

12345

www.internetwatcher.com

Download a free trial version of Internet Watcher, an Internet-filtering program that blocks many of the ads that pop up on your computer as you browse the Web. Also provides tools for sharing a broadband connection among networked computers, increasing the speed of your Internet connection, censoring sites, blocking cookies, and more.

Privacy Rights Clearinghouse

12345

www.privacyrights.org

Privacy Rights Clearinghouse is a nonprofit consumer education and advocacy group that is dedicated to helping keep personal information private. Here, you can learn tips and tricks for keeping your personal information secure both on and off the Internet. Site features content in both English and Spanish.

SpyBot

12345

www.safer-networking.org

Are you afraid that somebody or some website has installed spyware or annoying adware on your computer that is following your web wanderings and inundating your computer with annoying pop-up ads? Then download SpyBot from this site, install it, and check your system. SpyBot can track down most spyware and adware and automatically remove it from your computer.

Spyware Encyclopedia

12345

www3.ca.com/securityadvisor/pest/search.aspx

Computer Associates Spyware Encyclopedia serves the Internet community by providing information on more than 20,000 Internet pests, including spyware, adware, and Trojan horses.

SpyWare Info

12345 RSS

www.spywareinfo.com

Many less-reputable companies on the Internet install unsolicited spyware and adware on your computer to follow your movements on the Web and bury you in annoying pop-up ads. This site provides the information, resources, and utilities you need to fight back.

TRUSTe

12345

www.truste.com

A site for web publishers and consumers, advising everyone on privacy issues. Consumers can learn how to best protect themselves from sharing too much information when online, and publishers can learn how to safeguard information provided by visitors.

Webroot

12345

www.webroot.com

Webroot sells software that protects your identity and provides security by preventing websites from viewing the cookies and history of previous web searches that reside on your computer. You can download a 30-day free trial of the Window Washer software to clean your hard drive. Features several other Internet security, censoring, and privacy programs, too.

SEARCH ENGINES

About.com

12345

www.about.com

About.com isn't really a search engine as much as it is an online know-it-all site. More than 500 experts contribute content to this site, covering almost every topic imaginable, or at least the top most requested topics on the Web. When you search a topic, you typically receive an article from one of the experts along with links to other information and resources.

AltaVista

12345

www.altavista.com

AltaVista is a well-established search tool that indexes billions of web pages, MP3 audio, video clips, news, images, and other data. It also features a directory you can browse, phone books for looking up people and businesses, and a translation tool so you can sort of make sense of foreign language pages.

Ask.com

www.ask.com

While most search engines determine the relative relevance of a web page according to the number of times it is accessed or the number of sites that link to it, Ask.com determines relevance based on a page's rank in its community or category. What this boils down to is that you might get some different search results when you search at Ask.com than you get when you use the more popular search engines. Ask.com provides a collection of search tools that enable you to perform the following focused searches: Web, Images, News, Maps & Directions, Local, Weather, Encyclopedia, Shopping, Desktop, and Blogs & Feeds.

Dogpile

12345

www.dogpile.com

One of our favorite search engines, Dogpile combines the power of several search engines, including Google and Yahoo!, to generate more results than you would otherwise receive using any individual search engine. You can perform a Web search, People search, or Business search; search for web pages, images, audio clips, video clips, or news on the Web; or check out the joke of the day. You can also download and install the Dogpile search toolbar to add to your browser for quick access.

Best Google.com

12345

www.google.com

Google is unmatched in terms of the depth and breadth of its searches and the tools it offers. The opening page is deceptively simple, prompting you to type a word, phrase, or other character string to begin your search, but behind the scenes, Google offers a well-stocked toolbox of web accessories. Just above the search box are links for special searches: Images, Groups (discussion forums), News (actual news stories from around the world), Froogle (for shopping), and Maps (to search for neighborhood stores, areas, and attractions). Click the More link for additional tools, some of which are still in development but all of which are intriguing.

Lycos.com

www.lycos.com

Lycos is a capable search engine with several tabs that enable you to perform targeted searches: Web, People, Yellow Pages, Shopping, Images & Audio, and Classifieds. The opening page presents featured content, including News, Entertainment, Music, and Games; featured services, including blogs and personal websites; and Lycos 50, the top 50 web searches of the day.

Mamma

www.mamma.com

Mamma is the self-proclaimed "mother of all search engines." It's actually a metasearch engine, which gathers hits from other search engines and compiles them in a single collection for your perusal. Tabs enable you to perform specific searches: Web, News, Images, White Pages, and Yellow Pages. You can purchase Mamma wear and accessories through Cafepress.com. Site also features a utility for searching your desktop for misplaced files and email messages.

MetaCrawler

www.metacrawler.com

MetaCrawler is the search engine of search engines; that is, it searches the results of several other search engines, including Yahoo!, Google, Ask Jeeves, and About, and provides a list of links that match your search terms. MetaCrawler features a web search, Yellow Pages, and White Pages and can find web pages, audio and video clips, images, and news. You can also set your search preferences and perform more advanced searches to limit or broaden the results.

MSN.com

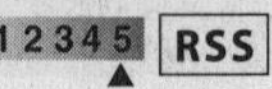

www.msn.com

MSN's opening page is quite impressive, providing summaries of the top news stories of the day along with links to other popular content areas and providers. At the top of the page is the search engine part, where you can search for web pages, news, images, misplaced items on your computer's desktop, or articles in Encarta (Microsoft's encyclopedia). MSN also features a downloadable toolbar you can add to your desktop.

Northern Light

www.northernlight.com

If you *need* a search engine for your business or website, Northern Light can help develop a custom search engine for your needs. Visit this site for more information.

Search Engine Watch

www.searchenginewatch.com

To obtain the latest news, information, and reviews of current Internet search engines, visit this site. This site also features a collection of web search tips.

A B C D E F G H I J K L M N O P Q R S T U V W X Y Z

A B C D E F G H I J K L M N O P Q R S T U V W X Y Z

Yahoo!

1 2 3 4 5

www.yahoo.com

Yahoo! is unique in that it uses not only automated search tools to track down pages but also human beings. For many years, Yahoo! was the unchallenged champion of search engines, providing users an easy way to navigate through category listings to find the best sites. You can still use this approach by clicking the Directory tab. The opening page displays a standard search box into which you type your search entry, but you can click other tabs to search for images, video, audio, local stores and attractions, news, and shopping. If it weren't for Google, Yahoo! would be our choice as Best of the Best search tool.

SECURITY/VIRUS HOAXES

McAfee AntiVirus

1 2 3 4 5

www.mcafee.com

Home of McAfee VirusScan, one of the most popular antivirus programs on the market. Here, you can learn about the latest virus scares, find out whether a reported virus is really a hoax, and download the latest virus definitions. You can also check out McAfee's firewall program to protect your system from hackers. Click the Threat Center link for timely hacker and malware reports.

Panda Software

1 2 3 4 5

www.pandasoftware.com

Panda specializes in antivirus and Internet security software. Here, you can learn about Internet threats, Panda Software products, and what you can do to protect your computer and Internet connection from security breaches.

> **Tip:** Scroll down the page and click the link for Panda ActiveScan to have your computer scanned for viruses for free.

Best Symantec AntiVirus Research Center

1 2 3 4 5

www.symantec.com/avcenter/index.html

Download detailed information on the latest virus definitions, find out what to do about them, browse the encyclopedia of online viruses and hoaxes, and visit the Reference area for answers to commonly asked questions. If someone sends an email to you, warning you of a new virus, be sure to check this site to make sure the virus warning isn't a hoax. This is an extensive listing. You can purchase Symantec products here, from firewalls to virus scanners, as well as purchase updates to your existing Symantec products. You can also purchase a family Internet security system that helps defend your PC against Internet threats and protects your children against inappropriate online content.

Symantec Security Check

1 2 3 4 5

www.security.symantec.com

Is your computer protected against unauthorized access over the Internet? If you're not sure, you can have it checked at this site. A complete report tells you just how safe your Internet connection really is and provides information on how to secure your connection.

Trend Micro: Scams and Hoaxes

1 2 3 4 5

www.trendmicro.com/vinfo/hoaxes/default.asp

If something pops up on your computer and looks a little suspicious or too good to be true, visit this site to look it up and determine exactly what's going on. Trend Micro catalogs common scams and hoaxes and provides a tool that enables you to search its databases for scams and hoaxes by name.

VirusList.com

www.viruslist.com

VirusList.com from Kasperksy Labs features the latest information on viruses, hackers, spam, and other threats to Internet privacy and security. This site includes a virus encyclopedia that covers various topics related to malware (viruses, spyware, and so on), including where it lives, what it is, who creates it, and what to do if your computer is infected. You can choose to view content in any of five languages: English, Russian, Polish, French, or German.

WEB PAGE DEVELOPMENT

1-2-3 ASPX

www.123aspx.com

Huge directory of Active Server Pages (ASP) information, technology, and tools. Find books, tutorials, discussion groups, code libraries, and other resources

AJAX

www.ajax.org

AJAX (Asynchronous JavaScript And XML) is "a web development technique used for creating interactive web applications. With AJAX, user interfaces from within the browser can use web services as their data source to store and retrieve information." This site is the official AJAX special interest group site, and when we visited, it had little to offer except a brief explanation of AJAX. By the time you visit, the site might have much more in place.

ASP Resource Index

www.aspin.com

A type of focused search engine for programmers, providing Active Server Pages (ASP) components, applications, scripts, tutorials, and references. Users can search the information reviews, ratings, price, or software version. Scroll down the page for links to additional resources in the following categories: References, Books & Media, Community, and Other ASP Sites.

ASP Today

www.asptoday.com

This online programmers' tool provides useful ASP columns written by programmers for programmers. A growing list of more than 1,300 articles offer practical ASP-related techniques, tips, and tricks that don't take much time to read.

ASPWire

www.aspwire.com

Stay current on ASP-related news at this site, which offers new product announcements, product reviews, articles, books, seminars, and ASP website announcements.

Bare Bones Guide to HTML

www.werbach.com/barebones

When you need instructions and advice in developing HTML web pages, this is the place to go. In addition to the Bare Bones Guide, this site features a FAQ and links to other useful resources.

Brainjar

www.brainjar.com

Brainjar features experiments in web programming and includes tutorials, technical articles, and examples.

Builder.com

www.builder.com

Builder.com, from CNET Networks, is a developer's forum that covers web and database development and object-oriented programming for Windows and UNIX/Linux platforms.

CGI Resource Index

1 2 3 4 5

www.cgi-resources.com

Access a collection of more than 4,600 premade CGIs, articles, and documentation in 360 categories.

Database Journal

1 2 3 4 5 RSS

www.databasejournal.com

Database Journal provides up-to-date news and articles regarding database servers. Current and archived news and reviews are available, and be sure to sign up for the free newsletter.

developerWorks: Java Technology

1 2 3 4 5 RSS

www-130.ibm.com/developerworks/java

Learn more about Java technology and how to use it at IBM's site. Pick up tools and code, read instructional articles, and stay current on the latest Java announcements.

DevChannel

1 2 3 4 5 Blog

www.devchannel.org

DevChannel is the "central news and reference resource for developers interested in core technology topics." Here, you can find articles, interviews, daily news updates, access to SourceForge projects, Freshmeat downloads, and Slashdot discussions. Come here to share information and resources with other developers.

DevX

1 2 3 4 5 RSS

www.devx.com

Serving the programming community, DevX is a commercial site that provides developers with the information, technology, and resources they need to create websites, applications, and e-commerce solutions for their clients. Resources for .NET, ASP, C++, DHTML, Java, XML, wireless, and more.

Dreamweaver

1 2 3 4 5

www.adobe.com/products/dreamweaver

You'll find articles, tutorials, tech support and downloads, and other resources to help you with Adobe's Dreamweaver.

FreeScripts

1 2 3 4 5

www.FreeScripts.com/scripts

Download free CGI scripts here. You'll be able to add a footer, have visitors rate an item on your site, and much more.

The HTML Writers Guild

1 2 3 4 5

www.hwg.org

A nonprofit organization for web authors, the guild provides members with tools and resources to improve their skills, including a lengthy list of web authoring classes available online. Be sure to check out all the upcoming events, seminars, and workshops.

Jars.com

1 2 3 4 5

www.jars.com

Search this Java review site for product and site information. You can also sign up to be a Jars reviewer and help to rate resource submissions.

Java.sun.com

1 2 3 4 5

www.java.sun.com

Go to the source for Java information, including support, tutorials, product information, APIs, downloads, and discussions, as well as plenty more.

Matt's Script Archive

1 2 3 4 5

www.scriptarchive.com

Search this site for free CGI scripts and link to other sites in search of what you're looking for. Check out the bulletin boards, web discussion forums, Matt's free Perl CGI scripts, and free C++ CGI scripts. Also get help from this site.

.NET

www.microsoft.com/net

Learn all about Microsoft's new software technologies for "connecting your world of information, people, systems, and devices." Microsoft's .NET initiative is designed to blur the lines between personal computers, networks, the Internet, and wireless communication devices, including cellular phones.

Page Resource.com

www.pageresource.com

Novice web page creators will want to drop in for tutorials on HTML and JavaScript. Information on DHTML, CGI, and Perl, plus web design guidelines.

Perl.com

www.perl.com

The O'Reilly and Associates Perl site is the premier site for learning about Perl. Provides links for documentation, training, downloads, books, FAQs, and other resources focusing on Perl.

PHP

www.php.net

Official site of PHP (Hypertext Preprocessor), this site features an introductory tutorial, an online manual, and other assistance to help web developers get up to speed with the PHP scripting language. Site also contains announcements of upcoming events and links to other useful PHP sites.

Python.org

www.python.org

Since its introduction, Python has been the programming language of choice for many developers. It's easy to learn, supports integration with other languages, and comes complete with a robust collection of standard libraries. At this official Python site, you can learn more about this language and its benefits, obtain the documentation you need to get started, access free downloads, and swap information with a community of enthusiastic Python developers.

ScriptSearch

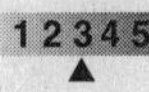

www.scriptsearch.com

Search by keyword, language, or category to find free CGI scripts. This site claims to be the largest archive.

SiteExperts.com

www.siteexperts.com

Online community of web page and website developers. Variety of discussion groups and resources for developers.

SQL Server Magazine

www.windowsitpro.com/SQLServer

This online magazine provides programmers with SQL news, how-to articles, and resources. Book and product reviews are just two of the helpful listings here. This site also links to Fatbrain.com, where you can purchase books and other printed materials.

Best W3 Schools

www.w3schools.com

W3 Schools is unmatched in breadth and depth of instructional tutorials and tools for developing websites and individual pages. This site covers it all: HTML, XHTML, XML, CSS, JavaScript, DHTML, VBScript, WML, SQL, ASP, PHP, .NET, Flash, and a host of other topics and tools. And if this gets too heavy for you, take a break and read the joke of the day.

Web Developer's Virtual Library

www.wdvl.com

This excellent resource for web developers provides quick access to discussion forums, software reviews, tutorials, guides for authoring and design, and a good collection of feature articles.

A B C D E F G H I J K L M N O P Q R S T U V W X Y Z

WebDeveloper.com

1 2 3 4 5

www.webdeveloper.com

WebDeveloper.com centers around a heft collection of discussion forums. Forums are grouped into three main categories—Client Side, Server Side, E-Commerce, and Etc.—with several forums included in each category. Site also features a collection of articles, script downloads, and links to other useful developer sites.

Webmonkey.com

1 2 3 4 5

www.webmonkey.com

A comprehensive resource for web developers, filled with how-to articles on web design, authoring, multimedia, e-commerce, programming, and jobs. You can browse the content at this site according to your level of expertise: Beginning, Builder, or Master. Site also features two well-stocked libraries: a How-To Library and a Resource Library.

Webmonkey for Kids

1 2 3 4 5

www.webmonkey.wired.com/webmonkey/kids

Children can learn how to create their very own websites here. This site features four sections: Lessons, Projects, Playground, and Tools.

WEB PAGE SOFTWARE & RESOURCES

Adobe

1 2 3 4 5

www.adobe.com

Adobe is home to some of the most popular and powerful web page development tools, including Shockwave, Flash, and Dreamweaver. If you want to make sites that are animated and interactive, this is the place to find the tools you need to achieve your goal. You can even download trial versions of Adobe products so you can test them out before you buy.

CoffeeCup Software

1 2 3 4 5 RSS

www.coffeecup.com

A complete line of web page design, creation, and management software, including CoffeeCup HTML Editor, Firestarter, WebCam, and GIF Animator. Download free shareware versions of these programs to take them for a test drive or order full versions online. Excellent site design has a clean, sleek appearance that's easy to navigate.

CoolPage

1 2 3 4 5

www.coolpage.com

CoolPage is a web page design and creation tool for beginners that enables drag-and-drop placement of objects on a page. This page-layout program provides all the tools you need to construct, format, and publish your page on the Web. Here, you can learn more about the program and download a free trial version.

Developers Network

1 2 3 4 5

www.msdn.microsoft.com

Developers Network contains plenty of news, feature, and how-to articles, as well as technical notes, training information, and guidance.

FrontPage

1 2 3 4 5

www.office.microsoft.com/en-us/FX010858021033.aspx

The home of Microsoft's website creation and management software provides a brief introduction to FrontPage, a gallery of ideas, how-to articles, tips and tricks, free downloads, and online technical support.

HTML Goodies

1 2 3 4 5

www.htmlgoodies.com

Tutorials, tips, and advice for both beginners and experts presented in a simple and straightforward manner.

Pagetutor.com

www.pagetutor.com

Excellent collection of HTML tutorials written in plain English. Download the shareware version of PageTutor.

Sausage Software

Sausage Software is the developer of HotDog, one of the most popular web page creation and publishing programs around. Think of it as a desktop publishing program for the Web that's easy to use. This site features access to all Sausage Software's products, including HotDog Professional, FlashPoint (for creating Flash animations), HotDog PageWiz, HotFTP (for performing FTP file transfers), and HotDog Junior (for kids). At this site, you can learn more about these programs and download free trial versions.

SitePal

www.oddcast.com/sitepal

Add an animated, automated version of yourself or someone else to your website who greets visitors and responds to their questions. The creators of this intriguing product are eager to convince you that this will have an immediate and positive impact on sales. Visit this site for an overview, a free trial, and a quote.

Slashdot

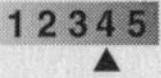

www.slashdot.org

At this site billed as News for Nerds, you can pick up techie news, articles, and reviews. Lots of reviews and a lengthy message thread here.

XMetal

www.xmetal.com

XMetal makes creating web pages as easy as creating documents in a desktop publishing program. Here, you can download a shareware version of the program or purchase a copy. Additional resources are also available.

A B C D E F G H I J K L M N O P Q R S T U V W X Y Z

INVENTIONS AND INVENTORS

The American Experience

1 2 3 4 5 (rating: 3)

www.pbs.org/wgbh/amex/telephone/sfeature

Sponsored by PBS, this site offers short essays on several inventions, such as the can opener, blue jeans, the Frisbee, the feather duster, the gas mask, the blood bank, and the oil burner. You can also find links to the rest of the PBS site, including the PBS shop and programming schedule.

Edison National Historic Site

1 2 3 4 5 (rating: 3)

www.nps.gov/edis/home.htm

Visit the site of one of the greatest inventors of our time, go on a virtual tour of his laboratory, read his biography, check his long list of patents, visit the photo gallery, and much more.

Enchanted Learning: Inventors and Inventions

1 2 3 4 5 (rating: 3)

www.enchantedlearning.com/inventors

Enchanted Learning is responsible for this page on inventors and inventions, where you can explore topics from A to Z, by time periods starting with the 1300s and earlier, or by category, including clothing, medicine, and science and industry.

Engines of Our Ingenuity

1 2 3 4 5 (rating: 3)

www.uh.edu/admin/engines/engines.htm

Produced by Oxford University, John H. Lienhard's radio program series about engines tells the story of how our culture is formed by human creativity and invention. You can purchase the book *The Engines of Our Ingenuity* from this site.

Franklin Institute

1 2 3 4 5 (rating: 3)

www.sln.fi.edu

The Franklin Institute, in Philadelphia of course, features this site where you can learn about and explore the world of science and inventions. This site features some content about Ben Franklin and his inventions, but the Franklin Institute is more of a full-featured science museum. You'll find plenty here for science buffs, teachers, parents, and students.

InventNet

1 2 3 4 5 (rating: 3)

www.inventnet.com

News summaries and postings on topics of interest to inventors, including law and politics. This site supports inventor's rights.

Inventors Assistance Resource Directory

1 2 3 4 5 (rating: 3)

www.inventored.org

A decent list of inventor support groups with local U.S. contact information. References listed here include how to promote your invention and how to contact an attorney to protect your invention.

Inventors' Digest Online

1 2 3 4 5 (rating: 3)

www.inventorsdigest.com

This site is designed for anyone who has ever said, "I've got a great idea...now what do I do?" It's also *the* spot for anyone who's searching for the next *hot* product! Check out the magazine site and then follow the links to the wonderful world of invention! Clothing items available here, too.

 Lemelson Center

www.invention.smithsonian.org/home

The Jerome and Dorothy Lemelson Center for the Study of Invention and Innovation is a branch of the Smithsonian Institution. The center's mission is to "document, interpret, and disseminate information about invention and innovation, to encourage inventive creativity in young people, and to foster an appreciation for the central role invention and innovation play in the history of the United States." Here, you can find exhibits on everything from Thomas Edison to electric guitars and quartz watches. Special areas are available for students, teachers, historians, inventors, and reporters.

Lemelson-MIT Program

www.web.mit.edu/invent

Visit MIT's invention website, where you can learn about the Lemelson-MIT award program, find out who's the inventor of the week, check on high school programs, and find links to dozens of other inventor resources. This site also features a game and trivia area and an outstanding Inventor's Handbook that covers everything from explaining what makes something "intellectual property" to how to raise the capital you need to bring your invention to fruition.

National Inventor Fraud Center

www.inventorfraud.com

The NIFC is dedicated to educating inventors so they can profit from their inventions and avoid becoming a victim of fraud. Here, you can find a beginner's guide called Inventor First Steps, learn about patent protection, find out how to profit from your invention and license it, and obtain links to legitimate patent resources and invention services.

National Inventors Hall of Fame

www.invent.org

Alphabetic index of inventors. Each link has a short biography, picture, and patent numbers of the inventor. Site also features programs, workshops, contests, and attractions for all ages. However, we think the designers need to invent a more intuitive user interface for this site. Trying to find what you're looking for is more challenging than coming up with a marketable new invention.

New Inventors

www.abc.net.au/newinventors

New Inventors is a TV show that introduces inventors and inventions originating from Australia, the country purported to have the most inventors per capita of any nation. Here, you can search for an invention that appeared on the show, vote for your favorite invention, apply to include your invention on the show, or visit the message boards to share your interest in the show with like-minded folks.

Nikola Tesla

www.neuronet.pitt.edu/~bogdan/tesla

This site is dedicated to one of the most important and least known American inventors, Nikola Tesla. Here, you can find a brief biography of this intriguing inventor along with information on his activity at the 1893 World's Fair, his contributions to the invention and promotion of alternating current over direct current for distributing electricity, and much more.

PatentCafe.com

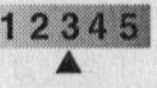

www.patentcafe.com

Learn more about patenting and protecting your idea with information from this site, as well as locating professionals to assist you. Find manufacturers, government assistance, and attorneys. Click the link for the Kids' Cafe or go directly to kids.patentcafe.com to visit the area specifically designed for K–12 inventors.

Top Ten African American Inventors

1 2 3 4 5

www.teacher.scholastic.com/activities/bhistory/inventors

This Scholastic site presents an excellent introduction to the top African American inventors, including George Washington Carver, Elijah McCoy, and Dr. Patricia E. Bath. Visit this site to learn where the expression "the real McCoy" came from.

Totally Absurd Inventions

1 2 3 4 5

www.totallyabsurd.com/absurd.htm

Floating Furniture, the Pet Petter, the Putt 'n Reel...the goofiest inventions that were actually awarded patents are all here and quite amusing. What's even funnier is that you might notice some products coming out that use these ideas, such as the Fingertip Toothbrush. Some of these sounded so weird that we looked up the patent numbers at the U.S. Patent Office—many of the patent numbers we checked were bona-fide patents!

United Inventors Association

www.uiausa.com

United Inventors Association is "a nonprofit inventor support group serving the invention community since 1990." The association's goal is to help the U.S. Patent and Trademark Office and the U.S. Federal Trade Commission "bring an end to the questionable services of many so-called invention promotion companies." This is an excellent place for inventors to gather to exchange advice, support one another, and learn how to spot patent scams.

U.S. Patent and Trademark Office

1 2 3 4 5

www.uspto.gov

For more than 200 years, the basic role of the U.S. Patent and Trademark Office (PTO) has remained the same: to promote the progress of science and the useful arts by securing for limited times to inventors the exclusive right to their respective discoveries. Check out this site to see how to register your invention idea and get a patent.

Related Site

www.uspto.gov/go/kids

JAILS

360degrees

www.360degrees.org

Collection of interviews and taped audio diaries gathered from inmates, correctional officers, lawyers, judges, parole officers, parents, victims, and others whose lives have been affected by the criminal justice system. As you listen to each individual's story, you can take a 360-degree tour of the individual's personal space—the jail cell, office, living room, or other environment in which the person spends most of his or her time.

American Correctional Association

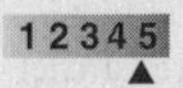

www.aca.org

This is the online home of the oldest and largest international correctional association in the world. Here, you can find information about membership, conferences, standards and accreditation, professional development and workshops, government and public affairs, and much more. You can also look for work in the Job Bank.

American Jail Association

www.corrections.com/aja

This site is the Internet home of the American Jail Association (AJA), a "national, nonprofit organization that exists to support those who work in and operate our nation's jails and is the only national association that focuses exclusively on issues specific to the operations of local correctional facilities." Here, you can find information about the organization and its conferences, training materials, and awards.

American Probation and Parole Association

www.appa-net.org

APPA focuses on probation, parole, and community corrections in the United States and its territories and Canada. Here, you can learn how to become a member and take advantages of the many services and training opportunities the APPA has to offer.

Correctional Education Association

www.ceanational.org

The CEA is a not-for-profit organization that serves and supports those who provide education and training to staff and administrators of correctional institutions. Visit this site to become a member and learn about the various services the CEA offers.

Best Corrections Connection

12345

www.corrections.com

This site is a weekly news source and online community for corrections professionals. Here, you can find articles about corrections institutions, a buyer's guide covering more than 1,000 industry products and services, hundreds of job openings, open discussion forums, and more. The directory features categories including Education, Food Service, Health Care, International, Juvenile, Privatization, Student, and Technology. This one-stop site provides everything a corrections professional needs laid out in an easily accessible format, making it our choice for Best of the Best jail site.

A B C D E F G H I J K L M N O P Q R S T U V W X Y Z

Federal Bureau of Prisons

1 2 3 4 5

www.bop.gov

Home of the U.S. Department of Justice Federal Bureau of Prisons, this site describes the mission and vision of the Bureau and provides an inmate search tool to help visitors find out where a particular inmate is incarcerated. Visitors may be monitored, so be careful what you look for.

JUSTNET: Justice Information Network

www.nlectc.org

This program, from the National Institute of Justice, provides technology assistance, training, testing, evaluation, and other services for the criminal justice system. The site also features success stories and links to other criminal justice resources on the Internet.

National Institute of Justice

www.ojp.usdoj.gov/nij

The NIJ is the research, development, and evaluation arm of the Justice Department. This page features NIJ news, events, funding opportunities, and links to NIJ publications. You can learn how to become a member and check out other services and opportunities provided by the NIJ.

Officer.com

www.officer.com

Created and owned by officer James Meredith, this comprehensive law enforcement resource site is dedicated to serving the law-enforcement community. Hundreds of links to agencies, associations, departments of correction, most-wanted lists, police supply stores, and much more. Lots of content is related to the latest technology.

Prisontalk

1 2 3 4 5

www.prisontalk.com

Prisontalk is a huge collection of discussion forums that address all aspects of prison life, including visitation rights, phone privileges, diseases, the drug war, and relationships. Friends and relatives can use the forums to communicate with their imprisoned loved ones, to have their questions answered, and to find assistance.

> **Tip:** Be sure to check out the rules for posting and the various FAQs before you begin posting your own messages.

Related Site

www.ojp.usdoj.gov/bjs/jails.htm

Stanford Prison Experiment

www.prisonexp.org

Philip Zimbardo and a handful of other researchers and assistants at Stanford decided to re-create the conditions at Abu Ghraib prison in Iraq to see what would happen if you put good people in an evil place. Visit this site to learn about the experiment, witness the results, and view a slide show and short video clips of some of the disturbing scenes.

U.S. Bureau of Justice Statistics

1 2 3 4 5

www.ojp.usdoj.gov/bjs/correct.htm

This site tracks and makes available to the public statistics concerning adult correctional populations, jail facilities, trends, and other information pertinent to crime and correctional institutions in the United States. Also covers capital punishment, probation, and parole.

JANITORIAL

Housekeeping Channel

www.housekeepingchannel.com

The Housekeeping Channel is the place to go for articles, tips, tools, and supplies to keep every room in your house sparkling clean and disinfected. Here, you can find dozens of discussion forums where you can swap cleaning secrets with other housekeepers, tune into HC TV for streaming video tutorials and tips, listen to HC Radio while you work or relax, or refer to the HC-Pedia to look up terminology and obtain additional instructions and tips. This site provides great information to a wide audience in way that makes it easy to track down everything you need to know about cleaning every room in your house.

Janitorial Bidding Guide

www.janitorialbidding.com

Thinking of starting your own janitorial service? Then visit this site to find out about a video that can help you land lucrative service contracts.

ServiceAid

www.serviceaid.net

ServiceAid provides service to the service industry, including janitorial, lawn care, and plumbing businesses. It places your business on the Internet and provides your custom site with the tools your clients need to schedule appointments and contact you hassle-free.

SERVICES

ABM Janitorial Services

www.abm.com

One of the largest janitorial and building maintenance companies in the country, ABM caters to large corporations. Provides services to companies in more than 40 states and employs more than 73,000 people. ABM also provides other services, including engineering, elevator, parking, and security.

Jani-King

www.janiking.com

Jani-King is a successful franchise operation that caters to corporate clients. Jani-King handles the contracting and then uses local franchise owners to do the cleaning. Here, you can check out the various services Jani-King offers and learn more about franchising and career opportunities.

Maid Brigade

www.maidbrigade.com

Maid Brigade operates more than 350 cleaning services across the United States, Canada, and Ireland. Here, you can search for a local Maid Brigade office, schedule a housecleaning, or find out about franchising opportunities. Site also features some excellent home cleaning tips.

Molly Maid

www.mollymaid.com

Another home-cleaning franchise devoted to handling the housework for its clients. Search for a Molly Maid near you or check out the franchise opportunities.

Vanguard Cleaning Systems

www.vanguardcleaning.com

Featuring office-cleaning services for businesses and corporations, Vanguard provides commercial-cleaning services to more than 28,000 corporate customers through more than 600 independent franchises.

SUPPLIES

Carolina Janitorial & Maintenance Supply

www.cjms.com

Complete selection of cleaning equipment and supplies for professionals. Brooms, mops, paper products, disinfectants, deodorizers, window-cleaning supplies, and anything else you need to keep things clean and shiny. Good customer service reputation, too.

CyberClean

www.cyberclean.com

Well-stocked collection of cleaning supplies and equipment. Everything from brooms to wastebaskets. Shop online and have your order shipped directly to you.

Dirt Happens

www.dirthappens.com

When dirt happens, shop at this site for everything you need to clean it up. Dirt Happens is a wholesale distributor of professional floor care products, carpet care products, floor machines, waste receptacles, window cleaning equipment, and many specially formulated cleaning chemicals for your unique environment.

Discount Janitorial Supplies

www.discountjanitorialsupply.com

Discount Janitorial Supply carries "thousands of commercial quality janitorial supplies for business, janitorial contractors, government, schools, and everyday home use." Place an order online, and have it shipped that day to your door from one of 27 locations in the United States.

> **Tip:** Check out the Rapid Awards Points Program to earn back some money while you shop.

HighPower Supplies

www.higherpowersupplies.com

Pressure washers and supplies, painting equipment, janitorial equipment and supplies, storage containers, safety equipment, and more.

J&R Supply

www.jandrsupply.com

J&R Supply has all the janitorial equipment and supplies you need, along with great service and prices and an excellent return policy. Best of all, the site is easy to navigate. After opening the home page, scroll down for links to various categories of equipment and supplies: Brooms, Brushes, and Accessories; Chemicals; Facility Maintenance; Floor Maintenance; and more. Discounts and free shipping for large orders.

Jani-Mart.com

www.jani-mart.com

Online janitorial supply warehouse featuring a complete stock of cleaning supplies. Trash cans and liners, paper products, mops and buckets, and more. Food service items available, too. Ships orders from any of 22 locations nationwide.

Twin Supply

www.twinsupply.com

Twin Supply is a NY-based company that carries janitorial supplies, office supplies, food service supplies, party supplies, professional cutlery, coffee urns, pizza supplies, commercial kitchen equipment, baby-changing stations, and equipment replacement parts.

JETSKI

International Jet Sports Boating Association

www.ijsba.com

IJSBA is the worldwide sanctioning body for jet boat racing. Here, you can learn the rules and regulations, check race schedules and events, find out how to get started in racing, and locate the nearest jet boat racing school. Whether you're a fan or a participant, you will find plenty of interesting information at this site.

Best jetski.com

www.jetski.com

Dedicated to everything dealing with personal watercraft, this site provides a list of places to ride, a customizable ride calendar for logging events, model specs, club information, chatrooms, message boards, classifieds, and much more.

JetSki News

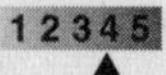

www.jetskinews.com

Personal website built and maintained by Christopher Riley to support the Jet Ski community. Site features news, comparisons, product reviews, rider profiles, discussion forums, free downloads, games, quizzes, and more. A great place to learn about Jet Skiing and other personal watercraft sports, gather information and advice, share your enthusiasm with fellow fans of the sport, and just hang out and have fun.

Kawasaki

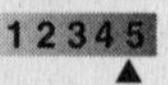

www.kawasaki.com

Kawasaki features a slick site that showcases its entire line of recreational vehicles, including its Jet Ski watercraft. You can check out the various models of one-, two-, and three-passenger watercraft available at this site. You can also join the owner's club, shop online for accessories, or register for the free newsletter.

Personal Watercraft Illustrated

www.watercraft.com

Online version of the popular magazine for personal watercraft enthusiasts. The site offers articles, product reviews, message boards, and online shopping (mostly for videos). Also provides some information on upcoming events. When you enter the site, the top of the main page contains some links to timely information, but when you scroll down, you'll find a lot of dated links, many of which don't work.

Powerski Jetboard

www.powerski.com

Powerski manufactures an interesting device called the Jetboard, which is like a motorized surfboard with a handle.

SBT on the Web

www.sbtontheweb.com

SBT carries a complete line of remanufactured engines, cranks, and parts for Sea-Doo, Jet-Ski, WaveRunner, and other PWC (personal watercraft). Site also features technical support, customer support, and discussion forums, where you can learn more about the inner workings of your PWC and have your questions answered.

Sea-Doo

12345 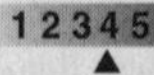

www.sea-doo.com

Home of some of the most popular lines of jetskis and waverunners on the market. Visit the virtual showroom to check out the current offerings. From the showroom, you can click a Jetski or Waverunner to view a brief description of it and check out the manufacturer's suggested retail price, check out the specs, view photos of the craft from different angles, check out reviews, or download a printable brochure. This site is sleek and easy to navigate.

Yamaha

12345

www.yamaha-motor.com

On display at this site are all of Yamaha's recreational vehicles, including its WaveRunners. Click the WaveRunners link to check out the latest models. This site also provides a search tool to locate local dealers, parts, and service. Shop online for apparel and accessories, obtain financing, and even check out the latest press and product reviews.

JEWELRY

Blue Nile

12345

www.bluenile.com

Fine jewelry with a focus on wedding and engagement rings. Great place to shop for that special gift. Some excellent information on how to select quality jewelry, evaluate diamonds and pearls, and understand the differences of various precious metals.

Diamond-Guide

12345

www.diamond-guide.com

From the home page, click the Learning Center link to access illustrated tutorials that show you how to evaluate diamonds, pearls, and colored stones. Also provides tips on caring for and traveling with jewelry.

Best DiamondReview.com

12345

www.diamondreview.com

Providing independent, unbiased research on diamond jewelry, this site is the favorite hangout for many diamond jewelry enthusiasts and professionals. Features a four-step process to becoming an enlightened buyer: read the tutorial, ask questions, find a jeweler, and then research prices. Easy to navigate and packed with useful information for consumers, this site is an easy Best of the Best pick.

ice.com

12345

www.ice.com

Shop by price or browse the online catalog to check out ice.com's wide selection of rings, necklaces, bracelets, watches, and other jewelry. Free shipping on orders more than $100, plus a 30-day money-back guarantee.

Jewelry Central

www.jewelrycentral.com

This huge online jewelry store is well organized, enabling you to browse various sections, including Rings & Bands, Earrings & Studs, Bracelets & Bangles, and Necklaces & Pendants. You can also shop by material: gold, platinum, silver, diamond, gemstone, or pearl. This site can even suggest gift ideas.

Jewelrylist.com

www.jewelrylist.com

You can shop online for jewelry at this site, which provides a single storefront for numerous jewelry stores. You can click links in any of several categories, including bridal jewelry, diamonds, precious metals, and gemstones. When you click a link, items from a featured store appear at the top of the page followed by links to other stores that carry items that fit the description you clicked. You can then order items directly from that store.

Jewelry Mall

www.jewelrymall.com

As you might guess from its name, Jewelry Mall features links to other online jewelry stores. However, it functions as much more than a referral site. It also features useful articles, including *Gem Buying Tips, Care & Lore*, and a *Diamond Buying Guide.*

Mondera

12345

www.mondera.com

Collection of fine jewelry worn by royalty and celebrities worldwide. Here, you can create your own custom ring by selecting a stone and setting. Get expert advice on how to choose quality jewelry and spot the phony stuff.

APPRAISAL

American Society of Appraisers

12345

www.appraisers.org

Home of the ASA, one of the top two organizations responsible for setting guidelines for professional appraisers. Click Find an Appraisal Expert to search for an ASA-approved appraiser in your area.

Appraisal Foundation

12345

www.appraisalfoundation.org

The Appraisal Foundation is a federal not-for-profit educational organization devoted to developing and promoting standards for valuation and defining the necessary qualifications for appraisers in various areas. This site features tabs for News, Events, USAP/Standards, and Education/Qualifications. From the home page, you can click a link to find an appraiser or learn how to become an appraiser. Here, you can find information on jewelry appraisal and on other forms of appraisal, including real estate.

How to Choose a Jewelry Appraiser

www.palagems.com/choosing_an_appraiser.htm

Excellent article that reveals the guidelines you should follow when selecting an appraiser. Article covers cost of the appraisal, questions to ask, common terminology and certifications, what a proper appraisal should contain, and stories of people who've gotten ripped off by phony appraisers.

International Society of Appraisers

12345

www.isa-appraisers.org

Home of the ISA, one of the top two organizations responsible for setting guidelines for professional appraisers. Click Find an Appraiser to search for an ISA-approved appraiser in your area.

DESIGNER & DESIGNERS

Abrasha's Gallery

12345

www.abrasha.com

Intriguing gallery of jewelry created from combinations of precious and nonprecious metals, stones, and other materials. When we visited the site, it hadn't been updated for some time, but the styles on display are still more modern than what you see in your average jewelry store.

Bernardine Fine Art Jewelry

12345

www.bernardine.com

Bernadine Fine Art Jewelry features a wide selection of unique rings, necklaces, and earrings, but you can also commission custom designs to have jewelry artist Nancy Bernardine design and create a one-of-a-kind piece.

Castor Jewelry.com

12345

www.castorjewelry.com

Browse the collection of beautiful and unique jewelry pieces or contact Tom Castor to have him draw up a design for you. Computerized illustrations provide you with a clear image of the design before you decide whether to have it made.

JewelrySupply.com

www.jewelrysupply.com

Create your own earrings, necklaces, rings, and other jewelry. At JewelrySupply.com, you can find all the tools and materials you need to start designing and creating your own custom jewelry. Lots of materials for beading.

Maui Divers Jewelry

www.mauidivers.com

Maui Divers Jewelry carries a wide selection of Hawaiian jewelry complete with plenty of black coral, Tahitian black pearl, and other precious materials you may not find at a more conventional jewelry store.

Polished & Put-Together

www.p-pt.com

When you're looking for something unique, check out Polished & Put-Together, where you can find one-of-a-kind and limited edition rings, necklaces, earrings, and other pieces. You can also contact a designer to work out a custom design.

Rhino Jewelry Design

www.rhino3d.com/jewelry.htm

Rhino is a modeling software program that runs under Windows and enables jewelry designers to express their visions on a computer screen as 3D models. This is a great tool for professional designers to design custom jewelry, show their designs to prospective clients, and land a contract before production begins. After the customer approves the design, you can print a 3D rendering of the model or export the design to a CAM (computer-aided manufacturing) program to produce the model for casting. Site features a gallery, free downloads (for trial and evaluation), support, training, and other resources.

REPAIR

RGM Watch Repair and Restoration

www.rgmwatches.com/repair.html

Repair and restoration service for high-quality Swiss watch brands.

ToolsGS

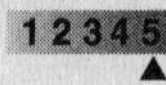

www.toolsgs.com

ToolsGS carries a wide selection of tools for jewelry making and repair, watch repair, and wood carving.

A B C D E F G H I J K L M N O P Q R S T U V W X Y Z

JOBS/EMPLOYMENT

Adventures in Education

1 2 3 4 5

adventuresineducation.org

Adventures in Education designed this site to help junior high and high school students and their parents plan their careers and educational paths, calculate the costs, and secure financial aid.

AdvisorTeam

1 2 3 4 5

www.advisorteam.org

AdvisorTeam offers a selection of web-enabled products and services for academic, corporate, and government organizations to assist in evaluating employee temperaments for optimum team building and communications. By subjecting employees to a few tests, AdvisorTeam is able to pigeonhole employees into one of four temperament categories: Artisan, Guardian, Idealist, or Rational. Visit this site to learn more about the company and its products and services.

Career Center

1 2 3 4 5

www.career.emory.edu/Students/CareerDev.htm

A step-by-step procedure that can help you define your career planning process. It is recommended that each step be followed sequentially.

CareerJournal from the Wall Street Journal

1 2 3 4 5 RSS

www.careerjournal.com

Excellent collection of articles and tips on finding your dream job. Salary and hiring information, job search tool, resumé database, discussion groups, and more.

Career Key

1 2 3 4 5

www.careerkey.org

Visit this site to fill out an online form that helps determine the type of career that's right for you. This site also offers plenty of additional advice on how to make the best career choice. Includes information on various careers, including salary, job outlook, and training.

Careers.org

www.careers.org

This site is a great resource center if you're looking for a job or a new career. Many links with many inspiring ideas!

JobStar Central

1 2 3 4 5

jobstar.org

JobStar Central is the site to visit before you start looking for a job. This site features resumés, career guides, salary information, secrets and tips about how to find hidden jobs, and an Ask Electra Q&A area.

Related Site

jobstar.org/tools/career/spec-car.htm

Mapping Your Future

1 2 3 4 5

www.mapping-your-future.org

Mapping Your Future's mission is to counsel students and families about college, career, and financial aid choices through a state-of-the-art, public-service website. This site is also available in Spanish.

Monster Message Boards

discussion.monster.com/messageboards/Index.asp

Don't let your career just drift aimlessly. Get advice on planning and managing your career and any specific problems you have in one of the many message boards. Sponsored by Monster.com.

Occupational Outlook Handbook

www.bls.gov/oco/home.htm

Excellent career resource. Find out information about different occupations, industry outlooks, and more. Information is provided by the Bureau of Labor Statistics.

Self-Assessment Career Survey

mois.org/moistest.html

If you are interested in finding out what careers you might like to pursue, take a few moments and complete this brief survey of career cluster area interests.

WEDDLE's

www.weddles.com

WEDDLE's is "a research, publishing, consulting, and training firm dedicated to helping people and organizations maximize their success in recruiting, retention, job search, and career self-management." This site is designed for corporate recruiters, HR professionals, staffing firms, independent recruiters, job seekers, and career activists; in other words, for everyone involved in hiring or being hired. Click the Tips for Success link to find tips for job hunters and recruiters. The Associations link is also particularly useful in helping track down various associations in specific fields—more than 1,500 associations are listed.

Workplace Fairness

www.workplacefairness.org

If your boss or company is giving you the shaft, visit this site to learn your rights as an employee and find out where to go to get help. This site organizes its content into four distinct areas: Your Rights, News and Issues, Resources, and Take Action. Workplace Fairness is a not-for-profit group dedicated to establishing and enforcing workplace policies that are fair and productive for all involved.

COMPANY INFORMATION

Hoovers

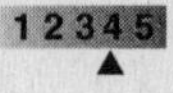

www.hoovers.com/free

If you're thinking about applying for a job at a specific company and you don't know where the company is located, what it does, or who you should contact, go to Hoovers online, and do a little free research. You can search the Hoovers directory by company name or ticker symbol to pull up a full report on the company.

JobStar: Researching Companies

jobstar.org/hidden/coinfo.php

The JobStar site looks less than impressive on its surface, but it provides an excellent guide for researching companies online. The guide leads you step by step through the process and provides links at every step to sites that can help you with your research.

NationJob

www.nationjob.com

NationJob is an online employment service that helps companies find employees and helps employees find jobs. Here, you can search for specific jobs or click the Company Directory link to pull up an alphabetic list of companies sponsored by NationJob. If you find a company you like, you can then click a link to find out more about submitting an application or resumé. Site also features a free career test, a salary wizard, and additional job-search resources.

PR Newswire

www.prnewswire.com

PR Newswire is "the global leader in news and information distribution services for professional communicators." Here, you can find late-breaking information for just about every major corporation and business. Companies use PR Newswire to distribute their press releases, and journalists come here to get the official word from companies on their current activities. As a job hunter, you can use this site to dig up a little extra information on a company you're interested in working for.

Vault.com

1 2 3 4 5

www.vault.com

Search for jobs by city or job function, research specific companies, get up-to-date industry news, and sign up to receive Vault.com's e-newsletters. Find out what you're worth, too, and network with other members. More information on specific companies and what you can expect to make than you'll find almost anywhere else.

Wet Feet

1 2 3 4 5

www.wetfeet.com

Wet Feet is an online job recruitment service that helps companies more effectively fill their openings with qualified personnel and helps job seekers find rewarding, well-paying positions. If you're about to enter or reenter the job market or are thinking about changing careers, Wet Feet can provide the information, resources, and job prospects you need. Before starting your job search, stop by Wet Feet to research various career choices and get the inside scoop on specific industries, such as consulting and hiring companies.

EMPLOYEE INCENTIVES

CorporateRewards.com

1 2 3 4 5

www.corporaterewards.com

When you want to reward your employees without giving them a permanent pay raise or increasing their benefits, consider gift certificates. CorporateRewards.com specializes in programs powered by the GiveAnything.com Universal Gift Certificate platform, which features gift certificates that recipients can use at hundreds of their favorite stores.

CTM Incentives

1 2 3 4 5

www.ctm-incentives.com

A leading developer of online rewards and loyalty programs, NetCentives provides you with a way to build stronger relationships with customers and employees, by recognizing and rewarding the behavior you want to continue.

Pros and Cons of Pay for Performance

1 2 3 4 5

hr.monster.com/articles/incentiveprograms

This excellent article explores the benefits and drawbacks of employee incentive programs. Does dispensing food to a rooster every time he pecks the piano guarantee that he'll soon play Beethoven? Read this article to find out what the author of it thinks and to pick up some tips on making sure that your rewards program doesn't end up punishing your employees.

HUMAN RESOURCE ASSISTANCE

BASIC

1 2 3 4 5

www.basicflex.com

Benefit Administrative Services International Corporation, BASIC for short, is a human resource service company many employers use to administer their benefits programs. Thousands of employers rely on it to administer and provide various services. If you run a company that is looking to outsource its benefits program, BASIC can handle the job.

Human Resource Executive Online

www.hreonline.com

Human Resource Executive is a magazine for human resource managers. This site provides access to much of the content that's available in the magazine along with additional features. Here, you check out the latest news and analysis, read feature stories, visit the technology center or the legal clinic, or use the HR Internet Search to track down additional resources online.

Office of Personnel Development

www.opm.gov

The Office of Personnel Management is the federal government's human resource agency, in charge of "building a high-quality and diverse workforce" for the federal government. Here, you can learn about employment, benefits, and career opportunities.

Primavera Systems

www.evolve.com

Primavera Systems, Inc. is "the world's leading project and portfolio management software company, providing the software foundation that enables all types of businesses to achieve excellence in managing their portfolios, programs, projects and resources." Here, you can learn more about Evolve, its products and services, and the success that its clients have achieved through teaming up with Evolve.

Society for Human Resource Management

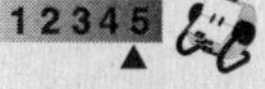

www.shrm.org

The Society for Human Resource Management (SHRM) is "the world's largest association devoted to human resource management." At this site, you can learn more about the organization, access a huge knowledgebase of HR information and resources, learn about HR consulting and technology, watch free SHRM webcasts, and much more. HR professionals will want to bookmark this site for quick return visits.

Top Echelon

www.topechelon.com

Top Echelon serves recruiters, companies, and job seekers by pooling information on candidates and trying to link them with matching potential employers.

Workforce Management

www.workforce.com

Workforce Management is a human resource magazine packed with articles on what's currently happening in the world of hiring, firing, benefits management, employee incentives, workforce development, and other issues regarding gainful employment and human resources management. The opening page contains news items and feature articles with links to other areas on the site, including a Research Center, Community Center, Vendor Directory, HR Management, and Legal Insight.

Workstream

www.workstreaminc.com

Workstream is a workforce management company that provides services to all those involved in the workforce: HR professionals, their suppliers, third-party recruiters, and job seekers. Workstream offers recruitment services, outplacement services, job databases, and more.

JOB-HUNTING TIPS

JobHuntingTips.com

www.job-hunting-tips.com

JobHuntingTips.com is packed with advice and tips on how to build and manage your career and land your next job. Content is organized in centers, including CV and Career Centre (curriculum vitae, resumés, and cover letters), Interview Centre, First Job Centre, Work from Home, and Insider Secrets (free ebook). Some excellent guidance and tips, no matter what kind of job you're looking for.

JobHuntersBible

www.jobhuntersbible.com

This site is designed to function as a supplement to the bestselling self-help book *What Color Is Your Parachute?* by Dick Bolles. Resources are generally divided into two sections: the Net Guide, which provides information on how to manage your job hunt, and the Parachute Library, which contains articles from Dick Bolles and his friends.

WorkSource

12345

https://fortress.wa.gov

Washington state has put together and maintains this website as a service to both workers and employers. The opening page provides a short search form you can fill out to search for job openings in your area of expertise or interest. Along the left is a navigation bar that provides quick access to several of the most popular features of the site, including classified ads, government jobs, and education. To the right of the job search form are links to other useful tools and resources, including Quick Guides (for job searching, posting resumés, submitting cover letters, and so forth), Job Fair Calendar, Skills Center, and Training Programs. Although some of the features are useful only for finding employment in Washington state, some information and resources are useful for anyone who's looking for a job.

JOB SEARCH

6Figurejobs.com

www.6figurejobs.com

Research jobs, find recruiters, and have your resumé seen by some of the top companies at this site for experienced professionals.

Academic Employment Network

12345

www.academploy.com

Search for education positions by state or position at this teaching-focused employment site.

America's Job Bank

12345

www.ajb.dni.us

One of the largest job banks around, this site provides access to the job listings of the public employment services in each state. Search by word, keyword, or state to find many potential jobs. Site also features an array of tools and guides to help you stage an effective job search, including information on how to compose a resumé and cover letter, and an online coach.

Best Jobs USA

12345

www.bestjobsusa.com

Best Jobs USA is an excellent job bank site that doesn't get as much press as Monster.com or CareerBuilder.com, but is just as or even more impressive. Here, you can search for jobs, post a resumé, check out a list of the top 50 companies to work for, and read some excellent articles about finding a job, advancing your career, and assessing your prospects.

Black Collegian Online

12345

www.black-collegian.com

Career site for African American students and professionals. Searchable jobs database, resumé bank, internship listings, graduate schools, and study abroad.

Career Builder

12345 RSS

www.careerbuilder.com

Billed as a "Mega Job Search," Careerbuilder.com has an active, continuously updated database of hundreds of thousands of jobs from more than 25,000 companies. Search the database, post your resumé, and build your career.

CareerShop.com

12345

www.careershop.com

A job search site that offers to email you jobs that match your qualifications and interests, as well as allow you to search the jobs database. You'll also find streaming video job tips and news.

CollegeGrad.com

12345

www.collegegrad.com

If you're a college student or recent college graduate, this is the site to go to find entry-level jobs and advice on how to turbo charge your job search. Site features a search form along with several special features, including Preparation, Job Search Advice, Resumés, Interview Prep, and Relocation Center.

College Recruiter

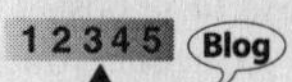

www.adguide.com

Jobs for college students, graduates, and recent grads. Entry-level work and career opportunities. Searchable database of jobs categorized by job type and location.

Computer Jobs

12345

www.developers.net

IT professionals can create a job profile and then receive emails regarding jobs posted that match their profile. Limited to programming and computer positions.

EmploymentGuide.com

12345

www.employmentguide.com

On this site, you can post your resumé, search the current job listings, visit the Education Center to learn about courses and programs that can help you land a job or advance your career, check out job fairs, obtain career advice, use the Salary Wizard to determine how much you're worth (as an employee), and much more.

Federal Government Job Search

12345

www.fedworld.gov/jobs/jobsearch.html

Looking for that cushy, secure government job you've always wanted? Look no further. Just plug in the desired geographical location of where you want to work and a descriptive word or two about the desired position, and this site can hook you up with the perfect position. Site also features links to the top government sites, science and tech sites, and other resources.

FlipDog.com

www.flipdog.com

Featuring a database of hundreds of thousands of jobs from more than 30,000 employers, FlipDog has become one of the most popular sites for job hunters. Search the database, post your resumé, or contact a headhunter. Useful tutorials on resumé writing and distribution.

Related Sites

www.heidrick.com

www.execunet.com

HotJobs.com

hotjobs.yahoo.com

Search thousands of jobs by keyword, location, or company in just about every type of job. You can save your recent searches and store a collection of customized resumés online, and browse through a database full of job leads.

> **Tip:** Click the Career Tools tab for a collection of tools that can help you manage and advance your career, including guides for creating a resumé, successfully navigating an interview, networking, and a salary calculator.

A B C D E F G H I J K L M N O P Q R S T U V W X Y Z

Job Bank USA

12345

www.jobbankusa.com

Employment and resumé information services to job candidates, employers, and recruitment firms. Job meta-search feature accesses large Internet employment databases.

jobhunt.org

12345 

www.job-hunt.org

jobhunt.org provides a directory that's designed to filter out the crummy job search sites and provide links to only the best job hunting sites and resources on the Web. Site also features an excellent selection of articles on job hunting and interviewing.

Jobs.com

12345

www.jobs.com

At Jobs.com, you can search for a specific job by keyword or browse for jobs by state or category.

Linkedin

12345

https://www.linkedin.com

Linkedin is an online networking service that enables you to leverage the power of your current contacts to establish your ultimate contacts. Whether you are looking for a new job or are trying to expand your business, Linkedin can help you find and get in touch with the people you need to contact.

Best Monster.com

12345

www.monster.com

Receive daily emails of job summaries that match what you're looking for, from part-time to full-time in a range of career fields. You can search up-to-date databases for job openings nationwide in virtually any field and make online applications to those jobs. Post your resumeé on the site and have prospective employers come to you! This site's popularity in itself is enough to warrant it the Best of the Best designation, but it also features an easy-to-use interface and some of the best career information around.

Monstertrak

12345

www.monstertrak.com

One of the few sites established especially for new college grads, Monstertrak is the result of a partnership with more than 800 career centers and alumni associations. Find listings and network with helpful grads.

Netshare

12345

www.netshare.com

More than 1,800 elusive six-figure executive positions are listed here. By subscribing to the site, you have access to all the best-paying jobs, plus some helpful information on how to tailor your cover letter and resumé and give yourself the best chance of landing that dream position. Recruiters can post job openings for free. Visitors can search the database for free, but contact information is blocked; you must subscribe to the service to obtain all the available information.

Quintessential Careers

12345

www.quintcareers.com

Whether you are entering the job market for the first time or are thinking about changing jobs for any reason, you can find the information and resources you need to execute a successful employment search. The opening page enables you to search for specific positions wherever you plan to live and work. It also provides links to other areas of the site, where you can access the career toolkit, obtain tips for writing resumés, get the latest job market data, ask the Career Doctor for advice, and much more.

Ryze

www.ryze.com

Business networking site that enables registered users to "meet other people in the high-tech, finance and digital media industries and develop long-term business relationships with them." The site includes an events calendar, message board, private messaging facilities, home pages, and a contact manager.

Spencer Stuart Talent Network

www.spencerstuart.com

Spencer Stuart is a global headhunter, a talent-management organization that specializes in senior executive searches and board director appointments. It is focused on the long-term success of its clients. You can learn more about the available services, join the talent pool, or become a Spencer Stuart client online at this site.

Telecommuting Jobs

www.tjobs.com

Check here for current news on the telecommuting phenomenon and find potential job opportunities online.

TrueCareers

www.truecareers.com

Dedicated to the new job hunter, TrueCareers provides information on job fairs, available positions, and has an online resumé builder. Great place for new college grads to find premium openings at major corporations.

Vets4Hire.com

www.vets4hire.com

Whether you're a veteran of the armed services or seeking to hire veterans, check out this site. Vets4Hire is committed to connecting veterans who are looking for work with companies who are looking to hire qualified veterans. This site also features articles both for job seekers and employers and some cool tools, including a free personality assessment.

Related Site

www.vetjobs.com

Workopolis

www.workopolis.com

This is the home of Canada's biggest job search site. Here, you can search for a job, post a current job opening, and check out the resource site for information, advice, and other articles and resources.

JOB-SHARING TIPS

Job Share Guidebook

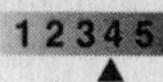

www.pao.gov.ab.ca/staff/flexible-work/jobshare/index.html

This guidebook was developed to address job sharing in Alberta, Canada, public service, but it provides excellent information and advice for any employer who is considering offering job-share opportunities and for any employee who's thinking about job sharing.

Job Sharing

wlb.monster.com/articles/jobsharing

Excellent article on the pros and cons of job sharing and how different companies implement job-sharing programs in different ways.

U.S. Department of Labor

www.dol.gov/dol/topic/workhours/jobsharing.htm

Short article by the U.S. Department of Labor that describes job sharing and some of the benefits those who promote job sharing claim it offers.

Woman's Work

12345

www.womans-work.com

Featuring more than 25,000 professional flexible jobs, including job-share, telecommuting, and work-at-home opportunities, this is a great place for working mothers and anyone seeking alternative work arrangements to start searching for a job. Search the database or post your resumé. Some excellent articles on job sharing and salary and benefit expectations, too.

Related Site

www.womans-work.com/job_share_search.htm

Work & Family Connections

12345

www.workfamily.com

Work & Family Connections is dedicated to helping "employers create a workplace that is both supportive and effective, a workplace that ensures that your investment in employees pays off, a work environment with a dual agenda—one that meets business goals and also allows employees to meet their personal goals." Employers can find plenty of tips on this site for making their workplaces family friendly. Site also features a directory of more than 100 links to other sites that offer related content.

Work/Life Options Job-Sharing Guide

12345

opm.gov/Employment_and_Benefits/WorkLife/WorkplaceFlexibilities/jobshare/index.asp

From the U.S. Office of Personnel Management, this job-sharing guide is designed to assist other government agencies in establishing family-friendly workplaces by making full utilization of all the personnel flexibilities and resources available.

Best WorkOptions.com

12345

www.workoptions.com

Devoted to promoting alternative work arrangements, WorkOptions.com provides information on job sharing, part-time positions, compressed work weeks, telecommuting, and flex time. For about $30, you can order the Flex Success Proposal Blueprint to pitch your work arrangement idea to your current employer.

JOURNALISM

American Journalism Review

www.ajr.org

This is the online home of *American Journalism Review* magazine, a publication that covers news and addresses journalistic issues in print, television, radio, and online media. Here, you can read articles from the most recent edition, check out the archives for previous articles and columns, and explore additional resources. The site also features some lighthearted journalistic humor.

> **Tip:** In the navigation bar on the left, the News Sources buttons take you to directories of links to the home pages for major newspapers, magazines, TV networks, and radio stations.

Columbia Journalism Review

12345

www.cjr.org

Home of "America's premiere media monitor." CJR is a watchdog organization that monitors the press in all its broadcasting forms: newspapers, magazines, radio, television, and the Internet. Tries to keep the press honest. Great collection of links to online versions of the most popular newspapers, magazines, and TV stations.

 High School Journalism

12345

www.highschooljournalism.org

Presented by the American Society of Newspaper Editors, this site is designed to encourage and support high school journalists and journalism teachers. Students can find articles on journalism, post questions to professional journalists, take a journalism quiz, and find links to high school newspapers. Teachers will find journalism lesson plans, links to support organizations, and other resources for teaching the craft. Visitors can also check into scholarships and colleges that offer journalism degrees. This Best of the Best site has something to offer anyone interested in journalism.

Investigative Reporters and Editors

www.ire.org

Located at the Missouri School of Journalism, IRE provides support, education, and resources for investigative reporters, editors, and others who are interested and involved in investigative journalism. At this site, you can read the history of the organization; learn how to become a member; find out about workshops and seminars; access investigative articles, tipsheets, and guides; dip into the campaign finance information center; and much more.

JournalismJobs.com

12345

www.journalismjobs.com

In partnership with the *Columbia Journalism Review*, this site is dedicated to helping journalists find jobs. Job listings for newspapers, magazines, radio, TV, and online broadcasters are available. Articles on freelancing, salary expectations, journalism style, and more.

JournalismNet

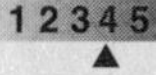

www.journalismnet.com

If you plan on becoming a successful investigative journalist, then you need to know how to dig up information on people, places, and events. This site presents a host of techniques for searching effectively on the Web.

A B C D E F G H I J K L M N O P Q R S T U V W X Y Z

Journalism.org

www.journalism.org

Devoted to improving the quality of journalism, Journalism.org highlights daily news stories that represent issues in journalism and provides an extensive collection of articles relating to journalism. Discussion forums allow members to debate and discuss current issues. Its annual report on the state of the news media is particularly revealing and informative. This site also provides information about the Project for Excellence in Journalism as an initiative by journalists to clarify and raise the standards of American journalism.

NewsLink

newslink.org

Links to newspapers, magazines, radio stations, and TV networks from all around the globe.

Newspaper Association of America

www.naa.org

NAA is a not-for-profit organization that focuses on newspaper marketing, public policy, diversity, industry development, operations, and readership. This site's home page features news about the newspaper industry along with links to various NAA resources, including its Federation Networking Directory, Vendor Links, and Newspaper University.

North Gate: Berkeley's Graduate School of Journalism

journalism.berkeley.edu

Journalism news from around the world, plus information on Berkeley's Graduate School of Journalism, including admissions policies, students, faculty, and resources.

Poynter.org

www.poynter.org

Home of the Poynter Institute, "a school for journalists, future journalists, and teachers of journalism." Here, you can learn more about the Poynter Institute's many seminars, find out about journalism conventions across the country, access online journalism tutorials, read award-winning reports and commentary, and much more.

Reporters Committee for Freedom of the Press

www.rcfp.org

The Reporters Committee for Freedom of the Press is a not-for-profit organization that works to provide free legal assistance to journalists. If you're a reporter who is being taken to court over a story you wrote, contact the RCFP for help.

Society of Professional Journalists

www.spj.org

Dedicated to the preservation of the free press as a cornerstone of democracy in the United States, this site is maintained to help defend the First Amendment rights and to promote high standards in journalism. Here, you can catch the top news stories regarding journalism topics, find out more about careers in journalism, learn about SPJ's programs for journalists, and even enter a contest for a chance to win a prestigious SPJ award in journalism.

Walter Cronkite School of Journalism & Mass Communication

cronkite.asu.edu

Named after the former managing editor of *CBS Evening News with Walter Cronkite*, the Cronkite school is one of the largest of its kind in the nation. This site features information about the school plus a collection of articles dealing with current issues relevant to journalism.

Writers Write Journalism Resources

www.writerswrite.com/journalism

Excellent collection of articles and links to other sites where journalists can find additional resources. Find journalism schools, read headlines, or join a discussion group.

1-800-GOT-JUNK?

www.1800gotjunk.com

Need to get rid of some junk? Contact America's largest junk removal service to have it hauled away. Here, you can find service center locations or even sign up for your own franchise.

Imagination Factory

www.kid-at-art.com

The Imagination Factory inspires kids to recycle by transforming their junk into art. Here, you can find dozens of ideas for creative projects and plenty of inspiration to come up with your own ideas. This site also features a good collection of links to related sites on the environment and art.

Junk Food Blog

www.junkfoodblog.com

If you're tired of eating soy cheese and trying to nourish yourself with carrot sticks and celery, then visit the Food Blog. Here, you can find out about the latest junk food hitting the market, so you can gobble up additional fat, sugar, salt, corn syrup, and all that other wonderful stuff we love to eat.

Junk Science

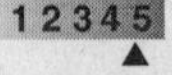

www.junkscience.com

With the motto "All the Junk That's Fit to Debunk," Junk Science calls into question many claims in the mainstream media that are supposedly backed up by scientific evidence, such as the environmental benefits of the Kyoto Protocol. The site is created and maintained by Steven Milloy, author of *Junk Science Judo: Self-Defense Against Health Scares and Scams*, and Barry Hearn.

Junk Yard Dog

www.junkyarddog.com

Free search tool for finding used auto, truck, and motorcycle parts. Fill out a part request and have Junk Yard Dog submit the request to its nationwide network of junk yards. Great way to locate those hard-to-find parts without rummaging through your local junkyard.

Junk Yard Parts Online

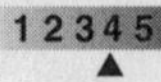

www.junk-yard-hotline.com

Looking for a part for your 67 Chevy? Then turn to Junk Yard Parts Online, a huge database of used car parts from junkyards all across the country. You specify the part you want and how much you're willing to pay, and this site contacts dealers to have them contact you via email, fax, or phone with their quotes.

Best Junkyard Wars

school.discovery.com/networks/junkyardwars/

Home of the Emmy-nominated television show, where engineers, mechanics, and the average Joe face off to see who can turn the most miserable pile of junk into something that does what it's supposed to do in 10 hours or less. This site is designed specifically to help teachers bring the Junkyard Wars concept into their classrooms. Here, you can find a collection of classroom videos, a teacher challenge, junkyard fun, an activities library, and much more.

A B C D E F G H I J K L M N O P Q R S T U V W X Y Z

Stop the Junkmail

1 2 3 4 5

www.stopthejunkmail.com

Service that sends email notices to specified companies on your behalf to tell them to stop sending flyers, catalogs, credit card applications, and other unsolicited junk to your home. Costs $19.95 to join.

Technology Recycling

1 2 3 4 5

www.techrecycle.com

Technology Recycling is a company that helps other companies in more than 200 cities properly dispose of their computers and other high-tech equipment. They disassemble the gadgets they collect, destroy any data they might contain, reprocess any materials they can salvage (including metals and glass), and properly dispose of the rest. They don't accept used computers as donations; companies must pay for the service.

KIDS

Amazon Interactive

12345

www.eduweb.com/amazon.html

Avoid the mosquitoes and piranhas. Explore the Amazon online. Here, you'll find answers to the most common questions about the Amazon, such as, "How rainy is the rainforest?" and "Who lives there?"

Animaland

www.animaland.org

Great site for young children to start exploring the wonderful world of animals. Everything from stories about animals to animal cartoons, pet care tips, career ideas, and Ask Azula's Q&A section.

American Library Association: Links to Kids Sites

www.ala.org/ala/alsc/greatwebsites/greatwebsiteskids.htm

When you're looking for great, clean, safe areas on the Web specifically designed for children and teenagers, this directory of sites from the American Library Association is the place to go. It features links to many of the best children's websites, grouped by categories including animals, the arts, history and biography, literature and languages, and sciences. Most of the sites are a barrel of fun in addition to exhibiting various degrees of educational merit.

America's CryptoKids: Future Codemakers & Codebreakers

12345

www.nsa.gov/kids

The National Security Agency/Central Security Service created and maintains this site to encourage young people to sharpen their minds by learning to make and break secret codes. Here, kids can access Codes and Ciphers (a brief introduction to codes and tools for deciphering them, plus a glossary of terms), Games & Activities (brainteasers, cryptograms, and other fun stuff), Student Resources (resources, museum, and high school and college programs), and character biographies (profiles of the cartoon characters that host the site). Very cool site.

Arthur

12345

pbskids.org/arthur

Join Arthur, Prunella, and the rest of the gang as they get themselves in emotional jams, learn important life lessons, and build character. Based on the children's books by Marc Brown. This site features links for friends, games, printable items, e-cards, and more.

Arts and Kids

12345

www.artsandkids.com

Enter the art contest and have your artwork featured in an online gallery for everyone to enjoy. Or play the puzzle game by putting all the pieces together in the correct order. A good site for encouraging kids to paint and draw.

Artsonia

12345

www.artsonia.com

Artsonia is a great way to encourage kids to draw and paint and for schools and parents organizations to do a little fundraising in the process. Here's how it works: Parents and teachers can upload a child's artwork to add it to the online art museum, where visitors can view the creations. If a visitor (typically a parent or grandparent) is dazzled by a piece of artwork, the visitor can then order a copy of it or a keychain, mug, T-shirt, or other item that prominently displays the artwork. The school earns 15 percent of all purchases. Cool, huh?

Awesome Library

www.awesomelibrary.org

A World Wide Web digital library for children in grades K–12. Contains information in the categories of art, science, social studies, miscellaneous, and so on. Within each category, several specific topics are featured to simplify searching.

BAM! (Body and Mind)

www.bam.gov

The Centers for Disease Control and Prevention created and maintain this site to keep kids informed of health issues, disease prevention, hygiene, nutrition, and safety. Site is colorful, interactive, fun, and easy to navigate. Along the top of the opening page is a navigation bar that provides quick access to the main sections of the site: Diseases, Food & Nutrition, Physical Activity, Your Safety, Your Life, and Your Body. Site features a game room, quizzes, and an activity calendar, along with plenty of material to help teachers incorporate lessons into their curriculum.

Bill Nye the Science Guy's Nye Labs Online

www.billnye.com

A companion site to the educational television show *Bill Nye the Science Guy*, Nye Labs Online features daily home science demonstrations, a forum for asking Bill questions, episode guides, teaching materials, and related show resources.

Captain Planet

www.captainplanetfdn.org

Information about the cartoon's characters and an episode guide. Learn more about the Captain Planet Foundation, whose mission is to fund and support hands-on environmental projects for children and youth. The objective of this foundation is to encourage innovative programs that empower children and youth around the world to work individually and collectively to solve environmental problems in their neighborhoods and communities.

Channel One

www.channelone.com

Online version of the popular Channel One broadcasting service that pipes news and current events into classrooms across America. At this site, kids can find information and commentary on various issues that relate to their generation. Check out the latest headline news, listen to music, find out the latest sports scores and highlights, play online games, enter contests, and much more.

Chateau Meddybemps

www.meddybemps.com

Chateau Meddybemps features "uncommon amusements for grown-ups and children." The fun and games area offers interactive games and ideas for activities and crafts. You can check out Beantime Stories for children's stories that are entertaining for all ages.

Chem4Kids

www.chem4kids.com

A tour of key concepts in chemistry written for kids. The site also contains separate sections for physics, biology, astronomy, and geography that visitors can go to for similar instruction. Interesting and entertaining.

ChessKids

www.chesskids.com

This site introduces kids to chess and teaches parents how to teach their kids how to play this classic game of strategy.

Children's Express UK

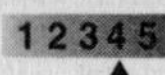

www.childrens-express.org

Online children's news organization, based in the United Kingdom, and devoted to helping children ages 8 to 18 learn through journalism. Over 10 years, the staff has published more than 1,000 stories. Read some of the latest stories here.

Colgate Kid's World

12345

kids-world.colgate.com

This site contains information about cavity prevention, games, stories, a coloring book, interesting information, and pictures from around the world.

CollegeBound Network

12345

www.collegebound.net

Working in partnership with colleges, universities, corporations, military branches, and educational companies, CollegeBound Network has created a stimulating community for teenagers to hang out and expand their horizons. Great resource for high school students who are considering college.

Cool LEGO Site of the Week

12345

www.lugnet.com/cool

Check out LUGNET to see the amazing things kids and adults are creating with LEGO bricks these days—not just the Lunar Lander you had as a kid. Also features links to other LEGO pages.

The Crayola Home Page

12345

www.crayola.com

Everything you always wanted to know about crayons and all the fun things you can do with them. You can buy Crayola products, from crayons and markers to clothing items you can color. You'll also find a gift idea link to help you choose an age-appropriate gift. Site features a Crayola navigation bar with a clickable crayon for each area: Coloring & Activities, Arts & Crafts, Card Creator, The Crayola Store.com, Color Corner, The Crayola FACTORY, Where to Buy, Helpful Information, and Lesson Plans. Great site for kids, teachers, and parents!

Cyber Stacks for Kids

12345

www.boulder.lib.co.us/youth/links.html

A site provided by the Boulder, Colorado, Public Library that includes links for learning about cultures, reference resources, games, a meeting place, and a science center. Also links to other fun places for children.

Cyberkids

12345

www.cyberkids.com

Lots of fun stuff for kids. Check out the newest articles, reviews, and fiction. Kids can even submit their own work to be published. There's fun stuff, too, such as magic tricks and a game section full of goodies.

Diary Project

12345 

www.diaryproject.com

The Diary Project encourages teenagers to express their personal views and insights on specific topics. Here, you can read what other teenagers have written or submit your own original entry. Technically, this isn't a blog, but it's close enough to call it a blog.

Discovery Channel: Discovery Kids

12345 

kids.discovery.com

The Discovery Channel provides some of the best and most interesting educational programs for children and teens, including Croc Files, Kenny the Shark, Endurance, and Scout's Safari. This site features information about each show, plus games, activities, and other fun, educational material.

Disney

12345 

disney.com

Great place for kids to explore, this site is packed with online games, information about Disney TV shows and movies, kids clubs, family crafts and party planners, vacations, and more. Site is attractive, easy to navigate, and packed with great, interactive content.

Dr. Seuss: Seussville

12345

www.seussville.com

Home of *The Cat and the Hat* and all the other beloved Dr. Seuss stories, this site carries visitors to Seussville, where they can read Dr. Seuss's biography, have fun on the playground, shop online, or check on upcoming events. Very well-designed, engaging site.

Eco-Kids

12345

www.ecokids.ca

This site features ecological activities to teach children about recycling and composting. You can use the navigation bar near the top of the opening page to navigate the site or mouse over objects in the beaver's den to explore features and then click the desired object. Areas include Play & Learn, EcoKids Club, Have Your Say (discussion boards), Eco Calendar, Feedback, and Teachers & Parents. Opening page also offers a Fact of the Day.

edbydesign.com

12345

www.edbydesign.com/kidsact.html

This site features educational games designed for children between the ages of 5 and 12. Here, you can play scrambler puzzles; practice mathematical skills; and publish your own stories, jokes, riddles, and poems online. Also provides resources for teachers and parents of children with special needs.

Eddy the Eco-Dog

12345

www.eddytheeco-dog.com

Eddy the Eco-Dog teaches kids about the environment. Kids can go to four "surfermania" areas by guessing the right password. After they're in, they can find all sorts of cool places to go. They can send postcards to friends, learn more about Eddy, and sign Eddy's guest book so that he can write to them. Cool joke machine is also featured.

EPA Global Warming for Kids

12345

www.epa.gov/globalwarming/kids

Excellent site from the EPA introduces kids to the topic of global warming. Here, kids can learn what global warming is, the difference between weather and climate, the meaning of "greenhouse effect," and what we can do to help. Site also features content specifically for teachers.

FirstGov for Kids

www.kids.gov

This site was developed and is maintained by the Federal Citizen Information Center to provide links to Federal kids' sites along with some of the best kids' sites from other organizations all grouped by subject. Links are grouped by category, covering everything from Arts and Careers to State Sites and Transportation. Each link is annotated, so you know what you're getting before you get there.

The Froggy Page

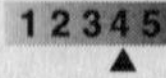

www.frogsonice.com/froggy

Everything that kids want to know about frogs! Kids can listen to frog sounds, read frog tales from all over the world, and look at frog pictures. Older kids will appreciate the scientific amphibian section, which includes frog anatomy and dissection as well as detailed scientific information on frogs and other amphibians from all over the world. Be sure to check out the creative and unique T-shirts and sweatshirts available for purchase.

F.U.N. Place

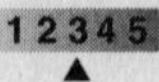

www.thefunplace.com

FUN, short for Families United on the Net, is a gathering place for parents and children to share thoughts, ideas, and talents. This site also provides links to plenty of resources, including a parenting guide, recipe database, and bulletin boards.

Games Kids Play

1 2 3 4 5

www.gameskidsplay.net

Looking for some games to teach your kids? Or perhaps you want to find out the complete verse to a rhyme that's stuck in your head. Well, you've come to the right place. This site provides rules for hundreds of children's games, as well as rhymes to accompany some of them. A great parenting, camping, or scouting resource.

Girls Only

1 2 3 4 5

www.gogirlsonly.org

This Girl Scout–sponsored page helps girls (aged 5 to 11) learn how to do things, such as build their own web page and become a scout. Navigation bar that runs across the top of the page provides easy access to the main areas of the site: games, quizzes, girl talk (message boards and polls), spotlight, about me, and what's up.

A Girl's World Online Clubhouse

1 2 3 4 5

www.agirlsworld.com

A world created especially for girls, this site features advice, pen pals, online diaries, chat, and a class on babysitting. Articles on women's health issues, a recipe collection, and games are also featured.

GoCityKids

1 2 3 4 5

www.gocitykids.com/choose

Are you looking for places to take your kids that are fun and educational? Then look to GoCity Kids for information on parks, stores, professional services, restaurants, babysitters, places to stay, entertainment, and other great places and services. GoCityKids can help parents navigate large metropolitan areas without spending a great deal of time researching. Whether you live in or near one of the cities the directory includes, or are planning a trip to one of them, you will find the directory most useful.

Goosebumps

1 2 3 4 5

place.scholastic.com/goosebumps/index.htm

Home of the popular collection of spooky *Goosebumps* books for kids by R. L. Stine. Visit this site to contact the author, play games, watch video clips, and more.

Headbone Zone

1 2 3 4 5

www.headbone.com

Play games, enter contests, ask questions and get advice, read about celebrities, express your opinions, and chat with friends—all from Headbone.com. Parents should supervise activity in the chat areas.

> **Tip:** Site has some annoying pop-up ads that tend to blend in with the pages. Click the X button in the upper-right corner of the pop-up window to close the ad.

Kidland

1 2 3 4 5

www.kidland.com

Kids can leap from site to site with Webbie, an animated frog. This site contains an index of kids' sites, activities, books, cartoons, educational information, games, and other topics related to children.

Kids Domain

1 2 3 4 5

www.kidsdomain.com

Kids will enjoy playing online games or learning some new craft projects at this site, which has lots of children's activities.

Kids' Place

1 2 3 4 5

www.eduplace.com/kids

Houghton Mifflin's Kids' Place is designed specifically for children in grades K–8. Features three distinct areas—School Books, Games, and Brain Power—that provide many fun and educational activities.

Kids Planet

www.kidsplanet.org

This site encourages kids to become defenders of the planet by educating them about endangered species and the interrelationships of species. This site features articles, games, interactive lessons, and engaging activities.

Kids' WB!

12345

kidswb.warnerbros.com

Kids' WB! is the children's programming service of The WB (Warner Bros) Network, the number-one broadcast network for kids. This site features all of your favorite Saturday morning cartoon shows along with games, videos, free downloads, and music. The opening page also displays a schedule of shows for this coming Saturday.

Kids-Korner.com

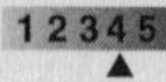

www.kidskorner.com

Hangout for kids age 14 and under, this site features an entertainment center, complete with games, movie reviews, and book reviews. Also features a game of the week, site of the week, and search tool for finding kid-safe sites.

KidsCom.com

12345

www.kidscom.com

KidsCom.com features an incredible collection of online activities and interactive tools for kids of all ages. Site features Games, the IS (Idea Seekers) Universe, Chat (including chat rooms and message boards), Make Friends (where you can create your own web pages or C-cards or find a pen pal), and Create (where you can make a scrapbook, tell a story or joke, or mix your own music). And that's just a sampling of what this site has to offer. Very attractive design, easy to navigate, and packed with features.

Kidsites

www.kidsites.org

Excellent directory of sites specifically for kids, teachers, and parents. Sites are grouped by category, including Toddlers, Preschoolers, Primary, Family & Parenting, Teachers, and Shopping Online.

KidSites.com

www.kidsites.com

Directory of hundreds of the best websites for kids.

KidsHealth.org

12345

kidshealth.org

This site contains interactive articles about medicine, surgery, parenting, and children's healthcare. The site is divided into sections for parents, teens, and kids, with the content tailored accordingly. It's a nice option for parents who want to give their kids good health information that they can access without Mom and Dad having to lecture them.

The LEGO Company

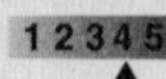

www.lego.com

The official LEGO universe: products, services, LEGOLAND, company history, and recent press releases. You can purchase LEGO toys from this site and have them shipped worldwide!

MaMaMedia.com

www.mamamedia.com

A kid-safe, entertaining site that offers kids the chance to create website collections, design their own multimedia characters and stories, and enjoy computer clubs and interactive chat with other kids. Links to another site for older kids.

A B C D E F G H I J K L M N O P Q R S T U V W X Y Z

Mark Kistler's Imagination Station

12345

www.draw3d.com

Learn how to draw in 3D with online drawing lessons from this famous public television art teacher.

Mojo's Musical Museum

12345

www.kididdles.com/museum

Can't remember the words to your favorite kid songs? Then look them up at Mojo's Musical Museum. If you know the title, you can search for it by name. If you don't know the title, browse the index, search through the subject index, or check out the song of the day.

Mr. Rogers' Neighborhood

pbskids.org/rogers

The famous Mr. Rogers has a website, sponsored by PBS. You can take a peek inside Mr. Rogers' house, sing along with the song list, and visit the neighborhood of make-believe. This site also includes a video tribute to Mr. Rogers, along with information for parents on how to help their children approach this site and the *Mr. Rogers' Neighborhood* series since the death of Mr. Rogers.

MysteryNet's Kids Mysteries

12345

Kids.MysteryNet.com

Offers mysteries, stories, tricks, and contests for kids. Also features online Nancy Drew mysteries and maze adventures.

Nabisco World

12345

www.nabiscoworld.com

Great collection of online games divided into categories including arcade, sports, puzzle & board, and multiplayer. Register for prizes or just find out about Nabisco's collection of tasty snacks.

National Gallery of Arts

12345

www.nga.gov/kids

The National Gallery of Arts hosts this site to pique children's interest in the arts, educate them about some of its exhibits, and provide interactive art activities to hone their skills and provide some basic instruction. Anyone can visit this site to learn more about the museum's exhibits, check its calendar of events, learn about upcoming films for kids, explore some family activities, and sign up to receive the newsletter via email.

National Geographic for Kids

12345

www.nationalgeographic.com/kids

National Geographic has a solid reputation for producing consistently high-quality photos and publications, and this site reinforces that reputation. From this site, you can access the magazine, feature stories, games, activities, experiments, a cartoon factory, and much more. Site is colorful, interactive, easy to navigate, and offers a tremendous collection of timely, accurate, and engaging information. Site also features homework help plus resources for parents and teachers.

Nick Jr.

www.nickjr.com

Nickelodeon features this site for preschoolers and their parents. Site features information about the many entertaining and educational shows for preschoolers, along with games, crafts, and activities to encourage families to play, learn, and create together. Excellent site.

Noggin

www.noggin.com

Noggin, from the creators of Nickelodeon, bills itself as preschool on TV and on the computer. Of course, on the Internet, it is much more interactive, featuring games, stories, puzzles, and other interactive educational features to keep kids entertained while teaching them the basics.

The NoodleHead Network

www.noodlehead.com

The NoodleHead Network is an award-winning video company based in Burlington, Vermont. It produces, markets, and distributes educational videotapes created from a kid's view. Kids play an integral role in the creation of each tape—from script development to acting to editing. Then a group of "ex-kids"—writers, producers, and educators—translate those ideas into unique videos that educate and inspire.

OLogy

www.ology.amnh.org

If you think science is no fun, check out this site sponsored by the American Museum of Natural History. Here, you can study genetics, astronomy, and paleontology in a fun-filled environment, and learn some interesting facts by playing a robust selection of trivia games.

Paw Island

www.pawisland.com

Paw Island is a magical island world inhabited by cats and dogs. In this special world, all the adult pets have jobs, roles, or responsibilities on the island. More importantly, they are all able to teach the island's younger pets the difference between right and wrong. Features activities, games, cartoons, and online shopping.

PBS Kids

pbskids.org

Sing and dance to PBS tunes with your favorite characters, play any of the 47 different games available, or print out pages to color featuring more PBS characters. This site is rich with PBS characters and activities.

Pojo.com

www.pojo.com

Pojo.com is "the Internet's premiere location for the most popular of gaming issues." Visitors can check out Pojo's online bookstore or connect with other gamers and collectors in a host of message boards related to popular game crazes, including Pokemon, Digimon, Dragon Ball Z, Gundam, Magic: The Gathering, and Harry Potter.

Reach for the Sky

rfts.worldarcstudio.com

Site developed for young adults (ages 11–18) to motivate them to achieve their full potential. Features actual career stories and information to help teens in choosing an appealing career to pursue and avoid some of the traps that all too frequently sabotage the potential of our youth.

Reading Rainbow

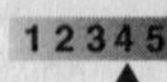

gpn.unl.edu/rainbow

Home page of the *Reading Rainbow*, devoted to encouraging reading and writing in young children. Find a complete *Reading Rainbow* book list plus lesson plans and study guides. Books, videos, and other items available online.

Sesame Workshop

www.sesameworkshop.org

Kid city! This site features stickers, games, gadgets, and puzzles. The Parent's Toolbox offers tips and tactics from *Sesame Street Parents*, plus email from Elmo, games, stories, coloring, Muppet profiles, show information, and trivia. You'll also find activities, crafts, and recipes.

SFS Kids

www.sfskids.com

Created and maintained by the San Francisco Symphony, this site is dedicated to providing a place for kids and families to learn more about music. Here, you can check out a selection of instruments, learn the basics of reading music, compose your own tunes, and send audio postcards to your friends and family via email.

SmartGirl

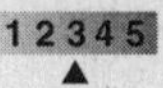

www.smartgirl.org

This all-girl teenage hangout features articles dealing with issues that many teenagers face, including sexuality, sports, school issues, family problems, and depression. Also provides reviews of books, beauty aids, music, and magazines. Creative writing forum where teen girls can showcase their works, plus an anonymous Speak Out section.

Soap Bubbles

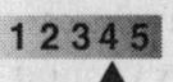

www.exploratorium.edu/ronh/bubbles

Bubbles! Bubbles everywhere! Kids love bubbles, and this educational site will teach them everything about the chemistry that makes up bubbles. Get your summer bubble recipe here. The site also includes links to other bubbly sites.

Sports Illustrated for Kids

www.sikids.com

Very cool site with sporting information geared toward kids and youths. Just like the adult *Sports Illustrated* magazine, this online version offers detailed articles about sporting events, sports heroes, and more. This version not only covers football, baseball, and other mainstream sports, but skateboarding and other "X" sports, too.

Squigly's Playhouse

www.squiglysplayhouse.com

Squigly's Playhouse is a great place to visit on a rainy day. It features games, crafts, jokes, pencil puzzles, coloring pictures, brainteasers, and more—something for everyone, especially the younger crowd.

Stone Soup

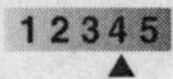

www.stonesoup.com

Magazine written and illustrated by writers and artists ages 8 to 13. Children can send in their own manuscripts for possible publication. It inspires young writers and contains beautiful stories written by young people.

Stories from the Web

www.storiesfromtheweb.org

Stories from the Web encourages readers and aspiring writers ages 0–14 to read and, if desired, submit their original reviews, stories, poetry, and songs for display in the gallery.

StreetPlay.com

www.streetplay.com

Drop that mouse, turn off the TV, and hit the streets for some good old-fashioned fun with your neighborhood pals. This site celebrates the games your parents grew up with—stickball, handball, hopscotch, jump rope, and marbles, to name a few. Provides rules for most games and plenty of photos that show you how to play many of the featured games.

Surfnet Kids

www.surfnetkids.com

Barbara J. Feldman put together this site as a safe place for kids, parents, and teachers to find the best websites for kids. Barbara is a syndicated columnist, a parent, and an experienced web surfer who acts as your guide. Scroll down for a list of Website Reviews for Kids, Parents, and Teachers; a Directory of Site Reviews; a Directory of Kids Games; and Recent Blog Entries from My (Barbara's) Other Sites. Each link is annotated with Barbara's commentary.

A B C D E F G H I J K L M N O P Q R S T U V W X Y Z

Thomas the Tank Engine Page

12345

www.hitentertainment.com/thomasand-friends

Calling all *Thomas the Tank Engine* fans! Read stories, play games, and have fun. You can also design your own My Thomas page.

Time for Kids

12345

www.timeforkids.com/TFK

This online magazine is written and produced by the *Time* magazine folks. This is a site where your kids can get the latest on their favorite music, film, or TV artists, as well as get the latest news on current events. They can also add their opinions in Kids' Views on the News.

USFA (United States Fire Administration) for Kids

12345

www.usfa.fema.gov/kids/flash.shtm

Kids can visit this site to learn about fire safety basics, including home fire safety, smoke alarms, and escaping from a fire. Site also features games, puzzles, and coloring pages.

VolcanoWorld

12345

volcano.und.nodak.edu

An educational place for kids to learn all about volcanoes. This site contains experiments, images, and data (all pertaining to volcanoes), and an area where kids can learn where the latest volcanic eruptions have occurred. The Kids Door opens into a world of art, quizzes, and virtual field trips. Site features the latest news on active volcanoes, keeping visitors informed concerning recent eruptions.

What Kids Can Do

12345

www.whatkidscando.org

Stories from around the country about kids who work with teachers or other adults for the public good.

The White House for Kids

www.whitehouse.gov/kids

Kids tour the White House and learn about the location and history of the White House. Kids can learn about children and pets who grew up and lived in the White House, and even write to the president, the vice president, and the first lady using special email addresses!

Why Files

12345

whyfiles.org

Each week a new report is presented and explained using scientific theory—"the science behind the news." Search the archives to read past articles and send in your own questions. Excellent, timely articles on scientific matters related to quality of modern human existence.

Best Wild World of Wonka

12345

www.wonka.com

Willie Wonka and his chocolate factory have built a home on the Web. Visit the wacky Wonka, take a tour of the Chocolate Factory, read the joke of the day, play several games, or download the free screensaver or wallpaper. You and your kids both will love this Best of the Best site!

Yahooligans

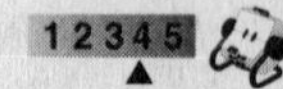

www.yahooligans.com

Website search engine for children that contains sections devoted to history, the arts, politics, computers and games, entertainment, sports and recreation, daily news, events, weather, and comics. Also features a school section that contains programs and homework answers.

KIDS' INTERNET GAMES

Bonus.com

12345

www.bonus.com

Bonus.com is a one-stop website for family games and entertainment. It functions as a secluded safe zone on the Internet, where kids can wander around without their parents worrying that they might be wandering off. Here, you can find hundreds of games, puzzles, and fun, interesting activities for the entire family. Several companies sponsor the site, so you will see advertising displayed in a bar at the top of the site, and you can expect a few more intrusive pop-ups, but the game selection is incredible.

Best Candystand

12345

www.candystand.com

Sponsored by the likes of Lifesavers, Nickelodeon, CapriSun, and Jello, Candystand is one of the best free game sites on the Web, featuring dozens of arcade games, card games, puzzles, multiplayer games, and sports games. The games are kind of cheesy, which makes them even more attractive. You have to log in to play, but you can then register to win valuable prizes.

CBC.CA/Kids/Games

12345

www.cbc.ca/kids/games

Visit this site to play Mr. Meaty: The Game and dozens of other games in the following categories: Action, Show Games, Classics, and Puzzles. This site, from the Canadian Broadcasting Company, also offers free downloads of desktop wallpapers, screensavers, and icons.

Centipede

12345

www.wzzm13.com/games/centipede.html

Compared to modern video games, this game is somewhat of a joke, but if you'd like to play one of the most popular games of the good ol' days, visit this site and play a couple rounds of Centipede.

The Codebook

12345

www.codebook.se

Serious Macintosh game players survive with cheats that get them extra lives, unlimited funds, hints, walkthroughs, and so on. Check this site for the cheats you need for your game.

DreamWorks Kids

12345

www.dwkids.com

DreamWorks, the computer animation company that's produced classics such as *Wallace & Gromit: The Curse of the Were-Rabbit*, *Shrek*, and *Madagascar* has created and maintains this site to offer fans games, crafts, and puzzles designed to entertain and educate. Visitors can also sign up to receive a newsletter via email, and parents can visit to download a free learning guide.

Escape from Knab

www.escapefromknab.com

A money-management Shockwave game for kids.

FamilyFun.com

12345

familyfun.go.com/games

Excellent collection of games for the whole family. Many of the games at this site are intended to be played by two or more people to encourage family bonding through play. Site also features an impressive collection of arcade games, word games, puzzles, and card and board games.

Funbrain.com

www.funbrain.com

More than 30 different online games. Kids can click on their age group or search by category to find a game they want to play.

Funschool

12345

www.funschool.com

Fun, educational games for preschool kids up to sixth grade. Games and activities are grouped by age. Site also features some free downloads and printable activities, arcade games, puzzles, board games, and teacher features.

Junior Achievement TITAN

12345

titan.ja.org

Kids over 13 are invited to play Junior Achievement's business simulation game, where they can play the role of CEO and compete against other young business tycoons.

Kaboose Games

resources.kaboose.com/games

Kaboose Games is a directory of some of the best games and gaming sites on the Internet. Scroll down for categories and then follow the trail of links to the desired game or gaming site.

KidsCom Games

12345

www.kidscom.com/games/games.html

Lots of fun stuff for kids of all ages! This is the place to find video game information. You'll find easy games, challenging games, Shockwave games, Java games, and more. Share tips and tricks about your favorite games on the GameTalk message boards.

Millsberry.com

12345

www.millsberry.com

From General Mills, this site has fun games featuring Lucky Charms, Trix, Cheerios, and Fruit Roll-Ups. This site also offers other activities kids will enjoy.

PBS Kids Games

12345

pbskids.org/games.html

PBS offers some fun, mind-challenging, interactive games at this site, including a collection of games from Barney & Friends, Caillou's jigsaw puzzles, Mister Rogers' Neighborhood Peek-a-Boo, and many more.

playkidsgames.com

12345

www.playkidsgames.com

Educational games that kids can play with their parents. Play Subtraction Pinball, Whack a Mole Alphabet, Musical Memory Turtle, and more.

Shockwave Games

12345

www.shockwave.com

Shockwave is famous for animating web pages, so it should be no surprise that game developers are drawn to it. Here, you can play a wide selection of Shockwave games, everything from puzzles and parlor games to arcade games and interactive shoot-'em-ups. Some games might be too violent for younger children, but many are directed specifically at the younger crowd.

Warner Brothers Games Gallery

12345

www2.warnerbros.com/web/games/index.jsp

Find popular Warner Brothers characters such as the Animaniacs, Wile E. Coyote, and the rest of the Looney Toons clan. You'll also find many Shockwave games.

WebChess

12345

www.june29.com/Chess

WebChess is a website that allows two individuals to play chess over the Web. You can come and join in a game, wait for an opponent, or just watch the other games being played.

Zeeks.com

1 2 3 4 5

www.zeeks.com

Lots of activities for kids, from games to puzzles to projects and more. In addition to games, kids can chat, create their own calendar, and get answers to questions they submit. Some annoying pop-up ads.

SAFE SURFING

Ask for Kids

1 2 3 4 5

www.askforkids.com

If you type in a question in plain English, Ask for Kids finds one website that answers the question. In some cases, you need to rephrase your question slightly to get the answer you want, but Ask for Kids will prompt you.

Related Site

www.rcls.org/ksearch.htm

Ben's Guide to U.S. Government for Kids

bensguide.gpo.gov/subject.html

This site features an extensive directory of websites created by various U.S. government agencies specifically for kids. Browse through the directory or click a link for the desired age group: K–2, 3–5, 6–8, 9–12, or P&T (parents and teachers).

Blog Safety

1 2 3 4 5

www.blogsafety.com

More and more kids and teenagers are blogging at sites such as MySpace and LiveJournal, and give out a lot more personal information than they should. This site reveals the dangers of blogging and offers guidance and tips on how to blog safely.

Chat Danger

www.chatdanger.com

Chat Danger is for parents who need to know how to protect their children from the potential dangers of online chat rooms. This site presents a couple real stories to wake parents up to the dangers and provides advice on how to keep their children from falling victim to online predators.

The Children's Partnership

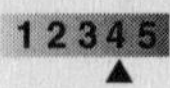

www.childrenspartnership.org

How do you keep your child safe online? This site, from the Children's Partnership, the National PTA, and the National Urban League, can help. Site offers an online safety PowerPoint presentation, a parents' guide to the Internet, and other articles and resources to help parents raise happy, well-adjusted children.

CyberPatrol

1 2 3 4 5

www.cyberpatrol.com

CyberPatrol is a software program that monitors Internet use and censors content that's inappropriate for kids. You can visit this site to download a free trial version of the software or to explore other resources. Click the Online Safety tab to access links to Safe Surfing Tips, Safety Program, and other Useful Links. Safe Surfing Tips is a guide to the World Wide Web for kids, parents, and teachers. It features links to sites that are safe for kids ages 6 to 16+. A great way for teachers and parents to safely introduce children to the Internet.

CYBERsitter

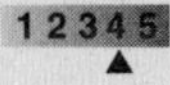

www.solidoak.com

CYBERsitter enables parents to limit their children's access to objectionable material on the Internet. Parents can choose to block, block and alert, or simply alert them when access is attempted to these areas. Working secretly in the background, CYBERsitter analyzes all Internet activity. Download a free trial from the website, and then you can choose to purchase it later.

A B C D E F G H I J L M N O P Q R S T U V W X Y Z

A B C D E F G H I J K L M N O P Q R S T U V W X Y Z

GetNetWise

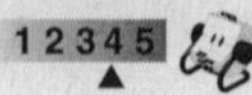

www.getnetwise.org

More than just a search engine, GetNetWise is a resource for parents to help kids have safe, educational, and entertaining online experiences. You'll find a glossary of Internet terms, a guide to online safety, directions for reporting online trouble, a directory of online safety tools, and links to safe sites for kids to visit.

> **Tip:** Click the Kids' Safety link to access an Online Safety Guide, Tools for Families, Web Sites for Kids, and Reporting Trouble.

ICRA

www.icra.org

The Recreational Software Advisory Council is an independent, nonprofit organization based in Washington, D.C., that empowers the public, especially parents, to make informed decisions about electronic media by means of an open and objective content-advisory system. Useful information specifically for kids, too.

JuniorNet

www.juniornet.com

This site provides lots of games and activities by established publishers for children ages 3 to 12. Only registered members from within a closed network can access JuniorNet.

KidsClick!

sunsite.berkeley.edu/KidsClick!

Search engine created by librarians for kids to help children and teenagers do their research on the Web in a safe, secure environment. Hundreds of links to interesting sites arranged in easy-to-navigate categories and subcategories.

Net-Mom

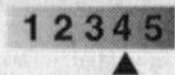

www.netmom.com

An excellent resource site from Jean Armour Polly, author of *Internet Kids* and *Family Yellow Pages.* Her book can be ordered via links to Amazon.com or Borders.com. You'll also find the 100 Hot Family Sites.

Net Nanny

www.netnanny.com

A software filter that prevents pornographic material from being shown on your computer and restricts access to files on your computer desktop. You can order the software at this site for $39.95 and download it immediately, or have it shipped to you.

Safe Surf

www.safesurf.com

SafeSurf has developed an Internet rating system that alerts parents when inappropriate material is available on a website and then filters out sites that the parents do not want their kids to see. Excellent tip on shutting down your browser when being harassed by a never-ending barrage of pornographic windows.

SafeKids.Com

12345

www.safekids.com

Find tips, advice, and information on searching safe sites, as well as links to family-friendly sites and search engines.

SafeTeens.com

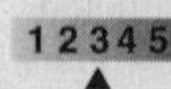

www.safeteens.com

A guide to teen safety on the Internet. This site not only offers ways to keep teens safe while using the Internet, but it also supplies many good websites that teens will find interesting or helpful. You can also subscribe to a free newsletter when you visit this site.

Best StaySafe.org

www.staysafe.org

Staysafe.org is "an educational site intended to help consumers understand both the positive aspects of the Internet as well as how to manage a variety of safety and security issues that exist online." Content is organized by age group with a couple extra categories: Kids, Teens, Parents, 50+, Community, and Toolbox. The Community link takes you to a page where you can get information and tips on how to collaborate with others to keep the Internet safe and protect your information and your children. The Toolbox link opens a page that reveals technologies and procedures for protecting your data and kids and discouraging online predators, crooks, and vandals.

Web Wise Kids

1 2 3 4 5

www.webwisekids.com

Internet safety and computer usage tips from Tracey O'Connell-Jay, founder and director of Web Wise Kids. She offers some really good tips, such as keeping your computer in an easily supervised area and establishing rules for computer use and Internet surfing.

SITES BY KIDS

Amazing Kids

1 2 3 4 5

www.amazing-kids.org

Amazing kids do some amazing things and create some amazing Web pages. Here, you can find links to some of those pages, stories about what some amazing kids have accomplished, and even submit content to have it included on the site.

Kids Space

www.kids-space.org

Kids Space is a website of kids, by kids, and for kids, where kids can hang out, express themselves, share their knowledge and insights, communicate with one another, and have fun in a safe environment. Opening page displays a graphic of a dollhouse with rooms populated with objects you can click to move from one area of the site to another.

Kidz Café

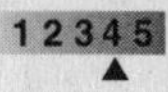

www.kidzcafe.org

Kidz Café is devoted to showcasing the works of talented kids on the Internet. Here, kids can share their original artwork, stories, poems, recipes, and other creations with other kids all around the world. This site features several sections, including Kidz Activities, Kidz Gallery, and Kidz Storytime. To contribute, you can email your artwork or stories or mail entries to the addresses provided at this site.

ThinkQuest Library

www.thinkquest.org/library

The ThinkQuest Library features over 5,500 websites created by students from around the world as part of a competition. This site organizes the links by category, including Arts & Entertainment, Books & Literature, Geography & Travel, Math, and Science & Technology. Each link is annotated, so you know what the site is about before you click its link. Many of the links are old, but some are fairly current.

World Wide Art Gallery

www.theartgallery.com.au/kidsart.html

At the World Wide Art Gallery, you can view an impressive collection of original children's graphic art and learn more about art and artists.

ZOOM

1 2 3 4 5

pbskids.org/zoom

ZOOM is a site for kids by kids (more than five million at last count) that features games, activities, information about the show (on PBS), and printable items including cards, signs, and activities booklets.

KNITTING

Artfibers Fashion Yarn

12345

www.artfibers.com

Displays hundreds of unique fashion yarns in knit swatches and offers ideas for using these yarns to create stylish projects.

elann.com

12345

secure.elann.com

elann.com offers "captivating yarns at irresistible prices," along with free patterns, a chat center, and a swap center. Company also carries a wide selection of books, patterns, needles, tools, samples, and gifts. Site includes a search tool and index to make tracking down products much easier.

Free Patterns

12345

www.freepatterns.com

Free Patterns offers free patterns for knitting, crocheting, cross-stitch, quilting, sewing, and other crafts. You do need to register and download Adobe Reader to be able to view and print patterns, but after you're set up, you have access to hundreds of free, high-quality patterns.

Frugal Knitting Haus

12345

www.frugalhaus.com

This online knitting store offers a wide selection of knitting and crocheting patterns, as well as needles and supplies. In addition, you can find knitting pattern books that give ideas for the use of leftover yarn. The store also offers free patterns.

The Garter Belt

12345 Blog

www.thegarterbelt.com

The Garter Belt features a collection of designs and patterns that you can order and download online. Each design is a printable PDF file that provides a photo of the item and complete instructions. Site has a nice, clean design that features excellent photos of the finished products.

Knit 'N Style

12345

www.knitnstyle.com

This is the online version of the knitting magazine, complete with pattern photos and information, as well as knitting links and articles.

Knit Picks

12345

www.knitpicks.com

Knit Picks "was formed as a separate division of Crafts Americana Group in 2002 with the purpose of connecting knitters with a wide selection of yarn, knitting books, needles, and accessories at great prices." Knit Picks carries a wide selection of yarns, needles, and accessories; books and patterns; and projects and tools. You can browse for items or search the catalogue by keyword or item number.

Knitting Universe

12345

www.knittinguniverse.com

This is a comprehensive site for anyone interested in knitting. Learn about yarns; get tips, tricks, and techniques; and shop for yarns and patterns online. Download free patterns, too. You can also subscribe to *Knitter's Magazine*. Excellent resource for beginners and experts alike!

Knitty

1 2 3 4 5

www.knitty.com

Knitty is a magazine about knitting—not only about knitting caps, gloves, and scarves, but also very cool blouses, sweaters, skirts, and even bracelets. At this site, you can read feature articles, access patterns, check the archives for articles from previous editions, read and post messages in the coffee shop, and shop online.

kpixie

1 2 3 4 5 Blog

www.kpixie.com

"Rock your stash" with kpixie, a company that specializes in hard-to-find yarns, ranging from imported bamboo and paper yarns to American-raised wool, recycled silk, and hand-tied scarf yarns with lots of sparkle. Here, you can also find a wide selection of patterns, needles, knit kits, and accessories.

LearnToKnit

1 2 3 4 5

www.learntoknit.com

Beginners will want to make LearnToKnit their first stop on their long journey to knitting. Learn the difference between knitting and crocheting, understand the basics, get started, and then check out the projects when you're ready.

Best Learn to Knit at Lion Brand Yarn

1 2 3 4 5 Blog

learntoknit.lionbrand.com

Excellent and comprehensive illustrated guide to knitting. This online instruction manual covers everything from casting on and learning the knit and purl stitches to grafting with the kitcheners stitch—29 chapters in all. Along the left side of the page, you'll find links to dozens of other helpful resources and online guides including, Learn to Crochet, Knit/Crochet FAQ, Knit/Crochet Abbreviations, Free Patterns, and links to the online store where you can purchase yarn, needles, and other supplies and accessories.

Staceyjoy's Knitting Stitch Portfolio

www.redlipstick.net/knit

Features an index of downloadable Fair Isle patterns and notes—with cable and machine tuck patterns.

Vogue Knitting

www.vogueknitting.com

Whether you're a novice knitter or an experienced pro who yearns to move beyond knitting stodgy old sweaters and scarves, this site offers everything you need. Click the How To tab for excellent illustrated instructions on how to knit. Click the Magazine tab to learn what the latest edition of *Vogue Knitting* has to offer. Click the Books tab to check out a large selection of books for sale. Site also features Links to other knitting sites, Exclusives (printable PDF files with instructions and charts for knitting projects), and Corrections (for any erroneous information that happens to end up in one of the books or magazines).

> **Tip:** Click the How To tab and then click the Glossary link for a great collection of knitting and crocheting terms and abbreviations and their definitions.

Webs: America's Yarn Store

1 2 3 4 5

yarn.com

Located in Northampton, Massachusetts, Webs offers hand knitters, machine knitters, and weavers a complete selection of yarns and equipment for their crafts by mail order from its store.

The Woolery

www.woolery.com

Since 1981, The Woolery has been a catalog mail-order supplier of spinning wheels, looms, related supplies, books, dyes, and fibers for crafters and artists. Now all its resources are at your disposal online. You can even read the site in French if you prefer.

Yesterknits

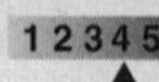

www.yesterknits.com/setup.html

You'll find tens of thousands of vintage knitting and crocheting patterns at this Scotland-based company's site. Search the patterns, or just look at the most popular ones, and then buy them via mail.

You Knit What??

youknitwhat.blogspot.com

Commentary from an incredulous knitter on some of the designs she has witnessed and attempted through her years as a devoted knitter. Very entertaining.

LANDSCAPE

Best Cultural Landscape Foundation

1 2 3 4 5

www.tclf.org

This site, which is visually stunning, addresses landscaping from the perspective of public parks, historic sites, gardens, scenic highways, college campuses, farmland, cemeteries, and even industrial sites. Check out the In the News section for the latest information, or sign up to receive the Foundation's free e-newsletter.

EPA Green Landscaping with Native Plants

1 2 3 4 5

www.epa.gov/greenacres

This site encourages everyone—from home gardeners to facilities managers at corporations—to consider adding native plants and wildflowers to a garden to beautify the environment and to attract butterflies and other animals and insects. To accomplish this, the site has helpful how-to information, an Ask-the-Expert area, a landscaping video, and basic information on why native plants are more beneficial to the environment.

Landscape Architecture Guide

1 2 3 4 5

gardenvisit.com/landscape

For everything related to landscape architecture—including garden design, career and job information, history and theory, and a list of the 100 best landscape architecture books—visit this site. Be sure to click on the Products link for reviews and photographs of hundreds of related items and tools.

Landscaping for Energy Efficiency

1 2 3 4 5

www.pioneerthinking.com/landscape.html

Are you looking for cost-effective yet eye-pleasing ways to lower your energy bills? This site gives advice on how to plant trees, shrubs, vines, grasses, and hedges for reducing heating and cooling costs, while also bringing other improvements to your community. Reader tips included.

Landscaping to Attract Birds

1 2 3 4 5

www.bcpl.net/~tross/by/attract.html

Tells visitors how to plant birdbaths and feeders and situate trees and flowers to attract the denizens of the air. Also contains descriptions of the benefits of landscaping for birds, plants for wild birds, and information for getting started, as well as a reading list and a link to other files on backyard birding.

LAWN CARE

American Lawns

1 2 3 4 5 RSS

www.american-lawns.com

This site is a great resource for anyone looking to improve his or her own lawn. Here, you will find information on the different types of turf, how to deal with weeds, and feature length articles on all sorts of lawn care–related topics. Want to know what to look for when buying new plants from a nursery, or how to improve your nighttime garden with landscape lighting? If so, this site is for you. There's even a featured article titled "5 Steps to a Lush, *Almost* Perfect Lawn."

Organic Lawn Care

1 2 3 4 5

www.richsoil.com/lawn

Learn how to reduce or eliminate your lawn's addiction to expensive and environmentally harmful chemicals. Step-by-step instructions on lawn care and weed and pest control.

Outdoor Power Equipment Institute

opei.mow.org/consumer/index.asp

A mega-database of outdoor equipment, including reviews and guides on the use and maintenance of lawn mowers and other outdoor power equipment. Excellent list of Earth-friendly yard-care tips, plus information on mower safety and links to related websites.

Best Scotts Lawncare Page

www.scotts.com

The home of Scotts fertilizers, this site shows you how to maintain your lawn's health through the proper use of chemical fertilizers. Some excellent information on the basics of seeding, mowing, and watering. Provides a maintenance schedule showing when you should fertilize.

Yardcare.com

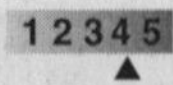

www.yardcare.com

All your lawn-care questions are answered at this site created and maintained by Toro. Learn everything from selecting grass seed to setting your mower to the proper height. Tips for controlling weeds, revitalizing a dying lawn, dealing with grubs and other pests, and reducing lawn maintenance, and the latest yard-care trends are also featured on this site.

PLANNING

3D Garden Composer

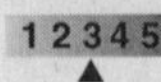

www.gardencomposer.com

Home page of one of the best gardening and landscaping programs on the market. 3D Garden Composer helps you design your garden on your computer and provides an encyclopedia covering more than 9,000 plants. At this site, you can view demos of the program, check out a photo gallery, and even order the program online. Links to FAQs, general information, and support.

Developing the Landscape Plan

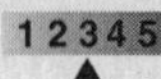

muextension.missouri.edu/xplor/agguides/hort/g06901.htm

Pointers to keep in mind while drawing up your own plan for your yard. Site also features events and calendars, news and publications, and access to a searchable database.

Landscape Design—Do It Yourself

www.the-landscape-design-site.com/landscapeplanning.html

Steve Boulden of S&S Designed Landscaping runs this site, where you'll find a lot of great information about landscape planning, including basic design principles, ideas, pictures, focal points, analysis, and more. Click on the Materials link at the top of the page for free landscape design ideas, advice, and resources.

SHRUBS

Colorado State University Gardening & Horticulture

1 2 3 4 5

www.coopext.colostate.edu/4DMG/Trees/Shrubs/shrubs.htm

Maintained by a group of Colorado-based master gardeners, this site has more information about shrubs than any other site we could find. From data about air pollution that affects shrubs to fall, winter, and spring pruning tips, this site has it all. Although of primary use to people residing in the Rocky Mountain states of Colorado, Wyoming, and Utah, much can be gleaned for other parts of the country, too, from this comprehensive text-based site.

Do It Yourself.com's Shrubs Page

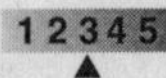

www.doityourself.com/scat/treesandshrubs

Brought to you by one of the Web's largest home improvement and home-repair libraries, this page is a launching pad for all things shrubs. Here, you will find information on planting, pruning, equipment, and maintenance and care.

Planting Techniques for Trees and Shrubs

1 2 3 4 5

buncombe.ces.ncsu.edu/depts/hort/hil/hil-601.html

Last revised in 1997, this one-page site provides a nice overview of planting techniques for both trees and shrubs.

University of Saskatchewan Trees and Shrubs Page

1 2 3 4 5

www.gardenline.usask.ca/trees/index.html

This page, maintained by the University of Saskatchewan, is a nice starting point for information about planting, maintaining, and moving shrubs.

TREES

American Forests

1 2 3 4 5

www.americanforests.org

This nonprofit organization is dedicated to reforestation as well as the preservation of the nation's forests. Learn how to become part of the group's efforts to plant millions of trees and why this effort is so important. You'll also find interesting information on historical trees.

The Bonsai Site

1 2 3 4 5

www.bonsaisite.com

A useful site for anyone interested in learning about bonsai. Includes helpful links to FAQs, bonsai history, tools, and supplies.

Best Global Trees Campaign

1 2 3 4 5

www.globaltrees.org

A wonderful site dedicated to raising awareness about a campaign to save the world's threatened and endangered tree species. This site is packed with educational resources, tree profiles, and suggested readings about trees and their conservation.

How to Prune Trees

1 2 3 4 5

www.na.fs.fed.us/spfo/pubs/howtos/ht_prune/prun001.htm

From the U.S. Forest Service, this site features a complete guide to pruning trees, including information on how and why pruning helps maintain the health and appearance of the tree.

TreeHelp.com

1 2 3 4 5

www.treehelp.com

Everything you need to know about caring for mature trees, including how to prune trees, identify and treat diseases, prevent insect infestations, and much more. This site also offers a selection of tree care products. Search the Arborist Directory for more information about trees in your state.

A B C D E F G H I J K M N O P Q R S T U V W X Y Z

LANGUAGES/LINGUISTICS

Center for Applied Linguistics

www.cal.org

CAL is dedicated to "improving communication through better understanding of language and culture." Here, you can find a comprehensive list of past and ongoing projects at CAL, plus a database packed with language resources and an online store for purchasing books. Some CAL publications are free. Links to job listings.

Child Language Development

www.kidsource.com/ASHA/child_language.html

Q&A list discussing issues concerning language development in children. Addresses everything from the concept of language to the parents' role in helping children develop. Sponsored by the American Speech, Language, Hearing Association.

Ethnologue: Languages of the World

1 2 3 4 5

www.sil.org/ethnologue

If you've ever wanted to know what people are saying all over the world, this is the place to come. This site includes a detailed study of the names, number of speakers, location, dialects, linguistic affiliation, multilingualism of speakers, and much more information on more than 1,000 languages. A searchable database and clickable maps are provided to help you find just the language you are looking for. A bibliography, publications, and software tools are also available.

iLoveLanguages

1 2 3 4 5

www.ilovelanguages.com

This site contains more than 2,000 links to language resources, such as online language lessons, translating dictionaries, native literature, translation services, software, language schools, and jobs. Excellent site for students and teachers of linguistics and foreign languages.

Language Miniatures

home.bluemarble.net/~langmin

Biweekly essays about the social, political, historical, and structural aspects of language. Past articles have addressed such topics as female grammar, animal language, and computer speech recognition. Find links to 11 categories and all Language Miniatures.

Best Linguist List

www.linguistlist.org

Linguist List is the world's largest linguistics resource and database in the world, "dedicated to providing information on language and language analysis, and to providing the discipline of linguistics with the infrastructure necessary to function in the digital world." Here, you can find people and organizations, jobs, calls and conferences, publications, language resources, text and computer tools, mailing lists, and more. Join the Linguist List to receive special member benefits.

Linguistic Society of America

www.lsadc.org

The Linguistics Society of America is dedicated to promoting and supporting the scientific study of languages. Here, you can find out more about the organization. Point to About Linguistics to view a menu of options including Linguistics News, the Discipline of Linguistics, FAQs, Fields of Linguistics, and Videos on the Web. Jobs, resources, and membership are also listed.

A B C D E F G H I J K L M N O P Q R S T U V W X Y Z

Loglan

www.loglan.org

Loglan is an artificial human language originally designed/invented by the late James Cooke Brown in the late 1950s. This site details the construction and usage of this language. An HTML primer to learn Loglan and sample texts are also available.

Semiotics for Beginners

www.aber.ac.uk/media/Documents/S4B/semiotic.html

As the title suggests, this site provides an online course in the study of signs and communication in society (semiotics). Here, you get an introduction to this discipline, current applications and research, and lists of suggested reading material. Also includes a message board and a chat room.

Virtual Foreign Language Classroom

www.nvcc.vccs.edu/vflc/links.htm

This virtual classroom from the Virginia Community College System and Distance Learning facility provides links to other sites relating to culture, instruction, and other language resources designed to enhance the learning of foreign languages. Links are organized into three categories: Courses and Instruction, Language Resources, and Culture. Registered faculty members can read and post messages in the Forum.

WordSmith Tools

www.lexically.net/wordsmith

Wordsmith Tools is an integrated suite of programs for looking at how words behave in texts. It is intended for linguists, language teachers, and others who need to examine language as part of their work. Download a full demo version from this site at the Oxford University Press. Includes FAQs. Demos also available in French and German.

CHINESE

Best Chinese Outpost

www.chinese-outpost.com/language

If you've always wanted to learn Mandarin Chinese, this site is for you. Here, you will find information on Chinese pronunciation, characters, and grammar. Click on the Characters link for a nice overview on the basic strokes or click on Pronunciation for information on the tones of Mandarin Chinese.

Learning Chinese

www.chinapage.com/learnchinese.html

A jumping-off point for anyone interested in speaking or reading Chinese. Click on the A Is for Love link for interactive flash cards, or on Listening to the sound of Chinese to hear a few sample words being spoken.

Omniglot's Chinese Script and Language Page

www.omniglot.com/writing/chinese.htm

A comprehensive and easy to follow site covering the origins of writing in China, the Chinese writing system, the evolution of Chinese characters and numerals, and more. There's even an overview of Braille for Chinese.

Zhongwen.com

zhongwen.com

This site present a series of zipu or "character genealogies" that show graphically the interconnections between over 4,000 characters according to the Shuowen Jiezi and subsequent research by etymologists.

A
B
C
D
E
F
G
H
I
J
K
L
M
N
O
P
Q
R
S
T
U
V
W
X
Y
Z

ENGLISH

African American Vernacular English

12345

www.une.edu.au/langnet/aave.htm

AAVE (African American Vernacular English), commonly referred to as Ebonics, is a form of English spoken primarily by African Americans. This article focuses on the possible origins of AAVE. Includes information on the background, vocabulary, sounds, and grammar of Ebonics.

The American-British British-American Dictionary

12345

www.peak.org/~jeremy/dictionary/chapters/introduction.php

A fun and handy reference for Americans traveling in Britain or Britons traveling in America. This dictionary includes American-to-British and British-to-American words and their definitions. A fun resource with references, jokes, accents and dialects, and more.

Australian Slang

12345

www.koalanet.com.au/australian-slang.html

A site containing an Australian-English slang and phrase dictionary. You'll find hundreds of colorful Australian phrases here. If you're planning a trip to Australia anytime soon or just want to know how far "back of Bourke" is, check out this site. Includes links to other pertinent information about Australia.

The Collective Nouns

12345

www.ojohaven.com/collectives

If a group of fish is called a *school* and a group of lions equals a *pride*, what is the name of a group of whales? Would you believe a *pod*? This fun site catalogs many collective nouns—many of them humorous. For example, you might see a colony of penguins, a siege of herons, a bunch of things, or a giggle of girls. Submissions of collective nouns are accepted at this site.

Best Common Errors in English

12345

www.wsu.edu/~brians/errors/errors.html

A fascinating little site. Based on Washington State University Professor of English Paul Brains' book, *Common Errors in English Language*, this site features hundred upon hundreds of words that are commonly misused or misspelled.

Grammar and Style Notes

12345

andromeda.rutgers.edu/~jlynch/Writing

Quick! What's the difference between *affect* and *effect*? Jack Lynch has the answer, and he's offered it up on this site, an online guide to the complexities of English grammar. Lynch clearly explains the differences between commonly confused words, defines terms such as *dangling participle*, and offers his own opinions on a variety of style issues. A list of writing guides and links to online grammar sources are also included.

SlangSite

12345

www.slangsite.com/slang/G.html

This extensive dictionary of slang will make you wonder if you really understand English. Some examples are *mack daddy*, *rawk*, *faboo*, and *quazzle*.

WordNet

12345

wordnet.princeton.edu

A lexical reference work, WordNet is designed to map out the relationships and connections between words and their synonyms. Created by the Cognitive Science Laboratory at Princeton University, this site was developed as an educational tool for improving vocabulary and reading comprehension. A FAQs page is included.

FARSI

Easy Persian

1 2 3 4 5

www.easypersian.com

Easy Persian is a mostly free site that offers lessons, drills, and resources for anyone learning Farsi. Many of this site's lessons include audio files, which can be very helpful when attempting to learn a new language.

Farsi Dictionary

1 2 3 4 5

www.farsidic.com

A simple, easy-to-use dictionary. Just enter an English word and click the Look It Up button for the matching word in Farsi. No bells or whistles, just a solid and reliable English-to-Farsi and Farsi-to-English dictionary.

QuickFarsi.com's English-Farsi Translation Services

1 2 3 4 5

quickfarsi.com

Need a contract, research paper, or personal letter translated from Farsi to English or from English to Farsi? If so, this site is for you. QuickFarsi.com accepts requests for bids via email, fax, or traditional mail, and will even provide you with a free, no-obligation price quote. There's even a section on this site where you can learn more about the Farsi language and the people who speak it.

Teachionary: Farsi Word Sets

1 2 3 4 5

www.sprex.com/teachionary/Farsi.html

A very cool little site. If you learn best by hearing and then repeating what you've heard, you'll really appreciate this site. Click on any of the 15 categories and listen to words spoken in Farsi. Click on the Guess button on any of the inside pages to test yourself on what you've leaned.

FRENCH

Basic French Word List

1 2 3 4 5

mypage.bluewin.ch/a-z/cusipage/basicfrench.html

Wondering how to say everything in French? Visit this site for a list of the 1,047 most basic English words and their French translation.

French Language Course Page

1 2 3 4 5

www.jump-gate.com/languages/french

This site features nine easy to follow lessons for learning French. From articles and genders to sentence structure, this site has it all, for free.

Online French Dictionary

1 2 3 4 5

www.freedict.com/onldict/fre.html

A free online dictionary that allows you to convert English words into their French equivalent, and vice versa.

Why Study French

1 2 3 4 5

www.fll.vt.edu/French/whyfrench.html

On this page, Virginia Polytechnic Institute and State University's Associate Professor of French, Richard Shryock, makes a convincing argument for studying French. If you're on the fence about combining French with business, information technology, or international studies, be sure to visit this site.

GENERAL LANGUAGE AND LINGUISTICS

ERIC Clearinghouse on Languages and Linguistics

1 2 3 4 5

www.cal.org/resources/update.html

The ERIC Clearinghouse on Languages and Linguistics is operated by the Center for Applied

Linguistics, a private nonprofit organization. This site provides a wide range of services and resources for language educators, including a FAQs list, directory of resources, online newsletter, the *CAL Digest*, and information teachers need to know about teaching languages.

Forum for Modern Language Studies

12345

fmls.oupjournals.org

Forum for Modern Language Studies is a journal that contains "articles on all aspects of literary and linguistic studies, from the Middle Ages to the present day." At this site, you can access articles from the current issue, browse the archive, find submission copies, subscribe to the journal, and order back issues. There's also information and instruction for authors who want to submit an article.

Language Map

12345

www.mla.org/census_map

Select a language, select a state, and this site displays a map showing the number of people in various areas of the selected region in the United States that speak the language you specified.

Modern Language Association

12345

www.mla.org

Since 1883, the Modern Language Association has promoted the study and teaching of language and literature. Here, you can learn more about the MLA and the MLA Style, shop online at the bookstore, check convention dates, and peruse the professional resources. A job information list is included.

The Translator's Home Companion

12345

www.lai.com/companion.html

Sponsored by the Northern California Translators Association, the Translator's Home Companion provides a guide to resources for professional translators. Links to online translation resources, such as dictionaries, are listed on this site. Translation news, product information, reviews, and organizations can also be found here. Looking for work? Subscribe to the translator jobs newsletter.

GERMAN

German for Travelers

12345

www.germanfortravellers.com

This site features free lessons, a members-only section, a community area where you can connect with other people learning and studying the German language, and much more.

German News and Newspapers

libraries.mit.edu/guides/types/flnews/german.html

If you already speak and read German, this site is for you. Here, you will find an extensive list of German newspaper and magazine websites, all of which are written in German.

German Studies Web

12345

www.dartmouth.edu/~wess

An interesting site that is designed to provide access to scholarly resources in German studies, including all German-speaking countries. This site's offerings have undergone an intense selection and evaluation process, making them up-to-date and relevant to anyone studying German.

New English-German Dictionary

12345

www.iee.et.tu-dresden.de/cgi-bin/cgiwrap/wernerr/search.sh

Use this site to translate English words into German and German words into English. According to the site, this free online dictionary contains more than 200,000 translations.

GREEK

English-Greek Dictionary

12345

www.lib.uchicago.edu/efts/Woodhouse

Unlike other online translation dictionaries, this one, based on S. C. Woodhouse's *A Vocabulary of the*

Attic Language, reveals not just the word you're looking for in textual form but also as the word appeared in the aforementioned book. If all online dictionaries were like this one, perhaps everyone would be more interested in etymology.

Greek Alphabet

12345

www.greek-language.com/alphabet

The Greek alphabet shown on this page reveals both the English and Greek upper- and lowercase letter, along with modern Greek pronunciation for each. At the bottom and to the side of this are links to additional Greek language resources.

Greek Language Courses in Greece

12345

www.languagesabroad.co.uk/greek.html

Studying the Greek language online is one thing; traveling to Greece to learn it firsthand is another! Visit this site to learn about Greek language schools in Athens, Thessaloniki, and Crete; and while you're on the site, request a brochure or sign up for a free e-newsletter.

Best Greek and Latin Language Resources

12345

www.cs.utk.edu/~mclennan/OM/grk-lat.html

Managed by Bruce MacLennan of the University of Tennessee, this page is a jumping-off point for lots of interesting information about the ancient Greek language. Here, you will find links to dictionaries, books, ancient Greek alphabetic numerals, and more.

ITALIAN

Istituto Il David Italian Language School

12345

www.davidschool.com

Officially authorized by the Italian Ministry of Education, this school—located in Florence, Italy—offers standard and intensive group and one-on-one Italian language lessons. Additional classes are offered in Italian cooking and wines, business, fashion, and art history and painting. Information on enrollment, prices, accommodations, and dates is available on this site, as are tests and quizzes on general Italian language knowledge.

Italian-Language-Study.org

12345

www.italian-language-study.org

To learn more about the Italian language, its roots and origins, and even statistics on the number of people who speak Italian, visit this site. Click on the Alphabet link for the reduced Latin Italian alphabet or the Modern Italian link for an overview of how this romance language evolved.

Best Learn Italian - From the BBC

www.bbc.co.uk/languages/italian

This site contains a treasure trove of fun and useful information about the Italian language. Presented by the BBC, here you can find everything from holiday phrases and slang to basic grammar and information about living and working in Italy. Be sure to click on the Cool Italian link for audio files or the Gauge Your Level link for a self-test. As they say in Italy, this site should make you *sono strafelice.*

R-O-Matic Italian/English Dictionary

12345

www.aromatic.com/itaeng

For a simple, easy-to-use English-to-Italian and Italian-to-English dictionary, visit this site. You can even add words of your own to the dictionary if you find it to be lacking.

JAPANESE

BJT: Business Japanese Proficiency Test

12345

www.jetro.go.jp/en/bjt

The BJT is a test that measures and evaluates your Japanese communication skills, with a specific emphasis on business-related situations. If you are learning Japanese as a foreign (or as a second) language, and you are a considering conducting in Japan, you should use this site to register to take the BJT.

StudyJapanese.org

1 2 3 4 5

www.studyjapanese.org

StudyJapanese.org was started by a Swede who, in his own words, is "just trying to learn Japanese." Included are lessons, flash cards, information on Japanese grammar, and more.

Best Tada Taku's Glossary

1 2 3 4 5

www.jandodd.com/japan/glossary.htm

Travel writer Jan Dodd brings us this contemporary Japanese glossary of terms and words. Packed with nearly 1,000 entries, this site is a must read for anyone interested in popular Japanese words and phrases.

Your Name in Japanese

1 2 3 4 5

www.japanesetranslator.co.uk/your-name-in-japanese

A fun little site. Enter your first name and click the Translate button for how your name appears when written in Japanese.

LEARNING LANGUAGES

CLAS: Chinese Learner's Alternative Site

1 2 3 4 5

www.sinologic.com/clas

CLAS offers the Chinese learner great resources. In addition to the standard fare of vocabulary words and dictionaries, CLAS offers information on the latest happenings in Chinese language and culture. Including links to Chinese history, religion, philosophy, and more.

Dutch 101

1 2 3 4 5

www.forbeginners.info/dutch

Learn basic Dutch vocabulary and grammar. Unfortunately, this site provides little direction on proper pronunciation.

French Language Course

1 2 3 4 5

www.jump-gate.com/languages/french

An online course in the French language. The course consists of nine lessons and some additional vocabulary. In addition to the lessons, you'll find a section describing French expressions and idioms. Also included are pointers to other French language and culture sites.

Focal an Lae: The Word of the Day in Irish

1 2 3 4 5

w3.lincolnu.edu/~focal

Focal an Lae, literally "the word of the day" in Gaelic, is a site devoted to the Gaelic language spoken in Ireland. It includes back issues of *Focal an Lae* in case you have missed them or just want to build your vocabulary. The site also features other valuable Gaelic language resources such as a list of useful phrases and links to other Gaelic information sites. A good site for beginners.

Foreign Languages for Travelers

1 2 3 4 5

www.travlang.com/languages

A useful site featuring phrases in several languages that can be used by people who are planning trips abroad. Languages covered include Spanish, Portuguese, German, French, and Dutch. Sound clips demonstrating pronunciation can also be found on the site. Markets a line of text-based and voice-recognition translating devices and other translation tools, including translating dictionaries for more than 35 languages.

Gaelic Languages Info

1 2 3 4 5

www.ceantar.org

Collection of resources and pointers for learners and speakers of Irish Gaelic. Resources include links to Irish Gaelic websites, software, and online dictionaries. Although this site mainly lists information relevant to Irish Gaelic, it also includes some information on other Gaelic languages such as Scottish and Manx. There is also a link for information for teachers and linguists.

Learning Catalan on The Internet

12345

www.catalunya-lliure.com/curs/catala.html

This site is a nice starting place for those who are interested in learning Catalan. Included is a brief tutorial, Catalan dictionaries, and links to classes and more information about the language.

A Welsh Course

12345

www.cs.cf.ac.uk/fun/welsh/Welsh.html

A course in the Welsh language. Welsh is a language related to the Gaelic languages of Ireland and Scotland, primarily spoken in Wales. The course is geared toward beginners with an emphasis in developing conversational skills. The site also provides links to other Welsh resources on the Web.

RUSSIAN

English Russian Dictionary

12345

www.russianlessons.net/dictionary/dictionary.php

Just as its name suggests, this site allows you to enter the English spelling of a word and in return receive its Russian equivalent. Very simple and easy-to-use site.

Institute of Modern Russian Culture (IMRC)

www.usc.edu/dept/LAS/IMRC

Augment your Russian language studies with a visit to the IMRC website. Here, you will learn about Russian culture through paintings, illustrations, and photographs. Managed by the University of Southern California, this site offers a wealth of archived materials from both published and unpublished artists.

Lexiteria's Russian Grammar Reference

12345

www.alphadictionary.com/rusgrammar

This site's owner, Pennsylvania-based Lexiteria Corporation, specializes in the creation and maintenance of translation online dictionaries and word lists. Their Russian site, although not particularly appealing on a visual level, far exceeds our expectations from a content perspective, Here, you will find the Cyrillic alphabet, rules of Russian spelling and punctuation, verbal accent patterns, and lots of information on Russian nouns, adjectives, pronouns, and word formation. A must see for anyone serious about studying Russian.

Best MasterRussian.com

12345

masterrussian.com

According to this site, "You don't need to get a Russian visa and buy a ticket to Moscow to learn Russian." MasterRussian.com helps you by providing free grammar and vocabulary tips, and offers opportunities to practice speaking and reading Russian, all the while learning about Russian culture and people. Other site features include free tests and quizzes, homework help, online forums and discussion boards, and three different pronunciation guides.

SIGN LANGUAGE

American Sign Language Browser

commtechlab.msu.edu/sites/aslweb/browser.htm

A very cool site. Maintained by the Michigan State University's Communication Technology Laboratory, this site features thousands of short video clips of ASL signs. From "A Lot" to "Zigzag," if you want to see how to sign it using ASL, this site is for you.

Best National Association of the Deaf

12345 Blog RSS

www.nad.org

The 125-year-old National Association of the Deaf (NAD) is committed to promoting, protecting, and preserving the rights and quality of life of deaf and hard of hearing individuals throughout the United States. A tremendous amount of information and resources can be found on this site, including current data on legal rights, advocacy opportunities, and networking events. Click on the Inside NAD link for membership information or on Advocacy Issues for the latest news on matters of importance to the deaf and hearing impaired.

Sign Language Associates

12345

www.signlanguage.com

If you need a sign interpreter for an upcoming event, or if you yourself are interested in securing sign interpretation jobs, visit this site. Sign Language Associates (SLA) is the oldest and most successful private sign interpreting service provider in the United States. Here, you will find contact information for SLA, job openings, seminar descriptions, and links of interest to deaf consumers.

SignWriting.org

12345

www.signwriting.org

According to this site, "SignWriting is a writing system which uses visual symbols to represent the handshapes, movements, and facial expressions of signed languages. It is an "alphabet"—a list of symbols used to write any signed language in the world." Here, you will learn all about SignWriting and find lots of interesting articles and resources for SignWriting yourself.

SPANISH

Don Quijote

12345

www.donquijote.org

Don Quijote offers several programs for learning Spanish in Spanish-speaking locations, including Granada, Tenerife, Barcelona, and Madrid. There's no better way to learn Spanish than to immerse yourself in it, and there's no better place to immerse yourself than in a country where Spanish is the native tongue. You can also use this site to learn Spanish at home using the online tools. Check out this site to find programs, prices, and schedules.

ForoDeEspanol.com

12345

www.forodeespanol.com

Moderated entirely by volunteers, this site's main feature is its 20+ forums where you can learn and practice your Spanish composition skills with other learners from across the world. Site forums focus on grammar and word games, teaching Spanish as a foreign language, sports, books and films, Spanish for business interactions, societal debates, poetry, and music and songs, just to name a few.

Learn Spanish

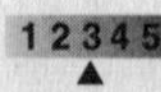

www.studyspanish.com

Learn some basic Spanish vocabulary, grammar, and phrases. Premium pay services are available for the more serious language student. CDs and audio tapes are also available. Also includes a free membership option.

Online Spanish-English Dictionary

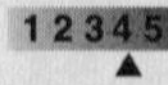

education.yahoo.com/reference/dict_en_es

Maintained by the same folks who publish the American Heritage Dictionary, this site—which is part of Yahoo.com's Education section—allows you to enter a word in either English or Spanish and receive either the Spanish or English translation, both in written and audio form. There are also English and Spanish indexes, which make finding certain words easy.

Best Spanish-Kit's Spanish Learning Tools

12345

www.spanish-kit.net

Spanish-Kit.com is a free educational resource for anyone serious about learning Spanish. Here, you will find lots of information about Spanish grammar and vocabulary, along with a nice collection of Spanish readers that can be downloaded in their entirety free of charge. Launched in 2005, this site is still in its infancy and appears to be growing by leaps and bounds every day.

LAW

ClassActionAmerica.com

www.classactionamerica.com

Learn about ongoing and upcoming class action lawsuits and see if you're eligible to cash in on the billions of dollars a year that go unclaimed. You must sign up to become a member to receive information.

CourtTV

www.courttv.com

CourtTV is a premier cable channel that focuses on all aspects of the criminal justice system. It features fictional shows, actual trials, legal commentary, investigative reports, and documentaries. This site also includes an online store where you can purchase DVDs and TV show merchandise as well as newsletters and a link to jobs available at CourtTV.

divorceLAWinfo.com

www.divorcelawinfo.com

If you're contemplating divorce, you might want to read through the FAQs regarding divorce at this site, which is managed by a legal forms company. You can also hear more about how to represent yourself in a divorce, purchase divorce and separation agreement forms online, and learn about other services available from this company to assist you in getting a divorce. Links to different state divorce laws are also included.

Federal Bureau of Investigation

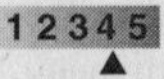

www.fbi.gov

Take a look at the FBI's most wanted list or the monthly list of new criminals at this site, where you can also learn about the agency's activities and where kids can have fun finding out more about crime detection and law enforcement. Up-to-date information on the FBI's mission to combat terrorists as well. A well-organized, comprehensive site. For kids areas, click the Visit Our Kids' Page link and then click the desired age group: K–5th Grade or 6–12 Grades.

FindLaw.com

www.findlaw.com

Like Yahoo! for the law, FindLaw gives you access to virtually any information that's law related, some free and some at a fee. Download forms, search databases of past cases, scope out professional development opportunities, and a lot more at this site. You can also browse legal information on bankruptcy, civil rights, real estate, and more. Also provided is a search tool for finding a lawyer in your area.

FreeAdvice

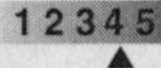

www.freeadvice.com

Explore a wide range of legal topics, research a particular issue, post a message in one of the many Q&A forums, or join a legal chat. Great place for the general public to find information on legal issues. You can also find a lawyer when you search by topic and state.

Internet Legal Resource Guide

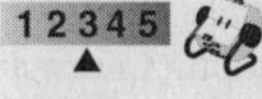

www.ilrg.com

Visitors will find more than 4,000 links to sites around the globe related to the law and the legal profession. Easy to navigate design makes this site simple for anyone to use.

A B C D E F G H I J K L M N O P Q R S T U V W X Y Z

Law Books

12345

www.claitors.com

Purchase law books as well as legal products and supplies at this site. Claitor's also offers one of the largest inventories of government books and papers available for purchase.

LawGuru.com

12345

www.lawguru.com

Have a legal question you'd like the answer to? You'll probably find it at this site in the FAQs section, by searching more than 35,000 legal questions and answers in the bulletin board section (BBS), by searching the more than 500 search engines at the site, or by asking an attorney directly on the BBS system. You can also find thousands of legal forms that may purchased on this site.

Lawyers.com

12345 RSS

www.lawyers.com

Excellent site for tracking down lawyers near you who specialize in various aspects of the law, such as disability, divorce, bankruptcy, and so on. Lawyer.com also provides information on how to select and work effectively with a lawyer who's right for you, and how to better understand whatever legal issue you are currently facing. Use this site to research and browse legal topics, gain access to legal tips, or contact a lawyer.

National Consumer Law Center (NCLC)

12345

www.consumerlaw.org

The National Consumer Law Center works to protect the rights of vulnerable, low-income Americans. This site features publications, information on conferences and training programs, and advice for attorneys and consumers. NCLC job listings are also available through this site.

Best National Crime Prevention Council (NCPC)

12345

www.ncpc.org

Most famous for its "McGruff, the crime dog" campaign to prevent crime, the NCPC site provides information about its programs and upcoming public service announcements. It has a section just for kids, as well as training tools and program ideas to help keep you and your family safe. Excellent site design combined with relevant information for regular people make this an easy Best of the Best pick.

Pritchard Law Webs

www.lawmoose.com/internetlawlib/1.htm

A legal resource originally established by the U.S. House of Representatives as a means of making the law more accessible to average citizens, the website is now managed by a private company. On it, you'll find searchable databases to seek out legal cases of interest, check laws by subject, read laws sorted by state or country, as well as find several other ways to track down law information of interest. Includes information on treaties and international law, law schools and libraries, and legal profession directories.

United States Code

12345

assembler.law.cornell.edu/uscode

Sponsored by Cornell University's Law School, you can use this site to search the entire U.S. code by title and section at this site. This version is generated from the most recent version made available by the U.S. House of Representatives.

WWW Virtual Library–Law

12345

www.law.indiana.edu/v-lib

Search the Indiana University virtual law library by typing in a keyword, or start with a pop-up menu of standard topics, such as business law, contracts, or family law. Or search by information type, such as state government or federal government. A simple, easy-to-use site with a straightforward way to start looking for information.

CYBER LAW & CYBERSPACE ISSUES

Allwhois.com

www.allwhois.com

Type in a website URL and find out who owns it, who registered it, and where the organization is located. A handy resource for anyone needing to know more about a particular site.

Electronic Commerce and Internet Law Resource Center–Perkins Coie, LLP

www.perkinscoie.com

The case digest at Perkins Coie's website aims to provide background information on international cases that impact cyber law issues. The resource center offers recent articles on Internet law. You can also find out about recent litigation in which the firm represented Internet-related clients.

GigaLaw

www.gigalaw.com

Attorney Doug Isenberg created this site to call attention to various news stories about legal issues pertaining to the Internet. GigaLaw.com provides links to current stories about a wide range of topics, including blogging, intellectual property rights, FTC regulation of data brokers, taxing the Internet, and regulating spam. The site features news, articles, a reference library, and discussion forums.

Internet Library of Law and Court Decisions

www.phillipsnizer.com/internetlib.htm

Phillips Nizer, LLP, makes this extensive Internet Library of Law and Court Decisions accessible to all. Simply click a topic for a list of laws and court decisions that apply to the selected topic. This site is excellent for researching Internet law and pinpointing precedents. You can even receive e-mail updates from the site on the latest developments in Internet Law by subscribing to the Internet Law Update electronic newsletter.

Kuesterlaw Technology Law Resources

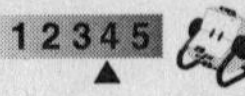

www.kuesterlaw.com

This site is a comprehensive resource for "technology law information, especially including patent, copyright, and trademark law." Created and maintained by Jeffrey R. Kuester, this site also provides a directory of helpful government resources.

LAW SCHOOLS

Association of American Law Schools

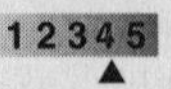

www.aals.org

A nonprofit association of 166 law schools. The purpose of the association is "the improvement of the legal profession through legal education." Use this site to order mailing labels all member institutions, download a free directory of law school deans and professors, and read special reports on issues related to law school education.

Columbia Law School

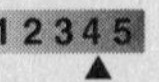

www.law.columbia.edu

Learn more about the resources, students, and faculty at Columbia University through the law school's website. A scrolling Columbia Law news function enables you to click on a story to learn more, and lots of information is available for prospective students.

FindLaw for Students

stu.findlaw.com

FindLaw is a search tool that can help users track down legal resources. FindLaw for students limits the search to law schools and resources connected to law schools, including prelaw, legal careers, and the bar exam. When you don't know where to look for a piece of legal information, check out this site.

Franklin Pierce Law Center

www.fplc.edu

If you're considering law school, check out the Franklin Pierce Law Center. This website provides information about its classes, admission policy, financial aid opportunities, and other features. It also offers additional online resources.

Harvard Law School

www.law.harvard.edu

Whether you're considering a legal career and want to know more about attending the oldest law school in the country or are interested in finding out about jobs at Harvard Law School, this website can tell you just about anything you need to know. Learn more about the admissions process, career counseling, students, faculty, facilities, programs, and publications. You can even guide yourself through an online walking tour of the Law School campus.

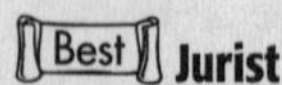 Jurist

jurist.law.pitt.edu

The University of Pittsburgh School of Law manages this site, which was set up to assist law students and teachers alike stay current on legal information and to share ideas on legal events and rulings of the day.

Kaplan Test Prep and Admissions

www.kaptest.com

From Kaplan, everything you need to know about the LSAT and law school—including scoring, sections, and dates and registration—is available. Click on the More link next to Law. The site also includes links to help you the through law school admissions process and applying for financial aid. Access to law schools and law student resources can also be found on this site.

Law School Admission Council Online

www.lsac.org

If you're planning on going to law school, one of your first hurdles, after you get your undergraduate degree, is to get a decent score on your LSAT. The LSAC (Law School Admission Council) can help you prepare for the test and take care of all the other aspects of applying for admission and financial aid. It can even help you find accredited schools.

Law School Discussion.org

www.lawschooldiscussion.org

Law school discussion forums cover topics such as selecting a law school, taking the LSAT, finding law school rankings, and obtaining letters of recommendation. Links to other resources, including blogs and book reviews are available on this site.

LawSchool.com

www.lawschool.com

Impressive collection of news reports, articles, and resources relating to law schools. Find law school rankings, tips on preparing for exams, law reviews, bar exam information, and more. Links to additional resources on prelaw and other topics.

Stanford Law School

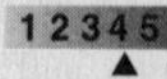

www.law.stanford.edu

Admissions, administrative, and faculty information are all available at Stanford Law School's site, which also provides school news and information about upcoming events.

University of Chicago Law School

www.law.uchicago.edu

A complete guide to applying to and attending the University of Chicago Law School, with information about the process for prospective students,as well as information for current students on upcoming events at the school.

Yale Law School Home Page

www.law.yale.edu

Find everything you wanted to know about this highly competitive law school at its website, which features admissions information, faculty and student data, a library overview, law school publications, and information about life as a Yale Law School student.

LEGAL ORGANIZATIONS

ACLU Freedom Network

RSS

www.aclu.org

The home page for the American Civil Liberties Union takes you to the latest happenings from Congress and what's happening in the nation's courts. You can also join the ACLU, browse its cyberstore, and read about current events. Other links take you to highlights of cases in which the ACLU is involved.

Best American Bar Association (ABA)

www.abanet.org

The American Bar Association web site has a number of great features, including links to information about the various programs of the ABA (each entity has its own link), a calendar of events, and information of general interest to the public.

American Immigration Lawyers Association (AILA)

www.aila.org

Links to information about the AILA, membership information, and AILA conferences can be found on this robust site. Also, writings about immigration as it pertains to the United State of America, the role of immigration lawyers, and recent legislative affairs that affect immigration law, can be found on this site. Provided, too, is a searchable index of AILA members and immigration lawyers on the Web.

Association of Corporate Counsel

www.acca.com

At the official site of the Association of Corporate Counsel, members of the organization can network with fellow corporate attorneys, find a local chapter, investigate professional conferences, and access information services.

Association of Trial Lawyers of America

www.atlanet.org

Exchange information and ideas with fellow members of the ATLA, find a lawyer, look into conferences and professional development opportunities, get up-to-date information on recent court decisions, and learn more about member benefits at this site.

National Association of Attorneys General

www.naag.org

Visit this site to learn more about the role of the attorney general in your state, and catch up on recent legal decisions and actions taken by the National Association of Attorneys General. Click on the Attorneys General link for an updated list of state AGs.

National District Attorneys Association (NDAA)

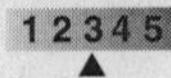

www.ndaa-apri.org

Members of the NDAA can find out about upcoming conferences, publications, and resources, all of which are available on this site. Click on Links to find resources related to child abuse, gun violence prosecution, hate crimes, traffic laws, and preventing violence against women.

National Lawyers Association (NLA)

www.nla.org

The National Lawyers Associations was founded by attorneys for attorneys "who do not want their bar association taking stands on issues without their prior approval." Here, you can learn more about the organization, read related articles, become a member, and join in spirited discussions of various issues affecting lawyers and the legal profession.

LEGAL PUBLICATIONS

ALSO (American Law Sources Online!)

www.lawsource.com/also

Although this site may not be the most visually appealing site on the Net, it does contain a wealth of information, including a comprehensive, uniform, and useful compilation of links to all online sources of American law that are available without charge. Source documents are stored in various file formats in many separately maintained databases located in several countries. Scroll down the home page to find links to information from each state.

American Bar Association Journal

www.abanet.org/journal

The American Bar Association publishes its own journal, and this is the online home of that journal. This site features current news items that attorneys will probably find interesting. Visit this site to subscribe to the *Journal*, check the FAQs or alerts, and peruse the latest news from the world of law.

European Journal of International Law

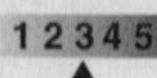

www.ejil.org

Website of one of the world's leading international law journals. An integral part of the *European Journal of International Law,* this website provides many features unavailable in the printed version of the journal, including links, e-newsletters, and a discussion area.

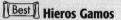

Best Hieros Gamos

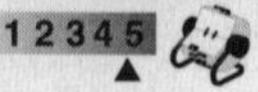

www.hg.org

Comprehensive resource for legal professionals, law students, and persons seeking law-related information. Links include employment, bar associations, legal associations, law schools, publishers, law firms, law sites, government sites, vendors, and online services. The site is available in English, Spanish, German, French, and Italian.

Law.com

www.law.com

Updated daily, this site "connects legal professionals to more than 20 award-winning national and regional legal publications online, including The American Lawyer, The National Law Journal, New York Law Journal and Legal Times." Articles on high-profile cases and suits, courtroom updates, and new rulings are just some of the interesting and resourceful links you'll find on this site. Also included is access to national legal journals online, the marketplace, an employment center, and law firms online.

Law Journals and Publications

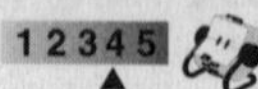

www.ilrg.com/journals.html

The Internet Legal Research Group has assembled this collection of links to more than 100 law journals and publications on the Web.

Law Library of Congress

www.loc.gov/law/public/law.html

Internet home of the world's largest law library, with a collection of more than two million volumes spanning the ages and covering virtually every jurisdiction in the world.

TheLawyer.com

www.the-lawyer.co.uk

This U.K.-based legal site offers news on the profession, reports on special sectors, and job openings.

Lawyers Weekly

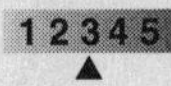

www.lawyersweekly.com

Lawyers Weekly brings tens of thousands of readers up-to-the-minute news on the cases and developments that directly affect their legal practice. This site provides insight from the country's leading experts on how to win more cases, avoid malpractice traps, practice more efficiently, and prosper. Focuses on small law firms.

National Law Journal

www.law.com/jsp/nlj/index.jsp

Stay current on legal issues through this print and online publication by reading the latest news and searching past issues. Use this site to access white papers, search for legal experts, find a court reporter, search for verdicts, look up legal terms, and buy books and other related products.

Nolo Press

www.nolo.com

Publishing legal information in plain English for more than 30 years, Nolo Press has empowered average citizens to understand and fight for their rights. Here, you'll find Nolo's Legal Encyclopedia, a law FAQ, financial calculators, resources for various types of cases and legal issues, and a wide selection of Nolo Press books, which you can purchase online.

LITERATURE

American Authors on the Web

www.lang.nagoya-u.ac.jp/~matsuoka/AmeLit.html

Search the lengthy list of American authors alphabetically to learn more about the individuals and their work. Some authors feature ongoing discussion groups that you can join. Also included are links to related websites.

American and English Literature Resources

library.scsu.ctstateu.edu/litbib.html

This extensive bibliography of resources pertaining to American and English literature attempts to zero in on the best resources available on the Web, including where you can find electronic versions of classic texts and the home pages of various authors. Sites are organized first by American literature and then by English literature. These main categories are further subdivided by genre.

Bartleby.com

12345

www.bartleby.com

This site bills itself as "the preeminent publisher of literature, reference and verse providing students, researchers, and the intellectually curious with unlimited access to books and information on the Web, free of charge." In other words, this site provides the electronic texts of many classical literary works—poems, plays, novels, and short stories. It's also a great place to find biographies of your favorite authors. This site also includes searchable databases of reference, verse, fiction, and nonfiction.

Bibliomania

bibliomania.net

This ultimate source of information for book buyers, sellers, and collectors is "intended to inform and educate book enthusiasts so that they can make wise decisions in their internet transactions." Includes links to book awards, book collecting, book fairs, and more.

BookNotes

www.booknotes.org/home/index.asp

"A companion Website to C-SPAN's Sunday author interview series, BookNotes." Find out which author will be appearing on this week's show, watch a video clip of the interview, and scan the online resource section to read first chapters of featured books or to look at transcripts of past interviews.

BookWire Index–Author Indexes

www.bookwire.com

An index of author and literature sites that can be searched and accessed via BookWire. A huge resource of useful sites, including reviews, book lists, forums, and publishers home pages.

Best Candlelight Stories

www.candlelightstories.com

This award-winning site is a repository for children's online literature. From Rumpelstiltskin to Thumbelina, you can read your children these online classics. Included is a bookstore, international gallery, and spelling machine game. Story and illustration submissions are welcome. This site links to Amazon.com, where you can purchase books. Good site for teachers.

Comparative Literature Studies

12345

www.cl-studies.org

Comparative Literature Studies is "a journal devoted to the comparative research in literary history, the history of ideas, critical theory, studies between authors, and literary relations within and beyond the Western tradition." Here, you can check out the titles of the articles in the current edition, search the archives, and choose to subscribe to the journal.

Critical Reading: A Guide

12345

www.brocku.ca/english/jlye/criticalreading.html

Professor John Lye has developed this critical reading guide for his first-year literature students. It provides a step-by-step, disciplined approach to interpreting literary works. If you already graduated from college, you'll probably read this thinking, "Why didn't my teacher tell me this?"

éCLAT

ccat.sas.upenn.edu/Complit/Eclat

ÉCLAT (Essential Comparative Literature And Theory) is a directory of comparative literature sites, programs, and resources on the Web.

The Electronic Text Center at the University of Virginia

12345

etext.lib.virginia.edu

This excellent and thorough site contains thousands of texts, in modern, early modern, and middle English, plus French, German, Japanese, and Latin. Here, you'll find fiction, science fiction, poetry, theology, essays, histories, and many other types of materials. Although a huge number of these texts are freely available, some texts are available only to users at the University of Virginia; the licensors of these texts have not permitted the university to make them widely available.

Literary Criticism

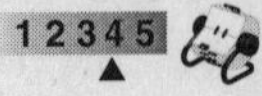

www.ipl.org/div/litcrit

This is the Internet Public Library's directory of literary criticism, which points the way to critical and biographical websites about authors and their works that you can browse by author, by title, or by nationality and literary period. Great site for researching the existing criticism about a specific literary work.

Literary Resources on the Net

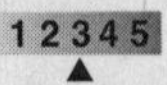

andromeda.rutgers.edu/~jlynch/Lit

This directory of literary resources maintained by Jack Lynch of Rutgers University features links related to various literary periods and nationalities, including Classical, Biblical, Medieval, Renaissance, Romantic, Victorian British, American, and Women's Literature and Feminism. Also includes links to literary theory.

The Literature Network

12345

www.online-literature.com

The Literature Network is a cool place to hang out and learn about the most famous authors and their works. Scroll down the page to view a list of links to authors, and then click the author of your choice to view a brief biography and links to his or her most famous literary works, if they're available. This site also has links to quotes, Shakespeare, and more; a Literature Forum is also available if you have questions about literature. The site is constantly acquiring new texts, so check back often.

Literature.org–The Online Literature Library

12345

www.literature.org/authors/baum-l-frank/the-wonderful-wizard-of-oz

Part of the Knowledge Matters Ltd. literacy series, this site offers the complete text of *The Wonderful Wizard of Oz*, linkable by chapter. Also offered are other titles by L. Frank Baum in the *Wizard of Oz* series.

A B C D E F G H I J K M N O P Q R S T U V W X Y Z

Michigan eLibrary

12345

mel.lib.mi.us

A project sponsored in part by Michigan's libraries, this site includes collections of online excerpts, stories, and reports in categories such as education, humanities and the arts, and science and the environment. It also includes a reference desk as well as a periodicals section.

The Mystery Books

12345

www.bookspot.com/mystery.htm

Bookspot's mystery books features links to a Mystery Guide, a Bloodstained Bookshelf, The Thrilling Detective, and other mystery literature sites you might find interesting. There are also links to authors, publishers, and reviews.

Related Site

www.cluelass.com

Nobel Laureates

12345

nobelprize.org/literature/laureates

Complete list of winners of the Nobel Prize in Literature from 1901 to the present. Click an author's name to access the author's biography, bibliography, acceptance speech, and other resources.

Project Gutenberg

12345

www.gutenberg.org

This award-winning site contains a collection of electronically stored books, mostly classics, which you can download for free and view offline. The online book catalog lets you browse by author, title, or language. Gopher searches for your favorite author reveal various options for downloading.

Pulitzer Prizes

12345

www.pulitzer.org

Search the archive to find names of Pulitzer Prize winners since the awards' inception, read about the history of the awards, and download entry forms for consideration this year.

The Romance Reader

12345

www.theromancereader.com

Before you buy that next romance novel, scan the thousands of reviews available at this site, which is dedicated to romance novel fans worldwide. While you're at the site, you can read biographical information, learn more about other members' interests and feedback, and share your thoughts on the quality of recent romance titles you've read. The *TRR Newsletter* provides updates and reviews.

Victorian Women Writers

12345

www.indiana.edu/~letrs/vwwp

From Indiana University, this great site features scads of nineteenth-century texts. The works, selected with the assistance of the university Advisory Board, include anthologies, novels, political pamphlets, religious tracts, children's books, and volumes of poetry and verse drama. Searchable database is also included on this site.

MAGIC

All Magic Guide

12345

allmagicguide.com

Learn new magic tricks, find out about upcoming TV and radio programs on magic, shop for magic tricks, and get firsthand advice on performing magic from fellow magicians.RELATED

David Blaine

12345

www.davidblaine.com

David Blaine, the masochist of magic, has made quite a name for himself by trying to freeze, starve, drown, and otherwise torture himself in the name of magic. But he's one of the best sleight-of-hand magicians in the business. Here, you can check out his official site and find out about his latest antics

Earth's Largest Magic Shop

12345

www.elmagicshop.com

You can find lots of stuff for everyone, from the beginner to the professional. Check out the Beginner's section and the Free Trick area.

Best eCardTricks

12345

www.ecardtricks.com

eCardTricks features video demonstrations of card tricks and instructions on performing the tricks. This site also offers an online version of the shell game, in which you try to outsmart the computer, and a crystal ball you can use to peer into your future. Links to other magic sites and stores round out the selection, making this full-featured site our selection as Best of the Best for magic.

Ellusionist

12345

www.ellusionist.com

Brad Christian and the rest of team Ellusionist can help you learn some amazing sleight-of-hand illusions you can perform anywhere, and you can order the training DVDs online. This site features easy, one-click access to several sections, including Store, Forums, Free Stuff, and Magic Reviews. You can see some of the tricks in action and preview the training videos before buying them.

eyetricks.com

12345

www.eyetricks.com

eyetricks.com specializes in optical illusions, but it also features a fair share of brain teasers, games, 3D oddities, and other mind-warping illusions. The opening page displays links to several optical illusions along with a link to the complete index of optical illusions. This site also features links to magic stores, its magic shop, freebies, and other related sites.

HappyMagic.com

12345

www.happymagic.com

The folks at HappyMagic have done the sifting for you; you don't have to worry about getting a trick that you will just throw in a drawer and never use again.

International Conservatory of Magic

www.magicschool.com

This site contains more than 2,000 pages of magic. I.C.O.M Online provides comprehensive, first-class instruction in the art of being a magician, offering personal live instruction via lecture tours, 24-hour-a-day website-based text and virtual lessons, Internet chat, and live Web audio lectures. All aspects of magic are covered, including sleight of hand, illusion, presentation, showmanship, promotion, and theory.

MAGIC

www.magicmagazine.com

The largest-selling magic journal in the world. Get a taste of the magazine here. If you like what you see, you can subscribe easily.

Magic Directory

www.magicdirectory.com

If you're looking for magic, magicians, tricks, or something else related to the world of magic and you don't know where to start, start here. This vast directory of links can help you track down just what you need. Links are organized in categories including Magic Tricks, Magicians, and Magic Publications. Or, you can enter a search term to search the entire directory or only a specified category.

Magic Show

www.allmagic.com

This site features a host of magic tricks grouped by Diversions, Card Magic, Stage Magic, and Close-Up Magic. Each link calls up an article that explains a specific trick. Nice, clear photos show you, in addition to telling you how to perform the trick.

Magictricks.com

www.magictricks.com

Online magic store with many sources of magic history, museums, facts, and places to visit.

TV Magic Guide.com

www.tvmagicguide.com

Here, you can check the TV listings for the upcoming week to learn about scheduled magic programs and interviews with magicians. Some free video clips are available to advertise videos that are for sale.

MANGA (SEE GRAPHIC NOVELS)

MAPS

David Rumsey Historical Map Collection

12345

www.davidrumsey.com

With a focus on rare eighteenth and nineteenth century North and South American cartographic historical materials, this online collection features more than 6,400 maps, which you can view by using your web browser, via Java, or by using a special GIS viewer that features map overlays. The collection also features historical maps of the world, Europe, Asia, and Africa. A great place for geography teachers to introduce students to cartography.

Finding Your Way with Map and Compass

12345

www.erg.usgs.gov/isb/pubs/factsheets/fs03501.html

Detailed instruction on the use of maps and compasses from the U.S. Geological Survey Department. Also includes the fundamentals of topographical map making and scale.

Best Google Earth

12345

earth.google.com

If you haven't yet checked out Google Earth, you're the only one on the planet who hasn't, so get to it. Google Earth is a free utility you can download and install on your computer and pull up satellite images, maps, and 3D images of just about anywhere in the world simply by specifying the address or location. Anyone in the world can contribute content to Google Earth. Google Earth combines the power of the Google search engine with the vast resources on the Web, including satellite images, maps, and photographs, to present a searchable database of the earth's surface. At this site, you can download and install the free version of Google Earth and use it to take a virtual tour of the globe.

Google Maps

12345

maps.google.com

Google Maps provides street maps and driving directions for various towns and cities. For a map of an area type in the desired location and click Search. For driving directions, click the Driving Directions link and then enter the address of your starting location and desired destination and click Search. You can also enter a search string, such as "hotels in chicago" to bring up a map showing the locations of popular hotels in the Chicago area.

> **Tip:** On Google's opening search page, you can type an address in the Search box and press Enter to call up a link to a map.

GraphicMaps.com

12345

www.graphicmaps.com/graphic_.htm

Custom map company features downloadable maps you can use in PowerPoint presentations, on websites, in real estate businesses, and so forth. Maps are much more basic, making them perfect for use in presentations.

MapQuest

1 2 3 4 5

www.mapquest.com

Excellent and resourceful guide for those who are planning to travel in North America. Has travel guides, trip information, clickable maps, directions, and so much more. Share plans and tips with fellow vacationers, get relocation information, or order a road atlas on CD-ROM. Although Google Earth has earned its spot as the best of the best website in the Maps group, MapQuest is still much better at helping you plot a route from point A to point B.

Maps.com

1 2 3 4 5

www.maps.com

Huge map and travel store, where you can purchase and download printable maps or order printed maps.

Maps of the United States

1 2 3 4 5

www.lib.utexas.edu/maps/united_states.html

High-quality electronic maps cataloged by state from the Perry-Castañeda Library Map Collection. Most maps in PDF format.

National Geographic's Map Machine

1 2 3 4 5

plasma.nationalgeographic.com/mapmachine

Unique interactive map that can zoom in on any location in the United States. Simply type the name of a location—city, state, country, or ZIP code—and press Enter, and the Map Machine pulls up a list of links to all sorts of interesting maps, including street maps, aerial maps, satellite maps, and census maps. Excellent little kiosk for exploring an area from different angles.

Windows Live Local

1 2 3 4 5

local.live.com

Microsoft's Windows Live Local map site helps you route your journey from point A to point B anywhere in the United States. This trip tick program provides some additional tools, including a scratch pad, pushpin locators, and Windows Live Local help to bring you up to speed.

MARKETING

Adweek Online

12345

www.adweek.com

Adweek Online is the electronic edition of a popular print magazine that focuses on advertising and marketing. It features the inside scoop on what's going on in the advertising and marketing departments of high-profile companies and corporations.

antfarm interactive

12345

www.antfarminteractive.com

This is the home of antfarm interactive, one of the more Internet-savvy brand-building and strengthening companies on the Web. If you're looking to build a brand presence, antfarm interactive can help.

Brandweek Magazine

12345

www.brandweek.com

Brandweek covers news and information about the U.S. marketing industry and focuses on all levels of the brand activation process. The magazine features several special reports every year, including Marketers of the Year, Next Generation Marketers (under 40), Guerrilla Marketers, and Superbrands. Its writers and editors focus on the top 2,000 brands that spend $250 billion on media in the United States each year. Excellent website both in content and design.

ClickZ Network

12345 Blog RSS

www.clickz.com

ClickZ is the "largest resource of interactive marketing news, information, commentary, advice, opinion, research, and reference in the world, online or off." This site presents its content in several sections including News, Experts, Stats, Features, and Resources. Excellent site for marketing professionals.

CommerceNet

www.commerce.net

Provides its users with a list of more than 20,000 commercial Web URLs, an 800-numbers directory, and a list of Internet consultants. Daily news updates keep users informed of events on the Internet.

Direct Marketing Association

12345

www.the-dma.org

The Direct Marketing Association (The DMA) is the largest trade association for businesses that are interested and involved in direct, database, and interactive global marketing. Here, you can learn more about the DMA, become a member, and access its services.

DMI Music & Media Solutions

12345

www.dmiworldwide.com

DMI Music & Media Solutions takes an innovative approach to marketing by helping clients use music to connect consumers to their products. They've worked with Victoria's Secret, United Airlines, Purina, and other large companies to introduce music into their marketing plans with great success.

ESOMAR

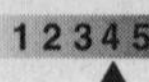

www.esomar.org

ESOMAR is an international organization of marketing and opinion research and professions. ESOMAR is devoted to promoting the use of opinion and market research to improve decision making in both business and society at large.

The GreenBook

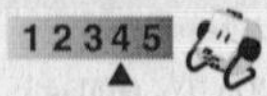

www.greenbook.org

Looking for a marketing research firm? Then the *GreenBook* should be your first stop. It is the annual directory of marketing research firms that can be ordered in print form here or searched free online.

Guerrilla Marketing

www.gmarketing.com

Read daily or bimonthly material from Jay Conrad Levinson, Mr. Guerrilla Marketing, as well as search the site's archives for useful guerrilla marketing strategies detailed by other marketing pros. You can find plenty of information here, as well as details on Jay's latest book and several audio recordings of interviews with Jay.

KnowThis.com

www.knowthis.com

A reference site consisting of thousands of sites having to do with marketing, advertising, and promotion. Get a basic course in marketing or delve deep to find out what an effective website looks like. Whether you're a marketing student or professional, you can find plenty of excellent, up-to-date information at this site, our Best of the Best selection in the Marketing category.

> **Tip:** KnowThis contributes information on marketing to the WWW Virtual Library. Click the WWW Virtual Library icon in the upper-right corner of the opening page to access information in a host of other subject areas.

LitLamp

www.litlamp.com

Learn how to promote your business by sponsoring an organization. LitLamp is a community of more than 30,000 sponsors and agencies that offer advertising in exchange for sponsorships.

Marketing

www.marketingclick.com

Marketing professionals can access the latest industry news, feature articles, and other information about Internet marketing, direct marketing, public relations, promotions, and advertising at this site, which provides a research library, discussion forums, and buyers' guides.

MarketingTerms.com

www.marketingterms.com

This list of marketing terms is an excellent reference tool for students of Internet marketing. This site includes links to Web hosting definitions, Internet marketing terms and acronyms, marketing education, and other marketing references. A good place to start searching for information.

MRA: Marketing Research Association

www.mra-net.org

Dedicated to "advancing the practical application, use, and understanding of the opinion and marketing research profession," MRA features research tools, publications about marketing and opinion polls, software tools, and more. Distance-learning programs, video training, and a career guide are also available.

Reveries.com

www.reveries.com

Available only online, this marketing magazine reads less like a marketing magazine and more like a newspaper focused on the oddest daily stories. But that's the point behind this innovative marketing rag—it flings open the curtains to reveal the most intriguing consumer behavior that's currently acting itself out in the marketplace. Even if you're not in marketing, check out this site to wash the cobwebs out of your brain.

Sales and Marketing Executives International

www.smei.org

Sales & Marketing Executives International (SMEI) is "the only worldwide knowledge-growth and relationship-building forum created for sales and marketing executives. SMEI fills a void by providing a personal and professional community devoted to providing knowledge, growth, leadership and connections between peers in both sales and marketing." This site features more than 200,000 searchable articles covering all areas of sales and marketing.

Sales and Marketing Management Magazine

www.salesandmarketing.com

This is the website of *Sales and Marketing Management* magazine, which is devoted to providing its readers with "easy access to the most relevant trends, strategies, exclusive research, expert voices, and cutting-edge case studies designed to help them sell more, manage better, and market smarter." Here, you can read sample articles and sign up for a subscription.

MARRIAGE

Alliance for Marriage

12345

www.allianceformarriage.org

Married couples are often too busy trying to make it through the day to support pro-marriage legislation. The Alliance for Marriage promotes pro-marriage legislation to prevent overtaxing couples and families and support families in their quest to strengthen their family bonds. Here, you can learn more about the alliance and what its doing on the behalf of married couples and families. Site also features some excellent and timely articles on the topic of marriage.

American Association for Marriage and Family Therapy

12345

www.aamft.org

AAMFT represents "the professional interests of more than 23,000 marriage and family therapists throughout the United States, Canada and abroad." For marriage counselors, family therapists, and others in the marriage and family therapy field, this site offers a wealth of information about upcoming events, seminars, legislation, and other resources and news of interest. Couples and families can also find some solid information about what marriage and family therapy can do to help and search for a therapist near them.

BellaOnline Marriage Site

12345 RSS

www.bellaonline.com/site/marriage

This site offers some excellent and timely articles about marriage. To go directly to a topic of interest, click one of the links in the Subjects column off to the left. Or, check out the feature articles on the right.

Best Divorce Busting

12345

www.divorcebusting.com

If your soul mate has ever told you, "I love you but I'm not in love with you anymore," then visit this site for a translation of what that means and what you and your significant other can do to revitalize the passion you once felt for one another. At this site, Michele Weiner-Davis singlehandedly confronts rampant divorce in the United States by encouraging couples to stay together and work together to deepen their relationships and improve their sex lives. Visit this site to test your relationship IQ, read up on the Divorce Remedy, sample some chapters from Michele's many books, and find out about other products and services that can help you get your marriage back on track.

Smart Marriages

12345

www.smartmarriages.com

Smart Marriages is the Internet home of the Coalition for Marriages, Family and Couples Education. This site functions as an online kiosk and meeting place for couples to locate marriage and relationship counselors, find relationship courses and workshops, and assist marriage counselors and other interested professionals in their pursuit of continuing education. Site features cartoons, quotes, and even an Ask Dr. Romance area.

Worldwide Marriage Encounters

12345

www.wwme.org

Worldwide Marriage Encounter "offers a weekend experience designed to give married couples the opportunity to learn a technique of loving communication that they can use for the rest of their lives." If your marriage isn't exactly on the rocks, but you want to add back that spark you felt when you first met, a weekend marriage encounter might just do the trick. Visit this site to learn more about these encounters and find one near you.

MARTIAL ARTS

Century Fitness

www.centuryfitness.com

Mega-store for exercise and fitness products, this site features a martial arts section, where you can shop for everything from uniforms and sparring gear to weapons and nutritional supplements.

Martial Arts Books and Videos

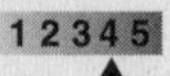

www.turtlepress.com

Dozens of free martial arts video clips, book excerpts, and articles, plus martial arts books and videos for sale.

MartialArts.org

www.martialarts.org

MartialArts.org is a well-designed site devoted to introducing and educating visitors to the various styles of martial arts. However, this site offers a wide variety of content for beginners, experts, students, and teachers. It includes information on the martial arts business, articles on instruction and school management, tips on diet and fitness, and much more. If you have a broadband connection, check out the Media tab for a host of training video clips and audio clips.

MartialArtsMart.com

store.martialartsmart.net

More than 3,000 pieces of martial arts equipment, accessories, and supplies are available here. Choose from Chinese, Japanese, Filipino, Korean, and Thai martial arts.

Best MartialInfo.com

www.martialinfo.com

This huge information kiosk for everything related to martial arts, features articles, biographies, descriptions of the various styles, photo galleries, and videos. Search for instructors, shop for equipment and clothing, read product reviews, and much more. If you're interested in martial arts, be sure to bookmark this site for quick return visits.

Qi: The Journal of Traditional Eastern Health and Fitness

www.qi-journal.com

Features in-depth information on Chinese culture, traditional medicine, and research; links; a calendar of events; *Qi Journal* articles; and a complete catalog of items related to the internal martial arts, Chinese culture, and the traditional healing arts.

Real Combat Online

www.kungfuonline.com

This site is for hardcore, brutal, hand-to-hand combat. On the other hand, it's realistic and an excellent source for law enforcement.

TigerStrike.com

1 2 3 4 5

www.tigerstrike.com

Whether you need uniforms, sparring gear, weapons, or other martial arts equipment or apparel, this site claims that it can provide your order faster and cheaper than anyone else can.

CAPOEIRA

Capoeira Arts

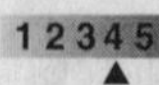

www.capoeiraarts.com

Capoeira Arts is a "colorful multipurpose global village where you can sip a cappucino to the rhythmic beat of a berimbau. Most of the time you can watch a Capoeira class practicing sweeps, high kicks and handstands. You can consume your meal to the mesmerizing background of the musical instruments and chanting." At this site, you can sample the ambience and purchase many of the same products that you can pick up at the village in Berkeley, California: music, books, videos, and instruments. You can also find out about classes being offered.

Capoeira.com

www.capoeira.com

Capoeira.com is an online community of Capoeiristas who regularly post articles and photos related to the topic on this central meeting place. If you're interested in hanging out with fellow Capoeiristas, this is the place for you. Tabbed navigation makes it easy to move from one section to the next: Welcome, Articles, Calendar, Forum, Gallery, and Sign Up!

Capoeirista.com

www.capoeirista.com

This site doesn't look like much when you first open the page, but it offers a great primer on capoeirista. Site includes a glossary, brief history, a list of capoeirista masters, links to music, and a respectable directory of schools listed by country. Beginners should check out the FAQs to get up to speed. Discussion forums can also help you connect with others who are interested in capoeirista.

Planet Capoeira.com

www.planetcapoeira.com

Planet Capoeira is a magazine devoted to the study and practice of Capoeira. At this site, you can subscribe to the magazine, but the site offers little in the way of articles from the magazine. The purpose of the site is to encourage and support the capoeira community. Here, you can find discussion forums, blogs, an online store, and more.

JUDO

International Judo Federation

www.ijf.org

This site has background information on the federation, as well as judo regulations, history, national bodies, and tournament results. Site also features video clips of recent competitions.

Kodokan Judo Institute

www.kodokan.org

Home of the Kodokan Judo Institute, this site provides information about the institute and the origin of Kodokan Judo. Links to other judo sites, information about upcoming events, and an online store are all featured here.

USA Judo

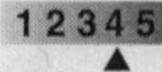

www.usjudo.org

The national governing body for the sport of judo in the United States, USA Judo is responsible for selecting and preparing teams for international competition. Here, you can learn more about the organization, its teams and coaches, tournament results, and more.

JUJITSU

International Ju-Jitsu Federation

1 2 3 4 5

www.jjifweb.com

The JJIF is "the international forum for Ju-Jitsu where the National Official Sport Authorities can debate issues related to the practice of Ju-Jitsu in order to establish International Programmes and activities, and in order to elect the institutions, which will implement them." This site features general information about Ju-Jitsu, news, a calendar, membership information, competitions, games, and referees.

Ultimate Jujitsu

1 2 3 4 5

www.ultimatejujitsu.com

Ultimate Jujitsu focuses on promoting and supporting a community interested in exchanging information on jujitsu. Hence, the site opens with access to its discussion forums. You can click the Information link to display a brief history of jujitsu or click Techniques for links to one-page illustrated cheat sheets on specific techniques. Site also features information on worldwide events, book reviews, and a gallery.

KUNG FU

Authentic Kung Fu

1 2 3 4 5

www.authentickungfu.com

This site presents some good information on the Authentic Kung Fu Association, on Praying Mantis and Wing Chun Kung Fu, on Tai Chi Chuan, and on the philosophy behind the martial arts.

Chinese Kung Fu Wu Su Association

1 2 3 4 5

www.kungfu-wusu.com

One of the few martial arts academies in the West that offers instruction in traditional Chinese kung fu. View a schedule of events and FAQ and meet Grandmaster Alan Lee and other masters of the temple.

Kung Fu Magazine

1 2 3 4 5

ezine.kungfumagazine.com

This online version of *Kung Fu* magazine provides information and entertainment related to the Chinese martial and healing arts. Online features of the magazine include the e-zine, Kungfu Forums, Kungfu resources, and more.

SHOTOKAN

Shotokan Karate of America

1 2 3 4 5

www.ska.org

A nonprofit karate organization founded in 1955 by Tsutomu Ohshima, who is also recognized as the chief instructor of many other national Shotokan organizations worldwide. Some excellent background information to get visitors up to speed.

TAE KWON DO

General Tae Kwon Do Info

1 2 3 4 5

www.barrel.net

Covers tae kwon do techniques, competitions, history, and belt requirements; includes links.

A B C D E F G H I J K L M N O P Q R S T U V W X Y Z

A B C D E F G H I J K L N O P Q R S T U V W X Y Z

Unofficial Tae Kwon Do Hyung Resource Page

1 2 3 4 5

tkd.paperwindow.com

Descriptions of many of the forms you need to know to master tae kwon do. This site's mission is to provide serious students of Tae Kwon Do with information that augment the instruction they already receive and provide jumping-off points from which students can pursue their many varied interests across the full spectrum of tae kwon do.

The World Taekwondo Federation

1 2 3 4 5

www.wtf.org

The World Taekwondo Federation is "the International Federation governing the sport of Taekwondo and is a member of the Association of Summer Olympic International Federations. Whether you're a competitor or a fan, you can find plenty of information at this site concerning the background of taek won do and the rules that govern competitions. Site also provides details about upcoming events.

TAI CHI

International Taoist Tai Chi Society

1 2 3 4 5

www.taoist.org

Founded by Master Moy Lin-Shin, this international society is dedicated to making Taoist tai chi available to everyone. If you're interested in learning Tai Chi, this is a great place to gather information and find out where to go for more in-depth instruction.

Taoism and the Philosophy of Tai Chi Chuan

1 2 3 4 5

www.chebucto.ns.ca/Philosophy/Taichi/taoism.html

Comprehensive history of Taoism showing the connection between Taoism and tai chi. The site design could use some work, but the content is solid.

Wudang.com

1 2 3 4 5

www.wudang.com

This beautiful site contains information about the history, practice, and philosophy of tai chi and several other martial arts.

MATHEMATICS

AAA Math

12345

www.aaamath.com

This site features hundreds of pages that teach basic math skills to students in grades K–8. Each page provides an explanation of the basic concept being taught, interactive practice, and several challenge games. Subjects covered range from addition and subtraction to algebra and statistics.

American Mathematical Society

12345

www.ams.org

Home of the American Mathematical Society. Offers professional memberships. Publishes electronic journals; books on math; and the fee-based MathSci database, which features comprehensive coverage of research in mathematics, computer science, and statistics.

Ask Dr. Math

12345

mathforum.org/dr.math/dr-math.html

Math question and answer page, where you can post your math question to have it answered by a student or professor at Drexel University. Before posting a question, browse the archive to see if it has already been answered.

eFunda

12345

www.efunda.com

Short for engineering fundamentals, eFunda provides more than 30,000 pages packed with basic information about engineering, along with a collection of engineering calculators. Here, you can find information about materials, designs, manufacturing processes, along with unit conversions, formulae, and basic mathematical principles. Several conversion programs are available that you can download and install on your Palm computer.

Egyptian Mathematics

12345

www.eyelid.co.uk/numbers.htm

Learn about the Egyptian math system and how the Egyptians used math in their architecture. Free Egyptian temples screensaver. Links to Amazon.com for online shopping.

Eric Weisstein's World of Mathematics

12345

mathworld.wolfram.com

This comprehensive encyclopedia of mathematics includes hundreds of definitions and explanations of topics ranging from algebra and geometry to calculus and discrete math. Excellent reference book for math students and teachers. Hosted and sponsored by Wolfram Research, Inc., makers of *Mathematica*, "the world's most powerful and flexible software package for doing mathematics."

ExploreLearning.com

12345

www.explorelearning.com

This site features online, interactive math and science activities, called Gizmos, that cover linear equations, quadratic equations, complex numbers, trigonometry, and more.

FigureThis!

12345

www.figurethis.org

This site features math challenges for all members of your family. Sections include Teachers Corner, Family Corner, Challenge Index, and Math Index. Site is bilingual in English and Spanish.

goENC

12345

www.goenc.com

Supports improving teaching and learning of math and science in secondary schools. Offers links to other Internet resources. Presents online catalog and databases, as well as a collection of Internet software and information. Great site for math teachers.

Best HotMath.com

12345

hotmath.com

Based on a study that math students learn most effectively when they see half of their homework problems worked out and explained to them, Math.com features answers and explanations to the odd-numbered problems in most math textbooks. Help is offered for a wide range of the most challenging math courses, including Pre-Algebra, Algebra I, Algebra II, Geometry, Trigonometry, Precalculus, and Calculus. Visitors simply click a link for the subject, click a link for the textbook they're using, and then start working through problems. For complete access, the site charges a reasonable fee.

Interactive Mathematics Online

12345

library.thinkquest.org/2647/main.htm

Learn more about what you can do with algebra, geometry, trigonometry, and chaos theory at this fun site. Check out the Cool Java Stuff page and make your own stereograms.

MegaMathematics!

12345

www.cs.uidaho.edu/~casey931/mega-math/menu.html

MegaMathematics! is directed toward middle-school and high-school students and is designed to present various math topics in innovative ways. Topics include Untangling the Mathematics of Knots and Algorithms and Ice Cream for All. And who said mathematicians didn't have a sense of humor?

National Council of Teachers of Mathematics

12345

www.nctm.org

The National Council of Teachers of Mathematics is dedicated to providing vision, leadership, and resources to math teachers of primary and secondary students to ensure quality math instruction for all students. This site provides tips and curriculum guidelines for elementary, middle school, and high school math teachers.

PSU Math–Mathematics Websites

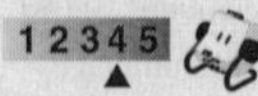

www.math.psu.edu/MathLists/Contents.html

This site provides a robust collection of links to website for the mathematically inclined. Sites are grouped by categories including Mathematics Department Web Servers (by country), societies and associations, journals, subject areas, and software. If you're a serious student or professor of mathematics, this site is a great place to start your search.

ALGEBRA

Algebra Help

12345

www.algebrahelp.com

This site provides a collection of lessons, calculators, and worksheets to assist students and teachers of algebra. Great resource for students when their teacher is not readily available and their parents have forgotten everything they learned about algebra in high school.

Algebra Homework Help

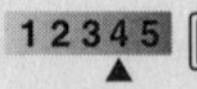

www.algebra.com

At Algebra Homework Help, students can get the assistance they need for any level of algebra instruction. Lessons are grouped by level, starting with pre-algebra and moving up to algebra II. Site features math homework solvers, lessons, and free online tutors.

S.O.S. Mathematics Algebra

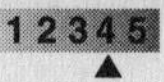

www.sosmath.com/algebra/algebra.html

Get basic definitions and tools for various math topics, from integers to quadratic equations and factors. This is a comprehensive site with lots of good information and links, designed primarily as a refresher course for adults who forget what they once knew.

CALCULUS

Calculus Help

www.calculus-help.com

Michael Kelley, author of *The Complete Idiot's Guide to Precalculus* offers his expertise free of charge to all calculus-challenged students. Here, you can check out the Problem of the Week, access some tutorials and other "fun" stuff, and find out more about Mike's books. Site also features a directory of math-related links you can follow to expand your knowledge.

COW (Calculus On the Web)

www.math.temple.edu/~cow

Clickable volumes of calculus lessons for students at any level. Lessons cover Precalculus, Calculus, Linear Algebra, Number Theory, and Abstract Algebra. Self-contained modules deliver lessons in an easily digestible format.

Karl's Calculus Tutor

www.karlscalculus.org

Karl's Calculus Tutor shows students, step-by-step how to work out a host of sample problems. Here, you can find "coverage of limits, continuity, derivatives, related rates, optimization, L'Hopital's rule, integration, and much more." If you're struggling with a certain aspect of calculus, this is a good place to go for help.

MathGV Function Plotting Software

www.mathgv.com

MathGV features a downloadable program for plotting two-dimensional, parametric, polar, and three-dimension functions—something every college-level calculus student can really use. When I visited the site, MathGV was offering the program for free but plans were in the works to begin selling a commercial version.

CHAOS

Chaos Hypertextbook

hypertextbook.com/chaos

Glenn Elert composed "this book for anyone with an interest in chaos, fractals, nonlinear dynamics, or mathematics in general." As he describes it, "It's a moderately heavy piece of work, requiring a bit of mathematical knowledge, but it is definitely not aimed at mathematicians. My background is in physics and I use mathematics extensively in problem solving. Like many educated people, I also enjoy math as a diversion. This is the audience I am writing for." Book consists of four chapters: Mathematical Experiments, Strange & Complex, About Dimension, and Measuring Chaos. Several appendixes are also included.

Chaos at Maryland

www-chaos.umd.edu/chaos.html

Provides information on the various applications of chaos theory, including dimensions, fractal basin boundaries, chaotic scattering, and controlling chaos. Includes online papers, a searchable database, and general references. Also offers the Chaos Gallery. Be sure to check here for dissertation help!

Non-Linear Lab

www.apmaths.uwo.ca/~bfraser/nll/version1

The Non-Linear Lab is devoted to expanding the study of chaos beyond the focus of most novice students—the study of fractals. When you reach the page, you're greeted with a brief description of the site. Scroll down to access a clickable table of contents to help you navigate the site.

Open Directory: Chaos & Fractals

dmoz.org/Science/Math/Chaos_and_Fractals

Excellent directory of sites dealing with chaos theory and fractals. Links to more than 300 sites grouped by Chaos, Fractal Art, and Software.

FRACTALS

Fractal eXtreme

www.cygnus-software.com

FX (Fractal eXtreme) is "a fractal exploration program that draws pictures of the Mandelbrot set and other fractals on your PC and allows you to explore these fractals by zooming and panning toward interesting areas with your mouse or keyboard." Here, you can learn more about the program, purchase it, and discover more about chaos theory and fractals.

Fractal Websites

www.fractaldomains.com/html/sites.html

Excellent directory of fractal websites and galleries. Sites are organized by Galleries and Fractal Information.

GEOMETRY

Sacred Geometry

www.intent.com/sg

Interested in the metaphysical aspect of numbers and shapes in nature? Then visit this site, where math and spirituality meet. If you know a student who's less than enthused when it comes to studying geometry, this site provides plenty to turn a jaded mind into an eager learner.

Science U: Geometry Center

www.scienceu.com/geometry

Science U's Geometry Center is packed with information and interactive activities for beginning-level geometry students. Content is presented in categories, including Interactive, Activities, Articles, Classroom, and Facts & Figures. Site also features a search tool for tracking down specific topics.

MATHEMATICIANS

Biographies of Women Mathematicians

www.agnesscott.edu/lriddle/women/women.htm

Comprehensive collection of biographies of women mathematicians organized by alphabet, chronology, and birthplace. Site includes a brief biography for each featured mathematician along with a photograph and enables you to look up birth and death anniversaries, awards, and prizes.

Indexes of Biographies

www-gap.dcs.st-and.ac.uk/~history/BiogIndex.html

Very basic but comprehensive index of the world's most famous mathematicians organized alphabetically and historically. Site also features a chronology and timeline, a search form, birthplace map, and a Mathematician of the Day.

NUMERIC ANALYSIS

Math Forum: Numeric Analysis

12345

mathforum.org/advanced/numeric.html

This site features links to various websites and resources that deal specifically with numeric analysis. Great place to start your search.

SIAM (Society for Industrial and Applied Mathematics)

12345

www.siam.org

SIAM's mission is "to ensure the strongest interactions between mathematics and other scientific and technological communities through membership activities, publication of journals and books, and conferences." Here, you can learn more about the organization and its members and about upcoming conferences and events, search for jobs and internships, check out the journal and book lists, and read up on SIAM news.

STATISTICS

Create a Graph

12345

nces.ed.gov/nceskids/graphing

Excellent online graphing tool leads students step-by-step through the process of creating Bar, Line, Area, Pie, and X-Y graphs. Graphs are completely customizable and printable, and because the NCES (National Center for Education Statistics) uses graphs to analyze education data, they have plenty of great examples in how graphs can be applied to real-life situations. A tabbed interface enables students to quickly and easily design a graph, enter data and labels, preview the graph, and then print or save it.

Interactive Statistical Calculation Pages

12345 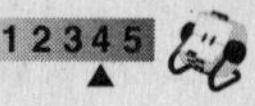

statpages.org

The Interactive Statistical Calculation Pages project "represents an ongoing effort to develop and disseminate statistical analysis software in the form of web pages." This site contains links to hundreds of pages that contain computational software tools for analyzing data.

Math, Statistics, and Computational Science

12345

math.nist.gov

Diverse collection of resources related to mathematics from the National Institute of Standards and Technology. For statistics, check out the NIST/SEMATECH Engineering Statistics Handbook and the Statistical Reference Datasheets.

The Statistics Home Page

12345

www.statsoft.com/textbook/stathome.html

This site features an online version of the textbook *Statistics: Methods and Applications*—a popular textbook used in both undergraduate and graduate college level statistics courses. Simply click a button for the desired chapter to start learning statistics online. Each chapter contains hyperlinks of key concepts and terms that you can click to obtain more information.

TRIGONOMETRY

S.O.S. Mathematics

12345

www.sosmath.com/trig/trig.html

Beginning students of trigonometry will find this site useful. It provides lessons on basic trigonometry, explaining angle measures and trigonometric functions and equations. Also features a table of trigonometric identities, and instructions on how to solve equations. Visitors can also explore sections on Calculus and Trigonometry and Hyperbolic Trigonometry.

MEDIATION

American Arbitration Association

12345

www.adr.org

According to the American Arbitration Association, this site is "the most comprehensive site for up-to-the-minute information about mediation, arbitration, and other forms of alternative dispute resolution (ADR)." Here, you can learn more about the AAA and its services; file a case online; access resources on various types of arbitration, including commercial, consumer, employment, and health care; check out the rules, guides, and fact sheets; and download some useful forms.

Conflict Research Consortium

12345

conflict.colorado.edu

The Conflict Research Consortium takes a multidisciplinary approach to conflict resolution, focusing on "finding more constructive ways of addressing difficult, long-term, and intractable conflicts, and getting that information to the people involved in these conflicts so that they can approach them in a more constructive way." Here, you can find conflict resolution sites, databases, publications, conference information, and links.

Best Federal Mediation and Conciliation Services (FMCS)

12345

www.fmcs.gov

Agency of the U.S. government that handles arbitration and mediation of labor disputes and contract negotiations. Here, you can learn the basics of mediation through the FMCS FAQ, learn about the agency's history and what it can do to help you mediate conflicts in your business, and locate additional resources, including articles and useful links to other mediation sites. Site also features success stories of situations in which FMCS assisted in the mediation. This well-designed site is packed with useful information and links, making it our choice for Best of the Best in the Mediation category.

Guide to Alternative Dispute Resolution

12345

www.hg.org/adr.html

From Hieros Gamos, "the comprehensive legal site." This site offers current legal and mediation news. Many links to other mediation information sites and legal professionals who can assist in mediation and other areas of law.

JAMS ADR

12345

www.jamsadr.com

Learn about alternative dispute resolution (ADR), find out about JAMS, discover why you should use the JAMS service, determine when you should contact JAMS, and find an office or panelist near you.

Mediate.com

12345

www.mediate.com

Mediate.com is one of the most popular mediation sites on the Web, featuring a dizzying collection of articles, advice, and resources on all aspects of mediation. Just point to Sections to view the list of areas on the site; they cover everything from attorneys to youth and schools and include topics on diversity, health care, probate, and workplace. You can browse the online library, peruse the marketplace, find training, or hang out in the discussion forums.

MEDICINE

CareMark.com

12345

www.caremark.com

Get your prescriptions filled, purchase cosmetics, and buy any other product that you would normally find in a traditional drugstore. Also provides tools for researching prescription medications.

CVS/Pharmacy

12345

www.cvs.com

A quicker way to get your CVS prescription refilled—online. Log onto the site and specify the prescription you want refilled and the store that has the record, and your order will be ready for pickup when you arrive. While you're at the site, you can also check prices on other prescriptions and in-store specials, read health-related articles, and find the CVS nearest you. If you have a digital camera, you can also upload your snapshots for online "film" processing.

drugstore.com

12345

www.drugstore.com

Purchase health, beauty, and nutrition products, as well as prescription medicines, online at this site. A great selection of products, from shampoos to suntan lotion to vitamins, at reasonable prices. Helpful articles and tips help you improve your health and appearance.

Eckerd.com

12345

www.eckerd.com

Get your prescription filled and delivered directly to your doorstep from Eckerd's, where you can also research medicines or ask the pharmacist a question. Health and beauty supplies are offered here, too, as well as vitamins, household goods, baby care items, and photo developing. You can also locate a store near you at the site.

familymeds.com

12345

www.familymeds.com

Click on a common health problem, such as snoring or a sprain, and get more information on typical causes and suggested solutions to each from the site's pharmacist. You can then order the recommended products right from the site.

Medicine Shoppe

12345

www.medshoppe.com

In addition to ordering health products at this site, you can learn more about various diseases and illnesses and ways you can avoid them, read health news, and search the Reuters Drug Database. The emphasis is on learning to stay healthy rather than on product sales, which is nice.

Rite Aid

12345

www.riteaid.com

In addition to having a prescription filled, asking a pharmacist a question online, buying products, and scanning health databases online, you can also locate a nearby Rite Aid location and check for current specials and discounts.

SavOn.com

12345

www.savon.com

A fully stocked online drug store. Get product information here and then purchase the products online from this site. Lots of merchandise to choose from, including baby supplies, cosmetics, and vitamins.

Walgreens

12345

www.walgreens.com

Walgreens carries a wide selection of products ranging from prescription and over-the-counter drugs to vitamins, beauty products, household items, and electronics. You can browse the shelves by category, search the site for specific products, have your prescriptions refilled online, and even upload photos for processing. Site also features a comprehensive Health Library, where you can learn more about specific medical conditions.

> **Tip:** Before you shop at your local Walgreens, scroll to the bottom of the page and click Weekly Ad to see what's on sale, create a shopping list, and print coupons.

DRUG INFORMATION

FDA: Food and Drug Administration

12345

www.fda.gov

The FDA is in charge of testing and approving the manufacture, distribution, and use of pharmaceuticals. Here, you can look up information on any medications that have come under the FDA's scrutiny. This is an excellent site to research drug alerts and get the facts about potentially harmful or rumored-to-be-harmful medications and counterfeit medications.

National Library of Medicine

12345

www.nlm.nih.gov

The National Library of Medicine is the largest biomedical library in the world. Although it serves the medical community, it also assists consumers in evaluating sources of information so they can conduct their own research. Here, you can find a history of medicine and online exhibitions, health news and alerts, and information on diseases and prescription medications (via Medline Plus).

RxList.com

12345

www.rxlist.com

Excellent site for researching specific prescription medications. Provides information on indications, dosages, side effects, warnings, interactions, and more. You can take a quiz to test your medical knowledge or submit a question to have it answered.

SafeMedication.com

12345

www.safemedication.com

SafeMedication.com is a site created and managed by pharmacists to provide patients with the prescription information they need to take their medications properly, become aware of potential side effects, and avoid dangerous drug interactions. This is a great site to visit when you lose the prescription information your pharmacist sent home with you.

FIRST-AID INFORMATION

1st Spot First Aid

12345

1st-spot.net/topic_firstaid.html

Find out how to treat basic injuries or conditions, such as heatstroke or frostbite, with the help of this site. You'll also find basic first aid guidance and answers to first aid questions. This site also offers invaluable information about what to keep in a first aid kit.

American College of Emergency Physicians

12345

www.acep.org

Everything you need to know about preventing emergencies and responding to emergencies when they happen. Find out what you need to pack in a first aid kit for your home and learn how to prepare an emergency-response plan. Site features a special area for patients and consumers.

Anaphylactic Treatment Guidelines

1 2 3 4 5

www.anaphylaxis.com

Learn about the preferred treatment for severe allergic reactions. Links to EpiPen, an auto-injector that administers epinephrine, the definitive emergency treatment for severe allergic reactions. Anyone who suffers from life-threatening allergies should bookmark this page.

HealthWorld First Aid

1 2 3 4 5

www.healthy.net/clinic/firstaid

This site from HealthWorld provides quick access to treatment for animal bites, burns, choking, drug overdoses, shock, sunburn, and a host of other emergency health conditions.

Mayo Clinic's First-Aid Guide

1 2 3 4 5

www.mayoclinic.com/findinformation/firstaidandselfcare/index.cfm

In an emergency, you don't want to be looking up instructions on the Web; the Mayo Clinic recommends that you seek professional help immediately. If you're trying to bone up on your knowledge of first-aid treatment, however, this is a great place to do it. Here, you can find instructions for a wide range of emergency health conditions, including anaphylaxis, frost bite, heat stroke, and tick bites. Dozens of conditions are covered.

MEDICAL RESOURCES

The AAMC's Academic Medicine Website

1 2 3 4 5

www.aamc.org

The Association of American Medical Colleges site lists and provides links to accredited U.S. and Canadian medical schools, major teaching hospitals, and academic and professional societies. It provides the latest information on news and events, includes AAMC publications and information, and presents research and government relations resources. Also includes information and links to education, research, and healthcare.

American Lung Association

1 2 3 4 5

www.lungusa.org

Here, you can find information on the ALA (including research programs, grants, and awards), as well as the American Thoracic Society (the international professional and scientific society for respiratory and critical care medicine). Read the ALA's annual report. Check out information on asthma, emphysema, and other lung diseases; tobacco control; and environmental health. This is a great resource for parents of children with asthma. You'll also find information on volunteer opportunities, special events, and promotions, as well as an extensive list of related links.

BBC Science & Nature: Human Body & Mind

1 2 3 4 5

www.bbc.co.uk/science/humanbody

This site takes you on a virtual tour of the human body and mind. Here, you can build your own skeleton, stretch muscles, arrange internal organs, take the senses challenge, play the nervous system game, and much more. Also explores issues dealing with psychology and the functioning of the human brain.

Centers for Disease Control and Prevention

1 2 3 4 5

www.cdc.gov

Provides links to the CDC's 13 centers, institutes, and offices, and a search engine to quickly locate your point of interest. Includes geographic health information and pinpoints certain disease outbreaks in the world. Also makes vaccine and immunization recommendations. Provides information on diseases, health risks, and prevention guidelines, as well as strategies for chronic diseases, HIV/AIDS, sexually transmitted diseases, tuberculosis, and more. Also offers information on specific populations, such as adolescent and school health, infants' and children's health, and women's health. Offers helpful links to publications, software, and other products. Also provides scientific data, surveillance, health statistics, and laboratory information.

A B C D E F G H I J K L M N O P Q R S T U V W X Y Z

drkoop.com

1 2 3 4 5

www.drkoop.com

Dr. Everett C. Koop was the closest thing the United States ever had to a Surgeon General who was able to achieve celebrity status. This site, which is not associated with the good Dr. Koop, manages to help him retain some of his celebrity status nevertheless. This site provides solid health advice and information for consumers. Several sections are available, including News Archive, Animations, Health Videos, Health Tools, and Procedures. You can also subscribe to a free newsletter.

HealthWorld Online

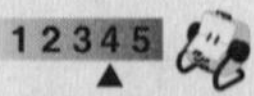

www.healthy.net

HealthWorld Online is a huge directory of health information and resources available 24 hours a day. The opening page displays a graphic representation of HealthWorld, consisting of a University, health news center, nutrition center, clinic, alternative medicine dome, and other virtual buildings. You can navigate the site using this map or by clicking links in the list on the left, including Wellness Test, Health Conditions, Healthy Child, and Expert Columns. Scroll down the page to access a more detailed list of links for each category.

MedLine Plus

www.medlineplus.gov

Find information on diseases, conditions, and health issues by searching the comprehensive database. You can also track down drug information, hospitals, doctors, and organizations that specialize in a particular condition. This site is created and maintained as a service of the National Library of Medicine and the National Institutes of Health, so you can trust that the information you receive is coming from a reliable source.

National Center for Complementary and Alternative Medicine (NCCAM)

nccam.nih.gov

Given the host of alternative treatments available for just about every illness and ailment you can name, determining which ones are effective, which ones are useless, and which ones are downright dangerous is a huge challenge. Fortunately, NCCAM constantly monitors and assesses the effectiveness of alternative and complementary therapies and posts the information on its website. Here, you can sort out effective therapies from dangerous quackery.

National Organization for Rare Disorders, Inc. (NORD)

www.rarediseases.org

NORD consists of more than 140 not-for-profit voluntary health organizations serving people with rare disorders and disabilities. Read the Orphan Disease Update newsletter or search the rare disease database, the NORD organizational database, or the orphan drug designation database for information on specific rare disorders. A rare or orphan disease affects fewer than 200,000 people in the United States. There are more than 5,000 rare disorders that affect 20 million Americans. This site includes links to various support groups.

New England Journal of Medicine

content.nejm.org

A comprehensive site from the famed journal. You can find present and past issues of the journal here, as well as up-to-date medical information on a wide variety of topics. This site is a must for anyone interested in the medical field.

Plink: The Plastic Surgery Link

www.nvpc.nl/plink

Offers a collection of plastic surgery-related links, targeting physicians and interested laypersons. Includes hospital web pages, journals, books, and general information. Also provides information on societies, departments, physicians, private clinics, conferences, research, and residencies.

Student Doctor Network

www.studentdoctor.net

The Student Doctor Network (SDN) is "a nonprofit website, dedicated to the pre-health and health professional student community," whose mission it is to help students select and prepare for various professional careers in health. Site includes plenty of useful resources, but also acts as a forum where professionals and students can meet to exchange information.

U.S. Department of Health and Human Services

12345

www.os.dhhs.gov

The U.S. Department of Health and Human Resources has put together this excellent online kiosk of information relating to a wide range of health topics, including Diseases & Conditions, Health & Safety, Families & Children, Aging, and Drug & Food Information.

Visible Human Project

www.nlm.nih.gov/research/visible/visible_human.html

Three-dimensional representations of the human body, with visualizations of the dissectible human, software tools, and other areas.

Best WebMD

www.webMD.com

A site connecting consumers and health professionals, WebMD aims to provide patients with more information about their healthcare, as well as to help prevent problems by providing useful health-related articles and advice. Online support groups are also available here for topics such as quitting smoking and dieting. This essential medical encyclopedia makes it easy to research symptoms, diseases, prescription medications, and other health-related topics. An easy Best of the Best pick in the Medical Resources category.

NURSING
(SEE NURSING)

PAIN MANAGEMENT

American Academy of Pain Management

www.aapainmanage.org

A site for healthcare professionals and consumers suffering from chronic pain, providing both with the opportunity to connect and learn more about pain management techniques. Consumers can click the Patients link to search the database for a qualified pain management professional and access a directory of links to other sites that provide more specific information about pain management.

American Chronic Pain Association

www.theacpa.org

The American Chronic Pain Association (ACPA) is a nonprofit, tax-exempt organization whose members provide a support system for those suffering with chronic pain through education and self-help group activities. Find out how to join by visiting this site.

Mayo Clinic Pain Center

 RSS

www.mayoclinic.com/health/pain/PN99999

At the Mayo Clinic Pain Center, patients suffering from chronic pain can research various methods for alleviating and managing their pain. Site covers Pain Medications; Ointments, Injection Therapy, and Surgery; Alternative Care, and Self Care. You can click Ask a Specialist to locate answers to previously posted questions or to post your own question.

Pain.com

www.pain.com

This site offers a world of information on pain, including information about pain products and the companies that make them, pain resources, a collection of original full-text articles on pain and its management by noted pain professionals, and much more! Site offers CME/CPE/CE credit for healthcare professionals.

Partners Against Pain

www.partnersagainstpain.com

At this site patients, caregivers, and health care providers are encouraged to partner in the fight against pain by promoting standards of pain care. The site's table of contents includes pain assessment, regulatory issues, and education center. Also features a useful glossary of terms and some free guides you can order by registering.

StopPain.org

1 2 3 4 5

www.stoppain.org

StopPain.org is dedicated to helping patients alleviate their chronic, nonmalignant pain through all available and effective means, including pain medication, palliative care (in a home, hospital, or hospice setting), psychological interventions (including hypnosis, biofeedback, and psychotherapy), rehabilitative therapies (including physical and occupational therapy), injections, implants, and complementary therapies (including acupuncture and massage). Finding the information you need at this site can be a bit of a challenge, but the site features quality content, including a multimedia library.

MEMORY

Human Memory

1 2 3 4 5

memory.uva.nl

The Psychology Department at the University of Amsterdam has put together this Human Memory page to provide visitors with various memory tests and then teach them techniques for improving their memory.

Memory Improvement Techniques

1 2 3 4 5

www.mindtools.com/memory.html

This site explains techniques that can help improve memory "when studying for exams or in situations where you need to remember detailed, structured information." Site features dozens of free tips and techniques along with links to additional resources that can help you whip your mind and memory into tip-top condition.

Best Memory Loss & the Brain

1 2 3 4 5

www.memorylossonline.com

Memory Loss & the Brain is "a free publication of the Memory Disorders Project at Rutgers-Newark, which is partially supported by donations from two private foundations. The online version of *Memory Loss & the Brain* is sponsored by a grant from the Johnson and Johnson Family of Companies." Here, you can find the latest information and discoveries related to the brain and its capacity to remember stuff. Site also features a robust glossary, additional resources, and tips for improving your memory.

A B C D E F G H I J K L M N O P Q R S T U V W X Y Z

MEN & MEN'S ISSUES

Dr. Warren Farrell

www.warrenfarrell.com

Author of *Why Men Earn More*, in addition to several other books dealing with men and men's issues, Dr. Farrell hosts this site to help men and women develop a deeper understanding and appreciation of the male perspective. Here, you can find out why Warren is the way he is, when and where he'll be speaking, and how to hire him to be an expert witness in custody cases or gender pay discrimination. You can also visit to read the article of the month, check out his collection of audio tapes (based on his books), and explore links to other valuable resources.

Fathering Magazine

www.fathermag.com

A site that indexes a huge range of fatherhood topics, from custody issues to second families, to a father's relationship with a son or daughter. News, information, and discussions galore. Well worth a visit.

Best GQ Magazine

www.gq.com

Male-oriented magazine that's primarily directed toward the professional, sophisticated male features photos, cultural commentary, celebrity profiles, political articles, and plenty of style advice to help the modern male remain in tune to the latest developments in culture and style.

> **Tip:** Women can click the Women link at the top of the page to go to Style.com, the online home of *Vogue* and *W*.

The Male Affirmative Resource Center

www.themenscenter.com

The Male Affirmative Resource Center is dedicated to helping men "find male-positive resources, information, and support." This site features local, state, national, and international indexes; a news ticker; discussion forums; and chat areas. It also features a list of men's events and a bookstore.

The Mankind Project

www.mkp.org

A nonprofit training organization that seeks to help men make better decisions about how they live their lives, to help them connect with their feelings, and to lead lives of integrity. The site provides information on upcoming Warrior training weekends and the organization's mission.

Maxim Online

www.maximonline.com

Men's magazine that focuses on the four primary male interests: girls, entertainment, sports, and humor.

Men Stuff

1 2 3 4 5 ▲

`www.menstuff.org`

An educational website with information on more than 100 topics related to men's issues, such as circumcision, divorce, fathers, and sexuality. Provides a nonjudgmental environment where men can learn more about becoming better fathers, husbands, and human beings; find out more about male health issues, including testicular cancer and sexual dysfunction; and stay informed about other current issues relating to male health and well-being. When dealing with just about any issue related to being a man, there's no better site in this category.

MensActivism.org

1 2 3 4 5 ▲ Blog

`www.mensactivism.org`

MensActivism.org "tracks news and information about men's issues from around the world," focusing on "promoting activism in support of men's rights and equality." Here, you can read the organization's philosophy and FAQs, access the news stories, submit a story, or connect with other men's issues activists in the chatrooms.

National Fatherhood Initiative

1 2 3 4 5 ▲

`www.fatherhood.org`

In an effort to counteract the trend toward fatherlessness in families, this site provides support, information, and advice to fathers to help get and keep them connected to their children.

MEN'S HEALTH

Best CDC: Men's Health

www.cdc.gov/men/tips.htm

The Centers for Disease Control sponsor this site specifically devoted to men's health and related issues. Site covers men's health issues from A to Z, tips for establishing a healthy lifestyle, a quiz to test your health IQ, statistics, and links to related sites. The What's New area keeps visitors posted concerning the latest developments in the health field that address the most persistent and serious health issues affecting men. Excellent information in a format that makes it easy to find just the information you need.

Men's Fitness

www.mensfitness.com

The online edition of this monthly men's magazine offers personal health articles and discussion areas, including training, nutrition, sex and behavior, sports and adventure, and gear. You can also subscribe to the print version from this site.

Men's Health Network

www.menshealthnetwork.org

Men's Health Network (MHN) is a nonprofit organization dedicated to keeping men, boys, and families informed about various health issues related to the male population. Physicians, researches, public health workers, and other individuals and health professionals contribute to the site. Here, you can find out more about the organization, subscribe for its newsletter, and find links to other helpful sites. Some annoying pop-ups, but otherwise this site is an excellent, reliable resource for men's health issues.

Men's Health Week

www.menshealthweek.org

Celebrated every year during the week leading up to Father's Day, Men's Health Week is intended to "heighten the awareness of preventable health problems and encourage early detection and treatment of disease among men and boys." Here, you can learn more about the organization and the various events it has planned for the upcoming Men's Health Week.

Viagra

www.viagra.com

Take the self-screening questionnaire at this site to find out whether you're likely to be suffering from erectile dysfunction. If you are, you'll want to read more at the site about Viagra, how it works, and whether it's likely to help or if you should take it.

A B C D E F G H I J K L M N O P Q R S T U V W X Y Z

MENTAL HEALTH DISORDERS

AtHealth.com

12345

www.athealth.com

For the general public, this site features a Consumers area, where you can find excellent descriptions of nearly every mental disorder, including a description of the disorder and possible treatments, organized in a Q&A format. The Practitioner area provides more in-depth information on prescriptions and other treatment recommendations, but it requires you to register.

The Center for Mental Health Services

12345

www.mentalhealth.org

The CMHS National Mental Health Services Knowledge Exchange Network (KEN) provides information about mental health via toll-free telephone services, an electronic bulletin board, and publications. KEN is for users of mental health services and their families, the general public, policy makers, providers, and the media. It gives you information and resources on prevention, treatment, and rehabilitation services for mental illnesses.

Internet Mental Health

www.mentalhealth.com

Find what you need to know about mental health, including the most common mental health disorders, diagnoses, and most-prescribed medications. Also check out the several links to related sites and information. This site also has an online magazine with editorials, articles, letters, and stories of recovery.

Mental Health InfoSource

12345

www.mhsource.com

This site contains sections regarding disorders and drugs, 600 links on mental health, a mental health professional directory, and more. Use the search tool to track down information on the particular mental health topic in which you're interested. Check out the A to Z Disorders Index for information about a specific disorder.

Mental Health Matters

www.mental-health-matters.com

A directory of resources related to mental health and mental illness, including alternative treatments, emotional support, mental health law, community and government agencies, statistics, support groups, and more. The listings are updated regularly to stay current.

Mental Health Net

mentalhelp.net

Get information on disorders such as depression, anxiety, panic attacks, chronic fatigue syndrome, and substance abuse. You can also get access to professional resources in psychology, psychiatry, and social work; journals; and self-help magazines. Plus, you can read articles containing the latest news and developments in mental health.

National Alliance for the Mentally Ill (NAMI) Home Page

12345

www.nami.org

Browse through a host of articles brought to you by NAMI. Learn about the latest treatments and therapy; health-insurance issues; the role of genetics;

typical Q&As; and related bills, laws, and regulations. Look into NAMI's campaign to end discrimination against the mentally ill and ways you can help. Take advantage of Helpline Online, where volunteers talk with you about mental illnesses and the medications that treat them. Examine the scientific aspects of mental illness. Get the facts on depression, schizophrenia, brain disorders, and several more.

Best National Institute of Mental Health

1 2 3 4 5

www.nimh.nih.gov

The NIMH site provides news about mental health research, reports, and clinical trials, both for mental health professionals and members of the public. Excellent place to visit for late-breaking news and discoveries related to a wide range of mental health issues. One of the most valuable offerings on this site are the publications, which you can download for free. Each brochure is packaged as a PDF file that contains the bare essentials of what you need to know to understand a specific mental health disorder, effective treatment options, and the prognosis.

National Mental Health Association

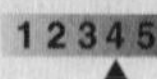

www.nmha.org

Information about the organization and its network of hundreds of affiliates. This site includes mental health fact sheets, pamphlets, news releases, legislative alerts, and more.

Psych Central

psychcentral.com/disorders

Comprehensive list of mental health disorders along with quizzes, medications, book reviews, and other helpful resources. Excellent place to learn the signs, symptoms, and treatments for a wide range of mental health disorders.

AGORAPHOBIA

Agoraphobia Insight

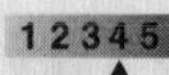

www.anxietyinsight.com

Agoraphobia Insight offers basic information about agoraphobia, anxiety, and panic disorders. Here, you can find a definition of agoraphobia, learn about its symptoms, and discover various treatment options. Site also features an informative FAQs.

ANOREXIA NERVOSA *(SEE MENTAL HEALTH DISORDERS—EATING DISORDERS)*

ANXIETY & PANIC DISORDERS

Anxiety Disorders Association of America

www.adaa.org

ADAA provides help for those suffering from anxiety disorders. At this site, you can research the most common manifestations of anxiety, take a self-test, explore effective treatments, learn of upcoming clinical trials, find a therapist, and explore other hot topics.

Anxiety Panic Attack Resource Site

www.anxietypanic.com

This site is packed with information, personal stories, advice, articles, and descriptions of various medications and treatments that can help with anxiety and panic attacks. Chatrooms and questionnaires are available for members. Updated daily.

Anxiety Panic Internet Resource

1 2 3 4 5 Blog RSS

www.algy.com/anxiety

A self-help guide for those suffering from anxiety and/or panic disorders. This site addresses the causes of and treatments for panic attacks, phobias, extreme shyness, obsessive-compulsive behaviors, and generalized anxiety that disrupt the lives of an estimated fifteen percent of the population. If you or someone you love suffers from an anxiety or panic disorder, visit this site for relief and help.

National Panic & Anxiety Disorder News

1 2 3 4 5

www.npadnews.com

This site features a robust collection of articles on the latest developments related to panic and anxiety disorders.

ATTENTION DEFICIT HYPERACTIVITY DISORDER

A.D.D. Warehouse

1 2 3 4 5

www.addwarehouse.com

This site features an online catalog of books, videos, training tools, games, and assessment products on ADD and ADHD and related problems for parents, educators, health professionals, children, and adults.

ADD FAQ

1 2 3 4 5

www.faqfarm.com/Health/ADD

This frequently asked questions (FAQ) list addresses the background, testing, treatments, and resources dealing with Attention Deficit Disorder. This is a great place to start researching ADD.

ADD/ADHD Links Pages

1 2 3 4 5

user.cybrzn.com/~kenyonck/add/Links

This page offers myriad annotated and categorized ADD/ADHD links as well as a link to a page with all the links listed alphabetically. The list includes links to sites about different facets of living with ADD/ADHD.

ADDitude.com

1 2 3 4 5

www.additudemag.com

Home of ADDitude magazine, where you can find information about ADD in adults and children from experts and from those who are dealing with this condition themselves or with a family member.

ADD Warehouse

1 2 3 4 5

addwarehouse.com

If you're looking for books, videos, or training programs to help deal with ADD, ADHD, or other developmental disorders, look no further than this site. Place your order online, over the phone, or via fax.

Best Attention Deficit Disorder Association

1 2 3 4 5

www.add.org

This extremely comprehensive site on the topic of ADD features a great collection of articles and fact sheets on ADD and ADHD, suggestions on organization and time management, insights and tips on how to deal with workplace issues, specific details about coaching, help with legal issues, the latest information on current treatments, and much more. When you reach the home page, click the Articles link to get started. This site also presents information about membership and upcoming conferences. Its searchable directory can help you locate psychiatrists, counselors, coaches, legal assistance, and more. If you or a loved one suffers from ADD or ADHD, bookmark this Best of the Best site now.

CHADD: Children and Adults with Attention-Deficit/Hyperactivity Disorder

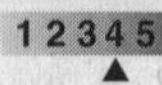

www.chadd.org/index.htm

Sponsored by CHADD, the nation's leading nonprofit ADHD group, this site features the latest information about ADHD diagnosis, treatment, and legislation. You can find the answers to most of your questions in CHADD's FAQs, sign up for its newsletter, become a member, or even find out about local CHADD support groups.

Christian ADHD Alternative Treatment List

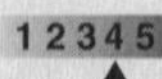

www.christianadhd.com

This online support group and resource center provides information for those suffering from ADD, ADHD, and related psychological illnesses and for the guardians or parents of ADHD children. It provides a Christian perspective that reassures visitors that their illness is not a punishment for something they've done.

Internet Special Education Resources

www.iser.com

This site focuses on helping parents find local special education professionals who can help with learning disabilities and Attention Deficit Disorder assessment, therapy, advocacy, and other special needs.

AUTISM & ASPERGER'S SYNDROME

Asperger and Autism Information

12345

www.maapservices.org

MAAP (More advanced individuals with Autism, Asperger syndrome, and Pervasive developmental disorder) "is a nonprofit organization dedicated to providing information and advice to families. Here, you can find the latest information about Autism and Asperger's Syndrome, locate additional resources near you, check out some free publications, and learn more about your legal rights or the rights of a loved one.

Autism Research Institute

www.autismwebsite.com

Dr. Bernard Rimland is one of the leading authorities on autism research and treatment. This site provides access to a vast collection of articles, publications, and other resources related to autism.

Autism.tv

www.autism.tv

Cutting-edge site features a collection of podcasts and webcasts dealing with autism, including channels from the DAN! conference, Autism Technology, and Autism Today. Some channels are pay per view.

DANconference.com

12345

www.danconference.com

DAN! (Defeat Autism Now!) "is dedicated to educating parents and clinicians regarding biomedical-based research, appropriate testing, and safe and effective interventions for autism." Here, you can learn more about the organization and conference dates.

BIPOLAR DISORDER (SEE ALSO MENTAL HEALTH DISORDERS—DEPRESSION)

BPSO: Bipolar Significant Others

www.bpso.org

BPSO provides "information and support to the spouses, families, friends and other loved ones of those who suffer from bipolar disorder (manic-depression)." The resources at this site are designed to help family and friends of those who have bipolar disorder "cope with behaviors that sometimes arise from the illness, better understand our own reactions, and determine how we may best support our loved ones in their efforts to understand and live with this often terrible disease." Site also features a useful directory of links to other bipolar sites.

Bipolar World

www.bipolarworld.net

Bipolar World is dedicated to those who are living with bipolar disorder. This site provides information about bipolar disorder and its treatment and enables visitors to communicate with others who are living with the disorder. Visit this site regularly to obtain late-breaking news about discoveries and treatments, read personal stories, find community support, and learn about legislation that can protect your rights. Site also features chatrooms and discussion forums.

Child & Adolescent Bipolar Foundation

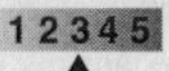

www.bpkids.org

The Child & Adolescent Bipolar Foundation "educates families, professionals, and the public about pediatric bipolar disorder; connects families with resources and support; advocates for and empowers affected families; and supports research on pediatric bipolar disorder and its cure." Point to the Learning Center link to obtain information about pediatric bipolar disorder, connect to the advocacy center, view a timeline of the history of bipolar disorder, or find a doctor or support group in your area.

Cyclothymic Disorder

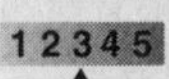

www.psycom.net/depression.central.cyclothymia.html

Cyclothymia is considered a milder form of bipolar disorder in which mood swings occur more frequently but are less intense. Here, you can learn more about cyclothymia including the diagnostic criteria and most effective treatments.

McMan's Depression and Bipolar Web

www.mcmanweb.com

John McManamy, a journalist diagnosed with bipolar disorder, has been writing about his experiences with the disorder and his insights into treatments for several years. At this site, you can read several of McManamy's articles, connect with others in the online forums, subscribe to McManamy's newsletter, and find links to a host of other resources on the web.

Pendulum Resources: The Bipolar Disorder Port

www.pendulum.org

A departure point for learning everything you need to know about bipolar disorder (manic depression). Find out about the diagnostic criteria for bipolar disorder, the latest medications and treatments, and ongoing studies. Includes links to other sites, books, articles, and even some jokes.

CONDUCT DISORDER

American Academy of Childhood & Adolescent Psychiatry

www.aacap.org/publications/factsfam/conduct.htm

This site provides an excellent introduction to conduct disorder, describing its symptoms along with some basic information on treatments.

Clinical Guide to Conduct Disorder

dcfswebresource.prairienet.org/resources/conductdisorder_guide.php

This is a outstanding, clinical description of conduct disorder and Oppositional Defiant Disorder, which includes an overview of symptoms and diagnosis, assessment, and treatments.

ConductDisorders.com

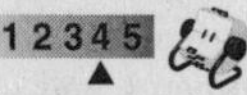

www.conductdisorders.com

If you're a parent trying to raise a challenging child, visit ConductDisorders.com to connect with other parents who are willing to share their stories, support you, and offer advice from life in the trenches. Click the Links button for a directory of additional websites.

Oppositional Defiant Disorder (ODD) and Conduct Disorders

12345

www.klis.com/chandler/pamphlet/oddcd/oddcdpamphlet.htm

A free, online book that covers ODD and conduct disorders in some depth. Features several intriguing vignettes, a list of symptoms to look for, and various available treatments (medical and nonmedical).

CYCLOTHYMIC DISORDER *(SEE MENTAL HEALTH DISORDER—BIPOLAR DISORDEER)*

DELIRIUM

Delirium

12345

www.clevelandclinicmeded.com/diseasemanagement/psychiatry/delirium/delirium.htm

Online publication from the Cleveland Center defines delirium, explores its prevalence and pathophysiology, describes its signs and symptoms, and reveals various treatments that have proven to be somewhat effective. Clickable table of contents helps you go directly to the topic that interests you most. Site also provides some clickable references to articles.

Patient Family Guide to Delirium

12345

www.psych.org/psych_pract/treatg/patientfam_guide/Delirium.pdf

12-page introduction to the topic of delirium for patients who suffer from it and their loved ones. Site covers signs and symptoms, treatments, and prognosis.

DEMENTIA

Dementia.com

12345 RSS

www.dementia.com

Dementia.com is a one-stop kiosk where you can obtain news and information on the latest discoveries and treatments for this often debilitating disease. Resources are grouped by categories, including About Dementia, Caring for Dimentia, News, Literature, Community, and Resources. Click the Caring link for a brief primer on dementia along with tips. To take a quiz, click the Community link.

Dementia on the Neurology Channel

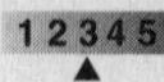

www.neurologychannel.com/dementia

Pretty good overview of dementia includes a description of the signs and symptoms, the different types of dementia, and possible causes.

DEPRESSION

All About Depression

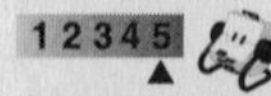

www.allaboutdepression.com

This excellent site provides information about all forms of depression, including bipolar depression, dysthymia, postpartum depression, and seasonal affective disorder. Tabbed interface helps you quickly move to your area of interest: Causes, Diagnosis, Treatment, Medication, Special Topics, and Resources. On the Resources tab, you can find a directory of links to other sites that focus on depression. Site also features online self-tests and workshops, discussion forums, and special sections for friends and family. You can register to receive the AAD newsletter.

Coping with Depression Fallout

www.depressionfallout.com

Learning how to cope with someone who is depressed and how it affects you is the focus of this site, which is based heavily on the book, *How You*

Can Survive When They're Depressed. Not a lot of information, but one of the few sites to recognize the impact depression has on others.

Depressed Anonymous

12345

www.depressedanon.com

Depressed Anonymous was formed to provide therapeutic resources for depressed individuals of all ages. Check out the newsletter for mental health professionals and depressed or recovering individuals. Practice the 12-step program to recovery.

Best Depression and Bipolar Support Alliance

12345

www.dbsalliance.org

Find information about clinical depression, dysthymic disorder, major depression, bipolar disorder, treatments, as well as self-help resources online. Read general articles about depression and other mood disorders, find a local support group, or research a specific topic. You can also buy books from the online store. Whether you're suffering from clinical depression or have a loved one who suffers from a serious psychiatric disorder, this is the best place to start your research.

depression-screening.org

12345

www.depression-screening.org

Sponsored by the National Mental Health Association with support from Eli Lilly and Company, this site provides a survey you can complete to determine whether you have common symptoms of depression. It is careful to mention that this is no diagnosis, but the results can help you determine whether you need a more-thorough evaluation.

National Institutes of Mental Health: Depression

12345

www.nimh.nih.gov/HealthInformation/Depressionmenu.cfm

Read the National Institutes of Mental Health (NIMH) brochure on depression and how to deal with it. This brochure provides descriptions of and treatments for major depression, dysthymia, and bipolar disorder (manic depression) for both the depressed person and those around him or her. This site also provides links to additional resources and to a special area for kids.

Psychology Information Online

12345

www.psychologyinfo.com/depression

Plenty of information about the symptoms of depression, causes, treatments, as well as descriptions of the many types of depression. Also, find out how common it is in various groups, such as in women and teenagers.

Teen Depression

12345

www.teen-depression.info

Depression might manifest itself differently in teens than it does in adults. This site can help you develop your own personal program of prevention, detection, and treatment. This site also covers bipolar disorder in teens and teen suicide.

EATING DISORDERS

American Anorexia Bulimia Association of Philadelphia

12345

www.aabaphila.org

Great resource for individuals confronting eating disorders. Also contains information for professionals who treat eating disorders and information for friends and families who are affected.

Anorexic Web

12345

www.anorexicweb.com

Designed and written by a recovering anorexic, the site aims to provide understanding to those fighting eating disorders through information, photos, and reflective poems. Unlike more medically oriented sites, this one speaks directly to those afflicted with eating disorders. And, because this site has been developed by a recovering anorexic, it provides a nonjudgmental forum that is highly empathetic.

A B C D E F G H I J K L M N O P Q R S T U V W X Y Z

Binge Eating Disorders

12345

win.niddk.nih.gov/publications/binge.htm

This site addresses binge eating disorders by providing information to help identify the problem. Directions on getting help are also provided.

Center for Eating Disorders

12345

www.sjmcmd.org/eatingdisorders

A resource for gathering information on eating disorders. Includes FAQs and discussion groups for the eating disorder sufferer. Questions asked here are answered.

Eating Disorders Association (EDA)

12345

www.edauk.com

Very informative site for both young and older people who suffer from or are interested in learning more about eating disorders. Provides a cool interactive flip-card tool for determining if you have an eating disorder and provides general information about the various eating disorders. Features some poetry and other inspirational material plus links to other resources.

Eating Disorders Online.com

eatingdisordersonline.com

This site provides information to help recognize if you or someone you know has a problem with eating. At the end of each brief article is a list of local organizations available to help individuals cope and treat their illness.

Eating Disorders Resource Centre

12345

www.uq.net.au/eda/documents/start.html

This site provides information about eating disorders and periodic newsletters about treatment options.

Girl Power! Bodywise

12345

www.girlpower.gov/girlarea/bodywise/eatingdisorders/anorexia.htm

The U.S. Department of Health and Human Services has set up this anorexia site specifically for kids of all ages, especially girls. Bodywise provides basic information on anorexia along with real-life stories from girls who suffer from the disorder.

National Eating Disorder Association

12345

www.nationaleatingdisorders.org

This site, created and maintained by the NEDA (National Eating Disorders Association) offers information, help, and referrals for those suffering from a wide range of eating disorders, including anorexia, bulimia, and binge eating. It also provides information for those concerned with body image and weight issues. NEDA is the largest nonprofit organization in the United States that focuses on eating disorders.

National Women's Health Association

12345

www.4woman.gov/faq/easyread/anorexia-etr.htm

This site provides an excellent overview of anorexia and bulimia, including common causes and signs. It also contains an illustrated map of the body that shows the effects of eating disorders on various parts of the human anatomy. You can scroll down to the bottom of the page for a list of additional resources.

The Renfrew Center Foundation

12345

www.renfrew.org

Get answers to your questions about eating disorders, downloadable educational materials, information about treatment options and current research studies, and view a list of recommended books and other resources. You can even submit a question online.

Best Something Fishy

1 2 3 4 5

www.something-fishy.org

A site full of information related to symptoms, treatments, variations on eating disorders (EDs), and physical problems as a result of EDs, as well as advice for doctors, friends, and family members to help those struggling with the disorder. You can buy music and other small gift-type items. A percentage of the proceeds from every sale goes to support nonprofit organizations.

OBSESSIVE-COMPULSIVE DISORDER

Obsessive-Compulsive Disorder for Kids

1 2 3 4 5

kidshealth.org/kid/health_problems/learning_problem/ocd.html

Excellent overview of OCD written specifically to help children understand the disorder. Article describes obsessions and compulsions in an easily digestible format and goes on to explain various available treatments.

Obsessive-Compulsive Disorder (OCD) Screening Quiz

1 2 3 4 5

psychcentral.com/ocdquiz.htm

If you suspect that you or a loved one suffers from OCD, visit this site to take a screening quiz and determine whether you or your loved one needs to consult with a specialist.

Obsessive-Compulsive Foundation

1 2 3 4 5

www.ocfoundation.org

Learn about the different classifications of OCD and the treatments that have been effective. Find out the causes and symptoms of the disease, as well as how to get help. Find out whom to contact for more information.

OPPOSITIONAL DEFIANT DISORDER *(SEE MENTAL HEALTH DISORDER—CONDUCT DISORDER)*

PANIC DISORDER *(SEE MENTAL HEALTH DISORDERS—ANXIETY & PANIC DISORDERS)*

PARANOIA

Paranoia and Paranoid Disorders

1 2 3 4 5

www.nmha.org/infoctr/factsheets/paranoia.cfm

Good fact sheet introducing paranoia. Site defines paranoia, describes its symptoms, explores potential causes, and explains the treatment approach.

Useful Information on Paranoia

1 2 3 4 5

www.hoptechno.com/paranoia.htm

Excellent article on paranoia that includes some brief narratives of paranoid episodes. Article also explains the diagnostic criteria and treatment options and explains the link between paranoia and schizophrenia.

PERSONALITY DISORDERS

Borderline Personality Disorder

1 2 3 4 5

www.bpdcentral.com

Site focuses on borderline personality disorder, covering everything from diagnosis and treatment to finding legal help. Check out the FAQs tab to learn the bare essentials. The information at this site is directed more toward the loved ones of those who suffer from BPD.

Mayo Clinic: Personality Disorders

1 2 3 4 5 ▲

www.nmha.org/infoctr/factsheets/paranoia.cfm

Outstanding information on various personality disorders from a trusted source of medical information. This site provides an overview of personality disorders, describes the common signs and symptoms, explains the screening process, presents treatment options, and reveals potential complications.

National Education Alliance for Borderline Personality Disorder

1 2 3 4 5 ▲

www.borderlinepersonalitydisorder.com

The National Education Alliance for Borderline Personality Disorder's mission is "to raise public awareness, provide education, promote research on borderline personality disorder, and enhance the quality of life of those affected by this serious mental illness." Here, you can find resources for families and doctors, a list of upcoming events, some free publications, and information about the alliance.

National Mental Health Association: Personality Disorders

1 2 3 4 5 ▲

www.nmha.org/infoctr/factsheets/91.cfm

Excellent fact sheet introduces visitors to the various personality disorders along with their diagnosis and treatment.

Personality Disorder Test

1 2 3 4 5 ▲

www.4degreez.com/misc/personality_disorder_test.mv

Do you suspect that you or a loved one has a personality disorder? Then visit this site to take a test and find out if you or your loved one fits the diagnostic criteria. Of course, no online test can determine whether you have a psychiatric or psychological condition, but the test can help you determine whether you or your loved one needs to consult a doctor. The test results show whether or not you're likely to suffer from a personality disorder and show you which personality disorder(s) are more likely affecting you.

Personality Disorders

1 2 3 4 5 ▲

www.focusas.com/PersonalityDisorders.html

This site covers a wide range of personality disorders, including anti-social, borderline, histrionic, obsessive-compulsive, paranoid, and schizoid. Good overview of personality disorders in general, but doesn't go into much depth.

POST-TRAUMATIC STRESS DISORDER

The American Academy of Experts in Traumatic Stress

1 2 3 4 5 ▲

www.aaets.org

Read articles from *Trauma Response*, the official publication of the Academy. Articles cover a wide range of trauma: trauma as a result of combat, domestic violence, plane disasters, terrorist acts, natural disasters, rape, divorce, school violence, and more. You can examine case studies and profiles, learn exactly what post-traumatic stress disorder is, look at what causes it, and learn about the various treatments that have been administered.

David Baldwin's Trauma Information Pages

1 2 3 4 5 ▲

www.trauma-pages.com

David Baldwin's site features useful information about dealing with post-traumatic stress disorders. Through these papers, Baldwin explores what goes on in the brain biologically during traumatic experiences, which psychotherapies are most effective in dealing with these disorders and why, and how one can best measure the clinical effectiveness of these treatments. Excellent bibliography with links to Amazon.com for online shopping.

International Society for Traumatic Stress Studies

www.istss.org

Excellent resource for professionals who specialize in diagnosing, treating, and researching traumatic stress. Not much here for those who suffer from it.

National Center for Post-Traumatic Stress Disorder

www.ncptsd.va.gov

The National Center for Post-Traumatic Stress Disorder (PTSD) has a mission: "To advance the clinical care and social welfare of America's veterans through research, education, and training in the science, diagnosis, and treatment of PTSD and stress-related disorders." Even if you're not a veteran, you can pick up plenty of useful and current information about traumatic stress disorder. Site features several categories, including Topics, Facts, Publications, and Documents. PTSD assessments are also available online.

PSYCHOSIS

Early Psychosis Prevention and Intervention Centre

1 2 3 4 5

www.eppic.org.au

EPPIC (Early Psychosis Prevention and Intervention Centre) "aims to facilitate early identification and treatment of psychosis and therefore reduce the disruption to the young person's functioning and psychosocial development." At this site, you can learn more about psychosis, including what you can do to help someone suffering from psychosis.

Psychosis–Glossary

www.aacap.org/about/glossary/Psychos.htm

Informative article on psychosis explaining that psychosis is a common symptom of several mental disorders, including schizophrenia and bipolar disorder. Article defines delusions and hallucinations.

SCHIZOPHRENIA

The Experience of Schizophrenia

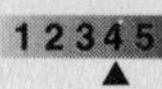

www.chovil.com

Ian Chovil describes his firsthand experience living with schizophrenia and provides guidance on treatments that others may find helpful.

NARSAD: National Association for Research on Schizophrenia and Depression

www.narsad.org

"NARSAD's mission is to raise funds for psychiatric brain disorder research for scientists worldwide, in an effort to find the causes, better treatments, and eventual cures for these disorders." Click the Disorders & Conditions link to navigate to the specific disorder for which you want more information.

Best Schizophrenia.com

www.schizophrenia.com

Schizophrenia.com lives up to its self-proclaimed status as the World's Number 1 Schizophrenia website, providing an overview; a description of signs, symptoms, and causes; treatments; success stories; and much more. Site offers information that's helpful not only for people suffering from schizophrenia but also for loved ones. You can take an early screening test online, check out the discussion forums, and keep abreast of the latest developments in treatment. This outstanding site is up-to-date, packed with useful information, and easy to navigate.

Schizophrenics Anonymous

sanonymous.com

Schizophrenics Anonymous is a self-help group for those suffering from schizophrenia. Site offers some general information about schizophrenia and related conditions but is more useful as a networking tool.

World Fellowship for Schizophrenia and Allied Disorders

www.world-schizophrenia.org

WFSAD (World Fellowship for Schizophrenia and Allied Disorders) is "dedicated to lightening the burden of schizophrenia and allied disorders for sufferers and their families." Click the Disorders link to begin learning about schizophrenia and related disorders. The Resources link leads you to a list of other websites devoted to mental health issues and schizophrenia in particular. Some excellent information on stigmas, how to overcome them, and how to advocate for fair treatment.

TOURETTE'S SYNDROME

The Facts About Tourette's Syndrome

members.tripod.com/~tourette13

Good overview of Tourette's syndrome helps those who are unfamiliar with the disorder get up to speed in a hurry. Dispels common myths and misconceptions about Tourette's.

Tourette's Syndrome Association, Inc.

www.tsa-usa.org

At this site, TSA provides an excellent collection of articles and other resources for those suffering from Tourette's syndrome and their friends and families. Site is organized into several sections, including News & Events, Medical & Treatment, Medical Education, Living with TS, Newly Diagnosed, and Clinical/Counseling. Special area for kids.

Tourette's Syndrome Information Support Site

1 2 3 4 5 Blog

www.tourettes-disorder.com

This site is devoted to giving hope to those who are living with Tourette's syndrome. Site offers basic information on Tourette's, including diagnostic criteria and available treatments, along with links to discussion groups, support groups, and fun stuff. If you're looking for an understanding community to support you, this is the place to go.

Tourette's Syndrome Plus

1 2 3 4 5

www.tourettesyndrome.net

This site covers Tourette's syndrome along with other disorders that commonly affect children and adolescence. For every condition described on the site, you'll also find articles and files relating to school-related issues in the Education section of the site. Don't miss the general Behavior section, where you can find topics of concerns to parents and teachers of children with these childhood-onset conditions or disorders. Excellent collection of articles.

A B C D E F G H I J K L M N O P Q R S T U V W X Y Z

MEXICO

Best Access Mexico Connect

1 2 3 4 5

www.mexconnect.com

Access Mexico Connect is "a monthly, electronic magazine devoted to providing quality information about and promoting Mexico to the world. The magazine is supported by a searchable and cross-indexed database of over 12,000 articles and 2,700 photographs." Site also features discussion forums related to specific areas inside Mexico. Some features are available only to subscribers.

CIA World Factbook: Mexico

1 2 3 4 5

www.cia.gov/cia/publications/factbook/geos/mx.html

The CIA World Factbook is an excellent research resource for learning about a country, its people, its geography, its resources, and other facts and statistics. This page is a great place to launch any investigation into Mexico.

> **Tip:** Icons appear next to each topic of interest. A description of each icon appears at the top of the page, but you can rest the mouse pointer on an icon to view its name.

Mexico for Kids

1 2 3 4 5

www.elbalero.gob.mx/index_kids.html

For an excellent introduction to Mexico, visitors of all ages should visit this site. Here, you can learn about Mexico's history and government, explore its various states, wonder at its amazing biodiversity, and play some online games. You can browse the site in any of four languages: English, Italian, Spanish, or French.

MexOnline

1 2 3 4 5

www.mexonline.com

Comprehensive travel directory for anyone who's planning a trip to Mexico. Site covers Activities, Food & Drink, History, and more. Check out the message boards to get inside tips from others who have traveled the country.

A B C D E F G H I J K L M N O P Q R S T U V W X Y Z

MOTIVATIONAL & SELF-IMPROVEMENT INFORMATION

AchievementRadio.com

www.achievement-radio.com

Internet radio station that focuses on "personal success, positive living, and self-improvement." Features top motivational speakers giving free advice.

Deepak Chopra

12345

www.chopra.com

This is a one-stop shopping website for those seeking self-improvement. Pick up the tip of the day, the quote of the day, the vegetarian recipe of the week, and plenty of other spiritual guidance at Deepak Chopra's site, which includes information about his personal growth workshops and materials. You can also ask him a question and learn more about the Center for Well Being. Order books, candles, spices, and food supplements here.

Dr. Phil

12345

www.drphil.com

A popular guest on the Oprah Winfrey show until he received his own show, Dr. Phil's in-your-face approach encourages people to "Get Real, Get Smart, and Get Going." Here, you can learn more about the show and about Dr. Phil and his books; you can learn about upcoming shows; you can shop for merchandise online; and you can even learn what to do to get on the show. Discussion forums enable you to connect with other fans of Dr. Phil's, and you can start your own online diary for private use or to share with visitors at the site. Very classy site packed with useful information and easy to navigate.

John Gray

12345

www.marsvenus.com

Take John Gray's Personal Success Block Buster questionnaire to get feedback on what areas of your life are holding you back from total success. Then read about all of his books, upcoming conferences, and recent magazine columns on relationships and parenting. Purchase books, audio and videotapes, CDs, and games at this site.

Les Brown

www.lesbrown.com

Find a quote that speaks to you in Les's Success Quotes section of the site, or read Les's bio, find out about upcoming speaking engagements, read essays, and post a message on the message board.

MotivationalQuotes.com

12345

www.motivationalquotes.com

Huge collection of motivational quotes, prayers, and positive affirmations. The site is devoted to promoting positive thinking.

Motivational Speakers

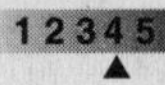

www.speakersla.com

Learn about the Distinguished Speakers Series and "Experience a season of heroes and legends. You'll be moved, you'll be challenged, you'll leave *inspired*!" Purchase tickets to the series from this website.

Self-Growth.com

www.selfgrowth.com

This site offers a plethora of self-help and personal growth resources. You can find hundreds of articles, more than 4,000 links, IQ tests, a free newsletter, inspirational quotes, and much, much more.

Successories.com

www.successories.com

Successories is dedicated to helping organizations and individuals realize their full potential. This company believes that motivation originates with attitude, grows in response to goals, and endures when reinforced through exposure to insightful ideas in your environment. The unique collection of themed merchandise is designed to promote a positive outlook; celebrate human achievement; and inspire excellence in your career, your business, and your life.

Suze Orman

www.suzeorman.com/home.asp

This site is the home of money-management guru Suze Orman, author of *The Money Book for the Young Fabulous and Broke*, which provides practical advice on holding on to what you have and achieving your personal financial goals and other goals relating to your family. At this site, you can find books and other products, sign up to receive a newsletter, check out her program schedule, and much more.

Tony Robbins: Resources for Creating an Extraordinary Quality of Life

www.tonyrobbins.com

Home page of motivational guru Anthony Robbins. Learn about upcoming events, browse through his products and order them online, read the results he's achieved, visit daily for the day's "Daily Action," find out about coaching support, and more.

Zig Ziglar

www.zigziglar.com

Sign up to get a free Zig newsletter, listen to clips from the speaker, and get more information on Zig Ziglar and his programs here. Books, videos, and gifts can all be purchased from the website.

MOTORCYCLES/CHOPPERS

AFMWeb (American Federation of Motorcyclists)

www.afmracing.org

Focuses on motorcycle road racing. Offers a new racer school, practice information, and a schedule of races. Also includes a FAQs area, a rulebook, links, membership information, race results, and a classified section.

American Motorcyclist Association

www.ama-cycle.org

Promotes the interests of motorcycle enthusiasts. The site includes AMA pro and amateur racing information, travel, and more.

BMW Motorcycles

12345

www.bmwmotorcycles.com

The official BMW motorcycles website, this visually appealing site is full of fun animation and solid information about BMW motorcycles. Learn about the complete line of BMW bikes, check out the gear and accessories, find a local dealer, and get financing information.

Ducati

www.ducati.com

At Ducati, you can locate a dealer, check out late-breaking Ducati racing news, browse the newest line of Ducati motorcycles, access information about Ducati service, explore the culture and heritage of Ducati from the 1920s to now, join the Ducati community, download wallpaper and other freebies, or shop for accessories online.

Best Harley-Davidson

12345

www.harley-davidson.com

Official site of Harley-Davidson—the products, the company, and the experience. Check out the current models; find a dealer; and see what kind of new clothing, accessories, and gifts are available. You can even get information about investing in the Harley-Davidson company. This site's sleek design and comprehensive offerings make it the best commercial motorcycle site on the Web.

Honda Motorcycles

12345

powersports.honda.com

Get a preview of the newest Honda models, and get your racing news and schedule here, as well as information on special deals and events sponsored by Honda. You can also learn more about patented Honda racing innovations.

Horizons Unlimited

12345 Blog

www.horizonsunlimited.com

When motorcycle traveling is in your blood, there's not much you can do to quell the urge, so visit this site for some ideas on where you can explore next. This site is dedicated to fostering a community of motorcycle travelers and providing them with the information and resources they need to find the best places to go and the best places to stay and eat along the way. This site provides plenty of information on trip planning, traveler's tales, links to other sites, and online forums in several languages.

Indian Motorcycles

1 2 3 4 5

www.indianmotorcycle.com

Home of America's oldest brand of motorcycle. Check out the latest line of Indian motorcycles, view a history of the company from 1900 to present, find a dealer, or copy free ride maps.

Kawasaki.com

1 2 3 4 5

www.kawasaki.com

Find out about special deals on Kawasaki wheels, order Kawasaki clothing and accessories online, and stay on top of Kawasaki news and promotions.

motogranprix.com

www.motogp.com/en/motogp

If you follow the Motorcycle Grand Prix, you'll want to bookmark this page. Features calendar of races, race results, current standings, news, information about the riders and teams, and much more.

Motorcycle Online

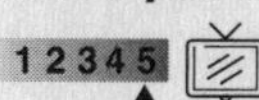

www.motorcycle.com

Motorcycle Online includes feature articles and classifieds, plus a museum and bulletin board. Read product reviews, get repair tips, share information with other motorcycle enthusiasts, and hear about next year's models at this site.

Motorcycle Riders Foundation

1 2 3 4 5

www.mrf.org

This Washington, D.C.-based bikers advocacy site offers news from D.C., MRF reports, a message board, national motorcycle laws, and links for information and research.

Two Wheel Freaks

1 2 3 4 5

www.2wf.com

Huge resource for everything related to motorcycles, this site covers racing, culture, bike tests, repair and maintenance, stunt riding, and more. Staffed by motorcycle owners and enthusiasts, dedicated to providing the best information in an irreverent and entertaining format. Discussion groups are also available.

Yamaha

1 2 3 4 5

www.yamaha-motor.com

Home of Yamaha Motor Company, makers of motorcycles, snowmobiles, Jet Skis, boats, golf carts, and other popular recreational motor vehicles. Here, you can check out the latest motorcycle models and find a dealer near you.

MOVIES/FILMS

CinemaNow!

www.cinemanow.com

CinemaNow! is an online video distributor, sort of an online pay-per-view service. You register with CinemaNow!, find a movie you want to watch, order and pay for the movie, download it to your computer, and then watch it as much as you want. The movies you find are the same ones you might get via pay-per-view or at your local video rental store. Some free independent films for download.

E! Online

movies.eonline.com

You're sure to be up to speed on all the movie industry dirt with the help of this site, which offers celebrity news, movie release information and rankings, movie synopses, and box office reports.

Film Affinity

www.filmaffinity.com

At Film Affinity, you register and enter your ratings for a selection of movies. The site searches its database of other registered users, finds your movie soul mates, and consults their ratings to find other movies that might appeal to your tastes. Pretty cool concept, and cool site.

Film Bug: Guide to the Movie Stars

12345

www.filmbug.com

Filmbug "has an extensive database with biographies of over 9,000 actors, directors, screenwriters, and other celebrities." You can search for a star by name or browse the directory from A to Z. Also features a Movies tab you can use to search for your favorite stars by movie or TV series.

Best Internet Movie Database

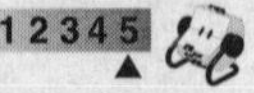

imdb.com

The online authority for all things related to movies and film, this comprehensive directory allows you to track down movies and trivia by movie title, director, or actor. Want a list of all the movies in which Robert De Niro appeared? Then search for "Robert De Niro" to pull up a list of this master's films. Check out the new releases, top videos on DVD and VHS, top rated movies of all time in various categories, and independent movies. You can tour the photo gallery, play movie trivia games online, and visit the message boards to keep in touch with fellow movie buffs. With its no-frills presentation, excellent search tools, and comprehensive database of movie trivia, this site has no equal.

Movies.com

movies.go.com

Are you planning a movie night? Then get it right at Movies.com. Here, you can find movie reviews, trailers, theater times and locations, DVDs and videos, and everything else related to movies. This site focuses on new releases.

FESTIVALS

Cannes Film Festival

www.festival-cannes.fr

If you can't make it to France for the Cannes Film Festival, this is the next best thing. At this site you can explore the award winners for feature films, short films, and Cannes classics from 1946 to the current year; meet the juries who were in charge of selections for each year; view the official awards;

check out some of the major events in and around the festival; and more. Great site for film buffs.

Sundance Film Festival

festival.sundance.org

Robert Redford's Sundance Film Festival now has a website, where you can learn more about this important festival and check out what's happening at Sundance when the festival is in full swing.

Nonstop Film Festivals

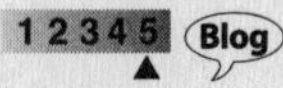

www.filmfestivals.com

If film festivals are your thing, Nonstop Film Festivals is the place to be. This site features a clearinghouse of information on film festivals around the world. Content is provided in several sections, including Films, Festivals, People, and Awards. If you're sponsoring a film festival you want to promote, you can list it here.

Tribeca Film Festival

www.tribecafilmfestival.org

Robert De Niro's own Tribeca Film Festival is on the web, and you can visit it here to view video clips, obtain ticket information, and learn more about this year's upcoming festival.

INDEPENDENT FILMS

AtomFilms

www.atomfilms.com

AtomFilms features on-demand viewing of more than 1,500 world-class game, film, and animation titles. Genres include animation, comedy, music, extreme, action, and drama. Collectively, more than 20 million entertainment fans visit the AtomFilms and Shockwave sites each month to check out what they have to offer. Very cool streaming video.

BMW Films

bmwfilms.com

If you're interested in short films created by some of Hollywood's finest talents, check out this site.

IFILM

www.ifilm.com

Online video library packed with short downloadable movies and movie clips broken down into several categories, including Action, Animation, Comedy, Drama, Erotica, Gay & Lesbian, and Sci-Fi. Check out the top short films and trailers, or browse the categories for a complete selection.

IndieFilmSpot

www.striketheset.com

IndieFilmSpot provides independent film makers an online distribution channel for their works. To view the movies, you must register and pay for your membership. Price per clip varies depending on whether you are a standard or monthly user.

Richmond Moving Image Co-Op

www.rmicweb.org

Flicker festivals have cropped up all around the nation, providing budding filmmakers the chance to produce their own short flicks (under 15 minutes) and show them to real live audiences. This site is the home of the Richmond Flicker, located in Richmond, Virginia, and the James River Film Festival. Here, you can learn about upcoming festivals, check the schedule, and even download programs from past festivals. Do you have a movie you want to show? Click the SUBMIT YOUR FILM link and learn where to mail your footage. *RMIC* is a great source of information about alternative films. You can read about filmmakers, find out what's showing where, and download images from films.

UndergroundFilm.org

www.undergroundfilm.org

UndergroundFilm.org is a nonprofit company dedicated to helping independent filmmakers distribute their creations to audiences via the Web. Here, you can download independent films, watch them, and then come back and comment on them on the message boards. Great place for filmmakers and audience members to interact and share insights.

REVIEWS

Agony Booth

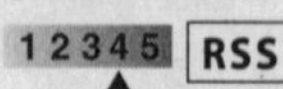

www.agonybooth.com

If you have ever been subjected to an awful movie and kind of enjoyed wallowing in it by discussing its failures on so many levels, then the Agony Booth might just be the place for you. Here, rogue reviewers trash the worst that the movie industry has to offer—all in good humor, of course.

Rotten Tomatoes

www.rottentomatoes.com

Rotten Tomatoes, created by movie buff Senh Duong, is the advice you need *before* you see a movie. With critiques of more than 120,000 titles and critical reaction from the nation's top print and online film critics, you can hardly go wrong seeing a recommended movie. The site's unique Tomatometer tallies the votes pro and con, and summarizes them to give you a quick freshness rating—over 60 percent is basically equivalent to a thumbs up. Very cool site.

Real Guide Home

movies.real.com

Read reviews of top movies and new releases, watch clips and movie trailers, read interviews with the stars, and find out about upcoming projects.

Metacritic

12345 RSS

www.metacritic.com

Are you looking for a movie review for a newly released flick? Then look no further. For every movie featured on the site, Metacritic pulls together reviews from the top film critics, provides a brief synopsis of each critic's opinion of the flick, and provides a link for accessing the full review. Metacritic also tallies the ratings to determine a "metascore" that reflects the collective rating from all critics. Recently, Metacritic has started rating CDs and games, too.

Roger Ebert

rogerebert.suntimes.com

If you rely on Roger Ebert's reviews to guide your movie selections, check out this site where he posts his reviews online. In addition to Ebert's movie reviews, you can check out his list of all time great movies, peruse the movie glossary, read the latest news from the film festivals, and get Oscar updates.

STUDIOS

20th Century Fox

12345

www.foxmovies.com

A&E

12345

www.aetv.com

DreamWorks

12345

www.dreamworks.com

First Look Features

12345

www.flp.com

Fox Searchlight

1 2 3 4 5 Blog

www.foxsearchlight.com

Gaumont

1 2 3 4 5

www.gaumont.com

HBO

1 2 3 4 5

www.hbo.com

Lionsgate

1 2 3 4 5

www.lionsgatefilms.com

MGM & Orion Pictures

1 2 3 4 5

www.mgmua.com

Miramax

1 2 3 4 5

www.miramax.com

New Line Cinema

1 2 3 4 5

www.newline.com

Paramount

1 2 3 4 5

www.paramount.com

Showtime

1 2 3 4 5 RSS

www.sho.com

Sony Pictures

1 2 3 4 5

www.sonypictures.com/movies/index.html

Turner Classic Movies

1 2 3 4 5 RSS

www.tcm.com

United International Pictures

1 2 3 4 5

www.uip.com

Universal Pictures

1 2 3 4 5

www.universalpictures.com

Universal Studios

1 2 3 4 5

www.universalstudios.com

Walt Disney Studios

1 2 3 4 5

disney.go.com/disneypictures/index.html

Warner Bros. & Castle Rock

1 2 3 4 5

www2.warnerbros.com

THEATERS

Cinemark & IMAX

1 2 3 4 5

www.cinemark.com

Find out what's showing at your local Cinemark or IMAX Theater, check on showtimes, and find out about money-saving deals. Site links to IMDB for information about specific movies.

Fandango

www.fandango.com

Fandango is a search tool for tracking down local theaters that are playing the movies you want to see. You simply specify the movie you want to see and your location (city and state or ZIP code). Fandango displays the location of movie theaters in your area that are playing the movie, complete with showtimes. You can often order tickets online and even obtain driving directions from your home to the theater. Trailers are offered for most movies.

> **Tip:** If you have a wireweb browser, type mobile.fandango.com into the browser to access Fandango wireless.

Hollywood.com

www.hollywood.com

is more than a tool for finding theaters in your area that are playing the movies you want to see. When you perform a search, the resulting page enables you to view trailers, clips, and still photos; read a review of the movie; jump to the movie's official site; and obtain even more information about the movie. Site features the latest Web offerings, including blogs, podcasts, webcasts, and RSS feeds. You can even create your own fan site. Outstanding site offers plenty in a format that's easy to navigate.

Moviefone

movies.aol.com

Moviefone is a service that enables you to locate theaters that are playing the movies you want to see. You search for the movie along with your ZIP code or city and state, and Moviefone locates the nearest theaters playing the movie. Assuming the theater supports it, you can order tickets online. Trailers are offered for most movies.

Regal Cinemas

www.regalcinemas.com

If you have a Regal Cinema, United Artists Theatre, or Edwards Theatre in your area, you can go online to find out which movies are playing at the local theater and then check showtimes. Regal works through Fandango for ordering tickets online. Trailers are offered for most movies.

MUSEUMS

Children's Museum of Indianapolis

12345

www.childrensmuseum.org

The Children's Museum of Indianapolis is one of the top children's museums in the world, featuring exhibits specifically geared to get kids interested in the various branches of science and technology. At this site, you can tour the museum's exhibits (past and present), play games online, learn how to get more out of your museum visit, shop at the museum store, and more. Special areas are available for teachers and parents.

Exploratorium

www.exploratorium.edu

Website of the Exploratorium, a unique museum housed inside San Francisco's Palace of Fine Arts, which features more than "650 science, art, and human perception exhibits." Founded by noted physicist Dr. Frank Oppenheimer, this site is devoted to nurturing people's curiosity about the world around them. Here, you can check out various online exhibits and learn more about the museum.

MuseumStuff.com

www.museumstuff.com/shop

Directory of online museum stores, many of which feature online shopping. Search for a museum store by entering a keyword or browse by categories, such as Art and Design, History, and Science.

National Museum of the American Indian

www.nmai.si.edu

The National Museum of the American Indian is the Smithsonian's sixteenth museum, and it is comprised of three facilities—in New York, Maryland, and Washington, D.C. Here, you can learn more about the museum, its collections, its exhibits, and its educational activities and events.

ARCHITECTURE

The Chicago Athenaeum: The Museum of Architecture and Design

www.chi-athenaeum.org

The Chicago Athenaeum features "Landmark Chicago," the first permanent exhibition celebrating Chicago's position as the world capital of historical and contemporary landmarks of modern architecture. This site contains information and photos from this exhibit, as well as other details about the museum, its exhibits, and its upcoming schedule.

Getty Center

www.getty.edu

Home of the Getty Center, in Los Angeles, "one of the largest privately funded architectural complexes ever designed and constructed in a single architectural campaign." Check out a gallery from more than 600 photographers whose work is in the Getty Museum's collection.

National Building Museum

www.nbm.org

The National Building Museum presents permanent exhibitions about the world we live in, from our homes and offices to our parks and cities. This site has online excerpts of exhibits past and present, as well as information about books that complement them. It also offers summaries from "The Urban Forum," a program designed to explore issues related to the design, growth, and governance of American cities. Stop by this site to find the museum's hours of operation and location.

The Octagon Museum

www.archfoundation.org/octagon

The Octagon is the museum is "the oldest museum in the United States dedicated to architecture and design." Here, you can explore various architectural designs and discover how these designs influence the way we live.

The Skyscraper Museum

www.skyscraper.org

This not-for-profit corporation is devoted to the study of high-rise buildings, past, present, and future. The site celebrates New York City's rich architectural heritage. Here, you can learn more about the organization and its projects and events.

ART

American Visionary Art Museum

www.avam.org

The world's largest grassroots art exhibition, located in Baltimore's Inner Harbor. Some stuff for kids, such as the Make Your Own Robot game.

The Andy Warhol Museum

www.warhol.org

This site is part of the Carnegie Museums of Pittsburgh; it features a guided tour of the museum itself (opened in 1994), which features images and biographical information regarding Andy Warhol. It also describes the work of the Archives Study Center, which collects and preserves anything to do with Warhol's life and work. A calendar details upcoming exhibitions and events. Links to various Andy Warhol stores, where you can purchase T-shirts, posters, prints, and more.

Artcyclopedia

www.artcyclopedia.com

An art search engine that lets you track down art information by artist, movement, medium, subject, or nationality. It also offers information on museums and other art links.

The Art Institute of Chicago

12345

www.artic.edu

Comprising both a museum and an art school, the institute's site contains everything you always wanted to know about the museum, including information about exhibits and collections, the history and layout of the museum, publications and press releases, gift shop items, and Institute membership information. You can also view art and play games related to art here. Special area for kids and families.

Asian Art Museum of San Francisco

www.asianart.org

This is the largest museum in the Western world devoted to the arts and cultures of Asia. This site provides information about exhibits and programs at the museum, as well as job openings there. Art is organized by country or region.

Cincinnati Art Museum

www.cincinnatiartmuseum.com

This site features a virtual tour of the museum's collections, children's activities, general information, and much more. Be sure to check out the museum's online gift store for gift items.

The Columbia Museum of Art

12345

www.colmusart.org

The museum's exhibits contain European and American fine and decorative art representing a time period of nearly seven centuries. Its public collections of Renaissance and Baroque art include works by Botticelli, Boucher, Canaletto, Tintoretto, and many others. The museum's online magazine,

Collections, will alert you to recent acquisitions, a calendar of events, staffing changes, and additional newsworthy tidbits about the museum, located in Columbia, South Carolina.

Fine Arts Museums of San Francisco

www.thinker.org

Search more than 82,000 images from the deYoung Museum and the Legion of Honor, the two museums that comprise the Art Museums of San Francisco, as well as browse information about current and upcoming exhibitions. You can even create your own online gallery using any selection and arrangement from the collection of 82,000 images.

Guggenheim Museums

www.guggenheim.org

Site contains information about five museums: the Solomon R. Guggenheim Museum on Fifth Avenue in New York City; the Guggenheim Museum SoHo on Broadway in New York City; the Guggenheim Museum in Bilbao, Spain; the Peggy Guggenheim Collection in Venice, Italy; and the Deutsch Guggenheim Berlin. Includes some great photos of the museums and their exhibits. Some information on programs for children and families.

Harvard University Art Museums

www.artmuseums.harvard.edu

This is the website for the Harvard University Art Museums—the Fogg Art Museum, the Busch-Reisinger Museum, the Arthur M. Sackler Museum, and the Strauss Center for Conservations—all in Cambridge, Massachusetts.

Indianapolis Museum of Art

www.ima-art.org

The nation's seventh largest general art museum has permanent collections of African, American, Asian, contemporary, decorative, and European art, as well as a textiles and costumes collection, prints, drawings, and photographs. The IMA complex is surrounded by a 152-acre park, including 50 intensively landscaped acres that are accessible to the public.

J. Paul Getty Museum

1 2 3 4 5

www.getty.edu/museum

Learn about the Getty Museum's collection of artworks, which include antiquities, decorative arts, medieval manuscripts, European paintings, sculptures, drawings, and photographs. Get an overview of the exhibitions and check out the calendar of upcoming events. The online gift store offers everything from hats and T-shirts to calendars, cards, and posters.

The Kemper Museum of Contemporary Art

1 2 3 4 5

www.kemperart.org

This site includes a calendar of events, the history and architecture of the museum, images from the collection, and a guest book. The museum boasts a notable Georgia O'Keeffe collection, several watercolors of which can be viewed at this site.

Le Louvre

1 2 3 4 5

www.louvre.fr

This official site of the famous museum, the home of the *Mona Lisa*, includes information about the museum's seven departments: Oriental Antiquities (with a section dedicated to Islamic Art); Egyptian Antiquities (with a section dedicated to Coptic Art); Greek, Etruscan, and Roman Antiquities; Paintings; Sculptures; Objets d'Art; and Prints and Drawings. The site includes many details (small sections of paintings, enlarged so you can see them better) from the museum's collections. Take some cool QuickTime virtual tours of the museum.

Los Angeles County Museum of Art

1 2 3 4 5

collectionsonline.lacma.org

The Los Angeles County Museum of Art has a collection of more than 100,000 works. Here, you can find more than 50,000 of them online. You can search the site by artist or browse the three main collections: Center for Art of Americas, Center for European Art, and Center for Asian Art. If you're navigating via the map on the opening page, you should know that when you point to a center, such as the Center for Art of Americas, a menu opens that provides graphic representations of your choices. Hover the map over each choice to display a text label describing it.

Best Metropolitan Museum of Art, New York

1 2 3 4 5

www.metmuseum.org

One of the largest art museums in the world, The Met's collections include more than two million works of art—several hundred thousand of which are on view at any given time—spanning more than 5,000 years of world culture, from prehistory to the present. Stay updated on upcoming exhibitions and buy museum products online. This site has an attractive design, is easy to maneuver, and features a huge collection of quality photographs that make visiting this site the next best thing to being there.

Museum of Bad Art

1 2 3 4 5

www.museumofbadart.org

The Museum of Bad Art is dedicated to the collection, preservation, exhibition, and celebration of bad art. The site contains many examples of bad art, including one rather amusing piece entitled "Sunday on the Pot with George." Be sure to check out the MOBA gift store, where you can purchase miniature art reproductions!

Museum of Fine Arts, Boston

1 2 3 4 5

www.mfa.org

This museum prides itself on exhibiting art that is "past and present, old and new, plain and fancy," including masterpieces by Renoir, Monet, Sargent, Turner, Gauguin, and others. The site hosts an online exhibition and contains links to samples from upcoming exhibits. Learn about upcoming exhibitions and purchase museum products online.

Museum of Fine Arts, Houston

1 2 3 4 5

mfah.org

The Museum of Fine Arts, Houston site, includes visuals and information about the permanent collection, traveling exhibitions, events, and educational programs. Collections with online links include African sculpture, American painting, ancient art, decorative arts, Impressionist painting, twentieth-century sculpture, and films.

Museum of Modern Art, New York

1 2 3 4 5

www.moma.org

This site displays samples from current and future exhibits, as well as from MOMA's permanent collection, which includes paintings and sculptures, drawings, prints and illustrated books, architecture and design, photographs, and film and video. The collection includes exceptional groups of work by Matisse, Picasso, Miró, Mondrian, Brancusi, and Pollock. It also contains links to online projects as well as other websites created in conjunction with the Museum of Modern Art and its exhibits. A wealth of information is available about this New York City landmark. Be sure to check out the online gift store.

National Gallery of Art

1 2 3 4 5

www.nga.gov

The National Gallery of Art is located in Washington D.C., but no matter where you live, if you have a computer and an Internet connection, you can tour the gallery's vast collection right here. Peruse the collection by category, take a guided tour, check out the exhibitions, learn more about the collection, and even shop online. Younger kids will find the special NGA for Kids area quite appealing; you can go there directly by typing www.nga.gov/kids/.

National Gallery of Canada

1 2 3 4 5

national.gallery.ca

The National Gallery of Canada is the permanent home of Canada's exceptional national art collection, which includes Canadian art, Inuit art, contemporary art, as well as European, American, and Asian art. With text descriptions in both French and English, this well-designed site showcases this large gallery housing the Canadian national art collection.

Royal Ontario Museum

12345 RSS

www.rom.on.ca

This large museum has Greek, Roman, and Far Eastern art, archaeology, and natural sciences collections, as well as Native ethnology and natural history collections. Virtual exhibits include educational activities such as games, quizzes, and QuickTime movies, as well as online artifact identification and curatorial research.

The San Francisco Museum of Modern Art

12345

www.sfmoma.org

Information about the museum's collection of modern and contemporary artwork is available, including exhibition details, a calendar of events, and educational programs. Information about the rental gallery can also be found here.

The Smithsonian Institution

12345

www.si.edu

The 150-year-old Smithsonian Institution comprises the National Portrait Gallery, the National Museum of American Art, the National Air and Space Museum, the Sackler Gallery, the Cooper-Hewitt Museum of Design, the National Museum of American History, the National Museum of Natural History, and more. You can search this comprehensive site using an A–Z subject index and learn about events and activities. Special areas just for kids.

Web Gallery of Art

12345

www.wga.hu/index1.html

The Web Gallery of Art boasts a collection of more than 11,600 digital reproductions of European paintings and sculptures from 1150 to 1800 A.D., along with commentary and biographies of many of the artists. Search for a specific piece or take a guided tour through the gallery. This site is somewhat off the beaten track, but well worth the detour.

HISTORY & CULTURE

Morikami Museum and Japanese Gardens

12345

www.morikami.org

The only museum in the United States dedicated exclusively to the living culture of Japan, this museum contains a rare Bonsai collection of miniature trees and has beautiful Japanese-style landscaping. Sample photos from the museum's exhibits of Japanese arts, crafts, and artifacts are included at this site.

Museum of Tolerance

12345

www.wiesenthal.com/mot

Take an online tour of this interactive museum that focuses on prejudice and racism in America, as well as the horrors of the Holocaust, as examples of inhumanity. Read biographies of children of the Holocaust, which are updated daily, and make arrangements to visit the Los Angeles museum in person.

National Civil Rights Museum

12345

www.civilrightsmuseum.org

The National Civil Rights Museum presents a timeline of the civil rights struggle relating to African-Americans, with emphasis on the significant events of the 1950s and 1960s. Take an online tour or get more information about the facility at the website.

UCLA Fowler Museum of Cultural History

12345

www.fowler.ucla.edu/incEngine

UCLA's Fowler Museum "celebrates the world's diverse cultures and rich visual arts, especially those of Africa, Asia, Oceania, Native, and Latin America," through exhibitions and publications.

A B C D E F G H I J K L M N O P Q R S T U V W X Y Z

United States Holocaust Memorial Museum

www.ushmm.org

This museum is an international resource for the development of research on the Holocaust and related issues, including those of contemporary significance. Includes a photographic, film, and video archive. The site contains links to museum resources and activities, as well as to related organizations and an internship program.

Wright Brothers Aeroplane Company and Museum of Aviation

1 2 3 4 5

www.first-to-fly.com

Enjoy hands-on aviation fun at this museum, which offers virtual adventures and expeditions in four Wright brothers' planes, as well as historical information. The site contains a lot of information about planes and aviation that is perfect for students.

NATURAL HISTORY

American Museum of Natural History

1 2 3 4 5

www.amnh.org

The museum's collections include the world's largest collection of fossil mammals, dinosaurs, insects, invertebrates, and more. The site lists a few of its thousands of research projects, along with some photos. The museum displays a wide range of temporary exhibits, which also can be explored at this site. Search the site to find specific information about animals of interest.

Related (Kid) Site

www.ology.amnh.org

The Carnegie Museum of Natural History

1 2 3 4 5

www.carnegiemuseums.org/cmnh

Founded in 1895, the Carnegie Museum of Natural History is one of the nation's leading research museums and is renowned for its Dinosaur Hall. This page was established to provide news of the museum's events, as well as developments in the field of natural history in general. It is divided into 13 different and wide-ranging scientific sections, from anthropology and birds to minerals and nature reserves.

The Cleveland Museum of Natural History

1 2 3 4 5

www.cmnh.org

This museum has more than one million specimens in the fields of anthropology, archaeology, astronomy, botany, geology, paleontology, zoology, and wildlife biology. It also has educational programs and links to exhibits and museum news.

The Field Museum

www.fieldmuseum.org

Use this site to find out what's new at Chicago's Field Museum, which has featured Sue, the largest, most complete T-Rex exhibit in the world; the Dead Sea Scrolls; and maneless tigers, called Tsavos. This is one of the largest and most diverse museums in the world. Site also features some cool interactive presentations to engage visitors of all ages.

Florida Museum of Natural History

1 2 3 4 5

www.flmnh.ufl.edu

With more than 16 million specimens, this is the largest museum of natural history in the southern United States. This site features descriptions of its collections in both the Department of Anthropology and the Department of Natural Sciences, which include mammals, birds, fossils, plants, and more.

Natural History Museum of Los Angeles County

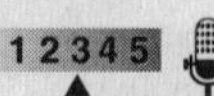

www.lam.mus.ca.us

Descriptions of current and upcoming exhibits at the museum, plus a calendar of events, information on membership and group visits, and a few online presentations.

A B C D E F G H I J K L M N O P Q R S T U V W X Y Z

Natural History Museum in the United Kingdom

12345

www.nhm.ac.uk

This site defines and explains each of the museum's five main departments and also discusses its six focus areas for research. For each department (Botany, Zoology, Entomology, Paleontology, and Mineralogy), the site provides photos and details about several ongoing research projects at the museum.

Smithsonian National Museum of Natural History

12345

www.mnh.si.edu

This extensive site has everything you ever wanted to know about this museum. Read about museum exhibitions, such as the return of Ishi, Echinoderms, and the giant squid. Online exhibits relate to global warming, hologlobes, and cross-roads of continents, among others.

Swedish Museum of Natural History

12345

www.nrm.se

The largest museum in Sweden, it has more than 18 million objects and is one of the 10 largest natural history museums in the world. The page is divided into the following categories: Research, Exhibitions, Events and Education, Cosmonova (one of the most modern Omni-max theaters in the world), and Administration and Service. You can navigate the site in English or Swedish.

University of California Museum of Paleontology

12345

www.ucmp.berkeley.edu

UCMP is dedicated to "investigating and promoting the understanding of the history of life and the diversity of the Earth's biota through research and education." Here, you can learn more about its programs and activities and access introductions to many of its most intriguing exhibits.

PHOTOGRAPHY & FILM

Berkeley Art Museum/Pacific Film Archive

12345

www.bampfa.berkeley.edu

The visual arts center of the University of California at Berkeley, the UAM/PFA is noted for its thought-provoking exhibitions of both art and film. The museum website contains online versions of current and former exhibitions.

California Museum of Photography

12345

www.cmp.ucr.edu

This site contains photos, descriptions, and other information from exhibits at this museum, as well as links to a museum store, with copies of featured photos from the exhibit for sale. (Items in the store link to Amazon.com, where you can place your order.)

George Eastman House: International Museum of Photography and Film

12345

www.eastmanhouse.org

Take a look at the timeline of photography, learn more about the photographic and film exhibitions, and find out about upcoming workshops at this museum.

International Center of Photography

12345

www.icp.org

Established to collect twentieth-century works, this center has a special emphasis on documentary photography. The center, located in New York City, also teaches all levels of photography. Site contains photos from special exhibits.

A B C D E F G H I J K L M N O P Q R S T U V W X Y Z

A B C D E F G H I J K L

National Museum of Photography, Film, and Television

12345

www.nmpft.org.uk

This museum contains varied displays, interactive features, large and small screens, and constantly changing special exhibitions, events, theater, and education. Catch up on online research projects and learn about upcoming exhibitions here.

Smithsonian Photographs Online

12345

photo2.si.edu

This site makes the photographic offerings of the Smithsonian available online. Browse the contents or search a huge library of photographs by keyword.

Related Site

smithsonianimages.si.edu

Underwater Photography: Philip Colla

www.oceanlight.com

Gallery of some of the most beautiful underwater photos covering all aspects of marine life and ecology by Philip Colla. If you have a publication that requires some top-notch undersea photos, this is the place to purchase a license for some of the best photos you'll find.

ORGANIZATIONS

American Association of Museums

www.aam-us.org

This organization provides a focal point for professionals in museum and museum-related fields, and currently has more than 16,000 members. Every type of museum is represented in its membership, from arboretums to youth museums. Site links to membership information, newsletters, and a bookstore.

Group for Education in Museums

www.gem.org.uk

Group for anyone concerned with education in museums. Site contains links to excerpts from the quarterly newsletter, the annual *Journal of Education in Museums*, and other publications. Also contains links to lists of museums.

The Museum Security Network

www.museum-security.org

This initiative by security managers of leading Dutch museums aims to present a global platform for all aspects of museum and art security. The site has articles about security matters, law links, and searchable databases. Also links to other similar sites.

SCIENCE & TECHNOLOGY

Adler Planetarium and Astronomy Museum

www.adlerplanetarium.org

This web home of the Alder Planetarium and Astronomy Museum features astronomy FAQs, a Skywatchers Guide, and information about what you can see at this Chicago facility. Though it's no substitute for a visit to the museum, this site provides a preview of what you can find at the museum and in your own star-gazing adventures. If you're interested in downloading podcasts, go directly to www.adlerpodcast.com.

The Exploratorium

www.exploratorium.edu

The Exploratorium is a collage of 650 interactive exhibits in the areas of science, art, and human perception. It provides access to and information about science, nature, art, and technology. The site has online versions of exhibits and tons of other scientific information.

N O P Q R S T U V W X Y Z

The Museum of Contemporary Ideas

1 2 3 4 5

www.superfictions.com

This unique museum delves into the worlds of the visual arts, the philosophy of science, architecture, technology, performing arts, and off-planet systems.

The Museum of Science and Industry, Chicago

www.msichicago.org

This site contains online exhibits that provide a sample of the experiences available at the museum. For many of the newer exhibits, the website enables you to take a virtual tour—through viewing either photographs or a brief video clip. It also provides Omnimax film clips and educational resources for teachers, as well as exhibit schedules and general information about the Chicago area.

National Museum of Science and Technology, Canada

1 2 3 4 5

www.science-tech.nmstc.ca

This museum was created to explore "the transformation of Canada." Different subjects of the museum include agriculture, communications, energy, forestry, graphic arts, transportation, and many others. Links and descriptions are provided for all subjects as well as for behind-the-scenes information such as restoration.

Oregon Museum of Science and Industry

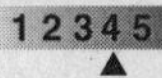

www.omsi.edu

Observe vibrations and sound waves in the museum's Electronics Lab or weave your own piece of the Web in the Computer Lab. This site provides links to all the museum's main areas, complete with photos and descriptions of many exhibits. You can find a lot of great information at this site.

Questacon: National Science and Technology Centre

www.questacon.edu.au

This site includes fun activities and links for Australia's national science museum. You can take a virtual tour of the galleries and explore the hands-on zone, all without leaving the comfort of home (or paying for a trip to Australia).

Shedd Aquarium

www.sheddaquarium.org

Find out about animals and exhibits at this Chicago aquarium, where you can Ask Shedd about an aquatic topic, such as caring for a home aquarium, or a particular animal at the aquarium.

Stephen Birch Aquarium Museum

www.aquarium.ucsd.edu

Part of the Scripps Institution of Oceanography, this aquarium offers volunteer opportunities, educational programs, and summer learning adventures. This home page provides information about all these, plus links to what's new at the aquarium and membership information.

MUSIC

BUYING CDS

Amazon.com

1 2 3 4 5

www.amazon.com

Amazon.com is the largest online department store on the planet, and it features a huge collection of both new and used CDs. A great selection combined with good prices and great service makes this an excellent place to shop.

Barnes & Noble.com

1 2 3 4 5

music.barnesandnoble.com

This popular bookstore has been selling CDs for quite some time; check out the selection and prices and place your order online.

BestBuy.com

1 2 3 4 5

www.bestbuy.com

The largest consumer electronics store in the nation now delivers a huge collection of CD and DVD titles at competitive prices.

Bleep

1 2 3 4 5 RSS

www.warprecords.com/bleep

Warp Records in Britain features this online music store where you can purchase entire albums or individual tracks in MP3 format for less than the cost of those same tracks on CD. Check out the featured albums, choose to browse by artist, or search for a particular artist or album.

Blue Vision Music

1 2 3 4 5

www.bluevisionmusic.com

Specializing in original contemporary music for kids, this online store offers a small collection of tapes, CDs, and books featuring the work of James Coffey. Sample some of the songs directly from the site (in AU format—requires a plug-in or player). The Kid's Club section offers some interesting activities for the younger set (QuickTime or other movie viewer required).

Buy.com

1 2 3 4 5

www.buy.com

Pick a category of music and then search for particular artists or albums. On the right side of the site, you can find out which albums and singles are at the top of the charts. Buy.com provides free shipping, too.

CD Baby

1 2 3 4 5

www.cdbaby.com

Online music store specializing in CDs from independent artists. If you recorded a CD, CD Baby can help you sell it online. You can even sample one or two songs from a CD before you decide to purchase it.

CD Universe

1 2 3 4 5

www.cduniverse.com

CD Universe promises the most music at the best prices. The interface is particularly easy to use, with graphics augmented by text to explain the purpose of each section. (You don't need to spend as much time roaming around to find the section you want.) Interested in the top-flight artists in each genre? Check out the Charts section.

f.y.e.: for your entertainment

12345

www.fye.com

f.y.e. offers a vast collection of CDs, videos, downloadable tracks, games, and other media items for purchase. You can shop online, search for a store near you, and find out about upcoming events.

Rasputin Music

12345

www.rasputinmusic.com

When you're tired of shopping at the standard online mega-music stores, check out Rasputin Music to experience a refreshing ambience. The online store is easy to navigate, enabling you to browse the collection by genre or search for specific artists or albums. This site also features reviews written by the staff, used CDs and DVDs, coupons, and more.

Sam Goody Music

12345

www.samgoody.com

Just about every type of music for every possible taste is available here. This online extension of Sam Goody's brick-and-mortar stores offers CDs, tapes, and videos, and sheet music.

Sony Music Store

12345

www.sonymusicstore.com

A division of Sony Music Entertainment, Inc., that's dedicated to delivering thousands of CD and DVD titles directly to the consumer at bargain prices. Children can click the Kids Corner link for special selections.

TowerRecords.com

12345

www.towerrecords.com

Search for particular bands or types of music, or just browse the listings to find something of interest. The site offers CDs for under $7 and new releases you'll want to pay attention to. You can also listen to tracks before you buy them.

Wherehouse.com

12345

www.wherehouse.com

Wherehouse.com carries all forms of entertainment media—movies, music, and games, in various forms including CDs and DVDs, new and used. Wherehouse.com will also take your old, used stuff off your hands and give you in-store credit so you can afford replacements. This site is one of the easiest to navigate. The opening Music page features a search box to locate CDs by title or artist, a list of genres you can browse, feature items, bestsellers, and a search box in which you can type the title of a used CD you want to sell to see how much Wherehouse.com will give you for it.

BUYING MP3S

ARTISTdirect

12345 RSS

listen.artistdirect.com

ARTISTdirect introduces fans to original artists, both in music and video, through free audio and video clips, reviews, and other promotional material that encourages fans to head to the stores to buy the artists' CDs, DVDs, MP3 tracks, apparel, and other products. In other words, this site features a huge selection of freebies. Use the navigation bar at the top to access news; shop for CDs, apparel, or accessories; browse by genre (styles); listen to the top downloads; or watch the top music videos.

audiogalaxy

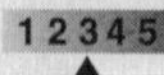

`www.audiogalaxy.com`

audiogalaxy is a weird site that doesn't seem to know what it wants to be when it grows up. You can browse the site by music category or search for specific artists or albums. Most artists or albums have links to download sample tunes, but the links might or might not work depending on the copyright restrictions; the links that do work are the ones that allow you to order the CD online. This site also features links to online music auctions.

BuyMusic@Buy.com

`www.buy.com`

BuyMusic is a section of the Internet superstore Buy.com, which carries everything from computers to cameras to toys. Click the Music link to download audio clips for less than a dollar per track. You can search for specific albums, artists, or tracks, or browse the collection by genre.

eFolkMusic.com

`www.efolkmusic.org`

eFolkMusic is a not-for-profit group that digitizes and distributes music clips from various folk artists. You join eFolkMusic for an annual fee After you're a member, you can download a limited number of tracks for free and pay for others at discount prices. Most of the money goes to the artists.

eMusic

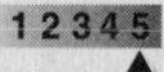

`www.emusic.com`

At eMusic, you can start downloading free MP3s right away—after you register, that is. You get a specified number of free downloads and a couple of weeks to decide whether you want to continue using the service. If you cancel the service in the specified time period, you still get to keep the tunes you downloaded and you don't have to pay the registration fee. Fees vary depending on the membership you choose, which controls the number of tunes you get to download each month.

Epitonic.com

`www.epitonic.com`

Unlike many music download sites that push the top 20 tunes and music videos, Epitonic.com searches the dark corners of the music world for lesser-known artists in an attempt to deliver their goods to potential fans. Here, you can find a great collection of original and unique music to sample from artists that few have ever heard of...yet. Very cool site for those who want something off the main music highway.

Furthur Network

`www.furthurnet.com`

Many performers and bands encourage their fans to share their recordings of live shows. Furthur Network enables fans to do this online via special peer-to-peer network sharing. Visit this site to download the software and hook up with thousands of fans to share your recordings of live shows. If you're a taper or want to hook up with some tapers, this is the place to be.

iMesh

`www.imesh.com`

This site features file-swapping software, similar to Kazaa and Morpheus, that enables users to swap files (usually MP3 music files) and chat online. To keep everything legal, iMesh continues to work on establishing distribution agreements with copyright holders.

Best iTunes

`www.apple.com/itunes`

iTunes is Apple's jukebox for Mac and Windows machines. With it, you can store, play, and manage your entire music collection on your computer and transfer audio clips between your computer and iPod. You can also use iTunes to burn tracks to recordable CDs and to stream audio between computers on a local network. If you have an iPod and a computer, you should definitely visit this site to download and install iTunes on your PC or Mac. Now iTunes also features videos.

liveplasma

www.liveplasma.com

liveplasma features one of the more interesting music search interfaces on the Web. Here, you enter the name of your favorite artist, and liveplasma displays a solar system of artists and groups whose sound might appeal to you. You can then click links to order CDs online. Cool concept.

MP3.com

www.mp3.com

MP3.com was one of the first companies to push sample MP3 clips on the Internet. Now it's owned by CNET and is a more of a music review/referral service. Here, you can download and play sample music videos and tracks, read news and reviews of your favorite artists and albums, check out reviews of the latest MP3 players to hit the market, and connect with other listeners and fans in the discussion forums. When you want to purchase MP3 clips, CDs, or MP3 players, MP3.com shuffles you off to other sites where you can purchase the items you want.

Napster

www.napster.com

Originally the most popular place on the Internet for swapping MP3 music clips with other music lovers, this service has undergone major renovation to make it legal. Napster no longer is an MP3 file-sharing program, but a service that enables you to download a certain number of tracks for a monthly fee. Select from more than 1,000,000 tracks!

Rhapsody

www.rhapsody.com

Rhapsody provides a music-on-demand subscription service complete with Internet radio featuring more than 80 stations. You can listen to the radio while you work or play on your computer, and even skip songs you don't like. To download tunes to your computer, you must sign up for a monthly subscription; you can then pick the artists and songs you want to hear, download clips, and for less than a buck a track you can burn tracks to CDs. Rhapsody provides you with unlimited playback time for the selected songs.

URGE

12345

www.urge.com

URGE is MTV's answer to Apple's iTunes. Here, you can purchase individual tracks for less than and subscribe to the service for additional perks and lower rates. When we visited the site, URGE was offering a free 14-day subscription.

Virgin Digital

www.virgindigital.com

Virgin Digital provides its own digital music player for Windows that enables you to tune in to online radio stations, create your own music library and playlists, and experience digital music and videos on your computer. You can join the Music Club and pay a monthly subscription fee for unlimited playback while you are a member; but if you want to own tracks, transfer them to an MP3 player, or burn them to CDs, you must purchase them for about one dollar per track.

INFORMATION, NEWS, & REVIEWS

Alternative Press Online

1 2 3 4 5

altpress.com

Read reviews of your favorite alternative bands, buy a back issue of an AP or preorder an upcoming one, make a custom CD, or add your two cents to the online reviews and discussions here.

AMG All Music Guide

1 2 3 4 5

allmusic.com

All Music Guide offers music and game reviews, biographies of performers, ratings, images, titles, and credits for current and out-of-print works. Links to Barnes & Noble to provide online shopping.

ANTI-

1 2 3 4 5

www.anti.com

ANTI- is all about "real artists creating great recordings on their own terms." If you want to find out what the top artists are doing outside of mainstream music, visit this site. Here, you find well-written, insightful reviews of CDs and free downloads along with related articles and tour dates, when available.

Billboard Online

www.billboard.com

This site offers fast and easy access to *Billboard* magazine's huge electronic library. Charts and articles from the current issue are available to visitors. Site also features news and reviews, featured artists, awards, chatrooms, online puzzles, and much more.

ICE Online

1 2 3 4 5

www.icemagazine.com

Based on the printed publication. The site offers a free trial subscription and provides information and exclusive articles on upcoming album releases. Also includes release dates that are updated weekly.

Latin Music Online

1 2 3 4 5

www.lamusica.com

The popularity of Latin music continues to grow in the United States. This site is well designed and packed with quality news and features surrounding Latin music. Links to Amazon for shopping.

Launch Your Yahoo! Music Experience

launch.yahoo.com

This is Yahoo!'s pop music site, where you can find articles about your favorite musicians, groups, and CDs. Features music videos, exclusive online radio stations, downloadable music clips, and much more.

MetaCritic

www.metacritic.com/music

MetaCritic features reviews of films, DVDs/videos, music, games, and books. Check out the Music section for reviews of recently released CDs including their MetaScore, an indication of the overall rating of each CD.

MTV

www.mtv.com/music

MTV used to focus on music. Now it focuses on a generation, feeding it whatever entertainment it seems to hunger for. However, if you go directly to the Music section, you can return to the MTV of the good old days and access music, music videos, reviews, artist biographies, photos, and much more.

MuchMusic

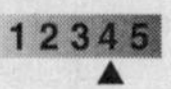

www.muchmusic.com

MuchMusic is "a Canadian network dedicated to providing an entertaining, informative, and engaging look at popular music as it happens. Our revolutionary approach to television allows our viewers to get up close and personal with their favorite artists, acts and entertainers through original programming features, concerts, specials, live daily news hits, interactive television, wireless communication and unique web-only content." At this site, you can get the latest news and information about your favorite artists and access content you can't get anywhere else.

Music Critic

www.music-critic.com

You can find reviews of music, movies, games, and beer at this site. Links to Amazon.com, where you can purchase many of the items reviewed.

Music Yellow Pages

musicyellowpages.com

Search the more than 40,000 listings in 400 categories related to the music, pro audio, lighting, and entertainment industries. Find suppliers online free or order the print edition for a fee.

MustHear

www.musthear.com

This site for those with discerning tastes features reviews of albums that you simply must hear. Scroll to the bottom of the opening page for access to the button that takes you to a list of available reviews.

NME

12345

www.nme.com

The online home of *NME* (New Musical Express) magazine, this site features music news, reviews, concert information, charts, and much more. Bulletin boards and chat provide a means of interacting with fellow fans, and NME Radio plays in the background, so you can listen while you explore the site. The site has an attitude that's not the best for young children.

NY ROCK

www.nyrock.com

Daily rock-and-roll updates, reviews, and articles with that New York flair. Categorized by band, this site also offers gossip, news, and RealAudio sound clips.

Rock on TV

www.vh1.com/artists/rock_on_tv

Learn which artists will be appearing on TV this week by clicking either on the performer name or the day of the week you're interested in hearing about. You can also catch up on music news and music club information. This site is divided into three areas: RockOnTV, MusicNewswire, and the CD Club Web Server.

RollingStone.com

www.rollingstone.com

This is the online home of *Rolling Stone* magazine. The site contains most of the news, reviews, charts, and interviews available in the print edition. It also includes an area where users can comment on movies, music, and more. Free downloadable MP3 clips, video clips, and a huge photo gallery make this one of the best hangouts for rock fans.

SPIN.com

www.spin.com

SPIN magazine covers and promotes "all the music that rocks." Here, you can find news, feature articles, album reviews, and *SPIN*'s photo gallery. You can also tune into *SPIN* radio online. If you have a cellular phone, check out the SPIN Mobile area to learn how to access *SPIN* when you're on the road.

VH1.COM

www.vh1.com

Read daily reviews at the online version of this cable station, where you can also get music news, find concerts coming to your area, and learn what's on tap tonight on VH1.

VIBE

www.vibe.com

A hip-hop online magazine that features daily entertainment updates, preview videos and audio clips, and archives of past issues.

World Café

worldcafe.org

Home of the *World Café*, a public radio show that provides an avenue for up-and-coming musicians to showcase their stuff. Hosted by David Dye, the show consists of a low-key interview intermixed with songs. Links to interviews that you can listen to online. Search for artists, buy CDs, enter contests, or find a local radio station that plays the show.

LYRICS

A–Z Lyrics

www.azlyrics.com

If you want to learn a song but you can't catch all the lyrics from listening to it, turn to A–Z Lyrics to find the complete text. Here, you can browse lyrics by artist or group.

Burt Bacharach: A House Is Not a Home Page

www.bacharachonline.com

Provides lyrics, biography, news, audio files, lyrics, chord sheets, and news about songwriter Burt Bacharach. Includes articles, pictures, and a list of hit songs. Also provides links to sites where you can purchase Bacharach's music.

Led Zeppelin Lyrics

www.alwaysontherun.net/ledzep.htm

This site contains the lyrics to many Led Zeppelin songs. Just click the song title and read the lyrics. The links will take you to a master index of lyrics for many groups.

Lyrics.com

www.lyrics.com

Lyrics.com offers a searchable database of a fairly large, but by no means comprehensive, collection of pop, rock, and rap song lyrics.

LYRICS Download.com

www.lyricsdownload.com

LYRICS Download.com is a community of lyric sharers who post the lyrics to their favorite songs to share with fellow fans. Here, you can search a database of lyrics for more than 600,000 songs.

Lyrics Search Engine

lyrics.astraweb.com

This no-nonsense site features a search box which you can type the name of a song or artist into to begin your search. It's not the best for browsing; but if you know what you're looking for, this tool can find it for you.

Musicnotes.com

musicnotes.com

Download digital sheet music to your PC for a small fee, print it, and play it. Choose from a huge selection of today's pop hits to classical selections. Search by title, artist, or composer to find exactly what you're looking for.

National Anthems

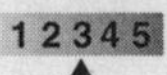

www.lengua.com/hymnen.htm

The national anthems of many countries are available here. You can find them in their original form or with an English translation. Click the speaker to hear the anthem you've chosen. This is a growing site, so you might want to contribute any information you have about other national anthems, their lyrics, music, or history.

MP3SHARING/ SEARCH ENGINES

AltaVista Audio File Search

www.altavista.com/audio/default

AltaVista is an outstanding search engine that features a special search tool for audio files. It can track down audio store in several different formats, including MP3, WAV, WindowsMedia, AIFF, and RealAudio.

theinfo.com

www.theinfo.com/music

A music search engine that allows you to put all your criteria in one screen. You can also find music and links to buy it direct from online stores such as Amazon.com.

Kazaa

www.kazaa.com

This Internet file-sharing program enables users to swap files, including games, audio clips, video clips, and shareware over the Internet. Relies on the honor system to prevent users from breaking copyright laws. If you install the free version, bear in mind that you will be inundated with pop-up ads. To avoid the pop-ups, purchase Kazaa Plus.

Morpheus

www.morpheus.com

Morpheus is a file-sharing program that many users employ to swap audio clips, video clips, and software. Much of the sharing that goes on is either illegal, unethical, or both. To stay legal, honor the copyrights of original artists.

MP3 Nexus

www.bigg.net

Download players, search other MP3 sites for music, get the latest digital music news, and download songs for your personal enjoyment.

MP3Nut

www.mp3nut.com

Huge, searchable database of MP3 files. A little difficult to maneuver at first; but if you read the screens and follow the instructions, this might just turn out to be your favorite MP3 site on the Web.

MP3Search.com

www.mp3search.com

MP3Search.com can help you track down audio recordings stored in a variety of popular formats, including MP3. You can search by artist or title. You typically need to scroll down to the bottom of the page to access the results of a search to get past all the advertising and disclaimers, but you should eventually find a Download Now link that you can right-click and choose to download and save to your computer.

MPEG.ORG

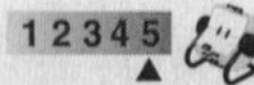

www.mpeg.org

A directory of links to MP3 sites with downloadable music as well as MP3 news and information.

Search MP3

www.searchmpthree.com

This search engine allows you to search for songs and music videos created by various artists and placed on the site for promotional purposes. You can also purchase CDs through links to Amazon.com.

Best Singing Fish

1 2 3 4 5

search.singingfish.com

Singing Fish is *the* place to go to search for free audio and video clips on the Web. By entering specific search criteria, including the type of media you're looking for (audio or video), the duration (any length, greater than 1 minute, or greater than 3 minutes), the format (MP3, Windows, Real, or QuickTime), and the category (for example, music or movies), you can perform a target search of items by song title or artist. Consider setting the duration to >1 or >3 minutes to avoid getting a bunch of links to 30-second sample clips offered by many commercial music sites.

MUSIC EVENTS

Blues Festivals

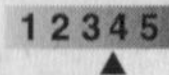

www.bluesfestivals.com

A fantastic site full of listings and links to blues festivals nationwide. Bookmark this one; it's a must for any true blues fan

Festivals.com

1 2 3 4 5

www.festivals.com

Festivals.com is "the largest resource on the Internet for information about community festivals, fairs and special events." It lists more than 40,000 community events from around the world. You can search for a specific event by keyword, browse by category, or click the map of the United States to browse by state. Although the selection of festivals includes more than music festivals, this is often a good place to start.

JamBase

www.jambase.com

JamBase features the work of improvisational groups and artists and encourages fans to *go see live music*! Here, you can read concert and CD reviews, find out about upcoming concerts, check out the news wire, and enter contests for the chance to win great prizes.

Mardi Gras Official Website

1 2 3 4 5

www.mardigrasday.com

Although it is now known primarily as a drunkfest, Mardi Gras includes some fantastic music and draws musicians from all over to join in the festivities. Check out this site for details, schedules of music events, instructions on how to plan parties for various age groups, and more. Some stuff just for kids and teens. Teachers who want to introduce their students to Mardi Gras will also find some useful tools and information.

Mojam

1 2 3 4 5

www.mojam.com

Find music events by searching the database for cities, venues, or artists. Or click on one of the lists of top tours, or new tours, to find out where the groups are headed. You can also learn more about what events are coming up in major U.S. cities simply by clicking on the city name. If you're a band or promoter, you can add information about an upcoming event to the calendar, too.

Pollstar: The Concert Hotwire

www.pollstar.com

This online weekly media magazine geared for the concert industry publishes several industry directories, performer tour histories, mailing labels, and directories on disk. Search the site for upcoming concert information by band name or venue.

Ticketmaster.com

www.ticketmaster.com

Find music and sporting events, as well as upcoming theater and comedy performances, by searching the Ticketmaster site by keyword, artist, or location. You can then charge your tickets by phone or purchase your tickets online.

Related Site

tickets.msn.com

TicketWeb

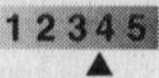

www.ticketweb.com

Online box office that simplifies the process of obtaining tickets to concerts, plays, museums, and other interesting and entertaining places and events.

tkt.com

www.tkt.com

Scalper (a.k.a. *ticket broker*) website, where you can buy or sell tickets to some of the top events at astronomical prices.

Related Sites

www.tixx.com

www.ticketsnow.com

MUSIC GENRES—ALTERNATIVE

Alternative Addiction

www.alternativeaddiction.com

Alternative Addiction features news, music, and videos of popular and upcoming alternative bands along with AA Radio, where you can tune in to listen or watch online. Plenty of articles and reviews.

AlternativeMusic.com

www.alternativemusic.com

AlternativeMusic.com is "a place where people can find and buy almost any piece of alternative music they want." Company promises great service and a wide selection and offers weekly international and dance releases, along with previews.

Ink Blot Magazine: Deep Coverage of Great Music

www.inkblotmagazine.com

Ink Blot online music magazine features album reviews, band interviews, music industry gossip, RealAudio music clips, pictures, and much more. This e-zine is biweekly and free.

Insound

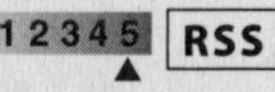

www.insound.com

Insound is an web-based mail-order company that specializes in distributing the music of independent artists. Here, you can sample tracks and order CDs online.

ModernRock.com

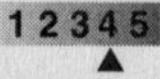

modernrock.com

ModernRock.com features news, reviews, and charts for the top alternative rock bands.

Nettwerk Productions

www.nettwerk.com

Home of Nettwerk Records, a company that produces recordings for many of the top alternative artists. Here, you can browse the directory of Nettwerk's artists from A to Z.

Sub Pop Records Online

1 2 3 4 5

www.subpop.com

This site, the online home for Sub Pop Records, covers the underground Seattle music scene. Get reviews and hear samples of hot upcoming bands and artists, find out about tours and appearances, and check out the links to fun stuff. Lots of free downloads.

MUSIC GENRES— BLUEGRASS

Banjo Tablatures and Bluegrass Information

1 2 3 4 5

www.bluegrassbanjo.org

Banjo newsletter recommended for all banjo pickers features tablatures for three-finger, clawhammer, and jazz banjo players.

Blistered Fingers

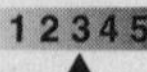

www.blisteredfingers.com

Site of all information related to June and August Blistered Fingers Family Bluegrass Festival (Waterville, Maine). In addition to festival information, you can send information if you'd like to be part of the open stage segment, find other links, and subscribe to the newsletter.

BlueGrassRoots Master Catalog Search

members.tripod.com/~kc4vus/roots.html

Enormous database of bluegrass musicians and record labels. Search the database for your favorite musician, band, or album. You can also search by the label or the year. A master catalog is available for download.

Bluegrass Unlimited

1 2 3 4 5

www.bluegrassmusic.com

This home of *Bluegrass Unlimited* magazine provides an image of the current month's issue along with a list of the top five songs, bluegrass music awards, reviews, pictures, and more.

Bluegrass World

1 2 3 4 5

www.bluegrassworld.com

You can find bluegrass musicians, festivals, merchandise, record companies, catalogs, radio stations, and bluegrass music links all in one place.

Canyon Country Bluegrass Festival

1 2 3 4 5

www.canyoncountrybluegrass.com

This is home to Canyon Country Bluegrass Festival information. Located in Pennsylvania's "Grand Canyon," this festival has been celebrated for more than 10 years.

Central Texas Bluegrass Association

1 2 3 4 5

www.centraltexasbluegrass.org

Offers information about the Central Texas Bluegrass Association, a nonprofit corporation. Includes a calendar of events, as well as workshop and membership information.

Huck Finn's Country and Bluegrass Jubilee!

12345

www.Huckfinn.com

This country and bluegrass festival in Southern California lasts three days and also includes horseback riding, clogging, catfish fishing, boating, and crafts. Make a reservation, check the maps on how to get there, and check out the activities available.

iBluegrass Magazine

12345

www.ibluegrass.com

Listen to Bluegrass music as you scope out this site for chat, news, and festival information from its vast database, or search for a new band to listen to. You can also list festivals or bands you're involved with free by uploading information to the onsite database.

Intermountain Acoustic Music Association

12345

www.xmission.com/~iama

Nonprofit organization devoted to promoting and preserving acoustic music, including bluegrass, folk, and old-time music. The IAMA sponsors various seminars, workshops, and concerts; check out the event calendar for dates and locations. There's also a monthly newsletter for members—become one by filling out the online form and sending in your membership fee.

International Bluegrass Music Association

12345

www.ibma.org

The IBMA's mission is to promote bluegrass and expand its popularity. Obtain membership information, read the latest news, or visit the International Bluegrass Museum.

Society for the Preservation of Bluegrass Music in America

12345

www.spbgma.com

SPBGMA is dedicated to preserving the tradition of bluegrass music in the United States. At this site, you can find a printable order form for the *100 Classic Bluegrass and Folk Songs* book, a calendar of events and festivals, current awards, a Hall of Greats, information about the organization.

Sugar Hill Records

12345

www.sugarhillrecords.com

Sugar Hill Records is one of the top labels for bluegrass artists. Here, you can explore the work of its many artists and groups, check on tour dates, browse the catalog, shop online, and tune in to Sugar Hill Radio, an all-bluegrass-all-the-time Internet radio station (with a subscription to Radio Free Virgin Royal).

Top 100 Bluegrass Sites

12345

www.bluegrassrules.com/top100.asp

Directory of the "best" 100 bluegrass sites is a great place to start looking for information about various bands and festivals. Most of the sites you're directed to are the official sites of the top bluegrass bands, where you can sample music, check for tour dates, and view photos.

Tottenham Bluegrass Festival

12345

www.tottenhambluegrass.ca

Everything you want to know about the Tottenham Bluegrass Festival (Ontario, Canada). Find out location, ticket price, and performance schedule.

Washington Bluegrass Association

1 2 3 4 5

www.washingtonbluegrassassociation.org

Extensive listing of links to bluegrass performance schedules, artists, and associations. You can also find teachers and membership information.

Welcome to Planet Bluegrass!

1 2 3 4 5

www.bluegrass.com

Blue Planet Music, organizers of the legendary Telluride Bluegrass Festival, is now online. The site contains a festival schedule and information, as well as information about Blue Planet recordings and its mail-order operation. You can also buy posters, T-shirts, tickets, and other merchandise from the secure server.

MUSIC GENRES— CHRISTIAN MUSIC

CCM Magazine.com

1 2 3 4 5 Blog RSS

www.ccmcom.com

Read about provocative Christian musicians in the news section or read music reviews, listen to clips by Christian bands, or join in discussions going on at the site. You can also find interesting feature articles about bands on tour and Christian musicians in general. When you want to know what's going on in the Christian music scene, this is the place to go.

Christianity Today: Music Section

1 2 3 4 5 RSS

www.christianitytoday.com/music

Christianity Today has a music section that's quite impressive, providing links that enable you to browse by artist, read reviews and interviews, shop online for CDs, and check out a list of the top Christian music performers. This page is better than most websites that are exclusively devoted to Christian music.

ChristianMusic.org

1 2 3 4 5 Blog

www.christianmusic.org

ChristianMusic.org features Christian music news and highlights, reviews, top Christian music songs, discussion forums, information about upcoming Christian music concerts, and much more.

Christian Music Resources

1 2 3 4 5 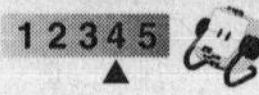

www.guitarsite.com/christian.htm

Excellent collection of links to various Christian music resource sites on the Web.

Jamsline: The Christian Music Info Source

1 2 3 4 5

www.jamsline.com

This site offers hundreds of titles for purchase, including songs from Amy Grant, Jars of Clay, Anointed, and more.

MUSIC GENRES— CLASSICAL

Adante: Everything Classical

1 2 3 4 5

www.andante.com

Excellent online store for classical music. Site features its magazine, a music room, and a boutique. In the music room, you can search for selections by composer, partner, genre, work, performer, instrument, and ensemble. Several selections you can listen to for free. You can also tune into Adante radio for streaming broadcasts of classical music.

American Classical Music Hall of Fame

1 2 3 4 5

www.americanclassicalmusic.org

The official home of the American Classical Music Hall of Fame features photos and biographies of inductees along with a sampling of their musical achievements. You can also learn about the Hall of Fame and obtain instructions on how to explore this site more fully.

The Classical Guitarist

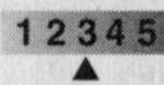

www.guitarist.com/cg/cg.htm

The Classical Guitarist features classical guitar sheet music and MIDI files, a beginner's page, a guide to classical guitar in Portland Oregon, and a directory of links to other classical guitar sites.

The Classical MIDI Connection

www.classicalmidiconnection.com/cmc

Contains a load of classical MIDI sequences for your listening pleasure. You can browse the site and listen to or save any of the sequences available. This site is well organized, and you can search via composers as well as musical style.

Classical Music Archives

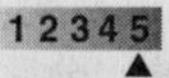

www.classicalarchives.com

For a mere $25 a year, this site provides access to more than 38,000 full length classical music recordings from more than 2,000 of the world's most famous and gifted composers. This site also features biographies, commentary, and a special learning center. The discussion forums provide an online hangout for classical music fans and experts to exchange information and share their enthusiasm for classical music. Excellent site. Bravo!

Classical Music of the WWW Virtual Library

www.gprep.org/classical

A huge resource of information available for you to read, just like at a traditional library. Search the database to learn more about particular classical composers or music, learn about classical music organizations, find out about discussion forums, brush up on music techniques, or peruse many other subcategories.

Classical Net

www.classical.net

Classical Net is a classical music directory featuring "more than 3,200 CD/DVD/Book reviews, as well as 6,000 files and over 4,000 links to other classical music websites." Content is organized in sections including Basic Repertoire List, Classical CD Buying Guide, Composers Works & Data, and Books & Scores.

Classical USA

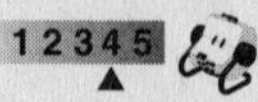

classicalusa.com

This site features reviews of more than 1,000 CDs, 4,800 files, and more than 2,600 links to other classical music websites. Very comprehensive directory to all things classical on the Web, including film and video, opera theater and song, and music publications.

Essentials of Music

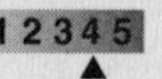

www.essentialsofmusic.com

This is an excellent site for music students and even casual listeners to become acquainted with and begin to appreciate classical music. It features three areas: Eras, Composers, and Glossary.

Gramophone

www.gramophone.co.uk

Online version of the internationally acclaimed magazine, this site features incisive articles on current classical music recordings, orchestras, and performances. Interviews, profiles, editor's choice top 10 recordings, information about competitions and industry news, and more. Also provides online discussion forums.

Klassikne

12345

www.culturekiosque.com/klassik

An online magazine for classical music fans, including articles, performer and composer interviews and biographies, reviews, and schedules. Some articles appear in both French and English. Don't leave without checking out the list of the 101 best vintage recordings.

The Mozart Project

www.mozartproject.org

The Mozart Project is the work of Steve Boerner, who has assembled an excellent collection of resources for students and fans of Mozart's work. Site features a biography, composition, selected essays, a bibliography, and an annotated directory of links to other useful sites.

MusicOnline Classical Music Directory

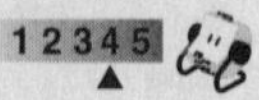

www.musicalonline.com

Comprehensive directory to classical music resources on the Internet, including schools, museums, journals, music theory, scholarly works, competitions, scholarships, and much more.

New York Philharmonic

www.newyorkphilharmonic.org

Information for fans and friends of the New York Philharmonic, including educational guides, historical information, ticket information, and news releases. Kids are welcome to visit this site or the site designed specifically for them at www.nyphilkids.org.

Piano Nanny

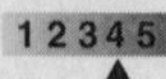

www.pianonanny.com

Always wanted to learn how to play the piano but never had the time to learn? This site provides piano lessons online. Each lesson takes about 35 minutes to complete (you must have QuickTime installed).

Sony Classical

12345

www.sonybmgmasterworks.com

Sony Entertainment's classical music site, where you can learn about Sony's classical artists, check out their CDs, listen to sample sound clips, view photos, and find out about upcoming tours.

Symphony Orchestra Information

www.hoptechno.com/symphony.htm

Find information on the major symphony orchestras in the world. Organized by geographical area, this site includes historical background, websites, email addresses, and concert schedules of many major symphony orchestras.

XLNC1.org

www.xlnc1.org

Excellency One is an Internet radio station based in Chula Vista, California, that plays classical music from its database of more than 400 pieces. Check in here to find the best stream for your location.

Related Sites

www.chopin.org

www.edepot.com/beethoven.html

www.sai-national.org/phil/composers/composer.html

MUSIC GENRES—COUNTRY

Country Music Awards

12345

www.cmaawards.com

Home of the Country Music Awards, this site provides information about the top-rated country music stars and songs. Here, you can find out about the upcoming Country Music Awards, check out the nominees, and look up the winners of awards.

CMT.com

www.cmt.com

Read feature articles about your favorite country music stars, find new albums slated for release, download country music clips from your favorite artists, and read country music news. Also features audio and video clips, message boards, and ringtones. CMT has become an award-winning centerpiece of the country music community, and it offers plenty of high-quality content for country music fans on this outstanding site. Country music fans of all ages will want to bookmark this site for return visits.

GAC TV: Great American Country TV

www.countrystars.com

GAC TV is the premier TV channel for country music and its performing artists. Here, your can check out the programming schedule, find news about your favorite country music artists, join the GAC club, shop online, tune into country radio stations online, and even download some free ringtones and games for your cell phone.

History of Country Music

12345

www.roughstock.com/history

Focuses on influential country artists as far back as the beginning of country music itself. Features history on artists such as Roy Acuff, Hank Williams, Gene Autry, Patsy Cline, Charley Pride, and more. Includes country styles such as Western swing, urban cowboy, honky-tonk, the Nashville sound, and others.

Jack Ingram

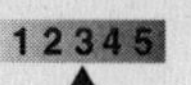

www.jackingram.net

Nice-looking site that provides tour dates, a link for buying CDs, and a link for signing up for a newsletter but not much else.

Women of Country

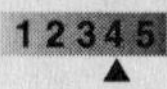

www.womenofcountry.com

When you're looking for information on female country stars, this is the place to go. The opening page covers featured artists and provides links to reviews, interviews, news, fan club information, and much more.

MUSIC GENRES—ETHNIC

Afro-Caribbean Music

www.afromix.org

Yes, you can find reggae music here, but you'll also find everything from Afro Funk to Ziglibithy to suit your musical tastes. Explore Africa and the Caribbean by artist, geographical location, and style. You'll also find a list of African/Caribbean nightclubs and restaurants in Paris. This site, available in both English and French, is nicely organized, with colorful 3D musical notes indicating the sections. You'll find an excellent page of links to related web resources along with a blogosphere.

Ari Davidow's Klezmer Shack

www.klezmershack.com

Focuses on the klezmer musical blend of traditional Jewish folk music, blues, and jazz. You can find articles, artist profiles, CD reviews, concert and festival information, a guide to radio programs, and contact information for klezmer musicians. You'll also find links to sites where you can buy klezmer CDs and a great annotated section on other klezmer-related resources on the Web.

Caribbean Music

www.crsmusic.com

CRS Music in Barbados is *the* record label for Caribbean music. Here, you can check out Caribbean music news, search for CDs and artists, read and post messages in the discussion forums, check on upcoming events, and shop for CDs online.

Charts All Over the World

www.lanet.lv/misc/charts

This site features links to more than 800 music charts from all over the world, organized by country.

Dirty Linen

www.dirtynelson.com/linen/73toc.html

Dirty Linen is an online magazine for folk and world music. At its home page, you can find a table of contents, a list of back issues, a "gig guide," and more. Well worth checking out. You can also subscribe to the regular magazine and have it delivered to you every other month.

The Flamenco Guitar

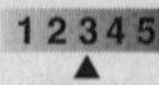

www.guitarist.com/fg/fg.htm

More information on flamenco, with an introduction for beginners. Discographies for both dancers and guitarists and MIDI sound files are available. You'll also find dozens and dozens of links to related sites.

Folk Australia

folkaustralia.com

This site covers Australian folk music and even offers a search feature. You'll also find interviews, news of local folk clubs in the Sydney area, and links to folk music sites in Australia, Ireland, the United Kingdom, and the United States. You can find short bios of Australian folk musicians, news of upcoming festivals and events, and "folksy" organizations, all in a clear, nicely organized format.

Irish and Celtic Music on the Internet

www.celticmusic.com

CelticMusic.Com, an online magazine, focuses on Celtic music. Check out the site's magazine index for a helpful listing of back issues and links to the home pages of featured artists. The site also includes sheet music for traditional tunes, reviews of recent CDs, audio excerpts (for the titles with dancing musical notes next to them), and more in the Virtual Tunebook section.

JewishMusic.com

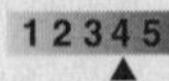

www.jewishmusic.com

Offers a wide variety of Jewish music selections. You'll find an online catalog and links to other Jewish music sites. There are a few articles, too, and an artists section with links to their home pages. Check out the RealAudio library.

KiwiFolk: Folk and Acoustic Music in New Zealand

kiwifolk.org.nz

This site organizes a wealth of information about New Zealand folk and acoustic music. You can find upcoming events, festival news, bios of "kiwi" artists, and links to related pages.

Mbira

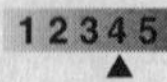

www.mbira.org

This page is an excellent introduction to mbira, the traditional music of Zimbabwe. It also covers Shona traditions, customs, and literature as they relate to mbira. You can listen to a sampler of mbira music and check out the calendar of events.

Music in Scotland

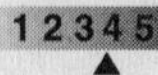

www.musicinscotland.com

This Scottish music site promotes music and musicians who have a Celtic connection to a worldwide audience, including Scottish, Irish, Cape Breton, French, and Spanish musicians. This site provides an excellent introduction to Scottish music and provides links to many additional resources.

Norwegian Music Information Centre

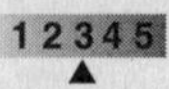

www.mic.no

You can find all kinds of information on Norwegian music here—biographies on many composers; articles covering Norwegian music history, early and church music, and more recent pop, rock, and jazz; information on festivals and other events; and links to many related sites. Site is also available in English.

Peruvian Music

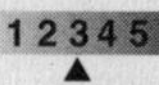

www.musicaperuana.com/english/song.htm

This page has sound files of Andean flute and guitar music as well as links to related Peruvian music topics. The opening page offers three language selections: Spanish, French, and English.

Puro Mariachi

www.mariachi.org

You can find just about everything you wanted to know about mariachi music here, including a history of mariachi, recommended books and CDs, and the lyrics to just about every Mexican song ever written, alphabetized by first line of the song. There are also dozens and dozens of links to Mexican music and cultural sites.

Songs of Indonesia

www.geocities.com/SoHo/1823

This is an archive of Indonesian songs, divided into pop, traditional, and national songs, some in MIDI format. You can find links to related sites, too.

Temple Records

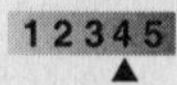

www.templerecords.co.uk

Provides home site and online ordering for Temple Records, which specializes in Scottish traditional music. Includes an online catalog, artist descriptions, and ordering information.

Welcome to Bali & Beyond

www.balibeyond.com

Bali & Beyond is a Los Angeles–based performing arts company inspired by the culture of Indonesia, which plays Gamelan music. The ensemble tours nationwide, featuring a variety of music, theater, and educational presentations. This colorful site contains lots of information about upcoming concert schedules and events. Check out the Kechat section for background on the Indonesian culture and music, and Maria's Corner for all kinds of interesting gift items.

World Music Store

www.worldmusicstore.com

The World Music Store carries music from all over the world. The opening page displays a map of the world with designated hotspots. Simply click a hotspot to view a list of countries in that area and then click the country of your choice to view a list of available CDs.

MUSIC GENRES—JAZZ

BBC Music–Jazz

www.bbc.co.uk/music/jazz

The BBC features this introduction to jazz, which includes news, reviews, sample audio clips, and artist profiles. Site also features an artist search and an album search.

All About Jazz

www.allaboutjazz.com

This site features a huge collection of information and resources about jazz, including reviews, interviews, profiles, columns, information about jazz around the world, various guides including directories for jazz festivals and artists, discussion forums, and much more. Whether you're already a jazz aficionado or are just beginning to become interested, this site provides heaping servings of everything jazz.

Down Beat Magazine

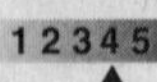

www.downbeat.com

The place to go for the latest news, reviews, and information about your favorite jazz bands and artists.

Jambands

www.jambands.com

Jambands isn't the glitziest website around, but its packed with news, commentary, photos, and reviews galore. Anyone who's interested in a wide range of music should visit this site to see what's happening in the most happenin' areas of the music community.

JAZZ

www.pbs.org/jazz

This is the home of the PBS-sponsored movie *JAZZ*, by Ken Burns, where you can find biographies of famous jazz musicians, transcripts of many of the interviews, audio samples (in the Jazz Lounge), a jazz timeline, and a special area just for kids.

Jazz Corner

www.jazzcorner.com

This comprehensive jazz kiosk provides links to individual artists' home pages, a calendar of jazz events for most states, a photo gallery, interviews, reviews, news, and a discussion area.

Jazz Online

www.jazzonln.com

Watch live online video of some of your favorite jazz performers, such as Chick Corea and Kenny Garrett, among others; listen to jazz clips; check out the hottest jazz albums on the top five lists; read feature articles on jazz performers; and get the latest music news. Features a Jazz 101 class for beginners.

Best The Jazz Review

1 2 3 4 5

www.jazzreview.com

Listen to audio reviews, post your own review of particular pieces, read others' reviews, check out a featured artist, and listen to featured performers as part of the "CD of the Week." This site features jazz interviews and reviews, news, biographies, eCards, links to other jazz sites, a club finder, a concert search, artist events, photography, and just about anything else a true fan of jazz could ever want. Site provides an easily accessible navigation bar off to the left and is packed with quality content, making it an easy selection as our Best of the Best Jazz music site.

Jazz Roots

12345

www.jass.com

A great history site offering a musical timeline showing the extension of jazz music nationally, as well as archives containing bios of musicians and photos. A nice overview of the growth of this musical genre.

A Passion for Jazz

www.apassion4jazz.net

This site features a little of everything related to jazz, focusing on jazz history and education. Here, you'll find links for a jazz timeline, jazz improvisation, jazz festivals, posters and photos, theory books, fake books, sheet music, and more. You can also shop online for apparel and gift items and explore links to other excellent jazz sites.

Red Hot Jazz Archive

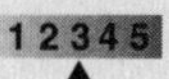

www.redhotjazz.com

Search for information on jazz bands, musicians, and films at this site, which provides plenty of information about the rise of jazz prior to 1930. You can also search for information about essays.

MUSIC GENRES—OPERA

The Aria Database

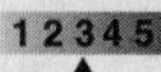

www.aria-database.com

Would you like to be able to search for information on a particular aria, opera, or composer? This is the place. Search by name, opera, language, or voice type. The database includes MIDI files of some of the music, libretti, translations, and more. Mozart and Verdi are featured, but many other composers are also included. Related links also featured.

Báthory Erzsébet: Elizabeth Báthory

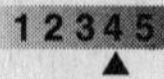

bathory.org

If you're at all interested in how an opera came to be, visit this site. In the Cologne Journal section, Dennis Báthory-Kitsz describes the plans for this semihistorical opera in progress. Check out the history, the bibliography, and, of course, the castle photos.

FanFaire

12345

ffaire.com

A e-zine by and for fans of opera and classical music, updated quarterly, with reviews, slide shows, pictures, and embedded sound files. For best viewing, you'll need a fairly fast modem and a recent version Internet Explorer. Be prepared for sound at a substantial volume; the Java applets might reset your volume levels.

Los Angeles Opera

12345

www.losangelesopera.com

If you're planning a visit to the Los Angeles area, or you live there, and you're looking for an engaging cultural experience, check out the Los Angeles Opera website, where you can learn about upcoming shows, brush up on opera basics, research the history of the Los Angeles opera and the biographies of some of its most famous performers, and much more. You can even take a virtual tour of the grounds and facilities. Nice combination of classical and modern at this site.

The Metropolitan Opera

12345

www.metoperafamily.org

The Metropolitan Opera Family of Websites features links to the Metropolitan Opera, The Opera Shop, The Guild, Education, and Opera News. Click the Metropolitan Opera link to explore the season, buy tickets, learn how to support the Met, discover the basics of opera, research the history of the Met, and more. Whether you're already a fan of the opera or are looking for an engaging cultural experience, visit this site to enhance what already promises to be a soul-deepening excursion. Excellent resources for those who need assistance in honing their tastes.

New York City Opera

12345

www.nycopera.com

Information and current schedules for the world-famous New York City Opera. Includes performer biographies.

OPERA America

12345

www.operaamerica.org

OPERA America is an organization that serves the field of opera by providing informational, technical, and administrative resources to the public in regard to opera. Its mission is to promote opera as exciting and accessible to individuals from all walks of life. The site includes information about advocacy and awareness programs, professional development, an artists database of OPERA America members, and a season and schedule database. Special area with resources for K–12 and other opera newcomers.

Opera Glass

opera.stanford.edu

Enjoy this ever-expanding site of links to opera information on the Web. Opera companies, opera people, and more help to comprise this comprehensive site.

Opera News Online

www.metoperafamily.org/operanews/index.aspx

An electronic publication of the Metropolitan Opera Guild, Inc. Historical and musical analyses, performance reviews, profiles and interviews, and more. Visitors are welcome to pop in and scope out selected news and articles before subscribing. A subscription gives you access to the full magazine online and via mail.

The Opera Schedule Server

www.fsz.bme.hu/opera

A searchable database providing information about what's playing at opera houses all around the world.

Operabase

www.operabase.com

Detailed information on broadcast and performance schedules, festivals, and events; opera houses; reviews; and links. Includes opera timelines for viewers seeking a little history. Databases are searchable by singer, conductor, producer, composer, and more. A complete and complex site, available in seven languages.

Opera for Kids

www.operaforkids.org

Information about FBN Productions' operas for kids. This site is designed more for teachers to learn about productions that they can offer to their students.

OperaNet Magazine

www.culturekiosque.com/opera

An online magazine for opera fans, featuring performer interviews, articles, schedules, and reviews of performances and recordings.

OperaStuff.com

www.operastuff.com

OperaStuff.com features an extensive directory of links to various opera resources on the Web. Links are organized by category including Opera Singers,

A B C D E F G H I J K L M N O P Q R S T U V W X Y Z

Opera Links, Opera Companies, and Singer Resource, making it easy to browse for content. Site also provides a search dialog box, which enables you to perform more focused searches.

Royal Opera House

12345

www.royalopera.org

The Royal Opera House, in Covent Garden, London, is the home of the Royal Opera, the Royal Ballet, and the Orchestra of the Royal Opera House. Here, you can check the schedule for the upcoming season and the following season, book tickets online, find out about backstage tours, research performers, and read up on the Royal Opera House. Site is easy to navigate and accented with some excellent photographs.

San Francisco Opera

12345

www.sfopera.com

This site features information about the San Francisco Opera, including upcoming performances, ticket information, and opera basics.

Seattle Opera

12345

www.seattleopera.org

Get free previews of upcoming performances, learn more about opera stories, find ticket information, and make arrangements to attend a performance at the Seattle Opera, all from the company's website. The background music and singing at this site are a nice touch.

Sydney Opera House

12345

www.sydneyoperahouse.com

Learn more about this Australian cultural landmark, its history, and its future performances. This site also sports a nice shopping site where you can purchase CDs, videos, and Australian-related music gifts. Special areas for kids.

MUSIC GENRES—POP MUSIC

The Beatles LOVE Cirque Du Soleil

12345

www.beatles.com

The closest thing you'll ever get to the Beatles getting back together is getting your hands on one of their old LP's and listening to it over and over. The next best thing might just be the Cirque Du Soleil resurrection of the band and its music and spirit on stage. At this site, you can get a brief glimpse of what the show promises to deliver along with a backstage pass to the making of the show.

MUSIC SOFTWARE: MP3 PLAYERS, RIPPERS, AND BURNERS

iTunes

12345

www.itunes.com

iTunes is Apple's jukebox for Mac and Windows machines. With it, you can store, play, and manage your entire music collection on your computer and transfer audio clips between your computer and iPod. You can also use iTunes to burn tracks to recordable CDs and to stream audio between computers on a local network. If you have an iPod and a computer, you should definitely visit this site to download and install iTunes on your PC or Mac.

Magix Music Maker

12345

www.magix.com

Find lots of software to make your own music, including children's music, music for your website, ringtones, or to learn how to play an instrument. You can also download MP3 files.

MusicMatch

1 2 3 4 5 RSS

www.musicmatch.com

Home of one of the most popular MP3 players, rippers, and burners around. With MusicMatch, you can transform audio clips on CDs into MP3 clips, arrange MP3 clips to create your own playlists, and burn your playlists to create custom CDs.

QuickTime

1 2 3 4 5

www.apple.com/quicktime

Download QuickTime at this site so that you can view videos on your computer. You'll also find some of the top music videos available for downloading and viewing here. Site also features a huge collection of movie trailers.

RealPlayer

1 2 3 4 5

www.realplayer.com

Tune into more than 3,200 radio stations and get clear audio and bright video, free upgrades, and more when you purchase RealPlayer from realplayer.com. This site also offers other Real products that can enhance your listening and viewing experience. Free version also available for download. Check it out!

Roxio

1 2 3 4 5

www.roxio.com

Home of Roxio's popular Easy CD Creator software, which allows you to duplicate CDs, copy data files to recordable discs, transform CD tracks into MP3 clips, play MP3 clips on your PC, and burn your own custom playlists to audio CDs. Excellent program for managing your digital music collection and easy to use.

Shareware Music Machine

www.hitsquad.com/smm

A large collection of downloadable music software for use in recording and playing music with your computer. Instructions and assistance provided by the webmasters.

Shockwave.com

1 2 3 4 5

www.shockwave.com

Download Shockwave and Flash Player for free so that you can view games, presentations, and animations in all their glory on other sites. Excellent collection of free games.

WinAmp

www.winamp.com

WinAmp is an online media player, ripper, and CD burner. WinAmp Free enables you to download free audio and video clips from the WinAmp site and play them on your computer, tune in to several Internet radio and TV stations, and create your own custom media library. WinAmp Pro, which costs about $15, enables you to rip tracks from your CDs and convert them to MP3 clips and burn MP3 clips (that you rip or download from the Internet) to recordable CDs. This site also features a Games area, free audio and video clips, and discussion forums.

Windows Media Player

1 2 3 4 5

www.microsoft.com/windows/windowsmedia/default.aspx

With Windows Media Player, you can tune in to online radio stations, download and play audio and video clips, create custom playlists, rip tracks off

CDs you own, and burn tracks to recordable CDs. If you have a PC that's running Windows, you probably have Windows Media Player installed on your computer, but do you have the latest version? Run Windows Media Player and click Help, About Windows Media Player to view the version number. Then check this site to determine the latest version and download it if necessary. If you don't have Windows Media Player, you can download it from this site for free.

MUSIC: INSTRUMENTS

8th street.com

www.8thstreet.com

Search the online database for virtually any type of musical instrument or equipment and find guaranteed lowest prices as well as free shipping when you order from the site. Whether you need amps, drums, or professional recording gear, you can find it at this site.

Accordions International

www.accordioninfo.com

Accordion music has come a long way since Lawrence Welk. This manufacturer even offers MIDI kits for electronic accordions. Read about the Concerto, the world's first digital/acoustic accordion. Other types of new—as well as used—instruments are also available. Order merchandise by phone, fax, or mail.

The Barrel Organ Museum

www.organito.com.ar

The barrel organ has a fascinating history that constitutes more than just the prototypical organ grinder. If you've never seen a barrel organ (other than in the movies), be sure to visit this museum, located in Argentina. Scroll down the opening page and click the link for the desired language: Spanish, Italian, English, French, German, Dutch, or Japanese.

Fender

www.fender.com

Fender guitars have a strong worldwide reputation for quality. At this site, you can check out the latest Fender guitars, amps, and other equipment, find a dealer near you, check out other resources, and shop online.

Gear4Music

www.gear4music.com

This site features musical instruments and equipment at bargain prices. Products are categorized as Instruments, Live, Studio, and Computer to make it easier to find the equipment you need for a specific purpose. This is a British store, so prices are in pounds and euros.

Gibson Musical Instruments

www.gibson.com

Get information on Gibson guitars, locate local dealers, and buy and sell Gibson equipment online at the Gibson site.

Guitarsite.com

www.guitarsite.com

If you're into guitar music—playing, recording, or listening—check out this site. You can find hundreds of listings for guitar shops, guitar chords, guitar dealers, guitar publications, guitarists...you get the idea. But it's not just guitars—everything musical seems to be included. Some bonus items are also available, including a list of guitar jokes.

Guitar: WholeNote.com

www.wholenote.com

WholeNote is dedicated to fostering a community of guitar aficionados for sharing musical knowledge. WholeNote provides an ever-evolving, always expanding music instruction book that you can play at your own speed. Site features a guitar store, composer software, groove builder, instruction, MP3s, tablatures, and much more. Whether your pick, pluck, or strum a guitar, this site is for you, no matter what your level of expertise.

Hubbard Harpsichords, Inc.

1 2 3 4 5

www.hubharp.com

Hubbard sells complete harpsichords but also sells kits. The company's weekend workshops can help you to put together your own kit, with Hubbard's help, at a price that's substantially reduced from that of a completely assembled instrument. This site offers details about all the Hubbard products and services, as well as books, CDs, news, events, and general information.

The Internet Cello Society

1 2 3 4 5

www.cello.org

With more than 14,000 members in more than 80 different countries, this organization is an international "cyber-community of cellists." Learn about the society, connect with other musicians, check out the links, and play the many RealAudio sound files.

LOOPLABS

1 2 3 4 5

www.looplabs.com

Featuring an online music mixer, this site enables visitors to mix their own collection of recorded sounds to create original recordings. You'll feel like you're in a professional recording studio! After you have recorded your tune, you can upload it to share with others online.

Mid-East Mfg. Co.

1 2 3 4 5

www.mid-east.com

This site offers a large selection of ethnic musical instruments: sitars, bagpipes, lyres, ocarinas, doumbeks, and many others. Specials, seconds, and repairs—some at great prices—have their own page. Addresses of regional showrooms and related links are also included.

The Music House

1 2 3 4 5

www.musichouse.com

Based in Lake Forest, California, this company provides a wide variety of instruments and sheet music to commercial establishments or educational institutions. The service is particularly useful to small music stores that don't have the space or capital to keep a large inventory. Music House School Affiliates can rent or purchase band and orchestral instruments and receive funding assistance.

Rhythm Fusion–Musical Instruments from Around the World

1 2 3 4 5

www.rhythmfusion.com

Looking for sound makers from around the world? Then this is your site. You can purchase doumbeks, African drums, rattles, wind instruments, gongs, and much more by clicking on the icon of each type of instrument.

Unicorn Strings Music Company

1 2 3 4 5

unicornstrings.com

This company specializes in bowed psalteries. You might have seen these unusual instruments in magazines and on TV, such as on the popular science fiction show *Babylon 5*. From this site, you can learn about the company, the instrument and how it's played, the music it produces, and, of course, how to get one.

Yamaha

1 2 3 4 5

www.yamaha.com

Yamaha is a world-renowned manufacturer of musical instruments and other audio products for professionals and consumers alike. Here, you can check out the latest product lines, read reviews, find local dealers, and download some free ringtones.

ORGANIZATIONS AND CLUBS

AMC: American Music Conference

www.amc-music.com

AMC is a nonprofit educational organization dedicated to promoting music, music making, and music education to the general public through several educational institutions nationwide. Visit the site to learn more about the group's research and educational programs.

American Federation of Musicians of the United States and Canada

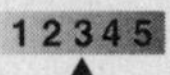

www.afm.org

Professional union of musicians, full- and part-time, as well as students, in all genres. The AFM's goal is to improve musicians' working conditions and wages, and to support the arts and arts education. The Current Events section includes important industry news; the Hiring Musicians section describes how to hire a musician and provides links to booking agents and local musicians. Check the site list for links to related organizations, affiliates, and offerings for young musicians.

American Pianists Association

www.americanpianists.org

The American Pianists Association (APA) is devoted to "discovering, promoting, and advancing the careers of world-class, classical and jazz pianists, who are citizens of the United States between the ages of 18 and 30, through competitions, performance tours, and educational programs." Here, you can learn more about the association and about its programs, competitions, and awards. We're not impressed with the navigation tools at this site—you need to mouse over the squares on the opening page to find out what each one links to.

American Society of Composers, Authors, and Publishers

www.ascap.com

Read *Playback* magazine, ASCAP's member magazine at the site, which addresses licensing issues of interest to independent creative artists. You can also get membership information. You'll certainly want to visit the ASCAP café online, where you can pick up survival tips, hear success stories, solicit expert opinions from those who've been there, and access streaming radio and podcasts.

BMI.com

bmi.com

BMI is a nonprofit organization representing hundreds of thousands of songwriters, composers, and music publishers in all genres. This site provides a searchable database of its more than three million works. Check the Legislative Update section to keep up-to-date with the latest on copyright laws and other legislation related to intellectual property. The Recommended Reading section tracks all sorts of information on the BMI membership, along with books and articles of interest to the community. The Licensing and Songwriters' Toolboxes provide a wealth of useful material for the professional involved in the music field.

Creative Musicians Coalition

www.aimcmc.com

This international organization represents independent artists and record labels producing music in more than two dozen different styles. On the site, you'll find a directory of artists and the AfterTouch catalog. Search by artist, style, or label. The Showcase section offers reviews and samples of new music (some might require plug-ins). Are you ready to experiment?

Grammy.com

www.grammy.com

Home of the Grammy Awards, the premier awards organization in the recording industry. This site provides information about the National Academy of Recording Arts & Sciences, Inc., also known as the Recording Academy. This group is "dedicated to improving the quality of life and cultural condition for music and its makers." Here, you can find out about the upcoming Grammy Awards, check out the nominees, and look up the winners.

Just Plain Folks

www.jpfolks.com

Just Plain Folks is an "ever growing group of songwriters, recording artists, music publishers, record labels, performing arts societies, educational institutions, recording studios and engineers, producers, legal professionals, publicists and journalists, publications, music manufacturers and retailers and about every other type of member of the music industry." Here, you can learn more about the organization, begin networking with its members, and share your enthusiasm of song and music with some down-to-earth recording professionals.

Ladyslipper Music

www.ladyslipper.org

Nonprofit music organization dedicated to "heightening public awareness of the achievements of women artists and musicians, and expanding the scope and availability of musical and literary recordings by women." Here, you can tune into *Ladyslipper* magazine and shop for CDs released by a vast assortment of female recording artists in an extensive list of categories.

NAMM

www.namm.com

Home of the International Music Products Association, NAMM represents more than 7,700 retailers, manufacturers, wholesalers, and publishers in the United States and 85+ other countries. Here, you can learn about upcoming events, including trade shows and the summer session; access resources; and learn about NAMM's current and upcoming projects.

National Music Publisher's Association

www.nmpa.org

NMPA is a strong defender of copyrights, particularly for the music industry, representing more than 800 music publishers. Here, you can learn more about the organization and how it has helped the music industry.

New Media Consortium

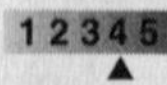

www.nmc.org

The NMC is a nonprofit "consortium of nearly 200 leading colleges, universities, museums, corporations, and other learning-focused organizations dedicated to the exploration and use of new media and new technologies. Here, you can check out the gallery of cutting-edge creations, learn about upcoming events and projects, and explore the organization in greater depth.

Recording Industry Association of America

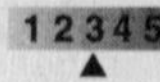

www.riaa.com

The RIAA is a trade association representing the U.S. sound recording industry. The thrust of this site is the themes of antipiracy and artistic freedom. Plenty of interesting reading on these and other topics, as well as a searchable database of gold and platinum record winners, and a short list of related links. This site also features information for parents.

Rhythm and Blues Foundation

www.rhythm-n-blues.org

Founded by Bonnie Raitt, the Rhythm and Blues Foundation is an independent nonprofit service organization with a worldwide reputation for meeting the needs of former rhythm and blues artists. Visitors can explore the R&B Timeline, sample recordings in the Sound Room, sign up to receive an email newsletter, learn more about the organization, and shop online. When we visited the site, the most promising features—the R&B Timeline and the Sound Room—were under construction.

Wolverine Antique Music Society

www.shellac.org/wams

Presents the Wolverine Antique Music Society. Focuses on the preservation of music originally recorded for 78rpm records. Offers much to the 78 collector and early jazz aficionado. Contains many articles on the music, collecting, and all sorts of technical and resource information pertaining to antique audio. Also contains information on the early record labels, 78 album cover art, and sound clips.

Women in Music

www.womeninmusic.com

Women in Music (WIM) is a nonprofit organization with the goal of supporting the efforts and careers of women in the music industry. Numerous programs are offered at this site, including referrals, newsletters, seminars and workshops, insider's tips, and more. Events and industry news sections provide useful updates on music-related activities. You can also order apparel and other merchandise from this site, join the organization, and make donations online.

RADIO SITES

All Songs Considered

www.npr.org/programs/asc

Home of National Public Radio's music broadcasts, this site provides an on-demand archive of musical pieces featured on NPR's popular radio show. Features a handful of music videos, too.

BBC Radio 4 Website

www.bbc.co.uk/radio4

The British Broadcasting Company is famous worldwide for its news coverage as well as in-depth reports on science, nature, history, religion, and more. Its comedy specials and dedication to preserving drama and the other arts also add to its allure. At this site, you can access much of what the BBC has to offer via its radio programming; plus you can quickly link to its television offerings.

Best The Bob Rivers Show

www.bobrivers.com

Bob Rivers as Weird Al Yankovic. Features downloadable hits such as "12 Days of Layoffs" and "50 Ways to Feed My Brother." Site is packed with recordings from the show, jokes, song lyrics and recordings, and much more. Every radio station should have a complementary website that's as attractively designed and packed with as much free stuff as this. Outstanding.

BRS Web-Radio Directory

www.web-radio.com

Directory of thousands of radio stations that broadcast on the Web. You can view the complete directory or browse stations by call letters, states, countries, or format, or view a list of stations that broadcast exclusively over the Internet.

CBC Radio

www.cbcradio3.com

This is the online radio station of CBC Radio-Canada, Canada's National Public Broadcasting network. As soon as you connect, the music starts playing. Click the Table of Contents link on the left of the page to view additional content, including articles, photos, and links to other online music sites.

Classic FM

www.classicfm.com

If you're a fan of classical music, tune in to Classic FM, where you can listen to streaming audio broadcasts of classical tunes along with commentary. Tune in to Classic TV to watch shows about your favorite composers and other topics related to classical music.

Earth & Sky Radio Series

www.earthsky.com

Every day Deborah Byrd and Joel Block discuss scientific issues that affect our lives on this science radio series heard by millions of Americans on more than 950 commercial and public stations across the country. The online shop offers many gift ideas that you can buy from the website.

Hearts of Space

www.hos.com

Home of Hearts of Space, a combination record label and radio show syndication company. Here, you can sample the works of various recording artists, listen to Internet radio stations, and learn more about the company and its services.

KAOS: Welcome to KAOS!

www.kaosradio.org

KAOS is a radio station located at Evergreen State College in Olympia, Washington. It offers traditional and popular music of America and the world, including jazz, classical, swing, blues, soul, rap, R&B, Celtic, new acoustic and electronic music, Native American, Spanish language, rock, and Broadway music. You'll also hear comedy, radio theater, stories from *Pacifica News* and the *Monitor Press*, and news on public affairs. The site includes an on-air schedule, bios of the programmers, and descriptions of the programs. You'll also see KAOS's listing of the current top 30 songs.

KEXP

www.kexp.org

At this site, you can listen to KEXP out of Seattle, check its daily programming schedule, listen to archived programs and live performances, read reviews of new albums, find out about upcoming concerts and events, and much more.

KPIG Radio Online

www.kpig.com

Tune into the web version of this California radio station that aims to be a throwback to the 60s and 70s when DJs added personality to their broadcasts. Check the site for the station's playlist, which varies from 50s music forward, information on DJs, and an active community of fans you can chat with. Be sure to check out the calendars and T-shirts available for purchase from this site.

Live365

www.live365.com

Live365 features the largest network of Internet radio stations on the Web providing everything from music stations to talk radio and special broadcasts. To start browsing, simply click the link for the desired genre, including Alternative, Comedy, Hip Hop, Classical, Reggae, Pop, and Rock. Click the More link for a complete offering of links, including Talk and Government. When you don't know where to tune in, stop here for a complete directory.

MITList of Radio Stations on the Internet

www.radio-locator.com/cgi-bin/home

Find stations broadcasting on the Web by typing in a city and state, or the call letters, and you'll quickly find out where you can tune in to the broadcast. The database contains more than 10,000 stations, so there's a fair chance the one you want is here.

NPR: National Public Radio Online

www.npr.org

This site lets you listen to NPR news on the hour. View summaries of programs and then listen to them, or check out some of the special highlighted stories that you might have missed. Check out the information on the news magazines, talk shows, and cultural and information stories you can listen to—among them, *All Things Considered, Morning Edition, Car Talk,* and *Jazz from Lincoln Center.*

Premiere Radio Networks

www.premrad.com

You'll find a large selection of syndicated talk, music, and entertainment shows that air on Premiere Radio Networks' radio waves here on their web version. Search the channels to find the type of programming you want to listen to and then tune in.

Public Radio Exchange

www.prx.org

PRX (Public Radio Exchange) is a service that links public radio program producers with stations to assist in the distribution and peer review of programs. Register and you can listen to new shows before they are broadcast on the radio and offer your own feedback. Station managers can choose to license shows.

Public Radio Fan

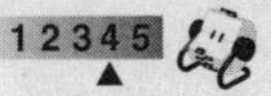

www.publicradiofan.com

This site features a public radio programming guide for stations across the United States. Many program listings contain links that take you directly to the radio station's website, where you can "tune in" to the program. When you connect, make sure you enter your time zone to obtain an accurate programming schedule.

RadioTower

www.radiotower.com

Searchable directory of more than 8,000 online radio sites. Search by category (genre), country, or station.

SHOUTcast

12345

www.shoutcast.com

SHOUTcast is "Nullsoft's Free Winamp-based distributed streaming audio system" that thousands of broadcasters around the world use to broadcast their radio stations on the Web. Here, you can search the SHOUTcast directory for the station you want to listen to.

Transom

www.transom.org

Billing itself as "A Showcase & Workshop for New Public Radio," Transom features a diverse collection of in-depth, behind-the-scenes reports about real-life events and concerns. When you're tired of hearing the same old news reports and nightly specials, check out Transom for some more unique offerings. You can even record your own stories and submit them for inclusion on this site.

World Radio Network Online

www.wrn.org

WRN offers a global perspective on current world events and updates you on news from your homeland. It also covers arts and culture, music, sports, science, and more. WRN via cable, satellite, local AM/FM, and the Internet is used as an educational resource by schools, colleges, and universities. You'll also find WRN schedules and learn how to listen to live newscast audio streams in RealAudio and StreamWorks 24 hours a day from many of the world's leading public and international broadcasters.

WTOP

www.wtopnews.com

WTOP online is Washington D.C.'s source for news, sports, and weather on the Internet. At this site, you can read local, national, and world news stories; check Washington's traffic, weather, and sports; look into science, health, and entertainment; and tune in to WTOP to listen to its live broadcast.

Yahoo! Launchcast

launch.yahoo.com/launchcast

Yahoo! Launchcast enables you to tune in more than 100 exclusive commercial-free radio stations, create your own custom radio station based on the genres you prefer, and search for song lyrics while you listen.

Youth Radio

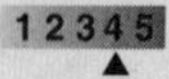

www.youthradio.org

Youth Radio is dedicated to providing young people with the training and opportunities to become successful as radio producers, broadcasters, and in other radio broadcasting roles. Here, you can check out the work of some of the talented individuals involved with Youth Radio.

MYSTERY

ClueLass

12345 Blog RSS

www.cluelass.com

ClueLass is "the longtime screen alias of Kate Derie, a writer/editor/website designer/publisher who lives in Tucson, Arizona, with her husband and her Bernese Mountain Dog." Kate and her fellow cronies maintain this site to keep mystery fans posted of the latest happenings and creations in the world of mystery. Site also features a Mystery FAQ that tackles the most frequently asked questions about the mystery genre and several of the most prominent people working within that genre.

Independent Mystery Publishers

12345

www.mysterypublishers.com

IMP is a group of "independent publishers of mystery and suspense fiction and related nonfiction who share information, trade ideas, and work together on marketing projects." Here, you can learn more about the group and how to become an active member. If you're a writer dabbling in creating your own mystery novel, this is a great place to connect with others who share your interest and enthusiasm and who know the ropes.

Masterpiece Theatre & MYSTERY!

12345

www.pbs.org/wgbh/masterpiece

The PBS *MYSTERY!* series presents top-notch British mysteries. Here, you can learn how the show came into being, learn the program history, research detectives, play *MYSTERY!* games, find out about the American *Mysteries* series, discuss episodes online, and shop for merchandise. You can also check the broadcast schedule and see what's in the works for the upcoming season.

Mysterious Bookshop

12345

www.mysteriousbookshop.com

Located at 58 Warren Street in New York, the Mysterious Bookshop is "the oldest mystery specialist book store in America." It promises to offer the "best in mystery, crime, suspense, espionage, and detective fiction." Store carries signed first editions, rare and collectible books, staff favorites, collectibles, and other merchandise for mystery fans the world over. You can even shop online.

Mystery Guide

12345

www.mysteryguide.com

The Mystery Guide features more than 700 original reviews of mystery novels, a list of new mystery titles, author interviews, trivia questions, and ratings. You browse for books by genre, including Caper, Forensic, Political, SF Mystery, Suspense, and Thriller.

Mystery Ink

12345

www.mysteryinkonline.com

Mystery Ink features book reviews, author interviews, some reference materials, book awards, and links to other quality mystery sites, most of which are the sites of accomplished mystery authors.

Best Mystery Net

12345

www.mysterynet.com

Mystery Net is "the place for online mysteries and mystery games." The site features See-n-Solve, Solve-it, Twist, and Flash mysteries, Get-a-Clue mini-mysteries, and Teasers by Members. You can "sign up for the free monthly email mystery and receive a Solve-it each month." What's most impressive about this site is not the design, but the breadth of content it offers. Whether you have a preference for TV mysteries, mystery movies, books, or games, this site has something to offer, along with an active online community, complete with discussion forums. Special area for kids' mysteries, too.

The Mystery Reader

www.themysteryreader.com

The Mystery Reader features reviews of mystery novels from several categories, including Police/Detectives, Thrillers, Suspense, Cozy Mysteries, Historical Mysteries, Romance Mysteries, and Eclectica. Site also features an alphabetic list of the top authors in the genre. The list of eagerly awaited titles and the Booksigning Tales are woefully out of date, but the site is still well worth the visit for mystery novel fans.

Mystery Readers International

www.mysteryreaders.org

With mystery readers from all 50 of the United States and 18 foreign countries, Mystery Readers International is the largest group of its kind in the world and includes readers, fans, critics, editors, publishers, and writers. Here, you can track down local reading groups, obtain contact information for a host of mystery periodicals, locate local bookstores that are known to carry a wide selection of mystery novels, read reviews of the latest mystery novels, and much more.

Stop, You're Killing Me!

www.stopyourekillingme.com

If you're trying to track down a mystery novel, this should be your first stop to solving the mystery. Site features a searchable/browsable cross-index of mystery, intrigue, and suspense novels. You can search by author, character, or location; check the FAQ to find answers to questions about the site; or sign up to receive the newsletter via email. Site also features a directory of links to other mystery websites, author websites, and resources and references.

Top Mystery

www.topmystery.com

Top Mystery is dedicated to guiding visitors to the best that the mystery genre has to offer—the best books, best movies, and links to the best sites. The alphabetic button bar that runs across the top of the home page helps you navigate an alphabetic listing of the top mystery authors, providing a brief biography of each author. Site also features links to online versions of classic mystery novels along with a discussion forum.

MYTHOLOGY

Dictionary of Greek and Roman Myths

12345

www.online-mythology.com

If you need to look up information about a god, goddess, hero, or heroine of Greek or Roman mythology, this is the place for you. Site provides an alphabetic list of characters from Achelous to Venus.

Egyptian Mythology

12345

touregypt.net/gods1.htm

Good introduction to Egyptian mythology covers the main gods and their primary places of worship, the roles that kings played in promoting their pet mythological figures, and the Egyptian myth of creation.

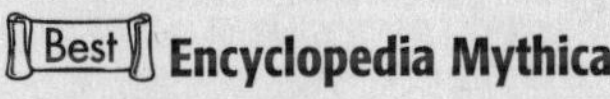

Best Encyclopedia Mythica

12345 RSS

www.pantheon.org

Huge online encyclopedia provides extensive coverage of mythology related to various countries, eras, and cultures. The encyclopedia lets you explore Aboriginal, African, Celtic, Greek, Roman, Native American, Mayan, and Japanese mythology just to name a few of the more popular traditions. If you think you already know your mythology, try your hand at the Myth Quiz. Special interest areas include a Bestiary, Legendary Heroes, an Image Gallery, and Genealogical Tables. Whether you need to do a little research for a school project or simply need to explore your mythological roots, this site offers up the information you need.

Joseph Campbell Foundation

12345

www.jcf.org

Joseph Campbell, the most renowned mythologist ever, has done more to disperse the wisdom of mythology than the mythologians themselves. Here, you can learn more about Joseph Campbell and his works, find out about upcoming events and roundtable discussions, find answers to the most commonly asked questions, and find out how to contact the foundation.

Myth and Culture

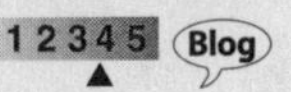

12345 Blog

www.mythandculture.com

If you're interested in learning about the role of myth in culture, this is a great site to begin your research. Site features a clear definition of "myth" and a discussion of cultural mythology, explores personal mythology and dreams, and investigates the link between religion and mythology. The site design is a little clunky, but the content is solid.

Mythology

12345

www.windows.ucar.edu/cgi-bin/tour_def/mythology/mythology.html

Don't let the long site address or the fact that this site was last updated more than six years ago discourage you from visiting it. This is one of the best designed mythology sites on the Web, and it takes an interesting approach to connecting the various mythological traditions—by looking at how they interpreted heavenly objects. Site features links to the Sun, Moon, Earth, Solar System, and Constellations. It describes Classical Mythology, investigates Family Trees, and explores World Mythology. Visitors can access additional features through the navigation bar near the bottom of the window.

Mythus: Comparative Mythology

1 2 3 4 5

`mythus.com`

This is the home page of Verlyn Flieger, comparative mythologist who specializes in the study of J. R. R. Tolkein. Here, you can read descriptions of several of her books and find links to other important books on Tolkein.

Myth Web

1 2 3 4 5

`www.mythweb.com`

The Myth Web is an excellent resource for anyone studying Greek mythology. Site focuses mainly on characters in Greek mythology—gods and heroes. For a more extensive list of characters, click the Encyclopedia link. The Today link shines a spotlight on one of the more famous characters.

Norse Mythology

1 2 3 4 5

`www.ugcs.caltech.edu/~cherryne/mythology.html`

Nothing fancy here, just an incredibly good introduction to Norse mythology along with links to some excellent stories about mythological figures and the Norse way of looking at the world. Site features links for Mythic Figures, Creation, Cosmology, Ragnarok, Valkyrie, Berserker, Chronology, Links, and Sources. Great place to start researching Norse mythology.

THEOI Project

1 2 3 4 5

`www.theoi.com`

"A comprehensive guide to the Gods (*Theoi*), Spirits (*Daimones*), and Monsters (*Theres*) of ancient Greek mythology and religion." Site features a bestiary, various family trees, a map of the kingdoms commonly mentioned in Greek mythology, a photo gallery of the gods and various heroes, a bibliography, and links to other useful mythology sites.

A B C D E F G H I J K L M N O P Q R S T U V W X Y Z

NATURE

Audubon Nature Institute

12345

www.auduboninstitute.org

Audubon Nature Institute, located in New Orleans, Louisiana, is a collection of zoos and parks dedicated to nature. Each zoo and park has its own area on this site—to go to the desired area, simply point to Your Visit and click the link for the desired area. If you're planning on visiting the Nature Institute, don't miss the Upcoming Events page, where you can find the dates and times of special events.

BBC Nature Site

www.bbc.co.uk/sn

The British Broadcasting Company's Nature site is packed with articles and presentations about animals and the environment. Check out this week's nature special, take the daily quiz, subscribe to the newsletter, check out the birdcam, or browse the site for nature information that catches your eye. The opening page offers a few Highlights (special stories), or you can choose to browse the site by content category, including Animals, Prehistoric Life, Human Body & Mind, Space, and Hot Topics. Site also features some excellent online games for naturalists of all ages.

Becoming Human

www.becominghuman.org

Documentary, news, commentary, and reference library designed to help visitors more fully comprehend human evolution.

Denver Museum of Nature & Science

www.dmns.org

The Denver Museum of Nature & Science offers "a variety of exhibitions, programs, and activities to help Museum visitors experience the natural wonders of Colorado, Earth, and the universe." Here, you can explore a collection of current, upcoming, and online exhibitions; check out what's playing when at the IMAX theater and what's happening at the planetarium; learn more about educational programs at the museum; and much more.

Best eNature

www.enature.com

This for-profit site, owned and operated by the National Wildlife Federation, features a huge collection of wildlife resources for novice and expert alike. Find field guides for more than 5,500 animal and plant species, learn about birding, find out how to create your own nature habitats in your yard, get answers from the experts, and much more. This site covers the birds, the bees, the butterflies, the lizards, and a wide array of other known creatures, plants, and living organism on this planet, making it our pick for Best of the Best nature site.

English Nature

www.english-nature.org.uk

English Nature is committed to protecting and enhancing English landscapes and wildlife and promoting countryside access and recreation. This site features English nature news, a map with the locations of nature preserves and wildlife habitats, resources for schools and teachers, an online image library, and a red kites webcam, to name only a few of the special features and content areas.

Natural Resources Defense Council

www.nrdc.org

Interested in preserving our natural resources and ensuring the survival of all living species? Then check out the NRDC's official website, where you can learn more about conservation and wildlife preservation. The NRDC is one of the most active environmental action organizations on the planet, and this site provides an excellent overview of the top issues, including global warming, air and water pollution, fish and wildlife preservation, and toxic chemicals and other waste products. What we found most impressive at this site is its huge collection of practical guides that teach what the average person needs to know to live a greener lifestyle. Site content is offered in both English and Spanish.

Nature

www.nature.com

This online version of *Nature* journal provides free access to many of the features and articles covered in the journal, plus a whole lot of extras, including blogs, Podcasts, and Web feeds. Subscribers obtain full access to the site. Covers the latest nature news, giving a more scientific perspective.

Nature Canada

www.cnf.ca

Nature Canada's mission is "to conserve and protect nature—Canada's natural diversity of plant and animal species and their environment." Use the navigation bar near the top of the page to skip to access a collection of menus with options for pulling up specific content. Menus include Endangered Species, Nature Education, Parks and Protected Areas, Bird Conservation, The Nature Network, and Support Us. You can also click the Search option to track down specific information on the site.

> **Tip:** Click Nature Education, click Nature Watch, and click one of the Nature Watch program icons to obtain a printable PDF document that helps you learn about one aspect of the environment and collect data about it for scientists to study.

NatureServe.org

www.natureserve.org

NatureServe.org offers scientific information about endangered species and threatened ecosystems to help with conservation efforts in the New World—Canada, the United States, and Central and South America. Here, you can find information about the organization, research tens of thousands of species and ecosystems, and obtain other useful information.

Notebaert Nature Museum

www.chias.org

The Chicago Academy of Sciences Peggy Notebaert Nature Museum is dedicated to fostering "environmental learning through the exhibits and education programs of the Museum and through the Academy's collections, research, symposia, publications, events, and other activities." By studying the effects of global environmental issues on the Midwest, the organization attempts to "build an understanding of global environmental issues." Before visiting the museum, visit this site to learn a little about the museum's main attractions. Site also features some resources for teachers.

PBS Nature Site

www.pbs.org/wnet/nature

For more than 20 years, the PBS *Nature* series has informed and entertained its viewers through its premier nature programming. You can now access much of the information presented in these shows online. The site features a searchable database of past programs, information on upcoming programs, a video database, puzzles, interactive games, and e-postcards you can send to friends and relatives.

RainforestWeb.org

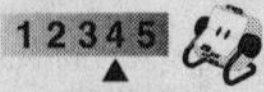

www.rainforestweb.org

Concerned about preservation of the rainforests? Then visit this site to learn more about rainforests and the projects that threaten their very existence. Learn why rainforests are important, what's happening to them, why they're being destroyed, and what you can do to help. This site functions primarily as a gateway to other websites that offer content related to rain forest conservation.

Sierra Club

www.sierraclub.org

The Sierra Club is one of the oldest grass-roots environmental activist groups. Its website encourages you to enjoy the great outdoors, take action to preserve our natural resources, and join or donate to the Sierra Club to help the organization fight for environmental-friendly legislation. Great place for environmental activists to keep abreast of current issues.

WWF

www.panda.org

WWF (formerly known as the World Wildlife Fund) is an independent conservation organization that's "active in over 90 countries and can safely claim to have played a major role in the evolution of the international conservation movement." With an emphasis on saving existing habitats, including both plants and animals, this is a great place for environmental activists to visit. Learn about the group's activities and programs and how you can join WWF in its conservation efforts.

NEEDLECRAFTS

A to Z Needlepoint

1 2 3 4 5

www.a-z-needlepoint.com

Online store that carries a wide selection of needlepoint canvases, yarns, threads, accessories, kits, video tapes, and other related items. Scroll down for a list of the 20 most popular needlepoint designers, where you can shop for designs by designer rather than category.

The Angel's Nook

1 2 3 4 5

www.theangelsnook.com

The Angel's Nook is an online store that carries a wide selection of kits and patterns for counted cross stitch, stamped cross stitch, needlepoint, and embroidery. Store also carries felt kits, beginner kits, punch needle, and rubber stamps.

Bird Cross Stitch

1 2 3 4 5

www.birdcrossstitch.com

If you like birds and you enjoy cross stitching, this site helps you merge the two interests. Site offers "free cross stitch patterns of hummingbirds and other birds, as well as a bluebird alphabet, ladybug alphabet, butterfly patterns, and southwest designs." You'll also find a couple cross stitch tutorials.

Embroidery.com

1 2 3 4 5

www.embroidery.com

Embroidery.com is an online store that carries a huge collection of designs, threads, sewing supplies, furniture, apparel, software, and equipment. Site also features some free designs. For instructions on how to embroider, click Ideas & Education. This opens a page with links to videos, help files, a project gallery, and some tips and techniques.

Embroidery Online

1 2 3 4 5

www.embroideryonline.com

Embroidery Online is a store where you can purchase embroidery designs and supplies, download free project ideas and instructions, and register to receive free embroidery tips via email.

FreeEmbroideryStuff.com

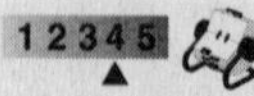

www.freeembroiderystuff.com

Self billed as "The Internet resource for the embroidery industry," this site features links to free embroidery designs, software, catalogues, and articles. Site also features an Embroidery Forum, where you can exchange messages with other embroiderers; a Digitizer's Corner, where you can locate a digitizer; and a Technician's corner, where you can search for a local sewing machine technician and get tips on how to properly maintain your machine. Click Embroidery Links for links to other embroidery sites.

Husqvarna

www.husqvarnaviking.com

Husqvarna Viking is a manufacturer of hi-tech sewing machines that not only sew but also embroider. The machines are programmable, automating much of the process. When you reach the home page, click the icon for your country and then click Embroidery to view long list of links to embroidery topics, including News, Machines, Software, Clubs, and Free Designs.

Janome

12345

www.janome.com

Janome is a sewing machine company that specialize in hi-tech machines that automated the embroidery process. Here, you can check out the latest machines and accessories, find project ideas, download free designs, take a few free lessons, learn new techniques, and order additional software for your machine.

Megrisoft Embroidery Digitizing

12345

www.megrisoft.com

Megrisoft is a custom embroidery design digitizing service, which can transform your hand-drawn or computer-generated art or your photos into digitized renderings that you can load into your hi-tech sewing machine. Here, you can check out what Megrisoft has to offer and even download a free digitized designs.

Best National NeedleArts Association

12345

www.tnna.org

The National NeedleArts Association defines "needleart" as "any form of hand technique utilizing a needle and some type of fiber, yarn, or thread in an effort to create a final product that may be both functional and attractive." Remaining in line with that definition, this site features content related to needlepoint, embroidery, crochet, knitting, and cross stitch. Here, you can find a clear definition of each needleart, search for NeedleArt shops and events near you, and learn more about your favorite needlearts.

Needlepoint.com

12345

www.needlepoint.com

Needlepoint.com is an online store that carries a wide selection of canvases, accessories, and kits. The preview photos of the products are a little dinky, but are of high enough quality to help you select items. Site also features a Stitcher's Gallery, where you can check out the work of other needlepointers.

PatternsOnline

12345

www.patternsonline.com

If you're looking for cross stitch patterns, PatternsOnline should be your first stop. This online store has a selection of more than 5,000 cross stitch patterns that you can purchase and immediately download and print. No waiting, no shipping charges, and you can print as many copies of the pattern as you like or even resize the pattern for different applications.

The Stitchery.com

12345

thestitchery.com

The Stitchery.com is an online store that carries a wide selection of needlecraft items and kits. Whether you're interested in cross stitch, embroidery, needlepoint, or quilting, you'll find plenty of products and accessories at this site. You can also register to receive email notices of the latest specials.

NETWORKING

3Com

1 2 3 4 5

www.3com.com

3Com Corp., a manufacturer of networking hardware, allows people who visit the company's site to learn about employment opportunities, browse company products, and get customer support.

Cable Digital News

1 2 3 4 5 Blog RSS

www.cabledigitalnews.com/

An "online publication providing news and analysis of the cable industry's evolving communications and entertainment services and infrastructure." Site features sections on High-Speed Data, VoIP, Video, Multimedia, and Home Networking. Plenty of links to industry sites and vendors are also available.

Cisco Connection Online

1 2 3 4 5

www.cisco.com

Cisco Systems, Inc., is the worldwide leader in networking for the Internet. Cisco products include routers, LAN and ATM switches, dialup access servers, and network management software. Cisco Systems news and product/service information are available on this site. The opening page is packed with links for information, products, services, technology, and training.

Consortium for School Networking

1 2 3 4 5

www.cosn.org

The Consortium for School Networking (CoSN) is a national nonprofit organization that promotes the use of information technologies and the Internet in K–12 education to improve education. School districts, state and local education agencies, nonprofit educational organizations, and other companies and individuals in the consortium work together to achieve its goals.

Emulex Network Systems

www.emulex.com

This company designs and produces hardware and software for network access, communications, and time management. Products specialize in the management of data between computers and peripheral equipment. The site includes detailed product listings, upgrade programs, technical support, and a company profile.

HELIOS Software

www.helios.de

HELIOS Software is a leading developer of "high-performance networking and client/server software products for Macintosh, DOS/Windows PCs, and UNIX." Check out the FAQs section, read the latest news, and see the specials HELIOS is offering.

Hitachi Data Systems (HDS)

1 2 3 4 5 Blog

www.hds.com

Learn about Hitachi Data Systems products and services targeting the IT needs of large enterprises.

Home Network Security

www.cert.org/tech_tips/home_networks.html

How secure is your home network? Check this site to find out and to learn about network security in a home or small-business environment. This site begins with an introduction to home security and then discusses available technology, specific risks, and actions you can take to secure your network.

A B C D E F G H I J K L M N O P Q R S T U V W X Y Z

How Home Networking Works

12345

computer.howstuffworks.com/home-network.htm

Excellent illustrated introduction to home networking from the experts who show how just about everything works—HowStuffWorks.com. Site covers standard Ethernet networks, wireless networking, power line and phone line networking, routers, firewalls, and more. If you're intimidated by the idea of networking two or more computers at home or for your small business, check out this site to get up to speed in a hurry.

Hughes Network Systems

12345

www.hns.com

The Hughes Network Systems home page presents the company's networking and telecommunications products and services. Job listings, general corporate information, and online customer support are also provided.

Hummingbird Ltd.

12345

www.hummingbird.com

Delivers enterprise software solutions to simplify business transactions on the Internet and empower users to get their jobs done more easily and accurately.

IBM Networking Hardware

12345

www.networking.ibm.com

IBM offers several networking options for businesses and corporations, including wireless networking, IBM eServer networking, and storage networking, along with a wide selection of networking hardware (controllers, adapters, and Token Ring). Scroll down the page for information on emerging technologies.

Interphase Corporation

12345

www.iphase.com

Products for mass storage and high-speed networks. You'll find links to products, support, news, and employment opportunities.

InterWorking Labs

12345

www.iwl.com

Offers Test Suite software products that test SNMP network hardware, such as routers, printers, hubs, servers, and UPSs. Find out about the company's products, download a free SNMP test suite demo, and contact IWL staff.

Intranet Journal

www.intranetjournal.com

Visitors to this site can learn about current intranet standards, intranet security and software, planning, tools, and more. An intranet FAQ, message boards, and an events calendar keep you abreast of what's happening in the world of intranet technology and development.

IT Architect

www.itarchitect.com

This site is the online version of *IT Architect* magazine, a publication on the cutting edge of network and Internet technology. Here, you can sample some articles from the current and past editions, exchange information and ideas in the discussion forums, access free tutorials, and learn about technologies that are creating the most buzz.

A B C D E F G H I J K L M N O P Q R S T U V W X Y Z

IT Toolbox

1 2 3 4 5 Blog RSS

networking.ittoolbox.com

IT Toolbox (Information Technology Toolbox) links millions of IT specialists and information resources to serve the IT community, especially in terms of helping them make the best IT decisions for their specific applications. IT Toolbox empowers IT professionals to "evaluate vendors, plan and manage projects, solve problems, stay current, and manage their careers." This site features more than two dozen knowledge bases, several discussion forums where you can collaborate with other members, blogs, weekly newsletters, and a job center. For IT professionals, especially network administrators, this site features excellent information and tools for networking and security.

ITPRC.com

1 2 3 4 5

www.itprc.com/nms.htm

The goal of this site is to provide a one-stop shop for information technology professionals to find technical information on data networking. You'll find links to a large collection of networking-related information as well as links to career management information and professional discussion forums. Nothing fancy, just links to excellent resources and tools.

Jini Connection Technology

1 2 3 4 5

wwws.sun.com/software/jini

Official page of Sun Microsystems networking technology, Jini. This site features technical specifications, white papers, patches and other downloads, developer tools, and tutorials. Jini network technology provides a simple infrastructure for delivering network services and for creating spontaneous interaction between programs that use these services. The site has many articles and stories about Jini as well as more-extensive definitions.

Kinesix

1 2 3 4 5

www.kinesix.com

Manufacturer of Sammi, which enables you to integrate network applications without writing any network or graphical user interface code. The site has several links to places where you can learn more about Sammi, including current users, tech support, employment opportunities, and more. Kinesix has a couple other development tools for real-time applications over network and Internet connections, too.

Lancom Technologies

1 2 3 4 5

www.lancom-tech.com

Lancom Technologies provides all the courseware you need to become CNA or CNE certified. Here, you can order the Hands-On Linux Course, a Linux Video Tutorial, and Instructor Support Materials.

Linksys Online

1 2 3 4 5

www.linksys.com

This site is the home page for Linksys, a manufacturer of high-speed networking and connectivity products, specializing in wireless networking configurations for homes and small businesses. Visitors to this site can learn about company products and receive technical support and free software upgrades.

Lucent

1 2 3 4 5

www.lucent.com

Lucent has been one of the main producers of networking and telecommunications equipment and technology. Visit this site to learn more about Lucent's products and services.

Microsoft Servers

www.microsoft.com/servers

Interested in Microsoft networking products? Then visit this site, where Microsoft showcases its network server software. Here, you can find information about Microsoft's .NET Enterprise family of servers, including BizTalk, Commerce, Exchange, Internet Security, and Mobile Information servers. Obtain product information, find out where you can purchase products, get technical support, download patches, and much more.

Netgear

www.netgear.com

Whether you have a large corporate network or just a home or small office network, you will find what you need here. This site complements itself with many useful and informative articles and documents on the subject of networking. If you have Netgear products, this is a great place to find support and free updates.

NetWare Connection

www.nwconnection.com

Magazine for Novell networking professionals. Covers products, technical issues, and industry news. The site includes current and archived issues, a magazine subscription form, and an online bookstore. Here, you can find a selection of free and timely articles, interviews, and industry news.

Network Computing Magazine

www.nwc.com

IT professionals will want to bookmark this online version of *Network Computing* magazine. Here, you can find the latest networking news and reviews, read late-breaking industry news, learn how to perform specific networking tasks, download networking tools and toolkits, and much more. Additional benefits are available for subscribers.

Network Professionals Association

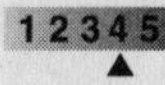

www.npanet.org

NPA is a nonprofit association for network professionals that encourages adherence to a Code Of Ethics, self-regulation, and vendor neutrality. The NPA focuses on helping network professionals fully develop their skills and talents and ensures the integrity of the profession.

Network Security Library

secinf.net

This site features a directory of network security information and resources, including hundreds of articles, FAQs, white papers, and books. Network professionals are encouraged to submit additional resources to grow the library.

Network World

www.networkworld.com

Network World claims to be "The Leader in Network Knowledge," and from the looks of its site, we agree. Down the center of the page runs highlights of the most timely and popular content, including breaking news, information on new products, a list of hot topics, top five blogs and opinion columns, featured white papers, and sponsored links. A navigation bar runs down the left side of the page, providing quick access to Research Centers (Applications, Convergence, Network Management, Security, Wireless/Mobile, and more), News, Events, Vendor Solutions, and Site Resources (product tests, buyers guides, encyclopedia, and more). Site sports an attractive design that's easy to navigate and packed with excellent information and resources.

Nortel Networks

www.nortelnetworks.com/index.html

Nortel is "a recognized leader in delivering communications capabilities that enhance the human experience, ignite and power global commerce, and secure and protect the world's most critical information. Serving both service provider and enterprise customers, Nortel delivers innovative technology solutions encompassing end-to-end broadband, Voice over IP, multimedia services and applications, and wireless broadband designed to help people solve the world's greatest challenges." At this site, you can learn more about Nortel products and how to implement their network architecture into your business, explore solutions, get training and support, and even read up on a few case studies.

Novell, Inc.

www.novell.com

A leader in networking software provides information on new products, online technical support, and different networking solutions for business and government. Site features three main areas: Products & Solutions, Service & Support, and Partners & Community.

> **Tip:** Click the Glossary link at the bottom of the page to access a comprehensive glossary of networking terms.

Plaintree Systems

www.plaintree.com

Plaintree Systems specializes in developing infrared wireless networking solutions, which are popular options for campus networks, Internet service providers (ISPs), other service providers, and airports. Visit this site to see whether infrared networking might be the best solution for you, to check out some case studies, and to explore available products.

Practically Networked

www.practicallynetworked.com

This excellent resource for IT and networking professionals features articles and reviews of the latest equipment and technologies along with dates and reports about important conferences. Includes separate sections for IT Management, Networking & Communications, Web Development, Hardware & Systems, and Software development.

Proxim

www.proxim.com

Proxim is "a global pioneer in scalable broadband wireless networking systems, from Wi-Fi to wireless Gigabit Ethernet, for communities, enterprises, governments, and service providers." At this site, you can learn more about the company and its products, obtain training and support, and find out where to go to buy Proxim products and services.

Softlinx, Inc.

www.softlinx.com

Softlinx develops integrated document management, fax server and email management applications, automated application data delivery, and email storage systems for mid-size to large corporations and service providers. Here, you can learn more about Softlinx products, services, solutions, and customers.

TechFest–Networking Protocols

www.techfest.com/networking/prot.htm

TechFest.com is a website created and maintained by a technology professional who works in the computer networking industry to help others find "good technical information on all topics relating to networking and computer technology." Links are organized in four main categories: Networking, Computer Hardware, Computer Software, and Electronics. You can also submit links for consideration.

USB

www.usb.org

Information about the Universal Serial Bus interface and the various standards, including USB 1.0, USB 2.0, Wireless USB, and USB On-the-Go. Also features technical specifications and other resources for developers.

> **Tip:** Click About USB-IF, click Frequently Asked Questions, click FAQ: Support and Installation, and click USB Evaluation Utility to download a free utility that tells you which USB standard, if any, your computer supports.

Vicomsoft

www.vicomsoft.com

Vicomsoft develops "award-winning software solutions for both education and business users." Its software is designed primarily to "protect children from unsuitable Internet content, provide advanced firewall protection, and manage IP networks." Content at this site is presented in two sections: Education and Business.

Wi-Fi Net News

www.wifinetnews.com

Wi-Fi Net News is a blog that focuses on the latest news and information in the world of Wi-Fi networking from the people most involved in it. Here, you can learn about the latest high-tech breakthroughs in wireless networking and various applications for the new technology. You can also obtain behind-the-scenes reports of what's going on at the companies driving the new technology.

WindowsNetworking.com

www.windowsnetworking.com

WindowsNetworking.com is dedicated to providing free late-breaking technical information for network administrators. From this site, you can access the Admin Knowledge Base, Articles & Tutorials, Author backgrounds, a Hardware section, several sections devoted to specific Windows networking topics, Message Boards, Newsletters, and a Software section.

Related Sites

www.msexchange.org

www.isaserver.org

www.windowsecurity.com

www.serverfiles.com

www.ntfaxfaq.com

Zhone Technologies

www.zhone.com

Zhone's "Single Line Multi-Service architecture (SLMS) allows carriers to concurrently deliver voice, new premium data, and video services over copper or fiber access lines" and re-invent the way they provide service to their customers. Here, you can find out more about Zhone Technologies products, services, and solutions.

NEW AGE

AzNewAge

12345

www.aznewage.com

A vast amount of new age religion and philosophy information with links to other Arizona sites. It will take you hours to go through all the information provided by this site, which covers religion, healing, philosophy, theology, politics, sex, and even income taxes.

Eckankar

12345

www.eckankar.org

Eckankar is a new age religion that focuses on returning to god through an expanded consciousness of your life experiences. Here, you can learn more about the religion and what it has to offer.

How to Talk New Age

12345

www.well.com/user/mick/newagept.html

Learn new age lingo, from a humorous standpoint. Site features an alphabetic list of common terms and phrases, including Astrology, Numerology, and Whole Earth. Serious followers of new age disciplines probably should avoid this site.

International Center for Reiki Training

12345

www.reiki.org

The International Center for Reiki Training promotes becoming more in tune with spiritual consciousness (REI) to properly guide our life energy force (KI) to affect positive personal and global change. Visit this site to learn more.

Llewellyn Online

12345

www.llewellyn.com

Llewellyn Online is dedicated to serving the trade and consumers worldwide with options and tools for exploring new worlds of mind & spirit, thereby aiding in the quests of expanded human potential, spiritual consciousness, and planetary awareness." Get a free copy of *New Worlds*, a catalog that covers the widest range of new age subjects, from astrology and psychic development to yoga, healing, personal transformation, modern magic, the paranormal, Wicca, and beyond. Includes a special area for teens and young adults. Great place to find books on various new age topics.

New Age Center, Sedona, Arizona

12345

www.sedonanewagecenter.com

Many believe that Sedona, Arizona, is a special spiritual place, where you can plug into vortex energy flows. At this site, you can visit one of Sedona's top new age stores online and see what it has to offer. Use the navigation bar on the right to access Events Calendar, Psychic Readers, Weekly Horoscope, Sedona Vortex Info and Tours, New Age Music, and more. Site also features some useful information if you're planning a visit to Sedona.

New Age Online Australia

12345

www.newage.com.au

This site contains a huge amount of free-to-read new age and spiritual information covering astrology, Wicca and Pagan spirituality, UFOs and ETs, ascension, earth changes, channelings, crystals, dreams, divination, angels, magic, karma, meditation, healing, and much, much more. Excellent article with links to additional resources on sustainable living.

A B C D E F G H I J K L M N O P Q R S T U V W X Y Z

New Age Retailer

1 2 3 4 5

`www.newageretailer.com`

This site is the Internet home of the top-selling publication for retail distributors of new age products—*New Age Retailer* magazine. The mission of this magazine is to present information and resources for new age stores.

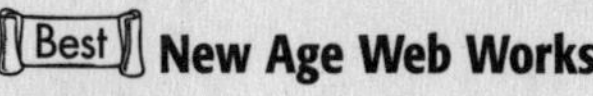

New Age Web Works

1 2 3 4 5

`www.newageinfo.com`

New Age Web Works is one of the Internet's leading sources "of information about alternative health, new thought religions, environmental issues, spirituality, and metaphysical sciences. Content is presented in departments, which you can quickly access using the navigation bar on the left: Alternative Health, Environment, Metaphysical, New Spiritual, Pagan, Forbidden Knowledge, and Ancient Wisdom. On the right is a list of the week's newest articles. Scroll down the page and look on the left for a list of links to the most popular new age pages.

NewAgeJournal.com

1 2 3 4 5

`www.newagejournal.com`

This online magazine features articles about various New Age topics, along with free daily horoscopes and a brief primer on New Age beliefs and lifestyles. On the left is a list of featured articles. On the right are additional links for accessing archived articles, writer's guidelines, new age web works, and new age travel.

Real Music

1 2 3 4 5

`www.realmusic.com`

Real Music features more than 100 new age albums from more than 20 international artists. Its artists regularly chart on Billboard' Magazine's New Age Chart. If you are looking for relaxing, spiritually uplifting music, this is the site for you.

Salem New Age Center

1 2 3 4 5

`www.salemctr.com/newage`

Offers FAQs on the new age movement and meditation, lists of popular new age books, articles on ET human origins, and a free email newsletter.

Tools for Transformation

1 2 3 4 5

`www.trans4mind.com`

This site is dedicated to promoting the continued evolution of humans in mind, body, and spirit. Here, you can find articles, resources, courses, and other tools that can help you achieve self-fulfillment in all aspects of your being.

NEWS

AME Info

www.ameinfo.com

AME Info features business news for the Middle East. Here, you can find an excellent collection of articles on energy, education, economy, healthcare, real estate, and other topics related to business in the Middle East.

Arts & Letters Daily

www.aldaily.com

Comprehensive digest and directory of news, book reviews, essays, and opinions gathered from the top newspapers, magazines, radio programs, news services, and other media sources around the world. Features gobs of information in an easy-to-access format.

Atlantic Unbound

12345

www.theatlantic.com

Sample in-depth articles on politics, society, arts, and culture from this print magazine. Back issues are archived.

CBC.ca News

www.cbc.ca

CBC (Canadian Broadcasting Corporation) created and maintains this news site to keep Canadians living both home and abroad informed about local, national, and international news. CBC Newsworld is Canada's "leading source for live news coverage, award-winning documentaries. and distinctive current affairs programming with a unique Canadian perspective."

Congressional Quarterly

www.cq.com

Comprehensive news and analysis of what's happening in the corridors of power. The site follows Congress, the federal government, and political events.

Best Google News

news.google.com

Google News acts as a portal to up-to-the-minute news stories from more than 4,500 news and information sources around the world. On the front page, you find summaries of the headline news along with links to the sources from which Google obtained the stories. On the left side of the page are links to World News, National News, Business, Science, Sports, Entertainment, and Health. Along the right side of the page are links to more headline news stories along with links to people who are making the news. You can customize the page and even sign up to have alerts about specific news stories emailed to you.

Harper's

www.harpers.org

Aims to provide readers with a window on the world by exploring nonmainstream topics. Find a magazine index and subscription details here.

Internet Public Library

www.ipl.org/div/serials

The Internet Public Library offers this directory of online magazines that fall into several categories, including Arts & Humanities, Business & Economics, Computers & the Internet, Education, and Health & Medical Services. Links to Kids and Teens areas.

MagazinesAtoZ.com

www.magazinesatoz.com

Use this directory of more than 1,300 magazines, catalogs, and periodicals to track down the desired publication. This site also features a search tool to find specific articles within magazines.

The Nation

www.thenation.com

Weekly selected news articles and commentary from the well-known liberal magazine, along with book and movie reviews, analysis of cultures and ideas, and much more.

National Journal

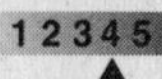

nationaljournal.com

Formerly *PoliticsNow*, *National Journal* contains many of the features that made *PoliticsNow* one of the most popular sites on the Web, including the Poll Track database, the "Buzz" insider columns, and the *Almanac of American Politics*. Also, it contains *Earlybird*, an early morning digest of hot political news; *Buzz Columns*, a "daily dose of analysis and commentary on Congress"; and *Daybook*, a daily planner for upcoming political and policy events in the capitol.

National Review

www.nationalreview.com

This site is filled with opinions and features from the popular United States conservative magazine. Tabbed navigation provides quick access to articles and commentary in the following five areas: Today, Politics, Culture, Financial, and Books. Site also features a live blog feed.

The New Republic

www.tnr.com

Daily top stories and blog postings from writers at *The New Republic*. Site also features sections on Politics and Books & the Arts along with links to your favorite columnists and a link for downloading the current issue.

News Directory

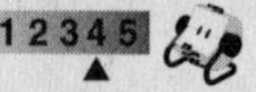

newsdirectory.com

This site features an extensive directory of magazines grouped by categories, including Arts & Entertainment, Business, Science, Sports, and Travel. Also features a directory of newspapers grouped by country and broadcasting stations. Excellent site for tracking down a broad selection of offerings.

Newsweek

www.newsweek.com

Read this week's top stories; check daily news updates; log in with your questions for upcoming Live Talk segments on controversial topics; and read regular columns about international issues, business, society, political campaigns, and more. You'll definitely be caught up on current events after visiting this site!

A B C D E F G H I J K L M N O P Q R S T U V W X Y Z

Popular Science

www.popsci.com

This website comes to you compliments of the editors of *Popular Science* magazine. Find out what's new in the automotive, computer, electronics, home technology, and science fields. Plus, get other articles from the magazine, various buying guides, and helpful links. Excellent articles coupled with outstanding graphics make this a top site.

RushLimbaugh.com

www.rushlimbaugh.com

You love him or you hate him, but now you can do that 24/7 at the Rush Limbaugh site. Here, you can follow the stories that Rush himself is following, learn more about his radio broadcast, research in the Limbaugh Library, shop at the RIB store, or order a subscription to the Limbaugh Letter. This is a great place for fans to hang out and for liberals to get to know their sworn enemy.

TIME

www.time.com

Puts the news in context with full text of the print magazine each week. This site is updated throughout the day and cross-referenced. Use the navigation bar on the left to access the main sections of the site: Nation, World, Biz & Tech, Arts, Science & Health, Specials, and Photos. The opening page features the current cover story along with Hot Topics, Analysis and Opinion, and Pictures of the Week. Includes a link to *TIME for Kids* and links to CNN for videos and webcasts.

U.S. News & World Report

www.usnews.com

U.S. News & World Report is one of the most trustworthy news magazines on the market. Here, you can sample the current edition of the magazine, read up on late-breaking headline news, and read a smattering of articles in the five main sections of the magazine: Nation & World, Inside Washington, Health, Money, and Opinion. This site also features the *U.S. News & World Report* rankings and "best of" lists that help readers find the best colleges and graduate schools, hospitals and health plans, places to work, and leaders.

USA Weekend

12345

www.usaweekend.com

USA WEEKEND is a small magazine that many local newspapers slip into the weekend editions of their papers. It features articles on entertainment, fitness, finance, and current events; interviews; games; recipes; and other entertaining stuff, much of which is available at this site.

The Utne Reader

www.utne.com

The reader's digest of the alternative press, the *Utne Reader* wanders off the mainstream track to provide articles about topics you won't find covered in *Time, Newsweek*, or most other news magazines you can find on the grocery store shelves.

The Weekend Australian

www.theaustralian.news.com.au

This web home of Australia's national daily newspaper features headline news, sports, business, opinion, and much more. You can browse the stories or click a link from the navigation area on the left side of the page to call up a specific section of the paper.

The Weekly Standard

12345 Blog

www.weeklystandard.com

The online version of this right-leaning magazine contains samplings of news and commentary. Features from previous issues are included, along with an excellent collection of current editorials.

Yahoo! News

news.yahoo.com

Yahoo! News gathers news stories and commentary from the top media sites around the world and delivers it to a single location, so you don't have to hunt for it yourself. The opening page displays headline stories and feature articles, and you can click a tab to get the type of news you want: U.S., Business, World, Entertainment, Sports, Tech, Politics, Science, Health, or Travel. When you click a tab, links appear below the tab to help you focus in on exactly what you want; for example, if you click the World tab, the following links appear—Middle East, Europe, Latin America, Africa, Asia, Canada, Australia, and Antarctica.

Related Site

news.yahoo.com/rss

ZDNet–PC Magazine

www.pcmag.com

You will find all kinds of current information about computers on this site, including late-breaking news, articles, product reviews, and free downloads. By becoming a registered member, you will receive free email, software, and the free magazine. The site is well designed, with the information presented in a way that makes it easy to find and easy to navigate.

RESOURCES

Accuracy in Media

www.aim.org

Accuracy in Media is "a nonprofit, grassroots citizens watchdog of the news media that critiques botched and bungled news stories and sets the record straight on important issues that have received slanted coverage." Here, you can find out which media channels are broadcasting the most propaganda and find out the truth behind some of the more slanted stories that make the headlines.

American Journalism Review

www.ajr.org

This site provides a comprehensive review of news media, including magazines, newspapers, TV, radio, and websites; more links to industry-related sites; a job search tool for journalists; links to journalism organizations and media monitors; links to journalist tools, including dictionaries, style guides, and a thesaurus; information about journalism awards; and much more. If you're a journalist or aspiring journalist, bookmark this site for frequent future visits.

American Society of Newspaper Editors

www.asne.org

The American Society of Newspaper Editors is "a membership organization for daily newspaper editors, people who serve the editorial needs of daily newspapers, and certain distinguished individuals who have worked on behalf of editors through the years." The opening page presents you with a navigation bar you can use to jump to the main sections of the site, including Diversity, Careers, Credibility, and First Amendment.

Associated Press

www.ap.org

Associated Press is "the backbone of the world's information system serving thousands of daily newspaper, radio, television, and online customers with coverage in all media and news in all formats. It is the largest and oldest news organization in the world, serving as a source of news, photos, graphics, audio, and video for more than one billion people a day." At this site, you can check out the latest headline news or browse content by media type: Photo, Audio, Video, RSS, and Podcast. The navigation bar at the left offers various entry points to learn about and access AP services.

CyberJournalist.net

www.cyberjournalist.net

CyberJournalist.net offers a forum for exploring and discussing the influence of the Internet and other communication technologies and trends have on the media. Site offers "tips, news, and commentary about online journalism, citizen's media, digital storytelling, converged news operations, and using the Internet as a reporting tool." Excellent site for bloggers and for traditional media people to converge and hash out some of the issues surrounding blogging and the media. Site also features links to news websites that feature podcasts and RSS feeds.

Editor & Publisher

12345

www.editorandpublisher.com

Editor & Publisher is a journal for the news media industry that covers "all aspects of the North American newspaper industry, including business, newsroom, advertising, circulation, marketing, technology, online, and syndicates. The opening page features several articles from the current edition, along with columns and a few biographies of news people in the news. A navigation bar on the right provides quick access to the journal's departments: Business, Ad/Circ, Newsroom, Online, Technology, and Syndicates.

The Feedroom

www.feedroom.com

The Feedroom is a company develops broadband video broadcasting solutions to companies that need to get their message out to the masses. Here, you can learn more about the Feedroom's products, services, and solutions.

Freedom Forum

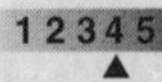

www.freedomforum.org

The Freedom Forum is "a nonpartisan foundation dedicated to free press, free speech, and free spirit for all people. The foundation focuses on three priorities: the Newseum, the First Amendment, and newsroom diversity." Here, you can find a good selection of articles and opinions on first amendment rights and the importance of fostering diversity in the newsroom.

indianz.com

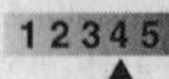

www.indianz.com

You'll find news, information, and entertainment provided from a Native American perspective. In addition to national news, this site offers headlines from tribes across the country, as well as more in-depth reports on issues that directly impact Native American communities.

Info Today

www.infotoday.com

This site provides numerous articles, product reviews, case studies, evaluations, and informed opinions about selecting and using electronics products. Written for the busy information professional.

Mirror Syndication International

www.mirrorpix.com

Features more than 250,000 newspaper pictures online plus an offline library of more than 3 million pictures, which it offers for sale to businesses and private customers. The site accepts credit cards.

Newseum

12345

www.newseum.org

Visit the Newseum to read the headlines of more than 400 newspapers around the world, play the Newsmania Quiz Game, and check out the Newseum's virtual exhibits of the media coverage surrounding many of history's top stories.

> **Tip:** Near the top of the opening page is a navigation bar that looks sort of like a filmstrip. Rest the mouse pointer on a frame in that strip to find out what it is, and then click it if you want to go there.

A B C D E F G H I J K L M N O P Q R S T U V W X Y Z

NewsLink

newslink.org

An index of national and foreign newspapers, campus newspapers, dailies, nondailies, and alternative press. Covers newspapers, magazines, radio, TV, and blogs. You can browse the collection by state and city, by type of coverage or media type (newspaper, magazine, TV, and so on), or search the site for a specific news source by name.

oneworld.net

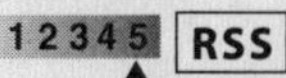

www.oneworld.net

This super-site of information is dedicated to reporting on global development issues, such as education, migration, or children's rights. In addition to news reports, you'll find searchable archives, opportunities for chat, and discussion forums. Links to various editions worldwide in several different languages.

The Write News

www.writenews.com

This site features news, information, and resources for professionals in the media and in publishing. Provides more than 1,000 links to the most valuable resources on the Web, along with links to gobs of blogs.

SERVICES

allAfrica.com

allafrica.com

This leading provider of African news and information posts more than 700 stories daily in English and French and features a searchable archive of more than 400,000 articles. Visit this site to access the latest African headline news, sports, and editorials, along with business and stock market reports, currency information, health alerts, and more.

Aljazeera

english.aljazeera.net/HomePage

Aljazeera is the news service of choice for most of the Arabic world. Here, you can find news from around the world, commentary, special reports, political cartoons, polls, and other newsworthy items.

BBC News

news.bbc.co.uk

Updated every minute, the British Broadcasting Channel (BBC) site has a definite international slant to its reporting, which runs the gamut from international politics to sports and celebrities. The BBC offers balanced coverage, a comprehensive approach, an excellent design, and an easy-to-navigate layout.

Business Wire

www.businesswire.com

Business News distributes news to the media locally, nationally, and worldwide. This wire service offers customized news-release distribution to the news media, online services, the Internet, and the investment community. Membership required.

Crayon

crayon.net

Nifty free tool for managing news on the Web. Create your own newspaper with links to sources that interest you.

Federal Communications Commission

www.fcc.gov

Federal Communications Commission (FCC) online serves as a forum for public discussion concerning FCC issues (including broadcasting). It contains current legislation, full text of relevant speeches, agenda, and the FCC daily digest, along with lists of email addresses to which you can send comments and concerns about television.

InfoBeat

www.infobeat.com

Find out about InfoBeat's personalized news service. This service will deliver news customized to your stated preferences by email so that you don't have to search around on the Web and gather articles yourself.

The Paperboy

www.thepaperboy.com

Check this service's "top drawer" to find top news sources or browse newspaper listings by country. Excellent collection of the world's most popular newspapers, plus the search tools you need to track down the stories you want.

PBS: Online NewsHour

www.pbs.org/newshour

News features and analysis, complete with online forums for discussion of the issues of the day. Subscriptions for email news delivery also are available.

PR Newswire

www.prnewswire.com

PR Newswire describes itself as "the leading source of immediate news from corporations worldwide for media, business, the financial community, and the individual investor." Click Today's News for headline news along with a collection of links to help you limit the scope of the news to one of the following areas: Breaking News, Company News, Agency News, Feature News, or News Photos. You can access the news in several different languages by clicking the International link and clicking the desired language. You can also visit this site to distribute press releases; click Send Release.

Reuters

www.reuters.com

Reuters, a leading news and information company, fulfills the business community's and news media's financial, multimedia, and professional information needs. At this site, you can get online news or learn more about Reuters. Reuters offers news feeds for business news, investing, and U.S. and international news.

Best Rocketinfo

www.rocketinfo.com

Upon reaching the opening page, click Search News, RSS, and Blogs. The resulting page displays an RSS news feed search tool that you can use to track down sites that offer RSS feeds of text-based stories, blogs, audio, or video. Down the middle of the page, you can find a selection of stories currently making the headline news. You can use the search tool near the top of the page to track down specific feeds or use the navigation bar on the left to browse available feeds. Running down the right side of the page are ads that keep the service free. Rocketinfo enables you to search more than 16,000 continuously updated news sources from around the world. With RSS news feeds gaining in popularity, a site like this that enables users to track down feeds with a click of a button is well deserving of the Best of the Best website designation in the category of News Services.

Sympatico NewsExpress

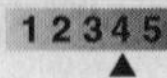

news.sympatico.msn.ca/Home/

MSN's Canadian news service featuring news headlines, editorials, stories, and features, plus updates, local coverage, and current affairs and events. Site's content is offered in both English and French.

A B C D E F G H I J K L M N O P Q R S T U V W X Y Z

United Press International (UPI)

www.upi.com

Avoid the middlemen and get the news where the news services get their news, the UPI wire service. This site posts up-to-the-minute news on business, sports, current events, politics, science, technology, and more.

WebClipping.com

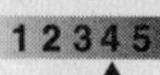

www.webclipping.com

WebClipping.com is a service that automatically monitors 20,000 top Web-based publications, 1.5 billion web pages, 90 real-time streaming newswires, and 63,000 Usenet newsgroups for name, brand, or trademark information, and delivers a complete report of anything it finds to you via email. If you're in business and you want to find out what people are saying about you and who's saying it, you may find the service valuable. Prices, services, and research tools are listed.

U.S. NEWS MEDIA

abcNEWS.com

abcnews.go.com

This home site of ABC's award-winning *World News Tonight* with Charles Gibson puts the day's top stories within reach of a single mouse click. Check U.S. and international news, stock market updates, politics, weather, sports, and more. Links to other ABC news shows, including *Good Morning America*, *20/20*, and *Primetime*.

CBS News

www.cbsnews.com

Visit Dan Rather's home on the Web to check out today's headline news. Focuses mainly on U.S. news, but covers international issues, business and stock market news, and investigative stories, too. Use the navigation bar at the top of the home page to find more information on World news, Science and Technology, HealthWatch, and Entertainment. Links to *60 Minutes*, *48 Hours*, and *The Early Show*.

Christian Science Monitor

www.csmonitor.com

Comprehensive national and international coverage from the online version of this award-winning newspaper. Use the navigation bar at the top of the page to check out World News, U.S. News, Commentary, Work & Money, Learning, Living, and more. This newspaper provides a balanced view on most issues.

CNN Interactive

www.cnn.com

Get all the top news stories at your fingertips, or delve into weather, sports, science and technical news, travel, style, show business, health, and earth topics. Many stories have accompanying QuickTime video segments. This site also describes what CNN has to offer on television.

Disaster News Network

www.disasternews.net

Comprehensive source of primarily United States disasters, response news, and volunteer needs. Some coverage of international disasters and relief efforts, too. You'll find organization links, ways you can help, and the latest stories.

ESPN.com

www.espn.com

You can view game scores and statistics, get sports news, participate in fan polls, interact with other sports lovers, buy tickets online for sports events, visit the training room, and much more.

A B C D E F G H I J K L M N O P Q R S T U V W X Y Z

FoxNews.com

www.foxnews.com

For a more conservative approach to the news and editorials of the day, visit the FoxNews website. Here, you can check out national and international news, get weather forecasts for your area, keep abreast of the current political scene, and check in on entertainment options. Hardcore conservatives should check out the link to the *O'Reilly Factor*.

> To access the blogs, point to Opinion, in the navigation bar near the top of the opening page. To access RSS feeds, point to Services.

Los Angeles Times

www.latimes.com

Includes local news as well as national coverage of major stories, in-depth features, pictures, and classifieds. This website's no-frills approach to headline news coupled with a comprehensive list of links to various feature articles make it our choice as Best of the Best. However, there are so many excellent candidates in this category that we had a tough time selecting only one.

MSNBC

www.msnbc.msn.com/

MSNBC, one of the top cable news stations, is also a leader on the Web, featuring this news site, where you can access late-breaking headline news, weather, and sports; live video feeds; blogs; sudoku and crossword puzzles; business news; entertainment; and much more. You can configure your news page by entering your ZIP code, to get local news and weather, and up to three ticker symbols to display stock quotes.

New York Times

www.nytimes.com

Home of one of the world's most famous broadsheets, featuring local and national sports and news, as well as coverage of international issues. Covers the entire range of news, including national and international news, business, sports, weather, politics, science, technology, entertainment, education, health, and editorials.

NPR

www.npr.org

National Public Radio broadcasts. Listen to the most recent or past broadcasts including *All Things Considered, Morning Edition, Science Friday, Talk of the Nation*, and NPR's hourly newscast.

San Jose Mercury News

www.mercurynews.com/

Up-to-the-minute news on computers and technology, sports, national issues, and business from this Silicon Valley community paper. As you might expect from a Silicon Valley newspaper, this site offers cutting-edge features, including blogs, podcasts, live video feeds, and RSS news feeds.

USA Today

www.usatoday.com

The first full-color national paper to hit the market, this online version of *USA Today* features the top news, money, sports, and life reports across the nation. When you'd rather look at pictures than read lengthy reports, *USA Today* is the place for you.

Wall Street Journal Interactive

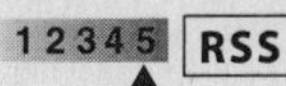

online.wsj.com/public/us

If you think the *Wall Street Journal* is for guys who wear expensive suits, visit this site to have your preconceptions erased. WSJ features some of the best investigative reporting, analysis, and writing of any newspaper in the United States, and you can access much of it online. You must subscribe, for about $60 per year, but you can check it out for free.

Washington Post

www.washingtonpost.com

Includes most of the print features from this daily, which is known for its political coverage. This site also offers weather, style, technology, and a place for chat.

WEBZINES

Asia Pacific News

www.apn.btbtravel.com

Browse through the top 50 news agencies and newspapers in the Asia Pacific region. Also offered are links to shopping and employment sites.

Drudge Report

www.drudgereport.com

Internet scandalmonger Matt Drudge tracks the latest gossip from Capitol Hill, Hollywood, and beyond. Links to international news sources and columnists can also be found here.

The Economist

www.economist.com

Weekly magazine from the United Kingdom features insightful articles about economic issues from around the world and analysis on how these issues affect the global economy. Here, you can sample articles and columns from the current edition and use the navigation bar on the left to access specific articles for different economic hotspots, including the United States, Europe, Asia, Middle East & Africa, and Britain.

Emerging Markets

www.emergingmarkets.org

Emerging Markets is an information kiosk "for investors, bankers, and brokers working in the debt markets of the developing world." Its editorial staff gathers information from various sources around the world (Euromoney plc, ministries of finance, central banks, academics, bankers, and economists) and supplements it with contributions "from the leading voices on developing country economies."

Jane's Defence Weekly

jdw.janes.com

Jane's Defence Weekly features news and analysis related to military issues and events from around the world. Here, you can find out about recent arms deals, experimental military technology, planned troop deployments, and rising geopolitical threats. Think of it as your own personal Intel network. At this site, you can sample a selection of articles, but for the good stuff, you must subscribe, and it's not cheap.

Jane's Foreign Report

www.foreignreport.com

Offers predictions and analyses on foreign diplomacy, political developments, economic policies, and business. Subscribe for weekly briefings.

Salon.com

www.salon.com

An intelligent, provocative online magazine that presents the latest news, reviews, and analysis in a variety of content areas including Arts & Entertainment, Life, News, People, and Politics. Winner of several awards for site design and content as well as journalism. Subscribe to the site for ad-free access or watch an ad for temporary free access.

A B C D E F G H I J K L M N O P Q R S T U V W X Y Z

Slate

12345 RSS

slate.msn.com

Hard-hitting online magazine that pulls no punches when it comes to criticizing politicians and policies. Behind-the-scenes reviews of international happenings and their effects on life in the United States. Features business, sports, and technology sections, too. Lots of ads.

The Smoking Gun

www.thesmokinggun.com

This online tabloid masquerading as the home of an investigative journalism site provides background reports covering the latest celebrity and political scandals. Check out the day's featured document or click the Archives link for a list of previous investigations.

Veterans News and Information Service

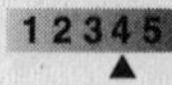

www.vnis.com

Browse through this comprehensive news and information resource for military veterans. It includes news from the Navy, the Marines, and the Coast Guard.

WEBZINE

www.webzine2005.com

WEBZINE is "a real world, face-to-face celebration of independent publishing on the Internet. It's part panel discussions and speakers, part workshops and much freeform collaboration, schmoozing and after-party boozing. The panel discussions aim to inspire, the workshops are hands-on forums of learning and the Master's Lounge is the unstructured place to share knowledge, ideas and URLs." If you're interested in independent publishing on the Web, check out this rag-tag group of hi-tech journalists.

NONPROFIT & CHARITABLE ORGANIZATIONS–RESOURCES

BoardSource

12345

www.boardsource.org

If you need to assemble a board of directors for your nonprofit agency, this is the place to go. Features books, training, Board Q&As, and membership information.

Charity Village

12345

www.charityvillage.com

This Charity Village offers a bonanza of information for Canadian nonprofits—"more than 3,000 pages of news, jobs, information and resources for executives, staffers, donors, and volunteers." If philanthropy and volunteerism are part of your world, this is your place.

The Chronicle of Philanthropy

12345

philanthropy.com

Summaries of articles published in the *Chronicle*'s print version. Browse the site to find information on gifts and grants, fundraising, management, and technology of interest to nonprofit organizations.

> **Tip:** Chronicle of Philanthropy also features a fairly extensive list of job openings at not-for-profit organizations.

Council on Foundations

12345

www.cof.org

A membership association composed of more than 2,000 grant-making foundations and giving programs from around the world (independent, corporate, and public). COF provides leadership expertise, legal services, and networking opportunities to its members. The site also promotes accountability among member foundations.

Foundation Center

12345

www.fdncenter.org

For grant seekers and grant makers, this site contains information on libraries and locations, training and seminars, funding trends and analyses, the fundraising process, and publications and CD-ROMs. Also, it includes a searchable database and an online reference desk. If you're in charge of writing grants and tracking down donors for your not-for-profit organization, this should be the first stop on your journey.

Foundation Finder

12345

lnp.fdncenter.org/finder.html

This Foundation Center search page can help you find addresses and phone numbers for more than 86,000 grant makers in the U.S.—including private foundations, community foundations, grant-making public charities, and corporate giving programs.

IRS: Charities

1 2 3 4 5

www.irs.gov/charities

If you're running a not-for-profit organization, you'd better file the right forms with the IRS to establish and maintain your tax-exempt status. This site provides information and guidance from the IRS on how to handle this important paperwork. The navigation bar at the top of the opening page enables you to quickly access the information you need based on the type of organization you're running: Charitable Organizations, Churches and Religious Orgs, Contributors, Other Non-Profits, Political Orgs, and Private Foundations.

John D. and Catherine T. MacArthur Foundation

1 2 3 4 5

www.macfdn.org

One of the nation's 10 largest foundations, MacArthur today has assets of $5 billion and issues grants totaling more than $200 million annually. The Foundation seeks the development of healthy individuals and effective communities, peace within and among nations, responsible choices about human reproduction, and a global ecosystem capable of supporting healthy human societies. It pursues this mission by supporting research, policy development, dissemination, education and training, and practice.

National Committee on Planned Giving

1 2 3 4 5

www.ncpg.org

The National Committee on Planned Giving is the professional association for people whose work includes developing, marketing, and administering charitable planned gifts. Those people include fundraisers for nonprofit institutions and consultants and donor advisors working in a variety of for-profit settings.

Nonprofit Gateway

1 2 3 4 5 RSS

www.firstgov.gov/Business/Nonprofit.shtml

Learn more about government support for nonprofit groups by clicking on federal government agency names at this simple site that's packed with valuable information.

Nonprofit Genie

1 2 3 4 5

www.genie.org

Sponsored by C-MAP, the California Management Assistance Partnership, this site is dedicated to providing the nonprofit community the information and resources it needs to succeed. Features a hot topic and cool site of the week, a useful collection of nonprofit FAQs, a monthly newsletter, and links to other nonprofit resources on the Web.

The Nonprofit Resource Center

www.not-for-profit.org

Directory of websites that can help you form, manage, maintain, and secure funding for your not-for-profit organization. Links are grouped in five categories: Legal & Boards of Directors; Support Organizations; Finance, Accounting, & General Management; Fundraising; and Marketing & People Management.

NPO-NET

1 2 3 4 5

npo.net

This site is primarily a resource for Chicago-area nonprofit organizations, but also enables you to search for grants and grant makers, information on fundraising and philanthropy, training for nonprofit management, nonprofit discussions, and more.

Philanthropy.org

1 2 3 4 5

www.philanthropy.org

This site is the home of the Center for the Study of Philanthropy (CSP), which was founded in September 1986. CSP is devoted to providing an ongoing national and international forum for research, discussion, and public education on philanthropic trends. The home page contains links to Research on Philanthropy, Multicultural Philanthropy, International Philanthropy, and Women's Philanthropy.

Tech Soup

12345 RSS

www.techsoup.org

Nonprofits need technology, too, and this site shows them where to obtain hardware, software, and technical advice free or at bargain rates. A wide range of users will find the technical support area useful, and if you would like to donate used computer equipment, this site can help you find centers that accept used equipment and deliver it to nonprofits that need it.

ASSOCIATIONS

Alliance for Nonprofit Management

12345

www.allianceonline.org

The Alliance for Nonprofit Management is devoted to helping nonprofits fulfill their missions by providing them with the information, resources, and leadership they need. Site features information about the alliance and its conferences and events, a list of frequently asked questions (and their answers), publications, information on how the alliance can help you start and maintain your organization, and a Career Bank where you can search for a job at a nonprofit organization.

Independent Sector

12345

www.independentsector.org

Independent Sector is the headquarters of a group of about 550 organizations that work together for charities, foundations, and corporate giving programs in the United States. The group sponsors research programs; fights for public policies that support a dynamic, independent sector; and creates "unparalleled resources so staff, boards, and volunteers can improve their organizations and better serve their communities." Site features some good general articles on giving and donating along with member profiles, publications, and information about the annual conference and other events.

CHARITABLE CONTRIBUTIONS

American Institute of Philanthropy

12345

www.charitywatch.org

Find out about this organization, the charities it tracks, and its philosophy on rating. You'll also find articles on charitable giving. Click the Tips link to get 10 tips for giving wisely.

America's Charities

12345

www.charities.org

America's Charities is dedicated to "developing the spirit of caring and sharing at the workplace, by providing employers and employees with efficient, effective, low-cost workplace charitable giving campaigns; offering a broad range of charity choices that reflect the diversity of the American people; and providing member charities with the financial resources required to meet human service needs." This site features an index of U.S. charitable organizations, searchable by charity type (education, environment, health, human services, civil and human rights, and so on).

BBB Wise Giving Alliance

12345

www.give.org

BBB Wise Giving Alliance carries information for hundreds of top nonprofits that solicit contributions across the United States. Here, you can find out how your favorite charity is spending your donation, get tips for giving wisely, keep abreast of news and alerts, inquire about a not-for-profit organization or file a complaint, or download an enrollment form to list your not-for-profit organization with BBB Wise Giving Alliance.

Charitable Choices

12345

www.charitablechoices.org

Look here for information on more than 300 nonprofit organizations. Most of the charities listed are based in the Washington, D.C., area. Many international organizations are also represented.

Charity Navigator

www.charitynavigator.org

When you know the cause you want to support but you don't know which organization is most worthy of your financial support, check out the Charity Navigator. Here, you can find ratings of more than 5,000 worthy charities. Search by name, category, or region. Site also features a list of the top 10 charities, philanthropy news, tips for giving wisely, and some feature articles on giving and noble causes.

The CharityNet

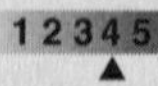

www.charitynet.org

This super-site provides resources for the international nonprofit community and its contributors.

GuideStar

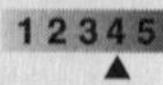

www.guidestar.org

Links to the latest articles in the popular press about nonprofits and philanthropy. Also, access the Search for a Non-Profit database, which contains more than 1.5 million nonprofit organizations. You can search by type, city and state, revenue range, or keyword.

The Hunger Site

12345

www.thehungersite.com

By just visiting this site and clicking a button, you can help donate food to needy areas and countries. The site's sponsors fund the work of the group, so there is no cost to you. The site has delivered millions of tons of food to starving people in more than 74 different countries around the world.

Independent Charities of America

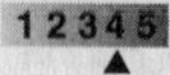

www.independentcharities.org

A nonprofit organization that prescreens high-quality national and international charities and presents them for your giving consideration. Click on a category (Children, Animals, Environment) or click on Charity Search to search by name or keyword.

JustGive.com

12345

www.justgive.org

If you would like to make a donation to a nonprofit organization but are not sure just who to give to and which organizations are legitimate, check out this site. JustGive is a nonprofit organization dedicated to connecting people with the charities and causes they care about. JustGive also features charity baskets, each of which distributes your overall contribution to four related charities. Baskets include Animals, Hunger, Peace, Earth, and Children. Site serves more than 1,000,000 legitimate nonprofit organizations and ensures that your contribution goes toward a good cause.

Network for Good

www.networkforgood.org

Network for Good aims to be a central resource connecting individuals who want to volunteer or donate financially to local organizations of interest. To find a volunteer opportunity, specify your location and the type of work you'd like to do, and Network for Good can help you find suitable opportunities in your neighborhood. To donate money, you can search for a charity by name or browse the site for ideas.

Philanthropy Roundtable

12345

www.philanthropyroundtable.org

The Philanthropy Roundtable is based on the premise that "voluntary private action offers the best means of addressing many of society's needs." This site offers articles of interest to donors, corporate giving representatives, foundation staff and trustees, and trust and estate officers.

A B C D E F G H I J K L M O P Q R S T U V W X Y Z

World Vision

www.worldvision.org/worldvision/master.nsf

World Vision is "a Christian relief and development organization dedicated to helping children and their communities worldwide reach their full potential by tackling the causes of poverty." Here, you can learn more about the organization, sponsor a child, read about disaster relief opportunities, and check out the WV annual report. Features a newsletter and a domestic projects database.

FUNDRAISING

Fund-Raising.Com

www.fund-raising.com

Fund-Raising.Com is an online community dedicated to helping nonprofit organizations discover and develop practical, unique fundraising activities. The opening page presents three main areas: Knowledge Base (with general fundraising tips), Fundraising Ideas, and Fundraising Tips (more tips). Site also offers Featured Fundraisers, a Fundraising Directory, and a Fundraiser Forum (where you can connect with others to exchange ideas).

Fund$Raiser Cyberzine

www.fundsraiser.com

Fundraising ideas, information, and resources. Only the current issue is online. Back issues may be ordered on disk.

Grassroots Fundraising Journal

www.grassrootsfundraising.org

Grassroots Fundraising Journal offers "practical tips and tools to help you raise money for your organization." Contents at this site are presented in three main areas: Magazine, Fundraising How-To, and About Us. The Magazine links enable you to sample articles from the current and past issues of the journal. Fundraising How-To has an excellent article for beginners and additional resources.

Schoolpop

www.schoolpop.com

Hundreds of shops are linked through this site, which provides up to 60 percent of the purchase proceeds to fund the work of more than 50,000 schools and other nonprofit organizations. Choose an organization to support, or pick a shop to buy from and whenever you purchase anything from one of the member stores, a percentage of your purchase goes to the nonprofit of your choice. Major retailers are involved, including eBay, Staples, Best Buy, and Coldwater Creek, and there is no additional cost to the consumer.

ORGANIZATIONS

Adobe Community Relations

www.adobe.com/aboutadobe/philanthropy/main.html

This corporate philanthropy arm of Adobe is primarily interested in supporting nonprofit health and human service organizations that, in turn, provide help to disadvantaged youth, the homeless, victims of abuse, and so on.

AT&T Foundation

www.att.com/foundation

This site is the company's philanthropic arm that helps people to lead self-sufficient, productive lives. AT&T is particularly interested in projects that involve technological innovation. Its four program areas are Education, Civic Programs, Arts and Culture, and Community Service.

Ben and Jerry's Foundation

www.benjerry.com/foundation

Ben and Jerry's Foundation seeks programs concerned with societal, institutional, and environmental change. The foundation's particular areas of interest are children and families, disenfranchised groups, and the environment. The site also describes restrictions, types of grants, and ways to apply.

A B C D E F G H I J K L M N O P Q R S T U V W X Y Z

Benton Foundation

www.benton.org

Concerned with the information infrastructure. Among the foundation's projects: communications policy and practice, a report on public opinion of library leaders' visions of future, children's programs, the arts, and public interest organizations.

Carnegie Foundation

www.carnegie.org

Grant-making foundation dedicated to enhancing knowledge. Currently supports education and healthy development of children and youth, preventing deadly conflict, strengthening human resources in developing countries, and other special projects. Learn how to submit a proposal, search for grant opportunities, and check out the proposal guidelines. If you're planning on writing a grant proposal, check out this site before you start. You'll save yourself some time and frustration.

Children's Miracle Network (CMN)

www.cmn.org

Find out what this organization does to help nonprofit children's hospitals. Learn how you can become involved in supporting its mission. Search for your community's local CMN affiliate if you are most interested in giving where you live and in helping critically ill children.

Commonwealth Fund

www.cmwf.org

Conducts research on health and social policy issues. Programs include improving healthcare services, improving the health of minority Americans and the well-being of the elderly, developing the capacities of children and young people, and improving public spaces and services.

Goodwill Industries International

www.goodwill.org

Provides employment and training services, and removes barriers for people with disabilities. The site contains information on the organization and its charitable works, current news, and more. Also, it enables you to find a donation center, a retail location, and a Goodwill store in your area.

Habitat for Humanity International

www.habitat.org

Learn about the efforts of this organization to build affordable homes for the needy. You'll find information on where the organization builds, how it works, and how you can support its work—either by volunteering locally or donating.

Junior Achievement

www.ja.org

Find out more about Junior Achievement's efforts to introduce students in grades K–12 to the free-enterprise system by establishing for-profit businesses in local communities. Search the site to find a JA chapter near you.

Best Rotary International

12345

www.rotary.org

Are you a business leader searching for something more to life? Do you want to give back to your community and make the world a better place? Then consider becoming a Rotarian. Rotary International is a worldwide organization of business and professional leaders who provide humanitarian services and uphold high ethical standards in their profession. Their well-designed website is packed with information about the organization and ways you can become a member. Find a Rotary chapter in your area, learn about Rotary initiatives, download forms and information, and become a member.

United Way of America

1 2 3 4 5

national.unitedway.org

An organization embracing local community-based United Way groups, made up of volunteers, charities, and contributors. This site contains information on several of the United Way's programs, including Mobilization for America's Children and the United Way partnership with the National Football League. The site also includes news, a United Way FAQs sheet, and a description of how United Way works.

VOLUNTEERING

20 Ways for Teenagers to Help Other People by Volunteering

1 2 3 4 5

www.bygpub.com/books/tg2rw/volunteer.htm

This page shows teenagers 20 ways to volunteer their time to help other people.

Advice for Volunteers

1 2 3 4 5

www.serviceleader.org/advice/index.html

Information on finding the right volunteer opportunity and making the most out of your volunteer activities and efforts can be found on this site.

Corporation for National and Community Service

1 2 3 4 5 RSS

www.cns.gov

Official site of the AmeriCorps, Senior Corps, and Learn and Serve America, this government site is dedicated to encouraging and supporting volunteerism in America.

Energize

1 2 3 4 5

www.energizeinc.com

Energize, Inc. is a company that specializes in volunteerism training, consulting, and publishing, helping volunteer organizations establish, maintain, and grow their volunteer corps. Here, you can find various articles on volunteerism, research the library, search the referral network, and take advantage of the collective wisdom of others working in the field.

Global Volunteers

1 2 3 4 5

www.globalvolunteers.org

Global Volunteers is an effort to achieve worldwide peace by partnering volunteers with local hosts and sponsors, who all work together on a project. The site provides information on the work of this organization and includes a volunteer application. You can also access a map (one of the United States and the other of the world) with country sites you can click to learn more about volunteer opportunities in specific countries.

Idealist

1 2 3 4 5

www.idealist.org

Global clearinghouse of nonprofit and volunteering resources. Search or browse through more than 50,000 organizations in more than 165 countries. Find volunteer opportunities worldwide, particular programs, services, books, videos, articles, or materials for nonprofits, and more. Idealist is a project of Action Without Borders and includes a special area for kids and teens.

Best Peace Corps

1 2 3 4 5

www.peacecorps.gov

U.S. government-supported volunteer organization with participants involved in projects in more than 130 countries. President Kennedy founded the Peace Corps in 1961 to provide help and assistance to underdeveloped countries. Since then, thousands of people from diversified cultural groups have served in the Peace Corps. The Peace Corps has three main goals: to help people in countries that are interested, to promote a better understanding of Americans, and to promote a better understanding of other people in other countries and societies. On this site, you can find out how and why you might want to volunteer.

A B C D E F G H I J K L M N O P Q R S T U V W X Y Z

Points of Light Foundation

12345

www.pointsoflight.org

This nonprofit organization located in Washington, D.C., is devoted to energizing thousands of volunteers to chip in their time and expertise to address and resolve many of the world's most pressing problems. At this site, you learn what you can do to help the cause.

SERVEnet

www.servenet.org

Enter your ZIP code at the SERVEnet site to post and find volunteer and career opportunities in your local area. In addition to searching for volunteer opportunities that make the best use of your interests and skills, you can find service news, events, best practices, and other resources.

VISTA—Volunteers in Service to America

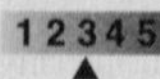

www.friendsofvista.org

One of America's oldest volunteer organizations, founded during the Kennedy years, this site provides the volunteer with useful information about what the organization does and how you can join. A great way to volunteer your time.

Volunteer Today

www.volunteertoday.com

This monthly gazette features news, articles, event schedules, and an archive, as well as recruiting, retention, and training information. Good directory of additional resources.

Volunteerism in Canada

www.volunteer.ca/index-eng.php

This site features some of the benefits of volunteering and provides a directory of organizations in Canada that are in need of volunteers.

VolunteerMatch

www.volunteermatch.org

This ambitious project has more than lived up to its potential, enabling volunteers to find many thousands of volunteer opportunities all over the United States. Organizations might post both ongoing and one-time projects, allowing volunteers from several key cities to find just the opportunity they are looking for.

Volunteers of America

www.voa.org

Services, news, and policy positions from one of America's largest and most comprehensive charitable, nonprofit human service organizations.

Wilderness Volunteers

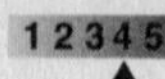

www.wildernessvolunteers.org

This nonprofit organization promotes volunteer service in U.S. wildlands, parks, and reserves. The site details registration information, leadership qualities, meals, and activities. Must be 18 or older to volunteer.

NURSING

American Association of Neuroscience Nurses

12345

www.aann.org

American Association of Neuroscience Nurses (AANN) is a specialty organization serving nurses worldwide. Its site offers membership info, a bulletin board, resources, a job mart, and more.

AllHeart.com

12345

www.allheart.com

A shopping site for nurses and the medical profession. Order scrubs, stethoscopes, and much more from this site. You can also request a bid on a volume order.

allnurses.com

12345

allnurses.com

allnurses.com is a community of more than 135,000 nurses involved in more than 350 different topic discussions. Site also features nursing news.

American Association of Colleges of Nursing

12345

www.aacn.nche.edu

Overview of the American Association of Colleges of Nursing. Upcoming conferences, educational standards and special projects, CCNE accreditation and publications, position statements, and a CareerLink are all included. Navigation bar that runs down the left side of the opening page provides quick access to the different content areas of this site.

American Association of Critical-Care Nurses

12345

www.aacn.org

American Association of Critical-Care Nurses (AACN) "is committed to providing the highest quality resources to maximize nurses' contribution to caring and improving the healthcare of critically ill patients and their families." The opening page displays dozens of links grouped by category, including Clinical Practice, Public Policy, Certification, Education, and Research. Tabbed navigation at the top of the page and a navigation bar that runs down the left side of the page make it easy to move around this site and find the desired information and resources.

American Nurses Association

12345

www.nursingworld.org

The ANA represents the nation's 2.9 million registered nurses. The site lists addresses of state nursing associations, meetings and events, and links to important reference sources.

Cool Nurse

12345

www.coolnurse.com

If you're an adolescent or teenager who has questions about sexuality, drugs, and health, you might be a little hesitant to ask your doctor. To get reliable information in an unintimidating format, check out Cool Nurse. The opening page offers some feature articles along with a navigation bar on the left that provides quick access to the main content areas, including First Aid, Looking Good, Mental Health, Sex Stuff, Substance Abuse, STDs, and Your Social Life. Site also features quizzes, discussion forums, hotline numbers, and a glossary.

A B C D E F G H I J K L M N O P Q R S T U V W X Y Z

Cybernurse.com

www.cybernurse.com

Resource page for nurses, with extensive information related to careers, a search function, and related links. Use the navigation bar on the left to access various resources, including Student Nurses, Cybernurse Forums, Live Chat, Nursing Careers, Nursing Humor, and Nursing Hangman.

Discover Nursing

www.discovernursing.com

Discover Nursing is part of a Johnson & Johnson campaign to secure and improve the future of nursing as a career. If you're considering a career in nursing, this is the site for you. Here, you can learn about the profession and why the nursing profession is in dire need of qualified personnel. The site also points you in the direction of the top nursing schools and shows you how to secure financial aid. This site also offers recruiting materials and information on nursing specialties.

Interfaith Health Program

www.ihpnet.org

Interfaith Health Program believes that faith-based groups can work within a community to ensure that every single member of that community obtains the healthcare services they need. This site explains IHP and offers a searchable database to access real-life examples of the healthcare model it supports. You'll also find an archive of articles, news on the program's research, and health resource links.

National Association of Pediatric Nurse Practitioners

www.napnap.org

NAPNAP is dedicated to "promoting optimal health for children through leadership, practice, advocacy, education and research." If you're a pediatric nurse, this site offers information and resources you will probably find quite useful. Content is organized in four main sections: Practice, Advocacy, Education, and Research. Site includes a Career Resource Guide, a Practice FAQ, a Continuing Education Center, and more.

> **Tip:** If you're a parent, click the Practice tab and click Patient Information/Education to access a page of links to sites that provide information and guidance on common childhood health conditions.

NP Central

www.npcentral.net

Information for and about nurse practitioners, including a directory of links to sites, job announcements, education resources, and professional bodies.

Nurse Options USA

www.nurseoptions.com

Sign up for an email listing of positions for RNs and nurse management or learn about extra income opportunities. Submit your profile.

Nurse Recruiter

www.nurse-recruiter.com

Excellent job site for nurses groups job openings by category, including Hospital, Nursing Home, Travel Nursing, Office Nursing, Camp Nursing, and RN Jobs. Simply pick the desired category and then specify a location, position, and optional keywords to zero in on the perfect position.

NurseWeek.com

www.nurseweek.com

This site contains nursing articles, editorials, continuing education programs, nursing events, career advancement information, and employment opportunities. Excellent place for nurses to go for career information, information on continuing education courses, and news relating to the nursing field.

NurseZone

12345

www.nursezone.com

NurseZone is an "online nursing community, dedicated to meeting the personal and career needs of today's nurses and nursing students." Here, you can explore "the latest in health care news, devices and technology, advice by industry experts, as well as career information and thousands of nursing jobs." This site addresses the concerns and needs of most professional nurses and features a Career Center, Relocation Center, Student Nurse Center, and information on Education and Development.

NursingCenter.com

12345

www.nursingcenter.com

Packed with articles, inside information, and links to additional nursing resources on the Web, this site is an excellent resource kiosk for nurses. Includes recommended reading, information on professional development and continuing education, career guides, a job center, links to the nursing community, and links to online stores where you can purchase nursing apparel and other nursing-related items.

Nursing Education of America

12345

www.nursingeducation.org

This site offers info on NEA and its accredited continuing education programs for nurses.

Best Nursing Spectrum

12345

www.nursingspectrum.com

The Nursing Spectrum is an online news and information kiosk for professional nurses and students. Here, you can find articles about the latest topics in the nursing profession, along with links to educational opportunities and financial aid, career management resources, and discussion boards where you can connect with other nurses. This site features a weekly guest lecture and a Question and Answer area. If you're a nurse or planning on going to school to become a nurse, this is a great site to check out. Use the navigation bar that runs down the left side of the page to jump to Regional News, Nurse Community, Jobs/Employers, Education/CE, Career Management, Student's Corner, and other content areas.

Nursing Standard

12345

www.nursing-standard.co.uk

Hailing from the United Kingdom, this site is *Nursing Standard* magazine's home on the Web. Specializes in helping nurses find resources on professional development, nursing courses, and jobs.

Procare USA

12345

www.procareusa.com

Places American and Canadian RNs throughout the United States. Read about the employment search and hiring packages.

Registered Nurses

12345

www.bls.gov/oco/ocos083.htm

The U.S. Department of Labor created and maintains this page to inform visitors of the nature of the work and provide various labor statistics concerning careers as a registered nurse. High school or college students who are weighing their career options and considering a career in the medical field should check out this site.

School Nurse

12345

www.schoolnurse.com

Excellent resource for school nurses keeps them abreast of the major health issues in schools, current trends, and health alerts. Site includes a library, book store, and fun stuff.

WholeNurse

12345 RSS

www.wholenurse.com

Provides information to nurses, patients, and medical personnel of all types in an effort to keep up with the growing amount of information posted online.

NUTRITION (SEE DIET & NUTRITION)

A
B
C
D
E
F
G
H
I
J
K
L
M
N
O
P
Q
R
S
T
U
V
W
X
Y
Z

OCEANS

Aquatic Network

12345 RSS

www.aquanet.com

This site functions as an information server for the aquatic world, providing information on aquaculture, conservation, fisheries, marine science and oceanography, maritime heritage, ocean engineering, and seafood. You can purchase everything from books to fish on this site!

Enchanted Learning's Guide to the Oceans

12345

www.enchantedlearning.com/subjects/ocean

This site is one of the best sites for children to begin their exploration of the oceans and the plant and animal life that live below sea level. Here, kids can learn about waves, tides, coral reefs, tidal zones, ocean explorers, and much more. They can also print diagrams to label and color and download instructions for fun and interesting projects.

National Oceanic and Atmospheric Administration

www.noaa.gov

This home of the NOAA is packed with information not only about ocean weather patterns and currents but also about fisheries, fishery management, preservation of coastal environments and coral reefs, and explanations of navigational tools and techniques. This site is easy to navigate and features a hefty collection of colorful photos.

Related Sites

www.oceanservice.noaa.gov

www.coralreef.noaa.gov

Oceana

12345

www.oceana.org

Oceana is a group of marine scientists, economists, lawyers, advocates, and activists dedicated to winning "specific and concrete policy changes to reduce pollution and to prevent the irreversible collapse of fish populations, marine mammals, and other sea life." At this site, you can learn what you can do to help, both as a consumer and as a more active participant. Site offers some interesting and timely articles to keep you informed and organizes its content by geographical location: North America, South America, and Europe.

The Ocean Alliance

12345

www.oceanalliance.org

The Ocean Alliance is focused on protecting and conserving whales through research and international education initiatives. Here, you can follow the voyage of the Odyssey as it carries out its five-year mission to study the seas. You can learn more about the Ocean Alliance and its goals. You can contribute to the organization. You can even shop online.

The Ocean Channel

www.ocean.com

This site features the latest news, studies, and warnings about the condition of the earth's oceans. Here, you'll find information about ocean travel, a gallery of ocean photos, Poseidon's library of sea stories, and links to hundreds of sites featuring everything from ocean gear to conservation groups.

A B C D E F G H I J K L M N O P Q R S T U V W X Y Z

The Ocean Conservancy

www.oceanconservancy.org

The Ocean Conservancy is dedicated to protecting and preserving the world's oceans, its resources, and its countless inhabitants. Here, you can learn more about the issues that threaten the health and survival of our oceans and what you can do to help.

OceanLink

oceanlink.island.net

OceanLink is packed with information and resources for enthusiastic ocean explorers of all ages. Click Ocean Info to access more than a dozen links for a variety of fascinating ocean topics; click AquaFacts for the latest news and trivia about ocean life; or click Records to find out which marine creature is the largest or smallest, which can dive the deepest, which is the fastest, and which is the slowest. This site also features an excellent glossary.

Ocean's Futures Society

www.oceanfutures.org

From Jean-Michel Cousteau, the Ocean's Futures website is designed to educate visitors about the beauty and power of the ocean and its inhabitants and encourage people to protect and preserve the world's oceans and ocean inhabitants. Kids will particularly love this site because Ocean's Futures has partnered with Nick.com, Paramount Pictures, and the creator of SpongeBob SquarePants to include content directed particularly for young ocean lovers. Well-designed, easy to navigate, and packed with useful information, this site is our favorite, although the Ocean Channel is quite good, too.

Planet Ocean

school.discovery.com/schooladventures/planetocean

Engaging introduction to the oceans for children of all ages. At this site, you get a general overview of the oceans along with descriptions of the oceans more interesting inhabitants: the blue whale, the barracuda, the tube worm, and some additional marine megastars. Site also features some tips for teachers.

Scripps Institution of Oceanography

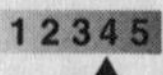

sio.ucsd.edu

This is the Internet home of the world famous Scripps Institution of Oceanography, a part of the University of California, San Diego campus. Scripps has a 100-year history of helping various countries around the world research and solve problems relating to the oceans. Here, you can find information about the various programs and research projects that the Scripps Institution is involved in and explore its diverse collection of marine species and geophysical data. Its library is also searchable online.

SeaWeb

www.seaweb.org

SeaWeb is dedicated to raising awareness of the world oceans and sea life and the threats they face in the modern world in the hopes that greater awareness will inspire people to do what they can to conserve the world's oceans. Here, you can learn more about SeaWeb and its programs, read the latest information about the oceans, and find out what you can do to help.

SeaWorld

www.seaworld.org

This site is a great place for kids to learn about animals both in the oceans and on land. It's also a great place for teachers to obtain resources for their biology and science classes. Downloadable, printable teacher guides are available for all ages of students from kindergarten up to 12th grade and cover a variety of topics ranging from arctic wildlife to sharks, wetlands, and species diversity. Parents can also obtain information about various adventure camps designed for kids.

Stephen Birch Aquarium Museum

www.aquarium.ucsd.edu

Stephen Birch Aquarium Museum is part of the Scripps Institution of Oceanography. This aquarium has information about volunteer opportunities, educational programs, and summer learning adventures. Here, you can also find links to what's new at the aquarium, membership information, ocean quizzes, and articles and videos about various species of marine animals.

Surfrider Foundation USA

www.surfrider.org

Surfrider Foundation is a nonprofit group dedicated to protecting, preserving, and restoring the world's oceans and beaches. At this site, you can learn about the group's strategic initiatives, find late-breaking news on ocean pollution and conservation, and learn more about beach preservation.

Titanic, the Official Archive

www.titanic-online.com

This site explores the history of the *Titanic* from its conception and building to the time it sank and its discovery at the bottom of the ocean. This site also provides information about the passengers and crew and descriptions and photos of many of the artifacts collected during the discovery. You can shop for *Titanic*-related merchandise online.

Whales Online

www.whales-online.org

This information site is dedicated to the "conservation of whales, dolphins, and porpoises in the Southern Hemisphere." Here, you can find information about whales, dolphins, and porpoises by region; obtain information about responsible whale and dolphin watching; and learn about the numerous threats that our oceans and whales face.

Woods Hole Oceanographic Institution

www.whoi.edu

Woods Hole Oceanographic Institution is a private, not-for-profit organization that studies the oceans and attempts to develop solutions for the most serious problems threatening the health of our oceans. At this site, you can learn about the Woods Hole programs and research projects, about the many interesting research vessels and vehicles (submersibles), and about its educational program offerings. This site also features fascinating articles about current expeditions and other ocean-related topics.

OFFICE MANAGEMENT

Apple's Office Management Software

12345

www.apple.com/business/basics/productivity.html

If you're running a business on Apple computers, this is the site to go to find all of the software you need for office management and productivity.

Entrepreneur.com

12345 Blog

www.entrepreneur.com

Entrepreneur.com is dedicated to helping small businesses grow. Here, you can find articles on various office management topics, including hiring and training employees, insuring your business, honing your management skills, managing a family business, and expanding to international markets.

IRS Small Business Site

12345

www.irs.gov/businesses/small

One of the biggest headaches you face when you own your own business results from various tax issues. At this site, the IRS offers to help small-business owners make sense of the various tax rules and regulations. This site features a virtual classroom plus articles on employer ID numbers; employment taxes; rules for opening, operating, and closing a small business; and rules that govern how you can depreciate your business assets. And if you're already familiar with the basics, this site can quickly bring you up to speed on the annual changes to the tax laws. Content is offered in both English and Spanish.

Kaufmann eVenturing

12345 Blog

www.eventuring.org

Kauffman eVenturing is "a trusted guide for entrepreneurs on the path to high growth. The site provides original articles, written by entrepreneurs for entrepreneurs, and aggregates 'the best of the best' content on the Web related to starting and running high-impact companies." The opening page displays a clickable index of topics along with a navigation bar that provides easy access to other features, including an excellent glossary of business terms.

Microsoft Office Online

12345

office.microsoft.com

If your business uses Windows PCs, you'll want to bookmark this home page for Microsoft Office Online. In addition to providing information about various Microsoft Office products and updates, this site features articles and tips for using those products in an office setting.

Small Business Administration

12345

www.sba.gov

The Small Business Administration is a federal organization developed to promote small businesses. Here, you can find links to all the information and resources you need to start, finance, manage, and grow your small business. Content is organized into five areas: Starting, Financing, Managing, Business Opportunities, and Disaster Recovery.

Startup Journal

1 2 3 4 5 RSS

www.startupjournal.com

Wall Street Journal's center for entrepreneurs offers all the information and tools you need to start your own business. Running down the center of the page are feature stories about small-business success, trends, and other items of interest. Running down the left side of the page is a navigation bar that provides quick access to franchise opportunities, business-planning tools, and other Wall Street websites. Use the tabs that run along the top of the page to jump to your area of need or interest: Columnists, How-To, Ideas, Franchising, Financing, E-Commerce, or Running a Business.

Scroll down the opening page for additional treats, including podcasts, discussions, Startup Journal Reports, a Q&A, and interactive quizzes.

OFFICE SUPPLY STORES

abcoffice.com

www.abcoffice.com

This online office supply store carries more than paper and staples. It also carries some of the heavy-duty items that large offices require, including display cases, payroll clocks, shrink wrap equipment, and much more. Streaming video demos of selected products are available along with the Ask Dave Blog.

BusinessSupply.com

www.business-supply.com

This site offers convenient, one-stop shopping for the business supplies, office machines, and business furniture you need to keep your small business or large office. Browse the store by category or search for specific items.

BuyerZone.com

1 2 3 4 5 RSS

www.buyerzone.com/office_equipment

Resources for becoming a more-informed purchaser of office equipment, focusing primarily on electronic equipment, including copiers, printers, fax machines, and shredders. Features buyer's guides, articles, and newsletters. Obtain free quotes on equipment purchases from several online stores. Whether you manage your own small office or offices for a large corporation, you'll find plenty of excellent information and deals on this site.

Home Office Direct

1 2 3 4 5

www.homeofficedirect.com

Online office furniture warehouse features a wide selection of desks, computer desks, computer carts, office chairs, and accessories.

Independent Stationers Online

1 2 3 4 5

www.office-plus.com

This online newsletter promises to keep you up to date on the latest in the office products industry—hot topics, products, reviews, and more. Also, get the details on the OP Office Plus cooperative and its network of dealers.

MicroCenter

1 2 3 4 5

www.microcenter.com

MicroCenter is a great place to shop for bargains on office equipment and supplies, particularly computer equipment and printer supplies. Here, you can search for stores near you or order products online.

A B C D E F G H I J K L M N O P Q R S T U V W X Y Z

Office Depot

12345

www.officedepot.com

Office Depot offers a wide range of office supplies including office furniture, office stationery, and mailroom supplies. Shoppers can search for items by Office Depot's product number, the manufacturer's model number, or the UPC or bar code number found on products. The site also features an online Office Depot credit card application and a store locator to help shoppers find the Office Depot closest to them.

OfficeFurniture.com

12345

www.officefurniture.com

Search for modular furniture, filing cabinets, seating, and accessories for your office at OfficeFurniture.com, where you should have no problem finding an office furniture solution that fits your budget.

OfficeMax OnLine

12345

www.officemax.com

Shop through various categories of office equipment, supplies, and services in the OfficeMax, CopyMax, and FurnitureMax sections. If your business has more than 50 office employees, you can sign up to join the OfficeMax Corporate Direct program for perks and savings. Well-designed site makes it easy to find products. Here, you can also find bargains available only online.

Ontime Supplies

12345

www.ontimesupplies.com

Ontime Supplies promises low prices and rush delivery to ensure that you have the supplies you need when you need them. Tabbed navigation makes it easy to browse this online store, or you can shop for specific products by name, manufacturer, or category. You can also check your order status online.

PRIME Office Products

12345

ecom.primeop.com

This online office supply superstore offers a wide selection of office supplies in several categories, including Binders/Supplies, Computer Supplies, Filing Supplies, Furniture, Mail & Packing, and Office Equipment, to name only a few. Shop online and have your supplies delivered right to your door.

Quill Office Products

12345

www.quillcorp.com

Quill Corporation is a business-to-business direct marketer of office supplies, computer supplies, and office machines. It serves schools, businesses, associations, institutions, and professional offices in the United States. Quill offers free-gift deals to promote many of its products and features an Office Insider area where you can pick up valuable office tips.

Staples, Inc.

12345

www.staples.com

Although most people are familiar with this office-products superstore, not as many are aware of the company's website. Locate the store nearest you, look over special deals for contract and commercial customers (government, healthcare, and educational accounts), and don't forget to check out the job postings! Fill in your snail mail info for a copy of the Staples catalog or order all your supplies and equipment online and have them shipped to your door. Staples offers reasonable prices, a wide selection, and easy-to-use order forms, along with online rebates for some of the products you purchase.

USPS Shipping Supplies Online

12345

shop.usps.com

If you have a busy office—at home or otherwise—this site will save you a lot of time. You can order supplies and packing materials, and you can send Priority Mail, Express Mail, Global Mail, and even Global Express Guaranteed. This provides a convenient way to do your shipping and receiving functions.

Viking Direct

www.viking-direct.co.uk

If you visit Europe frequently, perhaps on business trips, or you live in the area, this is a great place to order your supplies. You can also order from any other country. Just keep in mind that, if you are traveling, this resource is available to you. Viking is an online mail order facility offering everything from office supplies to office machines.

RESOURCES & TIPS

123 Sort It

www.123sortit.com

If you feel as though you could use some help in organizing your home or office, you'll definitely want to visit this site. Here, you'll find some great ideas for getting more organized—finding your desk, reducing clutter, and managing your paperwork more efficiently. You can also buy some tools to help you stay on top of your mess.

AllBusiness.com

www.allbusiness.com

AllBusiness.com is "an online media and e-commerce company that operates one of the premier business sites on the Web." Entrepreneurs, consultants, and business professionals can visit this site to learn tricks for saving time and money through expert advice and practical solutions. Site features plenty of how-to articles, business forms, contracts and agreements, expert advice, blogs, business news, business directory listings, product comparisons, business guides, a small business association, and more.

CheckWorks.com

www.checkworks.com

Order your business or personal checks straight from the printer and get a huge selection of styles at a reasonable price.

morebusiness.com

Blog

www.morebusiness.com

morebusiness.com is an information site created and maintained by entrepreneurs for entrepreneurs. Here, you can find excellent advice and how-to information on creating your own business and marketing plans, starting your own business, incorporating, building a website, securing financing, managing your business, and more. Site also offers some financial calculators.

Office.com

www.office.com

This site pulls together news specific to your industry, ways to network with your peers, business management advice, and details on which suppliers to use. With this site's help, you can save time and money looking for qualified vendors. You can also learn more about getting started with e-commerce.

SmallBizManager

smallbizmanager.com

This site acts as an information kiosk for small-business owners, providing links to everything from office supply stores to legal services. If you're running a small business and can't find what you need, this is a great place to start.

United States Postal Service ZIP Code–Look-Up

12345

zip4.usps.com/zip4

Type in the address, city, or office location and the U.S. Postal Service's ZIP code look-up software will provide the ZIP-plus-four code. Using this service is much easier than using the print directory—and you can be sure it's always up-to-date.

Zairletter

12345

www.zairmail.com/Default.asp

Direct mail service. Download templates from this site to create professional-looking letters, postcards, flyers, and brochures; then have them printed, folded, and mailed, all by Zairletter. You design the message and let the experts at the site get it out quickly and economically.

ORIGAMI

Joseph Wu's Origami Page

12345

www.origami.as

This site features the origami art of Joseph Wu, along with links to sites where you can find other origami creations and instructions. Crisp, clear photos of some of these amazing creations will inspire awe in some visitors and the desire to create in others.

Origami

12345

www.origami.com

Alex Barber created and maintains this site to offer visitors a glimpse of his origami gallery along with free diagrams (in PDF format), links to other origami sites, a search tool for origami books (in and out of print), and a discussion mailing list.

Origami for Everyone

12345

origami.iap-peacetree.org

Origami for Everyone serves up its content in three languages: English, German, and Swedish. Simply click the link for the desired language and start exploring the site. The main page provides a brief introduction to the site along with a navigation bar you can use to jump to other areas: Gallery, Basics, Traditional Models, My Own Designs, and Links. Some excellent guides for beginners along with unique models that will impress even the most experienced origami aficionado.

Origami Underground

12345 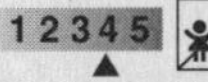

underground.zork.net

If you're looking for erotic origami, this is the site for you. Simply scroll down the page and click the name of the desired model to access photos, diagrams, and instructions. If you've designed an erotic origami model, you can submit it at this site. Site also features a list of recommended books.

Best Origami USA

12345

www.origami-usa.org

Origami USA surpasses other websites in this category in both breadth and depth. Site features a navigation bar on the left with links to Events, Resources (including Models and Discussion), Fun Stuff (Fold This! and Puzzles), Shopping, and About Us (information on contacting and joining Origami USA). This site continues to grow with the addition of diagrams, resources, and puzzles, and offers a searchable index, links to other origami sites, and an online lending library for members.

Paperfolding.com

12345

www.paperfolding.com

Eric Andersen created and maintains this site to offer visitors some math mixed with origami. Here, you'll find model diagrams, photos, and a brief history of origami. Site provides links to other useful sites, although many of the links are out of date.

International Osteoporosis Foundation

12345

www.osteofound.org

The International Osteoporosis Foundation (IOF) is "an international non-governmental organization dedicated to advancing the understanding of osteoporosis and promoting prevention, diagnosis, and treatment of the disease worldwide." Site features a useful guide called Osteoporosis: What You Need to Know, information for health professionals, links to related sites, and more.

OSTEOPOROSIS

Best Medline Plus: Osteoporosis

12345

www.nlm.nih.gov/medlineplus/osteoporosis.html

Medline Plus is a trustworthy source of medical information on just about every health topic. The Osteoporosis page features news, timely information from the NIH (National Institutes of Health), Overviews, Diagnosis/Symptoms, Treatments, and Prevention. Site offers some excellent (though somewhat lengthy) videos, interactive tutorials, information on clinical trials and the latest research, and information specific to women, men, and kids.

National Osteoporosis Foundation

12345

www.nof.org

The National Osteoporosis Foundation's mission is "to prevent osteoporosis, to promote lifelong bone health, to help improve the lives of those affected by osteoporosis and related fractures, and to find a cure." This site provides information about the foundation along with tips for preventing bone loss, information for patients, and a search tool for tracking down a qualified doctor.

Osteoporosis: Medications and Other Treatments

12345

www.womenshealthchannel.com/osteoporosis/treatment.shtml

From the Women's Health Channel comes this collection of articles and information on osteoporosis. Content features an overview, an explanation of causes and risk factors, information on symptoms and diagnosis, descriptions of various tests used for screening, and information on medical and surgical treatments and prevention strategies.

PAINTING

Artist & Craftman Supply Online

12345

artistcraftsman.com

Artist & Craftman Supply Online is the place to go for painting supplies, equipment, and accessories. Larry Adlerstein, founder and president, travels around the globe in a constant search to acquire accurate and timely information and discover the best products. The company's goal is "to give artists the option of as many different brands, as many different colors, and as many types of materials as we possibly can find" and offer them at bargain-basement prices. This site offers a list of more than three dozen art supply categories for you to browse through, along with a blog and an Ask Our Experts feature. Site also carries art supplies for young, budding artists.

Elin Pendleton: Free Oil Painting Lessons

12345

www.elinart.com/pages/lsnstilloil.html

Elin Pendleton provides this tutorial that shows you how she moves from an original idea, through the entire process as she paints in her studio. At this site, you can view additional samples of Elin's inspired artwork.

FARP: A Diminutive Survival Guide to Oil Painting

12345

elfwood.lysator.liu.se/farp/oil/oils.html

If you're into fantasy art and you'd like some practical tips from an accomplished artist who's learned his art in the trenches, check out this Diminutive Survival Guide to Oil Painting. Here, you'll find a brief overview to get you started along with a collection of survival guides, discussion groups, reviews of oil painting books, and a collection of original artwork. Site provides its own search tool, but finding stuff can still be quite a challenge—this site is packed with stuff.

Interactive Art School: Free Lessons

12345

www.interactiveartschool.com/free-art-lessons.html

The Interactive Art School provides you with nine free lessons to inspire you to take up a paint brush, stretch a canvas, and start painting. Lessons include a sample critique, an introduction to form, the secret of making a "real" painting, using ovals and other basic shapes to create paintings, and the basics of composition. You can register for a full six-lesson course. Click Art Links for a directory of links to other art-related websites.

Oil Painting Techniques

12345

www.oil-painting-techniques.com

Oil Painting Techniques features a collection of about 30 pages on various oil painting topics, including Art History, Aesthetics, Composition, Color Theory, Glazing, Portraits, Landscapes, Framing, and Selling Your Work. Excellent resource for oil painters, regardless of their level of expertise. Each page covers a single topic in pretty good detail and provides a short directory of links to other related sites.

Pearl Paint

12345

www.pearlpaint.com

Pearl Art and Craft supply has been offering a wide selection of supplies to artists at great prices for more than 70 years. Site features a navigation bar that enables you to search by brand from A to Z, or you can browse by category, including Paints, Brushes, Canvas/Painting Surfaces, Easels, and Furniture/Equipment.

If Pearl Paint has a store near you, click the Flyer link to learn about specials. Or, click E-Specials to learn about bargains you can get only online.

WatercolorPainting.com

12345

www.watercolorpainting.com

WatercolorPainting.com is an outstanding illustrated guide that provides step-by-step tutorials to help visitors master a wide variety of techniques. Site features watercolor tutorials, step-by-step paintings, a learning center with a vast collection of additional guides, an excellent collection of links to other high-quality watercolor websites, and a fairly extensive glossary of terms. If you want to learn how to paint with watercolors, this is definitely the Best of the Best place for you.

PARENTING

Canadian Parents Online

1 2 3 4 5

www.canadianparents.com

This excellent resource covers everything from preconception tips to raising tweeners and teenagers. Chatrooms and message boards help parents join forces in the challenging field of parenting. Online experts offer tips and hints on topics such as packing a healthy lunch and raising children with special needs. Links to stores where you can purchase products online.

Caring for Kids

1 2 3 4 5

www.caringforkids.cps.ca

The Canadian Pediatric Society has developed this Caring for Kids site to educate parents on how to raise healthy children and to keep parents informed of the latest information, alerts, and product recalls that apply to the health and safety of their children. Areas at this site include Pregnancy & Babies, When Your Child Is Sick, Teen Health, Immunization, Behavior & Development, Health Eating, and Keeping Kids Safe. Excellent site for parents, especially first-time parents.

Facts for Families

1 2 3 4 5

www.aacap.org/info_families

The American Academy of Child and Adolescent Psychiatry (AACAP) developed *Facts for Families* to provide concise and up-to-date information on issues that affect children, teenagers, and their families. Find out about depression in teens, ways to help your teen with stress, manic-depressive illness in teens, normal adolescent development, ways to deal with teens and eating disorders, and so on.

Family Education Network: A Parenting and Education Resource

1 2 3 4 5

www.familyeducation.com/home

Articles and advice from experts. Psychologists and pediatricians answer questions from parents. Users can find schools in their area that provide online access by using the search feature at this site. Kids can obtain homework help and check out some interesting activities. Content is organized by age group: Your Child 0–6, Your Child 7–11, and Your Child 12–18.

Family Resource Center

1 2 3 4 5 Blog RSS

www.familyresource.com

The Family Resource Center features a wide range of information, tools, and resources for all aspects of family life, including relationships, pregnancy, parenting, health, finance, and lifestyles. Click the Parenting link near the top of the page to access articles in dozens of categories, including Activities, Behavior Issues, and School and Learning. This site even features podcasts of *The Family Report.*

FamilyTime

1 2 3 4 5

www.familytime.com

Articles and advice from experts on how to better organize your family and the time you spend together. Tools for meal planning, keeping a calendar, and saving money are featured, along with plenty of useful tips.

Girl Power! Campaign

1 2 3 4 5

www.girlpower.gov

This is the official site of Girl Power, a national public education campaign sponsored by the

Department of Health and Human Services to encourage 9- to 13-year-old girls to make the most of their lives.

iParenting.com

12345 Blog RSS

www.iparenting.com

From conception to birth to teen years, you'll find helpful articles and guidance from other parents who've dealt with similar issues. Point to the Parenting link near the top of the page to open a menu of options for different stages in parenting: Preconception, Pregnancy, Babies, Breastfeed, Toddlers, and so on, up to Teenagers. Site also features a mom of the month, a dad of the month, discussion forums, and a hefty collection of lifestyle sites.

John Rosemond

12345

www.rosemond.com

Syndicated columnist and child-rearing expert John Rosemond has encouraged parents to take the lead for years and avoid the unpleasantries of having children rule the roost. Now you can read his weekly column online, check out his speaking schedule, take a peak at John's insightful thought for the day, and link to Rosemond parent groups at Yahoo!.

KidSource

12345

www.kidsource.com

KidSource provides information on parenting that covers all stages of development from newborn up to K–12 and all aspects of parenting. Parents will find links to dozens of articles on parenting and kids can try many of the suggested activities. This site has been created and is maintained by parents to help provide parents with the information and resources they need to become more-effective caregivers.

Mothering Magazine

12345

www.mothering.com

Mothering magazine encourages mothers to adopt a natural living approach to raising a healthy family. Here, you can find articles on how to protect your child from injury and disease without relying too heavily on vaccines and other heavy-duty medical interventions. This site also encourages families to moderate their TV watching and video game play, eat healthy, and meditate. Some excellent information and suggestions even for those who do not completely embrace the natural-living approach.

The National Parenting Center

12345

www.tnpc.com

Founded in July 1989, The National Parenting Center (TNPC) has become one of America's foremost parenting information services. Dedicated to providing parents with comprehensive and responsible guidance from the world's most renowned child-rearing authorities, The National Parenting Center invites parents to expand their parenting skills and strengths. Also, learn about product recalls at this site and chat online with other parents.

NCF—National Center for Fathering

12345

www.fathers.com

The NCF mission is to inspire and equip men to be better fathers through fathering research and inspiration. Here, you'll find hundreds of articles for nearly every fathering situation, tips for dads, and information on programs and training available to help make dads better fathers.

Parenthood.com

12345

www.parenthood.com

Parenthood.com brings you a one-stop source for articles, expert advice, and feedback from other parents on issues related to pregnancy, labor, baby care, and parenting at all levels of childhood and adolescent development. Experts, chat, and greeting cards are available at this site. If you're expecting or have recently given birth, you can register to get an email newsletter tailored to your stage of pregnancy or your baby's age. Site also features a photo gallery and a section on Nutrition & Food.

Parenting.com

12345 Blog RSS

www.parenting.com/parenting

Parenting.com is dedicated to "making pregnancy and parenthood smarter, saner, and easier." This site focuses on parenting in the early years, but is planning to expand its coverage to raising teenagers. This site also features chat areas and message boards. Scroll down the page to find the Ages & Stages Shortcut buttons that enable you to quickly access age-related content with a click of a button.

Parenting.org

12345

www.parenting.org

Created and maintained by the Girls and Boys Town National Resource and Training Center, this site is designed to help parents deal with the day-to-day care taking, guidance, and development of their children. Resources are organized by age group, as follows: precious beginnings (0–4), discovery years (5–9), tween years (10–14), and taking flight (15–19). Also features a site for professionals.

Parents-Talk.com

12345

www.parents-talk.com

Parents-Talk is an online parenting magazine that features expert advice and access to several parenting message boards. A section on Through Kids' Eyes features kids' insights into various issues and kids' recommendations on toys and other products supposedly designed for kids. The parenting message boards encourage parents to trade secrets and support one another through the difficult process of parenting children and young adults. Site also features games for kids.

Positive Parenting

12345 Blog

www.positiveparenting.com

The Positive Parenting site is dedicated to providing resources and information to make parenting more rewarding, effective, and considerably easier. Site also features a bookstore with a good collection of books on positive parenting.

The WholeFamily Center

12345

www.wholefamily.com

Forum for learning strategies for resolving the tensions arising in family life. Each center has real-life dramas you can listen to on RealAudio. The site features just about all the information that families and teens, especially, have questions about. You'll find sections on school, sexuality, a crisis center, ways to deal with relationships, feelings and emotions, substance abuse, and what kids like to do—just hang out.

Working Mother

12345

www.workingmother.com

Website of *Working Mother* magazine, this site offers working mothers advice on how to establish a health balance between family and career. Here, you can sample content from the current issue.

ADOLESCENTS

About Parenting Teens

12345

parentingteens.about.com/mbody.htm

You can learn a lot about parenting on this site from expert human guides and get hot news, helpful advice, and invaluable links to other sites that contain similar information.

ADOL: Adolescence Directory On-Line

12345

education.indiana.edu/cas/adol/adol.html

This electronic guide to information on adolescent issues is a service of the Center for Adolescent Studies at Indiana University.

Campaign for Our Children

12345

www.cfoc.org

News, facts, and statistics about teenage pregnancies, with resources for parents and teachers. Click Teen Guide to jump to the page specifically about parenting teenagers.

Dear Lucie

www.lucie.com

Lucie Walters writes a syndicated teen advice column. This site offers advice to teens on subjects such as sexuality, depression, alcohol, pregnancy, romance, eating disorders, and parents. The site contains an archive of past columns. Scroll down for links to specific topics of interest.

Drug Testing

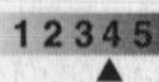

rapiddrug.com

Are your kids on drugs? This site offers drug-testing kits that include simple dipsticks to test for marijuana and five-panel test kits to check for THC, cocaine, opium, meth, and amphetamines.

Family Development Program: Parenting Teens Publications

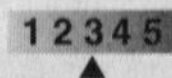

ceinfo.unh.edu/Family/Parent.htm

This site lists publications about parenting teens. Each publication focuses on a specific aspect: physical changes, emotional changes, cognitive changes, and changes in relationship dynamics.

KidsHealth.org: For Teens

kidshealth.org/teen

Brought to you by AI duPont Hospital for Children in Delaware. Teens can come here and get answers to questions or concerns that they haven't wanted to talk about. Topics include issues such as health, sex, food, sports, and school. A separate section has been created for parents who need a resource for concerns about their own teen.

Kotex.com

www.kotex.com

This is a great commercial site that deals with sensitive issues regarding women's health. Take your daughter here when the time is right or let her explore it on her own.

Tip: Go to www.girlspace.com to access the site specifically designed for younger women.

National Families in Action

www.nationalfamilies.org

National Families in Action is a national drug education, prevention, and policy center based in Atlanta, Georgia. The organization was founded in 1977. Its mission is to help families and communities prevent drug abuse among children.

ParenTalk Newsletter: Adolescence

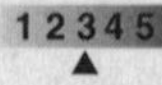

www.tnpc.com/parentalk/adoles.html

Advice about parenting your teen: keeping the lines of communication open, talking about sex and drugs, dealing with rebellion, dealing with divorce, discussing suicide, and more.

Raising Successful Teenagers

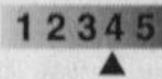

www.childdevelopmentinfo.com/parenting/teens.shtml

Raising Successful Teens is dedicated to providing parents with the information and resources they need to help teens with challenging issues and assist them in achieving their full potential. Site features a Parenting 101 guide, tips on helping to build self-esteem, guidance on dealing with angry children, and a host of other areas focused on the major challenges of raising a teenager.

Talking with Kids About Tough Issues

www.talkingwithkids.org

Tips and resources for talking with your kids about tough issues, especially violence, alcohol, sex, HIV/AIDS, and terrorism. Request booklets and read Q&As to see the recommendations for helping teens deal with these important issues.

Teen Challenge World Wide Network

www.teenchallenge.com

Education about drug culture and abuse, including the latest statistics, outreach programs, and local information.

Teen Help

www.vpp.com/teenhelp

Support network for teenagers and parents dealing with issues confronting adolescents. Includes links and a hotline.

BABIES AND TODDLERS (SEE ALSO, BABIES)

Baby Bag Online

www.babybag.com

This website is a resource for parenting and childcare. Visitors can post birth announcements, read stories, and access articles and links on topics ranging from health and safety to pregnancy, childbirth, and behavioral issues. Some excellent advice from experts.

BabyCenter

www.babycenter.com

Offers information on pregnancy, baby care, and nutrition as well as a guide to baby names and a pregnancy timeline. Users can personalize the page by entering their baby's due date or birth date.

BabyPlace

www.baby-place.com

This site features more than 100,000 pages of baby-related content and more than 2,500 links to other sites that its editors have personally reviewed. Offers information on pregnancy, parenting, health, games, and even jokes. Baby Place Mall provides links to online stores where parents can shop.

CribLife 2000

www.criblife2000.com

Dedicated to helping parents reduce babies' exposure to harmful chemicals and other dangers related to cribs. Read a history of Sudden Infant Death Syndrome (SIDS) and learn about safe crib practices and products.

Dr. Greene: Toddlers

Blog

www.drgreene.com

A pediatrician dispenses advice on handling temper tantrums, surviving the terrible twos, teaching sharing, stopping biting, and all sorts of other questions and concerns that specifically apply to toddlers. The page address given here takes you to the opening page. To get to the toddlers area, click Ages and Stages, and then click Toddlers.

eToys

www.etoys.com

Huge online toy store, featuring recommendations, bargains, a catalog, and a searchable database. Items are sorted by age group and by category: dolls, collectible toys, video games, and so on. Great place for kids to go shopping, too; just make sure your child doesn't have your credit card number.

FindCareNow

www.findcarenow.com

This site features a childcare search tool to match parents with nannies and other childcare providers. You can also find several good articles and tips on childcare and parenting.

KidSource: Toddlers

www.kidsource.com/kidsource/pages/toddlers.html

Advice and reference material on health, learning, and development. The site also includes information on positive discipline.

Live and Learn

12345

www.liveandlearn.com

Contains links to education resources, free software, and online games, plus information on age-appropriate toys and child safety. In addition, the site provides a good list of teaching sites.

National Organization of Mothers of Twins Clubs

12345

www.nomotc.org

Find facts and figures related to the incidence of multiple births as well as local support organizations and resources to aid in meeting the distinctive developmental needs of twins. Some excellent advice from other parents of twins and parenting experts on how to raise well-adjusted twins. Information on the organization's annual conference is also available.

Best Pampers Parenting Institute

12345

www.pampers.com

Advice for parents about child development, health, and skincare—plus a guide to Pampers products. When you first arrive at the site, click the desired country/language (you have several from which to choose). The next page features a navigation bar with buttons for the various stages of a baby's development, from Pregnancy to Preschooler, so you can access content that focuses on your baby's current needs. Site is well designed and packed with reliable and current information and plenty of tips for new parents.

Parenting Toddlers

12345 Blog RSS

www.parentingtoddlers.com

This site focuses specifically on parenting toddlers in a way that helps parents retain their sanity and raise well-adjusted kids who are able to achieve their full potential. Articles on this site cover toddler safety, potty training, disciplining your toddler, and engaging your toddler in activities and crafts.

Parents.com

12345

www.parents.com

Feature articles from this print publication cover topics such as parents-to-be, travel, development, health and safety, fun, and food. "Ask the Expert" gives you the chance to have your specific question answered.

Zero to Three Policy Center

12345

www.zerotothree.org

The Zero to Three Policy Center maintains the Zero to Three Policy Network—a "nationwide effort to improve the quality of care for children up to age three." Visit this site to learn about the campaign, to search for quality childcare, or to join in the movement. If you're a parent getting ready to search for quality childcare, visit this site to learn how to evaluate a childcare provider.

K–6

About Child Parenting

12345

childparenting.about.com

About's Child Parenting section covers just about every topic imaginable that's related to raising children K–6. Learn some arts and crafts ideas, get help for raising children with special needs, and learn how to deal with specific problems that commonly arise.

Boy Scouts of America

12345

www.scouting.org

This organization's home page describes the Cub Scouts and Boy Scouts and their programs. The site also covers joining and volunteering for parents and kids, and offers a catalog of merchandise. Find a BSA council in your area using the locator provided.

A B C D E F G H I J K L M N O P Q R S T U V W X Y Z

Child & Family Web Guide

cfw.tufts.edu

The Child & Family Web Guide, created and maintained by graduate students and faculty at Tufts University, is a directory of websites on topics of interest to parents and professionals. The goal of the site is to present links to those sites that provide the most reliable and valuable information on parenting and childcare.

ClubMom

www.mom.com

Read interesting articles on raising children today, chat with moms facing similar situations as you, and get and give advice on parenting subjects. Also, tune in to live chats with experts.

Expect the Best from a Girl

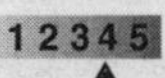

www.academic.org

Provides ways to encourage your daughter to develop competence and self-confidence—particularly in science, math, and technology.

FamilyFun

12345

family.go.com

This is a great place for parents and kids to go when they're "bored." This site is packed with ideas for fun crafts and activities. When I visited just before April Fool's Day, the site featured a collection of 35 pranks that parents could play on their children. Very current information presented in an easily accessible and fun format! Site also features basic parenting tips.

HELP for Parents

12345

www.helpforfamilies.com

A great resource from Dr. Tim Dunnigan, where you can learn effective discipline techniques. Visiting this site is just like going to a good parenting class—without having to leave your house.

K-6 Parenting

www.way2hope.org/k-6_parenting.htm

Just the thing all parents love—advice on how to raise kids from someone who doesn't have kids.

Kids Camps

12345

www.kidscamps.com/special_needs/learning_disab_add.html

The Internet's most comprehensive directory of traditional and specialty overnight camps. The camp caters to those with learning difficulties and offers tours and experiences for children, teenagers, and families.

KidsHealth.org

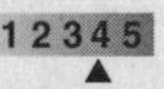

www.kidshealth.org

Looking for expert health information for the entire family? KidsHealth.org has the latest on everything from chicken pox to dyslexia, in easy-to-read articles for kids, teens, and parents.

MOST–Mothers of Supertwins

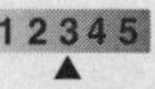

www.mostonline.org

MOST is "a network of families with triplets, quadruplets and more, providing information, resources, empathy, and good humor during pregnancy, infancy, toddlerhood and school age." Mothers of triplets or more will want to commiserate with other moms in the same situation through this site's message boards. The site also has a quarterly online magazine and access to shopping sites that will fit your particular needs. You must become a member to shop at the online store.

National AfterSchool Association

www.naaweb.org

When your child is school aged, one of the biggest worries is not what your child does in school but what he or she does after school. This site is dedicated to helping teachers, policy makers, administrators, and others who provide or should provide after-school activities ensure that the after-school activities are safe, fun, and valuable. Here, you can learn more about the organization's accreditation programs, conferences, affiliates, and publications.

National Head Start Association

12345

www.nhsa.org

The National Head Start Program is a school readiness program that provides "comprehensive education, health, nutrition, and parent involvement services to low-income children and their families." Here, you can learn more about the program, determine whether your family qualifies for it, and find out what you can do to help.

National Network for Child Care: School Age Child Development

12345

www.nncc.org

Excellent collection of articles on all stages of childhood development from infant to primary school, plus groupings of articles on special topics, such as brain development, aggression, social skills, depression, and assessing a child's abilities.

Parenting Pipeline

12345

www.ext.nodak.edu/extnews/pipeline

Online newsletters from the North Dakota State University Extension Service. Very good developmental information for parenting elementary-age and junior high school children.

Parenting Young Children

12345

lancaster.unl.edu/famliv/parenting/young_children

Online guide packed with articles specifically for parents of young children. Articles include Dealing with Tantrums, Contracting with Your Child, Effective Ways to Guide Children, and many more.

SINGLE PARENTING

Christianity Today: Single Parenting

12345

www.christianitytoday.com/parenting/features/single.html

Christianity Today's Single Parenting area provides several articles to help single parents raise their children and deal with common issues, especially those relating to teenagers. Articles are dated, but still relevant.

Living with a Single Parent

12345

kidshealth.org/kid/feeling/home_family/single_parents.html

Excellent article for kids discusses the challenges of living with a single parent and provides advice on how to cope. When you're done reading this article, click the More Articles Like This tab for additional advice.

Making Lemonade

12345

makinglemonade.com

This site, created by single parent and webmaster Jodi Seidler is dedicated to helping single parents effectively raise and enjoy their children while at the same time maintaining their own emotional well-being and expanding their social circles. Read articles in the archives, check out single parent-related links, and share your war stories and triumphs with other single parents at this site.

Mothers Without Custody

12345

www.proactive-coach.com/divorce/mothers

A support and resource organization for this much-overlooked segment of the single-parent population. Provides a forum for discussing issues.

Parent Alienation Syndrome

12345

www.familycourts.com

If you're a parent who has experienced or is in the process of an ugly divorce, and you've found that your once loving and adoring children now despise you, you're not alone. Thousands of parents are feeling the same devastating emotions, sometimes referred to as *parent alienation syndrome.* Visit this site to learn more about it and what you can do to help you and your child work through it.

Parenting SOLO for Singles

12345

www.solosingles.com/ssparent

Extensive directory of information and resources for single parents covers everything from making time for yourself to building your child's self-esteem.

Parents Without Partners

12345

www.parentswithoutpartners.org

Locate a PWP chapter near you. The site has many features and is concerned with problems of bringing up children alone—especially the emotional conflicts of divorce, never being married, separation, or widowhood. PWP is an international organization that provides real help in the way of discussions, professional speakers, study groups, and publications. The site is well designed, and you will enjoy looking through it. You'll find a news section, a newsletter, and you can shop at the Mall from such companies as Amazon.com.

ParentsWorld.com

12345 RSS

www.parentsworld.com

This site features articles and commentary on child support, dating, parenting, and other topics relevant to parenting, especially single parenting. You can also find discussion forums for meeting and talking with other parents, a recipe area, a FAQs list, e-cards, and more.

Single and Custodial Fathers' Network

12345

www.scfn.org

Support organization for single and remarried fathers with custodial care. Find information on work and parenting issues, a mailing list, and chat.

Single Parent Central

12345

www.singleparentcentral.com

Get news and information about trends in single-parenting families, share advice and wisdom, learn about ways to save money, and find links to other related sites. Site features an excellent collection of little known facts and insightful articles.

SingleParentMeet

12345

www.singleparentmeet.com

Online dating service for single parents. Here, you can browse pictures and video, chat online in real time, and communicate anonymously until you're ready to meet someone of interest.

Single Parents Association

12345

www.singleparents.org

Single Parents Association (SPA) is a nonprofit organization devoted to providing single-parent families educational opportunities and fun activities through its national headquarters and local chapter network.

SingleParent Tips

12345 RSS

singleparent.lifetips.com

This site is packed with solid tips for single parents grouped in 20 categories including Child Care, Divorce, Family Fun, and Raising Teens. Although many of the tips are just as valuable for two-parent households, many apply specifically to single parenting.

A B C D E F G H I J K L M N O Q R S T U V W X Y Z

SPECIAL NEEDS

Arc

1 2 3 4 5

www.thearc.org

The Arc "advocates for the rights and full participation of all children and adults with intellectual and developmental disabilities." Here, you can find out more about the organization, track down local chapters, and find instructions on how to work the system to most effectively address your needs. Scroll down the page for some valuable free resources, including state-specific family resource guides and Medicare fact sheets.

Children with Disabilities Information

1 2 3 4 5

www.childrensdisabilities.info

This site is maintained by parents who are raising a child with disabilities, so it contains plenty of information from those who actually face the day-to-day struggles. Although the information focuses primarily on problems that arise due to premature birth, the site also addresses other disabilities and more general topics. You can also find book reviews, interviews, discussion links, and other resources.

Children with Spina Bifida

1 2 3 4 5

www.waisman.wisc.edu/~rowley/sb-kids/index.htmlx

Promotes information sharing between parents. The site provides news and research updates, details of problems, a list of related organizations, and a directory of links to other resources.

Cleft Lip: Wide Smiles

1 2 3 4 5

www.widesmiles.org

Formed to ensure that parents of cleft-affected children do not have to feel alone. Chat online with parents or read the files.

ConductDisorders.com

1 2 3 4 5

www.conductdisorders.com

You can join the parents' support group here. Also, read articles that may help you understand and better deal with your child's conduct difficulties. Find out about treatment programs and scan the bookstore for suggested resources you may want to read.

Council for Exceptional Children

1 2 3 4 5

www.cec.sped.org

The Council for Exceptional Children is an organization dedicated to improving educational outcomes for students with disabilities. Users can access a database of professional literature, information, and resources, and find out about financial aid opportunities for education.

Down Syndrome

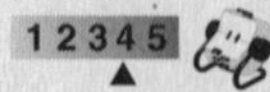

www.downsyndrome.com

This forum for sharing experiences and information about Down Syndrome features a family chat area, a bulletin board, and an online magazine.

Dyslexia: The Gift

1 2 3 4 5

www.dyslexia.com

Provides information about the positive side of learning disabilities and remedial teaching methods suited to the dyslexic learning style.

Family Village

1 2 3 4 5

www.familyvillage.wisc.edu

Virtual community for persons with mental retardation and other disabilities, their families, and those who provide services and support. From the shopping mall, you can buy anything from canes and walkers to clothing, computers, software, and footwear.

A B C D E F G H I J K L M N O P Q R S T U V W X Y Z

Federation for Children with Special Needs

12345

www.fcsn.org

The Federation for Children with Special Needs is "a center for parents and parent organizations to work together on behalf of children with special needs and their families." Here, you can learn about the Federation and explore its health and education programs.

Genetic Alliance

12345

www.geneticalliance.org

The Genetic Alliance is an advocacy group working with and on behalf of those who have genetic diseases. As a coalition of hundreds of genetic advocacy organizations, health professionals, clinics, hospitals and companies, the Alliance works "to accelerate translational research; improve the climate for the development of technologies; encourage cohorts for clinical trials; increase the availability of linked, annotated biological resources; and ultimately lead to improved human health."

Hydrocephalus Association

12345

www.hydroassoc.org

This site provides publications, conference details, and links for people with hydrocephalus, their families, and health professionals.

Individualized Educational Program (IEP)

12345

www.ed.gov/parents/needs/speced/iepguide/index.html

If you are the parent of a child who has special needs in school, the first step you want to take is to develop an Individualized Educational Program (IEP) for your child. This site provides a comprehensive guide for developing, implementing, and maintaining an effective IEP along with a list of links to additional resources.

Internet Resources for Special Children

12345

www.irsc.org

This site features a catalog for parents and professionals in relation to child disabilities, disorders, and healthcare. Huge collection of links broken down into categories including Adaptive Equipment & Technologies, Diseases & Conditions, Sports & Recreation, Learning Disabilities, and more than a dozen more. Great place to start researching any topics relating to children with special needs.

Make-a-Wish Foundation of America

12345

www.wish.org

This site outlines the history of this organization, which grants wishes to children with life-threatening medical conditions. You'll also find details about activities in the works.

National Academy for Child Development (NACD)

12345

www.nacd.org

The NACD provides data and support for learning disorders, including ADD and mental retardation. Find out more about the organization and its products and services at this site. You can order CDs, audio tapes, and special software from the site.

National Information Center for Children and Youth with Disabilities (NICHCY)

12345

www.nichcy.org

The National Information Center for Children and Youth with Disabilities provides facts about referrals, education, and family issues. The site can help you locate the organizations and agencies within your state that are working on disability-related issues. Kids who visit the site may want to click the Zigawhat! link to access an area specifically designed for kids with disabilities.

PCI Publishing

12345

www.pcicatalog.com

This site offers a catalog for children and adults with special educational needs. Topics include life skills, transition, inclusion, and communication. The site sells a variety of learning products for children, including games and books. You can purchase online.

Premature Baby Premature Child

12345

www.prematurity.org

This volunteer website is dedicated to providing parents with the information and resources they need to care for their premature babies and deal with the challenges parents face throughout the development of their children. The site encourages parents and professionals to advocate for their children so that they have the resources they need to achieve their full potential.

Sibling Support Project

12345

www.thearc.org/siblingsupport

Dedicated to brothers and sisters of people with special health and developmental needs. Here, you can learn more about the project and its sibling workshops and connect with others who are living with similar situations in their homes.

SNAP Online: Special Needs Advocate for Parents

12345

www.snapinfo.org

An online resource for information, education, advocacy, and referrals for families with special needs children of all ages and disabilities.

Special Needs Children Site

12345 RSS

www.bellaonline.com/site/specialneedschildren

Bella Online features an area specifically for parents who have special needs children. The page displays a collection of feature articles along with a list of clickable topics, including Advocacy; Behavior, Communication, and Discipline; Family Support; and Inclusive Education. Many of the topics focus on a specific disability, such as Down Syndrome and ADD/ADHD. Site also features discussion forums.

United Cerebral Palsy

12345

www.ucpa.org

This national group provides education and research services to people with disabilities, their families, the public, and other organizations. Good place to go for information and assistance with all disabilities, not just cerebral palsy. Click Parenting & Families for specific information on parenting a child with cerebral palsy.

STAY-AT-HOME PARENTS

Bizy Moms: A Complete Resource for Work-at-Home Moms

12345

www.bizymoms.com

Business ideas for moms working from home. Also included are FAQs and insights into the book *The Stay at Home Mom's Guide to Making Money from Home.*

Home-Based Working Moms

12345

www.hbwm.com

Association for mothers and fathers working from home. Find out about membership and get tips and ideas for your business. This site offers a great collection of tips and articles.

HomeJobStop

12345

homejobstop.com

HomeJobStop.com is devoted to helping telecommuter wannabes achieve their dreams of establishing a successful career working at home. Think of it as a placement service for telecommuters. This site does not advertise the usual work-at-home chain letter and pyramid schemes, commercial advertisements disguised as job ads, or other scams.

Main Street Mom

1 2 3 4 5

www.mainstreetmom.com

This online network for stay-at-home moms features an excellent collection of articles and resources on everything from personal finance management to parenting, gardening, and cooking. Most of the content is intended for traditional moms who stay at home and raise the kids.

Miserly Moms: Stay-At-Home Mom (SAHM) Links

1 2 3 4 5

www.miserlymoms.com

The author of this site says, "Staying at home with your children is one of the best things you can do for them. In order to help you with this goal, I have compiled the following list of some of the best SAHMs links that can be found." This attractive, well-organized site is full of useful stuff.

Slowlane.com

1 2 3 4 5

www.slowlane.com

Searchable online resource for stay-at-home dads and primary caregivers and their families. Includes articles primarily written by stay-at-home dads. Also includes media clips and links to hundreds of other resources on the Web. Online chat and discussion groups to help stay-at-home dads keep from becoming agoraphobic.

SOHO Parenting Center

1 2 3 4 5

www.sohoparenting.com

The SOHO Parenting Center is dedicated to helping parents deal with the emotional aspect of parenting. Here, you can join a parents' circle where you can obtain the support, encouragement, and advice you need to deal with the daily emotional challenges of parenting children and teenagers. The SOHO Parenting Center offers several workshops along with links to other useful sites.

Strategies for Financing Stay-at-Home Parenting

1 2 3 4 5

www.careerjournal.com/myc/workfamily/20040708-todorova.html

If you're a stay-at-home parent who's having a tough time making ends meet or you're currently working and wondering whether you can afford to stay at home to care for the kids, then read this article for ideas on how to smooth the transition financially.

WAHM (Work at Home Moms)

1 2 3 4 5

www.wahm.com

For mothers working from home, this site offers advice on balancing mothering and work, as well as access to a network of "web moms." Register for the weekly newsletter to receive the latest news and job listings via email each week.

Work at Home Parents

1 2 3 4 5

www.work-at-home-parents.com

Work at Home Parents provides you with the resources you need to choose the right business opportunity for you. Also provides information about scams and ways to avoid falling for a scam.

Working at Home: A Primer

1 2 3 4 5

www.clubmom.com/display/222977

Good article covering the challenges of working at home and providing guidance at how to work at home most effectively.

STEPPARENTING

CoMamas.com

1 2 3 4 5

www.comamas.com

Can an ex-wife (biological mother) and new wife (stepmother) get along well enough to raise a well-adjusted child? Well, the creators of this site did it;

A B C D E F G H I J K L M N O P Q R S T U V W X Y Z

and if you're in a similar situation, they might be able to offer the advice and guidance you need to succeed, or at least tone down the conflict.

Second Wives Club

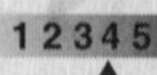

www.secondwivesclub.com

Support and advice with a healthy attitude for women who are involved in blended families or living as second wives.

Shared Parenting Information Group

home.clara.net/spig

Find guidelines for separated parents, parenting plans, and FAQs about joint custody. The site includes articles and resources on shared parenting.

Stepfamily Association of America

www.saafamilies.org

Support organization for stepfamilies and blended families. The site includes featured articles, book reviews, and some interesting facts and statistics.

Stepfamily Network

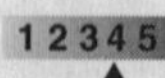

www.stepfamily.net

Includes some useful links on how to get support along with a collection of discussion forums to encourage online sharing of information and insights. Find info on the volunteer network and get answers to your questions at this site.

The Stepfamily Zone

www.stepfamily.asn.au

This excellent and up-to-date site from Australia focuses on all aspects of stepparenting and the blended family. The front page contains several current articles on stepfamilies, such as how to fix a broken stepfamily and stories about real families who are facing the challenges of adjusting to a new life. This site also provides links to books, book reviews, courses, support groups, discussion forums, and other relevant resources on the Web.

Stepparent Adoption

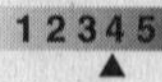

step-parent.adoption.com

Stepparenting adoption, the most common form of adoption, occurs when "a stepparent assumes financial and legal responsibility for his/her spouse's child(ren), and the noncustodial parent is released from all parenting responsibilities." Here, you can learn more about stepparent adoption and how to proceed legally.

PARKS

American Park Network

www.americanparknetwork.com

Consult maps and look at the scenery for any of America's national parks. Historical and educational notes are included for each park. Participate in online discussions about camping and exploring these national resources.

California State Parks

12345

www.parks.ca.gov

California State Parks "contains the largest and most diverse natural and cultural heritage holdings of any state agency in the nation, including underwater preserves, reserves, and parks; redwood, rhododendron, and wildlife reserves; state beaches, recreation areas, wilderness areas, and reservoirs; state historic parks, historic homes, Spanish era adobe buildings, including museums, visitor centers, cultural reserves, and preserves; as well as lighthouses, ghost towns, waterslides, conference centers, and off-highway vehicle parks." Click Find a Park to search for a specific park or browse the database of parks.

Campgrounds by City

www.campgrounds-by-city.com

Huge, searchable directory of campgrounds and state parks. You can search the directory by state or by type of park, look up summer camps for kids, access a checklist of camping supplies, or shop online for camp gear.

Canyonlands

12345

www.canyonlands-utah.com

Utah's largest national park is profiled at this site. You'll find accommodations, various area destinations, tours, campgrounds, and travel resources via the site.

Colorado State Parks and Outdoor Recreation

12345

parks.state.co.us

Information on parks in Colorado, including recreational activities and fees. This site also provides information on seasonal jobs, a park finder, trail maps, news, and online activities for kids.

Death Valley National Park

12345

www.desertusa.com/dv/du_dvpmain.html

Visitors to this website will find a virtual visitor's center for Nevada's Death Valley National Park. Information on weather, temperature, activities, accommodations, and fees is included, as are maps and a guide to desert wildlife. You can also communicate with others at the Desert Talk message board and mailbag. Be sure to visit the Trading Post for some shopping fun!

Discover Banff

12345

www.discoverbanff.com

A comprehensive guide to travel in Banff, Canada, is available at this site. It offers information on Banff and Jasper Parks, dining, tours, accommodations, equipment rentals, seasonal activities, and links to related sites.

Fodor's National Parks

www.fodors.com/parks

Information on lodging, camping, and dining facilities at America's national parks from Fodor's, featuring maps and photos of each park.

Glacier National Park

www.nps.gov/glac

This site describes Glacier National Park, which covers more than one million acres of forests, lakes, meadows, and high rocky peaks in the northwest part of Montana. You'll learn that 70 species of mammals and 260 species of birds contribute to the spectacular diversity of life preserved in the park. You can select any state on this site to locate a national park of your choice.

GORP: U.S. National Parks and Reserves

gorp.away.com/gorp/resource/us_national_park/main.htm

Features a state-by-state list of national parks in the United States. Users can click on a park to obtain specific information on visitor centers and facilities such as hiking, climbing, and camping. Free registration is required before you can view the pages.

GORP: Wilderness Area List

gorp.away.com/gorp/resource/US_Wilderness_Area/main.htm

Tourist information and tips about U.S. national forests and wildlife refuges. Free registration is required before you can view the pages.

Grand Canyon Official Tourism Page

www.thecanyon.com

This site provides all the tourism information you'll need when visiting Grand Canyon National Park. You'll get all the standard information on what to do and where to go, stay, eat, and shop. Plus, read news bits, get weather info, see photographs, read anecdotes, and learn all about the local area. A great resource. The site also offers a great shopping mall where you can buy everything from wonderful jewelry to Native American art, and you can shop online as well as at the park.

Harper's Ferry NHP Virtual Visitor Center

www.nps.gov/hafe/home.htm

The John Brown–led insurrection against slavery, in Harper's Ferry in 1859, later spawned the National Park Service's Harper's Ferry (West Virginia) Virtual Visitor Center, which is located at the confluence of the Potomac and Shenandoah rivers. These pages help you learn about or plan a trip to the area, plus give you insightful lessons on a part of our national heritage.

L.L. Bean's Park Search

www.llbean.com/parksearch

A park-search service covering 1,500 U.S. national and state parks, forests, wildlife refuges, and other public recreation lands. You can search by park name, activity, or state. A handy site with volumes of information and many photos.

Maps of United States National Parks and Monuments

www.lib.utexas.edu/maps/national_parks.html

The University of Texas at Austin has put its map collection online. Maps are listed alphabetically or by park region. The site also contains maps of national historic and military parks, memorials, and battlefields.

Mesa Verde National Park

www.mesaverde.org

This site provides a wealth of information on the Mesa Verde National Park in Colorado, delves into the archaeology of the ancestral Puebloans, and covers the ancient—as well as the modern—culture of the area. Check out the electronic bookstore, which sells park-related materials.

A B C D E F G H I J K L M N O P Q R S T U V W X Y Z

Mount Rainier National Park

12345

www.mount.rainier.national-park.com

This unofficial guide to Mount Rainier National Park features information on the park's history, visitor services, trails, and more.

National Parks Conservation Society

12345

www.npca.org

The National Parks Conservation Society is dedicated to preserving the U.S. National Park System now and for all future generations. From this site, you can choose to explore the parks, learn more about wildlife preservation, check out the coastal areas and marine life, visit Alaska, learn about cultural diversity across the nation, and find out what you can do to help conserve these valuable natural resources.

National Parks and Wildlife Service

12345

www.nationalparks.nsw.gov.au

The National Parks and Wildlife Service is a park service and conservation organization in New South Wales, Australia. Here, you can check out the parks in New South Wales, explore their cultural heritage, explore nature and conservation topics, and find out how the Australian government is working to preserve its parks and wildlife. Site also features 360-degree panorama views of selected parks.

New Mexico State Parks

12345

www.emnrd.state.nm.us/nmparks

The New Mexico State Parks site contains information on and a detailed map of each park, as well as month-by-month listings of park events, fees, and regulations for park and boating use.

Northwest Trek

12345

www.nwtrek.org

This wildlife park is located in Tacoma, Washington; its site contains a virtual tour of the park, news on current special events, an animal trivia quiz, general park information, and information for teachers and group leaders.

Olympic National Park

12345

www.northolympic.com/onp

This site provides dozens of links to information on Olympic National Park in the Pacific Northwest, which has 4,000,000 visitors annually. Also included is a link to a virtual tour of the park and special content for kids. All the information you need in one spot.

Best PARKNET: The National Park Service Place

12345

www.nps.gov

A mandatory stop for anyone interested in our national parks. This is the National Park Service's home page, a searchable site that links to NPS sites for all the parks. Besides finding data on any individual park, you can read special travel features and learn about such topics as natural resources in the parks and America's histories and cultures—plus visit the Park Store. If you're planning a nature vacation, be sure you check out this Best of the Best site.

Petrified Forest National Park

12345

www.nps.gov/pefo

The Petrified Forest National Park protects one of the largest, most spectacular tracts of petrified wood in the nation. This site gives a history of the area as well as other useful information.

Saguaro National Park

12345

www.saguaro.national-park.com

If you're planning a trip to Tucson, Arizona, consider including the Saguaro National Park on your itinerary, and if you do decide to visit the park, visit this site first to access information about activities, fees, and camping; trail maps; biking trails; self-guided field trips; and much more. Site design is second rate compared to other sites in this category, but the content is solid.

A B C D E F G H I J K L M N O P Q R S T U V W X Y Z

A B C D E F G H I J K L M N O P Q R S T U V W X Y Z

South Carolina State Parks

12345 RSS

http://www.southcarolinaparks.com/park-finder/park_locator.aspx

Listing of state parks in South Carolina with photos, descriptions, and recreational information on each.

Texas State Parks

12345

www.tpwd.state.tx.us/park/parks.htm

This page lists Texas' state parks and historic sites, providing information about accommodations, activities, and regulations in each park.

U.S. National Parks

12345

www.us-national-parks.net

List of national parks in the United States with photos and information on each, including the address; camping, hiking, and lodging guides; park details; maps; and skiing, rafting, and visitors' guides. This main site and each of the park sites it points to aren't the most impressive in terms of design, but the coverage is fairly extensive.

Yellowstone Net

12345

www.yellowstone.net

Site recommended by *USA Today* and others. Visit Yellowstone Net for all kinds of information on the park, news, photos, specialty stores, reservations, related links, and access to the Yellowstone Net community. Check it out.

Yosemite Park

12345

www.yosemitepark.com

Delaware North Companies, a hospitality provider who has a contract with the national park system, created and maintains this site to introduce tourists to the various sites and amenities that Yosemite National Park has to offer. This appealing site presents a park overview, information about Yosemite lodging, park activities, dining and shopping, special events, gifts and memories, special offers, news releases, and search/index categories for you to explore.

PEDIATRICS

Best American Academy of Pediatrics

12345

www.aap.org

Established primarily for pediatricians seeking to provide the best care for their patients, the AAP site provides research papers; free access to Medline, the medical database; and information on professional opportunities. Parents will find the section on You and Your Family particularly useful; it's packed with safety information, product recalls, parenting guidelines, and tips to help make your parenting experience more fulfilling and successful.

American Board of Pediatrics

12345

www.abp.org

The American Board of Pediatrics is dedicated to establishing high standards for pediatricians and evaluating pediatricians who apply for certification. At this site, pediatricians and medical students can learn more about the board, residency training, and the certification process. Parents can use the search tool to find a certified pediatrician by location. The site also provides links to other resources.

American Pediatric Society/Society for Pediatric Research

12345

www.aps-spr.org

At this site, you can find information about both the American Pediatric Society and the Society for Pediatric Research. This site contains links to abstracts, awards, newsletters, the Pediatric Research Foundation, announcements and positions, publications, programs and grants, student research programs, and other resources. If you're a pediatrician, you will definitely want to visit this site, but there's not much here for parents or caregivers.

Canadian Pediatric Society

12345

www.cps.ca/english/index.htm

This site, designed for pediatricians and others who are involved with child healthcare, provides information about the Canadian Pediatric Society, publications and other resources, professional development, programs, and advocacy. The Media Centre features a host of media resources pediatricians can use in their practice to help educate parents and patients.

Children with Diabetes

12345

www.childrenwithdiabetes.com/index_cwd.htm

Anyone who has diabetes or who has a child with diabetes needs to visit this site. It is packed with information and has real-time chatrooms. This site strives to be the online community for kids, families, and adults with diabetes.

Contemporary Pediatrics

12345

www.contemporarypediatrics.com

Contemporary Pediatrics is a magazine that "offers pediatric health providers continuing education on the prevention, diagnosis, and management of illness and behavior problems in infants, children, and adolescents through review articles that address practical clinical concerns. One article each month carries CME credit." Visit this site to sample articles from the current edition, explore the site's mysteries and quandaries, pick up a few clinical tips, ask a featured expert, and more.

Dr. Greene's HouseCalls

www.drgreene.com

Get helpful hints from this pediatrician. Need some advice from a kid pro? Submit a question online, search through topics relating to developmental stages, or just read up on Dr. Greene's featured articles. This site is a friendly resource for any parent.

GeneralPediatrics.com

generalpediatrics.com

Designed to be a starting point for general pediatrics information on the Web. Find resources suitable for patients and physicians.

I Am Your Child

www.iamyourchild.org

Designed to give information about children from before birth through three years of age, this quality site has much to offer parents of young children. The site is tuned in to the issues of child development in this age group and offers information from "The Experts."

India Parenting

www.indiaparenting.com

Comprehensive healthcare guide for parents and pediatricians. Explains common childhood diseases and treatments, provides home remedies and commonsense treatments, and provides guidelines on nutrition and prescription medications. The preponderance of pop-up ads at this site is annoying.

Johns Hopkins Children's Center

www.hopkinschildrens.org

Johns Hopkins Children's Center is one of the premier pediatric health centers in the world. Here, you can find a specialist, request an appointment, learn everything you need to know about your visit from A to Z, search for a center that's nearest you, and look up childhood medical conditions to find out which division of the center treats it.

KidSource Online

www.kidsource.com

Good collection of articles and other resources relating to child rearing and healthcare. Covers everything from summer planning and homework helpers to health and safety issues. Some book reviews that might interest kids.

La Leche League International

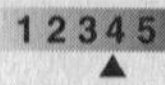

www.lalecheleague.org

Home to the international, nonprofit, nonsectarian organization that promotes the health benefits of breastfeeding and provides lactation support for women who want to breastfeed. The site also provides healthcare professionals with continuing education opportunities and the latest research on lactation management. Find information about local chapters of La Leche League, too.

MedlinePlus Doctor and Dentist Directories

www.nlm.nih.gov/medlineplus/directories.html

Enables you to locate dentists, physicians, healthcare providers, and hospitals in your area based on your specific healthcare needs.

Medscape: Pediatrics

www.medscape.com/pediatricshome

Medscape, part of WebMD, provides medical information and educational resources for physicians and the general public. Its Pediatrics Home Page focuses on specific issues and conditions that pediatricians must deal with in their practices and health concerns that parents may have concerning their children.

A B C D E F G H I J K L M N O P Q R S T U V W X Y Z

National Childhood Cancer Foundation

12345

www.curesearch.org

This site gives details of the programs and activities of this organization, which supports pediatric cancer treatment and research projects.

Pediatric Infectious Disease Journal

12345

www.pidj.com

This journal, a publication of Lippincott Williams & Wilkins, focuses on infectious diseases in children. Professionals can visit this site to subscribe to the journal, access abstracts and articles, and even submit articles for publication.

Related Sites

www.pids.org

www.espid.org

Pediatrics in Review

12345 RSS

pedsinreview.aapjournals.org

Pediatrics in Review provides continuing education articles and resources for pediatricians. By subscribing, pediatricians can gain full access to the journal, which includes special features, such as Back to Basics (refresher courses), Consultation with the Specialist (specialists' perspectives on a range of topics), What's New (breakthroughs), and Index of Suspicion (to test diagnostic skills).

PETS

AnimalNetwork

12345

www.animalnetwork.com

Looking for a magazine about your favorite pet? Then check out this site. Here, you'll find magazines for every pet imaginable, from dogs and cats to fish and reptiles. You can even find magazines about horses. Free trial subscriptions available if you subscribe online.

Breederlink.com

12345

www.breederlink.com

Breederlink.com is "a comprehensive pet search index where you can search our yellow pages for all of your pet needs." Site provides quick access to pet related links organized in categories including Pet Breeders, Pet Services, Pet Supplies, and Pet Products. You can browse the collection of links or search for a specific item or animal.

PAWS: Pets Are Wonderful Support

12345

www.pawssf.org

PAWS is a nonprofit organization that explores and promotes the benefits of dogs, cats, and other pets in improving the quality of life for those with AIDS and other diseases. The Education area provides information on the potential benefits and risks of pet ownership. Other areas include Donate, Volunteer, Calendar, and Shop.

Pets4You

12345

www.pets4you.com

This site functions as a directory of breeders and shelters where you can find pets for purchase or adoption. Here, you can view pictures of puppies, dogs, kittens, cats, birds, reptiles, and other exotic breeds. Site also provides a searchable listing of trainers, supplies, and services.

Travel Pets

12345

www.travelpets.com

If you like to hop in the car (or on a plane) with your pet and travel around, you might find that after you reach your destination, you can't find a hotel or motel that will accept your pet. At Travel Pets, you can search specifically for places in the United States and Canada that accommodate pets. This site also features travel tips and a traveler's checklist. When you return from your trip, consider revisiting the site to post photos of your pet in transit.

The Virtual Pet Cemetery

12345

www.mycemetery.com/pet/index.html

All pet owners must eventually deal with the loss of a pet. The Virtual Pet Cemetery offers a place to give your pet a virtual burial and to say your goodbyes. This site has numerous touching accounts of people and the pets they lost. The site has won many awards.

Yahoo! Pets

12345

pets.yahoo.com

Yahoo! Pets focuses on dogs and cats but offers information and resources on other pets, too. Dog lovers will find plenty of articles about selecting the right breed, caring for your dog, and properly training your dog. Cat owners will find answers to their questions about behavior issues, nutrition, and helping a new cat adjust to a new home. Site also offers information about adopting animals.

CATS (SEE CATS)

DOGS (SEE DOGS)

FISH (SEE FISH/ AQUARIUMS)

EXOTIC

Bella Online: Exotic Pets Site

www.bellaonline.com/site/exoticpets

Why *Bella*, a magazine for women, would have an entire area set aside for information about exotic pets is beyond us, but they do, and it offers up some pretty good articles and a collection of links to other useful sites.

Dr. Jungle's Animal World

www.animal-world.com

Dr. Jungle's Animal World introduces visitors to all sorts of exotic pets, including freshwater and saltwater fish, reef fish, birds, small mammals, and reptiles. Here, you can learn about specific animals and environments, find out which animals make good pets and which ones don't, get detailed information on how to care for a wide variety of pets, and gather a collection of insightful tips.

Exotic Pet Co

1 2 3 4 5

exoticpetco.com

Cheryl Morgan founded Exotic Pet Co to help "independent breeders, zoos, and individual pet lovers from all over the globe find the exotics for which they are searching." Site features several tabs to help you narrow your search: Large Mammals, Small Mammals, Primates, Birds/Reptiles, Hoof Stock, and Available Animals. If you're looking for a specific animal, Cheryl can help you track it down.

Best Exotic Pet Vet

1 2 3 4 5

www.exoticpetvet.net

Created and maintained by exotic pet veterinarian Margaret A. Wissman, D.V.M., and Bill Parsons, M.S., this site is offered as a gift to the pet community and features an extensive collection of information and tips on properly caring for exotic animals, including birds, primates, reptiles, and other small animals. You can also find guidance at this site for helping select good exotic pets for children. Veterinarians can also visit the site to obtain expert advice from a top exotic pet vet. Because of the breadth and depth of information offered at this site, it's well deserving of our Best of the Best designation in the Exotic Pets category.

S&S Exotic Animals, Inc.

1 2 3 4 5

www.sandsexoticanimals.com

Exotic animal store in Huston that carries a well-stocked inventory of exotic pets, including birds, mammals, lizards, snakes, and turtles. You can also find all the cages, food, and other supplies and accessories you need to care for your exotic pet along with care sheets that provide basic instructions.

PET CARE

American Animal Hospital Association (AAHA)

1 2 3 4 5

www.healthypet.com

AAHA offers pet care tips, answers to FAQs on care and illnesses, and a library of articles on topics from behavior to nutrition. At first glance, the site looks a little sparse, but click on the Pet Care Library link, and you'll see links to all sorts of tutorials and articles on pet care and training. Click the Coloring link to view printable posters for kids to color. Check the FAQs for answers to common questions or subscribe to the Pet Planet newsletter.

American Pet Association

12345

www.apapets.org

The American Pet Association is dedicated to promoting responsible pet ownership through action, services, and education. You will find lots of useful information here to help you assist your pet in leading a more peaceful, safe, and enjoyable coexistence with you. Information here is interesting, informative, and useful for pet owners of all types.

Animal Health Information

12345

www.avma.org/careforanimals/animatedjourneys/pethealth/pethealth.asp

Get info on dental care, pet population control, and vaccinations. Learn how to deal with diseases such as heart disease, heartworm disease, cancer, Lyme disease, parasites, toxoplasmosis, and rabies.

The AVMA (American Veterinary Medical Association) Network

12345

www.avma.org

The American Veterinary Medical Association answers questions on pet care, selection, and loss, and how your veterinarian helps you enjoy your pet. The Kids' Korner includes pictures you can print out for your kids to color. Each picture includes an activity or advice on feeding, training, or basic care. This site is extremely attractive, well organized, and offers a wealth of information.

> **Tip:** Pet owners can go to the main AVMA page and then scroll down for links to "public resources" or go directly to the AVMA Care for Pets site at www.avma.org/care4pets.

CyberPet

12345

www.cyberpet.com

Directory to resources on the Web for cat and dog owners and breeders, including healthcare, selection and training articles, products, and services. Pet fanciers, exhibitors, owners, and breeders will find something here.

DoctorDog.com: Cat and Dog Supplies and Pet Health Care

12345

www.doctordog.com

Huge collection of dog and cat healthcare and pet supplies, including leashes, toys, shampoos, rug cleaners, and more, plus some resources on general healthcare issues.

The Humane Society of the United States: Pet Care

12345

www.hsus.org/pets/pet_care

The Humane Society of the United States offers dozens of articles on a wide range of pet care topics. Here, you can also find additional information on adopting pets, becoming an activist to promote the humane treatment of all animals, and donate online to help the organization protect animals more effectively.

NetPets

12345

www.netpets.com

A resource for dog, cat, horse, fish, and bird owners. The site includes information about pet health and nutrition, and offers an events calendar, a library of articles, and a list of animal shelters by state.

Pet Care and Wildlife Information

12345

www.klsnet.com

This reference provides information on caring for all sorts of pets, including exotic fish, reptiles, and amphibians. Also provides information about caring for dogs, cats, and other furry creatures.

ThePetCenter.com

12345

www.thepetcenter.com

Information about general healthcare issues relating primarily to dogs and cats. Some specific information about various diseases and treatments and what you can expect if your pet must undergo surgery. Excellent tutorials on how to attract natural wildlife to your back yard. Animal lovers of all types should check out this site. Links to other sites to purchase pet supplies.

Pet Columns from University of Illinois College of Veterinary Medicine (CVM)

1 2 3 4 5

www.cvm.uiuc.edu/petcolumns

Search by keyword or by most recent to least recent articles for authoritative articles on pet care, common problems, and their management. Also, the site provides links to the University of Illinois CVM and the Continuing Education Public Extension Service.

PetEducation.com

1 2 3 4 5

www.peteducation.com

This site was created by vets to provide information on caring for your pet, so you'll find tons of articles to scan. There are also pet services directories, a veterinary dictionary, answers to frequently asked questions, quizzes, and the latest pet news. Tabbed navigation makes it easy to focus on the information you need for the type of pet you have.

Pet Plan Insurance

1 2 3 4 5

www.petplan.com

Pet Plan Insurance, a Canadian company, offers health insurance policies for your cat and dog to protect them in the event of accident, illness, or disease. Having pet insurance is becoming increasingly common, because people don't want to have to choose between saving their beloved pet or putting it down because they can't afford the medical price tag.

Related Site

www.petinsurance.com/

PetNet

1 2 3 4 5

www.petnet.com.au

Australia's Petcare and Advisory Service has information for pet lovers everywhere, including Selectapet, plus a guide to local services. By using Selectapet, you can be sure that you are ready to get a pet and find which breeds are best suited to your lifestyle, budget, and temperament. Site also features valuable information on properly caring for your pet.

PetPlace.com

1 2 3 4 5 RSS

www.petplace.com

Whether your pet is well or sick, you'll find this site a handy reference. Wellness tips will help keep your pet healthy, and the illness information will assist in assessing what might be wrong when Fido starts acting funny. You can also store your pet's medical information at the site for easy access in a central spot. This site features more than 5,000 veterinarian-approved articles on pet selection, care, and training.

Pets Need Dental Care, Too

1 2 3 4 5

www.petdental.com

This site makes you aware of potential problems with your pets caused by dental situations, just as with humans. Dental problems can cause serious health problems in addition to painful tooth loss or gum disease. If your pet is acting strangely or seems to be ill for no apparent reason, you should check out this site. Special area for kids includes the animated Pete & Gigi show, a coloring book, and a trivia quiz.

PetSage–Pet Care Products

1 2 3 4 5

www.petsage.com

PetSage offers "holistic and healthier choices for your companion animals, from diet—the foundation of health—to complementary and alternative therapies." PetSage introduces you to holistic products and treatments that can help improve your pet's overall health and well-being. The site offers a lot of information about raising and caring for pets. Check out the Q&A area for common questions from pet owners answered by experts.

Veterinary Oncology

12345

www.vetmed.lsu.edu/oncology

This veterinary hospital of Louisiana State University has information for owners about the diagnosis and treatment of cancer in animals.

VeterinaryPartner.com

12345

www.veterinarypartner.com

The most effective way to properly care for your pet is to team up with your veterinarian. By properly caring for your pet at home and taking your pet to see your veterinarian for vaccinations and regular checkups, you can keep your pet healthy and happy and extend its life. At this site, information and assistance is two steps away—click a species on the left and then click the tab for the desired information: Behavior, Health, Diseases, or Drugs. Or, you can choose to search for a specific topic. Site offers information on the care of dogs, cats, reptiles, and small mammals. Unfortunately, when we visited, the site had no information about the care of birds.

PET SUPPLIES

Cardinal Pet Products

12345

www.cardinalpet.com

Try tea-tree spray for flea-bite dermatitis, hot spots, and dry skin irritation, or check out the oatmeal shampoo for dry, itchy skin and skin irritations. Or maybe your pet just needs the herbal shampoo for cleaning and deodorizing. The cedar shampoo and cedar spray kill infestations of insects (these are natural, nontoxic alternatives to chemical insecticides). Try the herbal collar to repel insects. A glossary of herbs and botanicals is included. These products are not sold online, but you can look at a list of local outlets that sell them.

Doctors Foster and Smith

12345

www.petwarehouse.com

A mail-order catalog company that specializes in aquatic, bird, dog, cat, reptile, small animal, and pond products at factory direct prices. Pet Warehouse also includes a pharmacy where you can purchase prescription medications at a discount.

Nature's Pet Marketplace

12345

www.naturespet.com

Offers natural and holistic products. This site includes homeopathic remedies, dog and cat food, vitamin and herbal supplements, grooming and skin care products, and flea and tick remedies. Also offers a natural line of bird food and supplements. The site includes descriptions and explanations of holistic products as well as other information.

Pet Experts, Naturally!

12345

www.pet-experts.com

About pets, animals, wholesale, natural pet products, and discount animal supplies. Dog, cat, bird, fish, reptile, iguana, and even ferret supplies can be found here.

Pet Market

12345

www.petmarket.com

Search for discount pet supplies and learn about the most popular products for your dog, cat, bird, or other friend. Pet Market promises competitive prices, a wide selection, and excellent service.

PETCO

12345

www.petco.com

Read articles about dog care, such as how to safely trim your pooch's nails. Learn whether putting your pet in a kennel is harmful and search for pet services and products all at this one place. PETCO carries a huge inventory of a wide variety of pet products for dogs, cats, fish, reptiles, birds, and other small animals and includes a link you can click to obtain adoption information. Click the Pet Care link to obtain pet care guides and articles.

PetFoodDirect.com

12345

www.petfooddirect.com/store

Order pet foods and accessories online and have them shipped to your doorstep. Food, health products, toys, and treats are all found here. Site features a selection of more than 11,000 pet products.

PetSmart

12345

www.petsmart.com

Huge online pet store and pet information kiosk. Whether you own a dog, cat, bird, fish, reptile, or rodent, you can find all the supplies and accessories you need right here. Features basic care instructions, feeding calculators, information on illnesses and treatments, instructions on choosing the right animal for you, and much more.

ThatPetPlace.com

12345

www.thatpetplace.com

This pet supply superstore carries everything for almost every pet imaginable at great prices. Features accessories for dogs and cats, fish, birds, reptiles, and other small creatures. Includes a few articles on caring for and training pets. Easy to navigate.

Wyld's Wingdom, Inc.

12345

www.wingdom.com

Specializes in exotic pets and pet bird products. Offers bird food, bird toys, and bird-related products. Wyld's doesn't sell directly to the public, but these products may be at your local pet store.

Related Sites

www.petsafe.net

www.pet-expo.com/birdbird.htm

www.coolpetstuff.com

A B C D E F G H I J K L M N O Q R S T U V W X Y Z

PHILOSOPHY

Academic Info: Philosophy

www.academicinfo.net/phil.html

An extensive directory of sites on the study of philosophy. Includes sections on specific philosophical topics and general reference sources.

American Philosophical Organization

www.apaonline.org/apa

If you're a philosopher, you should definitely visit this site to obtain information on how to become a member of this professional organization. When you're a member, you gain full access to the site, including access to job postings; the APA Newsletters; and Grants, Fellowships, and Prizes.

Dharma the Cat

12345

www.dharmathecat.com

Dharma the Cat blends humor and spirituality into a cartoon that takes visitors "on the rocky path to nirvana with a Buddhist cat, a novice monk and a mouse hell-bent on cheese." Here, you get to dabble in Eastern philosophy and Buddhism; read articles and anecdotes about coping with life; and remain engaged and entertained while stimulating your brain cells with thought-provoking insights and ideas.

Ephilosopher

www.ephilosopher.com

Ephilosopher is "a web community dedicated to philosophical thinking," where you can submit articles and news stories, post links, use the philosophy forums chat, subscribe to blogs, and more." Site features news, announcements, jobs, discussion forums, links to other resources, humor, and games.

EpistemeLinks.com: Philosophy Resources on the Internet

12345

www.epistemelinks.com

Site features thousands of sorted links to philosophy-related sites. Links are divided into categories including philosophers, philosophy texts, publications, newsgroups, and job postings. Shop for books via a link to Amazon.com. Excellent starting point for any philosophical research project.

Internet Encyclopedia of Philosophy

12345

www.utm.edu/research/iep

Excellent alphabetic listing of philosophers and philosophical problems, concepts, and theories. Click a letter to get started and then follow the trail of links to the desired philosopher, problem, concept, or theory. Excellent place to do research, particularly for beginning students of philosophy.

Nietzsche Page at Stanford

12345

plato.stanford.edu/entries/nietzsche

Excellent overview of Friedrich Nietzsche's life, publications, and ideas. Features a substantial bibliography plus links to other useful Nietzsche sites. Part of Stanford's Encyclopedia of Philosophy.

No Dogs or Philosophers Allowed

www.nodogs.org

The brainchild of Milk Bottle Productions, No Dogs or Philosophers Allowed is "a live call-in show which brings together academics, activists, and lay thinkers to discuss the pressing issues raised by the human condition." Here, you can learn more about the show, view the weekly video, take the No Dogs Quiz, and engage in some mindful pleasures.

The Philosophical Gourmet Report

12345

www.philosophicalgourmet.com

Contains the national rankings of graduate schools of analytic philosophy in the United States. Also includes foreign rankings. Highly detailed. Great resource for helping philosophy grads track down the best grad schools in their field.

Philosophy Around the Web

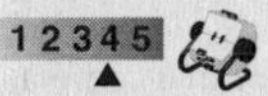

users.ox.ac.uk/~worc0337/phil_index.html

Striving to be a central gateway to philosophy information on the Web, users can learn the basics of philosophy, find useful links, check out sites by topic, scan educational institution and individual web pages, and much more.

Philosophy Now

12345

www.philosophynow.org

This online version of *Philosophy Now* features articles on various philosophical topics and problems, commentary, a letter column called "Dear Socrates," introductions to various periods in philosophical thought, and much more. This is one of the more rationally organized sites in the philosophy category, and reveals the many practical applications of and current issues influenced by the pursuit of philosophical understanding.

Plato's Dialogues

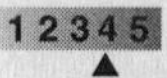

plato-dialogues.org

Brief biography of Plato's life, including his works, plus English translations of Plato's dialogues, including *The Crito, The Phaedo, The Phaedrus, The Symposium*, and *The Republic*.

PSYCHE

12345

psyche.cs.monash.edu.au

PSYCHE is an interdisciplinary journal of research and consciousness. The site provides direct access to *PSYCHE*'s archives. Also contains a FAQs area associated with the journal.

Questia: Philosophy

12345

www.questia.com/library/philosophy

Questia, the "World's Largest Online Library," offers a clickable table of contents that covers all areas of philosophy, including Western and Eastern thought, and provides links to the various eras covering everything from ancient philosophy to 20th century and contemporary thought. Click Philosophers to obtain links to pages on the most influential philosophers. When you find the content you're looking for, you usually gain access to an electronic version of a full-length book on the topic.

Best The Radical Academy

radicalacademy.com

The Radical Academy is an ongoing discussion of philosophy, politics, and the human condition. Site offers a huge collection of information and articles that covers the entire history of philosophy and highlights the philosophers who've had the greatest influence. Here, you can find Adventures in Philosophy (a history of philosophy and the doctrines of the major philosophers), the Classic Philosophers Series (history by era and the most influential philosophers in each era), a glossary of philosophical terms, a list of philosophical quotations, and much more.

Stanford Encyclopedia of Philosophy

plato.stanford.edu

Features an indexed dynamic encyclopedia in which each entry is maintained and kept up-to-date by an expert or group of experts in the field of philosophy. This is a work in progress, and many of the philosophers and concepts listed in the comprehensive index are not covered in the encyclopedia. However, the coverage that is provided is exceptional.

Theosophical Society

12345

www.theosociety.org

The society was founded in 1875 in an effort to promote the expressed awareness of the oneness of life. This site links to descriptions of foundational, esoteric texts by Blavatsky and others. Acts as a guide for personal exploration of truth.

A B C D E F G H I J K L M N O Q R S T U V W X Y Z

PHOTOGRAPHY

CAMERAS

Abe's of Maine

1 2 3 4 5

www.abesofmaine.com

Promising prices of up to 50 percent off retail, Abe's specializes in selling camera equipment and supplies online from the store in Brooklyn, New York.

Ace Index

1 2 3 4 5

www.acecam.com

Use the Ace index to find manufacturer sites, dealer sites, used equipment sites, photo labs, and much more.

AGFA Digital Cameras

1 2 3 4 5

www.agfa.com

Which digital camera is right for you? Check out AGFA's product line. This site has a search feature that allows you to search for information, and the company offers commercial services such as those offered to the newspaper industry.

Beach Photo & Video

1 2 3 4 5

beachphoto.com

Whether you need a photo restored or are in the market for a used camera, Beach Photo is likely to provide the services you need. Buy new or used equipment here, and have film processed or printed, too.

Camera Review.com

1 2 3 4 5

www.camerareview.com

Specify the features you're looking for in a camera, and the database will provide a list of camera models that meet your criteria. You can also look at the online rankings of the most popular cameras, according to people who own and use them. Then compare features of two or more cameras side by side to help in making your purchase decision.

CameraWorld

1 2 3 4 5

www.cameraworld.com

This enormous online camera warehouse is stocked with everything a novice or expert photographer needs: digital cameras, film cameras, a wide variety of camcorders, lenses, film, light meters, books, and more.

Complete Guide to Digital Cameras and Digital Photography

1 2 3 4 5

www.shortcourses.com

A free online course on digital photography. A gallery of images taken with a digital camera is included. This is an information-packed site!

Digital Camera Imaging Resource Page

1 2 3 4 5 RSS

www.imaging-resource.com

Digital cameras, features, specs, reviews, and sample images for most brands and models are available at this site.

Digital Camera News

12345

www.steves-digicams.com/diginews.html

A great overview of the latest digital camera products. The site also includes information on related software and updates. It includes the Picture of the Day, submitted by viewers. The site comes from Steve's Digicams.

Digital Camera Resource Page

www.dcresource.com

The Digital Camera Resource page posts current information and reviews. This is a popular site for digital camera buffs, current owners, and potential owners. It is well designed and easy to navigate. In the site's own words, "The Digital Camera Resource Page, founded in 1997, is designed to be an unofficial resource for current or future owners of digital cameras. It is aimed more towards the consumer end, rather than the high end." This site does not sell anything or promote anything but rather offers current information on digital cameras. Site also features a good directory of links to major camera manufacturer websites.

Digital Photography Review

www.dpreview.com

A complete digital camera resource that carries information about hundreds of digital cameras and accessories. Includes product news, galleries, forums, a buying guide, and a glossary.

EarthCam

www.earthcam.com

Want to watch the world go by while sitting at your computer? Then tune in to these webcams positioned at major metropolitan areas around the world: New York, Chicago, Las Vegas, Moscow, and Quito, to name a few. You can also poke around people's kitchens and offices, tattoo shops, and anywhere else people choose to photograph other people and places and broadcast them on the Web.

Focus Camera & Video

12345

www.focuscamera.com

Bills itself as the #1 deep discount source for every photographic, sports optic, astronomical, and video camera item for more than 30 years. One of America's largest-stocking photo and optics dealers, with thousands of items in stock.

HowStuffWorks: How Digital Cameras Work

12345

www.howstuffworks.com/digital-camera.htm

If you're curious as to how digital cameras capture and store images, this site provides an easily understandable explanation.

Megapixel.net

12345

www.megapixel.net

Like most good photography sites, this one offers photography articles, discussion forums, product reviews, and tips and techniques for improving your skill.

PC Photo Review

12345

www.pcphotoreview.com

Digital camera site offers news, reviews, guides, tips, and forums.

Photo.net

12345

www.photo.net

Pages and pages of camera-related commentary. For example, "What Camera Should I Buy?" explores some options (view cameras, medium-formats, SLRs, and even lowly point-and-shoots are covered) and some opinions. This site contains a ton of handy tips: recommended films, ritzy frame shops, places to shop for cameras, places to send your slides for processing, and so on.

Ritz Camera

12345

www.ritzcamera.com

A network of e-commerce websites, including Ritz Camera, Wolf Camera, Photography.com, and other businesses, this site offers a huge selection of cameras and provides easy browsing. Stop by the Learning Center to learn more about various photographic products and services and then check out the special coupons and deals available at Ritz Camera.

DIGITAL PHOTOGRAPHY

Canvas on Demand

12345

www.canvasondemand.com

Canvas on Demand is a service that can transform a photograph into an oil-on-canvas work of art with more depth and definition than is possible in a photo. A little pricey, but unique.

Digital Photography Challenge

12345

www.dpchallenge.com

Join Digital Photography Challenge to pick up photography tricks and techniques, enter your photos in competitions, and challenge your knowledge of photography. Site features several photo galleries, forums where you can read and post messages, tutorials, advice, and much more. Members can even sell their prints online!

Digital Photography Tips

12345 Blog

www.macdevcenter.com/pub/a/mac/2002/10/22/digi_photo_tips.html

This page offers 10 tips for improving the quality of your digital photos along with a link for ordering the author's book.

Digital Photography Weblog

12345 Blog RSS

digitalphotography.weblogsinc.com

This site features ongoing discussions of digital cameras, equipment, accessories, and software; provides how-to instructions; offers current news related to digital photography; and includes a good collection of tips and techniques to assist visitors in improving their photographs. You'll also find plenty of sample photographs at this site, as you may have guessed.

HP Digital Photo Activity Center

12345

h10050.www1.hp.com/activitycenter/us/en

If you have a printer that's capable of photo printing, check out some of what HP has to offer in papers and other products that can help you transform your photos into creative keepsakes.

Internet Brothers: Digital Photography Tips and Techniques

12345

internetbrothers.com/phototips.htm

At this site, the Internet Brothers team up to provide you with an excellent introduction to digital photography that can smooth the transition between old film photography and cutting-edge digital technology. Here, you learn the basics, find out how to pick a camera that's right for you, get tips on how to take high-quality photos, and gather techniques for editing out imperfections.

Lexar: Digital Photography Tips

12345

www.lexar.com/dp/tips_lessons/index.html

Lexar, one of the leading manufacturers of high-quality digital cameras, offers dozens of tips and tutorials written by experienced professionals to help you take the best digital photos and edit and enhance them to make them even better. Articles cover a wide variety of topics, from basic photography and memory card management to taking high-quality shots under water. Whether you're a rank beginner or a professional who's trying to master a new technique, this site can help guide you to success.

Photographysites.com

www.photographysites.com

A thematic photography directory designed to "promote the exchange of traffic among similar types of online photo galleries." Here, you'll find a collection of sites grouped into several categories, including landscape, nature, wildlife, fine art, travel, nude, documentary, and digital stock. Site enables photographers to post their work at one site and have their work automatically linked to many other photography websites.

ONLINE SHARING

Club Photo

1 2 3 4 5

www.clubphoto.com

Club Photo can transform film into digital images or work directly with the digital image files stored on your digital camera. Simply send in your film or upload the files, use Club Photo's software to edit and enhance the photos, and then share them online with friends and family or order prints, cards, calendars, mugs, T-shirts, and other items right online. This site introduces you to the process and makes it easy to upload and edit photos and order prints and other products.

Kodakgallery.com

1 2 3 4 5

www.kodakgallery.com

With Kodakgallery.com, Kodak's online photo sharing and print service, you can send in a roll of film or upload digital photos from a digital camera to the service. The site allows you to share your photos with others by creating an online photo album and/or order prints, greeting cards, and other items. Kodak offers free software to help you upload your photos to the service, and to crop and enhance your photos before ordering prints.

PhotoWorks

1 2 3 4 5

www.photoworks.com

Another popular online digital photo processing site, PhotoWorks allows you to send in a roll of film or upload photos you have taken with your digital camera and then edit, enhance, and share photos online. If desired, you can order photo prints, greeting cards, custom calendars, and other items that display your photos. This service is great for creating keepsakes and gifts!

SmugMug

www.smugmug.com

SmugMug is a digital photo/video sharing service that enables you to share photos and video clips with friends and relatives and/or market them online. For about $40 per year, you can store an unlimited number of photos and have up to 2 gigabytes of traffic per month—that's about 20 to 30 thousand photo views per month. This site has an elegant design that is easy to navigate. For another $20 per year, you can bump up your storage, double your traffic, and add video clips. Professionals can opt for the high-end package that provides unlimited access and enables them to sell their photos online for about $150 a year.

Snapfish.com

1 2 3 4 5

www.snapfish.com

Whether you snap photos using a 35mm camera with film or a high-tech digital camera, Snapfish can develop your film for you, create a set of prints, put together an online photo album, and provide the tools you need to create professional photo albums, mugs, greeting cards, T-shirts, and other creative items. Snapfish even provides the software you need to enhance your images before you make prints!

Yahoo! Photos

12345

photos.yahoo.com

Yahoo! Photos enables you to upload an unlimited number of photos, order prints and pick them up at your local Target store within an hour of ordering, and "share photos through email, in real time using Yahoo! Messenger with Voice, or even from your mobile phone with Yahoo! Mobile." You can also have your photos transferred to calendars, photo albums, greeting cards, mugs, and other merchandise.

RESOURCES

American Museum of Photography

12345

www.photographymuseum.com

This site provides a beautifully displayed collection along with information and services for researchers and collectors. It also contains information on preservation and a newsletter.

Apogee Photo

12345

www.apogeephoto.com

Dedicated to entertaining and informing photographers of all ages, this site offers high-quality articles and columns about photography. Features basic instructions on taking pictures, techniques for novice and advanced photographers, information about digital imaging, and more. Also provides links to workshops, books, and schools that may be of interest to readers

BetterPhoto.com

12345

www.betterphoto.com/home.asp

This excellent source for novice photographers features scads of information about photography basics, plus online workshops that lead you step-by-step through the process of learning new techniques. Created and maintained by Jim Miotke, author of *Absolute Beginner's Guide to Taking Great Photos*, this site also provides a Q&A section, discussion forums, and a buyer's guide. Links to Amazon.com, where you can purchase cameras and accessories online.

Focus on Photography

12345

www.azuswebworks.com/photography

Lots of information on the processes and techniques of modern photography. A wealth of technical information is available. This site is wonderful in its simplicity because the information is easy to find. This makes it a gem for the amateur and professional alike. You'll find everything from the basics to the more complicated techniques such as lighting and composition. You'll also find a section with sample pictures, references, and an excellent FAQs section.

George Eastman House: Timeline of Photography

12345

www.eastmanhouse.org

An overview of the history of photographic images from the fifth century B.C. until the present along with some online photo galleries. Visitors are invited to post photographs of their pets. The information is presented in list style or by time periods. The site is from the George Eastman House.

Getty Images

12345

creative.gettyimages.com/photodisc

Looking for high-quality digital images for use in an upcoming marketing campaign? Then search this site by keyword to find images that may fit your needs. You can purchase more than 100,000 images on disc using secure card services.

History of Photography

12345

www.rleggat.com/photohistory

Information on some of the most significant processes used during the early days of photography, in addition to pen-portraits of many of the most important photographers of the period. Site design is a little dated, but the content is still relevant and informative.

International Center of Photography

1 2 3 4 5

www.icp.org

ICP's mission is to "present photography's vital and central place in contemporary culture, and to lead in interpretation issues central to its development." View online exhibitions and learn more about the work of this organization.

Knowledgehound

1 2 3 4 5

www.knowledgehound.com/topics/photogra.htm

Knowledgehound features links to articles and other resources on various aspects of photography, including equipment (cameras and film), technique (digital photography, aerial photography, and nature photography), and general topics (including photography primers). Site offers some excellent tips and tutorials.

KODAK: Taking Great Pictures

1 2 3 4 5

www.kodak.com/US/en/nav/takingPics.shtml

This handy guide to taking better pictures provides tips, techniques, and "problem picture remedies," for any level of photographer. Online tutorials discuss fundamentals of photography, including lighting, composition, and basic darkroom techniques. Sample photos show you how the pros do it, and a selection of reference materials is always on hand to help you with technical terminology and concepts.

Luminous Landscape

1 2 3 4 5

www.luminous-landscape.com

The Luminous Landscape is the self-proclaimed "most comprehensive site devoted to the art of landscape, nature and documentary photography using digital as well as traditional image processing techniques." It's not commercial, so you won't be inundated with ads. Instead, the site provides more than 2,000 pages of articles, tutorials, product reviews, and actual photographs. This site features excellent information from experienced photographers around the world.

Masters of Photography

1 2 3 4 5

www.masters-of-photography.com

Browse the list of famous photographers and click on someone of interest to view his or her photos and read articles on that individual's background and training.

National Geographic

1 2 3 4 5

www.nationalgeographic.com/photography/camerabag

Promoting its belief that photography is more about pictures than it is about technology and fancy equipment, this site shares some of the secrets of great photography from the masters of high-quality images—*National Geographic*'s photo engineering department. This area contains two links: one for shop talk and the other for hot photography tips.

New York Institute of Photography

1 2 3 4 5

www.nyip.com

This is the online home of the world's oldest photography school. Here, you can learn about the courses offered at NYIP, read articles on various topics, and check out reviews of the latest gear. Site also features photo contests.

Online Photography Courses

1 2 3 4 5

www.photo-seminars.com/pscampus.htm

Online courses and workshops. This site also offers one-on-one instruction—lessons on all subjects and photography on all levels. You can purchase books, videos, and other related items through the online store using secure card services.

Photo Arts

1 2 3 4 5

www.photoarts.com

View exhibitions of work by contemporary and fine art photographers; take a look at what some online galleries have to offer; and read the *PhotoArts Journal* for up-to-date news, reviews, and more beautiful photo art.

Photography Review

1 2 3 4 5 RSS

www.photographyreview.com

Learn photography skills from fellow photographers, check out product reviews of cameras by consumers and professionals, as well as other photography equipment, and then scan the online swap sheet to find good used gear. The site is "By photographers for photographers," leaning more toward an advanced audience. Content is organized into several areas: Reviews, Shop, Share, and Learn. The Learn area features buying guides, photo lessons, how-to's, and additional links.

Photolinks Database

www.photolinks.com

Searchable directory of photography-related websites. Because this site focuses on photography, it can provide a more up-to-date and comprehensive listing of photography sites than you'll find at a general search site, such as Google. Free listings for photography-related websites are available.

PhotoSecrets

www.photosecrets.com

Learn how to take and sell travel photos at this site, which offers travel photography guidebooks for sale. The tips are definitely worth a look.

PhotoSig

www.photosig.com

PhotoSig was designed by Willis Boyce to "give photographers the opportunity to display their photographs, have them evaluated and critiqued by others, and improve their photographic skills through constructive criticism." Amateur and expert photographers are welcome to post their photographs, hone their skills, and help other photographers improve their techniques.

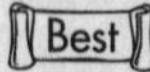

PopPhoto.com

1 2 3 4 5

www.popphoto.com

This online home of *Popular Photography & Imaging* magazine offers photography news, feature stories, tests and product reviews, photography tutorials, and plenty of high-quality images that will dazzle you. The opening page presents an excellent collection of information and resources, but you can also browse the site using the tabs near the top of the page: Popular Photography, American Photo, Tests & Reviews, Buyer's Guide, How To, Galleries, Forums, Contests, and Mentor Series.

Professional Photographers of America

www.ppa.com

Search the database of member professional photographers to find one you like. Learn about upcoming educational opportunities and events, as well as PPA member benefits. You can also pick up creative ideas for making your family photos more memorable and your wedding photos smashing.

Shutterbug Online

1 2 3 4 5

www.shutterbug.net

Shutterbug Online is the web version of one of the most popular magazines for photography enthusiasts, and it's packed with loads of free information, lessons, tips, and product reviews. The site opens with a featured news story and a product review. Running across the top of the page is a navigation bar, which provides quick access to various content areas of the site: Equipment Reviews, Techniques, Forums, Picture This, Galleries, Vote, Contests, Links, and Refresher Courses. For a more detailed listing of available content, scroll down the opening page and use the links on the right side of the page to navigate the site.

PODCASTS

Best Apple iTunes: Podcasts

www.apple.com/itunes/podcasts

From the company that created the podcast craze comes this site where you can download a copy of iTunes (for your Mac or Windows PC) and use it to subscribe to and play your favorite Podcasts and transfer Podcasts to you iPod to take them on the road. This site also features a Resources area where you can learn everything you need to know about Podcasts. The Resources area contains the following links: Overview, User Tips, Tutorials, FAQ, iPod 101, Mac Users, and Windows Users.

Digital Podcast

www.digitalpodcast.com

Directory of podcasts that enables you to browse by category, including Art, Business and Finance, Games, Books, Movies and Entertainment, Politics, and Science.

DopplerRadio

www.dopplerradio.net

Doppler is a podcast aggregator—a software tool that enables you to subscribe to podcasts, and then it automatically downloads updated podcast content to your iPod or MP3 player so you can listen to it at your convenience. Here, you can download Doppler, check out recommended podcasts, and access the list of FAQs.

FeedValidator.org

feedvalidator.org

To create your own podcast for broadcasting audio and other content on the Web, you need to create an RSS, ATOM, or other properly formatted file type that podcast aggregators can identify and process. FeedValidator enables you to validate RSS and ATOM files after you create them to ensure that they are properly formatted.

iLounge

www.ilounge.com

If you own an iPod or are thinking about purchasing one, this iLounge is a great place to go for independent information on Apple Computer's digital audio players, accessories, and related software. Site features news, articles, free music, reviews, FAQs, discussion forums, software, and a photo gallery that showcases the iPod around the world. When you want to know the latest information about the iPod and iPod accessories and software, visit this site.

IndieFeed

blindingflashes.blogs.com/indie_feed

IndieFeed enables you to download and play free music from independent artists via the IndieFeed playlists. Each recording you download is preceded by a brief introduction on the artist and where you can go to purchase the music. This provides a refreshing alternative to commercial-laden radio stations that often don't even mention the artist or group performing the music. Excellent way to discover new artists.

iPodder.org

www.ipodder.org

iPodder.org features a small program, called iPodder, that you can download and run on your computer to automatically download files, typically audio files, from various websites directly to your MP3 player so that you can listen to them later. But this site provides much more than a program that enables you to receive podcasts; it also includes a directory of more than 5,000 sites that feature podcasts, so you can find the content you want.

Juice

juicereceiver.sourceforge.net

Juice is the official home of the software of the same name, offered for free by sourceforge.net. Juice is a podcast receiver that enables you to download, store, and play podcasts on your computer to create your own custom audio programming. Here, you can learn more about Juice and podcasts in general and download the latest version for several platforms, including Windows, Linux, and Mac OS X.

NIMIQ

www.nimiq.nl

NIMIQ is a podcast aggregator for Windows. It enables you to subscribe to podcasts and download updated content from podcasts directly to your iPod or MP3 player. At this site, you can download a free copy of NIMIQ, read up on NIMIQ and various podcast topics, and access a variety of recommended podcasts.

Pod101

www.pod101.com

If you're new to the concept of podcasts, this is the site for you. It opens with a brief definition of podcasts and provides a few samples. When you're ready to start listening to podcasts, check out the step-by-step instructions on how to obtain the required software and subscribe to the desired content. If you want to create your own podcasts, this site provides instructions for that, too.

Podcast Alley

www.podcastalley.com

Podcast Alley is "the podcast lovers portal. Featuring the best podcast directory and the top 10 podcasts (as voted on by the listeners)." Site also features podcast software, a podcast forum, and additional podcasting information.

Podcast Bunker

www.podcastbunker.com

Unlike most podcast directories, Podcast Bunker opts for quality over quantity. Instead of trying to list every podcast on the Web, the folks at Podcast Bunker evaluate new podcasts for audio quality and content and post links to only the best podcasts they find. Here, you can browse those sites by category (requires you to log in). Site also features an excellent collection of tips and tools for creating your own high-quality podcast.

Podcast Central

www.podcastcentral.com

Podcast Central organizes its content in four categories. The Podcasts category functions as a directory of podcasts. Resources features the information and tools you need to create your own podcasts. Ipodders offers links to software for transferring podcasts to your MP3 player. And Contact Us provides a link to contact the Webmasters at this site. Casual users typically visit this site to scope out their favorite podcasts.

podcast.net

www.podcast.net

When you're ready to begin downloading podcasts to your iPod or MP3 player, check out podcast.net for a directory of podcasts that are currently available. This site features links to hundreds of podcasts conveniently organized by category, or you can search for a specific podcast by name. Site also features links to several podcast applications, including iPodder, Doppler, and ipodderX. If you have a website that features a podcast, you can add it to the directory.

Podcast Network

www.thepodcastnetwork.com

Podcast Network is an online directory of podcasts. This site's creators review the podcasts before listing them on the site to ensure some level of quality control.

Podcasting News

www.podcastingnews.com

Podcasting News is a podcast directory, news, and resource center all rolled into one. Here, you can check out the latest podcasting gear and technology, read articles, browse the directory, connect with other podcast aficionados in the discussion forums, and locate tools and tips for creating your own podcasts.

Podcast Tutorial

www.feedforall.com/podcasting-tutorial.htm

FeedForAll is an RSS feed-creation tool that enables you to prepare content for podcasts. This site features a tutorial that leads you step-by-step through the process of using FeedForAll. You can also download the software at this site.

Podcast Reviews

podcastreviews.net

Which podcasts are cool? Which are crud? This site evaluates podcasts and provides recommendations.

Podfly

www.podfly.com

Podfly is a blog that features articles, interviews, and podcast reviews.

Yahoo! Podcasts

podcasts.yahoo.com

Yahoo!, already considered one of the premier search engines for web pages, applies its power to the podcast arena, enabling you to search for the podcasts that you're interested in listening to or browse the directories. Yahoo! also presents you with a small selection of recommended podcasts and a list of the most popular and the most highly rated podcasts.

POETRY

Bad Poetry Page

1 2 3 4 5

www.coffeeshoptimes.com/badpoet.html

Coffee Shop Times is an online cultural hangout for the alternative crowd. Here, the folks of CST treat you to some really bad poetry. If you come across a really bad poem somewhere else, consider posting it here for consideration.

Bartleby.com Verse

1 2 3 4 5

www.bartleby.com/verse

Thousands of poems by hundreds of famous poets are available at this site, where you can search for poets by name or poems by title or browse through the available collections and anthologies. Best of all, access to the poems is completely free!

Eserver Poetry Collection

1 2 3 4 5

eserver.org/poetry

The Eserver Poetry Collection features representative works from some of the world's well-known British and American poets. Site also features essays and humorous works plus links to other excellent poetry sites.

Fooling with Words with Bill Moyers

1 2 3 4 5

www.pbs.org/wnet/foolingwithwords

This online version of the PBS special provides an overview and lesson plans that can help teachers encourage student interest in poetry. An overview and three lesson plans are available. More than a dozen contemporary poets are featured, along with videos of the poets reading their poems. This excellent introduction to poetry benefits not only younger students, but also anyone interested in gaining a greater appreciation of poetry.

Giggle Poetry

1 2 3 4 5

www.gigglepoetry.com

Giggle Poetry introduces young children to poetry in a way that most kids find to be fun and engaging. This site features colorful cartoons, poetry games and ratings, school poems, favorite poems, instructions on writing nursery rhymes and limericks, and much more.

Haiku Society of America

1 2 3 4 5

www.hsa-haiku.org

If haiku is your poetry of choice, check out the Haiku Society of America's website, where you can check out sample verse, learn about various contests, access teacher resources, and sign up to become a member.

Poetry 180

1 2 3 4 5

www.loc.gov/poetry/180

Sponsored by the Library of Congress, Poetry 180 is designed to make it easy for students, particularly high school students, to read or listen to at least one poem a day during the school year. Simply type the number of the poem you want to hear and click Go.

Best Poetry Archives

1 2 3 4 5

www.emule.com/poetry

The Poetry Archives is devoted to preserving and making available to students, educators, and others interested in poetry the works of the classic poets. You can search the database by first line, author, or poem title. Active discussion forums can help you track down other poetry and learn more about poetry. The Top Poems list ranks poems by popularity, and the Top Authors list ranks poets by popularity. All original poems are no longer copyrighted, but any translations included may be copyrighted. Also includes a shopping area for purchasing classic poetry collections.

Poetry.com

1 2 3 4 5 (rating: 4)

www.poetry.com

Sponsored by the International Library of Poetry, Poetry.com's goal is to "eliminate the traditional barriers that prevent most people from having their message heard." Visit this site to enter your poems in one of the biggest poetry contests in the world for a chance to win cash prizes. Site also features information about rhyming and poetry techniques, a list of the 100 greatest poems ever written, a quiz to test your poetry IQ, and much more.

Poetry Daily

1 2 3 4 5 (rating: 4)

www.poems.com

This site features a new poem every day from a contemporary poet and provides information about the poet and any poetry that he or she has published. You can browse the archives for previous featured poetry.

Poetry Express

1 2 3 4 5 (rating: 3)

www.poetryexpress.org

Poetry Express features 15 poems that you can write simply by following the step-by-step instructions given at this site. The site uses various techniques to inspire you to create something that is your own unique poetic expression.

PoetryFoundation.org

1 2 3 4 5 (rating: 4) RSS

poetryfoundation.org

PoetryFoundation.org is "one of several efforts underway by the Poetry Foundation to strengthen the reciprocal relation between poetry and its audience." Site is update every week in an effort to provide visitors with news and articles that foster their enthusiasm for poetry. This site contains "an archive of more than 3,000 contemporary and classic poems in English by more than 250 poets, which includes poems and essays from back issues of *Poetry* magazine." Here, you'll find poems both in text form and as audio recordings, many of which are read by the poets who penned them. Visitors are encouraged to search the site, read and listen to the poetry, and comment on what they find.

Poetry Magazine

1 2 3 4 5 (rating: 3)

www.poetrymagazine.org

Poetry magazine is dedicated to publishing the best verse being written today, "regardless of where, by whom, or under what theory of art it is written." Here, you can sample content from the current and past issues of the magazine, check out the features poet and prose writer, and read the letter of the month.

PoetryPoetry

1 2 3 4 5 (rating: 3)

www.poetrypoetry.com

Dedicated to the art of spoken word poetry, this site features an excellent collection of audio recordings showcasing the performance poetry of original poets from across the country.

Poetry Slam, Inc.

1 2 3 4 5 (rating: 4)

www.poetryslam.com

Poetry Slam is the art of spoken word performance poetry, and this site is its official home on the Web. Poetry Slam, Inc. encourages performance poets and organizers to join in its grassroots movement by creating registered poetry slams in their towns or cities. Here, you'll find a Slam FAQ (frequently asked questions), information about the current year's National Poetry Slam, a list of Poetry Slam venues around the country, free audio and video clips of top performers, discussion forums, chatrooms, and much more. You can even shop online for Slam CDs, books, t-shirts, and other paraphernalia.

Related Sites

www.nuyorican.org

www.austinslam.com

www.chicagopoetry.com

www.gotpoetry.com

www.e-poetry.de

www.slamnation.com

The Poetry Society of America

12345

www.poetrysociety.org

The Poetry Society of America is dedicated to stirring up interest and enthusiasm in all forms of poetry—written and spoken word. Its Poetry in Motion project places poems in buses and subways, and currently reaches more than 10 million Americans on a daily basis. Here, you can learn more about the organization and its members and programs, enter the chapbook contests, learn about upcoming events, and order books online.

Poets.org

12345

www.poets.org

Poets.org, created and managed by the Academy of American Poets, features more than 1,400 poems, essays about poetry, biographies of more than 450 poets, and RealAudio recordings of more than 100 poems read by the composing poet or other poets. Here, you can learn about the academy and its programs, share your own work, find local poetry resources and events, and explore the rhythms and sounds of the contemporary poetry scene.

slampapi.com

12345

www.slampapi.com

This is the official digital hangout of Marc Smith, who catalyzed the slam poetry movement and continues to spread the (spoken) word. Here, you can check out information about upcoming events at the Green Mill, read a selection of poems, learn about slam shows and other performance poetry events around the country, submit an article for publication on the site, or contact Marc personally. This site provides a good feel for the family nature of the Poetry Slam and its commitment to allowing people to voice their opinions, even if those opinions are highly critical of slam.

World of Poetry

12345

www.worldofpoetry.org

Billing itself as "the first digital poetry anthology," The World of Poetry is a project that's designed to pick up where The United States of Poetry left off. The project pairs up filmmakers with poets from across the country and around the world to record poets composing, performing, and teaching their art. The ultimate goal is to create a digital video library of hundreds of the best, most original contemporary poets. Selected clips, along with narration, will be compiled into a one-hour PBS special called *World of Poetry*. Here, you can learn more about the project and access the official website for The United States of Poetry.

POKER

Poker.com

www.poker.com

Poker.com is a place to go to play poker online and learn more about the game. Before you ante up at this site, use the navigation bar on the left to pull up the Getting Started and How to Play pages, which introduce you to the basics. You can start playing at any time by clicking Play Now! The navigation bar also contains links you can click to find out about tournaments and promotions. Beginners will want to scroll down the page to the Poker Info options in the navigation bar. Here, you'll find a Poker Glossary, Rules of Poker, Winning Poker Hands, the History of Poker, and much more. If you become a regular player, you'll probably want to join the community of players and hang out in the discussion forums for some lively banter. Even if you choose not to play online, you'll find plenty of quality information at this site.

Best Poker Pages

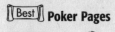

www.pokerpages.com

Poker Pages is an online kiosk to everything that's happening in the world of poker, online and off. The opening page looks like an overstuffed buffet of information and options, including top tournament results, leaderboards, feature articles, statistics, featured players, and a host of other current topics and information. Across the top of the page is a navigation bar that provides quick access to the main areas of the site: Worldwide Tournaments, Cardroom Directory, Poker Articles, Poker Players, Poker Information, Skill League, and Freeplay Poker.

> **Tip:** Beginners should scroll down the left side of the page for Poker Basics links: Poker Rules, Glossary, Hand Ranking, Poker Strategy, Crossword Puzzle, and Poker School Online.

PokerRoom.com

www.pokerroom.com

PokerRoom.com is an online poker game site, where you can pit your skills against other players in a variety of card games, including black jack and Texas Hold 'em. The site and games are developed and maintained by people with genuine knowledge and interest in poker, and the site enables you to connect with other players and establish friendships in the poker community. Site also features games developed for mobile phones.

Poker Stars

www.pokerstars.com

PokerStars is an online poker room, where you can play against some of the best players from around the world. Site offers free user-friendly poker software and a wide variety of poker tournaments. PokerStars claims that it "qualifies more players for the World Series of Poker, World Poker Tour, and European Poker Tour than anywhere else." Here, you can also obtain tournament results and statistics.

Poker-Strategy.org

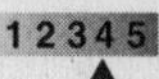

www.poker-strategy.org

Poker-Strategy.org is a great place to learn the basics of various poker games and hone your strategy for playing online poker. Site also features links to online poker games.

Poker Tips

www.pokertips.org

Poker Tips is packed with strategy, tips, and information for poker players at all levels. Site features a poker strategy section, which is essentially "a crash course chock full with poker tips designed to improve your poker skills." You can read and post messages in the discussion forum to get more advice or tips, do a little table talk, or here the latest goings on from other players. Site also features online poker reviews, so you can find the best places to play online.

World Poker Tour

www.worldpokertour.com

The World Poker Tour sparked a poker frenzy across the United States and around the world by broadcasting the top players in action to TV viewers everywhere. World Poker Tour features "a collection of prestigious tournaments played in top casinos and card rooms across the globe, including the glamorous Bellagio in Las Vegas and the Aviation Club de France in Paris." Tournaments eventually lead up to a grand finale in which the winner pockets more than $1 million. This site offers information about the show and its hosts, a behind-the- scenes look at how to play poker, bios of featured players, rules, tips, fun facts, odds calculators, leader boards, gobs of video footage, and much more. Few poker enthusiasts could visit this site and be disappointed.

World Series of Poker

www.worldseriesofpoker.com

World Series of Poker is one of the first poker competitions to spark interest in poker across the United States. Here, you can learn more about the tournament, follow its progress (when the tournament is in full swing), and check the final standings when it's over. Not much additional information about poker or how to play.

A B C D E F G H I J K L M N O Q R S T U V W X Y Z

POLITICS

The American Spectator

12345 Blog RSS

www.spectator.org

The American Spectator is a monthly magazine that goes behind the scenes in Washington politics to reveal what's really going on. The articles are seasoned with a good dose of edgy humor and bare-knuckled analysis, making them fun to read as well as informative.

Capitol Hill Blue

12345 Blog

www.chblue.com

Capitol Hill Blue provides no-holds-barred coverage of late breaking stories in Washington politics. When you want insider information with some savvy commentary, this is the site to visit. Capitol Hill Blue takes a skeptical view of Washington politics, trusting few of the policymakers who run the lives of the U.S. citizens.

Contacting the Congress

12345

www.visi.com/juan/congress

Find a congressperson's email address, website, or ground address by typing in that person's name or clicking on the state he or she represents. You can also key in your ZIP code to identify your representative and find his or her email address. There are more than 500 email addresses on the site and 500 more web page addresses.

Council on Foreign Relations

www.cfr.org

Are you interested in U.S. foreign relations? Then check out this official site of the Council on Foreign Relations, where you can find out the latest information on the United States' relationships with other countries, including Russia, Britain, Egypt, Saudi Arabia, Iraq, Iran, Pakistan, and others. Learn what current and former presidents, national security advisors, and other leaders are thinking about U.S. foreign policy and politics.

FactCheck.org

12345

www.factcheck.org

When you want the facts without the spin about various politicians, go to FatCheck.org. This nonprofit organization is dedicated to keeping politicians honest, or at least making sure that the voters have access to the facts. When one politician quotes another, did he or she get the quote right? Does a particular political advertisement properly present the facts? Find out all that and more at this site.

The Hill

12345 Blog

www.thehill.com

Web home of *The Hill*, "a nonpartisan, nonideological weekly newspaper that describes the inner workings of Congress, the pressures confronting policy makers and the many ways—often unpredictable—in which decisions are made." If you're interested in the inner workings of Congress and other government leaders and are looking for behind-the-scenes coverage of current political events, this is the site for you.

Meetup

12345

www.meetup.com

Meetup is a service that enables local interest groups to set a time and place for their meetings. Although not strictly political, in election years many of the more popular groups that arrange to meet on Meetup are interested in a specific candidate. All sorts of local groups form at Meetup, including poker groups, goths, movie buffs, and subculture groups.

New York Times: Politics

www.nytimes.com/pages/politics/

Political page of the *New York Times* features late-breaking stories related to United States politics, foreign policy, and legislation. Here, you'll find plenty of stories told in text as well as in audio and video clips. Site features a list of the most popular stories based on the most e-mailed about, the most blogged, and the most searched.

Office of the Clerk On-Line Information Center

12345

clerkweb.house.gov

Take a virtual tour of the House chamber, obtain copies of bills and House documents, and find historical information about the House of Representatives.

opensecrets.org

12345

www.opensecrets.org

Are your senators and congressional leaders in the pockets of large corporations and special interest groups? Check this site to find out. This site is created and maintained by the Center for Responsive Politics, a watchdog group that follows the money in Washington, D.C., to find out where it's going and why, and to keep citizens informed.

Related Site

www.capitaleye.org

Opinion Journal

12345

www.opinionjournal.com

Opinion Journal is the *Wall Street Journal*'s editorial page site, featuring commentary and analysis on politics and policy, business, and society. The editorial philosophy that steers the content of the columns stresses the need to inform the public but also to sharpen the political debate on important issues of the day.

Political Money Line

12345

www.fecinfo.com

Home of the Federal Election Commission, this site provides citizens with information on campaign contributions from corporations, PACs, and other sources. If you're wondering where the money flows in Washington, D.C., check out this site.

Politics1.com

12345 Blog

www.politics1.com

A bipartisan blog that aims to inform Americans regarding the political process and issues being discussed. Get campaign information, updates on current debates, and sign up for the Politics1 newsletter. Very active blog.

Power Line

www.powerlineblog.com

Blog written by John H. Hinderaker, Scott W. Johnson, and others covering income inequality, income taxes, campaign finance reform, affirmative action, welfare reform, and race in the criminal justice system. Here, you can check out their latest analysis of top political issues of the day.

RealClearPolitics

12345 Blog

www.realclearpolitics.com

RealClearPolitics is a blog that features current news, political analysis, commentary, and opinion polls from various newspapers and other resources around the world. Whether you're wondering what's going on in Washington or China, this site provides the insights you need to develop an in-depth understanding.

A B C D E F G H I J K L M N O P Q R S T U V W X Y Z

Best SpeakOut–Politics, Activism, and Political Issues Online

1 2 3 4 5

www.speakout.com

SpeakOut.com is an opinion research company started by Ron Howard, a guy who wanted to speak out and make his opinions known to the government but didn't have a clear idea about how to go about expressing himself to the people who could really help him. So, Ron started this site to help other aspiring activists figure out how to make their voices heard. SpeakOut gives you an opportunity to let your thoughts and opinions be known using the site's online polls. The site provides you with the information and activism tools needed to speak out on such subjects as political and social issues, elections, political parties, the government, and democracy. When you feel as though you can't sit still and remain silent while other people are making decisions that negatively affect your life, check out this Best of the Best site and get involved!

Town Hall

www.townhall.com

Town Hall features conservative news and information and provides a forum for discussing the top issues of the day. Visit this site for an earful on taxes, pro-life, liberals, and other issues that conservatives like to talk about.

Vote.com

www.vote.com

Vote.com presents a list of current hot issues you can read about and cast a vote for or against. Vote.com passes the poll results on to Congress and other leaders so that your voice can be heard.

washingtonpost.com OnPolitics

www.washingtonpost.com/politics

Home of the *Washington Post*, one of the most popular newspapers on Capitol Hill, this site provides headline news about what's going on in the capitol. In addition, you can find out about upcoming elections, election results, lobbying efforts, campaign contributions, and other political topics. You can even cast your vote in the daily poll.

Welcome to the White House

www.whitehouse.gov

A rich site filled with information about the White House, including background information on the president and vice president and their families. It provides access to government services, news regarding what's happening at the White House this week, historical information, and access to White House documents.

POLITICAL CAMPAIGNS

California Voter Foundation

1 2 3 4 5

www.calvoter.org

If you're a California citizen and you feel obligated to cast your vote in the next election, visit this site first to get the information you need to make an informed choice. Here, you can find the most current voter guide along with information about the latest initiatives. Pull up the campaign promises archive to see whether your local politicians are delivering on their word.

Campaign Finance Reform

www.brookings.org/GS/CF/CF_HP.HTM

This site's goal is to improve the quality of debate on campaign finance reform so that a workable approach can be passed by Congress and signed into law by the president. Examine new approaches to reform. Check out articles analyzing the proposed reforms, related opinion pieces, and proposals to Congress. Go to the Public Forum on Campaign Finance Reform to view others' ideas, analyses, and opinions.

Campaigns and Elections

12345

www.campaignline.com

Campaigns and Elections Online is a magazine for political professionals. You can check out the changing odds on major national, state, and local races across the country. Browse any of the following sections: National Directory of Public Affairs; Lobbying; and Issues Management Consultants, Products, and Services. Or, check out the Political Analysis section. Get a subscription to *Campaign Insider*, a weekly newsletter for political consultants and committees. The site also includes *C&E's Buyers Guide*, information on telephone services, media placement, direct-mail services, fundraising, and more.

C-SPAN Networks

www.c-span.org

Check out the C-SPAN schedules (C-SPAN and C-SPAN2) and content, explore the Public Affairs Video Archives, or listen to the *Washington Journal* program. Explore today's headlines from papers such as the *Washington Post, San Francisco Examiner, Chicago Sun-Times*, and more. C-SPAN in the Classroom is a great link for teachers and students. C-SPAN's Majic Bus travels on tours such as one chronicling the history of civil rights in the Deep South. *C-SPAN Online Live* lets you watch events as they are happening (such as news conferences). Check out the *Booknotes* program, which presents America's finest authors discussing reading, writing, and the power of ideas. Get information on the U.S. House schedule and weekly committee hearings.

Elections

12345

www.multied.com/elections

This presidential elections statistics site is presented by MultiEducator. Check out colorful graphs of the electoral votes cast in presidential elections from 1789 to the present. Download photos of scenes from American history and read selected documents (such as the Articles of Confederation and the Civil Rights Act of 1957). The MultiEducator American History product lets you access events chronologically, alphabetically, or by topic. Access facts about major events in U.S. history and get extensive information about each of the presidents. Audio-visuals highlight major periods in U.S. history, and video clips showcase achievements and tragedies. This site links to HistoryShopping.com, where you can purchase learning materials online.

Federal Election Commission (FEC)

12345

www.fec.gov

This is the official site for the Federal Election Commission (FEC), which was established to administer and enforce the Federal Election Campaign Act (FECA). The site is filled with tons of useful information that can be searched by state, party, office, or name. Very useful for research on political subjects, for entertainment, or just for informative reading on how the political system works.

The Gallup Organization

www.gallup.com

The people who practically invented the political public-opinion poll bring you a site that lets you study all the political trends for the entire election season. Gallup Polls, press releases, and special reports on key social and business-related issues are presented. Get information and poll results on current events.

IRS: Political and Lobbying Activity

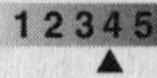

www.irs.gov/charities/charitable/article/0,,id=120703,00.html

This page from the IRS describes the rules and regulations that govern taxation of political donations and gift giving.

The National Journal

nationaljournal.com

The National Journal provides commentary, news, and resource materials on politics and policy. It offers online delivery of most National Journal Group daily publications—*CongressDaily*, *The Hotline*, *American Health Line*, *Greenwire*, and *Technology Daily*. It includes a database of polling results and trends. It also offers the *Almanac of American Politics* as well as schedules for Congress.

Pew Research Center

people-press.org

Independent organization that "studies attitudes toward press, politics, and public policy issues." This site includes survey results and an index of public attention to major news stories.

Political Information

www.politicalinformation.com

If you're looking for information on politics for whatever reason, this site provides a quick way to find almost everything that you need. This site gathers news and headlines from more than 5,000 selected policy and political websites and presents you with a couple dozen links to the top news stories from around the world, the top political stories, and selected feature stories. The site's creators describe the site as "indispensable resource for journalists, political professionals, students and political junkies around the world."

Project Vote Smart

www.vote-smart.org

Project Vote Smart tracks the performance of more than 12,000 political leaders—the president, congresspersons, governors, and state legislators. Get information on issue positions, voting records, performance evaluations, campaign finances, and biographies. Enter your ZIP+4 code, and the search engine looks up who represents you and gives you the relevant details and statistics. Alternatively, track the performance of the Congress. Find out how candidates stood on issues before they were elected and see how your Congressperson voted on a bill. Track the status of legislation as it works its way through Congress; read the text of a bill; and find out whether a bill has had committee action, whether it is scheduled for a hearing or a vote, and whether your congressperson is a cosponsor.

> **Tip:** To obtain your ZIP+4 code, go to zip4.usps.com.

Rasmussen Reports

1 2 3 4 5

www.rasmussenreports.com

This site features opinion polls and approval ratings for politicians, products, celebrities, and just about anything else about which people commonly have opinions. Site also features selected news stories.

Roll Call

1 2 3 4 5 RSS

www.rollcall.com

Biweekly newspaper covering Congress. Site presents its content in several areas, including News, Opinion, Politics, Around the Hill (rumors and insider talk), and Congressional Clearinghouse.

Smith & Harroff Political Advertising

1 2 3 4 5

www.smithharroff.com/polcampaigns.htm

If you're gearing up to campaign for office, where do you go to put together the required advertising? Smith & Harroff is one company that you can try. Visit this site to browse through a list of clients and to find out what the company has to offer.

THOMAS: U.S. Congress on the Internet

1 2 3 4 5

thomas.loc.gov

What's going on in the United States Congress? THOMAS can tell you. The THOMAS World Wide Web system, developed and maintained by the Library of Congress provides free access to congressional records and bills that have passed or are in the process of being developed and approved. Site also features some excellent tutorials to bring students up to speed on how the government works.

A B C D E F G H I J K L M N O P Q R S T U V W X Y Z

POLITICAL PARTIES

The American Party

1 2 3 4 5

www.theamericanparty.org

Home of The American Party, a conservative organization devoted to free trade, clean living, and strong families. Visit this site to learn more about the party and its principles, read the party's platform for the upcoming election, view a calendar of events, and check out the list of officers.

The Christian Coalition

1 2 3 4 5 Blog

www.cc.org

CC members fight for laws they feel promote the Christian agenda and fight against those that do not. This site has reports on every relevant law, as well as how each member of Congress voted. The pages include family resources, articles on American Christians, and more.

College Republican National Committee

1 2 3 4 5

www.crnc.org

Home of the nation's largest, oldest Republican student organization, this site features information about the CRNC, news related to the organization, and membership information. Use the online form to register to vote.

Communist Party

1 2 3 4 5

www.cpusa.org

The Communist Party, no longer affiliated with the Communist Party in Russia, runs few of its own candidates but is responsible for trying to influence politicians and voters through its grass-roots activism. Here, you can learn more about the party and how it stands on various issues, most of which are economic in nature.

The Democratic National Committee

1 2 3 4 5 Blog

www.democrats.org/index.html

Read news from the DNC, browse through the archives, and learn where the Democratic Party stands on various issues. You can also read through the current year of DNC press releases. This site includes information on various Senate hearings, as well as a guide to Republican campaign finance abuses. The site also includes Democratic National Committee FAQs. The Get Active! section tells you how to join the DNC, volunteer, and register to vote.

Directory of U.S. Political Parties

www.politics1.com/parties.htm

Excellent directory of political parties in the United States. This site covers the two major parties, Republican and Democrat, along with lesser-known parties listed in alphabetic order. Here, you can read a brief description of each party and find a link, if available, to its website.

GOP.com

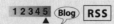

1 2 3 4 5 Blog RSS

www.rnc.org

GOP.com is the home of the Republican National Committee, more often referred to as Republicans. Here, you can learn the Republican stance on current issues, read up on the latest political news stories and storms, learn how to get involved on the state level, register to vote, sign up to volunteer, donate online, find out more about the Republican Party, check out the blogs, and even create your own MyGOP website.

Green Party USA

1 2 3 4 5 RSS

www.gpus.org

This site is one in a chain of Green Party sites. It revels in some of the past actions of the Green Party, such as Ralph Nader's candidacy for president, but it also reaches beyond that election to highlight current Green Party issues, activism, and campaigns. Site also features the 10 values of the Green Party. If you're interested in supporting environmental causes and consumer activism, check out this site.

The John Birch Society

12345

www.jbs.org

The JB Society makes Republicans look like a bunch of long-haired liberals. This site discusses their opinions of "less government, more responsibility," and offers a FAQs area, a newsletter, commentary on pending legislation, and more.

Libertarian Party Headquarters

12345

www.lp.org

The Libertarian Party is dedicated to lessening the influence of government on people's lives and helping people take more responsibility for their actions. This site is dense with Libertarian issues and positions.

Reform Party Official Website

12345

www.reformparty.org

If there's an aspect to politics and government that can be reformed, this party wants to reform it. The party's platform is wide, but highlights include disallowing all gifts and junkets, requiring the White House and Congress to have the same retirement and healthcare plans as the rest of us, shortening campaigns to four months, changing Election Day to a Saturday or Sunday so working people can vote more easily, and more.

U.S. Peace Government

www.uspeacegovernment.org

Formerly the Natural Law Party, the U.S. Peace Government has built its foundation in nature and quantum physics, in an attempt to build a government that's in concert with the flow of nature. Sounds a bit like Buddhism.

Workers World Party

RSS

www.workers.org

This anti-capitalist, pro-Socialist Party believes that capitalism rests on the foundation of the wealthy few oppressing the multitudes of poor. The party calls for the workers of the world to unite against imperialist policies worldwide.

Young Democrats of America

www.yda.org

Young Democrats of America is the official youth arm of the Democratic party. The organization is open to anyone under the age of 36 who affiliates with the Democratic Party. This site features information about state and local chapters, provides instructions on how to create a new chapter, and keeps you informed of any caucuses scheduled for your areaVisit this site to learn about the hottest issues and what you can do as a Democrat to swing the vote in your favor.

PREGNANCY & BIRTH

About.com–Pregnancy/Birth

1 2 3 4 5

pregnancy.about.com

Even if you're just starting to think about getting pregnant, this site is a great resource. From conceiving to experiencing pregnancy and getting ready for the big day, this site just about has it all. You'll find lots of information, opportunities for sharing and learning from other parents, and places to buy all the baby stuff you need.

Ask Noah About: Pregnancy, Fertility, Infertility, Contraception

1 2 3 4 5

www.noah-health.org/en/pregnancy

Extremely comprehensive site provided by New York Online Access to Health (NOAH). Information is provided on virtually any and every topic or question you might have regarding reproduction and parenting. The site has a no-frills look but is well organized and full of useful information.

Best American Pregnancy Association

1 2 3 4 5

www.americanpregnancy.org

The American Pregnancy Association is "a national health organization committed to promoting reproductive and pregnancy wellness through education, research, advocacy, and community awareness." This site covers all aspects of pregnancy from preventing pregnancy to improving your chances of becoming pregnant. Also features topics on adoption, pregnancy wellness, prenatal testing, pregnancy loss, and women's health. Site includes a pregnancy calculator and links to news and resources. The APA also provides a 1-800 number you can call to talk to a reproductive educator. Very comprehensive site with an attractive design that's easy to navigate.

ePregnancy.com

1 2 3 4 5

www.epregnancy.com

As this site claims, "from before pregnancy to after birth," you'll find helpful articles, interactive features to chat with and meet other women like you, links to useful resources, as well as shopping solutions for you and your baby.

Fit Pregnancy

1 2 3 4 5

www.fitpregnancy.com

Read articles at this site and learn about eating right, exercising, keeping your mind and body fit, and understanding you and your baby. You can also Ask the Experts for pregnancy advice. This site is for pregnant women and those trying to get pregnant.

Healthy Pregnancy

1 2 3 4 5

www.4woman.gov/Pregnancy

Part of the National Women's Health Information Center, this Healthy Pregnancy section is designed to educate women about health issues relating to pregnancy and birth. This site covers everything from pregnancy planning and fertility, through the various stages of pregnancy, and how to prepare and care for your new baby. Includes a pregnancy quiz, an ovulation calculator, a due date calculator, and a childcare provider checklist, along with other tools and information.

Labor of Love

1 2 3 4 5

www.thelaboroflove.com

Pregnancy and parenting website with message boards, tips, birth stories, pen pals, and an online magazine.

Medline Plus: Pregnancy

www.nlm.nih.gov/medlineplus/pregnancy.html

The National Institutes of Health's Medline Plus provides a cornucopia of information and resources about all health-related matters, including pregnancy. This pregnancy area features a huge collection of reliable medical advice for expectant parents grouped in categories that include Latest News, Overviews, Diagnosis/Symptoms, Prevention/Screening, Health Check Tools, and Nutrition. Many of the articles cited here contain links to other reliable pregnancy sites and health centers.

National Campaign to Prevent Teen Pregnancy

www.teenpregnancy.org

The National Campaign to Prevent Teen Pregnancy is dedicated to reducing the number of teen pregnancies by one third between the years 1996 and 2005. This site provides information for teenagers, parents, teachers, healthcare workers, and policy makers. You can also visit this site to obtain posters, stickers, and other materials for your school or organization.

OBGYN.net

www.obgyn.net/women/pregnancy/pregnancy.htm

OBGYN.net is an extensive online directory of pregnancy information and resources covering everything from amniocentesis to toxoplasmosis.

Pregnancy Daily

pregnancydaily.com

Sign up to receive your pregnancy daily update, telling you how old your fetus is in days and what's going on with your pregnancy that day. More than 500 entries guide you from pregnancy to birth. Site also features links to parenting magazine sites that can keep you informed at all stages of your child's development.

Pregnancy-info.net

www.pregnancy-info.net

This site features links to dozens of articles for expecting parents, including articles on complications, childcare, and becoming a first-time father. You can also create your own free blog that you can personalize with your own design elements, photographs, and special words.

Pregnancy Magazine

www.pregnancymagazine.com

This online version of *Pregnancy* magazine offers a few sample articles from the current edition along with a form you can fill out to subscribe to the magazine.

Pregnancy.org

12345

www.pregnancy.org

Online community of parents who gather to support each other and educate one another to raise their children. Here, you'll find pregnancy information, a pregnancy calendar, growth charts, fun games, bulletin boards, question and answer areas, and much more.

Pregnancy Today

pregnancytoday.com

Pregnancy information including news, discussion boards, resources, lifestyle issues, expert advice, and more.

StorkNet

www.storknet.com

One-stop web station for pregnancy, childbirth, breastfeeding, and parenting information. Excellent articles on how to keep yourself and your baby healthy during pregnancy.

A B C D E F G H I J K L M N O P Q R S T U V W X Y Z

SureBaby.com

12345

www.surebaby.com

SureBaby.com focuses on the early signs of pregnancy and various pregnancy-detection techniques to help moms-to-be know as early as possible that they might need to watch their health for the baby's sake. This site features a list of top 10 signs of pregnancy and early pregnancy along with information on infant and baby development, a pregnancy calendar, early pregnancy tests, a list of baby names, ideas for baby shower games, an informative baby care guide, and information on getting pregnant.

Weight Gain Estimator

12345 RSS

www.babycenter.com/calculator/1522.html

Type in your height (in inches) and weight (in pounds) to obtain an estimate of how much weight you will gain by the time you are ready to give birth.

West Side Pregnancy Resource Center

12345

www.wprc.org/pregnancy.phtml

The Westside Pregnancy Resource Center serves to "inform, encourage, and assist women and their families by providing quality services within a caring environment that will promote their social, physical, emotional, spiritual health and well-being." Here, you can find a stock of information and resources covering topics that describe the various development stages of your unborn child, prenatal testing and screening, pregnancy health risks, single parenting, and how to keep yourself and your baby healthy during pregnancy.

BIRTH & BABIES

BabyUniverse.com

12345

www.babyuniverse.com

Get advice on what you *really* need for a baby; then read product reviews and order just about everything from this site. You'll find strollers, car seats, cribs, gift ideas, and lots more.

BabyZone

12345

babyzone.com

A handy reference tool that covers all stages of pregnancy and birth from preconception to parenting. You can also shop online with a large selection of baby clothes, educational toys, and some baby gift ideas in case you can't make up your mind about what to get. You can also read about adoption, birth stories, and baby names, and you can ask an expert.

Birth Psychology

12345

www.birthpsychology.com

Provides information on prenatal and perinatal psychology and health. Find out what affects the psychology of the fetus inside the womb, traumas that can damage the vulnerable psyche, and treatments to help heal mental and emotional damage. This site features personal stories, expert articles, and late-breaking news.

Breastfeeding.com

12345

www.breastfeeding.com

You'll be amazed at all the information you can find here on breastfeeding. You'll find answers to questions about supply, technique, development, working while breastfeeding, and much more. You can even buy breast pumps, watch video clips of babies, find a local lactation consultant, and join discussions with other moms and dads. Site also serves up some fun and humor.

Childbirth.org

12345

www.childbirth.org

Search this huge site to get answers to all your questions about childbirth, including episiotomies, doulas, depression, and diapering. You'll find all these topics here.

CONTRACEPTION & ABORTION

Abortion Clinic Directory

www.abortionclinic.org

Reproductive choices and information. Users can search for providers of various reproductive services, including adoption, abortion (medical or surgical), or family planning. Site also offers information on RU-486 and STDs as well as an article on the effects of abortion on men.

AbortionFacts.com

www.abortionfacts.com

AbortionFacts.com presents information defending both sides of the abortion issue—pro-choice and pro-life, encouraging visitors to draw their own conclusions, but definitely leaning toward the pro-life perspective. You can check out the various popular arguments, obtain statistics and quick facts, learn about contraceptives and adoption options, and perform other research.

ACLU Reproductive Rights

www.aclu.org/reproductiverights/index.html

Plenty of information about the ACLU's position on reproductive freedom, including regularly updated news on abortion, court cases, legislation, recommended book list, ACLU materials on abortion, and links to other sites.

Contraception.net

www.contraception.net

When you're considering your contraceptive options, you may not be aware of all the available options. This site covers everything from abstinence to oral contraceptives, IUDs, condoms, and vaginal rings. Here, you can learn the pros and cons of various contraceptive methods and learn how to discuss your options with your doctor.

ContraceptionOnline.org

1 2 3 4 5

www.contraceptiononline.org

Baylor College of Medicine offers this online educational resource "for health care providers and health educators seeking the latest information on reproductive health, family planning, and contraception." Here, healthcare providers and educators can obtain up-to-date and practical educational tools and materials.

Ethics Updates

ethics.sandiego.edu/Applied/Abortion/index.asp

A comprehensive resource of information regarding current legislation on abortion, public opinion poll results and statistics, and links to other websites about abortion. Site includes some video clips of talks and presentations.

NARAL Pro-Choice America

www.prochoiceamerica.org/

NARAL's Pro-Choice America is dedicated to keeping voters throughout the United States informed about the reproductive rights they have any threats to limit those rights. Through voter education and activism, NARAL's pro-choice movement works to expand reproductive rights to give women a choice while working to promote contraception as the first and most important choice.

National Abortion Federation

www.prochoice.org

This site is divided into the following categories: Abortion Fact Sheets, If You're Pregnant, Voices of Choice, Clinic Violence, Media Center, Legal Issues, Get Involved, Take Action, Contributions, and Join NAF.

National Right to Life

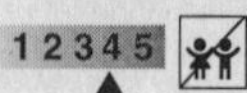

www.nrlc.org

This site offers a pro-life perspective on abortion and other right-to-life issues. This organization is one of the largest pro-life groups in the United States. The site includes information about what you can do to help support the cause and allows you to add your email address to its mailing list.

Best Planned Parenthood Federation of America, Inc.

12345

www.plannedparenthood.org

A source for sexual health information for women. Topics covered include abortion, birth control, brochures and products, parenting and pregnancy, pro-choice advocacy, women's health, and more. You'll also find links, fact sheets, FAQs, a guide for parents, job listings, and a nurse practitioner program. The online store offers books and pamphlets about Planned Parenthood as well as branded items such as T-shirts and coffee cups. Spanish translations are also available. Excellent content combined with an easily navigable format make this a hands-down choice for Best of the Best.

Planned Parenthood Golden Gate

12345

www.ppgg.org

Home of the largest not-for-profit birth-control and reproductive healthcare organizations in the world. This site is devoted to helping educate women, men, and teenagers to make responsible decisions about their own sexuality and reproductive choices. Learn more about Planned Parenthood's medical services and education programs, shop its secure online store, donate online, or learn how to become a Planned Parenthood activist.

Teenwire

12345

www.teenwire.com

Planned Parenthood designed this site to answer the questions and concerns of teens and their families. It addresses birth control for teens, body changes, dating and relationships, staying healthy, testing your sex IQ, and helps you figure out what to do if you're pregnant.

INFERTILITY

About Infertility

infertility.about.com

Directory of articles and resources relating to infertility and techniques and drugs that can increase your chances of conceiving.

American Fertility Association

www.theafa.org

Dedicated to increasing the awareness and understanding of infertility and related issues, AFA features support groups for couples who have trouble conceiving. AFA also advocates health insurance to cover infertility. At this site, you can learn more about the AFA support groups, join discussion forums, chat with other couples who are dealing with infertility, and read the Facts and FAQs for additional information.

Fertility Friend

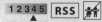

www.fertilityfriend.com

This site specializes in helping you "chart your way to conception." Here, you can find an ovulation calculator, BBT (basal body temperature or temperature at rest) chart and analysis, tips on increasing your chances of conception, and more. You must sign up for the free service because Fertility Friend is offered only for those who are trying to conceive.

Fertility Plus

www.fertilityplus.org/toc.html

Read articles about basic fertility issues, such as low-tech ways to conceive and ovulation predictor kits, as well as more-advanced topics. Check out fertility FAQs, see the fertility resource list, and chuckle at the humor section.

Infertility: A Couple's Survival Guide

www.drdaiter.com/table.html

Learn the basics regarding infertility, ovulation, the pelvis, and sperm here—to increase your odds of getting pregnant.

Infertility Treatments

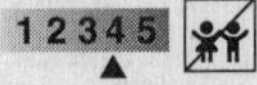

www.ihr.com/infertility

Take a quick online tour of infertility treatments and options. Or gather more in-depth information on the various options. You can also get book references and check out links. You'll find lots of useful medical overviews.

The InterNational Council on Infertility Information Dissemination (INCIID)

www.inciid.org

This nonprofit consumer advocacy group aims to inform couples of their options regarding infertility treatments. Features essays, articles, commentaries, and fact sheets on infertility, plus a searchable directory of fertility experts. The site also includes interactive discussion forums and chatrooms.

IVF.com

www.ivf.com

Dr. Mark Perloe has compiled information in areas of women's health including infertility, polycystic ovaries, IVF, endometriosis, and pelvic pain treatment options. Information is offered in the form of articles. Discussion transcripts are available to aid couples in understanding their treatment options.

Mayo Clinic: Infertility

www.mayoclinic.com/health/infertility/DS00310

This section at the Mayo Clinic websites covers a variety of topics on infertility, including signs and symptoms, causes, risk factors, screening and diagnosis, treatment, and coping with infertility.

Medline Plus Infertility Resources

www.nlm.nih.gov/medlineplus/infertility.html

Reading room packed with news and articles pertaining to infertility divided into categories including News, General Overviews, Anatomy/Physiology, Clinical Trials, Diagnosis, Treatment, and much more. Excellent place to start researching infertility and finding ways to treat it.

RESOLVE: The National Infertility Association

www.resolve.org

You'll find infertility support and information at this organization's site. You can read the online guide, access a helpline to find local organizations to assist you, as well as contact a community of people to help you make choices regarding fertility treatments, adoption, surrogacy, or the decision to remain childless.

Shared Journey

www.sharedjourney.com

A valuable collective resource for information on infertility. Here, you can find answers to your questions as well as support and information regarding current technology being used to achieve the goal of parenthood.

MIDWIFERY

American College of Nurse-Midwives

12345

www.midwife.org

American College of Nurse-Midwives (ACNM) is dedicated to "promoting the health and well-being of women and infants within their families and communities through the development and support of the profession of midwifery as practiced by certified nurse-midwives, and certified midwives." Most of the information and resources at this site are intended for midwives, but you can click the

Consumer Information link or go to www.mymidwife.org for general information about midwives, everyday health, and information on caring for your baby. You can also access a searchable directory of midwives at this site.

DONA (Doulas of North America) International

1 2 3 4 5

www.dona.org

DONA International is "the oldest, largest, and most respected doula association in the world," and is dedicated to ensuring the proper training and continuing education of doulas (women who assist couples in pregnancy, labor, birth, and postpartum period) around the world. Although most of the information at this site is specifically for doulas, the site features a For Mothers & Families menu with links to pages that provide information, questions, and answers about doulas.

Doula Network

1 2 3 4 5

doulanetwork.com

Doula Network offers an excellent description of what a doula is and does along with additional information about pregnancy and childbirth. Site features two areas: one for consumers and one for doulas. The consumer area provides information about doulas along with a search tool that can help you locate a doula in your area. The doula area provides instructions on how to get listed in the doula directory.

Midwifery Information

www.moonlily.com/obc/midwife.html

Whether you're interested in becoming a midwife or are one already, you'll enjoy this site's wealth of information on the topic. It offers articles, links, current news and information, and lots of resources.

Midwifery Today

www.midwiferytoday.com

Midwifery Today is a journal written by midwives for midwives and doulas to cultivate a community of those with shared interests and experiences in the birthing experience. Here, you can read stories, research studies that support the practice of midwifery, and find books that might help the families you serve. If you're expecting, you can visit this site to search its directory of qualified midwives and doulas or just learn a little more about your delivery options.

MISCARRIAGE

American Pregnancy Association: Miscarriage

1 2 3 4 5

www.americanpregnancy.org/pregnancycomplications/miscarriage.html

Excellent article from the American Pregnancy Association that covers several topics related to miscarriages: why they occur, the chances of having a miscarriage, the warning signs, the different types, prevention, treatment, and emotional treatment.

Hygeia

www.hygeia.org

Hygeia is an international community of families grieving from the loss of a child. Here, you'll find original poetry of loss and hope, medical information about maternal and child health, and the opportunity to share your stories and share your experience of lost parenthood with thousands of registered families worldwide.

MEND (Mommies Enduring Neonatal Death)

12345

www.mend.org

MEND is "a Christian, nonprofit organization that reaches out to families who have suffered the loss of a baby through miscarriage, stillbirth, or early infant death." Here, you can subscribe to the group's bi-monthly newsletters, learn about its two annual commemorative ceremonies, and find out more about its support groups in the Dallas/Fort Worth metroplex and its chapters in northwest Arkansas, Kansas, Houston, and Georgia.

Miscarriage Association

12345

www.miscarriageassociation.org.uk

The Miscarriage Association is located in the United Kingdom and offers help and support to those who have recently experienced a miscarriage. The association has more than 150 volunteers available to answer calls and provide support and counseling, and all these volunteers have been through the experience themselves.

M.I.S.S.–Mothers In Sympathy & Support

12345

www.missfoundation.org

At this site, you can find a support group, a place for sharing experiences, as well as articles, poetry, and information for professionals and families in grief. Special areas to help bereaved children cope.

SHARE

www.nationalshareoffice.com

Sign up for the SHARE newsletter for grieving parents, link with other parents suffering the same loss, read articles that may help, and find support groups.

PRESIDENTS & RULERS

American Presidents: Life Portraits

www.americanpresidents.org

C-SPAN created and maintains this site to provide visitors with in-depth portraits of the lives of the presidents of the United States. For each president, the site presents biographical facts, key events, presidential places, and reference material. You can also tour presidential and vice presidential grave sites, watch program video, access lesson plans, view the portrait gallery, and more. To get started, click the Pick a President menu and click the name of the desired president.

British Prime Ministers

www.number10.gov.uk/output/page123.asp

Direct from 10 Downing Street comes a "detailed look at all the prime ministers who have been successful or infamous, short-lived failures or history makers." At this site, you can learn about each prime minister from childhood to his or her eventual demise, read their more memorable quotations, discover quirky facts about them, and explore their careers and family life. This site lists the PMs in chronological order according to the date on which they took office. This site even accounts for missing days, when Britain had no one at the helm.

Emperors of Sangoku: China, India, and Japan

www.friesian.com/sangoku.htm

This site provides an overview of the history of China, India, and Japan by era and emperor. Scroll down the page for a complete index.

Related Sites

www.infoplease.com/ipa/A0775280.html

www.answers.com/topic/rulers-of-japan

France Rulers

 RSS

www.infoplease.com/ipa/A0107521.html

infoplease presents this list of the rulers of France from 751 to the present organized by era. For most rulers, you can click a link that displays additional information, including a biography and links to additional information.

Germany: Chancellors

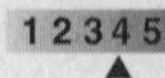

www.nndb.com/gov/754/000051601

This site lists the chancellors of Germany from 1871 to the present. Click a chancellor's name to pull up a page that presents a picture of the chancellor, a brief biography, and a collection of additional information. Some pages contain links to additional resources.

Related Sites

www.terra.es/personal2/monolith/gdr.htm

www.bundeskanzlerin.de

Best POTUS: Presidents of the United States

www.ipl.org/div/potus

POTUS, created and maintained by the IPL (Internet Public Library), presents a good collection of information about every president of the United States, including background information, election results, cabinet members, notable events, and some points of interest on each of the presidents. Site also provides links to biographies, historical documents, audio and video files, and other presidential sites. This is an excellent point of departure whether your research needs are light or heavy.

The Presidents of the United States

12345

www.whitehouse.gov/history/presidents

From the White House comes a complete list of the presidents of the United States from George Washington to the current president. You can display the list alphabetically or by date. When you click a president, you get a brief biography of the selected president describing the major events and accomplishments during that term in office. Site also presents links to kids' biographies of presidents, biographies of the first ladies, and a kid's quiz to test your knowledge.

Prime Ministers of Canada

12345

www.primeministers.ca

This site offers a brief biography of each of Canada's prime ministers, along with an in-depth analysis of the eight most influential prime ministers in Canada's history, providing "glimpses into their personalities and estimates of their contributions by leading historians, journalists, and political colleagues." Site includes plenty of information, graphics, and audio clips to keep visitors engaged and informed.

Russian Leaders

12345

en.wikipedia.org/wiki/List_of_Leaders_of_Russia

Wikipedia features a list of leaders of Russia, the Soviet Union, and the RSFSR, and Russian presidents. List is organized by era, so you can focus in on the group of leaders in the desired era.

A B C D E F G H I J K L M N O P Q R S T U V W X Y Z

PSYCHIATRY (SEE ALSO MENTAL HEALTH DISORDERS)

A B C D E F G H I J K L M N O P Q R S T U V W X Y Z

American Academy of Child & Adolescent Psychiatry

12345

www.aacap.org

The American Academy of Child & Adolescent Psychiatry focuses the diagnosis, treatment, and ongoing care of children and adolescents who have psychiatric disorders, including ADD/ADHD, depression, bipolar disorder, schizophrenia, and conduct disorders. This site features information for everyone involved in the treatment, including medical students, psychiatrists, psychologists, counselors, and family members. If you're a consumer, click the Facts for Families & Resources link to obtain information that's relevant to you.

American Journal of Psychiatry

12345 RSS

ajp.psychiatryonline.org

The *American Journal of Psychiatry* is "the most widely read psychiatric journal in the world." Here, professionals in the field of mental health can find the online version of the journal, designed to keep them up-to-date on all aspects of psychiatry, including medication and other treatment innovations and forensic, ethical, economic, and social topics. Feature articles present overviews and in-depth analysis of psychiatric syndromes and issues. You can browse the content by issue, subject, or section; search for articles by author or keyword; check out the current issue; preview features issues, and explore key features of AJP Online.

American Psychiatric Association

12345

www.psych.org

The American Psychiatric Association is a professional organization with more than 35,000 U.S. and international member physicians, who "work together to ensure humane care and effective treatment for all persons with mental disorder, including mental retardation and substance-related disorders." This site features information on advocacy, education, ethics, research, psychiatric practice, and careers; a list of district and state branches; a newsroom; a calendar of events and conferences; and additional resource links. Must be a member to access most of the information and resources on this site.

Best Archives of General Psychiatry

12345 RSS

archpsyc.ama-assn.org

The *Journal of the American Medical Association* presents this online version of its *Archives of General Psychiatry Journal*, a must-read for the psychiatric community. This site features highlights from the current edition along with a link you can click to view the entire table of contents of the current issue. Site also features e-mail lists, information on how to subscribe to the journal, and information for writers and contributors. You must be a subscriber to access the full text or PDF versions of the articles.

Tip: Scroll down the page to find the link for Past Issues.

Journal Watch Psychiatry

1 2 3 4 5

psychiatry.jwatch.org

Journal Watch Psychiatry reviews the latest clinical psychiatric research being published and presents its findings on this site and in its printed journal to keep clinicians informed concerning the latest findings, alerts, and breakthroughs in the field. Each month, the editors summarize 15 to 17 of the most important studies and provide commentary to translate the findings into plain English.

ParentsMedGuide.org

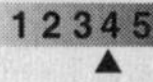

www.parentsmedguide.org

If your child has been diagnosed as suffering from depression, check out this site to learn more about the potential risks and benefits of anti-depressant medications for your child.

Psychiatry Source

1 2 3 4 5

www.psychiatrysource.com

Psychiatry Source is "an international resource for healthcare professionals with focus on Bipolar Disorder, Schizophrenia, Depression and Anxiety." Site features news, congressional reports, an events calendar, case studies, treatment guidelines, and a collection of links to additional related sites. Visitors must register to gain access.

A B C D E F G H I J K L M N O P Q R S T U V W X Y Z

PSYCHOLOGY

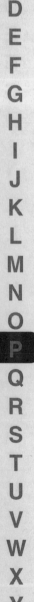

American Psychological Association

1 2 3 4 5 RSS

www.apa.org

Some excellent articles on general psychological and mental health issues of current interest, plus a consumer health guide, searchable psychologist directory, and information about the APA.

Dr. Grohol's Psych Central

psychcentral.com/resources

Search psychology topics organized alphabetically to find articles on subjects such as manic depression, obsessive-compulsive disorder, abuse, and many others. You can jump into live chats at the site for more discussion, take online quizzes, access a medication library, read book reviews, get the latest news in the field, and more.

Encyclopedia of Psychology

1 2 3 4 5

www.psychology.org

Excellent online directory for psychiatrists, psychologists, students, and patients. Not technically an encyclopedia, this site provides links to more than 2,000 other sites.

Galaxy Psychology

1 2 3 4 5

www.galaxy.com/galaxy/Social-Sciences/Psychology.html

Links to a variety of online psychology sites. Also listed are hypnosis, psychologists, and self-help site links.

A Guide to Psychology and Its Practice

1 2 3 4 5

www.guidetopsychology.com

This guide provides "free information about the practice of clinical psychology." You can click a subject category to browse the site or use the Subject Index to help track down more specific information. Topics include Psychological Practice, Clinical Issues, Social Issues, Personality and Identity, Stress Management, and Self Help.

National Association of Cognitive Behavioral Psychology

1 2 3 4 5

www.nacbt.org

One of the most effective nonmedication treatments for a host of mental health disorders is cognitive behavioral therapy. At this site, you can learn about the various types of CBT and the critical components that make it effective. Site also features a small directory of links to other CBT sites.

PSYbersquare

1 2 3 4 5

www.psybersquare.com

"Whether you need help at home or at work, in the bedroom or the board room, the exercises and events at PSYbersquare can help you achieve and win in the game of life," claims Dr. Mark Sichel, an experienced therapist and the originator of the site. This site features some excellent articles on psychological disorders, advice on how to deal with family dysfunctions, self-assessment tests and interactive exercises to help you deal with panic and anxiety, and instructions on how to raise a child who's free from addictions. Content is organized into areas, which include Me, Us, Work, Family, Women, Men, Anxiety, and Depression. Links to Amazon.com, where you can purchase recommended books.

PsychCrawler

www.psychcrawler.com

Developed by the American Psychological Association, PsychCrawler is a search tool for articles, news, information, and resources specifically related to psychology. If you can't find what you're looking for at other sites, try looking for it here. When we visited the site, it was under construction, but it should be up and running by the time you read this.

Psychology.com

www.psychology.com

Find a therapist or ask a therapist a question online at this site, which also offers tests and games to help you learn more about yourself, articles on useful concepts and techniques, and tips on dealing with stress and other issues.

Psychology.net

www.psychology.net

Headline news about current events and issues relating to psychology. Links to Amazon.com to search for books on various psychology topics.

Best Psychology Today

12345

cms.psychologytoday.com

Psychology Today is the most popular psychology magazine on the planet, covering all topics related to psychiatric care and therapy. Here, you can access many of the articles in current and past editions, locate psychiatrists and psychologists near you, take self-tests to identify potential mental health problems, and access additional resources. This site offers an outstanding guide to help you find a qualified therapist; a Diagnosis Dictionary to assist you in determining if you or a loved one have the symptoms of a major psychological disorder; topic areas that focus on everything from addictions and anxiety to sex and stress; information on a wide variety of complementary healthcare treatments; and self-tests for Career, Health, IQ, Personality, and Relationships.

Psychology Works

www.cpa.ca/factsheets/main.htm

This site features a collection of fact sheets on various psychological disorders along with the psychological treatment options that are most effective in treating each disorder. Each fact sheet contains a brief description of the disorder and its symptoms followed by treatment options. Some pages contain links to additional related sites.

School Psychology Resources Online

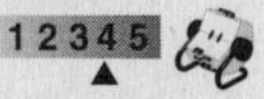

www.schoolpsychology.net

Good resource for school-related psychology programs. The links are vast and include mental retardation, eating disorders, substance abuse, the gifted and talented, mood disorders, and much more. This site also offers links to journals and articles, as well as many links to related sites.

Self-Help Magazine

www.selfhelpmagazine.com

E-zine that has more than 300 professionals who contribute to its issues. Offers articles, classifieds, reviews, banner ads, and many links to related information. This site also has *psychtoons* and postcards. You can subscribe to a free newsletter, too.

Social Psychology Network

www.socialpsychology.org

The Social Psychology Network is the largest social psychology database on the Internet, serving up more than 13,000 links related to psychology. The links offered on this site cover social psychology topics, doctorate programs, research groups, professional journals, teaching resources, textbooks, and online psychology journals. If you're interested in topics related to social psychology (the study of how and why individuals behave a certain way in a group setting), visit this site.

PUBLICATIONS

JOURNALS & EZINES

The Angling Report Newsletter

1 2 3 4 5

www.anglingreport.com/index.htm

This newsletter from the traveling fisherman covers tackle, fishing equipment, fishing info, and fishing hot spots. Great information for light-tackle and fly-fishing enthusiasts.

BestEzines–Choose Your Ezines Wisely

emailuniverse.com/bestezines

Why waste time searching for e-zines on the Internet when you can find them on BestEzines.com? This site offers hundreds of free e-zine subscription opportunities. You can choose from the best ones, but first you should check out the many articles and advice on the subject. Don't clutter your mailbox with worthless junk when you can have the best and most useful to you.

Body Modification Ezine

www.bmezine.com

Body Modification Ezine (or BME for short) features articles on tattooing, body piercing, sarification, and other body art. Content on this site consists primarily of stories and galleries, but also contains a BME encyclopedia, warnings, a FAQs area, and community links.

Exemplaria

1 2 3 4 5

web.english.ufl.edu/exemplaria

A journal of theory in medieval and Renaissance studies, *Exemplaria* is based at the University of Florida. Read articles concerning literature and culture from the formative Middle Ages.

Ezine-Universe.com

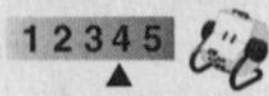

new-list.com

Searchable and browsable directory of e-zines. E-zines are grouped into categories including Arts and Humanities, Business and Economy, Entertainment, Government, Health, and more.

E-zineZ

1 2 3 4 5

www.e-zinez.com

The E-ZineZ site is dedicated to helping you produce and publish an Internet email newsletter. It begins by offering an online tutorial and individual articles on planning, producing, and promoting your e-zine. This site is very helpful!

The Gay and Lesbian Review

glreview.com

Considered the premier journal for gay and lesbian studies, *The Gay and Lesbian Review* is now online. You'll find indexes, articles, and excerpts in the area of sexuality from big-name scholars, such as Camille Paglia and Edmund White.

Ovid

12345

www.ovid.com

This site scans medical journals daily and compiles them into reports on specific medical topics that are then emailed to individuals who've requested them. Sign up here to be on the list for the most up-to-date medical information on AIDS, women's health, cardiology, and several other topics.

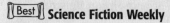

Best Science Fiction Weekly

12345 RSS

www.scifi.com/sfw

This electronic sci-fi magazine covers books, movies, TV, games, artwork, merchandise, and even some interviews. This popular site among sci-fi buffs includes a "news of the week" feature, which informs readers about current events in the sci-fi world. The site is easy to navigate and features interesting letters from readers and other visitors. The design and content here are top notch, earning this site our Best of the Best designation in the Journals & E-zines category.

Wine and Dine E-Zine

12345

www.winedine.co.uk

This site covers wine and restaurant reviews. One item of particular interest is the New Restaurant review, which is quite extensive. Site has a nice, clean, streamlined design and excellent content.

MAGAZINES

Advertising Age

www.adage.com

Advertising Age is an online magazine that features stories from around the world related to advertising. Here, you can learn about the most inventive advertising campaigns and marketing strategies and tune into business news that's often related to advertising. Site also enables you to join the AdAge mailing list.

The Atlantic Online

12345

www.theatlantic.com

This is the online home of the *Atlantic Monthly*, one of the most popular magazines in the United States. In addition to providing subscribers with an online version of the *Atlantic Monthly*, this site features back issues to 1995 along with hundreds of articles selected from past issues. This site also offers additional coverage of books, literature, and culture and an interactive forum, Post & Riposte.

BYTE Magazine

www.byte.com

Contains a five-year, searchable archive of BYTE Magazine. Enter a search term, and presto! Articles that include the term you entered appear in an easy-to-retrieve format. You can download files and shareware mentioned in BYTE articles and download BYTE's benchmark tests. This valuable site is worth a bookmark in your browser software.

Car Collector

12345

www.carcollector.com

Car Collector Magazine online features back issues, advertising information, subscription information, and automotive news.

Computerworld Online

www.computerworld.com

Computerworld is "the most trusted source for the critical information needs of senior IT management at medium-size to large companies." IT managers can access this online version of the magazine for articles on hi-tech topics, including IT

A B C D E F G H I J K L M N O P Q R S T U V W X Y Z

Management, Networking, Security, Software, and Storage; discover the latest hardware and software options; stay on top of security threats; and remain in the loop about what's happening at the top tech companies.

Cosmopolitan

  RSS 

www.cosmomag.com

Pick up weekly tips to improve your love life and career, check your horoscope, and offer advice to other readers facing agonizing situations. This site is an encapsulated version of the print magazine, but entertaining nonetheless.

Discover Magazine

12345

www.discover.com

Discover online is a science magazine that includes text of issues, photos, links related to articles, and a subscription service. This cool site features engaging content that's highly informative. Unfortunately, you have to subscribe to the magazine to get the full versions of the articles.

Editor & Publisher

12345

www.editorandpublisher.com

Editor & Publisher magazine online offers selected articles from the printed version of the magazine as well as web-only content. It also offers comprehensive coverage of new media news and trends affecting the newspaper industry.

Esquire

12345

www.esquireb2b.com

Online version of one of the most popular men's magazine—*Esquire.* Find out what's stylish and what's not; who's hot and who's not; and how to take care of yourself, your money, and your body; and how to seduce your lover.

E.W. Scripps

www.scripps.com

This site is the online face of media giant E.W. Scripps. Scripps-Howard owns more than a dozen daily newspapers, more than a half dozen television networks, and a host of other media outlets you might want to check out.

Fantasy and Science Fiction Magazine

www.sfsite.com/fsf

Founded in 1949, Fantasy and Science Fiction magazine is "the award-winning SF magazine which is the original publisher of SF classics like Stephen King's Dark Tower, Daniel Keyes's Flowers for Algernon, and Walter M. Miller's A Canticle for Leibowitz." Visit this site to find out what's in the current issue or to subscribe to the magazine or order back issues.

Folk Roots

www.frootsmag.com

This site provides the condensed, electronic version of *Folk Roots.* It features its guide to folk and world music events in Britain and Europe, CD reviews, charts of bestselling music, a play list from *Folk Roots* radio program on the BBC World Service, a complete table of contents from the current issue, and much more.

Forbes

www.forbes.com

Stay up-to-date on the day's financial and investing news with Forbes.com, analyze your holdings, get stock advice from Streetwalker, and play the Forbes Investment Challenge to earn a chance at a new laptop computer.

Fortune

www.fortune.com

Daily business reports and articles from the print magazine. Get company profiles, tips on investing, small-business information, and career leads. Also features top executives, top companies, and a list of the best companies to work for.

Glamour

us.glamour.com

Read some of this month's articles online, check out fashion do's and don'ts, and post your opinion for the benefit of *Glamour*'s editors.

Harper's

12345 RSS

www.harpers.org

One of the most popular magazines in the United States, *Harper's* features literature, politics, culture, and the arts. At this site, you can check out the table of contents of the current issue, sample some of *Harper's* best cartoons, and check out the contents of past issues.

HotWired

hotwired.wired.com

The slickest magazine in the industry has a web page with articles on culture, politics, and technology. You can sample articles from the current edition or subscribe online for wider access.

HOW Magazine

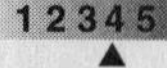

www.howdesign.com

HOW magazine "provides graphic-design professionals with essential business information, covers new technology and processes, profiles renowned and up-and-coming designers, details noteworthy projects, and provides creative inspiration." Site features news, guidance, and advice; information on upcoming conferences and competitions; a discussion forum; and web polls.

Internet Public Library

12345

www.ipl.org/div/serials

Internet Public Library contains a directory of online magazines organized by category. Follow the trail of links to locate the desired publication.

Internetweek Online

internetweek.cmp.com

A colorful site with news for corporate network managers. This publication provides testing, reviews, industry news, and funny tidbits on the world of networking and information management. Use the navigation bar at the top of the page to access the main content areas: News, Trends, Hands On, Blog, Product Finder, Internet Business, Software, Security, and Web Dev.

LIFE Magazine

12345

www.life.com/Life

LIFE "features the country's finest photographers and writers telling the most compelling stories of our times." But *LIFE* isn't just about presenting the lives of others—it's about inspiring readers to make a fuller life of their own by presenting them with great ideas for the weekend, your two favorite days of the week. Check out this site to sample some of the stories and photographs from the current issue.

MacWorld

www.macworld.com

MacWorld is the premier magazine for Macintosh computers, users, and buyers. *MacWorld* online enables you to search past issues and read articles. It also provides Internet tips, product reviews, industry news, newsletters, forums, and a pricefinder. If you own a Mac, bookmark this site.

Magazine CyberCenter

www.magamall.com

Get information on magazines, such as where to buy them locally, how to subscribe, and how to get back issues. Search by magazine category or name to find what you're looking for.

MakeZine.com

www.makezine.com

If you're a MacGyver type who likes to fiddle around in the garage and tinker with contraptions, visit MakeZine.com for some ideas and guidance to inspire you. This site is loaded is "loaded with exciting projects that help you make the most of your technology at home and away from home."

Metagrid

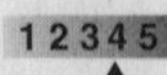

www.metagrid.com

Metagrid is a searchable, browsable directory of more than 8,000 online newspapers magazines. You can search by keyword, browse by country, or look at a list of the top 30.

MotherJones.com

www.mojones.com

Mother Jones is a magazine of investigation and ideas for independent thinkers. Provocative articles inform readers and inspire action toward positive social change. Colorful and personal, this magazine challenges conventional wisdom, exposes abuses of power, helps redefine stubborn problems, and offers fresh solutions. The discussion forum encourages visitors to share their views with one another on a variety of issues. Winner of several awards for excellence in publishing and journalism.

Motorcycle Online

www.motorcycle.com

This online magazine covers all aspects of motorcycles, including new model reviews, daily news, technical help, pictures, and tours.

Ms. Magazine

www.msmagazine.com

Ms. was "the first U.S. magazine to feature prominent American women demanding the repeal of laws that criminalized abortion, the first to explain and advocate for the ERA, to rate presidential candidates on women's issues, to put domestic violence and sexual harassment on the cover of a women's magazine, to feature feminist protest of pornography, to commission and feature a national study on date rape, and to blow the whistle on the undue influence of advertising on magazine journalism." Visit this site not only to read some of the best feminist articles currently on the Web, but also to tap into the women's movement and become an outspoken activist.

New Yorker

www.newyorker.com

For decades, the *New Yorker* has informed, entertained, and introduced people from all over the world to some of the up and coming literary artists of the time. At this site, you can sample some of what the *New Yorker* has to offer and explore past issues.

NewsLink

newslink.org

Find online versions of many of the most popular newspapers, magazines, and blogs or search for a topic to find articles in one or more of the online publications.

Newsweek

www.newsweek.com

Catch this week's news on the *Newsweek* online site, read feature articles on everything from politics and culture to science and medicine, get travel tips, view selected videos, and access Web exclusives. If you like *Newsweek*, you'll love this site. Visitors must subscribe to the site for the weekly podcast.

People

people.aol.com/people

Get a rundown of the articles in this week's issue of the popular entertainment magazine, *People*, as well as special subscription offers.

PM Zone

popularmechanics.com

Popular Mechanics online provides movies, pictures, and information about new and useful products and technology. Site also features some excellent and practical how-to articles for the weekend mechanic.

Popular Science

www.popsci.com

Articles from the magazine's current issue, links, and message forums are available here, along with practical hands-on instructions in the How2.0 area. Articles cover a wide range of hi-tech topics including Computers & Electronics, Science, Aviation & Space, Automotive Technology, Technology, and Medicine.

Rolling Stone

www.rollingstone.com

Stay in tune to top musical acts, read music news, and even upload your demo tape for review by *Rolling Stone* critics! You'll also find video-on-demand of stars you love and a schedule of upcoming music webcasts.

Runners World

www.runnersworld.com

Race results, tips from top athletes, info on biomechanics and injury prevention, and articles from the print magazine are at this site. Don't miss the daily tips.

Science Magazine Home

www.sciencemag.org

You will find many interesting articles from this magazine and learn how to subscribe to the print magazine. The site contains current articles and an archive of previous articles.

ScienceDaily Magazine—Your Link to the Latest Research News

www.sciencedaily.com

ScienceDaily is a free, advertising-supported online magazine that presents late-breaking news about the latest discoveries and hottest research projects in everything from astrophysics to medicine to zoology. The site also provides a nice search feature and a picture of the day.

Scientific American

1 2 3 4 5  

www.sciam.com

Scientific American is the premier science magazine for the general public. Features the latest news in the world of science, covering everything from anthropology to zoology. Good collection of articles on recent discoveries in space, on earth, and undersea. Covers medical breakthroughs, environmental debates, strange phenomena, and daily occurrences that you might not understand, such as what happens when you get a sunburn. If you're a scientist at heart, this is the site for you, even if you didn't do all that well in your high school chemistry class.

SciTech Daily Review

1 2 3 4 5 Blog

www.scitechdaily.com

Comprehensive digest and directory of science and technology articles pulled from the top scientific publications around the world. Covers everything from the latest feats accomplished by computer hackers to the way a doctor's bedside manner can affect the recovery rates of his or her patients. This publication takes no sides and presents a balanced selection of the latest data in science, technology, and medicine.

Shutterbug

1 2 3 4 5

www.shutterbug.net

Photography information and source magazine, with articles, reviews, and back issues available online.

SkiNet

1 2 3 4 5

www.skinet.com

The editors of *Ski* magazine and *Skiing* magazine present snow reports, resort profiles, gear information, and news. When we visited this site, it was closed for renovation, but it should be up and running and much improved by fall 2006.

Sky & Telescope Online

1 2 3 4 5

skyandtelescope.com

Sky Publishing Corporation provides astronomical news and calendars, product reviews, viewing tips, and special pages. Excellent how-to information is also available for novice astronomers.

Smoke Magazine

www.smokemag.com

The distinctive lifestyle magazine is geared to the cigar and pipe enthusiast. Includes cigar reviews, FAQs, and discussion forums.

Surfer Magazine

  RSS

www.surfermag.com

At this site, you can read recent surfing headlines, ask the surf doctor, see QuickTime movies, and select stories from the print magazine.

Tennis Magazine

www.tennis.com

Comprehensive tennis resource that includes the latest news and results from grand slams and other tournaments, along with rankings, and stats.

> **Tip:** Scroll down the page to access links for free instructions—either as explained and illustrated in articles or through free video clips.

Time Magazine

www.time.com/time

If you like *Time* magazine, you'll love this site. It features a sampling of articles from the current and past issues covering national and international news, business and technology, arts and culture, and science and health, with plenty of analysis and commentary thrown in to influence your opinions. Site also features a link for *Time for Kids*.

TravelASSIST Magazine

travelassist.com/mag/mag_home.html

This online magazine contains articles on travel and travel spots around the United States and the world. It includes back issues for online reading.

Twins Magazine

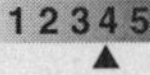

www.twinsmagazine.com

This site includes tidbits, resources, articles, and more from the magazine's current issue.

Vanity Fair

www.vanityfair.com

A quick glance at the cover of *Vanity Fair* might make the casual observer think that the magazine was little more than an upscale version of *People.* But if you can get past the slick fashion ads, you'll find that the magazine has some well-done articles and exposés on business, politics, and culture. This site features a selection of articles and commentaries from the magazine along with a discussion forum and other features that take you beyond the contents of the magazine.

Vogue

www.style.com/vogue

Home of *Vogue* magazine. See a listing of the current month's magazine content with brief descriptions. The site also offers links to nutrition, fitness, and weight loss information. It includes forums, a chatroom, and other Condé Nast publications.

Windows IT Pro

www.windowsitpro.com

The *Windows IT Pro* magazine network is "the leading independent, impartial source of practical, technical information to help IT professionals better understand and manage the Windows and SQL Server enterprise." Here, Windows IT professionals can access articles on hot topics, including Active Directory, Migration, Networking, Security, and Web Administration. Many articles are accessible only for *Windows IT Pro* subscribers.

Wine Spectator

www.winespectator.com

A comprehensive magazine covering wine, food, and travel. Site offers opinion and commentary (much of it via blogs), news and features, wine ratings (some free, others for members only), vintage charts, and daily wine picks.

Wood Online

www.woodmagazine.com

Wood magazine covers the world of woodworking from A to Z and includes how-to project instructions, techniques, tool reviews, wood technology, and lumber kits. Site features free tips and downloadable plans, lively and informative discussion forums, primers on woodworking basics, and much more. If you're a carpenter or want to take up woodworking as a hobby, this is a great place to find just the information you need.

Worth Online

www.worth.com

Provides daily market snapshots, a message board, and financial intelligence online. Whether you're looking for help spotting trends in the marketplace or you're trying to figure out how to retire on your life savings, this site offers plenty of excellent information and advice.

ZDNet

www.zdnet.com

One of the PC world's premier websites, ZDNet features product reviews, industry news, downloadable shareware, and great leads on computing deals. Site features plenty of blogs and video clips, along with insight and guidance from the leading tech gurus.

QUILTING

The AIDS Memorial Quilt

12345

www.aidsquilt.org

Description of the AIDS Memorial Quilt Project, including its history, purpose, and display schedule. You'll find a nice gift shop or online store from which you can purchase clothes, videos, books, posters, postcards, and other such items. The site is well designed and easy to navigate and features information about the AIDS Memorial Quilt Project.

Bryer Patch Studio

12345

www.bryerpatch.com

Bryer Patch Studio offers a collection of FAQs (and their answers) to a wide range of quilting topics, including Computers & Quilting, Dyeing and Painting, Quilt Care, Storing Quilts, and Pricing and Selling Quilts. You can also shop online for inkjet kits (to create your own patterns), fabric, posters, and quilts.

Canadian Quilters' Association

12345

www.canadianquilter.com

Learn about this association, check out the schedules for upcoming events, paste a message on the quilting board, and peruse the extensive list of quilting links.

Free Quilt Ideas

12345

www.freequiltideas.com

If you want to quilt but don't want to shell out money for patterns, check out these free patterns first. Here, you'll find dozens of free patterns complete with instructions.

From the Heartland

12345

www.qheartland.com

Sharlene Jorgenson created and maintains this site to provide her fans and quilting enthusiasts with the patterns, instructions, and products they need to create beautiful quilts. Here, you can order TV books and videos, template sets, notions, quilting stencils, and patterns. Site also features a list of frequently asked questions, along with their answers.

Jinny Beyer Studio

12345

www.jinnybeyer.com

Quilting instruction, monthly patterns, quilting tips, and a quilters' showcase, as well as Jinny Beyer's own range of quilting fabrics and a selection of free patterns. Site is nicely designed, offers excellent information, and is updated regularly.

Martingale & Company

12345

www2.martingale-pub.com

Looking for books on quilting? Then this site is your source. Search for a particular book or scan the database of titles. You'll also find free quilting patterns for download. Martingale & Company is the largest publisher of quilting books and is responsible for publishing more than 700 books on the subject.

McCall's Quilting Magazine

12345

www.mccallsquilting.com

McCall's Quilting is one of the top quilting magazines around. A few minutes at this site proves why. Here, you can find settings and a huge collection of tips, current articles, back issues, lessons, bonus patterns, a kids corner, vintage quilt patterns,

patterns and instructions for quick quilts, a newsletter you can register to receive via email, and much more. Site also features discussion forums and chat rooms where you can gather around with other quilting enthusiasts to share your interests, get help, and ask and answer questions.

National Quilting Association

12345

www.nqaquilts.org

The National Quilting Association, a nonprofit organization that was founded in 1970, works to promote every aspect of quilting, including everything from creating quilts to collecting and preserving quilts. Visit this site to learn more about the organization and its programs and services.

Patchwork Mountain

12345

www.patchworkmountain.com

Patchwork Mountain carries more than 1,000 of quilting fabrics, plus hundreds of other quilting supplies, including books, kits, hangers, and notions.

Piecemakers

12345

www.piecemakers.com

You'll definitely want to check out the calendar quilts this group designs and sells; they're extraordinary. At this site, you can buy quilting supplies and kits, pick up free stuff, and just learn more about quilting. California residents might want to find the group's location and class schedule.

Planet Patchwork

12345

planetpatchwork.com

This comprehensive site for quilters includes reviews of quilting software, books, and products, plus links and excellence awards. Running down the center of the page are links to feature stories. Along the left side of the page is a navigation bar that provides access to specific areas of the site, including Block of the Month, Mystery Quilt, Quilt Gallery, Quilters, Essays, For Beginners, and Techniques. You can also find discussion forums and plenty of links to additional quilting sites.

The Quilt Channel

12345 Blog RSS

www.quiltchannel.com

This quilting blog/hub provides a searchable database for quilting-related queries, or you can click on one of the subject categories to get started. You'll find connections to anything quilting related you could desire: people, sites, tips, organizations, shopping resources, and more.

The Quilter Magazine

12345

www.thequiltermag.com

The Quilter Magazine caters to the needs of quilters, needlecrafters, and fiber artists, providing them with a selection of quilting projects both large and small in traditional and contemporary designs. The magazine also features how-to articles on various techniques from the experts.

Quilters Online Resource

12345

www.nmia.com/~mgdesign/qor

Meet pen pals, look at patterns, scan project ideas, read software reviews, or enjoy the photo gallery. Check out the beginners section. If you are a busy quilter, this site is probably your best bet because it is quick loading, with only a few graphics, but the ones here are effective in leading you to the information you need. This site is easy to navigate and has many useful features. These features include a section for beginners (well suited for a general quilting audience), a project section, pen pals section, an email card section, quilting styles section, and a pattern page. You'll also find links to sites where you can make online purchases.

Quilter's Review

12345

www.quiltersreview.com

Quilter's Review presents a collection of reviews related to all sorts of quilting products, including rulers, books, and magazines. Site also features a hefty collection of quilting and computer tips along with a newsletter, discussion forums, and online polls.

Quilters Village

www.quiltersvillage.com

This magazine shop for quilters provides links to Primedia's four quilting magazines: *Quilter's Newsletter Magazine, McCall's Quilting, Quiltmaker*, and *Quick Quilts*. In addition to links to the various magazine sites, the navigation bar at this site includes links to Basic Lessons, QV Patterns, a Newsletter Archive, and Quilting Offers.

Quilting Arts Magazine

www.quiltingarts.com

Quilting Arts Magazine features articles on artists, quilting, embroidery, doll making, and other creative activities that require sewing. This site features a FAQ list, information about quilting contests, a quilters' bazaar, message boards, and more.

Quilting with a Passion

quiltingpassion.com

Comprehensive directory of free patterns and other quilting resources on the Web. Find more than 2,100 free patterns! Subscribe to the Quilting Passion newsletter, check out the forum gallery, download a free quilted calendar Windows desktop, or take a quilting class. You'll find plenty to keep you busy (and interested) at this site!

Quiltmaker Magazine

www.quiltmaker.com

Quiltmaker is the magazine for quilting enthusiasts, no matter what their level of skill. Site offers scads of patterns, tips, and techniques. Use the navigation bar that runs down the left side of the page to go to any of the following areas on the site: Back Issues, Basic Lessons, Contests, Gizmos & Gotta Haves, Motifs, Patterns, and Tips & Techniques, to name a few.

QuiltWear.com

www.quiltwear.com

Quiltwear.com sells women's and children's clothing patterns and embellishments of interest to quilters, sewers, and crafters.

World Wide Quilting Page

www.quilt.com

This, the oldest and largest quilting site on the Web, has hundreds of pages of instructions, patterns, show listings, store listings, guild listings, famous quilters' pages, a bulletin board, a trading post, classifieds for quilters, and lots more.

A B C D E F G H I J K L M N O P Q R S T U V W X Y Z

QUOTATIONS

Advertising Quotes

1 2 3 4 5

advertising.utexas.edu/research/quotes

Jef Richards, associate professor of Advertising at the University of Texas at Austin, has collected a set of quotations about the world of advertising. The index includes more than 60 subcategories. Highlights along the way include Billboards, Critics, Evil, Fantasy and Dreams, Honesty, Manipulation, Morality and Ethics, Puffery, Sex, and Value.

Amusing Quotes

1 2 3 4 5

www.amusingquotes.com

Read some funny quotes from some of the funnier people in history, including W. C. Fields, Will Rogers, Erma Bombeck, and Bill Cosby.

Annabelle's Quotation Guide

1 2 3 4 5

www.annabelle.net

Browse quotes by topic or author, sign up to receive a weekly featured quote, and check out the quotation bookstore to find just the right book of sayings.

Bartlett's Familiar Quotations

1 2 3 4 5

www.bartleby.com/100

The 10th edition of John Bartlett's famous book, published in 1901, has been converted to HTML format and posted to the Web by Project Bartleby, an extensive web-based literature library established by Columbia University. Collection includes more than 11,000 quotations.

Creative Quotations

1 2 3 4 5

creativequotations.com

A comprehensive quotation site that can be searched/perused in multiple ways: by different thematic concepts, keyword, or author. Also included are areas for quotational poetry, a thematic quotation calendar, and quotations from famous individuals born on the current date. Well worth a visit.

Daremore Quotes

1 2 3 4 5

www.daremore.com/quosoft.html

This siteoffers daily inspirational messages for women, providing a different quote on users' desktops every day. You can download new messages monthly, or you can drop by the site at any time to peruse the entire list.

Dictionary of Quotations

1 2 3 4 5

www.quotationreference.com

The Dictionary of Quotations is set up to look like an actual book, complete with a table of contents. When you first open this site, click the book title to access the table of contents. From here, you have one-click access to new quotes, an author index, and a subject index, among other sections of the site.

Follow Your Dreams

1 2 3 4 5

www.followyourdreams.com/food.html

Inspirational quotations. Includes hundreds of quotations about courage, persistence, happiness, the purpose of life, and more from famous people throughout history.

Freeality Search

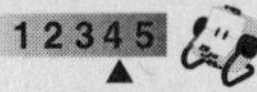

www.freeality.com/phrases.htm

Search for words, phrases, and quotations at a list of sites, which should provide a wide range of quotes to choose from.

Idiomsite

www.idiomsite.com

Has anyone ever told you you're "as cute as a bug's ear?" Here, you can find the meanings and origins of the most common English idiomatic expressions.

Mathematical Quotation Server

math.furman.edu/~mwoodard/mquot.html

"Life is good for only two things, discovering mathematics and teaching mathematics." Read this quotation from Siméon Poisson and other famous mathematical quotations at the Mathematical Quotation Server. Here, you can view a random quotation, search for a specific quotation, or browse quotations alphabetically by the name of the speaker.

MemorableQuotations.com

www.memorablequotations.com

Huge collection of quotations categorized by discipline (or profession), country, historical period, and author. No search tool to zero in on a specific quote, but a great place to browse for wise tidbits and sage advice. Lots of pop-ups.

Quotation Center

cyber-nation.com/victory/quotations/subjects/quotes_subjects_a_to_b.html

Provided by Cyber Nation, this collection of more than 54,000 quotes meant to empower and motivate is quite impressive. You can choose from just about any topic available, alphabetized by category.

Quotations Archive

www.aphids.com/quotes/index.shtml

The Quotations Archive is a searchable database of quotations for every occasion. You can browse the collection by subject or author or use the search tool to find a specific quote.

> **Tip:** Click the Related Websites link for links to more quotation sites.

Quotations of William Blake

www.memorablequotations.com/blake.htm

This page offers, in somewhat of a hodgepodge, a list of quotations by the radical poet.

Quotations Page

www.quotationspage.com

This searchable collection of quotations includes quotes of the day, links to other quotation resources, and the opportunity to submit quotations.

Quotegeek.com

www.quotegeek.com

Find quotes for term papers or schoolwork, or just for fun, from Literature and Personalities to Movies and TV. Scan quotes relevant for the season and find which are the most popular.

Best Quoteland.com

www.quoteland.com

One of the better-looking quote sites, Quoteland.com enables visitors to browse for quotes by topic or author or by category, including Motivational, Art, Dreams, Love, Sports, and Literary. Special features include Identify a Quote, Rate a Quote, and Suggest a Quote. Discussion forums round out the site, enabling visitors to connect to fellow quotation lovers. We particularly like this site because it provides so many different ways to search for quotations.

A B C D E F G H I J K L M N O P Q R S T U V W X Y Z

QuoteWorld.org

12345

www.quoteworld.org

Tens of thousands of famous quotations. Search for a specific quote by author or subject, check out the quotation of the day, browse the quotations by topic or author, see quotes in context, or check out the discussion area to post a quote or ask someone for help in tracking down a quote. This site's comprehensive collection of famous quotes combined with its powerful search tools make it one of the best quotation sites on the Web.

Quotez

12345

www.geocities.com/Athens/Oracle/6517

This site features more than 5,000 quotations arranged into more than 500 subjects by some 800 authors (including more than 100 by Shakespeare alone). Can't find what you're looking for? Fill out the form provided; the folks at this site will conduct a search for you and post your request to the alt.quotations newsgroup for quotation nuts to respond to.

Women's Quotes

12345

wisdom_quotes.tripod.com/blqulist.htm

Free online database of quotations by historic and contemporary women. You can browse the collection by author, but the site provides no search tool or option to browse by topic.

RAILROADS

AAR: Association of American Railroads

12345

www.aar.org

Representing North America's freight railroads and Amtrak. Strives to help make the rail industry increasingly safe, efficient, and productive. Here, you can examine statistics, position papers, and links collections.

Abandoned Railroads of the United States

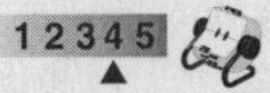

www.abandonedrailroads.com

This ever-expanding site presents the locations and stories of various abandoned railroad routes throughout the United States. Site features a good directory of links to other historical sites and rails-to-trails programs where you can obtain more information. Here, you can also find tips for locating abandoned railroad lines in your neighborhood. Most of the information on this site is from railroad hunters.

Alaskan Railroad

12345

www.alaskarailroad.com

The Alaskan Railroad transports freight and passengers across this northernmost United States. Here, you can find out about rail tours and freight services, corporate information, the company's real estate department and ongoing projects, job opportunities, and more. You can also shop online at the gift store.

Best Amtrak

12345

www.amtrak.com

Check departure and arrival times for Amtrak trains, find the station nearest to you, check fares and schedules, plan a trip, and search for specials. If you like riding the train, you'll love the convenience of this site. And if you have a PDA, this site features a tool that enables you to access schedules and other information from your PDA.

BNSF Railway

12345

www.bnsf.com

If you're looking for affordable shipping throughout the central and midwestern United States, BNSF Railway might offer the solution you need. At this site, you can check out BNSF's shipping routes and prices, learn about new services, and find out what BNSF offers to help your business succeed. Site is bilingual in English and Spanish.

Conrail

12345

www.conrail.com

The United States government created Conrail (a.k.a. Big Blue) to maintain railroad freight service between the northeastern and midwestern United States. Conrail now serves New Jersey, Philadelphia, and Detroit. Here, you can learn more about the history of Conrail, explore details about its freight service, get fact sheets and performance reports, and check for job openings.

CSX

1 2 3 4 5

www.csx.com

CSX is a freight transportation company that ships raw materials and products across the eastern United States. Here, you can learn more about the company and the services it provides, visit the help center, check out the job board, and visit areas specific to your industry.

Federal Railroad Administration

1 2 3 4 5

www.fra.dot.gov

Home of the U.S. government's organization for ensuring and improving railroad safety. Visit this site for a brief history of the administration and see what it's doing to make train travel safer.

Freightworld

1 2 3 4 5

www.freightworld.com/railroads.html

Provides links to websites for freight railroad companies throughout the world, organized by region.

Great American Station Foundation

1 2 3 4 5

www.reconnectingamerica.org

Dedicated to fostering community growth and enhance railroad travel, the Reconnecting America is responsible for organizing the restoration and rebuilding of many train stations in major metropolitan areas across America, as well integrating the various transportation networks that help us get around. Visit this site to learn more about the organization and its ongoing projects.

The Historical Website

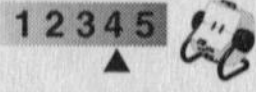

www.rrhistorical.com

If you are interested in railroading, this is the first site you should visit because it contains extensive information about railroading, including information about the history of railroading, clubs, organizations, and technical societies.

History of Railroads and Maps

1 2 3 4 5

memory.loc.gov/ammem/gmdhtml/rrhtml/rrintro.html

This site, maintained by the Library of Congress, illustrates the early days of the railroad and its expansion from the eastern United States to the west. As such, it represents an important historical record of expansion, settlement, and industrialization. It also shows how mapmaking techniques have evolved over the years.

Railroad Network

www.railroad.net

Railroad Network is a creation of Mike Roque, whose love for trains was inspired by the commuter trains in his hometown of Mount Vernon, New York. Mike later moved to upstate New York, where he became interested in freight trains and model railroading. This site features discussion forums, articles, photos, event announcements, links, and a store where you can shop for shirts, coffee mugs, and other souvenirs.

RailServe

www.railserve.com

A railroad site's catalog that enables visitors to search by a specific keyword to find all rail-related sites or to browse by category, such as antiques, newsgroups, or passenger transit. Thousands of links.

Steam Locomotives

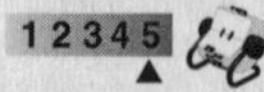

www.steamlocomotive.com

If you're interested in researching steam locomotives, this is a great site. Here, you'll find a directory of survivors with information on where they're currently stored, historical information, wheel arrangements, steam engine types, virtual tours (of museums and other places where you can find steam locomotives), and a list of steam engine builders and engine specifications.

TrainWeb

trainweb.com

Train Web invites visitors to hop aboard this portal for all things related to trains. Here, you'll find "information on train travel, model railroading, railfan, and railroad industry information including Amtrak train travelogues, railroad photographs, model train building tips, and more."

Union Pacific Railroad

www.up.com

The official Union Pacific site, containing service reports, the *INFO Online* magazine, facts, and figures and history, as well as plenty of corporate information regarding getting a job here and doing business with the company. Site offers a special area for the general public that provides information on safety, a history of UP with photographs, employment opportunities, and an online store where you can purchase gifts and memorabilia.

REAL ESTATE

BUYING/SELLING

Americas Virtual Real Estate Store

1 2 3 4 5

www.americas-real-estate.com

This site enables For Sale by Owner sellers to list their homes on the MLS (multiple listing service) for a flat fee and attempt to sell their homes online without paying an agent commission. House hunters can also visit this site to check out listings of homes for sale.

Century 21

1 2 3 4 5

www.century21.com

Aimed at property buyers and sellers. An online Property Search lets you search by state, city, or ZIP code. You provide input, and every listing matching your criteria pops up. Click on Tips and Terms and find answers to FAQs and the Real Estate Glossary, which defines more than 900 real estate terms. Site also features useful guides for both buyers and sellers.

Coldwell Banker

www.coldwellbanker.com

Before you invest time in searching for a new home, try out Coldwell Banker's Personal Retriever service that assists you in determining what features you need in a home. Then search the Coldwell Banker database of more than 200,000 homes and make use of the online concierge service to get settled with less hassle. This site presents some excellent articles and video on how to find and buy your dream home for less money and how to get more when you sell.

The Commercial Network

1 2 3 4 5

www.tcnworldwide.com

TCN Worldwide Real Estate offers "comprehensive commercial real estate transaction, management, and consulting services." Site focuses on commercial, not residential real estate in North America, the Pacific Rim, Latin America, Europe, and other countries. In addition to listing properties for sale or lease in more than 150 locations, the site offers an online referral information service and a database that helps members pinpoint market values and property trends worldwide.

Domania.com

1 2 3 4 5

www.domania.com

Before selling or buying a home, do your homework at this site. Check comparable home prices, determine how much equity you have built up in your home, check mortgage rates, use the online calculators, and much more. Cool tool helps you find out the actual sales price of recently purchased homes in your area. This site is attractive, easy to navigate, and packed with powerful tools and great information for both sellers and buyers, making it our pick for Best of the Best.

ERA

1 2 3 4 5

www.era.com

This site opens with six options, but most users need only one of the first two: Buy a Home or Sell a Home. Simply point to the option to display a complete menu of suboptions and then click the desired suboption. The site is packed with information and tools, including a searchable directory of open houses, a property search, a resource center, and a collection of financial calculators.

GMAC Real Estate

12345

www.gmacrealestate.com

GMAC, a division of General Motors Corporation, purchased Better Homes and Gardens Real Estate in 1998, and has provided real estate and relocation services to customers ever since. Here, you can learn more about the services GMAC Real Estate offers, search for a local office, and access a collection of useful tools, including a mortgage calculator, refinance calculator, school reports, city reports, and relocation crime lab. Not the best site on the block.

HomeBuilder.com

12345

www.homebuilder.com

This site offers advice, tools, and resources to find a new home, home plans, or a builder. To find a new home, you simply specify the desired location and type of home (new construction or manufactured home), and have the site search for you. Scroll down the page for additional tools and information, including home plans, home security, find local merchants, and advice and ideas. Site also features special areas for real estate professionals and builders.

HomeFair.com

12345

www.homefair.com

The calculators and research tools available at this site will be a big help to anyone looking for a home, including crime statistics, moving estimates, and school reports, to name just a few. You also can get information on home-related services, such as decorating, moving, home improvement, financing, and gardening.

HomeGain

12345

www.homegain.com

Use HomeGain's Valuation Tool to find out what your home's worth and then select an agent that's just right for you using the Agent Evaluator. You'll also find consumer guides to home buying and selling in the site's library, along with plenty of additional tools and information. Note that you will have to register to use the site's resources.

HomeLife Real Estate

12345

www.homelife.com

This site features three areas that are particularly helpful for home buyers, home sellers, and home owners. For example, the area for home buyers includes tips, a buyer's guide, a property search tool, and a free home buyer service. For sellers, HomeLife features a list of tips, a seller's guide, and a free home evaluation.

Home Plans

12345

www.homeplans.com

Looking for plans for your dream home? Then search at this site. Here, you can enter a few specifications, including number of bedrooms and baths, to pull up a list of prospective plans. Site also features a resource center, tabs for obtaining customized plans and project plans, and a tab for books and other project planning products.

Homeseekers.com

12345

www.homeseekers.com

Search for a home in a particular city or region and track down an agent to assist you in finding a new home, or use the information pulled from 175 multiple listing services to assess the value of your home before deciding to put it on the market. You also can shop for a mortgage and other home-related services and look for foreclosure properties.

HUD: U.S. Department of Housing and Urban Development

12345 

www.hud.gov

Created and maintained by the U.S. government, HUD's online site provides some valuable information for anyone who's planning to buy or sell a home. Check out a list of questions you should ask before purchasing a home, learn your rights as a home buyer, find out how much house you can afford, and much more. This site also features some excellent advice on how to deal with foreclosures.

A B C D E F G H I J K L M N O P Q R S T U V W X Y Z

International Real Estate Digest

12345

www.ired.com

Looking for an independent and all-inclusive source of real estate information? This mega-site is it. The IRED Real Estate Directory offers nearly 50,000 links to real estate websites worldwide and can be searched by state, country, or category. If you're buying a home, selling a home, or just interested in real estate information in general, this site offers just about everything you want to know. Great collection of articles, especially for real estate professionals.

MSN Real Estate

12345

realestate.msn.com

MSN Real Estate provides a searchable database of U.S. real estate listings, complete with neighborhood demographics. It contains information on the home-buying process, including negotiating and financing. Visitors can prequalify or apply for a loan online. Also features advice on home décor, cooking and entertainment, and home improvement and repair. Very comprehensive, nicely designed site.

NewHomeNetwork.com

12345

www.newhomenetwork.com

A site for new home builders and buyers, visitors can search the database of available homes in cities across the country. In addition to basic home and community information, you can learn about school districts and mortgage estimates and see floor plans and photos. A clickable map of the United States provides quick access to the real estate classifieds of the major newspapers around the country.

Nolo.com–Real Estate

12345

www.nolo.com/category/re_home.html

This self-help legal site can assist you in learning more about the process of buying and selling real estate, as well as commercial space and rental property. Read articles, do research, and turn to Auntie Nolo with questions you can't seem to find the answer to. Features online mortgage calculators, too.

Owners.com

12345

www.owners.com

Owners.com provides a searchable, national database of homes for sale by owners and foreclosure properties. It also provides reports on school districts, real estate glossaries, and mortgage calculators. Excellent real estate hub for buyers and sellers alike.

RalphRoberts.com

12345 Blog

www.ralphroberts.com

Ralph R. Roberts, CRS, GRI, is a highly sought-after speaker, consultant, author, and personal coach. Since he first started selling real estate in 1979, Ralph has sold more than 10,000 homes, propelling *Time* magazine to name him "the best-selling REALTOR in America." Here, Ralph offers to buyers and sellers some free advice and guidance along with links to list your home or find a home in the Detroit area. Click Ralph's Blog link for even more great content.

Real Estate Center Online

12345

recenter.tamu.edu

This is the comprehensive source for all things related to Texas real estate. An excellent site design allows viewers to browse efficiently through myriad materials, including numerous publications, statistical data, an extraordinary collection of real estate articles—even annual and monthly building permit statistics for all 50 states.

RealEstateabc.com

12345

realestateabc.com

Whether you're buying your first house or trying to become a real estate broker, this site has all the information and resources you need to be successful. Check out the learning library to learn all about mortgages and financing, use the calculators to crunch your numbers, read the latest news about interest rates and the direction they're going, check out the directories to locate properties or find and agent. This is a great place to research comparable properties in your area to determine the fair market value of a house you're planning to buy or sell.

REALTOR.com

1 2 3 4 5

www.realtor.com

This official site of the National Association of REALTORS is jam packed with useful information and tips for home buyers and sellers alike. Tabbed navigation makes it easy to jump to the main content areas: Find a Home, Rentals, Home Finance, Moving, and Home & Garden. Here, you can find a Real Estate 101 primer for both buyers and sellers, a tool for searching for home anywhere in the country, an estimator for determining the current value of a home you want to sell, tips for making your home worth more, a resource center for real estate professionals, and much more. Site also posts current mortgage interest rates.

Realty Times

realtytimes.com

Realty Times is the top "real estate news site on the Internet and is fast becoming one of television's most informative real estate news programs." Here, you can find plenty of articles and videos from the top agents and other professionals in the real estate industry along with tips on how to save money when you purchase a property and make more money when you sell. Site also posts the latest mortgage interest rates and links to the top news stories in real estate.

REMAX Real Estate Network

www.remax.com

REMAX is one of the top real estate agencies in the United States. Here, you can find links to residential and commercial property, a property search tool, a luxury home search, a searchable directory of REMAX agents, a Real Estate 101 primer, mortgage tools, and moving assistance.

SellMyHome101.com

1 2 3 4 5

www.sellmyhome101.com

Whether you plan to do it yourself or hire a realtor, this site offers advice about how to prepare your home to sell—including how tidying up the garage and adding fresh flowers in strategic spots to help you market your house.

Zillow

1 2 3 4 5 Blog

www.zillow.com

Zillow is dedicated to empowering home buyers, sellers, and owners by providing them with a zillion data points concerning home values. Site features three main areas—one for buyers, one for sellers, and one for owners. It offers data and free home valuations for over 65 million properties. At Zillow, you simply specify the address of the house, including the city, state, and ZIP code, and Zillow serves up a host of information, including photos in many cases. You can even check out the homes of your favorite celebrities and find additional articles on home valuations on how to choose comparable properties for more accurate valuations.

FINANCING/ MORTGAGES

ABN-AMRO

1 2 3 4 5

www.mortgage.com

Your "home for home loans" provides online access to the wide array of home lending products and services offered by ABN AMRO Mortgage. At Mortgage.com, you can apply for a new mortgage, refinance your home, access information on your current mortgage, check current rates, and much more. Features a low-cost closing, so you can often save money right from the start.

Amortization Schedule

12345

www.mortgageloan.com

No-frills site packed with useful information and tools. Scan current interest rates by state or use one of several financial calculators. Here, you can learn how much your monthly mortgage payment will be based on the amount financed, the interest rate, and the amount of the loan. Use the Early Mortgage Payoff calculator to see whether you can pay off your mortgage early. The site can also put you in contact with several mortgage companies to have them bid for your business.

Related Site

www.cmacmi.com

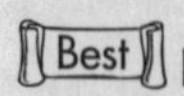 Bankrate.com

12345

www.bankrate.com/brm

Bankrate, is "the Web's leading aggregator of financial rate information. Bankrate's rate data research offering is unique in its depth and breadth. Bankrate continually surveys approximately 4,800 financial institutions in all 50 states in order to provide clear, objective, and unbiased rates to consumers." This site features an excellent collection of the latest and reliable news, information, and advice on a wide selection of topics, including mortgages, student loans, credit card debt, CDs, and interest rates. Bankrate also keeps its eyes on the feds to provide you with a heads up on moves that could affect your future financial portrait. Articles are well written, and information is easy to find.

BestRate

12345

www.bestrate.com

Tired of groveling for money? Do you want lenders to compete for *your* business? Then try BestRate. Just fill out a form online, and BestRate picks four of the best offers from more than 600 lenders nationwide to present to you. Site also posts the current interest rates and provides visitors with a collection of useful calculators and other tools.

California Association of Realtors Online

  RSS

www.car.org

The official publications of the California Association of Realtors offer articles, industry news, legal information, and more. The site also provides an index to previous issues and links to other publications.

Countrywide Financial

12345

www.countrywide.com

One of the largest mortgage companies in the United States, Countrywide allows consumers to apply for mortgages online. You can also find information about homeowner's insurance and home refinance here. Site also features a collection of articles, tools, and advice that can help you make savvy financial choices.

Ditech

12345

www.ditech.com

One of the most popular online loan services on the Web, Ditech features the tools and forms you need to research and secure a first or second mortgage or other type of loan from the convenience of your home. At this site, you can check the current rates, apply for a loan, check your loan status 24 hours a day, and chat live with a representative.

E-Loan

12345

www.e-loan.com

Apply for a mortgage or refinance online and learn whether you qualify. Rates are competitive and the process is fast. Good collection of financial calculators to show you how different interest rates and payment schedules can affect your monthly payment.

Fannie Mae Home Page

www.fanniemae.com

The nation's largest source of home mortgage funds, Fannie Mae works to expand affordable housing opportunities for all. The Fannie Mae site is as diverse as the company. Viewers can search the listing of Fannie Mae properties for sale, read up on the latest news for lenders, or review the latest housing and market outlook.

> Click Homepath for an article with links to additional information to help buyers purchase the right home and find competitive financing.

Federal Home Loan Banks

www.fhlbanks.com

Sponsored by the government but privately financed, Federal Home Loan Banks supports thousands of banks, credit unions, and savings companies as they supply mortgage loans to consumers. They provide lending support for most of the mortgages written in the United States.

FHA Today!

www.fhatoday.com

FHA Today! is a division of HCI Mortgage that specializes in processing FHA loans. Here, you can learn more about the benefits of FHA loans and determine whether you qualify. This site answers some of the most common questions people have about FHA loans, describes the loan process, and enables you to apply for an FHA loan online.

Freddie Mac Home Page

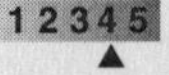

www.freddiemac.com

Established to support home ownership and rental housing, Freddie Mac has helped to finance one in six American homes. The site explains Freddie Mac's role in housing finance, offers investor information on mortgage-backed securities, offers a listing of Freddie Mac homes for sale throughout the country through its HomeSteps link, and much more. Check out the links under Buying and Owning a Home.

HUD Housing FHA Home Page

www.hud.gov/offices/hsg/index.cfm

Information at this site is geared toward businesses and consumers, with lots of helpful information on buying or renting single and multifamily dwellings. Visitors to the site might also search a directory of HUD housing, participate in online forums, or review a number of related websites. Site also features a good article on predatory lending.

Inman News Features

www.inman.com

A wellspring of real estate news and trends, Inman News offers extensive coverage of the industry with features and daily mortgage reports. Another plus: Featured articles from past issues are archived for weeks at a time on this site.

Interest.com

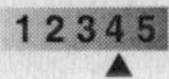

mortgages.interest.com

Comparison shop mortgage rates for your area and then consider all your options. Tips and advice at the site will help you decide when to refinance, whether you'll qualify for a standard mortgage, and what kinds of incentives might be available if you're a first-time home buyer. Site also offers a collection of mortgage calculators and a glossary that can help you decipher cryptic real estate lingo.

LendingTree.com

www.lendingtree.com

LendingTree.com can fix you up with a great deal on a loan, whether you need money to finance a mortgage, purchase a car, pay tuition, consolidate your debt, or start a business. Just fill out a brief application online, and LendingTree.com will provide you with offers from four lenders. LendingTree.com can also help you find homeowner's insurance, an automobile warranty, or a real estate agent. The Knowledge Center features some resources that can assist you with buying or selling a home.

LoanWorks.com

1 2 3 4 5

www.loanworks.com

Apply online and get an answer in five minutes regarding your mortgage status. The Quick Price feature gives you an instant rate quote. An excellent service for real estate professionals to go to secure loans for their clients. Site also features a few pages devoted to current market conditions to keep you posted of the ever-changing landscape of mortgage interest rates.

Mortgage 101

1 2 3 4 5

www.mortgage101.com

Search interest rates by ZIP code; apply for pre-approval; or check out the E-Guides for information on calculators, appraisals, bankruptcy, credit, and down payments. Excellent place for first-time home buyers to go to better understand the home-buying process and access the information and tools they need to successfully finance their first home purchase.

Mortgage Bankers Association

www.mbaa.org

Mortgage Bankers Association provides its members with the tools and resources they need to maintain and grow their lending institutions. Although most of the information and resources on this site cater to industry professionals, a small Consumer section on the opening page provides access to a Home Loan Learning Center, LenderCareers, and a Free Homebuyer Education Course.

Mortgage Payment Calculator

1 2 3 4 5

www.homefair.com/homefair/usr/mortcalcform.html

You can use this page to help determine the amount of your monthly payment. Simply enter the amount of your proposed mortgage, the term of the loan, and your interest rate to check your approximate monthly payment. Then try it at different rates and different terms to see how they will affect your budget.

Mortgage-Net

1 2 3 4 5

www.mortgage-net.com

Use this page to determine the amount of income you need to afford the home of your choice, verify local mortgage rates, get a copy of your credit report, and more. This site has a wealth of mortgage trend information. Click Top 10 Mistakes to view a list of 10 no-no's when you're buying a home.

MortgageQuotes.com

1 2 3 4 5

www.mortgagequotes.com

This site features a Daily Mortgage Commentary to keep you informed of the latest trends in mortgage interest rates, along with a collection of calculators and tools to find the best loan for your situation and financial situation. You can obtain free quotes for purchasing a home, refinancing, debt consolidation, home equity, and new construction. Site also features school reports, free moving and insurance quotes, and a Mortgage 101 primer to bring you up to speed on the various types of available mortgages and what you need to watch out for.

MortgageSelect.com

1 2 3 4 5

www.mortgageselect.com

Easy-to-use mortgage finder displays today's current interest rates and lets you quickly apply for a loan online. Answer a few questions to have a loan officer call you with additional information or chat with a representative online. Click Tools & Calculators to assess your current financial position and analyze various loans. If you apply for a loan, you can return to the site to check on the status of your application.

Mortgage Tips

1 2 3 4 5

www.lowermybills.com/tipsadvice/mortgage.jsp

LowerMyBills.com features an excellent collection of mortgage tips that can help you trim the costs of financing your home purchase. Site covers a host of topics, including how to evaluate terms and rates, the pros and cons of adjustable rate mortgages, prepayment penalties, and interest-only loans.

PlanetLoan

1 2 3 4 5

www.planetloan.com

PlanetLoan is a search tool for finding local mortgage lenders. You simply select your state of residence and specify the type of loan desired (for example, Purchase, Refinance, or Auto). Planet Mortgage displays a list of local lenders. Select a lender and enter the requested information to have the lender contact you with more information. Some excellent articles and tools to help you make well-informed financial decisions.

QuickenMortgage.com

1 2 3 4 5 RSS

www.quicken.com/mortgage

Quicken, developer of some of the top-selling finance software for individuals and small businesses, is in the mortgage loan business, and you can check out what it has to offer at this site. Tabbed navigation provides you with quick access to the main content areas: Refinance, Home Purchase, Home Equity, Calculators, Loan Options, Bad Credit, and Rates. Site also features articles and advice for home buyers and owners.

SunTrust Mortgage

1 2 3 4 5

www.suntrustmortgage.com

Current mortgage interest rates, prequalifying information, calculators, a library of information, and more. You can also locate a loan officer near you. SunTrust offers a StepOne feature that enables you to secure pre-qualification for a loan online.

Related Sites

www.lendamerica.com

www.mgic.com

www.alaska.net/~premier

FLIPPING

Flip That House

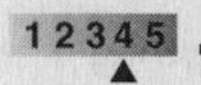  

home.discovery.com/tuneins/flipthathouse/flipthathouse.html

Discovery Channel's *Flip That House* makes its Internet home on this website, where you can play a preview video and check the date, time, and description of the upcoming episode.

Flip This House

1 2 3 4 5

www.aetv.com/flip_this_house/index.jsp

This is the official home of Rich Davis' popular show on AE called *Flip This House.* Here, you'll find episode descriptions, team member bios, tips, and before and after photos to inspire you, teach you the basics, and alert you to some of the inherent risks. Site also features discussion forums.

A B C D E F G H I J K L M N O P Q R S T U V W X Y Z

Flipping Houses

1 2 3 4 5

www.rateempire.com/flipping/reflipping.html

RateEmpire presents an excellent article on flipping houses along with links to other related articles.

How to Flip Houses

1 2 3 4 5 RSS

www.howtofliphouses.com

Gerald Romine, real estate professional and house flipper, teaches some of his secrets to flipping houses and investing in foreclosure properties.

FRAUD

Chicago Tribune's Mortgage Fraud Series

1 2 3 4 5 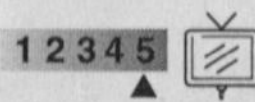

www.chicagotribune.com/news/specials/broadband/chi-mortgagefraud,0,1052574.htmlstory

Chicago Tribune reported a series of articles on mortgage fraud and other real estate scams in the Chicagoland area that resulted in homeowners losing their properties to con artists and neighborhoods falling into ruin. This excellent series reveals some of the real estate con artist's favorite tricks and the often devastating consequences of real estate fraud.

Best FlippingFrenzy.com

1 2 3 4 5 Blog

flippingfrenzy.com

Real estate scam buster Ralph Roberts created and maintains this site to educate the real estate industry as well as consumers about the prevalence of fraud in the real estate industry. This site contains a steady flow of news articles from around the country on the latest real estate scams, provides 10 tips for avoiding real estate and mortgage fraud, and provides a link you can click to report suspected fraudulent activity. Site also features links to other fraud-related sites.

Mortgage Fraud Blog

1 2 3 4 5 Blog RSS

www.mortgagefraudblog.com

Real estate attorney and fraud expert Rachel Dollar created and maintains this site to cast a light on some of the shady schemes that real estate con artists use to rip off lenders and unsuspecting homeowners. This blog features up-to-the-minute postings of the latest scams and on efforts to detect and shut down fraudulent schemes and educate professionals and consumers on the risks.

The Prieston Group's Mortgage Fraud Page

1 2 3 4 5 

mortgagefraud.squarespace.com

The Prieston Group is "a diversified mortgage risk management consulting company" that set up this site to keep lenders and other real estate professionals informed of current mortgage fraud scams and various tools and methods available to prevent mortgage fraud. Site also offers a collection of links to related mortgage fraud websites and blogs.

RELOCATION SERVICES

AIM Relocation

1 2 3 4 5 

www.aimrelocation.com

AIM Relocation offers a one-stop kiosk to all the resources you need to plan and execute a successful move. Here, you'll find a clickable list of resources, including Relocation Services, Community Links, Real Estate for Sale, Apartments for Rent, Corporate Housing, Moving and Storage, Schools/Colleges, and Travel & Lodging.

Apartments for Rent Online

1 2 3 4 5

www.forrent.com

Apartments for Rent Online is a listing of apartments and homes available across the United States. Users can search alphabetically; by amenities; or by state, city, and neighborhood. Visitors also can submit online ads.

Employee Relocation Council (ERC)

12345

www.erc.org

This site covers myriad relocation and human resource issues, from transfer costs to family concerns. Sections include information on ERC, a Relocation Career Hotline, Research and Publications, and more.

ExecuStay Inc.

12345

www.execustay.com

Find temporary housing accommodations nationwide at this site. ExecuStay (by Marriott) offerings range from fully furnished apartments to private homes, complete with linens, electronics, and cable television.

Moving.com

12345

www.monstermoving.com

Moving.com is an online relocation guide that contains more than 100,000 links to moving services, along with a fine collection of articles and tools "designed to reduce the time, cost, and stress associated with moving." Users can find links to real estate, careers, education, travel, taxes, insurance, mortgage, and rental sites. The database can be searched by subject, city, or state. You'll even find resources for childcare information and links for making the move easier for your kids. If an international move is in your future, this site can help with that, too.

Moving Local

12345 Blog RSS

movinglocal.com

Moving Local handles residential and commercial moving and storage and can provide you with a quote within 24 hours. Site also contains how-to articles on how to estimate the total cubic feet and weight of the items you want to move and provides packing tips.

Relocate America

12345

www.relocate-america.com

When you want to move but you're not sure where, check out Relocate America. This site provides information on towns and cities across the United States. Simply click the desired state, click a county, and click a town or city in that county for a brief description of the community. By entering your email address, you can obtain a listing of homes or rentals currently on the market.

The Relocation Wizard

12345

www.homefair.com/homefair/wizard/?NETSCAPE_LIVEWIRE.src

Answer the questions, submit your information to the wizard, and receive a suggested timeline. Find out what to do to help make your move go smoothly. Good selection of calculators for analyzing salary issues, moving costs, home affordability, and more. Links to school reports, city reports, and crime reports for most cities and towns.

RelocationCentral.com

12345

www.relocationcentral.com

RelocationCentral is a searchable directory of apartments for rent. If you're planning a big move and haven't yet purchased a home or found an apartment to reside in your destination, this site can book you into a rental unit. The site can also help you furnish your new digs with rental furniture.

Rent.net

12345

www.rent.net

This site offers a variety of rental and relocation resources broken into different categories of interest. Visitors will find a section geared to seniors, another on vacation rentals, one on furnished suites, and more. There are also sections on movers, truck rental, furniture rental, city guides, and insurance and auto information, along with a good collection of rental tips and other resources.

RPS Relocation Services

12345

www.rpsrelocation.com

RPS directs you to the resources and services that can actually help you though the actual process of moving, but this site also features tools and calculators to help you find the best place to move and plan for the transition. Tools include a relocation timeline, community comparison, home price check, salary calculator, address changer, and school statistics.

Salary Calculator

12345

www.homefair.com/homefair/calc/salcalc.html

If you make $45,000 per year living in Atlanta, Georgia, and would like to move to Seattle, Washington, how much would you need to make per year to maintain your current lifestyle? This site will tell you...and probably shock you.

The School Report

12345

www.homefair.com/sr_home.html

Offers school comparisons by city or county. Pick a state and a city or county, and up pops a report listing the various school districts, along with information about the total number of students, average student-to-teacher ratio, and average class size.

SchoolMatch

12345

www.schoolmatch.com

Find a school or system anywhere in the United States using the free online directory here, or buy an instant school evaluation.

TIMESHARES

2nd Market Timeshare Resales

12345

www.2ndmarkettimeshares.com

Bid on timeshare auctions here or search through available timeshare opportunities for more information. This site also provides a timeshare advisor to assist you in finding a good vacation match. Site also features a FAQ.

Hotel Timeshare Resales

12345

www.htr4timeshare.com

This site's entire focus is Marriott, Hilton, and Four Seasons hotel timeshares. It offers listings to browse and information explaining why you should choose this company to buy a timeshare property.

RCI vacationNET

12345

www.rci.com

Resort Condominiums International (RCI) offers a searchable online directory of more than 3,700 resorts around the world affiliated with its timeshare exchange program. The site also includes travel tips, a tour of featured resorts, and a section explaining vacation ownership.

Sell My Timeshare Now!

12345

www.sellmytimesharenow.com

If you have a timeshare to sell or rent or are looking for a timeshare to buy or lease, check out this site, where you can often purchase timeshares for half of what you'd pay by purchasing them directly from a timeshare resort. Site also features FAQs for buyers and sellers.

Stroman

12345

www.stroman.com

Search this site to learn more about available timeshares for sale by looking through the catalog of properties and reading up on the buying and selling process. Thousands of resort timeshares are also available. Site also features FAQs for buyers and sellers, a timeshare glossary, information on current trends, timeshare articles, and a list of the top 10 best-selling resorts. This is a great place to go not only to find timeshares but also to do some research before you invest.

TimeLinx

12345

www.timelinx.com

Fully searchable database, containing information on more than 3,500 timeshare resorts worldwide for exchange, resale, and rental. Includes membership details and featured resorts.

The Timeshare Beat

12345

www.thetimesharebeat.com

The Timeshare Beat is an online magazine for those who own and manage timeshare properties all over the world. This magazine has feature articles about the best areas to own timeshare properties along with up-to-date travel information and plenty of insightful articles and tips to help you get the most out of your timeshare and timeshare vacations. Site also features some useful tools, including a currency exchange calculator, a world clock, a calendar, traveler alerts, and a timeshare glossary.

Timeshare User's Group

12345

www.tug2.net

TUG (Timeshare User's Group) collects information, reviews, and ratings for more than 2,000 timeshare locations and provides information to its members along with area activities, restaurants, and sites to see. TUG is a great resource both for those who already own a timeshare and for those who are thinking of buying into a timeshare.

TimeSharing Today

12345

www.timesharing-today.com

The online edition of this magazine includes extensive classifieds, sample articles, and resort reviews to assist timeshare owners in getting the most out of their properties and facilitate sales and exchanges. This site features valuable articles about resort destinations, plus tips and advice on exchanging, buying, and selling timeshares. Also offers straightforward resort reviews from owners on exchange, and much more. The classified ads list hundreds of units for sale, rent, or trade.

Vacation Timeshare Rentals

12345

www.vacationtimesharerentals.com

Vacation Timeshare Rentals features classifieds where you can list timeshare property to sell or rent or find properties that are for sale or rent. You can search for timeshares by location, resort, city, ID, most popular, and newest. When we visited this site, it had a listing of more than 27,000 timeshare units worldwide.

REFERENCE

DICTIONARIES AND THESAURI

Acronym Finder

12345

www.acronymfinder.com

The Acronym Finder provides more than 485,000 common acronyms, abbreviations, and initialisms for a wide range of subjects in a searchable database.

Acronyms and Abbreviations

12345

www.ucc.ie/cgi-bin/acronym

Can't remember an acronym's meaning, like whether you should call A.A. or AAA when your car won't start? This easy-to-use site can help you out of your dilemma. Just type in the letters you're trying to decipher, and the acronym lookup site gives you an immediate definition.

ARTFL Project: Roget's Thesaurus Search Form

12345

humanities.uchicago.edu/orgs/ARTFL/forms_unrest/ROGET.html

The American and French Research on the Treasury of the French Language (ARTFL) Project, located at the University of Chicago, has provided this online version of Roget's Thesaurus. The interface is simple: Type the word you want, and the form will return synonyms and antonyms. Back up to humanities.uchicago.edu/orgs/ARTFL/ for more resources.

Cambridge Dictionaries

12345

dictionary.cambridge.org

This site gives you searchable access to several Cambridge Learner's dictionaries (for people who are learning English), including the *Cambridge Dictionary of American English, Advanced Learner's, Learner's, Idioms, Phrasal Verbs, French/English*, and *Spanish/English*. Site also features activities and worksheets and resources for teachers.

The Cook's Thesaurus

12345

www.switcheroo.com

Search this database for more information about ingredients and cooking tools. You'll find definitions, uses, pictures, and common substitute information for each category.

Dictionary of Cell and Molecular Biology

12345

www.mblab.gla.ac.uk/~julian/Dict.html

Searchable cell biology index. The online counterpart to *The Dictionary of Cell and Molecular Biology, Third Edition*, plus some additions.

Dictionary.com Definitions

12345

dictionary.reference.com

Type a word and press Enter to view a list of definitions for that word. Site also features a thesaurus and encyclopedia.

Dictionary.com Translation

dictionary.reference.com/translate/text.html

Translate any word, phrase, or sentence from English to a long list of languages, including French, German, Italian, Spanish, and Portuguese, or to English from the same languages.

Merriam-Webster Online

www.m-w.com

In addition to a dictionary and a thesaurus, you'll find a word of the day, word games, a spelling bee hive, and a word to the wise. Tabbed navigation provides quick access to other reference tools, including Merriam-Webster for Kids, Merriam-Webster Collegiate, Merriam-Webster Unabridged, and Encyclopedia Brittannica.

Online Dictionaries and Glossaries

www.rahul.net/lai/glossaries.html

Access dictionaries to assist in translating documents in foreign languages to English, or from English to something else. A long list of languages are covered.

Thesaurus.com

www.thesaurus.com

This is the complete thesaurus. You can browse alphabetically, choose one of the six classes of words, or type in a word to search. Then click the word and receive a list of synonyms. Site also features links to a dictionary, encyclopedia, word of the day, a translator, and daily puzzles.

TravLang's Translating Dictionaries

dictionaries.travlang.com

Access a long list of translating dictionaries at this site, offering translations to and from many foreign languages.

The Word Wizard

wordwizard.com

Not a dictionary in the strictest sense, but a site where words are celebrated. You must register to participate, but there are contests with prizes and just plain fun stuff to do with words. You also can Ask the Word Wizard for help with definitions, usage, or word origins.

yourDictionary.com

www.yourdictionary.com

yourDictionary.com is "a language products and services company that maintains the most comprehensive and authoritative language portal on the Web with more than 2500 dictionaries and grammars in over 300 languages, games that build language skills, and a forum (The Agora) for discussing language issues with the logophile community." Special topic glossaries are also available for business, law, medicine, sports, and humor.

ENCYCLOPEDIAS

Answers.com

www.answers.com

Answers.com bills itself as "the world's greatest encyclodictionalmanacapedia." One of the leading information sites on the Internet, Answers.com offers a searchable "collection of over three million answers drawn from over 60 titles from brand-name publishers, as well as original content created by Answers.com's own editorial team." This extensive reference site presents content in a host of categories, including business, health, travel, technology, science, entertainment, arts, and history.

Britannica.com

www.britannica.com

This official Encyclopedia Britannica website offers little in the way of free information. By subscribing to the site, however, you gain full access to Britannica's resources, including its search tool, interactive multimedia presentations, and in-depth articles. Here, you can find out more about Britannica's online and print publications and register for a free trial.

Encarta Online

encarta.msn.com

Encarta is a complete reference library, including an encyclopedia, dictionary, thesaurus, and world atlas. It also features quizzes, top 10 lists, and areas for students and educators.

> **Tip:** Click the Multimedia link for access to educational audio and video clips, photos, charts, interactive tools, thematic maps, and much more.

Encyclopedia.com

www.encyclopedia.com

Encyclopedia.com features more than 57,000 up-to-date articles from the Columbia Encyclopedia, Sixth Edition. The site links each article to newspaper and magazine articles, illustrations, maps, and other resources via HighBeam Research.

Related Site

www.bartleby.com/65

Encyclopedia Mythica

www.pantheon.org/mythica.html

This encyclopedia of mythology contains more that 6,800 articles about mythology from all over the world and throughout history. Popular areas include Greek, Roman, Egyptian, Chinese, and Japanese mythology. Site also offers a MythQuiz feature that enables you to test your knowledge.

Encyclopedia Smithsonian

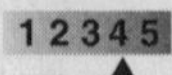

www.si.edu/resource/faq/start.htm

The Encyclopedia Smithsonian covers a wide range of topics from aeronautics to zoology. The encyclopedia functions as a portal to various Smithsonian resources that cover the selected topic along with links to other resources on the Web.

Grolier Encyclopedia

1 2 3 4 5

go.grolier.com

Grolier is a respected resource for encyclopedia articles and other reference tools, and now you can access this information online, assuming you choose to subscribe to the site. This site features special areas for librarians, teachers, parents, and students.

infoplease.com

www.infoplease.com

Comprehensive, searchable research library provides convenient access to various almanacs, a dictionary, an encyclopedia, and an atlas. Research history and geography and look up information on any country in the world. Also features biographies, weather reports and information, business and entertainment news, and a FactMonster area just for kids.

Medline Plus

www.nlm.nih.gov/medlineplus/encyclopedia.html

Medline Plus is a medical encyclopedia provided as a free service by the U.S. National Library of Medicine and the National Institutes of Health. This illustrated encyclopedia "includes over 4,000 articles about diseases, tests, symptoms, injuries, and surgeries," along with a good collection of medical photographs and illustrations.

Webopedia.com

1 2 3 4 5

www.webopedia.com

Is there a computer acronym, term, or concept that has you stumped? Then turn to the Webopedia to decipher it. Just type the entry and press Enter to find a complete definition. Most definitions also include a collection of links to other resources where you can find additional information.

Wikipedia

1 2 3 4 5

en.wikipedia.org

Wikipedia is a free, comprehensive online encyclopedia that students young and old will find indispensable. Wikipedia features more than a million articles in the English version alone, and continues to grow as volunteers contribute additional information. Here, you can search for specific articles, browse by topic, and contribute to the encyclopedia with your own unique knowledge and expertise. Because volunteers contribute articles, some content is open for debate, but you can find many insightful articles that include facts you can find nowhere else.When an article is accepted, it becomes its own "wiki," a unique section in this tapestry of information. Visitors can then add to the wiki or submit corrections and updates to it to fine-tune the content. The Wikipedia includes articles in a host of languages, including English, French, German, Russian, Polish, Chinese, Spanish, and Portuguese.

> **Tip:** After clicking the desired language, scroll down the page and click the Help Desk link for more information about Wikipedia and how to submit content, corrections, and additions.

World Book Encyclopedia

1 2 3 4 5

www.worldbookonline.com

This is the online version of the popular print encyclopedia, featuring access to all articles in the print edition plus additional articles that do not appear in the print edition. The online version also features some media content, such as video and interactive presentations that the print version is incapable of presenting. Excellent resource tool for students, teachers, and just about anyone who's curious. To access any of the content, you must subscribe to the site.

LIBRARIES

American Library Association

1 2 3 4 5 Blog RSS

www.ala.org

The American Library Association is "the oldest and largest library association in the world, with more than 64,000 members. Its mission is to promote the highest quality library and information services and public access to information. ALA offers professional services and publications to members and nonmembers, including online news stories from American Libraries and analysis of crucial issues from the Washington Office." Site features professional tools, information on upcoming conferences and events, and area for library education and careers, and the information and encouragement you need to advocate for your library and others. Librarians in the United States should bookmark this site for return visits.

The American War Library

1 2 3 4 5

members.aol.com/veterans

This library contains data on every military conflict in which the United States has been involved since the founding of the country. It also offers a veterans' registry, a photo archive section, and many other areas of benefit to veterans and their families.

Awesome Library for Teens

1 2 3 4 5

www.awesomelibrary.org/student5.html

Directory of links for teenagers and teachers organized by categories, including Games, Projects, English, Mathematics, Science, Leadership, Friends, and more.

Bartleby.com

1 2 3 4 5

www.bartleby.com

Bartleby is a great place to go for electronic versions of texts and to learn more about your favorite authors and literary works. Content is divided into four main sections: Reference, Verse, Fiction, and Nonfiction. The Reference section contains an incredible collection of reference books, including the *Farmer's Almanac*, *.98King James Bible*, *World Fact Book*, *Strunk's Style*, and *Gray's Anatomy*, to name a few.

Bibliomania: The Network Library

1 2 3 4 5

www.bibliomania.com

With more than 2,000 complete classic novels, articles, poems, and short stories in HTML and PDF formats, this is a great place to get that classical education you always wanted but never found the time for. You can purchase some of these books online using secure card resources.

Center for Research Libraries

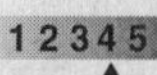

www.crl.edu

An international not-for-profit consortium of colleges, universities, and libraries that makes available scholarly research resources to users everywhere. At this site, you can search the collections.

HighBeam Research

www.highbeam.com

This unique library assistant, made up of partnerships with newspapers and magazines, provides a searchable index of articles from both current and past issues. You simply enter a keyword or phrase, and the e-librarian tracks down the resources for you. Provides free abstracts, but to access entire articles, you must subscribe to the service. Free seven-day trial.

INFOMINE

12345

infomine.ucr.edu

INFOMINE is a resource library primarily for faculty, researchers, and students at the university level. Here, you'll find online library card catalogs, electronic journals, searchable databases, mailing lists, articles, and more. Covers a wide selection of subjects from visual and performing arts to business and agriculture.

Internet Public Library

www.ipl.org

Includes resources for children, teenagers, and adults. The reference center allows you to ask questions of a real librarian (not a computer). The youth services and teen divisions have links to both books and other resources, such as writing contests, college information, science projects, and author question-and-answer sessions. A section is also devoted to information for librarians and other information professionals. Other features include tutorials, an exhibit hall, a reading room with browsable full-text resources, links to web search engines, and a multiuser object-oriented (MOO) environment for browsing the library.

The Library of Congress

www.loc.gov

Provides access to the Library of Congress online catalog and other databases. For librarians, this site includes valuable information about Library of Congress standards for cataloguing, acquisitions, and book preservation. You'll find frequently asked reference questions; links to international, federal, state, and local government information; links to Internet search engines and meta-indexes; a link to the U.S. Copyright Office home page; and information about Library of Congress special events and exhibits.

Library Spot

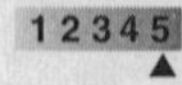

www.libraryspot.com

This online reference desk provides access to libraries, as well as answers to questions about a host of subjects, organized into categories. Established for students and teachers, but accessible to everyone.

Libweb–Library Servers on the Web

sunsite.berkeley.edu/Libweb

Find information from libraries in more than 135 countries. Site provides access to more than 7,500 pages. Use a keyword to locate a particular library location or system, or scan the long list.

Lightspan

12345

www.lightspan.com

Lightspan features a proven model available for educators that gives them an integrated set of products to assess students, align curricula to meet state standards, instruct students to successfully meet or exceed the standards, evaluate your program, and continue professional development in your system. You must subscribe to the site to access its content.

Medical/Health Sciences Libraries on the Web

www.lib.uiowa.edu/hardin-www /hslibs.html

A state-by-state listing of all medical and health science libraries on the Net. You'll find sections for foreign countries, plus an extensive listing of links.

National Archives and Records Administration

www.archives.gov/index.html

Includes both searchable and browsable services for locating government information via the Government Information Locator Service (GILS). Has links to the Federal Register, the National Archives and Records Administration Library, and the presidential libraries. The Presidential Libraries page also includes the addresses, phone numbers, fax numbers, email addresses, and links to the home pages for the presidential libraries. Also has links for genealogical research.

National First Ladies' Library

www.firstladies.org

Explores lives of our first ladies and their contributions to history. Contains bibliographies, press releases, a newsletter, a photo album, and Saxton McKinley house information.

The National Sporting Library

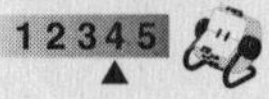

www.nsl.org

Containing more than 15,000 volumes on such topics as horse racing, breeding, shooting, foxhunting, angling, polo, sporting art, and more, the NSP serves as a resource for both the interested browser and the serious researcher. With books going back to the 1500s, the library is a storehouse of historical information on these sports. The emphasis is on horse-related sports, plus other sports closely related to the country life, so team sports such as baseball are not included. Site also features a good directory of links to other related resource websites.

OCLC Online Computer Library Center, Inc.

www.oclc.org/home

Contains information that is especially useful for librarians and other information professionals. Has links to OCLC documents and forms, a search engine for searching OCLC information, and demonstrations of OCLC services. Actual logon to some OCLC services is available by subscription only.

Portico: The British Library

www.bl.uk

Portico is the online information server for the British Library. From this point, you gain access to the online catalogs, lists of services, collections, and digital library. The site is beautifully rendered, with some documents (including images of actual pages) already available or in progress.

Smithsonian Institution Libraries

12345

www.sil.si.edu

Includes links to the various Smithsonian museums, a search engine for locating information within the Smithsonian, information about visiting Washington, D.C., information explaining how to become a member of the Smithsonian, a map showing the locations of most of the Smithsonian Museums, and a browsable shopping area.

Special Libraries Association

www.sla.org

The SLA consists of special librarians who are employed as information specialists by private businesses, governments, colleges, museums, and associations. This site is designed to promote the Special Library and to promote and advertise SLA membership benefits.

A B C D E F G H I J K L M N O P Q R S T U V W X Y Z

Sport Information Resource Center

12345

`www.sirc.ca`

NASLIN was developed to facilitate the spread of sports information among sports librarians, archivists, and others through publications, conferences, and educational programs. SPORTDiscus Online, the largest database of its kind, offers coverage of sports, fitness, and recreation-related publications. SPORTDiscus indexes more than 700,000 resources and "a wide range of information published in magazines and periodicals, books, theses, and dissertations, as well as conference proceedings, research papers, and videotapes." Daily, monthly, and annual subscriptions to the service are available.

The Sunnyvale Center for Innovation, Invention & Ideas

12345

`www.sci3.com`

Established by a unique arrangement between the United States Patent and Trademark Office and the City of Sunnyvale, California, the center is able to provide patent and trademark information and research to the entire western United States as well as to Pacific Rim countries. This is the only office of its kind in the western United States that can provide PTO information outside the Washington, D.C., area.

U.S. Department of Education (ED)

12345

`www.ed.gov/index.jsp`

Explore the U.S. Department of Education's home page, discover information about its offices and programs, and learn how to get assistance from the department. Lots of information and resources for research and education.

U.S. National Library of Medicine

12345

`www.nlm.nih.gov`

Search the library's free online health information library, Webline, or clinical trials information database for a better understanding of issues surrounding your personal health.

Web Library Directory

12345

`travelinlibrarian.info/libdir`

This site features a searchable/browsable directory of links to more than 8,800 library websites in 130 countries. Click a country name to locate a list of links to libraries in that country. Most of the countries currently represented are European (both East and West) and North American, although a few Asian, Middle Eastern, and South American countries are represented. Also has links to other library-related resources.

WWW Virtual Library

`vlib.org/Overview.html`

Extensive directory of reference materials organized by category, including Agriculture, Computing, Education, Humanities, Law, Science, and Society.

PHONE BOOKS

555-1212.com Area Code Lookup

12345

`www.555-1212.com`

Search by city or state name for U.S. or Canadian area codes, or browse by area code or state name. Returns area code and corresponding city/state. Area code links lead to a business directory where you can browse by category or search by business name.

AnyWho Toll-Free Directory

12345

`www.tollfree.att.net/tf.html`

Toll-free phone number directory set up by company name, city, state, and/or category. This site also features a reverse lookup feature, which enables you to search for a person's name by entering the person's phone number.

InfoSpace.com

12345

infospace.com

An information portal that gives you access to several information resources, from White and Yellow Page listings to maps and directions, city guides, weather, and many shopping options, all in one spot.

The Internet 800 Directory

12345

inter800.com

Searchable by keyword and state. Returns businesses matching the search criteria and their corresponding 800 telephone numbers, up to a maximum of 100 businesses.

PhoNETic

12345

www.phonetic.com

If you've ever come across a phone number expressed in alphabetic letters without the numeral equivalent next to it, you know how frustrating it can be to dial the "number." At this site, you can type in the alphabetic phone number to get the numeric equivalent and vice versa. Also includes information about obtaining phonetic telephone numbers and an explanation for why calculator and telephone keypads are different.

SuperPages.com

12345

www.superpages.com

Find the names and locations of businesses using this search engine, which accepts the business name, category, city, and/or state. Search also can be narrowed by using the ZIP code, area code, street name, or map location. Search returns the name, address, and telephone number of businesses matching search criteria. Option is available for seeing business locations on a map.

Switchboard

12345

www.switchboard.com

Search for either businesses or people. For people searches, enter the last name, first name, city, and/or state to receive the name, address, and phone number of all people matching the search criteria. For business searches, enter the company name, city, and/or state to return the name, address, and phone number of all businesses matching the search criteria. Registered users might also personalize and update their own listings. This is another highly recommended site for researchers and those persons interested in finding quick information about companies and businesses.

RESEARCH HELP

Academic Info

12345

www.academicinfo.net

A subject directory of Internet resources tailored to the university community. Each subject entry contains an annotated list of links to general websites for the field and links to more specialized resources.

Academy of Achievement

www.achievement.org

The Academy of Achievement features the stories of influential figures from the twentieth century who have been successful in their fields. When you click the name of an influential figure, you typically get a biography along with links to play short audio and video clips. Site also presents a collection of inspirational books, and you can access an online mentor program.

Almanac of Policy Issues

www.policyalmanac.org

This site features "background information, archived documents, and links on major U.S. public policy issues." Links are grouped by category, including Criminal Justice, Education, Environment, Social Welfare, and World: Foreign Affairs and National Security.

A B C D E F G H I J K L M N O P Q R S T U V W X Y Z

Biographical Dictionary

12345

www.s9.com/biography

Short biographies of more than 28,000 remarkable men and women who have shaped the world from ancient times to the present, searchable by name, birthday, date of death, profession, famous works, achievements, and other keywords.

CAIRSS for Music

12345

imr.utsa.edu/CAIRSS.html

Bibliographic database of music research literature covering music education, psychology, therapy, and medicine. Database includes citations from more than 1,300 different journals, including 18 primary journals.

CIA World Factbook

12345

www.odci.gov/cia/publications/factbook

The CIA World Factbook provides ethnographic, scientific, political, and geographic information about the world's countries and regions. This is an excellent resource for travelers and for students who are curious about key information and statistics about a particular country.

The Consumer Information Center

12345 RSS

www.pueblo.gsa.gov

Federal consumer publications are available at this site. Choose from eight categories or view those most recently featured by the media. Full-text versions are available online and can be viewed at no charge. You also can purchase printed copies. The site also offers a search option to make retrieving information easier.

Defense Almanac

12345

www.defenselink.mil/pubs/almanac

The U.S. Department of Defense created and maintains this almanac to inform citizens of military statistics, including general forces, special operations forces, aircraft, ships, submarines, missiles, ground combat systems, finances, organization, and much more. Whether you're a concerned citizen or a journalist or student who needs up-to-date military statistics, this site can provide you with the information you need.

Dismal Scientist

12345 RSS

www.economy.com/dismal

If you're looking for global economic news and analysis, this is the site to visit. Here, you'll find tools, analyses, and message boards to share your thoughts and opinions with others.

Fact Monster

12345

www.factmonster.com

Fact Monster is a research tool for kids from infoplease. This site features a homework center, timelines, almanacs, atlas, dictionary, encyclopedia, biographies, games, quizzes, and additional tools and cool stuff.

FedWorld.gov

12345

www.fedworld.gov

This site provides a list of links to various United States federal offices and administrations to make it easier for citizens to find the information they need.

General Research Resources

12345

www.uwc.edu/library/subject.htm

This University of Wisconsin online library of resources is organized by subject, including everything from anthropology to zoology. Provides links to additional university databases and search tools, too.

Internet FAQ Archives

12345

www.faqs.org/faqs

Thousands of websites feature FAQs (frequently asked questions lists) designed to help new visitors get up to speed in a hurry with the design or content of the site. The Internet FAQ Archives is a searchable/browsable directory of these FAQs.

iTools.com

12345

www.itools.com

Using fill-in-the-blank forms, you can search through dictionaries and thesauri; find acronyms or quotations; translate words between English and French and English and Japanese; find maps, area codes, and 800 numbers; look up currency exchange rates and stock quotes; and even track packages through the United States Postal Service, UPS, and FedEx.

Librarian's Index

lii.org

When you need research assistance, a qualified librarian is the first person you should see. At the Librarian's Index, you get a virtual librarian. This site features links to thousands of "high-quality websites carefully selected, described, and organized by our team of librarians. Topics include current events and issues, holidays and seasons, helpful tools for information users, human interest, and more." You can also subscribe to receive a weekly newsletter with the latest collection of new links.

Martindale's: The Reference Desk

www.martindalecenter.com

The Martindale Center features a rich directory of reference resources including a language center, science center, computer and Internet center, conversion tables, translators, world maps, constitutions, historical links, and just about anything else you might need to complete a research project. This site points you to some of the best educational resources that the Web has to offer. It's not fancy; but if you need information and don't know where to find it, Jim Martindale's links can point the way.

MegaConverter

12345

www.megaconverter.com

A collection of calculators and converters of measures, weights, and units is available at this site. For instance, users can convert miles to kilometers, gallons to liters, and years to seconds. Ancient measuring systems also can be converted.

Morse Code and the Phonetic Alphabets

12345

www.scphillips.com/morse

Contains the phonetic alphabets in British English, American English, international English, international aviation English, Italian, and German—and the Morse code equivalent for all letters plus some punctuation marks.

National Geographic Map Machine

12345

www.nationalgeographic.com/resources/ngo/maps

The *National Geographic* Map Machine is much more than your average road map or satellite image. The opening page presents you with a map of the world. Click the area in which you're interested and then keep clicking areas to zoom in on the specific location. This gives you a detailed roadmap of the selected area, which is fairly standard stuff. What's unique about this site is that it provides you with a robust collection of other map types. Click the Satellite tab to view a satellite image of the area. Click the Physical tab to view topography. Click More Theme Maps for additional maps, including Weather, Natural Disasters, Farming & Natural Resources, Population Density, and Trip Planning.

The Nobel Foundation

12345

nobelprize.org

In addition to offering a list of present winners, this official site presents a searchable database for past winners, games for teenagers, simulations, and more. Also offers a biography of Alfred Nobel and discusses his motivations for founding the prizes, in addition to explaining how Nobel laureates are nominated and selected.

Old Farmer's Almanac

12345 RSS

www.almanac.com

The *Old Farmer's Almanac* is North America's oldest continuously published periodical, providing information on weather and soil conditions since 1792. The online version offers weather forecasts, agricultural reports, herbal cures and treatments, and a host of additional information and practical wisdom.

Best refdesk.com

12345

www.refdesk.com

This site bills itself as a "one-stop reference for all things Internet." Although it is mainly a collection of links, it maintains a thorough and comprehensive database of references on a vast array of subjects. This site is one of our favorites, especially because we're writers and it provides quick reference to everything from grammar usage to the Library of Congress. Reported to be used by many professional people as well as just about everyone else, including government officials. If you need to do some quick and accurate research, we highly recommend this site as being your first stop.

Reference Tools

12345

www.lib.washington.edu/research

This extensive collection of links to a variety of reference materials from libraries to encyclopedias includes categories for particular grades, including Grads, Undergraduates, and Visitors & K12.

THOR: The Virtual Reference Desk

12345

thorplus.lib.purdue.edu

This information-rich site at the Purdue University Library provides references to many web resources, including government documents, information technology, dictionaries and language references, phone books and area codes, maps and travel information, science data, time and date information, and ZIP and postal codes.

U.S. Census Bureau

12345

www.census.gov

The U.S. Census Bureau provides population figures, economic indicators, and demographic information at this site. The site features an internal search engine to allow users to find census data more easily.

UTLink: Resources by Subject

12345

www.library.utoronto.ca

The University of Toronto Library maintains this site, which offers lists of resources, at U of T and beyond, in academic fields ranging from aboriginal educational resources to zoology. Nicely designed site packed with tools to simplify your research.

Vital Records Information: United States

12345

vitalrec.com

This page "contains information about where to obtain vital records from each state, territory, and county of the United States." You can also search public records (birth, death, marriage certificates, divorce decrees, and so on) for just about any citizen of the United States. To obtain records, you must pay up front for the search.

World Population

12345 RSS

www.census.gov/main/www/popclock.html

This site offers an estimate of the current world population at the time you access it.

International Association of Reiki Professionals

12345

www.iarp.org

The International Association of Reiki Professionals (IARP) is "the professional association of the global Reiki community, joining together thousands of members in fifty countries, working together to give Reiki a strong voice and wide reaching healing effects throughout the world." Reiki practitioners can find a host of useful information and resources, including articles, a research library, *Reiki Times* magazine, liability insurance, benefits, and much more. Site also features a searchable directory of Reiki practitioners and teachers.

REIKI

The International Center for Reiki Training

www.reiki.org

The International Center for Reiki Training is dedicated to teaching this holistic Japanese healing art. Here, you can learn what Reiki is, gather some free learning materials, order books and tapes online, access a good collection of articles and stories, and much more.

Best Reiki.nu

www.reiki.nu

Goran Sandwall, Reiki Master/Teacher, created and maintains this site to introduce visitors to Reiki history and practice. Here, you can find a discussion of Reiki symbols, a Reiki FAQ, articles on the importance of breathing correctly and drinking water, and reviews of Reiki books with links to order books through Amazon.com.

Click How to Use Reiki to learn the basics of performing a Reiki treatment on yourself or someone else.

The Reiki Page

reiki.7gen.com

The Reiki Page introduces Reiki to newcomers, guides recipients on how to benefit most from Reiki treatments, and provides information for practitioners.

RELATIONSHIPS

AdoringYou.com

1 2 3 4 5

love.adoringyou.com

Whether you're just experiencing puppy love or are in a long-term relationship, this site can help you stoke the fires of romance and strengthen your relationship with your mate. Site features love advice, dating tips, romantic ideas, e-cards, love tests, love poems and quotes, horoscopes, and an excellent collection of articles and tips. The ads on this site might intrude on your romantic interlude.

Dr. Phil

1 2 3 4 5

drphil.com

Dr. Phil offers his practical, confrontational wisdom on relationship issues at this site. Here, you can pick up some advice and tips on how to repair and strengthen your relationships with your mate, your children, your parents, and yourself.

The Five Love Languages

1 2 3 4 5

www.fivelovelanguages.com

Dr. Gary Chapman, author of the bestseller *The Five Love Languages*, created and maintains this site to remind people that everyone has their own preferred methods of giving and receiving love. Here, Dr. Chapman defines the five love languages and begins to take you on a journey of how you and your mate can identify the love languages that each of you prefers to speak and hear. Click Relationship Interests in the navigation bar on the left to skip to your area of interest: Marriage, Men, Resolving Conflict, Separation, Family Relationships, Parenting, Communication, Singles, Anger Management, or Relating to God. We loved the content on this site, but the awkward use of frames makes navigation difficult.

GrowthClimate

1 2 3 4 5

www.growthclimate.com

GrowthClimate is dedicated to individuals who are involved in a relationship with an abusive mate. This site offers online tests that can help you assess the current condition of your relationship and predict where it's likely to end up if something doesn't change. Site features relationship health tests for relationships, singles, and pornography addiction; educational materials; and information on receiving a personal consultation with a qualified counselor.

Home & Family Network

1 2 3 4 5

www.homeandfamilynetwork.com/relationships/relationshipadvice.html

The Home & Family Network offers this page to assist those in long-term relationships with overcoming relationship issues and strengthening their bonds of intimacy. Content includes tips for men, tips for women, couple time, sex and intimacy, a relationship Q&A, relationship tests, a marriage quiz, a cheating quiz, and much more.

Best MarsVenus.com

1 2 3 4 5

www.marsvenus.com

If you enjoyed John Gray's *Men Are from Mars, Women Are from Venus*, you'll love this site. In addition to gaining access to a host of books, tapes, and relationship therapy sessions, this site connects you to a dynamic community of men and women who are struggling together to fine-tune their relationships and carry them to the next level. You can read their stories or submit your own. Site also features a newsletter, a Q&A area, lots of free articles, relationship tests, a romance planner, and gender humor.

RELIGION

Academic Info: Religion

www.academicinfo.net/religindex.html

This site contains an extensive directory of websites devoted to world religions. Especially useful for the academic study of comparative religions.

Adherents–Religion Statistics and Geography

12345

www.adherents.com

This site offers insight into the growing collection of church memberships and religion inherent statistics. It provides more than 43,000 statistics for more than 4,200 faith groups from all major and most minor religions. Very statistical.

 BBC World Service–Religions of the World

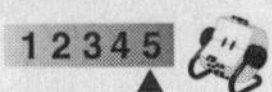

www.bbc.co.uk/religion/religions

BBC's World Religions site presents introductions and insights into a host of popular religions from atheism to Zoroastrianism and everything in between, including Buddhism, Christianity, Hinduism, Islam, Judaism, Mormon, Paganism, and Taoism. Each link takes you to a separate page that provides a brief description of the religion, its history and founder, its beliefs, and its form of worship. Site also provides a collection of links to other sites that provide more-detailed information.

beliefnet

beliefnet.com

Nonsectarian religious site devoted to keeping believers and non-believers informed about their beliefs. Covers everything from atheism and Christianity to Earth-based (pagan) religions. Additional sections explore the link between religions and marriage, sexuality, politics, and more. Take online quizzes, check out the message boards, or join a meditation or prayer group online.

Encyclopedia of Religion and Society

12345

hirr.hartsem.edu/ency

Huge online reference that covers most of the world's religions and belief systems.

Heroes of Faith

12345

www.myhero.com/faith/faith_content.asp

This site, which promotes no specific religion, features founders of the world's great religions along with individuals whose words and deeds qualify them to be considered heroes of faith.

Internet Encyclopedia of Philosophy

12345

www.utm.edu/research/iep

Excellent alphabetic listing of philosophers and philosophical problems, concepts, and theories. Click a letter to get started and then follow the trail of links to the desired philosopher, problem, concept, or theory. Excellent place to do research, particularly for beginning students of philosophy.

Religion News Service

www.religionnews.com

The Religion News Service provides a daily newsletter featuring unbiased coverage of religion, ethics, and spiritual issues from a secular viewpoint.

religion-online.org

1 2 3 4 5

www.religion-online.org

This site features the full text of more than 5,700 articles and chapters of books composed by some of the most recognized religious scholars in the world. The texts cover a wide range of topics, including the Old and New Testament, Theology, Ethics, History and Sociology of Religion, Communication and Cultural Studies, Pastoral Care, Counseling, Homiletics, Worship, Missions, and Religious Education.

Religion and Philosophy Websites

www.chowan.edu/acadp/Religion/websites.htm

Links to many religion and philosophy websites compiled by Chowan College.

ANCIENT

Ancient Religions and Myths

1 2 3 4 5

www.meta-religion.com/World_Religions/Ancient_religions/ancient_religions.htm

Huge collection of articles, stories, and myths related to ancient world religions organized by geographical location. Some of the entries are fairly short and shallow, but the site provides an excellent collection that's updated regularly.

Antiquity Online

1 2 3 4 5

fsmitha.com/h1

Search this site or scan the major subcategories for information about ancient history, philosophy, and religions, with an emphasis on historical significance and events of the times. The site has many documents and other information tracing the religious philosophy from ancient times to later years. The site is easy to navigate and has maps, images, and testimonials about the information provided here. You can read how religious ideas more than likely developed in "cave-dweller" days of ancient persons and how they evolved over time. Although not one of the "flashier" sites, it provides an intriguing look at the historical aspects of religion.

The Egyptian Book of the Dead

1 2 3 4 5

www.touregypt.net/bkofdead.htm

Learn all about the ancient Egyptians' view on death and the afterlife. The Book of the Dead is here in its full-translated glory, everything from "Hymn to Osiris" to "Making the Transformation to the Crocodile God."

Hellenic Macedonia

1 2 3 4 5

www.macedonian-heritage.gr/HellenicMacedonia/index.html

This site provides a comprehensive multimedia history of Macedonia covering "the political and economic history of the region, every form of culture and civilization, virtual visits to monuments, towns, and other attractions, and a variety of special topics."

ATHEISM

American Atheists

www.atheists.org

Information about atheism, separation of church and state, legal battles, school prayer, and biblical contradictions. Features an online store, a magazine, and plenty of up-to-date news articles on legislation and events related to atheism in the United States.

Atheism Central for Secondary Schools

1 2 3 4 5

www.eclipse.co.uk/thoughts

This excellent introduction to atheism explains the basis for most atheists' beliefs in the nonexistence of God (or of a god who intervenes in our lives).

Atheist Alliance

www.atheistalliance.org

Reach out to other atheists through this site, which aims to educate the public about the dangers of authoritarian religions through articles, books, links to other websites, and reference material.

The Infidel Guy Show

www.infidelguy.com

Reginald Vaughn Finley, self-described instigator of cognitive dissonance, is the Infidel Guy, a hardcore atheist who attempts to free the people from what he sees as the intellectual shackles of religions and other doctrines. Here, you can listen to Reginald's radio show, view his webcasts, check out his beliefs, and join an active community of atheists.

The Secular Web

www.infidels.org

A page of interest to atheists, agnostics, humanists, and freethinkers. Links to a variety of Internet resources, including Usenet newsgroups, IRC channels, and other web pages. The library contains several documents, historical and otherwise.

BUDDHISM

Buddhanet.net

buddhanet.net

This site, affiliated with a nonprofit organization, has a huge amount of information about the teachings of Buddha, links, chat, books about Buddhism, articles, and much more. You're likely to find everything you wanted to know about Buddhism at this attractive site.

New Kadampa Tradition

www.kadampa.net

This Mahayana Buddhist organization aims to preserve and promote the essence of Buddha's teachings in a form suited to the Western mind and way of life. This site offers information on books, meditation programs, and a directory of NKT centers.

Resources for the Study of Buddhism

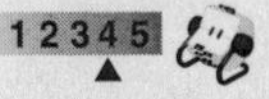

online.sfsu.edu/~rone/Buddhism/Buddhism.htm

Learn about basic Buddhist teachings through links and web references offered at this site, which contains helpful sites for children and adults.

tharpa.com

www.tharpa.com

Online bookstore for some of the best books on Buddhism and meditation. The site also features weekly snippets of wisdom, informative articles, and 500 glossary terms with definitions.

Tricycle Review

www.tricycle.com

Tricycle Review is America's leading Buddhist magazine, a publication intended to express Buddhist perspectives and practices to Western cultures. Here, you can find an excellent collection of articles from the magazine, along with blogs, audio teachings, discussion forums, personals, classifieds, and links to related sites.

A B C D E F G H I J K L M N O P Q R S T U V W X Y Z

CHRISTIANITY

American Baptist Churches USA Mission Center Online

1 2 3 4 5

www.abc-usa.org

Contains information about local American Baptist churches and American Baptist Green Lakes Conferences as well as national, international, and educational ministries.

Answers in Action

1 2 3 4 5

answers.org

Seeks to train Christians to "adopt and promote a Christian world view in every area of their lives." Features book reviews, information on contemporary issues, the Bible, Christian apologetics, and cults.

Augustine

1 2 3 4 5

ccat.sas.upenn.edu/jod/augustine.html

Contains translations and texts of Augustine, one of Christianity's most gifted and disciplined thinkers. Also includes other research materials and reference aids, and papers from an online seminar and images.

Baker Book House

1 2 3 4 5

www.bakerbooks.com

Baker Book House publishes approximately 200 Christian books a year in the categories of fiction, nonfiction, children's books, academic textbooks, and references. It also sells BakerBytes reference software. Published authors include Ruth Bell Graham and Robert Schuller, among others. Read excerpts from the latest publications online.

The Best Christian Links

www.tbcl.com

Extensive directory of the best Christian sites on the Web divided into categories including Art & Culture, Churches, Fellowship & Fun, and Spiritual Growth.

Bible Gateway

1 2 3 4 5 Blog RSS

bible.gospelcom.net

This award-winning site provides a search form for the Bible and handles many common translations. Lets you conduct searches and output verses in French, German, Swedish, Tagalog, Latin, or English. Also features audio versions of the Bible and its many passages, both Old and New Testaments.

Catholic Online

1 2 3 4 5

www.catholic.org

Bills itself as the "world's largest and most comprehensive Roman Catholic information service," and upon visiting this site, we would have to agree. This site provides a huge collection of current articles, along with message centers, forums, and research materials related to Roman Catholicism. You'll also find information about Catholic organizations, dioceses and archdioceses, publications, software, and doctrines.

Center for Reformed Theology and Apologetics (CRTA)

1 2 3 4 5

www.reformed.org

A nonprofit organization committed to the dispersal of online resources for the edification of believers of a Calvinist leaning. Links to articles on apologetics, the Bible, reformed books and commentaries, Calvinism/soteriology, Christianity and science, and so on. Searchable.

Christian Articles Archive

www.joyfulheart.com

Contains articles for Christian newsletters, religious periodicals, brochures, and sermon illustrations. Also provides information about using Internet email conferencing for Christian teaching and discipleship.

The Christian Missions

www.sim.org

This site offers the Great Commission Search Engine, which enables you to search for Christian missions all over the world. Site also features a SIM for Kids area.

Christianbook.com

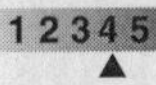

www.christianbook.com

Huge online bookstore specializing in books and other publications dealing with Christianity and related topics. Sells CDs, videos, and Christian gifts as well.

Christianity.com

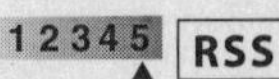

new.christianity.com

Christianity.com is a Christian resource hub where you can find articles, Bible study tools and quizzes, devotionals, community forums, and much more. Christianity.com's goal is to become the place where Christians start their day and where seekers begin their spiritual journeys.

Christianity Today

www.christianitytoday.com

Christianity Online is a Christian service featuring news about current events and politics, interviews with Christian musicians, and links to other Christian magazines. Visitors also can search a database of thousands of Christian websites.

crosswalk.com

www.crosswalk.com

Crosswalk offers Christians access to a directory of more than 20,000 Christian sites, news, information, Bible study tools, chat and discussion forums, a Bible search directory, and much more. But there's also a community to join and entertainment to be had here through the learning and sharing that takes place.

The Five Points of Calvinism

www.gty.org/~phil/dabney/5points.htm

R.L. Dabney discusses Calvinism without making use of the well-known acrostic. He discusses original sin, effectual calling, God's election, particular redemption, and perseverance of the saints. Footnotes follow.

Glide Memorial Church

www.glide.org

San Francisco's "church without walls" has a long history of serving the downtrodden outcasts of our society from the hippies and Black Panthers in the 1960s, Vietnam protestors in the 1970s, AIDS victims in the 1980s, crack addicts in the 1990s, and all people suffering from socio-economic problems into the twenty-first century. Here, you can learn more about Glide and how you can help.

GodWeb

www.godweb.org

In an effort to bring together an online Christian congregation, this site offers sermons, scripture studies, a multimedia Bible, and movie reviews.

Gospelcom.net

www.gospelcom.net

One of the best all-around Christian websites in this section, Gospelcom.net features a verse of the day, a daily devotional, mission news, ministry features, articles on how to become closer to God, and suggestions for youth ministry. Very solid site that's easy to navigate and serves the needs of the modern Christian. Scroll down for links to Christian radio stations and the joke of the day. Site also features online chat.

GraceCathedral.org

www.GraceCathedral.org

Visit San Francisco's Grace Cathedral Episcopal Church online, listen to services via its webcast, check out the media center, read interviews with spiritual leaders, and even take a virtual tour of the church without stepping foot in San Francisco.

Greater Grace World Outreach

www.ggwo.org

An international ministry with links to associated ministries such as *The Grace Hour International Radio Show*, missionary outreaches, and the Maryland Bible College and Seminary. This site also contains daily faith thoughts and information about upcoming conferences.

Greek Orthodox Archdiocese of America

www.goarch.org/en/resources

Provides information about Orthodox Christianity, the Greek Orthodox Archdiocese, the online chapel, Orthodox Christian resources, Orthodox Christian organizations, the Ministry Outreach Program, and more.

Harvest Online

www.harvest.org

Provides the history of the Harvest Christian Fellowship. Includes dates for upcoming Harvest Crusades, along with information about *A New Beginning with Greg Laurie* broadcasts.

Jesus Army

www.jesus.org.uk

What is the Jesus revolution? Find out on this award-winning British-based site. Contains an electronic magazine and many pictures.

Jesus Fellowship

jf.org

A family church, a Christian teaching center, a covenant community, a worldwide outreach center, a campus ministry, a neighborhood Bible fellowship, and much more. Links to Miami Christian University, where you can earn theological degrees online.

Jesus Film Project

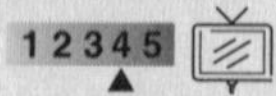

www.jesusfilm.org

Presents the Campus Crusade for Christ's Jesus Film Project. Includes well-designed graphics pages. Offers links to other Campus Crusade for Christ sites in the United States and abroad. You can view the movie in streaming video in just about any language on the planet.

Logos Research Systems

www.logos.com

An electronic publishing firm that offers CD-ROMs of biblical translations, ranging from the King James to the Revised Standard Version. Also includes many other titles.

Monastery of Christ in the Desert

www.christdesert.org/pax.html

Benedictine monks share their monastery via this beautiful website. Read up on their lives, listen to their chants, research their monastic studies, and even shop at the online gift store for books, prints, and other items.

Presbyterian Church USA

1 2 3 4 5

www.pcusa.org

Contains news from the Presbyterian News Service, reports and proceedings of the General Assembly, mission news, religious humor, and the PresbyNet conferencing system. There also are links to other Presbyterian-related sites, such as the web pages of local churches.

Project Wittenberg

1 2 3 4 5

www.iclnet.org/pub/resources/text/wittenberg/wittenberg-home.html

This award-winning site provides the thoughts of Martin Luther online. Plans to accumulate all of Luther's work, along with that of other theologians, and make them accessible to anyone who's curious to learn more about the Lutheran history and beliefs.

Religious Society of Friends

www.quaker.org

Offers a large directory of links about Quakers on the Web. Includes links to sites focusing on Quaker schools, journals, the American Friends Service Committee, genealogy sites, Quaker history, newsgroups, and more.

Scrolls from the Dead Sea

1 2 3 4 5

www.ibiblio.org/expo/deadsea.scrolls.exhibit/intro.html

This exhibit from the Library of Congress (reorganized by Jeff Barry) is a great scholastic site, containing the published text of the Qumran scrolls, commonly known as the Dead Sea scrolls. Bible scholars have studied these works extensively. The site offers a link to the Expo Bookstore, where you can purchase a printed copy of the exhibition catalog.

The Spurgeon Archive

1 2 3 4 5

www.spurgeon.org

This award-winning site is a collection of resources by and about Charles H. Spurgeon, English preacher and theologian. Contains information on his personal library, the full text of his sermons, his writings, and excerpts from *The Sword and the Trowel* and *The Treasury of David.*

The Trumpet

www.thetrumpet.com

The Trumpet, formerly *Plain Truth,* is a Christian fundamentalist news magazine that reports the news as an unfolding of biblical prophecy. If you're tired of reading the same old news with the same old slant, turn to *The Trumpet* for a more divine perspective.

Vatican

www.vatican.va

Online home of the Roman Catholic Church, this site takes you on a virtual tour of the Vatican, where you can access the latest news, perform research in the Vatican library and secret archives, tour the Vatican museums, read about past popes and the current pope, and much more.

World Religions Index

wri.leaderu.com/osites.html

This site provides you with an insight into the many religions and religious organizations of the world and offers to answer many interesting questions that you might have—for example, "Do all religions point to the same truth and do all religions lead to God?"

CULTS

FACTnet

www.factnet.org

Read news reports and suggestions of mind control and cult activity at this site, which aims to protect the freedom of the mind. Learn about psychological coercion, cult groups, and mind control here. Content is updated regularly with the latest news and analysis.

Ms. Guidance on Strange Cults

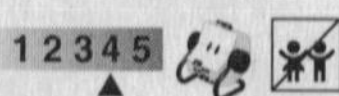

www.t0.or.at/msguide/devilgd1.htm

A plethora of links to all sorts of cult subjects. Several cult categories are addressed, including generic magic, paganism, freemasons, Gnostics, and many more.

Rick A. Ross Institute of New Jersey

www.rickross.com

The Rick A. Ross Institute of New Jersey presents this "database of information about cults, destructive cults, controversial groups and movements." Here, you can explore a massive "archive that contains thousands of individual documents including news stories, research papers, reports, court documents, book excerpts, personal testimonies and hundreds of links to additional relevant resources."

Steven Alan Hassan's Freedom of Mind Center

12345

www.freedomofmind.com

Steven Alan Hassan is a noted expert on cults and mind control. At this site, he seeks to educate others on the dangers of cults and other organizations that take away the power of free thinking. Here, you can find help for yourself or a loved one. A special area is also available for mental-health professionals to educate them of the risks of cults.

HINDUISM

Bhagvat Gita

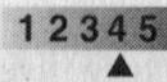

www.iconsoftec.com/gita

For students of Hinduism's most revered scripture, this site offers the Bhagvat Gita in the original Sanskrit, available in both PostScript and PDF formats. Also offers Arnold's complete English translation.

Hindu Kids

www.hindukids.org

Parents and kids who are interested in Buddhist philosophy, culture, and practice should check out this site. Site features an interactive map you can click to go to various areas on the site, including Learn, Pray, Play, Stories, Festivals, and Shop.

Hindu Resources Online

www.hindu.org

This site features a directory to information and resources related to Hinduism. The opening page provides an excellent definition of what it means to be Hindu.

Hindu Universe: Hindu Resource Center

www.hindunet.org

Learn about upcoming events, get the latest news about Hinduism and India, and stay connected to Hindu practices and teachings. In addition to Hindu history, philosophy, and wisdom, this site is packed with annoying ads.

Hinduism Online

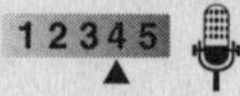

www.himalayanacademy.com

Created and maintained by the Himalayan Academy, this site provides a basic introduction to Hinduism, plus links to *Hinduism Today* magazine, Hindu books and art, the Hawaii Ashram, and other resources.

Hinduism Today

www.hinduismtoday.com

Learn all the basics of Hinduism at this informative site, which also offers books and other resources on the subject. Shopping mall provides links to stores where you can shop online for everything from books to gemstones.

iskon.com

www.iskcon.com

iskcon.com is "the official website of the International Society for Krishna Consciousness," which is better known as the Hare Krishna movement. Use the navigation bar at the top of the page to hop to the desired content area: Worldwide (Hare Krishna centers around the world), Culture (brief introduction to the group's practices), News (news, information, commentary, photos), ICJ (the *Iskon Communications Journal*), or Education (books, audio tapes, and other learning materials).

Understanding Hinduism

12345

www.hinduism.co.za

This site explores many aspects of Hinduism, including its founder, beliefs, practices, and customs. The navigation bar on the left offers dozens of links to topics including marriage, mathematics, calendars, Karma, Dharma, and food charts. Nothing fancy here, just great information and a lot of it.

ISLAM

Al-Islam

12345

www.al-islam.org

This site serves as a means of introducing Islam to you, and provides you with options for exploring this religion further. If you are a Muslim, this site serves as a repository for advancing your knowledge about Islam.

Answering Islam: A Christian-Muslim Dialog

12345

answering-islam.org.uk

This site provides answers, supported by Biblical scripture, to many of the arguments proposed by Muslim scholars that Islam is the one true faith. The creators of this site encourage visitors to examine the evidence themselves, and question it, before determining for themselves what they believe is true. Site also features a handful of links to related sites.

Illustrated Guide to Understanding Islam

12345

www.islam-guide.com

This site features a guide for those who wish to learn more about Islam, its holy book (the Koran), and its people (Muslims). This is an online book divided into clickable chapter titles.

International Association of Sufism

12345

www.ias.org

This site explores the teachings and precepts of Sufism. Offers many pages of information, pictures, and links intended to spread Sufi teachings of the brotherhood of man and the philosophy that self-understanding leads to a deeper understanding of the divine.

Islam 101

12345

www.islam101.com

Islam 101 is devoted to teaching visitors about Islam and "its way of life, civilization, and culture." Content at this site is divided into sections including Islamic Theology, Human Relations, Select Disciplines, and Comparative Religion.

Islam and Islamic Studies Resources

www.arches.uga.edu/~godlas

This site features a hefty collection of links to Muslim news, religion, politics, history, lives, art, and spirituality. Navigation is a bit clunky, but the site functions as a fairly good portal to online resources.

IslamiCity in Cyberspace

www.islam.org

Includes overview of doctrine, Quran; news, culture, education, and political information; downloadable radio/TV broadcasts (free software download); online shopping; a chat room; a virtual Mosque tour; web links; and a matrimonial service. Heavy coverage of Middle East politics. The site also features excellent information on understanding Islam.

Muslim Life in America

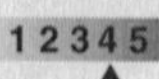

usinfo.state.gov/products/pubs/muslimlife

Maintained by the U.S. Department of State, this site is dedicated to promoting a greater understanding of Muslim people in the United States and elsewhere. Features a photo gallery, electronic journals, and links to other websites and publications. Content at this site is available in several languages: English, French, Russian, Arabic, Chinese, and Persian.

Online Islamic Bookstore

www.sharaaz.com

Provides information about the store's books, tapes, and software. Offers links to Islamic sites and book reviews of important books. Its aim? "To encourage the Muslim community to read again. To assert the importance of spiritual knowledge especially in this modern age."

Radio Islam

www.radioislam.com

Radio Islam is a daily Muslim call-in talk show out of Chicago that offers news, insights, commentary, and advice to followers of Islam. Here, you can tune in and listen to the broadcasts and feature presentations. Site also features links to Muslim Melodies and the Quran (audio readings of the Quran).

JUDAISM

Chabad-Lubavitch in Cyberspace

www.chabad.org

Chabad's mission is to "utilize Internet technology to unite Jews worldwide, empower them with knowledge of their 3,300 year-old tradition, and foster within them a deeper connection to Judaism's rituals and faith." This site has a nice design with a three-column format. In the left column is a navigation bar with links to the main content areas, including Magazine, Parshah, Calendar, Holidays, Daily Studies, Judaism 101, Spirituality, Women, Society & Living, Kids Zone, and Audio & Video. The center column offers featured articles and links to the more popular areas on the site. The right column presents an audio class, a calendar, and links to Chabad in the media. This is a great site to visit to view the Jewish perspective on current events.

Conversion to Judaism

www.convert.org

Anyone considering a conversion to Judaism should read the material offered on this site, which is organized in a FAQ format, making it easy to track down answers to some of the basic questions about Judaism and the process of conversion from another religion.

Jewish America

1 2 3 4 5

www.jewishamerica.org/ja/index.cfm

The aim of this site is to establish a community of Jews in America and provide them with the forum they need to dynamically discuss current issues. Site features a good collection of articles on Jewish continuity, heritage, tradition, and history, with a little humor tossed in for good measure. You can also find a small collection of discussion forums.

Jewish Encyclopedia

1 2 3 4 5

www.jewishencyclopedia.com

This is the home of the 12-volume Jewish Encyclopedia, first published between 1901 and 1906, consisting of more than 15,000 articles and illustrations. Great place to go to learn about early Jewish history, culture, and religion.

Jewish Theological Seminary

1 2 3 4 5

www.jtsa.edu

Represents this conservative seminary online. Provides a wealth of resources and links to conservative Jewish synagogues and institutions.

Jewish Virtual Library

www.jewishvirtuallibrary.org

The Jewish Virtual Library is an incredible monument to Jewish history and achievement. The library's resources cover history, women, the Holocaust, travel, the relationship between Israel and the United States, maps, politics, biographies, and more. Site also features and excellent directory of links to other sites.

> **Tip:** When we visited the site, the opening page presented a link called Myths & Facts, which links to an online book by Michael Bard presenting the Jewish position on the Middle East conflict between the Israelis and the Palestinians.

Jews for Judaism

1 2 3 4 5

www.jewsforjudaism.org

Through education and community, this site is working to counter attempts by Christians to convert Jewish believers. It provides resources, links, and information about local groups and counseling for those who might be interested.

Judaism 101

1 2 3 4 5

www.jewfaq.org

This site is an online encyclopedia of Judaism, covering "Jewish beliefs, people, places, things, language, scripture, holidays, practices and customs." The purpose is simply to inform and educate Jews and non-Jews about the religion by answering frequently asked questions.

Judaism and Jewish Resources

shamash.org/trb/judaism.html

Quite possibly the most complete source of Jewish information and Jewish-related links on the Web. Lists of links include media, singles groups, communities, newsgroups, reading lists, museums, and commerce sites.

MavenSearch

www.maven.co.il

Searchable directory for links to all things Jewish. Type a keyword or phrase to search the directory or browse by category. Categories include Communities, Travel and Tourism, Israel, Holocaust, Shopping & Gifts, and much more.

MyJewishLearning

1 2 3 4 5 RSS

www.myjewishlearning.com

This transdenominational website is dedicated to helping visitors deepen their knowledge and understanding of all aspects of Judaism. Here, you can find sections on History & Community, Daily Life

& Practice, Holidays, the Jewish Lifecycle (rituals for various stages in one's life), Texts, Ideas & Beliefs, and Culture. Site also features a glossary and a discussion area.

ORT

12345

www.ort.org

Coined from the acronym of the Russian words *Obschestvo Remeslenovo i zemledelcheskovo Trouda,* meaning The Society for Trades and Agricultural Labour, ORT is a worldwide education and training organization. At this site, you can learn more about ORT and its programs and schools.

Shamash

12345

shamash.org

This award-winning site run by the Jewish Internet Consortium offers links to various Jewish religious organizations ranging from Hillel to the World Zionist Organization. Includes FAQs pertaining to various facets of Judaism.

Shtetl: Yiddish Language and Culture

www.ibiblio.org/yiddish/shtetl.html

Shtetl means "small town" in Yiddish. This site aims to be a virtual small town on the Web. Provides information on Yiddish culture, as well as resources that point toward a wide range of links ranging from recommended books to kosher recipes.

Torah.org

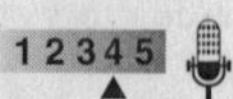

www.torah.org

This site provides Jewish educational material through article and reference archives, program and speaker information, and popular email classes.

Virtual Jerusalem

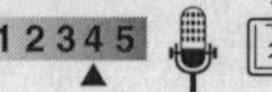

www.virtualjerusalem.com

Virtual Jerusalem offers updated news and information about Judaism and Israeli life, with departments for news, travel, technology, holidays, and entertainment. Site also features bulletin boards, live chat, and a Jewish email directory.

PRAYER

24-7 Prayer

www.24-7prayer.com

24-7 Prayer is a grassroots movement to encourage people to form prayer teams around the world to pray for the world.

Catholic Prayers

www.yenra.com/catholic/prayers

A treasury of Catholic prayers.

Evangelical Lutheran Church of America

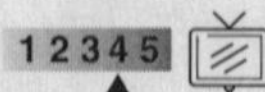

www.elca.org/prayer

The Lutheran Church created and maintains this site to enable visitors to post prayer requests and stories of answered prayers. Site also features instructions on how to meditate, a prayer for healing, prayer resources, and daily devotions.

International Prayer Network

www.victorious.org/prayer

The 24-hour International Prayer Network is one of the world's largest Christian prayer fellowships, with worldwide volunteers interceding for prayer requests from all over the globe.

A B C D E F G H I J K L M N O P Q R S T U V W X Y Z

LivePrayer

www.liveprayer.com

LivePrayer bills itself as "the first global prayer meeting." Here, you can fill out a prayer request online to have someone pray for you seven days a week. Site also offers audio and video clips of various prayers, devotionals, and sermons.

Lutheran Prayer Ministries

web.wt.net/~wayne/halpm.html

Learn how to start a prayer ministry and find useful resources and links at this site.

National Day of Prayer

www.ndptf.org

The first Thursday in May is the National Day of Prayer. This site encourages people to pray on this day and to organize other groups to pray. Includes a recommended prayer written specifically for this day.

Sacred Space

www.sacredspace.ie

Visit this site for an invitation to pray along with a group of Irish Jesuits. Features a prayer of the day in 20 languages plus a link to a site where you can pray with the pope.

World Ministry of Prayer

www.religiousscience.org/wmop_site

This site allows you to pray with a live person over the telephone or by email. It also has a prayer requests section and a catalog from which you can order from a large selection. Offers support through prayer.

World Prayer Network

www.worldprayer.org

This site is interested in uniting the world in prayer. Offers you the opportunity to pray with thousands of others with the same concerns and problems.

World Prayers

www.worldprayers.org

World Prayers features a collection of life-affirming players from various spiritual visionaries past and present. Here, you can spin the prayer wheel for a random prayer, browse selected prayers for peace, search for a prayer by name, or browse the index.

RETIREMENT

401K Center for Employers

1 2 3 4 5

401kcenter.com

Helps employers formulate a 401K plan by providing information on the six plan functions. Features plan overviews, Q&As, and contact numbers.

AARP WebPlace

1 2 3 4 5 Blog RSS

www.aarp.org

The home page for the American Association of Retired Persons provides information on the group's membership benefits, public policy positions, and volunteer programs. It also includes fact sheets on health, money, retirement, and other topics. As soon as you retire (possibly even before you retire), become a member of AARP and start taking advantage of what it has to offer. AARP is one of the most vocal advocates of senior citizen rights in the United States.

American Association of Homes and Services for the Aging

1 2 3 4 5

www2.aahsa.org

The American Association of Homes and Services for the Aging is an advocacy group composed of more than 5,600 nonprofit nursing homes, retirement communities, and other senior housing facilities. This site features a database of available senior housing.

Ameriprise

1 2 3 4 5

www.ameriprise.com

This instructional site, maintained by Ameriprise (formerly an American Express investment group), provides information on retirement savings, tax planning, and insurance buying.

CNN/Money Magazine Retirement

1 2 3 4 5 RSS

money.cnn.com/retirement

Retirement accounts, retirement planning, and living in retirement...it's all here at CNN and *Money* magazine's retirement site. This site also features a retirement calculator, a retirement guide, and additional tools and resources to help you plan for and make the most of your retirement years—financially, anyway.

ElderNet

1 2 3 4 5

www.eldernet.com

This comprehensive web index offers links to sites for the elderly, along with descriptions of each site. Incorporates health, finance, law, retirement, and lifestyle advice for seniors. Use tutorials, find activities, search resources, and read tips. After you click the Come In link on the opening page, the site presents a clickable map that takes you to your area of interest.

Forbes Retirement Planning

1 2 3 4 5

www.forbes.com/retirement

Forbes, one of the most highly respected personal finance magazines, features this area to focus on retirement planning. Here, you can find excellent articles on current issues, advice on how to maximize your retirement savings, special reports on various investment options, and much more.

Guide to Retirement Living

RSS

`www.retirement-living.com`

Comprehensive listing of living and healthcare options for retired people in the Mid-Atlantic states. Site also features a good collection of articles on a wide variety of retirement topics, including health, money, and legal issues.

Railroad Retirement Board

12345

`www.rrb.gov`

The Railroad Retirement Board is an independent federal agency whose job it is to "administer comprehensive retirement-survivor and unemployment-sickness benefit programs for the nation's railroad workers and their families, under the Railroad Retirement and Railroad Unemployment Insurance Acts." Here, you can learn more about the agency and tap its resources.

Retire Early

`www.retireearlyhomepage.com`

This site is dedicated to helping those who wish to retire early achieve their dreams. Most of the content presented here was presented elsewhere. The creator of this site brings it altogether to provide the tools and resources people need to plan for early retirement.

Retirement Calculators

`www.bhbt.com/pgs/calc_frame.html`

What will your expenses be after you retire? Are you saving enough to retire comfortably? What will your income be after you retire? Find answers to all of these questions and more by using Bar Harbor Bank and Trust's online retirement calculators.

Retirement Net

12345

`www.retirenet.com`

Retirement Net claims to be the "world's leading online retirement resource." This site enables you to search for retirement communities that match your interests and lifestyle. Browse through categories by lifestyle or search for a specific community.

Retirement with a Purpose

12345

`www.retirementwithapurpose.com`

You might have retired from your job, but you haven't retired from life. At this site, you can learn what you can do during your retirement to make the world a better place. Content at the site is organized by channel, including Home, Adventure, Advice, Grandparenting, Finance, Health, Transitions, and Relationships. If you're retired or are about to retire and are concerned about issues that commonly affect retired persons, check out this site.

Retirement Research Foundation

12345

`www.rrf.org`

This is the nation's largest private foundation devoted to aging and retirement issues. Explore funding interests, guidelines, FAQs, and what's new.

Seniors-Site.com

12345

`www.seniors-site.com`

Features information and bulletin boards on topics for seniors, including finance, education, death and dying, retirement, nursing homes, and nutrition.

Social Security Retirement Planner

12345

www.ssa.gov/retire2

The Social Security Retirement Planner "provides detailed information about your Social Security retirement benefits under current law and points out things you may want to consider as you prepare for the future." Here, you can find your retirement age, play with the numbers using the benefits calculator, learn about various Social Security benefits, find out what happens after you retire, and much more. You can also apply for benefits online and access a list of frequently asked questions.

Best Third Age

12345 Blog RSS

www.thirdage.com

Third Age is an e-zine aimed at those baby boomers who are starting their fifth decade. It includes articles on investing, love and relationships, health and fitness, hobbies, and technology. It also includes a chat room, discussion forums, and advice columns. We found this site to offer the most comprehensive coverage of issues related to retirement and aging, including health, money, work, relationships, sex, beauty, fashion, and recreation. Site also features expert advice and a list of the ten most frequently accessed articles.

WiredSeniors

12345

www.seniorssearch.com

This directory provides links to more than 5,000 sites geared toward the over-50 age group. Topics include history, health and fitness, hobbies, grandparenting, genealogy, travel, senior discounts, retirement, volunteering, and more.

ROCK CLIMBING

Best ABC of Rock Climbing

1 2 3 4 5

www.abc-of-rockclimbing.com

ABC of Rock Climbing provides you with "everything related to rock climbing and other essentials of the sport such as styles and techniques." Tabbed navigation provides quick access to information articles, news, a gear and equipment shop, a directory of holidays and travel services, and a dynamic community of rock climbers. Here, you'll find basic training for beginners along with techniques and tips for the more advanced climber. Site is attractive, easy to navigate, and packed with great information, equipment, and travel guides, making it an easy pick as Best of the Best in the Rock Climbing category.

American Mountain Guides Association

1 2 3 4 5

www.amga.com

The AMGA's site is aimed mostly at the climbing professional, with pages about courses and certification, but it is helpful to regular climbers with a page of referrals to certified guides. You can search the directory of guides by discipline or location.

American Safe Climbing Association

1 2 3 4 5

www.safeclimbing.org

Dedicated to making the sport of climbing safer, the ASCA replaces unsafe bolts and anchors at many popular climbing sites, such as Yosemite, Red Rock, and Joshua Tree, and educates climbers on safe climbing techniques. Check out this site for bolt information, fall forces, rebolting techniques, safe climbing techniques, and more. The site also provides a list of climbing routes that the ASCA has rebolted.

Big Wall Climbing Web Page

www.bigwalls.net

Diehard climbers will appreciate a home page dedicated to intense, multiday climbs; read about different walls, as well as stories of individual climbs. Answers the big question: What about when you need to go?

Bouldering

www.bouldering.com

Bouldering is primarily an online store that carries a wide selection of high-quality gear for rock climbers. Site also features videos and blogs.

Climber's First Aid

1 2 3 4 5

www.outdoor-resources.com/cfa.html

This web page is aimed at outdoor enthusiasts—climbers, hikers, bikers—and promotes the purchase of *Climber's First Aid: What to Do While Waiting for Help.* The book is printed on tear-resistant, water-resistant stock so that it will be rugged enough to take along on your wilderness adventures.

The Climbing Dictionary

1 2 3 4 5

www.rockclimbing.com/articles/term.php

This dictionary of rock climbing features a clickable alphabetic list of more than 240 terms and definitions covering everything from "A vue" to "zipper."

Climbing Online

www.climbing.com

Climbing magazine's home on the web features the latest climbing news, feature stories, product reviews, and online tutorials. Learn the basics or go beyond the basics with the latest techniques. Special how-to sections on dealing with rock and dealing with ice, plus dozens of technical tips and links to other rock-climbing resources on the Web (many to sites that feature webcams of popular climbing destinations) make this site one of the best in this category.

GORP–Climbing

12345

gorp.away.com/gorp/activity/climb.htm

Read articles organized by topic, such as gear, know-how, and location, to improve your skill level and prepare for your next climb. You'll also find information on trips you might want to consider. Lots of inspiring photos and helpful tips for both novice and expert climbers.

GPS Rock Climbing Guide

12345

www.colororange.com

This site, maintained by climber Jacques Rutschmann, provides geographic coordinates of rock-climbing areas (and hot springs) in the United States, Europe, and the rest of the world.

Joshua Tree Rock Climbing School

12345

www.rockclimbingschool.com

Learn how to climb from some of the top climbers in the world at one of the most popular climbing sites in the world, Joshua Tree National Park, located in southern California. This site provides information on the various rock-climbing courses offered at the school, plus brief biographies of the instructors and information about accommodations.

Nova Online: Lost on Everest

www.pbs.org/wgbh/nova/everest

PBS's *Nova* followed an expedition up the world's highest mountain, and every aspect of the climb can be found on this site. The series originally followed the climbers live in real time.

Online Climbing Guide

12345

www.onlineclimbing.com

This site, created by rock climbers for rock climbers, represents a community effort by climbers to provide a comprehensive directory of places to climb. Includes directions to favorite climb sites, photos, difficulty ratings, and more. Search for sites by state. Also features a directory of climbing gyms organized by state.

Rock & Ice: The Climber's Magazine

www.rockandice.com

Home of *Rock & Ice* magazine, this site provides a preview of the contents of the current issue and enables you to subscribe online.

Rock Climbing Australia

www.climbing.com.au

Site features a collection of articles on the science of rock climbing—studies on the effects of rock climbing and on the safest, most effective techniques. If you're planning on doing some rock climbing down under, the Aussie Crag Guide can help you locate the best places to climb.

RockClimbing.com

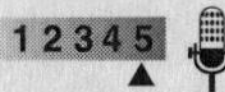

www.rockclimbing.com

A super climbing website complete with climbing routes for the most popular sites around the world, gear shopping, partner connecting, discussions, photos, and information on climbing techniques to improve your skill. This site's mission is to provide rock-climbing enthusiasts with the information and resources they need to fully enjoy the sport and foster a community in which rock climbers the world over can share their knowledge and enthusiasm.

RockList

www.rocklist.com

Long lists of cliffs, climbing gyms, alpine clubs, e-zines, literature, expeditions (including Everest), gear manufacturers, mountain information, and more. Search by geographical area anywhere in the world. Great site for finding places to climb.

Sportrock Climbing Centers

12345

www.sportrock.com

This sport climbing company offers several climbing facilities in the mid-Atlantic states. Here, you can find a Sportrock climbing center near you, get information on instruction for kids and beginners, and check membership rates.

Touchstone Climbing and Fitness

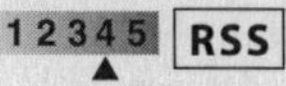

www.touchstoneclimbing.com

Touchstone Climbing and Fitness operates several indoor rock climbing facilities in the San Francisco area. Here, you can check out what the facilities offer and where they're located. Site also features some valuable training tips.

RODEO

American Junior Rodeo Association

1 2 3 4 5

www.ajra.org

The AJRA was begun when its founder went to rodeos and thought how unfair it was that kids were competing with adults, and so would never win, despite giving it their all. This page has a history of the AJRA, a schedule of competitions, results, standings, age divisions, a newsletter, and much more.

Billy Joe Jim Bob's Rodeo Links Page

www.gunslinger.com/rodeo.html

Perhaps the most complete rodeo index on the Web. Billy Joe Jim Bob takes great care to include links for every rodeo, rodeo association, and rodeo site he could find, which ends up being a whole lot of links!

Houston Livestock Show and Rodeo

1 2 3 4 5

www.hlsr.com

The Houston Livestock Show and Rodeo is one of the main rodeo attractions in the country, and you can learn more about it right here. This site features a year-round events calendar, information about the livestock and horse shows, a store where you can shop for merchandise, facts and FAQs, and much more.

Janet's Let's Rodeo Page

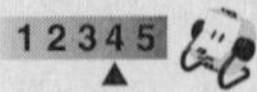

www.cowgirls.com/dream/jan/rodeo.htm

Janet's page has pictures, links to other rodeo sites, a long list of articles, and countless answers to her question, "What do cowgirls dream about?"

Mesquite Championship Rodeo

1 2 3 4 5

www.mesquiterodeo.com

Mesquite, Texas, 15 minutes outside Dallas, hosts this rodeo every Friday and Saturday night, where kids not only are welcome but also compete in events such as the Mutton Bustin' Event and the Kids Calf Scramble. This site features an events calendar, seating chart, rodeo standings, online ticket ordering, and a store where you can purchase merchandise.

Professional Bull Riders, Inc.

www.pbrnow.com

Professional Bull Riders, Inc., owned and operated by more than 700 professional bull riders, is dedicated to convincing the world that bull riders are mainstream athletes worthy of the attention and respect that other professional athletes receive. This site introduces you to the bulls and riders, provides information on tours and events, offers current rankings, and provides plenty of photos and videos to engage and entertain. Very well-designed site.

Best ProRodeo.com

prorodeo.org

The Professional Rodeo Cowboys Association's official website, ProRodeo.com provides up-to-date information about the latest rodeo competitions across the country. Read about your favorite rodeo riders, find the tour standings and scoreboard, check out the injury reports, learn of upcoming televised events, and even flip through some action photos. You can shop online at ProRodeo Merchandise, become a member, and even check out the media library. Packed with useful information in an easy-to-navigate format, this site is the hands-down winner of the Best of the Best award.

Tip: If you're new to rodeo, scroll down to near the bottom of the navigation bar on the left and click Event Descriptions to learn the lingo and how events are scored.

Slam! Sports Rodeo

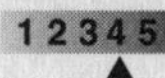

www.canoe.ca/SlamRodeo/home.html

Interested in what happened at rodeo tournaments last night or want to know more about your favorite rodeo stars? Check Slam! Sports Rodeo for all your rodeo news needs. Slam also covers other sports.

Women's Pro Rodeo Association

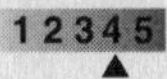

www.wpra.com

The Women's Professional Rodeo Association was formed in 1948 by a group of Texas ranch women who wanted to "add a little color and femininity to the rough-and-tumble sport of rodeo." At this site, you can view standings, results, a schedule of competitions, information about the division tour, and a history of rodeo.

A B C D E F G H I J K L M N O P Q R S T U V W X Y Z

ROMANCE

Alive with Love

www.alivewithlove.com

Author and romantic relationship expert Kara Oh maintains this romance directory to help couples stoke the romantic fires of their relationships. Here, you can find links to several sites on the Web that offer tips and advice on romance, dating and relationships; techniques for becoming more beautiful, sexy, and sensual; love tests; and advice on how to create love and passion. You'll also find a link to Kara's blog. Most of the links take you to sponsor sites, but a few of them offer advice from Kara herself.

eHarlequin

1 2 3 4 5

www.eharlequin.com

Harlequin Enterprises Limited is "the global leader in series romance and one of the world's leading publishers of women's fiction," publishing more than 115 titles a month in 25 languages in 94 international markets on 6 continents. Here, you can check out Harlequin Enterprises selection of books, shop online, meet your favorite authors online, and even learn how to write romance novels yourself.

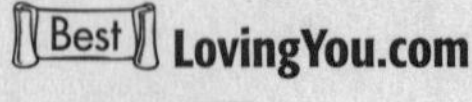

LovingYou.com

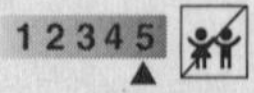

www.lovingyou.com

When you want to romance your partner, check out this site for ideas, advice, inspiration, dedications, gifts, and vacations. Site features an idea of the day, poem of the day, quote of the day, advice forums, love quizzes, lovescopes, love tasks, fun and games, and a host of articles that can transform a half-hearted lover into a sizzling Don Juan.

The Romance Club

1 2 3 4 5

www.theromanceclub.com

The Romance Club is dedicated to readers of romance novels. Here, you'll find book reviews, author interviews, and information about your favorite romance book author. Site also features a newsletter to keep fans posted of new releases and eagerly anticipated novels.

The Romance Reader

1 2 3 4 5

www.theromancereader.com

If you're into romance novels, check this site for reviews of the latest books on the market. Reviews are organized by genre, including Historical, Contemporary, Time Travel & Fantasy, Category, Regency, and Eclectica. Site also features author interviews, information on upcoming titles, an online contest, author contact information, and more.

Romance Tips

1 2 3 4 5

www.romancetips.com

This site features a huge collection of romance tips presented in four categories: Singles, Dating, Engagement, and Marriage. Tips in the Marriage category are wisely broken down into subcategories: Newlyweds, Husbands, Wives, and With Kids. The romantic ambience of this site is ruined by a constant barrage of advertisements, but it does provides some useful advice.

SCI-FI & FANTASY

Analog Science Fiction and Fact

1 2 3 4 5 Blog

www.analogsf.com

The popular *Analog* magazine is online here, offering samples of its columns and stories. *Analog* places equal emphasis on the terms *science* and *fiction*, in an attempt to provide a more realistic view of how science might develop in the future and be applied to improve the human condition. At this site, you can check out some columns and story excerpts from the magazine.

Asimov's Science Fiction

1 2 3 4 5 Blog

www.asimovs.com

Home of *Asimov's Science Fiction* magazine, which reviews the Best of the Best new science fiction publications and presents some of its own. Learn about the awards it has won, its authors, and other information about the magazine. Read some science fiction short stories from some of the best sci-fi writers in the business.

Classic SciFi

1 2 3 4 5

classicscifi.com

Classic SciFi covers movies and features, presents sci-fi TV listings, offers links to other sci-fi websites, and contains a list of events such as upcoming movie release dates. For each movie covered in the Movie area, this site provides links to Amazon.com and AllPosters.com, where you can purchase the movie or poster online.

> **Tip:** This is one of the best places to go to get TV listings of sci-fi shows and movies. Click TV Listings and use the resulting page to check out today's listings or look up listings later in the week.

Comics2Film

1 2 3 4 5 RSS

www.comics2film.com

Comics2Film specializes in information about comics that have been made into movies, including *Spiderman* and *X-Men*. The opening page contains news and announcements that fans might find particularly interesting. Site also contains galleries, discussion forums, and links to other related sites.

Dark Horse

1 2 3 4 5

www.dhorse.com

Dark Horse is the publisher of some classic comics, including Star Wars, Conan, Hellboy, and Usagi Yojimbo. Here you can check out the comics and download freebies including screensavers and wallpaper. Click Things from Another World to shop online for collectibles, apparel, and other merchandise. The DH Entertainment area features movies based on Dark Horse comics. And the DH Gallery features DH comics, books, and other products and resources.

Dark Shadows Online

1 2 3 4 5

www.darkshadowsonline.com

Premiering in 1966 on ABC television, this show was a soap opera based on ghouls, goblins, vampires, and the like. This site includes a history of the show, a cast list and information about what the cast members are doing now, a photo gallery, collectibles you can order online, features including trivia, information on festivals, links to DVDs and books you can order online, and links to other *Dark Shadows* sites (including the home pages of several cast members).

Related Sites

www.collinwood.net

users.rcn.com/mfmiozza

Daystrom Institute Technical Library

12345

www.ditl.org

The Daystrom Institute is a repository for all the technical information dealing with the various Star Trek episodes. Covers ships, personnel, weapons, stations, battles, lineage, size charts, and much more.

Encyclopedia of Fantastic Film and Television

12345

www.eofftv.com

This site provides in-depth coverage on specific science fiction movies and TV shows. It takes a story, such as Dr. Jekyll and Mr. Hyde, and covers all versions of the story in movies and on TV, all around the world, to show the various ways it has been adapted. Casual sci-fi fans might find this coverage a little heady, but it hooks hardcore fans. Click Updates and then click Top 100 Reviews, to view a list of the 100 most frequently reviewed sci-fi websites.

FanGrok

www.robbiesoft.co.uk/FanGrok

A U.K. online e-zine that satirizes sci-fi television. Some of the articles are funny; be sure to check out the *Telletubbies Exposed!* issue.

Fanspeak

12345

www.cinescape.com/0/Fanspeak.asp

Cinescape offers this collection of subsites run by sci-fi and comic book fans "who love a particular genre property so much, they themselves have become experts on such diverse topics as *Batman, Godzilla, Star Wars,* and the *X-Files.*" At these fan sites, you can gather current news, reviews, and information about your favorite shows, movies, heroes, superheroes, and villains and join in discussions with fellow fans.

Feminist Science Fiction, Fantasy, and Utopia

12345 Blog

www.feministsf.org/femsf/index.html

Created and maintained by Laura Quilter, this site provides information about feminist themes in science fiction literature; reviews; a checklist of feminist science fiction, fantasy, and utopian stories; a list of anthologies; links to research guides; and much more. Site design makes finding specific content a real chore, but the site offers some excellent content and links to additional resources on the Web and through listservs.

Forrest J. Ackerman Official Site

12345

4forry.best.vwh.net/foyer.shtml

This is the award-winning web home of the biggest science fiction fan ever and the creator of *Famous Monsters* magazine. Here you can peruse the library or art gallery or visit Ack in his office. The site is also accented with several challenging puzzles.

Global Episode Opinion Survey

12345

www.geos.tv

You hate (or love) a particular episode of your favorite sci-fi television show. Are you curious whether others agree or disagree? Then join GEOS, where you and others around the world can give opinions and rate the shows and their episodes. Site features some excellent search tools along with TV listings of current sci-fi shows, news, and feature articles about casts, crews, and stars.

The Hitchhiker's Guide to the Galaxy: The Movie

12345

hitchhikers.movies.go.com

This is the official website of the movie version of *The Hitchhiker's Guide to the Galaxy*, the cult classic radio comedy by Douglas Adams that eventually was published as a book. With the movie version, this can no longer be referred to as one of the great sci-fi movies that was never made. Visit this site to view the trailer and other movie clips, nab some free downloads (wallpapers, screensavers, buddy icons, posters, and so forth), check out the photo gallery, play games, or learn more about the characters in the movie.

Look What I Found in My Brain!

lucysnyder.blogspot.com

Look What I Found In My Brain! features "essays, movie and book reviews, humor, weird science facts, odd fiction, and maybe the stray poem." Almost everything you find on the site has been written by sci-fi enthusiast Lucy A. Snyder, but she occasionally presents offerings from guest writers. Site also features cat facts and humor.

Lord of the Rings Movie Site

www.lordoftherings.net

Home of one of the most popular movie series of all time, this site provides a virtual tour of the films and the legend. Check out movie trailers; learn more about the cast and crew; find late-breaking news and upcoming events; explore the well-stocked photo and video libraries; and even download free screensavers, desktop wallpaper, and other goodies.

The Matrix

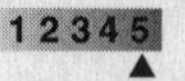

whatisthematrix.warnerbros.com

Fans of *The Matrix* will want to enter this virtual tour of the movie set to experience *The Matrix* in a completely new way. Read interviews with the cast and crew, view photos from the set, take 3D tours of the deck of the *Nebuchadnezzar*, flip through the comics, and more. One of the best new science fiction movies has the best science fiction website, too. It will keep visitors of all ages busy for hours.

Satellite News

www.mst3kinfo.com

Satellite News is the official home of the retired TV show *Mystery Science Theater*, on which the characters made fun of old sci-fi and horror movies from a space station. This site contains a history of the show, information about its creators and cast, and a host of news and information about sci-fi movies and the actors who starred in them. Site also features a FAQs area, an area to swap episodes with other fans, descriptions of what the show's creators and cast members are doing now, and information about all the movies shown on Mystery Science Theater.

Science Fiction Book Club

www.sfbc.com

Save up to 65 percent on science fiction books by becoming a member of the Science Fiction Book Club. This book club carries top titles and the latest publications.

Science Fiction Crowsnest

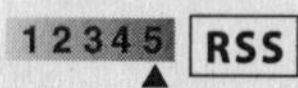

www.sfcrowsnest.com

Stephen Hunt's Science Fiction Crowsnest offers news, interviews, and editorials related to all things sci-fi. The opening page is packed with reviews of books, movies, and TV shows. The site also features online games, chat and discussion forums, and a website directory that makes it easier to locate specific articles. When we visited the site, it also had its fair share of annoying pop-up ads.

Science Fiction and Fantasy Research Database

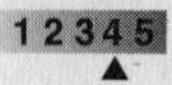

lib-oldweb.tamu.edu/cushing/sffrd

Compiled by Hal W. Hall, this database provides online access to more than 73,000 historical and critical items about science fiction, fantasy, and horror (in that order).

Science Fiction and Fantasy World

www.sffworld.com

Featuring more than 10,000 pages of science fiction and fantasy, this is one of the largest science fiction sites on the Web. Read some of the latest short stories and poems, check out the interviews, or visit the discussion forums to share your science fiction enthusiasm with other fans. The site also provides a directory of TV and movie listings, book reviews and excerpts, e-zines, a Fun Zone (where you can discuss humorous topics or join in role-playing games), and an art gallery with more than 1,000 sci-fi sketches and paintings. You can even submit your own writings for consideration.

Science Fiction and Fantasy Writers of America (SFWA)

12345

www.sfwa.org

Sci-fi writers will find this site, and this nonprofit organization, a big help in improving their writing skills and improving the financial rewards of writing science fiction. The site provides writing tips as well as model contracts to follow, document formatting guidance, and a regular bulletin for members.

Science Fiction Museum and Hall of Fame

12345

www.sfhomeworld.org

The Science Fiction Museum and Hall of Fame (SFM) is a "nonprofit organization created to inspire new generations to reach beyond the present, imagine the future, and explore the infinite possibilities of the universe." This site offers information about the museum, including its location and hours of operation; several online exhibits, Homeworld, Fantastic Voyages, Brave New Worlds, and Them; information about special educational programs the museum offers; membership information; and a calendar of events.

Science Fiction Weekly

12345 RSS

www.scifi.com/sfw

Weekly news, articles, features, interviews, and reviews. The site also features a games column, letters from fans, On Screen information about programs on television and in the movies, a Cool Stuff column, and a site-of-the-week feature.

SciFan

12345

www.scifan.com

SciFan offers science fiction fans plenty of reading material, from magazine subscriptions and books. Search the sci-fi author database to track down those titles you haven't read yet and then link to a bookstore to order it.

www.scifi.com

This site from the Sci Fi channel offers up lots of sci-fi adventures to explore. Between online programming and TV and movie reviews, you'll find plenty of unique and fascinating story lines to follow. You can also get sci-fi news, clips of animated features, movie trailers, and interviews. One of the top features of this site is the Scifipedia, and extensive online encyclopedia of science fiction that covers Anime, Art, Audio, Comics, ETs and UFOs, Games, Literature, Movies, TV, and more. Scroll down to the Did You Know? section for some interesting trivia. This site's excellent design, high-quality content, and up-to-date information combine to help this site earn our Best of the Best designation in the Science Fiction category.

The Sci-Fi Site

www.sfsite.com

Book reviews, news, and resources. This great site has lots of book reviews, opinion pieces, author interviews, fiction excerpts, author and publisher reading lists, and a variety of other wonderful features. You'll find a comprehensive list of links to author and fan tribute sites, SF conventions, movies, TV, magazines, e-zines, writer resources, publishers, and small press sites.

SciFi Source

www.scifisource.com

Excellent directory of hand-picked sci-fi and fantasy websites organized by categories, including Actors & Actresses, Books & Authors, Conventions & Events, Fantasy, and Science & Technology, to name a few. Here you can find links to more than 2,400 science fiction sites.

SFF Net

www.sff.net

This is the science fiction and fantasy website "for people who like to read," particularly for people who like to read genre fiction, including science fiction, fantasy, horror, romance, mystery, and young adult fiction. SFF Net's goal is to bring together writers, editors, publishers, and readers in an online community that benefits them all.

SF-Lovers

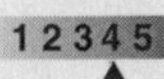

www.noreascon.org/users/sflovers/u1/web

An extensive collection of links to sci-fi resources on the Net. Subject areas include other archives and resource guides, authors, bibliographies, movies, and more. You can also subscribe to the SF-Lovers digest to receive your SF news via email. Click the Reference link for links to additional information sites on the Web for art, books, sci-fi fans, films, space sites, and TV shows.

Sky Captain and the World of Tomorrow

skycaptain.com

This is the official website of the movie *Sky Captain and the World of Tomorrow*, starring Gwyneth Paltrow, Jude Law, and Angelina Jolie. Here you can view a synopsis of the movie, listen to the soundtrack, view a movie trailer and behind-the-scenes footage, learn more about the characters, grab some free downloads, or play the game. This site has a high coolness rating.

Star Trek

www.startrek.com

Provides a good amount of information and links to many sites that cover the television, film, and cultural phenomenon that is *Star Trek*. This site includes pictures, sounds, quotes, fan information, and TV listings, a daily video clip and photo, a daily word and trivia, a quote of the day, and a daily reminder. You can also sign up for the newsletter and shop for *Star Trek* apparel and memorabilia online.

Star Wars Official Site

www.starwars.com

Star Wars fans will want to bookmark this site, which serves up everything you need to know about the *Star Wars* series. Features movie clips, well-stocked photo galleries, interviews with the creators and cast, and much more. Material is organized by episode, making it easy to find what you want. You can even shop online for *Star Wars* apparel and collectibles.

The TV Sci-Fi and Fantasy Database

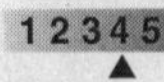

www.pazsaz.com/scifan.html

If you can't remember the name of a particular episode, or when it ran, just check with the database. It lists the name and original air date of more than 70 different shows. Note that no information about the episode is given. Comes in full-graphical and less-graphical versions.

Van Helsing Fan Site

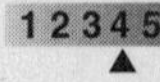

www.vanhelsingfan.com

This is the fan site for the movie version of *Van Helsing*, starring Hugh Jackman and Kate Beckinsale. Site features three main areas: Movie (characters, synopsis, goofs, trivia, and other facts about the movie), Media (gallery, fan art, wallpaper, video clips, icons, and so on), and Interactive (games, puzzles, fan fiction, and other interactive content).

Virus

1 2 3 4 5

www.virusthemovie.com

This official site offers information on the cast and crew of this action/science fiction movie. Photos, movie trailer, and games.

World Science Fiction Society

1 2 3 4 5

www.wsfs.org

The World Science Fiction Society is the group that chooses the recipient of the coveted Hugo Awards for science fiction achievement. It also determines the locations and committees for the annual World Science Fiction Conventions (the Worldcons), attends those Worldcons, and chooses "the locations and Committees for the occasional North American Science Fiction Conventions (the NASFiCs). (A NASFiC is held in North America in any year where the Worldcon is outside of North America.)"

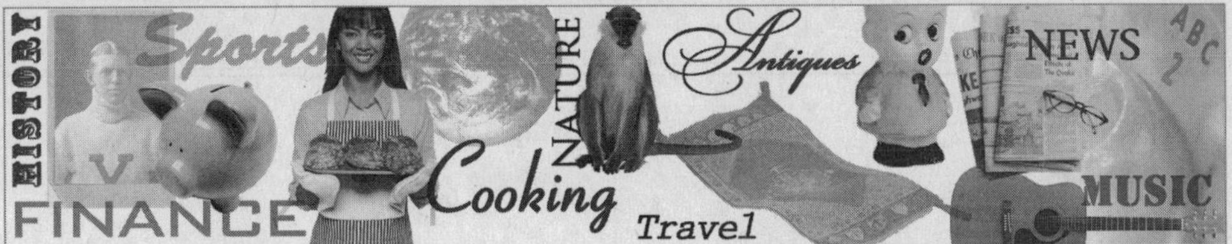

SCRAPBOOKING

Addicted to Scrapbooking

12345

www.addictedtoscrapbooking.com

Addicted to Scrapbooking bills itself as "the Largest Scrapbooking Store on the Web." Here you can find more than 250,000 scapbook layouts and search for supplies and equipments at more than 100 stores online, all through this one convenient shopping mall. You can shop by category or use the site's search tool to hunt for specific products by keyword.

Computer Scrapbooking

12345

www.computerscrapbooking.com

If you have a computer and you'd rather lay out your scrapbook pages on screen rather than on paper, visit this site to learn the tricks of the trade. Here you'll find plenty of articles and tutorials to get you started and learn new techniques, download some free patterns and clip art, access some excellent free fonts, check out some creative layouts, sign up for the mailing list, and find links to other related sites.

Creative Memories

12345

www.creativememories.com

Creative Memories is a scrapbook company that offers not only the supplies you need to get started, but also professionally trained consultants who can guide you through the design process and demonstrate techniques to simplify the various tasks involved. Site features a page where you can check out the company's products and services and an idea center where you can check out some sample layouts.

Tip: Click the Idea Center link and then click Tips and Resources for journaling and photography tips.

Best Scrapbook.com

12345 Blog

www.scrapbook.com

Scrapbook.com is a family run business in Mesa, Arizona, devoted to guiding people through the memory preservation process and keeping them motivated to document their lives and the lives of their loved ones. This site offers all the tools, supplies, and instructions you need to get your scrapbook hobby up and running and sharpen your skills. Here you'll find more than 200,000 sample layouts to inspire you, discussion forums with more than 1.5 million tips and suggestions, a well-stocked library of additional articles and tips, tens of thousands of scrapbook-related blogs, online instruction, and more. You can shop for items by category, brand, or theme, and even set up your own My Place area on the site to showcase your creations.

Scrapbooking 101

12345

www.scrapbooking101.net

Scrapbooking enthusiast LeNae Gerig offers to help novice scrapbookers get started at this site and teach a few tricks to the more experienced hobbyist. Site features general information, a list of supplies and equipment, tips about photos, basic techniques, instructions on using patterned paper, a layout of the month, and an article of the month.

A B C D E F G H I J K L M N O P Q R S T U V W X Y Z

Scrapbooking.com

1 2 3 4 5

scrapbooking.com

Scrapbooking.com is an online scrapbooking magazine packed with articles, project ideas, sample layouts, and activities for the whole family, along with online shopping for supplies. Down the middle of the page runs a column of feature articles, complete with a summary of each article and a link you can click to view the entire article. Along the left side of the page is a navigation bar that provides quick access to Newsletters, Product Demos, Contests, Coupons, the Store Directory, Community (bulletin boards, calendar, and free scrapbook galleries), and more.

ScrapbookingTop50

1 2 3 4 5

www.scrapbookingtop50.com

If you're looking for more scrapbooking sites than the selection we offer in this category, go to ScrapbookingTop50 to discover links to the top sites for buying supplies and equipment. Many of these sites also offer free layout ideas, tips, and instructions to get you started.

Scrapjazz

1 2 3 4 5

www.scrapjazz.com

This site features a collection of more than 100,000 scrapbook layouts, along with gobs of tips and instructions. You can search the Layout Gallery for a specific type of layout, browse the collection by theme or technique, read product reviews, take a brief course in Scrapbooking 101, share ideas and tips on the message boards, enter an online contest, sign up for the free newsletter, and much more. This site offers everything you need to get started and hone your skills as a scrapbook hobbiest.

SELF-HELP (SEE MOTIVATIONAL & SELF-IMPROVEMENT)

SENIORS

AARP

www.aarp.org

This user-friendly site contributes to AARP's goal of allowing senior citizens to lead the rich and fulfilling lives that they are accustomed to—not only by staying well informed, but also by staying active. Site features several areas including Member Discounts and Services; Issues and Elections; Learning and Technology; Health; Family, Home and Legal; Money and Work; Travel; and Fun and Games.

Administration on Aging (AOA)

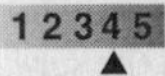

www.aoa.dhhs.gov

AOA is a federal agency serving as an advocate for older Americans and issues that concern them. The site provides a lot of background information on the Older Americans Act, as well as practical information for senior citizens and their caregivers—a resource directory, list of local agencies providing senior services, news, and health information.

AgeNet

12345

www.agenet.com

Seniors and their family members will find information at this site both interesting and useful. Topics covered include health, insurance, finance, drugs, and caregiver support. You can use the Social Security estimator, for example, to estimate the value of benefits you should receive at retirement or try out some brain exercises to improve your mental faculties. This site's comprehensive collection of resources for seniors combined with an inviting presentation makes this one of the better senior sites on the Web.

Best Aging in the Know

12345

www.healthinaging.org/agingintheknow

Aging in the Know, "Your Gateway to Health and Aging Resources on the Web," was created and is maintained by the American Geriatrics Society Foundation for Health in Aging (FHA) to provide seniors and their caregivers with up-to-date information on health and aging. Click Topics at a Glance to access a clickable table of contents on the top health issues related to aging. The Topics at a Glance section is presented in three main headings: How We Age, Health Care Decisions and Issues, and Elder Health at Your Fingertips. This gets you up to speed in a hurry on the main topics and enables you to quickly dip into a topic area of interest. Site also provides a What to Ask? feature that can help you communicate effectively with your healthcare provider and an online directory of links to related, high-quality sites. You can also explore the latest research developments at this site.

Alliance for Retired Americans

www.retiredamericans.org

The Alliance for Retired Americans is a national organization for retired citizens of the United States. Created by the AFL-CIO, the Alliance works to promote legislation that "protects the health and

A B C D E F G H I J K L M N O P Q R S T U V W X Y Z

economic security of seniors, rewards work, strengthens families, and builds thriving communities." Think of it as a union for retired workers, a way for retired workers to fight for their rights and have their voices heard. This is a great place for seniors to go to find out about government goings on that can affect their lives.

Alzheimer's Association

1 2 3 4 5

www.alz.org

This national nonprofit organization provides support to those afflicted with Alzheimer's as well as their caregivers. AA funds Alzheimer's research, which is documented at the site, and offers support and resources to help families cope with this illness. Great place to check up on the latest medications and treatments.

American Association of Homes and Services for the Aging

1 2 3 4 5

www2.aahsa.org

Visit this site for a listing of member facilities. Includes assisted living, nursing homes, and retirement communities.

American Geriatrics Society

1 2 3 4 5

www.americangeriatrics.org

The American Geriatrics Society is a group of healthcare professionals dedicated to improving the health and well-being of the elderly. Here you can learn more about the organization, check out the AGS newsroom and publications, or click Patient Education to go to the Aging in the Know site, which is covered earlier in this category.

Assisted Living Foundation

1 2 3 4 5

www.alfa.org

Detailed description from the Assisted Living Federation of America (ALFA). This organization represents more than 6,000 for-profit and not-for-profit providers of assisted living, continuing care retirement communities, independent living, and other forms of housing and services. Founded in 1990 to advance the assisted living industry and enhance the quality of life for the approximately one million consumers it serves, ALFA broadened its membership in 1999 to embrace the full range of housing and care providers who share ALFA's consumer-focused philosophy of care. The site includes an online bookstore from which you can order ALFA's books and other related items.

BenefitsCheckUp

1 2 3 4 5

www.benefitscheckup.org

BenefitsCheckUp is an online screening program to help adults over the age of 55 determine their qualifications for federal, state, and selected private and public benefit programs. Visit this site, fill out a form, and the site displays a list of the programs for which you qualify, along with a detailed description of each program, contact information, and the materials you need to apply for each program.

Centers for Medicare and Medicaid Services

1 2 3 4 5

www.cms.hhs.gov

The Centers for Medicare and Medicaid Services are part of the U.S. Department of Health and Human Services and are responsible for helping those who qualify for Medicare and Medicaid obtain the services and assistance they need. This site features all the manuals and forms you need to determine whether you qualify for benefits and then apply for those benefits. Site also offers general information about Medicare coverage and health plans and discussion forums where you can find answers to your questions.

Elderhostel

1 2 3 4 5

www.elderhostel.org

With the fundamental belief that no one should ever stop learning, this site provides access to resources around the world to continue your education (for adults age 55 and over). Here you can investigate more than 8,000 learning adventures in all 50 states and more than 90 foreign countries. Trips focus on history, culture, nature, music, outdoor activities such as walking and biking, individual skills, crafts, and study cruises.

Eldercare Locator

www.eldercare.gov

The Eldercare Locator is a public service of the U.S. Administration on Aging designed to "connect older Americans and their caregivers with sources of information on senior services. The service links those who need assistance with state and local area agencies on aging and community-based organizations that serve older adults and their caregivers." Site also offers a toll-free number you can call to talk with an actual living human being.

ElderWeb

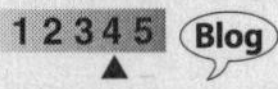

www.elderweb.com

ElderWeb is an online directory for the elderly, focusing mainly on healthcare. It includes hand-picked links to resources on long-term healthcare along with a searchable database of organizations devoted to long-term healthcare for the elderly. Areas on the site include Aging, Care, College Programs, Elder Law, Medicaid, Medicare, Technology, and Transportation, to name a few. Site also features articles, reports, announcements, and events.

FirstGov for Seniors

www.firstgov.gov/Topics/Seniors.shtml

FirstGov is the U.S. government's attempt to provide easy online access to information for its citizens. This area of FirstGov is devoted to serving the specific needs of the country's senior citizens. Here you'll find links to government sites and services for consumer protection, employment and volunteerism, education, health, travel, taxes, and much more.

Friendly4Seniors Websites

www.friendly4seniors.com

This site simply offers links to sites that are of interest to seniors. Choose your topic—Government, Financial, Housing, Medical, and many more—click and find what you're looking for. More than 2,000 senior-related listings that are reviewed and approved before being added to the list.

Grand Times

www.grandtimes.com

An e-zine dedicated to the needs of active retirees. Articles are grouped by category: Cooking, Finance & Law, Grandparenting, Health, Nostalgia & Fiction, Personality Profiles, Pets & Wildlife, Relationships, and Travel. Site also offers links to Free Legal Advice, Free Maps & Directions, Free Games, and Personal ads. You can shop online for gifts for your grandkids.

HomeStore.com Senior Living

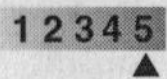

www.seniorhousingnet.com/seniors

This site has gathered a wide range of lifestyle options so family members and seniors can easily sort through retirement communities, assisted living, nursing homes, and home healthcare. Search through more than 55,000 listings!

Tip: Click Evaluate Your Needs to access an online screening tool that can help you determine the type of housing you need.

HUD for Senior Citizens

www.hud.gov/groups/seniors.cfm

The U.S. Department of Housing and Urban Development has created this section specifically to inform senior citizens of their housing options and help them find suitable places to live. Information to help seniors stay in their current homes, find apartments to rent, find retirement or nursing homes, locate organizations to stay active, and much more. Features related information on senior jobs, links to other resources on the Web, and links to other government agencies that address the needs of seniors.

Life Extension Foundation

www.lef.org

Anyone looking to slow the aging process will want to visit this site for research and medical news regarding life extension and aging. You can also purchase products and learn about membership in LEF.

A B C D E F G H I J K L M N O P Q R S T U V W X Y Z

Lifesphere

1 2 3 4 5 RSS

www.lifesphere.org

Lifesphere.org is "a nonprofit, continuum of services provider dedicated to helping older adults live to their highest potential as individuals who seek independence, good health, and personal fulfillment." Here you can investigate Lifesphere's retirement communities of Maple Knoll Village and the Knolls of Oxford, two senior centers: Sycamore Senior Center and Anderson Senior Center, a Senior Service Program Maple Knoll Senior Services and three affordable HUD Residences, LifeSphere Home Health Services, WMKV 89.3 FM Radio Station, a Montessori Child Center, consulting services, and much more.

Medicare.gov

1 2 3 4 5 RSS

www.medicare.gov

This is the official U.S. government site for people with Medicare insurance. Here you can learn about your benefits, file a claim or appeal online, look into long-term care benefits, explore your plan choices, report an address change, and much more. Site also provides information on general healthcare and wellness issues and a collection of search tools to help you locate healthcare providers, hospitals, nursing homes, and other useful information and resources.

National Council on Aging

1 2 3 4 5

www.ncoa.org

The National Council on the Aging "is a national network of organizations and individuals dedicated to improving the health and independence of older persons and increasing their continuing contributions to communities, society, and future generations." Here you can learn about the various programs that the NCOA supports, along with publications, events, advocacy, and research.

National Institute on Aging

1 2 3 4 5

www.nia.nih.gov

This site has a wealth of information for anyone interested in assessing his or her risk of being afflicted with Alzheimer's disease, researching treatments, as well as learning to cope with caring for someone with the disease. Site offers free publications in English and Spanish and announcements of clinical trials.

The National Senior Citizens Law Center

1 2 3 4 5

www.nsclc.org

The National Senior Citizens Law Center advocates, litigates, and publishes on low-income elderly and disability issues including Medicare, Medicaid, SSI, nursing homes, age discrimination, and pensions. Free publications are available on several topics of interest to seniors, including 20 Common Nursing Home Problems—and How to Resolve Them.

New LifeStyles

1 2 3 4 5

www.newlifestyles.com

New LifeStyles Online, a complete guide to senior housing and care options, lists all state-licensed senior housing facilities in the major metropolitan areas nationwide.

Senior.com

1 2 3 4 5

www.seniornews.com

Senior.com is an online community for seniors with the goal of "providing our members with a safe community to communicate with family and friends, to research information, and to purchase items in a secured environment." Site features four main areas: Travel, Family, Recreation, and News. When we visited the site, it was under construction, but it should be up and running by the time you read this.

The Senior Information Network

1 2 3 4 5

www.senior-inet.com

Senior Information Network is the premier high-tech source for obtaining information about Senior Support Services across the United States. The body of the community web pages is designed to provide you with a list of those people and agencies that can provide services for seniors in each community.

Senior Sites

12345

www.seniorsites.com

This site lists more than 5,000 nonprofit housing and services for senior citizens in the United States, Guam, and Puerto Rico. Also includes national and state resources.

SeniorJournal.com

12345

www.seniorjournal.com

This news and information kiosk for seniors covers everything from health to politics. Check here for information on healthcare for seniors, legislation, Social Security and Medicaid information, and much more.

SeniorNet

12345

www.seniornet.org

SeniorNet's mission is to "provide older adults education for and access to computer technology to enhance their lives and enable them to share their knowledge and wisdom." The site supports this effort through online programs, discussions, news, and special offers available only on the Internet.

seniorresource.com

12345

www.seniorresource.com

A resource for seniors considering all their housing options, with information about alternatives and links to supporting services, such as financing, mortgages, and retirement communities.

SeniorsSearch.com

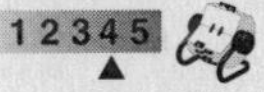

www.seniorssearch.com

A comprehensive search engine developed specifically for the over-50 crowd. Find merchants, information sources, and services organized by category. You'll also find senior media, such as senior radio, that provide programming information.

Social Security Online

12345

www.ssa.gov

Official website of the Social Security Administration. Includes announcements and reports on issues related to Social Security, contact information, and regular updates.

Third Age

12345 Blog RSS

www.thirdage.com

This site is a must-visit for baby boomers. It provides information, insights, interactive guides, and assessments on finances, beauty and health, personal growth, spirituality, relationships, and much more. Members can join in the lively online chats and post and peruse personal ads. Site also features free community workshops and a list of the ten most popular articles on the site.

Transitions, Inc. Elder Care Consulting

12345

www.asktransitions.com

Transitions locates and arranges services for older adults and their caregivers. Company representatives assess needs, hold seminars, and provide eldercare counseling. Through the navigation bar that runs down the left side of the page, you can quickly access Tips & Tools (to find elder care information, guides, check lists, articles, and stories), Ask Grandma (to get answers to frequently asked questions), Care Talk (to find answers to even more questions posted in the discussion forum), Caregiving Guide (for senior caregivers), and more.

Wired Seniors

12345

www.wiredseniors.com

Wired Seniors is a portal for tech-savvy seniors. Here you'll find links to a member page, Seniors Home Exchange (timeshare opportunities), SeniorsMatch.com (dating service for the over 50 crowd), Seniors Travel Guide, Seniors Radio (for online radio stations that may appeal to seniors), Discussion Forums, and more.

SEWING

American Sewing Guild

12345

www.asg.org

The American Sewing Guild is dedicated to keeping the tradition of sewing alive through education and support of those who sew and those who want to learn the craft. Here you can learn more about the organization, join up, get annual conference information, explore links to local chapters and dozens of informative sewing sites, and learn about contests and awards.

Cranston Village

12345

www.cranstonvillage.com

Home of the oldest fabric printing company in the United States, this site features suggestions for crafts and quilts, plus a history of the Cranston Print Works Company.

The Fabric Club

12345

www.fabricclub.com

Order a wide variety of fabrics from this site, which advertises wholesale prices. Search by type of fabric or use, such as home decorating or quilting, and order as many or as few yards as you need.

Fabrics.net

12345

www.fabrics.net

An information resource for sewers in search of particular fabrics, as well as individuals and vendors who have fabrics to sell. You can learn all about various types of fabrics and then look for sources in the database or shop online.

Fashion Fabrics Club

12345

www.fashionfabricsclub.com

Looking for unique, high-quality fabrics for your next sewing project? Then visit the Fashion Fabrics Club and check out its selection.

Fiskars

12345

www.fiskars.com

You'll find plenty of information about the many types of Fiskars brand scissors at this site, which also has many project ideas and tips. You'll also find links to related sites, such as crafts, special rebates or deals, and news about Fiskars.

Best Home Sewing Association

12345

www.sewing.org

Dedicated to "Get People Sewing," this site encourages visitors to take up a needle and thread and start stitching their own clothes. This site is packed with tutorials covering sewing techniques for both novice and intermediate stitchers, plus plenty of sewing projects, tips, and advice for sewers of all ages. Excellent place for both children and adults, women and men, to learn how to start sewing. With its appeal to such a wide audience and its comprehensive sewing information and instructions, we couldn't help but name this site Best of the Best in the Sewing category.

Jo-Ann Fabric and Crafts

12345

www.joann.com

Official site for Jo-Ann Fabric and Crafts stores. Find your local store, enter a drawing, subscribe to the store newsletter, visit the investor relations page, find out about in-store specials, or post a message in Message Central to ask questions or share tips. Best of all, visit the creative center for loads of crafts and sewing ideas and information. You can purchase all your supplies and equipment at this mega sewing store, including thread and fabric, needles, sewing machines, patterns, and machine embroidery and digital designs.

Lily Abello's Sewing Links

www.lilyabello.com

For sewing links and books, or button crafts, visit Lily's simple but abundant site. Here you can find more than 950 links to the best sewing-related sites on the Web.

Nancy's Notions

www.nancysnotions.com

A catalog of sewing, serging, and quilting notions. Also the home of *Sewing with Nancy* (the longest-running sewing show on PBS). At this site, you can purchase Nancy's books, videos, and kits; shop for machines, accessories, and supplies; and explore a collection of free projects, tips, and creative ideas.

Sew News

www.sewnews.com

Read articles from this sewing magazine, share information and ideas with others through the discussion forums, and link to other sewing sites through this one. Site includes free patterns, a Sew News Library, a Sewing Q&A, and Hot Picks! (recommended websites).

Sewing.com

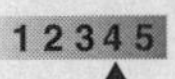

www.sewing.com

Find sewing instruction from other sewing community members as well as links to sites providing lessons. You'll also find book reviews, articles, and discussions. Comprehensive sewing dictionary, too. The site design is a little substandard, but the content is excellent.

A Sewing Web

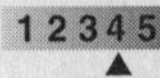

www.sewweb.com

Provides quality industrial sewing supplies to professional sewers all over the world, including industrial sewing thread, sewing machine presser feet, sewing accessories, and more.

Threads Magazine

www.taunton.com/threads/index.asp

Threads is the creative forum where people who sew and love to work with fabrics and fibers share their knowledge. The Feature Library offers links for Sewing Basics, Garment Construction, Fabric, Fitting, and more. Packed with step-by-step instructions, tips from the experts, and online videos that show you how it's done.

Wild Ginger Software

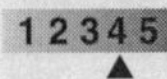

www.wildginger.com

Home of Wild Ginger Software, a company that develops sewing software for customizing patterns. You can download a free demo at this site and order products online.

MACHINES

Baby Lock

www.babylock.com

Learn more about Baby Lock brand machines, find projects you can complete with your Baby Lock, check out available software and download updates for any software you already own, and locate local dealers and events.

> **Tip:** Click the Projects button to access an excellent collection of free projects.

Bernina USA

12345

www.berninausa.com

This site is way more than a manufacturer's website designed to show off its products. It also offers education, tips, and free projects to help you get the most out of your Bernina sewing machine. The Online Classes are free—PDF files that provide fully illustrated instructions on sewing, serging, and embroidering skills and techniques. You can also check out the Sewing Studio for basic instructions, tips, and creative ideas.

Brother

12345

www.brother-usa.com/homesewing

Brother is best known for its typewriters and printers, but it also manufactures a collection of high-quality sewing machines. Here you can learn more about Brother's current line of sewing and embroidery machines. You can also shop for software and supplies, download free designs, explore techniques and creative ideas, and join the Brother Club to share your sewing enthusiasm with others.

Creative Feet

12345

www.creativefeet.com

Founder of the company, Clare Rowley-Greene, invented Creative Feet to enable visually impaired individuals to sew using a standard sewing machine. Since creating the first presser feet designs, Clare has widened her focus to create presser feet that simplify the sewing of specialized stitches. The site offers information about the presser feet designs, as well as other sewing products, such as books and videos.

Elna USA

12345

www.elnausa.com

Developers of sewing machines, sergers, embroidery machines, presses, and sewing accessories. Site offers product information, dealer locations, and an excellent collection of free projects. Check out the FAQs for answers to common questions about sewing, embroidery, quilting, and Elna software.

How Stuff Works

12345

home.howstuffworks.com/sewing-machine.htm

Ever wonder how a sewing machine works? Check out this site for an explanation that helps you wrap your brain around the concept. A few pages into the article, you'll discover a cool animation of just how a sewing machine performs its magic.

Husqvarna Viking

12345

www.husqvarnaviking.com

Learn more about Husqvarna, its products, and dealers, as well as educational retreats and free projects available at the site. On its surface, this site appears to be little more than a promotional site for Husqvarna Viking sewing machines; but if you dig a little deeper, you'll find a vast collection of online tutorials, tips, and techniques to help you get the most out of your sewing machine and inspire your own creative visions. In the navigation bar on the left, simply click your sewing area of interest: Sewing, Embroidery, or Quilting, and start exploring.

Mr. Vac and Mrs. Sew

12345

www.mrvacandmrssew.com

Mr. Vac and Mrs. Sew specialize in vacuum cleaners and sewing and embroidery machines, both new and used. They also carry a wide selection of embroidery designs, software, and supplies; sergers; and buttons. If you need anything related to sewing or embroidery, this is the place to go.

Pfaff Sewing Machines

12345

www.pfaff.com

This official corporate site for Pfaff sewing machines introduces you to the Pfaff product line of sewing, embroidery, overlock, and quilting machines and places you in touch with a community of Pfaff enthusiasts through its Pfaff Club, Pfaff Chat, and Pfaff Sewing Stars areas. Site also features a collection of free designs and a model selector to help you choose the right machine for your needs.

Sewing Machine Outlet

12345

www.sewingmachineoutlet.com

Source for new and used sewing machines, needles, sewing machine parts, and more.

Singer Machines

12345

www.singerco.com

If you're in the market for a Singer sewing machine, this site can take you on a tour of the various models and their features and steer you toward a local dealer. This site also features an excellent collection of reference guides, tutorials, and illustrated instructions on how to use your machine to its full potential. You can also explore a hefty collection of free project ideas and designs.

White Sewing

12345

www.whitesewing.com

White Sewing has a reputation for manufacturing sewing machines and sergers that are easy to use. Here you can explore the various models and explore a good collection of free project ideas. The Education area is a little disappointing.

PATTERNS

Butterick

12345

www.butterick.com

This site features an online version of Butterick's pattern catalogue, from which you can order products online. Patterns are grouped in categories, making it easy to find just what you're looking for.

Dress Forms and Pattern Fitting Online

12345

www.dressformdesigning.com

Learn patented Body Drafting and Clone Yourself techniques along with other tools and techniques, take design and sewing classes at home, schedule a sewing-and-design workshop in your area, or order videos online. This site is created by the "fit obsessed" for the "fit obsessed."

McCall's Pattern Catalog

12345

www.mccall.com

McCall's is one of the top pattern designers, and now you can check out its huge collection of patters online from McCall's, Butterick, and Vogue. When you click the McCall's link, the resulting page presents a list of pattern categories, including Evening/Prom/Bridal, Dresses, Tops/Vests, Skirts/Pants, Juniors, and Costumes, to name only a few. Click Sewing Sites for an extensive directory of some of the top sewing sites on the Web. Click Retailers to find a local pattern store that carries McCall patterns. Site also contains valuable size charts.

Sewingpatterns.com

12345

www.sewingpatterns.com

Huge collection of sewing patterns from several of the most popular companies, including McCall's, Simplicity, Vogue, Butterick, Kwik Sew, and New Look.

Simplicity

www.simplicity.com

Flip through the latest Simplicity pattern book for ideas for this season's fashions and get sewing help online here. You have to dig pretty deep into the site to find patterns, but the site offers an excellent collection of patterns along with photos that help you preview how they look on real people. What we found most impressive at this site is that it offers some excellent instructions and tips on sewing basics and dress fitting along with an Idea Exchange area and Simplicity Classroom, which offers a good collection of free projects.

Vintage Pattern Lending Library

www.vpll.org

The Vintage Pattern Lending Library "preserves, archives, and replicates historic fashion patterns from 1840 through 1950, vintage sewing publications, and fashion prints of the past." By ponying up for a membership, you can borrow items from the library, or you can purchase the patterns you want. Site features an online catalog and photo gallery. Great place to go if you need some period designs for a play.

Wildly Wonderful Wearables

www.wwwearables.com

Wildly Wonderful Wearables is an online company that specializes in sewing patterns and notions. The site also features some excellent primers and tutorials on sewing and a gallery where you can check out some cool designs.

SEXUALITY

The American Association of Sex Educators, Counselors, and Therapists (AASECT)

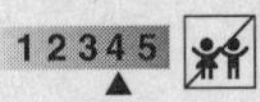

www.aasect.org

AASECT's website features a therapist locator as well as a list of FAQs about human sexuality, links to other sites, and information about how to become a certified sex educator, counselor, or therapist.

Better Sex University

www.bettersex.com/t-bsu-university.aspx

Better Sex University is the sex education area of the Better Sex site, a store where you can purchase vibrators, videos, movies, and sex kits. The University features a good collection of articles on how to improve your lovemaking along with a dictionary and some short courses. Site also features a Sex IQ test, a Q&A area, and information from the sexperts.

Coalition for Positive Sexuality

www.positive.org/Home

Subtitled "sex ed for your head," this site is an honest affirmation of safe sex between consenting individuals, primarily teenagers. Content is offered in both English and Spanish.

Dr. Laura Berman

www.drlauraberman.com

This is the official website of Dr. Laura Berman, expert in female sexual dysfunction and other areas of human sexuality that specifically affect women. This site features a Passion Portfolio, Sex Toy Finder, Position Finder, and online Journal, Sex & Intimacy Tips, Real Advice from Real Women, and more. Very classy site with reliable and accurate information and advice.

Gender and Sexuality

eserver.org/gender

This page publishes texts that address gender studies and homosexuality studies, with a particular focus on discussions of sex, gender, sexual identity, and sexuality in cultural practices.

Go Ask Alice!: Sexuality

www.goaskalice.columbia.edu/Cat6.html

Read frequently asked questions about male and female anatomy and sexual response at this site.

Gottman Institute

www.gottman.com

The Gottman Institute offers weekend and week-long workshops to help couples remain satisfied and fulfilled in their long-term monogamous relationships. The website includes quizzes and tips on relationships and an online store where you can shop for books, audiocassettes, videos, and other helpful products.

HealthySex.com

www.healthysex.com

At this site, Wendy Maltz, MSW, offers information and articles about healthy sexuality, sexual fantasies, mid-life sexuality, sex abuse, and more. You can also order books and tapes online.

A B C D E F G H I J K L M N O P Q R S T U V W X Y Z

Helen Fisher

helenfisher.com

This website discusses Dr. Fisher's findings on love, sex, and evolution.

HisandHerhealth.com

www.hisandherhealth.com

Read current research findings regarding male and female reproductive health and sexuality, as well as joining in chat, asking the doctor for guidance, and scanning articles and news.

HowToHaveGoodSex.com

www.howtohavegoodsex.com

Founded by Alex Robboy, LCSW, HowToHave GoodSex.com features sex education and tips, a glossary of common terms, questions and answers, plus information about workshops and an online store where you can order videos and toys. The site design is a little lacking, but the content is excellent.

Impotence Specialists

www.impotencespecialists.com

Find an impotence specialist online, read through FAQs about impotence and potential treatments, or post a question for a doctor on the bulletin board and check back for an answer.

intimategifts.com

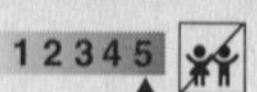

www.intimategifts.com

Order sex toys, books, lubricants, videos, and other accessories and gifts for loving couples here. Site features sex toy guides to help you select the right product for you and your partner.

iVillage: Love & Sex

love.ivillage.com

iVillage features this excellent site to address the most engaging and pressing topics about love and sexuality. The opening page presents a preview of feature articles, along with a navigation bar that enables you to quickly jump to specific content areas, including Singles & Dating, Love & Marriage, Understanding Men, Common Problems, Sex, Quizzes, Message Boards, Hot Stuff, From Contributors, and Free Newsletters. Excellent site for couples to explore their sexuality together.

Kinsey Home Page

www.indiana.edu/~kinsey

Visit Indiana University, home of the Kinsey Institute, where the sexual revolution of the 1960s found fuel, or at least permission, to begin. Here you can learn about the Kinsey Institute and its services and events, tour the library catalog and the gallery, view publications and other resources, and learn about educational opportunities at the institute.

Nerve.com

www.nerve.com

Online magazine that celebrates the beauty and absurdity of sex through thought-provoking and funny articles on various topics relating to human relationships and sexuality. View photographs, read personal essays, check out *Nerve*'s fiction and poetry, check out the personals, get advice, or visit the message boards to view questions and opinions from other fans of *Nerve*.

Pat Love & Associates

www.patlove.com

This is the home page of Dr. Pat Love, author of *Hot Monogamy*. At this site, you can learn more about Dr. Love and her approach, research current studies on relationships and sexuality, take relationship quizzes, and find out more about available seminars and workshops.

Scarleteen

www.scarleteen.com

Billed as "sex education for the real world," Scarleteen functions as an information kiosk and sexual myth-buster all in one. Site covers anatomy, safe sex practices, reproduction, infections, sexual politics, and more. The Crisis Hotline area provides excellent information for how to deal with abuse and other crises, and you can shop online for a few essentials, such as Scarleteen T-shirts and undies. Site also features discussion forums.

Sexual Health InfoCenter

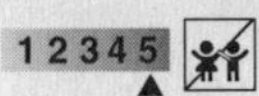

www.sexhealth.org

Online reading room for everything related to human sexuality. Guides on how to have better sex, sex and aging, STDs, safe sex, sexual dysfunction, and birth control. Discussion forums make it easy to obtain answers to your most pressing and personal questions. Links to intimategifts.com for online shopping. With its extensive coverage of nearly every topic relating to human sexuality, this is one of the better sexuality sites, although when we visited, the video links were dysfunctional.

SexualHealth.com

www.sexualhealth.com

You'll find lots of questions regarding sex, as well as answers from professionals, to help you understand your own issues and options. You can post your own questions, get recommended reading, and scan articles on sex topics.

Sexuality.org

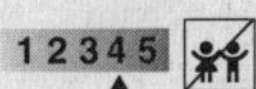

www.sexuality.org

You'll find articles and material designed to educate and inform visitors regarding sexuality issues. This site offers technique tips, book reviews, and event information.

Sexuality Forum

www.askisadora.com

Check the article archive for sexuality subjects you're interested in and, if you don't find what you're looking for, post a question to the public forum. You can also buy products that have been carefully selected by Isadora, the site's host.

Sexuality Information and Education Council of the U.S.

www.siecus.org

SIECUS is a national nonprofit organization that affirms that sexuality is a natural and healthy part of living. Provides information for parents and teens in an easy-to-understand format that's designed to educate visitors about sexuality and safe sex practices.

SexWithoutPain.com

www.sexwithoutpain.com

This site takes a multidisciplinary approach to the causes and treatments of pain associated with sexual intercourse.

Teen Sexuality

teensexuality.student.com

Teen Sexuality is "dedicated to straight, gay, lesbian, and bisexual teens and college students. It's a place for sex education and advice." This site features discussion forums and chat, surveys, polls, articles, and advice. This is area on The Student Center website, which you can visit by going directly to www.student.com.

Woman Spirit

www.Womanspirit.net

Dr. Gina Ogden, author of *Women Who Love Sex: An Inquiry into the Expanding Spirit of Women's Erotic Experience*, provides information on female sexuality and spirituality. Here, you also can join a reader's forum to exchange ideas with others, find a calendar of events and information about books and articles, access resources for counseling, and check out links to other websites.

SHOPPING

ActivePlaza

12345

www.activeplaza.com

ActivePlaza provides a "unique combination of searchable online shopping catalog, online shopping mall, and shopping directory." At this site, you can search for products carried by the top online merchants to help you find the best deals.

Best Amazon.com

12345

www.amazon.com

This well-known online bookstore offers just about every title under the sun, as well as videos, music, software, electronics, gardening equipment, toys, kitchen paraphernalia, and more at some of the best prices you can find. Amazon partners up with individual sellers to offer used books, movies, and other items, and it monitors the merchants to ensure they are providing quality service. Amazon's incredible selection of products coupled with its low prices and consistently high-quality service earn it our Best of the Best rating for the Shopping category.

> **Tip:** Click the Associates link at the bottom of the opening page to learn how you can earn a referral fee by selling Amazon.com products on your website.

Buy.com

12345 RSS

www.buy.com

Buy videos, music, software, books, games, computers, electronics, and travel services at a discount from this site. Pick a category and search the database to find the product you're looking for.

CatalogLink

12345

www.cataloglink.com

Select the catalogs you want to receive from the categories at this site to help you with your home shopping. You'll also find several links to the companies' home pages for online shopping.

Half.com

12345

half.ebay.com

Buy items (new or used) at 50 percent off or more from individuals who have them available. At this site, unlike an auction, you're guaranteed to get the product if it's advertised. Books, music, movies, and games are available. You can also sell products through this site, which is part of the eBay family of stores.

Home Shopping Network

12345

www.hsn.com

If you traded in your TV for a computer, you can still shop at the Home Shopping Network by visiting this site online. Shop by category, search for specific items, or browse through the most-popular featured products.

iQVC

12345

www.qvc.com

The granddaddy of home shopping networks. You can buy clothing, jewelry, electronics, home décor items, office supplies, fitness equipment, and more at this site.

Lycos Shopping Network

1 2 3 4 5

shop.lycos.com

A good point of entry, this site includes an impressive list of shopping categories as well as special features such as Aardvark, the online shopping experience with gifts for pets and the people who love them, and Andy's garage, gift ideas for men. Find the department store you're looking for from here.

msn Shopping

1 2 3 4 5

eshop.msn.com

The Microsoft Network features its own online shopping site, where you can find deals on just about any product, including computers and electronics, apparel, furniture, books, jewelry, and automotive equipment, just to name a few. This site boasts a collection of more than 30 million products and 7,000 stores. Great place to do a little comparison shopping.

Netmarket.com

1 2 3 4 5

www.netmarket.com

Search this database of hundreds of thousands of items to find what you're looking for. Daily special deals offer great prices, and you can sign up for a personal shopper to take care of your shopping for you. The site's goal is to save you time by bringing together tons of merchandise at great prices. For the best prices, you need to pony up a membership fee.

Target

1 2 3 4 5

www.target.com

A sharp site detailing all of Target's programs and offerings, such as the Lullaby Club, Club Wedd, Take Charge of Education, School Fundraising Made Simple, 5% Back to the Community, TREAT-SEATS, the Target Guest Card, and various guest services. You can even access sound clips of new music available at Target.

CLOTHING

BabyStyle

1 2 3 4 5

www.babystyle.com

This website features clothing and accessories for expectant mothers and their babies. This store also carries books, toys, bedding, and other items for babies and kids.

Bloomingdale's

1 2 3 4 5

www.bloomingdales.com

Includes online shopping, shopping by catalog, and shopping by personal shopper. The events page tells about upcoming sales and seasonal happenings in its various stores. Get design and style tips from the Home Design Experts page.

Coldwater Creek

1 2 3 4 5

www.coldwatercreek.com

Coldwater Creek specializes in casual clothing, accessories, and gifts that reflect the wide-open nature of the Rocky Mountains and the echoes of Native America.

DELiAs.com

1 2 3 4 5

www.delias.com

Request a catalog or shop online referring to catalog pages or a clothing item. You can also hang out in the lounge and chat, look at pictures, and enter contests. Popular with high school girls.

Designer Outlet.com

1 2 3 4 5

www.designeroutlet.com

Every two weeks, new designer fashions are made available at this site, which aims to bring designer samples and overstocks to the world. Search by category, look at photos of items for sale, or sign up for a personal shopper to keep her eyes open for that perfect item.

Dillard's

1 2 3 4 5

www.dillards.com

Dillard's is a retail department store where you can find fashion apparel and home furnishings. Here you can shop different areas including Women, Cosmetics, Shoes, Juniors, Children, Men, Home & Leisure, and Gifts. Wedding and Gift registries are also available, along with a store locator.

Eddie Bauer

1 2 3 4 5

www.eddiebauer.com

Search the site to check out Eddie Bauer's latest casual wear for men and women, request a catalog, or see what's on sale this week.

Fashionmall.com

1 2 3 4 5

www.fashionmall.com

Shop by brand, category, or style for fashions from a wide variety of merchants online. You can also enter drawings for free merchandise, check out recommended purchases, and tune in for chats with designers and celebrities.

HerRoom.com

1 2 3 4 5 Blog

www.herroom.com

No matter what kind of undergarment you prefer, underwire bras, thongs, or half-slips, this is the site you'll want to check out. Search for products by brand, style, or size.

L.L. Bean

1 2 3 4 5

www.llbean.com

Search L.L. Bean's selection of apparel and sporting gear online.

Lands' End

1 2 3 4 5

www.landsend.com/cd/frontdoor

Lands' End, owned by Sears Roebuck and Company, offers decorations, kids' stuff, pet gifts, home accessories, and more. A good-quality mail order merchandiser with a nicely designed website.

Lane Bryant

1 2 3 4 5

www.lbcatalog.com

For women who wear sizes 14W and up, Lane Bryant is one of the more popular stores to shop. Here, you can access the Lane Bryant catalog and place your order online.

Neiman Marcus

1 2 3 4 5

www.neimanmarcus.com

Neiman Marcus is *the* store for fashion apparel, shoes, handbags, jewelry, and accessories. The site features a personal shopper who can provide fashion advice via chat or email. Check out the latest trends in fashion and order right online.

Nordstrom

1 2 3 4 5

www.nordstrom.com

Nordstrom is a fashion store for men, women, and children. It's a little pricey, but it carries a wide selection of the latest fashions along with shoes, jewelry, handbags, perfumes, and beauty aids. A gift area helps you find the perfect gift and even have it wrapped and shipped. If you're looking for a deal, click the Sale tab.

COMPARISON BOTS

BizRate

1 2 3 4 5

www.bizrate.com

Comparison-shopping service that helps you find the best prices from online merchants who carry the products you want. Features customer ratings, too, to help you find online stores that offer reliable customer service.

Bottomdollar

www1.bottomdollar.com

Bottomdollar is a no-frills product search tool that enables you to search for specific products or browse by categories, including Apparel, Computers, Home & Garden, Jewelry & Watches, and Video Games, to name a few. Lots of electronics gadgets and gizmos.

Epinions

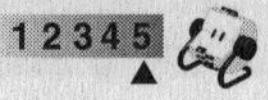

www.epinions.com

Epinions not only locates products at the best prices but it also provides merchant ratings from customers, so you know you're buying from reputable dealers. You can search all categories or limit your search to cars, books, movies, electronics, or a host of other categories.

mySimon

www.mysimon.com

Search for products by keyword or brand and then let MySimon provide you with a list of online merchants who carry it and their quoted price. Great product descriptions.

NexTag

www.nextag.com

Unlike other comparison-shopping sites, this site lets you negotiate with sellers after collecting total quoted prices from several. Sellers are online merchants and individuals.

Pricegrabber.com

www.pricegrabber.com

Find the stuff you want for the best price on the Web. Search for specific products or browse through several categories. Pricegrabber finds the store that offers the item for the best price. Enter your ZIP code to add shipping and handling charges.

PriceSCAN.com

www.pricescan.com

PriceSCAN.com is a service that searches for products at the best prices or for products with comparable functionality. Unlike most other price-comparison services on the Web, PriceSCAN.com does not limit its searches to web-based stores. Its staff also gathers information from vendors, catalogs, and magazine ads to help you track down the best price anywhere.

Productopia

www.productopia.com

Read user reviews and join in product discussions before searching the site for a purchase. You'll also find recommended gifts to get you started.

RoboShopper.com

1 2 3 4 5

www.roboshopper.com

Pick a category, pick a product, and RoboShopper presents you with the merchants carrying that product and the associated price. You can then jump from site to site, comparing total product cost information.

Shopping.com

www.shopping.com

Choose a product, and Shopping.com searches for the best prices among many online merchants and auctions. If you're not ready to buy right away, Shopping.com will keep you posted on specials and new options.

A B C D E F G H I J K L M N O P Q R S T U V W X Y Z

DISCOUNT STORES

Costco

12345

www.costco.com

Learn all about Costco and its member benefits, locate a Costco near you, purchase a membership, and shop securely with Costco Online. Also find out what's new at the club and sign up to be notified of special offers by email.

Overstock.com

12345

www.overstock.com

Search for brand-name bargains at this site, which offers just about everything—from computers to home décor to clothing—at a discount. Overstocked merchants mean great deals for consumers. Check out the Liquidation and Clearance Bins for bottom basement prices.

Sam's Club

12345

www.samsclub.com

Learn all about Sam's Club and member benefits, locate a Sam's Club near you, purchase a membership, and shop securely with Sam's Club Online. Also find out what's new at the club and join the Product Forum.

SmartBargains

12345

www.smartbargains.com

SmartBargains offers deals on overstocked and discontinued items. Here you can search for specific products or browse categories including Art & Prints, Bedding & Bath, Electronics, and Jewelry & Watches, to name a few. The opening page contains links to items that are commonly searched, including gifts for upcoming holidays.

Wal-Mart Online

12345

www.wal-mart.com

Find Wal-Mart product and price information at this site, and order your goodies online. Search the store for what you want; you'll be rewarded with photos and details on each item. Also, locate the Wal-Mart nearest you.

JEWELRY (SEE JEWELRY)

PERFUME

FragranceNet

12345

www.fragrancenet.com

FragranceNet boasts that it is "The world's largest discount fragrance store." With more than 1,000 genuine brand names at up to 70 percent off retail, it might well be. The attractive, well-designed site also offers free gift wrapping and free shipping, a gift reminder service, a search engine, and the chance to enter to win a $100 shopping spree, and more.

Perfumania

12345

www.perfumania.com

Perfumania is an online discount store that specializes in colognes and perfumes, cosmetics and skincare products, and other related products for men, women, and children. The company also offers gift sets, gift wrapping, a Gifting Center, and featured products for him and for her.

Perfume Center

12345 RSS

www.perfumecenter.com

This store offers hundreds of original brand-name fragrances for both men and women. You can place your order online or call the toll-free phone number, which is prominently featured on the opening page.

Perfume Emporium

1 2 3 4 5

`www.perfumeemporium.com`

Perfume Emporium carries a complete line of good-smelling stuff, including men's cologne, women's perfume, and candles. It also carries skin-care products and jewelry. You can search for specific items, browse by category, or check out the specials. Site also features a gift finder and a gift minder to remind you of upcoming dates, such as birthdays and anniversaries. Free beauty tips are also available.

Smell This

1 2 3 4 5

`www.smellthis.com`

The folks at this site are not shy about their philosophy, which is, in a nutshell, "perfume sucks." Smell This is the alternative line of fragrance products for the mind, body, and home. These scents are based on familiar smells we all identify with, such as baby powder, the beach, canned peaches, cut grass, soda pop fizz, fresh towels, chocolate brownies...you get the idea. You can order online, read through FAQs, find a store that carries the line, and more.

Uncommon Scents

1 2 3 4 5

`uncommonscents.com`

Specializing in luxurious, natural, custom-scented body care products for more than a quarter of a century. Choose from more than 50 custom fragrances inspired by nature or shop for natural bath and body care products from around the world. Toll-free phone *and* fax ordering available in addition to the online shopping option. Most products can be custom scented at no additional charge to you!

SEARCH ENGINES

Buyer's Index

1 2 3 4 5

`www.buyersindex.com`

Search 20,000 shopping sites and mail order catalogs offering more than 300 million products for consumers and businesses. Use keywords, product names, or company names to begin your search.

Froogle

1 2 3 4 5

`froogle.google.com`

Google's shopping site, Froogle, can help you track down products from various online merchants, and even sort your search results by price. Simply type a description of the item you're looking for and click the Search Froogle button. You can then sort by price (low-to-high or high-to-low) or enter a specific price range to limit the results. You can also browse Froogle by category.

InternetMall.com

1 2 3 4 5

`www.internetmall.com`

Comparison shop by searching through categories of products and services at this site, or link to other shopping sites of interest.

ShopGuide

1 2 3 4 5

`www.shopguide.com`

When you search this site, which consists of more than 20,000 online store sites all rolled into one, you'll find what you're looking for and learn about specials, discounts, coupons, freebies, and incentives. Site also enables you to browse for products by category.

Shopzilla

1 2 3 4 5

`www.shopzilla.com`

Shopzilla is a powerful shopping search tool with an index of approximately 30 million products from more than 60,000 stores. Here you can find almost any product being sold on the Web at the lowest price, check out product reviews, and research customer reviews of stores before placing your order.

Yahoo! Shopping

1 2 3 4 5

`shopping.yahoo.com`

Yahoo! Shopping gives you three ways to shop. You can search for specific items, browse by category, or check out the featured products on the opening page. This site can connect you to millions of products sold at more than 100,000 different sites.

SPECIALTY

Crate and Barrel

www.crateandbarrel.com

Opened in 1962 as a family business, Crate and Barrel is well known for carrying a wide range of unique, high-quality furniture and housewares. If you're getting married or expecting a baby, consider registering online to give your friends and relatives an easy way to purchase just what you need.

eBags.com

1 2 3 4 5

www.ebags.com

This site specializes in bags of all types—for computers, clothes, and sporting gear. You can find wallets, duffel bags, and bags for kids in all materials.

Fogdog Sports

1 2 3 4 5

www.fogdog.com

Basketball, baseball, and football fans will want to check out this site for the equipment they need to play well. But there is plenty of other gear for sports enthusiasts who like golf, badminton, tennis, and just about every other sport around. Apparel, equipment, and footwear can all be found here.

Gothic Clothing and Jewelry

www.blackrose.co.uk

Complete line of gothic clothing and jewelry for both men and women, including dresses, corsets, lingerie, skirts, bags, and hats.

Harry and David

1 2 3 4 5

www.harryanddavid.com

This site belongs to the company that has the best pears found anywhere in the world. Anything you order here will be appreciated and devoured.

Ikea.com

1 2 3 4 5

www.ikea.com

Request a copy of this year's catalog of inexpensive but well-designed furniture from IKEA or search the online product listings. You can also locate a store nearest you and get technical assistance in assembling your purchases.

Reel.com

1 2 3 4 5

www.reel.com

Movie buffs will want to check out this site for access to more than 100,000 movies and DVD titles available for purchase through Amazon.com. The site provides lots of assistance to help you decide which movies to buy through the use of reviews, interviews with stars, trailers, and synopses. Hollywood Video is the second largest video store chain in the United States, next to Blockbuster, with more than 1,800 video superstores.

Sailor Moon Specialty Store

1 2 3 4 5

japanimation.com/sm

One-stop shopping for apparel, jewelry, dolls, books, videos, games, and other Sailor Moon items.

The SPORTS Authority

1 2 3 4 5

www.thesportsauthority.com

Brand-name sporting good merchandise is available at this site in more than 1,000 categories, for just about every activity imaginable. Apparel, equipment, and footwear are all here. You'll also find an auction section where you can bid on used equipment.

World Traveler Luggage and Travel Goods

1 2 3 4 5

www.worldtraveler.com

A discount site for online ordering of sporting goods, luggage, business and computer cases, and travel accessories. Shop by product or by brand—whichever you find easier. Lowest, direct-to-consumer prices on major brands. Money-back guarantee.

SKATING

Black Diamond Sports

12345

www.skatepro.com

A huge selection of skates and parts are available at this site, as well as special deals and closeouts. Also provides a map of skate parks in and around Palo Alto, California.

International Skating Union

12345

www.isu.org

The International Skating Union is the governing body for world skating competitions, including figure skating, synchronized skating, and speed skating. Here you can check out the history of the organization, read the latest news and announcements, check world standings, research various skating rules, and more.

Riedell Skates

12345

www.riedellskates.com

Get information about Riedell skates for hockey, figure skating, inline skating, speed or roller skating, and pick up some tips and techniques for improving your performance, selecting boots and blades, getting a proper fit, and caring for your skates.

FIGURE SKATING

Figure Skater's Website

12345

www.sk8stuff.com

This site was created and is maintained by a figure skating enthusiast for skaters, coaches, parents, and others who are involved in the sport. Opening page presents news and announcements. Along the left side of the page is a navigation bar that provides access to additional resources, including Rules & Regulations, Skate Exchange, Official's Focus, Where to Get It, Fun & Games, and Links.

International Figure Skating Magazine (IFS)

12345 Blog RSS

www.ifsmagazine.com

Get the scoop on the latest news in figure skating through the online version of this print magazine. Read about the stars, their challenges, results of recent competitions, and sporting news; then share your enthusiasm with other fans in the discussion forums.

SkateWeb

12345

www.frogsonice.com/skateweb

SkateWeb is the website for skaters as well as figure skating fans. Here you can learn of upcoming events and past results, locate official websites of your favorite skaters, find clubs and rinks, track down pro shops, and much more. SkateWeb functions both as a comprehensive directory of skate sites and resources and as an electronic publication of news and articles.

Stars On Ice

12345

www.starsonice.com

Learn more about the cast of skaters in this year's Stars on Ice performance and get news regarding the tour. You can also get ticket information and performance dates.

Best U.S. Figure Skating

1 2 3 4 5

www.usfigureskating.org

U.S. Figure Skating is the governing body for the sport of figure skating in the United States. This site features news, athlete biographies, events and results, programs, articles from the skating magazine, and much more. You can find out how figure skating competitions are judged and scored. Excellent information organized in an easily accessible format and accented with some great graphics and photos all contribute to earning this site our Best of the Best award in the Skating category.

World Skating Museum

1 2 3 4 5

www.worldskatingmuseum.org

The World Figure Skating Museum & Hall of Fame is "the international repository for the sport of figure skating" and is "dedicated exclusively to the preservation and interpretation of the history of figure skating." Here you'll find some useful information to help you plan a visit to the museum and a link you can click to learn about the latest group of inductees to the Hall of Fame, but not much else.

INLINE SKATING

Get Rolling

1 2 3 4 5

www.getrolling.com

Find out about skating books, classes, camps, workshops, magazines, and more through the resources section of this site, which was established to help all skaters improve their skill and enjoyment of the sport. Site features some excellent video tutorials to help you master basic moves.

International Inline Skating Association

1 2 3 4 5

www.iisa.org

Learn to skate, find places to skate safely, pick up rules of the road, meet fellow skaters—all through this site. In addition, you can get news and information about the sport. Lots of information you'll want to look into.

LandRoller Skates

1 2 3 4 5

www.landroller.com

Get ready to toss your old inline skates in the dumpster, because LandRoller skates are taking the market by storm. These skates have oversized wheels, mounted on an angle, that provide skaters with superior balance and a smoother ride over nearly every common skating surface. LandRoller skates look a little funny, but so did the first airplanes. The company claims that one ride on these wild-looking skates is enough to convert the most vociferous critic into an avid advocate.

Rollerblade

1 2 3 4 5

www.rollerblade.com

Rollerblade, the world leader in the inline skate market, has created "one of the fastest-growing sports in the world," popular not only as off-season training devices for hockey players, but also as a trend-setting way to keep fit and trim. At this site, you can check out the latest line of products, find local and online dealers, track down places to skate in your area, read up on some tips for beginners, and play some free online games.

Skatepile.com

1 2 3 4 5

www.skatepile.com

One-stop shop for inline skates, parts, accessories, and videos. Features advice from the masters, profiles of some of the best inline skaters around, videos, trick tips, setup tips, and a photo gallery. For skates, accessories, and tips, there's no better place on the Web. To get to the tips, photos, videos, and such, open the Choose a Webzine Category list and click the desired option.

Zephyr Inline Skate Tours

1 2 3 4 5

www.zephyradventures.com

Get information about skating tours and vacations here, where you can request a guide by mail or scan the basic details online.

ROLLER SKATING

Finding a Roller Skating Rink

www.seskate.com/rinks/index.html

The biggest challenge to mastering the sport of roller skating may just be finding a roller rink near you. This site can help.

National Museum of Roller Skating

www.rollerskatingmuseum.com

The National Museum of Roller Skating created and maintains this site to introduce visitors to the museum and provides the museum's location and hours. Scroll down the page for links to Facts, Education, Exhibits, and Join. The site design and navigation are not the most intuitive; but if you need to do some research on the history of roller skating, this is the place to go.

Roller Skating Association

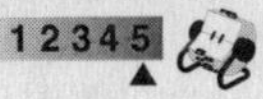

www.rollerskating.org

Roller Skating Association International is "a trade association representing skating center owners and operators; teachers, coaches and judges of roller skating; and manufacturers and suppliers of roller skating equipment." The opening page presents a link to enter the site and links to enter the four main areas of the site: Find a Skating Center Near You; Association and Membership; Games, Music, Promos and More; Roller Skating Suppliers and Manufacturers (where you can search for products and services by category). Site has a nice design, is easy to navigate, and offers great information for roller skaters and all those involved in the industry.

USA Roller Sports

www.usarollersports.org

USA Roller Sports (USARS) is "dedicated to creating, enhancing and conducting the best competitions and programs for roller sports." At this site, you'll find information on speedskating, figure skating, inline hockey, hardball hockey, recreation, and skateboarding for skaters at levels ranging from beginner to skilled athlete. If you have a skating club or organization and want to be involved in national competitions and social events, visit this site to gather the information and resources you need to get it rolling.

SPEED SKATING

BONT

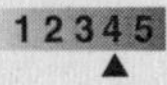

www.bont.com

BONT is the world's leading manufacturer of handmade speed skates (both ice and inline skates). Here, you can check out the latest products, shop for BONT apparel, read and post messages on the message boards, find special deals on BONT skates and accessories, shop online, and learn about upcoming meets and competitions.

GreatSkateWolverineSpeedTeam.com

www.greatskatewolverinespeedteam.com

This site, created and maintained by one of Michigan's top speedskating teams is primarily for team members and fans, but it also contains some excellent information for anyone interested in speedskating. Here you'll find an extensive directory of speed skating links, some outstanding speedskating tips and tricks, and lots of information about the team and its members and coaches.

> **Tip:** Click the Skating Links link and then under Speed Skating News and Information, click the Grow Inline Speed, to access an area at the site that provides information on starting a team, training, coaching, and getting the right equipment.

Speedskating.com

12345

www.speedskating.com

Very active bulletin board that caters to the speedskating community. Discussion forums cover both inline speedskating and ice speedskating. Here, you can share your enthusiasm for the sport, ask questions, and post comments and replies.

U.S. Speedskating

12345

www.usspeedskating.org

U.S. Speedskating is the governing body for speedskating in the United States. Here you can find the latest news and results, information about upcoming events, entry forms, biographies of U.S. Speedskating athletes, and additional information. Some member-only services include links to the Speedskating Hall of Fame, the record books, and the skate loan program.

SKIN CARE/COSMETICS

Acne Treatment

12345

www.acnetreatment.com

Basic information about diet, prescription drugs, over-the-counter products, stress, and other factors.

Avon

12345

shop.avon.com

Having trouble finding the Avon Lady in your neighborhood? Then go directly to Avon online. Avon carries a complete line of beauty aids, cosmetics, and jewelry. Shop online and have your order shipped to your door.

The Body Shop

12345

www.thebodyshop.com

The Body Shop is a cosmetic company devoted to environmental causes. Here you can shop for a wide selection of bath and beauty products, including skin-care products, makeup, home fragrances, and accessories. Site also features a store locator so you can shop locally at The Body Shop and try before you buy.

Cosmetic Connection

12345

www.cosmeticconnection.com

Read feature articles on beauty trends, techniques, application tips, and other seasonable information in the articles section, and then search for product reviews in the library before investing your hard-earned money in products that don't work as you want them to. Sign up for the free cosmetics report newsletter to get the skinny on the products you've been hearing about.

Cosmetic Mall

12345

www.cosmeticmall.com

Shop by brand or department, such as face or aromatherapy, for your favorite products. Or get advice and tips on what you should be using.

Dermatology Images: University of Iowa

12345

tray.dermatology.uiowa.edu/DermImag.htm

The Image Database of the Department of Dermatology of the University of Iowa provides you with information about common skin disorders and images of what they look like. This site will help you to identify most forms of skin problems, but you should consult your dermatologist if you think you have a problem. Nevertheless, the site is informative. Not for those with weak stomachs.

Best Dermatology Medical Reference

12345

www.emedicine.com/derm/index.shtml

Information on acne, contact dermatitis, scabies and other conditions. This site isn't the usual "flashy" web page, but it does have all or most c the information you would need to know abou skin care, with many interesting articles on the ject. Just a few of the many subjects discussed include Allergy and Immunology, Bacterial Infections, Cosmetics, Diseases of the Dermis, Fungal Infections, and Pediatric Diseases. Eacl ject is categorized alphabetically, which makes easy to find. This site is directed more toward fessional dermatologists rather than the gener public.

A B C D E F G H I J K L M N O P Q R S T U V W X Y Z

drugstore.com

1 2 3 4 5

www.drugstore.com

Search for skin-care products by use or brand here and have them shipped directly to you. Fragrances and cosmetics are also available here.

Faceart

1 2 3 4 5

www.faceart.com

Created by makeup junkies for makeup junkies, this site features articles on creative makeup projects. Sections on eye art, lip art, hair art, and more. Read the feature articles, find answers to your makeup questions, or order the makeup video to learn from the pros.

M-A-C Cosmetics

1 2 3 4 5

www.maccosmetics.com

If you're looking for a new, stunning look, visit M-A-C Cosmetics to check out cutting-edge makeup looks and check out the artists who designed them. At this site, you can also shop online, find a store that carries M-A-C products near you or email one or more of the face artists. When we visited the site, the Live Chat area was not accessible.

Mary Kay

1 2 3 4 5

www.marykay.com

Learn how to get the look you want with makeup through the Virtual Makeover section of this site, which shows you pictures of models having make-up applied in various ways. You can also learn more about various Mary Kay products and locate a local consultant, if you don't already have one.

Merle Norman Cosmetics Studio

1 2 3 4 5

www.merlenorman.com

Merle Norman develops its own line of skin-care and cosmetic products. This site features a store locator that enables you to find a Merle Norman Cosmetics Studio near you. You can also click the Products tab to check out various cosmetic products including cleansers, toners, lipsticks, and eye shadows.

National Rosacea Society

1 2 3 4 5

www.rosacea.org

Information on the skin problem, including the Rosacea Review, a hotline, and a special area for patients that includes a definition of the condition, photos of symptoms and treatment results, a rosacea FAQ, a diary booklet, a list of common triggers and treatments, and more.

Neutrogena

1 2 3 4 5

www.neutrogena.com

Skin-care products, special offers, and advice. S.O.S. section lists links to common skin problems; click a link to find solutions and products that can help. If the problem you have is not listed, click the Ask Neutrogena link to post the question to a dermatologist.

Sephora

1 2 3 4 5

www.sephora.com

Search for products to address your beauty challenges by typing in keywords, or looking by brand. You'll find beauty tips and trends, gift ideas, and product information galore. Sephora is the leading retail beauty chain in Europe and is building a strong market in the United States. Discover more about the company and its innovative stores, and learn more about Sephora's family of companies, including Sephora.com, Sephora USA, and the parent company, LVMH.

> **Tip:** If you're looking for a Sephora store near you, click Sephora Stores in the navigation bar at the top of the page.

Skin Care Campaign

1 2 3 4 5

www.skincarecampaign.org

The Skin Care Campaign is a not-for-profit organization working to represent the interests of all of those who suffer from skin-care conditions in the United Kingdom. Site features an extensive list of skin conditions, and for each provides a description, causes, symptoms, treatments, and information on where to go for additional help.

SkinCarePhysicians.com

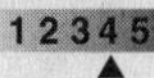

www.derm-infonet.com

Developed by the Academy of Dermatology, this site provides patients and doctors with up-to-date information on the diagnosis, treatment, and management of common skin conditions, including acne, eczema, psoriasis, rosacea, and skin cancer.

Skin Care Tips

1 2 3 4 5

www.lhj.com/home/Skin-Care-Tips.html

This site features links to skin-care articles that have appeared in the *Ladies Home Journal.*

Skin Culture Peel

www.skinculture.com

Skin Culture Peel manufactures and sells skin-peel products. This site features an online form you can fill out to determine your skin type, information about skin peels, and an online store where you can purchase various skin-peel products.

Skin Store

1 2 3 4 5

www.skinstore.com

This huge online store carries a robust collection of skin-care products. You can search for a specific product or browse by skin condition, men's products, best sellers, current promotions, great gifts, or manufacturer. Site also features and education center where you can learn more about skin conditions and skincare and obtain live assistance online.

SNOW SKIING

Altrec.com

12345

www.altrec.com/shop/dir/ski

Skiing, snowboarding, cycling, hiking, hunting, fishing, and other outdoor adventure sports. Altrec carries all the gear you need for most adventure sports, including skiing. The site also features some excellent articles and gear reviews.

Austria Ski Vacation Packages

www.snowpak.com/snowpak/resorts/austriaresorts.html

Part of the Snow Pak Online site. Get quotes for ski vacation packages in Austria and plan your dream vacation. Be sure to register for full-color brochures to be mailed to you and check out the live resort cams and RealAudio snow reports.

Big Bear Mountain Resorts

www.bigbearmountainresorts.com

Big Bear Mountain Resorts in Big Bear, California, built and maintains this site to introduce skiers, snowboarders, and other active vacationers to its many attractive features and outdoor activities. Use the navigation bar at the top of the page to quickly access the site's main areas: Summer Activities, Activities Report, Cams/Photos, Rates/Hours, Maps, and Season Passes. The site's content changes depending on the season. We visited this site during the summer, when the site was advertising its summer fare.

Boston Mills-Brandywine Ski Resort

www.bmbw.com

Located in the Cleveland/Akron area of Ohio, these two ski resorts operate jointly. Check out their website for powder and weather reports, available services, rental fees, night skiing information, live webcams, and lots more.

Cool Works' Ski Resorts and Ski/Snowboard Country Jobs

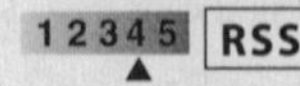

www.coolworks.com/skirsrts.htm

Ever wondered how those ski instructors get such cool jobs? Check out this site. Pick a state. Pick a resort. Pick a job. Spend the winter playing at your dream job. You'll also find links to other cool jobs in state parks, on cruise ships, and in camps. Definitely check this out.

GoSki.com

www.goski.com

Get more information about ski resorts around the world, plan your next ski vacation, look at product reviews, check the weather, and check the headlines before you head out.

ifyouski.com

www.ifyouski.com

ifyouski.com is "Britain's busiest specialist skiing website," offering information on chalet, apartment, and hotel holidays from 40 major and specialist ski tour operators; snow reports and webcams from the top resorts; ski instructions, techniques, and tips; snow ski gear reviews, and a community section with weekly newsletters, competitions, and polls.

K2 Skis

12345

www.k2skis.com

Visit this site to check out the complete line of K2 skis and other gear and use the Dealer Locator to find a dealer near you. Site features excellent graphics and product descriptions to help you pick the right products.

OnTheSnow.com

www.onthesnow.com

OnTheSnow.com is an information kiosk for snow skiers and snowboarders. It includes information on snow conditions and weather, live webcams (for many of the featured resorts), and events; travel information; news; a community center; and links to other snow sites. The opening page contains a quick snow report finder, and members provide a hefty collection of reviews.

Outdoor REVIEW

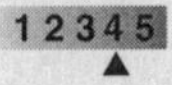

www.outdoorreview.com

Read or write your own reviews of skis, gear, and resorts. You can also pick up some basic skiing tips, chat with other skiers, check road reports, submit photos from mountains you've skied, and link to other hot sites.

Salomon Sports

www.salomonsports.com

Home of some of the most popular skis and snowboards, this site provides product information, information about famous skiers, and links to Salomon ski magazines and sites.

SkiCentral

www.skicentral.com

Check out the Best of the Best search and index site for skiers and snowboarders on the Internet. Here, you'll find more than 3,500 pages covering more than 80 snowsport topics, including snowsport sites, ski reports, resorts, snowcams, travel packages, equipment, and more. So, before planning your trip to the "white mountains of fun and pleasure," check out what this site has to offer.

Categories include Snowsport Sites, Find Gear, Resort Lodging, Ski Packages, Free Ski Photographs, Resorts & Travel, Lodging, Trip Planning, Skiing, Snowboarding, Snow Reports, Snowcams, News & Views, Sites by Region, Contests, Employment, and even Trail Maps.

Ski.com.au

www.ski.com.au

If you're planning a ski trip to Australia, visit this site first. Here you'll discover everything you need to plan your trip and secure reservations. Site features accommodations, reports, live webcams, weather information, news, retail guides for gear and guides, and more.

Skiing in Jackson Hole

www.jacksonholenet.com/ski

Extensive information about travel and lodging, the usual weather and powder reports, and information about four different ski resorts: Snow King, Grand Targhee, Jackson Hole, and White Pine. You'll also find a unique bit of information about ski safety, road safety, and spring skiing safety—along with tips on keeping warm.

SkiMaps

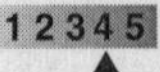

www.skimaps.com

SkiMaps.com offers "the largest collection of ski maps and ski area data on the World Wide Web." Here you can locate ski maps of the top ski resorts in the United States, Canada, and other countries around the world. Site also features news, discussion forums, and a Gear link that connects you to Altrec for online shopping.

SkiSnowboard.com

12345

www.skisnowboard.com

If you're looking for a place to ski or snowboard, this should be the first place you turn. Here you can find the best resorts for skiing, snowboarding, cross-country skiing, snowshoeing, and other snow sports around the world. Site also features a small collection of news stories on skiing and snowboarding.

SnoCountry Mountain Reports

12345

www.snocountry.com

SnoCountry Mountain Reports specializes in providing up-to-date information on ski resorts in the United States, Canada, Europe, and the southern hemisphere. Site also features specific reports for cross-country skiing along with other areas, including an equipment center, information on nutrition and skin care, and articles on family skiing and ski gear.

Stowe Mountain Resort

12345

www.stowe.com

Find out about upcoming package deals at Stowe, Vermont. The latest weather and powder conditions are here, along with FAQs, information about lessons, and directions to the resort.

The U.S. Ski Home Team Page

12345 RSS

www.usskiteam.com

The official page for the U.S. Ski Team. Stay informed about all the doings of the ski team all the time, not just during the Olympics. There's also World Cup news, selection criteria, and more official news. Excellent Disabled section specifically for paralympians.

SNOWMOBILING

American Snowmobiler Magazine

1 2 3 4 5 RSS

www.amsnow.com

Up-to-date information about snowmobiling and the snowmobile industry. Includes current news, a racing guide, a travel guide, product reviews, discussion forums, and more.

Arctic Cat

1 2 3 4 5

www.arctic-cat.com

Arctic Cat company's official site, with product information on snowmobiles, watercraft, and ATVs—plus safety information, dealer links, and a search tool for looking up parts.

International Snowmobile Manufacturers Association

1 2 3 4 5

www.snowmobile.org

Timely information about the sport of snowmobiling in North America and Europe. Features articles, stats and facts, and information on snowmobile safety. Links to other sites, too.

Maine Snowmobile Connection

www.sledmaine.com

Accommodations, trail reports, clubs, sled rentals, and other information for would-be Maine snowmobilers and other winter sports enthusiasts.

Michigan Snowmobiling

1 2 3 4 5

www.fishweb.com/recreation/snowmobile/snowmobiling.html

This site, intended to promote snowmobiling in the state of Michigan and foster a respect for the "beauty we invade," offers Michigan snow and trail reports, featured regions, rentals, stops, and stories.

Minnesota Snowmobiling

1 2 3 4 5

www.dnr.state.mn.us/snowmobiling/index.html

The Minnesota Department of Natural Resources created and maintains this site to promote snowmobiling in Minnesota, inform visitors of the regulations and code of conduct they must follow, and provide important safety tips and techniques. This site also presents several guides and maps to help you find the best places in Minnesota to go snowmobiling.

Ontario Snowmobiling

1 2 3 4 5

www.ontariosnowmobiling.com

This site, built and maintained to promote snowmobiling in Ontario, offers a good directory of links to other sites organized by category, including Accessories, Clubs/Associations, Dealers, Destinations, Tours, and Magazines.

Polaris Industries

1 2 3 4 5

www.polarisindustries.com/en-us/vehicles

Maker of snowmobiles, watercraft, and ATVs. Product information, latest news, annual report, and employment opportunities. Check out the Buying Tools link for free brochures and other information.

Ski-Doo

12345

www.ski-doo.com

Official site for Ski-Doo snowmobile manufacturer. Includes product information, safety tips, and links. Click the Cool Stuff link to shop for Ski-Doo toys, watches, gifts, and novelties.

Snowmobile Online

12345

www.off-road.com/snowmobile

Read the latest snowmobiling news, stay up-to-date on land use issues that threaten snowmobilers' access to parks and other areas, find places to ride, read product reviews and lots of other information about snowmobiling here.

SnowmobileWorld.com

12345

www.snowmobileworld.com

SnowmobileWorld.com features discussion forums, a tech center complete with how-to articles, a community center, and a link to CafePress.com (SW Store), where you can purchase Snowmobile World.com apparel and other items. Visit the multimedia area for free screensavers. Some valuable How-To articles are also available.

Snowmobiling.net

12345

www.snowmobiling.net

Snowmobilers can visit this site to load up on links, classified ads, electronic shopping services, message boards, and news.

SnowTracks

www.snowtracks.com

SnowTracks is the top site for snowmobile enthusiasts throughout the United States and Canada. Here you can find snowmobiling reports and trail conditions for the United States and Canada, trail maps, classifieds, news, a calendar of events, race information, live webcams, tech tips, discussion forums, and online chat. This is a great place to go to gather information and tips and join an active community of snowmobile enthusiasts.

World Snowmobile Association

12345

www.wsaracing.com

The WSA organizes, promotes, and runs ATV and snowmobile races, including the Snocross series. Here you can learn more about the various competitions, check out the schedule of upcoming races, register online, view racer profiles and standings, and even shop for insurance. Special areas are available for racers and spectators. You can also shop online for DVDs, transponders, WSA gear, and other items. Content at this site varies based on the season. Click the Snowmobile Tour tab for snowmobile content or the ATV Tour tab to learn more about ATV races and competitions.

Yamaha Motor Corporation

12345

www.yamaha-motor.com

Official corporate site of Yamaha Motor Corporation, USA, maker of snowmobiles, watercraft, ATVs, boats, racing karts, and more. Includes product and competition information.

SOCCER

American Youth Soccer

12345 Blog

soccer.org

American Youth Soccer is dedicated to making soccer a more fair and enjoyable game by encouraging players, coaches, and parents to follow its five philosophies: Everyone plays (at least half of each game), Balanced teams (to even out the competition), Open registration (interest and enthusiasm are the only prerequisites to playing), Positive coaching (encouragement rules), and Good sportsmanship (no whining and complaining). Visit this site to learn more about the organization and its guiding principles and its programs and events. Members can create and maintain their own blogs at this site.

ATL World Soccer News

12345

www.wldcup.com

Offers world soccer news, commentary, statistics, and scores. During the World Cup, you'll want to bookmark this site for the latest stories, scores, and team standings.

ESPN Soccer

soccernet.espn.go.com

ESPN is the leading sports broadcasting company in the world, and its Soccer site doesn't disappoint. We visited this site during the height of World Cup competition and found it packed with the most up-to-date scores, stats, standings, and stories. When we visited, you could use the navigation bar at the top of the screen to quickly jump to your area of interest: Live Scores, Schedules, Groups, Teams, Stats, Players, Venues, History, Qualifying, Boards, Fantasy, and More. When the World Cup isn't in full swing, the site features content organized in the following categories: Live Scores, England, Europe, UEFA Champions League, World Cup, US Home, MLS, and NCAA.

Best FIFA Online

www.fifa.com

Official page of soccer's world governing body provides coverage of competitions, press releases, a newsletter, and rules updates. Content is presented in English, German, French, and Spanish. During the World Cup, you can view photos and videos. The navigation bar at the top of the screen enables you to quickly jump to your area of interest: News, Men's & Youth, Women's, History of Football, Developing the Game, FIFA Fair Play, Marketing & TV, Media Service, FIFA Organisation, and Regulations & Directories.

FIFA World Cup

fifaworldcup.yahoo.com

Home of the biggest soccer tournament in the world, this site provides coverage of the most recent World Cup soccer games. Provides a preview of upcoming matches, scores and coverage of recent matches, video highlights, online message boards, and more. Site also features a Fun and Games area and special offerings to keep mobile web users in the loop.

Goal.com

www.goal.com

Goal.com is one of the most comprehensive resources for soccer news, photos, statistics, scores, standings, trades, and other soccer information.

The opening page presents headline news along with links for internationals, championships, hot topics, news, multimedia, and community. Content is offered in Italian, English, German, Spanish, French, Japanese, Russian, Chinese, and Thai. Excellent articles, photos, and feature stories.

InternetSoccer.com

1 2 3 4 5

www.ussoccerplayers.com

Late-breaking soccer news and scores plus a searchable index of teams and players. Search for news by continents, countries, competitions, or leagues. This site also features an excellent resource center for players, coaches, and parents; a Fun Zone with games and puzzles; newsletters; message boards; and player columns. Whether you're a fan of the game or you just enjoy playing, you'll find this to be one of the top soccer sites.

Major League Soccer (MLS)

www.mlsnet.com

Get stats, schedules, results, rankings, team information, and images of the players and videos of some of the best shots this season. Site also offers fantasy soccer and features for mobile Internet users. Site is bilingual in English and Spanish.

Soccer.com

1 2 3 4 5

www.soccer.com

Soccer.com is an online store where you'll find all the soccer gear, accessories, and attire you'll need to look and play like a real soccer professional.

SoccerAmerica.com

1 2 3 4 5

www.socceramerica.com

This is the online home of *SoccerAmerica* magazine. Here you can find top stories and feature articles, a soccer camp directory, a college guide, a FAQs area, and a tournament schedule. At the top of the page are a collection of links to various leagues and tournaments; click a link to display a list of articles that relate to it. If you like what you see, you can subscribe to the magazine online.

Soccer Camps

www.soccer-camps.com

This site offers a searchable online directory of soccer camps along with registration and pricing information, schedules, and just about anything else you need to know about soccer camps, with dozens of camps listed and organized by state.

Soccer Information Systems

www.soccerinfo.com

Contains a database of information relating to amateur soccer. Topics include high school soccer, coaching, recruiting, soccer writers, and camps.

Soccer-Sites

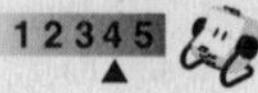

www.soccer-sites.com

Soccer-Sites claims to be your central starting point for the top soccer/football-related sites all over the world. Search the database using keywords to find a site quickly. Sites are updated regularly.

Soccer Times

1 2 3 4 5

www.soccertimes.com

Up-to-date news on the latest in U.S. and international soccer. Check on your favorite teams and players, explore NCAA soccer, get information on U.S. national teams, and keep abreast of the happenings at the World Cup Soccer tournament.

Soccer Tutor

1 2 3 4 5

www.soccertutor.com

Whether you are a player or a coach, you will find the techniques, training, and tips to carry your soccer play to the next level. Here you can take a free tour of the service to see what it has to offer, sign up for a free trial, and then subscribe to the service when you see how much it really has to offer. Nice design and great content.

United States Soccer Federation

www.ussoccer.com

The official site of the U.S. soccer governing body. It provides a history of soccer in the United States, an Olympic recap, a quarterly soccer e-zine, and more. Coaches and referees will find training advice and tips here, too.

U.S. Youth Soccer

12345

usyouthsoccer.org

History of the association, an events calendar, a catalog of U.S. Youth Soccer materials, and addresses of groups across the United States. Site features special content for players, coaches, and parents, along with information about available youth soccer programs. Site also offers content in Spanish.

World Soccer Page

www.wspsoccer.com

The World Soccer Page gives you plenty of information about U.S. and international soccer teams, players, games, news, and merchandise. Site also offers lively discussion boards where you can share your opinions and insights with other soccer fans from around the world. Click Games to predict the outcomes of scheduled games and pit your predications against the predications of other fans to see who's the most soccer savvy.

SOCIAL WORK/SERVICES

AAMFT

1 2 3 4 5

www.aamft.org

The American Association for Marriage and Family Therapy (AAMFT) is "the professional association for the field of marriage and family therapy, representing the professional interests of more than 23,000 marriage and family therapists throughout the United States, Canada, and abroad." This site features information on marriage and family therapists and a practice strategy newsletter.

ADEC

1 2 3 4 5

www.adec.org

The Association for Death Education and Counseling created and maintains this site for professionals, providing information on conferences, workshops, certification, and publications. If you're struggling with the loss of a loved one, click the Coping with Loss link to access links to articles and other related websites.

The Carter Center

1 2 3 4 5

www.cartercenter.org

The Carter Center, a project spearheaded by former president Jimmy Carter and first lady Roslyn, is "committed to advancing human rights and alleviating unnecessary human suffering" throughout the world. Visit this site to get information about their current and past work, as well as to find out what you can do to help.

Catholic Charities USA

1 2 3 4 5

www.catholiccharitiesusa.org

Largest social services organization in America. The site provides descriptions of programs and contact details for local agencies.

Council on Social Work Education

1 2 3 4 5

www.cswe.org

Council on Social Work Education (CSWE) is "a national association that preserves and enhances the quality of social work education for practice that promotes the goals of individual and community well-being and social justice." If you're a therapist or social worker, you'll want to bookmark this site, where you can obtain information about continuing education, accreditation, and various projects that the CSWE sponsors.

International Federation of Social Workers

1 2 3 4 5

www.ifsw.org

The International Federation of Social Workers (IFSW) is a worldwide organization "striving for social justice, human rights and social development through the development of social work, best practices, and international cooperation between social workers and their professional organizations." Here you can learn more about the IFSW, find out about upcoming events, read various news stories, or check the international job board.

A B C D E F G H I J K L M N O P Q R S T U V W X Y Z

National Association of Alcoholism and Drug Abuse Counselors (NAADAC)

1 2 3 4 5

`naadac.org`

Learn about the NAADAC and its membership, certifications, products, services, resource links, and more. Site also features a newsletter.

National Association of Social Workers

1 2 3 4 5

`www.naswdc.org`

With more than 153,000 members, the National Association of Social Workers is the largest organization of social workers in the world. Here you can learn more about the organization and check on its continuing education and credentialing programs. Waste no time on the opening page. Instead, click your desired area of interest in the navigation bar on the right: Aging, Behavioral Health, Children And Families, or Health. This delivers a page with a real navigation bar that can help you more effectively navigate the site.

The National Coalition for the Homeless

1 2 3 4 5

`www.nationalhomeless.org`

With the primary goal of abolishing homelessness in mind, this group relates tales of people's struggles with homelessness and provides links to information on recent developments and legislation that pertain to homelessness.

The New Social Worker Online

1 2 3 4 5

`www.socialworker.com`

The New Social Worker is a magazine that helps keep social workers informed of the latest developments and treatment approaches in social work. This site also offers job listings, a lively discussion forum, and additional resources to help social workers develop their skills and further their careers. You can subscribe online for the full print edition, the digital replica edition, or the free monthly newsletter.

New York State Dep... Assistance

1 2 3 4 5

`www.dfa.state.ny.us`

Formerly the Departmen... have two categories to ch... Temporary and Disabilit... Children and Family Ser... area, you can explore the... and services.

Best Social Work ... Websites

1 2 3 4 5

`gwbweb.wustl.edu/websites.html`

This directory of services, put together by Washington University in St. Louis, feature... excellent directory of links to social work a... services sites on the Web, categorized into ... groups covering everything from Abuse an... Violence to Women's Issues. This list of res... addresses health issues, psychiatric illnesses... ities, family crises, counseling, housing, veterans issues, and much more. When you're looking for help, this is the Best of the Best places to start.

SocialService.com

1 2 3 4 5

`www.socialservice.com`

Social workers and other social service professionals looking for a job will want to start here to find a new position, whether you're looking for something in mental health, domestic violence, children, outreach, or just about any other specialty. Employers can also post openings for access by professionals nationwide.

Social Work Access Network

1 2 3 4 5

`cosw.sc.edu/swan`

This site functions as a portal to other social work websites and resources. You can browse by category including Schools of Social Work, Upcoming Conferences, Social Work Organizations, and Social Work Publications. This site is maintained by faculty and students of the University of South Carolina. It also contains links to social work resources at the University, including information about its Master's in Social Work (MSW) and Ph.D. programs.

Social Work Search

1 2 3 4 5

www.socialworksearch.com

Socialworksearch.com provides social workers and related professionals with a search tool and directory of more than 1,500 different web pages of services and websites devoted solely to the social work profession. You can search for a specific resource by keyword, browse the categories, check out the top 50 social work websites, vote on your favorite site, or even add your site to the directory. If you're a social worker, bookmark this site for repeat visits.

U.S. Department of Health and Human Services

1 2 3 4 5

www.os.dhhs.gov

The government's principal agency for protecting the health of Americans and providing essential human services, especially for those who are least able to help themselves. The agency oversees more than 300 programs. Families who need assistance should check this site first to learn about available benefits and services.

U.S. Department of Labor: Social Workers

1 2 3 4 5

www.bls.gov/oco/ocos060.htm

The U.S. Department of Labor releases statistics and information for a wide range of careers, including social work. If you're considering becoming a social worker, check out this site to learn about the nature of the work and working conditions, the training you'll need, job prospects, average earnings, and related occupations.

SOFTBALL

Amateur Softball Association

1 2 3 4 5

www.softball.org

The Amateur Softball Association (ASA) is the strongest softball organization in the country and is the national governing body of softball in the United States, regulating competition "to ensure fairness and equal opportunity to the millions of player who annually play the sport." If you're looking for information about the game of softball—fastpitch, slowpitch or modified, men's or women's, adult or youth—you've come to the right place. Lots of links to other softball sites too.

American Fastpitch Association

1 2 3 4 5

www.afasoftball.com

The American Fastpitch Association maintains this site as a service to its members. The site features information on tournaments, tournament results, the AFA Rulebook, an umpire membership application, and player profiles.

Best ISF: International Softball Federation

1 2 3 4 5

www.internationalsoftball.com

This bilingual site (English and Spanish) is the home of the governing body of international softball, "as recognized by the International Olympic Committee (IOC) and the General Association of International Sports Federations (GAISF)." This site features information about the organization, the rules it sets, and upcoming and ongoing tournaments it sponsors. Tournaments include the Olympic games, the Slow Pitch World Cup, the Seniors Softball World Cup, and the World Masters Games. Free subscription to the ISF newsletter, plus online shopping for ISF merchandise. With all it has to offer, this site is the Best of the Best softball sites on the Web.

Tip: On the opening page, in the Welcome area, click the What Softball Is link to get a two-page PDF brochure that lays out the basics.

National Fastpitch Coaches Association

1 2 3 4 5

www.nfca.org

The NFCA is "a professional growth organiza[illegible] for fastpitch softball coaches from all competitive levels of play." Site features a members' area, convention information, details about the Leadoff Classic, a scoreboard, information about college fastpitch, and much more. If you coach fastpitch softball, visit this site to become a member and join the fastpitch coaches' community.

National Pro Fastpitch

1 2 3 4 5

www.profastpitch.com

This official site of the National Pro Fastpitch league provides information about the league, its president, and its future. Site includes information about teams, players, schedules, standings, statistics, and more. Here you can also find a Fan Zone with photos and polls and a Kids Zone with fun and games.

NCAA Women's Softball

1 2 3 4 5

www.ncaasports.com/softball/womens

National Collegiate Athletic Association's official site for women's softball. Includes a schedule, ticketing information, results, and previews. This site is well designed and easy to navigate and has great graphics with lots of information about softball. Some of the many features are rankings, teams, history, places to purchase tickets, and information about NCAA championships. Plus, you can purchase merchandise from an online store.

NZ Softball–New Zealand

1 2 3 4 5

www.softball.org.nz

Get a new perspective on the old baseball game by visiting this site somewhere down under—namely, New Zealand. This official New Zealand Softball website features plenty of information on tournaments, club tournaments, tournament records, player stats, and the softball World Series. Players, coaches, and umpires will also find plenty of useful resources at this site.

Senior Softball

1 2 3 4 5

www.seniorsoftball.com

Learn more about tournaments, rules, tours, and news regarding senior softball here.

Slow Pitch Softball History Page

1 2 3 4 5

www.angelfire.com/sd/slopitch

This site features softball national championship and World Series history. Also contains an excellent directory of links to other softball-related sites.

Softball on the Internet

1 2 3 4 5

www.softball.com

Softball information and an online catalog with products. Facts about gear, an Ask the Umpire section, and a toll-free number for ordering. Enter tournament dates into the directory.

SoftballSearch.com

1 2 3 4 5

softballsearch.eteamz.com

SoftballSearch.com is an excellent directory of softball-related websites organized by category, including Announcements, Camps and Clinics, Software and Rules, Tournaments, and Slowpitch Teams, to name only a few. Site also features links to discussion boards and sites that provide fastpitch and slowpitch tips and drills.

U.S.A. Softball Official Site

1 2 3 4 5

www.usasoftball.com

Fans of the U.S.A. Men's and Women's softball teams should bookmark this site to keep abreast of the latest news and developments. Provides information about and coverage of the Olympic Games, Pan American Games, and ISF World Championships. Includes "rosters, player and coach biographies, competition schedules, statistics and live play-by-play updates," when available.

A B C D E F G H I J K L M N O P Q R S T U V W X Y Z

SUICIDE PREVENTION

Best American Association of Suicidology

12345

www.suicidology.org

American Association of Suicidology (AAS) promotes research, public awareness programs, public education, and training for professionals and volunteers to build an understanding of and help prevent suicide. AAS also serves as a national clearinghouse for information on suicide. Although this education and resource group doesn't provide direct services, the home page contains a toll-free hotline number you can call for help, along with a page that provides guidance on what to do if you suspect a loved one or acquaintance of being suicidal. Click About Suicide to access this page. By clicking Prevention, you can access a small directory of links to sites with additional information. Content at this site is particularly useful for counselors, crisis center workers, doctors, and other professionals who deal with suicide on a regular basis.

American Foundation for Suicide Prevention (AFSP)

12345

www.afsp.org

The American Foundation for Suicide Prevention funds research, education, and treatment programs. The site includes such categories as Depression, Survivor Support, and Assisted Suicide.

Befrienders International

12345

www.befrienders.org

Locate one of the 400 Befrienders centers worldwide providing a sympathetic ear and suicide intervention based on listening therapy. Articles on helping a suicidal friend or family member, warning signs of suicide, suicide statistics, and more.

Community Lifelines

12345

www.communitylifelines.ca

Online brochures cover such issues as dealing with suicidal thoughts, helping a depressed person, and coping with grief in the aftermath. Click Resources to access the brochures.

Covenant House

12345

www.covenanthouse.org/nineline/index.html

Young people can contact the telephone advice line and locate help centers across the country, and parents can also get assistance. Two hotline numbers are available—one for support in English and one for Spanish.

National Strategy for Suicide Prevention

12345

www.mentalhealth.samhsa.gov/suicideprevention

The National Strategy for Suicide Prevention (NSSP) represents "the combined work of advocates, clinicians, researchers and survivors around the nation," and is designed to be "a catalyst for social change with the power to transform attitudes, policies, and services." Here you'll find a suicide hotline, free fact sheets, statistics on the deleterious effects of suicide on communities and the nation, state prevention programs, featured publications, and the latest news and resources.

National Suicide Prevention Lifeline

12345

www.suicidepreventionlifeline.org

The National Suicide Prevention Lifeline's mission is "to provide immediate assistance to individuals in suicidal crisis by connecting them to the nearest available suicide prevention and mental health service provider through a toll-free telephone number: 1-800-273-TALK (8255). It is the only national suicide prevention and intervention telephone resource funded by the federal government." This site also offers free brochures and other publicity materials, both in Spanish and English, to assist community leaders in getting the word out and letting people know they have a number to call for help.

SAVE: Suicide Help

1 2 3 4 5

www.save.org

Practical advice for dealing with suicidal feelings, helping someone who is suicidal, and dealing with the grief when someone close to you commits suicide. Hosted by Suicide Awareness Voices of Education (SAVE). This site also features a useful list of symptoms and danger signs that can help you identify a potential crisis. It also provides a toll-free suicide hotline number you can call in the event that you or a loved one is overcome by suicidal thoughts.

SFSP: Suicide Prevention

1 2 3 4 5

www.sfsuicide.org

Home of San Francisco Suicide Prevention, the oldest crisis hotline in America. Choose Suicide Facts and then click Myth or Fact Quiz for a series of statements and see how much you really know about spotting the warning signs for suicide. A 24-hour telephone crisis line is available.

Suicide Facts

1 2 3 4 5

www.cdc.gov/ncipc/factsheets/suifacts.htm

From the Centers for Disease Control, this site seeks to dispel myths about suicide and keep the populace informed concerning the facts. This is a basic fact sheet providing links to cited references, but it also provides suicide prevention strategies and links to other resources on the Web.

Suicide Prevention Advocacy Network

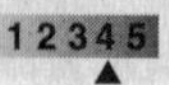

www.spanusa.org

The Suicide Prevention Action Network (SPAN USA) is a nonprofit organization "dedicated to preventing suicide through public education and awareness, community action and federal, state and local grassroots advocacy." Join the national campaign to reduce suicide rates. Find out how to be a community organizer and read the SPANUSA newsletter.

Yellow Ribbon Suicide Prevention Program

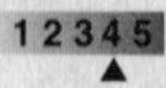

www.yellowribbon.org

This site is for both parents and teens, but the program is designed for young people. It teaches teens how to recognize the symptoms of depression in their friends and gives them ideas what they can do to help their friends get the help they need.

TABLE TENNIS

Butterfly Online

12345

www.butterflyonline.com

Butterfly is one of the major manufacturers of table tennis equipment in the world. At this site, you can find information about recent and upcoming tournaments, table tennis news, rules of the game, coaching tips, and player profiles; plus, you can browse through the huge collection of paddles, tables, balls, accessories, robots, and other equipment and accessories.

Classic Hardbat Table Tennis

12345

www.hardbat.com

Learn about hardbat table tennis—the rules, ratings, photos, and player profiles. Sign up for the newsletter or check out the upcoming events and tournament results at this site. Some great video clips are also available.

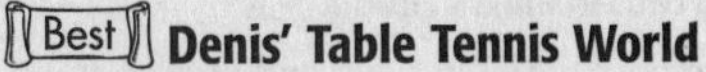

Denis' Table Tennis World

12345 RSS

www.tabletennis.gr

Prematch, match, and postmatch tips by Dimosthenis E. Messinis, Ph.D. Huge collection of resources with an easy-to-use navigation bar on the left containing sections on Articles-Tips, Exercises, Basics, Equipment, Rules, and even video clips. Quizzes, FAQs, interviews, world rankings, awards, and more provide a one-stop kiosk for everything a table tennis enthusiast needs to know. The Best of the Best table tennis sites in the group.

International Paralympic Table Tennis Committee

12345

www.ipttc.org

The official governing body for the disabled table tennis—both wheelchair and standing disabled. Site provides up-to-date information, including player rankings.

International Table Tennis Federation

12345

www.ittf.com

Browse through this online magazine for the latest world competition results and profiled players. Also includes links to other table tennis sites.

Megaspin.net

12345 RSS

www.megaspin.net

Check out table tennis rules, rankings, links, the picture gallery, news, and updates. Subscribe to the free newsletter to keep abreast of the latest news and upcoming events, or shop online for paddles, balls, and other table tennis accessories. This excellent site was barely edged out in the running for the Best of the Best prize, so be sure to check it out. Don't miss the Ping Pong Matrix video.

National Collegiate Table Tennis

12345

www.nctta.org

National Collegiate Table Tennis is devoted to promoting the sport of table tennis at the college level. This site features tournaments and results, standings, information about teams and players, player ratings, a discussion forum, and more.

North America Table Tennis, Inc.

www.natabletennis.com

Find out about the Stiga North American Teams Championships, one of the largest table tennis championships in the world, and about the Stiga North American Tour. Also provides information about the AAU Junior Olympics and the ACUI/NCTTA collegiate events and other NATT events. Provides a calendar of events, plus an online store where you can register for tournaments and purchase NATT apparel and used tables.

Ping-Pong.com

12345

www.ping-pong.com

Ping-Pong.com is the official website of the leading manufacturer of table tennis tables in North America. Here, you can check out its products, find local dealers that carry these tables, get game rules and troubleshooting advice, download PDF versions of the manuals, access a small list of FAQs, and find a handful of links to other table tennis sites.

The Sport of Table Tennis

12345

library.thinkquest.org/20570

Excellent information organized in a Q&A format for anyone interested in taking up the game of table tennis. Answers the questions: What is table tennis? How do I play? What do I need? Where do I play? Also provides tips, table tennis facts, table tennis terms, and a discussion board.

Table Tennis

12345

tabletennis.about.com

Find out lots of interesting facts from this complete table tennis community with an expert guide, forum, chats, links, bimonthly newsletter, weekly features, coaching tips, and much more.

Total Table Tennis

12345

www.totaltabletennis.com

Total Table Tennis is an online store that features a wide selection of quality table tennis products at excellent prices. If you're in the market for a table, paddle, balls, nets, or other table tennis equipment, sales representatives can help guide you to products that are best for your level of play and budget. You can search for a specific item or browse the store for robots, tables, and accessories.

USA Table Tennis

12345

www.usatt.org

Check here for news on the USA Nationals and browse through the Tournament Information Guide. Investigate the information on clubs, hot spots to play, equipment, dealers, USATT rules, upcoming tournaments, and results. Learn how to become a USA Table Tennis member. You can get information on table tennis rules in the Stump the Ump section or browse through the current and past issues of *USA Table Tennis* e-zine.

World Table Tennis News

12345

www.worldtabletennis.com

This site provides the latest news and information about competitive table tennis tournaments around the world, along with a handful of links to other table tennis sites.

TATTOOS/BODY ART

Altered Body

www.alteredbody.com

Altered Body is "an online resource for tattoo, body piercing and body painting information and picture galleries." Site features a search tool that can help you track down tattoo, piercing, and body painting designs, supplies, and services.

Body Art Studios

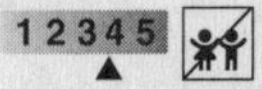

www.bodyartstudios.com

Body Art Studios, a posh tattoo and body-piercing parlor in Brooklyn, New York, presents this site to introduce visitors to its services. Here, you can browse the tattoo or body-piercing galleries, learn about the studio and the artist, and email the proprietor to set up an appointment.

Body Jewelry

www.bodyjewelry.com

Body Jewelry is an online store that offers a huge selection of unique sterling silver design and surgical steel body jewelry and accessories. If you can't find what you're looking for, simply email the company for assistance in finding it.

Earth Henna Kits

www.earthhenna.com

If you're into henna body painting, this is the site for you. Here, you'll find the kits, inks, and stencils to do both basic and intricate designs. Site also features several well-stocked galleries of tasteful photos, a history of henna, instructions on the use of henna, and a collection of links to other related sites. A video demonstration is also available.

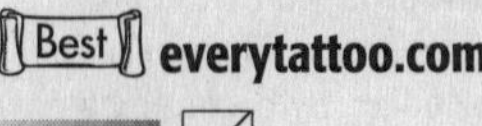

Best everytattoo.com

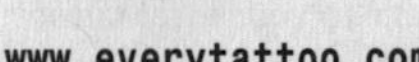

www.everytattoo.com

everytattoo.com is one of the best places to go to find tattoo designs. Designs are grouped in categories including Arm Bands, Dragons, Females, Japanese, Mermaids, Warriors, and Yin and Yang. Site also can also direct you to local tattoo parlors, magazines and books, stories, and conventions. You can hang out in the discussion forums, get aftercare advice, research local laws and regulations governing tattoo parlors in your area, register to upload pictures of your tattoos or original designs, and much more. This site does have some annoying pop-ups and other advertisements, but it's packed with great information and graphics. Also covers piercings.

Kingpin Tattoo Supply

www.kingpintattoosupply.com

If you're a tattoo artist looking for a wide selection of supplies and equipment at reasonable prices, check out Kingpin Tattoo Supply. This online store carries everything you need, including tattoo machines; tubes, tips, and grips; needles and needle heads; inks; medical supplies; piercing equipment; and more.

Tattoo Fun

www.tattoofun.com

If you'd like to try a tattoo or body ornament without making a lifelong commitment to it, check out this site. Here, you'll find a vast collection of temporary tattoos and body jewelry that doesn't require a needle of any sort. This company also carries henna body painting kits. Before you leave, check out the tattoo stories.

Tattoodles

www.tattoodles.com

Tattoodles is positioning itself as the ultimate online resource and community center for tattoo artists and enthusiasts. Here, you'll find a huge gallery of "flash" (designs) grouped by category, including Animals, Celtic, Fantasy, Floral, Kanji, Traditional, Tribal, and Zodiac. By becoming a paying member, you can download printable versions of your favorite designs to take to your local tattoo artist and get inked. Site also features a magazine and discussion forums and a bunch of cool free stuff, including desktop wallpaper.

TAXES

1040.com

12345

www.1040.com

1040.com is an online tax kiosk where you can find the forms and filing information you need to complete and submit your taxes. Site features one-click access to find a form, file online, a tax calendar, a tax estimator, filing addresses, related links, and a free 1040.com email.

Bankrate.com

12345

www.bankrate.com/brm/news/news_taxes_home.asp

Excellent income tax information and tips for individuals and small-business owners. Read articles that help you track down your refund, estimate your withholding tax, claim tax credits, realize the benefits of itemizing, deduct mortgage interest, and much more.

Citizens for Tax Justice

12345

www.ctj.org

This nonprofit organization does research to support its advocacy of a fairer tax code for middle- and low-income families, closing corporate tax loopholes, reducing the federal deficit, and requiring the rich to pay their fair share.

eSmartForms

12345

www.etaxforms.com

Tired of filling out those paper forms and mailing your tax return? Then do it online. This site features two simple, inexpensive ways to file your tax return electronically: either complete the "paperwork" online using web-based forms or download the forms you need, in Microsoft Word format. Complete the forms and upload to submit them. Cost is $15 or less.

Essential Links to Taxes

12345

www.el.com/elinks/taxes

Taxpayer tips and information on income tax preparation assistance, rules, tax code, financial planners and tax preparers, forms (from W-2 to Form 1040), publications, instructions, deductions, and filing.

Forbes: Taxes

12345

www.forbes.com/taxes

Forbes is one of the top personal finance and investment magazines in publication. Here, you can access several excellent articles on a variety of currently hot tax topics. Sometimes, Steve Forbes himself pops up to introduce the latest topic of interest.

H&R Block

12345

www.hrblock.com

Although you'll find plenty of information here to help you get better rates on credit cards, mortgages, and loans, the tax information is the most helpful. Use the Withholding Calculator to figure out how much you should be having taken out of your paycheck. Or find out the status of your refund check. Features tax news and tips, a year-round tax planning guide, a tax calendar, information about new tax laws, a well-stocked library of tax forms and IRS publications, and hundreds of tax-saving tips. Very attractive site, easy to navigate, and packed with the great tax information. Content is also offered in Spanish.

IRS: Internet Revenue Service

12345

www.irs.gov

The IRS site provides everything you need to become an informed taxpayer. Search the site for specific information or for downloadable, printable tax forms you might have trouble finding at your local post office or library, or you can choose to file your return online. The site also provides news about the IRS and tax legislation, along with information specifically for individuals, businesses, nonprofit organizations, and tax professionals. Learn about the earned income tax credit, tax scams and frauds, and your rights as a taxpayer.

IRS News

12345

www.irs.gov/newsroom/index.html

The IRS News page provides news, tips, places to go for help, online forms, links, information about record keeping, descriptions of common tax scams, and more.

Kiplinger Online

www.kiplinger.com

For more than 80 years, Kiplinger has been providing cutting-edge information and advice for financial management and investment. Check out this site for some free offerings. Includes business forecasts, news of the day, financial advice, tax news and advice, and investment and retirement information. Additional services for paying members. The site features no specific tax area, so you'll have to search for what you want.

MoneyCentral on Taxes

12345 RSS

moneycentral.msn.com/tax/home.asp

Information on tax planning and preparation, tax estimators, deduction finder, tax IQ test, Q&A, and information on reducing your tax burden. Site also features guidance on what to do if you're getting audited.

Best SmartMoney.com Tax Center

12345 RSS

www.smartmoney.com/tax

This informative site offers tax strategies and tools to help save you money. Areas at this site include Tax Worksheets; Tax Basics: Advice, Home and Family Taxes; Work and Business Taxes; Tax Basics: Filing; and more. Site also features a primer on tax credits for a variety of situations and several calculators to help you estimate taxes and discover vulnerable areas. Scroll down the page to use the index to find the information you need. All content is organized in easily recognizable categories, making it easy to navigate the site.

SmartPros Accounting

12345

accounting.smartpros.com

Download federal and state tax forms and publications, file your taxes electronically, or find an accountant to handle your taxes for you.

State and Local Taxes

12345 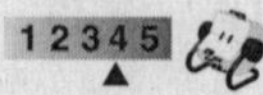

www.taxsites.com/state.html

State tax resource with general locators, current tax issues, organizations, and more. This site has dozens of useful and informative links to information about tax preparation, tax changes and updates, and more.

State Sales Tax Rates

12345

www.taxadmin.org/FTA/rate/sales.html

Simple table that shows sales tax rates for all 50 states.

Tax Analysts

12345

www.tax.org

Tax Analysts is "a nonprofit, nonpartisan organization fostering informed debate on federal, state, and international tax policy." The group encourages "development of tax systems that are fair, simple, and economically efficient." Here, you can find a good collection of information and resources on state, federal, and international tax issues.

Tax Glossary

12345

taxes.yahoo.com/glossary

Long list of terms you might encounter on your tax return along with a precise definition of each term. Running down the left side of the page is a navigation bar that provides quick access to additional tax information and resources, including forms, calculators, calendars, rates, basics, tips, and more.

Tax Guide for Investors

www.fairmark.com

Fairmark Press has created and maintains this site to help inform taxpayers of their options and of the latest tax legislation that might affect them. Tabbed navigation provides one-click access to a tax help center, Roth IRAs, options, capital gains, information on kids and college, and a message board. You can also peruse the tax and finance library and order books online. Some excellent articles and tips; but if you want something more in depth, you'll need to order one or two of the books.

The Tax Prophet

www.taxprophet.com

The Tax Prophet Robert L. Sommers of San Francisco, California, created and maintains this site to provide helpful articles on taxes as well as FAQs and tax-related links.

Tax Resources on the Web

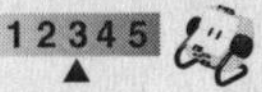

taxtopics.net

A simple-to-navigate yet comprehensive site that allows you to click on keywords, such as kiddy tax or dividends, and find links to sites with useful information on the subjects.

Tax Sites

www.taxsites.com

A site full of web-based tax and accounting resources, which you an access by clicking on a keyword.

TaxFoundation.org

www.taxfoundation.org

Dedicated to translating the overly complex and cryptic income tax code into something the average taxpayer can understand, TaxFoundation.org publishes reports that explain in plain English what taxpayers need to know. The foundation also answers tax questions from individuals and the media. This site also features headline tax news and commentary.

TaxHelp Online.com

www.taxhelponline.com

Get tax help online to address your individual concerns and situation. Find out what to do if you owe back taxes, or if you haven't filed in years, as well as how to handle just about any situation, including the infamous audit.

TurboTax

www.turbotax.com

This is the home of the most popular tax software in the United States. You can complete and submit your tax return right on the Web and use several of TurboTax's most popular calculators, including Tax Estimator. Site also provides access to IRS forms, a tax-prep checklist, tips and resources, information about tax law changes, and more.

United States Tax Code Online

www.fourmilab.ch/ustax/ustax.html

Provides interactive access to the complete text of the U.S. Internal Revenue Code.

Yahoo! Finance Tax Center

taxes.yahoo.com

Yahoo! Finance provides an online kiosk where you can get all the tax forms, information, and tools you need to calculate your tax liability and pay your fair share of the taxes. Includes tax calculators, federal and state forms, a beginner's guide, tax tips, and a whole lot more.

TEACHING

Activity Search

12345

www.eduplace.com/activity

A searchable database of 400 original K–8 classroom activities and lesson plans for teachers and parents.

American Federation of Teachers

12345

www.aft.org

Representing one million teachers and educational staff members, the AFT site (part of the AFL-CIO) provides teaching news, reports, and resources. This site also has many downloadable files concerning information that teachers will be interested in, plus information for parents.

ArtsEdge

12345

artsedge.kennedy-center.org/artsedge.html

ArtsEdge, sponsored by the Kennedy Center and maintained by MCI, is devoted to helping educators teach the arts more effectively. Teachers will find a pre-established curriculum, lesson plans, teaching materials, and activities available for download, as well as helpful web links, publications, and professional development information. The site also features a NewsBreak section, which provides up-to-date information on what's happening in the arts and education. Well presented and packed with useful tools.

Classroom CONNECT

12345

www.classroom.net

This business unit within Harcourt, Inc. is dedicated to helping schools incorporate the Internet into their curricula. Provides professional development and online curriculum resources that foster the use of computers and the Internet in core subjects, including math, language arts, science, and social studies.

DiscoverySchool.com

12345

school.discovery.com

DiscoverySchool.com is a place where teachers and parents can gather fresh ideas for presenting material to budding students. Site features special areas for teachers, including Lesson Plans and Teacher Tools. You can also check out educational programming on the Discovery Networks (Discovery Channel, TLC, Animal Planet, Travel Channel, and Discovery Health), shop at the Teacher's Store, check out the Curriculum Center, or select a homework helper. Site also features Brain Boosters, a clip art center, a puzzlemaker, a science fair center, and study starters.

Edheads

12345

www.edheads.org

Edheads partners up with various schools to provide interactive educational programming for students that is designed to help students achieve state standards. Several engaging online presentations are available here, including virtual knee surgery, weather, and simple machines. Teacher guides are available to help teachers incorporate the programming into their curriculum.

Education.com

12345

www.education.com

This site features a few news stories on topics in education along with a clickable list of the 10 most searched for topics on the site, but it's primarily a directory of links to other sites. Point to the

Directory link to display a menu of categories, including After School, Communities, Curriculum, Foreign Language, Pre-12 School Data, and Reference. Click the desired category to obtain a list of links to sites with related information and resources. Site also features some articles on parenting topics.

Education Index

12345

www.educationindex.com

Education Index is "an annotated guide to the best education-related sites on the Web." Links are grouped by subject and life stage, so you can find what you're looking for quickly and easily. Let Web Weasel be your guide. Click Coffee Shop to register and start chatting with other educators about topics of interest.

Education Place

www.eduplace.com

Focused on education for K–8 students, this site provides teachers with resources for professional development and offers some lively activities for the classroom. Special sections for students and parents, too.

Education Week on the Web

www.edweek.org

Education Week is a newspaper dedicated to America's education community. The paper covers "local, state, and national news and issues from preschool through the 12th grade." At this site, you can find many of the articles published in *Education Week* and *Teacher Magazine*, along with a Research Center and job listings for K–12 positions.

Education World

www.education-world.com

Education World is a powerful and free search engine focused on providing information to educators, students, and parents. Use the keyword search, browse by category, or join the Educators' Forum, a message board system to dialogue with educators around the globe. Reviews of 20 education sites are posted each month. Content is organized in the following categories: Lesson Planning, Administrator's Desk, School Issues, Professional Development, Technology Integration, and EdWorld at Home. Site also features classroom-to-home communication tools to help teachers keep in touch with parents.

Educational Resources

12345

www.edresources.com

Educational Resources provides teaching professionals with products and services needed to help students meet and exceed learning standards. You can search for products and services by keyword, department, publisher, grade, and platform or browse the collection by clicking one of the subject links in the navigation bar on the left.

Best Educator's Reference Desk

12345

eduref.org

This site is a goldmine for educators at all levels. Its resource collection contains links to more than 3,000 resources, including Internet sites, educational organizations, and electronic discussion groups. Its Lesson Plan collection features more than 2,000 lesson plans submitted by teachers from all across the United States. It's now the home of the ERIC Database, the world's largest source of educational information, including one million abstracts of documents and journal articles on education research and practice. Current information is provided in an easily accessible format at this Best of the Best site!

Federal Resources for Educational Excellence (FREE)

www.ed.gov/free

FREE makes hundreds of Internet-based education resources supported by agencies across the U.S. federal government easier to find. This is an excellent resource for teachers and students, as well as parents who choose to homeschool their children.

A B C D E F G H I J K L M N O P Q R S T U V W X Y Z

Global SchoolHouse

1 2 3 4 5

www.globalschoolnet.org/GSH

One-stop shopping for Internet-based projects of interest to K–12 educators and parents. Encourages and assists teachers in working collaboratively no matter where they're located geographically. Site features more than 2,000 collaborative projects.

goENC.com

1 2 3 4 5

www.goenc.com

Get K–12 math and science teaching support, including the newest ideas in approaches and material for teaching the subjects, and professional development support through publications and discussions. Paid subscribers have access to information about more than 27,000 print and multimedia curriculum resources and professional development materials.

Harcourt School Publishing

1 2 3 4 5

www.harcourtschool.com

A site that blends interactive learning for kids in grades pre-K–6 with resources for teachers and parents—all to complement Harcourt Brace school publications.

> When you reach the opening page, click The Learning Site link for online educational activities for students.

Intel Education Initiative

1 2 3 4 5

www97.intel.com/education

Intel provides curriculum in support of math and science education as well as information on competitions, scholarships, events, and more. Good information for teachers and students.

Kathy Schrock's Guide for Educators

1 2 3 4 5

school.discovery.com/schrockguide

Hosted by DiscoverySchool.com, Kathy Schrock's Guide for Educators is a directory of online resources for teachers. Dozens of links to teaching sites are grouped by category including Subject Access, Teacher Helpers, and Search Tools.

Lesson Plans Page

1 2 3 4 5

www.lessonplanspage.com

More than 2,500 lesson plans that are helpful for anyone in pre-K–12 education. Simply select your subject and your grade level to display a hefty list of links to lesson plans organized by category, such as math, science, English, music, computers and the Internet, social studies, art, physical education, and other subjects.

McGraw-Hill School Division

1 2 3 4 5

www.mmhschool.com

Web-based teaching resources for reading/language arts, mathematics, health, social studies, music, bilingual studies, and professional development. This site is the brainstorm of Macmillan/McGraw-Hill, the elementary school publishing unit of McGraw-Hill, and is one of the better-designed sites I've seen. McGraw-Hill is dedicated to educating children and to helping educational professionals by providing the highest quality services. The site is divided into sections called "islands," with one for parents, teachers, and students. Very well designed and worth the visit.

National Education Association

1 2 3 4 5

www.nea.org

The NEA site provides education statistics, reports, information on grants, events, legislative action, and much more information on the state of education. Site features special areas for Members & Educators, Parents & Community, Issues in Education, and a Legislative Action Center. The opening page also presents several feature articles, some of which are very inspirational.

New York Times Learning Network

1 2 3 4 5

www.nytimes.com/learning

Challenge your students to the daily news quiz or the word of the day. Science Q&A, Ask a Reporter, and a crossword puzzle are additional learning opportunities posted at this site. Teachers gain access to lesson plans and lesson plan archives. If you're looking to inspire your students to read more and participate in lively discussions of current events, this site is the ultimate tool to helping you do just that.

PBS Teacher's Source

1 2 3 4 5

www.pbs.org/teachersource

PBS offers a special area just for teachers on its site that contains featured lessons and activities, along with a directory of lessons and activities for specific subjects, including arts, literature, health and fitness, math, science, and social studies. Simply select a subject, select a grade level, and click Go. You can also register to have custom content delivered the next time you visit this site.

The Puffin House

1 2 3 4 5

www.puffin.co.uk

The Puffin House contains information about Penguin children's books. It includes activities for children, teachers' resources, and a searchable database of the full range of book titles. Don't miss the animated presentation "How a Book Is Made." This is an excellent primer for anyone who's thinking of writing a book.

Scholastic.com

1 2 3 4 5

teacher.scholastic.com/index.htm

Lots of great information to be incorporated into lesson plans as well as news regarding the latest teaching tools and methods, such as software and books. Great place to visit for students, teachers, and parents, but especially for teachers. You can simply click a grade level for access to teaching ideas for that grade or scroll down the page for a list of tools and other resources.

Teachers.net

1 2 3 4 5

www.teachers.net

Self-described as "The ultimate teacher's resource," this site encourages and supports teacher communication and collaboration. Features message boards, chat rooms, a schedule of online teacher meetings, libraries of teacher-submitted lesson plans and curricula, and more. To stay in touch with other teachers worldwide and work together to improve education, check out this site.

Technical Education Research Centers (TERC)

1 2 3 4 5

www.terc.edu

TERC is dedicated to building and fostering learning communities "in which learners from diverse communities engage in creative, rigorous, and reflective inquiry as an integral part of their lives," especially in terms of science an math. TERC is committed to achieving this vision by improving mathematics and science teaching and learning through collaboration, research, innovation, and implementation of programs designed to achieve its goals. At this site, you can learn more about the organization and its many areas of expertise and find out how it can collaborate with your school or other learning community to increase student performance in math and science.

U.S. Department of Education–Funding Opportunities

1 2 3 4 5

www.ed.gov/fund/landing.jhtml

Any teacher looking for funding will find it well worthwhile to visit this site for information about funding sources, tips on applying for an educational grant or financial aid, contract information, and upcoming opportunities.

A B C D E F G H I J K L M N O P Q R S T U V W X Y Z

USA Today Education

12345

www.usatoday.com/educate/home.htm

Join Experience Today to get your students involved in reading and understanding issues covered in the media. A four-page lesson plan accompanies a subscription to *USA Today* to assist teachers in making use of editorial content. Site also features link to the core subject areas.

Virtual Reference Desk

12345 Blog

www.webjunction.org/do/Navigation?category=11649

The primary purpose of this site is to provide librarians with the information, resources, and community support to build and maintain relevant, vibrant, and sustainable libraries in their communities. You can search the site for specific content or click one of the following tabs to browse through the offerings: Policies and Practices, Technology Resources, Buying and Funding, Services to Libraries, Learning Center, and Community Center.

TEENS

Bolt

www.bolt.com

Bolt is a popular blogging community for high school and college kids, where they can express their opinions freely on virtually any topic, post their photos and homespun videos, and share their favorite music and stories. Bolt bloggers can also network and meet new friends through forums, chat, or instant messaging. Almost all the content comes from members, not adults.

CyberTeens

www.cyberteens.com

Contests, interviews, art, and chat. Anyone can visit the message boards and browse messages posted by members, but if you want to participate, you must register and then sign in. Site also features links to other cool teen sites.

Favorite Teenage Angst Books

www.grouchy.com/angst

The teenage years are a tough transitional period in which painful self-discovery leads to tremendous anxiety. Here, you can browse the bookshelves to check out books that express and explore teenage angst. You also have the opportunity of meeting the authors and other creative folks.

Girls Life Magazine

www.girlslife.com

A magazine for girls and teens, featuring entertainment, news, advice, beauty tips, and more. Subscription information is available. The site contains a one-stop shopping mall just for girls.

GirlSite

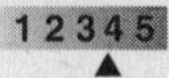

www.girlsite.org

GirlSite is a nonprofit organization dedicated to providing girls with the inspiration, resources, and support they need to discover and develop their own inner talents. This site features articles by various contributors who are meant to inspire, encourage, and inform young women.

Best IPL Teen Division

www.ipl.org/div/teen

A large collection of teen resources for doing homework, researching papers, career pathways, clubs, dating, health, and much more. If you are a teen, this site has information on all the things you would normally be interested in, such as arts and entertainment, college, high school, books, music, clubs, organizations, computers and the Internet, money matters, and homework. If you're looking for some easy answers—and who isn't—this is the place you can come to and ease your mind. The site also hosts a teen advisor who will help you with your problems and a Procrastinator area where you can find plenty to do to keep you from doing your homework on time. One of the more positive hangouts for teens on the Web.

Kiwibox

12345

www.kiwibox.com

Kiwibox is an online magazine specifically for teenagers. It features articles on the top teenage celebrities, information on concerts, articles on the latest fashions and trends, horoscopes, contests, online games, advice, and more.

A B C D E F G H I J K L M N O P Q R S T U V W X Y Z

LIQUIDGENERATION.com

www.liquidgeneration.com

Edgy and irreverent, this site pokes fun at the establishment with its singing celebrity karaoke machine, disgusting how-to videos, and *LiquidGeneration EXPOSED* tabloid.

Listen Up!

www.listenup.org

Listen Up! is a PBS program that "connects youth producers and their adult mentors from around the country to exchange work, share experiences and learn from one another." This site helps young filmmakers learn techniques from experienced mentors. You can find out more about Listen Up!, its national programs and distribution support, festival opportunities, and funding.

MyFuture

12345

www.myfuture.com

Resources to help high school students plan for their future. Includes information about saving money, choosing careers, creating resumes, investigating military opportunities, understanding alcoholism, buying cars, finding scholarships, and dating.

Next Step Magazine

www.nextstepmagazine.com

What's your next step after high school? Visit this site to explore your options, especially if you're planning to attend college. Here, you'll find some excellent articles to help ease the transition from high school to college and secure funding to pay for your college years. Content at this site is presented on several tabs, including College-Univ, Career Center, Students, Parents, and Counselors. Site also features a word of the week and an online poll.

SmartGirl

12345

www.smartgirl.org

SmartGirl, founded by Isabel Walcott, is now owned and maintained by the University of Michigan. Obviously focused on teenage girls, it features a newsletter, advice column, surveys, a place to submit original poetry or prose, and various product reviews.

TechnoTeen

technoteen.studentcenter.org

Super site for teens features a student center, relationship questionnaires, teen horoscopes and jokes, chat rooms and discussion forums, a date finder, and much more. Some stuff is not suitable for younger teens.

Teen Advice Online

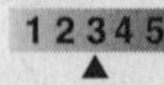

www.teenadviceonline.org

Counseling center where you can get help from a team of nonprofessional counselors age 13 years and older. Meet the volunteer counselors, read articles on various teenage-related issues, or post your question to get some free advice.

Teen Ink

www.teenink.com

Teen Ink is a monthly magazine and website written by teenagers for teenagers. Site features opinions, interviews, fiction, nonfiction, poetry, an art gallery, college reviews, movie reviews, and much more. This site also provides links to several writing contests for poetry, prose, and interviews.

Teenager Driving Contract

www.legalnews.net/drivingK.htm

Is your child enrolled in a driver's education course? Then before he or she receives a license, visit this site to obtain a legal agreement that spells out the rules of the road in detail. This agreement has plenty of built-in humor, too.

Teenager E-Books

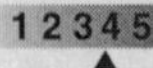

www.hopcottebooks.com/ebooks/teenager.html

Electronic books written for the teenage audience. Includes a photo of each book's cover plus a brief description of the plot.

Teenagers Today

teenagerstoday.com

Information for parents about raising their teenage children. Site also features an Expert Q&A, instructions on how to become and remain Web Savvy, and Online Diaries.

TeenLink

teenlink.nypl.org

The New York Public Library created and maintains this excellent site specifically for teenage readers. Site features access to the library's online search tools, a list of new books along with reviews, announcements of special library events, homework help, sample tests, library lingo, transcripts of live interviews with authors, a special area that deals with teen life issues, and much more.

Teenmag.com

www.teenmag.com

This e-zine for teenagers features news about teen celebrities and musical groups, an advice column, style and beauty tips, online questionnaires and polls, a prom primer, and much more. Primarily suited for teenage girls.

TeenPeople.com

www.teenpeople.com/teenpeople

People magazine for teenagers is online with this sleek site that features news about celebrities most teens care about. Celebrity news, hot styles, online games, and chat rooms make this a great teen hangout.

TeenReading

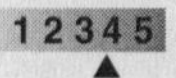

www.ala.org/ala/yalsa/teenreading/teenreading.htm

This American Library Association website is devoted to encouraging teenagers to read. Includes a recommended reading list, a top 10 list, and tips on how to encourage teens to read.

WireTap

www.alternet.org/wiretap

WireTap is an online news magazine created by socially conscious youth for socially conscious youth. It features "investigative news articles, personal essays and opinions, artwork and activism resources that challenge stereotypes, inspire creativity, foster dialogue and give young people a voice in the media." Here, visitors can read articles about environmental and political issues; learn about events sponsored by WireTap; check the classifieds for job opportunities; get involved in WireTap campaigns; read reviews of books, films, and albums; read poems and short stories; and peruse the gallery of photos, graffiti, and drawings.

Xenith.net

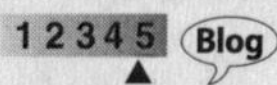

www.xenith.net

Xenith.net is a virtual hangout for teenagers who want to express themselves through their poetry, prose, or graffiti, or want to see what others their age have to say. Very active message boards, where you can get peer feedback on your writing, and a media store that features brief book reviews. When we visited this site, it was under construction with a posted promise that the site would soon be back...all purty and stuff.

Youth Outlook

www.youthoutlook.org

Youth Outlook is an online magazine/blog that features interesting and often humorous articles written by teenagers on various topics. The opening page is well designed; but when you get past that, the pages are kind of drab, supposedly to help them load faster. If you stick with it, though, you'll find plenty to keep you engaged, informed, and entertained.

A B C D E F G H I J K L M N O P Q R S T U V W X Y Z

TELEVISION

BBCi

www.bbc.co.uk

Home of British Broadcasting Corporation's interactive website, BBCi provides the latest headline news and sports; TV and radio programming information; and information on concerts, nightclubs, and other entertainment offerings.

E! Online

www.eonline.com

TV fans will want to bookmark this site, home of E!, the source for the latest news about everything in the entertainment industry. Here, you can find the latest news and gossip about your favorite celebrities and the hottest TV shows, movies, and recording artists. Read TV, movie, and CD reviews; take online quizzes and compete in trivia contests; check out the latest movie trailers and music clips; and find recent interviews with the top stars.

HBO: Home Box Office

www.hbo.com

Home of the *Sopranos, Sex and the City, Six Feet Under, Entourage,* and other award-winning shows, this site provides information about the various HBO original series, premier movies, sports specials, HBO documentaries and films, and much more. Here, you can get a sneak preview of your favorite shows and movies and go behind the scenes with your favorite HBO celebrities.

Networks

ABC	abc.com
ABC Family	abcfamily.go.com
A&E	www.aetv.com
AMC	www.amctv.com
Animal Planet	animal.discovery.com
BET	www.bet.com/bethome
Biography	www.biography.com
BRAVO	www.bravotv.com
Cartoon Network	www.cartoonnetwork.com
CBS	www.cbs.com
Cinemax	www.cinemax.com
CMT	www.cmt.com
CNBC	moneycentral.msn.com/investor/home.asp
CNN	www.cnn.com
Comedy Central	www.comedycentral.com
Court TV	www.courttv.com
C-SPAN	www.c-span.org
Discovery Channel	www.discovery.com
Disney Channel	www.disney.go.com/disneychannel
DIY Network	www.diynetwork.com
Encore	www.encoretv.com
E!	www.eonline.com
ESPN	espn.go.com
ESPN Classic	sports.espn.go.com/espn/classic/index
ESPN2	sports.espn.go.com/espntv/espnNetwork?networkID=2
Fit TV	fittv.discovery.com
Food Network	www.foodtv.com
FOX	www.fox.com
FOX Movie Channel	www.thefoxmoviechannel.com
FoxNews	www.foxnews.com
FX	www.fxnetwork.com
Gameshow Network	www.gsn.com
Golf Channel	www.thegolfchannel.com
Hallmark Channel	www.hallmarkchannel.com
HBO	www.hbo.com

HGTV	www.hgtv.com
History Channel	www.historychannel.com
i (independent TV)	www.ionline.tv
Indie Film Channel	www.ifctv.com
Lifetime	www.lifetimetv.com
MSNBC	www.msnbc.msn.com
MTV	www.mtv.com
NBC	www.nbc.com
Nickelodeon	www.nick.com
Outdoor Life	www.olntv.com
Oxygen	www.oxygen.com
PBS	www.pbs.org
Sci-Fi	www.scifi.com
Showtime	sho.com
SpeedTV	www.speedtv.com
STARZ!	www.starz.com
TBS Superstation	www.tbs.com
TCM	turnerclassicmovies.com
TLC	tlc.discovery.com
TNT	www.tnt.tv
Travel	travel.discovery.com
TV Land	www.tvland.com
UPN	www.upn.com
USA	www.usanetwork.com
VH1	www.vh1.com
WB	www.warnerbros.com
WE!	www.we.tv
Weather	www.weather.com
WGN	wgntv.trb.com

New York Times: Television

www.nytimes.com/pages/arts/television/index.html

From the *New York Times* Arts section comes this excellent collection of news, reviews, and interviews related to television shows and their stars.

Pentagon Channel

www.pentagonchannel.mil

The Pentagon Channel broadcasts military news and information for the 2.6 million members of the U.S. armed forces through programming, including Department of Defense news briefings, military news, interviews with top defense officials, and short stories about the work of our military. Here, you can tune in to the Pentagon Channel, download free podcasts, read program summaries, and check the program schedule.

Television Without Pity

www.televisionwithoutpity.com

Satirical recaps of television shows for the pure pleasure of lambasting the worst that TV has to offer.

Titan TV

www.titantv.com

Titan TV is a television programming guide with muscle. Here, you can search up to two weeks of program listings, complete with program descriptions, view the listing by category (news, sports, comedy, and so on), sign up for reminders, learn about new stations that might be available in your area, and much more.

TiVo

1 2 3 4 5

www.tivo.com

Are you busy whenever your favorite shows are on? Are you tired of programming your VCR to record them just so you can search your tapes later to find out what you recorded? Then consider TiVo, a system that lets you record up to 140 hours of TV shows to watch at your convenience and replay whenever you like. This site tells you what TiVo is all about, lets you order it online, and shows you how to set up the system.

Best TV Guide Online

www.tvguide.com

Can't find your television guide? Then tune in to the home page of one of the most popular magazines in the country, *TV Guide*. Click the TV Listings link, enter your ZIP code, make a few other selections, and you get an onscreen listing of all the TV shows of the day. This site also features news about your favorite shows, gossip about your favorite stars, a movie guide, a guide to the soaps, and much more. Shop the online store for collectors' items, special CDs and DVDs, and other items. If you spend more than an hour a day in front of the tube, you'll want to bookmark this Best of the Best site for your future reference.

TV History: The First 75 Years

www.tvhistory.tv

This site chronicles the first 50 years of TV history, starting with the "Mechanical Age" just prior to 1935, when inventors developed the first working models and going up to the year 2000. Content focuses primarily on the development of TV sets. Some good photos.

TV Land

www.tvland.com

Do you miss those TV shows from yesteryear? Can't live without *The Dick Van Dyke Show*, *Leave It to Beaver*, and *Get Smart*? Then check out TV Land's home on the Web, where you can learn more about these shows, download complete TV listings, and even shop online for TV Land apparel and paraphernalia.

TV Party

www.tvparty.com

Online museum of the best (and worst) in TV over the past 40 years. If you become nostalgic over the old TV shows, this is the site for you. Go behind the scenes with the site's creator and host, Billy Ingram, to listen to the gossip; explore the scandals; and view some of the best dancing, drama, comedy, and action clips from the shows that made TV what it is today. This site has some annoying pop-up ads, but we're guessing that's the price for free admission.

Ultimate TV

www.ultimatetv.com

Ultimate TV provides television shows on demand by recording your favorite shows to disk. You simply set up a schedule of what you want to record and then play back the show when *you're* ready to view it. Visit this site to learn more about this revolution in TV viewing.

Variety.com

www.variety.com

Variety.com is the online version of *Variety*, a magazine that features news and information about the entertainment industry, including television and movies. Here, you can find the latest news, special reports, links to blogs, articles about your favorite celebrities, and much more. If you're in the industry, you can take advantage of several tools, including Variety careers, the Showbiz Calendar, and the Slanguage glossary of insider terms.

Yahoo! TV

tv.yahoo.com

Yahoo! TV features daily TV listings along with daily picks, news and gossip, ratings, a TV database, and a special area just for soap opera fans.

Zap2it

www.zap2it.com

Zap2it is based on the premise that there are more and more TV shows and movies to watch and less and less time to find quality material. This site features TV listings plus information and reviews of shows and movies. Content is organized into several areas, including TV, movies, news, DVD, video, games, community, and photos. Enter your ZIP code to obtain local information.

TENNIS

American Tennis Professionals

www.atptennis.com/en

If you're a fan of men's tennis, American Tennis Professionals is the place to be when you're not watching the action. This site features tour news, events information, player profiles, rankings, statistics, a multimedia area, and pro shop. Content is offered in both English and Spanish.

CBS SportsLine: Tennis

www.sportsline.com/tennis

Daily news and tournament results, plus special features and columns relating to the game of tennis. Some areas require membership. The site has a shopping area where you can purchase tennis rackets and other tennis-related products.

Davis Cup

12345

www.daviscup.com

The Davis Cup pits country against country in a tennis shootout to determine the best tennis team in the world, and here you can learn more about the current Davis Cup competition and its illustrious history. Site features easy navigation via drop-down menus for draws and results, teams, ranking, and information about the Davis Cup, among other options. Also features a photo gallery.

GoTennis

www.gotennis.com

TennisFinder.com is "the world's most powerful and easy to use Tennis Partnering solution available online." If you love tennis, but you're having trouble hooking up with partners with similar skill levels, join the TennisFinder.com community. Site also features news, photos, tournament information and tickets, a message board, and a tennis mall.

International Tennis Federation Online

www.itftennis.com

Official site of the world governing body for tennis. Includes results and rankings. Want the latest news about tennis-related events? This site has much to offer in the way of the latest news, rules and regulations, and even the latest facts and figures.

Tennis Canada

www.tenniscanada.com

Canadian tennis rankings plus player information and tournament news. Site content is presented in both French and English.

TennisOne

www.tennisone.com

TennisOne is an online magazine primarily for tennis players and coaches. Articles focus on techniques, conditioning, tips, insights into the game, and advice on how to get more out of the game and improve your chances of winning. Some excellent videos demonstrate techniques. Site also features product reviews from the pros.

Tennis Online

www.tennisonline.com

Tennis Online keeps its eye out for the top tennis sites on the Web and gathers them in this directory. You can search for specific content by keyword or browse the sites by category, including Camps,

A B C D E F G H I J K L M N O P Q R S T U V W X Y Z

Clubs & Resorts, Equipment, Players, and Tournaments.

Tennis: A Research Guide

www.nypl.org/research/chss/grd/resguides/tennis

Bibliography on general tennis works from the New York Public Library, with links to more specific bibliographies. References to biographies, histories of the game, tennis instruction and literature, and periodicals.

Tennis Server

tennisserver.com

Features, equipment tips, and links to other tennis sites.

Tennis Warehouse

1 2 3 4 5

www.tennis-warehouse.com

This online tennis store carries a wide selection of everything you need to play tennis and look the part: racquets, apparel, shoes, bags, strings, grips, balls, books, videos, and more.

Tennis Welcome Center

www.tenniswelcomecenter.com

The Tennis Welcome Center is dedicated to promoting tennis and encouraging visitors to pick up a racket and start playing. Here, you'll find the benefits of tennis, an excellent FAQ on how to get started, and a search tool that can help you track down a Tennis Welcome Center near you.

United States Professional Tennis Association (USPTA)

www.uspta.org

Find a pro in your area for instruction, find out when this year's conferences and conventions are being held, and learn all about being a USPTA member here.

Tip: Some of the best content on this site is buried. Click Tennis A–Z, and then click Lessons Online and click Video.

United States Tennis Association

1 2 3 4 5

www.usta.com

Web home of the USTA, this site is dedicated to promoting and developing tennis. The USTA is the first governing body for tennis. At this site, you'll find news about the latest tournaments, information about various tennis leagues, tennis rules and regulations, and even some online games.

USA Today: Tennis

www.usatoday.com/sports/tennis/tennis.htm

Includes ATP and WTA results, rankings, money leaders, archived stories, and the latest news.

U.S. Open

www.usopen.org

Home of the major tennis event in the United States, this site features a history of the event, statistics and records, information on past champions, and much more for tennis players and fans alike. You can also shop online for U.S. Open apparel and accessories.

Best Wimbledon

www.wimbledon.org

This is the official site of the All England Lawn Tennis and Croquet Club and the Wimbledon Championships. This site offers news and feature stories, a visitor's guide, ticket information, history, statistics, standings, results, and information about the museum. You can shop online for hats, shirts, and other apparel and accessories. Add all that to a great-looking site, and you have the winner of our Best of the Best award for Tennis sites.

WTA Tour

www.wtatour.com

The WTA Tour is "the world's premier professional sport for women." In a typical year, more than 1,400 players representing 75 nations compete for more than $60 million in prize money at 63 events in 35 countries. This site offers a schedule, rankings, news, profiles, pro shop, and multimedia clips.

Yahoo! Tennis News

sports.yahoo.com/ten

The Yahoo! Tennis News page features headline news, opinions, rankings, schedules, scores, results, photos, and much more. Covers both men's and women's tennis.

THEATER & MUSICAL

Albany, New York Theatre and the Arts

12345

metro-links.com/AlbanyNewYork/EntertainmentTheTheaterTheArts.htm

This site provides a directory of arts and theater offerings in Albany, New York.

American Conservatory Theater

12345

www.act-sfbay.org

This acclaimed training institution and regional theater offers information on its upcoming schedule, performers, past productions, and mission here. You can purchase single tickets online to some productions.

American Repertory Theatre

12345

www.amrep.org

Interviews with casts and playwrights, previews of upcoming shows, and synopses and reviews of past productions.

American Theater Web

12345

americantheaterweb.com

American Theater Web presents news, reviews, and feature stories related to theaters and productions in the United States. From the opening page, you can search for a specific theater or show or find out what's happening by region, check out the headline stories, read theater news clippings that are updated daily, and customize the site to deliver information that's representative of your region.

American Variety Stage

12345

lcweb2.loc.gov/ammem/vshtml/vshome.html

Vaudeville and Popular Entertainment, 1870–1920. Online exhibition from the Library of Congress.

Backstage

12345 Blog

www.backstage.com

Backstage is a resource for actors. Here, you can find news stories and feature articles about the craft, learn how to obtain the training you need, find out about casting calls, chat with fellow actors, and more.

Broadway.com

12345

www.broadway.com

What's playing on Broadway? What's playing Off Broadway? Visit this site to find out. This site features headline news, columns, features and reviews, photos, recommended shows, hotel packages, dinner packages, programs, and more. Great place to go if you're planning a trip to New York and would like to take in a show. Special area is also available for teachers.

Broadway Online

12345

www.broadwayonline.com

This site, created by Broadway Worldwide, a company that produces high-quality recordings of live Broadway shows, presents this hi-tech, multimedia site to introduce visitors to its collection of DVD recordings. When you click the link for a show, a window appears that enables you to check out the cast and scenes and preview the video.

Broadway Play Publishing, Inc.

12345

www.BroadwayPlayPubl.com

This company, which adapts American plays, has a search engine and several related links. You can order books, plays, musicals, one-act collections, and play anthologies. See the adaptations of American classics and check out the photo gallery.

The Children's Theatre

12345

www.thechildrenstheatre.com

The Children's Theatre in Cincinnati runs plays in a real theater space that are geared specifically for children. Here, you can learn more about this theater and what it has to offer. Links to Ticketmaster to purchase tickets.

ChildrensTheatrePlays

12345

www.childrenstheatreplays.com

This site features stage plays for children, young audiences, and families, including *Snow White*, *Cinderella*, and *The Wizard of Oz*. This site is a great place for theater producers, directors, drama coaches, and teachers to find scripts for their productions.

Current Theatre

12345

theater.nytimes.com/pages/theater/index.html

Theater reviews from the *New York Times*.

Educational Theatre Association

12345

www.edta.org

The Educational Theatre Association sponsors theatre festivals for students and professional development programs for theatre teachers, produces a magazine and a quarterly journal, and performs several other varied tasks to support the theatre community—especially teachers and students. Content at this site is presented in several areas, including Visitor, Thespian Troupe Sponsor, Thespian, and Individual Adult Member.

English Actors at the Turn of the Century

12345

www.siue.edu/COSTUMES/actors/pics.html

This straightforward, interesting site provides colorful, full photographs of twentieth-century actors in their roles. Just click an actor or movie, and you're there. See many old actors including Maud Jeffries in *Herod*, Sir Henry Irving in *As You Like It*, and George Alexander in *If I Were King*.

Grand Theatre

12345

www.grandtheatre.com

Check out this London, Ontario, Canada's theater website to learn more about the renovated theater and upcoming performances, and to catch a glimpse of the ghost of the theater's founder, Ambrose Small, who haunts the theater and the site, it seems. You can get ticket purchase information here and do a little shopping online.

League of American Theatres and Producers

12345

www.livebroadway.com

On behalf of its members, the League of American Theatres and Producers "negotiates collective bargaining agreements with all theatrical unions and guilds; coordinates industry-wide marketing initiatives and corporate sponsorships; oversees government relations for the Broadway industry; maintains relevant research archives and databases; and supports charitable efforts for the benefit of the entire theatrical community." At this site, you can find out what's currently playing on Broadway; learn about events, programs, and services; access a professional development area; and much more.

Live Design

12345

livedesignonline.com

Selected articles from the print version of the highly respected magazine for behind-the-scenes theater professionals, including lighting, sound, and production designers, and costume and makeup professionals.

London Theatre Guide Online

12345

www.londontheatre.co.uk

Use this handy page to find information on West End shows, the Royal National Theatre, and other London theaters. Includes addresses, seating arrangements, reviews of current shows, ballet and opera listings, and a monthly email update service. You can find out the current costs of tickets and where to purchase them, as well as do some shopping by linking to other sites such as Amazon.com.

Related Site

www.officiallondontheatre.co.uk

Musicals.net

1 2 3 4 5

musicals.net

This site lists about 80 popular musicals and plenty of new ones coming up. Click a musical's name to list links, lyrics, media clips, notes, synopses, and tons of other information.

Now Casting

1 2 3 4 5

www.nowcasting.com

Searchable database brings together actors, casting directors, managers, and agents to help filmmakers create films and to find appropriate jobs for actors.

Best Playbill Online

1 2 3 4 5

www.playbill.com

The electronic version of the famous print publication that focuses on Broadway and Off-Broadway theaters. You can purchase tickets online, read reviews, and learn about the stars behind the top productions. Site also features interactive polls and quizzes, an awards database, seating charts, restaurant and hotel guides, and a well-stocked directory of links to other useful theater sites. Excellent site with a strong content offering. Join the Playbill Club to become eligible for significant discounts on tickets.

The Public Theater

1 2 3 4 5

www.publictheater.org

The Public Theater presents full seasons of new plays and musicals as well as Shakespeare and other classics at its Manhattan location. Find out how to get there, what shows the troupe will be performing, who's in the cast, and how you can support this group.

Put on a Play

1 2 3 4 5

www.writewords.org.uk/articles/theatre1.asp

Excellent overview of the step-by-step process you need to follow to produce your own play.

Roundabout Theatre Company

1 2 3 4 5

www.roundabouttheatre.org

Find out more about this classic theater group, upcoming shows, subscriptions that give members access to additional private performances (Theatre-Plus), its history, and ways you can subscribe. Links to other sites to purchase tickets.

Screen Actor's Guild

1 2 3 4 5

www.sag.com

Online site of the Screen Actor's Guild, the largest professional actors' advocacy group. Read news about SAG and its events, view a calendar of upcoming events, and get leads on talent agents. Professional actors and casting agents should bookmark this site.

Shakespeare: Subject to Change

1 2 3 4 5

www.ciconline.org/bdp1

This intriguing site, hosted by Cable in the Classroom, explores the various ways that Shakespeare's original texts might have been changed by typesetters, editors, directors, and others to provide us with the texts that many assume to be Shakespeare's original writings. Along the way, the site explores Shakespeare's language and points out some interesting facts about how well versed this playwright really was. This site is well designed and features engaging Flash presentations.

Shakespeare Theatre

shakespearedc.org

Information about the Washington, D.C.–based Shakespeare Theatre, including upcoming performances, cast bios, job listings and internships, and acting classes. Links to Tickets.com for purchasing tickets.

SITCOM

www.dangoldstein.com/sitcom.html

Information on the SITCOM program of improvised half-hour shows that mimic rehearsed and planned TV comedy. Provides a blend of structuralist literary criticism and artificial intelligence, a live show that converts audience suggestions into full-length, improvised TV sitcoms that unfold live on stage.

TheaterMania.com

RSS

www.theatermania.com

If you live in or near a major city, including New York, Chicago, or San Francisco, TheaterMania.com can help you find ticket information for plays and other theater performances. Site also features articles and reviews, ticket discounts, and a special area for kids' shows. Very classy site with excellent information.

Tony Awards Online

www.tonys.org

The Tony Awards program isn't strictly about musicals, of course—plenty of wonderful dramas and comedies take awards in their own categories—but the Tonys are always a guide to what's good in musicals on stage. Go to this site for a variety of entertainment: contests, games, a chat page, lists of award winners (and nominees, depending on the season), theater news, and other interesting sections. The site is very well designed and has a variety of information about the Tonys.

WWW Virtual Library Theatre and Drama

vl-theatre.com

This site features a comprehensive directory of theater-related resources on the Web, including plays, monologues, conferences, journals, mailing lists, and message boards.

TOYS

Archie McPhee

12345

www.mcphee.com

Home of the Lunch Lady action figure, avenging unicorn playset, and gummy bacon, this novelty store carries a good collection of fun stuff that's a little on the wild side.

AreYouGame.com

12345

www.areyougame.com/interact/default.asp

Choose an age group; favorite type of activity, such as brainteasers; or game, such as Monopoly, and AreYouGame will recommend specific games and puzzles for your child, or child at heart. Learn about new games or order well-known favorites at this site, which has an extensive collection of games for almost any age group.

Boardgames.com

12345

www.boardgames.com

A huge selection of board games is available here, from children's games to adult, strategy, or electronic handheld. You'll find current popular games such as Millionaire and Scrabble, but there are many, many others to buy or give as gifts. This site is well designed and easy to navigate. Better and easier than shopping at the mall. If you are into games of all kinds and would rather spend your time playing them than shopping in faraway crowded malls, this site is the place to get them. You can shop from the convenience of your own home, look at the games online, and read the descriptions at your leisure. You'll also find a lot of useful information about all the games here.

BRIO

12345

www.brioplay.com

Learn all about how BRIO wooden toys are constructed, about the many types, and the awards the toys have won. You can request a catalog be mailed to you or conduct an online toy search here to find what you're looking for. The site contains a feature that enables you to find out where to buy BRIO toys near you.

The Copernicus

12345

www.copernicustoys.com

A store specializing in toys for adult imagination and education for all levels: optical illusions, craft kits, puzzles, and the like. You can email for a complete catalog. The Copernicus sells toys both retail and wholesale.

Creativity for Kids

12345

www.creativityforkids.com

A wonderful craft activities supplier. Choose craft projects by age or type—such as glass beads, ceramics, or stitchery—to find a long list of products that match the criteria. Although you can't buy the products at this site, if you enter your ZIP code, the site will create a list of local stores that carry what you're looking for, as well as online merchants.

Discovery Toys

12345

www.discoverytoysinc.com

Check out the latest toys from this company, which creates toys appropriate for a child's age and developmental state. Learn more about which toys are appropriate and find a local educational consultant you can buy from.

Disney Online Store

12345

disneyshopping.go.com

Offers a full online catalog of Disney merchandise with secure online purchasing. Here, you'll find Disney toys, swimwear and other apparel, bedding, movies and CDs, and more. You also can access the Disney Store "gift finder" service and a listing of Disney Store locations worldwide.

Engadget

www.engadget.com

This blog specializes in high-tech toys and other pricey gadgets. You can read through the articles in the main column on the left or go to a specific section by clicking its link. Sections focus on dozens of gadget categories, including cellphones, HDTV, GPS, peripherals, robots, wearables, and wireless.

Etch-a-Sketch

www.etch-a-sketch.com

Etch-a-Sketch is a classic toy that enables anyone who has decent artistic skills and excellent hand-eye coordination to doodle a sketch by turning only two knobs on the screen. Here, you can check out the entire Etch-a-Sketch family of products, pick up a few savvy tips, check out the Etch-a-Sketch art gallery (very impressive), play some cool online games, and become an official member of the Etch-a-Sketch Club.

Best eToys

www.etoys.com

Huge online toy warehouse featuring just about every toy imaginable. Shop for specific toys by keyword or phrase, or browse for toys by age, category, or brand name. eToys can even help you shop by providing a list of bestselling toys, video game reviews, and special offers. Here, you'll find toys and games, educational toys, books, videos, room décor for kids' rooms, a gift finder, party supplies, electronic games, movies and videos, PC games, and a clearance rack. Order toys online and have your order shipped right to your door.

EXTEX Toys

12345

www.extextoys.com

EXTEX Toys carries a wide selection of toys, especially for active kids. Here, you'll find trampolines, pogo sticks, stilts, scooters, skateboards, zip lines, moonshoes, and other items that your local toy store may not carry.

FAO SCHWARZ

www.faoschwarz.com

FAO SCHWARZ is an upscale toystore that carries a wide selection of toys from collectible action figures and dolls to toy trains and RC vehicles. You can browse the store by category or brand name, use the gift finder to track down the perfect gift, view the online catalogue, or order a printed catalogue.

Firebox.com

www.firebox.com

Toys for boys (older boys and men, that is). Firebox.com is a U.K. company that offers an excellent collection of toys for the gadget lover, including unique digital cameras, portable MP3 players, game pads, remote control vehicles, mini speakers, projection clocks, and all sorts of other gizmos. Shopping for the man who has everything? Then shop here.

Fisher-Price

www.fisher-price.com

Select the perfect product from the personal shopper, create your own online baby and gift registry, view more than 300 products in the Fisher-Price showroom, and more.

The Gallery of Monster Toys

members.aol.com/raycastile/page1.htm

The creator of this site says it best: "Vintage monster toys are typically overlooked by collectors, largely because they seem obsolete in today's world. The toys in this gallery are not, for the most part, 'slick' or 'hyper-detailed.' They are humble and imperfect. They depict flawed, tortured creatures. These toys capture a time when horror was fun." After searching through all the "monsters" of past, present, and maybe the future, you may want one of these cuddly creatures for your very own. You'll find some information and links where you can purchase these prize creatures. This site is nice to visit if for no other reason than it shows some great "monsters" that you might want to own.

Genius Babies.com

12345

www.geniusbabies.com

Whether you're looking for an activity for your toddler or a baby shower gift, you're likely to find one in your price range here. Choose by age or type of toy, such as play mats or puzzles. You might want to find out about the top sellers, which are listed at the site, too.

Gizmodo

12345 Blog

www.gizmodo.com

Gizmodo is a blog for tech-hungry gadget hounds. Site features short news stories about the latest gadgets and technology to hit the market or it least make it to the planning stage.

Hasbro World

12345

www.hasbro.com

Home to the makers of Action Man, Battleship, Collector's Corner, Monopoly, Risk, Scrabble, Trivial Pursuit, Yahtzee, and many more favorites. You'll find a nice selection of Hasbro toys here, such as G.I. Joe and all his accessories and equipment. The site includes a search feature to help you locate places where you can buy the toys.

Into the Wind

12345

www.intothewind.com

Claiming to be the world's largest kite seller, this site will teach you about flying a kite and give you lots of types to choose from for purchase. From flags and banners to wind socks to traditional or stunt kites, this site has them all. You can also join a discussion forum to chat with fellow kiters.

KB Toys

12345

www.kbtoys.com

Shop by age, price, or brand for the toy you want, or find out about this week's sales before you decide. This online KB Toys site has a wide selection of toys for all ages.

Latoys.com

12345

www.latoys.com

A wide selection of toys and brands is available here with plenty of pictures to guide you. Tabbed navigation gives you quick access to toys from specific manufacturers.

Learning Curve International

12345

www.learningcurve.com

Learn about the toy product lines that build on your child's expanding mobility and development. Starting with soft Lamaze toys for infants, you can move to more solid Ambi toys and into several other toy lines as your child ages. Select the product line you're interested in and then view all the available toys. The site has a feature to help you find out where to purchase these toys.

LEGO World

12345

www.lego.com

Aimed primarily at kids, this site lists the LEGO toy groups (LEGO, Duplo, and so on) and provides a parent guide, a web surfer's club (so kids can list or make their own LEGO sites), and games to play on the Internet. Also has listings of whom to contact to get the various toys in every country. You can also shop online if you prefer. One of the better sites on the Internet with great graphics and easy-to-navigate menus.

Little Tikes

12345

www.littletikes.com

View and listen to Little Tikes toys being used at this site, which shows you the complete 200+ toy line. Then you can shop at the nearest local store that carries what you need. You'll also find a list of hot toys and those on sale

Mastermind Educational Toys

12345

www.mastermindtoys.com

Mastermind specializes in educational toys for kids (ages 0 to 11+), although you'll find plenty of parents playing with this stuff. Site features three ways to shop—by age, toy category, or brand. Mastermind also offers gift wrapping, free eUpdates, reasonable shipping fees, and a store locator.

Mattel

12345

www.mattel.com

The official site of one of the worldwide leaders in the design, manufacture, and marketing of children's products, including such brand names as Barbie, American Girl, Hot Wheels, Fisher Price, and more. Most of the links at this site carry you to a site that focuses on the selected product line.

Nintendo

12345 RSS

www.nintendo.com

Home of the king of video games, this site is packed with information about the company and its products. Here, you can learn about the latest Nintendo game systems, explore the wide selection of available games, get technical support and customer service, and share your enthusiasm for Nintendo video games with other enthusiastic players. You can even play free online games, download free software, subscribe to the Nintendo newsletter, check out featured Nintendo sites, and get more information about Nintendo and its products than you could ever imagine. Very easy to navigate and packed with valuable resources for Nintendo fans.

Rokenbok

12345

www.rokenbok.com

Rokenbok Toys are for kids aged 5 and up and are designed to be expanded. You can build with them, add cars and trucks, as well as add radio-controlled pieces. Learn about the components and skills your child builds with each addition. A convenient deal locator will help you find your local source of toys and items for you to purchase.

Schylling

12345

www.schylling.com

If you're looking for classic toys like tea sets or Curious George playthings, you'll want to scan this online store first.

Sega

12345

www.sega.com

One of the top developers of digital games and gaming systems, Sega offers this site to keep its customers informed of the latest products and provide support. Here, you can search for games by title, platform, or recommended age; go directly to a game's page for hints and tips; search for support; or check out the message boards. As you would likely expect, this site is well designed and easy to navigate.

Toys for Tots

12345

www.toysfortots.org

The U.S. Marine Reserve program Toys for Tots is described in complete detail at this site. It goes into the history, the foundation that helps to support the program, its corporate sponsors, and most important, how you can help. Site also offers some toy safety tips for parents.

Toys R Us

12345

www.toysrus.com

Toys R Us, one of the most popular brick-and-mortar toy stores, also offers its products online at this site. Here, you can shop for toys by age, category, or brand name; check for clearance items; go directly to specialty stores, including Toys R Us exclusives; peruse the top sellers; use the gift guide to find the perfect gift; or search for a Toys R Us store near you.

Related Site

www.babiesrus.com

A B C D E F G H I J K L M N O P Q R S T U V W X Y Z

TRACK & FIELD

Armory Track & Field Center

1 2 3 4 5

www.armorytrack.com

The Armory in northern Manhattan is one of the fastest indoor tracks in the world. It is also the future home of the National Track & Field Hall of Fame. At this site, you can tour this old facility, research its history, and learn more about its programs.

Athletics Canada

1 2 3 4 5

www.athleticscanada.com

As the governing body for Canadian track and field, Athletics Canada's page focuses on Canadian athletes, records, rankings, events, coaching, and news. Bilingual—English and French.

Cool Running

1 2 3 4 5

www.coolrunning.com

Cool Running is an online resource for the running community, offering articles and advice on training, nutrition, and running gear, along with information and results of races in the New England area. You can shop online for Cool Running gear.

Everything Track and Field

1 2 3 4 5

www.everythingtrackandfield.com

Everything Track and Field is an online store where you can purchase equipment and supplies at reasonable prices. Site also features training zones for all track and field events, including pole vault, high jump, shot put, discus, sprints, middle distance, javelin, and hurdles.

High Jump

1 2 3 4 5

www.brianmac.demon.co.uk/highjump

This page presents an excellent primer on the high jump event, explaining the approach, takeoff, and flight; suggesting drills and evaluation tests; and providing links to several other high-jump-related pages and sites.

Related Sites

www.todd.acheson.com

www.dwightstones.com

International Association of Athletics Federations

1 2 3 4 5 RSS

www.iaaf.org

This home of the International Association of Athletics Federations provides news, results, athletic journals, calendars, world rankings, and much more. This is a great site to visit to check out official world records for various track events.

Kelly's Running Warehouse

1 2 3 4 5

www.kellysrunningwarehouse.com

At this site with more than 75,000 running shoes in stock at prices up to $50 off, runners will want to at least check the inventory here before their next purchase. You can shop online using 100 percent secure shopping and check out the top 10 bestselling shoes.

Road Runner Sports Shoe Store

12345

www.roadrunnersports.com

Research and buy sports shoes, including name brands such as Nike, Reebok, Adidas, and Puma. If you like to shop online, this site has a nice, well-organized, and easy-to-navigate online store.

Runner's Web

www.runnersweb.com/running.html

The Runner's Web "aims to provide a portal into the world of running—including athletics (track and field) and road running, triathlon, and adventure racing." Here, you'll find news, information on running competitions, and training advice and techniques. Site also features links to books, tapes, and other products.

Runner's World Online

12345

www.runnersworld.com

Home of the popular *Runner's World* magazine, this site features some of the best articles about track and field events, cross-country, and marathons. Free training log and workout regimens, training plans, and calculators. Shoe and treadmill reviews, treatments for injuries, nutrition information, and much more. Site also features discussion forums.

Running4.com

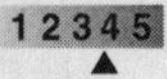

www.running4.com

Running4.com is an online training log by runners for runners. At this site, you can keep your own training log, read and post messages in the discussion forums, and read news stories on various running events.

Running Network

12345

www.runningnetwork.com

Get running tips, news, and links, as well as a track calendar and race results. This e-zine is dedicated to America's "grassroots runners." Here, you will find national and local running news, features, photos, extensive race results, a searchable calendar, training tips, clubs, stores, product reviews, and more.

Running and Track & Field

www.tflinks.com

This site features an excellent directory of articles, books, and links to other sites related to track and field. You can search for specific content by keyword or browse by category, including Athletes, Clubs, Competitions, Injuries, Statistics, and Training.

Shot Put

12345

www.brianmac.demon.co.uk/shot/index.htm

This page presents an excellent primer on the shot put event, explaining the grip, the stance, and the put; movement into the basic put; and the optimum projection angle; and providing links to several other shot-put-related pages and sites.

Sports Coach

12345

www.brianmac.demon.co.uk

Sports Coach creator Brian Mackenzie is "a Level 4 Performance Coach (UKA 4) and Coach Tutor Assessor with UK Athletics, the United Kingdom's National Governing body for Track and Field Athletics." Here, Brian offers his expertise free of charge to athletes and coaches, covering general topics on nutrition and training and providing primers on how to train and perform every track and field event, including running events, shot put, high jump, javelin throw, long jump, and pole vault. The site design isn't flashy, but the information is top notch.

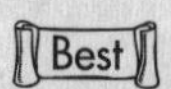 **Track and Field News**

12345

www.trackandfieldnews.com

Peruse past issues and check up on races, athletes, and records. The countless articles will keep die-hard runners busy until they're rested and ready to start running again. This site offers much for the online shopper, too. You can shop in a nice, easy-to-navigate online store and purchase everything from books to videos. You can review the latest issue of the magazine, see the men's world rankings by nation, search for articles of interest in the archive, and even check out the calendar and links to related sites. With all it offers and its pleasing presentation, this site grabs the gold.

Training for 400m/800m: An Alternative Plan

12345

www.oztrack.com/plan.htm

This site shares information gathered by its author regarding better methods to prepare an athlete to run in either the 400- or 800-meter medium sprints. The information includes specific training regimens.

USA Track and Field

12345

www.usatf.org

The official site of track and field's overseeing authority in the United States. These pages contain news, national and international records, race walking resources, masters racing, and race numerology.

USA Triathlon

12345

www.usatriathlon.org

This is the official home of the USA Triathlon team, which provides information on age groupings, elite athletes, coaching, news, information, rankings, rules, and much more. You can also shop for team merchandise online and explore a good collection of links to other triathlon sites.

TRAVEL & VACATION

ADVENTURE (SEE ADVENTURE TRAVEL/ECOTOURISM)

AIR TRAVEL

Airlines of the Web

12345

flyaow.com

Provides information about airlines, organized by geographic region. Also provides information about cargo airlines, newsgroups, and airports, as well as a good collection of tips for airline travelers.

AirSafe.com

www.airsafe.com

If you're worried about airline safety and security, this is the site for you. Here, you'll find tips on how best to deal with safety issues, terrorist threats, airport security, and baggage issues. Loads of tips available to make your air travel safer and make it proceed with fewer hassles. Get the latest safety statistics for various airlines and airplane models, plus additional travel advice. Before you head to the airport, head to this site.

Air Traffic Control System

12345

www.fly.faa.gov/flyfaa/usmap.jsp

This is the official site of the United States Air Traffic Control System. It contains a map of the United States with markers for each of the major airports. Simply click a marker to find out the status of the desired airport. If you don't see a marker for the airport you're interested in, you can search for an airport by name or select a region to zoom in on an area and display markers for more airports in that area.

Air Travel Health Tips

12345

familydoctor.org/455.xml

Familydoctor.org offers this page to help airline travelers have a healthy flight. Article discusses ear pain, jet lag, the importance of moving around on a long flight, and other issues.

Flight Arrivals

12345

www.flightarrivals.com

Real-time arrival and departure times for flights throughout the United States and Canada. Just type in the flight information and learn whether it's on time. Just the tool you need before heading to the airport to depart or to pick someone up.

Flyer Talk

12345

www.flyertalk.com

Flyer Talk is an online community where frequent flyers can meet to gab, exchange information and travel tips, and have their questions answered.

Seat Guru

12345

seatguru.com

Where should you sit on your next flight? Do you want a window seat? Quick access to the aisle? Plenty of legroom? A quiet seat? Tell Seat Guru the airline and aircraft you plan on flying, and let the Guru show you to your preferred seat.

Transportation Security Administration

12345

www.tsa.gov

Want to know the rules and regulations that govern passenger flights in the United States? Then check out this page from the Transportation Security Administration and obtain tips and tricks to make your progress through the security areas a little smoother. Site features key travel tips, a list of prohibited items, information for persons with disabilities and medical conditions, a list of frequently asked questions, and more.

AIRLINES (SEE AIR LINES)

BUDGET TRAVEL

11th Hour Vacations

1 2 3 4 5

`www.11thhourvacations.com`

Browse the available trips and cruises with departure dates in the next couple of weeks to find great deals. Whether you want to see New York City or Greece, you have a huge number of options to choose from. And the prices are reasonable. You can also enter your email to be alerted to deals on a particular destination.

Backpack Europe on a Budget

1 2 3 4 5

`www.backpackeurope.com`

Learn some of the strategies that can make it possible for you to backpack across Europe inexpensively. Find out about hostels, working abroad, and discount packages.

BargainTravel.com

1 2 3 4 5 RSS

`www.bargaintravel.com`

Find the best prices on vacation packages, car rentals, airfare, cruises, and hotels at this site.

BestFares.com

1 2 3 4 5

`www.bestfares.com`

Sign up for the BestFares weekly email to be alerted to special discount opportunities for Thursday through Tuesday travel. Some great deals you wouldn't have found anywhere else. This site also features some excellent travel resources, including a currency exchange calculator, worldwide weather report, ski report, fraud squad, and a list of attorneys general.

Budget Hotels

1 2 3 4 5

`www.budgethotels.com`

Find accommodations around the world at discount prices, as well as other travel bargains on cars and airfares here.

Busabout Europe

1 2 3 4 5

`www.busabout.com`

The economical alternative to rail travel, "Busabout is a freestyle travel network, designed exclusively for backpackers and independent travellers, offering a range of exciting travel experiences to suit all time constraints and budgets." Connects 50 cities in Europe and 41 destinations outside Europe by bus and other affordable transportation.

Council Travel

1 2 3 4 5

`www.statravel.com`

Offers discount and budget airfares, rail passes, hostel memberships, international student ID cards, and more, for student, youth, and budget travelers.

DiscountAirfares.com

1 2 3 4 5

`www.discountairfares.com`

Discount Airfares is a travel agent referral service. You enter your point of departure, destination, dates, and email address, and the site presents you with offers from five travel agents. You can also use other tools on the site to browse for low fares and offers.

Economy Travel

1 2 3 4 5

`www.economytravel.com`

Lowest international airfares on the Web, booked online. Consolidator fares, private fares, and low published fares, all on one site.

Expedia

1 2 3 4 5

www.expedia.com

Search for travel deals, make reservations, and shop around for special packages at Expedia. Expedia offers several ways to explore low fares. You can check for deals by destination; shop by theme (including beaches and romance); check out daily deals; or enter the desired departure point, destination, and dates, for free quotes.

Hostels.com

1 2 3 4 5

www.hostels.com

Find a hostel or low-cost hotel near where you're traveling and learn more about what to expect from experienced travelers at this site.

Hotels.com

1 2 3 4 5

www.hotels.com

Hotels.com focuses on accommodations, including suites, condos, and bed and breakfast deals, but the site also offers deals on airfare, car rentals, vacation packages, and cruises.

Hotwire.com

1 2 3 4 5

www.hotwire.com

Hotwire is dedicated to helping travelers fly, drive, and sleep cheap. On the opening page, you can search for bargains on airfare, car rentals, motel rooms, and cruises. Hotwire.com features tabs for easy navigation, including tabs for Weekend Getaways, Packages, and Deals & Destinations.

LastMinuteTravel.com

1 2 3 4 5

www.lastminutetravel.com

A site where you can find last-minute deals on airfare, hotels, cars, and cruises. You can browse for featured deals or enter your departure and destination points and dates to pull up a list of available options.

Lowestfare.com

1 2 3 4 5

www.lowestfare.com

If you're planning a vacation, cruise, or just a short trip into a neighboring state, you'll find a travel guide and a reservation section here and all at the lowest fares. Check out the fares here before planning your trip.

Moment's Notice

1 2 3 4 5

www.moments-notice.com

Check the daily specials to find last-minute travel deals at greatly reduced prices. Sign up for email alerts when travel bargains arise that meet your particular interests.

Orbitz

1 2 3 4 5 RSS

www.orbitz.com

Orbitz is "a leading online travel company offering leisure and business travelers a wide selection of low airfares, as well as deals on lodging, car rentals, cruises, vacation packages and other travel." Here, you can search for deals or have Orbitz notify you of deals via email, mobile phone, pager, or PDA. Orbitz can also notify you of delays or other events that may affect your trip.

> **Tip:** Click the My Trip tab to register and save your trip-planning information for later reference.

Priceline.com

1 2 3 4 5

www.priceline.com

Place a bid on airfare, hotels, and car rentals and see whether a company will accept it. If so, you can save hundreds or even thousands of dollars. Priceline also functions as a more standard deal hunter, enabling you to pull up a list of travel deals and select the desired offer...without having to post a bid.

A B C D E F G H I J K L M N O P Q R S T U V W X Y Z

SkyAuction.com

12345

www.skyauction.com

Bid on airfares, resorts, hotels, and car rentals starting at $1.

Travelocity

12345

www.travelocity.com

Full online travel service with information on destinations, travel bargains, and travel tips. You can even sign up to be notified when fares to a particular destination drop.

CAR RENTAL *(SEE CAR RENTAL)*

CAR TRAVEL

ASIRT: Association for Safe International Road Travel

12345

www.asirt.org

Want to know which countries are the most dangerous to drive in? You'll find such information here as well as other road information and safety data. Great site to visit if you're planning to study abroad or simply head out on a road trip in an unfamiliar country.

Auto Europe Car Rentals

12345 RSS

www.autoeurope.com

Auto Europe offers auto rentals, discounted airfare, and hotel packages worldwide. Check the Travel Specials to find this week's bargains.

BreezeNet's Rental Car Guide and Reservations

12345

www.bnm.com

A one-stop car rental site for quick online reservations to auto rental companies with airport service. Also includes coupons, discounts, and phone numbers.

Drive Europe

12345

www.driveeurope.com

If you're planning to tour Europe in a car, visit this site for some of the best driving tours around. Customized tours and event tours are also available. Site also features links to car and motor home rentals, apartment and villa rentals, Europe rail passes, and travel insurance.

Fun Roads

12345

www.funroads.com

Fun Roads is a travel site for RV travelers featuring travel ideas, RV parts and accessories, motor home service, tools for finding or selling an RV, and lots of travel tips and articles. If you own an RV, check out this site to learn how to get the most enjoyment out of your investment.

MomsMinivan

12345

www.momsminivan.com

Got kids? Then check out this site before you pack up to leave on your next cross-country excursion in the van. Here, you'll find more than 100 games and activities to keep babies, toddlers, and older kids entertained in the car or van.

Pet Car Travel Tips

12345 Blog

www.aspca.org/site/PageServer?pagename=pets_cartraveltips

The American Society for the Prevention of Cruelty to Animals created and maintains this page to provide pet owners with safety tips on how to travel safely with common pets in the car.

Road Trips

12345 Blog

www.roadtripusa.com

With the popularity of air travel and cruises, many people overlook the joyous adventures of affordable road trips. Here, you can check cross-country routes that have managed to avoid the devastation of development and retain their flavor.

Route 66

 RSS

www.historic66.com

Get your kicks on the famous roadway Route 66. This site is packed with photos, stories, and a wealth of helpful information. Also features a locator map.

Scenic Byways and Other Recreational Drives

www.gorp.com/gorp/activity/byway/byway.htm

Organized into categories such as Far West, Desert Southwest, Great Plains, and Great Lakes, this site helps you locate the scenic route to your destination. Contains links to a majority of the 50 states.

Traveling in the USA

www.travelingusa.com

These pages will help the U.S. traveler find information on parks, campgrounds, resorts, and recreation. From relief maps to kiddy activities, you'll probably satisfy your travel needs here. Also features links for Traveling Australia, Canada, and New Zealand.

CRUISES

Bargain Travel Cruises–Cheap Cruises

www.bargaintravelcruises.com

You can have a terrific vacation at the lowest possible cost by doing some research for the best possible deals available. You can take a bargain cruise by selecting from the best and cheapest available on this site. The site contains contact information on how to sign up for that trip of your dreams.

Carnival Cruises

www.carnival.com

Home of one of the most popular cruise lines in the world, this site provides quick quotes on the cost of your cruise. Just select a destination, specify the desired length of the cruise (in days), and pick a month. The site also provides information about destinations and guest services, group travel rates, and ways to finance your cruise. Also learn about job openings at this site.

Cruise.com

www.cruise.com

This site provides cruise reviews, statistics, and deals and offers to beat just about any offer you can find.

CruiseGuide

cruiseguide.net

At CruiseGuide, you can search for a cruise to practically anywhere in the world. You can search by destination, departure and return dates, duration, or cruise line.

Cruise Value Center

www.mycruisevalue.com

Find great values in cruises throughout the United States and the Caribbean here.

CruiseStar.com

www.cruisestar.com

In addition to cruise reviews and FAQs, you'll find discount cruises, last-minute deals, and bargains organized by cruise line.

A B C D E F G H I J K L M N O P Q R S T U V W X Y Z

Crystal Cruises

1 2 3 4 5

www.crystalcruises.com

Crystal Cruises has been voted the top cruise line for 10 consecutive years by readers of *Condé Nast Traveler* and *Travel + Leisure* magazines. Here, you can search for a cruise, explore destinations, learn about the various onboard activities and events, tour the ships, and get instructions and tips on how to plan and prepare for your trip.

Freighter World Cruises

1 2 3 4 5

www.freighterworld.com

Advertises Freighter World Cruises, Inc., a travel agency that focuses on freighter travel. Provides information on various freighter lines and their destinations. Cruise in economy style.

Holland America Line

1 2 3 4 5

www.hollandamerica.com

This site has information on Holland America Line's cruises to Alaska, the Caribbean, Hawaii, Asia and the Pacific, South America, Canada and New England, and Europe. You might request literature and order a video on your desired cruise destination.

i-cruise.com

1 2 3 4 5

www.icruise.com

i-cruise provides five ways to shop for cruises: by destination, departure port, sail date, cruise line, or cruise ship. Site also offers deals on airfare, which is sometimes included as part of the package.

Norwegian Cruise Line

1 2 3 4 5

www.ncl.com

Read about Norwegian Cruise Line destinations and music theme cruises, such as a big band cruise. Sample destinations are Mexico, Hawaii, Alaska, and the Caribbean. Find out about special deals.

Princess Cruises

1 2 3 4 5

www.awcv.com/princess.html

Cruise on the Love Boat to the Caribbean. Find out about special discounts, 50 percent or more. You can book your cruise online.

Royal Caribbean

1 2 3 4 5

www.royalcaribbean.com

Royal Caribbean is one of the top cruise liners in the world. At this site, you can explore a wide selection of cruises, get a feel for what a cruise might be like, and obtain tips on how to prepare for your cruise to make it a more enjoyable experience.

Schooner Mary Day

1 2 3 4 5

www.schoonermaryday.com

The Schooner Mary Day is a sailing cruise ship (windjammer) that carries couples, singles, and groups on three- to six-day cruises among the islands of Midcoast Maine. Here, you'll find online contact information for booking a cruise.

INFORMATION/TRAVEL TIPS

100% Pure New Zealand

1 2 3 4 5

www.newzealand.com/travel

New Zealand is a land of mountains, volcanoes, rain forests, beaches, and some of the most breathtaking scenery in the world. Visit this official travel site to get a small sample of the land, its people, and its culture. This site provides a history of New Zealand, key facts about it, a list of interesting destinations and activities, information on accommodations, and much more.

A&E Traveler

1 2 3 4 5

www.aetvtravel.com

Not your average travel agent, this travel site—maintained by A&E, the History Channel, and

Biography—is designed to help you plan trips to some of the more interesting points on the globe. Pick a country and an interest to view a list of available tours.

Abercrombie & Kent

12345

www.abercrombiekent.com

Luxury travel at its best. Visit this site and see how the other half lives. Travel through Scotland on the Royal Scotsman, with tours through England and Wales, or ride aboard the Venice-Simplon Orient Express. Enjoy gourmet dining and impeccable service. Go ahead—splurge!

Away.com

12345

away.com

Are you tired of the standard vacations to Florida, Hawaii, and other popular tourist destinations? Then check out Away.com for some unique ideas. Here, you can learn about trips to faraway places ranging from Alaska to Zimbabwe; search by activity to find archaeological trips, windsurfing hot spots, or ecological adventures; or search by interest to find inspirational destinations.

Citysearch

12345

www.citysearch.com

Whether you're going out of town or looking for the best dining, entertainment, and attractions near your home, let Citysearch be your guide. Here, you pick a city of your choice and view an online directory of restaurants, nightclubs, and events. Explore a little deeper and you can find the best bars, hotels, singles scenes, stores, spas, and health clubs.

Ecotourism Explorer

12345

www.ecotourism.org

Official website of The International Ecotourism Society (TIES), this site provides information about finding and using ecology-friendly lodging and travel services. Learn how to make ecologically responsible travel decisions, check out some sample trips, and learn more about ecotourism.

FamilyTravelForum

12345 RSS

www.familytravelforum.com

"Have Kids, Still Travel," is this site's motto, and members of FamilyTravelForum use this service to do just that. You can find help planning affordable family trips that everyone in your family will enjoy—or they'll at least need a pretty good excuse not to. Membership is about $4 per month ($10 for three months) and is well worth the cost, even if you use the service for a single trip.

Fodor's Travel Online

12345

www.fodors.com

Features guides to cities worldwide, travel chat, and resources. Also lets you custom-tailor a guide to more than 90 destinations worldwide.

Frommer's

12345 RSS

www.frommers.com

Frommer's produces some of the best travel guides available, and now you can get much of your travel information for free online. This site offers information on destinations and hotels, trip ideas, tips, deals and news, and an online bookstore where you can purchase a Frommer's guide to pack along with you on your trip. You can also book a trip online through one of Frommer's recommended travel sites.

IgoUgo

12345

www.igougo.com

Looking for travel advice from real people who traveled where you plan to go? Then look no further. IgoUgo features personal travel journals for more than 4,000 destinations written by hundreds of thousands of regular people who have actually visited those places. Find out about the best places to stay, the top restaurants offering the best value, interesting sites, and much more. Links to other services to book flights and cruises, rent automobiles, reserve a room, and more. Also features a good collection of photos of various destinations.

Journeywoman

12345

www.journeywoman.com

From where Queen Elizabeth buys her bras to how to stay healthy in Tibet to girls-only fly-fishing in the United States, *Journeywoman* dispenses valuable travel tips gathered from around the world. Written entirely from a female perspective.

Let's Go

12345 Blog

www.letsgo.com

Are you tired of site-seeing tours? Are you looking for a deeper travel experience? Then check out this Beyond Tourism site. Here, you can find trips that get you involved in the communities you visit. You can study abroad, work with children in Nepal, protect vegetation in Australia's bush country, promote human rights in South Africa, and much more. Great travel site for young adults who don't have a whole lot of money to spend on foreign travel.

Lonely Planet Online

12345 Blog RSS

www.lonelyplanet.com

Lonely Planet guidebooks have always catered to the budget traveler. At this site you can explore U.S. and world destinations. Simply click on a region, a country, or a city to get started. Read a selection from a book related to a journey that might be of interest, post messages for other travelers to respond to, check out the photo gallery, and lots more. You won't regret stopping at this site on the way to your next vacation.

> **Tip** Click the Travelcasts icon for free podcasts that introduce you to intriguing destinations around the world.

Luxury Link Travel Services

12345

www.luxurylink.com

Dedicated to the sophisticated traveler, this site features unique travel packages to countries all over the world. Here, you can find thousands of tours, cruises, specialty travel, hotels, resorts, inns, lodges, yacht charters, villas, spas, and more. Site features exclusive packages and best buys, as well as an auction area where you can bid on trip packages.

The North American Virtual Tourist

12345

www.virtualtourist.com/travel/North_America/TravelGuide-North_America.html

An incredible resource for North American travel! One click on the image map of North America will lead you to every Internet resource available for the selected state or region. This site is heaven for those looking for an all-encompassing site in the United States, Canada, or Mexico. Bookmark this site and visit frequently!

One Bag

12345

www.onebag.com

Learn how to travel light, with tips on what to pack and how to pack. You'll also find travel resource information, other tips on making travel easier, and a good annotated directory of links to related websites.

Pets Welcome

12345

www.petswelcome.com

Look through the Listings page to find hotels, bed and breakfasts, resorts, campgrounds, and beaches that are pet friendly. Learn from other pet owners who've traveled with their friends and share your advice with others in the discussion forums. This site even features tips on flying with your pet.

Premier Golf Classics Destinations

12345

www.premiergolf.com

Premier Golf Classics Destinations is the official travel website for the PGA. Here, golf enthusiasts can find travel packages to classic golf venues. If you're a golfer with some ready cash who wants to golf on the same courses as the pros, check out this site.

A B C D E F G H I J K L M N O P Q R S T U V W X Y Z

Rough Guides

1 2 3 4 5

www.roughguides.com

Rough Guides include "recommendations from shoestring to luxury and cover more than 200 destinations around the globe, including almost every country in the Americas and Europe, more than half of Africa and most of Asia and Australasia." This site features articles about traveling to exotic locations, whatever your travel budget may be. Learn more about restaurants, landmarks, the people, and things to do for many of the top destinations in the world.

Specialty Travel Guide

1 2 3 4 5

www.infohub.com/

Interesting site that organizes trips and tours by category, including Arts & Crafts, Boating & Sailing, Eco & Wildlife, Naturist, Railway Trips, and Scuba Diving. Here, you can explore various travel options, take an online quiz, hang out in the discussion forums, and look up offers on airfare, accommodations, and car rentals.

timeout.com

1 2 3 4 5

www.timeout.com

Get the latest information about bars, restaurants, nightlife, and more for dozens of the top cities in the world. Just click on London, Beijing, New York, Paris, or many others to get the inside scoop on the scene.

TRAVEL.com

1 2 3 4 5

www.travel.com

TRAVEL.com enables you to compare rates at major travel websites, enabling you to comparison shop for travel packages to nearly 900 destinations, including more than 100,000 hotel listings. Rates for vacation condos, bed and breakfasts, extended stay hotels with kitchenettes, hostels, resorts, and more are all available through this site. Here, you can also get travel advisories, weather information, as well as recreational, shopping, and real-time flight information at this site.

Travel Channel Online

   RSS

travel.discovery.com

Programming and schedules along with travel resources and travel chat from the folks who bring us the Discovery Channel. Choose to explore the site by destination or idea. Check out the live webcams and the interactive gallery, and use the free travel tools to plan your trip. Site features an excellent collection of destination guides.

Travel Medicine

1 2 3 4 5

www.travmed.com

Provides information about diseases, environmental concerns, and immunizations for travelers. Includes tips on what to pack in your travel medicine kit and concerns for pregnant women who are traveling. Features the 2001 edition of *International Travel Health Guide* in PDF format and a host of products you might want to stuff in your duffel bag.

The Travelite FAQ

1 2 3 4 5

www.travelite.org

Learn more than you probably ever wanted to know about packing tips. You'll find out about luggage, things to bring, packing methods, electrical appliances, accessories, and more.

Travellerspoint Travel Community

www.travellerspoint.com

Travellerspoint is an online community where world travelers can congregate and swap stories and tips about their favorite destinations. Site features discussion forums, blogs, photography, trip planning tools and tips, and links to other related travel sites.

TravelSource

1 2 3 4 5

www.travelsource.com

Includes information about different vacation packages and locations. Also provides links to travel agents and other travel resources to fine-tune your vacation plans. Whether you're looking to scuba dive, whitewater raft, take a cruise, or simply kick back, this site is your one-stop vacation planner. Site features interactive guides to 5,000 cities around the world.

TripAdvisor

www.tripadvisor.com

Unbiased reviews. of hotels, resorts, and vacations is TripAdvisor's specialty, but it does a great job of helping travelers come up with ideas for their next trips, too. You can check out trips to destinations all over the world, discover ways to travel more affordably, and find out the best places to stay. With TripAdvisor as your guide, you get the reliable advice you need to make the best choices.

Virtual Tourist

www.virtualtourist.com

Information and links about entertainment, media, business, culture, and traveling opportunities all over the world. Features separate tabs for travel guides, hotels, flights, and auctions. Also provides areas to hook up with other travelers and read and post messages. Almost all the reviews here are posted by world travelers and locals.

World Hum

www.worldhum.com

This unique travel site focuses less on commerce and more on human interaction, the stuff that makes most trips most memorable. Here, you'll find some of the best travel stories on the Web. This site encourages visitors to expand their horizons through travel and human interaction.

Zagat.com

www.zagat.com

You'll find more than 25,000 reviews for restaurants, nightclubs, hotels, and attractions around the world. Choose a city and you'll get recommendations for places to dine that evening.

INTERNATIONAL TRAVEL

AFRICANET

www.africanet.com

Use the search feature to track down just what you're looking for in the way of Africa travel information. Get in-depth information on many African countries and learn about recommended African sites to check out.

Airhitch

www.airhitch.org

This down-and-dirty site will help you learn how to travel to and within Europe for little money; it also offers other amazing travel deals. You might not have the coziest of accommodations, and you have to be flexible in considering destinations, but you can get to wherever it is you end up cheaply.

CDC (Centers for Disease Control and Prevention)

www.cdc.gov/travel

This U.S. government health agency is dedicated to preventing the spread of infectious diseases. This site provides useful, up-to-date information about health risks and disease outbreaks in areas all over the world. Find out which vaccinations you should receive and treatments you should pack before you leave for your trip. The site also provides up-to-date information about biological agents, such as anthrax.

Czech Info Center

www.czechinfocenter.com

A well-organized guide to the Czech Republic. Includes general information, bulletin boards (to help you find ancestors, for example), helpful travel information, and a section on the city of Prague

European Visits

www.eurodata.com

This "online magazine of European travel" offers articles on travel through Europe, as well as flight and hotel information. Get rail passes as well as guidebooks and maps online here, too.

Eurotrip.com

www.eurotrip.com

Anyone considering backpacking through Europe will want to start at this site for information on flying there cheaply, the hostels to stay in, things to see and do, packing tips, rail passes, and much more. Purchase your rail passes right online!

Eurotrotter

www.eurotrotter.com

For European travel, you'll find no better travel site than Eurotrotter. Simply click the desired destination country, and Eurotrotter presents you with a complete directory of available accommodations, restaurants, travel options, parks, museums, campgrounds, maps, and additional information about that country. It's almost as though you have a friend living in that country acting as your guide—however, Eurotrotter probably knows more than most friends do about what's available, and it can present the information in eight different languages.

FranceEscape

www.france.com

Informative site on planning a vacation in France. Includes studies in France, festivals, transportation, and classifieds.

Grand Circle Travel

www.gct.com/gcc/general

Grand Circle Travel functions as a worldwide hub to all destinations around the globe. Plan a trip to Asia, Europe, the South Pacific, Central or South America, North America, or Africa. Grand Circle Travel offers a wide selection of trip types, including river cruises, extended vacations, adventure trips, and European journeys. Grand Circle Travel attempts to provide its customers with meaningful, life-changing journeys.

Help for World Travelers

www.kropla.com

Find out the basics of electricity, phone usage, and Internet access in countries around the world. You'll want to know this stuff so you can use your modem and blow dry your hair after you get there.

Hobo Traveler

Blog RSS

www.hobotraveler.com

"A hobo travels to work. A tramp travels and won't work. A bum neither travels nor works." Here, Andy, a self-proclaimed hobo, presents his travel diary along with tips on more than 150 subjects related to travel. If you want to travel the world on a limited budget and work along the way, this is a great site for learning how to do it.

Inn26

www.inn26.com

Finding flights is usually not much of a problem, but finding just the right accommodations when you reach your destination can be quite a challenge. At Inn26, you can select from a wide range of accommodation types, including bed and breakfasts, motels, guest houses, campgrounds, apartments, villas, and hostels. Site also contains links for travel packages, car rentals, nightlife, and other related links.

International Travel and Health

www.who.int/ith

This World Health Organization's publication on world health and infectious diseases is an invaluable resource for world travelers. This site features information on traveling by air, environmental health risks, travel accidents, infectious diseases, and more. Search by country to determine specific health risks for a particular region.

International Travel Guide for Mallorca and the Balearic Islands

12345

www.mallorcaonline.com

Check out this international travel guide for Mallorca and the Balearic Islands to plan your next trip to Spain.

International Travel Maps and Books

12345

www.itmb.com

International Travel Maps and Books, Canada's largest supplier of maps, prepares detailed travel maps and guides of countries and regions around the world. Visit this site to order the map(s) and travel guides you need.

International Travel News

12345

www.intltravelnews.com

This site provides travel tips, reviews of various travel services, and recommendations from real-world travelers.

Kintetsu International Travel

12345

www.kintetsu.com

This Japanese international travel company, at home in the United States, offers full-featured services for travel to and around Japan. Here, you can find out about flights, Japan rail passes, hotel reservations, meetings and incentives, and more. Site also features a flight tracker.

Mexico Travel Guide

12345

www.go2mexico.com

If you're planning a trip to Mexico, check out this site first. The opening page presents a clickable map of Mexico, so you can quickly jump to your preferred destination. Site also features travel tips, a Spanish Helper, Mexico articles, and additional links to explore.

Monaco Online

12345

www.monaco.mc

Presents the principality of Monaco and its tourism, business, and motor racing. Includes English and French versions.

Planeta

12345

www.planeta.com

Environmentally aware travelers will want to check out Planeta, which is a guide to ecologically and environmentally responsible travel through South America and the Caribbean. This site serves as a central repository for travel that explores conservation and local development issues. Contributors include travel operators, environmentalists, and fellow travelers.

Rick Steves' Europe Through the Back Door

www.ricksteves.com

Learn what Rick Steves means about traveling Europe through the "back door," at his site, which contains information gleaned from his travel books as well as information on upcoming European trips that he manages. Site also offers some free audio tours of Rick's favorite destinations and attractions.

Salzburg, Austria

12345

www.salzburg.com/tourismus_e

Provides seasonal tourist information about Salzburg, Austria, and its surrounding regions. Offers alternatives to traditional holiday plans when abroad (in German and English).

Sri Lanka Internet Services

12345

www.lanka.net

The Sri Lanka web server page with links to travel and business guides, maps, gems, news, and Internet access information.

TravelAdvice.net

12345

www.travel-advice.net

TravelAdvice.net is a British site that provides advice and warnings about travel to various countries around the world. Content is organized into several areas, including Essential Advice (health & safety, embassies & visas, travel delay information, and travel insurance), Holiday Ideas, Getting There, Where to Stay, and Travel Information. Site also includes links to U.K. airport guides.

United States State Department Travel Warnings and Consular Info Sheets

12345

travel.state.gov

Provides up-to-date information for international travelers, including warnings, entry requirements, medical requirements, political status, and crime information for travel sites abroad. Also includes the location of the U.S. embassy in each country. Countries are easy to find in an alphabetic index.

Universal Currency Converter

12345

www.xe.com/ucc

Presents the exchange rate for 90 currencies. Don't be taken for an ignorant tourist and robbed blind when touring another country. If you need to know what Indian rupees are worth in Dutch guilders, this site will not let you down. Exchange rates are updated daily.

Vancouver, British Columbia

12345

www.city.vancouver.bc.ca

Provides FreeNet's information and links about Vancouver. Also offers links to the British Columbia home page and other Canadian home pages.

ISLAND TRAVEL

All-Inclusives Resort and Cruise Vacation Source

12345

www.allinclusivereservations.com

This site offers information on Caribbean and Mexican cruises and resorts as well as vacation information about Alaska, the Panama Canal, and Hawaii. The All-Inclusives offer is to give you all services with one payment, and you can sit back and enjoy your trip without worrying about attached costs.

America's Caribbean Paradise

12345

www.usvi.net

Provides information about the Virgin Islands, including wedding and vacation information, holidays, carnivals and other events, and weather forecasts. Also offers a section on real estate, vacation rentals, recipes, and Caribbean products.

Club Med

12345

www.clubmed.com

Locate a Club Med location that meets your needs for a particular type of vacation and activities, find out more about the atmosphere there, check on current deals, and even take a 360-degree look at some of the beaches.

Elite Island Resorts

12345

www.eliteislandresorts.com

This site presents a collection of posh island resorts on the Caribbean islands of Antigua, Palm Island, St. Kitts, St. Lucia, and Tortola.

A B C D E F G H I J K L M N O P Q R S T U V W X Y Z

Fiji Islands Travel Guide

12345

www.bulafiji.com

Created and maintained by the Fiji Visitors Bureau, this site features information about the Fiji islands, its main attractions, and its history and culture. Site also provides information about health, geography, currency, activities, accommodations, and transportation. If you're thinking of visiting the Fiji islands, this should be your first stop on the way.

Galveston Island Official Tourism Site

12345

www.galvestontourism.com

Your official site for information about Galveston, Texas, including maps, weather reports, activities, attractions, restaurants, and entertainment. You can even reserve a room online or check out the scenery and activity around Galveston Island with the webcams!

Hideaway Holidays: Travel Specialists to the Pacific Islands

12345

www.hideawayholidays.com.au

Specialist tour wholesaler to the exotic islands of the South Pacific. Air/land inclusive or land-only packages. Inquiries welcome from anyone.

Islands.com

12345

www.islands.com

Islands.com bills itself as "the Leading Guide to Island Travel," and for the most part, it lives up to this billing by covering travel to islands all around the world, including Key West, Martha's Vineyard, Ireland, Bora Bora, and New Zealand.

Isles of Scilly Travel Centre

12345

www.islesofscilly-travel.co.uk

Sea and air services to the Isles of Scilly from southwest United Kingdom. Pictures and information about these subtropical islands.

Maui Travel & Tourism

12345

www.maui.worldweb.com

A full-blown interactive guide to Maui. This main page provides a brief introduction to Maui. You can then scroll down for an extensive directory of links to help plan your trip.

NetWeb Bermuda

12345

www.bermuda.com

Offers links to Bermuda travel and cultural information. Also serves as an advertising site for Bermuda businesses.

Virgin Islands

12345

www.virginisles.com

This is a comprehensive guide to touring the U.S. Virgin Islands. It includes information about beaches, restaurants, hotels, and resorts. Special areas are offered specifically for St. Croix, St. Thomas, and St. John. Site also features facts about the island and recommended activities, if you're looking to do more than simply relaxing in paradise.

World Beaches

12345

www.surf-sun.com/worldbeaches.html

This site can help you choose the perfect coastal destination. It links to sandy sites throughout the United States and around the world.

LODGING

1st Traveler's Choice

12345

www.virtualcities.com/ons/0onsadex.htm

Information on lodging across the United States, Canada, and Mexico. Search by state, province, type, or languages spoken by innkeepers. Includes *Country Inns* magazine, the *Inn Times*; virtual cities' trade show; and a gourmet directory of hundreds of recipes from innkeepers. New inns added weekly

Alaskan Cabin, Cottage, and Lodge Catalog

12345

www.midnightsun.com

The Alaskan Cabin, Cottage, and Lodge Catalog is a comprehensive listing of all the wilderness cabins, cottages, and lodges in the state of Alaska. It includes a listing of nearly 200 U.S. Forestry Service recreation cabins in the Tongass and Chugach National Forests.

all-hotels.com

12345

www.all-hotels.com

This site aims to provide a one-stop-shop for hotel reservations, centralizing information about hotels worldwide in one place. Get information on available hotels and rooms for cities around the world and book online when you find what you want. More than 100,000 hotels all over the world in the database.

Choice Hotels

12345

www.hotelchoice.com

More than 5,000 of the Choice Hotels International are available from this site, which includes branches of Econolodge, Clarion, Comfort Inn, and more. Reservations are available from this site.

Colorado Vacation Guide

12345

www.coloradoadventure.net

The leading source for Colorado campgrounds, cabins, lodges, and dude ranches. Includes Colorado recreation, vacations, adventures, and fun things to do.

Cyber Rentals

12345

www.cyberrentals.com

Looking for a really "quiet" and private vacation spot? Why not rent a home, condo, or villa for your vacation and enjoy a home away from home? This site provides you with plenty of resources for just such a vacation and many of them at bargain prices. Features more than 21,000 available accommodations worldwide.

Hotelguide.com

12345

www.hotelguide.com

Look at a map of most major cities worldwide here to find the locations of hotels before booking a room. Then search the database to find available rooms and book online at one of more than 85,000 hotels listed for savings of up to 50 percent. You can also get information on vacation packages, such as golf outings, and link to other vacation and travel sites.

InnSite

12345

www.innsite.com

Search more than 50,000 pages of bed and breakfast listings to find one in 50 countries worldwide that meets your needs. For more detailed feedback about locations, you might want to visit the discussion groups to chat with fellow travelers.

International Bed and Breakfast Guide

12345

www.ibbp.com

National and international B&Bs dot this site. Countries featured other than the United States include Canada, Great Britain, New Zealand, and Argentina.

Lake Tahoe's West Shore Lodging

12345

www.tahoecountry.com/wslodging.html

Bed and breakfasts, guesthouses, and lodges along Lake Tahoe's tranquil West Shore offer visitors peaceful settings and a taste of Old Tahoe.

Lodging Guide World Wide

12345

www.lgww.com

It's not called the Lodging Guide World Wide for nothing. Reservations in most major cities around the world can be made here. You can search for a lodging by type and location or browse by state and city.

A B C D E F G H I J K L M N O P Q R S T U V W X Y Z

LodgingGuide

12345

lodgingguide.com

The LodgingGuide website "features not just hotels, but beds and breakfasts, vacation rentals, all-inclusives and more" from countries all around the world. Search for a specific location or simply browse the offerings starting with a country and then zeroing in on a specific location. Site also features links for a DiningGuide, EventGuide, NightGuide, and RetailGuide, along with a list of the top hotel destinations.

Lodgings International

12345

www.lodgingsinternational.com

Lodgings International is a directory of accommodations around the world, including "bed and breakfasts, inns, guest houses, lodges, villas, homes, beach houses, self-catering vacation rentals, condominiums, apartments, farmstays, retreats, cottages, hotels, motels, beach resorts, and ranches." You can search the directory by geographical location.

The National Lodging Directory

12345

www.guests.com

The National Lodging Directory, a user-friendly site, contains listings for hotels, motels, bed and breakfasts, and vacation rental property located in the United States. You can make online reservations on most client sites.

Professional Association of Innkeepers International

12345

www.paii.org

You'll find more than just the *Innkeeping Weekly* at this site, but do look at that, too. The book *So You Want to Be an Innkeeper* is available from this site, as are stimulating articles such as "Cutting Deals with Unlikely Allies" and B&B management tips.

Travel Web

12345

travelweb.flexrez.com/tweb

This huge travel monster provides information about more than just lodging. This site features a unique selection of independent hotels to help you keep away from the lodging machine of franchised establishments, if that's what you're looking for; however, you can find chain hotels here, too.

Vacation Direct

12345

www.vacationdirect.com

Vacation Direct can put you in contact with beachfront property owners who want to rent out their homes, villas, apartments, condos, or townhouses directly and usually for much less than you would pay for a hotel room.

West Virginia Lodging Guide

12345

wvweb.com/www/travel_recreation/lodging.html

West Virginia Lodging, a visitors guide to WV accommodations, includes bed and breakfasts, camping, hotels, motels, resorts, and vacation properties. You can browse by region or by the desired type of accommodation.

TRAIN TRAVEL

Amtrak

12345

www.amtrak.com

The country's foremost train authority, Amtrak, is accessed through this page. Find everything from the latest high-speed train information to travel tips and reservations on this useful home page. Promotional offers, student discounts, senior discounts, child fares, disability discounts. Check the site regularly because seasonal fare specials vary.

European and British Rail Passes

12345

www.eurail.com

Provides information on the Eurail Pass and rail passes for other countries such as Germany, Austria, Italy, Czech Republic, and Scandinavia. This site is a must for those considering traveling Europe by Eurail.

Grand Canyon Railway

12345

www.thetrain.com

Read about the historic Grand Canyon Railway. This site lists timetables and fares, travel packages, and weather information. The opening graphic is wonderful, and when you "climb aboard," listen for the train whistle blowing.

Orient-Express Trains & Cruises

12345

www.orient-expresstrains.com

View a slide show to get a sense of the experience of traveling cross-country via the Orient Express and other trains and cruise ships. You can also look at the route each train travels and get information on upcoming trips. Whether you want a luxury ride through the United Kingdom, Southeast Asia, Australia, or Europe, there are several relaxed and luxurious rides to choose from.

Train Traveling

12345

www.traintraveling.com

Train Traveling is a one-stop location for news and information concerning train travel around the world, including Europe, United Kingdom and Ireland, Canada, United States, Australia and New Zealand, Latin America, and Africa. Site covers intercity rail, local transit, rail tours, and tour trains. Site also features links to a language translator, currency converter, and a world clock.

VIA Rail Canada

12345

www.viarail.ca/en.index.html

Canada's rail system. Here, you'll find senior rates, student rates, a frequent traveler program, the CanRailPass, and information about various outdoor adventures in Canada.

U.S. TRAVEL

Alabama Wonder Full

12345

www.touralabama.org

This site created and maintained by the Alabama Department of Tourism & Travel is your travel guide to the best that Alabama has to offer you as a tourist. You can find out about activities that match your interests, special attractions and events, maps, accommodations, and more.

Alaskan Travel Guide

12345

www.alaskan.com

Find out all about travel in and around Alaska here, from where to stay, what to see, which parks to visit, and much more. Use the travel planner to sketch out your visit and to consider specific types of vacations.

The Arizona Guide

12345

www.arizonaguide.com

The official site for the Arizona Office of Tourism organized by region in text and imagemap format. Provides up-to-date weather information, maps, and state information. The site contains a list of destinations and activities and offers a travel service, trip planner, interactive state map, and even a free travel kit.

Arkansas: The Natural State

12345

www.arkansas.com

This exhaustive tourism guide of Arkansas provides information on state parts, outdoor recreation, history and heritage, arts and entertainment, lodging and dining, and a calendar of events. Features some free Arkansas screensavers and desktop wallpaper, plus an area for kids stuff and information about group travel.

Atlanta Travel Guide

1 2 3 4 5

www.atlanta.net

Take a virtual tour of Atlanta, Georgia, a big city filled with southern hospitality. This site features an area for tourists as well as information about business conventions and relocating to Atlanta.

Blue Ridge Country

1 2 3 4 5

www.blueridgecountry.com

Read the current issue of this travel magazine dedicated to the Blue Ridge Mountain region, see photos of the area, get advice on travel routes, and read the birding guide to learn more about native species. Lots of interesting articles that will pique your interest in this area.

California Travel Guide

1 2 3 4 5

www.visitcalifornia.com/state/tourism/tour_homepage.jsp

If you're thinking of visiting or moving to California, visit this site first to find maps, activities and attractions, lodgings, information about national parks and museums, and much more. The Maps area provides a detailed state map, regional maps, and city maps, along with maps of the best drives in California. Click Lodgings & Reservations to find places to stay including hotels, motels, RV parks, bed and breakfast inns, youth hostels, and state and federal park camping facilities. Site also features an area just for kids and the California Store, where you can shop for apparel, souvenirs, and books.

Cambridge, Massachusetts

www.cambridgema.gov

Features Cambridge resources and more. Offers information on the city's art, entertainment, museums, tourism, and general information for those looking to relocate. You can even tune into the city council's webcast.

Cincinnati Vacation Gateways

1 2 3 4 5

cincinnati.com/getaways

If you're thinking about traveling in the United States, why not visit one of the most beautiful and exciting places in the Midwest—Cincinnati, Ohio? You can spend a day at Kings Island with the kids, stay at one of dozens of luxury hotels, and dine in some of the finest restaurants in the country. Stay awhile and watch the Bengals football team play or maybe even spend a day watching the world-famous Cincinnati Reds play baseball. In the site's own words, the service will customize an "À la carte" vacation that is just right for you. This service can provide you with hotel accommodations, tickets to events and attractions, sporting events, museums, and much, much more. This is your complete online shopping mall for a wonderful vacation in Cincinnati.

Colorado.com

1 2 3 4 5

www.colorado.com

Request the official Colorado state guide to what's going on there or search the site for activities, view the state map to choose a destination, or search the city directory to find items of interest by location. There's also a seasonal directory to activities statewide and a kids area. You'll definitely want to stop here before finalizing your plans for a trip to Colorado.

George Washington's Mount Vernon Estate

1 2 3 4 5

www.mountvernon.org

Take a virtual tour of Mount Vernon or get information on visiting the estate in person. You can also find information from the library and archaeological digs on the premises.

TheGrandCanyon.com

1 2 3 4 5 RSS

www.thegrandcanyon.com

Need to know more about the Grand Canyon? You'll find maps, tour information, lodging and camping details, weather information, and more to help you get the most out of your trip here.

A B C D E F G H I J K L M N O P Q R S T U V W X Y Z

Idaho

1 2 3 4 5

www.state.id.us/tourism_transport

Provides information on regional attractions, state parks, and national forests; a calendar of events; and more general information on the state of Idaho.

Iowa Tourism Office

1 2 3 4 5

www.traveliowa.com

One of the better state-run sites on the Web, this site features a navigation bar on the left that contains links for Things To Do, Accommodations, Getting Around, Facts and Fun, a Media Center, and much more.

Las Vegas

1 2 3 4 5

www.vegas.com

Includes a wide range of vacation-planning information concerning Las Vegas, ranging from hotel information and reservations to show schedules, sports, conventions, betting tips, employment opportunities, and business services. Content is presented in several areas, including Search Hotels, Bestselling Shows, Vegas Guide, Vegas Events, Vegas Video, and Vegas.com tools. Whether you're looking to gamble, take in the top shows, or kick back in one of America's most exciting cities, this site can help you find just about everything you need to plan your trip.

Louisiana Travel Guide

1 2 3 4 5

www.louisianatravel.com

Request a free travel kit to learn more about all there is to do and see in Louisiana, or search online for ideas for family outings, outdoor fun, landmarks, restaurants, and accommodations. Succulent photos of Cajun cuisine will make you hungry for a trip to Louisiana.

Michigan: Travel Michigan

1 2 3 4 5

travel.michigan.org

Offers comprehensive information on what Michigan has to offer, such as local news and events, sightseeing, travel, entertainment, shopping, and more. Site also offers a list of the top destinations in Michigan and some deals that can trim your travel expenses. Be sure to visit this site before you travel Michigan.

Minneapolis

1 2 3 4 5 RSS

www.minneapolis.org

The official site of the city of Minneapolis, the city of lakes. Contains a searchable database for narrowing the scope of your search for travel information whether you're in town for a convention or on vacation with the family. From accommodations to dining and entertainment, it's all right here.

Nashville Scene

1 2 3 4 5

www.nashscene.com

An award-winning online newspaper providing the traveler a guide to dining and events in Nashville, Tennessee, in addition to offering some insight into the Tennessean mindset and culture.

Nebraska Travel and Tourism

1 2 3 4 5

visitnebraska.org

A well-presented documentation of the attractions, campgrounds, hotels, and tourist sites of Nebraska presented in a colorful interface organized by locale and topic. Click the Travel Planner to start planning your vacation, or, if you're planning on doing a driving trip through Nebraska, click the Scenic Byways link. Site also offers some free stuff, including a screensavers, wallpaper, jigsaw puzzles, eCards, and video postcards.

New Jersey and You

1 2 3 4 5

www.state.nj.us/travel

Explore New Jersey at this website to find out about the main attractions, events, and accommodations. Features sections on the arts, family recreation, romantic getaways, historical sites, outdoor recreation, shopping, and sports. Virtual tours are available for the main attractions.

New Mexico: America's Land of Enchantment

1 2 3 4 5

www.newmexico.org

A traveler's guide to New Mexico. Provides information about culture, outdoor activities, area ruins, regional events, and skiing. Also includes maps, brochures, and historical tidbits for travelers. Click Plan a Trip to get started.

New York State

1 2 3 4 5

www.iloveny.com

Get travel ideas by region as well as accommodation and activities suggestions at this site, where you'll see photos of the varied landscape in New York state. Check the schedule of state events and attractions, too.

NH.com: New Hampshire

1 2 3 4 5

www.nh.com

A comprehensive guide to the state of New Hampshire, including information about tourism, historical legacy, local happenings, and everything else under the sun.

Oregon: Travel Information

1 2 3 4 5

www.traveloregon.com

The Travel Oregon website provides an interactive map you can click to explore Oregon before you actually go there and scope out the places, attractions, and events you want to explore. Site also provides tools to help you find places to stay and things to do.

Santa Fe, New Mexico, Travel Information

1 2 3 4 5

www.santafe.org

Excellent guide for tourism and business travel for Santa Fe, New Mexico. Click Visitors to access a directory of restaurants, art galleries, museums, motels, and more. Site also enables you to book a room online.

Seattle.com

1 2 3 4 5

www.seattle.com

Serves as a guide to events, restaurants, accommodations, shopping, sports, and nightlife in the greater Seattle area.

> Scroll down to the bottom to view a good collection of links to other cities organized by state.

South Dakota World Wide Website

1 2 3 4 5

www.travelsd.com

This official travel site for South Dakota is replete with travel information, including area attractions, available accommodations, events, state parks, outdoor recreation, and travel tips available from an accurate clickable imagemap. Site also features a trip planner and special deals. Click I Want to Visit to start exploring the main attractions and activities.

Utah! Travel and Adventure Online

1 2 3 4 5

www.utah.com

Visit the Rocky Mountains, sand dunes, and Salt Lake of Utah via a virtual tour. This site also provides general tourist information, including maps and travel tips. Find out about a selection of vacation packages ranging from guided adventures to traditional family adventures. A visually breathtaking site not to be missed.

Virginia Is for Lovers

1 2 3 4 5

www.virginia.org

An eye-pleasing site containing general tourism information in addition to recreational activities, places to stay, restaurants, local events, theme attractions, and other points of interest in the state for lovers.

Washington, D.C.

1 2 3 4 5

www.district-of-columbia.com

Look at some of the most popular attractions and activities in Washington and get the editor's picks for hotels and restaurants. Recreation and travel into the area are also covered at this comprehensive site.

WorldWeb.com

1 2 3 4 5

www.usa.worldweb.com

WorldWeb.com features "information about American attractions, activities, weather, restaurants, transportation, tours, events, shops, and more." The opening page presents you with a travel directory that gives you one-click access to the information and resources you need to plan your trip to the United States or Canada. Site also offers maps, photos, travel articles, an itinerary maker, and a currency exchange calculator.

The Yankee Traveler

1 2 3 4 5

www.yankeemagazine.com/travel

Provides a compilation of travel-related sources of New England. Includes state web pages, information on Cape Cod and the islands, bed and breakfast inns, and map links. Also provides information about real estate, local businesses, and more. You can start exploring the site by clicking a state on the map, clicking one of the state links, or typing the name of a specific location. At this site, you can also book a hotel room or reserve a rental car.

WEEKEND GETAWAYS

Cheap Weekend Getaways

1 2 3 4 5 Blog

www.smartertravel.com/weekend-getaways

This site offers affordable weekend getaways. You can search by destination, check out specials from the site's sponsors, get travel advice on how to properly time your getaway, and explore featured getaways that might be a little more pricey.

Concierge Travel

1 2 3 4 5

www.concierge.com

Concierge.com is dedicated to helping the sophisticated traveler envision, plan, and execute the ideal vacation or getaway. Concierge.com features award-winning magazine media, including the *Condé Nast Traveler* Gold List, Hot List, Spa Poll, and Ski Poll, along with in-depth insider guides.

EscapeMaker Weekend Getaway Ideas

1 2 3 4 5

escapemaker.com

When you need to get away for the weekend, but you're not sure where to go, visit EscapeMaker, where you can find ideas for weekend getaways on the East Coast of the United States.

Lovetripper

1 2 3 4 5 RSS

www.lovetripper.com

Lovetripper specializes in romantic weekend getaways, honeymoons, and destination weddings. Here, you can find everything you need to plan your trip, including information on getaway destinations, resorts, and hotels. Site also features a how-to guide for planning a honeymoon and marriage rules and regulations for different areas around the globe.

Romantic Weekend Getaways

1 2 3 4 5

honeymoons.about.com/od/weekendgetaways/a/Romance_Weekend.htm

About's guide to honeymoons and weekend getaways recommends some romantic getaways for couples, along with links you can click to learn more about her suggestions. This site explores the pros and cons of various romantic getaways and reviews the recommended options.

Sandals Resorts

12345

www.sandals.com

Features information on tropical hideaways on the enchanted isles of Jamaica, Antigua, St. Lucia, and the Bahamas, created exclusively for couples.

site59.com

12345

www.site59.com

If you're not the type to plan your trip ahead of time, Site59 is the place for you. Named after the 59th minute, this site assumes that you've waited until the last minute to start planning your trip. Just choose the desired destination, and Site59 will assemble a travel package for you, including airline tickets, car rentals, and room reservations at a reasonable price. The departure points are limited to major cities, but except for that minor drawback, the site features an interesting approach to last-minute travel plans.

TotalEscape

12345

www.totalescape.com

Get away from it all by traveling to the most interesting sites in and around California. TotalEscape is California's guide to "local adventures, area activities, and cool places" off the beaten track, including areas where you can rent houseboats. Excellent collection of photos and links of the best places to go to and things to do to recharge your batteries. Links to Amazon.com for shopping.

Trip Spot

12345

www.tripspot.com/getawayfeature.htm

Travel planning central for your weekend getaways—airlines, hotels, maps, city guides, destination ideas, and much more!

VacationIdea.com

12345

www.vacationidea.com/Weekend_Getaways.html

VacationIdea.com features an entire page full of weekend getaway ideas. Browse by ideas, destinations, cities you want to get away *from*, or activities. Special ideas are available for romantic getaways and quick getaways, too.

Washington Post Weekend Getaways Guide

12345

www.washingtonpost.com/wp-adv/specialsales/virtualvacation/weekend.html

Guide to weekend getaways in and around Washington, D.C. Provides information on scenic events, fun and educational activities, recreation, lodging, and restaurants. Features links to the most popular vacation spots in the Washington, D.C., area.

UFOS

Coast to Coast AM with George Noory

www.coasttocoastam.com

Coast to Coast AM is the UFO/conspiracy theory radio program made famous by radio talk show host Art Bell. Art Bell has since retired, but now George Noory is at the mike, continuing the tradition. This features program information, a comprehensive library and photo gallery, and audio recordings of past shows. Focuses on UFOs, extraterrestrial beings, paranormal phenomena, and conspiracy theories.

CSETI–The Center for the Study of Extraterrestrial Intelligence

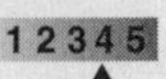

www.cseti.org

This is the site of the only worldwide organization dedicated to establishing peaceful and sustainable relations with extraterrestrial life forms. The organization was founded in 1990 for this specific purpose. This site also has products you can purchase, a schedule of events, and membership information.

CSICOP

www.csicop.org

Hundreds of thousands of people have reported alien abductions, viewings of UFOs, visits by ghosts, and other paranormal experiences, but are these honest, verifiable accounts? The Committee for the Scientific Investigation of Claims of the Paranormal (CSICOP) checks these reports to determine their validity. This site keeps you informed of what the skeptical, scientific community has concluded about many of the most popular claims. Special features include HoaxWatch, SKEPTIC Bibliography, Skeptic's Toolbox, and Klass Files.

International UFO Museum & Research Center

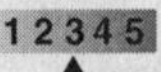

www.iufomrc.com

Learn more about the infamous Roswell, New Mexico, incident of 1947 at this site, which hopes to educate and inform the public about UFOs. The library provides UFO-related articles and research. Sales in the gift shop support the work of this organization. Take a virtual tour of the museum, check out the exhibits, and read about upcoming events. There are also links to the City of Roswell and other museums in New Mexico.

Best The J. Allen Hynek Center for UFO Studies

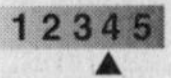

www.cufos.org

This organization is dedicated to exploring and studying reports of UFOs and is asking for help in keeping its files current. You can search the archive of articles and UFO sightings, as well as add to them with your own stories and reports. You can also read about famous sightings here. UFO FAQs also available in Spanish, French, Dutch, Italian, and Portuguese.

The Center for UFO Studies (CUFOS) is an international group of scientists, academics, investigators, and volunteers dedicated to the continuing examination and analysis of the UFO phenomenon. The purpose of this organization is to promote serious scientific interest in UFOs and to serve as an archive for reports, documents, and publications about the UFO phenomenon.

Kidnapped by UFOs?

www.pbs.org/wgbh/nova/aliens

The *Nova Online!* program on abductions is likely the best, most balanced presentation available on the topic of UFO abductions. Features a balanced view by providing expert opinions from the two conflicting camps: believers and skeptics. Read an interview with Carl Sagan, Philip Klass, or Bud Hopkins.

MUFON

1 2 3 4 5

www.mufon.com

Dedicated to the "systematic collection and analysis of UFO data with the ultimate goal of learning the origin & the nature of the UFO phenomenon." Here, you can report a sighting, get the latest UFO news and information, find out more about MUFON, join MUFON, and purchase UFO books and other publications online. Check out the FAQs, UFO Fast Facts, and the events calendar.

National UFO Reporting Center

1 2 3 4 5

www.ufocenter.com

The latest sightings reported to the National UFO Reporting Center. Have you seen a UFO? Then you can file a report at this site, too, or by calling the site's Hotline telephone number. Read about recent activities and highlights and peruse the Data Bank.

Rense.com

1 2 3 4 5

www.rense.com

The Jeff Rense radio show has a home on the Web, and this is it. Here, you'll find unfiltered news covering all sorts of topics including mainstream news stories, UFO and alien reports, and plenty of conspiracy theories. Watch a secret NASA video about UFOs and check out the UFO event maps.

U UFO Database

1 2 3 4 5

www.larryhatch.net

This database contains 20 years' worth of information on UFO sightings around the world. Filtered out of the database are any hoaxes and reports that have little evidence to back them up. Included are reports of UFOs of all sizes and shapes and of alien abductions that have some level of truth. You can browse by world map, regional map, or thematic map. Find out how to report a UFO sighting and click on the selected links for more UFO information.

UFO Info

1 2 3 4 5

www.ufoinfo.com

Get updates regarding sightings and abduction reports, news from around the world, publications, books, TV and radio programs devoted to UFOs, links, and other related articles and information about the site and how it functions (with the help of volunteers around the world). You can purchase dozens of books, CDs, and DVDs related to this subject from the online e-store by using secure credit card ordering. Need to report a sighting? Use the sighting report form to send information online.

UFO Roundup

1 2 3 4 5

ufoinfo.com/roundup

The latest weekly sightings roundup from Joseph Trainor. This Australian site offers lots of books, CDs, and videotapes in its online store. Most of these are through such online retailers as Amazon.com. You'll also find about 20 UFO-related reports. These professional, authentic reports are factual, straightforward, and interesting. This is an excellent source for UFO-related materials. Find links to space exploration sites and more.

UFO Seek

www.ufoseek.com

Comprehensive directory of UFO and paranormal information and resources. Search the directory by keyword or phrase, or browse by categories including alien abductions, near death experiences, and millennium prophecies, to name just a few. There is also a UFO Seek message board.

U.S. GOVERNMENT INFORMATION/ SERVICES

Center for Defense Information

www.cdi.org

The Center for Defense Information (CDI) "is dedicated to strengthening security through: international cooperation; reduced reliance on unilateral military power to resolve conflict; reduced reliance on nuclear weapons; a transformed and reformed military establishment; and, prudent oversight of, and spending on, defense programs." At this site, you can check out the latest information on the hot spots in defense, including arms control, arms trade, the Middle East, nuclear issues, space security, and terrorism. There are also newsletters and information about how you can support CDI.

Related Site

www.whitehouse.gov/response

Central Intelligence Agency

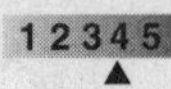

www.cia.gov

Learn all about the CIA, what it does, how to be considered for employment, which agencies report into it, what announcements the organization has made recently, and what publications it has produced. Links to the CIA Factbook and an index of articles are included. You'll also find FAQs and related links here.

Citizenship and Immigration Services

uscis.gov/graphics

Formerly the Immigration and Naturalization Service, the USCIS manages immigration and citizenship services and enforces immigration laws. Here, you can find immigration forms, information about fees and fingerprinting, details concerning immigration laws, a guide to the United States for new immigrants, and more. Interested in working for the U.S. federal government? Check out the USAJobs link for available positions.

Congressional Budget Office

12345

www.cbo.gov

If you wonder where all the facts and figures about government income and spending come from, most of them probably come from the Congressional Budget Office. Here, you can find the monthly budget report, budget projections, economic projections, historical data, and much more. Site also features a Visitor's Gallery, where you can learn more about the Congressional Budget Office. Job opportunities, internships, and fellowships are also available here.

DefenseLINK

www.defenselink.mil

The Department of Defense is responsible for providing the military forces needed to deter war and protect the security of our country. Visit this site to learn of the latest progress in the war on terrorism and on those countries that threaten our homeland security. You can also search for civilian jobs, browse through photos, and read special reports.

A B C D E F G H I J K L M N O P Q R S T U V W X Y Z

Department of Commerce

1 2 3 4 5

www.commerce.gov

Responsibilities include expanding U.S. exports, developing innovative technologies, gathering and disseminating statistical data, and predicting the weather. Find information about economic growth, free trade, and international outreach here. You can also review job listing if you're looking for a government job.

Department of Education

1 2 3 4 5

www.ed.gov

The mission of the Education Department is to ensure equal access to education and to promote educational excellence for all Americans. Information is available for students, parents, teachers, and administrators. In particular, you'll find listings for financial aid, grants and contracts, research statistics, policies, and programs. A job link is also provided for anyone interested in working for the U.S. Department of Education.

Department of Energy

1 2 3 4 5

www.energy.gov

The U.S. Department of Energy (DOE) works to foster a secure and reliable energy system and to be a responsible steward of the nation's nuclear weapons. There is information available for educators, students, and kids. Links to the environment, energy efficiency, and national energy labs are here, too, as are DOE job listings.

Department of Health and Human Services

1 2 3 4 5 RSS

www.os.dhhs.gov

Health and Human Services is responsible for protecting the health and well-being of Americans through programs such as Medicare and disease research to aid in prevention. The website provides information about the wide range of HHS programs, from disease and conditions, safety and wellness, families and children, disasters and emergencies, and more. Information on employment and training opportunities can also be found here.

Department of Homeland Security

1 2 3 4 5

www.dhs.gov

Created in response to the attack on 9-11, the Department of Homeland Security (DHS) is responsible for ensuring the safety of U.S. citizens against attacks from foreign countries and from terrorists at home and abroad. This department is also responsible for keeping citizens informed and helping them prepare for potential attacks. Information and links to emergency and disaster-related information, travel and transportation, immigration and borders, and more can be found on this site. Careers with the DHS are also listed.

Department of the Interior

1 2 3 4 5

www.doi.gov

The Department of the Interior protects and provides access to our nation's natural and cultural heritage. Part of this mission involves honoring our responsibilities to Native American tribes. Find information about the National Park Service, Bureau of Reclamation, U.S. Fish & Wildlife Service, Bureau of Indian Affairs, and more. There are also links to pages for children, teachers, and jobseekers.

Department of Justice

1 2 3 4 5

www.usdoj.gov

As the largest law firm in the nation, the Department of Justice (DOJ) serves as counsel for its citizens. It represents them in enforcing the law in the public's interest. Other information includes current news and job listings with the DOJ.

Department of Labor

1 2 3 4 5

www.dol.gov

The Department of Labor helps to prepare Americans for work and attempts to ensure their safety while on the job. Read topics concerning wages, health plans and benefits, and unemployment insurance. Also includes information for workers, employees, and jobseekers.

Department of State

12345

www.state.gov

The Department of State is the institution for the conduct of American diplomacy, a mission based on the role of the secretary of state as the president's principal foreign-policy adviser. Search information about issues and the press, travel and business, and youth and education. Current news items are also included.

Department of Transportation

12345

www.dot.gov

Serves as the focal point in the federal government for the coordinated national transportation policy and safety efforts. Read about topics on airline issues, drug and alcohol testing rules, and motor carrier companies. Special features include scenic byways, rail safety technology, national road closure information, and more. Looking for a job with the DOT? Check out their careers link, too.

Department of the Treasury

12345

www.ustreas.gov

The Department of the Treasury has a long history of managing the government's finances; promoting a stable economy; and helping to ensure a safer America promoting a prosperous and stable American and world economy, manage the government's finances, safeguard the financial systems, protect government leaders, secure a safe and drug-free America, and build a strong institution. On this site, you will find direct links to taxpayer information, buyers and collectors, money management, FAQs, and job opportunities. The entire site is also available in Spanish.

Department of Veterans Affairs

12345

www.va.gov

The Department of Veterans Affairs (VA) website is a resource of information on VA programs, benefits, and facilities worldwide. View VA jobs, the Kids page, VA organizations, and business opportunities.

Environmental Protection Agency

12345

www.epa.gov

Learn about pending environmental legislation, recent reports and updates regarding hazardous substances, speeches and testimony, emerging environmental issues, and more at this site. There is a special Kids page where kids can learn all about the environment. A career page and FAQs also included.

Federal Bureau of Investigation

12345

www.fbi.gov

Learn all about the FBI. Read the FBI's Most Wanted Fugitives list, see what investigations are underway, learn about the Freedom of Information Act, and more. You can also learn how to apply for a job with the FBI. This site also includes a page for kids.

Federal Citizen Information Center

12345

www.pueblo.gsa.gov

The folks with all the free publications. Most can be obtained online from the website. You can read these free publications or order them online. You can get information on dozens of topics, including consumer help, education, employment, federal programs, food, health, housing, money, recalls, travel, and scams/frauds. Read through the list of FAQs, and check out links to more great information.

Federal Trade Commission

12345 RSS

www.ftc.gov

Learn about what this agency does to protect consumers and educate yourself about protection through articles and publications, news releases, legal action reports, and other information about the inner workings of this organization. On this site, you can read about the history of the organization, learn about the Fair Credit Reporting Act, find jobs at the FTC, or file a complaint. The entire site is also available in Spanish.

A B C D E F G H I J K L M N O P Q R S T U V W X Y Z

FedStats

1 2 3 4 5

www.fedstats.gov

Statistics from more than 100 government agencies. Many agencies provide statistical reports in the form of downloadable PDF files only. Also provides links to several kids pages.

FedWorld Information Network

1 2 3 4 5

www.fedworld.gov

Search for documents, reports, and forms generated by U.S. government agencies through this searchable site. You can also use this site to search for jobs with the federal government, look for government research and development publications, and view full texts of U.S. Supreme Court decisions.

FirstGov

1 2 3 4 5 RSS

www.firstgov.org

Billing itself as "Your First Click to the U.S. Government," this site acts as an information kiosk to help citizens, businesses and not-for-profits, and other government agencies find their way around Washington, D.C. Here, you can start your search to find out how to secure government benefits, find a government job, check your Social Security status, apply for student loans, and access other federal government services. This official site of the U.S. government is intended to put government within easy reach of its citizens and reduce some of the paperwork involved.

MarineLINK

1 2 3 4 5

www.usmc.mil

Learn what it takes to be a Marine; stay current on Marine news; read about commemorative events for veterans, current leadership, history, and traditions; and find out how to be considered for the Marines. View publications and promotional videos. Comprehensive information on all things related to the Marines can be found at this site.

Peace Corps

1 2 3 4 5

www.peacecorps.gov

Read stories of true Peace Corps volunteer adventures, learn about what it means to be a volunteer, how you can become a volunteer, and apply for the opportunity online. Learn more about the Peace Corps by reading the history pages. Don't want to join? You can still work for the Peace Corps; just click on the agency job link for more information. French and Spanish versions of this site are also available.

U.S. Army

www.army.mil

Read about the leadership and management of the Army as well as news regarding current issues and events, find out what it means to be in the Army and where installations are, and get access to an archive of Army information you can search. Find out how you can support the troops, and read soldier stories.

U.S. Navy

www.navy.mil

Learn all about the Navy, its ships and submarines, job opportunities, and news here, where you can also post a question to be answered by a naval officer. You can also view photos of ships and subs. Interested in a Navy career? This site has the information you need; just click on the Careers link.

United States House of Representatives

1 2 3 4 5

www.house.gov

Find out what issues are being debated on the House floor this week, check on the voting histories of current representatives, and find out who your local representative is. You can also write to that individual through the site. Search feature allows you to find a bill or a law, voter information, or learn more about the legislative process. Looking for a job? A link to employment with the U.S. House of Representatives is also available.

United States Senate

www.senate.gov

Search the site for your senator or for the specifics of a bill recently passed or under consideration, and view images of fine art on display in the Senate art collection. You can also research legislation and records and learn about the committee system. Visitor information is available.

Welcome to the White House

www.whitehouse.gov

Lots of information about the White House, the current president, and the vice president; access to White House documents, statistics and reports, and issues of the day; as well as information about how the government works and how to track down services you might be entitled to. You'll also find information about touring the White House, including a map and information for those who are handicapped or have special needs. You will find information about the president and other government leaders, as well as news, history, and information for kids. A listing of current news articles is included, and the entire site is also available in Spanish.

VEGETARIAN (*SEE COOKING & RECIPE–VEGETARIAN*)

VETERAN & MILITARY ORGANIZATIONS

Air Force Association

www.afa.org

The AFA is "an independent, nonprofit, civilian aerospace organization that promotes public understanding of aerospace power and national defense." At the site, visitors can learn more about this organization; get information on legislative affairs; find out about membership; and access the online library, links, and event details. Information on awards, scholarships, and grants is also available through this site.

American Battle Monuments Commission

www.abmc.gov

Visit this site to learn more about the work of this commission to honor our war dead, including accessing the names of the hundreds of thousands of war dead since 1917. The site also provides information on national commemorative events scheduled throughout the year. An employment page and FAQs are also included.

The American Legion

www.legion.org

This site offers information about the American Legion's patriotic programs, including education and scholarships, Boy Scouts, flag protection, and more. Also covers veteran health issues. The American Legion was chartered by Congress in 1919 as a patriotic, mutual-help, wartime veterans' organization. Since then, the Legion has offered many services to its members, such as making sure veterans are treated fairly in hiring, getting medical attention, and receiving their rights for serving their country. There are approximately 15,000 Legion posts worldwide with nearly 3 million members. Information about the Legion's programs, membership, and scholarships is also available here.

AMVETS

1 2 3 4 5

www.amvets.org

AMVETS is a nonprofit organization devoted to supporting the U.S. military and its veterans. AMVETS also provides community services that enhance the lives of U.S. citizens. At this site, you can learn more about the organizations and its various programs. Employment information can also be found on this site.

Army and Air Force Exchange Service

1 2 3 4 5

www.aafes.com

AAFES operates close to 11,000 facilities worldwide, supporting 25 separate businesses in 25 countries, as well as in every state. Military personnel can access their accounts online, check out weekly specials, and find locations. Purchase gifts for our troops and find military gifts and collectibles.

A B C D E F G H I J K L M N O P Q R S T U V W X Y Z

Defend America

www.defendamerica.mil

Visit this site to learn the latest information about the U.S. war on terrorism and its efforts in reigning in rogue regimes. You can also visit this site to sign a card thanking our service men and women for fighting to protect the United States. You will also find links to all branches of the military, government sites, and information about how you can support the troops.

Department of Veterans Affairs

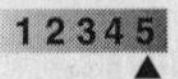

www.va.gov

An up-to-the-minute report about where veterans can go to find out about benefits, facilities, and special programs available to them. There is also information for jobs with the VA, veteran data, and a page for kids. Apply online for compensation and benefits and vocational rehab and employment services.

Disabled American Veterans

www.dav.org

The DAV is a nonprofit organization of more than one million veterans disabled during war. The primary work of the DAV is fighting for and obtaining benefits from various government agencies on behalf of disabled veterans. Veterans need not be members to qualify for this free assistance. The website describes the work the organization does and how individuals can support it. Read more about the DAV's services, learn about legislation, or become a volunteer.

Gulf War Veteran Resource Pages

www.gulfweb.org

This site is focused on providing useful information for Gulf War veterans. You'll find links to FAQs about chronic fatigue syndrome, Veterans Affairs medical centers, and information about chemical warfare and mustard gas. You'll also find a newsletter from Gulf veteran organizations and other support sources. Join a discussion forum or sign up for a referral to the National Gulf War Resource Center.

Korean War 50th Anniversary

korea50.army.mil

Learn more about the history of this conflict and commemorative events surrounding it at this site, where you'll also find images, first-hand interviews, and a Hall of Honor.

Best Military.com

www.military.com

This choice for Best of the Best military sites would make any general proud. It is well designed, up-to-date, and packed with the best information, most interesting articles, and most insightful U.S. military commentary on the Web. Here, young men and women can learn the benefits of serving in the various branches of the military; and all those interested can check out the latest military news, intel, rumors, and opinions. Military books, humor, movies, and everything else you can think of that's related to the military is covered here. Military.com boasts a membership of more than three million and supports all branches of the military—those on active duty, veterans, retirees, reservists, members of the National Guard, defense workers, family members, prospective military personnel, and military enthusiasts. Also includes information on how to find a job, the GI Bill, and tuition assistance, and more.

Military USA

www.militaryusa.com

Military USA is an organization that locates veterans worldwide. The site includes the company's mission, a national reunion registry, a Vietnam veterans database, and a listing of FAQs.

MOAA

1 2 3 4 5

www.moaa.org

An independent, nonprofit organization, MOAA (Military Officers Association of America) is dedicated to serving the members of the uniformed services—active, inactive, and retired, National Guard, and Reserve—and their families, and survivors. MOAA works to preserve earned entitlements and maintain a strong national defense. Six out of 10 retired officers belong to MOAA, as do more than 30,000 active-duty officers. Become a member and join online. Check out the services available including healthcare, educational assistance, finance, and more.

National Coalition for Homeless Veterans

1 2 3 4 5

www.nchv.org

This site provides links to veteran and related organizations, including All Things Military, AMVETS Blinded Veterans Association, Disabled American Veterans, Gulf War Veteran Resource, Jewish War Veterans of the USA, Military Order of the Purple Heart, National Veterans Legal Service Program, and more. Information is also available for homeless veteran services, how you can get involved, and how you can make a donation.

Paralyzed Veterans of America

1 2 3 4 5

www.pva.org

Paralyzed Veterans of America is a congressionally chartered organization devoted to helping veterans who have suffered spinal cord injuries. Members can obtain information and assistance on securing quality healthcare, benefits, and the rights and opportunities they deserve. Site also features updates on medical breakthroughs for treating spinal cord injuries. Provides information for members and spouses, research and education, and the PVA and Capitol Hill. Find out how you can support veterans or apply for a scholarship.

Soldier City

1 2 3 4 5

www.soldiercity.com

Online Army and Navy store with many items for sale, from bags and packs to clothing, flags, and more. Click on the links at the top of the page to access stores related to each military branch.

U.S. Department of Housing and Urban Development Veteran Resource Center (HUDVET)

1 2 3 4 5

www.hud.gov/offices/cpd/about/hudvet/index.cfm

HUDVET provides assistance in securing home mortgages and receiving HUD services through local assistance centers. The website offers information on resources and publications of use to veterans. Learn how you can apply for grants, or find an internship or job with HUD.

Veterans News and Information Service

1 2 3 4 5

www.vnis.com

VNIS is a comprehensive Internet resource for military veterans who are searching for the latest news and information regarding the military veteran community, including Navy, Air Force, Marine Corps, and Army news. Find information about VA home loans, the GI Bill, and other military loans.

VFW: Veterans of Foreign Wars

1 2 3 4 5

www.vfw.org

Dedicated to remembering and supporting U.S. veterans, the VFW is the nation's oldest major veterans' organization. At this site, you can learn more about the organization and its programs and find links to other veterans' organizations and support groups. Learn how you can join the VFW and receive member benefits.

Vietnam Veterans of America

www.vva.org

Founded in 1978, Vietnam Veterans of America (VVA) is "the only national Vietnam veterans organization congressionally chartered and exclusively dedicated to Vietnam-era veterans and their families." This not-for-profit group addresses issues that relate specifically to Vietnam veterans. At this site, you can learn more about the organization, its objectives, and the benefits that Vietnam vets are entitled to. You can also learn more about how to join the VVA and locate a local chapter.

Related Site

www.nps.gov/vive

A B C D E F G H I J K L M N O P Q R S T U V W X Y Z

VETERINARY MEDICINE

AAHA HealthyPet.com

12345

www.healthypet.com

This association of veterinary care providers seeks to help consumers identify qualified hospitals to care for their pets as well as provide basic pet-care information through its online library. Kids will enjoy printing out and coloring in the coloring page, and owners will appreciate the newsletter and FAQs.

American College of Veterinary Surgeons

12345

www.acvs.org

Find out why your pet might need a specialist surgeon and what board certification means. Search the directory for a surgeon near you. Information for veterinary professionals, including continuing education and employment opportunities. Find additional information about the ACVS's mission, research grants, and a newsletter.

Best American Veterinary Medical Association

12345

www.avma.org

The association's official site presents articles from the *Journal of American Veterinary Medical Association,* along with an animal health database, veterinary industry information, and pet-care advice. This site features a lot of news and stories about animals and animal care as well as vet resources and has a members center and a list of allied organizations. The site is well designed and easy to navigate, and you won't have any problems in finding information about animal care here. Career information and employment opportunities are also available on this site.

AVA Online

12345

www.ava.com.au

The Australian Veterinary Association provides online employment, education, and conference references on veterinary medicine. The site also has the latest news stories, current issues, articles on the rural sector, a search engine, and related links. Become a member by using the application form available here.

Center for Veterinary Medicine

12345

www.fda.gov/cvm/default.html

The U.S. Food and Drug Administration's Center for Veterinary Medicine (CVM) "regulates the manufacture and distribution of food additives and drugs that will be given to animals." Regulated items include pet foods and drugs as well as livestock feed and drugs for poultry, cattle, swine, and other farm animals. FAQs and employment information are also available here.

Department of Animal Science: Oklahoma State University

12345

www.ansi.okstate.edu

This site provides information about the Oklahoma State School of Veterinary Science. A map of the campus, descriptions of current research, student resources, and course information are included. Also read information about production and management, the *Animal Science Research Report,* and search job listings.

Interna tional Veterinary Information Service

1 2 3 4 5

www.ivis.org

IVIS is a nonprofit organization dedicated to providing up-to-date information for veterinarians, vet students, scientists, and researchers around the world. You can register for free to gain immediate access to all information, including the library and employment information at the IVIS classified ad section.

Kentucky Equine Research

1 2 3 4 5

www.wehn.com

This site is a resource for equine veterinarians, featuring a bulletin board for exchanging ideas on equine health. Other resources include an archive of the journal *Equine Review* and a calendar of upcoming conferences. Search by regions of North America, Australasia, and International. News and job opportunities are also listed here.

Merck Veterinary Manual

1 2 3 4 5

www.merckvetmanual.com

The Merck Veterinary Manual is one of the most comprehensive reference resources for veterinarians, featuring more than 12,000 articles and 1,200 photos and illustrations. Topics include behavior, circulatory system, pharmacology, and nervous system, to name only a few. Also includes access to reference guides, scholarship programs, and links to other veterinarian-related associations.

Murdoch University: Division of Veterinary and Biomedical Sciences

1 2 3 4 5

www.vetbiomed.murdoch.edu.au

This site, maintained by the Division of Biomedical Sciences at Murdoch University in Western Australia, has information on the school, its programs, faculty, staff, students, studies, alumni, computer-aided learning, and activities, along with a search engine. Read about the Veterinary Trust to learn more about activities and how you can help.

NOAH: Network of Animal Health

1 2 3 4 5

www.avma.org/noah/noahlog.asp

Created and maintained by the American Veterinary Medical Association, NOAH is a network that connects veterinarians "to colleagues, board-certified specialists, and a variety of online-interactive veterinary professional resources." NOAH is designed to provide veterinarians with easy access to the information and resources they need to treat their patients more effectively. To access NOAH, you must be a member of the AVMA and have a login name and password.

OncoLink: Veterinary Oncology

1 2 3 4 5

www.oncolink.com/types/section.cfm?c=22&s=69

This site, provided by the veterinary hospital of the University of Pennsylvania, has information about the diagnosis and treatment of cancer in animals. Read related topics on risk and prevention, screening, treatment options. Have a question? Ask the experts.

Veterinary Pet Insurance

1 2 3 4 5

www.petinsurance.com

Find out why you might want to consider buying pet insurance and the types of insurance products available, how the policy works, and what's covered; then enroll online if you like. Read the FAQs and learn the myths and facts about pet insurance.

Washington State University College of Veterinary Medicine

1 2 3 4 5

www.vetmed.wsu.edu

This site provides a virtual tour of veterinary hospital and service units. Admissions, undergraduate and graduate programs, continuing education, and research are also covered at this site. Request information and apply online.

VIDEO & MULTIMEDIA

Film Festival Today

12345

www.filmfestivaltoday.com

Film Festival Today is an online magazine that features news and announcements from more than 1,600 film festivals around the world along with information for independent filmmakers on topics including new technologies, digital video, DVD rushes, casting agents, financial shortcuts, contract glitches, and tips on working with the unions. Read the Features section for articles, FFT dailies, and archives. Go to Resources for more information on foundations and grants.

Oddcast

12345

www.oddcast.com

Oddcast is a multimedia service company that develops tools such as the Avatar to help media moguls create and roll out interactive, on-demand media products for broadcasting over the Web. At this site, you can check out some of the many tools that Oddcast has developed, learn more about how the company has helped other media companies develop award-winning media products, and even enter some online contests. Careers with Oddcast are also described here.

Without a Box

12345

www.withoutabox.com

Service designed for upcoming filmmakers, Without a Box helps aspiring filmmakers submit their films to various festivals, including Cannes. As a filmmaker, you can submit one video, one press kit, and a single application to Without a Box to have your film distributed to multiple film festivals around the world. Find a listing of upcoming film festivals and events, and competitions. Job opportunities also available.

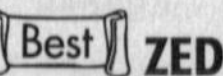 ZED

zed.cbc.ca/go.ZeD?page=home

ZED provides a place where artists can test the boundaries of genre, contributing work in any medium or collection of media they desire. ZED features music, film, video, performance art, visual art, word, and spoken-word forms of expression and exhibits these creations online at this site. Very easy to navigate, packed with original material, and ever evolving, ZED earns a spot as our Best of the Best Site for Video and Multimedia.

DVD

DVD FAQ

12345

www.dvddemystified.com/dvdfaq.html

This site features answers to frequently asked questions about DVD technology, covering everything from definitions and maintenance to compatibility issues.

DVD Price Search

12345

www.dvdpricesearch.com

A site that compares the total cost of purchasing a particular DVD across several sites, telling you which merchant offers you the best deal. The site doesn't sell movies; it just tells you which online merchant has the lowest price. Special offers and coupons are available. Find information on the top DVDs and upcoming and new releases.

dvdfile.com

1 2 3 4 5

www.dvdfile.com

Join in discussions about DVD movies, hardware, and software at this site, which also features industry news, reviews, movie release information, and a long list of movies currently available for rent or purchase in DVD format. Find out information on just about any movie, DVD, or software that you might have an interest in and order online. The site also has interesting information on the most current movies and music.

Netflix.com

1 2 3 4 5

www.netflix.com

This site offers a movie-recommendation search engine and Cinematch, which enables you to see movie suggestions that are geared to your specific preferences. In addition to offering movie reviews, the site also offers online rentals, access to what's playing when at your local theater, ticket sales, and streaming movies. Choose from more than 60,000 movies and 200 genres. Free trial memberships are frequently available.

MULTIMEDIA SEARCH ENGINES

120Seconds.com

1 2 3 4 5

www.120seconds.com

Offbeat Canadian radio station/media kiosk where you can access all sorts of entertaining audio and flash clips, animation shorts, games, news briefs, and funny stories. Even with a speedy cable-modem connection, downloads can take eons.

Lycos Entertainment

multimedia.lycos.com

Lycos is an excellent general-purpose web search engine, but it also features a separate search tool specifically for tracking down media files, including movie trailers, slide shows, music videos, and animation clips. Search top box office movies and entertainment news.

Real.com

1 2 3 4 5 RSS

guide.real.com

Search for videos and music at this site, which offers a wide range of things to listen to and watch. For movies, you can catch trailers and information about the latest releases, view interviews and animated features, or watch business and educational pieces. For videos, you can look for a particular title for download or research top box office hits and site favorites. Download free games and listen to free radio.

Singing Fish

1 2 3 4 5

search.singingfish.com

For multimedia search engines, Singing Fish has no equal. Clickable check box options enable you to quickly select the type of media—music, movies, radio, TV, news, sports, or finance. You can also specify the file format you want (MP3, Real, Windows, or QuickTime) and specify the desired length of the clips.

VIDEO

Amazon.com

1 2 3 4 5

www.amazon.com

Amazon.com features a huge collection of videos in categories ranging from Action & Adventure to Yoga. Here, you can find VHS or DVD versions of movies, exercise videos, educational videos, indie films, and much more. Search for specific movies by name, director, or favorite actor or browse by category.

> **Tip:** Create your own Wish List—save items you want to purchase, or have someone else purchase for you. After you open a personal account, your information will be saved for future use.

A B C D E F G H I J K L M N O P Q R S T U V W X Y Z

A B C D E F G H I J K L M N O P Q R S T U V W X Y Z

Blockbuster

12345

www.blockbuster.com

Search Blockbuster's database of videos and DVDs for purchase, get news on upcoming releases, learn who won the latest video awards, and watch short films online. There's also a news section called Latest Scoop to keep you in the know regarding the movie industry. Sign up for a free trial offer to have DVDs delivered right to your door (includes free shipping on more than 55,000 titles).

Buy.com

12345

www.buy.com

Search for videos to buy at a discount here, and find out about new releases and top rentals before making your selection. Browse by category, purchase gift certificates, and set up a wish list.

Hollywood Video

12345

www.hollywoodvideo.com

Hollywood Video is a video store that features a huge collection of DVDs for rent or purchase. You can search for movies, check out the recommendations, find special offers, see which movies will be coming soon, and more. At the My Hollywood area, you can create your own wish list, rate movies, and check on movies you've rated. Gift certificates are available for purchase here.

Outpost

12345

www.outpost.com

At Outpost, you can search for specific movies by title or browse by categories, including Action/Adventure, Anime, Collector Sets, Comedy, Family, and Science Fiction. The categories are somewhat limited, making it difficult to browse for movies, but if you know specifically what you want and you want more mainstream DVD selections, Outpost has a good collection.

Reel.com

12345

www.reel.com

Information kiosk for movies on DVD and VHS. Find out about new releases, check out the movie reviews, and even go behind the scenes in Hollywood to learn about your favorite celebrities and their latest projects. A kids section lets parents know what new movies are available. Links to Amazon.com for purchasing videos.

Suncoast Video

12345

www.suncoast.com

Suncoast Video is one of the most popular and well-stocked DVD and VHS video stores around. Here, you can shop online, search for movies by title or person (actor or director, for example), and locate some deals on the bargain rack. Suncoast also carries a good collection of anime. Check out new releases, purchase used DVDs at bargain prices, and purchase gift certificates here.

Things from Another World

12345

www.tfaw.com

Looking for classic movies you can't find elsewhere? Then turn to tfaw.com for the best movies from the past. You can search for specific movies by title or browse by date, genre, brand, series, or title. Both DVD and VHS formats are available. The opening page is excellent for specific searches, but if you want to browse, click the DVD or VHS tab near the top of the page for a list of clickable categories. Find out about new releases, and set up a wish list for your favorite movies.

VITAMINS & SUPPLEMENTS

eNutrition.com

1 2 3 4 5

www.enutrition.com

Get tips for managing your weight and improving your health. Also find information on sports nutrition, body and senses, and vitamins through useful short articles at the site. And then buy the products you need to get the results you want, such as appetite suppressants, vitamins, meal replacements, and much more, organized by brand and category. Also includes a listing of top-selling brands.

Medline Plus

www.nlm.nih.gov/medlineplus/vitaminsandminerals.html

Medline Plus covers all aspects of human health. This particular page focuses on vitamins and supplements. Site features the latest reports and warnings on various vitamins and minerals along with links to other useful sites. This site also has information on health-related topics, drugs and supplements, a dictionary, encyclopedia, directory, and other resources.

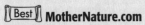

Best MotherNature.com

1 2 3 4 5

www.mothernature.com

This site offers a plethora of "natural" products and services aimed at helping you have a healthier lifestyle. You can research health issues, use a Supplement Planner to determine what vitamins are best for you, read customer reviews of products, and purchase vitamins and supplements online. Organic and kosher items are also available, as is information on homeopathy, aromatherapy, sexual health, and pet care. With its huge product line, excellent search tools, and simplified order forms, this site earns its place in the Best of the Best club.

Nature Made

1 2 3 4 5

www.naturemade.com

Nature Made is a large manufacturer of vitamin, mineral, and herbal supplements. Here, you can learn about its products, shop online, research various wellness topics, and check out the wellness profile for your sex and age group. You can search products by name, category, and common needs. Search the map to find retail stores that carry Nature Made products in your area, and Ask the Expert for advice on health, wellness, nutrition, and vitamins and supplements.

Pharmaton

1 2 3 4 5

www.pharmaton.com

Features a collection of natural healthcare products and dietary supplements, including ginsana, ginkoba, and flexium. Read the answers to question about the use of these products in the FAQ section.

Puritan's Pride

1 2 3 4 5

www.puritan.com

Shop online for vitamins, minerals, and other dietary supplements. This site includes health, fitness, and consumer information; a nutrient database; and a listing of live chat events. Top categories include Omega 3 and calcium products, C vitamins, antioxidants, and more. Read about health topics such as recipes, herbal remedies, and homeopathy.

vitacost.com

1 2 3 4 5 Blog

www.vitacost.com/healthshop.html

The site provides information and all-natural products for sale. Read articles in a wide array health topics; view vitamins and supplements; check out the Herbs, Diet, Sports Nutrition, Bath & Beauty, Emergency & Survival, Sexual Health, and other sections. Kosher products are also available for purchase.

VitaminShoppe.com

1 2 3 4 5

www.vitaminshoppe.com

Shop by brand name or product to find vitamins, nutritional supplements, and herbal products here. Find hot new products and weekly specials. Click on the links at the top of the page for information about weight management, sports nutrition, personal care, and books.

VOLLEYBALL

American Volleyball Coaches Association

1 2 3 4 5

www.avca.org

The AVCA site provides up-to-date results, job openings, available playing dates, educational materials, and articles on sports medicine and coaching. If you're interested in becoming a member of AVCA, you can join online. Read information about the AVCA awards, hall of fame, news, and convention. Career resources are also listed.

American Wallyball Association

1 2 3 4 5

www.wallyball.com

Wallyball is volleyball played on a racquetball court. Use this site to read the game's rules, order supplies and equipment, find out where you can play, and get details about different leagues and tournaments. Sign up for free membership registration online.

Best FIVB WWW Home Page

1 2 3 4 5

www.fivb.ch

The FIVB (*Fédération Internationale de Volleyball*) is the governing body of international volleyball. Use this site to learn more about upcoming events and tournaments, worldwide beach volleyball, FIVB meetings, program development, and educational and promotional material. Download the latest issue of *World Volley News.* As the home for the governing body of international volleyball, this site has an edge over the other sites in this category, but its design and content also contribute to making it the Best of the Best site in its class.

NCAA Men's and Women's Volleyball

1 2 3 4 5

www.ncaasports.com

The National College Athletic Association's official site includes information about all NCAA sports, including volleyball. After you pull up the NCAA home page, click the Volleyball link in the navigation bar on the top and click the desired section: Men's volleyball can be found under Spring Sports; women's volleyball can be found under Fall Sports. Schedule and ticketing information can also be found here.

USA Volleyball

1 2 3 4 5

www.usavolleyball.org

Links to youth and Junior Olympic teams as well as rosters for top men's and women's teams (U.S. and international). Read the latest volleyball headlines, shop for volleyball gear, and find out which teams won.

Volleyball.com

1 2 3 4 5

www.volleyball.com

You'll find indoor and outdoor volleyball gear for sale here; tips for improving your form; information on where to play locally; and rankings, schedules, bios, and stats on AVP, college, and Olympic volleyballers. The volleyball forum lets you express your opinion and get advice from fellow volleyball fans. Get the lowdown on training and techniques, building a court, and the history of volleyball.

Volleyball Hall of Fame

12345

www.volleyhall.org

Read the sport's and the hall's history, view photos, see who's been inducted into the hall, send feedback, buy a centennial volleyball, find out how you can support the Volleyball Hall of Fame, and study a map showing where the hall is located in Holyoke, Massachusetts.

Volleyball Magazine

12345

www.volleyballmag.com

Coverage of the sport from the beaches to the hardwood courts. Scores, player features, and forums for volleyball players are included in this site, along with information on subscription. Peruse the archives and read about the current month's features. Includes links to volleyball-related sites.

WAR

America's Wars

www.multied.com/wars.html

History Central provides overviews of the various wars and conflicts that the United States has been involved in, starting with the American Revolution and leading up to Operation Enduring Freedom. When you click a link for a particular war, a page appears with links that provide a brief overview or timeline of the war. Click a link for additional information. The coverage is not very comprehensive; but if you're looking for overviews, this is a great place to start.

AntiWar.com

www.antiwar.com

AntiWar.com features a huge collection of articles and reports on current wars in an attempt to convince nations, particularly the United States, to avoid war at all costs.

Cost of War

costofwar.com

Created and maintained by the National Priorities Project, this site displays a running tab of how much it costs the United States to wage war, both in financial costs and the burden on our communities and on the world.

DEBKAfile

12345

www.debka.com

To find out what's really going on in Israel and the rest of the Middle East, check out the DEBKAfile. This independent Internet publication features investigative reports and analysis focusing on "international terrorism, intelligence, international conflicts, Islam, military affairs, security and politics." Israeli-based, DEBKAfile is updated seven days a week in both English and Hebrew.

DefendAmerica

www.defendamerica.mil

DefendAmerica is the U.S. Department of Defense news site designed to keep citizens informed concerning progress in the war on terror. Site features a link to various ways citizens can support the troops, profiles of various military personnel, lists of fallen warriors, and links to the home pages of the various branches of the military.

GlobalSecurity.org

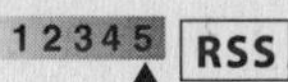

www.globalsecurity.org

GlobalSecurity.org is dedicated to making the world a more secure place by keeping people informed about what's really going on. Here, you can learn about special weapons, intelligence, homeland security, space, and cyberspace security. Some of the information is understandably less than forthcoming, but this site does provide a great deal of useful military data.

Imperial War Museum

12345

www.iwm.org.uk

This British site covers the major wars of the twentieth century, addressing all aspects of the war, abroad and at home. Here, you can view the history of the weapons of war, find out how war affected those on the homefront, and peruse various historical documents. An excellent place to go to research World War I and World War II.

Institute for War and Peace Reporting

www.iwpr.net

In an attempt to present both sides of the story and provide a balanced view of what's going on in the hot spots around the globe, the Institute for War and Peace Reporting features perspectives that commonly pitch intent against reality. Site is accessible in several languages and seeks assistance from anyone who can contribute information or expertise.

Jane's Information Group

www.janes.com

Jane's Information Group provides intelligence and analysis on national security issues, risks, and international defense to governments, militaries, business leaders, and academics in more than 180 countries. Here, you can access some of the less-classified information, see what Jane's Information Group has to offer, and open an account to gain full access.

Strategy Page

www.strategypage.com

If modern military strategy interests you, check out the Strategy Page, where you can find out what's currently working and not working in the war on terrorism and other conflicts. This site goes behind the scenes to provide visitors with the news that most sources don't make available to the public. The site's design is not award winning, but the information available here is something you can't get anywhere else!

Stratfor Security Consulting Intelligence Agency

www.stratfor.com

Stratfor is a security consulting intelligence agency that business, trade associations, government agencies, and individuals rely on daily to provide "timely, accurate global intelligence, analysis, and forecasting for making their most important strategic decisions." Here, you can sample a small collection of the type of information Stratfor supplies, but only subscribers get the in-depth reporting and analysis for which Stratfor is known. Subscriptions are pricey for the average person; but if you're in a position where you need accurate information and analysis of global events, the service is well worth the price.

AMERICAN CIVIL WAR

AmericanCivilWar.com

americancivilwar.com

Excellent site for learning about the people who were involved in the Civil War and the major events that define it. Feature indexes include a timeline of the Civil War, State Battle Maps, Women in the War, Battle Statistics, and more. A list of the major players and major battles is also included, plus a collection of recommended books and other resources.

The American Civil War Home Page

sunsite.utk.edu/civil-war

Huge directory of American Civil War resources on the Web includes links to music of the era, information about the secession crisis leading up to the war, articles about the presidential elections, images from the war, biographies of those involved, and much more. Nothing fancy here, but the site is updated regularly and features an extensive directory for serious researchers.

Civil War Book Review

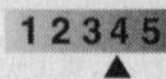

www.cwbr.com

This site features reviews of books about the Civil War and interviews with the authors. The opening page displays a list of reviews available in the current issue, but you can click the Past Issues link to check out books that were previewed in earlier issues.

Best CivilWar.com

RSS

www.civilwar.com

This site features a detailed history of the American Civil War, starting with a timeline of the major events to help you put all the details in perspective.

You can browse through battles by chronology or date; tour battlefields, cemeteries, forts, historic parks, monuments, and museums; listen to the favorite songs of the North and South; and view government documents, personal diaries, and letters from the time. If you're looking to do some research on the American Civil War, make this Best of the Best site your first stop.

The Civil War Home Page

www.civil-war.net

This site is dedicated to all the participants, both North and South, of the great American Civil War. It features a wide range of documents, such as Abraham Lincoln's Emancipation Proclamation and Sullivan Ballou's letter to his wife, a timeline of events leading up to the Civil War, a searchable database of more than 1,000 photos, an index to other Civil War sites on the Web, and much more.

The United States Civil War Center

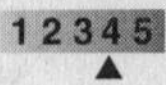

www.cwc.lsu.edu

The United States Civil War Center (USCWC) promotes the study of the American Civil War from various perspectives and disciplines. Here, you can find an index of resources on the Web along with a cemetery database, events calendar, questions page, and virtual exhibits.

COLD WAR

Berlin Wall Online

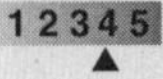

www.dailysoft.com/berlinwall

This site features an interactive history of the Berlin Wall from the time it was built in 1961 to the reunification of East and West Germany in 1990. Links to various areas at the site include Facts, FAQ, Memories, Photographs, and a Timeline.

Best CNN Interactive: Cold War

1 2 3 4 5

www.cnn.com/SPECIALS/cold.war

If you never did grasp what the Cold War was all about, how it started, the tactics involved, and how and why it was eventually resolved, check out CNN Interactive's online special. Here, you can navigate interactive maps, witness rare video footage, read the biographies of the key players, access declassified documents, and tour the Cold War capitals through 3D animations. You can explore this site in any number of ways: access the site one episode at a time, relive the Cold War experience, peruse the knowledge bank, discuss and debate topics online with other interested visitors, take the Cold War Challenge, or view the notes and tips for educators. This site is attractive, easy to navigate, and packed with intriguing information.

The Cold War Museum

1 2 3 4 5

www.coldwar.org

The Cold War Museum consists of a timeline of the Cold War from the 1940s to the 1990s. When you click a decade, a page pops up that includes the key events or individuals in that decade who shaped the Cold War. Click an event or key player to read more. The site also features a Cold War Trivia game to test your history knowledge. Although this site focuses on the Cold War, the site does an excellent job of bridging the Cold War to current events, demonstrating how Cold War developments continue to influence modern politics and military.

Cold War Policies: 1945–1991

history.acusd.edu/gen/20th/coldwar0.html

This site features a basic timeline of the Cold War, starting in Yalta, and ending with the aftermath in the Clinton era. Scan the timeline to get an overview of the events leading up to and contributing to the Cold War and then click individual links in the timeline to learn more. Most of the links call up pages with both text and photos to give you a clear understanding of a particular event.

The National Archives Learning Curve: The Cold War

1 2 3 4 5

www.learningcurve.gov.uk/coldwar/default.htm

This cool, interactive site provides an overview of the Cold War that questions the date on which it really began, along with other commonly held theories. The site's goal is to provide facts and various theories and then leave it up to you to draw your conclusions. Asking tough questions and taking a skeptical view of popular theories is what makes this site much more intellectually interactive than most of the Cold War sites you might encounter. That, coupled with the attractive design and easy-to-use interface, makes this site a close runner up as the Best of the Best in the Cold War category.

National Atomic Museum

1 2 3 4 5

`www.atomicmuseum.com`

The National Atomic Museum features a history of nuclear science and the global politics that drove its development. Here, you can learn about some of the exhibits at the museum and obtain information about the museum, including its location and hours of operation.

KOREAN WAR

History Central: The Korean War

1 2 3 4 5

`www.multied.com/korea`

History Central has done an outstanding job of chronicling the Korean War, from the causes leading up to it to the peace talks that followed it. Site consists of about 20 links, each of which opens a short article on the selected topic along with a photo or two. Not very in depth, but it provides an excellent overview of the war.

Korean War Commemoration

1 2 3 4 5

`korea50.army.mil`

This site commemorates the 50th anniversary of the Korean War. Here, you can find a brief history of the Korean War along with some direct observations from veterans, a chronology of the war, biographies of some of the key figures, maps, photos, and other tidbits.

> **Tip:** When you visit this site, click Enter Site, click History, and then click one of the links that borders the main graphic in the center of the page. The navigation bar at the top isn't the best tool around.

The Korean War

1 2 3 4 5

`www.korea-war.com`

Ed Evanhoe, life member of the Special Forces and Special Operations Associations, created and maintained this site, which features an excellent collection of information about the Korean War. Learn the history and facts about the "Forgotten War," find out which countries were involved, join the discussion lists, and check out some additional recommended reading.

Korean War: The Forgotten War

1 2 3 4 5

`www.military.com/Content/MoreContent1?file=index`

Military.com provides an excellent overview of the Korean War from beginning to end. Links on the left provide an outline of the presentation, and text and photos appear on the right.

Korean War Project

1 2 3 4 5

`www.koreanwar.org`

This site is dedicated to providing support for veterans and family members of the Korean War and to researchers and students of military history. Here, you can find help searching for those killed or missing in action and information about a particular unit. Find out about reunions and possibly even organize one yourself.

VIETNAM WAR

Vets with a Mission

1 2 3 4 5

`www.vwam.com/vets/hisintro.html`

Vets with a Mission is an organization of Vietnam veterans and nonveterans who are committed to "bringing healing, reconciliation and renewal to the people of Vietnam." Site features a breakdown of the various groups that populate Vietnam, a brief early history of the country, a description of the Tet Offensive, and descriptions of what the various branches of the U.S. military did during the War. Site also features projects, photos, and an online store.

Vietnam Online

12345

www.pbs.org/wgbh/amex/vietnam

This site looks back at the most unpopular war in U.S. history. It provides a brief introduction by David McCullough, a biography of the major players in the war, an interactive timeline, reflections from those who were involved at the time, specific notorious events, and a list of references. The tone of this site is one of regret and sadness at the losses both sides experienced.

Vietnam Veterans Memorial

12345

www.virtualwall.org

The Virtual Wall is the online version of the Vietnam Veterans Memorial. Here, veterans are listed in alphabetic order, so you can quickly look up their names, remember their service to the United States, and contribute to their memorials.

Best The Vietnam War Pictorial

12345

www.vietnampix.com

This site provides a highly graphical tour of the Vietnam War—"From the Delta to the DMZ, From Politics to Hippies, This Is the Fire in the Jungle." This site is not intended to provide an accurate documentation of the history of the war, but to provide a graphic tour of the conditions that both sides were subjected to. Tim Page took most of the intense photos that are displayed here. The tour leads you through six sections: Background, Machines, Faces, Hippies, Under Fire, and Life and Sorrow.

The Wars for Viet Nam: 1945–1975

12345

vietnam.vassar.edu

This site, based on course materials developed by Robert Brigham for his senior seminar on the Vietnam War at Vassar College, gives students the opportunity to study official documents related to the war. This site provides an excellent overview of the Vietnam War, including events that led up to it, and features links to the official documents used in Robert Brigham's seminar. Don't miss the Resources link for additional information and resources accessible on the Web.

WAR ON TERRORISM

America's War Against Terrorism

12345 

www.lib.umich.edu/govdocs/usterror.html

From the University of Michigan Library comes this comprehensive directory of links to various sites that offer information related to America's War on Terrorism. Site covers events from September 11, 2001 to the present and touches on all areas of the War on Terrorism, including the September 11th Attack and Its Aftermath, Intelligence, Terrorism Suspects, the Afghan War, Counterterrorism, and Other Countries Involved.

Best BBC News War on Terror

12345 

news.bbc.co.uk/2/hi/in_depth/world/200/war_on_terror/default.stm

The opening page at this site features a collection of links related to the War on Terror, including a timeline of Bin Laden's activities and terrorist network, a guide to key suspects, information on the possible whereabouts of Bin Laden, reports and analysis of the Madrid blasts, an analysis of U.S. strategy in the War on Terror, and much more. Very thorough and up-to-date reports and analysis presented in an attractive, multimedia format.

CNN: War Against Terror

12345 

www.cnn.com/SPECIALS/2001/trade.center

CNN created and maintains this site to keep visitors informed about the progress on the U.S. War on Terrorism, which began with the bombing of the World Trade Center on September 11, 2001. This site features a timeline of events, history and news about the war in Afghanistan and the war in Iraq, interactive areas with maps and photos, CNN's video coverage, and an excellent collection of information on related topics.

United States of America: National Security

1 2 3 4 5 RSS

www.whitehouse.gov/infocus/nationalsecurity/index.html

For the latest information on U.S. strategy for fighting the War on Terror, go to the White House itself. At this site, the White House delineates its National Security Strategy to keep U.S. citizens aware of what their government is doing to keep them safe. Site also features links to other areas that may be of interest, including the Department of Homeland Security's website.

Washington Post: War on Terror

1 2 3 4 5

www.washingtonpost.com/wp-dyn/nation/specials/attacked

The *Washington Post*'s War on Terror page offers the latest news and updates related to America's War on Terror. Coverage includes the wars in Afghanistan and Iraq, terror trials, a history of the 9/11 attacks, progress on the hunt for Bin Laden, and much more.

WORLD WAR I

Encyclopedia of the First World War

1 2 3 4 5

www.spartacus.schoolnet.co.uk/FWW.htm

If you're looking for a comprehensive resource on World War I and you don't mind getting bogged down at a site that's somewhat difficult to navigate, you will find this encyclopedia of the First World War most informative. Here, you can find a complete timeline of events leading up to and through the war, a list of the countries involved and their roles in the war, assessments of the allied armed forces and the central powers, and much more.

Best FIRST WORLD WAR.COM

1 2 3 4 5

www.firstworldwar.com

This site features extensive coverage of World War I, starting with events leading up to the war and proceeding to its end. Site features text, commentary, photos, and even audio clips. A navigation bar on the left side of the page makes it easy to move through the various areas of the site: How It Began, The Battles, Who's Who, War Timeline, Maps, Encyclopedia, Weapons of War, Prose and Poetry, and more. Excellent site that promises to get even better over time.

The Great War

1 2 3 4 5

www.pbs.org/greatwar

Home of the PBS special *The Great War and the Reshaping of the 20th Century*, this site features an interactive timeline of the war, maps and locations, interviews with 20 of the top World War I historians, and recaps of the 8 episodes that made up this award-winning show. You can also order the video collection and book online.

War Times Journal: The Great War

1 2 3 4 5

www.wtj.com/wars/greatwar

This site features a list of archives and articles about World War I. Archives include High Adventure, The Grand Fleet, The Red Fighter Pilot, and Germany's High Seas Fleet. Articles cover the Königsberg Incident, The Western Front, The Eastern Front, and Dark Autumn: The 1916 German Zeppelin Offensive. Most articles include photos and illustrated maps.

World War I Document Archives

1 2 3 4 5

www.lib.byu.edu/~rdh/wwi

Volunteers have compiled this extensive library of World War I documents, including treaties, diaries, commentaries, biographies, and links to other WWI sites. Excellent place to go for in-depth research.

World War I: Trenches on the Web

1 2 3 4 5

www.worldwar1.com

This site focuses on the "people, places, and events that comprised one of the worst calamities of modern history." Scroll down the page to access the links for navigating the site. You can then head out to the reference library, view selected tours of this site, the 1914–1918 super search facility, the WWI discussion forum, or the St. Mihiel Trip Wire.

A B C D E F G H I J K L M N O P Q R S T U V W X Y Z

World War One

www.bbc.co.uk/history/war/wwone

The BBC has put together an incredibly informative and moving site dealing with all aspects of World War I. When you land on the shores of this site, forget about the navigational links on the left—they're for other areas of the BBC's history site. The main area of the home page provides links to the major campaigns and battles, other geographical areas where the war was waged, revolutions in Russia, debates of the time, and more. Off to the right, you can find links to a timeline and a multimedia center, where you can view photos, listen to audio clips, and play animations of the battlefronts.

WORLD WAR II

Axis History Factbook

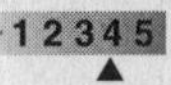

www.axishistory.com

This site is not a pro-Nazi site, but it does focus on the history of the Third Reich. Here, you'll find links to the Axis countries, to equipment used in the war, to various museums, and to information on the Allied countries.

Second World War Encyclopedia

www.spartacus.schoolnet.co.uk/2WW.htm

Incredibly comprehensive resource on World War II that features a complete timeline of events leading up to and through the war; a list of the countries involved and their roles in the war; lists of U.S., British, French, Russian, German, and Japanese military leaders; information on the air war and the sea war; descriptions of French and German resistance; and much more. Without a navigation bar to help you quickly return to the main sections of this site, it is a little difficult to navigate; but if you're looking for in-depth coverage of World War II, you'll find it here.

U.S. National World War II Memorial

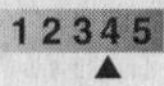

www.wwiimemorial.com

The World War II memorial honors the 16 million people who served in the armed forces of the United States during World War II, the more than 400,000 who died, and the millions who supported the war effort from home. Visit this site to learn more about the memorial and what you can do to show your support.

War Times Journal: World War II

12345

www.wtj.com/wars/wwtwo

This site features a list of current and archived articles about World War II. Articles include "The Normandy Landing," "Marine Scout on Saipan," "The Sinking of the Hyuga and Tone," and "Thunder Gods and Kamikazes." Archived articles include "The Bombing of Hiroshima." Most articles include photos and illustrated maps. The Flash animated map of the Normandy invasion is particularly well done.

World War 2 Timeline

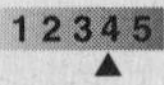

www.worldwar-2.net

This site features a fairly extensive timeline and history of World War II, covering the war in Europe, the Holocaust, the war at sea, the war in the desert, the war in Asia and the Pacific, and how the war affected the Americas. Click the World War 2 on Film link to order World War II videos from Amazon.com.

World War Two

www.bbc.co.uk/history/war/wwtwo

The BBC has designed an engaging and informative site dealing with all aspects of World War II. Ignore the links on the left side of the home page—they're for other areas of the BBC's history site. The main area of the home page provides links to The War Abroad, The Battle of the Atlantic, The Battle of Britain, The Secret War, Politics and Personalities, The Holocaust, and more. Off to the right, you can find links to a timeline and a multimedia center where you can view photos, listen to audio clips, play animations of the battlefronts, and even watch brief video clips.

WATCHES

Fossil

1 2 3 4 5

www.fossil.com

Fossil is one of the cooler sites in the Watch category. It offers the standard fare, enabling you to browse its current designs of both men's and women's watches, but this site also allows you to search online for accessories and apparel, design a watch, enter the Fossil Tin design contest, and shop for watches according to your preferred "vintage."

Rolex

1 2 3 4 5

www.rolex.com

Rolex watches have earned the highest reputation for both quality craftwork and design. Here, you can explore the latest collections of Rolex watches for both men and women, investigate Rolex ambassadors (artists, athletes, and celebrities who sport the Rolex brand), learn more about the Rolex institute, and find out more about Rolex's sponsorship of various athletic events and competitions.

Swatch.com

1 2 3 4 5

www.swatch.com

From the makers of the original Swiss Army Knife comes this site that introduces visitors to its latest line of Swatch watches. Here, you can check out the latest models, shop at the online store, get technical and customer service, find local stores that carry Swatches, and enter online contests.

Tag Heuer

1 2 3 4 5

www.tagheuer.com

Tag Heuer watches are top-of-the-line timepieces—attractively designed and engineered to perfection. Here, you can learn more about the brand, browse the current collections of both men's and women's models, and find authorized dealers.

Timex

1 2 3 4 5

www.timex.com

One of the most popular watch manufacturers, Timex created and maintains this site to introduce its latest models to customers. Here, you can find everything from basic watches to self-winding models and models that can measure your distance, speed, heart rate, and altitude. You can browse the collection by clicking Mens, Womens, Kids, New Products, or Gifts in the navigation bar at the top of the page. You can also find instructions for operating your watch.

Watch Repair FAQ

1 2 3 4 5

elginwatches.org/help/watch_repair.html

This is a good Q&A page on watch repair providing both short and long answers to the most frequently asked questions.

Watches Planet

1 2 3 4 5

www.watchesplanet.com

Watches Planet is a huge online store that carries a wide selection of quality watches for both the budget-conscious and the money-is-no-object crowd. You can search for a specific watch by keyword or model or browse the collection by manufacturer. Site also features separate areas for men's and women's watches and a selection of watches that make great gifts regardless of how much you're willing to spend.

WATER SPORTS

RAFTING

American Whitewater Resources Online

12345

www.americanwhitewater.org

Find out all the specifics about the rivers you will be rafting on before planning your experience. The mission of the AWA is to conserve and restore America's whitewater resources and to enhance opportunities to enjoy them safely. You'll find all kinds of help and information here, especially on safety and what is being done to save the whitewater ways.

GORP: Paddlesports

12345

www.gorp.com/gorp/activity/paddle.htm

GORP's paddlesports site is part of a larger network of sites devoted to outdoor recreation. Here, find out what is featured in the rafting news. Jump to river sites all over the country and the world. Learn how to keep from capsizing, get information on clubs, find books and other media about rafting, and join an online forum devoted to whitewater fans who have shared interests. You'll need to be a member to access most of the quality information.

International Rafting Federation

12345

www.intraftfed.com

The International Rafting Federation is a group of national rafting organizations that are collectively dedicated to ensuring "rafting's future and that of international competition." Site provides links to rafting champs and competitions, guides and guiding, members, newsletters, and the A River Somewhere area (which contains general information and photos related to rafting).

Northwest River Supplies

12345 Blog

www.nrsweb.com

Shop the online rafting catalog or surf the online classifieds to locate used equipment. You can also join the discussions and check out other river-rafting links here.

Riversearch

12345 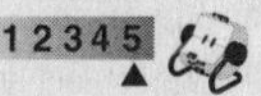

www.riversearch.com

Click on the online map to locate the best rivers for rafting near you as well as outfitters equipped to guide you.

White Water Photos

12345

www.mywhitewaterphotos.com

A photographer's paradise. This site has a great photo gallery that features the American Rivers, Kern River, Merced River, and Pigeon River. If you plan on rafting any of these whitewater rivers, check out this site to learn more about photograph packages of your trip.

Wild and Scenic Rivers

12345

www.nps.gov/rivers

The Wild and Scenic River Act in 1968 called for preserving rivers and their natural environments. This site tells you the history of the act. An exceptional part of this site's information, however, is in the listings of rivers by state, which is fairly exhaustive. Also, find out how you can get involved with agencies whose goal it is to uphold the Wild and Scenic River Act.

Wildwater Rafting

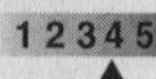

www.wildwaterrafting.com

For whitewater rafting in eastern Tennessee or western North and South Carolina, visit this site. Wildwater Rafting, Ltd. offers a variety of adventure rafting trips for people of all ages. Here, you can also find out about reservations policies, how to dress for a trip, trip pricing, and adventure specials.

Wildwater Rafting in Canada

www.wildwater.com

Wildwater Rafting in Canada is a rafting outfitter near Banff, Alberta, Canada, that guides rafters on adventures in the Kicking Horse River. Here, you can learn more about the company and its trips, check out the rapids ratings, and learn about special offers.

Windfall Rafting

www.windfallrafting.com

Learn more about rafting at this Maine outfitter, which also can provide accommodations and a travel planner. Get more information here or request a brochure.

ROWING

Amateur Rowing Association

www.ara-rowing.org

Home of the governing body of the sport of rowing in Great Britain, this site features information on coaching, development, and competitions. Features a brief article on the history of rowing, plus water safety codes and guidelines. Site also offers an excellent directory of links to other rowing sites.

Independent Rowing News

www.rowingnews.com

Independent Rowing News is a magazine by rowers for rowers. This site lets visitors sample some articles from the current issue, subscribe online, download free desktop wallpaper, and read and post articles in the discussion forums. Click Daily Dose of Rowing for announcements of events and competitions. We would have liked to have seen a little more content from the magazine.

NCAA Women's Rowing

www.ncaasports.com/rowing/womens

This site offers news, feature articles, photos, results, and race recaps for college women's rowing competitions.

Paddling@about.com

paddling.about.com

This site offers comprehensive information about rowing that covers canoes, kayaks, and rafts. Features news, results, links, a chat room, a bulletin board, magazines, outfitters, stores, and more.

River and Rowing Museum

www.rrm.co.uk

Home of the River and Rowing Museum Henley on Thames, this site provides a brief introduction to the museum, along with a few virtual tours, to encourage you to visit. Includes information about various educational programs provided by the museum.

Row Works

www.rowworks.com

The Row Works Clothing Company makes top-quality suits, shorts, winter gear, insulating Lifa Bodywear, and other fine rowing accessories.

Row2K.com

www.row2k.com

Updated daily, sometimes multiple times a day, this site features an excellent collection of news, results, interviews, and general information about the sport of rowing. Here, you can also find an extensive list of rowing camps, online polls, a calendar of upcoming events and competitions, feature stories, several galleries packed with photos, classified ads, and a respectable directory of links to other rowing sites.

Rower's World

rowersworld.com

Comprehensive rower's resource contains news and regatta results, a glossary of terms and rules, images and email postcards, and classifieds. The site is well designed and easy to navigate, which makes finding the information that you want almost as much fun as rowing itself. You'll find a nice search feature that will help you find what you want, a section with diaries and columns, and lots of stories, and you can even shop at an online store for items you may want to purchase.

Rowing FAQ

www.ruf.rice.edu/~crew/rowingfaq.html

Extensive collection of basic rowing information and terminology. Includes contact information for some of the larger rowing associations.

The Rowing Service

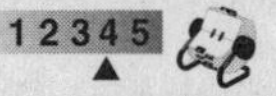

users.ox.ac.uk/~quarrell

This British page offers news, crew notices, race reports, coaching and technical information, and more. Site is a little archaic and not the easiest to navigate, but it features a treasure-trove of information and links to related resources on the Web.

RowingLinks—The Internet's Definitive Source for Rowing Links

www.rowinglinks.com

You can find all kinds of links to sites about the fine art of rowing your boat. Offers information about the sport all around the globe.

Simply OarSome

www.oarsome.com.au

This Australian company has been supplying the Australian Rowing Team since 1989. You can view its entire catalog and order all the gear online. You'll also find WWW rowing links and results from major rowing events.

USRowing

www.usrowing.org

Home of the organization that's dedicated to promoting and supporting the sport of rowing in the United States. Here, you can learn more about the organization and its members, get the latest rowing news and results, view a list of upcoming USRowing events, obtain information about the national team, and more.

Vespoli USA

www.vespoli.com

This commercial site promotes Vespoli racing shells. It discusses the shells' speed and value as well as the company's quality assurance and service.

WorldRowing.com

www.fisa.org

Home of the *Fédération Internationale des Sociétés d'Aviron* (FISA, in French), or the English equivalent International Federation of Rowing Associations. FISA is the international governing body of the sport of rowing. This site provides information about the organization, the events and competitions it sponsors, rowing news from *World Rowing Magazine*, competition results and standings, best times, and much more. Also features a photo gallery, a list of the top rowers, and an online version of FISA's rulebook. Links to stores where you can purchase FISA apparel online. Links to the World Champion Sports Network for webcasts.

WWW Virtual Library: Rowing

archive.museophile.sbu.ac.uk/rowing

Features a comprehensive rowing directory. It includes information about regattas, Olympic results, and links to rowing publications and newsgroups.

SCUBA DIVING

Aqua Lung

12345

www.aqualung.com

More than 60 years ago, Jacques Cousteau and Emile Gagnan developed the first aqua-lung. Since then, an entire company has sprouted up, offering a complete line of diving equipment. Visit this site to check out Aqua Lung's product line, use the interactive equipment selector, or find a dealer near you.

Beneath the Sea

www.beneaththesea.org

BTS is a not-for-profit organization that works toward increasing awareness of the earth's oceans and the sport of scuba diving. BTS helps promote the protection of marine wildlife via grants to other nonprofit groups. Includes links to seminars, workshops, mailing lists, and other diving-related sites.

DAN: Divers Alert Network

12345

www.diversalertnetwork.org

Divers Alert Network (DAN) is "a non-profit medical and research organization dedicated to the safety and health of recreational scuba divers and associated with Duke University Medical Center (DUMC)." Site features a navigation bar on the left that contains links for Membership, Insurance, Diving Medicine, Medical Research, Training & Education, and a Product Catalogue.

Deep Sea Divers Den

12345

www.divers-den.co

Based in Far North Queensland, Australia, Deep Sea Divers Den includes scuba diving to the Great Barrier Reef. Offers scuba diving courses in Cairns, Australia, at all levels, as well as one-day trips to the Great Barrier Reef for snorkelers and divers. PADI certification is available. You are asked to email for information on registering or signing up for the courses and other activities.

Doc's Diving Medicine

faculty.washington.edu/ekay

Dedicated to undersea medicine and issues of diving safety for sport and professional divers. This site offers information on diving safety and links to other sites where you can learn even more.

Gooddive.com

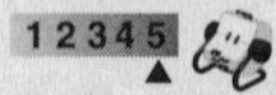

www.gooddive.com

Gooddive.com is "a scuba diving portal made for divers and professionals," both beginners and advanced. This site offers an excellent directory of links to scuba diving sites. The Gooddive team of professional divers and enthusiastic hobby divers hand pick all links, which are organized by category, including Vacation, Equipment, Dive Guide, Maps, Classifieds, Free Stuff, and Photo Gallery.

HSA: Handicapped Scuba Association

www.hsascuba.com

This organization is dedicated to making scuba more accessible to people with physical challenges, and its site appears to be updated frequently. It offers a quarterly journal, travel schedule, guides to wheelchair-accessible dive resorts, an HSA instructor locator page, and training course information for divers interested in becoming HSA dive instructors.

NAUI Online

www.naui.org

This is the National Association of Underwater Instructors website, where serious scuba divers can obtain the information they need. Site features a dive center locator, trainer locator, product catalog, information on NAUI courses, and much more.

PADI: Professional Association of Diving Instructors

www.padi.com

A fantastic site with current information. Updated daily, this site offers the usual dive center listings, BBSes, product catalogs, news, and course listings, and a wide range of information beyond the usual. Also provides plenty of information about PADI diving certification. Site content is divided into three areas: Start Diving, Keep Diving, and Teach Diving. Great site for both novice and expert scuba divers and their instructors.

Scuba Central

scubacentral.com

A goodpoint of entry for all scuba divers, this site provides a directory of the top scuba links and travel resources. Site also features a great article on debunking scuba diving fears that dispels common myths to allay the fears of those who are considering testing the waters.

Best Scuba Diving Magazine

www.scubadiving.com

Scuba Diving magazine is a publication that introduces divers to the best diving destinations, explains techniques and tips to help you dive safely and enjoyably, offers a great collection of underwater photographs in every issue, provides gear reviews, and presents news and information about divers and tours. At this site, you can sample articles and photos from the magazine and use the navigation bar at the top of the opening page to skip to your desired area of interest: Gear, Travel, Community (discussion forums, contests, and top 10), Training, and Photo/Video (tips and techniques for taking photos and recording video under water).

Scuba Schools International

www.ssiusa.com

Scuba Schools International provides scuba diving education and training through its international network of affiliates. The organization sets the standards by which its affiliates operate, ensuring quality and safety throughout its schools. At this site, you can learn more about SSI's system of training and can search for diver services, dive leader services, and dealer services.

Scuba Yellow Pages

www.scubayellowpages.com

Search this worldwide directory to find contacts and suppliers for all your scuba diving needs—from tour operators to airlines to clubs and certifications. The site also offers tons of information, a divers directory, a search feature to help you quickly locate information, email, and lots of divers' resources. If you're interested in diving for fun or profit, this is the place to locate equipment you need and other resources to make your dive much more successful no matter what your reason for diving.

ScubaDuba

www.scubaduba.com/index.html

Encourages active participation from divers. Requests that visitors submit diving-related articles or stories of interest. It offers classified ads, a buddy directory, a chat room, and photos. Here, you can search through more than 1,600 listings.

A B C D E F G H I J K L M N O P Q R S T U V W X Y Z

Skin Diver Online

www.skin-diver.com

With destination guides, gear info, instruction how-tos, and shopping options, you'll want to see what's here. Features interesting articles from *Skin Diver* magazine, Ask the Pro questions and answers, and medical information.

Sport Diver

1 2 3 4 5

www.sportdivermag.com

Read feature articles from this magazine about dive spots, track down dive operators and hotels, and get gear and instruction information. Learn about diving and the beautiful places you might want to experience. Very flashy site design makes you want to dive right in.

Sub-Aqua Association

www.saa.org.uk

Visit this home of "the friendliest divers in the world." This organization was founded more than 20 years ago by various British dive clubs to promote diving issues nationally. The site is professional and detailed, including a URL minder service to notify you via email any time the site is updated.

YMCA Scuba Program

www.ymcascuba.org

A good source of general information, such as a list of courses offered at the Y. This site also contains instructions on how to replace a lost C-card, which is a requirement for any diver. This site offers a quarterly journal, too, along with special areas for diabetic and asthmatic divers.

SNORKELING

About Snorkeling

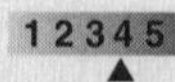

scuba.about.com/od/snorkelskills/a/snorkelingtips.htm

About's Scuba Diving Guide provides you with seven tips for snorkeling safely and having fun doing it. Site also features a small collection of links to other About snorkeling content, including a primer on how to teach kids to snorkel and a list of suggested reading.

Beachfront Snorkeling

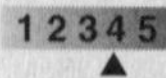

www.bfsng.com/snorkel

Beachfront Snorkeling's mission is "to become the starting point for snorkeling information on the Web," providing information on snorkeling, snorkeling locations, and snorkeling equipment. Site features maps and directions, snorkeling techniques and tips, dive guides, photos and photo tips, and a respectable directory of links to other top snorkeling websites.

BSAC Snorkeling

www.bsacsnorkelling.co.uk

BSAC (British Sub Aqua Club) presents this site to introduce water lovers to the underwater world of snorkeling. Site covers First Steps, Training, Activities, and Advice. Site features an excellent collection of snorkeling games that can help you hone your skills while having fun.

Snorkeling Basics

www.tomzap.com/snorkel.html

Good article on snorkeling basics explains mask and snorkel selection criteria, the purpose of fins, how to use your mask and snorkel, how to clear your ears, snorkeling hazards, snorkeling at night, and selecting a good site to snorkel.

A B C D E F G H I J K L M N O P Q R S T U V W X Y Z

SURFING

Board Building

www.viser.net/~anthwind

This library of links related to surfboard building includes links to board design, shaping, repair, tools, and fins. Includes a section on CAD (computer-aided drafting).

Closely Guarded Secrets of the UK Surfing World

www.britsurf.org/UKSurfIndex

A thorough and well-designed site for surfing in the United Kingdom. Features include listings of surf clubs and schools, an online surf shop, links to surfing magazines and the British Surfers Association, and much more.

Coastal British Columbia

www.surfingvancouverisland.com

This great site gives you all kinds of information about surfing. Even if you don't want to go surfing in British Columbia, you should check out the great pictures and information on this page. It has weather and wave information as well as good stories, photos, and other sporting information. If you like to surf and are interested in more information about some of the best surfing locations, enjoy a good story, and want to see photos of what you can expect when you get there, this is the site to find out about all that. It also has a free classified ad section for you.

International Surfing Museum

www.surfingmuseum.org

At this site, you can view the collection of surf films, surf music, surfboards, and memorabilia. Visit the current exhibit, too. If you like this site, consider becoming a member.

SG Magazine

www.sgmag.com

SG (Surfer/Snowboarder/Skater Girl) magazine is devoted to women who love to surf, snowboard, and skate. Site features a good collection of photos and videos, a Babewatch area, feature stories, industry news and links, travel reports, and more.

Surf World Museum–Torquay

www.surfworld.org.au

Located in Australia's surfing capitol, Torquay, Australia, the Surf World museum is the self-proclaimed "largest surfing and beach culture museum in the world." Here, you can check out its exhibits and even view new and vintage surf movies to relive the golden era of surfing in Australia.

Surfermag.com

www.surfermag.com

The *Surfermag* site features up-to-the-minute headlines and pictures, video clips of surfers in action, a bulletin board, product reviews, a surf report, an online surf shop, plenty of excellent photos, and subscription information. Use the navigation bar at the top of the page to jump to the desired content: Video, Features, Photos, Radio, Community, Magazine, Travel, or Fantasy Surfer (a fantasy surfer contest for men or women).

Surfing Magazine

www.surfingthemag.com

Surfing Magazine offers feature articles, news, wave reports, photos, and videos. You can preview the current issue of the magazine and subscribe online. Site also features links to its sister magazines that cover snowboarding, skateboarding, and biking.

Surfing in South Africa

www.wavescape.co.za

This site offers you an extensive guide to surfing in South Africa with travel information, surfing spots, photos, daily surf reports, stories, cartoons, surfer slang, and a lot more. You can access the various content areas through the navigation bar at the top of the opening page: Arrivals, Departures, Spots, Surf Report, Photos, Chat, Gear, or Tidings. Site also offers plenty of surfer stories and profiles. Don't ignore the navigation bar at the bottom of the page.

Surfline

www.surfline.com

Billing itself as "The Best Place on the Net to Get Wet," this site provides up-to-date reports and live webcams of the best places to surf worldwide. The site also features product reviews and plenty of articles about surfing and the world's top surfers. Along the left side of the page is a navigation bar that contains the names of the top surfing destinations all around the world. Simply click the name of a destination to receive a beach report detailing the surfing conditions. The Surfology area contains an excellent collection of surfing tips and technique along with a Surfology glossary. Before you head to the beach, check out this site, so you can "know before you go."

Surfrider Foundation USA

www.surfrider.org

The Surfrider Foundation is a nonprofit group dedicated to protecting, preserving, and restoring the world's oceans and beaches. Its site includes daily surf reports, Coastal Factoids, policy updates, and an online membership form.

WSP Sports

www.wsp-sports.com

A thorough windsurfing database divided into organized categories. Board reviews, travel reviews, weather information, wind calculator, and links. Site covers wind surfing, kite boarding, and paddle sports.

SWIMMING

Australia Swimming

www.swimming.org.au

Australia Swimming is home to one of the top swim teams in the world. Here, you can learn about upcoming meets; get great information for swimmers, coaches, and parents (via the Club Swimming link); obtain team information and swimmer profiles; check out the photo galleries; and access audio and video clips in the Media Library.

CDC: Healthy Swimming

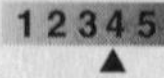

www.cdc.gov/healthyswimming

The Centers for Disease Control created and maintains this site to inform swimmers, coaches, parents, and poolkeepers on the essentials of water-transmitted diseases and how to prevent them. This site identifies common diseases, explains how they're spread and why chlorine doesn't kill them, and presents healthful practices to help prevent them.

D&J Sports

www.djsports.com

Speedo, Tyr, and Dolfin competition and fashion swimwear, plus caps, clothing, accessories, and other equipment. Use the secure online shopping cart.

FINA

12345 RSS

www.fina.org

FINA is the international governing organization of amateur aquatic sports. FINA, based in Switzerland, is a worldwide policy maker in all swimming, diving, synchronized swimming, water polo, open water, and Masters swimming sports. Read articles on the latest developments in aquatic sports. Check out the FINA calendar of events and find out the latest competition results. Learn about FINA's history, regulations, and members. You can also purchase related publications and videos from FINA.

International Swimming Hall of Fame

www.ishof.org

The International Swimming Hall of Fame is a not-for-profit educational organization. It annually honors the world's greatest aquatic heroes and preserves the sport's history. It serves as a worldwide focal point of swimming, diving, water polo, and synchronized swimming. Learn about the history of the Swimming Hall of Fame, the membership, and ways to make a donation. Includes a calendar of events, information on programs and activities, and an excellent directory of links to other swimming websites.

NCAA Men's Swimming and Diving

www.ncaasports.com/swimming/mens

National College Athletic Association official site. Includes schedules, ticket information, records, results, and previews.

NCAA Women's Swimming and Diving

www.ncaasports.com/swimming/womens

Official guide to the three divisions of the National College Athletic Association championships. Site features recaps, psyche sheets, and results.

STORMFAX Safe Ocean Swimming Guide

www.stormfax.com/safeswim.htm

This site discusses the major causes of accidents and ways you can avoid injury while enjoying your favorite activity. You learn about various dangerous surf conditions and even get the average water temperatures (by month) for various spots on the Atlantic coasts. You also learn how to use the Beaufort Wind Scale, which includes World Meteorological Organization wind descriptions and their effects on land and sea.

Swimmers Guide Online

www.swimmersguide.com

Contains a database of international, accessible, full-size, year-round pools (18,000+ currently). Each listing includes the name and address of the facility, contact and admission information, and a description of the facility.

Swimming Science Journal

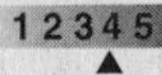

www-rohan.sdsu.edu/dept/coachsci/swimming/index.htm

This journal is divided into several parts, including the following: Swimming Science Abstracts, the Carlile Coaches' Forum, the Swimming Science Bulletin, DRUGS: The Crisis in Swimming, and How Champions Do It. The articles presented are drawn from the personal files of the editor. The contents usually are changed monthly and might or might not be thematic.

Swimming Teachers' Association

12345

www.sta.co.uk

The STA focuses on teaching aquatic skills, from basic water confidence to serious survival. Progressive challenges enable everyone—toddlers, teenagers, adults, the elderly, the handicapped, and the disabled—to get used to the water, enjoy it safely, and increase their fitness and water skills.

A B C D E F G H I J K L M N O P Q R S T U V W X Y Z

Ambitious, able swimmers can proceed to competition lifeguard and teaching levels. The STA discusses new ideas on coaching in swimming, diving, water polo, and lifesaving. Read a history of the STA and learn about the examinations, certificates, and awards available. Learn about STA membership, the membership goals, and the fees.

Swimming World Magazine

1 2 3 4 5 RSS

www.swiminfo.com

This online magazine caters to recreational swimmers as well as world-class competitors. Includes water workouts for specific purposes, products, results, tips on technique, and records.

> **Tip:** Click Time Conversions to access a utility that enables you to compare record times in events run in a yard-based versus a meter-based pool.

SwimNews Online

1 2 3 4 5 RSS

www.swimnews.com

This e-zine of the printed version presents breaking news, meet results, world rankings, and special events. Read the current issue of the magazine or browse through the archives of back issues. Use the search engine to specify a swimmer's last name or country and then view that swimmer's biography. Check out the swimming calendar of events or visit the Shopping Mall to order clothing, equipment, accessories, or training software.

United States Masters Swimming

1 2 3 4 5

www.usms.org

An organized program of swimming for adults. Anyone can join USMS. It has grown to more than 42,000 men and women from age 18 to over 100 and offers a variety of programs for the swimming enthusiast. Here, you can find information on membership, Health & Fitness, Training, Competition, and Local Programs, along with Articles & Publications.

USA Swimming

1 2 3 4 5 RSS

www.usaswimming.org

USA Swimming is the national governing body for competitive swimming in the United States. Get information on USA Swimming, which formulates the rules, implements policies and procedures, conducts national championships, disseminates safety and sports medicine information, and chooses athletes to represent the United States in international competition. You'll also find the latest swimming news, meet results, records, Olympic games information, and several swimming discussion forums you can participate in.

WebSwim

1 2 3 4 5

www.webswim.com

WebSwim is an online community of swimmers where you can read and post messages in several discussion forums, including On the Deck, Training Sessions, I Wanna Know, and Book Shop.

WATER-SKIING

American Barefoot Club

1 2 3 4 5

barefoot.org

A division of USA Water-Ski, ABC is dedicated to promoting the sport of barefoot skiing for individuals at all ability levels. Here, you can learn more about the organization, get the latest news, check up on U.S. competitions, hang out in the Barefoot chat room, check rankings, explore links to other barefoot water-skiing sites, and more.

Aquaskier

1 2 3 4 5

www.aquaskier.com

Aquaskier opens with a page of interesting articles on various water-skiing topics and presents a navigation bar on the left of the page that provides links to other sites organized by category, including Barefooting, Disabled, Fitness Training, Hydroplaning, Jumping, Kneeboarding, Show Skiing, Ski Racing, and Wakeboarding. Site also covers a collection of other water sports, including parasailing.

A B C D E F G H I J K L M N O P Q R S T U V W X Y Z

International Water Ski Federation

www.iwsf.com

Includes information on the IWSF World Cup, a calendar, World Junior Championships, and more. Covers water-skiing, wakeboarding, racing, and barefoot skiing. Here, you can also explore the rules of competitive water-skiing and check the rankings of the top water-skiers in the world.

National Show Ski Association

showski.com

If water-skiing with one foot hooked on the bar or as part of a pyramid sounds like fun to you, consider joining the NSSA. The association's site has a schedule of events, results of the Nationals tournament, show ski humor, news, photos, links, and more.

National Water Ski Racing Association

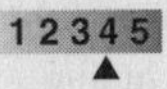

www.nwsra.net

News, schedule of events, results, rankings, and more. Sport division of the American Water Ski Association.

Planet Waterski

www.planetwaterski.com

Up-to-date list of upcoming water-skiing competitions around the world covers racing, barefoot, kneeboard, wakeboard, cable, and tournament events. Features event results and recommended places to ski, plus a fairly good collection of links to other ski resources on the Web.

USA Water Ski/American Water Ski Association

www.usawaterski.org

The official site of the U.S. water-skiing's governing body. Keep up to date on upcoming competitions and read the latest news on who's making headlines in this sport. This site provides information on sport skiing, show skiing, wakeboards, collegiate skiing, kneeboards, ski racing, barefoot skiing, and disabled skiers.

Wakeboarding Magazine

www.wakeboardingmag.com

Wakeboarding magazine presents news; feature articles; gear and boat reviews; instructions on wakeboarding, wakeskating, and boating; classifieds; announcements of upcoming events and competitions; photos and videos; discussion forums; and sample articles from its printed publication. Here, you'll also find links to related sites.

WaterSki Online

www.waterskimag.com

WaterSki Online is the Internet home of *WaterSki* magazine. Here, you can find buyer's guides, free product information, how-to articles, videos, photo galleries, screensavers, discussion forums, lifestyle articles, and much more concerning the sport and culture of waterskiing. Very well-designed site packed with useful information and adorned with high-quality photos.

World Water Ski Racing

www.skirace.net

This site is the official home of the International Water Ski Federation (IWSF) web portal for water ski racing. Here, you can subscribe to the "world's most popular water ski racing newsletter (WWSR), which is read by world champion water skiers and officials." You can also connect with other water-ski racing enthusiasts in the discussion forums. This site features news, information on upcoming races, a Q&A on how to get started in the sport, links to equipment manufacturers and dealers, feature articles on the top competitors, photos, and movies.

WEATHER & METEOROLOGY

Best AccuWeather.com

www1.accuweather.com

Watch the animated weather map of the United States to see what patterns might affect your plans. You can also type in your ZIP code to get your local forecast. This site is the world's weather authority for weather information in your area, including five-day forecasts. Not only that but you can get weather forecasts for almost any city that you might be interested in traveling to. Lots of weather news and information, video forecasts, podcasts, and blogs.

Atlantic Tropical Weather Center

www.atwc.org

Provides links to sites with the latest hurricane information and other weather information dealing with tropical cyclones. Also offers images, data, pictures, meteograms, models, and satellite loops. Not the best site for the average person looking for a weekend weather report; but if you're a weather geek, this site offers plenty of links to in-depth resource sites.

CNN Weather

www.cnn.com/WEATHER

Get your weather from CNN with full weather-related stories, information, and maps. This site also features information on severe weather conditions and fires, special reports (including allergy, beach, and ski reports), and safety tips.

Defense Meteorological Satellite Program

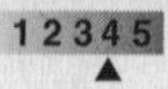

dmsp.ngdc.noaa.gov/dmsp.html

Two satellite constellations of near-polar orbiting, sun-synchronous satellites that monitor meteorological, oceanographic, and solar-terrestrial physics environments. Features currently occurring meteorological phenomena.

El Niño

www.elnino.noaa.gov

The National Oceanic and Atmospheric Administration has created and maintains this site to provide information about El Niño, including what it is and how it affects our weather. Also provides links to other El Niño sites.

Florida Weather Monitor

12345

www.hurricaneadvisories.com

Florida weather, radar, and satellite images; tropical weather information; and surf reports.

Intellicast

12345

www.intellicast.com

Serves as guide to weather, ski reports, and ocean conditions. Provides information for weather novices and professionals. New to Intellicast are health and travel reports. Also, check out its forecasts for national parks.

My-Cast Weather

www.my-cast.com

My-Cast weather delivers a personalized, up-to-the minute weather report to your desktop or web-enabled mobile phone. My-Cast offers free weather reports on the Web for registered users. My-Cast also offers special wireless products for pilots (My-Cast Pilot), anglers and hunters (Weather Scout), and Mobile My-Cast (for mobile phone users). You simply enter your location, and My-Cast delivers weather reports specifically for your area.

National Hurricane Center Tropical Prediction Center

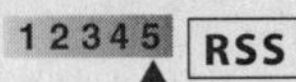

www.nhc.noaa.gov

Contains resources for the researcher, advanced student, and hobbyist interested in the latest information on tropical weather conditions, as well as archival information on weather data and maps. Provides links to other NOAA information and satellite data.

National Severe Storms Laboratory

www.nssl.noaa.gov

Provides information about the laboratory, including current research and programs. Does not offer specific information on severe weather but does provide links to sites that do. Also includes an extensive list of links to web literacy sites.

National Weather Center: Interactive Weather Center

iwin.nws.noaa.gov/iwin/graphicsversion/bigmain.html

A "user-friendly interface to the weather," with raw data from a telecommunications gateway, satellites, and other multilayered links. We found the site to be anything but user-friendly. The opening page is less than intuitive, but the site does offer some useful information for those who are a little more knowledgeable about the weather. Site offers reports on local, national, and international weather along with special reports for agriculture, aviation, and severe weather. Good place to get National Weather Center Alerts.

National Weather Service

www.nws.noaa.gov

Provides all information output by the National Weather Service (NWS), including national and international weather in graphical and textual formats, and information about regional offices. Also offers links to NOAA and other NWS programs. This is the official site of the National Weather Service, which is part of the National Oceanic and Atmospheric Administration. The site is clean, well organized, and easy to navigate. You don't have to wait for the latest weather bulletins from all around the country. The NWS provides weather, hydrologic, and climate forecasts and warnings for the United States and adjacent waters and oceanic areas. This is a good site to bookmark for quick weather forecasts and urgent bulletins such as tornado and severe storm information. Here, you'll find current information for such purposes as knowing when you are in danger from severe weather, planning trips, and for general interest.

Ocean Weather

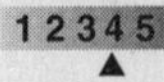

www.oceanweather.com

Ocean Weather uses a unique hindcasting approach to forecast ocean weather, including winds, waves, and surf. At this site, you can obtain current ocean data for various areas worldwide. Ocean engineers will want to check out OSMOSIS, Ocean Weather's software for developing hindsight forecasts.

UM Weather

cirrus.sprl.umich.edu/wxnet

UM Weather attempts to list every weather-related link on the Internet. Includes not only WWW sites, but also FTP, Gopher, and Telnet sites. Includes commercial sites as well as educational and governmental sites. Visit this site to check the latest forecasts and weather conditions or to skip to other weather sites on the Web in order to further your knowledge.

WeatherBug

www.aws.com

Provides national weather information from images and webcams to textual data. Also presents a photo gallery of severe weather by storm chasers throughout the country. Download the WeatherBug to have up-to-the-minute weather forecasts and information beamed to your desktop. WeatherBug was developed specifically for the education market to help teachers use real-world weather conditions for lessons in math, science, and geography. WeatherBug's scope has widened to include tools for consumers, business users, and government agencies.

Weather Channel

www.weather.com

The average human being can access just about everything they need to know about the weather through this site, which is one of the best on the Web. Simply enter your city name or ZIP code and click Go for a three-day forecast. Site also features health reports, travel advisories, traffic reports, forecasts for weddings and sporting events, recreation planners, garden planners, world weather reports, special features for mobile phones, satellite and Doppler weather maps (both stationary and in motion), and a tool that enables you to build your own custom weather page. As your contribution to the site, you have to put up with a moderate number of pop-up ads.

The Weather Underground

www.wunderground.com

Nationwide weather forecasts and information, including temperatures, visibility, wind strength and direction, heat index, wind-chill factor, humidity, dew point, and more. Click the desired state on the map or find forecasts by city or ZIP code. Site also offers features for web-enabled cell phones.

Weather World

www.ems.psu.edu/WeatherWorld

Weather World is an interesting site created and maintained by students and faculty at Penn State. Inspired by Charles Hosler, a professor of meteorology who was on the receiving end of a terrible TV weather forecast, this site attempts to provide more accurate information. This site features a climate watch, world temperatures, a 30-day forecast that's built a little bit on hindsight, a virtual tour of the studio, an anchor morph, trivia quizzes, and other wacky stuff.

WeatherOnline!

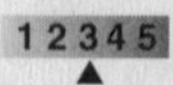

www.weatheronline.com

Get forecasts complete with weather graphics for any part of the United States. Just type in a ZIP code, city, or state to find weather and condition information and forecasts for the region. This site bills itself as "the most comprehensive weather site online." We found the site to be slightly above average.

Yahoo! Weather

weather.yahoo.com

If you're a frequenter of Yahoo!, check out its weather site. Here, you can search for a weather report by city or ZIP code or browse by country, view a current satellite image, register for mobile weather updates and alerts, view weather videos and maps, and get special alerts (including pollen, mosquito, and gardening, and fitness forecasts).

A B C D E F G H I J K L M N O P Q R S T U V W X Y Z

WEBCASTING

Digital Webcast

www.digitalwebcast.com

Digital Webcast is an online magazine for webcast developers. It features articles, product reviews, interviews, tips and techniques, and other content related to developing high-quality webcasts.

Discovery Education: United Streaming

12345

www.unitedstreaming.com

Discovery Education offers this site, complete with tools, tutorials, and other instructional materials to assist teachers in tapping the educational power of streaming video productions. Through the program promoted at this site, teachers can "gain access to a rich collection of more than 50,000 video segments from among 5,000 full-length educational videos from Discovery School and other award-winning producers—with more than 1,000 new titles added every year." Schools and homeschoolers are encouraged to subscribe. You can look up your school to find out whether it's already a subscriber.

International Webcasting Association

www.webcasters.org

The International Webcasting Association is "a forum for all companies involved in this digital revolution to promote webcasting and streaming media." Its founding members include tech giants Akamai, Apple Computers, Globix, Intervox Communications, Microsoft, Morgan Stanley Dean Witter, and Real Networks. At this site you can find membership information, discussion forums, webcaster news, a calendar of upcoming events, and a soon-to-be-implemented discussion forum.

QuickTime for Developers

12345 RSS

developer.apple.com/quicktime

Apple's QuickTime is one of the most popular players for streaming audio and video. Apple created and maintains this site specifically to help developers produce streaming audio and video content and broadcast it to web users. Site features a Getting Started area with a complete learning path to help developers get up and running in a hurry. Site also offers articles, sample code, a resource library (documentation, technical notes, and Q&A), related links, and mailing lists.

Real Networks

www.realnetworks.com/resources/index.html

Much of the streaming audio and video on the Web plays on a Real player. This site, from Real Networks is designed to assist developers in learning the tools and techniques necessary to produce RealAudio and RealVideo broadcasts. Here, you'll find content presented in several areas, including Starting Out, Production Topics, Delivery Topics, Tutorials, Code Samples, Documentation, SDKs, Tools & Plug-ins, and Security. Tutorials are, of course, presented as streaming video broadcasts.

Streaming Media World

12345

streamingmediaworld.com

Streaming Media World is an online magazine for those who develop and implement streaming audio and video productions. Content is presented in several areas including Audio (tools and methods for creating, serving, and playing live or recorded web

A B C D E F G H I J K L M N O P Q R S T U V W X Y Z

audio files), Video (tools and methods for finding, making, and serving videos), Flash (tools and techniques for creating and serving scalable Flash animations), and SYMM and SMIL (technologies for synchronizing audio and video components). Site features fundamentals, resources, and discussion forums.

Best StreamingMedia.com

www.streamingmedia.com

StreamingMedia.com provides industry news, information, articles, directories, and services for online broadcasters and others who need to keep up on the ever-changing technology. The site features "thousands of original articles, hundreds of hours of audio/video content, breaking news, research reports, industry directory, and case studies that showcase the latest real-world streaming media implementations." This is a great site to visit to witness real world implementations of streaming media technology and applications.

WebCasting.com

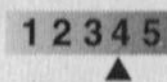

www.webcasting.com

WebCasting.com is a company based in Dallas, Texas, that specializes in developing webcast and podcast solutions for corporate, government, and faith-based communications organizations. WebCasting.com can handle both the hosting and production needs of its clients. Here, you can find out more about available services and use the online WebCasting Wizard to get a free quote in hours instead of days. Site also offers a toll-free telephone number so that you can call for a free consultation.

Windows Media Developer Center

msdn.microsoft.com/windowsmedia

Many sites that offer streaming video broadcasts serve them up in the Windows Media Player format. This site provides developers with the tools, resources, instructions, and tips they need to develop Windows media files and broadcast them on the Web. Click Understanding to get an overview of Windows media and the technologies that make it work. Click Digital Media Technology Pages to access resources for developing software applications and devices that support digital media. Site also features technical articles, downloads, samples, and a Community area where you can communicate with other developers in the discussion forums.

you-niversity.com

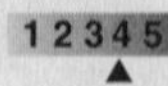

www.you-niversity.com

you-niversity.com features software and services for producing high-quality webcasts for educational and business applications. With you-niversity tools, you can broadcast live events, conferences, lectures, and slide shows over the Web.

WEDDING PLANNING

Ask Ginka

www.askginka.com

Pick a nationality, religion, theme, or holiday and have Ginka track down the services, products, and resources you need to plan the wedding, bridal shower, or birthday party of your dreams. Ginka features a directory of more than 20,000 links!

The Best Man

www.thebestman.com

Has your buddy designated you to be the best man at his wedding? If you've never done it before, you may be wondering just what you're supposed to do. This site provides a list of your duties as best man, help for planning the bachelor party, information on tuxedos, and tips on how to compose a successful toast.

Bliss! Weddings

www.blissweddings.com

Bliss! Weddings is built around a community of brides-to-be and newlyweds involved in lively discussion forums that cover every aspect of weddings—from bridal showers and bachelor parties to wedding and honeymoon plans. At the top of the page, you can select a subject area from the Plan Your Wedding menu to access articles, guides, tips, discussion forums, and products related to the subject. You can also select a planner from the Download a Free Planner menu to open a printable PDF planner for weddings and bridesmaids and a list of questions to ask consultants, florists, caterers, and photographers. Scroll down the page for links to discussion forums, interactive tools, feature articles, the Ask the Expert area, bride ideas, and how-to videos. This site is packed with free advice and plenty of products that can simplify and enhance your wedding planning, making it a close runner up for our selection as Best of the Best website in a competitive category.

Bridalink Store

www.bridalink.com

The Bridalink site is an online store that prides itself on its selection of cheap, personalized wedding favors along with other essential wedding reception items, such as cameras, place card holders, wedding cake serving sets, and toasting glasses. This store also carries attendant gifts, apparel, jewelry and accessories, items for the ceremony itself, and wedding planner tools. In addition, visitors can register for monthly giveaways.

Brides.com

12345

www.brides.com

Brides.com, the Internet home of *Modern Bride* magazine, features sections covering just everything related to weddings: Fashion, Beauty, Wedding Style, Planning, and Travel. Site also presents feature articles on a wide range of topics, a searchable/browsable directory of local resources, a host of discussion forums, well-stocked photo galleries, and Today's Brilliant Idea. You can subscribe to the magazine online using secure credit card resources.

> **Tip:** Scroll down the page for quick links to Wedding Dresses, Songs, Invitations, Favors, Vows, Flowers, Cakes, and Real Weddings.

Brides and Grooms

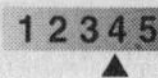

www.bridesandgrooms.com

Marriage and wedding guide with articles on everything from wedding photography tips and selecting music to last-minute questions you might have before you tie the knot. Along the right side of the page are links to several wedding services and products that can help enhance your wedding, before, during, and after the ceremony.

Great Bridal Expo

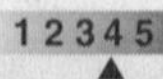

www.greatbridalexpo.com

This site features information about the Great Bridal Expo, a bridal show that tours to various cities throughout the United States. From this site, you can find out more about the Expo's exhibitors, special events, dates, and locations throughout the United States. You can even order tickets for the show online!

Grooms Online

www.groomsonline.com

The ultimate wedding site for men, Grooms Online provides helpful wedding information written in a tone especially designed for men, along with a huge directory of links that can help you find everything a groom or best man needs to plan. Use the navigation bar at the top of the screen to quickly jump to your area of interest: Groomsmen Gifts, Wedding Planning, Best Man, Bachelor Party, Tuxedo & Style, Honeymoon, or Directory.

The Knot: Weddings for the Real World

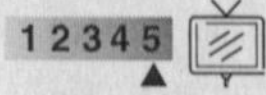

www.theknot.com

This site is an excellent wedding resource: 3,000+ wedding-related articles, 6,000 searchable gown pictures, how-tos, plus daily hot tips, discussion forums, and special personalized planning tools. This is definitely one of the most comprehensive, useful bridal planning sites on the Web. The site offers much in the way of helping you to plan your wedding, and you can even shop online for just about everything you will need.

Today's Bride Online Magazine

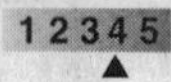

www.todaysbride.com

Today's Bride magazine's website is very user-friendly, including a search engine to help you find specific topics and a navigation bar on the left that contains links to categories of products and services offered by various online merchants. Categories cover everything from Alterations and Beauty Salons to Videography. Although this magazine focuses on helping brides in northeastern Ohio, many of its articles and other offerings are useful no matter where you live.

Ultimate Internet Wedding Guide

www.ultimatewedding.com

This site is built around an extensive directory of links to wedding products and services on the Web, but it also features a collection of excellent articles and tips on wedding planning, a list of top songs, wedding prose and poetry, vows and ceremonies, a photo gallery, ideas for wedding favors, discussion forums, and live chat areas.

USA Bride

www.usabride.com

Wedding planning help for brides and grooms, including gift and shower ideas, wedding songs, frugal wedding tips, and more. This site also features some excellent lists, including Guest Gripes: 10 Wedding Day Don'ts, So You're Getting Married: 5 Things to Think About, and 20 Ways to Panic-Proof Your Wedding Day.

Video In Production

www.videoinproduction.com

If you're planning on getting married in the Chicagoland area and would like to have your wedding day memories preserved on video DVD or VHS tape, check out this site and give the guys at Video In Production a call. Video In Production professionally records your wedding day, edits the video and mixes it with music, still shots, and other media to give you a keepsake that will last a lifetime.

Wedding Bells

1 2 3 4 5

www.weddingbells.com

Wed-zine that takes a thorough and stylish approach to wedding planning for both brides and grooms. Content is presented in several areas, including Get Started, Celebrate, Style, Grooms, and At Home. Most of the content focuses on style.

Best The Wedding Channel

www.weddingchannel.com

The Wedding Channel is an all-encompassing wedding resource. It contains the following wedding-related sections: My Tools, Planning, Fashion & Beauty, Local Vendors, Registry, Wedding Shop, Guest Hotels, Honeymoon, Community, and TV. Click My Tools to access a planning checklist, a link for creating your own wedding website, a Save-the-Date eCard to send to desired guests, a guest list manager, a budge calculator, an online scrapbook maker, and a shopping list. Click Planning to take a three-step tutorial on how to proceed with formulating and executing your wedding plans: Get Ideas, Get Advice, and Get It Done. With its powerful planning tools and great advice, this site edged out several other Wedding Planning sites in a competitive category.

Wedding Photography—Advice for the Bride and Groom

members.aol.com/anorama

This site offers some advice about selecting a wedding photographer for the special event. You should choose with care because you get only one shot at it and you want the best pictures possible.

WeddingSolutions.com

1 2 3 4 5

www.weddingsolutions.com

WeddingSolutions.com is a full-service wedding planning site. Tabbed navigation provides easy access to the My Wedding area (your customized wedding plan), fashion and beauty (for both bride and groom), local vendors, reception sites, honeymoon sites, shopping sites, a registry, and discussion forums. Site also features a photo galleries and a free wedding website.

WedNet

www.wednet.com

Contains numerous wedding-related articles with tips for every aspect of wedding planning. In addition, you can search for other Internet resources and wedding vendors, visit the WedNet library, and even register for a free subscription to a monthly newsletter.

A B C D E F G H I J K L M N O P Q R S T U V W X Y Z

WEIGHT LOSS

American Dietetic Association

12345

www.eatright.org

The American Dietetic Association is the largest organization of food and nutrition professionals in the United States, "translating the science of nutrition into practical solutions for healthy living." Here, you'll find plenty of healthy lifestyle tips, nutrition fact sheets, a Good Nutrition Reading List, the famous Food Guide Pyramid, and plenty of additional resources for consumers and nutritionists.

Ask Dr. Weil

12345

www.drweil.com

Learn more about Dr. Andrew Weil's approach to health by combining Western thinking and traditional medical perspectives. At the site, you can learn how to eat healthier, how vitamins and herbs can improve your health, and where to find natural foods. If you're looking for a sensible guide to natural, holistic health, Dr. Weil is the doctor to see.

Best of Weight Loss

12345

bestofweightloss.com

The Best of Weight Loss is a directory maintained by specialists in weight-loss physiology, weight management, exercise programs, and Internet research. Here, you can find reviews on the latest diets, a list of frequently asked questions, tips, calculators, success stories, and additional information and resources.

CyberDiet

12345

www.cyberdiet.com

Cyberdiet features an excellent collection of nutritional information, interactive tools, discussion groups, and other information and resources to enable users to develop and stick to a customized weight loss and management program. Here, you can access a daily food planner and assessment tools, find your nutritional profile, grab recipes and exercise tips, and much more.

The Diet Channel

12345

www.thedietchannel.com

The Diet Channel features an excellent introduction to the most popular diets. Here, you can look up diets by category, including Online Diets, Meal Planning Diets, Weight Loss Programs, Diet and Fitness Plans, Diets by Food Group, Diets by Food Type, Diets in the News, Popular Diets, and Weight Loss (patches, pills, tips, and other interventions). This site is riddled with ads for too-good-to-be-true weight loss programs, so it's a little difficult to tell just how unbiased the content really is; but if you're looking for a brief description of a new diet, this is a good place to check.

Doctor's Guide to Obesity

12345

www.docguide.com/news/content.nsf/PatientResAllCateg/Obesity?OpenDocument

The latest medical news and information for patients or friends/parents of patients diagnosed with obesity-related disorders. Site also features a collection of links to related discussion forums and websites.

Best eDiets.com

12345

www.ediets.com

eDiets enables you to explore a wide variety of diet, meal planning, and weight loss programs, choose the desired program, and obtain a customized plan and weekly menus that best fit your personality, lifestyle, and goals. Enter your email address, age, sex, height, and weight for a free profile and newsletter. eDiets.com provides reliable information about the leading diets, along with several online tools, including a nutrition tracker, recipe conversion calculator, and fat counter. You'll find plenty of articles to inspire you to create and stick to a diet and exercise plan that's right for you. Additional support is available in the discussion forums. We like this site because it goes beyond the fad diets to review less popular diet and weight-loss plans, including the Mayo Clinic Plan and the Vegetarian Plan.

Fast Food Facts

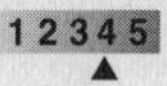

www.foodfacts.info

Click on a fast food restaurant name and type in a product to find out the breakdown of calories, fat, sodium, carbohydrates, and more. Or find out what products fit your diet by selecting a restaurant and setting limits on calories or sodium. Site also features news articles on various developments in the fast food industry, many of which are very positive. Warning: You might lose your appetite after seeing how fattening some items are.

Jenny Craig

12345

www.jennycraig.com

Home of one of the most popular weight loss programs, this site features Jenny Craig's story, success stories of people who have followed the program, weight loss programs and support for members, and online shopping. Become a member to access the recipe database and use the Jenny Craig eTools and custom meal planner.

L A Weight Loss Centers

12345

laweightloss.com

L A Weight Loss is a diet and exercise plan designed to help you shed weight without having to give up your unique lifestyle. This site introduces you to the program, offers success stories, and provides three content areas to help you begin your personal weight loss program: Healthy Eating, Healthy Living, and Health Tools, including a BMI calculator.

Natural Nutrition

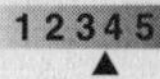

www.livrite.com

Learn all about natural nutrition, its basic philosophy, and tips for eating better with whole grains. This site contains lots of articles to read, recipes to copy, and directories of natural food stores and merchants online. If you're committed to following the nutritional advice of the Food and Drug Administration, this isn't the site for you.

Nutrisystem

12345

www.nutrisystem.com

Home of the popular Nutrisystem weight loss program. Here, you can learn more about the program, sign up for a free membership, and shop online for products. Nutrisystem offers several programs: Women, Women over 60, Men, Men over 60, Type-II Diabetic, and All Vegetarian. On the opening page, you can enter your sex, height, date of birth, current weight, and how much weight you'd like to lose to receive a free diet analysis.

Prevention.com—Weight Loss and Fitness

12345

www.prevention.com

With 100 diet tips, a meal planner, calorie calculator, and workout and weight quizzes, you're sure to be inspired to start that weight-loss program you've been meaning to. Lots of helpful advice and strategies from the publishers of *Prevention* magazine.

After reaching the home page, click the Weight Loss or Fitness tab to start your journey. Articles offer practical advice that you can start putting to work right away along with plenty of advice and alerts to keep you from trying anything that might be dangerous. Site also features a weight loss simulator to help you envision the new you.

Shape Up America

12345

www.shapeup.org

Safe weight management and physical fitness programs for one and all. Although not one of the flashier sites on the Internet, this site has some useful information that will assist you in losing and controlling weight. Click Shape Up! for access to several content areas: Fitness Center, Breakfast Benefits, Shape Up & Drop 10 Cyber Kitchen, Body Fat Lab, 10,000 Steps, and Support Center. Click Prevention and Rx to learn more about childhood and diabetic-induced obesity, get an obesity assessment, and explore additional resources.

Weight Watchers

12345

www.weightwatchers.com

Learn about Weight Watchers programs around the world at this site, which will also tell you about Weight Watchers' proprietary 1-2-3 Success Plan. The navigation bar at the top of the screen leads you to the main content areas on this site: The Plan, Food & Recipes, Healthy & Fit, Success Stories, Community, and Marketplace. Site features some excellent Q&A articles, engaging quizzes, lively discussions, and a huge database of recipes. Some features on this site are available only to registered users, but registration is free.

HealthCentral

www.healthcentral.com

12345 RSS

www.healthcentral.com

If you're looking for health and wellness information, it's likely you'll find it here, along with just about anything else you need to know about nutrition, health, eating right, vitamins, and more. This site offers a great collection of columns, library articles, and tools to help you treat your body better. You can browse the content at this site using various navigation tools. Click Symptoms A–Z to trace your symptoms back to possible causes and treatment options or check out the Health Library for a complete index of conditions. The People's Pharmacy can lead you to natural prevention and treatment approaches and the Rx Information link can assist you in learning more about medications your doctor recommended. This site also features a good collection of videos, 3D animations, in-depth reports and a host of other useful features that are too numerous to mention.

WINE

Ambrosia

www.ambrosiawine.com

Check out the top 10 purchased wines, talk wine with other wine lovers, and order wine from the site or request a catalog. Site also features a Wine 101 primer for novice enthusiasts.

Bordeaux

www.bordeaux.com

Take a tour of the Bordeaux countryside and learn how this wine is made. Find tips on enjoying Bordeaux wine and hosting a wine-tasting party. Learn what restaurants are "Bordeaux-friendly" and how to read a Bordeaux wine label. Also, learn the basics of grape varieties (Merlot, Cabernet, Semillon, and so on) and investigate the buyer's guide and vintage chart, as well as recipes for French cuisine. Or check out the glossary of basic wine terms.

Buyers and Cellars Wine Education

www.wineeducation.com

This site focuses on wine education. It helps you gain the confidence to enjoy wine and feel comfortable ordering it. You'll learn how to find bargain wines, distinguish the characteristics of different grapes, determine the correct temperature to serve wine, and more.

Edgerton's Wine Price File

www.wineprices.com

This site showcases software for serious wine collectors to help manage wine inventory and keep track of aging. Software includes a wine database, a view of your cellar, and *The Wine Price File* book for sale online.

Fetzer Vineyards

www.fetzer.com

This producer of organically farmed wines is the sixth-largest premium winery in the country. In addition to checking out Fetzer's wine, you can find out more about its environmental policies.

Food and Wine Access

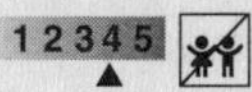

www.foodandwineaccess.com

Keep abreast of upcoming wine-tasting events and festivals, read wine and restaurant reviews, and get the lowdown on past events.

Food & Wine Magazine

www.foodandwine.com

You can find wines, foods, recipes, and more at this colorful, comprehensive site. Be sure to check out the store where you can purchase everything from mustard to cookbooks. Even if you already subscribe to the magazine, you should check out this site—it includes content not available in the magazine.

Geerlings & Wade

www.geerwade.com/gw/default.asp

Select a wine by region, flavor, or price and then purchase it from this site, which also offers accessories and wine gifts.

Global Wine Club

www.clubsofamerica.com

Part of the Clubs of America series. With each month's shipment, clients receive two different bottles of rare wine, many from small award-winning wineries around the world. Included in each shipment is *Wine Expeditions*, the Club newsletter, offering insights on the monthly selections. You'll also have an opportunity to order your favorite wines at discounted prices.

Gruppo Italiano Vini

www.gruppoitalianovini.com

This company not only produces and distributes Italian wine, it also manages historic wine cellars. Here, you can learn more about the many fine wines this winery produces.

Internet Guide to Wine and Frequently Asked Questions

www.sbwines.com/usenet_winefaq

This site features an online book that touches on the most common topics related to making and enjoying wine. Read a general introduction about what wine is. Learn how wine is made, aged, and stored. Learn the proper way to drink wine and get tips on buying wine. Check out the varieties of wine and tour wine countries in France, California, and Canada. The site design could use some work, but the content is great.

Into Wine

www.intowine.com

Introduction to the wonderful world of wines, this site provides information on various wine regions, explains how wine is made, provides instructions on how to properly store wine, shows you how to enjoy wine, and more.

K&L Wine Merchants

www.klwines.com

Named as the best wine shop on the Internet by *Money* magazine and one of the top 10 wine retailers in the nation by the publishers of the *Wine Spectator*.

Kahn's Fine Wines

www.kahnsfinewines.com

Wines, gourmet foods, cigars, and more can all be ordered online from this wonderful website. Kahn's Fine Wines, which has been a retail liquor and wine business in Indianapolis for more than 20 years, now specializes in fine wine. Site also features a small collection of links to other fine wine websites.

Kendall Jackson Wineries

www.kj.com

This site offers a host of valuable content areas that you can quickly access through the navigation bar at the top of the screen: Wines (Kendall Jackson wines), Learn (terminology, winemaking, and more), Wine & Food (recipes, a wine and food pairing guide, and an entertainment planner), Wine Club (get specials), and Events (the Tomato Festival and other events).

Marilyn Merlot

www.marilynmerlot.com

Order special collector's editions of Marilyn Merlot wines. You can purchase these wines online, but the price is pretty steep—some sell for more than $600 per bottle!

Merryvale Vineyards

www.merryvale.com

Features articles, reviews, recipes, and wine pairings. Click the Fun Stuff link for e-postcards, the wine trivia challenge, and weekend wine events. Site also offers a Trade site where dealers can find fact sheets, sell sheets, and press kit materials.

Napa Valley Virtual Visit

www.napavalley.com

Explore various Napa Valley wineries or purchase wines and wine-management software. This site provides sightseeing, dining, and catering ideas, as well as current events. If you're looking to make a real visit, check out the information about accommodations. Also contains links to other valley sites.

Ronn Wiegand, Master of Wine

www.ronnwiegand.com

Ronn Wiegand, the first person in the world to hold the Master of Wine and Master Sommelier wine titles, routinely tastes more than 5,000 wines every year. Here, Ronn offers a bit of his wine wisdom and expertise through a subscription newsletter and a collection of wine guides and wine charts you can purchase online. You can also learn how to hire Ronn as a consultant.

Spanish Wines

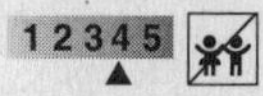

www.spanishwinesonline.co.uk

Spanish Wines is a specialist importer of Spanish wines and food. Here, you'll find information about its wide selection of imported products, along with profiles, vintages, storage tips, and common wine terms.

Sutter Home

www.sutterhome.com

Sutter Home created and maintains this site to introduce visitors to its selection of fine wines. When you verify that you're over 21 years of age, the site displays a page that enables you to check out its current wines, order products online, and read feature articles about a variety of topics related to wine, including cooking with wine and starting your own wine and reading club.

Vampire Vineyards

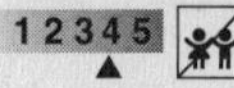

www.vampirewine.com

The Vampire line of wines is imported from Transylvania, Romania, and includes Merlot, Pinot Grigio, Pinot Noir, Sauvignon Blanc, and Cabernet Sauvignon. You also can purchase unique Vampire Vineyards merchandise, including posters, baseball hats, T-shirts, and wine glasses.

Wine Access

www.wineaccess.com/pvt/my-wineaccess.tcl

A complete guide for all wine lovers. Extensive information highlighted by a wine selection tool. Designed for everyone from the experienced collector to the interested beginner. Check out the list of top-rated wines and the Q&A list, and put together your own wine portfolio.

The Wine Broker

www.winebroker.com

Contains wine and wine-related information for all types of wine lovers, from casual to connoisseur. The site offers holiday gift packages, a monthly wine club, a list of rare wines, wine trivia, and more.

Wine Enthusiast

www.wineenthusiast.com

This site sells wine-related accessories, from cellars to corkscrews to cigars. Of course, it also sells wine itself, including specials and samplers. Sign up for a free catalog.

Wine Institute

www.wineinstitute.org

The Wine Institute is a not-for-profit organization that speaks and acts on behalf of the California wine agency. It promotes positive legislation for wine growers, makers, and related businesses; seeks to expand market opportunities; works to improve media relations; and acts in other ways to support the California wine industry.

Best Wine Lover's Page

www.wineloverspage.com

Frequently updated notes and advice on wines of good value are backed by an online wine-tasting tutorial, wine FAQs, vintage charts, interactive discussions, and more. Click the Wine Chat link to learn about upcoming chat sessions with respected wine connoisseurs. Wine questionnaire, wine lexicon, winegrape glossary, and other resources make this the most comprehensive wine site on the Web.

Wine Messenger

www.winemessenger.com

A wine retailer that features wines from small growers all over the world. Site offers some excellent general information about wines and wine tasting along with a food-pairing guide.

Wine on the Web: The Talking Wine Magazine

www.wineontheweb.com

Independent, international Internet publication with vintage charts, a searchable and alphabetized database, and wine news. Includes columns by The Flying Wine Man and The American Wine Guy. Devoted to helping wine consumers find the best wines in their price range. Site is up-to-date.

Wine-Searcher

www.wine-searcher.com

Wine-Searcher is designed to help wine enthusiasts find reputable Web-based dealers that carry their favorite wines. Merchants place their lists on Wine-Searcher so the wines can be more easily found via this site than with traditional Internet searches. Each offer is dated and is either updated or removed at regular intervals.

Wine Spectator

www.winespectator.com

Find answers to nearly every question you can think up about wine and wine tasting. You'll find a searchable database of wine information, wine ratings, news, a library, and forums. Links to retail sites that specialize in wine and wine-related products.

Wine: UC Davis Department of Viticulture and Enology

wineserver.ucdavis.edu

The home page of the Department of Viticulture and Enology at UC Davis, the oldest wine and grape research institution in the world, offers information about wine science, home winemaking, wine extension classes, wine literature, wine weather, wine aroma, wine URLs, wine and health, wine and travel, and more.

WineBusiness.com

winebusiness.com

Claiming to be the largest wine-related site on the Web, WineBusiness.com provides news and information for people working in the wine industry. Site features daily industry news; information on winemaking and grape growing; and reports on sales, marketing, business, and technology. Here, you can also check out the classified ads and look for a job in the industry.

Wine.com

www.wine.com

Home to the largest wine retailer in the United States, Wine.com features a huge wine cellar with a selection of more than 10,000 wines. Here, you can find wine reviews, a FAQ list, accessories, gift certificates, special deals, and more.

Wines on the Internet

www.wines.com

An excellent resource for wine-related topics. Provides links to online wineries and vineyards, features a virtual tasting room, and includes other notes of interest for the connoisseur and novice wine drinker alike. Also details upcoming events for wine enthusiasts and links to reputable online wine sellers.

Zachys Online

www.zachys.com

This online wine cellar features a huge collection of the finest wines in the world. This site features a searchable wine index, gifts and accessories, auctions, and special events. You can even ask for help in selecting a particular wine.

Related Sites

www.americanwineries.org

www.invinoveritas.com

www.wonderwine.com

www.wineaustralia.com.au

WOMEN/WOMEN'S ISSUES

AFL-CIO: Working Women Working Together

1 2 3 4 5 ▲ (4)

www.aflcio.org/women

Working women will want to check out the AFL-CIO's site devoted to supporting working women for facts and figures regarding working women and the children they support. You can also get information on how to become more active in supporting legislation for working women. Fill out the survey and find out more about upcoming conferences, too.

American Association of University Women (AAUW)

1 2 3 4 5 ▲ (4)

www.aauw.org

The American Association of University Women is a national organization that promotes education and equity for all women and girls. This website describes AAUW issues, research programs, grants and fellowships, membership information, and much more.

American Women's History

1 2 3 4 5 ▲ (3)

www.mtsu.edu/~kmiddlet/history/women.html

American Women's History is a research tool for those who are interested in studying the history of women in the United States. You can browse the index of materials by subject or state and learn research techniques for locating additional primary and secondary sources.

Amnesty International USA Women's Human Rights

1 2 3 4 5 ▲ (4) RSS

www.amnestyusa.org/women

Read about the poor conditions and situations women around the world face and learn more about what you can do to change it.

Artemis Search for Women's Studies Programs

1 2 3 4 5 ▲ (4)

www.artemisguide.com

A database of nearly 400 U.S. women's studies programs, listed alphabetically with brief descriptions and the opportunity to link to the specific college or university for more information.

Association for Women's Rights in Development

1 2 3 4 5 ▲ (4)

www.awid.org

The Association for Women's Rights in Development (AWID) is "an international membership organization connecting, informing, and mobilizing people and organizations committed to achieving gender equality, sustainable development, and women's human rights." Here, you can learn more about the organization and its goals, learn about membership and volunteer opportunities, view a list of frequently asked questions, access valuable information and resources on women's rights, and read and post messages in the group's discussion forums.

AWARE

www.aware.org

Learn more about the importance of self-protection and defense, strategies you can use, and places to go for instruction.

BizWomen

www.bizwomen.com

BizWomen provides an online interactive community for successful women in business to communicate, network, exchange ideas, and provide support for each other via the Internet. BizWomen also provides you with an Internet presence with your online business card, a colorful online brochure, or interactive catalog to make your products and services available online.

The Business Women's Network Interactive

www.bwni.com

The Business Women's Network the Business Women's Network is dedicated to helping thousands of professional women around the globe find solutions and rewarding opportunities. As the site claims, "Whether you're starting a business, climbing the corporate ladder, working towards career satisfaction and work life effectiveness, or running a leading organization, BWN has the resources and contacts you need to succeed." This site features a newsletter, a calendar of events, a directory of more than 6,500 national and international women's business organizations, profiles of outstanding businesswomen, and a host of opportunities for women to connect with others and contribute to the growing community of women in business.

CatalystWomen.org

www.catalystwomen.org

Catalyst reports on the state of women in business, providing research summaries and reports to help companies improve conditions and opportunities for women. Learn more about recent reports and recommendations made by Catalyst.

A Celebration of Women Writers

digital.library.upenn.edu/women

Celebration of Women Writers recognizes the contributions of women writers throughout history. This site provides a comprehensive listing of links to biographical and bibliographical information about women writers, and complete published books written by women. See What's New! for the most recent authors and books added to the listing. This is not only a great site for writers but for those wanting to break into the writing field. It has a lot of useful information for others doing research in this field and for the general public.

Center for Reproductive Law and Policy

www.crlp.org

This site provides a review of women's reproductive freedom in six countries around the world: Brazil, China, Germany, India, Nigeria, and the United States. Each country's pertinent laws and policies are discussed on a wide range of topics.

Chistell Publishing

www.chistell.com

This site contains books written by African American women about women's issues. Both informative and inspirational.

Diotima: Women and Gender in the Ancient World

www.stoa.org/diotima

This website is intended to serve as a resource for anyone interested in patterns of gender around the ancient Mediterranean and as a forum for collaboration among instructors who teach courses about women and gender in the ancient world. Includes research articles, course materials, a comprehensive bibliography, and more.

A
B
C
D
E
F
G
H
I
J
K
L
M
N
O
P
Q
R
S
T
U
V
W
X
Y
Z

Expect the Best from a Girl

12345

www.academic.org

This site prepared by the Women's College Coalition contains information about what parents and others can do to encourage girls in academic areas, particularly math and the sciences. Includes a listing of programs and institutes that can be contacted.

Feminist.com

12345

feminist.com

Feminist.com is a site aimed at helping women network more effectively on the Internet. Includes the abridged text of articles and speeches, women's health resources, women-owned businesses, links, and *lots* more!

Related Site

feminist.com//market/wombus/

Feminist Arts-Music

12345

www.feminist.org/arts/linkmusic.html

An annotated list of feminist musicians, with links to the artists' home pages and fan club pages where you can get more information.

Feminist Majority Foundation Online

12345 RSS

www.feminist.org

This site contains information on government actions for and against women, an online discussion group, publication information, and much more. There is also a shopping area where you can purchase feminist gifts, clothing, and other items.

Girl Power!

12345

www.girlpower.gov

The national public education campaign sponsored by the Department of the Health and Human Services to help encourage and empower 9- to 14-year-old girls.

Girls Incorporated

12345

www.girlsinc.org

An organization dedicated to "helping girls become strong, smart, and bold." This site includes research and advocacy information, membership information, and more.

Global Fund for Women

12345

www.globalfundforwomen.org

The Global Fund for Women is an international organization that focuses on human rights for women. Includes information on supported programs, news articles, and a FAQ sheet and describes what you can do to help.

Human Rights Watch

www.hrw.org/women

Human Rights Watch is "the largest human rights organization based in the United States." A dedicated staff of activist lawyers, journalists, academicians, and other professionals "conduct fact-finding investigations into human rights abuses in all regions of the world" and then publish their findings in an attempt to promote justice and fairness for all human beings. This link takes you to the Human Rights Watch page that focuses specifically on women's rights. Here, you'll find news on the latest human rights violations directed toward women.

> **Tip:** Scroll down the page to find a list of Campaigns and Focus pages to determine what you can do to help advocate on various key issues.

iVillage.com: The Women's Network

www.ivillage.com

Find information about many subjects of interest to women, including relationships, money, work, and career, plus getting pregnant, raising children, and more. The opening page presents teasers of feature articles that you can click to read the full article, along with a list of women's magazines related to the site and links to the most popular areas on the site. You can use the navigation bar at the top of the screen to cruise to the desired content area: Beauty & Style, Health & Well-Being, Diet & Fitness, Love & Sex, Pregnancy & Parenting, Home & Food, Entertainment, and Magazines. Site also features interviews and video clips.

Lifetime Online

www.lifetimetv.com

This is the World Wide Web extension of Lifetime Television, the women's network. Provides information about Lifetime's television schedule and programs, as well as articles on health and fitness, parenting, sports, and more. Includes a searchable index of topics covered.

Machon Chana

www.machonchana.org

A women's institute for the study of Judaism. This nicely done site helps educate Jewish women about their religion and culture.

National Association for Female Executives

www.nafe.com

Offers links to online career and business resources as well as contacts for networking. The site also offers articles on entrepreneurial issues and information on the mission and benefits of the National Association for Female Executives.

National Museum of Women in the Arts

www.nmwa.org

Home of the only museum in the world dedicated to recognizing the contributions of women artists, this site provides a history of the organization, an online gallery complete with biographies of each featured artist, a library and research center, and much more.

The National Organization for Women (NOW)

RSS

www.now.org

This home page for NOW offers press releases and articles, information on issues NOW is currently involved in, information on joining (with email or web addresses for many local chapters), and the history of NOW. Also provided is a search form if you're looking for a specific topic at NOW's site.

National Partnership for Women & Families (NPWF)

www.nationalpartnership.org

The National Partnership for Women & Families is "a nonprofit, nonpartisan organization that uses public education and advocacy to promote fairness in the workplace, quality health care, and policies that help women and men meet the dual demands of work and family." Here, you can learn more about the organization and about legislation that affects families and find out how you can get involved to make a positive impact.

National Women's Hall of Fame

www.greatwomen.org

Find out who this year's Hall of Fame inductees are or browse the directory alphabetically to learn about all of the women who have been inducted in years past, play games and participate in exercises to increase your knowledge of the contribution great women have made, learn more about the work of this organization, and buy Hall of Fame merchandise here.

National Women's History Project

www.nwhp.org

Official website of the National Women's History Project, which originated Women's History month. Many interesting features here about the history of women and what they have contributed in the past. Educators might benefit from learning more about the significant impact women had on history and for which they have not received credit. This project aims to bring their contributions to light. The site offers information and resources and an online catalog of products for sale.

NEWoman

www.newomen.com

NEWomen is an online magazine that offers a substantial collection of articles, advice, and commentary on women's issues, along with women's health advice, beauty tips, and sex and dating articles.

NWSA–National Women's Studies Association

1 2 3 4 5

www.nwsa.org

The NWSA supports and promotes feminist teaching, learning, research, and many other projects. It provides professional and community service at the pre-K through post-secondary levels. It also provides information about the inter-disciplinary field of Women's Studies for those outside the profession. The organization publishes a newsletter called *NWSAction* and other publications. The *NWSA Journal*, an official publication of the National Women's Studies Association, publishes the most up-to-date interdisciplinary, multicultural feminist scholarship linking feminist theory with teaching and activism. NWSA has an annual conference that provides opportunities for teachers, students, activists, and others to share research findings, strategies, and ideas for effecting social change.

Office of International Women's Issues

www.state.gov/g/wi

The U.S. Department of State has created and maintains this website to promote awareness of women's issues in America and around the world and encourage citizen's to become more involved in helping promote equal and civil treatment of women of all nations.

Office of Women's Business Ownership

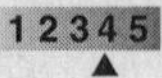

www.sbaonline.sba.gov/financing/special/women.html

Produced by the U.S. Small Business Association, this page provides information and resource links for women currently running or seeking to run small businesses in the United States.

OWBO Online Women's Business Center

1 2 3 4 5

www.onlinewbc.gov

OWBO promotes the growth of women-owned businesses through programs that address business training and technical assistance. You'll find a wealth of information here, including details on mentoring program opportunities, if you are in business or thinking about it.

Oxygen.com

www.oxygen.com

The online site with information for, by, and about women. Discuss issues of great importance, such as making the world a better place, to less important but perhaps equally interesting issues such as shopping, relationships, learning, sex, and more. Lots of chat and discussion opportunities, as well as interactive elements. The site also supports a shopping area for things you might need.

Shescape Online

www.shescape.com

www.shescape.com

Shescape is a dance show that celebrates lesbian culture. This site provides information about the show and includes an advice column, interviews, schedules of upcoming concerts and events, monthly horoscopes, health and fitness advice, and links to related sites. Links to MySpace.com for blogging.

Society of Women Engineers

12345

www.swe.org

Information about the society, plus a resumé database and job search help for female engineers. You can also subscribe to the group's magazine and find out how to submit articles for publication in it.

Spinsters Ink

12345

www.spinsters-ink.com

Spinsters Ink publishes novels and nonfiction works that deal with significant issues in women's lives from a feminist perspective. Included on the website are book reviews, ordering information, and submission information.

Sports Illustrated for Women

12345

sportsillustrated.cnn.com/siwomen

Stay up-to-date on the top women's sports stars and learn more about getting and keeping your body in shape.

TASC: The American Surrogacy Center, Inc.

12345

www.surrogacy.com

Comprehensive information on surrogate childbearing, including message boards, classified advertising, a directory of agencies and groups, and articles about surrogacy. Site also features support groups.

The United Nations and the Status of Women

12345

www.un.org/Conferences/Women/PubInfo/Status/Home.htm

This site from the United Nations provides information about what the UN has done since its inception to further the status of women. Included are conference findings, general articles, and commission reports.

WE: Women's Entertainment

12345 

www.we.tv

Home of the Women's Entertainment broadcasting company, which features programming specifically addressed to the female audience. Here, you can learn more about WE's various TV programs, including *Bridezillas*.

Web by Women, for Women

12345

www.io.com/~wwwomen

Lots of solid, unbiased, nonsleazy information about sexuality, pregnancy, contraception, and more. The site design is a little clunky, but the information remains useful and relevant.

WISE (Women's Initiative for Self Empowerment)

12345

www.wise-up.org

This site focuses primarily on domestic violence issues and providing "holistic and sustainable support services to women and children survivors of domestic violence and sexual assault; education to the public-at-large; advocacy with critical stakeholders; and training to service providers on the issues of domestic violence and sexual assault." This site features a list of programs and events, volunteer opportunities, jobs, and a photo gallery.

WomanOwned.Com–Business Information for Women Entrepreneurs

12345

www.womanowned.com

WomanOwned provides "information, tools, networking opportunities, and advice that have helped hundreds of thousands of women." Here, you'll find hundreds of articles, access to business tools and resources, and additional tools for networking with others in the business world online. This is a great place for women to learn how to start their own business, get it financed, and get support.

The Women and Politics Institute

12345

wandp.american.edu

Women and Politics is an academic journal published at West Georgia College in Carrollton, Georgia. The goal of the journal is to foster research and the development of theory on women's political participation, the role of women in society, and the impact of public policy upon women's lives. Included online are article abstracts, calls for papers, and subscription information.

Women and Social Movements in the United States: 1600–2000

12345

womhist.binghamton.edu

View United States history through the eyes of women instead of men, and see just how much women have contributed to the shaping of the nation. Site features several sections, including Documents, Teacher's Corner, and Search. A few additional links to related sites are also provided.

Women in Aviation History: The Ninety Nines

12345

www.ninety-nines.org/bios.html

At this site, you'll find biographies and tributes to the prominent women in the history of aviation, including Louise Sacchi, Fay Gillis Wells, and Bessie Coleman. Interesting!

Best Women's Human Rights Net

12345

www.whrnet.org

Women's Human Rights Net is very much like a global intelligence service on issues related to human rights for women. Here, you can find the latest news stories from around the world complete with analysis and commentary to place the information in the right context. The opening page displays a collection of late-breaking news and articles. You can use the navigation bar on the left to focus your search in the following content areas: Challenging Fundamentalisms, UN Conferences, Treaty Bodies and Instruments, HR Systems, Documents, Archives, and Links. With its thorough coverage of global issues affecting women's rights and its solid directory of links to other women's rights and advocacy sites, this site was an easy pick as Best of the Best in the Women's Issues category.

Women's Human Rights Resources

12345

www.law-lib.utoronto.ca/Diana

The Women's Human Rights Resources Programme (WHRR) "collects, organizes and disseminates information on women's human rights law to facilitate research, teaching, and cooperation," with an emphasis on selected international and Canadian topics. Here, you'll find a collection of websites, online documents, and bibliographies about women's human rights issues.

WomensNet

www.igc.or

Supports women's organizations worldwide and provides articles and links to information and resources for women's issues.

WomenWatch

12345

www.un.org/womenwatch

An overview of United Nations and regional programs dealing with women's rights and the advancement and empowerment of women, plus related news and statistics. Site features links to other U.N. websites, too.

Working Moms Refuge

12345

www.momsrefuge.com

Pick up tips and strategies for making the most of your time, from quick recipes to ideas for choosing a financial planner, at this site. Much of the content is geared to moms juggling childcare and work responsibilities, with chat and discussions forums available for commiserating and advice. Special area for dads is also available.

WWWomen!

www.wwwomen.com

A comprehensive search directory for information on issues of interest to women. WWWomen links users to chats, advice, site reviews, message boards, and websites about topics including health, religion, education, and feminism.

Yale Journal of Law and Feminism

www.yale.edu/lawnfem/law&fem.html

The Yale Journal of Law and Feminism is committed to publishing pieces about women's experiences, especially as they have been structured, affected, controlled, discussed, or ignored by the law. This website contains subscription information, access to past issues, and the chance to submit your own article or even order a T-shirt.

WOMEN'S HEALTH

Estronaut: Forum for Women's Health

1 2 3 4 5

www.womenshealth.org

Health and wellness page that focuses exclusively on women's health issues. The center column of this page presents news and articles on current health issues and breakthroughs. Use the navigation bar on the left to explore other content areas, including Sex, Gyny, Pregnancy, Eat, Body, Mind, Healthcare, Looks, and Move. You can mouse over a link in the navigation bar to find out where it'll take you.

Feminist Women's Health Center

1 2 3 4 5

www.fwhc.org

Feminist Women's Health Center is dedicated to building "a world where all women freely make their own decisions regarding their bodies, reproduction, and sexuality—a world where all women can fulfill their own unique potential and live healthy whole lives." This site features information on birth control, abortion, menstrual cycles, breast care, menopause, and other issues specifically related to women's health. Site also features special content for teenagers, a list of clinics and resources, a collection of inspirational poetry and stories, a news and views area, and a Q&A area.

Best National Women's Health Resource Center

1 2 3 4 5

www.healthywomen.org

The National Women's Health Resource Center (NWHRC), a nonprofit organization, is "the leading independent health information source for women. NWHRC develops and distributes up-to-date and objective women's health information based on the latest advances in medical research and practice." This site opens with a three-column page. Running down the middle is a collection of news and articles about the latest hot topics. Off on the left is a list of quick links to the most popular features, including Tool Kits (for common conditions), Health Women Take 10 (nutrition, health, and fitness tips), and other resources. The column on the right provides access to an alphabetic list of common conditions along with other features. Use the navigation tabs at the top of the page to jump to key content areas.

NBCC–National Breast Cancer Coalition

1 2 3 4 5

www.natlbcc.org

Learn more about this nonprofit advocacy organization and its efforts to eradicate breast cancer through action and public policy change. Join the organization or just learn more about breast cancer here through the breaking news section.

Women'sHealth

1 2 3 4 5

www.womenshealth.com

Women'sHealth features articles, advice, and treatment options for women who may benefit from various types of hormone replacement therapy. Heath topics cover anti-aging, bone health, menopause, natural HRT, perimenopause, premenstrual syndrome, restore testing, hysterectomy, skin care, and a special area for men.

WOODWORKING

Popular Woodworking

12345

www.popularwoodworking.com

This site is the Internet home of *Popular Woodworking* magazine. This site lets you sample from the magazine's content. Use the navigation bar on the left to jump to your desired area of interest: Tool Reviews, Free Project Plans, Select Articles, Searchable Links, Woodworking Schools, and Magazine Extras. Site also features a newsletter, bookstore, and other valuable information and resources.

WoodNet

12345

www.woodnet.net

More than 100 woodworking tips and techniques are available here to help you finish that project. You can also find out more about which tools are best for your job, exchange ideas in the discussion forums, and check out links to other woodworking sites.

WoodWeb

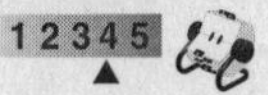

www.woodweb.com

Excellent directory of woodworking websites; provides links to woodworking information, resources, and products. Everything from adhesives and tools to software is available.

Woodworker's Central

www.woodworking.org

From the Woodworker's Website Association comes this handy website for woodworking enthusiasts. The site opens with a page that's chock full of links to practical information, including a wood sampler, a miter master (to take the guesswork out of your compound miters), a plan and article search (for free plans and tips), a tool survey (tool reviews), an accident survey (a database of suggestions on what not to do with your tools), and an online chat area (Wednesdays only). The site also features a navigation bar on the left that provides quick access to tools, safety information, videos, and other resources.

Best Woodworking.com

www.woodworking.com

This site features an awesome collection of articles, how-to tutorials, and tips on a wide range of woodworking topics. Tabbed navigation bar at the top takes you to the key content areas, including Home, Shop, Learn, Forum, Plans, and Links. The opening page presents introductions to the latest articles, which you can click to access the full versions. Areas on the opening page include forum (latest topics), current woodworking news, upcoming events, tools and gadgets, featured plan, and featured woodworker. You can pick up a lot of tips from expert woodworkers and even shop online for tools.

WRESTLING

Pro Wrestling Daily

1 2 3 4 5

www.prowrestlingdaily.com

Pro Wrestling Daily is a no-frills professional wrestling news and information site with dozens of links to current happenings and feature stories. Site also features a calendar, daily cartoon, previews, a photo gallery, recaps, results, and discussion forums.

Professional Wrestling Online Museum

1 2 3 4 5

www.wrestlingmuseum.com

If you're growing a little nostalgic over the real wrestlers of the good old days, visit the Professional Wrestling Online Museum. Here, you can research the past of your favorites, including Verne Gagne, Mad Dog Vachon, and Dick the Bruiser. Site features an alphabetic index of these classic grapplers, photo galleries, streaming audio, and a directory of links to related sites.

ProWrestling.com

www.prowrestling.com

Locate information on upcoming pro wrestling matches and TV programming, and read articles, get headline news, and stay up to date regarding your favorite wrestler's career here.

SLAM!

1 2 3 4 5

slam.canoe.ca/Slam/Wrestling

SLAM! Sports features this wrestling area where you can learn about WrestleMania, view wrestler bios and obituaries, visit the Hall of Fame, check up on news and rumors, browse the photo galleries, and chat with other fans.

TheMat.com

themat.com

Whether you're looking for collegiate, high school, youth, or women's wrestling, you'll find Olympic trial information, archives, results, and links here. This is also the home of USA Wrestling, the national governing body for freestyle and Greco-Roman wrestling in the United States. Here, you can learn more about the organization, event schedules, wrestling camps and clinics, international tours, and more. Shop online for USA Wrestling merchandise.

Total Nonstop Wrestling on Spike TV

www.tnawrestling.com

Spike TV is the most popular television network for professional wrestling and other bang-'em-up sports. Here, you can find out the latest about upcoming televised bouts and pay-per-view events, tour the photo archives, and get current news and results.

World Wrestling Entertainment

`www.wwe.com`

World Wrestling Entertainment is one of the top professional wrestling organizations in the world. Visit this site to learn more about the organization, its superstars, and upcoming events both on television and on pay per view. Chat areas and video games are also available.

WrestleZone

`www.wrestlezone.com`

Read the extensive list of headline wrestling news, stay updated on results and upcoming fights, and check out pics of your favorite guys and gals here.

Wrestling Planet

`www.wrestlingplanet.com`

Wrestling Planet is a professional wrestling site that features news, information, match results, and behind-the-scenes feature stories. Site also defines common wrestling jargon and reveals how wrestlers safely perform various tricks, such as throwing fireballs, striking one another with chairs, and bleeding. Discussion forums, wrestling schedules, and links to other pro-wrestling sites are also available.

Best Wrestling USA Magazine

1 2 3 4 5

`www.wrestlingusa.com`

Take a look at action photos, see results from college and high school matches, read articles, and find out about wrestling camps and just about anything else you might want to learn about junior high, high school, and collegiate wrestling. You can subscribe to the magazine, *Wrestling USA*, using a secured credit card connection. For coverage of real wrestling, this site has no match.

WRITING

11 Rules of Writing

1 2 3 4 5

www.junketstudies.com/rulesofw

Concise and practical tip list for punctuation, grammar, and clear writing. Also has links to other writing resources.

A+ Research and Writing

1 2 3 4 5

www.ipl.org/div/aplus

This resource for high school and college students includes guides for researching and writing academic papers. Also has research links.

About.com–Freelance Writers

1 2 3 4 5

freelancewrite.about.com

A great site for experienced and new freelance writers, providing writing gigs, tips for improving your writing abilities, contract help, and discussion opportunities. Go to the Jump Start section if you're new to freelancing or just jump right in to look for potential assignments. Find out what editors expect and learn from fellow writers based on their experiences.

Best AuthorLink!

1 2 3 4 5

www.authorlink.com

Authorlink, an award-winning Internet news/information/marketing service for the publishing industry, has been around for several years, which proves its viability. The service provides editors and agents fast access to prescreened professional fiction and nonfiction manuscripts that have been submitted by authors. Readers and writers can quickly order any titles from the secure e-store. These titles are available at major bookstores and online bookstores such as Amazon.com. Authorlink also has its own publishing imprint, Authorlink Press, which offers all the standard services including electronic press, short-run publishing services, and other services. If you are a writer or just interested in reading a good book, this is the site for you.

A+ Research and Writing

1 2 3 4 5

www.ipl.org/div/aplus

This resource for high school and college students includes guides for researching and writing academic papers. Also has research links.

Bartleby.com

1 2 3 4 5

www.bartleby.com

This site bills itself as "the preeminent publisher of literature, reference and verse providing students, researchers, and the intellectually curious with unlimited access to books and information on the Web, free of charge."

Business Writing Tips

1 2 3 4 5

www.basic-learning.com/wbwt/tip01.htm

Basic Learning Systems presents *Bull's Eye Business Writing*, a self-paced workbook that can help managers and others improve their business writing and all other written communications such as email, reports, letters, and so on. You can order some of the publications through the secure online store.

Children's Writing Resource Center

1 2 3 4 5

www.write4kids.com

Articles and recommendations for becoming a successful writer for children. Chat with other children's writers and illustrators.

IAAY Expository Writing Tutorial

1 2 3 4 5

www.cty.jhu.edu/writing

Home to John Hopkins' Institute for the Academic Advancement of Youth. This cool site provides expository writing instructions for kids in grades 6–12. Kids get to work with a more experienced writer as they explore the writing process. To participate, they must be enrolled in the tutorial to access the pages containing the assignments. Financial aid is available.

Indispensible Writing Resources

1 2 3 4 5

www.quintcareers.com/writing

This site features a directory of writing resources on and off the Web that can come in handy when you're writing a research paper. Includes links to writing labs, research-oriented search tools, writing-related websites, and style guides.

Proposal Writing

1 2 3 4 5

fdncenter.org/learn/shortcourse/prop1.html

This is an excellent article on how to write successful proposals, beginning with the process of gathering information.

Purdue Online Writing Lab (OWL)

1 2 3 4 5

owl.english.purdue.edu

Improve your writing with help from this online resource, where you'll also find handouts that might answer lots of your questions. But if not, turn to the Purdue experts for help.

RoseDog.com

1 2 3 4 5

rosedog.com

Post your work and get feedback or just exposure that might help boost your career. You'll also find information on literary agents here, too.

Screenwriters Online

1 2 3 4 5

screenwriter.com/insider

This is the only screenwriters' tutorial sponsored by professional screenwriters. It consists of a series of chat rooms, forums where screenplays are critiqued, the *Screenwriters Insider* newsletter, and interviews with professionals.

SPAN

1 2 3 4 5

www.spannet.org

SPAN is "a nonprofit trade association dedicated to advancing the interests and expertise of independent publishers and authors through educational opportunities and discounted services." If you're a writer looking for tips and techniques for publishing and promoting your own works, check out SPAN for guidance and resources.

Writers on the Net

1 2 3 4 5

www.writers.com

Pay-for-use tutoring and editing classes, and workshops led by experienced, published writers.

The Write News

writenews.com

This site presents everything you ever wanted to know about the publishing business. An online industry newsletter with more than 1,000 links for writers, agents, and publishers.

Writers Write

12345

www.writerswrite.com

Find writing jobs, improve your craft, and mingle with fellow authors here.

Writing Den

12345

www2.actden.com/writ_den

The Writing Den is designed for students from grade 6–12 who want to improve their writing skills. Site covers all aspects of writing from word choice to sentence and paragraph structure. Sections include Tips-O-Matic, Word-of-the-Day, and Teacher's Guide. Streaming audio narrations are also included.

Writing for Dollars

12345

www.writingfordollars.com

Searchable writer's guidelines database of paying markets. Find advice, publications, and resources for making money as a writer.

Writing-World.com

12345

www.writing-world.com

News articles, tips, and online classes for aspiring writers and for writers who want to further develop their talents.

Writing for the Web

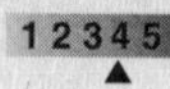

www.useit.com/papers/webwriting

People read differently on the Web than they do when reading printed publications, so writers need to adapt their material to the Web. Here, John Morkes and Jakob Nielsen publish the findings of their research on how people access information on the Web. Some excellent writing guidelines for web authors.

Xlibris

www1.xlibris.com

If you have a manuscript and are not sure how to go about getting it edited, illustrated, published, and marketed, check out this site. Xlibris provides complete services to authors to help them get their manuscripts to market to start generating royalties.

Young Authors Workshop

12345

www.planet.eon.net/~bplaroch

Resource for middle school students has sections for getting ideas, writing, editing, and publishing their work. Also has teacher resources.

YOGA

A2ZYoga

12345

www.a2zyoga.com

This excellent site covers a wide range of topics related to the philosophy and practice of yoga. It begins by providing answers to the three most common questions: How will yoga help me? Can I do yoga? What's the best yoga for me? The site covers the basics, including Getting Started, Practicing Yoga, Yoga Safety, and Yoga Poses. It also addresses common myths about yoga.

ABC of Yoga

www.abc-of-yoga.com

ABC of Yoga "covers a wide range of topics about the different aspects of Yoga such as the various yoga styles, postures, poses, and techniques." The opening page presents sections on Learn Yoga, Travel (yoga vacations), News, Shop, and Community. You can use the tabs that run across the top of the site to navigate to the desired section or use the links on the left for more precise navigation. Site covers basics, getting started, different styles, exercises and postures, and much more. Here, you can also find a directory of links to other yoga sites. Very complete and attractively designed site.

Body Trends

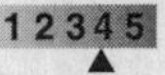

www.bodytrends.com/yoga.asp

You can order all your yoga-associated products from the BodyTrends.com site to get you started on the right stretch. The company offers such products as mats, bags, wedges, blocks, sandbags, straps, and numerous yoga-related videos.

Kundalini Support Center

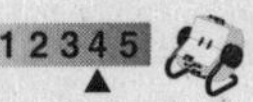

www.kundalini-support.com

Kundalini yoga focuses on awakening the spirit and increasing self-awareness of its practitioners. In some cases, the awakening experience of Kundalini can be quite intense and lead to complications. Here, you can find support and information to help you through the awakening and achieve the heightened awareness that Kundalini strives for. This site includes a survival guide, a list of Kundalini links and spiritual links, and a bibliography.

Sahaja Yoga Meditation

www.sahajayoga.org

Created by Shri Mataji Nirmala Devi in 1970, Sahaja yoga is a "method of meditation which brings a breakthrough in the evolution of human awareness." At this site, you can learn more about Sahaja meditation, read testimonials and health benefits, view a list of Q&As, check out the book reviews, and much more. Also provides information about Kundalini yoga.

Santosha.com

12345

www.santosha.com

Santosha.com is a commercial site where you can purchase yoga tools, supplies, books, and videos. Site also features some free information, including yoga postures, yoga sutras, and a Moksha journal.

Siddha Yoga Meditation

12345

www.siddhayoga.org

Learn what Siddha yoga is and find out about courses, news, and reading that might be of help, as well as centers that specialize in this type of yoga. The site also provides information on upcoming events and programs for youth. It also includes a nice online bookstore from which you can order related books.

Sivananda Yoga "Om" Page

12345

www.sivananda.org

A clearinghouse for information on yoga and Vedanta. The site has yoga exercise tips, a guide to higher consciousness, and biographies of Swami Vishnu and his guru, Swami Sivananda. From the home page, you can access the Five Points of Yoga and the Four Paths of Yoga for a fairly extensive illustrated guide to positions, exercises, and philosophy.

Step-by-Step Yoga Postures

12345

www.santosha.com/asanas

This site has a lot of useful information. One of the highlights is the listing of both the Sanskrit name and English translation. Choose from a long list of asanas and read step-by-step directions on how to achieve these yoga positions. Also read about meditation.

A World of Yoga

12345

www.yogaworld.org

At this site, you'll learn more about yoga techniques and how it can help you reach a higher state of consciousness, according to the site's host, Graham Ledgerwood. Find out about the eight main types of yoga and how they relate to an individual's spiritual path.

Yoga Alliance

12345

www.yogaalliance.org

Yoga Alliance is an international organization of yoga instructors and schools that deals with certification. Here, you can look up certified schools and instructors. If you're a yoga instructor, you can find additional services and support.

Yogabasics.com

12345

www.yogabasics.com

This beautifully designed site makes it easy to learn yoga basics and then move on to learn how to use yoga as a healing art. Four tabs on the opening page provide easy access to the major features at this site: Practice, Learn, Explore, Connect. Each tab pulls up a list of options—for example, when you click the Practice tab, a navigation bar appears that enables you to check out yoga postures, breathing techniques, meditation, and pose sequences. Clear graphics make it easy to understand the various positions. For even more content and features, subscribe for a premium membership.

> **Tip:** If you're a beginner, click the Learn tab and click History & Philosophy for a brief primer, and then click Chakras for a description of the seven chakras.

Yoga.com

12345

www.yoga.com

Yoga.com is primarily an online store, where you can purchase yoga books and videos, clothing, mats, and other items. However, it also features articles, instruction, a pose of the month, free downloads, discussion forums, and other content and services for the yoga community.

The Yoga Directory

www.yogadirectory.com

The Yoga Directory contains a list of yoga teachers, yoga centers, organizations, music, yoga therapists, health products, and yoga retreats, giving you just about everything you need to practice yoga.

Best Yoga Journal

www.yogajournal.com

Yoga Journal is a magazine, and you can subscribe to it at this site, but this site offers a lot of excellent information for free, even if you're not a subscriber. The opening page features a collection of articles from the current issue along with a photo gallery, expert advice, an online poll, and a calendar of events. Near the top of the page is a navigation bar that provides quick access to the many areas of the site, including New to Yoga, Poses, Practice, Health, Wisdom, and Meditation. The opening page also offers a Pose Finder, a Yoga 101 primer, Expert Advice, and a tool for finding yoga classes near you. Site has an attractive design, is easy to navigate, and features excellent content, making it an easy choice for Best of the Best in the Yoga category.

Yoga Site

www.yogasite.com

Great instructional material that tells and shows you, through drawings, about basic yoga positions. You also can read about yoga styles, review questions and answers posed regarding yoga, identify yoga-related organizations, and read about yoga therapy news. And if you still find you have unanswered questions about yoga, you'll find links to other yoga sites that might help.

Yoga Synergy

www.yogasynergy.com.au

Yoga Synergy was established in Newtown (Sydney, Australia) in 1984. The teaching represents a synthesis between traditional Hatha yoga and modern medical science and is designed to "enhance one's life by nurturing and generating the internal fire and life force that keeps us alive."

YOUTH ORGANIZATIONS

America's Promise

12345

www.americaspromise.org

After the Presidents' Summit for America's Future in 1997, America's Promise—The Alliance for Youth was founded to make children and youth a national priority. At this site, you can learn the five promises that the organization has made to America's children and youth and find out what you can do right now to help fulfill those promises.

Boy Scouts of America

12345

www.scouting.org

If you're a scout, you can use this site to learn about scouting programs, events, publications, merchandise, and awards, as well as to play fun games online. Anyone considering becoming a scout (boys age 7 to 20) or a scout leader will find this site informative.

Boys and Girls Clubs of America

12345

www.bgca.org

The Boys and Girls Club Movement is a nationwide affiliation of local, autonomous organizations working to help youth from all backgrounds (with special concern for those from disadvantaged circumstances) develop the qualities needed to become responsible citizens and leaders. Gameroom area is available for young visitors.

B'nai B'rith Youth Organization

12345

www.bbyo.org

B'nai B'rith is a "youth-led, worldwide organization which provides opportunities for Jewish youth to develop their leadership potential, a positive Jewish identity and commitment to their personal development."

CYO: Catholic Youth Organization

12345

www.cyocamp.org

Home of the Catholic Youth Organization–sponsored camps. Learn more about the CYO camps, meet the staff, check up on employment opportunities, and learn how to contact personnel via email.

Best Girl Scouts

12345

www.girlscouts.org

Learn all about the world's largest organization for girls, its programs, research activities, traditions, publications, and, of course, Girl Scout cookies. The site has a nice shopping mall where you can securely shop for most of the things any young woman would be interested in. There is also a helpful FAQs section if you have unanswered questions and online games and quizzes just for fun. The Girl Scouts are where girls turn to discover fun, friendship, and the power of girls together. They promote the theory that Girl Scouting gives girls opportunities to build skills for lifetime success in sports, science, and even in a Girl Scout cookie sale.

National 4-H Council

12345

www.fourhcouncil.edu

Whether you're considering joining 4-H, or if you're a 4-H alumnus, this site has information for you about current programs and initiatives, getting involved, and reconnecting with past 4-Hers. 4-H is dedicated to helping youth develop leadership skills while understanding and addressing important community issues.

National Association of Peer Programs

www.peerprograms.org

The National Association of Peer Programs (NAPP) is a nonprofit corporation whose mission is "to help adults establish, train, supervise, maintain, and evaluate peer programs." Here, you can learn more about the organization and how it can help you and your community build peer programs help the youth in your area who are at the greatest risk. When we visited, the site was working on including testimonials from people who have been helped by NAPP-sponsored peer programs.

National Mentoring Center

www.nwrel.org/mentoring/organizations.html

This site features links to various organizations that offer mentoring programs for youth, including Big Brothers Big Sisters of America, Public/Private Ventures, and The National Mentoring Partnerships.

Operation Fit Kids

www.acefitness.org/ofk/default.aspx

Operation Fit Kids is a program from the American Council on Exercise designed to make kids more active and to encourage proper nutrition. Here, you can find youth fitness facts, a youth fitness Q&A, exercise programs, and additional information and resources.

YMCA

www.ymca.int

Locate YMCA offices and hotels at this site, where you'll also learn more about the mission of this Christian organization and its programs. You can review the online magazine, *YMCA World*, and catch up on organizational news. You'll also find a directory of national and local associations.

Related Site

www.ymca.org

Young People's Ministries

www.gbod.org/youngpeople

Young People's Ministries is designed to connect young people in ministries with young people all over the world and strengthen the connection between the youth, God, and the church. Site features inspirational stories that show youth living their faith and making a difference in the world. Visit this site to learn how to get connected and find the support and inspiration you and your youth group needs to continue doing positive work to improve the world.

YouthLink

www.youthlink.org

YouthLink, a division of the Foundation of America, is geared toward youths and encourages their participation within their own communities by rewarding those who are selected with Youth Action Award grants.

ZOOS

The Albuquerque Aquarium

1 2 3 4 5

www.cabq.gov/biopark/aquarium/index.html

Take a fascinating journey through the marine habitats of the oceans at this fantastic aquarium in New Mexico. Many other features are available here, such as information about the zoo, the city, and other items you might be interested in.

American Zoo and Aquarium Association

1 2 3 4 5

www.aza.org

This is the flagship membership organization for zoological parks, aquariums, oceanariums, and wildlife parks in North America. Find out what they are all about, their members, publications, conferences, how to support their conservation and animal welfare work, and more.

Birmingham Zoo

1 2 3 4 5

www.birminghamzoo.com

The Birmingham Zoo is home to nearly 750 animals representing about 250 species, and attracts nearly a half million visitors annually. Although this site provides little information about the animals, it does provide the basic information you need to plan your visit to the zoo and learn about its many educational and volunteer programs.

The Bronx Zoo

1 2 3 4 5

www.bronxzoo.com

The Bronx Zoo is home to more than 4,000 animals, including some of the world's most endangered species. The zoo has more than 265 wooded acres devoted to spacious naturalistic habitats. The site is almost as impressive with abundant information about the zoo and what it provides.

Brookfield Zoo

1 2 3 4 5

www.brookfieldzoo.org

Brookfield Zoo, located on 200 wild acres just outside Chicago, uses this website to introduce visitors to many of its main attractions and its interesting inhabitants. Content is divided into four main sections—Information, Adventure Trail, Projects & Programs, and Support the Zoo. A Quick Links menu provides easy access to specific areas on the site. For information about a specific animal, scroll down the page and under Adventure Trail, click Field Guide to the Animals.

Cincinnati Zoo and Botanical Garden

1 2 3 4 5 

www.cincyzoo.org

Wander through this site to experience the Cincinnati Zoo and the world of nature. Find current events and discover what's new, learn about conservation and how you can help, get information on exotic travel programs, educate yourself about wildlife, and participate in the weekly animal/plant guessing game.

> **Tip:** Upon reaching the opening page, click the Exhibits/Gardens link at the top of the page and then click Animal Exhibits or Gardens on the left for a clickable map of the zoo's main attractions.

Cleveland Metroparks Zoo

1 2 3 4 5 

www.clemetzoo.com

Want to visit the rain forest? Tour the zoo? Learn about conservation? Get educated about the natural world? Read about research being conducted by zoo staff? You can do all this and more at the site of the Cleveland Metroparks Zoo. The opening page provides easy access to the four main content areas: Discover, Learn, Explore, and Protect.

The Dallas Zoo

12345

www.dallas-zoo.org

One of the best-looking websites featuring all the main attractions you can find at most zoos plus an aquarium. There's tons of information about the zoo and related subjects. Be sure to visit here before you go to the zoo. It's worth the effort just to visit the site, and after you do, you'll probably want to visit the zoo in person.

Denver Zoo

12345

www.denverzoo.org

Visitors can take a zoo tour and view short video clips of the animals, find operating hours and admission prices, or read about the conservation efforts of the Denver Zoo. Kids can click the Kids menu for quick access to information about special offerings at the zoo, including activities, parties, the carousel, and train rides.

Fort Worth Zoo

www.fortworthzoo.com

Zoo hours, a zoo map, educational opportunities, and special events are presented here. Visitors also can print games and puzzles from the Delta's Kids Page.

The Indianapolis Zoo

www.indianapoliszoo.com

The Indianapolis Zoo is one of the premier zoos in the country and features a unique Underwater Dolphin Dome. Click the Dolphin Adventure tab to learn more about it. Site features tabbed navigation along the top, providing quick access to Visitor Info, About Zoo and Gardens, Members, Education, Special Events, Corporate/Social Events, Work at the Zoo & Gardens, and Support the Zoo & Gardens. When you click a tab, another more detailed navigation bar appears on the left. Site features some good information and excellent photos, but the amount of information available about specific animals is a little disappointing.

Kids World 2000: Animals, Zoos and Aquariums

now2000.com/kids/zoos.shtml

A place where young cyber-travelers can find 50+ links to animals, zoos, and aquariums in the United States and overseas. Just click a link to jump to the site of your choice and learn all about the flora and fauna.

Lincoln Park Zoo

12345

www.lpzoo.com

This site presents an excellent introduction to the Lincoln Park Zoo in Chicago. The open page offers quick access to the main attractions along with a navigation bar at the top with links to Info (hours of operation, directions, and so on), Events (calendar, public programs, and private events), Animals (fact sheets and animal care), Education (public programs, school programs, and an educational game), Conservation & Science (what the zoo does and what we can do to help preserve wildlife), Support (how you can support the zoo), and Shop (buy stuff online).

The Los Angeles Zoo

www.lazoo.org

Opened in November 1966, the Los Angeles Zoo is home to more than 1,200 animals. This site includes a history of the zoo as well as visitor information, animal facts, excerpts from the zoo's quarterly magazine, a list of job opportunities, and a small collection of games.

> **Tip:** When you click Animal Facts on the opening page, the site presents information about only one animal. Scroll down to the bottom of this page and click on Click Here to View Other Animal Facts.

Memphis Zoo Home Page

www.memphiszoo.org

This site provides basic information about the Memphis Zoo, such as hours and prices, educational programs, special events, membership, the gift shop, the animal hospital, and the zoo's history. Good information mainly for those interested in visiting in person.

National Zoo

natzoo.si.edu

The Smithsonian Institution runs the National Zoological Park, the world's largest museum and research complex. The National Zoo is dedicated to "celebrating, studying, and protecting wild animals in their natural habitats." The actual zoo is a 163-acre zoological park in Rock Creek National Park in Washington, D.C., where the famous pandas, Tian Tian and Mei Xiang, call home. This website is packed with information about all sorts of wild animals, and the site is very attractive and easy to navigate. Visiting is like taking a trip to the zoo, except here you can learn much more about the various species.

The North Carolina Zoological Park

www.nczoo.org

If you'd like to get a glimpse of this zoo, click Visit the Zoo to get a park overview, a park map, photo tour, visitors' hints, and gift and food information. Click Animal Finder for vital statistics about an animal of interest; you can search for animals by name, browse a complete listing, or list them by exhibit. Site also features free stuff, including desktop wallpaper and online games.

Oakland Zoo

www.oaklandzoo.org

The Oakland Zoo created this website to encourage visitors to learn more about the zoo and its inhabitants and to support the zoo. The navigation bar on the left presents several options including About the Zoo, Animals A–Z, Education Programs, and Valley Children's Zoo. For a zoo that's located in a major city, this website is disappointing.

Oregon Zoo

www.oregonzoo.org

You can search this Portland, Oregon, zoo's site or just jump to one of the offered areas: About Our Zoo, About Our Animals, Visitor Information, What's Happening, Get Involved, Saving Species, Teachers and Educators, No Adults Allowed!, and more. There's something for everyone here. Click the Gallery link for access to the webcams, videos, and podcasts.

Philadelphia Zoo Online

www.phillyzoo.org

Besides the home page, this site offers an education page, a conservation page, an animals list, the PhillyZoo News page, and an online search engine. You also can enter the site index to get all kinds of information on animals, conservation activities, zoo facts, and more.

The Phoenix Zoo

www.phoenixzoo.org/zoo

The Phoenix Zoo has a stellar reputation as one of the best zoos in the country for kids. This site is a great place to go to orient yourself to the zoo before visiting it, but it offers little else. You won't find a tremendous amount of information about the zoo's inhabitants, for example.

Pittsburgh Zoo and Aquarium

www.pittsburghzoo.com

"Located approximately 5 miles east of downtown Pittsburgh, the Pittsburgh Zoo & PPG Aquarium is a 77-acre facility that is home to thousands of animals representing hundreds of diverse species." The opening page at this site presents a navigation bar off to the left, which you can use to skip to General Info, Wildlife (where you can look up an animal or find answers to common questions), Education (programs and activities), Conservation (recycling and other conservation projects and activities), Special Events (calendar of upcoming events), PPG Aquarium (where you can learn about coral and specific animals at the aquarium), Water's Edge (polar bears, sea otters, and walrus), and Kids' Kingdom (games and activities for young visitors).

The San Antonio Zoo

www.sazoo-aq.org

At this site, you can get a word from the director, learn what's new at the zoo, get general zoo information, tour the zoo, learn about the "adopt an animal" program, find out about zoo membership and employment opportunities, and access links to related sites. This site also features some online games for kids.

San Diego Zoo

www.sandiegozoo.org

The San Diego zoo has a reputation for being the best zoo in the world, and it continues its dedication to quality with this tech-savvy site. This is the only site in the Zoo category that features blogs, a robust collection of podcasts, and a huge assortment of videos, live webcams, and TV clips. The navigation bar that runs across the top of the page provides quick access to visitor information, a calendar of upcoming events, animal & plants (information, photos, webcams, and more), a kids area, education resources, and additional features.

San Francisco Zoo

www.sfzoo.org

For the past few years, the San Francisco Zoo has been undergoing some major renovations, including a recently expanded Children's Zoo and an all new Lipman Family Lemur Forest. At this site, you can learn about the latest developments; obtain visitor information; and learn about the various programs, exhibits, and activities sponsored by the zoo.

The St. Louis Zoo

www.stlzoo.org

You can do everything from plan your visit to the zoo to adopt an animal and much more. A beautiful site consisting of many rich features to make your visit more enjoyable, along with some fairly good information about specific animals complete with photos.

Woodland Park Zoo (Seattle, WA)

www.zoo.org

The Woodland Park Zoo in Seattle, Washington, maintains this site with a virtual tour; information on admission, conservation, and education; special events, the zoo store, and exhibits.

ZooWeb

www.zooweb.com

Excellent directory to zoo and aquarium websites from all over the world. The navigation bar on the left lets you jump to Top Sites, Zooper Sites, Zoo Groups (who's who in zoos), Zoo Games, and Zoo Cams. Running down the right side of the opening page is a list of Guest links. The center of the page contains some feature sites.

INDEX

A

abortion
- Abortion Clinic Directory, 713
- AbortionFacts.com, 713
- **ACLU Reproductive Rights, 713**
- Ethics Updates, 713
- NARAL Pro-Choice America, 713
- National Abortion Federation, 713
- **National Right to Life, 714**
- Planned Parenthood Federation of America, Inc., 714
- Planned Parenthood Golden Gate, 714
- Teenwire, 714

accessories (clothing). *See* jewelry; watches

accounting
- Accounting Terminology Guide, 1
- American Institute of Certified Public Accountants, 1
- CPA Directory, 1
- CPA Journal Online, The, 1
- SmartPros, 1

acting. *See* movies; theater

activism
- Activism.net, 2
- AlterNet, 2
- CorpWatch.org, 2
- Digital Freedom Network, 2
- Idealist.org, 2
- Indybay.org, 2
- PETA.org, 3
- Protest.Net, 3
- They Rule, 3
- tolerance.org, 3
- Voice of the People, 3
- World Connected, A, 3

acupuncture
- Acupuncture.com, 27
- Acupuncture/Acupressure Internet Resources, 27
- American Academy of Medical Acupuncture, 28
- American College of Acupuncture & Oriental Medicine, 28
- Blue Poppy Press, 28
- National Certification Commission for Acupuncture and Oriental Medicine, 28

ADD/ADHD (Attention Deficit Disorder/Attention Deficit Hyperactivity Disorder)
- A.D.D. Warehouse, 547
- ADD FAQ, 547
- ADD Warehouse, 547
- ADD/ADHD Links Pages, 547
- ADDitude.com, 547

addictions/recovery
- alcoholism, 4-8
- drugs, 5-8
- gambling, 6, 333
- general resources
  - *12 Step Cyber Cafe, 7*
  - *Addiction Intervention Resources, 4*
  - *Addiction Recovery Guide, The, 4, 8*
  - *Betty Ford Center, 8*
  - *D.A.R.E., 8*
  - *Get It Straight: The Facts About Drugs, 8*
  - *Indiana Prevention Resource Center, 8*
  - *Join Together Online, 8*
  - *Prevention Online, 9*
  - *Substance Abuse & Mental Health Services Administration, 9*
- sex, 6
- smoking, 6-7

adolescents. *See also* teens; children
- About Parenting Teens, 661
- ADOL: Adolescence Directory On-Line, 661
- alcohol and drug abuse/prevention, 4-8
- Awesome Library for Teens, 757
- Campaign for Our Children, 661
- Canadian Parents Online, 659
- Cool Nurse, 643
- Dear Lucie, 662
- Drug Testing, 662
- Facts for Families, 659
- Family Development Program: Parenting Teens Publications, 662
- Family Education Network: A Parenting and Education Resource, 659
- Family Resource Center, 659
- FamilyTime, 659
- Girl Power! Campaign, 659
- homework help, 255-256, 262
- iParenting.com, 660
- John Rosemond, 660
- KidsHealth.org: For Teens, 662
- KidSource, 660
- Kotex.com, 662
- Mothering Magazine, 660
- National Campaign to Prevent Teen Pregnancy, 711
- National Families in Action, 662
- National Parenting Center, The, 660
- NCF-National Center for Fathering, 660
- ParenTalk Newsletter: Adolescence, 662
- Parenthood.com, 660
- Parenting.com, 661
- Parenting.org, 661

Parents-Talk.com, 661
Planned Parenthood Federation of America, Inc., 714
Positive Parenting, 661
Raising Successful Teenagers, 662
Talking with Kids About Tough Issues, 662
Teen Challenge World Wide Network, 663
Teen Depression, 551
Teen Help, 663
Teen Sexuality, 809
Teenwire, 714
WholeFamily Center, The, 661
Working Mother, 661

adoption
Adopting.org, 10
Adoption Benefits: Employers as Partners in Family Building, 10
Adoption Guide, The, 10
Adoption Search, 10
Adoption Shop, 10
Adoption Today Magazine, 11
Adoption Travel, 10
Adoption.com, 10
AdoptUsKids, 11
Child Welfare Information Gateway, 11
Dave Thomas Foundation for Adoption, 11
Holt International Children's Services, 11
Independent Adoption Center: Open Adoptions for Birth Mothers and Parents, 11
National Adoption Center, 11
National Council for Adoption, 12
Our Chinese Daughters, 12
Precious in HIS Sight (Internet Adoption Photo Listing), 12
Stepparent Adoption, 672

adventure travel/ecotourism
Adventure Center, 13
Adventure Travel Tips, 13
Alpine Ascents International, 13
Backroads, 13
EarthRiver Expeditions, 13
GORPtravel.com, 13
Great Pacific Adventures, 13
iExplore, 13-14
Mountain Travel Sobek, 14
Outside Online, 14
Recreation.gov, 14
Rod and Gun, 14
Silver Lining Tours, 14
Smithsonian Journeys, 14
Storm Chasing Adventure Tours, 14
Walking Adventures International, 14

advice
All Experts, 15
Answer Bag, 15
Ask a Chef, 15
Daily Candy, 15
Dear Abby, 15
Dr. Laura, 15
Dr. Ruth Online!, 15
drDrew, 16
Elder Wisdom Circle, 16
Everything2, 16
Experts Exchange, 16
Femina, 16
Go Ask Alice!, 16
Kasamba, 16
KnowledgeHound, 16
Relationship-Talk.com, 17
Teen Advice Online, 17

Afghanistan, government information/services, 360

Africa
AFRICANET, 880
allAfrica.com, 629
Capoeira, 526
history, 376
Surfing in South Africa, 928

African-Americans
African American Vernacular English, 500
Black Collegian Online, 468
Chistell Publishing, 949
Eyes of Glory, 388
Martin Luther King, Jr. Day, 397
National Civil Rights Museum, 383, 571
Negro Baseball League, 82
Top Ten African American Inventors, 454
United Negro College Fund, 181

agoraphobia, 546

agriculture
Agricultural Network Information Center (AgNIC), 18
Agriculture in the Classroom, 18
Agriculture Online, 18
AgWeb, 18
American Dairy Science Association (ADSA), 18
American Egg Board, 18
American Farm Bureau: Voice of Agriculture, 18
American Farmland Trust, 19
Beef Home Page, 19
Ceres Online, 19
Economic Research Service (USDA), 19
Farm Safety 4 Just Kids, 19
FarmCredit, 19
Farmland Information Center, 19
Food and Agriculture Organization of the United Nations, 19
Gemplers.com, 19
GrainGenes, 19
House Committee on Agriculture, 20
John Deere-Agricultural Equipment, 20
Kansas City Board of Trade (Kansas City, Missouri), 20
National Agricultural Library (NAL), 20
National Corn Growers Association (NCGA), 20
National Pork Producers Council, 20
Old Farmer's Almanac, 763
Small Farm Today Magazine, 20
Sunkist, 20
Today's Market Prices, 21
USDA (United States Department of Agriculture), 21

AIDS/HIV treatment and prevention
AEGiS, 365
AIDS Education and Research Trust, 365
AIDS Outreach Center, 365
AIDS.ORG, 365
AIDSinfo, 365
Body: A Multimedia AIDS and HIV Information Resource, The, 365-366
Centers for Disease Control and Prevention: HIV, 366
Children with AIDS Project, 366
CPR for AIDS Patients, 367
HIV InSite: Gateway to AIDS Knowledge, 366
Magic Johnson Foundation, Inc., 366
Project Inform, 366
Stop AIDS Project, 366
UNAIDS, 366

air conditioning and heating (home)
AC Doctor, 406
American Society of Heating, Refrigerating, and Air-Conditioning Engineers, Inc., 406
Bryant Heating and Cooling Systems, 406
Carrier, 406
Lennox, 406
Trane, 406

airlines/air travel. *See also* budget travel
Aer Lingus, 22
Air Canada, 22, 143
Air Safe, 68
Air Traffic Control System, 871
Air Travel Health Tips, 871
Airfare.com, 77
Airlines of the Web, 871
AirSafe.com, 871
Alaska Airlines, 22
Aloha Airlines, 22
American Airlines, 22
ATA, 22
Austrian Airlines, 22
British Airways, 22
Cathay Pacific, 22
China Airlines, 22
Continental, 22
Delta SkyLinks Home Page, 69
Delta, 22
Flight Arrivals, 871
Flyer Talk, 871
Frontier, 22
Hawaiian Airlines, 22
JetBlue Airways, 22
Lufthansa, 22
Malaysia Airlines, 23
Mexicana Airlines, 23
Midwest Airlines, 23
New England Airlines, 23
Northwest, 23
Priceline.com, 78
Qantas Airlines, 23
Seat Guru, 871
Singapore Airlines, 23
SkyWest Airlines, 23
Southwest, 23
Spirit Airlines, 23
Transportation Security Administration, 871
Turkish Airlines, 23
United, 23
US Airways, 23

Alabama
Alabama Wonder Full, 887
Birmingham Zoo, 968

Alaska
Alaska Airlines, 22
Alaskan Cabin, Cottage, and Lodge Catalog, 885
Alaskan Railroad, 739
Alaskan Travel Guide, 887

alcohol. *See also* wines
Bombay Sapphire, 318
Intoximeters Inc. Drink Wheel Page, 318
Jack Daniels, 318
Jim Beam, 319
MixedDrink.com, 319
World's Best Bars, 319

alcoholism/recovery
12 Step Cyber Cafe, 7
Al-Anon, 4
Alateen, 4
Alcoholics Anonymous, 4
Betty Ford Center, 8
College Drinking Prevention Website, 4
Cool Spot, The, 5
Drinking: A Student's Guide, 5
DrinkWise, 5
National Institute on Alcohol Abuse and Alcoholism, 5
Sobriety and Recovery Resources, 5

algebra
Algebra Help, 530
Algebra Homework Help, 530
S.O.S. Mathematics Algebra, 531

allergies
Allegra: Allergy Answer Site, 24
Allergy Info, 24
Allergy Store, The, 24
Allergy, Asthma, and Allerpet, 24
American Academy of Allergy, Asthma, & Immunology Online, 24
DustFree.com, 24
food, 25, 323-324
HealingWell's Allergy Resource Center, 25
HowStuffWorks.com: Allergies, 25
National Institute of Allergy and Infectious Diseases, 25
Pollen, 25
Priorities, 25

alternative medicine
A2ZYoga, 963
ABC to Yoga, 963
acupuncture, 27-28
Alternative Health News, 26
Alternative Medicine Magazine Online, 26
AlternativeDr.com, 26
American Holistic Health Association, 26
aromatherapy, 28-29
Ayurveda Yoga Ultra-Nutrition, 26
Body Trends, 963
Chi-Lel Qigong, 26
chiropractors, 164-165
cleansing/detoxification, 29

HealthWorld Online, 26
herbalism, 30-31
homeopathy, 31-32
Kundalini Support Center, 963
Life Matters, 27
magnet therapy, 32
massage, 32-33, 101
Mayo Clinic: Complementary and Alternative Medicine, 27
National Center for Complementary and Alternative Medicine, 27
Natural Health and Longevity Resource Center, 27
New Age Web Works, 623
PetSage-Pet Care Products, 683
Qi: The Journal of Traditional Eastern Health & Fitness, 27
Reiki, 622, 764-765
Sahaja Yoga Meditation, 963
Santosha.com, 963
Siddha Yoga Meditation, 964
Sivananda Yoga "Om" Page, 964
Step-by-Step Yoga Postures, 964
Tai Chi, 528
WholeHealthMD.com, 27
World of Yoga, A, 964
Yoga Alliance, 964
Yoga Directory, The, 965
Yoga Journal, 965
Yoga Site, 965
Yoga Synergy, 965
Yoga.com, 964
Yogabasics.com, 964

alternative music
Alternative Addiction, 585
AlternativeMusic.com, 585
InkBlot Magazine: Deep Coverage of Great Music, 585
Insound, 585
ModernRock.com, 585
Nettwerk Productions, 586
Sub Pop Records Online, 586

Alzheimer's
Ageless Design, Inc., 34
Alzheimer Research Forum, 34
Alzheimer Society of Canada, 34
Alzheimer's Association, 34, 798
Alzheimer's Disease Education and Referral Center, 34
Alzheimer's Disease International, 34
Alzheimer's Foundation of America, 35
Alzheimer's Watch, 35
Healthy Aging, Geriatrics, and Elderly Care, 35
National Library of Medicine (NLM), 35

American Civil War
American Civil War Home Page, The, 914
AmericanCivilWar.com, 914
Civil War Book Review, 914
Civil War Home Page, The, 915
Guidon Books, 115
United States Civil War Center, The, 915

Americas, history of
Ancestors in the Americas, 377
Cultures & History of the Americas, 377
Hispanic History in the Americas, 377
History of the Americas, 377
Jaguar: Icon of Power Through Mayan History, 378

amusement and theme parks
Adventure City, 36
Amusement Park Physics, 36
Anheuser-Busch Theme Parks, 36
Canobie Lake Park, 36
Cedar Point, 36
Disney.com-The Website for Families, 36
Great Escape and Splashwater Kingdom, 36
Hershey Park, 37
LEGOLAND California, 37
Paramount Canada's Wonderland, 143
Paramount's Great America, 37
Paramount's Kings Island, 37
Sea World, 37
SeaWorld, 648
Six Flags Theme Parks, 37
Theme Park Review, 37
TouristFlorida.com, 79
Universal Studios, 37
Walt Disney World, 38

anatomy
Gray's Anatomy of the Human Body, 39
Human Anatomy at EnchantedLearning.com, 39
Human Anatomy Online, 39
Instant Anatomy, 39
WebAnatomy, 39

ancient history
Ancient Greece at the World History Compass, 377
Ancient Mexico, 385
Ancient Worlds, 377
BBC: Inside Ancient History, 378
Egyptian Mathematics, 529
Jaguar: Icon of Power Through Mayan History, 378

animals. *See also* insects; pets
Animaland, 477
Audabon Nature Institute, 611
Bat Conservation, 271
BBC Nature Site, 611
birds, 102-104
cats, 154-155
Coastal America Partnership National Web Site, 274
Conservation Breeding Specialist Group, 271
eNature, 611
English Nature, 611
fish, 37, 271, 314, 575, 647
Froggy Page, 480
horses, 415-417
Jaguar: Icon of Power Through Mayan History, 378
Kids Planet, 482
KnowledgeHound, 16
Landscaping to Attriact Birds, 495
National Audubon Society, 272
National Geographic for Kids, 483
National Wildlife Federation, 273
Natural Resources Defense Council, 612
Nature Conservancy, The, 273

NatureServe.org, 612
Ocean Alliance, The, 647
Pet Car Travel Tips, 874
PETA.org, 3
Pets Welcome, 878
SeaWorld, 648
Texas Parks and Wildlife, 425
U.S. Fish and Wildlife Service, 425
U.S. Fish and Wildlife Service-National Wetlands Inventory, 275
veterinary medicine, 681, 904-905
Whale Museum's Orca Adoption Program, The, 276
Whales Online, 649
Wildlife Conservation Society/Bronx Zoo, 273
World Wildlife Fund, 273
WWF, 613
zoos, 968-971

animation
American Royal Arts, 40
Animation Art, 184
Animation Library, 40
Animation World Network, 40, 184
anime, 41, 186
Archie, 184
Arthur on PBS, 477
Batman-Superman, 184
Big Cartoon Database, 184, 420
Captain Planet, 478
Cartoon Brew, 184
Cartoon Network.com, 185, 420
Cartoonster, 185
Chuck Jones Website, 40, 185
Comic Book Movies, 185
Computer Graphics World Magazine, 40, 185
Disney.com, 36, 186, 479
DreamWorks Kids, 487
EX: The Online World of Anime and Manga, 186
International Animated Film Society, 40, 186
International Museum of Cartoon Art, 186
Jerry Beck's Cartoon Research, 421
Kids WB!, 482
National Cartoon Museum, 421
Nick Jr., 483
Noggin, 483
PBS Kids, 484
Red Vs. Blue, 420
Sailor Moon Specialty Store, 816
Shark Tale, 186
Simpsons, The, 187
South Park, 187
Spongebob Squarepants, 187
Warner Brothers Games Gallery, 488

anime. *See also* manga
Anime Cafe, 41
Anime News Network, 41
Anime, 100, 41
Best Anime, 41
EX: The Online World of Anime and Manga, 186
theOtaku.com, 41
VIZ Media, 41

anorexia nervosa. *See* mental health, eating disorders

antiques
Antiquarian Booksellers' Association of America (ABAA), 114
Antiquenet.com, 42
Antiques and Collectibles Guide, The, 42
Antiques Council, The, 42
Antiques Roadshow, 42
Artnet.com, 42
automobiles, 58
Collectics, 172
Curioscape, 172
Early American History Auctions, Inc., 42
East Bay Book Search, 115
Eureka, I Found It!, 42
Finer Times, 42
GoAntiques, 43
Guidon Books, 115
ICollector.com, 43
Loganberry Books, 115
Maine Antique Digest, 43
Newel, 43
Tias, 43
Wolverine Antique Music Society, 603

antivirus software/resources
AVG AntiVirus, 196
McAfee AntiVirus, 446
McAfee.com, 196
Panda Software, 446
Symantec, 196
Symantec AntiVirus Research Center, 446
Symantec Security Check, 446
Trend Micro: Scams and Hoaxes, 446
VirusList.com, 446

anxiety and panic disorders
Anxiety Disorders Association of America, 546
Anxiety Panic Attack Resource Site, 546
Anxiety Panic Internet Resource, 547
National Panic & Anxiety Disorder News, 547

apartments. *See also* timeshares
Apartments for Rent Online, 750
ExecuStay Inc., 751
RelocationCentral.com, 751
Rental Decorating, 403

Apple computers
Macintosh, 190-191
troubleshooting, 198-199

appraisals (jewelry)
American Society of Appraisers, 462
Appraisal Foundation, 462
How to Choose a Jewelry Appraiser, 462
International Society of Appraisers, 462

aquariums. *See* fish/aquariums

arcade games. *See* games and puzzles

architecture. *See also* home, design
American Institute of Architects, The, 44
Arch Inform, 44
Architects USA, 44
Architectural Record, 44

A B C D E F G H I J K L M N O P Q R S T U V W X Y Z

Architecture Magazine, 44
Architecture.com, 44
Association of Collegiate Schools of Architecture, 44
Design Basics Home Online Planbook, 44
First Source Exchange, 45
Frank Lloyd Wright Home and Studio, 382
GreatBuildings.com, 45
Metropolis Magazine, 45
museums, 567-568
Pritzker Architecture Prize, The, 45

arctic and antarctica history
Antarctica History, 378
Antarctica: History and Exploration, 378
Arctic Studies Center, 378

Arizona
Arizona Guide, The, 887
AzNewAge, 622
Cliff Castle Casino, 152
Grand Canyon Railway, 887
Guidon Books, 115
New Age Center, Sedona, Arizona, 622
Phoenix Zoo, The, 970
TheGrandCanyon.co, 888

Arkansas
Arkansas Children's Hospital, 373
Arkansas: The Natural State, 887

Army (U.S.). ***See*** **military**

aromatherapy
Amateur Aromatherapy, 28
AromaWeb, 28
Canadian Association of Aromatherapists, 28
National Association for Holistic Aromatherapy, 28
Precious Aromatherapy, 29
World of Aromatherapy, A, 29

arts
Absolutearts.com, 46
animation, 40-41
architecture, 44-45, 382, 567-568
Art History Resources on the Web, 46
Art on the Net, 46
Artcyclopedia, 46
Arts and Kids, 477
ArtsEdge Network, 250, 846
Artsonia, 477
Atlantic Unbound, 624
Bird Art, 102
dance, 209-212
graphic design, 47
HotWired, 727
HOW Magazine, 727
Imagination Factory, 475
instruction/reference, 46-47
ItsRainingBargains, 78
Kidz Cafe, 491
KnowledgeHound, 16
Loganberry Books, 115
Mark Kistler's Imagination Station, 483
Michael's: The Arts and Crafts Store, 207
museums
American Visionary Art Museum, 568
Andy Warhol Museum, The, 568
Art Institute of Chicago, The, 568
Artcyclopedia, 568
Asian Art Museum of San Francisco, 568
Berkeley Art Museum/Pacific Film Archive, 573
California Museum of Photography, 573
Cincinnati Art Museum, 568
Columbia Museum of Art, The, 569
Fine Arts Museums of San Francisco, 569
George Eastman House: International Museum of Photography and Film, 573
Guggenheim Museums, 569
Harvard University Art Museums, 569
Indianapolis Museum of Art, 569
International Center of Photography, 573
J. Paul Getty Museum, 569
Kemper Museum of Contemporary Art, The, 569
Le Louvre, 569
Los Angeles County Museum of Art, 570
Metropolitan Museum of Art, New York, 570
Museum of Bad Art, 570
Museum of Fine Arts, Boston, 570
Museum of Fine Arts, Houston, 570
Museum of Modern Art, New York, 570
National Gallery of Art, 483, 570
National Gallery of Canada, 570
National Museum of Women in the Arts, 951
National Museum of Photography, Film, and Television, 574
Royal Ontario Museum, 571
San Francisco Museum of Modern Art, The, 571
Smithsonian Institution, The, 571
Smithsponianm Photographs Online, 574
Underwater Photography: Philip Colla, 574
Web Gallery of Art, 571
World Wide Art Gallery, 491
New Republic, The, 625
News Directory, 625
painting, 657-658
photography, 573-574, 688-694
posters, 176-177
Salon.com, 633
Teen Ink, 852
theater and musical, 860-863
Xenith.net, 853

Aruba, 151

Asia
China Airlines, 22
history, 379-380
Malaysia Airlines, 23
Singapore Airlines, 23

- Turkish Airlines, 23
- United Nations Economic Social Commission for Asia and the Pacific, 132
- VBT, 94

astrology. *See also* new age
- Astrology et al Bookstore, 114
- Astrology on the Web, 48
- Astrology Online, 48
- MSN Astrology, 48
- Yahoo! Astrology, 48

astronomy
- Adler Planetarium and Astronomy Museum, 574
- Amazing Space, 49
- American Astronomical Society, 49
- Astronomy for Kids, 49
- Astronomy Magazine, 49
- Astronomy Now On-Line, 49
- Astronomy Picture of the Day, 49
- BadAstronomy.com, 50
- Chandra X-Ray Observatory, 50
- Constellation X, 50
- Earth & Sky, 50
- Event Inventor: Web Sites for Space Mission Projects, The, 50
- Griffith Astronomy, 50
- High Energy Astrophysics Science Archive Research Center, 50
- HubbleSite, 50
- International Astronomical Union, 51
- Lunar and Planetary Sciences at NSSDC, 51
- Mount Wilson Obersvatory, 51
- NASA Earth Observatory, 51
- NASA History Office, 51
- NASA HumanSpace Flight, 51
- NASAKIDS, 51
- National Geographic Star Journey, 51
- SEDS Internet Space Warehouse, 52
- Sky & Telescope Online, 730
- Sky & Telescope, 52
- Star Stuff: A Guide to the Night Sky, 52
- Views of the Solar System, 52

atheism
- American Atheists, 768
- Atheism Central for Secondary Schools, 768
- Atheist Alliance, 769
- Infidel Guy Show, The, 769
- Secular Web, The, 769

Attention Deficit Hyperactivity Disorder. *See* ADD/ADHD

auctions
- Amazon Auctions, 53
- Andalé, 53
- AuctionAddict.com, 53
- Early American History Auctions, Inc., 42
- eBay Motors, 61
- eBay, 53
- Hertiage Rare Coin Gallery, 174
- ICollector.com, 43
- InetAuction, 53
- Internet Auction List, 53
- Maine Antique Digest, 43
- MastroNet, Inc., 53
- Overstock.com Auctions, 54
- Priceline.com, 54
- Sotheby's, 54
- U.S. Department of Treasury Auctions, 54
- uBid, 54
- Vendio Productions, 54
- Yahoo! Auctions, 54

audio books
- Audible, 112
- Audio Books on Compact Disc, 112
- AudioBooks Online, 112
- AudioBooks.com, 112
- Books on Tape, 112

audio. *See* electronics

Australia
- Australia Swimming, 928
- Australian Department of Foreign Affairs and Trade, 130
- Australian Slang, 500
- AVA Online, 904
- Deep Sea Divers Den, 924
- Folk Australia, 592
- government information/services, 360
- history, 380
- Murdoch University: Division of Veterinary and Biomedical Sciences, 905
- National Parks and Wildlife Service, 675
- New Age Online Australia, 622
- New Inventors, 453
- PetNet, 683
- Qantas Airlines, 23
- Questacon: National Science and Technology Centre, 575
- Rock Climbing Australia, 784
- Simply OarSome, 923
- Surf World Museum-Torquay, 927
- Sydney Hang Gliding Centre, 293
- Sydney Opera House, 597
- Weekend Australian, The, 626

Austria
- Austria Ski Vacation Packages, 824
- Austrian Airlines, 22
- Salzburg, Austria, 882

authors. *See also* literature; writing
- 11 Rules of Writing, 960
- About.com-Freelance Writers, 960
- American Authors on the Web, 514
- AuthorLink!, 960
- Bartleby.com, 960
- BookNotes, 514
- BookWire Index-Author Indexes, 514
- Celebration of Women Writers, A, 949
- Childen's Writing Resource Center, 961
- Chistell Publishing, 949
- Comparative Literature Studies, 515
- Dr. Seuss: Seussville, 480
- E-CLAT, 515
- Goosebumps, 481
- Literature.org The Online Literature Library, 515
- Nietzche Page at Stanford, 686
- Nobel Laureates, 516
- Plato's Dialogues, 687

Project Gutenberg, 516
Pulitzer Prizes, 516
Quotations of William Blake, 737
Romance Reader, The, 516
RoseDog.com, 961
Screenwriters Online, 961
Spinsters Ink, 953
Stories from the Web, 485
Victorian Women Writers, 516
Write News, The, 961
Writers Write, 962
Writing Den, 962
Writing for Dollars, 962
Writing for the Web, 962
Writing-World.com, 962
Xlibris, 962
Young Authors Workshop, 962

autism and Asperger's syndrome
Asperger and Autism Information, 548
Autism Research Institute, 548
Autism.tv, 548
DANconference.com, 548

automobiles. *See also* motorcycles; RC (Radio Control) cars
auto manuals, 66-67
buying online, 60-62
Car Collector, 725
car travel, 874-875
classic cars, 58, 62
clubs and organizations, 58-59
collectibles/collecting, 175-176
coupons, 78-79
Department of Transportation, 897
Henry Ford Estate: Fair Lane, 383
insurance, 429-431
manufacturers, 62-66
parts, 475
Popular Science, 626, 729
Priceline.com, 78
racing, 55-57
RedTagDeals.com, 79
rental, 151
repair, 66-67
Rokenbok Toys, 867
Teenage Driving Contract, 852

aviation
ACES HIGH: The Finest in Aviation Photography, 68
Air Affair, 68
Air Combat USA, 68
Air Force Association, 900
Air Force Link, 68
Air Traffic Control System, 871
Air Travel Health Tips, 871
Aircraft Images Archive, 68
Airfare.com, 77
airlines, 22-23, 68-69, 143, 871
AirSafe.com, 871
Amelia Earhart, 68
Aviation Museum Locator, 68
AVWeb, 68
ballooning, 75-76
Basics of Space Flight Learners' Workbook, 69
Boeing Company, The, 69
Embry-Riddle Aeronautical University, 69
FAA, 69
Fear of Flying, 69
Flight Arrivals, 871
Flight Safety Foundation, 69
Flyer Talk, 871
Helicopter Adventures, Inc., 69
Jesse Davidson Aviation Archives, 69
Landings, 70
Lockheed Martin, 70
NASA Home Page, 70
NASA Television, 70
National Aeronautic Association, 70
National Museum of the U.S. Air Force, 70
Pilot Shop, 70
Priceline.com, 78
Smithsonian National Air and Space Museum, 70
Student Pilot Network, 70
Transportation Security Administration, 871
Women in Aviation History: The Ninety Nines, 954
X Prize, 70

B

babies and toddlers. *See also* children
American Academy of Pediatrics, 71
Babies Online, 71
Babies Today Online, 71
Babies 'R' Us, 71
Baby Bag Online, 71, 663
Baby Beechnut, 71
Baby Center, 71, 663
Baby Name, 72
Baby Place, 72, 663
Baby Shower Gifts, 355
Baby Zone, 72
BabyStyle Clothes, 811
Caring for Kids, 659
CouponSurfer, 79
CribLife 2000, 663
Crying Babies, 72
Dr. Greene: Toddlers, 663
eToys, 663
Facts for Families, 659
Family Education Network: A Parenting and Education Resource, 659
Family Resource Center, 659
FamilyTime, 659
FindCareNow, 663
Genius Babies.com, 866
Gerber, 72
Huggies Baby Network, 72
iParenting.com, 660
ItsRainingBargains, 78
John Rosemond, 660
KidSource, 660
KidSource: Toddlers, 663
Learning Curve International, 866
Little Tikes, 866
Live and Learn, 664
Mastermind Educational Toys, 867
Mothering Magazine, 660
National Healthy Mothers, Healthy Babies Coalition, 72-73
National Organization of Mothers of Twins Clubs, 664

National Parenting Center, The, 660
NCF-National Center for Fathering, 660
Pampers Parenting Institute, 73, 664
Parenthood.com, 660
Parenting Toddlers, 664
Parenting.com, 661
Parenting.org, 661
Parents of Premature Babies, 73
Parents-Talk.com, 661
Parents.com, 664
Positive Parenting, 661
Pregnancy & Parenting, 73
pregnancy and birth, 73, 710-712
Sesame Workshop, 73
WholeFamily Center, The, 661
Working Mother, 661
Zero to Three Policy Center, 664

background checks
Background Check Gateway, 74
Check Point, 74
Discreet Research, 74
Docusearch, 74
Employment Background Checks, 74
KnowX, 74
National Association of Professional Background Screeners (NAPBS), 74

backpacking. *See also* hiking; mountain biking
Backpacker Magazine, 139
Backpacker.com, The, 139
Eastern Mountain Sports, 139
Leave No Trace, 139
Lightweight Backpacker, The, 139

ballet
American Ballet Theatre, 210
Ballerina Gallery, 210
ballet.com, 210
Boston Ballet, 210
CyberDance: Ballet on the Web, 211
International Dance Directory, 211
New York City Ballet, 211
Russian Classical Ballet, 211
San Francisco Ballet, 211

ballooning
Balloon Federation of America, 75
Balloon Life Magazine, 75
Balloon Pages on the World Wide Web, 75
Blast Valve, 75
Hot Air Ballooning, 75
Hot Air Balloons USA, 75
Jet Stream Information, 75
National Scientific Balloon Facility, 76
Nova's Online Balloon Race Around the World, 76

ballroom dancing
Arthur Murray, 211
Ballroom Dancers.com, 211
Dance Directory-Ballroom, 211
Take the Lead, 212
United States Amateur Ballroom Dancers Association, 212

banking
Bank of America, 304
Citibank, 304
E*TRADE Banking, 304
EH.net, 304
EverBank, 304
Export-Import Bank of the United States, 130
NetBank, 305
Wells Fargo, 305
World Bank Group, 132

bankruptcy
American Bankruptcy Institute, 224
Bankruptcy Action, 224
Bankruptcy: An Overview, 224
InterNet Bankruptcy Law Library, 224
Personal Bankruptcy Information, 224

bargains
Airfare.com, 77
Amazing-Bargains, 77
Birkenstock Express, 77
BookCloseOuts.com, 114
Bridal Bargains, 77
coupons, 77-80
CurrentCodes.com, 77
freebies, 77, 80
ItsRainingBargains, 78
LowerMyBills.com, 78
Overstock.com, 78
Priceline.com, 78
SalesCircular.com, 78
SecondSpin, 78
techbargains.com, 78

baseball
Babe Ruth League Official Website, 81
Baseball Almanac, 81
Baseball America, 81
Baseball Archive, 81
Baseball Links, 81
Baseball Think Factory, 81
Baseball-Reference, 81
college, 82
fantasy, 83-84
Little League Online, 82
Negro Baseball League, 82
professional
American League Websites, 83
Major League Baseball, 83
Minor League Baseball, 84
National League websites, 84
National Baseball Hall of Fame, 84
USA Today: Baseball Weekly, 84
WebBall, 171

basketball
Coaching Well Basketball Journal, 85
college, 86
FIBA: Federation International de Basketball Amateur, 85
Five Star Hoops, 85
Full Court Press, 85
Harlem Globetrotters Online, 85
National Wheelchair Basketball Association, 85
Power Basketball, 85

professional
Baskeball Daily, 87
Naismith Memorial Basketball Hall of Fame, 87
National Basketball Association, 87
NBA Development League, 87
NBA Eastern Conference Websites, 87
NBA Western Conference Websites, 87-88
WNBA Eastern Conference Websites, 88
WNBA Western Conference Websites, 88
Women's National Basketball Association, 88
Sports Illustrated Basketball, 86
USBasket, 86
women
Full Court Press, 85-86
National Basketball Association, 87
WNBA Eastern Conference Websites, 88
WNBA Western Conference Websites, 88
Women's National Basketball Association, 88
Beanie Babies (collectibles/ collecting)
Beanie Babies Official Club, 173
Beanie Babies: Wholesale and Retail, 173
Beanie History, 173
Ty's Beanie Site, 173
beer
Ale Street News, 89
All About Beer, 89
Badger Brewery, 89
Beamish & Crawford Brewery, 89
Beer Hunter, 89
Beer Institute Online, 90
Beer Me!, 90
Beer, Beer, and More Beer Home Brewing Supplies, 89
BeerAdvocate.com, 89
BeerBooks.com, 89
Brewers Association, 90
Bud Online, 90
Guinness, 90
Heineken, 90
Leinenkugel's Leinie Lodge, 90
Pabst Brewing Company, 90
Pub Brewing Company, The, 91
RealBeer.com: The Beer Portal, 91
Redhook Ale Brewery, 91
Sam Adams, 91
Siebel Institute of Technology, 91
Belgium, government information/services, 360
Bermuda, 884
beverages. *See* food and drink
bicycles
Adventure Cycling Association, 92
Aegis Bicycles, 92
Analytic Cycling, 92
Bianchi, 92
Bicycle Helmet Safety Institute Home Page, 200
Bicycling.com, 92
Bike Lane, 92
Bike Ride Online, 92
Cambria Bicycle Outfitters, 93
Competitive Cyclist, 93
Cycling Web, 93
Cyclingnews.com, 93
Lowrider Bicycles, 93
maintenance and repair, 94-95
mountain biking, 94-96
Pedestrian and Bicycle Information Center, 284
Performance Bicycles, 93
Schwinn, 93
Shimano, 94
Specialized, 94
Tour de France, 94
VBT, 94
VeloNews Interactive, 94
billiards
American Poolplayers Association, 97
Billiard Congress of America, 97
Billiards Digest Interactive, 97
Brunswick, 97
Illustrated Principles of Pool and Billiards, 97
McDermott Handcrafted Cues, 97
Pool Hall, 97
U.S. Billiard Association, 98
Women's Professional Billiard Association, 98
bingo
Bingo Bugle Online Newspaper, 99
Bingo Gala, 99
Bingo Novelty World, 99
Bingo Online, 99
Bingo Zone, 99
Bingo.com, 99
CyberBingo, 99
Dot-Bingo.com, 99
Instant Bingo, 100
Which Bingo, 100
biographies
Academy of Achievement, 761
Biographical Dictionary, 101, 762
Biographies of Women Mathematicians, 532
Biography Center, 101
Biography Maker, The, 101
Biography, 101
Indexes of Biographies, 532
Pulitzer Prize, The, 101
bipolar disorder. *See also* depression
Bipolar World, 549
BPSO: Bipolar Significant Others, 548
Child & Adolescent Bipolar Foundation, 549
Cyclothymic Disorder, 549
Depression and Bipolar Support Alliance, 551
McMan's Depression and Bipolar Web, 549
Pendulum Resources: The Bipolar Disorder Port, 549
birds
About Birding and Wild Birds, 102
All About Birds, 102

American Birding Association, 102
Bird Art, 102
Bird Song Matcher, 102
Bird Watchers Digest, 102
Birder, 102
Birding in British Columbia, 103
Birding.com, 103
Birds n Ways, 103
BIRDTALK.com Magazine, 102
Cockatiel Society, 103
Fabulous Kakapo (Strigops Habroptilus), The, 103
Field Guides, 103
Finch World, 103
Hot Spots for Birders, 103
Hotspot for Birds, 103
Landscaping to Attract Birds, 495
Life of Birds, 104
Majestic Macaws, 104
National Audubon Society, 104, 272
Optics for Birding, 104
PETBird, 104
Peterson Guide for Birds Online, 104
Wild Birds Unlimited, 104
Wyld's Wingdom, Inc., 685

bisexual issues. *See* gay/lesbian/bisexual/transgender issues

blindness
Guide Dogs for the Blind, 238
Helen Keller National Center for Deaf-Blind Youth, 218

blogs and blogging
blog hosting and tools, 106-107
directories and search engines, 105-106

bluegrass music
Banjo Tablatures and Bluegrass Information, 586
Blistered Fingers, 586
Bluegrass Unlimited, 586
Bluegrass World, 586
BlueGrassRoots Master Catalog, 586
Canyon Country Bluegrass Festival, 586
Central Texas Bluegrass Association, 586
Huck Finn's Country and Bluegrass Jubilee!, 587
iBluegrass Magazine, 587
Intermountain Acoustic Music Association, 587
International Bluegrass Music Association, 587
Society for the Preservation of Bluegrass Music in America, 587
Sugar Hill Records, 587
Top 100 Bluegrass Sites, 587
Tottenham Bluegrass Festival, 587
Washington Bluegrass Association, 588
Welcome to Planet Bluegrass!, 588

board games
Board Game Central, 338
Board Games at About.com, 338
BoardGameGeek, 338
Monopoly, 339
Official Worldwide Scrabble Home Page, 339

boats and sailing. *See also* cruises; rafting
1001 Boats for Sale, 108
American Sail Training Association, 108
American Sailing Association, 108
Boat Owners World, 108
Boating 4 Kids, 108
Boating Magazine, 108
Boats.com, 108-109
BoatSafeKids, 108
Discover Boating, 109
Good Old Boat Magazine, 109
International Jet Sports Boating Association, 459
JetSki News, 459
jetski.com, 459
Kawasaki, 459
Mark Rosenstein's Sailing Page, 109
Personal Watercraft Illustrated, 459
Powerski Jetboar, 459
Sailboats Inc., 109
SailNet, 109
SBT on the Web, 460
Sea-Doo, 109, 460
Titanic, the Official Archive, 649
U.S. Coast Guard Office of Boating Safety, 109
U.S. Sailing, 110
United States Power Squadrons Web Page, 109
Yachtingnet, 110
Yamaha, 460

body art/tattoos
Altered Body, 841
Body Art Studios, 841
Body Jewelry, 841
Earth Henna Kits, 841
everytattoo.com, 841
Kingpin Tattoo Supply, 841
Tattoo Fun, 841
Tattoodles, 842

bonds
Bond Market Association, 305
Bonds Online, 305
CNNfn Bond Center, 305
TreasuryDirect, 305

books. *See also* libraries (reference)
Amazing-Bargains, 77
American Library Association: Links to Kids Sites, 477
Arts & Letters Daily, 624
audio books, 112
auto manuals, 66-67
Awesome Library, 478
Baker Book House, 770
Bartleby.com, 757
BeerBooks.com, 89
bookstores, 114-118, 155
Broadway Play Publishing, Inc., 861
Christianbook.com, 771
CouponSurfer, 79
CurrentCodes.com, 77
Dr. Seuss: Seussville, 480
eHarlequin, 788
Engines of Our Ingenuity, The, 452

Favorite Teenage Angst Books, 851
Feminist Science Fiction, Fantasy, and Utopia, 790
general resources
American Booksellers Association, 111
Banned Books Online, 111
BookCrossing, 111
BookWire, 111
Children's Literature Web Guide (CLWG), 111
Conservation Online, 111
Great Books Foundation, 111
Hundred Highlights from the Koninklijke Bibliotheek, A, 112
Goosebumps, 481
graphic novels, 362
Harcourt School Publishing, 848
Harry Potter (Scholastic Books), 112
Henry Miller Library, 112
horror, 412-414
International Travel Maps and Books, 882
Law Books, 508
Lily Abello's Sewing Links, 803
literature, 514-516
Literature.org The Online Literature Library, 515
Look What I Found in My Brain!, 791
Martial Arts Books and Videos, 525
McGraw-Hill School Division, 848
mysteries, 607-608
Nation, The, 625
New Republic, The, 625
Newberty Medal, 252
Nobel Laureates, 516
online, 116-117
Online Islamic Bookstore, 776
PCI Publishing, 670
Plato's Dialogues, 687
Project Gutenberg, 117, 516
publishing, 117-118
Puffin House, The, 849
Pulitzer Prizes, 516
Reading Rainbow, 484
RedTagDeals.com, 79
reviews, 112-113
Romance Club, The, 788
Romance Reader, The, 788
Scholastic.com, 252, 849
sci-fi and fantasy, 791-794
SmartDivorce.com, 236
Teenager E-Books, 853
TeenLink, 853
Victorian Women Writers, 516
botanical gardens, 968
bowhunting, 423
bowling
Amateur Bowling Tournaments, 119
AMF Bowling Worldwide, 119
Bowl.com: Official Site of the United States Bowling Congress, 119
Bowler's Paradise, 119
Bowlers Journal International, 119
Bowling This Month Magazine, 119
Bowling World, 120
Bowling Zone, 120
Bowling.com, 119
BowlingIndex, 119
Brunswick Online, 120
Dick Ritger Bowling Camps, 120
Duckpin Bowling, 120
International Bowling Museum and hall of Fame, 120
LeagueSecretary.com, 120
PBA Tour, 120
Youth Bowling, 120
boxing
Boxing Game, 121
Boxing Monthly, 121
Boxing Talk, 121
Boxing Times, The, 121
Boxing: CBS SportsLine, 121
Cyber Boxing Zone, 121
Doghouse Boxing, 121
ESPN.com Boxing, 121
HBO Boxing, 122
International Boxing Hall of Fame, 122
International Female Boxers Association, 122
Max Boxing, 122
Showtime Championship Boxing, 122
USA Boxing, 122
World Boxing Association, 122
World Boxing Council, 122
boys. *See* children
Brazil
Capoeira, 526
government information/services, 360
buddhism
Buddhanet.net, 769
New Kadampa Tradition, 769
Resources for the Study of Buddhism, 769
tharpa.com, 769
Tricycle Review, 769
budget travel
11th Hour Vacations, 872
Backpack Europe on a Budget, 872
Bargain Travel Cruises-Cheap Cruises, 875
BargainTravel.com, 872
BestFares.com, 872
budget hotels, 872
Busabout Europe, 872
Cheap Weekend Getaways, 891
Council Travel, 872
Cruise Value Center, 875
DiscountAirfares.com, 872
Economy Travel, 872
Expedia, 873
Hostels.com,, 873
Hotels.com, 873
Hotwire.com, 873
LastMinuteTravel.com, 873
Lowestfare.com, 873
Moment's Notice, 873
Orbitz, 873
Priceline.com, 873
SkyAuction.com, 874
Travelocity, 874
budgeting
About Frugality, 330
BetterBudgeting.com, 330
Cheapskate Monthly, 330

Dollar Stretcher, 330
Frugal Shopper, The, 330
Frugal Village, 330

bugs. *See* insects

business

401K Center for Employers, 780
accounting, 1
Adoption Benefits: Employers as Partners in Family Building, 10
Advertising Age, 725
Advertising Quotes, 736
Association of Corporate Counsel, 511
background checks, 74
Better Business Bureau, 200
BizWomen, 949
Business Wire, 629
Business Women's Network Interactive, The, 949
Business Writing Tips, 960
CatalystWomen.org, 949
ConsumerWebWatch, 200
Corporate Watch, 201
CorpWatch.org, 2
Department of Commerce, 896
Department of the Treasury, 897
Dismal Scientist, 762
e-commerce, 241-243
Emerging Markets, 633
employee incentives, 466
Federal Trade Commission, 897
Forbes, 726
Fortune, 727
franchising, 126-128
general resources
411.com, 123
All Business Network, 123
BigBook, 123
Bigfoot, 123
BizWiz, The, 123
Brint.com, 123
Business 2.0, 123
Business Wire, 124
Business.com, 124
BusinessTown, 123
Businesstravelnet.com, 123
BusinessWeek.com, 124
CorporateInformation, 124
Dun & Bradstreet, 124
Fast Company, 124
Forbes Online, 124
Fortune.com, 124
Harvard Business Online, 124
Hoover's Online, 125
InfoSpace.com, 125
LEXIS-NEXIS Communication Center, 125
One Source, 125
STAT-USA, 125
Switchboard: The Internet Directory, 125
Telephone Directories on the, 125
The Industry Standard, 125
Web100: Big Business on the Web, 125
H. Wayne Huizenga School of Business and Entrepreneurship, 245
home-based businesses, 128-129
human resources, 466-467
insurance, 431-432
international businesses, 130-132
iTools.com, 763
janitorial, 457-458
Junior Achievement TITAN, 488
Junior Achievement, 640
Kansas City Board of Trade (Kansas City, Missouri), 20
marketing, 521-523
National Association for Female Executives, 951
National Partnership for Women & Families (NPFW), 951
News Directory, 625
Newsweek, 625
office management, 650-651
Office of Women's Business Ownership, 952
office supplies, 651-653
OWBO Online Women's Business Center, 952
patent information, 132-134
PR Newswire, 630
Slate, 634
small businesses, 129, 134-136
They Rule, 3
TIME, 626
Today's Market Prices, 21
U.S. News & World Report, 626
Utne Reader, The, 626
Vanity Fair, 731
WomanOwned.com-Business Information for Women Entrepreneurs, 953
Working Moms Refuge, 954
Working Wounded, 420
World Connected, A, 3
Worth Online, 732
Yahoo! News, 627

C

calculus

Calculus Help, 531
COW (Calculus On the Web), 531
Karl's Calculus Tutor, 531
MathGV Function Plotting Software, 531

California

Academy of Art University, 46
Adventure City, 36
amusement and theme parks, 37
Asian Art Museum of San Francisco, 568
Big Bear Mountain Resorts, 824
California Association of Realtors Online, 746
California Homeschool Network, 248
California Museum of Photography, 573
California State Parks, 673
California State Science Fair, 255
California Travel Guide, 888
California Voter Foundation, 705
City Lights Bookstore, 115
Exploratorium, 567

Fine Arts Museums of San Francisco, 569
Getty Center, 567
Griffith Observatory, 50
J. Paul Getty Museum, 569
Joshua Tree Rock Climbing School, 784
LA Blogs, 105
LEGOLAND California, 37
Los Angeles County Museum of Art, 570
Los Angeles Opera, 595
Los Angeles Times, 632
Los Angeles Zoo, The, 969
Mount Wilson Observatory, 51
Museum of Tolerance, 571
Natural History Museum of Los Angeles County, 572
Nietzche Page at Stanford, 686
North Gate: Berkeley's Graduate School of Journalism, 474
Oakland Zoo, 970
Public Health Institute, 373-374
Ralph's: First in Southern California, 322
San Diego Model Railroad Museum, 394
San Diego Zoo, 971
San Francisco Ballet, 211
San Francisco Museum of Modern Art, The, 571
San Francisco Opera, 597
San Francisco Zoo, 971
San Jose Mercury News, 632
Stanford Encyclopedia of Philosophy, 687
Stanford Law School, 510
Stanford Prison Experiment, 456
Stop AIDS Project, 366
Sunnyvale Center for Innovation, Invention & Ideas, The, 760
TotalEscape, 892
UCLA Fowler Museum of Cultural History, 571
Universal Studios, 37
University of California Museum of Palentology, 573
Yosemite Park, 676

cameras

Abe's of Maine, 688
Ace Index, 688
AGFA Digital Cameras, 688
Beach Photo & Video, 688
Camera Review.com, 688
CameraWorld, 688
Complete Guide to Digital Cameras and Digital Photography, 688
Digital Camera Images Resource Page, 688
Digital Camera News, 689
Digital Camera Resource Page, 689
Digital Photography Review, 689
EarthCam, 689
Focus Camera & Video, 689
HowStuffWorks: How Digital Cameras Work, 689
Megapixel.net, 689
PC Photo Review, 689
Photo.net, 689
Ritz Camera, 690

camping

Altrec.com, 137
American Park Network, 673
American Park Network-Camping, 137
backpacking, 139
California State Parks, 673
Camp-A-Roo, 137
Campfire Cooking, 137
Campground Directory, 137
Campgrounds by City, 673
Camping World Online, 137
Canyonlands, 673
Coleman.com, 137
Colorado State Parks and Outdoor Recreation, 673
Death Valley National Park, 673
Fodor's National Parks, 674
Get Knotted, 138
Glacier National Parks, 674
GORP: U.S. National Parks and Reserves, 674
GORP: Wilderness Area List, 674
Grand Canyon Official Tourism Page, 674
Harper's Ferry NHP Virtual Visitor Center, 674
hiking, 139-141
KOA Homepage, 138
L.L. Bean Welcome Page, 138
L.L. Bean's Park Search, 674
Maps of United States National Parks and Monuments, 674
Mesa Verde National Park, 674
Minnesota State Parks, 138
Mount Rainier National Park, 675
National Parks and Wildlife Service, 675
National Parks Conservation Society, 675
New Mexico State Parks, 675
Northwest Trek, 675
Ocean City, MD's Frontier Town Campground, 138
Olympic National Park, 675
Outdoor Action, 138
PARKNET: The National Park Service Place, 675
Petrified Forest National Park, 675
Saguaro National Park, 675
South Carolina State Parks, 676
Texas State Parks, 676
U.S. National Parks, 676
U.S. Scouting Project, 138
Visit Your National Parks, 138
Yellowstone Net, 676
Yosemite Park, 676

camps (summer)

American Camping Association, 142
Camp Channel, 142
Christian Camping International, 142
CYO: Catholic Youth Organization, 966
Kids Camps, 142, 665
Soccer Camps, 830
Summer Camps, 142

Canada

Air Canada, 22, 143
Alzheimer Society of Canada, 34

American Federation of Musicians of the United States and Canada, 601
Athletics Canada, 868
Birding in British Columbia, 103
Canada, 143
Canada.com, 143
Canadian Association of Aromatherapists, 28
Canadian Business Franchise Magazine, 127
Canadian Parents Online, 659
Canadian Pediatric Society, 677
Canadian Publishers' Council, 118
Canadian Quilters' Association, 733
Caring for Kids, 659
CBC Radio, 603
CBC.ca News, 624
Charity Village, 635
Child Crisis Network, 160
Chiropractic in Canada, 164
Citizenship and Immigration to Canada, 143
Coastal British Columbia, 927
Discover Banff, 673
Flight Arrivals, 871
government information/services, 360
Grand Theatre, 861
Healthy Ontario, 363
history, 381
Job Share Guidebook, 471
Montreal Official Tourist Info, 143
moreMontreal.com, 143
MuchMusic, 581
National Gallery of Canada, 570
National Museum of Science and Technology, Canada, 575
Nature Canada, 612
Newfoundland Backcountry, 140
North American Virtual Tourist, The, 878
Online Snowmobiling, 827
Ontario Science Centre, 143
Paramount Canada's Wonderland, 143
Prime Ministers of Canada, 719
Royal Ontario Museum, 571
Street Cents Online, 255
Sympatico NewsExpress, 630
Tennis Canada, 857
Toronto.com, 144
Tottenham Bluegrass Festival, 587
Trails.com, 96
University of Saskatchewan Trees and Shrubs Page, 497
UTLink: Resources by Subject, 764
Vancouver, British Columbia, 883
VBT, 94
VIA Rail Canada, 887
Volunteerism in Canada, 642
Wildwater Rafting in Canada, 922
Workopolis, 471

cancer
ACOR.org, 145
American Cancer Society, 145
animals, 905
Avon: The Crusade, 145
Breast Cancer Action, 145
Cancer Detection and Prevention, 145
Cancer Directory, 145
Cancer Facts, 145
Cancer Group Institute, 145
Cancer411.com, 146
Cancerbackup, 146
CancerCare.org, 146
CancerKids, 146
CancerNews on the Net, 146
CanTeen, 146
Community Breast Health Project, 146
Faces of Hope, 146
National Cancer Institute, 147
NBCC-National Breast Cancer Coalition, 956
OncoLink: University of Pennsylvania Cancer Center Resources, 147
Prostate.com, 147
Steve Dunn's Cancer Guide, 147
Susan G. Komen Breast Center Foundation, 147
Testicular Cancer Resource Center, 147

candy
Abbott's Caramels, 148
Altoids, 148
Bubblegum, 148
Candy Critic, 148
Candy Direct: World's Largest, 148
Candy USA, 148
Candy Wrapper Museum, 148
Candy's Apples, 148
Godiva Chocolatier, 149
Hershey Chocolate North America, 149
Hometown Favorites, 149
Kailua Candy Company, 149
Name That Candybar, 149
PEZ Candy, 149
Ultimate Bad Candy Website, The, 149

canoeing/kayaking
American Canoe Association, 150
Canoe & Kayak, 150
Paddling.net, 150
WetDawg.com, 150

Capoeira
Capoeira Arts, 526
Capoeira.com, 526
Capoeirista, 526
Planet Capoeira, 526

card games
Card Games Site, The, 339
Cardboard Cognition, 339
Download Free Games, 339
Freecell.com, 339
House of Cards, The, 339
Wizards of the Coast, Inc., 338

careers. *See* jobs/employment

cars. *See* automobiles; RC (Radio Control) cars

cartoons
American Royal Arts, 40
Animation Library, 40
Animation World Network, 40

anime, 41
Big Cartoon Database, 420
Calvin and Hobbes, 184
Cartoon Network, 420
CartoonBank, 420
Cartoonster, 185
Chuck Jones Website, 40
Comics.com, 185
Computer Graphics World, 40
Daryl Cagle's Pro Cartoonist Index, 421
Disney.com-The Website for Families, 36
Frown.com, The, 421
International Animated Film Society, 40
Jerry Beck's Cartoon Research, 421
MTNCartoons, 186
National Cartoon Museum, 421
Official Peanuts Website, 186
Todays Cartoon by Randy Glasbergen, 421
WebComics, 187

casinos
Caesar's Resorts, 152
Casino Center, 152
Casino City, 152
Cliff Castle Casino, 152
Golden Nugget, 152
Mississippi Casinos, 152
Peppermill Reno Hotel Casino, 152
Sands Hotel and Casino, 153
Spirit Mountain Casino, 153
Venetian, 153

Catalan (languages/linguistics). ***See*** **Spanish**

Catholicism
Catholic Charities USA, 832
Catholic Health Association, 373
Catholic Prayers, 778
CYO: Catholic Youth Organization, 966

cats
American Cat Fanciers Association, 154
Beware of Cat!, 154
Big Cats Online, 154
Castbuzz Bookstore, 155
Cat Fanciers Association, 154
Cat Fanciers, 154
Cat House (EFBC/FCC), 154
Cats Protection League, 154
CatToys.com, 155
DoctorDog.com: Cat and Dog Supplies and Pet Health Care, 682
How to Toilet-Train Your Cat, 155
Taking Care of Your Cat, 155
Virtual Kitty!, 155

CDs, buying
Amazon.com, 576
Barnes & Noble.com, 576
BestBuy.com, 576
Bleep, 576
Blue Vision Music, 576
Buy.com, 576
CD Baby, 576
CD Universe, 576
f.y.e.: for your entertainment, 577
Rasputin Music, 577
Sam Goody Music, 577
SecondSpin, 78
Sony Music Store, 577
TowerRecords.com, 577
Wherehouse.com, 577

celiac disease
Celiac Disease and Gluten-free Diet Support Center, 156
Celiac Disease Foundation, 156
Celiac Sprue Association, 156
GlutenFreedom.net, 156

censorship
Center for Democracy and Technology, 157
Electronic Frontier Foundation, 157
Freedom of Expression Links, 157
Index on Censorship, 157
National Coalition Against Censorship, 157
Project Censored, 157

Central America, history of, 377

Champ car racing series
Champcar World Series, 55
Newman/Hass Racing, 56

chaos mathematics
Chaos at Maryland, 531
Chaos Hypertextbook, 531
Non-Linear Lab, 532
Open Directory: Chaos & Fractals, 532

charities/nonprofit groups
Adobe Community Relations, 639
Alliance for Nonprofit Management, 637
America's Charities, 637
American Institute of Philanthropy, 637
AT&T Foundation, 639
BBB Wise Giving Alliance, 637
Ben and Jerry's Foundation, 639
Benton Foundation, 640
BoardSource, 635
Carnegie Foundation, 640
Charitable Choices, 638
Charity Navigator, 638
Charity Village, 635
CharityNet, The, 638
Children's Miracle Network (CMN), 640
Chronicle of Philanthropy, The, 635
Commonwealth Fund, 640
Council on Foundations, 635
Foundation Center, 635
Foundation Finder, 635
fundraising, 639
Goodwill Industries International, 640
GuideStar, 638
Habitat for Humanity International, 640
Hunger Site, The, 638
Independent Charities of America, 638
Independent Sector, 637
IRS: Charities, 636
John D. and Catherine T. MacArthur Foundation, 636
Junior Achievement, 640

JustGive.com, 638
National Committee on Planned Giving, 636
Network for Good, 638
Nonprofit Gateway, 636
Nonprofit Genie, 636
Nonprofit Resource Center, The, 636
NPO-NET, 636
Philanthropy Roundtable, 638
Philanthropy.org, 636
Rotary International, 640
Tech Soup, 637
United Way of America, 641
volunteering, 641-642
World Vision, 639

chats and social groups (Internet). *See also* instant messaging and telephony (Internet)
Bold Chat, 435
Chat-Zone, 435
Chathouse, 435
Cubic Space Main, 435
CyberTown, 435
mIRC, 435
MSN Groups, 436
SpinChat, 436
Talk City, 436
Worlds 3D Ultimate Chat Plus, 436
Yahoo! Chat, 436
Yahoo! Groups, 436

cheat codes (games)
1UP.com, 339
GameCube Code Center, 340
GameWinners.com, 340
Go! Go! Cheat Codes!, 340
IGN, 336

cheerleading
About Cheerleading, 158
American Cheerleader Junior Magazine, 158
American Cheerleader Magazine, 158
Cheerleading.net, 158
RAMGraphics: Spiritwear, 158
Team Cheer Online, 158
U.S. Open Cheerleading Competition, 158
Varsity.com, 158

chess
Caissa's Web Home Page, 159
Internet Chess Club, 159
This Week in Chess, 159
United States Chess Federation (USCF), 159

children. *See also* pediatrics; teens
AAA Math, 529
adolescents, 4-8, 551, 643, 659-663, 711, 714, 757, 809
adoption, 10-12
AKA: GIRL SKATER, 294
alcohol and drug abuse/prevention, 4-8
Amazon Interactive, 477
America's CryptoKids: Future Codemakers & Codebreakers, 477
America's Promise, 966
American Library Association: Links to Kids Sites, 477
American Youth Soccer, 829
Animaland, 477
Arthur on PBS, 477
Arts and Kids, 477
Artsonia, 477
Astronomy for Kids, 49
autism and Asperger's Syndrome, 548
Awesome Library, 478
Awesome Library for Teens, 757
BAM! (Body and Mind), 478
B'nai B'rith Youth Organization, 966
babies and toddlers, 71-73, 79, 355, 659-664, 710-712, 811, 866-867
Bill Nye the Science Guy's Nye Labs Online, 478
Boating 4 Kids, 108
BoatSafeKids, 108
BookHive, 113
books, 252
Boy Scouts of America, 664, 966
Boys and Girls Clubs of America, 966
British North America Philatelic Society Stamp Collecting for Kids, 177
business, 133, 308-309, 640
Camp-A-Roo, 137
Canadian Parents Online, 659
Candlelight Stories, 514
CanTeen, 146
Captain Planet, 478
Caring for Kids, 659
Center for Reproductive Law and Policy, 949
Channel One, 478
Chateau Meddybemps, 478
Chem4Kids, 478
ChessKids, 478
child abuse and missing children, 160-161
childcare, 162-163
Children Language Development, 498
Children's Express UK, 478
Children's Literature Web Guide (CLWG), 111
Children's Miracle Network (CMN), 640
Children's Museum of Indianapolis, 567
Children's Theatre, The, 861
Children's Writing Resource Center, 961
ChildrensTheatrePlays, 861
CIA History for Kids, 388
Colgate Kid's World, 479
CollegeBound Network, 479
Cool LEGO Site of the Week, 479
Cool Nurse, 643
Cool Spot, The, 5
Crayola Home Page, The, 479
Cyber Stacks for Kids, 479
Cyberkids, 479
CYO: Catholic Youth Organization, 966
Diary Project, 479
Discovery Channel: Discovery Kids, 479
Disney.com, 36, 186, 479
divorce and custody, 235-236
Drinking: A Student's Guide, 5
Earth & Sky, 50
Eco-Kids, 480
edbydesign.com, 480
Eddy the Eco-Dog, 480

Educational Theatre Association, 861
Enchanted Learning's Guide to the Oceans, 647
EPA Global Warming for Kids, 480
Expect the Best from a Girl, 665
Facts for Families, 659
Family Education Network: A Parenting and Education Resource, 659
Family Resource Center, 659
FamilyTime, 659
Farm Safety 4 Just Kids, 19
F.U.N. Place, 480
FirstGov for Kids, 480
FirstGov for Kids: Geography, 353
Froggy Page, 480
Games Kids Play, 481
games, 484-490
Girl Dating Tips, 215
Girl Incorporated, 950
Girl Power! Bodywise, 552
Girl Power! Campaign, 659
Girl Power!, 950
Girl Scouts, 966
Girl's World Online Clubhouse, 481
Girls Life Magazine, 851
GirlSite, 851
GoCityKids, 481
Goosebumps, 481
Great Books Foundation, 111
Harry Potter (Scholastic Books), 112
Headbone Zone, 481
health, 366-368, 371
Hindu Kids, 774
homework help, 255-256, 262, 529
Internet Safety, 489-491
iParenting.com, 660
John Rosemond, 660
Just 4 Girls, 481
K-6, 664-666
Kidland, 481
Kids Do Ecology, 275
Kids Domain, 481
Kids Domain Holidays, 397
Kids Planet, 482
Kids Learn About Diabetes, 229
Kids Walk to School, 284
Kids WB!, 482
Kids-Korner.com, 482
KidsCom.com, 482
Kidsgardening.com, 344
KidsHealth.org, 482
KidSites.com, 482
KidSource, 660
KidsRunning.com, 280
Kotex.com, 662
LEGO Company, The, 482
Literature.org The Online Literature Library, 515
Loganberry Books, 115
Luna Kids Dance Programs, 210
MaMaMedia.com, 482
Mark Kistler's Imagination Station, 483
Melpomene, 281
Mexico for Kids, 557
Mojo's Musical Museum, 483
Mothering Magazine, 660
Mr. Rogers' Neighborhood, 483
MysteryNet's Kids Mysteries, 483
Nabisco World, 483
NASAKIDS, 51
National 4-H Council, 966
National Association of Peer Programs, 967
National Gallery of Arts, 483
National Geographic for Kids, 483
National Mentoring Center, 967
National Parenting Center, The, 660
NCF-National Center for Fathering, 660
Nick Jr., 483
Noggin, 483
NoodleHead Network, The, 484
OLogy, 484
Operation Fit Kids, 967
Parenthood.com, 660
Parenting.com, 661
Parenting.org, 661
Parents-Talk.com, 661
Paw Island, 484
PBS Kids, 484
pediatrics, 677-679
Positive Parenting, 661
Reach for the Sky, 484
Reading Rainbow, 484
Safe Place, A, 239
SeaWorld, 648
Sesame Workshop, 484
Seussville, 480
SFS Kids, 484-485
single parenting, 666-667
SmartGirl, 485, 852
Soap Bubbles, 485
Soccer Camps, 830
special needs
ADD/ADHD (Attention Deficit Disorder/Attention Deficit Hyperactivity Disorder), 547
Arc, 668
Autism and Asperger's Syndrome, 548
bipolar disorder, 549
CancerKids, 146
Celiac Disease Foundation, 156
Children with AIDS Project, 366
Children with Diabetes Online Community, 228
Children with Diabetes Recipes, 228
Children with Disabilities Information, 668
Children with Spina Bifida, 668
Cleft Lip: Wide Smiles, 668
conduct disorder, 549, 668
Council for Exceptional Children, 668
deafness, 217-218
Disability.gov, 369
Down Syndrome WWW Pages, 370
Down Syndrome, 668
Dyslexia: The Gift, 668

A B C D E F G H I J K L M N O P Q R S T U V W X Y Z

Family Village, 668
Federation for Children with Special Needs, 669
Genetic Alliance, 669
Hydrocephalus Association, 669
Individualized Education Program (IEP), 669
Internet Resoource for Special Children, 669
Kids Learn About Diabetes, 229
LD Online, 369
Make-a-Wish Foundation of America, 669
Medical Alert Charms for Children, 229
Muscular Dystrophy Association, 371
National Academy for Child Development (NACD), 669
National Association for Visually Handicapped, 369
National Information Center for Children and Youth with Disabilities (NICHCY), 669
OCD (Obsessive-Compulsive Disorder), 553
PCI Publishing, 670
Premature Baby Premature Child, 670
Sibling Support Project, 670
SNAP Online: Special Needs Advocate for Parents, 670
Social Security Administration: Disability Benefits, 369
Special Needs Children Site, 670
UCPnet, 369
United Cerebral Palsy, 670
World Association of Persons with Disabilities, 369
youreable.com, 369
Spongebob Squarepants, 187
sports, 82, 170-171, 326
Sports Illustrated for Kids, 485
Star Stuff: A Guide to the Night Sky, 52
stay-at-home parents, 670-671
stepparenting, 671-672
Stock Market Game, The, 308
Stone Soup, 485
Stories from the Web, 485
summer camps, 142
Surfnet Kids, 485
TASC: The American Surrogacy Center, IUnc., 953
Teenmag.com, 853
Thomas the Tank Engine Page, 486
Time for Kids, 486
Twins Magazine, 731
U.S. Scouting Project, 138
U.S. Youth Soccer, 831
USFA (United States Fire Administration) for Kids, 486
VolcanoWorld, 486
web sites by kids, 491
web surfing, 489-491
Webmonkey for Kids, 450
What Kids Can Do, 486
White House for Kids, The, 486
WholeFamily Center, The, 661
Why Files, 486
Wild World of Wonka, 486
Working Mother, 661
Writing Den, 962
Yahooligans, 486
YMCA, 967
Yound People's Ministries, 967
Young Investor.com, 309
Youth Bowling, 120
Youth Radio, 606
YouthLink, 967

Chile, government information/services, 360

China
China Airlines, 22
Emperors of Sangoku: China, India, and Japan, 718
feng shui, 302
government information/services, 360
history, 379-380
Kung Fu, 527
Mah Jongg, 340-341
Our Chinese Daughters, 12
Tai Chi, 528

Chinese (languages/linguistics)
Chinese Outpost, 499
CLAS: Chinese Learner's Alternative Site, 504
Learning Chinese, 499
Omniglot's Chinese Script and Language Page, 499
Zhongwen.com, 499

chiropractors
American Chiropratic Association, 164
CHIROdirectory.com, 164
Chiropractic in Canada, 164
Chiropractic Internet Resources, 164
Chiropractic Resource Organization, The, 164
ChiroWeb, 164
ChiroStore Online, 164
International Chiropractors Association, 164
MyBackStore.com, 165
Spine-Health.com, 165
SpineUniverse.com, 165

choppers. *See* motorcycles

Christianity
American Baptist Churches USA Mission Center Online, 770
Answering Islam: A Christian-Muslim Dialog, 775
Answers in Action, 770
Augustine, 770
Baker Book House, 770
Best Christian Links, The, 770
Bible Gateway, 770
Catholic Online, 770
Center for Reformed Theology and Apologetics (CRTA), 770
Christian Articles Archive, 771
Christian Camping International, 142
Christian Coalition, The, 708
Christian Matchmaker, 214
Christian Missions, The, 771
Christian Science Monitor, 631
Christianbook.com, 771

Christianity Today, 771
Christianity Today: Single Parenting, 666
Christianity.com, 771
crosswalk.com, 771
Five Points of Calvinism, The, 771
Glide Memorial Church, 771
GodWeb, 771
Gospelcom.net, 771
GraceCathedral.org, 772
Greater Grace World Outreach, 772
Greek Orthodox Archdiocese of America, 772
Harvest Online, 772
International Prayer Network, 778
Jesus Army, 772
Jesus Film Project, 772
Logos Research Systems, 772
MEND (Mommies Enduring Neonatal Death), 717
Monastery of Christ in the Desert, 772
music, 588
Presbyterian Church USA, 773
Project Wittenberg, 773
Religious Society of Friends, 773
Scrolls from the Dead Sea, 773
Spurgeon Archive, The, 773
Trumpet, The, 773
Vatican, 773
World Religions Index, 773
World Vision, 639
YMCA, 967
Young People's Ministries, 967

cigars

Cigar Aficionado Magazine, 166
Cigar Friendly.com, 166
Cigar Nexus, 166
Cigar World, 166
Cigar.com, 166
Internet Cigar Group, 166
Smoke Magazine, 730
Top 25 Cigars, 166

civil rights

American Civil Liberties Union, The, 167
Amnesty International, 167
Birmingham Civil Rights Institute, 167
Cato Institute, 167
censorship, 157
Civil Rights Division (of the Department of Justice), 167
civilrights.org, 167
Law Research: The United States Department of Justice, 168
Minority Rights Group International, 168
National Civil Rights Museum, 168
Office of Civil Rights: U.S. Department of Education, 168

classical music

Adante: Everything Classical, 588
American Classical Music Hall of Fame, 588
Classical Guitarist, The, 589
Classical MIDI Connection, The, 589
Classical Music Archives, 589
Classical Music of the WWW Virtual Library, 589
Classical Net, 589
Classical USA, 589
Essentials of Music, 589
Gramophone, 589
Klassikne, 590
Mozart Project, The, 590
MusicOnline Classical Music Directory, 590
New York Philharmonic, 590
Piano Nanny, 590
Sony Classical, 590
symphony orchestra information, 590
XLNC1.org, 590

classifieds

Bargain Trade Online, 169
BuySellBid, 169
craigslist.org, 169
sell.com, 169
Trader Online, 169
Yahoo! Classifieds, 169

cleansing/detoxification

Arise & Shine Herbal Products, 29
Cleanse.Net, 29
Energise For Life Detox and Cleanse Guide, 29
HSP-Online.com, 29
WebMD.com: Detox Diets and Cleaning the Body, 29

clothing/fashion

accessories, 461-463, 920
advice, 15
BabyStyle, 811
Birkenstock Express, 77
Bloomingdale's, 811
Coldwater Creek, 811
Cosmopolitan, 726
D&J Sports, 928
DELiAs.com, 811
Designer Outlet.com, 811
Dillard's, 812
Dior.com, 300
Donna Karan, 300
Eddie Bauer, 812
ELLE.com, 300
Fashionmall.com, 812
Fogdog Sports, 816
Givenchy, 300
Glamour, 727
Gothic Clothing and Jewelry, 816
GQ Magazine, 542
HerRoom.com, 812
Hint Fashion Magazine, 300
Issey Mayake, 300
jewelry, 461-463
L.L. Bean Welcome Page, 138
L.L. Bean, 812
Lands' End, 812
Lane Bryant, 812
Metropolis Magazine, 45
Nordstrom, 812
Polo.com, 301
QuiltWear.com, 735
RAMGraphics: Spiritwear, 158
RedTagDeals.com, 79
Row Works, 922
Soldier City, 902
SPORTS Authority, The, 816

STYLE.com, 301
SwimNews Online, 930
Team Cheer Online, 158
Tommy Hilfiger, 301
Vogue, 301, 731
watches, 463, 920
Yves Saint Laurent, 301
ZOOZOOM.com Magazine, 301

coaching (sports)
Coaching Corner, 170
Coaching Well Basketball Journal, 85
eTeamz, 170
FIBA: Federation International de Basketball Amateur, 85
Five Star Hoops, 85
Football Drills, 170
MyCoachOnline, 170
National Alliance for Youth Sports, 170
Power Basketball, 85
SoccerROM, 170
Sports Coach, 171
WebBall, 171

coffees and teas
Cafe Maison Coffee Roasters, 319
China Mist Tea Company, 319
CoffeeAM.com, 319
Java Coffee & Tea Co., 319
Kona Coffee Times, 319
Orleans Coffee Exchange, 320
Peet's Coffee & Tea, 320
Starbucks, 320

coins (collectibles/collecting)
American Numismatic Association, 173
Coin Shows, 173
Coin Site, 173
Coin World, 173
CoinCollector.org, 174
CoinLink Numismatic and Rare Coins Index, 174
Forum Ancient Coins, 174
Heritage Rare Coin Gallery, 174
NumisMedia-Numismatic Interactive Network, 174
United States Mint, The, 174

Cold War
Berlin Wall Online, 915
CNN Interactive: Cold War, 915
Cold War Museum, The, 915
Cold War Policies: 1945-1991, 915
National Archives Learning Curve: The Cold War, The, 915
National Atomic Museum, 916

collectibles/collecting
antiques, 42-43
automobiles (toys), 175-176
Beanie Babies, 173
Beckett Collectibles Online, 172
coins, 173-174
Collectics, 172
CollectingChannel.com, 172
Collector Online, 172
Collectors Universe, 172
Collectors.or, 172
Curioscape, 172
dolls, 174-175
posters, 176-177
stamps, 177-178

colleges and universities
Academy of Art University, 46
ACHE: American College of Healthcare Executives, 371
American Association of Colleges of Nursing, 643
American Association of University Women (AAUW), 948
American College of Acupuncture & Oriental Medicine, 28
American College of Emergency Physicians, 269, 536
American College of Gastronenterology, 370
American College of Nurse-Midwives, 715
American College of Veterinary Surgeons, 904
Artemis Search for Women's Studies Programs, 948
Association of Collegiate Schools of Architecture, 44
Berkeley Art Museum/Pacific Film Archive, 573
Better Sex University, 807
Bigwords.com, 116
Boulder School of Massage Therapy, 32
Chaos at Maryland, 531
College Drinking Prevention Website, 4
College Republican National Committee, 708
CollegeBound Network, 479
CollegeHumor.com, 418
Colorado State Outdoor Adventure Programs, 288
Colorado State University Gardening & Horticulture, 496
Columbia Law School, 509
Culinary Schools, 204
Department of Animal Science: Oklahoma State University, 904
Dermatology Images: University of Iowa, 821
Electronic Text Center at the University of Virginia, The, 515
Embry-Riddle Aeronautical University Virtual Library, 69
Embry-Riddle Aeronautical University, 69
Expect the Best from a Girl, 950
financial aid and scholarships, 180-182
Franklin Pierce Law Center, 510
Gallaudet University, Washington, D.C., 218
General Research Resources, 762
general resources
ACT, 179
Campus Tours, 179
Chronicle of Higher Education, 179
College Answer, 179
College Board, 179
College View College Search, 179
Community Colleges, 179
Mapping Your Future, 179

mtvU, 180
Petersons.com: The College Channel, 180
Princeton Review Rankings, 180
Ulinks, 180
Xap, 180
Geography at the University of Buffalo, 353
graduate schools, 182-183
Harvard Gay & Lesbian Caucus, 347
Harvard Law School, 510
Harvard University Art Museums, 569
Indiana Prevention Resource Center, 8
Iowa State University's Tasty Insect Recipes, 428
Iowa State's Entomology Image Gallery, 428
job searches, 468-469
Lemelson-MIT Program, 453
Math Forum @ Drexel, The, 262
Murdoch University: Division of Veterinary and Biomedical Sciences, 905
Music Schools, 180
Nietzche Page at Stanford, 686
North Gate: Berkeley's Graduate School of Journalism, 474
OncoLink: University of Pennsylvania Cancer Center Resources, 147
Pet Columns from University of Illinois College of Veterinary Medicine (CVM), 683
Poynter.org, 474
Purdue Online Writing Lab (OWL), 961
reference libraries, 758
research help, 761
sports
baseball, 82
basketball, 86
football, 325
Stanford Encyclopedia of Philosophy, 687
Stanford Law School, 510
Technology Enhanced Learning and Research (TELR) at Ohio State University, 246
Tilburg University Marketing Journals, 132
U.S. College Hockey Online, 396
UCLA Fowler Museum of Cultural History, 571
University of California Museum of Paleontolgy, 573
University of California's Scripps Institution of Oceangraphy, 648
University of Chicago Law School, 510
University of Phoenix Online, 246
UTLink: Resources by Subject, 764
Washington State University College of Veterinary Medicine, 905
Wine: UC Davis Department of Viticulture and Enology, 946
WWW Virtual Library-Law, 508
Yale Law School Home Page, 511

Colorado
Boulder School of Massage Therapy, 32
Colorado State Outdoor Adventure Programs, 288
Colorado State Parks and Outdoor Recreation, 673
Colorado State University Gardening & Horticulture, 496
Colorado Vacation Guide, 885
Colorado.com, 888
Denver Museum of Nature & Science, 611
Denver Zoo, 969
Mesa Verde National Park, 674

comedy. *See* humor

comics, cartoons, and animation
American Royal Arts, 40
anime, 41, 186
Animation Art, 184
Animation Library, 40
Animation World Network, 40, 184
Archie, 184
Arthur on PBS, 477
Batman-Superman, 184
Big Cartoon Database, 184, 420
Calvin and Hobbes, 184
Captain Planet, 478
Cartoon Brew, 184
Cartoon Network.com, 185, 420
Cartoonster, 185
Chuck Jones Website, 40, 185
Comic Book Movies, 185
Comic Book Resources, 185
Comics.com, 185
Comics2Film, 789
Computer Graphics World Magazine, 40, 185
Dark Horse Comics Home Page, 185, 789
DC Comics, 185
Diamond Comic Distributor, Inc., 186
Digital Webring, 186
Disney.com, 36, 186, 479
Fanspeak, 790
graphic novels, 362
International Animated Film Society, 40, 186
International Museum of Cartoon Art, 186
Jerry Beck's Cartoon Research, 421
Kids WB!, 482
manga, 186, 362, 816
Marvel Comics, 186
MTN Cartoons, 186
National Cartoon Museum, 421
Nick Jr., 483
Noggin, 483
Official Peanuts Website, 186
PBS Kids, 484
Red Vs. Blue, 420
Sailor Moon Specialty Store, 816
Shark Tale, 186
Simpsons, The, 187
South Park, 187
Spongebob Squarepants, 187

Warner Brothers Games Gallery, 488
WebComics, 187
Zanadu Comics, 116

comparison bots
BizRate, 813
Bottomdollar, 813
Epinions, 813
mySimon, 813
NexTag, 813
Pricegrabber.com, 813
PriceSCAN.com, 813
Productopia, 813
RoboShopper.com, 813
Shopping.com, 813

computers
antivirus software/resources, 196, 446
buying/information resources, 188-189
BYTE Magazine, 725
Center for Machine Translation, 498
Computer Emergency Response Time, 269
Computer Gear, 355
Computer History Museum, 188
Computer Recycling, 276
Computer Scrapbooking, 795
Computerworld Online, 725
ConsumerWorld Bargains, 77
Experts Exchange, 16
games and puzzles, 334-341
hardware/software companies, 189-190
HotWired, 727
Internet FAQ Archives, 762
ItsRainingBargains, 78
job searches, 469
JokeWallpaper.com, 421
Longhorn Blogs, 105
Macintosh, 190-191, 198-199
MacWorld, 727
networking, 616-621
PCs, 191-192, 199
Pearson Technology Group, 118
Popular Science, 626, 729
programming languages, 193-196
SeniorNet, 801
software-downloads, 196-197
software-miscellaneous, 197-198
techbargains.com, 78
Technology Recycling, 476
troubleshooting, 198-199
Webopedia.com, 756
Windows IT Pro, 731
Wired Seniors, 801
ZDNet, 732
ZDNet-PC Magazine, 627

concerts
Blues Festivals, 584
Festivals.com, 584
JamBase, 584
Mardi Gras Official Website, 584
Mojam, 584
Pollstar: The Concert Hotwire, 585
Ticketmaster.com, 585
TicketWeb, 585
tkt.com, 585

conduct disorder
American Academy of Childhood & Adolescent Psychiatry, 549
Clinical Guide to Conduct Disorder, 549
ConductDisorders.com, 549
Oppositional Defiant Disorder (ODD) and Conduct Disorders, 550

conservation
American Farmland Trust, 19
Arbor Day Foundation, 271
Atlantic Salmon Federation, 271
Bat Conservation, 271
Butterfly Web site: Conservation and Ecology, The, 271
Coastal America Partnership National Web Site, 274
Conservation Breeding Specialist Group, 271
Conservation International, 272
Ducks Unlimited, 423
Earth Island, 272
Earthwatch, 274
Ecologia, 274
Ecology and Society, 274
Ecology Fund, 274
Ecology.com, 274
Environment Directory, The, 274
Environmental Education Resources, 272
green home, 272
Greenpeace, 274
Home Energy Saver, 275
International Ecotourism Society, 275
International Rivers Network, 272
Kids Do Ecology, 275
MrSolar.com, 272
National Audubon Society, 104
National Audubon Society, 272
National Oceanic and Atmospheric Administration, 272, 647
National Wildlife Federation, 273
Nature Conservancy, The, 273
Ocean Alliance, The, 273
RAINFORESTWEB.ORG, 273
Sierra Club, 275
Surfrider Foundation USA, 273
Texas Parks and Wildlife, 425
U.S. Fish and Wildlife Service, 425
U.S. Fish and Wildlife Service-National Wetlands Inventory, 275
Wildlife Conservation Society/Bronx Zoo, 273
World Wildlife Fund, 273

construction (home)
B4UBUILD.com, 399
Bricsnet, 399
Build.com, 399
Builder Online, 400
Building Industry Exchange, 400
BuildingCost.net, 400
Construction-Resource.com, 400
HomeBuilder.COM, 400
Housing Zone, 400
National Association of Home Builders, 400

consumer issues
- Better Business Bureau, 200
- Bicycle Helmet Safety Institute Home Page, 200
- Consumer Information Center, The, 762
- Consumer Law Page, The, 200
- Consumer World, 200
- ConsumerLine, 200
- ConsumerWebWatch, 200
- Corporate Watch, 201
- FDA Consumer Magazine, 201
- Federal Citizen Information Center, 201
- FirstGov for Consumers, 201
- Foundation for Taxpayer and Consumer Rights, 201
- Internet ScamBusters, 201
- National Consumer Law Center (NCLC), 508
- National Consumer Protection Week, 201
- National Consumers League, 201
- National Fraud Information Center, The, 202
- Street Cents Online, 255
- U.S. Consumer Product Safety Commission, 202

contraception
- Contraception.net, 713
- ContraceptionOnline.org, 713
- Planned Parenthood Federation of America, Inc., 714
- Planned Parenthood Golden Gate, 714
- Teenwire, 714

cooking and recipes. *See also* diet and nutrition; food and drink
- ADA Recipe of the Day, 228
- advice, 15
- American Egg Board, 18
- Arise & Shine Herbal Products, 29
- Baby Bag Online, 71
- Beef Home Page, 19
- Betty Crocker, 203
- Books for Cooks, 114
- Books for Cooks, 115
- Bread, 203
- Campfire Cooking, 137
- Chef Talk, 203
- Children with Diabetes Recipes, 228
- Chile Pepper Magazine, 203
- Cook's Thesaurus, The, 754
- Cookbooks Online Recipe Database, 203
- Cooking Couple Clubhouse Web site, 203
- Cooking Light, 203
- Cooks Online, 203
- Creole and Cajun Recipe Page, 204
- Culinary Schools, 204
- Culinary World Tour, 204
- Diabetic Gourmet Magazine, 229
- Dinner Co-Op, 204
- Epicurious, 204
- Fabulous Foods, 204
- FatFree Vegetarian Mailing List Archive, 204
- Food Allergy & Anaphylaxis Network, 25
- Food Allergy Initiative, 25
- Food Network, 204
- Global Gourmet, 317
- Gourmet Connection Network, 229
- Great Cookware, 317
- home-brewing (beer), 89-91
- Instawares: Restaurant Supply Superstore, 317
- KnowledgeHound, 16
- Kosher Express, 204
- Mushroom Recipes, 204
- National Pork Producer's Council, 205
- New England Lobster, 205
- Pasta Home Page, 205
- Prevention.com, 205
- Stuart's Chinese Recipes, 205
- TexMex, 205
- Top Secret Recipes, 205
- U-pons, 80
- WeightWatchers Recipes, 205

cosmetics/skin care
- Acne Treatment, 821
- Avon, 821
- Body Shop, The, 821
- Cosmetic Connection, 821
- Cosmetic Mall, 821
- Dermatology Images: University of Iowa, 821
- Dermatology Medical Reference, 821
- drugstore.com, 822
- Faceart, 822
- M-A-C Cosmetics, 822
- Mary Kay, 822
- Merle Norman Cosmetics Studio, 822
- National Rosacea Society, 822
- Neutrogena, 822
- Sephora, 822
- Skin Care Campaign, 823
- Skin Care tips, 823
- Skin Culture Peel, 823
- Skin Store, 823
- SkinCarePhysicians.com, 823

Costa Rica, government information/services, 360

country music
- CMT.com, 591
- Country Music Awards, 590
- GAC TV: Great American Country TV, 591
- History of Country Music, 591
- Jack Ingram, 591
- Women of Country, 591

coupons
- Ben's Bargains, 77
- Car-pons, 78
- ConsumerWorld Bargains, 77
- Cool Savings, 79
- Coupon Pages, 79
- CouponSurfer, 79
- Daily e-Deals, 79
- DealCatcher.com, 77
- Fat Wallet, 79
- MyCoupons, 79
- RedTagDeals.com, 79
- RoomSaver.com, 79
- TouristFlorida.com, 79
- U-pons, 80
- ValPak, 80

CPR. *See also* emergency services
- CPR for AIDS Patients, 367
- CPR, 367
- Learn CPR, 367
- Mayo Clinic First Aid Guide, 367

crafts. *See also* hobbies
American Sewing Guild, 802
Art Glass World, 206
Arts and Crafts Society, 206
Aunt Annie's Crafts, 206
Butterick, 805
Craft Fairs Online, 206
Craftster.org, 206
Cranston Village, 802
Creativity for Kids, 864
crocheting, 208
Do-It-Yourself Network, 206
Dress Forms and Pattern Fitting Online, 805
Fabric Club, The, 802
Fabrics.net, 802
Fashion Fabrics Club, 802
Fiskars, 802
Get Crafty, 206
Hands-on Crafts, 207
hobby shops and craft stores, 206
HobbyTown USA, 391
Home Sewing Association, 802
Jo-Ann Fabric and Crafts, 802
knitting, 492-494
Lily Abello's Sewing Links, 803
Longaberger Baskets, 403
McCall's Pattern Catalog, 805
Michael's: The Arts and Crafts Store, 207
Nancy's Notions, 803
needlecrafts, 614-615
origami, 655
quilting, 733-735
ReadyMade, 207
Sew News, 803
Sewing Web, A, 803
Sewing.com, 803
Sewingpatterns.com, 805
Simplicity, 806
Threads Magazine, 803
Vintage Pattern Lending Library, 806
Wild Ginger Software, 803
Wildly Wonderful Wearables, 806
woodworking, 731

credit counseling. *See also* frugal spending
123Debt.com, 222
American Consumer Credit Counseling, 222
American Debt Management Services, 222
AnnualCreditReport.com, 222
Bankrate.com, 222
bankruptcy, 224
Consumer Credit Counseling by Springboard, 222
credit cards, 224-225
Department of Veternas Affairs Debt Management, 223
Federal Trade Commission Credit Section, 223
foreclosures, 225
InfoHQ Online CPA, 223
Money Management International, 223
MSN Money: Savings and Debt Management, 223
National Foundation for Credit Counseling, 223
Smart Money, 223
Ten Strategies to Reduce Your Debt, 223-224
U.S. National Debt Clock, 224

criminal justice. *See also* law and legal issues
360degrees.org, 455
American Correctional Association, 455
American Jail Association, 455
American Probation and Parole Association, 455
Correctional Education Association, 455
Corrections Connection, 455
Federal Bureau of Prisons, 456
JUSTNET: Justice Information Network, 456
National Institute of Justice, 456
Officer.com, 456
Prisontalk, 456
Stanford Prison Experiment, 456
U.S. Bureau of Justice Statistics, 456

crocheting
Crochet Patternh Central, 208
Hip Vintage Crochet, 208
Learn to Crochet Easily, 208
NextStitch, 208
Smart Crochet, 208

cross-country running
Cool Running, 280
KidsRunning.com, 280
USATF on the Web, 280

cross-stitching. *See* needlecrafts

cruises
All-Inclusives Resort and Cruise Vacation Source, 883
Bargain Travel Cruises-Cheap Cruises, 875
Carnival Cruises, 875
Cruise Value Center, 875
Cruise.com, 875
CruiseGuide, 875
CruiseStar.com, 875
Crystal Cruises, 876
Freighter World Cruises, 876
Holland America Line, 876
i-cruise.com, 876
Norwegian Cruise Line, 876
Orient-Express Trains & Cruises, 887
Princess Cruises, 876
Royal Caribbean, 876
Schooner Mary Day, 876

cults
FACTnet, 774
Ms. Guidance on Strange Cults, 774
Rick A. Ross Institute of New Jersey, 774
Steven Alan Hassan's Freedom of Mind Center, 774

culture
Atlantic Online, The, 725
Atlantic Unbound, 624
gay/lesbian/bisexual/transgender issues, 348
Harper's, 727
KnowledgeHound, 16
museums, 571-572
Nation, The, 625
New York Times: Television, 855

Newsweek, 625
Salon.com, 633
TIME, 626
Vanity Fair, 731

current affairs
Atlantic Online, The, 725
Current Affairs, 382
eHistory: Middle East, 386
Harper's, 727
History in the News: The Middle East, 387
Middle East History & Resources, 387
New Yorker, 728
Newsweeks, 729
Politics and Current Affairs Forum, 382
Time Magazine, 730
Vanity Fair, 731

cyber law and cyberspace issues. *See also* law and legal issues
Allwhois.com, 509
Electronic Commerce and Internet Law Resource Center-Perkins Coie, LLP, 509
GigaLaw, 509
Internet Library of Law and Court Decisions, 509
Kuesterlaw Technology Law Resources, 509

Czech Republic, 880

D

dance
ANYTOWN: Stories of America, 209
ballet, 210-211
ballroom dancing, 211-212
BornToSalsa.com, 209
C.L.O.G., 209
Dance Magazine, 209
Dance Spirit, 209
Dance Teacher Magazine, 209
Dancer Online, 209
International Association of Gay Square Dance Clubs, 348
La Musica, 209
Luna Kids Dance Programs, 210
Pow Wow Dancing, 210
So You Think You Can Dance, 210
Voice of Dance, 210

darts
Crow's Dart Page, 213
Dart Bars, 213
Darts World Magazine, 213
Sewa-Darts, 213
Smilie Darts, 213
Top, 100 Darts Sites, 213
World Darts Federation, 213

dating. *See also* relationships; romance
advice/tips, 215-216
dating sites, 214
personals/services, 214-215
SingleParentMeet, 667

daycare providers
Administration for Children and Families, 162
AFDS, Inc., 162
Bright Beginnings Family Child Care, 162
ChildCareAware, 162
DaycareUniverse.com, 162
Individual States' Childcare Licensure Regulations, 163
Kiddie Campus U, 163
Monday Morning Moms, 163
NAEYC Accredited Centers, 163
National Association of Child Care Resource & Referral Agencies (NACCRRA), 163
National Network for Child Care (NNCC), 163

deafness
Alexander Graham Bell Association for Deaf and Hard of Hearing, 217
ASL Access, 217
Captioned Media Program, 217
Deaf Chat, 217
Deaf Resources, 217
Deaf.com, 217
DeafandHH.com, 217
deafkids.com, 217
DeafNation, 218
DeafZONE, 218
Gallaudet University, Washington, D.C., 218
GG Wiz's FingerSpeller, 218
HandSpeak, 218
Helen Keller National Center for Deaf-Blind Youth, 218
National Association of the Deaf (NAD), 218
National Institute on Deafness and Other Communication Disorders, 218
Oral Deaf Education, 218
SignWritingSite, 219
Zoos Software, 219

death and dying
ADEC, 832
Beyond Indigo, 220
Euthanasia World Directory, 220
GriefNet, 220
Hospice Foundation of America, 220
Hospice Net, 220
Hospice, 220
Life Extension Foundation, 799
Medline Plus: On Death and Dying, 221
National Hospice and Palliative Care Organization, 221
Seniors-Site.com, 781

debt management. *See also* frugal spending
123Debt.com, 222
American Consumer Credit Counseling, 222
American Debt Management Services, 222
AnnualCreditReport.com, 222
Bankrate.com, 222
bankruptcy, 224
Consumer Credit Counseling by Springboard, 222
credit cards, 224-225
Department of Veterans Affairs Debt Management, 223
Federal Trade Commission Credit Section, 223
foreclosures, 225
InfoHQ Online CPA, 223
LowerMyBills.com, 78
Money Management International, 223

MSN Money: Savings and Debt Management, 223
National Foundation for Credit Counseling, 223
Smart Money, 223
Suze Orman, 559
Ten Strategies to Reduce Your Debt, 223-224
U.S. National Debt Clock, 224

decks and patios
BestDeckSite, 401
ConcreteNetwork.com, 401
Deck Design, 401
DecKorators, 401
Hometime.com, 401
PatioPavers, 401
Treatedwood Home Page, 401

decorating/painting (home)
All-Home Decor, 401
American Society of Interior Designers, 402
Ballard Design, 402
Bed Bath & Beyond, 402
Better Homes and Gardens, 402
cMYVision, 402
CreateandBarrel.com, 402
Design Addict, 402
Designing Online, 402
EZblinds.com, 402
FurnitureFind.com, 403
FurnitureOnline.com, 403
Home and Garden Television (HGTV), 403
Home Fashion Information Network, 403
Longaberger Baskets, 403
No Brainer Blinds and Shades, 403
Pier 1 Imports, 403
Pottery Barn, 403
Rental Decorating, 403
Stencil Ease Home Decor and Craft Stencils, 404
Traditional Home Magazine, 404
unicaHOME, 404
UrbanScapes, 404

delirium, 550

dementia, 550

dentistry
Academy of General Dentistry, 226
American Academy of Cosmetic Dentistry, 226
American Dental Association, 226
American Dental Hygienists' Association, 226
Dentistry.com, 226
HealthWeb, 226
Pets Need Dental Care, Too, 683
Sports Dentistry Online, 227

depression. *See also* mental health
All About Depression, 550
Coping with Depression Fallout, 550
Depressed Anonymous, 551
Depression and Bipolar Support Alliance, 551
depression-screening.org, 551
McMan's Depression and Bipolar Web, 549
NARSAD: National Association for Research on Schizophrenia and Depression, 555
National Institutes of Mental Health: Depression, 551
Psychology Information Online, 551
Teen Depression, 551

dermatology
Dermatlogy Images: University of Iowa, 821
Dermatlogy Medical Reference, 821
National Rosacea Society, 822
Skin Care Campaign, 823
SkinCarePhysicians.com, 823

detoxification/cleansing
Arise & Shine Herbal Products, 29
Cleanse.Net, 29
Energise For Life Detox and Cleanse Guide, 29
HSP-Online.com, 29
WebMD.com: Detox Diets and Cleaning the Body, 29

diabetes
ADA Recipe of the Day, 228
ADA: American Diabetes Association, 228
Center for Disease Control Diabetes FAQ, 228
Children with Diabetes Online Community, 228
Children with Diabetes Recipes, 228
Diabetes Health Magazine, 228
Diabetes Insight, 229
Diabetes Mall, 229
Diabetic Gourmet Magazine, 229
Gourmet Connection Network, 229
Joslin Diabetes Center, 229
Kids Learn About Diabetes, 229
Medical Alert Charms for Children, 229
National Diabetes Education Program, 229
National Institute of Diabetes & Digestive & Kidney Disorders, 229

dictionaries and thesauri
Acronym Finder, 754
Acronyms and Abbreviations, 754
ARTFL Project: Roget's Thesaurus Search Form, 754
Cambridge Dictionaries, 754
Climbing Dictionary, The, 783
Dictionary.com Definitions, 754
Dictionary.com Translation, 755
iTools.com, 763
Merriam-Webster Online, 755
Online Dictionaries and Glossaries, 755
Thesaurus.com, 755
TravLang's Translating Dictionaries, 755
Word Wizard, The, 755
yourDictionary.com, 755

diet and nutrition. *See also* cooking and recipes; exercise and fitness; food and drink; health; weight loss

American Dietetic Association, 940

American Heart Association, 230

Arise & Shine Herbal Products, 29

Ask Dr. Weil, 940

Ask the Dietitian, 230

Best of Weight Loss, 940

Blonz Guide to Nutrition, Food, and Health Resources, 230

Celiac Disease, 156

Center for Science in the Public Interest, 230

Consumer Information Center: Food, 230

CyberDiet, 940

Diet Channel, The, 940

Dietsite.com, 230

Doctor's Guide to Obesity, 940

Dole 5 a Day, 230

eDiets.com, 231, 941

Energise For Life Detox and Cleanse Guide, 29

Fast Food Facts, 941

Feingold Association of the United States, 231

Food and Nutrition Information Center, 231

Food Pyramid, 231

HealthCentral, 942

Healthfinder, 231

HSP-Online.com, 29

Jenny Craig, 941

L A Weight Loss Centers, 941

LifeClinic, 231

Mayo Clinic Food & Nutrition Center, 231

Meals for You, 232

Natural Nutrition, 941

Nutrisystem, 941

Nutrition Cafe, 232

Nutrition Explorations, 232

Nutrition.gov, 232

Prevention's Healthy Ideas, 232

Prevention.com, 205

Prevention.com-Weight Loss and Fitness, 941-942

Self Magazine, 232

Shape Up America, 942

vitamins and supplements, 909-910

WebMD.com: Detox Diets and Cleaning the Body, 29

Weight Watchers, 942

WeightWatchers Recipes, 205

digital photography

AGFA Digital Cameras, 688

Canvas on Demand, 690

Complete Guide to Digital Cameras and Digital Photography, 688

Digital Camera Images Resource Page, 688

Digital Camera News, 689

Digital Camera Resource Page, 689

Digital Photography Challenge, 690

Digital Photography Review, 689

Digital Photography Tips, 690

Digital Photography Weblog, 690

HowStuffWorks: How Digital Cameras Work, 689

HP Digital Photo Activity Center, 690

Internet Brothers: Digital Photography Tips and Techniques, 690

Lexar: Digital Photography Tips, 690

Megapixel.net, 689

PC Photo Review, 689

Photographysites.com, 691

sharing photos online, 691-692

dinosaurs

BBC Walking with Dinosaurs, 233

Carnegie Museum of Natural History, The, 572

Dinosaur National Monument, 233

Dinosaurs: Facts and Fiction, 233

Discovering Dinosaurs, 233

Discovery Channel: When Dinosaurs Roamed America, 233

Extinctions.com, 233

Field Museum of Natural History, 233

Smithsonian NMNH Dinosaur Home Page, 234

disabilities

blindness

Guide Dogs for the Blind, 238

Helen Keller National Center for Deaf-Blind Youth, 218

Children's Miracle Network (CMN), 640

deafness

Alexander Graham Bell Association for Deaf and Hard of Hearing, 217

American Sign Language Browser, 505

ASL Access, 217

Captioned Media Program, 217

Deaf Chat, 217

Deaf Resources, 217

Deaf.com, 217

DeafandHH.com, 217

deafkids.com, 217

DeafNation, 218

DeafZONE, 218

Gallaudet University, Washington, D.C., 218

GG Wiz's FingerSpeller, 218

HandSpeak, 218

Hellen Keller National Center for Deaf-Blind Youth, 218

National Association of the Deaf (NAD), 218, 505

National Institute on Deafness and Other Communication Disorders, 218

Oral Deaf Education, 218

SignWritingSite, 219

Zoos Software, 219

Disability.gov, 369

Disabled American Veterans, 901

Down Syndrome WWW Pages, 370

Gimponthego.com, 374

A B C D E F G H I J K L M N O P Q R S T U V W X Y Z

Goodwill Industries International, 640
HSA: Handicapped Scuba Association, 924
International Paralympic Table Tennis Committee, 839
LD Online, 369
Muscular Dystrophy Association, 371
National Association for Visually Handicapped, 369
National Wheelchair Basketball Association, 85
Paralyzed Veterans of America, 369, 902
Social Security Administration: Disability Benefits, 369
UCPnet, 369
World Association of Persons with Disabilities, 369
youreable.com, 369

discount stores
Costco Online, 814
Overstock.com, 814
Sam's Club, 814
SmartBargains, 814
Wal-Mart Online, 814

distance learning
American Institute for Paralegal Studies, 245
ConferenceCalltraining, 245
Distance Education at a Glance, 245
Distance Education Clearinghouse, 245
Distance Learning and Online Education, 245
Distance Learning on the Net, 245
foreign languages, 247
H. Wayne Huizenga School of Business and Entrepreneurship, 245
Mindedge: Online Education, 246
Petersons.com: The Lifelong Learning Channel, 246
TEAMS Distance Learning, 246
Technology Enhanced Learning and Research (TELR) at Ohio State University, 246
United States Distance Learning Association, 246
University of Phoenix Online, 246
WorldWideLearn, 246

diving
NCAA Men's Swimming and Diving, 929
NCAA Women's Swimming and Diving, 929
scuba diving, 924-926
snorkeling, 926

divorce and custody
child support, 236
Children's Rights Council, 235
Divorce Busting, 524
Divorce Magazine, 235
DivorceCare Home Page, 235
divorceLAWinfo.com, 507
DivorceNet, 235
DivorceWizards, 235
FamilyLaw.org, 235
Men Stuff, 543
SmartDivorce.com, 236
stepparenting, 671-672

dogs
Adopt a Greyhound, 237
American Kennel Club (AKC), 237
DoctorDog.com: Cat and Dog Supplies and Pet Health Care, 682
Dog Breed Info Center, 237
Dog-Play, 237
Dog.com, 237
Dogs in Review, 237
GORP: Great Outdoor Recreation Pages, 238
Guide Dogs for the Blind, 238
iLoveDogs.com, 238
Next Day Pets, 238
Taking Care of Your Dog, 238
Terrific Pets, 238
Three Dog Bakery, 238

dolls (collectibles/collecting)
Alexander Doll Company, 174
American Girl, 174
Barbie.com, 175
Blythe Dolls, 175
collectiblestoday.com, 175
Corolle Dolls, 175
minishop.com, 175
Raggedy Ann & Andy Museum, 175
United Federation of Doll Clubs, Inc., The, 175

domestic violence
End Abuse, 239
National Coalition Against Domestic Violence, 239
National Network to End Domestic Violence, 239
Office on Violence Against Women, 239
Safe Horizon, 239
Safe Place, A, 239
WISE (Women's Initiative for Self Empowerment), 953

dream interrpretation
Dream Doctor, 240
Dream Moods, 240
Dreams Foundation, 240
International Association for the Study of Dreams, 240
Swoon@Glamour, 240

drinks. *See* food and drink

drug abuse/recovery
CrystalRecovery.com, 5
D.A.R.E., 8
Drugnet, 5
Get It Straight: The Facts About Drugs, 8
Marijuana Anonymous World Services, The, 8
Narcotics Anonymous, 5
National Institute on Drug Abuse, 8
Partnership for a Drug-Free America, 8
Substance Abuse Treatment Facility Locator, 6

drug information (medicine)
FDA: Food and Drug Administration, 536
National Library of Medicine, 536
RxList.com, 536
SafeMedication.com, 536

drugstores
CareMark.com, 535
CVS/Pharmacy, 535
drugstore.com, 535

Eckerd.com, 535
familymeds.com, 535
Medicine Shoppe, 535
Rite Aid, 535
SavOn.com, 535
Walgreens, 536
Dutch (languages/linguistics), 101 , 504
DVDs
Amazon.com, 907
Blockbuster, 908
Buy.com, 908
DVD FAQ, 906
DVD Price Search, 906
dvdfile.com, 907
Hollywood Video, 908
Netflix.com, 907
Outpost, 908
Reel.com, 816
Reel.com, 908
Suncoast Video, 908
Things from Another World, 908

E

e-commerce
Beginner's Guide to E-Commerce, 241
CommerceNet, 241
Doba.com, 241
E-Commerce Guide, 241
E-Commerce Times, 241
eBay, 241
eMarketer.com, 241
Emerging Enterprise, The, 242
Federal Trade Commission's E-Commerce Publications, 242
FreeMerchant.com, 242
Google AdSense, 242
Guide to E-Commerce, 242
Internet Marketing Center, 242
Internet.com, 242
Jupiter Direct Research, 242
Marketing Tips, 243
PayPal, 243
SellItOnTheWeb, 243
Sloan Center for Internet Retailing, 243
TechWeb, 243
Wilson: Web Marketing and E-Commerce, 243
Wired.com, 243
e-zines
Angling Report Newsletter, The, 724
BestEzines-Choose Your Ezines Wisely, 724
Body Modification E-zine, 724
E-zineZ, 724
Ezine-Universe.com, 724
Science Fiction Weekly, 725, 792
Wine and Dine E-Zine, 725
eating disorders
American Anorexia Bulimia Association of Philadelphia, 551
Anorexia Web, 551
Binge Eating Disorders, 552
Center for Eating Disorders, 552
Eating Disorders Association (EDA), 552
Eating Disorders Resource Centre, 552
Eating Disorders Online.com, 552
Girl Power! Bodywise, 552
National Eating Disorder Association, 552
National Women's Health Association, 552
Renfrew Center Foundation, The, 552
Something Fishy, 553
ecotourism. *See* adventure travel/ecotourism
Ecuador, government information/services, 360
education. *See also* teaching
A+ Research and Writing, 960
Activity Search, 846
Agriculture in the Classroom, 18
Amazing Space, 49
Amazon Interactive, 477
American Association of University Women (AAUW), 948
American Federation of Teachers, 846
Animaland, 477
Artemis Search for Women's Studies Programs, 948
ArtsEdge, 846
AskTheBrain, 260
Astronomy for Kids, 49
BAM! (Body and Mind), 478
Benjamin Franklin: Glimpses of the Man, 260
Bill Nye the Science Guy's Nye Labs Online, 478
BookHive, 113
Bugscope, 427
Buyers and Cellars Wine Education, 943
careers, 464
Chem4Kids, 478
Children's Museum of Indianapolis, 567
CIA History for Kids, 388
Classroom CONNECT, 846
CliffsNotes, 261
Community Learning Network, 261
Consortium for School Networking, 616
Council for Exceptional Children, 261
Council on Social Work Education, 832
D.A.R.E., 8
Dance Teacher Magazine, 209
Department of Education, 896
Discovery Toys, 864
DiscoverySchool.com, 846
distance learning, 245-246
Earth & Sky, 50
Eco-Kids, 480
edbydesign.com, 480
Eddy the Eco-Dog, 480
Edheads, 846
Education Index, 261, 847
Education Place, 847
Education Week on the Web, 847
Education World, 244, 847
Education.com, 846
Educational Resources, 847
Educator's Reference Desk, 847
Educause, 261
Encarta Online, 261, 756

Enchanted Learning: Inventors and Inventions, 452
Environmental Explorers Club, 276
EPA Global Warming for Kids, 480
Escape from Knab, 487
Expect the Best from a Girl, 950
experiential/outdoor, 286-291
Exploratorium, The, 567, 574
Family Education Network: A Parenting and Education Resource, 659
Federal Citizen Information Center, 897
Federal Resources for Educational Excellence (FREE), 847
FirstGov for Kids, 480
FREE: Federal Resources for Education Excellence, 261
Froggy Page, 480
Funschool, 488
Get It Straight: The Facts About Drugs, 8
Global SchoolHouse, 848
goENC.com, 848
GreatSchools.net, 244
Group for Education in Museums, 574
Harcourt School Publishing, 848
Healthy Pregnancy, 710
homeschooling, 247-248
homework help, 255-256, 262
IAAY Expository Writing Tutorial, 961
infoplease.com, 262
Intel Education Initiative, 848
Interactive Art School: Free Lessons, 657
international education, 249-250, 263
JASON, 244
Junior Achievement TITAN, 488
K-12, 250-259, 262, 529-530
Kathy Schrock's Guide for Educators, 848
Kid Info, 262
Kids Do Ecology, 275
Kids' Place, 481
KidsHealth.org, 482
Landmarks for Schools, 383
law schools, 509-511
LD Online, 369
Learning Curve International, 866
learning disabilities. *See* special needs children
Lesson Plans Page, 848
MarcoPolo, 244
Marshall Brain's How Stuff Works, 332
Mastermind Educational toys, 867
Math Forum @ Drexel, The, 262
Mathematical Quotation Server, 737
McGraw-Hill School Division, 848
Mexico for Kids, 557
NAEYC Accredited Centers, 163
NASA Education Sites, 262
National AfterSchool Association, 665
National Diabetes Education Program, 229
National Education Association, 244, 848
National Geographic for Kids, 483
National Head Start Association, 666
National Mentoring Center, 967
New York Times Learning Network, 849
NoodleHead Network, The, 484
Notebaert Nature Museum, 612
Nursing Education of America, 645
NWSA-National Women's Studies Associations, 952
Office of Civil Rights: U.S. Department of Education, 168
OLogy, 484
Oral Deaf Education, 218
PBS Teacher's Source, 849
PetEducation.com, 683
Peterson's Education Center, 262
PinkMonkey, 262
playkidsgames.com, 488
preschool, 259-260
Puffin House, The, 849
Purdue Online Writing Lab (OWL), 961
Reach for the Sky, 484
reference libraries, 758-760
Scholastic.com, 849
scifair.org, 262
Seniors-Site.com, 781
Smithsonian Journeys, 14
SparkNotes, 262
sports, 925, 929
Talking with Kids About Tough Issues, 662
Teachers.net, 849
Technical Education Research Centers (TERC), 849
Tutor.com, 262
U.S. Department of Education, 244
U.S. Department of Education-Funding Opportunities, 849
United Nations Cyberschool Bus, 263
USA Today Education, 850
USFA (United States Fire Administration) for Kids, 486
Virtual Reference Desk, 850
VolcanoWorld, 486
White House for Kids, The, 486
Why Files, 486
Wine: UC Davis Department of Viticulture and Enology, 946
WordNet, 500
Writers on the Net, 961
Writing Den, 962
Yahoo! Education Directory, 244-245
Young Investor, 245
YourDictionary.com, 263

Egypt
Egyptian Mathematics, 529
Egyptian Mythology, 609
Egyption Book of the Dead, The, 768
government information/services, 360

eldercare
AARP, 797
Administration on Aging (AOA), 797
AgeNet Eldercare Network, 264
AgeNet, 797
Aging in the Know, 797
Alzheimer's, 34-35, 798
American Association of Homes and Services for the Aging, 798
American Geriatrics Society, 798
Assisted Living Foundation, 798
BenefitsCheckUp, 798
CareGuide@Home, 264
Centers for Medicare and Medicaid Services, 798
ElderCare Advocates, 264
Eldercare at Home: A Comprehensive Guide, 264
Eldercare Locator, 264, 799
ElderWeb, 264, 799
FCA: Family Caregiver Alliance, 265
Friendly4Seniors Websites, 799
Health and Age, 265
HomeStore.com Senior Living, 799
HUD for Senior Citizens, 799
Life Extension Foundation, 799
Lifesphere, 800
Medicare.gov, 800
National Council on Aging, 800
National Institute on Aging, 800
National Senior Citizens Law Center, The, 800
New LifeStyles, 800
osteoporosis, 655-656
Senior Information Network, The, 800
Senior Sites, 801
Senior.com, 800
SeniorJournal, 801
seniorresource.com, 801
SeniorsSearch.com, 801
SeniorStore.com, 357
Social Security Online, 801
Third Age, 801
Transitions, Inc. Elder Care Consulting, 801

electrical (home)
DoItYourself.com Electrical and Electronics, 404
Electrical Safety Foundation, 404
Home & Family, 404
Home and Garden Television: Electrical, 405
HomeTips, 405
Saving Electricity, 405

electronics
Alpine of America, 266
Audio Ideas Guide, 266
Audio Video News, 266
Best Buy, 266
Bose Corporation, 266
Cambridge SoundWorks, 266
Chumbo.com, 188
Consumer Electronics Show, 266
Crutchfield, 267
Curcuit City, 266
Dynamism.com, 267
eCoustics.com, 267
Home Theater Magazine, 267
IEEE Home Page, 267
Internet Mall, 267
ItsRainingBargains, 78
Jerry Raskin's Needle Doctor, 267
Mega Hertz, 267
Nextag, 267
Phone Scoop, 268
Popular Science, 626, 729
Radio Shack, 268
Reviews at cnet.com, 268
Sony, 268
SoundStage, 268
techbargains.com, 78
TWICE: This Week in Consumer Electronics, 268
Unbeatable.com, 268

email
anti-spam resources, 434-435
Bigfoot, 438
emailaddresses.com, 438
Eudora, 438
Gmail, 438
Harness Email, 438
HTMail, 441
junk email, 476
Lycos Mail, 438
Lyris.net, 442
MSN Hotmail, 438
Netiquette, 438
opt-in email, 441-442
PostMasterDirect.com, 442
Talking Email, 439
Thunderbird, 439
Yahoo! Mail, 439
ZapZone Email, 439

embroidery. *See* needlecrafts

emergency services. *See also* CPR
911: National Emergency Number Association, 269
AfterDisaster, 269
American College of Emergency Physicians, 269
American Red Cross, 269
Computer Emergency Response Team, 269
FEMA: Federal Emergency Management Agency, 269
FireFighting.Com, 270
Lifesaving Resources, 270
Lifesaving Society (for Lifeguards), 270
Mountain Rescue Association, 270
Paramedic.com, 270
Rock-N-Rescue, 270

employment. *See* jobs/ employment

encyclopedias
Answers.com, 755
Britannica.com, 755
Encarta Online, 756
Encyclopedia Mythica, 609, 756
Encyclopedia of Religion and Society, 767
Encyclopedia Smithsonian, 756
Encyclopedia.com, 756
Grolier Encyclopedia, 756
infoplease.com, 756
Internet Encyclopedia of Philosophy, 767
Jewish Encyclopedia, 777

Judaism, 101, 777
Medline Plus, 756
Webopedia.com, 756
Wikipedia, 757
World Book Encyclopedia, 757

energy
Department of Energy, 896
Home Energy Saver, 275
MrSolar.com, 272
NEI: Nuclear Energy Institute, 276

engineering
eFunda, 529
Society of Women Engineers, 953

England. *See* United Kingdom

English (languages/linguistics)
African American Vernacular English, 500
American-British British-American Dictionary, The, 500
Australian Slang, 500
Collective Nouns, The, 500
Common Errors in English, 500
Grammar and Style Notes, 500
SlangSite, 500
WordNet, 500

entomology. *See* insects

environmental and global issues. *See also* adventure travel/eco-tourism; experiential/outdoor education; nature
Amazon Interactive, 477
American Farmland Trust, 19
BBC Nature Site, 611
Captain Planet, 478
conservation, 271-275, 425
CorpWatch.org, 2
Department of Energy, 896
Department of the Interior, 896
Eco-Kids, 480
Ecotourism Explorer, 877
Eddy the Eco-Dog, 480
Environmental Protection Agency, 897
EPA Global Warming for Kids, 480
Green Party USA, 708
Imagination Factory, 475
Junk Science, 475
Kids Planet, 482
KnowledgeHound, 16
Leave No Trace, 139
National Audobon Society, 104
National Fish & Wildlife Foundation, 314
National Geographic for Kids, 483
National Parks Conservation Society, 675
Natural Resources Defense Council, 612
NatureServe.org, 612
NHBS Environmental Bookstore, 115
Notebaert Nature Museum, 612
Ocean Alliance, The, 647
Ocean Channel, The, 647
Ocean Conservancy, The, 648
Ocean's Futures Society, 648
Oceana, 647
Planeta, 882
preservation, 275-276
RainforestWeb.org, 613
recycling, 276-277
SeaWeb, 648
Sierra Club, 613
Surfrider Foundation, 649
Technology Recycling, 476
United States Fish and Wildlife Service, 316
Wilderness Volunteers, 642
Woods Hole Oceanographic Institution, 649
WWF, 613

ethnic music
Afro-Caribbean Music, 591
Ari Davidow's Klezmer Shack, 591
Caribbean Music, 592
Charts All Over the World, 592
Dirty Linen, 592
Flemenco Guitar, The, 592
Folk Australia, 592
Irish and Celtic Music on the Internet, 592
JewishMusic.com, 592
KiwiFolk: Folk and Acoustic Music in New Zealand, 592
Latin Music Online, 580
Mbira, 592
Music in Scotland, 593
Norwegian Music Information Centre, 593
Peruvian Music, 593
Puro Mariachi, 593
Rhythm Fusion-Musical Instruments from Around the World, 600
Songs of Indonesia, 593
Temple Records, 593
Welcome to Bali & Beyond, 593
World Music Store, 593

etiquette
Emily Post Institute, 278
Etiquette Hell, 278
Golf Etiquette from the PGA, 278
Miss Manners, 278
Netiquette Home Page, 278
Original Tipping Page, 278

Europe
Aer Lingus, 22
Airhitch, 880
Backpack Europe on a Budget, 872
British Airways, 22
Drive Europe, 874
ESPN Soccer, 829
Europcar, 151
European and British Rail Passes, 886
European Visits, 881
Eurotrip.com, 881
Gateway to the European Union, 130
history, 384-385
Lufthansa, 22
Rick Steves' Europe Through the Back Door, 882
Turkish Airlines, 23
VBT, 94

European Union, government information/services, 360

exercise and fitness. *See also* diet and nutrition; health
24HourFitness, 279
Aerobics and Fitness Association, 279

A B C D E F G H I J K L M N O P Q R S T U V W X Y Z

American Council on Exercise, 279
American Heart Association: Exercise & Fitness, 279
Bally Total Fitness, 280
Calories Per Hour, 279
cross-country running, 280
Diet Detective, The, 280
Fitness Jumpsite, 280
Fitness Magazine, 281
Fitness Online, 281
Fitness Zone, 281
Fitness.com, 280
KidsHealth.org, 665
KidsHealth.org: For Teens, 662
martial arts, 525-528
Medline Plus Exercise & Fitness, 279
Melpomene, 281
Men's Fitness.com, 281, 544
Mirkin Report, 281
NetSweat, 281
Operation Fit Kids, 967
pilates, 282
President's Council on Physical Fitness and Exercise, 281
Prevention.com-Weight Loss and Fitness, 941-942
running, 729, 282-283
Shape Up America, 942
walking, 28, 284
weightlifting and bodybuilding, 281, 284-285
Why Exercise Is Cool, 280
yoga, 963-965

exotic pets
Bella Online: Exotic Pets Site, 681
Dr. Jungle's Animal World, 681
Exotic Pet Co, 681
Exotic Pet Vet, 681
S&S Exotic Animals, Inc., 681

experiential/outdoor education. *See also* environmental and global issues
ACCT: Association for Challenge Course Technology, 286
AEE: Association for Experiential Education, 286
AO: America Outdoors, 287
AORE: Association of Outdoor Recreation & Education, 287
CEO: Coalition for Education in the Outdoors, 287
EnviroEducation.com, 286
NAAEE: North America Association for Environmental Education, 287
NAI: National Association for Interpretation, 287
NRPA: National Parks and Recreation Association, 287
NYSOEA: New York State Outdoor Education Association, 288
Outdoor Ed, 286
outdoor education centers, 286-290
PPA: Professional Paddlesports Association, 288
ropes/challenge courses, 290-291
WEA: Wilderness Education Association, 288

extreme sports
Boardz, 291
EXPN Extreme Sports, 292
Extreme Sports Channel, 292
Extreme Sports Online, 292
hang gliding and paragliding, 293-294
Outside Online, 292
Parachute Industry Association, 292
PointXCamp, 292
Sandboard Magazine, 293
skateboarding, 294
skydiving, 294-295
snowboarding, 295-296

eye care
American Academy of Ophthalmology, 297
Eye Care America, 297
Eye Care Source, 297
Eye Injury First Aid, 297
Eyeglasses.com, 297
Financial Aid for Eye Care, 297
Finding an Eye Care Professional, 297
Macular Degeneration Foundation, 298
National Eye Institute, 298
Prevent Blindness America, 298

F

families. *See also* children; parenting; pregnancy and birth
AAMFT, 832
adoption, 10-12
American Association for Marriage and Family Therapy, 524
Center for Reproductive Law and Policy, 949
childcare, 162-163
divorce and custody, 235-236, 524
FamilyTravelForum, 877
gay/lesbian/bisexual/transgender issues, 347-348
genealogy, 351-352
Home & Family Network, 766
National Partnership for Women & Families (NPFW), 951
New York State Department of Family Assistance, 833
Smoke-Free Families, 7
Teenagers Today, 853
Work & Family Connections, 472
Work/Life Options Job-Sharing Guide, 472

fantasy sports
baseball, 83-84
ESPN.com Fantasy Sports, 299
Fantasy Sports Central, 299
Sandbox: Fantasy Sports, 299
SportsLine.com's Fantasy Page, 299

fantasy. *See* sci-fi & fantasy

farming
Agricultural Network Information Center (AgNIC), 18
Agriculture in the Classroom, 18
Agriculture Online, 18
AgWeb, 18
American Dairy Science Association (ADSA), 18

American Egg Board, 18
American Farm Bureau: Voice of Agriculture, 18
Ceres Online, 19
Economic Research Service (USDA), 19
Farm Safety 4 Just Kids, 19
FarmCredit, 19
Farmland Information Center, 19
Food and Agriculture Organization of the United Nations, 19
Gempler's, 19
GrainGenes, 19-20
John Deere-Agricultural Equipment, 20
Kansas City Board of Trade (Kansas City, Missouri), 20
National 4-H Council, 966
National Agricultural Library (NAL), 20
National Corn Growers Association (NCGA), 20
National Pork Producers Council, 20
Small Farm Today Magazine, 20
Sunkist, 20
Today's Market Prices, 21
USDA (United States Department of Agriculture), 21

Farsi (languages/linguistics)
Easy Persian, 501
Farsi Dictionary, 501
QuickFarsi.com's English-Farsi Translation Services, 501
Teachionary: Farsi Word Sets, 501

fashion/clothing
accessories, 461-463, 920
advice, 15
BabyStyle, 811
Birkenstock Express, 77
Bloomingdale's, 811
Coldwater Creek, 811
Cosmopolitan, 726
D&J Sports, 928
DELiAs.com, 811
Designer Outlet.com, 811
Dillard's, 812
Dior.com, 300
Donna Karan, 300
Eddie Bauer, 812
ELLE.com, 300
Fashionmall.com, 812
Fogdog Sports, 816
Givenchy, 300
Glamour, 727
Gothic Clothing and Jewelry, 816
GQ Magazine, 542
HerRoom.com, 812
Hint Fashion Magazine, 300
Issey Mayake, 300
jewelry, 461-463
L.L. Bean Welcome Page, 138
L.L. Bean, 812
Lands' End, 812
Lane Bryant, 812
Metropolis Magazine, 45
Nordstrom, 812
Polo.com, 301
QuiltWear.com, 735
RAMGraphics: Spiritwear, 158
RedTagDeals.com, 79
Row Works, 922
Soldier City, 902
SPORTS Authority, The, 816
STYLE.com, 301
SwimNews Online, 930
Team Cheer Online, 158
Tommy Hilfiger, 301
Vogue, 301, 731
watches, 463, 920
Yves Saint Laurent, 301
ZOOZOOM.com Magazine, 301

feminism. *See* women and women's issues

feng shui
American Feng Shui Institute, 302
Cyber Feng Shui Club, 302
Fast Feng Shui, 302
Feng Shui Times, 302

figure skating
Figure Skater's Website, 817
International Figure Skating Magazine (IFS), 817
SkateWeb, 817
Stars On Ice, 817
U.S. Figure Skating, 818
World Skating Museum, 818

Fiji Islands, 884

film. *See* movies/films

finance and investments. *See also* accounting
About Credit, 303
AgeNet, 797
banking, 304-305
bonds, 305
Campaign Finance Reform, 705
CreditReport.com, 303
debt management, 222-225
Department of the Treasury, 897
Dismal Scientist, 762
Emerging Markets, 633
Escape from Knab, 487
FarmCredit, 19
Forbes Online, 124, 726
Fortune.com, 124, 727
Friendly4Seniors Websites, 799
investments
10K Wizard, 306
American Association of Individual Investors, 306
Biospace, 306
Bivio, 306
Financial Engines, 306
Financial Times, 307
GreenMoneyJournal Online Guide, 307
Hoover's Online, 307
investment clubs, 306
Investopedia, 307
Investor's Business Daily, 307
Kiplinger, 307
Marketocracy, 307
Money Central, 307
Money Magazine, 308
Motley Fool's Guide to Investment Clubs, 306
Prophet.net, 308
Red Herring, 308
Reuters Investor, 308
RiskGrades, 308

Silicon Investor, 308
Stock Market Game, The, 308
StockTrack Portfolio Simulations, 309
TheStreet.com, 309
ValueEngine.com, 309
Yahoo! Finance, 309
Yodlee, 309
Young Investor.com, 309
IPOs (Initial Public Offerings), 310
iTools.com, 763
KnowledgeHound, 16
ManagingMyMoney.com, 303
Medicare.gov, 800
Microsoft Money Central's Planning Section, 303
Money Magazine's Money, 101 Tutorial, 303
mutual funds, 310-311
online trading, 311-313
Quicken.com, 304
retirement, 780-782
stocks, 313
Strategies for Financing Stay-at-Home Parenting, 671
Street Cents Online, 255
Student Loans and Education Financing, 258
Suze Orman, 559
Universal Currency Converter, 883
U.S. news & World Report, 626
World Bank Group, 132
Worth Online, 732
Young Investor, 245
financial aid and scholarships
Citibank StudentLoan.com, 180
College Is Possible, 180
eStudentLoan.com, 181
FAFSA (Free Application for Federal Student Aid), 181
fastWEB! (Financial Aid Search Through the Web), 181
FinAid!, 181
Financial Aid Resource Center, 181
Princeton Review, The, 181
Student Financial Assistance, 181
United Negro College Fund, 181
Welcome to the Harry Truman Scholarship Foundation, 182
Yahoo! Education: Financial Aid: College Aid Offices, 182
first-aid
1st Spot First Aid, 536
American College of Emergency Physicians, 536
Anaphylactic Treatment Guidelines, 537
HealthWorld First Aid, 537
Mayo Clinic's First-Aid Guide, 537
fish/aquariums
Albuquerque Aquarium, The, 968
American Zoo and Aquarium Association, 968
AquariumFish.net, 314
Aquatic Network, 647
Atlantic Salmon Federation, 271
Freshwater Aquariums, 314
Kids World 2000: Animals, Zoos and Aquariums, 969
National Fish & Wildlife Foundation, 314
Pittsburgh zoo and Aquarium, 971
Sea World, 37
Shedd Aquarium, 575
Stephen Birch Aquarium Museum, 649
U.S. Fish and Wildlife Service-National Wetlands Inventory, 275
fishing
Angling Report Newsletter, The, 724
eders.com, 315
Field & Stream Online, 315
Fishing.com, 315
FishingWorld.com, 315
Gulf Coast Angler's Association, 315
Nor'east Saltwater Online, 315
Rod and Gun, 14
Saltwater Sportsman, 316
Top Fishing Secrets, 316
United States Fish and Wildlife Service, 316
fitness. *See* exercise and fitness
flooring (home)
Armstrong Flooring, 405
Flooring America, 405
iFloor, 405
Pergo Laminate Flooring, 405
Woodfloors.org, 405
Florida
Florida Museum of Natural History, 572
Florida Weather Monitor, 932
TouristFlorida.com, 79
Universal Studios, 37
Walt Disney World, 38
flowers. *See* gardening; landscaping
folk music, 726
food and drink. *See also* cooking and recipes; diet and nutrition
advice, 15
alcohol, 318-319
Ale Street News, 89
All About Beer, 89
allergies, 25, 323-324
American Egg Board, 18
Baby Beechnut, 71
Badger Brewery, 89
Beamish & Crawford Brewery, 89
Beef Home Page, 19
beer, 89-91
BeerAdvocate.com, 89
BevNet, 317
candy, 148-149
Coca-Cola, 317
coffees and teas, 319-320
Coupon Pages, 79
Energise For Life Detox and Cleanse Guide, 29
FDA: Food and Drug Administration, 536
Gerber, 72
Global Gourmet, 317
gluten-free. ***See*** Celiac disease
Great Cookware, 317
groceries, 321-322
Harry and David Gourmet Food Gifts, 356, 816
HSP-Online.com, 29

Instawares: Restaurant Supply Superstore, 317
Iowa State University's Tasty Insect Recipes, 428
Junk Food Blog, 475
Maine Lobsters and New England Clambakes, 317
Millsbery.com, 488
Nabisco World, 483
Omaha Steaks, 317
organic foods, 322-323
Smucker's, 318
Snapple, 318
U-pons, 80
Wet Planet Beverages, 318
wines, 741, 943-947

football
American Football Coaches Association, 324
college, 325
Football Drills, 170
Football.com, 325
professional
Canadian Football League, 326
National Football League, 326
NFLPlayers.com, 327
Play Football: The Official NFL Site for Kids, 326
Pro Football Hall of Fame, 327

foreclosures
Foreclosure.com, 225
How to Avoid Foreclosure, 225
HUD (Housing and Urban Development), 225
National Consumer Law Center, 225

foreign languages
American Council on the Teaching of Foreign Languages, 247
Discovery Foreign Language Programs, 247
don Quijote, 247
Learn Spanish Online, 247
Lingolex, 247
Spanish Language Exercises, 247
World Language Resources, 247

foreign policy
Carnegie Council on Ethics and International Affairs, 328
Center for Security Policy, The, 328
CIA World Factbook, 353
CIA World Factbook: Mexico, 557
Council on Foreign Relations, 703
Department of State, 897
embassy.org, 328
Foreign Policy Association, 328
Foreign Policy in Focus, 328
Jane's Foreign Report, 633
National Security Archive, 388
NATO: The North Atlantic Treaty Organization, 329
U.S. Agency for International Development, 329
United Nations, The, 329

Formula One racing
Atlas F1, 56
Formula1.com, 56
ITV Formula, 1, 56
News on F1, 56
Shell and Ferrari Motorsports, 56

fractals, 532

France
Cannes Film Festival, 562
Corolle Dolls, 175
France Rulers, 718
FranceEscape, 881
government information/services, 360
history, 384
Le Louvre, 569

franchising (business)
American Association of Franchisees & Dealers, 126
Be the Boss, 126
BizBuySell, 126
Canadian Business Franchise Magazine, 127
Centercourt USA, 127
Federal Trade Commission: Franchises and Business Opportunities, 127
Franchise Handbook On-Line, The, 127
Franchise Registry, The, 127
Franchise Solutions, 127
Franchise Update, 127
Franchise Zone by Entrepreneur.com, 127-128
Franchise.com, 127
Franchising.com, 128
FRANInfo, 128
International Franchise Association, 128
USA Today Franchise Solutions, 128

fraud
Internet ScamBusters, 201
National Fraud Information Center, The, 202

free speech
Center for Democracy and Technology, 157
Electronic Frontier Foundation, 157
Freedom of Expession Links, 157
Index on Censorship, 157
National Coalition Against Censorship, 157
Project Censored, 157

freebies
#1 Free Stuff, 80
100 Hot Free Stuff, 80
Ben's Bargains, 77
Freaky Freddies Free Funhouse, 80
Free Site X, 80
Free Site, The, 80
FreeShop.com, 80
Refundsweepers.com, 80
seasonal and holiday freebies, 80

French (languages/linguistics)
Basic French Word List, 501
French Language Course, 501, 504
Online French Dictionary, 501
Why Study French, 501

frugal spending. *See also* debt management
About Frugality, 330
BetterBudgeting.com, 330
Cheapskate Monthly, 330
Dollar Stretcher, 330

Frugal Shopper, The, 330
Frugal Village, 330

fun sites
Al Lowe's Humor Site, 331
Burning Man, 331
Caricature Zone, 331
Comedy Central, 331
Dane Cook, 331
Extreme Funny Humor, 331
Fortean Times, 332
Marshall Brain's How Stuff Works, 332
SlashNOT, 332
Stupid.com, 332
Uncle Roy All Around You, 332
Worth1000.com, 332

fundraising
Fund$Raiser Cyberzine, 639
Fund-Raising.Com, 639
Grassroots Fundraising Journal, 639
Schoolpop, 639

G

Gaelic (languages/lingustics), 504

gambling. *See also* games and puzzles
addiction/recovery, 6, 333
casinos, 152-153
Gambling Online Magazine, 333
Mah Jongg, 340-341
online, 152, 333
poker, 701-702
tips/strategies, 333

games and puzzles. *See also* gambling
AreYouGame.com, 864
billiards, 97-98
bingo, 99-100
board games, 338-339, 864
Bonus.com, 487
Caissa's Web Home Page, 159
Candystand, 487
card games, 338-339, 701-702
CBC.CA/Kids/Games, 487
Centipede, 487
cheat codes, 336, 339-340
ChessKids, 478
Codebook, The, 487
DreamWorks Kids, 487
edbydesign.com, 480
Escape from Knab, 487
eToys, 663
FamilyFun.com, 487
Funbrain.com, 487
Funschool, 488
Games Kids Play, 481
Golden Tee, 358
Hasbro World, 866
Internet Chess Club, 159
Internet games, 159, 334-339
Junior Achievement TITAN, 488
JuniorNet, 490
Kaboose Games, 488
Kakuro, 340
KidsCom Games, 488
Mah Jongg, 340-341
Millsberry.com, 488
multi-user games, 337, 341
Nabisco Kids, 483
PBS Kids Games, 488
playkidsgames.com, 488
Pojo.com, 484
poker, 701-702
Shockwave Games, 488
Squigly's Playhouse, 485
StreetPlay.com, 485
Sudoku, 341
Thinks.com, 340
This Week in Chess, 159
triva games, 342
Uncle Roy All Around You, 332
United States Chess Federation (USCF), 159
video games, 188, 191, 336-341, 487, 867
Warner Brothers Games Gallery, 488
WebChess, 488
Zeeks.com, 489

gardening and landscaping
American Horticultural Society, 343
Better Homes and Gardens Online Garden Page, 343
botanical gardens, 968
Botany.com, 343
Burpee Seeds Home Page, 343
Butterfly Website, The, 427
Cortesia Sanctuary and Center, 343
Cultural Landscape Foundation, 495
Earthly Goods Online, 343
EPA Green Landscaping with Native Plants, 495
flowers, 345
Garden Humor, 344
Gardener's Supply Company, 344
GardenGuides, 344
GardenNet, 344
Gardenscape, 344
GardenWeb, 344
Gemplers.com, 19
Home and Garden Television (HGTV), 403
Kidsgardening.com, 344
Landscape Architecture Guide, 495
Landscaping for Energy Efficiency, 495
Landscaping to Attract Birds, 495
lawn care, 495-496
Missouri Botanical Gardens, 344
National Gardening Association, 344
New Jersey Weed Gallery, 345
Old Farmer's Almanac, 763
planning, 496
Secret Garden, 345
shrubs, 496-497
Smith & Hawken, 345
trees, 497
vegetables, 343

gay/lesbian/bisexual/transgender issues
AIDS Memorial Quilt, The, 733
colleges and universities, 347
crisis intervention and counseling, 347
Gay and Lesbian Review, The, 724
Gay Men's Health Crisis, 346

Gay.com, 346
GayScape, 346
home and family, 347-348
magazines, 349-350
media and culture, 348
PlanetOut, 346
political and legal issues, 349
PrideLinks.com, 346
Queer Resources Directory (QRD), 346
religion, 350
Shescape Online, 952
tolerance.org, 3
travel, 350

genealogy. *See also* history
Ancestry.com, 351
Beginner's Guide to Family Research, 351
Cyndi's List of Genealogy Sites on the Web, 351
Ellis Island, 351
Everton's Genealogical Helper, 351
Eyes of Glory, 388
Family Search, 351
FamilyTreeMaker.com, 351
Genealogy Home Page, The, 352
German Genealogy Resources, 352
JewishGen: The Home of Jewish Genealogy, 352
National Archives and Records Administration: Genealogy Page, 352
Origins.net, 352
Vital Records Information: United States, 352

Geography. *See also* maps
CIA World Factbook, 353
FirstGov for Kids: Geography, 353
GeoCommunity, 353
Geography at the University of Buffalo, 353
Geography World, 353
GPS Primer, 353
National Geographic, 353
Test Your Geography Knowledge, 354
USGS Learning Web, 354
WorldAtlas.com, 354

geometry, 532

Georgia
Atlanta Travel Guide, 888
Lookout Mountain Hang Gliding, 293

German (languages/lingustics)
German for Travelers, 502
German News and Newspapers, 502
German Studies Web, 502
New English-German Dictionary, 502

Germany
German Genealogy Resources, 352
Germany: Chancellors, 718
government information/services, 360
history, 385
Lufthansa, 22

ghosts
Halloween Ghost Stories, 413
Moonlit Road, The, 413
Obiwan's UFO-Free Paranormal Page, 413
Shadowlands: Ghosts & Hauntings, The, 413

gifts
ArtisanGifts.com, 355
Ashford.com, 355
Baby Shower Gifts, 355
Bath and Body Works, 355
Blue Mountain Cards, 355
Brookstone, 355
Computer Gear, 355
FragranceNet.com, 355
Gift Collector, 356
GiftCertificates.com, 356
Gifts.com, 356
Gump's, 356
Hammacher Schlemmer, 356
Harry and David Gourmet Food Gifts, 356
MarthaStewart.com, 356
Perfect Present Picker, 356
Perfumania.com, 356
RedEnvelope Gifts: The Right Gift, Right Away, 357
SeniorStore.com, 357
Sharper Image, 357Spencer Gifts, 357
Surprise.com, 357
Target.com, 357

girls. *See* children

global politics
Amnesty International USA Women's Human Rights, 948
AntiWar.com, 913
Carnegie Council on Ethics and International Affairs, 328
Center for Defense Information, 895
Center for Reproductive Law and Policy, 949
Center for Security Policy, The, 328
CIA World Factbook, 762
CIA World Factbook: Mexico, 557
Cold War, 915-916
Council on Foreign Relations, 703
DEBKAfile, 913
Department of State (U.S.), 897
eHistory: Middle East, 386
embassy.org, 328
Food and Agriculture Organization of the United Nations, 19
Foreign Policy Association, 328
Foreign Policy in Focus, 328
Global Fund for Women, 950
GlobalSecurity.org, 913
History in the News: The Middle East, 387
Human Rights Watch, 950
Jane's Foreign Report, 633
Korean War, 916
League of Nations Statistical and Disarmament Documents, 383
Middle East History & Resources, 387
Middle East: A Century of Conflict, The, 387
National Security Archive, 388
NATO: The North Atlantic Treaty Organization, 329
Newsweek, 625
Office of International Women's Issues, 952

Politics and Current Affairs Forum, 382
Stratfor Security Consulting Intelligence Agency, 914
terrorism, 917-918
TIME, 626
U.S. Agency for International Development, 329
U.S. News & World Report, 626
UNAIDS, 366
United Nations and the Status of Women, The, 953
United Nations Cyberschool Bus, 263
United Nations, The, 329
Utne Reader, The, 626
Vietnam War, 916-917
Women and Politics Institute, The, 954
Women's Human Rights Net, 954
Women's Human Rights Resources, 954
WomenWatch, 954
World Connected, A, 3
World Population, 764
World War I, 918-919
World War II, 919

gluten-free food and drink. *See* Celiac disease

golf
BadGolfMonthly.com, 358
Ben Hogan Golf Products, 358
FootJoy, 358
Golden Tee, 358
Golf Etiquette from the PGA, 278
Golf Tips Magazine, 359
Golf.com, 358
Golfcourse.com, 358
GolfGuideWeb.com, 358
Golfsmith, 359
GolfWeb, 359
LPGA.com, 359
Masters, The, 359
Open Championship, The, 359
PGA.com, 359
Premier Golf Classics Destinations, 878
USGA.org, 359

government (U.S.)
American Presidents: Life Portraits, 718
POTUS: Presidents of the United States, 718
Presidents of the United States, The, 719

government agencies (U.S.)
Administration on Aging (AOA), 797
BISNIS, 130
CDC's Tobacco Info-Quit Site, 7
Center for Defense Information, 895
Centers for Disease Control and Prevention: HIV, 366
Centers for Disease Control: Travel Health, 374
Centers for Medicare and Medicaid Services, 798
Central Intelligence Agency, 895
Child Welfare Information Gateway, 11
CIA History for Kids, 388
Citizenship and Immigration Services, 895
Civil Rights Division (of the Department of Justice), 167
Congressional Budget Office, 895
Congressional Quarterly, 624
Contacting the Congress, 703
Defense Almanac, 762
Department of Commerce, 896
Department of Defense, 895
Department of Education, 896
Department of Energy, 896
Department of Health and Human Services, 896
Department of Homeland Security, 896
Department of Justice, 896
Department of Labor, 896
Department of State, 897
Department of the Interior, 896
Department of the Treasury, 897
Department of Transportation, 897
Department of Veterans Affairs, 897
Disability.gov, 369
Environmental Protection Agency's Office of Water, 276
Environmental Protection Agency, 897
Export-Import Bank of the United States, 130
FAA, 69
FDA: Food and Drug Administration, 536
Federal Bureau of Investigation, 507, 897
Federal Bureau of Prisons, 456
Federal Communications Commission, 629
Federal Election Commission (FEC), 706
Federal Railroad Administration, 740
Federal Trade Commission's E-Commerce Publications, 242
Federal Trade Commission, 897
Federal Trade Commission: Franchises and Business Opportunities, 127
FedStats, 898
FedWorld Information Network, 898
FedWorld.gov, 762
FEMA: Federal Emergency Management Agency, 269
FirstGov for Consumers, 201
FirstGov for Seniors, 799
FirstGov, 898
FREE: Federal Resources for Education Excellence, 261
House Committee on Agriculture, 20
HUD for Senior Citizens, 799
HUD Housing FHA Home Page, 747
HUD: U.S. Department of Housing and Urban Development, 743
IRS, 843
IRS: Charities, 636
IRS: Political and Lobbying Activity, 706
Law Research: The United States Department of Justice, 168

Library of Congress, The, 758
MarineLINK, 898
Medicare.gov, 800
NASA Home Page, 70
NASA Television, 70
National Archives and Records Administration, 759
National Institutes of Health, 364
National Oceanic and Atmospheric Administration, 272, 647
Office of Civil Rights: U.S. Department of Education, 168
Office of Personnel Development, 467
Office of the Clerk On-Line Information Center, 704
OSHA (Occupational Safety and Health Administration), 373
Peace Corps, 898
President's Council on Physical Fitness and Exercise, 281
Railroad Retirement Board, 781
Recreation.gov, 14
Small Business Administration, 135
Social Security Administration: Disability Benefits, 369
Social Security Online, 801
Social Security Retirement Planner, 782
U.S. Army, 898
U.S. Census Bureau, 764
U.S. Consumer Product Safety Commission, 202
U.S. Department of Education, 244, 760
U.S. Department of Education-Funding Opportunities, 849
U.S. Department of Health and Human Services, 539, 834
U.S. Department of Labor: job sharing resources, 471
U.S. Department of Labor: Social Workers, 834
U.S. Department of State: Russian History, 388
U.S. Department of Treasury Auctions, 54
U.S. Fish and Wildlife Service, 425
U.S. Fish and Wildlife Service—National Wetlands Inventory, 275
U.S. International Trade Commission, 132
U.S. Navy, 898
U.S. Patent and Trademark Office, 454
USGS Learning Web, 354
United States Environmental Protection Agency, 276
United States Fish and Wildlife Service, 316
United States House of Representatives, 898
United States Postal Service ZIP Code—Look-Up, 654
United States Postal Service, 135
United States Senate, 899
United States State Department Travel Warnings and Consular Info Sheets, 883
United States Trade Representative, 132
USDA (United States Department of Agriculture), 21
USPS Shipping Supplies Online, 652
Welcome to the White House, 705, 899

government information/services
Afghanistan, 360
Australia, 360
Belgium, 360
Brazil, 360
Canada, 360
Chile, 360
China, 360
Costa Rica, 360
Ecuador, 360
Egypt, 360
European Union, 360
France, 360
Germany, 360
Greece, 360
Iceland, 360
India, 360
Indonesia, 360
Iran, 360
Iraq, 360
Israel, 360
Italy, 360
Japan, 360
Kenya, 360
Kuwait, 360
Lithuania, 360
Mexico, 360
Netherlands, 360
New Zealand, 360
Nigeria, 360
Pakistan, 361
Peru, 361
Russia, 361
Saudi Arabia, 361
South Africa, 361
South Korea, 361
Spain, 361
Thailand, 361
Turkey, 361
United Kingdon, 361

graduate schools
Accepted.com, 182
Advice for Undergraduates Considering Graduate School, 182
All About Grad School, 182
ETS Net, 182
Gradschools.com, 182
GradView, 182
GRE Online, 183
Kaplan Online, 183
Lawschool.com, 183

graphic design
American Institute of Graphic Arts (AIGA), 47
Freelance Designers Directory, 47
Graphic Artists Guild, 47
How Magazine's HowDesign.com, 47

graphic novels
Graphic Novel Review, 362
Manga Graphic novels, 362
NBM Publishing, 362
No Flying, No Tights, 362
Zanadu Comics, 116

Great Britain. *See* United Kingdom

Greece
- Ancient Greece at the World History Compass, 377
- Dictionary of Greek and Roman Myths, 609
- government information/services, 360
- THEOI Project, 610

Greek (languages/lingustics)
- English-Greek Dictionary, 502
- Greek Alphabet, 503
- Greek and Latin Language Resources, 503
- Greek Language Courses in Greece, 503

greeting cards, 355

groceries
- Albertsons.com, 321
- EthnicGrocer.com, 321
- Groceries-Express.com, 321
- NetGrocer, 321
- Peapod, 321
- Price Chopper Supermarkets, 321
- Ralph's: First in Southern California, 322
- Safeway, 322
- ThaiGrocer, 322
- Trader Joe's, 322
- Wild Oats, 322

Gulf War, 901

H

hang gliding and paragliding
- A-Z of Paragliding, 293
- Adventure Productions, 293
- All About Hang Gliding, 293
- BHPA, 293
- How Hang Gliding Works, 293
- Lookout Mountain Hang Gliding, 293
- Sydney Hang Gliding Centre, 293
- United States Hang Gliding Association, 294

hardware/software companies
- AMD, 189
- Apache Digital Corporation, 189
- Apple Computer Home Page, 189
- Dell.com, 189
- Gateway, 189
- Hewlett-Packard, 190
- IBM Corporation, 190
- Intel, 190
- MPC, 190
- Sony Style, 190
- Sun, 190
- Toshiba, 190

Hawaii
- Aloha Airlines, 22
- Big Island Mountain Biking Trail Guide, 95
- Hawaiian Airlines, 22
- Kailua Candy Company, 149
- Kona Coffee Times, 319
- Maui Travel & Tourism, 884

health
- Aetna InteliHealth, 363
- Air Travel Health Tips, 871
- allergies
  - *Allegra: Allergy Answer Site, 24*
  - *Allergy Info, 24*
  - *Allergy Store, The, 24*
  - *Allergy, Asthma, and Allerpet, 24*
  - *American Academy of Allergy, Asthma, & Immunology Online, 24*
  - *DustFree.com, 24*
  - *Food Allergy & Anaphylaxis Network, 25*
  - *Food Allergy Initiative, 25*
  - *HealingWell's Allergy Resource Center, 25*
  - *HowStuffWorks.com: Allergies, 25*
  - *Pollen, 25*
  - *Priorities, 25*
- alternative medicine
  - *acupuncture, 27-28*
  - *Alternative Health News, 26*
  - *Alternative Medicine Magazine Online, 26*
  - *AlternativeDr.com, 26*
  - *American Holistic Health Association, 26*
  - *aromatherapy, 28-29*
  - *Ayurveda Yoga Ultra-Nutrition, 26*
  - *Chi-Lel Qigong, 26*
  - *cleansing/detoxification, 29*
  - *HealthWorld Online, 26*
  - *herbalism, 30-31*
  - *homeopathy, 31-32*
  - *Life Matters, 27*
  - *magnet therapy, 32*
  - *massage, 32-33*
  - *May Clinic: Complementary and Alternative Medicine, 27*
  - *National Center for Complementary and Alternative Medicine, 27*
  - *Natural Health and Longevity Resource Center, 27*
  - *Qi: The Journal of Traditional Eastern Health & Fitness, 27*
  - *WholeHealthMD.com, 27*
- animals. *See* veterinary medicine
- BAM! (Body and Mind), 478
- cancer
  - *ACOR.org, 145*
  - *American Cancer Society, 145*
  - *Avon: The Crusade, 145*
  - *Cancer Detection and Prevention, 145*
  - *Cancer Directory, 145*
  - *Cancer Facts, 145*
  - *Cancer Group Institute, 145*
  - *Cancer411.com, 146*
  - *Cancerbackup, 146*
  - *CancerCare.org, 146*
  - *CancerKids, 146*
  - *CancerNews on the Net, 146*
  - *CancerTeen, 146*
  - *Community Breast Health Project, 146*
  - *Faces of Hope, 146*
  - *National Cancer Institute, 147*

OncoLink: University of Pennsylvania Cancer Center Resources, 147
Prostate.com, 147
Steve Dunn's Cancer Guide, 147
Susan G. Komen Breast Cancer Foundation, 147
Testicular Cancer Resource Center, 147
Caring for Kids, 659
CDC: Health Swimming, 928
children
American Academy of Pediatrics, 367
Arkansas Children's Hospital, 373
Child and Adolescent Health and Development, 367
Child Health Research Project, 367
Children with AIDS Project, 366
Children's Hospital and Regional Medical Center, Seatlle, 368
Children's Hospital Boston, 367-368
Children's Hospital of Philadelphia, The, 368
drSpock.com, 368
KidsHealth, 368
National Institute of Child Health and Human Development, 368
Riley Hospital for Children, 368
St. Jude Children's Research Hospital, 368
Sudden Infant Death Syndrome (SIDS) Information Home Page, 371
Climber's First Aid, 783
Colgate Kid's World, 479
CouponSurfer, 79
CPR, 367
Department of Health and Human Services, 896
diabetes
ADA Recipe of the Day, 228
ADA: American Diabetes Association, 228
Central for Disease Control Diabetes FAQ, 228
Children with Diabetes Online Community, 228
Children with Diabetes Recipes, 228
Diabetes Health Magazine, 228
Diabetes Insight, 229
Diabetes Mall, 229
Diabetic Gourmet Magazine, 229
Gourmet Connection Network, 229
Joslin Diabetes Center, 229
Kids Learn About Diabetes, 229
Medical Alert Charms for Children, 229
National Diabetes Education Program, 229
National Institute of Diabetes & Digestive & Kidney Disorders, 229
diet and nutrition
American Heart Association, 230
Ask the Dietitian, 230
Blonz Guide to Nutrition, Food, and Health Resources, 230
Center for Science in the Public Interest, 230
Consumer Information Center: Food, 230
DietSite.com, 230
Dole 5 a Day, 230
eDiets, 231
Feingold Association of the United States, 231
Food and Nutrition Information Center, 231
Food and Pyramid, 231
Healthfinder, 231
LifeClinic, 231
Mayo Clinic Food & Nutrition Center, 231
Meals for You, 232
Nuitrition.gov, 232
Nutrition Cafe, 232
Nutrition Explorations, 232
Prevention's Healthy Ideas, 232
Self Magazine, 232
Diet Detective, The, 280
disabilities
Disability.gov, 369
Down Syndrome WWW Pages, 370
Gimponthego.com, 374
LD Online, 369
Muscular Dystrophy Association, 371
National Association for Visually Handicapped, 369
Paralyzed Veterans of America, 369
Social Security Administration: Disability Benefits, 369
UCPnet, 369
World Association of Persons with Disabilities, 369
youreable.com, 369
diseases and conditions
American Cancer Society, 370
American College of Gastronenterology, 370
Arthritis Resource Center, 370
Association of Cancer Online Resources, 370
Down Syndrome WWW Pages, 370
Endometriosis, 370
Introduction to Skin Cancer, 370
MedicineNet.com, 370
Muscular Dystrophy Association, 371
National Organization for Rare Diseases, 371
National Osteoporosis Foundation, 371
National Prostate Cancer Coalition, 371
NewsRx, 371
StopPain.org, 371, 540
Sudden Infant Death Syndrome (SIDS) Information Home Page, 371
drkoop.com, 538
Drug Testing, 662

eCureMe Self Diagnosis, 363
eldercare
AARP, 797
AgeNet, 797
Aging in the Know, 797
Alzheimer's Association, 798
American Geriatrics Society, 798
Centers for Medicare and Medicaid Services, 798
ElderNet, 780
ElderWeb, 799
Friendly4Seniors Websites, 799
Healthy Aging, Geriatrics, and Elderly Care, 35
Lifesphere, 800
Medicare.gov, 800
National Institute on Aging, 800
osteoporosis, 655-656
Retirement with a Purpose, 781
SeniorJournal.com, 801
Third Age, 801
Estronaut: Forum for Women's Health, 956
eye care
American Academy of Ophthalmology, 297
Eye Care America, 297
Eye Care Source, 297
Eye Injury First Aid, 297
Eyeglasses.com, 297
Financial Aid for Eye Care, 297
Finding an Eye Care Professional, 297
Macular Degeneration Foundation, 298
National Eye Institute, 298
Prevent Blindness America, 298
Family Education Network: A Parenting and Education Resource, 659
FamilyDoctor.org, 363
Feminist Women's Health Center, 956
Go Ask Alice!, 16
Guide to Retirement Living, 781
healthcare administration and management
ACHE: American College of Healthcare Executives, 371
Agency for Health Care Administration, 371
American Association of Healthcare Administration Management, 372
Americfan Physical Therapy Association, 372
Health Economics, 372
Institute for Healthcare Improvement, 372
modernhealthcare.com, 372
HealthCentral, 942
HealthWeb, 363
HealthWorld Online, 538
Healthy Ontario, 363
HisandHerhealth.com, 808
HIV/AIDS treatment and prevention
AEGiS, 365
AIDS Education and Research Trust, 365
AIDS Outreach Center, 365
AIDS.ORG, 365
AIDSinfo, 365
Body: A Multimedia AIDS and HIV Information Resource, The, 365-366
Centers for Disease Control and Prevention: HIV, 366
Children with AIDS Project, 366
CPR for AIDS Patients, 367
HIV InSite: Gateway to AIDS Knowledge, 366
Magic Johnson Foundation, Inc., 366
Project Inform, 366
Stop AIDS Project, 366
UNAIDS, 366
institutes
Arkansas Children's Hospital, 373
Catholic Health Association, 373
OSHA (Occupational Safety and Health Administration) Web site, 373
Public Health Institute, 373-374
insurance
AFLAC, 372
America's Health Insurance Plans, 372
eHealthInsurance, 372
HealthInsuranceFinders.com, 373
HealthInsuranceInfo.net, 373
Insurance Fraud, 373
International Medical Group, 373
PacifiCare, 373
Interfaith Health Program, 644
International Travel and Health, 881
iParenting.com, 660
KidsHealth.org, 482, 665
KidsHealth.org: For Teens, 662
Kotex.com, 662
MayoClinic.com, 363
medical history
Center for Disease Control: Travel Health, 374
Gimponthego.com, 374
History of Medicine, 374
History of the Health Sciences Worldwide Links, 374
MDTravelHealth, 374
Travel Health Online, 374
Medical/Health Sciences Libraries on the Web, 759
MedLine Plus, 364, 538
Medscape, 364
Melpomene, 281
men
CDC: Men's Health, 544
Men's Fitness, 544
Men's Health Network, 544
Men's Health Week, 544
Viagra, 544
mental
ADD/ADHD (Attention Deficit Disorder/Attention Deficit Hyperactivity Disorder), 547

agoraphobia, 546
anorexia nervosa. ***See*** *health, mental, eating disorders*
anxiety and panic disorders, 546-547
AtHealth.com, 545
autism and Asperger's syndrome, 548
bipolar disorder, 548-551. ***See also*** *health, mental, depression*
Center for Mental Health Services, The, 545
conduct disorder, 549-550
delirium, 550
dementia, 550
depression, 549-551, 555
eating disorders, 551-553
Internet Mental Health, 545
memory, 541
Mental Health InfoSource, 545
Mental Health Matters, 545
Mental Health Net, 545
National Alliance for the Mentally Ill (NAMI) Home Page, 546
National Institute of Mental Health, 546
National Mental Health Association, 546
OCD (Obesessive-Compulsive Disorder), 553
paranoia, 553
personality disorders, 553-554
post traumatic stress disorder, 554-555
Psych Central, 546
psychiatry, 720-721
psychology, 722-723
psychosis, 555
schizophrenia, 555-556
Substance Abuse & Mental Health Services Administration, 9
suicide prevention, 837-838
Tourette's syndrome, 556
Mirkin Report, 281
MSN Health, 364
National Center for Complementary and Alternative Medicine (NCCAM), 538
National Healthy Mothers, Healthy Babies Coalition, 72-73
National Institutes of Health, 364
National Safety Council, 364
National Women's Health Resource Center, 956
NBCC-National Breast Cancer Coalition, 956
NOAH: New York Online Access to Health, 364
Operation Fit Kids, 967
Parenthood.com, 660
pregnancy and birth
About.com-Pregnancy/Birth, 710
American Pregnancy Association, 710
Ask Noah About: Pregnancy, Fertility, Infertility, Contraception, 710
BabyZone, 712
Birth Psychology, 712
Breastfeeding.com, 712
Childbirth.or, 712
Fit Pregnancy, 710
Healthy Pregnancy, 710
Medline Plus: Pregnancy, 711
OBGYN.net, 711
Pregnancy Daily, 711
Pregnancy Today, 711
Pregnancy-info.net, 711
Pregnancy.org, 711
StorkNet, 711
SureBaby.com, 712
Weight Gain Estimator, 712
West Side Pregnancy Resource Center, 712
Prevention Magazine, 364
Quackwatch, 364
Runners World, 729
Sexual Health infoCenter, 809
SexualHealth.com, 809
Third Age, 782
Travel Medicine, 879
U.S. Department of Health and Human Services, 539
U.S. National Library of Medicine, 760
vitamins and supplements
eNutrition.com, 909
Medline Plus, 909
MotherNature.com, 909
Nature Made, 909
Pharmaton, 909
Puritan's Pride, 909
vitacost.com, 910
VitaminShoppe.com, 910
WebMD, 365, 539
weight loss
American Dietetic Association, 940
Ask Dr. Weil, 940
Best of Weight Loss, 940
CyberDiet, 940
Diet Channel, The, 940
Doctor's Guide to Obesity, 940
eDiets.com, 941
Fast Food Facts, 941
Jenny Craig, 941
L A Weight Loss Centers, 941
Natural Nutrition, 941
Nutrisystem, 941
Prevention.com-Weight Loss and Fitness, 941-942
Shape Up America, 942
Weight Watchers, 942
Women'sHealth, 956
World Health Network, 365
Yahoo! News, 627
yoga
A2ZYoga, 963
ABC to Yoga, 963
Body Trends, 963
Kundalini Support Center, 963
Sahaja Yoga Meditation, 963
Santosha.com, 963
Siddha Yoga Meditation, 964
Sivananda Yoga "Om" Page, 964

Step-by-Step Yoga Postures, 964

World of Yoga, A, 964

Yoga Alliance, 964

Yoga Directory, The, 965

Yoga Journal, 965

Yoga Site, 965

Yoga Synergy, 965

Yoga.com, 964

Yogabasics.com, 964

heating and air conditioning (home)

AC Doctor, 406

American Society of Heating, Refrigerating, and Air-Conditioning Engineers, Inc., 406

Bryant Heating and Cooling Systems, 406

Carrier, 406

Lennox, 406

Trane, 406

herbalism

American Botanical Council, 30

Digestive System, 30

Henriette's Herbal Home Page, 30

Herb Research Foundation: Herbs and Herbal Medicine for Health, 30

Herb.org, 30

Herbal Encyclopedia, 30

Herbs First, 30

Medline Plus on Herbal Medicines, 30

National Center for Complementary and Alternative Medicine, 31

PlanetHerbs, 31

Rocky Mountain Herbal Institute, 31

Whole Herb Company, The, 31

hiking. *See also* backpacking; mountain biking

America's Roof, 139

American Hiking Society, 139

American Long Distance Hiking Association-West, 139

American Volkssports Association, 140

Appalachian National Scenic Trail, 140

Barefoot Hikers, 140

GORP-Great Outdoor Recreation Pages, 140

Great Outdoor Emporium Mall, 140

LightBackpacker.com, 140

Newfoundland Backcountry, 140

Superior Hiking Trail Association, 140

Trailplace, 141

Trails.com, 141

Washington Trails Association, 141

Yosemite Trails Pack Station, 141

Hinduism

Bhagvat Gita, 774

Hindu Kids, 774

Hindu Resources Online, 774

Hindu Universe: Hindu Resource Center, 774

Hinduism Online, 774

Hinduism Today, 775

iskon.com, 775

Understanding Hinduism, 775

history. *See also* antiques; genealogy

Africa, 376

America's Wars, 913

American Civil War, 914-915

American Experience, The, 452

American Variety Stage, 860

American Women's History, 948

Americas

Ancestors in the Americas, 377

Cultures & History of the Americas, 377

Hispanic History in the Americas, 377

History of the Americas, 377

Jaguar: Icon of Power Through Mayan History, 378

ancient

Ancient Greece at the World History Compass, 377

Ancient Mexico, 385

Ancient Worlds, 377

BBC: Inside Ancient History, 378

Egyptian Mathematics, 529

Jaguar: Icon of Power Through Mayan History, 378

arctic and antarctica, 378

Art History Resources on the Web, 46

Asia

AsianInfo.org, 378

East & Southeast Asia: An Annotated Directory, 379

East Asian History, 379

History of China, 379

Indian History, 379

Japanese History, 379

Korean History Project, 379

Most Comprehensive Reference on the Political History of Pakistan,The, 380

TravelChinaGuide: History, 380

Australia and Oceania, 380

baseball

Baseball Almanac, 81

Baseball Archive, 81

Baseball Think Factory, 81

Baseball-Reference, 81

National Baseball Hall of Fame, 84

Negro Baseball League, 82

Best of History Sites, 375

Biography, 101

Canada, 381

Cold War, 915-916

Computer History Museum, 188

Conversations with History, 375

Current Affairs, 382

David Rumsey Historical Map Collection, 519

dinosaurs

BBC Walking with Dinosaurs, 233

Dinosaur National Monument, 233

Dinosaurs: Facts and Fiction, 233
Discovering Dinosaurs, 233
Discovery Channel: When Dinosaurs Roamed America, 233
Extinctions.com, 233
Field Museum of Natural History, 233
Smithsonian NMNH Dinosaur Home Page, 234
Diotima: Women and Gender in the Ancient World, 949
documents and landmarks
American Memory, 382
Chronology of U.S. Historical Documents, A, 382
England Landmarks and Historical Sites, 382
Frank Lloyd Wright Home and Studio, 382
George Washington's Mount Vernon, 382
Guggenheim Museum, 382
History Ford Estate: Fair Lane, 383
Landmarks for Schools, 383
League of Nations Statistical and Disarmament Documents, 383
Moscow Landmarks, 383
Mount Rushmore, 383
National Civil Rights Museum, 383
National Parks and Monuments, 383
Our Documents, 383
Statue of Liberty-Ellis Island Foundation, 384
Susan B. Anthony House Museum and National Landmark, 384
Edison National Historic Site, 452
Ellis Island, 351
Encyclopedia Smithsonian, 756
Engines of Our Ingenuity, 452
English Actors at the Turn of the Century, 861
Europe, 384-385
Exemplaria, 724
EyeWitness to History, 375
France, 384
Franklin Institute, 452
George Eastman House: Timeline of Photography, 692
George Washington's Mount Vernon Estate, 888
Germany, 385
Grolier's Online: The American Presidency, 255
Historical Website, The, 740
History Channel, 375
History House, 375
History Matters, 375
History of Country Music, 591
History of Hanukkah, 397
History of Photography, 692
History On-Line, 376
History Place, 376
Imperial War Museum, 913
Indian Motorcycles, 561
Iran, 386
Irish History on the Web, 376
Italy, 385
Korean War, 916
Lemelson Center, 453
mathematics, 532
medical
Center for Disease Control: Travel Health, 374
Gimponthego.com, 374
History of Medicine, 374
History of the Health Sciences Worldwide Links, 374
MDTravelHealth, 374
Travel Health Online, 374
Mexico
Ancient Mexico, 385
History Channel: The History of Mexico, 385
History, Myths, Arts, and Traditions of Mexico, 386
Mexexperience, 386
Museum of the History of Mexico, 386
U.S. Mexican War, 386
Middle East
eHistory: Middle East, 386
History in the News: The Middle East, 387
History of Iran, 386
History of Israel and Palestine in Map Form, 387
Middle East History & Resources, 387
Middle East: A Century of Confilct, The, 387
Mountain Bike Hall of Fame, 95
museums
American Museum of Natural History, 572
Berkeley Art Museum/Pacific Film Archive, 573
California Museum of Photography, 573
Carnegie Museum of Natural History, The, 572
Cleveland Museum of Natural History, The, 572
Field Museum, The, 572
Florida Museum of Natural History, 572
George Eastman House: International Museum of Photography and Film, 573
International Center of Photography, 573
Morikami Museum of Japanese Gardens, 571
Museum of Tolerance, 571
National Civil Rights Museum, 168, 571
National Museum of Photography, Film, and Television, 574
Natural History Museum in the United Kingdom, 573
Natural History Museum of Los Angeles County, 572
National Inventors Hall of Fame, 453
National Museum of the American Indian, 567
Smithsonian National Museum of Natural History, 573
Smithsonian Natural History Museum, 376
Smithsonian Photographs Online, 574

Swedish Museum of Natural History, 573
UCLA Fowler Museum of Cultural History, 571
Underwater Photography: Philip Colla, 574
United States Holocaust Memorial Mueseum, 572
University of California Museum of Palentology, 573
Wright Brothers Aeroplane Company and Museum of Aviation, 572
NASA History Office, 51
National Archives and Records Administration, 759
National First Ladies' Library, 759
National Sporting Library, The, 759
National Women's History Project, 376, 951
personal history, investigating. ***See*** background checks
political campaigns, 706
Posters, Inc. Historical Posters, 176
presidents and rulers
American Presidents: Life Portraits, 718
British Prime Ministers, 718
Emperors of Sangoku: China, India, and Japan, 718
France Rulers, 718
Germany: Chancellors, 718
POTUS: Presidents of the United States, 718
Presidents of the United States, The, 719
Prime Ministers of Canada, 719
Russian Leaders, 719
Route 66, 875
Russia
Alexander Palace Websites, 387
Face of Russia, The, 387
History of Russia, 388
Moscow Landmarks, 383
U.S. Department of State: Russian History, 388
Slow Pitch Softball History Page, 836
Smithsonian Institution Libraries, 759
Smithsonian Institution, The, 571
Spain, 385
Steam Locomotives, 740
Taoism and the Philosophy of Tai Chi Chuan, 528
Tesla, Nikola, 453
Titanic, The Official Archive, 649
Top Ten African American Inventors, 454
Tour de France, 94
TV History: The First 75 Years, 856
Union Pacific Railroad, 741
United Kingdom, 384
United States
American Memory, 388
CIA History for Kids, 388
Eyes of Glory, 388
George Washington's Mount Vernon, 382
Henry Ford Estate: Fair Lane, 383
Mount Rushmore, 383
National Civil Rights Museum, 383
National Parks and Monuments, 383
National Security Archive, 388
National Trust for Historic Preservation, 389
Our Documents, 383
Outline of U.S. History, 388
Smithsonian National Museum of American History, 389
Smithsonian Natural History Museum, 376
Statue of Liberty-Ellis Island Foundation, 384
Susan B. Anthony House Museum and National Landmark, 384
TheHistoryNet, 388
USHistory.org, 389
Vietnam War, 916-917
Women and Social Movements in the United States: 1600-2000, 954
Women in Aviation History: The Ninety Nines, 954
world
Encyclopedia of World History, 389
History of the World Timeline, 389
HistoryWorld, 389
HyperHistory, 390
World History Archives, 390
World War I
Encyclopedia of the First World War, 918
FIRST WORLD WAR.COM, 918
Great War, The, 918
League of Nations Statistical and Disarmament Documents, 383
War Times Journal: The Great War, 918
World War I Document Archives, 918
World War I: Trenches on the Web, 918
World War One, 919
World War II, 919
HIV. *See* AIDS/HIV treatment and prevention
hobbies. *See also* crafts
A2Z Hobbies, 391
collectibles/collecting
Beanie Babies, 173
Beckett Collectibles Online, 172
coins, 173-174
Collectics, 172
CollectingChannel.com, 172
Collector Online, 172
Collectors Universe, 172
Collectors.org, 172
Curioscape, 172
dolls, 174-175
Hot Wheels/Matchbox Cars, 175-176
posters, 176-177
stamps, 177-178
Creativity for Kids, 864

eHobbies, 391
HOBBYLINC, 391
HobbyTown USA, 391
knitting
Artfibers Fashion Yarn, 492
elann.com, 492
Free Patterns, 492
Frugal Knitting Haus, 492
Garter Belt, The, 492
Knit 'N Style, 492
Knit Picks, 492
Knitting Universe, 492
Knitty, 493
kpixie, 493
Learn to Knit at Lion Brand Yarn, 493
LearnToKnit, 493
Staceyjoy's Knitting Stitch Portfolio, 493
Vogue Knitting, 493
Webs: America's Yarn Store, 493
Woolery, The, 493
Yesterknits, 494
You Knit What??, 494
Michael's Arts and Crafts Store, 207
model trains, 394
models, building, 393
origami, 655
quilting
AIDS Memorial Quilt, The, 733
Bryer Patch Studio, 733
Canadian Quilters' Association, 733
Free Quilt Ideas, 733
From the Heartland, 733
Jinny Beyer Studio, 733
Martingale & Company, 733
McCall's Quilting Magazine, 733
National Quilting Association, 734
Patchwork Mountain, 734
Piecemakers, 734
Planet Patchwork, 734
Quilt Channel, The, 734
Quilter Magazine, The, 734
Quilter's Review, 734
Quilters Online Resource, 734
Quilters Village, 735
Quilting Arts Magazine, 735
Quilting with a Passion, 735
Quiltmaker Magazine, 735
QuiltWear.com, 735
World Wide Quilting Page, 735
radio
Amateur Radio and DX Reference Guide, 391
ARRL: National Association for Amateur Radio, 391
eHam.net, 391
Ham Radio Outlet, 392
RC (Radio Control) vehicles, 392-393
scrapbooking, 795-796
Third Age, 782
woodworking, 731, 957

hockey
AHL: Offical American Hockey League Website, 395
ESPN Hockey Site, 395
Hockey Hall of Fame, 395
Hockey News Online, The, 395
Hockey's Future, 395
HockeyBrain, 395
Internet Hockey Database, 395
National Hockey League Players' Association, 395
NHL: Official National Hockey League Website, 396
Science of Hockey, 396
U.S. College Hockey Online, 396
USA Hockey, 396

holidays and celebrations
Christmas Around the World, 397
Fourth of July, The, 397
Hallmark.com, 397
Holidays on the Net, 397
KidProJ's Multicultural Calendar, 397
Kids Domain Holidays, 397
Martin Luther King, Jr. Day, 397
Passover on the Net, 398
Ramadan, 398
seasonal and holiday freebies, 80

home. *See also* gardening and landscaping; timeshares
American Association of Homes and Services for the Aging, 780
automation
EH (Electronic House) Publishing, 406
Home Automation, 407
Home Controls, Inc., 407
SmartHome.com, 407
X10, 407
businesses. ***See also*** small businesses
At-Home Based Business Online, 128
Bizy Moms, 128
Business Owners' Idea Cafe, 128
Getting New Business Ideas, 128
Jim Blasingame: The Small-Business Advocate, 129
PowerHomeBiz.com, 129
Pros and Cons of Working at Home, 129
Quatloos, 129
Small & Home Based Business Links, 129
Women's Work, 129
WorkAtHomeIndex.net, 129
WorkingFromHome.com, 129
buying/selling
Americas Virtual Real Estate Store, 742
Century 21, 742
Coldwell Banker, 742
Commerical Network, The, 742
Domania.com, 742
ERA, 742
GMAC Real Estate, 743
Home Plans, 743
HomeBuilder.com, 743

HomeFair.com, 743
HomeGain, 743
HomeLife Real Estate, 743
Homeseekers.com, 743
HUD: U.S. Department of Housing and Urban Development, 743
International Real Estate Digest, 744
MSN Real Estate, 744
NewHomeNetwork.com, 744
Nolo.com-Real Estate, 744
Owners.com, 744
RalphRoberts.com, 744
Real Estate Center Online, 744
RealEstateabc.com, 744
REALTOR.com, 745
Realty Times, 745
REMAX Real Estate Network, 745
SellMyHome101.com, 745
Zillow, 745

construction
Ask The Builder, 399
B4UBUILD.com, 399
Bricsnet, 399
Build.com, 399
Builder Online, 400
Building Industry Exchange, 400
BuildingCost.net, 400
Construction-Resource.com, 400
DoItYourself.com, 399
Habitat for Humanity, 399
HomeBuilder.COM, 400
Housing Zone, 400
National Association of Home Builders, 400

decks and patios, 401

decorating/painting
All-Home Decor, 401
American Society of Interior Designers, 402
Ballard Design, 402
Bed Bath & Beyond, 402
Better Homes and Gardens, 402
cMYVision, 402
CrateandBarrel.com, 402
Design Addict, 402
Designing Online, 402
EZblinds.com, 402
FurnitureFind.com, 403
FurnitureOnline.com, 403
Home and Garden Television (HGTV), 403
Home Fashion Information Network, 403
Longaberger Baskets, 403
No Brainer Blinds and Shades, 403
Pier 1 Imports, 403
Pottery Barn, 403
Rental Decorating, 403
Stencil Ease Home Decor and Craft Stencils, 404
Traditional Home Magazine, 404
unicaHOME, 404
UrbanScapes, 404

design. ***See also*** architecture
AARP: Universal Design, 407
Consumer's Guide to Energy Efficiency and Renewable Energy, 407
Design Basics Home Online Planbook, 44
Design Community Forums, 407
Home Planners, 407
HomePlans.com, 408
interior design, 410-411
New Home Source, 408
Punch Software, 408
Sustainable House Design, 408

eldercare, 34

electrical
DoItYourself.com Electrical and Electronics, 404
Electrical Safety Foundation, 404
Home & Family, 404
Home and Garden Television: Electrical, 405
HomeTips, 405
Saving Electricity, 405

financing/mortgaging
ABN-AMRO, 745
Amortization Schedule, 746
Bankrate.com, 746
BestRate, 746
California Association of Realtors Online, 746
Countrywide Financial, 746
Ditech, 746
E-Loan, 746
Fannie Mae Home Page, 747
Federal Home Loan Banks, 747
FHA Today!, 747
Freddie Mac Home Page, 747
HUD Husing FHA Home Page, 747
Inman News Features, 747
Interest.com, 747
LendingTree.com, 747-748
LoanWorks.com, 748
Mortgage Bankers Association, 748
Mortgage Fraud Blog, 750
Mortgage Payment Calculator, 748
Mortgage Tips, 749
Mortgage, 101, 748
Mortgage-Net, 748
MortgageQuotes.com, 748
MortgageSelect.com, 749
PlanetLoan, 749
Prieston Group's Mortgage Fraud Page, The, 750
QuickenMortgage.com, 749
SunTrust Mortgage, 749

flipping
Flip That House, 749
Flip This House, 749
Flipping Houses, 750
FlippingFrenzy.com, 750
How to Flip Houses, 750

flooring, 405
foreclosures, 225
fraud (real estate), 750
Habitat for Humanity International, 640

heating and air conditioning, 406
Home Energy Saver, 275
improvement and repair
Ace Hardware, 408
BobVila.com, 408
diyfixit, 408
Fiberglass Insulation by Owens Corning, 408
HandymanUSA, 409
Home Depot, 409
Homedoctor.net, 409
Hometime, 409
Ian Evans' World of Old Houses, 409
Lowe's Home Improvement Warehouse, 409
Natural Handyman, 409
Old House, The, 409
On the House with the Carey Brothers, 409
Pella Windows and Doors, 410
Remodeling Online, 410
This Old House, 410
Tools of the Trade, 410
Your New House with Michael Holigan, 410
inspection, 410
insurance, 432
KnowledgeHound, 16
plumbing, 411
relocation services
AIM Relocation, 750
Apartments for Rent Online, 750
Employee Relocation Council (ERC), 751
ExecuStay Inc., 751
Moving Local, 751
Moving.com, 751
Relocate America, 751
Relocation Wizard, The, 751
RelocationCentral.com, 751
Rent.net, 751
RPS Relocation Services, 752
Salary Calculator, 752
School Report, The, 752
SchoolMatch, 752
Sound Home Resource Center, 399

home-brewing (beer)
All About Beer, 89
Beer Me!, 90
Beer, Beer, and More Beer Home Brewing Supplies, 89
BeerAdvocate.com, 89
BeerBooks.com, 89
Brewers Association, 90
RealBeer.com: The Beer Portal, 91

homeopathy
abc Homeopathy, 31
Finding Professional Homeopathic Care, 31
Homeopathic FAQs, 31
Homeopathy Internet Resources, 31
Homeopathy Online, 31
National Center for Homeopathy (NCH), 32

homeschooling
A to Z Home's Cool Homeschooling Website, 247
California Homeschool Network, 248
Eclectic Homeschool Online, 248
Home School Foundation, 248
Home School World, 248
Homeschool Central, 248
Homeschool Legal Defense Association, 248
Homeschool.com, 248
HomeSchoolZone.com, 248
Oregon Home Education Network, 249

homework help (grades K-12), 255-256, 262, 529

horror
dark fantasy, 413
Dark Worlds, 412
ghosts, 413
Horror Writers Association, 413
Horror.com, 412
Horror.net, 412
HorrorChannel.com, 412
HorrorFind, 412
HorrorMovies.com, 412
Horrorview.com, 412
occult, 414
Upcoming Horror Movies, 413
vampires, 414

horses
American Paint Horse Association, 415
American Saddlebred Horse, The, 415
BarrelHorses.com, 415
Breeds, 415
Care for My Horse, 415
Choosing a Horse, 415
Churchill Downs, 416
EquiSearch, 416
Horse Behavior, 416
Horse Centric, 416
Horse Source, The, 416
HorseCity.com, 416
PBS's Nature: Horses, 416
TheHorse.com, 416
United States Dressage Federation, 417
WesternHorseman.com, 417

hotels/motels. *See* lodging

housekeeping. *See* janitorial

HTML (hypertext markup language), 448

human resources
BASIC, 466
Human Resource Executive Online, 467
Office of Personnel Development, 467
Primavera Systems, 467
Society for Human Resource Management, 467
Top Echelon, 467
Workforce Management, 467
Workstream, 467

human rights
AbortionFacts.com, 713
ACLU Reproductive Rights, 713
American Immigration Lawyers Association (AILA), 511
Amnesty International USA Women's Human Rights, 948
Amnesty International, 167
Association for Women's Rights in Development, 948

A B C D E F G H I J K L M N O P Q R S T U V W X Y Z

Center for Reproductive Law and Policy, 949
Digital Freedom Network, 2
Ethics Updates, 713
gay/lesbian/bisexual/transgender issues, 349
Global Fund for Women, 950
Human Rights Watch, 950
Minority Rights Group International, 168
NARAL Pro-Choice America, 713
National Abortion Federation, 713
National Right to Life, 714
Office of International Women's Issues, 952
United Nations and the Status of Women, The, 953
Women and Politics Institute, The, 954
Women's Human Rights Net, 954
Women's Human Rights Resources, 954
WomenWatch, 954
Workplace Fairness, 465

humor
Al Lowe's Humor Site, 331
Amusing Quotes, 736
Break.com, 418
Caricature Zone, 331
cartoons, 420-421
Chickenhead, 418
CollegeHumor.com, 418
Comedy Central, 331, 418
Comedy-Zone.net, 418
Cruel Site of the Day, 418
Dane Cook, 331
Darwin Awards, 418-419
Despair, Inc., 419
Extreme Funny Humor, 331
Garden Humor, 344
How to Talk New Age, 622
Humor, 100, 419
JibJab, 419
jokes
Aardvark Archie's Guide to Rude Humor, 418
Joke a Day, A, 421
Joke Frog, 421
Joke Yard, 422
Jokeathon, 421
JokeWallpaper.com, 421
Lots of Jokes, 422
Mefco's Random Joke Server, 422
Ray Owen's Joke a Day, 422
LaughNet, 419
Maxim Online, 542
Modern Humorist, 419
National Lampoon, 419
Onion, The, 419
Red Vs. Blue, 420
SITCOM Home Page, 863
SlashNOT, 332
Spencer Gifts, 357
Stupid.com, 332
Totally Absurd Inventions, 454
Un-Cabaret, 420
(un)Official Dave Berry Blog, The, 419
Weird Site, The, 420
Whitehouse.org, 420
Working Wounded, 420

hunting
Bowhunting.Net, 423
Bowsite, The, 423
Browning Home Page, 423
Buckmasters Magazine Online, 423
Clay Pigeon Shooting Association, 423
Ducks Unlimited, 423
Easton Archery, 423
Eders.com, 423
Field & Stream Online, 424
Hunting Information Systems: An Online Guide, 424
Hunting Trail WebRing, 424
Hunting.Net, 424
Idaho Archery, 424
Maine Guides Online, 424
MyOAN, 424
National Rifle Association, 424
North American Hunting Club, 425
Pearson Archery, 425
Rod and Gun, 14
Texas Parks and Wildlife, 425
U.S. Fish and Wildlife Service, 425

hypnosis. *See also* self-help and motivational
American Society of Clinical Hypnosis, 426
Hypnosis Motivation Seminar, 426
Hypnosis Online, 426
Hypnosis.com, 426
HypnosisDownloads.com, 426

I

Iceland, government information/services, 360

Idaho
Idaho Archery, 424
Idaho, 889
Yellowstone Net, 676

Identity Theft. *See* privacy (Internet)

Illinois
Adler Planetarium and Astronomy Museum, 574
Art Institute of Chicago, The, 568
Brookfield Zoo, 968
Chicago Athenaeum: The Museum of Architecture and Design, The, 567
Field Museum of National History, 233, 572
Illinois Institute for Addiction Recovery, 6
Lincoln Park Zoo, 969
Museum of Science and Industry, Chicago, The, 575
Notebaert Nature Museum, 612
NPO-NET, 636
Pet Columns from University of Illinois College of Veterinary Medicine (CVM), 683
Powell's Books, 116
Raggedy Ann & Andy Museum, 175
University of Chicago Law School, 510

immigration
American Immigration Lawyers Association (AILA), 511

Citizenship and Immigration to Canada, 143

income taxes. *See* taxes

independent film

AtomFilms, 563

BMW Films, 563

IFILM, 563

IndieFilmSpot, 563

Richmond Moving Image Co-Op, 563

UndergroundFilm.org, 564

India

Emperors of Sangoku: China, India, and Japan, 718

government information/services, 360

Indian History, 379

Indiana

Children's Museum of Indianapolis, 567

Indiana Prevention Resource Center, 8

Indianapolis Museum of Art, 569

Indianapolis Zoo, The, 969

Riley Hospital for Children, 368

WWW Virtual Library-Law, 508

Indonesia. *See also* Asia, history

government information/services, 360

Songs of Indonesia, 593

Welcome to Bali & Beyond, 593

infertility

About Infertility, 714

American Fertility Association, 714

Fertility Friend, 714

Fertility Plus, 714

Infertility Treatments, 715

Infertility: A Couple's Survival Guide, 715

InterNational Council on Infertility Information Dissemination (INCIID), The, 715

IVF.com, 715

Mayo Clinic: Infertility, 715

Medline Plus Infertility Resources, 715

RESOLVE: The National Infertility Association, 715

Shared Journey, 715

inline skating. *See also* roller skating

Get Rolling, 818

International Inline Skating Association, 818

LandRoller Skates, 818

Rollerblade, 818

Skatepile.com, 818

Zephyr Inline Skate Tours, 818

insects. *See also* animals

BugBios.com, 427

Bugscope, 427

Bugwood Network, 427

Butterfly Gardening, 345

Butterfly Web site: Conservation and Ecology, The, 271

Butterfly Website, The, 427

eNature.com, 427

Entomology Index of Internet Resources, 427

Forensic Entomology, 427

Insect Bites and Stings from Medline Plus, 428

Insecta-Inspecta.com, 428

Insectlopedia, 428

Insects Hotlist, 428

Iowa State University's Tasty Insect Recipes, 428

Iowa State's Entomology Image Gallery, 428

Spiders, 428

Yuckiest Site on the Internet, 428

instant messaging and telephony (Internet). *See also* chats and social groups (Internet)

America Online Instant Messenger, 439

iChat AV, 439

ICQ.com, 439

Instant Messaging Planet, 439

Jabber, 439

MSN Messenger Service, 440

Net2Phone, 440

Odigo.com, 440

PalTalk, 440

REBOL Internet Operating System, 440

Skype, 440

Trillian, 440

Yahoo! Messenger, 440

insurance

A.M Best Company, 429

AgeNet, 797

American Insurance Association, 429

Ameriprise, 780

automobiles

AAA.com, 431

Allstate, 431

Comparison Market, 431

eSurance, 431

GEICO Direct, 431

Insurance Institute for Highway Safety, 429

National Motor Club, 431

National Safety Council, 430

Progressive, 431

State Farm, 431

Chubb Group of Insurance Companies, 429

Claims, 429

companies

AIG, 431

Farmers Insurance, 431

Hartford, The, 432

MetLife, 432

Prudential, 432

Travelers, The, 432

health

AFLAC, 372

America's Health Insurance Plans, 372

eHealthInsurance, 372

HealthInsuranceFinders.com, 373

HealthInsuranceInfo.net, 373

Insurance Fraud, 373

International Medical Group, 373

PacifiCare, 373

homeowners/renters

Consumer's Guide to Homeowner's Insurance, 432

Insure.com: Renters Insurance, 432

Twelve Ways to Save Money on Homeowner's Insurance, 432
Independent Insurance Agents of America, 429
Insurance Information Institute, 429
Insure.com, 429
InsWeb, 430
IntelliQuote.com, 430
Medicare.gov, 800
National Association of Insurance and Financial Advisors, 430
National Association of Insurance Commissioners (NAIC), 430
National Student Services, Inc., 432
Nationwide Insurance, 430
Pet Plan Insurance, 683
QuickQuote, 430
State Insurance Regulators, 430
Veterinary Pet Insurance, 905

interior design
American Society of Interior Designers, 410
DoItYourself Interior Design, 411
Home Decor Advice, 411
Home Decorating Digest, 411
Interior Design, 411

international business
Australian Department of Foreign Affairs and Trade, 130
BISNIS, 130
Export-Import Bank of the United States, 130
Federation of International Trade Associations, 130
FinFacts, 130
Gateway to the European Union, 130
globalEDGE, 130
Infonation, 130
International Business Ethics Institute, 131
International Business Forum, 131
International Monetary Fund, 131
International Trade Center, 131
Internationalist, The, 131
JETRO (Japan External Trade Organizations), 131
Latin Trade, 131
Newsweek International Business Edition, 131
OverseasJobs.com, 131
Tilburg University Marketing Journals, 132
U.S. International Trade Commission, 132
United Nations and Business, 132
United Nations Economic Social Commission for Asia and the Pacific, 132
United States Council for International Business, 132
United States Trade Representative, 132
World Bank Group, 132
World Trade Organization, 132

international education
AFS Intercultural Programs, 249
American Councils for International Education, 249
Digital Education Network EduFund, The, 249
Exchange, 249
GoAbroad.com, 249
International Education Site, The, 249
NAFSA: Association of International Educators, 249
Rotary International Eastern States Student EXchange Program, Inc. (ESSEX), 250
Study Abroad Directory, 250

international politics
Amnesty International USA Women's Human Rights, 948
AntiWar.com, 913
Carnegie Council on Ethics and International Affairs, 328
Center for Defense Information, 895
Center for Reproductive Law and Policy, 949
Center for Security Policy, The, 328
CIA World Factbook, 353, 762
CIA World Factbook: Mexico, 557
Cold War, 915-916
Council on Foreign Relations, 703
DEBKAfile, 913
Department of State (U.S.), 897
eHistory: Middle East, 386
embassy.org, 328
Food and Agriculture Organization of the United Nations, 19
Foreign Policy Association, 328
Foreign Policy in Focus, 328
Global Fund for Women, 950
GlobalSecurity.org, 913
History in the News: The Middle East, 387
Human Rights Watch, 950
Jane's Foreign Report, 633
Korean War, 916
League of Nations Statistical and Disarmament Documents, 383
Middle East History & Resources, 387
Middle East: A Century of Conflict, The, 387
National Security Archive, 388
NATO: The North Atlantic Treaty Organization, 329
Newsweek, 625
Office of International Women's Issues, 952
Politics and Current Affairs Forum, 382
Stratfor Security Consulting Intelligence Agency, 914
terrorism, 917-918
TIME, 626
U.S. Agency for International Development, 329
U.S. News & World Report, 626
UNAIDS, 366
United Nations and the Status of Women, The, 953
United Nations Cyberschool Bus, 263
United Nations, The, 329
Utne Reader, The, 626
Vietnam War, 916-917

Women and Politics Institute, The, 954
Women's Human Rights Net, 954
Women's Human Rights Resources, 954
WomenWatch, 954
World Connected, A, 3
World Population, 764
World War I, 918-919
World War II, 919

international travel
AFRICANET, 880
Airhitch, 880
CDC (Centers for Disease Control and Prevention), 880
Czech Info Center, 880
European Visits, 881
Eurotrip.com, 881
Eurotrotter, 881
FranceEscape, 881
Grand Circle Travel, 881
Help for World Travelers, 881
Hobo Traveler, 881
Inn26, 881
International Travel and Health, 881
International Travel Guide for Mallorca and the Balearic Islands, 882
International Travel Maps and Books, 882
International Travel News, 882
Kintetsu International Travel, 882
Mexico Travel Guide, 882
Monaco Online, 882
Orient-Express Trains & Cruises, 887
Planeta, 882
Rick Steves' Europe Through the Back Door, 882
Salzburg, Austria, 882
Sri Lanka Internet Services, 882
TravelAdvice.ent, 883
United States State Department Travel Warnings and Consular Info Sheets, 883
Universal Currency Converter, 883
Vancouver, British Columbia, 883

Internet
anti-spam resources
ActivatorMail, 434
Antispam!, 434
CAUCE, 434
Fight Spam on the Internet, 434
FTC Spam Page, 434
GetNetWise: Spam, 434
SpamCon Foundation, 434
SpamCop, 435
chats and social groups. ***See also*** Internet, instant messaging and telephony
Bold Chat, 435
Chat-Zone, 435
Chathouse, 435
Cubic Space Main, 435
CyberTown, 435
mIRC, 435
MSN Groups, 436
SpinChat, 436
Talk City, 436
Worlds 3D Ultimate Chat Plus, 436
Yahoo! Chat, 436
Yahoo! Groups, 436
classifieds, 169
connection speeds
Broadband Home Central, 437
Broadbandwidthplace Speed Test, 437
DSL Reports Speed Test, 437
PC Pitstop Internet, 438
Toast.net Performance, 438
email
Bigfoot, 438
emailaddresses.com, 438
Eudora, 438
Gmail, 438
Harness Email, 438
HTMail, 441
Lycos Mail, 438
Lyris.net, 442
MSN Hotmail, 438
Netiquette, 438
opt-in email, 441-442
PostMasterDirect.com, 442
Talking Email, 439
Thunderbird, 439
Yahoo! Mail, 439
ZapZone Email, 439
European Telecommunications Institute, 433
gambling
Casino City, 152
Gambling-Win.com, 333
Gambling.com, 333
Gone Gambling, 333
Real Vegas Online, 333
games and puzzles
1MoreGame.com, 334
3D Realms, 334
Apple Corps, 334
Banja, 334
Big Fish Games, 334
Bonus.com, 487
Boxerjam.com, 334
BrettspielWelt, 334
Candystand, 487
CBC.CA/Kids/Games, 487
Centipede, 487
Chinook, 335
ClueMaster, 335
Codebook, The, 487
CoffeeBreakArcade, 335
Download Free Games, 339
DreamWorks Kids, 487
EA.com, 335
Escape from Knab, 487
FamilyFun.com, 487
FreeArcade.com, 335
Fruit Game, The, 335
Funbrain.com, 487
Funschool, 488
G4 Media Network, 335
Gamasutra, 335
GameColony.com, 335
Games Domain, 335
GamesIndustries.biz, 336
Gamespot, 336
GameSpy, 336
Gamesville, 336
GlobZ, 336
Homers, 336
IGN, 336

Junior Achievement TITAN, 488
Kaboose Games, 488
KidsCom Games, 488
Kids Domain Online Games, 337
Millsberry.com, 488
MSN Game Zone, 337
Multi-Player Online Games Directory, 337
multi-user games, 337, 341
NovaLogic, 337
PBS Kids Games, 488
playkidsgames.com, 488
PopCap Games, 337
SegaNet, 337
Shockwave Games, 488
Star Wars Galaxies, 337
There, 337
Velvet-Strike, 338
Warner Brothers Games Gallery, 488
WebChess, 488
World Village Games, 338
Yahoo! Games, 338
Yohoho! Puzzle Pirates, 338
Zeeks.com, 489
Grid Cafe, 433
HotWired, 727
instant messaging and telephony. **See also** Internet, chats and social groups
America Online Instant Messenger, 439
iChat AV, 439
ICQ.com, 439
Instant Messaging Planet, 439
Jabber, 439
MSN Messenger Service, 440
Net2Phone, 440
Odigo.com, 440
PalTalk, 440
REBOL Internet Operating System, 440
Skype, 440
Trillian, 440
Yahoo! Messenger, 440
Internet Architecture Board, 433
Internet Public Library, 727
Internet Resources for Special Children, 669
Internet ScamBusters, 201
Internet Storm Center, 433
Internet.com, 433
Internetweek Online, 727
InterNIC, 433
ISOC (Internet Society), 433
ISP (Internet Service Providers)
Directory, The, 436
Earthlink, 436
Free Internet Connections, 436
Free ISP Directory, 437
Free Site, The, 437
ISP Check, 437
ISP Planet, 437
Juno, 437
NoCharge.com, 437
PeoplePC, 437
kids, safety, 489-491
Net Nanny, 490
Safe Surf, 490
SafeKids.com, 490
SafeTeens.com, 490
StaySafe.org, 491
web sites by kids, 491
web surfing, 489
web surfing, 490
Web Wise Kids, 491
law
Allwhois.com, 509
Electronic Commerce and Internet Law Resource Center-Perkins Coie, LLP, 509
GigaLaw, 509
Internet Library of Law and Court Decisions, 509
Kuesterlaw Technology Law Resources, 509
MacWorld, 727
online telephone directories, 441
privacy. **See also** Internet, security/virus hoaxes
Ad Muncher, 442
Ad-Aware, 442
Anonymizer.com, 442
Anti-Phishing Workgroup, 442
BBBonline, 442
Center for Democracy and Technology, 442
CookieCentral.com, 443
CyberPatrol, 443
Electronic Frontier Foundation, 443
Fight Identity Theft, 443
How Not to Get Hooked by a 'Phishing' Scam, 443
ID Theft Affidavit, 443
Internet Watcher, 443
Privacy Rights Clearinghouse, 443
SpyBot, 443
Spyware Encyclopedia, 444
SpyWre Info, 444
TRUSTe, 444
Webroot, 444
search engines
About.com, 444
AltaVista, 444
Ask.com, 444
Dogpile, 444
Google.com, 445
Lycos.com, 445
Mamma, 445
MetaCrawler, 445
MSN.com, 445
Northern Light, 445
Search Engine Watch, 445
Yahoo!, 446
security/virus hoaxes. **See also** Internet, privacy
McAfee AntiVirus, 446
Panda Software, 446
Symantec AntiVirus Research Center, 446
Symantec Security Check, 446
Trend Micro: Scams and Hoaxes, 446
VirusList.com, 446
sharing photos online
Club Photo, 691
Kodakgallery.com, 691
PhotoWorks, 691
SmugMug, 691

Snapfish.com, 691
Yahoo! Photos, 692
Surfnet Kids, 485
web page development
1-2-3 ASPX, 447
AJAX, 447
ASP Resource Index, 447
ASP Today, 447
ASPWire, 447
Bare Bones Guide to HTML, 447
Brainjar, 447
Builder.com, 447
CGI Resource Index, 448
CoffeeCup Software, 450
CoolPage, 450
Database Journal, 448
Developers Network, 450
developerWorks: Java Technology, 448
DevX, 448
Dreamweaver, 448
FreeScripts, 448
FrontPage, 450
HTML Goodies, 450
HTML Writers Guild, 448
Jars.com, 448
Java.sun.com, 448
Macromedia, 450
Matt's Script Archive, 448
.NET, 449
PageResource.com, 449
Pagetutor.com, 451
Perl.com, 449
PHP, 449
Python.org, 449
Sausage Software, 451
ScriptSearch, 449
SiteExperts.com, 449
SitePal, 451
Slashdot, 451
SQL Server Magazine, 449
W3 Schools, 449
Web Developer's Virtual Library, 449
WebDeveloper.com, 450
Webmonkey for Kids, 450
Webmonkey.com, 450
XMetal, 451
Wi-Fi Planet, 434
World Wide Web Consortium, 434
Writing for the Web, 962
ZDNet, 732

inventions and inventors. *See also* science
American Experience, The, 452
Edison National Historic Site, 452
Enchanted Learning: Inventors and Inventions, 452
Engines of Our Ingenuity, 452
Franklin Institute, 452
InventNet, 452
Inventors Assistance Resource Directory, 452
Inventors' Digest Online, 452
Lemelson Center, 453
Lemelson-MIT Program, 453
National Inventor Fraud Center, 453
National Inventors Hall of Fame, 453
New Inventors, 453
Nikola Tesla, 453
PatentCafe.com, 453
Sunnyvale Center for Innovation, Invention & Ideas, The, 760
Top Ten African American Inventors, 454
Totally Absurd Inventions, 454
U.S. Patent and Trademark Office, 454
United Inventors Association, 454

investments. *See* finance and investments

Iowa
Dermatology Images: University of Iowa, 821
Iowa State University's Tasty Insect Recipes, 428
Iowa State's Entomology Image Gallery, 428
Iowa Tourism Office, 889

IPOs (Initial Public Offerings), 310

Iran
government information/services, 360
history, 386

Iraq, government information/services, 360

Ireland
Aer Lingus, 22
Beamish & Crawford Brewery, 89
FinFacts, 130
Irish and Celtic Music on the Internet, 592
Irish History on the Web, 376

IRL (Indy Racing League) series, 56

Islam
Al-Islam, 775
Answering Islam: A Christian-Muslim Dialog, 775
Illustrated Guide to Understanding Islam, 775
International Association of Sufism, 775
Islam and Islamic Studies Resources, 776
Islam, 101, 775
IslamiCity in Cyberspace, 776
Muslim Life in America, 776
Online Islamic Bookstore, 776
Radio Islam, 776
Ramadan, 398

island travel
All-Inclusives Resort and Cruise Vacation Source, 883
America's Caribbean Paradise, 883
Club Med, 883
Elite Island Resorts, 883
Fiji Islands Travel Guide, 884
Galveston Island Official Tourism site, 884
Hideaway Holidays: Travel Specialists to the Pacific Islands, 884
Islands.com, 884
Isles of Scilly Travel Centre, 884
Maui Travel & Tourism, 884
NetWeb Bermuda, 884
Virgin Islands, 884
World Beaches, 884

Israel
government information/services, 360
history, 387
Virtual Jerusalem, 778

Italian (languages/lingustics)
- Istituto Il David Italian Language, 503
- Italian-Language-Study.org, 503
- Learn Italian - From the BBC, 503
- R-O-Matic Italian/English Dictionary, 503

Italy
- Dictionary of Green and Roman Myths, 609
- government information/services, 360
- history, 385

J

jails
- 360degrees.org, 455
- American Correctional Association, 455
- American Jail Association, 455
- American Probation and Parole Association, 455
- Correctional Education Association, 455
- Corrections Connection, 455
- Federal Bureau of Prisons, 456
- JUSTNET: Justice Information Network, 456
- National Institute of Justice, 456
- Officer.com, 456
- Prisontalk, 456
- Stanford Prison Experiment, 456
- U.S. Bureau of Justice Statistics, 456

janitorial
- Housekeeping Channel, 457
- Janitorial Bidding Guide, 457
- ServiceAid, 457
- services
  - *ABM Janitorial Services, 457*
  - *Jani-King, 457*
  - *Maid Brigade, 457*
  - *Molly Maid, 457*
  - *Vanguard Cleaning Systems, 458*
- supplies
  - *Carolina Janitorial & Maintenance Supply, 458*
  - *CyberClean, 458*
  - *Dirt Happens, 458*
  - *Discount Janitorial Supplies, 458*
  - *HighPower Supplies, 458*
  - *J&R Supply, 458*
  - *Jani-Mart.com, 458*
  - *Twin Supply, 458*

Japan
- anime, 41, 186
- Emperors of Sangoku: China, India, and Japan, 718
- government information/services, 360
- history, 379
- JETRO (Japan External Trade Organizations), 131
- Judo, 526
- Jujitsu, 527
- Kakuro, 340
- Kintetsu International Travel, 882
- manga, 186, 362, 816
- Morikami Museum and Japanese Gardens, 571
- Shotokan (karate), 527
- Sudoku, 341
- Universal Studios, 37

Japanese (languages/lingustics)
- BJT: Business Japanese Proficiency Test, 503
- StudyJapanese.org, 504
- Tada Taku's Glossary, 504
- Your Name in Japanese, 504

Java (computer languages), 448

jazz music
- All About Jazz, 594
- BBC Music-Jazz, 594
- Down Beat Magazine, 594
- Jambands, 594
- Jazz Corner, 594
- Jazz Online, 594
- Jazz Review, The, 594
- Jazz Roots, 595
- JAZZ, 594
- Passion for Jazz, A, 595
- Red Hot Jazz Archive, 595

jetskis. *See also* boats and sailing
- International Jet Sports Boating Association, 459
- JetSki News, 459
- jetski.com, 459
- Kawasaki, 459
- Personal Watercraft Illustrated, 459
- Powerski Jetboard, 459
- SBT on the Web, 460
- Sea-Doo, 460
- Yamaha, 460

jewelry. *See also* body art/tattoos; watches
- Amazing-Bargains, 77
- appraisals, 462
- Blue Nile, 461
- designers, 462-463
- Diamond-Guide, 461
- DiamondReview.com, 461
- Gothic Clothing and Jewelry, 816
- ice.com, 461
- Jewelry Central, 461
- Jewelry Mall, 461
- Jewelrylist.com, 461
- Mondera, 462
- repair/restoration, 463

jobs/employment. *See also* real estate; relocation services
- Adventures in Education, 464
- AdvisorTeam, 464
- Career Center, 464
- Career Key, 464
- CareerJournal from the Wall Street Journal, 464
- Careers.org, 464
- company information, 465-466
- Cool Works' Ski Resorts and Ski/Snowboard Country Jobs, 824
- Department of Labor, 896
- developers.net: Jobs for Technical Professionals, 194
- EducationJobs.com, 250
- human resources, 466-467
- incentives, 466
- job sharing, 471-472
- JobStar Central, 464
- JournalismJobs.com, 473

A B C D E F G H I J K L M N O P Q R S T U V W X Y Z

Mapping Your Future, 464
Monster Message Boards, 465
NASE (National Association for the Self-Employed), 135
Occupational Outlook Handbook, 465
OSHA (Occupational Safety and Health Administration), 373
OverseasJobs.com, 131
Salary Calculator, 752
searches, 467-471
Self-Assessment Career Survey, 465
sharing, 471-472
Social Work Search, 834
SocialService.com, 833
WEDDLE's, 465
Working Wounded, 420
Workplace Fairness, 465

jogging. ***See*** **track and field**

jokes

Aardvark Archie's Guide to Rude Humor, 418
Joke a Day, A, 421
Joke Frog, 421
Joke Yard, 422
Jokeathon, 421
JokeWallpaper.com, 421
Lots of Jokes, 422
Mefco's Random Joke Server, 422
Ray Owen's Joke a Day, 422

journalism

AlterNet, 2
American Journalism Review, 473
Columbia Journalism Review, 473
High School Journalism, 473
Investigative Reporters and Editors, 473
Journalism.org, 474
JournalismJobs.com, 473
JournalismNet, 473
Newslink, 474
Newspaper Association of America, 474
North Gate: Berkeley's Graduate School of Journalism, 474
Poynter.org, 474
Reporters Committee for Freedom of the Press, 474
Society of Professional Journalists, 474
Walter Cronkite School of Journalism & Mass Communication, 474
Writers Write Journalism Resources, 474

Judaism

Ari Davidow's Klezmer Shack, 591
B'nai B'rith Youth Organization, 966
Chabad-Lubavitch in Cyberspace, 776
Converson to Jadaism, 776
Eyes of Glory, 388
History of Hanukkah, 397
Holocaust Chronicle, The, 385
Jewish America, 777
Jewish Encyclopedia, 777
Jewish Theological Seminary, 777
Jewish Virtual Library, 777
JewishGen: The Home of Jewish Genealogy, 352
JewishMusic.com, 592
Jews for Judaism, 777
Judaism and Jewish Resources, 777
Judaism, 101, 777
Kosher Express, 204
Machon Chana, 951
MavenSearch, 777
MyJewishLearning, 777
ORT, 778
Passover on the Net, 398
Shamash, 778
Shtetl: Yiddish Language and Culture, 778
Torah.org, 778
United States Holocaust Memorial Museum, 572
Virtual Jerusalem, 778

Judo

International Judo Federation, 526
Kodokan Judo Institute, 526
USA Judo, 526

Jujitsu

International Ju-Jitsu Federation, 527
Ultimate Jujitsu, 527

junk

1-800-GOT-JUNK?, 475
email, 476
Imagination Factory, 475
Junk Food Blog, 475
Junk Science, 475
Junk Yard Dog, 475
Junk Yard Parts Online, 475
recycling, 475
Technology Recycling, 476

K

K-12 (education)

ALA Resources for Parents and Kids, 250
ArtsEdge Network, 250
Awesome Library, 250
ClassroomConnectDirect.com, 250
Discovery Channel School, 250
Education Week News, 251
educational television

Bill Nye the Science Guy's Nye Labs Online, 253
Biography, 253
Cable in the Classroom, 253
ChannelOne.com, 253
Children's Television Workshop, 253
Discovery Channel, The, 254
KET: Kentucky Educational Television, 254
Merrow Report, 254
MyETV: South Carolina Educational TV and Radio, 254
Noggin, 254
PBS Teacher Source, 254
Stephen Hawking's Universe, 254
Street Cents Online, 255

EducationJobs.com, 250
EduHound, 251
Family Education Network, 251
FunBrain, 251

Global Online Adventure Learning Site, 251
homework help, 255-256, 262, 529-530
KidsBank.com, 251
Kindergarten Connection, 251
MarcoPolo, 244
Microsoft Education, 251
Montessori education, 257
Mr. Dowling's Virtual Classroom, 252
NASA John C. Stennis Space Center Education and University Affairs, 252
Newbery Medal, 252
On2, 252
private education, 258
public education, 259
Questacon: The National Science and Technology Center, 252
Questia: World's Largest Online Library, 252
Scholastic.com, 252
Science Source, The, 252
USA Today Education, 253
World Almanac for Kids, 253
Yahoo! Education Directory, 244-245
Yahoo! Education: K-12 Directory, 253

K-6 (children)
About Child Parenting, 664
Boy Scouts of America, 664
Child & Family Web Guide, 665
ClubMom, 665
Expect the Best from a Girl, 665
FamilyFun, 665
HELP for Parents, 665
K-6 Parenting, 665
Kids Camps, 665
KidsHealth.org, 665
MOST-Mothers of Supertwins, 665
National AfterSchool Association, 665
National Head Start Association, 666
National Network for Child Care: School Age Child Development, 666
Parenting Pipeline, 666
Parenting Young Children, 666

Kakuro (puzzles), 340

karate, Shotokan, 527

kayaking. *See* canoeing/kayaking

Kentucky
Churchill Downs, 416
Kentucky Equine Research, 905
KET: Kentucky Educational Television, 254

Kenya, government information/services, 360

kids. *See* children

knitting
Artfibers Fashion Yarn, 492
elann.com, 492
Free Patterns, 492
Frugal Knitting Haus, 492
Garter Belt, The, 492
Knit 'N Style, 492
Knit Picks, 492
Knitting Universe, 492
Knitty, 493
kpixie, 493
Learn to Knit at Lion Brand Yarn, 493
LearnToKnit, 493
Staceyjoy's Knitting Stitch Portfolio, 493
Vogue Knitting, 493
Webs: America's Yarn Store, 493
Woolery, The, 493
Yesterknits, 494
You Knit What??, 494

Korea
history, 379
Korean War, 901, 916
Tae Kwon Do, 527-528

Kung Fu
Authentic Kung Fu, 527
Chinese Kung Fu Wu Su Association, 527
Kung Fu Magazine, 527

Kuwait, government information/services, 360

L

landscaping. *See* gardening and landscaping

languages/linguistics
Catalan, 505. *See also* Spanish
Center for Machine Translation, 498
Children Language Development, 498
Chinese, 499, 504
Dutch, 504
English, 500
ERIC Clearinghouse on Languages and Linguistics, 501
Ethnologue: Languages of the World, 498
Farsi, 501
Foreign Languages for Travelers, 504
Forum for Modern Language Studies, 502
French, 501, 504
Gaelic, 504
German, 502
Greek, 502-503
iLoveLanguages, 498
Italian, 503
iTools.com, 763
Japanese, 503-504
Language Map, 502
Language Miniatures, 498
Linguist List, 498
Linguistic Society of America, 498
Loglan, 499
Modern Language Association, 502
Morse Code and the Phonetic Alphabets, 763
Online Dictionaries and Glossaries, 755
Russian, 505
Semiotics for Beginners, 499
sign language
Alexander Graham Bell Association for Deaf and Hard of Hearing, 217
American Sign Language Browser, 505
ASL Access, 217

Deaf Resources, 217
GG Wiz's FingerSpeller, 218
HandSpeak, 218
Helen Keller National Center for Deaf-Blind Youth, 218
National Association of the Deaf (NAD), 218
National Association of the Deaf, 505
Sign Language Associates, 506
SignWriting.org, 506
SignWritingSite, 219
Zoos Software, 219
Spanish, 506. ***See also*** Catalan
Tada Taku's Glossary, 504
Translator's Home Companion, The, 502
TravLang's Translating Dictionaries, 755
Virtual Foreign Language Classroom, 499
Welsh, 505
WordSmith Tools, 499

law and legal issues
Alzheimer's Foundation of America, 35
American Institute for Paralegal Studies, 245
background checks, 74
bankruptcy, 224
Center for Reproductive Law and Policy, 949
civil rights
American Civil Liberties Union, The, 167
Amnesty International, 167
Birmingham Civil Rights Institute, 167
Cato Institute, 167
Civil Rights Division (of the Department of Justice), 167
civilrights.org, 167
Law Research: The United States Department of Justice, 168
Minority Rights Group International, 168
ClassActionAmerica.com, 507
consumer issues, 200
criminal justice, 455-456
cyber law and cyberspace issues, 509
Department of Justice, 896
divorce and custody
child support, 236
Children's Rights Council, 235
Divorce Magazine, 235
DivorceCare Home Page, 235
DivorceNet, 235
DivorceWizards, 235
FamilyLaw.org, 235
divorceLAWinfo.com, 507
ElderNet, 780
Federal Bureau of Investigation, 507, 897
FindLaw.com, 507
fraud
Internet ScamBusters, 201
National Fraud Information Center, The, 202
FreeAdvice, 507
gay/lesbian/bisexual/transgender issues, 349
Homeschool Legal Defense Association, 248
Internet Legal Resource Guide, 507
KnowledgeHound, 16
Law Books, 508
law schools
Association of American Law Schools, 509
Columbia Law School, 509
FindLaw for Students, 509
Franklin Pierce Law Center, 510
Harvard Law School, 510
Jurist, 510
Kaplan Test Prep and Admissions, 510
Law School Admission Council Online, 510
Law School Discussion.org, 510
Lawschool.com, 183, 510
Stanford Law School, 510
University of Chicago Law School, 510
Yale Law School Home Page, 511
LawCatalog.com, 115
LawGuru.com, 508
Lawyers.com, 508
legal organizations
ACLU Freedom Network, 511
American Bar Association (ABA), 511
American Immigration Lawyers Association (AILA), 511
Association of Corporate Counsel, 511
Association of Trial Lawyers of America, 511
National Association of Attorneys General, 511
National District Attorneys Association (NDAA), 511
National Lawyers Association (NLA), 512
legal publications, 512-513
mediation, 534
National Consumer Law Center (NCLC), 225, 508
National Crime Prevention Council (NCPC), 508
National Senior Citizens Law Center, The, 800
patent law
All About Trademarks, 132
American Intellectual Property Law Association (AIPLA), 133
American Patent and Trademark Law Center, 133
British Library: Patents, The, 133
Delphion Intellectual Property Network, 133
General Information Concerning Patents, 133
Intellectual Property Mall, 133
InventNet, 452
Inventors Assistance Resource Directory, 452
KuesterLaw Resource, 133
Patent Act, 133
Patent and Trademark Office, 134

Patent Law Links, 134
PatentCafe.com, 453
U.K. Patent Office, 134
U.S.Patent and Trademark Office, 454
Pritchard Law Webs, 508
Retirement with a Purpose, 781
United States Code, 508
Workplace Fairness, 465
WWW Virtual Library-Law, 508
Yale Journal of Law and Feminism, 955

law enforcement
360degrees.org, 455
American Correctional Association, 455
American Jail Association, 455
American Probation and Parole Association, 455
Correctional Education Association, 455
Corrections Connection, 455
Federal Bureau of Prisons, 456
JUSTNET: Justice Information Network, 456
National Institute of Justice, 456
Officer.com, 456
Prisontalk, 456
Stanford Prison Experiment, 456
U.S. Bureau of Justice Statistics, 456

learning disabilities. *See* special needs children

lesbian issues. *See* gay/lesbian/bisexual/transgender issues

libraries (reference)
American Library Association, 757
American War Library, The, 757
Awesome Library for Teens, 757
Bartleby.com, 757
Bibliomania: The Network Library, 757-758
Center for Research Libraries, 758
HighBeam Research, 758
INFOMINE, 758
Internet Public Library, 758
Library of Congress, The, 758
Library Spot, 758
Libweb-Library Servers on the Web, 758
Lightspan, 758-760
Medical/Health Sciences Libraries on the Web, 759
National Archives and Records Administration, 759
National First Ladies' Library, 759
National Sporting Library, The, 759
OCLC Online Computer Library Center, Inc., 759
Portico: The British Library, 759
Smithsonian Institution Libraries, 759
Special Libraries Association, 759
Sport Information Resource Center, 760
Sunnyvale Center for Innovation, Invention & Ideas, The, 760
U.S. Department of Education (ED), 760
Web Library Directory, 760
WWW Virtual Library, 760

literature. *See also* authors; writing
America and English Literature Resources, 514
American Authors on the Web, 514
Bartleby.com, 514, 757
Bibliomania, 514
BookNotes, 514
BookWire Index-Author Indexes, 514
Candlelight Stories, 514
Celebration of Women Writers, A, 949
Children's Literature Web Guide (CLWG), 111
Comparative Literature Studies, 515
Critical Reading: A Guide, 515
E-CLAT, 515
Electronic Text Center at the University of Virginia, The, 515
Feminist Science Fiction, Fantasy, and Utopia, 790
Harper's, 727
Henry Miller Library, 112
horror
dark fantasy, 413
Dark Worlds, 412
Horror Writers Associaton, 413
Horror.net, 412
HorrorFind, 412
vampires, 414
Literary Criticism, 515
Literary Resources on the Net, 515
Literature.org The Online Literature Library, 515
Literture Network, 515
Michigan eLibrary, 516
mysteries
ClueLass, 607
Independent Mystery Publishers, 607
Mysterious Bookshop, 607
Mystery Guide, 607
Mystery Ink, 607
Mystery Net, 607
Mystery Reader, The, 608
Mystery Readers International, 608
Stop, You're Killing Me!, 608
Top Mystery, 608
Mystery Books, The, 516
New Yorker, 728
Newbery Medal, 252
Nobel Laureates, 516
Plato's Dialogues, 687
Project Gutenberg, 516
Pulitzer Prizes, 516
Roman Reader, The, 516
sci-fi and fantasy
Sci-Fi Site, The, 792
Science Fiction and Fantasy World, 792
Science Fiction and Fantasy Writers of America (SFWA), 792
Science Fiction Book Club, 791
Science Fiction Museum Hall of Fame, 792

SciFan, 792
SciFi Source, 793
SF-Lovers, 793
SF-Lovers, 794
SFF Net, 793
Victorian Women Writers, 516
Lithuania, government information/services, 360
lodging
1st Traveler's Choice, 884
Alaska Cabin, Cottage, and Lodge Catalog, 885
all-hotels.com, 885
Big Bear Mountain Resorts, 824
Boston Mills-Brandywine Ski Resort, 824
Budget Hotels, 872
Choice Hotels, 885
Colorado Vacation Guide, 885
Cool Works' Ski Resorts and Ski/Snowboard Country Jobs, 824
Cyber Rentals, 885
Elderhostel, 798
GoSki.com, 824
Hostels.com, 873
Hotelguide.com, 885
Hotels.com, 873
InnSite, 885
International Bed and Breakfast Guide, 885
Lake Tahoe's West Shore Lodging, 885
Lodging Guide World Wide, 885
LodgingGuide, 886
Lodgings International, 886
National Lodging Directory, The, 886
Priceline.com, 78
Professional Association of Innkeepers International, 886
RoomSaver.colm, 79
Sandals Resorts, 892
Stowe Mountain Resort, 826
Travel Web, 886
Vacation Direct, 886
West Virginia Lodging Guide, 886
Louisiana
Louisiana Travel Guide, 889
Mardi Gras Official Website, 584
Orlean Coffee Exchange, 320
Lutherans
Evangelical Lutherna Church of America, 778
Lutheran Prayer Ministries, 779
lyrics (music)
A-Z Lyrics, 582
Burt Bacharach's A House Is Not a Home Page, 582
Led Zeppelin Lyrics, 582
LYRICS Download.com, 582
Lyrics Search Engine, 582
Lyrics.com, 582
Musicnotes.com, 583
National Anthems, 583

M

Macintosh
Apple Insider, 190
Apple Links, 190
iLounge, 190
iPod Hacks, 191
Mac Addict, 191
Mac Design Online, 191
Mac Home, 191
Mac Update, 191
MacGamer.com, 191
Macintosh News Network, 191
Macworld, 191
troubleshooting, 198-199
magazines
365Gay, 349
ADDitude.com, 547
Adoption Guide, The, 10
Adoption Today Magazine, 11
Advertising Age, 725
Advocate, The, 349
Alternative Medicine Magazine Online, 26
American Cheerleader Junior Magazine, 158
American Cheerleader Magazine, 158
American Girl, 174
American Journalism Review, 473, 627
American Poolplayers Magazine, 97
American Snowmobiler Magazine, 827
American Spectator, The, 703
Analog Science Fiction and Fact, 789
Animation World Network, 40
Architecture Magazine, 44
Arts & Letters Daily, 624
Asimov's Science Fiction, 789
Associated Press, 627
Astronomy Magazine, 49
Atlantic Online, The, 112, 725
Atlantic Unbound, 624
Backpacker Magazine, 139
Balloon Life Magazine, 75
Baseball America, 81-82
Better Homes and Gardens, 402
Bicycling.com, 92
Billiards Digest Interactive, 97
BIRDTALK.com Magazine, 102
Blue Ridge Country, 888
Bluegrass Unlimited, 586
Boating Magazine, 108
Bowling This Month Magazine, 119
Boxing Monthly, 121
Brandweek Magazine, 521
Brides.com, 937
Buckmasters Magazine Online Web site, 423
Builder Online, 400
BusinessWeek.com, 124
BYTE Magazine, 725
Campaigns and Elections, 706
Canadian Business Franchise Magazine, 127
Canoe & Kayak, 150
Car Collector, 725
CartoonBank, 420
CCM Magazine.com, 588
Chi-Lel Qigong, 26
Chile Pepper Magazine, 203
Christianity Today: Music Store, 588

Christianity Today: Single Parenting, 666
Cigar Aficionado Magazine, 166
Climbing Online, 784
CNN/Money Magazine Retirement, 780
Columbia Journalism Review, 473
Computer Graphics World, 40, 185
Computerworld Online, 725
Concierge Travel, 891
Conservation Online, 111
Contemporary Pediatrics, 677
Cosmopolitan, 726
Dance Magazine, 209
Dance Spirit, 209
Dance Teacher Magazine, 209
Dancer Online, 209
Darts World Magazine, 213
Daryl Cagle's Pro Cartoonist Index, 421
Diabetes Health Magazine, 228
Diabetic Gourmet Magazine, 229
Digital Webcast, 935
Discover Magazine, 726
Divorce Magazine, 235
Dogs in Review, 237
Down Beat Magazine, 594
E.W. Scripps, 726
Editor & Publisher, 726
ELLE.com, 300
Entrepreneur.com, 134
EquiSearch, 416
Esquire, 726
Family Car Web Magazine, 67
Fantasy and Science Fiction Magazine, 726
Fathering Magazine, 542
FDA Consumer Magazine, 201
Field & Stream Online, 315, 424
Film Festival Today, 906
FineScale Modeler Magazine, 393
Fitness Magazine, 281
Fitness Online, 281
Folk Roots, 726
Forbes Retirement Planning, 780
Forbes, 726
Fortean Times, 332
Fortune.com, 124, 727
Gambling Online Magazine, 333
Gay Parent Magazine, 347
Girlfriends Magazine, 349
Girls Life Magazine, 851
Glamour, 727
Golf Tips Magazine, 359
Good Old Boat Magazine, 109
GQ Magazine, 542
Harper's, 624, 727
HighBeam Research, 758
Hinduism Online, 774
Hint Fashion Magazine, 300
Hockey News Online, The, 395
Home Theater Magazine, 267
HotWired, 727
How Magazine's HowDesign.com, 47
HOW Magazine, 727
Human Resource Executive Online, 467
iBluegrass Magazine, 587
Independent Rowing News, 922
Ink Blot Magazine: Deep Coverage of Great Music, 585
Interior Design, 411
International Association of Reiki Professionals, 764
International Data Group, 198
International Figure Skating Magazine (IFS), 817
International Table Tennis Federation, 839
Internet Public Library, 625, 727
Internetweek Online, 727
Investor's Business Daily, 307
IT Architect, 617
KidsRunning.com, 280
Kiplinger, 307
Knit 'N Style, 492
Knitty, 493
Kung Fu Magazine, 527
Ladyslipper Music, 602
LIFE Magazine, 727
Mac Home, 191
MacGamer.com, 191
Macworld, 191
MacWorld, 727
Magazine CyberCenter, 728
MagazinesAtoZ.com, 625
MakeZine.com, 728
Massage Magazine, 33
Maxim Online, 542
McCall's Quilting Magazine, 733
Men's Fitness.com, 281, 544
Metagrid, 728
Metropolis, 45
Money Magazine's Money, 101 Tutorial, 303
Money Magazine, 308
Mothering Magazine, 660
MotherJones.com, 728
Motorcycle Online, 561, 728
Mountain Bike Action, 95
Mountain Bike Magazine, 95
Ms. Magazine, 728
Nation, The, 625
National Geographic Map Machine, 520, 763
National Geographic Star Journey, 51
National Geographic, 353, 693
National Lampoon, 419
National Review, 625
NetWare Connection, 619
Network Computig Magazine, 619
New Age Retailer, 623
New Republic, The, 625
New Social Worker Online, The, 833
New Yorker, 728
NEWoman, 952
News Directory, 625
NewsLink, 629, 729
Newsweek International Business Edition, 131
Newsweek, 625, 729
Next Step Magazine, 852
NME (New Music Express), 581
Nor'east Saltwater Online, 315
Nursing Standard, 645

OperaNet Magazine, 596
Organic Gardening Magazine, 323
Outside Online, 14
PC World, 192
People, 729
Personal Watercraft illustrated, 459
Philosophy Now, 687
Planet Capoeira.com, 526
PM Zone, 729
Poetry Magazine, 699
PopPhoto.com, 694
Popular Science, 626, 729
Popular Woodworking, 957
Pregnancy Magazine, 711
Prevention Magazine, 205, 364
Prevention's Healthy Ideas, 232
Prevention.com-Weight Loss and Fitness, 941-942
Psychology Today, 723
QT Magazine, 350
Quilter Magazine, The, 734
Quilters Village, 735
Quilting Arts Magazine, 735
Quiltmaker Magazine, 735
Radio Control Car Action Magazine, 392
Radio Control Zone, 392
Remodeling Online, 410
Rock & Ice: The Climber's Magazine, 784
RollingStone.com, 581, 729
Runners World, 729, 869
Running Times, 283
SailNet, 109
Sandboard Magazine, 293
Sci-Fi Site, The, 792
Science Magazine Home, 729
ScienceDaily Magazine-Your Link to the Latest Research News, 729
Scientific American, 730
SciFan, 792
SciFi Source, 793
SciTech Daily Review, 730
Scuba Diving Magazine, 925
Self Magazine, 232
Self-Help Magazine, 723
Sew News, 803
SF-Lovers, 793
SG Magazine, 927
Shutterbug Online, 694
Shutterbug, 730
Skin Diver Online, 926
SkiNet, 730
Sky & Telescope Online, 730
Sky & Telescope, 52
Small Farm Today Magazine, 20
Smart Computing Magazine, 189
Smart Money, 223
Smoke Magazine, 730
SPIN.com, 582
Sport Diver, 926
Sports Illustrated: fantasy baseball, 83
Sports Illustrated Basketball, 86
Sports Illustrated College Basketball, 86
Sports Illustrated: College Baseball, 82
Sports Illustrated for Women, 953
SQL Server Magazine, 449
Stone Soup, 485
Streaming Media World, 935
STYLE.com, 301
Surfer Magazine, 730
Surfermag.com, 927
Surfing Magazine, 927
Swimming World Magazine, 930
SwimNews Online, 930
Swoon@Glamour, 240
Teen Ink, 852
TeenPeople.com, 853
Tennis Magazine, 730
TheHistoryNet, 388
Threads Magazine, 803
Time for Kids, 256, 486
Time Magazine, 730
Today's Bride Online Magazine, 938
Track and field News, 870
Traditional Home Magazine, 404
Transworld Skateboarding Magazine, 294
TravelASSIST Magazine, 731
Tricycle Review, 769
Trumpet, The, 773
TWICE: This Week in Consumer Electronics, 268
Twins Magazine, 731
U.S. News & World Report, 626
Union Pacific Railroad, 741
USA Weekend, 626
Utne Reader, The, 626
Vanity Fair, 731
Variety.com, 856
VIBE, 582
Vogue Knitting, 493
Vogue, 301, 731
Volleyball Magazine, 912
Wakeboarding Magazine, 931
Walking Connection, The, 284
WaterSki Online, 931
webzines
- *Asia Pacific News, 633*
- *Drudge Report, 633*
- *Economist, The, 633*
- *Emerging Markets, 633*
- *Jane's Defence Weekly, 633*
- *Jane's Foreign Report, 633*
- *Salon.com, 633*
- *Slate, 634*
- *Smoking Gun, The, 634*
- *Veterans News and Information Service, 634*
- *WEBZINE, 634*

Weekly Standard, The, 626
Whosoever, 350
Windows IT Pro, 731
Wine on the Web: The Talking Wine Magazine, 946
Wine Spectator, 731
Wired.com, 243
Wood Online, 731
Workforce Management, 467
Working Mother, 661
Worth Online, 732
ZDNet, 189, 198, 732
ZDNet-PC Magazine, 627
ZOOZOOM.com Magazine, 301

magic
- All Magic Guide, 517
- David Blaine, 517
- Earth's Largest Magic Shop, 517
- eCardTricks, 517
- Ellusionist, 517
- eyetricks.com, 517
- HappyMagic.com, 517
- International Conservatory of Magic, 518
- Magic Directory, 518
- Magic Show, 518
- MAGIC, 518
- Magictricks.com, 518
- TV Magic Guide.com, 518

magnet therapy, 32

Mah Jongg
- Mah Jongg Website, The, 340
- Mahjong Escape from Spin Top Games, 340
- Primary Games, 341

mail (junk), 476

Maine
- Abe's of Maine, 688
- Maine Antique Digest, 43
- Maine Guides Online, 424
- Maine Lobsters and New England Clambakes, 317
- Maine Snowmobile Connection, 827
- Schooner Mary Day, 876

Malaysia, 23. *See also* Asia, history

manga. *See also* anime
- EX: The Online World of Anime and Manga, 186
- graphic novels, 362
- Sailor Moon Specialty Store, 816

maps. *See also* Geography
- David Rumsey Historical Map Collection, 519
- Finding Your Way with Map and Compass, 519
- Google Earth, 519
- Google Maps, 519
- GraphicMaps.com, 519
- History of Railroads and Maps, 740
- International Travel Maps and Books, 882
- Language Map, 502
- MapQuest, 520
- Maps of the United States, 520
- Maps of United States National Parks and Monuments, 674
- Maps.com, 520
- National Geographic Map Machine, 520, 763
- National Geographic, 353
- SkiMaps, 825
- Windows Live Local, 520
- WorldAtlas.com, 354

marathons
- Marathon Training, 283
- New York City Marathon, 283
- Portland Marathon, 283

marketing
- Adweek Online, 521
- antfarm interactive, 521
- Brandweek Magazine, 521
- ClickZ Network, 521
- CommerceNet, 521
- Direct Marketing Association, 521
- DMI Music & Media Solutions, 521
- ESOMAR, 522
- GreenBook, The, 522
- Guerrilla Marketing, 522
- KnowThis.com, 522
- LitLamp, 522
- Marketing, 522
- MarketingTerms.com, 522
- MRA: Marketing Research Association, 522
- Reveries.com, 523
- Sales and Marketing Executives International, 523

marriage
- AAMFT, 832
- Alliance for Marriage, 524
- American Association for Marriage and Family Therapy, 524
- BellaOnline Marriage Site, 524
- divorce and custody
  - *child support, 236*
  - *Children's Rights Council, 235*
  - *Divorce Busting, 524*
  - *Divorce Magazine, 235*
  - *DivorceCare Home Page, 235*
  - *divorceLAWinfo.com, 507*
  - *DivorceNet, 235*
  - *DivorceWizards, 235*
  - *FamilyLaw.org, 235*
  - *SmartDivorce.com, 236*
- Five Love Languages, The, 766
- MarsVenus.com, 766
- Smart Marriages, 524
- Web by Women, foir Women, 953
- wedding planning
  - *Ask Ginka, 937*
  - *Best Man, The, 937*
  - *Bliss! Weddings, 937*
  - *Bridalink Store, 937*
  - *Brides and Grooms, 938*
  - *Brides.com, 937*
  - *Great Bridal Expo, 938*
  - *Grooms Online, 938*
  - *Knot: Weddings for the Real World, The, 938*
  - *Lovetripper, 891*
  - *Romantic Weekend Getaways, 891*
  - *Today's Bride Online Magazine, 938*
  - *Ultimate Internet Wedding Guide, 938*
  - *USA Bride, 938*
  - *Video In Production, 938*
  - *Wedding Bells, 939*
  - *Wedding Channel, The, 939*
  - *Wedding Photography-Advice for the Bride and Groom, 939*
  - *WeddingSolutions.com, 939*
  - *WedNet, 939*
- Worldwide Marriage Encounters, 524

martial arts. *See also* self-defense
- Capoeira, 526
- Century Fitness, 525
- Judo, 526
- Jujitsu, 527
- Kodokan Judo Institute, 526
- Kung Fu, 527
- Martial Arts Books and Videos, 525

MartialArts.org, 525
MartialArtsMart.com, 525
MartialInfo.com, 525
Qi: The Journal of Traditional Eastern Health and Fitness, 525
Real Combat Online, 525
Shotokan, 527
Tae Kwon Do, 527-528
Tai Chi, 528
TigerStrike.com, 525

Maryland
American Visionary Art Museum, 568
Chaos at Maryland, 531
Ocean City, MD's Frontier Town Campground, 138

Massachussets
Boston Ballet, 210
Boston Book Reivew, 113
Cambridge, Massachusetts, 888
Children's Hospital Boston, 367-368
Harvard Law School, 510
Harvard University Art Museums, 569
Materials Company of Boston, The, 257
Museum of Fine Arts, Boston, 570
Yale Law School Home Page, 511

massage
American Massage Therapy Association, 32
Associated Bodywork and Massage Professionals, 32
Body Therapy Associates, 32
Bodywork and Massage Information, 32
Boulder School of Massage Therapy, 32
Living Earth Crafts, 33
Massage Magazine, 33
Massage Network, 33
Massage Therapy, 33, 101
Massage Today, 33
Massage Warehouse, 33
Utah College of Massage Therapy, 33

mathematics
AAA Math, 529
algebra
Algebra Help, 530
Algebra Homework Help, 530
S.O.S. Mathematics Algebra, 531
American Mathematical Society, 529
Ask Dr. Math, 529
calculus, 531
chaos mathematics
Chaos at Maryland, 531
Chaos Hypertextbook, 531
Non-Linear Lab, 532
Open Directory: Chaos & Fractals, 532
eFunda, 529
Egyptian Mathematics, 529
Eric Weisstein's World of Mathematics, 529
ExploreMath.com, 529
FigureThis!, 529
fractals, 532
geometry, 532
goENC, 530
HotMath.com, 530
Intel Education Initiative, 848
Interactive Mathematics Online, 530
Math Forum @ Drexel, The, 262
mathematicians
Biographies of Women Mathematicians, 532
Indexes of Biographies, 532
MegaConverter, 763
Megamathematics!, 530
NASA Education Sites, 262
National Council of Teachers of Mathematics, 530
numeric analysis
Math Forum: Numeric Analysis, 533
SIAM (Society for Industrial and Applied Mathematics), 533
PSU Math-Mathematics Websites, 530
statistics, 533
trigonometry, 533

mediation
American Arbitration Association, 534
Conflict Research Consortium, 534
Federal Mediation and Conciliation Services (FMCS), 534
Guide to Alternative Dispute Resolution, 534
JAMS ADR, 534
Mediate.com, 534

medicine
AIDS/HIV treatment and prevention
AEGiS, 365
AIDS Education and Research Trust, 365
AIDS Outreach Center, 365
AIDS.ORG, 365
AIDSinfo, 365
Body: A Multimedia AIDS and HIV Information Resource, The, 365-366
Centers for Disease Control and Prevention: HIV, 366
Children with AIDS Project, 366
CPR for AIDS Patients, 367
HIV InSite: Gateway to AIDS Knowledge, 366
Magic Johnson Foundation, Inc., 366
Project Inform, 366
Stop AIDS Project, 366
UNAIDS, 366
allergies
Allegra: Allergy Answer Site, 24
Allergy Info, 24
Allergy, Asthma, and Allerpet, 24
American Academy of Allergy, Asthma, & Immunology Online, 24
Food Allergy & Anaphylaxis Network, 25
Food Allergy Initiative, 25
HealingWell's Allergy Resource Center, 25

HowStuffWorks.com: Allergies, 25
National Institute of Allergy and Infectious Diseases, 25
Priorities, 25

alternative
A2ZYoga, 963
ABC to Yoga, 963
acupuncture, 27-28
Alternative Health News, 26
Alternative Medicine Magazine Online, 26
AlternativeDr.com, 26
American Holistic Health Association, 26
aromatherapy, 28-29
Ayurveda Yoga Ultra-Nutrition, 26
Body Trends, 963
Chi-Lel Qigong, 26
chiropractors, 164-165
cleansing/detoxification, 29
HealthWorld Online, 26
herbalism, 30-31
homeopathy, 31-32
Kundalini Support Center, 963
Life Matters, 27
magnet therapy, 32
massage, 32-33
Mayo Clinic: Complementary and Alternative Medicine, 27
National Center for Complementary and Alternative Medicine, 27
Natural Health and Longevity Resource Center, 27
New Age Web Works, 623
PetSage-Pet Care Products, 683
Qi: The Journal of Traditional Eastern Health & Fitness, 27
Reiki, 622, 764-765
Sahaja Yoga Meditation, 963
Santosha.com, 963
Siddha Yoga Meditation, 964
Sivananda Yoga "Om" Page, 964
Step-by-Step Yoga Postures, 964
Tai Chi, 528
WholeHealthMD.com, 27
World of Yoga, A, 964
Yoga Alliance, 964
Yoga Directory, The, 965
Yoga Journal, 965
Yoga Site, 965
Yoga Synergy, 965
Yoga.com, 964
Yogabasics.com, 964

Alzheimer's, 34-35
American College of Emergency Physicians, 269
anatomy, 39
Ask Dr. Weil, 940
BAM! (Body and Mind), 478
cancer
ACOR.org, 145
American Cancer Society, 145
Avon: The Crusade, 145
Breast Cancer Action, 145
Cancer Detection and Prevention, 145
Cancer Directory, 145
Cancer Facts, 145
Cancer Group Institute, 145
Cancer411.com, 146
Cancerbackup, 146
CancerCare.org, 146
CancerKids, 146
CancerNews on the Net, 146
CanTeen, 146
Community Breast Health Project, 146
Faces of Hope, 146
National Cancer Institute, 147
NBCC-National Breast Cancer Coalition, 956
OncoLink: University of Pennsylvania Cancer Center Resources, 147
Prostate.com, 147
Steve Dunn's Cancer Guide, 147
Susan G. Komen Breast Center Foundation, 147
Testicular Cancer Resource Center, 147

CDC: Health Swimming, 928
celiac disease, 156
Climber's First Aid, 783
CPR, 367
dentistry, 226-227
Department of Health and Human Services, 896
dermatology
Dermatology Images: University of Iowa, 821
Dermatlogy Medical Reference, 821
National Rosacea Society, 822
Skin Care Campaign, 823
SkinCarePhysicians.com, 823

diabetes
ADA Recipe of the Day, 228
ADA: Americn Diabetes Association, 228
Central for Disease Control Diabetes FAQ, 228
Children with Diabetes Online Community, 228
Children with Diabetes Recipes, 228
Diabetes Health Magazine, 228
Diabetes Insight, 229
Diabetes Mall, 229
Diabetic Gourmet Magazine, 229
Gourmet Connection Network, 229
Joslin Diabetes Center, 229
Kids Learn About Diabetes, 229
Medical Alert Charms for Children, 229
National Diabetes Education Program, 229
National Institute of Diabetes & Digestive & Kidney Disorders, 229

diseases and conditions
- *American Cancer Society, 370*
- *American College of Gastroenterology, 370*
- *Arthritis Resource Center, 370*
- *Association of Cancer Online Resources, 370*
- *Down Syndrome WWW Pages, 370*
- *Endometriosis, 370*
- *Introduction to Skin Cancer, 370*
- *MedicineNet.com, 370*
- *Muscular Dystrophy Association, 371*
- *National Organization for Rare Diseases, 371*
- *National Osteoporosis Foundation, 371*
- *National Prostate Cancer Coalition, 371*
- *NewsRx, 371*
- *StopPain.org, 371, 540*
- *Sudden Infant Death Syndrome (SIDS) Information Home Page, 371*

Doc's Diving Medicine, 924

drug information
- *FDA: Food and Drug Administration, 536*
- *National Library of Medicine, 536*
- *RxList.com, 536*
- *SafeMedication.com, 536*

Drug Testing, 662

drugstores
- *CareMark.com, 535*
- *CVS/Pharmacy, 535*
- *drugstore.com, 535*
- *Eckerd.com, 535*
- *familymeds.com, 535*
- *Medicine Shoppe, 535*
- *Rite Aid, 535*
- *SavOn.com, 535*
- *Walgreens, 536*

eCureMe Self Diagnosis, 363

eldercare
- *Alzheimer's Association, 798*
- *American Geriatrics Society, 798*
- *Centers for Medicare and Medicaid Services, 798*
- *ElderWeb, 799*
- *Friendly4Seniors Websites, 799*
- *Life Extension Foundation, 799*
- *Lifesphere, 800*
- *Medicare.gov, 800*
- *National Institute on Aging, 800*
- *osteoporosis, 655*
- *osteoporosis, 656*

FamilyDoctor.org, 363

first-aid information
- *1st Spot First Aid, 536*
- *American College of Emergency Physicians, 536*
- *Anaphylactic Treatment Guidelines, 537*
- *HealthWorld First Aid, 537*
- *Mayo Clinic's First-Aid Guide, 537*

HealthCentral, 942

HealthWeb, 363

Healthy Ontario, 363

KidsHealth.org, 482

MayoClinic.com, 363

medical history, 374

medical resources
- *AAMC's Academic Medicine Website, The, 537*
- *American Lung Association, 537*
- *BBC Science & Nature: Human Body & Mind, 537*
- *Centers for Disease Control and Prevention, 537*
- *drkoop.com, 538*
- *HealthWorld Online, 538*
- *MedLine Plus, 538*
- *National Center for Complementary and Alternative Medicine (NCCAM), 538*
- *National Organization for Rare Disorders, Inc. (NORD), 538*
- *New England Journal of Medicine, 538*
- *Plink: The Plastic Surgery Link, 539*
- *Student Doctor Network, 539*
- *U.S. Department of Health and Human Services, 539*
- *Visible Human Project, 539*
- *WebMD, 539*

Medical/Health Sciences Libraries on the Web, 759

Medline Plus, 364

Medscape, 364

MSN Health, 364

National Institutes of Health, 364

nursing
- *AllHeart.com, 643*
- *allnurses.com, 643*
- *American Association of Colleges of Nursing, 643*
- *American Association of Critical-Care Nurses, 643*
- *American Association of Neuroscience Nurses, 643*
- *American Nurses Association, 643*
- *Cool Nurse, 643*
- *Cybernurse.com, 644*
- *Discover Nursing, 644*
- *Interfaith Health Program, 644*
- *National Association of Pediatric Nurse Practitioners, 644*
- *NP Central, 644*
- *Nurse Options USA, 644*
- *Nurse Recruiter, 644*
- *NurseWeek.com, 644*
- *NurseZone, 645*
- *Nursing Education of America, 645*
- *Nursing Spectrum, 645*
- *Nursing Standard, 645*
- *NursingCenter.com, 645*
- *Procare USA, 645*
- *Registered Nurses, 645*
- *School Nurse, 645*
- *WholeNurse, 645*

Ovid, 725

pain management
- *American Academy of Pain Management, 539*
- *American Chronic Pain Association, 539*
- *Mayo Clinic Pain Center, 540*
- *Pain.com, 540*
- *Partners Against Pain, 540*
- *StopPain.org, 371, 540*

Paramedic.com, 270

pediatrics
- *American Academy of Pediatrics, 71, 367, 677*
- *American Board of Pediatrics, 677*
- *American Pediatric Society/Society for Pediatric Research, 677*
- *Arkansas Children's Hospital, 373*
- *Canadian Pediatric Society, 677*
- *Caring for Kids, 659*
- *Child and Adolescent Health and Development, 367*
- *Child Health Research Project, 367*
- *Children with AIDS Project, 366*
- *Children with Diabetes, 677*
- *Children's Hosptial and Regional Medical Center, Seattle, 368*
- *Children's Hosptial Boston, 367-368*
- *Children's Hosptial of Philadelphia, The, 368*
- *Contemporary Pediatrics, 677*
- *CribLife 2000, 663*
- *Dr. Greene's HouseCalls, 678*
- *Dr. Greene: Toddlers, 663*
- *drSpock.com, 368*
- *Family Education Network: A Parenting and Education Resource, 659*
- *GeneralPediatrics.com, 678*
- *I Am Your Child, 678*
- *India Parenting, 678*
- *iParenting.com, 660*
- *Johns Hopkins Children's Center, 678*
- *KidsHealth.org, 368, 665*
- *KidSource, 678*
- *La Leche League International, 678*
- *Medline Plus: Pregnancy, 711*
- *MedlinePlus Doctor and Dentist Directories, 678*
- *Medscape: Pediatrics, 678-679*
- *National Childhood Cancer Foundation, 679*
- *National Healthy Mothers, Healthy Babies Coalition, 72-73*
- *National Institute of Child Health and Human Development, 368*
- *OBGYN.net, 711*
- *Parenthood.com, 660*
- *Parents of Premature Babies, 73*
- *Pediatrics in Review, 679*
- *Pregnancy & Parenting, 73*
- *Riley Hospital for Children, 368*
- *St. Jude Children's Research Hospital, 368*

Quackwatch, 364

reference libraries, 760

Travel Medicine, 879

veterinary
- *AAHA HealthyPet.com, 904*
- *American Animal Hospital Association (AAHA), 681*
- *American College of Veterinary Surgeons, 904*
- *American Veterinary Medical Association, 904*
- *Animal Health Information, 682*
- *AVA Online, 904*
- *AVMA (American Veterinary Medical Association) Network, The, 682*
- *Center for Veterinary Medicine, 904*
- *CyberPet, 682*
- *Department of Animal Science: Oklahoma State University, 904*
- *DoctorDog.com: Cat and Dog Supplies and Pet Health Care, 682*
- *Exotic Pet Vet, 681*
- *International Veterinary Information Service, 905*
- *Kentucky Equine Research, 905*
- *Merck Veterinary Manual, 905*
- *Murdoch University: Division of Veterinary and Biomedical Sciences, 905*
- *NOAH: Network of Animal Health, 905*
- *OncoLink: Veterinary Oncology, 905*
- *Pet Columns from University of Illinois College of Veterinary Medicine (CVM), 683*
- *PetPlace.com, 683*
- *Pets Need Dental Care, Too, 683*
- *PetSage-Pet Care Products, 683*
- *ThePetCenter.com, 682*
- *Veterinary Oncology, 684*
- *Veterinary Pet Insurance, 905*
- *VeterinaryPartner.com, 684*
- *Washington State University College of Veterinary Medicine, 905*

Viagra, 544

WebMD, 365

memory
- Human Memory, 541
- Memory Improvement Techniques, 541
- Memory Loss & the Brain, 541

men
- American Coalition for Fathers and Children, 236
- cancer, 147
- Dr. Warren Farrell, 542
- Esquire, 726
- Fathering Magazine, 542
- firebox.com, 865

GQ Magazine, 542
health, 544
Male Affirmative Resource Center, The, 542
Mankind Project, The, 542
Maxim Online, 542
Men Stuff, 543
MensActivism.org, 543
National Fatherhood Initiative, 543
NCAA Men's Swimming and Diving, 929
NCF-National Center for Fathering, 660
Pregnancy-info.net, 711
Single and Custodial Fathers' Network, 667

mental health
ADD/ADHD (Attention Deficit Disorder/Attention Deficit Hyperactivity Disorder), 547
agoraphobia, 546
anorexia nervosa. ***See*** mental health, eating disorders
anxiety and panic disorders
Anxiety Disorders Association of America, 546
Anxiety Panic Attack Resource Site, 546
Anxiety Panic Internet Resource, 547
National Panic & Anxiety Disorder News, 547
AtHealth.com, 545
autism and Asperger's syndrome, 548
bipolar disorder. ***See also*** mental health, depression
Bipolar World, 549
BPSO: Bipolar Significant Others, 548
Child & Adolescent Bipolar Foundation, 549
Cyclothymic Disorder, 549
Depression and Bipolar Support Alliance, 551
McMan's Depression and Bipolar Web, 549
Pendulum Resources: The Bipolar Disorder Port, 549
Center for Mental Health Services, The, 545
conduct disorder
American Academy of Childhood & Adolescent Psychiatry, 549
Clinical Guide to Conduct Disorder, 549
ConductDisorders.com, 549
Oppositional Defiant Disorder (ODD) and Conduct Disorders, 550
delirium, 550
dementia, 550
depression
All About Depression, 550
Coping with Depression Fallout, 550
Depressed Anonymous, 551
Depression and Bipolar Support Alliance, 551
depression-screening.org, 551
McMan's Depression and Bipolar Web, 549
NARSAD: National Associaton for Research on Schizophrenia and Depression, 555
National Institutes of Mental Health: Depression, 551
Psychology Information Online, 551
Teen Depression, 551
eating disorders
American Anorexia Bulimia Association of Philadelphia, 551
Anorexia Web, 551
Binge Eating Disorders, 552
Center for Eating Disorders, 552
Eating Disorders Association (EDA), 552
Eating Disorders Resource Centre, 552
Eating Disorders Online.com, 552
Girl Power! Bodywise, 552
National Eating Disorder Association, 552
National Women's Health Association, 552
Renfrew Center Foundation, The, 552
Something Fishy, 553
Internet Mental Health, 545
memory, 541
Mental Health InfoSource, 545
Mental Health Matters, 545
Mental Health Net, 545
National Alliance for the Mentally Ill (NAMI) Home Page, 546
National Institute of Mental Health, 546
National Mental Health Association, 546
OCD (Obsessive-Compulsive Disorder), 553
paranoia, 553
personality disorders
Borderline Personality Disorder, 553
Mayo Clinic: Personality Disorders, 554
National Education Alliance for Borderline Personality Disorder, 554
National Metnal Health Association: Personality Disorders, 554
Personality Disorder Test, 554
Personality Disorders, 554
post traumatic stress disorder
American Academy of Experts in Traumatic Stress, The, 554
David Baldwin's Trauma Information Pages, 554
International Society for Traumatic Stress Studies, 555
National Center for Post Traumatic Stress Disorder, 555
Psych Central, 546
psychiatry
American Academy of Child & Adolescent Psychiatry, 720
American Journal of Psychiatry, 720
American Psychiatric Association, 720

Archives of General Psychiatry, 720
Journal Watch Psychiatry, 721
ParentsMedGuide.org, 721
Psychiatry Source, 721
psychology
American Psychological Association, 722
Dr. Grohol's Psych Central, 722
Encyclopedia of Psychology, 722
Galaxy Psychology, 722
Guide to Psychology and Its Practice, A, 722
National Association of Cognitive Behavioral Psychology, 722
PSYbersquare, 722
PsychCrawler, 723
Psychology Today, 723
Psychology Works, 723
Psychology.com, 723
Psychology.net, 723
School Psychology Resources Online, 723
Self-Help Magazine, 723
Social Psychology Network, 723
psychosis, 555
schizophrenia, 555-556
Substance Abuse & Mental Health Services Administration, 9
suicide prevention
American Association of Suicidology, 837
American Foundation for Suicide Prevention (AFSP), 837
Befrienders International, 837
Community Lifelines, 837
Covenant House, 837
National Strategy for Suicide Prevention, 837
National Suicide Preventionl Lifeline, 837
SAVE: Suicide Help, 838
SFSP: Suicide Prevention, 838
Suicide Facts, 838
Suicide Prevention Advocacy Network, 838
Yellow Ribbon Suicide Prevention Program, 838
Tourette's syndrome, 556

meteorology. ***See*** **weather and meteorology**

Mexico
Access Mexico Connect, 557
CIA World Factbook: Mexico, 557
government information/ services, 360
history
Ancestors in the Americas, 377
Ancient Mexico, 385
Cultures & History of the Americas, 377
Hispanic History in the Americas, 377
History Channel: The History of Mexico, 385
History of the Americas, 377
History, Myths, Arts, and Traditions of Mexico, 386
Mexexperience, 386
Museum of the History of Mexico, 386
U.S. Mexican War, 386
Mexicana Airlines, 23
Mexico for Kids, 557
Mexico Travel Guide, 882
MexOnline, 557
North American Virtual Tourist, The, 878
Puro Mariachi, 593

Michigan
eLibrary, 516
Michigan Snowmobiling, 827
Michigan: Travel Michigan, 889

Middle East
Aljazeera News Service, 629
DEBKAfile, 913
history
eHistory: Middle East, 386
History in the News: The Middle East, 387
History of Iran, 386
History of Israel and Palestine in Map Form, 387
Middle East History & Resources, 387
Middle East: A Century of Conflict, The, 387

midwifery
American College of Nurse-Midwives, 715
DONA (Doulas of North America) International, 716
Doula Network, 716
Midwifery Information, 716
Midwifery Today, 716

military
Air Combat USA, 68
Air Force Association, 900
Air Force Link, 68
Aircraft Images Archive, 68
America's Wars, 913
American Civil War, 115, 914-915
American War Library, The, 757
Army and Air Force Exchange Service, 900
Cold War, 915-916
Cost of War, 913
Defend America, 901
DefendAmerica, 913
Defense Almanac, 762
DefenseLINK, 895
GlobalSecurity.org, 913
Imperial War Museum, 913
Jane's Defence Weekly, 633
Jane's Information Group, 914
Korean War, 901, 916
MarineLINK, 898
National Museum of the U.S. Air Force, 70
Pentagon Channel, 855
Soldier City, 902
Strategy Page, 914
terrorism, 917-918
U.S. Army, 898
U.S. Navy, 898
veterans affairs
AMVETS, 900
Department of Veterans Affairs, 897, 901

Department of Veteran Affairs Debt Management, 223
Disabled American Veterans, 901
Gulf War Veteran Resource Pages, 901
Military USA, 901
Military.com, 901
MOAA, 902
National Coalition for Homeless Veterans, 902
Paralyzed Veterans of America, 369, 902
U.S. Department of Housing and Urban Development Veteran Resource Center (HUDVET), 902
Veterans News and Information Service, 634, 902
Vets4Hire.com, 471
VFW: Veterans of Foreign Wars, 902
Vietnam Veterans of America, 903
Vietnam War, 916-917
World War I, 918-919
World War II, 919

Minnesota
MayoClinic.com, 363
Michigan Snowmobiling, 827
Minneapolis, 889
Minnesota State Parks, 138

miscarriage
American Pregnancy Association: Miscarriage, 716
Hygeia, 716
M.I.S.S.-Mothers In Sympathy & Support, 717
MEND (Mommies Enduring Neonatal Death), 717
Miscarriage Association, 717
SHARE, 717

missing children. *See* children, child abuse and missing children

Mississippi, 152

Missouri
International Bowling Museum and Hall of Fame, 120
Kansas City Board of Trade, 20
Missouri Botanical Gardens, 344
St. Louis Zoo, The, 971

models, building (hobbies)
FineScale Modeler Magazine, 393
Internet Hobbies, 393
Model-Ships, 393
Revell, 393
Testors, 393

Monaco, 882

Mongolia. *See* Asia, history

Montana, 676

Montessori education
American Montessori Society, 257
Association Montessori Internationale, 257
Center for Contemporary Montessori Programs, The, 257
International Montessori Index of Schools, 257
International Montessori Society, 257
Materials Company of Boston, The, 257
Montessori Foundation, The, 257
Nienhuis: Montessori Teaching Materials, 257

mortgages. *See* real estate, financing/mortgaging

motels/hotels. *See* lodging

motivational and self-improvement information. *See also* advice; hypnosis
AchievementRadio.com, 558
Deepak Chopra, 558
Dr. Phil, 558
John Gray, 558
Les Brown, 558
Motivational Speakers, 559
MotivationalQuotes.com, 558
Self-Growth.com, 559
Successories.com, 559
Suze Orman, 559
Tony Robbins: Resources for Creating an Extraordinary Quality of Life, 559
Zig Ziglar, 559

motorcycles
AFMWeb (American Federation of Motocyclists), 560
American Motorcyclist Association, 560
BMW Motorcycles, 560
Ducati, 560
Harley-Davidson, 560
Honda Motorcycles, 560
Horizons Unlimited, 560
Indian Motorcycles, 561
Junk Yard Dog, 475
Junk Yard Parts Online, 475
Kawasaki.com, 561
motogranprix.com, 561
Motorcycle Online, 561, 728
Motorcycle Riders Foundation, 561
Two Wheel Freaks, 561
Yamaha, 561

mountain biking. *See also* backpacking; hiking
Big Island Mountain Biking Trail Guide, 95
Bike Ride Online, 92
Cannondale, 93
Diamondback Bikes, 95
Dictionary of Mountain Bike Slang, 95
Dirt World, 95
International Mountain Bicycling Association, 95
Marin, 93
Merlin Bicycles, 93
Mountain Bike Action, 95
Mountain Bike Hall of Fame, 95
Mountain Bike Magazine, 95
Mountain Bike Trailsource, 96
Mountain Cycle, 96
Mountain Workshop Dirt Camp, 96
MTBR.com: The Ultimate Mountain Biking Resource, 96
Road Bike Review, 96
Rocky Mountain Bicycles, 96
Santa Cruz Bicycles, 96
Trails from Rails, 94
Trails.com, 96
Trek Bicycle Corporation, 94

Western Spirit Cycling, 96

movies/film

Amazon.com, 907
Blockbuster, 908
Buy.com, 908
Chumbo.com, 188
CinemaNow!, 562
Classic SciFi, 789
Comic Book Movies, 185
Comics2Film, 789
Disney.com-The Website for Families, 36
DreamWorks Kids, 487
DVD Price Search, 906
dvdfile.com, 907
E! Online, 562, 854
Encyclopedia of Fantastic Film and Television, 790
festivals
Cannes Film Festival, 562
Nonstop Film Festivals, 563
Sundance Film Festival, 563
Tribeca Film Festival, 563
Film Affinity, 562
Film Bug: Guide to the Movie Stars, 562
Film Festival Today, 906
Gallery of Monster Toys, The, 865
HBO (Home Box Office), 854
Hitchhiker's Guide to the Galaxy: The Movie, The, 791
Hollywood Video, 908
horror
Dark Worlds, 412
Horror.com, 412
Horror.net, 412
HorrorMovies.com, 412
Horrorview.com, 412
Upcoming Horror Movies, 413
independent film
AtomFilms, 563
BMW Films, 563
IFILM, 563
IndieFilmSpot, 563
Richmond Moving Image Co-Op, 563
UndergroundFilm.org, 564
Internet Movie Database, 562
Jesus Film Project, 772
Look What I Found in My Brain!, 791
Lord of the Rings Movie Site, 791
Matrix, The, 791
Movies.com, 562
museums
Berkeley Art Museum/Pacific Film Archive, 573
California Museum of Photography, 573
George Eastman House: International Museum of Photography and Film, 573
International Center of Photography, 573
National Museum of Photography, Film, and Television, 574
Smithsonian Photographs Online, 574
Underwater Photography: Philip Colla, 574
Nation, The, 625
Netflix.com, 907
Outpost, 908
Reel.com, 816, 908
reviews, 564
Rick's Movie Graphics and Posters, 176-177
Sci-Fi Site, The, 792
Science Fiction and Fantasy World, 792
Science Fiction Crowsnest, 791
Science Fiction Museum Hall of Fame, 792
Science Fiction Weekly, 725, 792
SciFi Source, 793
SCIFI.COM, 792
Screen Actor's Guild, 862
Screenwriters Online, 961
SF-Lovers, 793
Sky Captain and the World of Tomorrow, 793
Star Wars Official Site, 793
studios
20th Century Fox, 564
DreamWorks, 564
First Look Features, 564
Lionsgate, 565
MGM & Orion Pictures, 565
Miramax, 565
New Line Cinema, 565
Paramount, 565
Sony Pictures, 565
United International Pictures, 565
Universal Pictures, 565
Universal Studios, 37, 565
Walt Disney Studios, 565
Warner Bros. & Castle Rock, 565
Suncoast Video, 908
Take the Lead, 212
theaters
Cinemark & IMAX, 565
Fandango, 566
Hollywood.com, 566
Moviefone, 566
Regal Cinemas, 566
Things from Another World, 908
Top Mystery, 608
Van Helsing, 793
Variety.com, 856
Virus, 794

MP3s

buying
ARTISTdirect, 577
audiogalaxy, 578
BuyMusic@Buy.com, 578
eFolkMusic.com, 578
eMusic, 578
Epitonic.com, 578
Furthur Network, 578
iMesh, 578
iTunes, 578
liveplasma, 579
MP3.com, 579
Napster, 579
Rhapsody, 579
URGE, 579
Virgin Digital, 579
sharing/search engines, 583-584

multi-user games
- MPOGD, 341
- Multi-Player Online Games Directory, 337
- MultiPlayerGames.com, 341
- Play Free Online Games, 341
- Star Wars Galaxies, 337

multimedia. *See* video and multimedia

museums
- American Museum of Photography, 692
- architecture
  - *Chicago Athenaeum: The Museum of Architecture and Design, The, 567*
  - *Getty Center, 567*
  - *National Building Museum, 567*
  - *Octagon Museum, The, 568*
  - *Skyscraper Museum, The, 568*
- art
  - *American Visionary Art Museum, 568*
  - *Andy Warhol Museum, the, 568*
  - *Art Institute of Chicago, The, 568*
  - *Artcyclopedia, 568*
  - *Asian Art Museum of San Francisco, 568*
  - *Cincinnati Art Museum, 568*
  - *Columbia Museum of Art, The, 569*
  - *Fine Arts Museums of San Francisco, 569*
  - *Guggenheim Museums, 569*
  - *Harvard University Art Museums, 569*
  - *Indianapolis Museum of Art, 569*
  - *J. Paul Getty Museum, 569*
  - *Kemper Museum of Contemporary Art, The, 569*
  - *Le Louvre, 569*
  - *Los Angeles County Museum of Art, 570*
  - *Metropolitan Museum of Art, New York, 570*
  - *Museum of Bad Art, 570*
  - *Museum of Fine Arts, Boston, 570*
  - *Museum of Fine Arts, Houston, 570*
  - *Museum of Modern Art, New York, 570*
  - *National Gallery of Art, 570*
  - *National Gallery of Canada, 570*
  - *Royal Ontario Museum, 571*
  - *San Francisco Museum of Modern Art, The, 571*
  - *Smithsonian Institution, The, 571*
  - *Web Gallery of Art, 571*
- Aviation Museum Locator, 68
- Barrel Organ Museum, The, 599
- Candy Wrapper Museum, 148
- Children's Museum of Indianapolis, 567
- Cold War Museum, The, 915
- Computer History Museum, 188
- Denver Museum of Nature & Science, 611
- Encyclopedia Smithsonian, 756
- Exploratorium, 567
- Field Museum of Natural History, 233
- Guggenheim Museum, 382
- history and culture
  - *Morikami Museum and Japanese Gardens, 571*
  - *Museum of Tolerance, 571*
  - *National Civil Rights Museum, 571*
  - *UCLA Fowler Museum of Cultural History, 571*
  - *United States Holocaust Memorial Museum, 572*
  - *Wright Brothers Aeroplane Company and Museum of Aviation, 572*
- International Bowling Museum and Hall of Fame, 120
- International Boxing Hall of Fame, 122
- International Museum of Cartoon Art, 186
- International Surfing Museum, 927
- International UFO Museum and Research Center, 893
- Mark Rosenstein's Sailing Page, 109
- Mojo's Musical Museum, 483
- Motorsports Hall of Fame, 55
- Mountain Bike Hall of Fame, 95
- Museum of the History of Mexico, 386
- MuseumStuff.com, 567
- Naismith Memorial Basketball Hall of Fame, 87
- National Atomic Museum, 916
- National Baseball Hall of Fame, 84
- National Cartoon Museum, 421
- National Civil Rights Museum, 168, 383
- National Gallery of Arts, 483
- National Inventors Hall of Fame, 453
- National Museum of the American Indian, 567
- National Museum of the U.S. Air Force, 70
- National Museum of Women in the Arts, 951
- natural history
  - *American Museum of Natural History, 572*
  - *Carnegie Museum of Natural History, The, 572*
  - *Cleveland Museum of Natural History, The, 572*
  - *Field Museum, The, 572*
  - *Florida Museum of Natural History, 572*
  - *Natural History Museum in the United Kingdom, 573*
  - *Natural History Museum of Los Angeles County, 572*
  - *Smithsonian National Museum of Natural History, 573*
  - *Swedish Museum of Natural History, 573*
  - *University of California Museum of Paleontology, 573*

Notebaert Nature Museum, 612
organizations
American Association of Museums, 574
Group for Education in Museums, 574
Museum Security Network, The, 574
photography and film
Berkeley Art Museum/Pacific Film Archive, 573
California Museum of Photography, 573
George Eastman House: International Museum of Photography and Film, 573
International Center of Photography, 573
National Museum of Photography, Film, and Television, 574
Smithsonian Photographs Online, 574
Underwater Photography: Philip Colla, 574
Professional Wrestling Online Museum, 958
Raggedy Ann & Andy Museum, 175
River and Rowing Museum, 922
San Diego Model Railroad Museum, 394
science and technology
Adler Planetarium and Astronomy Museum, 574
Exploratorium, The, 574
Museum of Contemporary Ideas, The, 575
Museum of Science and Industry, Chicago, The, 575
National Museum of Science and Technology, Canada, 575
Oregon Museum of Science and Industry, 575
Questacon: National Science and Technology Centre, 575
Shedd Aquarium, 575
Stephen Birch Aquarium Museum, 575
Smithsonian Institution Libraries, 759
Smithsonian National Air and Space Museum, 70
Smithsonian National Museum of American History, 389
Smithsonian Natural History Museum, 376
Smithsonian NMNH Dinosaur Home Page, 234
Stephen Birch Aquarium Museum, 649
Surf World Museum-Torquay, 927
Susan B. Anthony House Museum and National Landmark, 384
Whale Museum's Orca Adoption Program, The, 276
music. *See also* podcasts; radio; theater and musical
alternative
Alternative Addiction, 585
AlternativeMusic.com, 585
Ink Blot Magazine: Deep Coverage of Great Music, 585
Insound, 585
ModernRock.com, 585
Nettwerk Productions, 586
Sub Pop Records Online, 586
Bird Song Matcher, 102
bluegrass
Banjo Tablatures and Bluegrass Information, 586
Blistered Fingers, 586
Bluegrass Unlimited, 586
Bluegrass World, 586
BlueGrassRoots Master Catalog Search, 586
Canyon Country Bluegrass Festival, 586
Central Texas Bluegrass Association, 586
Huck Finn's Country and Bluegrass Jubilee!, 587
iBluegrass Magazine, 587
Intermountain Acoustic Music Association, 587
International Bluegrass Music Association, 587
Society for the Preservation of Bluegrass Music in America, 587
Sugar Hill Records, 587
Top, 100 Bluegrass Sites, 587
Tottenham Bluegrass Festival, 587
Washington Bluegrass Association, 588
Welcome to Planet Bluegrass!, 588
CAIRSS for Music, 762
CDs, buying, 576-577
Christian
CCM Magazine.com, 588
Christian Music Resources, 588
Christianity Today: Music Section, 588
ChristianMusic.org, 588
Jamsline: The Christian Music Info Source, 588
classical
Adante: Everything Classical, 588
American Classical Music Hall of Fame, 588
Classical Guitarist, The, 589
Classical MIDI Connection, The, 589
Classical Music Archives, 589
Classical Music of The WWW Virtual Library, 589
Classical Net, 589
Classical USA, 589
Essentials of Music, 589
Gramophone, 589
Klassikne, 590
Mozart Project, The, 590
MusicOnline Classical Music Directory, 590
New York Philharmonic, 590
Piano Nanny, 590
Sony Classical, 590
symphony orchestra information, 590
XLNC1.org, 590

country
- *CMT.com, 591*
- *Country Music Awards, 590*
- *GAC TV: Great American Country TV, 591*
- *History of Country Music, 591*
- *Jack Ingram, 591*
- *Women of Country, 591*

DMI Music & Media Solutions, 521

E! Online, 854

ethnic
- *Afro-Caribbean Music, 591*
- *Ari Davidow's Klezmer Shack, 591*
- *Caribbean Music, 592*
- *Charts All Over the World, 592*
- *Dirty Linen, 592*
- *Flemenco Guitar, The, 592*
- *Folk Australia, 592*
- *Irish and Celtic Music on the Internet, 592*
- *JewishMusic.com, 592*
- *KiwiFolk: Folk and Acoustic Music in New Zealand, 592*
- *Latin Music Online, 580*
- *Mbira, 592*
- *Music in Scotland, 593*
- *Norwegian Music Information Centre, 593*
- *Peruvian Music, 593*
- *Puro Mariachi, 593*
- *Rhytm Fusion-Musical Instruments from Around the World, 600*
- *Songs of Indonesia, 593*
- *Temple Records, 593*
- *Welcome to Bali & Beyond, 593*
- *World Music Store, 593*

events
- *Blues Festivals, 584*
- *Festivals.com, 584*
- *JamBase, 584*
- *Mardi Gras Official Website, 584*
- *Mojam, 584*
- *Pollstar: The Concert Hotwire, 585*
- *Ticketmaster.com, 585*
- *TicketWeb, 585*
- *tkt.com, 585*

Feminist Arts-Music, 950

folk, 726

information, news, and reviews
- *Alternative Press Online, 580*
- *AMG All Music Guide, 580*
- *ANTI-, 580*
- *ICE Online, 580*
- *Latin Music Online, 580*
- *Launch Your Yahoo! Music Experience, 580*
- *MetaCritic, 580*
- *MuchMusic, 581*
- *Music Critic, 581*
- *Music Yellow Pages, 581*
- *MustHear, 581*
- *NME (New Music Express), 581*
- *NY ROCK, 581*
- *Rock on TV, 581*
- *RollingStone.com, 581*
- *SPIN.com, 582*
- *VH1.COM, 582*
- *VIBE, 582*
- *World Cafe, 582*

instruments
- *8th street.com, 599*
- *Accordions International, 599*
- *Barrel Organ Museum, The, 599*
- *Fender, 599*
- *Gear4Music, 599*
- *Gibson Musical Instruments, 599*
- *Guitar: WholeNote.com, 599*
- *Guitarsite.com, 599*
- *Hubbard Harpsichords, Inc., 600*
- *Internet Cello Society, The, 600*
- *LOOPLABS, 600*
- *Mid-East Mfg. Co., 600*
- *Music House, The, 600*
- *Rhythm Fusion-Musical Instruments from Around the World, 600*
- *Unicorn Strings Music Company, 600*
- *Yamaha, 600*

jazz
- *All About Jazz, 594*
- *BBC Music-Jazz, 594*
- *Down Beat Magazine, 594*
- *Jambands, 594*
- *Jazz Corner, 594*
- *Jazz Online, 594*
- *Jazz Review, The, 594*
- *Jazz Roots, 595*
- *JAZZ, 594*
- *Passion for Jazz, A, 595*
- *Red Hot Jazz Archive, 595*

Juliard Bookstore, 115

Lesbian and Gay Bands of America, 348

lyrics
- *A-Z Lyrics, 582*
- *Burt Bacharach: A House Is Not a Home Page, 582*
- *Led Zeppelin Lyrics, 582*
- *LYRICS Download.com, 582*
- *Lyrics Search Engine, 582*
- *Lyrics.com, 582*
- *Musicnotes.com, 583*
- *National Anthems, 583*

Mojo's Musical Museum, 483

MP3s
- *buying, 577-579*
- *sharing/search engines, 583-584*

Music Schools, 180

Nashville Scene, 889

opera
- *Aria Database, The, 595*
- *Bathory Erzsebet: Elizabeth Bathory, 595*
- *FanFaire, 595*
- *Los Angeles Opera, 595*
- *Metropolitan Opera, The, 595*
- *New York City Opera, 596*
- *OPERA America, 596*
- *Opera for Kids, 596*
- *Opera Glass, 596*

Opera News Online, 596
Opera Schedule Server, The, 596
Operabase, 596
OperaNet Magazine, 596
OperaStuff.com, 597
Royal Opera House, 597
San Francisco Opera, 597
Seattle Opera, 597
Sydney Opera House, 597
organizations and clubs
AMC: American Music Conference, 601
American Federation of Musicians of the United States and Canada, 601
American Pianists Association, 601
American Society of Composers, Authors, and Publishers, 601
BMI.com, 601
Creative Musicians Coalition, 601
Grammy.com, 602
Just Plain Folks, 602
Ladyslipper Music, 602
NAMM, 602
National Music Publisher's Association, 602
New Media Consortium, 602
Rhythm and Blues Foundation, 602
Wolverine Antique Music Society, 603
Women In Music, 603
pop, 597
radio sites
BBC Radio 4 Website, 603
Bob Rivers Show, The, 603
BRS Web-Radio Directory, 603
CBC Radio, 603
Classic FM, 604
Earth & Sky Radio Series, 604
Hearts of Space, 604
KAOS: Welcome to KAOS!, 604
KEXP Radio, 604
KPIG Radio Online, 604
Live365, 604
MITList Of Radio Stations On The Internet, 604
National Public Radio, 603
NPR: National Public Radio Online, 605
Premiere Radio Networks, 605
Public Radio Exchange, 605
Public Radio Fan, 605
RadioTower, 605
SHOUTcast, 605
Transom, 605
World Radio Network Online, 605
WTOP, 606
Yahoo! Launchcast, 606
Youth Radio, 606
Real Music, 623
Rolling Stone, 729
SecondSpin, 78
SFS Kids, 484-485
software
iTunes, 597
Magix Music Maker, 597
MusicMatch, 598
QuickTime, 598
RealPlayer, 598
Roxio, 598
Shareware Music Machine, 598
Shockwave.com, 598
WinAmp, 598
Windows Media Player, 599
Time Life, 118
Women in the Arts, 348
mutual funds
Brill's Mutual Funds Interactive, 310
Dreyfus Corporation, 310
Fidelity, 310
Janus Funds, 310
Morningstar, 310
Mutual Fund Investor, 310
Personal Fund, 311
ProFunds, 311
Putnam Investments, 311
T. Rowe Price, 311
TCW Mutual Funds, 311
Vanguards, 311
mysteries
ClueLass, 607
Independent Mystery Publishers, 607
Masterpiece Theatre & MYSTERY!, 607
Mysteries Bookshop, 607
Mystery Guide, 607
Mystery Ink, 607
Mystery Net, 607
Mystery Reader, The, 608
Mystery Readers International, 608
Stop, You're Killing Me!, 608
Top Mystery, 608
mythology
Dictionary of Greek and Roman Myths, 609
Egyptian Mythology, 609
Encyclopedia Mythica, 609, 756
Joseph Campbell Foundation, 609
Myth and Culture, 609
Myth Web, 610
Mythology, 609
Mythus: Comparative Mythology, 610
Norse Mythology, 610
THEOI Project, 610

N

NASCAR
Fox Sports NASCAR Site, 57
My Brickyard: Brickyard 400, 57
NASCAR.com, 57
national parks
American Park Network-Camping, 137
Death Valley National Park, 673
Fodor's National Parks, 674
Glacier National Parks, 674
GORP: U.S. National Parks and Reserves, 674
Grand Canyon Official Tourism Page, 674
Grand Canyon Railway, 887

Harper's Ferry NHP Virtual Visitor Center, 674
Maps of United States National Parks and Monuments, 674
Mesa Verde National Park, 674
Mount Rainier National Park, 675
National Parks and Monuments, 383
National Parks and Wildlife Service, 675
National Parks Conservation Society, 675
Olympic National Park, 675
PARKNET: The National Park Service Place, 675
Petrified Forest National Park, 675
Saguaro National Park, 675
Texas Parks and Wildlife, 425
TheGrandCanyon.com, 888
U.S. National Parks, 676
Visit Your National Parks, 138
Yellowstone Net, 676
Yosemite Park, 676

Native-Americans
indianz.com, 628
National Museum of the American Indian, 567

natural history museums
American Museum of Natural History, 572
Carnegie Museum of Natural History, The, 572
Cleveland Museum of Natural History, The, 572
Field Museum, The, 572
Florida Museum of Natural History, 572
Natural History Museum in the United Kingdom, 573
Natural History Museum of Los Angeles, 572
Smithsonian National Museum of Natural History, 573
Smithsonian Natural History Museum, 376
Swedish Museum of Natural History, 573
University of California Museum of Paleontology, 573

nature. *See also* environment; outdoors
Audabon Nature Institute, 611
BBC Nature Site, 611
Becoming Human, 611
Denver Museum of Nature & Science, 611
eNature, 611
eNature.com, 427
English Nature, 611
Natural Resources Defense Council, 612
Nature Canada, 612
Nature Journal, 612
NatureServe.org, 612
Notebaert Nature Museum, 612
RainforestWeb.org, 613
Sierra Club, 613
WWF, 613

Nebraska
Nebraska Travel and Tourism, 889
Omaha Steaks, 317

needlecrafts
A to Z Needlepoint, 614
Angel's Nook, The, 614
Bird Cross Stitch, 614
Embroidery Online, 614
Embroidery.com, 614
FreeEmbroideryStuff.com, 614
Husqvarna, 614
Janome, 615
Megrisoft Embroidery Digitizine, 615
National NeedleArts Association, 615
Needlepoint.com, 615
PatternsOnline, 615
Stitchery.com, The, 615

Netherlands
government information/services, 360
Heineken, 90
Hundred Highlights from the Koninklijke Bibliotheek, 112

networking
3Com, 616
Cable Digital News, 616
Cisco Connection Online, 616
Consortium for School Networking, 616
Emulex Network Systems, 616
HELIOS Software, 616
Hitachi Data Systems (HDS), 616
Home Network Security, 616
How Home Networking Works, 617
Hughes Network Systems, 617
Hummingbird Ltd., 617
IBM Networking Hardware, 617
Interphase Corporation, 617
InterWorking Labs, 617
Intranet Journal, 617
IT Architect, 617
IT Toolbox, 618
ITPRC.com, 618
Jini Connection Technology, 618
Kinesix, 618
Lancom Technologies, 618
Linksys Online, 618
Lucent, 618
Microsoft Servers, 619
Netgear, 619
NetWare Connection, 619
Network Computing Magazine, 619
Network Professionals Association, 619
Network Security Library, 619
Network World, 619
Nortel Networks, 620
Novell, Inc., 620
Plaintree Systems, 620
Practically Networked, 620
Proxim, 620
Softlinx, Inc., 620
TechFest-Networking Protocols, 620
USB, 621
Vicomsoft, 621
Wi-Fi Net News, 621
WindowsNetworking.com, 621
Zhone Technologies, 621

Nevada
- Death Valley National Park, 673
- Golden Nugget, 152
- Lake Tahoe's West Shore Lodging, 885
- Las Vegas, 889
- Peppermill Reno Hotel Casino, 152
- Venetian, 153

new age. *See also* alternative medicine; astrology
- AzNewAge, 622
- Eckankar, 622
- How to Talk New Age, 622
- International Center for Reiki Training, The, 622
- Llewellyn Onlne, 622
- New Age Center, Sedona, Arizona, 622
- New Age Online Australia, 622
- New Age Retailer, 623
- New Age Web Works, 623
- NewAgeJournal.com, 623
- Real Music, 623
- Salem New Age Center, 623
- Tools for Transformation, 623

New Hampshire
- Canobie Lake Park, 36
- NH.com: New Hampshire, 890

New Jersey
- New Jersey and You, 889
- New Jersey Weed Gallery, 345
- Rick A. Ross Institute of New Jersey, 774
- Sands Hotel and Casino, 153

New Mexico
- Albuquerque Aquarium, The, 968
- International UFO Museum and Research Center, 893
- New Mexico State Parks, 675
- New Mexico: America's Land of Enchantment, 890
- Santa Fe, New Mexico, Travel Information, 890

New York
- Albany, New York Theatre and the Arts, 860
- Bronx Zoo, The, 968
- Geography at the University of Buffalo, 353
- Great Escape and Splashwater Kingdom, 36
- Guggenheim Museum, 382
- Guggenheim Museums, 569
- International Center of Photography, 573
- Metropolitan Museum of Art, New York, 570
- Museum of Modern Art, New York, 570
- New York City Ballet, 211
- New York City Marathon, 283
- New York City Opera, 596
- New York Review of Books, 113
- New York State Department of Family Assistance, 833
- New York State, 890
- New York Times Book Review, 113
- New York Times, 632
- NOAH: New York Online Access to Health, 364
- NYSOEA: New York State Outdoor Education Association, 288
- Public Theater, The, 862
- Skyscraper Museum, The, 568
- Statue of Liberty-Ellis Island Foundation, 384
- Tribeca Film Festival, 563

New Zealand
- 100% Pure New Zealand, 876
- government information/services, 360
- history, 380
- KiwiFolk: Folk and Acoustic Music in New Zealand, 592
- VBT, 94

news
- AME Info, 624
- Arts & Letters Daily, 624
- Atlantic Unbound, 624
- BBCi, 854
- CBC.ca News, 624
- Congressional Quarterly, 624
- Google News, 624
- Harper's, 624
- Institute for War and Peace Reporting, 914
- Internet Public Library, 625
- MagazinesAtoZ.com, 625
- Nation, The, 625
- National Journal, 625
- National Review, 625
- New Republic, The, 625
- New York Times: Television, 855
- News Directory, 625
- Newsweek, 625
- Popular Science, 626, 729
- resources
  - *Accuracy in Media, 627*
  - *American Journalism Review, 627*
  - *American Society of Newspaper Editors, 627*
  - *Associated Press, 627*
  - *CyberJournalist.net, 628*
  - *Editor & Publisher, 628*
  - *Feedroom, The, 628*
  - *Freedom Forum, 628*
  - *indianz.com, 628*
  - *Info Today, 628*
  - *Mirror Syndication International, 628*
  - *Newseum, 628*
  - *NewsLink, 629*
  - *oneworld.net, 629*
  - *United Press International (UPI), 631*
  - *WebClipping.com, 631*
  - *Write News, The, 629*
- RushLimbaugh.com, 626
- services
  - *Aljazeera News Service, 629*
  - *allAfrica.com, 629*
  - *BBC News, 629*
  - *Business Wire, 629*
  - *Crayon, 629*
  - *Federal Communication Commission, 629*
  - *InfoBeat, 630*
  - *Paperboy, The, 630*
  - *PBS: Online NewsHour, 630*
  - *PR Newswire, 630*
  - *Reuters, 630*
  - *Rocketinfo, 630*
  - *Sympatico NewsExpress, 630*

U.S. News Media
- *abcNEWS.com, 631*
- *CBS News, 631*
- *Christian Science Monitor, 631*
- *CNN Interactive, 631*
- *Disaster News Network, 631*
- *ESPN.com, 631*
- *FoxNews.com, 632*
- *Los Angeles Times, 632*
- *MSNBC, 632*
- *New York Times, 632*
- *NPR, 632*
- *San Jose Mercury News, 632*
- *TIME, 626*
- *U.S. News & World Report, 626*
- *USA Today, 632*
- *USA Weekend, 626*
- *Wall Street Journal Interactive, 633*
- *Washington Post, 633*

Utne Reader, The, 626
webzines
- *Asia Pacific News, 633*
- *Drudge Report, 633*
- *Economist, The, 633*
- *Emerging Markets, 633*
- *Jane's Defence Weekly, 633*
- *Jane's Foreign Report, 633*
- *Salon.com, 633*
- *Slate, 634*
- *Smoking Gun, The, 634*
- *Veterans News and Information Service, 634*
- *WEBZINE, 634*

Weekend Australian, The, 626
Weekly Standard, The, 626
Yahoo! News, 627
ZDNet-PC Magazine, 627

newspapers
American Journalism Review, 473, 627
American Society of Newspaper Editors, 627
Arts & Letters Daily, 624
Associated Press, 627
Bingo Bugle Online Newspaper, 99
Bowling World, 120
Calvin and Hobbes, 184
CartoonBank, 420
Chicago Tribune's Mortgage Fraud Series, 750
Christian Science Monitor, 631
Collegiate Baseball Newspaper, 82
Columbia Journalism Review, 473
Comics.com, 185
Conservation Online, 111
Crayon, 629
Daryl Cagle's Pro Cartoonist Index, 421
Dear Abby, 15
Dear Lucie, 662
E.W. Scripps, 726
Editor & Publisher, 628
Education Week on the Web, 847
Financial Times, 307
High School Journalism, 473
HighBeam Research, 758
Hill, The, 703
Institute for War and Peace Reporting, 914
Investigative Reporters and Editors, 473
John Rosemond, 660
Journalism.org, 474
JournalismJobs.com, 473
JournalismNet, 473
Los Angeles Times, 632
Metagrid, 728
Mirror Syndication International, 628
Nashville Scene, 889
New York Times Book Review, 113
New York Times Learning Network, 849
New York Times, 632
New York Times: Politics, 704
News Directory, 625
Newseum, 628
Newslink, 474, 629, 729
Newspaper Advertising.com, 61
Newspaper Association of America, 474
North Gate: Berkeley's Graduate School of Journalism, 474
Onion, The, 419
Opinion Journal, 704
Paperboy, The, 630
Poynter.org, 474
Reporters Committee for Freedom of the Press, 474
San Jose Mercury News, 632
Society of Professional Journalists, 474
(un)Official Dave Barry Blog, The, 419
USA Today Education, 253, 850
USA Today Franchise Solutions, 128
USA Today, 632
USA Today: Baseball Weekly, 84
USA Today: Tennis, 858
Wall Street Journal Interactive, 633
Walter Cronkite School of Journalism & Mass Communication, 474
Washington Post Weekend Getaways Guide, 892
Washington Post, 633
washingtonpost.com OnPolitics, 705
Weekend Australian, The, 626
Writers Write Journalism Resources, 474

Nigeria, government information/services, 360

nonprofit and charitable organizations-resources
associations
- *Alliance for Nonprofit Management, 637*
- *Independent Sector, 637*

BoardSource, 635
charitable contributions
- *America's Charities, 637*
- *American Institute of Philanthropy, 637*
- *BBB Wise Giving Alliance, 637*
- *Charitable Choices, 638*
- *Charity Navigator, 638*
- *CharityNet, The, 638*
- *GuideStar, 638*

Hunger Site, The, 638
Independent Charities of America, 638
JustGive.com, 638
Network for Good, 638
Philanthropy Roundtable, 638
World Vision, 639
Charity Village, 635
Chronicle of Philanthropy, The, 635
Council on Foundations, 635
Foundation Center, 635
Foundation Finder, 635
fundraising
Fund$Raiser Cyberzine, 639
Fund-Raising.Com, 639
Grassroots Fundraising Journal, 639
Schoolpop, 639
IRS: Charities, 636
John D. and Catherine T. MacArthur Foundation, 636
National Committee on Planned Giving, 636
Nonprofit Gateway, 636
Nonprofit Genie, 636
Nonprofit Resource Center, The, 636
NPO-NET, 636
organizations
Adobe Community Relations, 639
AT&T Foundation, 639
Ben and Jerry's Foundation, 639
Benton Foundation, 640
Carnegie Foundation, 640
Children's Miracle Network (CMN), 640
Commonwealth Fund, 640
Goodwill Industries International, 640
Habitat for Humanity International, 640
Junior Achievement, 640
Rotary International, 640
United Way of America, 641
Philanthropy.org, 636
Tech Soup, 637
volunteering
20 Ways for Teenagers to Help Other People by Volunteering, 641
Advice for Volunteers, 641
Corporation for National and Community Service, 641
Energize, 641
Global Volunteers, 641
Idealist, 641
Peace Corps, 641
Points of Light Foundation, 642
SERVEnet, 642
VISTA-Volunteers in Service to America, 642
Volunteer Today, 642
Volunteerism in Canada, 642
VolunteerMatch, 642
Volunteers of America, 642
Wilderness Volunteers, 642
North Carolina
North Carolina Outward Bound, 289
North Carolina Zoological Park, The, 970
Norway, 593
numeric analysis
Math Forum: Numeric Analysis, 533
SIAM (Society for Industrial and Applied Mathematics), 533
nursing
AllHeart.com, 643
allnurses.com, 643
American Association of Colleges of Nursing, 643
American Association of Critical-Care Nurses, 643
American Association of Neuroscience Nurses, 643
American Nurses Association, 643
Cool Nurse, 643
Cybernurse.com, 644
Discover Nursing, 644
Interfaith Health Program, 644
National Association of Pediatric Nurse Practitioners, 644
NP Central, 644
Nurse Options USA, 644
Nurse Recruiter, 644
NurseWeek.com, 644
NurseZone, 645
Nursing Education of America, 645
Nursing Spectrum, 645
Nursing Standard, 645
NursingCenter.com, 645
Procare USA, 645
Registered Nurses, 645
School Nurse, 645
WholeNurse, 645
nutrition. *See* diet and nutrition

O

occult, 100, 414
OCD (Obsessive-Compulsive Disorder)
Obsessive-Compulsive Disorder (OCD) Screening Quiz, 553
Obsessive-Compulsive Disorder for Kids, 553
Obsessive-Compulsive Foundation, 553
Oceania, history of, 380
oceans. *See also* scuba diving
American Shore and Beach Preservation Association, 275
Aquatic Network, 647
Coastal America Partnership National Web Site, 274
Enchanted Learning's Guide to the Oceans, 647
National Oceanic and Atmospheric Administration, 272, 647
Ocean Alliance, The, 273, 647
Ocean Channel, The, 647
Ocean Conservancy, The, 648
Ocean Weather, 933
Ocean's Futures Society, 648
Oceana, 647
OceansLink, 648
Planet Ocean, 648
Scripps Institution of Oceangraphy, 648
SeaWeb, 648
SeaWorld, 648

Stephen Birch Aquarium Museum, 649
Surfrider Foundation USA, 273
Surfrider Foundation, 649
Titanic, The Official Archive, 649
Underwater Photography: Philip Colla, 574
Whale Museum's Orca Adoption Program, The, 276
Whales Online, 649
Woods Hole Oceanographic Institution, 649

ODD (Oppositional Defiant Disorder). *See* conduct disorder

office management
123 Sort It, 653
AllBusiness.com, 653
Apple's Office Management Software, 650
CheckWorks.com, 653
Entrepreneur.com, 650
IRS Small Business Site, 650
Kaufmann eVenturing, 650
Microsoft Office Online, 650
morebusiness.com, 653
Office.com, 653
Small Business Administration, 650
SmallBizManager, 653
Startup Journal, 651
United States Postal Service ZIP Code-Look-Up, 654
Zairletter, 654

office supplies
abcoffice.com, 651
Action Office Supplies, Inc., 651
BuyerZone.com, 651
Home Office Direct, 651
Independent Stationers Online, 651
MicroCenter, 651
Office Depot, 652
OfficeFurniture.com, 652
OfficeMax OnLine, 652
Ontime Supplies, 652
PRIME Office Products, 652
Quill Office Products, 652
Staples, Inc., 652
USPS Shipping Supplies Online, 652
Viking Direct, 653

Ohio
Boston Mills-Brandywine Ski Resort, 824
Cedar Point, 36
Children's Theatre, The, 861
Cincinnati Art Museum, 568
Cincinnati Vacation Gateways, 888
Cincinnati Zoo and Botanical Garden, 968
Cleveland Metroparks Zoo, 968
Cleveland Museum of Natural History, The, 572
Paramount's Kings Island, 37
Technology Enhanced Learning and Research (TELR) at Ohio State University, 246

online journals. *See* blogs and blogging

online shopping
Active Plaza, 810
Amazon.com, 810
BabyStyle Clothes, 811
Bloomingdale's, 811
Buy.com, 810
CatalogLink, 810
Coldwater Creek, 811
comparison bots, 813
DELiAs.com, 811
Designer Outlet.com, 811
Dillard's, 812
discount stores, 814
Eddie Bauer, 812
Fashionmall.com, 812
Half.com, 810
HerRoom.com, 812
Home Shopping Network, 810
iQVC, 810
L.L. Bean, 812
Lands' End, 812
Lane Bryant, 812
Lycos Shopping Network, 811
msn Shopping, 811
Neiman Marcus, 812
Netmarket.com, 811
Nordstrom, 812
perfume, 814-815
search engines, 815
speciality items, 816
Target, 811
SPORTS Authority, 816

online trading
CyberTrader, 311
E*TRADE, 312
Firstrade, 312
FOLIOfn, 312
Investing Online Resource Center, 312
Merrill Lynch Direct, 312
Morgan Stanley, 312
Online Trading Academy, 313
Schwab Online Investing, 313
Scottrade, 313
Wachovia, 313

opera
Aria Database, The, 595
Bathory Erzsebet: Elizabeth Bathory, 595
FanFaire, 595
Los Angeles Opera, 595
Metropolitan Opera, The, 595
New York City Opera, 596
OPERA America, 596
Opera for Kids, 596
Opera Glass, 596
Opera News Online, 596
Opera Schedule Server, The, 596
Operabase, 596
OperaNet Magazine, 596
OperaStuff.com, 597
Royal Opera House, 597
San Francisco Opera, 597
Seattle Opera, 597
Sydney Opera House, 597

Oregon
Oregon Home Education Network, 249
Oregon Museum of Science and Industry, 575
Oregon Zoo, 970
Oregon: Travel Information, 890
Portland Marathon, 283
Powell's Books, 116
Spirit Mountain Casino, 153

organic foods
- Campaign to Label Genetically Engineered Foods, 322
- Eden Foods, 323
- GAIAM.com Lifestyle Company, 323
- Organic Alliance, 323
- Organic Consumers Association, 323
- Organic Gardening Magazine, 323
- Organic Trade Association, 323
- Wild Oats, 322

origami
- Joseph Wu's Origami Page, 655
- Origami for Everyone, 655
- Origami Underground, 655
- Origami USA, 655
- Origami, 655
- Paperfolding.com, 655

osteoporosis
- International Osteoporosis, 655
- Medline Plus: Osteoporosis, 656
- National Osteoporosis Foundation, 656
- Osteoporosis: Medications and Other Treatments, 656

outdoors
- adventure travel/ecotourism, 13-14
- American Park Network, 673
- California State Parks, 673
- Campgrounds by City, 673
- camping, 137-141
- canoeing/kayaking, 150
- Canyonlands, 673
- Colorado State Parks and Outdoor Recreation, 673
- conservation, 19, 104, 271-275, 423-425
- Death Valley National Park, 673
- education, 286-291
- Finding Your Way with Map and Compass, 519
- Fodor's National Parks, 674
- Glacier National Parks, 674
- GORP: U.S. National Parks and Reserves, 674
- GORP: Wilderness Area List, 674
- Grand Canyon Official Tourism Page, 674
- Harper's Ferry NHP Virtual Visitor Center, 674
- KnowledgeHound, 16
- L.L. Bean's Park Search, 674
- Maps of United States National Parks and Monuments, 674
- Mesa Verde National Park, 674
- Mount Rainier National Park, 675
- mountain biking, 92-96
- National Parks and Monuments, 383
- National Parks and Wildlife Service, 675
- National Parks Conservation Society, 675
- New Mexico State Parks, 675
- Northwest Trek, 675
- Olympic National Park, 675
- Outside Online, 292
- PARKNET: The National Park Service Place, 675
- Petrified Forest National Park, 675
- rock climbing, 783-785
- Saguaro National Park, 675
- South Carolina State Parks, 676
- Texas Parks and Wildlife, 425
- Texas State Parks, 676
- U.S. Fish and Wildlife Service, 425
- U.S. National Parks, 676
- Yellowstone Net, 676
- Yosemite Park, 676

P

pain management
- American Academy of Pain Management, 539
- American Chronic Pain Association, 539
- Mayo Clinic Pain Center, 540
- Pain.com, 540
- Partners Against Pain, 540
- StopPain.org, 371, 540

painting (art)
- Artist & Craftsman Supply Online, 657
- Elin Pendleton: Free Oil Painting Lessons, 657
- FARP: A Diminutive Survival Guide to Oil Painting, 657
- Interactive Art School: Free Lessons, 657
- Oil Painting Techniques, 657
- Pearl Paint, 657
- WatercolorPainting.com, 658

painting/decorating (home)
- All-Home Decor, 401
- American Society of Interior Designers, 402
- Ballard Design, 402
- Bed Bath & Beyond, 402
- Better Homes and Gardens, 402
- cMYVision, 402
- CrateandBarrel.com, 402
- Design Addict, 402
- Designing Online, 402
- EZblinds.com, 402
- FurnitureFind.com, 403
- FurnitureOnline.com, 403
- Home and Garden Television (HGTV), 403
- Home Fashion Information Network, 403
- Longaberger Baskets, 403
- No Brainer Blinds and Shades, 403
- Pier 1 Imports, 403
- Pottery Barn, 403
- Rental Decorating, 403
- Stencil Ease Home Decor and Craft Stencils, 404
- Traditional Home Magazine, 404
- unicaHOME, 404
- UrbanScapes, 404

Pakistan
- government information/services, 361
- history, 380

Palestine, history of, 387

panic disorders. *See* anxiety and panic disorders

paragliding. *See* hang gliding and paragliding

paranoia, 553

parenting
- adolescents, 661-663
- adoption, 10-12
- babies, 71-73, 663-664
- Bizy Moms, 128
- Canadian Parents Online, 659
- Caring for Kids, 659
- childcare, 162-163
- Facts for Families, 659
- Family Education Network: A Parenting and Education Resource, 659
- Family Resource Center, 659
- FamilyTime, 659
- Fathering Magazine, 542
- gay/lesbian/bisexual/transgender issues, 347-348
- Girl Power! Campaign, 659
- Home & Family Network, 766
- Homework Help for Parents, 256
- iParenting.com, 660
- John Rosemond, 660
- K-6, 664-666
- KidSource, 660
- Men Stuff, 543
- Mothering Magazine, 660
- National Fatherhood Initiative, 543
- National Parenting Center, The, 660
- NCF-National Center for Fathering, 660
- Parenthood.com, 660
- Parenting.com, 661
- Parenting.org, 661
- Parents-Talk.com, 661
- Positive Parenting, 661
- single parenting, 666-667
- special needs children, 668-670
- stay-at-home parents, 670-671
- stepparenting, 671-672
- Teenagers Today, 853
- Twins Magazine, 731
- WholeFamily Center, The, 661
- Working Mother, 661

parks
- American Park Network, 673
- California State Parks, 673
- Campgrounds by Cit, 673
- Canyonlands, 673
- Colorado State Parks and Outdoor Recreation, 673
- Death Valley National Park, 673
- Fodor's National Parks, 674
- Glacier National Parks, 674
- GORP: U.S. National Parks and Reserves, 674
- GORP: Wilderness Area List, 674
- Grand Canyon Official Tourism Page, 674
- Harper's Ferry NHP Virtual Visitor Center, 674
- L.L. Bean's Park Search, 674
- Maps of United States National Parks and Monuments, 674
- Mesa Verde National Park, 674
- Mount Rainier National Park, 675
- National Parks and Wildlife Service, 675
- National Parks Conservation Society, 675
- New Mexico State Parks, 675
- Northwest Trek, 675
- Olympic National Park, 675
- PARKNET: The National Park Service Place, 675
- Petrified Forest National Park, 675
- Saguaro National Park, 675
- South Carolina State Parks, 676
- Texas State Parks, 676
- U.S. National Parks, 676
- Yellowstone Net, 676
- Yosemite Park, 676

party planning. *See* holidays and celebrations

patents
- All About Trademarks, 132
- American Intellectual Property Law Association (AIPLA), 133
- American Patent and Trademark Law Center, 133
- British Library: Patents, The, 133
- By KIDDS for KIDDS, 133
- Community of Science: U.S. Patent Search, 133
- Delphion Intellectual Property Network, 133
- General Information Concerning Patents, 133
- Intellectual Property Mall, 133
- InventNet, 452
- Inventors Assistance Resource Directory, 452
- KuesterLaw Resource, 133
- Lemelson Center, 453
- Lemelson-MIT Program, 453
- National Inventor Fraud Center, 453
- Patent Act, 133
- Patent and Trademark Office, 134
- PatentCafe.com, 453
- Patent Law Links, 134
- U.K. Patent Office, 134
- U.S. Patent and Trademark Office, 454

patios. *See* decks and patios

PCs
- Annoyances.org, 191
- GoToMyPC, 192
- Microsoft Product Support Services, 192
- PC Guide, 192
- PC World, 192
- PCs for Everyone, 192
- troubleshooting, 199
- Windows, 192
- WinPlanet, 192
- Woody's Watch, 192

pediatrics
- American Academy of Pediatrics, 71, 367, 677
- American Board of Pediatrics, 677
- American Pediatric Society/Society for Pediatric Research, 677
- Arkansas Children's Hospital, 373
- Canadian Pediatric Society, 677
- Caring for Kids, 659
- Child and Adolescent Health and Development, 367
- Child Health Research Project, 367

Children with AIDS Project, 366
Children with Diabetes, 677
Children's Hospital and Regional Medical Center, Seattle, 368
Children's Hospital Boston, 367-368
Children's Hospital of Philadelphia, The, 368
Contemporary Pediatrics, 677
CribLife 2000, 663
Dr. Greene's HouseCalls, 678
Dr. Greene: Toddlers, 663
drSpock.com, 368
Family Education Network: A Parenting and Education Resource, 659
GeneralPediatrics.com, 678
I Am Your Child, 678
India Parenting, 678
iParenting.com, 660
Johns Hopkins Children's Center, 678
KidsHealth, 368
KidsHealth.org, 665
KidSource Online, 678
La Leche League International, 678
Medline Plus: Pregnancy, 711
MedlinePlus Doctor and Dentist Directories, 678
Medscape: Pediatrics, 678
National Childhood Cancer Foundation, 679
National Healthy Mothers, Healthy Babies Coalition, 72-73
National Institute of Child Health and Human Development, 368
OBGYN.net, 711
Parenthood.com, 660
Parents of Premature Babies, 73
Pediatric Infectious Disease Journal, 679
Pediatrics in Review, 679
Pregnancy & Parenting, 73
Riley Hospital for Children, 368
St. Jude Children's Research Hospital, 368

Pennsylvania
American Anorexia and Bulimia Association, 551
Andy Warhol Museum, The, 568
Children's Hospital of Philadelphia, The, 368
Franklin Institute, 452
Hershey Park, 37
OncoLink: University of Pennsylvania Cancer Center Resources, 147
Philadelphia Zoo Online, 970
Pittsburgh Zoo and Aquarium, 971

perfume
FragranceNet, 814
Perfumania, 814
Perfume Center, 814
Perfume Emporium, 815
Smell This, 815
Uncommon Scents, 815

personal histories, investigating. *See* background checks

personality disorders
Borderline Personality Disorder, 553
Mayo Clinic: Personality Disorders, 554
National Education Alliance for Borderline Personality Disorder, 554
National Mental Health Association: Personality Disorders, 554
Personality Disorder Test, 554
Personality Disorders, 554

personals/services (dating)
2ofaKind Online, 214
Christian Matchmaker, 214
eCRUSH, 214
eHarmony.com, 214
LoveCity, 214
Match.com, 214
OkCupid!, 215

Peru
government information/services, 361
Peruvian Music, 593

pets. *See also* animals
birds, 102-104
Birds n Ways, 103
Breederlink.com, 680
caring for, 681-684
cats, 154-155
dogs, 237-238
exotic, 681
KnowledgeHound, 16
PAWS: Pets Are Wonderful Support, 680
Pet Car Travel Tips, 874
Pets Welcome, 878
Pets4You, 680
supplies, 684-685
Travel Pets, 680
Virtual Pet Cemetery, 680
Yahoo! Pets, 680

philanthropy. *See* nonprofit and charitable organizations

Philippines. *See* Asia, history

philosophy. *See also* religion
Absolutearts.com, 46
Academic Info: Philosophy, 686
American Philosophical Organization, 686
Dharma the Cat, 686
Ephilosopher, 686
EpistemeLinks.com: Philosophy Resources on the Internet, 686
Internet Encyclopedia of Philosophy, 686, 767
new age, 622-623
Nietzche Page at Stanford, 686
No Dogs or Philosophers Allowed, 686
Philosophical Gourmet Report, The, 687
Philosophy Around the Web, 687
Philosophy Now, 687
Plato's Dialogues, 687
PSYCHE, 687
Questia: Philosophy, 687
Radical Academy, The, 687
Religion and Philosophy Websites, 768
Stanford Encyclopedia of Philosophy, 687
Taoism and the Philosophy of Tai Chi Chuan, 528
Theosophical Society, 687

phone books. *See also* telephone directories
- 555-1212.com Area Code Lookup, 760
- AnyWho Toll-Free Directory, 760
- InfoSpace.com, 761
- Internet 800 Directory, The, 761
- PhoNETic, 761
- SuperPages.com, 761
- Switchboard, 761

photography
- ACES HIGH: The Finest in Aviation Photography, 68
- Aircraft Images Archive, 68
- American Museum of Photography, 692
- Apogee Photo, 692
- Astronomy Picture of the Day, 49
- BetterPhoto.com, 692
- cameras, 688-690
- Conservation Online, 111
- digital, 688-692
- Focus on Photography, 692
- George Eastman House: Timeline of Photography, 692
- Getty Images, 692
- History of Photography, 692
- International Center of Photography, 693
- Jesse Davidson Aviation Archives, 69
- Knowledgehound, 693
- KODAK: Taking Great Pictures, 693
- LIFE Magazine, 727
- Luminous Landscape, 693
- Masters of Photography, 693
- Mirror Syndication International, 628
- museums, 573-574
- National Geographic, 353, 693
- New York Institute of Photography, 693
- Online Photography Courses, 693
- Photo Arts, 693
- Photography Review, 694
- Photolinks Database, 694
- PhotoSecrets, 694
- PhotoSig, 694
- PopPhoto.com, 694
- Professional Photographers of America, 694
- sharing photos online, 691-692
- Shutterbug Online, 694
- Shutterbug, 730
- Wedding Photography-Advice for the Bride and Groom, 939
- White Water Photos, 921
- Worth1000.com, 332

pilates
- Balanced Body Pilates, 282
- Pilates Center, The, 282
- Pilates Method Alliance, 282
- Pilates Studio, 282
- Power Pilates, 282
- Winsor Pilates: Official Site, 282

ping-pong. *See* table tennis

plumbing
- Plumbing Tips, 411
- Plumbing, 101, 411
- theplumber.com, 411
- Toiletology, 101, 411

podcasts. *See also* music; radio
- Apple iTunes: Podcasts, 695
- Digital Podcast, 695
- DopplerRadio, 695
- FeedValidator.org, 695
- iLounge, 695
- IndieFeed, 695
- iPodder.org, 695
- Juice, 696
- NIMIQ, 696
- Pod101, 696
- Podcast Alley, 696
- Podcast Bunker, 696
- Podcast Central, 696
- Podcast Network, 696
- Podcast Reviews, 697
- Podcast Tutorial, 697
- podcast.net, 696
- Podcasting News, 697
- Podfly, 697
- Yahoo! Podcasts, 697

poetry
- Bad Poetry Page, 698
- Bartleby.com Verse, 698
- Boston Book Review, 113
- Eserver Poetry Collection, 698
- Fooling with Words with Bill Moyers, 698
- Giggle Poetry, 698
- Haiku Society of America, 698
- Isle of Lesbos, The, 348
- Look What I Found in My Brain!, 791
- Poetry Archives, 698
- Poetry Daily, 699
- Poetry Express, 699
- Poetry Magazine, 699
- Poetry Slam, Inc., 699
- Poetry Society of America, The, 700
- Poetry, 180, 698
- Poetry.com, 699
- PoetryFoundation.org, 699
- PoetryPoetry, 699
- Poets.org, 700
- slampapi.com, 700
- Teen Ink, 852
- World of Poetry, 700
- Xenith.net, 853

poker
- Poker Pages, 701
- Poker Stars, 701
- Poker Tips, 702
- Poker-Strategy.org, 701
- Poker.com, 701
- PokerRoom.com, 701
- World Poker Tour, 702
- World Series of Poker, 702

politics. *See also* Presidents and Rulers
- Activism.net, 2
- AlterNet, 2
- American Spectator, The, 703
- Atlantic Unbound, 624
- campaigns, 705-707
- Capitol Hill Blue, 703
- CIA World Factbook, 353
- Congressional Quarterly, 624
- Contacting the Congress, 703
- CorpWatch.org, 2
- Digital Freedom Network, 2
- FactCheck.org, 703
- gay/lesbian/bisexual/transgender issues, 349

global. ***See also*** foreign policy
- *Amnesty International USA Women's Human Rights, 948*
- *AntiWar.com, 913*
- *Carnegie Council on Ethics and International Affairs, 328*
- *Center for Defense Information, 895*
- *Center for Reproductive Law and Policy, 949*
- *Center for Security Policy, The, 328*
- *CIA World Factbook, 762*
- *CIA World Factbook: Mexico, 557*
- *Cold War, 915-916*
- *Council on Foreign Relations, 703*
- *DEBKAfile, 913*
- *Department of State (U.S.), 897*
- *eHistory: Middle East, 386*
- *embassy.org, 328*
- *Food and Agriculture Organization of the United Nations, 19*
- *Foreign Policy Association, 328*
- *Foreign Policy in Focus, 328*
- *Global Fund for Women, 950*
- *GlobalSecurity.org, 913*
- *History in the News: The Middle East, 387*
- *Human Rights Watch, 950*
- *Jane's Foreign Report, 633*
- *Korean War, 916*
- *League of Nations Statistical and Disarmament Documents, 383*
- *Middle East History & Resources, 387*
- *Middle East: A Century of Conflict, The, 387*
- *National Security Archive, 388*
- *NATO: The North Atlantic Treaty Organization, 329*
- *Newsweek, 625*
- *Office of International Women's Issues, 952*
- *Politics and Current Affairs Forum, 382*
- *Stratfor Security Consulting Intelligence Agency, 914*
- *terrorism, 917-918*
- *TIME, 626*
- *U.S. Agency for International Development, 329*
- *U.S. News & World Report, 626*
- *UNAIDS, 366*
- *United Nations and the Status of Women, The, 953*
- *United Nations Cyberschool Bus, 263*
- *United Nations, The, 329*
- *Utne Reader, The, 626*
- *Vietnam War, 916-917*
- *Women and Politics Institute, The, 954*
- *Women's Human Rights Net, 954*
- *Women's Human Rights Resources, 954*
- *WomenWatch, 954*
- *World Connected, A, 3*
- *World Population, 764*
- *World War I, 918-919*
- *World War II, 919*

Harper's, 727
Hill, The, 703
HotWired, 727
Idealist.org, 2
Indybay.org, 2
Meetup, 703
Nation, The, 625
National Journal, 625
National Organization for Women (NOW), The, 951
National Review, 625
New Republic, The, 625
New York Times: Politics, 704
Newsweek, 625, 729
Office of the Clerk On-Line Information Center, 704
opensecrets.org, 704
Opinion Journal, 704
parties, 708-709
Political Money Line, 704
Politics1.com, 704
Power Line, 704
RealClearPolitics, 704
RushLimbaugh.com, 626
Salon.com, 633
Slate, 634
SpeakOut-Politics, Activism, and Political Issues Online, 705
They Rule, 3
Time Magazine, 730
TIME, 626
tolerance.org, 3
Town Hall, 705
U.S. News & World Report, 626
United States House of Representatives, 898
United States Senate, 899
Utne Reader, The, 626
Vanity Fair, 731
Voice of the People, 3
Vote.com, 705
washingtonpost.com OnPolitics, 705
Weekly Standard, The, 626
Welcome to the White House, 705, 899
Whitehouse.org, 420
WireTap, 853
Women and Social Movements in the United States: 1600-2000, 954
Yahoo! News, 627

pool. *See* billiards

pop music, 597

post traumatic stress disorder
- American Academy of Experts in Traumatic Stress, The, 554
- David Baldwin's Trauma Information Pages, 554
- International Society for Traumatic Stress Studies, 555
- National Center for Post Traumatic Stress Disorder, 555

posters (collectibles/collecting)
- AllPosters.com, 176
- Art.com, 176
- Chisholm-Larsson Vintage Posters, 176
- PosterGroup.com, 176

Posters, Inc. Historical Posters, 176
Rick's Movie Graphics and Posters, 176-177

prayer
24-7 Prayer, 778
Catholic Prayers, 778
Evangelical Lutheran Church of America, 778
International Prayer Network, 778
LivePrayer, 779
Lutheran Prayer Ministries, 779
National Day of Prayer, 779
Sacred Space, 779
World Ministry of Prayer, 779
World Prayer Network, 779
World Prayers, 779

pregnancy and birth
About.com-Pregnancy/Birth, 710
American Pregnancy Association, 710
Ask Noah About: Pregnancy, Fertility, Infertility, Contraception, 710
BabyUniverse.com, 712
BabyZone, 712
Birth Psychology, 712
Breastfeeding.com, 712
Childbirth.org, 712
contraception and abortion, 713-714
Endometriosis, 370
ePregnancy.com, 710
Fit Pregnancy, 710
Healthy Pregnancy, 710
infertility, 714-715
Labor of Love, 710
Medline Plus: Pregnancy, 711
midwifery, 715-716
miscarriage, 716-717
National Campaign to Prevent Teen Pregnancy, 711
OBGYN.net, 711
Pregnancy Daily, 711
Pregnancy Magazine, 711
Pregnancy Today, 711
Pregnancy-info.net, 711
Pregnancy.org, 711
StorkNet, 711
SureBaby.com, 712
TASC: The American Surrogacy Center, Inc., 953
Web by Women, foir Women, 953
Weight Gain Estimator, 712
West Side Pregnancy Resource Center, 712

preschool
Chateau Meddybemps, 259
Everything Preschool, 259
FamilyEducation, 259
First-School, 259
KinderCare, 260
Perpetual Preschool, The, 260
Preschool Express, 260
Preschool Page, 260
PreschoolEducation.com, 260
ReadyWeb Home Page, 260
SuperKids Software Review, 260

preservation
American Shore and Beach Preservation Association, 275
Environmental Defense Fund, 275
Environmental Explorers Club, 276
Environmental Protection Agency's Office of Water, 276
NEI: Nuclear Energy Institute, 276
United States Environmental Protection Agency, 276
Whale Museum's Orca Adoption Program, The, 276

presidents and rulers
American Presidents: Life Portraits, 718
British Prime Ministers, 718
Emperors of Sangoku: China, India, and Japan, 718
France Rulers, 718
Germany: Chancellors, 718
Grolier's Online: The American Presidency, 255
Mount Rushmore, 383
National Archives and Records Administration, 759
National First Ladies' Library, 759
POTUS: Presidents of the United States, 718
Presidents of the United States, The, 719
Prime Ministers of Canada, 719
Russian Leaders, 719

privacy (Internet). ***See also*** **security (Internet)**
Ad-Aware, 442
Ad-Muncher, 442
Anonymizer.com, 442
Anti-Phishing Workgroup, 442
BBBonline, 442
Center for Democracy and Technology, 442
CookieCentral.com, 443
CyberPatrol, 443
Electronic Frontier Foundation, 443
Fight Indentity Theft, 443
How Not to Get Hooked by a 'Phishing' Scam, 443
ID Theft Affidavit, 443
Internet Watcher, 443
Privacy Rights Clearinghouse, 443
SpyBot, 443
Spyware Encyclopedia, 444
SpyWare Info, 444
TRUSTe, 444
Webroot, 444

private education
Council for American Private Education, 258
Eschoolsearch.com, 258
Independent Schools Association of the Central States, 258
New York State Association of Independent Schools, 258
Peterson's Education Center, 258
Private School Review, 258
Student Loans and Education Financing, 258
TABS-The Association of Boarding Schools, 258

programming languages (computers)
Active State, 193
Amzi! Prolog+Logic Server, 193

Applescript, 193
ASP Alliance, 193
ASP Free, 193
ASP, 101, 193
Borland C++, 193
Builder.com, 193
CGI Extremes, 194
CGI Resource Index, 194
Code Guru, 194
developers.net: Jobs for Technical Professionals, 194
EarthWeb, 194
eXtreme Programming, 194
Hotscripts.com, 194
HTML Center, 194
HTML Goodies, 194
HTML Guru, 195
HTML Help, 195
java.sun.com, 195
JavaScripts, 195
Linux Advisor, 195
Linux Planet, 195
MSDN Online, 195
Perl.com, 195
Perl: CPAN (Comprehensive Perl Archive Network), 195
Programmers' Heaven, 195
VBWire, 196
Visual Basic: Microsoft Visual Basic, 196
Webmonkey, 196

psychology

American Academy of Child & Adolescent Psychiatry, 549, 720
American Journal of Psychiatry, 720
American Psychiatric Association, 720
American Psychological Association, 722
Archives of General Psychiatry, 720
Dr. Grohol's Psych Central, 722
Encyclopedia of Psychology, 722
Galaxy Psychology, 722
Guide to Psychology and Its Practice, A, 722
Journal Watch Psychiatry, 721
National Association of Cognitive Behavioral Psychology, 722
ParentsMedGuide.org, 721
PSYbersquare, 722
PsychCrawler, 723
Psychiatry Source, 721
Psychology Today, 723
Psychology Works, 723
Psychology,net, 723
Psychology.com, 723
School Psychology Resources Online, 723
Self-Help Magazine, 723
Social Psychology Network, 723

psychosis

Early Psychosis Prevention and Intervention Centre, 555
Psychosis-Glossary, 555

public education

Center on Re-Inventing Public Education, 259
Parents for Public Schools, 259
Public Education Network, 259
Story of Public Education, The, 259

publications

journals and e-zines, 724-725
magazines, 725-732

publishing

Association of American Publishers, 117
AuthorLink!, 960
Baker Book House, 770
Bartleby.com, 960
Books @ Random, 117
Books AtoZ, 117
Broadway Play Publishing, Inc., 861
Canadian Publishers' Council, 118
eBook Directory, The, 117
Harcourt School Publishing, 848
Houghton Mifflin Company, 118
Independent Mystery Publishers, 607
International Data Group, 198
John Wiley & Sons, 118
McGraw-Hill Bookstore, 118
McGraw-Hill School Division, 848
Nolo Press, 513
Pearson Technology Group, 118
Perseus Books Group, 118
Publishers Marketing Association (PMA) Online, 118
Publishers Weekly, 118
RoseDog.com, 961
Time Life, 118
WEBZINE, 634
Write News, The, 961
Writing for Dollars, 962
Xlibris, 962
Young Authors Workshop, 962

puzzles

Kakuro, 340
Sudoku, 341
Thinks.com, 340
Yohoho! Puzzle Pirates, 338

Q

quilting

AIDS Memorial Quilt, The, 733
Bryer Patch Studio, 733
Canadian Quilters' Association, 733
Free Quilt Ideas, 733
From the Heartland, 733
Jinny Beyer Studio, 733
Martingale & Company, 733
McCall's Quilting Magazine, 733
Nancy's Notions, 803
National Quilting Association, 734
Patchwork Mountain, 734
Piecemakers, 734
Planet Patchwork, 734
Quilt Channel, The, 734
Quilter Magazine, The, 734
Quilter's Review, 734
Quilters Online Resources, 734
Quilters Village, 735
Quilting Arts Magazine, 735

Quilting with a Passion, 735
Quiltmaker Magazine, 735
QuiltWear.com, 735
World Wide Quilting Page, 735

quotations
Advertising Quotes, 736
Amusing Quotes, 736
Annabelle's Quotation Guide, 736
Bartlett's Familiar Quotations, 736
Creative Quotations, 736
Daremore Quotes, 736
Dictionary of Quotations, 736
Follow Your Dreams, 736
Freeality Search, 737
Idiomsite, 737
Mathematical Quotation Server, 737
MemorableQuotations.com, 737
Quotation Center, 737
Quotations Archive, 737
Quotations of William Blake, 737
Quotations Page, 737
Quotegeek.com, 737
Quoteland.com, 737
QuoteWorld.org, 738
Quotez, 738
Women's Quotes, 738

R

racing
auto racing
Andretti Home Page, 55
Auto Racing Daily, 55
CATCHFENCE.com, 55
Champ car series, 56
Champ cars, 55
Formula One, 56
Honda Racing, 55
IRL, 56
Motorsports Hall of Fame, 55
NASCAR, 57
NHRA Online, 55
Racecar, 55
bicycling
Analytic Cycling, 92
Bianchi, 92
Bicycling.com, 92
Bike Lane, 92
Bike Ride Online, 92
Cambira Bicycle Outfitters, 93
Competitive Cyclist, 93
Cycling Web, 93
Cyclingnews.com, 93
Shimano, 94
Specialized, 94
Tour de France, 94
VeloNews Interactive, 94
horse, 416
motogranprix.com, 561

radio. *See also* music; podcasts
AchievementRadio.com, 558
Amateur Radio and DX Reference Guide, 391
American Journalism Review, 627
ARRL: National Association for Amateur Radio, 391
Arts & Letters Daily, 624
Associated Press, 627
BBC Radio 4 Website, 603
Bob Rivers Show, Th, 603
BRS Web-Radio Directory, 603
Car Talk, 66
CBC Radio, 603
Classic FM, 604
Coast to Coast AM with George Noory, 893
Dr. Laura, 15
Earth & Sky Radio Series, 604
Earth & Sky, 50
eHam.net, 391
Engines of Our Ingenuity, 452
Federal Communication Commission, 629
Greater Grace World Outreach, 772
Ham Radio Outlet, 392
Hearts of Space, 604
KAOS: Welcome to KAOS!, 604
KEXP Radio, 604
KPIG Radio Online, 604
Live365, 604
Middle East: A Century of Conflict, The, 387
Mirkin Report, 281
MITList Of Radio Stations On The Internet, 604
MyETV: South Carolina Educational TV and Radio, 254
National Public Radio, 603
NewsLink, 629
NPR: National Public Radio Online, 605, 632
On the House with the Carey Brothers, 409
Premiere Radio Networks, 605
Public Radio Exchange, 605
Public Radio Fan, 605
Radio Islam, 776
RadioTower, 605
Rense.com, 894
RushLimbaugh.com, 626
SHOUTcast, 605
Transom, 605
World Radio Network Online, 605
WTOP, 606
Yahoo! Launchcast, 606
Youth Radio, 606

rafting. *See also* boating; sailing
American Whitewater Resources Online, 921
Gorp: Paddlesports, 921
International Rafting Federation, 921
RIVERSEARCH, 921
White Water Photos, 921
Wild and Scenic Rivers, 921
Wildwater Rafting in Canada, 922
Wildwater Rafting, 922
Windfall Rafting, 922

railroads
AAR: Association of American Railroads, 739
Abandoned Railroads of the United States, 739
Abandoned RailServe, 740
Alaskan Railroad, 739
Amtrak, 739
BNSF Railway, 739
Conrail, 739
CSX, 740

Federal Railroad Administration, 740
Freightworld, 740
Great American Station Foundation, 740
Historical Website, The, 740
History of Railroads and Maps, 740
model trains, 394
Railroad Network, 740
Railroad Retirement Board, 781
RailServe, 740
Steam Locomotives, 740
TrainWeb, 741
travel
- *Amtrak, 886*
- *European and British Rail Passes, 886*
- *Grand Canyon Railway, 887*
- *Orient-Express Trains & Cruises, 887*
- *Train Traveling, 887*
- *VIA Rail Canada, 887*
- *Wine Spectator, 731*

Union Pacific Railroad, 741

RC (Radio Control) vehicles

cars
- *Hobby People, 392*
- *Radio Control Car Action Magazine, 392*
- *Tower Hobbies, 392*

planes
- *Great Planes, 392*
- *Radio Control Zone, 392*
- *RC Plane Talk, 393*

real estate

buying/selling
- *Americas Virtual Real Estate Store, 742*
- *Century 21, 742*
- *Coldwell Banker, 742*
- *Commercial Network, The, 742*
- *Domania.com, 742*
- *ERA, 742*
- *GMAC Real Estate, 743*
- *Home Plans, 743*
- *HomeBuilder.com, 743*
- *HomeFair.com, 743*
- *HomeGain, 743*
- *HomeLife Real Estate, 743*
- *Homeseekers.com, 743*
- *HUD: U.S. Department of Housing and Urban Development, 743*
- *International Real Estate Digest, 744*
- *MSN Real Estate, 744*
- *NewHomeNetwork.com, 744*
- *Nolo.com-Real Estate, 744*
- *Owners.com, 744*
- *RalphRoberts.com, 744*
- *Real Estate Center Online, 744*
- *RealEstateabc.com, 744*
- *REALTOR.com, 745*
- *Realty Times, 745*
- *REMAX Real Estate Network, 745*
- *SellMyHome101.com, 745*
- *Zillow, 745*

financing/mortgaging
- *ABN-AMRO, 745*
- *Amortization Schedule, 746*
- *Bankrate.com, 746*
- *BestRate, 746*
- *California Association of Realtors Online, 746*
- *Countrywide Financial, 746*
- *Ditech, 746*
- *E-Loan, 746*
- *Fannie Mae Home Page, 747*
- *Federal Home Loan Banks, 747*
- *FHA Today!, 747*
- *Freddie Mac Home Page, 747*
- *HUD Housing FHA Home Page, 747*
- *Inman News Features, 747*
- *Interest.com, 747*
- *LendingTree.com, 747-748*
- *LoanWorks.com, 748*
- *Mortgage Bankers Association, 748*
- *Mortgage Fraud Blog, 750*
- *Mortgage Payment Calculator, 748*
- *Mortgage Tips, 749*
- *Mortgage, 101, 748*
- *Mortgage-Net, 748*
- *MortgageQuotes.com, 748*
- *MortgageSelect.com, 749*
- *PlanetLoan, 749*
- *Prieston Group's Mortgage Fraud Page, The, 750*
- *QuickenMortgage.com, 749*
- *SunTrust Mortgage, 749*

flipping
- *Flip That House, 749*
- *Flip This House, 749*
- *Flipping Houses, 750*
- *FlippingFrenzy.com, 750*
- *How to Flip Houses, 750*

fraud, 750

relocation services
- *AIM Relocation, 750*
- *Apartments for Rent Online, 750*
- *Employee Relocation Council (ERC), 751*
- *ExecuStay Inc., 751*
- *Moving Local, 751*
- *Moving.com, 751*
- *Relocate America, 751*
- *Relocation Wizard, The, 751*
- *RelocationCentral.com, 751*
- *Rent.net, 751*
- *RPS Relocation Services, 752*
- *Salary Calculator, 752*
- *School Report, The, 752*
- *SchoolMatch, 752*

timeshares
- *2nd Market Timeshare Resales, 752*
- *Hotel Timeshare Resales, 752*
- *RCI vacationNET, 752*
- *Sell My Timeshare Now!, 752*
- *Stroman, 753*
- *TimeLinx, 753*
- *Timeshare Beat, The, 753*

A B C D E F G H I J K L M N O P Q R S T U V W X Y Z

Timeshare User's Group, 753
TimeSharing Today, 753
Vacation Timeshare Rentals, 753
rebates. ***See*** bargains
recipes. ***See*** cooking and recipes
recycling
BioCycle: Journal of Composting and Organics Recycling, 276
Computer Recycling, 276
Earth 911, 276
Freecycle, 277
Imagination Factory, 475
Junkyard Wars, 475
Recycle City, 277
Recycle This!, 277
Recycler's World, 277
Shred-It Mobile Paper Shredding and Recycling, 277
Technology Recycling, 476
reference. ***See also*** writing
dictionaries and thesauri
Acronym Finder, 754
Acronyms and Abbreviations, 754
ARTFL Project: Roget's Thesaurus Search Form, 754
Cambridge Dictionaries, 754
Climbing Dictionary, the, 783
Dictionary.com Definitions, 754
Dictionary.com Translation, 755
iTools.com, 763
Merriam-Webster Online, 755
Online Dictionaries and Glossaries, 755
Thesaurus.com, 755
TravLang's Translating Dictionaries, 755
Word Wizard, The, 755
yourDictionary.com, 755
encyclopedias
Answers.com, 755
Britannica.com, 755
Encarta Online, 756
Encyclopedia Mythica, 609, 756
Encyclopedia of Religion and Society, 767
Encyclopedia Smithsonian, 756
Encyclopedia.com, 756
Grolier Encyclopedia, 756
infoplease.com, 756
Jewish Encyclopedia, 777
Judaism, 101, 777
Medline Plus, 756
Webopedia.com, 756
Wikipedia, 757
World Book Encyclopedia, 757
libraries
American Library Association, 757
American War Library, The, 757
Awesome Library for Teens, 757
Bartleby.com, 757
Bibliomania: The Network Library, 757-758
Center for Research Libraries, 758
HighBeam Research, 758
INFOMINE, 758
Internet Public Library, 758
Library of Congress, The, 758
Library Spot, 758
Libweb-Library Servers on the Web, 758
Lightspan, 758
Medical/Health Sciences Libraries on the Web, 759
National Archives and Records Administration, 759
National First Ladies' Library, 759
National Sporting Library, The, 759
OCLC Online Computer Library Center, Inc., 759
Portico: The British Library, 759
Smithsonian Institution Libraries, 759
Special Libraries Association, 759
Sport Information Resource Center, 760
Sunnyvale Center for Innovation, Invention & Ideas, The, 760
U.S. Department of Education (ED), 760
U.S. National Library of Medicine, 760
Web Library Directory, 760
WWW Virtual Library, 760
phone books
555-1212.com Area Code Lookup, 760
AnyWho Toll-Free Directory, 760
InfoSpace.com, 761
Internet 800 Directory, The, 761
PhoNETic, 761
SuperPages.com, 761
Switchboard, 761
research
Academic Info, 761
Academy of Achievement, 761
Almanac of Policy Issues, 761
Biographical Dictionary, 762
CAIRSS for Music, 762
CIA World Factbook, 762
Consumer Information Center, The, 762
Cook's Thesaurus, The, 754
Defense Almanac, 762
Dismal Scientist, 762
Fact Monster, 762
FedWorld.gov, 762
General Research Resources, 762
Internet FAQ Archives, 762
iTools.com, 763
Librarian's Index, 763
Martindale's: The Reference Desk, 763
MegaConverter, 763
Morse Code and the Phonetic Alphabets, 763
National Geographic Map Machine, 763

Nobel Foundation, The, 763
Old Farmer's Almanac, 763
refdesk.com, 764
Reference Tools, 764
THOR: The Virtual Reference Desk, 764
U.S. Census Bureau, 764
UTLink: Resources by Subject, 764
Vital Records Information: United States, 764
World Population, 764

Reiki
International Association of Reiki Professionals, 764
International Center for Reiki Training, The, 622, 765
Reiki Page, The, 765
Reiki.nu, 765

relationships. *See also* dating; romance
AdoringYou.com, 766
background checks, 74
Dr. Phil, 766
drDrew, 16
Everything2, 16
Femina, 16
Five Love Languages, The, 766
GrowthClimate, 766
Home & Family Network, 766
MarsVenus.com, 766
Men Stuff, 543
online
Facebook, 106
MySpace, 107
Relationship-Talk.com, 17
Third Age, 782

religion. *See also* philosophy
Academic Info: Religion, 767
Adherents-Religion Statistics and Geography, 767
ancient
Ancient Religions and Myths, 768
Antiquity Online, 768
Egyptian Book of the Dead, The, 768
Hellenic Macedonia, 768
atheism
American Atheists, 768
Atheism Central for Secondary Schools, 768
Atheist Alliance, 769
Infidel Guy Show, The, 769
Secular Web, The, 769
BBC World Service-Religions of the World, 767
beliefnet, 767
buddhism
Buddhanet.net, 769
New Kadampa Tradition, 769
Resources for the Study of Buddhism, 769
tharpa.com, 769
Tricycle Review, 769
Christianity
American Baptist Churches USA Mission Center Online, 770
Answering Islam: A Christian-Muslim Dialog, 775
Answers in Action, 770
Augustine, 770
Baker Book House, 770
Best Christian Links, The, 770
Bible Gateway, 770
Catholic Health Association, 373
Catholic Online, 770
Center for Reformed Theology and Apologetics (CRTA), 770
Christian Articles Archive, 771
Christian Camping International, 142
Christian Coalition, The, 708
Christian Matchmaker, 214
Christian Missions, The, 771
Christian Science Monitor, 631
Christianbook.com, 771
Christianity Today, 771
Christianity Today: Single Parenting, 666
Christianity.com, 771
crosswalk.com, 771
Five Points of Calvinism, The, 771
Glide Memorial Church, 771
GodWeb, 771
Gospelcom.net, 771
GraceCathedral.org, 772
Greater Grace World Outreach, 772
Greek Orthodox Archdiocese of America, 772
Harvest Online, 772
Jesus Army, 772
Jesus Film Project, 772
Logos Research Systems, 772
MEND (Mommies Enduring Neonatal Death), 717
Monastery of Christ in the Desert, 772
music, 588
Presyterian Church USA, 773
Project Wittenberg, 773
Religious Society of Friends, 773
Scrolls from the Dead Sea, 773
Spurgeon Archive, The, 773
Trumpet, The, 773
Vatican, 773
World Religions Index, 773
World Vision, 639
cults
FACTnet, 774
Ms. Guidance on Strange Cults, 774
Rick A. Ross Institute of New Jersey, 774
Steven Alan Hassan's Freedom of Mind Center, 774
Encyclopedia of Religion and Society, 767
gay/lesbian/bisexual/transgender issues, 350
Heroes of Faith, 767

Hinduism
Bhagvat Gita, 774
Hindu Kids, 774
Hindu Resources Online, 774
Hindu Universe: Hindu Resource Center, 774
Hinduism Online, 774
Hinduism Today, 775
iskon.com, 775
Understanding Hinduism, 775
Internet Encyclopedia of Philosophy, 767
Islam, 101
Al-Islam, 775
Answering Islam: A Christian-Muslim Dialog, 775
Illustrated Guide to Understanding Islam, 775
International Association of Sufism, 775
Islam and Islamic Studies Resources, 776
IslamiCity in Cyberspace, 776
Muslim Life in America, 776
Online Islamic Bookstore, 776
Radio Islam, 776
Ramadan, 398
Judaism
Ari Davidow's Klezmer Shack, 591
Chabad-Lubavitch in Cyberspace, 776
Conversion to Judaism, 776
Eyes of Glory, 388
History of Hanukkah, 397
Holocaust Chronicle, The, 385
Jewish America, 777
Jewish Encyclopedia, 777
Jewish Theological Seminary, 777
Jewish Virtual Library, 777
JewishMusic.com, 592
Jews for Judaism, 777
Judaism and Jewish Resources, 777
Judaism, 101, 777
Kosher Express, 204
MavenSearch, 777
MyJewishLearning, 777
ORT, 778
Passover on the Net, 398
Shamash, 778
Shtetl: Yiddish Language and Culture, 778
Torah.org, 778
United States Holocaust Memorial Museum, 572
Virtual Jerusalem, 778
new age
AzNewAge, 622
Eckankar, 622
International Center for Reiki Training, The, 622
Llewellyn Online, 622
New Age Center, Sedona, Arizona, 622
New Age Online Australia, 622
New Age Retailer, 623
New Age Web Works, 623
NewAgeJournal.com, 623
Real Music, 623
Salem New Age Center, 623
Tools for Transformation, 623
prayer
24-7 Prayer, 778
Catholic Prayers, 778
Evangelical Lutheran Church of America, 778
International Prayer Network, 778
LivePrayer, 779
Lutheran Prayer Ministries, 779
National Day of Prayer, 779
Sacred Space, 779
World Ministry of Prayer, 779
World Prayer Network, 779
Religion and Philosophy Websites, 768
Religion News Service, 767
religion-online.org, 768
World Prayers, 779
Zen Gardens, 345
research
Academic Info, 761
Academy of Achievement, 761
Almanac of Policy Issues, 761
Biographical Dictionary, 762
CAIRSS for Music, 762
CIA World Factbook, 762
Consumer Information Center, The, 762
Cook's Thesaurus, The, 754
Defense Almanac, 762
Dismal Scientist, 762
Fact Monster, 762
FedWorld.gov, 762
General Research Resources, 762
Internet FAQ Archives, 762
iTools.com, 763
Librarian's Index, 763
Martindale's: The Reference Desk, 763
MegaConverter, 763
Morse Code and the Phonetic Alphabets, 763
National Geographic Map Machine, 763
Nobel Foundation, The, 763
Old Farmer's Almanac, 763
refdesk.com, 764
Reference Tools, 764
THOR: The Virtual Reference Desk, 764
U.S. Census Bureau, 764
UTLink: Resources by Subject, 764
Vital Records Information: United States, 764
World Population, 764
retirement
401K Center for Employers, 780
AARP WebPlace, 780
American Association of Homes and Services for the Aging, 780
Ameriprise, 780
CNN/Money Magazine Retirement, 780
ElderNet, 780

Forbes Retirement Planning, 780
Guide to Retirement Living, 781
Railroad Retirement Board, 781
Retire Early, 781
Retirement Calculators, 781
Retirement Net, 781
Retirement Research Foundation, 781
Retirement with a Purpose, 781
Seniors-Site.com, 781
Social Security Retirement Planner, 782
Third Age, 782

rock climbing
ABC of Rock Climbing, 783
American Mountain Guides Association, 783
American Safe Climbing Association, 783
Big Wall Climbing Web Page, 783
Bouldering, 783
Climber's First Aid, 783
Climbing Dictionary, The, 783
Climbing Online, 784
GORP-Climbing, 784
GPS Rock Climbing Guide, 784
Joshua Tree Rock Climbing School, 784
Nova Online: Lost on Everest, 784
Online Climbing Guide, 784
Rock & Ice: The Climber's Magazine, 784
Rock Climbing Australia, 784
Rock-N-Rescue, 270
RockClimbing.com, 785
RockList, 785
Sportrock Climbing Centers, 785
Touchstone Climbing and Fitness, 785

rodeo
American Junior Rodeo Association, 786
Billy Joe Jim Bob's Rodeo Links Page, 786
Houston Livestock Show and Rodeo, 786
International Gay Rodeo Association, 348
Janet's Let's Rodeo Page, 786
Mesquite Championship Rodeo, 786
Professional Bull Riders, Inc., 786
ProRodeo.com, 786
SLAM! Sports Rodeo, 787
Women's Pro Rodeo Association, 787

roller skating. *See also* inline skating
Finding a Roller Skating Rink, 819
National Museum of Roller Skating, 819
Roller Skating Assocation, 819
USA Roller Sports, 819

romance. *See also* dating; relationships; sexuality
Alive with Love, 788
eHarlequin, 788
LovingYou.com, 788
Romance Club, The, 788
Romance Reader, The, 788
Romance Tips, 788

rowing
Amateur Rowing Association, 922
Independent Rowing News, 922
NCAA Women's Rowing, 922
Paddling@about.com, 922
River and Rowing Museum, 922
Row Works, 922
Row2K.com, 923
Rower's World, 923
Rowing FAQ, 923
Rowing Service, The, 923
RowingLinks-The Internet's Definitive Source for Rowing Links, 923
Simply OarSome, 923
USRowing, 923
Vespoli USA, 923
WorldRowing.com, 923
WWW Virtual Library: Rowing, 924

running. *See also* track and field
American Running Association, 282
American Track & Field, 282
cross-country, 280
Marathon Training, 283
New York City Marathon, 283
Portland Marathon, 283
Road Running Information Center, 283
Runner's Schedule, The, 283
Runner's Web, 283
Runner's World Online, 283
Running Network, 283
Running Times, 283
Venue Sports Inc., 283
WomenRunners.com, 283

Russia
government information/services, 361
history
Alexander Palace Websites, 387
Face of Russia, The, 387
History of Russia, 388
Moscow Landmarks, 383
U.S. Department of State: Russian History, 388
Russian Classical Ballet, 211
Russian Leaders, 719

Russian (languages/lingustics)
English Russian Dictionary, 505
Institute of Modern Russian Culture (IMRC), 505
Lexiteria's Russian Grammar Reference, 505
MasterRussian.com, 505

S

sailing. *See also* cruises; rafting
1001 Boats for Sale, 108
American Sail Training Association, 108
American Sailing Association, 108
Boat Owners World, 108
Boating 4 Kids, 108
Boating Magazine, 108
Boats.com, 108-109

BoatSafeKids, 108
Discover Boating, 109
Good Old Boat Magazine, 109
International Jet Sports Boating Association, 459
JetSki News, 459
jetski.com, 459
Kawasaki, 459
Mark Rosenstein's Sailing Page, 109
Personal Watercraft Illustrated, 459
Powerski Jetboar, 459
Sailboats Inc., 109
SailNet, 109
SBT on the Web, 460
Sea-Doo, 109, 460
Titanic, the Official Archive, 649
U.S. Coast Guard Office of Boating Safety, 109
U.S. Sailing, 110
United States Power Squadrons Web Page, 109
Yachtingnet, 110
Yamaha, 460

Saudi Arabia, government information/services, 361

schizophrenia
Experience of Schizophrenia, The, 555
NARSAD: National Association for Research on Schizophrenia and Depression, 555
Schizophrenia.com, 555
Schizophrenics Anonymous, 555
World Fellowship for Schizophrenia and Allied Disorders, 556

scholarships. *See* financial aid & scholarships

sci-fi and fantasy
Analog Science Fiction and Fact, 789
Asimov's Science Fiction, 789
Classic SciFi, 789
Comics2Film, 789
dark fantasy, 413
Dark Horse, 789
Dark Shadows, 789
Daystrom Institue Technical Library, 790
Encyclopedia of Fantastic Film and Television, 790
FanGrok, 790
Fanspeak, 790
Fantasy and Science Fiction Magazine, 726
Feminist Science Fiction, Fantasy, and Utopia, 790
Forrest J. Ackerman Official Site, 790
Global Episode Opinion Survey, 790
Hitchhiker's Guide to the Galaxy: The Movie, The, 791
Look What I Found in My Brain!, 791
Lord of the Rings Movie Site, 791
Matrix, The, 791
Red Vs. Blue, 420
Satellite News, 791
Sci-Fi Site, The, 792
Science Fiction and Fantasy Research Database, 791
Science Fiction and Fantasy Writers of America (SFWA), 792
Science Fiction and Fantasy World, 792
Science Fiction Book Club, 791
Science Fiction Crowsnest, 791
Science Fiction Museum Hall of Fame, 792
Science Fiction Weekly, 725, 792
SciFan, 792
SciFi Source, 793
SCIFI.COM, 792
SF-Lovers, 793
SFF Net, 793
Sky Captain and the World of Tomorrow, 793
Star Trek, 793
Star Wars Official Site, 793
TV Sci-Fi and Fantasy Database, The, 793
Van Helsing, 793
Virus, 794
World Science Fiction Society, 794

science. *See also* inventions and inventors
American Dairy Science Association (ADSA), 18
astronomy
Amazing Space, 49
American Astronomical Society, 49
Astronomy for Kids, 49
Astronomy Magazine, 49
Astronomy Now On-Line, 49
Astronomy Picture of the Day, 49
BadAstronomy.com, 50
Chandra X-Ray Observatory, 50
Constellation X, 50
Earth & Sky, 50
Event Inventor: Web Sites for Space Mission Projects, The, 50
Griffith Astronomy, 50
High Energy Astrophysics Science Archive Research Center, 50
HubbleSite, 50
International Astronomical Union, 51
Lunar and Planetary Sciences st NSSDC, 51
Mount Wilson Observatory, 51
museums, 574
NASA Earth Observatory, 51
NASA History Office, 51
NASA HumanSpace Flight, 51
NASAKIDS, 51
National Geographic Star Journey, 51
SEDS Internet Space Warehouse, 52
Sky & Telescope, 52
Star Stuff: A Guide to the Night Sky, 52
Views of the Solar System, 52
BBC Science & Nature: Human Body & Mind, 537
Becoming Human, 611

Bill Nye the Science Guy's Nye Labs Online, 253, 478
California State Science Fair, 255
Chem4Kids, 478
Children's Museum of Indianapolis, 567
Community of Science: U.S. Patent Search, 133
Denver Museum of Nature & Science, 611
Discover Magazine, 726
entomology. *See* insects
Exploratorium, 567
HotWired, 727
Intel Education Initiative, 848
Junk Science, 475
Medical/Health Sciences Libraries on the Web, 759
MegaConverter, 763
meteorology, 14
museums, 574-575
NASA Education Sites, 262
NASA John C. Stennis Space Center Education and University Affairs, 252
National Scientific Balloon Facility, 76
News Directory, 625
NHBS Environmental Bookstore, 115
Nova's Online Balloon Race Around the World, 76
OLogy, 484
Ontario Science Centre, 143
physics, 36
PM Zone, 729
Popular Science, 626, 729
Questacon: The National Science and Technology Center, 252
Science Magazine Home, 729
Science of Hockey, 396
Science Source, The, 252
ScienceDaily Magazine-Your Link to the Latest Research News, 729
Scientific American, 730
scifair.org, 262
SciTech Daily Review, 730
Sky & Telescope Online, 730
VolcanoWorld, 486
Yahoo! News, 627

Scotland. *See* United Kingdom

scrapbooking
Addicted to Scrapbooking, 795
Computer Scrapbooking, 795
Creative Memories, 795
Scrapbook.com, 795
Scrapbooking, 101, 795
Scrapbooking.com, 796
ScrapbookingTop50, 796
Scrapjazz, 796

scuba diving. *See also* diving; snorkeling
Aqua Lung, 924
DAN: Divers Alert Network, 924
Deep Sea Divers Den, 924
Doc's Diving Medicine, 924
Gooddive.com, 924
HSA: Handicapped Scuba Association, 924
NAUI Online, 925
PADI: Professional Association of Diving Instructors, 925
Scuba Central, 925
Scuba Diving Magazine, 925
Scuba Schools International, 925
Scuba Yellow Pages, 925
ScubaDuba, 925
Skin Diver Online, 926
Sport Diver, 926
Sub-Aqua Association, 926
YMCA Scuba Program, 926

search engines
120Seconds.com, 907
About.com, 444
AltaVista, 444
Ask.com, 444
Dogpile, 444
Google.com, 445
Lycos.com, 445, 907
Mamma, 445
MetaCrawler, 445
MSN.com, 445
multimedia, 907
Northern Light, 445
Real.com, 907
Search Engine Watch, 445
Singing Fish, 907
Yahoo!, 446

security (Internet). *See also* privacy (Internet)
McAfee AntiVirus, 446
Panda Software, 446
Symantec AntiVirus Research Center, 446
Symantec Security Check, 446
Symantec Trend Micro: Scams and Hoaxes, 446
VirusList.com, 446

self-defense, 949. *See also* martial arts

self-help and motivational information. *See also* advice; hypnosis
AchievementRadio.com, 558
Deepak Chopra, 558
Dr. Phil, 558
John Gray, 558
Les Brown, 558
Motivational Speakers, 559
MotivationalQuotes.com, 558
Self-Growth.com, 559
Successories.com, 559
Suze Orman, 559
Tony Robbins: Resources for Creating an Extraordinary Quality of Life, 559
Zig Ziglar, 559

senior citizens
401K Center for Employers, 780
AARP WebPlace, 780
AARP, 797
AARP: Universal Design, 407
Administration on Aging (AOA), 797
AgeNet, 797
AgeNet Eldercare Network, 264
Aging in the Know, 797
Alliance for Retired Americans, 797
Alzheimer's, 34-35, 798
American Association of Homes and Services for the Aging, 780, 798
American Geriatrics Society, 798
Ameriprise, 780
Assisted Living Foundation, 798

BenefitsCheckUp, 798
CareGuide@Home, 264
Centers for Medicare and Medicaid Services, 798
CNN/Money Magazine Retirement, 780
Elder Wisdom Circle, 16
ElderCare Advocates, 264
Eldercare at Home: A Comprehensive Guide, 264
Eldercare Locator, 264, 799
Elderhostel, 798
ElderNet, 780
ElderWeb, 264, 799
FCA: Family Caregiver Alliance, 265
FirstGov for Seniors, 799
Forbes Retirement Planning, 780
Friendly4Seniors Websites, 799
Grand Times, 799
Guide to Retirement Living, 781
Health and Age, 265
HUD for Senior Citizens, 799
Life Extension Foundation, 799
Lifesphere, 800
Medicare.gov, 800
National Council on Aging, 800
National Institute on Aging, 800
National Senior Citizens Law Center, The, 800
New LifeStyles, 800
Railroad Retirement Board, 781
Retire Early, 781
Retirement Calculators, 781
Retirement Net, 781
Retirement Research Foundation, 781
Retirement with a PurposeWeb site, 781
Senior Information Network, The, 800
Senior Living Alternatives, 799
Senior Sites, 801
Senior Softball, 836
Senior.com, 800
SeniorJournal.com, 801
SeniorNet, 801
seniorresource.com, 801
Seniors-Site.com, 781
SeniorsSearch.com, 801
SeniorStore.com, 357
Social Security Online, 801
Social Security Retirement Planner, 782
Third Age, 782, 801
Transitions, Inc. Elder Care Consulting, 801
Wired Seniors, 801

sewing
American Sewing Guild, 802
Cranston Village, 802
Fabric Club, The, 802
Fabrics.net, 802
Fashion Fabrics Club, 802
Fiskars, 802
Home Sewing Association, 802
Jo-Ann Fabric and Crafts, 802
Lily Abello's Sewing Links, 803
machines
Baby Lock, 803
Bernina USA, 804
Brother, 804
Creative Feet, 804
Elna USA, 804
How Stuff Works, 804
Husqvarna Viking, 804
Husqvarna, 614
Janome, 615
Mr. Vac and Mrs. Sew, 804
Pfaff Sewing Machines, 804
Sewing Machine Outlet, 805
Singer Machines, 805
White Sewing, 805
Nancy's Notions, 803
needlecrafts
A to Z Needlepoint, 614
Angel's Nook, The, 614
Bird Cross Stitch, 614
Embroidery Online, 614
Embroidery.com, 614
FreeEmbroideryStuff.com, 614
Husqvarna, 614
Janome, 615
Megrisoft Embroidery Digitizing, 615
National NeedleArts Association, 615
Needlepoint.com, 615
PatternsOnline, 615
Stitchery.com, The, 615
patterns
Butterick, 805
Dress Forms and Pattern Fitting Online, 805
McCall's Pattern Catalog, 805
Sewingpatterns.com, 805
Simplicity, 806
Vintage Pattern Lending Library, 806
Wildly Wonderful Wearables, 806
Sew News, 803
Sewing Web, A, 803
Sewing.com, 803
Threads Magazine, 803
Wild Ginger Software, 803

sexuality. *See also* romance
addictions, 6
American Association of Sex Educators, Counselors, and Therapists (AASECT), The, 807
Better Sex University, 807
Coalition for Positive Sexuality, 807
Contraception.net, 713
ContraceptionOnline.org, 713
Dr. Laura Berman, 807
Dr. Ruth Online!, 15
drDrew, 16
Gender and Sexuality, 807
Go Ask Alice!: Sexuality, 807
Gottman Institute, 807
HealthySex.com, 807
Helen Fisher, 808
HisandHerhealth.com, 808
HowToHaveGoodSex.com, 808
Impotence Specialists, 808
intimategifts.com, 808
iVillage: Love & Sex, 808
Kinsey Home Page, 808
Men Stuff, 543

A B C D E F G H I J K L M N O P Q R S T U V W X Y Z

Nerve.com, 808
Pat Love & Associates, 808
Planned Parenthood Federation of America, Inc., 714
Planned Parenthood Golden Gate, 714
Relationship-Talk.com, 17
Scarleteen, 809
Sexual Health infoCenter, 809
SexualHealth.com, 809
Sexuality Forum, 809
Sexuality Information and Education Council of the U.S., 809
Sexuality.org, 809
SexWithoutPain.com, 809
Teen Sexuality, 809
Viagra, 544
Web by Women, foir Women, 953
Woman Spirit, 809

ships. *See* boats and sailing

shoes

FootJoy, 358
Kelly's Running Warehouse, 868
Road Runner Sports Shoe Store, 869

shopping. *See also* jewelry

Active Plaza, 810
Adoption Shop, 10
Amazon.com, 810
ArtisanGifts.com, 355
Ashford.com, 355
Babies [quote]R[quote] Us, 71
Baby Center, 71
Baby Shower Gifts, 355
BabyStyle Clothes, 811
bargains, 77-80
bargainsOverstock.com, 78
Bath and Body Works, 355
Best Buy, 266
Bloomingdale's, 811
Brookstone, 355
Buy.com, 810
CatalogLink, 810
Circuit City, 266
clothing, 77-79, 138
Coldwater Creek, 811
comparison bots, 813
Computer Gear, 355
computers, 188-189
DELiAs.com, 811
Designer Outlet.com, 811
Dillard's, 812
discount stores, 814
drugstores, 535-536
Eddie Bauer, 812
Fashionmall.com, 812
FragranceNet.com, 355
frugal spending, 330
Gift Collector, 356
GiftCertificates.com, 356
Gifts.com, 356
groceries, 321-322
Gump's, 356
Half.com, 810
Hammacher Schlemmer, 356
Harry and David Gourmet Food Gifts, 356
HerRoom.com, 812
Home Shopping Network, 810
Internet Mall, 267
iQVC, 810
L.L. Bean, 812
Lands' End, 812
Lane Bryant, 812
LowerMyBills.com, 78
Lycos Shopping Network, 811
MarthaStewart.com, 356
msn Shopping, 811
music

CDs, 576-577
MP3s, 577-579

Neiman Marcus, 812
Netmarket.com, 811
Nordstrom, 812
Perfect Present Picker, 356
Perfumania.com, 356
perfume, 814-815
RedEnvelope Gifts: The Right Gift, Right Away, 357
search engines, 815
SeniorStore.com, 357
Sharper Image, 357
specialty

Crate and Barrel, 816
eBags.com, 816
Fogdog Sports, 816
Gothic Clothing and Jewelry, 816
Harry and David, 816
Ikea.com, 816
Reel.com, 816
Sailor Moon Specialty Store, 816
World Traveler Luggage and Travel Goods, 816

Spencer Gifts, 357
Surprise.com, 357
Target.com, 357, 811
video

Amazon.com, 907
Blockbuster, 908
Buy.com, 908
Hollywood Video, 908
Outpost, 908
Reel.com, 908
Suncoast Video, 908
Things from Another World, 908

Shotokan (martial arts), 527

sign language

Alexander Graham Bell Association for Deaf and Hard of Hearing, 217
American Sign Language Browser, 505
ASL Access, 217
Deaf Resources, 217
GG Wiz's FingerSpeller, 218
HandSpeak, 218
Helen Keller National Center for Deaf-Blind Youth, 218
National Association of the Deaf, 218, 505
Sign Language Associates, 506
SignWriting.org, 506
SignWritingSite, 219
Zoos Software, 219

Singapore, 23. *See also* Asia, history

single parenting

Christianity Today: Single Parenting, 666
Living with a Single Parent, 666
Making Lemonade, 666
Mothers Without Custody, 666

A
B
C
D
E
F
G
H
I
J
K
L
M
N
O
P
Q
R
S
T
U
V
W
X
Y
Z

Parent Alienation Syndrome, 667
Parenting SOLO for Singles, 667
Parents Without Partners, 667
ParentsWorld.com, 667
Single and Custodial Fathers' Network, 667
Single Parent Central, 667
Single Parents Association, 667
SingleParent Tips, 667
SingleParentMeet, 667

skateboarding
AKA: GIRL SKATER, 294
Skateboard.com, 294
Skatepark.org, 294
Transworld Skateboarding Magazine, 294
Tum Yeto, 294

skating
Black Diamond Sports, 817
figure skating
Figure Skater's Website, 817
International Figure Skating Magazine (IFS), 817
SkateWeb, 817
Stars On Ice, 817
U.S. Figure Skating, 818
World Skating Museum, 818
inline skating
Get Rolling, 818
International Inline Skating Association, 818
LandRoller Skates, 818
Rollerblade, 818
Skatepile.com, 818
Zephyr Inline Skate Tours, 818
inline skating. ***See also*** skating, roller
International Skating Union, 817
Riedell Skates, 817
roller skating
Finding a Roller Skating Rink, 819
National Museum of Roller Skating, 819
Roller Skating Association, 819
USA Roller Sports, 819
roller skating. ***See also*** skating, inline
speed skating
BONT, 819
GreatSkateWolverineSpeedTeam.com, 819
Speedskating.com, 820
U.S. Speedskating, 820

skiing
SkiNet, 730
snow skiing
Altrec.com, 824
Austria Ski Vacation Packages, 824
Big Bear Mountain Resorts, 824
Boston Mills-Brandywine Ski Resort, 824
Cool Works' Ski Resorts and Ski/Snowboard Country Jobs, 824
GoSki.com, 824
ifyouski.com, 824
K2 Skis, 825
OnTheSnow.com, 825
Outdoor REVIEW, 825
Salomon Sports, 825
Ski.com.au, 825
SkiCentral, 825
Skiing in Jackson Hole, 825
SkiMaps, 825
SkiSnowboard.com, 826
SnoCountry Mountain Reports, 826
Stowe Mountain Resort, 826
U.S. Ski Home Team Page, The, 826
water-skiing, 930-931

skin care/cosmetics
Acne Treatment, 821
Avon, 821
Body Shop, The, 821
Cosmetic Connection, 821
Cosmetic Mall, 821
Dermatology Images: University of Iowa, 821
Dermatology Medical Reference, 821
drugstore.com, 822
Faceart, 822
M-A-C Cosmetics, 822
Mary Kay, 822
Merle Norman Cosmetics Studio, 822
National Rosacea Society, 822
Neutrogena, 822
Sephora, 822
Skin Care Campaign, 823
Skin Care Tips, 823
Skin Culture Peel, 823
Skin Store, 823
SkinCarePhysicians.com, 823

skydiving
DropZone, 294
National Skydiving League, 294
Skydive!, 295
Skydiving Fatalities, 295
SkyPeople, 295
United States Parachute Association, 295

small business
IRS Small Business Site, 650
Small Business Administration, 650
SmallBizManager, 653

small businesses. *See also* home, businesses
products and services
AllBusiness.com, 134
CenterBeam, 134
Doba, 134
eFax.com, 134
entrepreneur.com, 134
Microsoft Small Business Center, 134
NASE (National Association for the Self-Employed), 135
Onvia, 135
Quicken Small-Business Center, 135
Small Business Administration, 135
Stamps.com, 135
United States Postal Service, 135
Visa Small-Business Center, 135

Small & home Based Business Links, 129
webstorefront support
aplus.net, 136
Bigstep.com, 136
Earthlink Business, 136
HostMySite.com, 136
PayPal, 136
ProStores, 136
TopHosts.com, 136
ValueWeb, 136

smoking, quitting
Action on Smoking and Health (ASH), 6
Campaign for Tobacco-Free Kids, 6
CDC's Tobacco Info-Quit Site, 7
Definition of Nicotine Dependence, 7
Nicorette, 7
Nicotine Anonymous, 7
Quit Smoking Support.com, 7
QuitNet, The, 7
QuitSmoking.com, 7
Smoke-Free Families, 7

snorkeling. *See also* diving; scuba diving
About Snorkeling, 926
Beachfront Snorkeling, 926
BSAC Snorkeling, 926
Snorkeling Basics, 926

snow skiing
Altrec.com, 824
Austria Ski Vacation Packages, 824
Big Bear Mountain Resorts, 824
Boston Mills-Brandywine Ski Resort, 824
Cool Works' Ski Resorts and Ski/Snowboard Country Jobs, 824
GoSki.com, 824
ifyouski.com, 824
K2 Skis, 825
OnTheSnow.com, 825
Outdoor REVIEW, 825
Saloman Sports, 825
Ski.com.au, 825
SkiCentral, 825
Skiing in Jackson Hole, 825
SkiMaps, 825
SkiSnowboard.com, 826
SnoCountry Mountain Reports, 826
Stowe Mountain Resort, 826
U.S. Ski Home Team Page, The, 826

snowboarding
Board the World, 295
Burton Snowboards, 295
Ski Central, 295
Snowboarding2.com, 296
Transworld Snowboarding, 296

snowmobiling
American Snowmobiler Magazine, 827
Arctic Cat, 827
International Snowmobile Manufacturers Association, 827
Maine Snowmobile Connection, 827
Michigan Snowmobiling, 827
Minnesota Snowmobiling, 827
Ontario Snowmobiling, 827
Polaris Industries, 827
Ski-Doo, 828
Snowmobile Online, 828
SnowmobileWorld.com, 828
Snowmobiling.net, 828
SnowTracks, 828
World Snowmobile Association, 828
Yamaha Motor Corporation, 828

soccer
American Youth Soccer, 829
ATL World Soccer News, 829
ESPN Soccer, 829
FIFA Online, 829
FIFA World Cup, 829
Goal.com, 829
InternetSoccer.com, 830
Major League Soccer (MLS), 830
Soccer Camps, 830
Soccer Information Systems, 830
Soccer Times, 830
Soccer Tutor, 830
Soccer-Sites, 830
Soccer.com, 830
SoccerAmerica.com, 830
SoccerROM, 170
U.S. Youth Soccer, 831
United States Soccer Federation, 831
World Soccer Page, 831

social work/services
AAMFT, 832
ADEC, 832
Carter Center, The, 832
Catholic Charities USA, 832
Council on Social Work Education, 832
International Federation of Social Workers, 832
National Association of Alcoholism and Drug Abuse Counselors (NAADAC), 833
National Association of Social Workers, 833
National Coalition for the Homeless, The, 833
New Social Worker Online, The, 833
New York State Department of Family Assistance, 833
Social Work and Social Services Websites, 833
Social Work Search, 834
Social Worker Access Network, 834
SocialService.com, 833
U.S. Department of Health and Human Services, 834
U.S. Department of Labor: Social Workers, 834

softball
Amateur Softball Association, 835
American Fastpitch Association, 835
ISF: International Softball Federation, 835
National Fastpitch Coaches Association, 835
National Pro Fastpitch, 835
NCAA Women's Softball, 835
NZ Softball-New Zealand, 836
Senior Softball, 836
Slow Pitch Softball History Page, 836

Softball on the Internet, 836
SoftballSearch.com, 836
U.S.A. Softball Official Site, 836

software
antivirus, 196
downloads
5 Star, 196
BlackICE Update Center, 196
Download.com, 196
freshmeat.net, 197
Happy Puppy, 197
Jumbo!, 197
Qwerks, 197
SnapFiles, 197
softpedia.com, 197
Tucows, 197
miscellaneous
Adobe, 197
Family Tree Maker Online, 198
International Data Group, 198
Lauria McCanna's Photoshop, Corel, Painter, and Paintshop Pro Tips, 198
Web Copier, 198
ZDNet, 198
software/hardware companies
AMD, 189
Apache Digital Corporation, 189
Apple Computer Home Page, 189
Dell.com, 189
Gateway, 189
Hewlett-Packard, 190
IBM Corporation, 190
Intel, 190
MPC, 190
Sony Style, 190
Sun, 190
Toshiba, 190

South Africa
government information/services, 361
Surfing in South Africa, 928

South America
Ancestors in the Americas, 377
Cultures & History of the Americas, 377
Hispanic History in the Americas, 377
History of the Americas, 377
Jaguar: Icon of Power Through Mayan History, 378
Planeta, 882

South Carolina
Columbia Museum of Art, The, 569
MyETV: South Carolina Educational TV and Radio, 254
South Carolina State Parks, 676

South Dakota, 890

South Korea, government information/services, 361

Spain
government information/services, 361
history, 385
International Travel Guide for Mallorca and the Balearic Islands, 882
Learning Catalan on The Internet, 505
Spanish Wines, 945

Spanish (languages/linguistics)
Don Quijote, 506
ForoDeEspanol.com, 506
Learn Spanish, 506
Online Spanish-English Dictionary, 506
Spanish-Kit's Spanish Learning Tools, 506

special needs children
ADD/ADHD (Attention Deficit Disorder/Attention Deficit Hyperactivity Disorder), 547
Arc, 668
Autism and Asperger's Syndrome, 548
bipolar disorder, 549
CancerKids, 146
Celiac Disease Foundation, 156
Children with AIDS Project, 366
Children with Diabetes Online Community, 228
Children with Diabetes Recipes, 228
Children with Disabilities Information, 668
Children with Spina Bifida, 668
Cleft Lip: Wide Smiles, 668
conduct disorder, 549, 668
Council for Exceptional Children, 668
deafness, 217-218
Disability.gov, 369
Down Syndrome WWW Pages, 370
Down Syndrome, 668
Dyslexia: The Gift, 668
Family Village, 668
Federation for Children with Special Needs, 669
Genetic Alliance, 669
Hydrocephalus Association, 669
Individualized Education Program (IEP), 669
Internet Resoource for Special Children, 669
Kids Learn About Diabetes, 229
LD Online, 369
Make-a-Wish Foundation of America, 669
Medical Alert Charms for Children, 229
Muscular Dystrophy Association, 371
National Academy for Child Development (NACD), 669
National Association for Visually Handicapped, 369
National Information Center for Children and Youth with Disabilities (NICHCY), 669
OCD (Obsessive-Compulsive Disorder), 553
PCI Publishing, 670
Premature Baby Premature Child, 670
Sibling Support Project, 670
SNAP Online: Special Needs Advocate for Parents, 670
Social Security Administration: Disability Benefits, 369
Special Needs Children Site, 670
UCPnet, 369

United Cerebral Palsy, 670
World Association of Persons with Disabilities, 369
youreable.com, 369

speed skating
BONT, 819
GreatSkateWolverineSpeedTeam.com, 819
Speedskating.com, 820
U.S. Speedskating, 820

sports. *See also* cheerleading; gambling
baseball
Babe Ruth League Official Website, 81
Baseball Almanac, 81
Baseball America, 81
Baseball Archive, 81
Baseball Links, 81
Baseball Think Factory, 81
Baseball-Reference, 81
college, 82
fantasy, 83-84
Little League Online, 82
Negro Baseball League, 82
professional, 83-84
WebBall, 171
basketball
Coaching Well Basketball Journal, 85
college, 86
FIBA: Federation International de Basketball Amateur, 85
Five Star Hoops, 85
Full Court Press, 85
Harlem Globeltrotters Online, 85
National Wheelchair Basketball Association, 85
Power Basketball, 85
professional, 87-88
Sports Illustrated Basketball, 86
USBasket, 86
women, 85-88
bowling
Amateur Bowling Tournaments, 119
AMF Bowling Worldwide, 119
Bowl.com: Official Site of the United States Bowling Congress, 119
Bowler's Paradise, 119
Bowlers Journal International, 119
Bowling This Month Magazine, 119
Bowling World, 120
Bowling Zone, 120
Bowling.com, 119
BowlingIndex, 119
Brunswick Online, 120
Dick Ritger Bowling Camps, 120
Duckpin Bowling, 120
International Bowling Museum and Hall of Fame, 120
LeagueSecretary.com, 120
PBA Tour, 120
Youth Bowling, 120
boxing
Boxing Game, 121
Boxing Monthly, 121
Boxing Talk, 121
Boxing Times, The, 121
Boxing: CBS SportsLine, 121
Cyber Boxing Zone, 121
Doghouse Boxing, 121
ESPN.com Boxing, 121
HBO Boxing, 122
International Boxing Hall of Fame, 122
International Female Boxers Association, 122
Max Boxing, 122
Showtime Championship Boxing, 122
USA Boxing, 122
World Boxing Association, 122
World Boxing Council, 122
coaching
Coaching Corner, 170
Coaching Well Basketball Journal, 85
eTeamz, 170
Federation International de Basketball Amateur, 85
Five Star Hoops, 85
Football Drills, 170
MyCoachOnline, 170
National Alliance for Youth Sports, 170
Power Basketball, 85
SoccerROM, 170
Sports Coach, 171
WebBall, 171
CouponSurfer, 79
Crow's Dart Page, 213
darts
Dart Bars, 213
Darts World Magazine, 213
Sewa-Darts, 213
Smilie Darts, 213
Top, 100 Darts Sites, 213
World Darts Federation, 213
diving
NCAA Men's Swimming and Diving, 929
NCAA Women's Swimming and Diving, 929
scuba diving, 924-926
snorkeling, 926
ESPN.com, 631
extreme
Boardz, 291
EXPN Extreme Sports, 292
Extreme Sports Channel, 292
Extreme Sports Online, 292
hang gliding and paragliding, 293-294
Outside Online, 292
Parachute Industry Association, 292
PointXCamp, 292
Sandboard Magazine, 293
skateboarding, 294
skydiving, 294-295
snowboarding, 295-296
fantasy
baseball, 83-84
ESPN.com Fantasy Sports, 299
Fantasy Sports Central, 299

Sandbox: Fantasy Sports, 299
Sportsline.com's Fantasy Page, 299

fishing
- *Angling Report Newsletter, The, 724*
- *eders.com, 315*
- *Field & Stream Online, 315*
- *Fishing.com, 315*
- *FishingWorld.com, 315*
- *Gulf Coast Angler's Association, 315*
- *Nor'east Saltwater Online, 315*
- *Rod and Gun, 14*
- *Saltwater Sportsman, 316*
- *Top Fishing Secrets, 316*

Fogdog Sports, 816

football
- *American Football Coaches Association, 324*
- *college, 325*
- *Football Drills, 170*
- *Football.com, 325*
- *professional, 326-327*

golf
- *BadGolfMonthly.com, 358*
- *Ben Hogan Golf Products, 358*
- *FootJoy, 358*
- *Golden Tee, 358*
- *Golf Etiquette from the PGA, 278*
- *Golf Tips Magazine, 359*
- *Golf.com, 358*
- *Golfcourse.com, 358*
- *GolfGuideWeb.com, 358*
- *Golfsmith, 359*
- *GolfWeb, 359*
- *LPGA.com, 359*
- *Masters, The, 359*
- *Open Championship, The, 359*
- *PGA.com, 359*
- *Premier Golf Classics Destinations, 878*
- *USGA.com, 359*

hockey
- *AHL: Official American Hockey League Website, 395*
- *ESPN Hockey Site, 395*
- *Hockey Hall of Fame, 395*
- *Hockey News Online, The, 395*
- *Hockey's Future, 395*
- *HockeyBrain, 395*
- *Internet Hockey Database, 395*
- *National Hockey League Players' Association, 395*
- *NHL: Official National Hockey League Website, 396*
- *Science of Hockey, 396*
- *U.S. College Hockey Online, 396*
- *USA Hockey, 396*

horse racing, 416

hunting
- *Bowhunting.Net, 423*
- *Bowsite, The, 423*
- *Browning Home Page, 423*
- *Buckmasters Magazine Online, 423*
- *Clay Pigeon Shooting Association, 423*
- *Ducks Unlimited, 423*
- *Easton Archery, 423*
- *Eders.com, 423*
- *Field & Stream Online, 424*
- *Hunting Information Systems: An Online Guide, 424*
- *Hunting Trail WebRing, 424*
- *Hunting.Net, 424*
- *Idaho Archery, 424*
- *Maine Guides Online, 424*
- *MyOAN, 424*
- *National Rifle Association, 424*
- *North Amerian Hunting Club, 425*
- *Pearson Archery, 425*
- *Rod and Gun, 14*
- *Texas Parks and Wildlife, 425*
- *U.S. Fish and Wildlife Service, 425*

ItsRainingBargains, 78

Maxim Online, 542

memorabilia, collecting, 172

National Sporting Library, The, 759

News Directory, 625

racing
- *auto racing, 55-57*
- *bicycling, 92-94*
- *motogranprix.com, 561*

rock climbing, 270

rodeo
- *American Junior Rodeo Association, 786*
- *Billy Joe Jim Bob's Rodeo Links Page, 786*
- *Houston Livestock Show and Rodeo, 786*
- *Janet's Let's Rodeo Page, 786*
- *Mesquite Championship Rodeo, 786*
- *Professional Bull Riders, Inc., 786*
- *ProRodeo.com, 786*
- *SLAM! Sports Rodeo, 787*
- *Women's Pro Rodeo Association, 787*

skating
- *Black Diamond Sports, 817*
- *figure skating, 817-818*
- *inline skating, 818*
- *International Skating Union, 817*
- *Riedell Skates, 817*
- *roller skating, 819*
- *speed skating, 819-820*

skiing
- *SkiNet, 730*
- *snow skiing, 824-826*
- *water-skiing, 930-931*

Slate, 634

snowmobiling
- *American Snowmobiler Magazine, 827*
- *Arctic Cat, 827*
- *International Snowmobile Manufacturers Association, 827*

Main Snowmobile Connection, 827
Michigan Snowmobiling, 827
Minnesota Snowmobiling, 827
Ontario Snowmobiling, 827
Polaris Industries, 827
Ski-Doo, 828
Snowmobile Online, 828
SnowmobileWorld.com, 828
Snowmobiling.net, 828
SnowTracks, 828
World Snowmobile Association, 828
Yamaha Motor Corporation, 828

soccer
American Youth Soccer, 829
ATL World Soccer News, 829
ESPN Soccer, 829
FIFA Online, 829
FIFA World Cup, 829
Goal.com, 829
InternetSoccer.com, 830
Major League Soccer (MLS), 830
Soccer Camps, 830
Soccer Information Systems, 830
Soccer Times, 830
Soccer Tutor, 830
Soccer-Sites, 830
Soccer.com, 830
SoccerAmerica.com, 830
SoccerROM, 170
U.S. Youth Soccer, 831
United States Soccer Federation, 831
World Soccer Page, 831

softball
Amateur Softball Association, 835
American Fastpitch Association, 835
ISF: International Softball Federation, 835
National Fastpitch Coaches Association, 835
National Pro Softpitch, 835
NCAA Women's Softball, 835
NZ Softball-New Zealand, 836
Senior Softball, 836
Slow Pitch Softball history Page, 836
Softball on the Internet, 836
SoftballSearch.com, 836
U.S.A. Softball Official Site, 836

Sport Information Resource Center, 760
Sports Dentistry Online, 227
Sports Illustrated for Kids, 485
Sports Illustrated for Women, 953
surfing, 273
tennis
American Tennis Professionals, 857
CBS Sportsline: Tennis, 857
Davis Cup, 857
GoTennis, 857
International Tennis Federation, 857
table tennis, 839-840
Tennis Canada, 857
Tennis Magazine, 730
Tennis Online, 857
Tennis Server, 858
Tennis Warehouse, 858
Tennis Welcome Center, 858
Tennis: A Research Guide, 858
TennisOne, 857
U.S. Open, 858
United States Professional Tennis Association (USPTA), 858
United States Tennis Association, 858
USA Today: Tennis, 858
Wimbledon, 858
Yahoo! Tennis News, 859

tennisWTA Tour, 859
The SPORTS Authority, 816
track and field
Armory Track & Field Center, 868
Athletics Canada, 868
Cool Running, 868
cross-country, 280
Everything Track and Field, 868
High Jump, 868
International Association of Athletics Federations, 868
Kelly's Running Warehouse, 868
Road Runner Sports Shoe Store, 869
Runner's World Online, 869
Runner's, 869
Running and Track & Field, 869
Running Network, 869
Running4.com, 869
Shot Put, 869
Sports Coach, 869
Track and Field News, 870
Training for 400m/800m: An Alternative Plan, 870
USA Track and Field, 870
USA Triathalon, 870

volleyball
American Volleyball Coaches Association, 911
American Wallyball Association, 911
FIVB WWW Home Page, 911
NCAA Men's and Women's Volleyball, 911
USA Volleyball, 911
Volleyball Hall of Fame, 912
Volleyball Magazine, 912
Volleyball.com, 911

water. ***See also*** boats and sailing
canoeing/kayaking, 150
diving, 929
jetskis, 459-460
rafting, 921-922
rowing, 922-924
scuba diving, 924-926

snorkeling, 926
Surfer Magazine, 730
surfing, 927-928
swimming, 928-930
water-skiing, 930-931
wrestling
TheMat.com, 958
Wrestling USA Magazine, 959
Yahoo! News, 627

Sri Lanka, 882

stamps (collectibles/collecting)
American Philatelic Society, 177
Antarctic Philately, 177
AskPhil, 177
British Library Philatelic Collections, 177
British North America Philatelic Society Stamp Collecting for Kids, 177
Joseph Luft's Philatelic Resources on the Web, 177
Open Source Directory of Philatelic Sites, 177
philbasner.com, 177
S.C. Virtes Stamps, 178
Stamp Finder.com, 178
Stamp Shows, 178
Stamps.net, 178
United States Postal Service, 178
Virtual Stamp Club, 178

statistics
Create a Graph, 533
FedStats Web site, 898
Interactive Statistical Calculation Pages, 533
Math, Statistics, and Computational Science, 533
Statistics Home Page, The, 533

stay-at-home parents
Bizy Moms: A Complete Resource for Work-at-Home Moms, 670
Home-Based Working Moms, 670
HomeJobStop, 670
Main Street Mom, 671
Miserly Moms: Stay-At-Home Mom (SAHM) Links, 671
Slowlane.com, 671
SOHO Parenting Center, 671
Strategies for Financing Stay-at-Home Parenting, 671
WAHM (Work at Home Moms), 671
Work at Home Parents, 671
Working at Home: A Primer, 671

stepparenting
CoMamas.com, 671-672
Second Wives Club, 672
Shared Parenting Information Group, 672
Stepfamily Association of America, 672
Stepfamily Network, 672
Stepfamily Zone, The, 672
Stepparent Adoption, 672

stocks
BusinessWeek Online Stocks, 313
Smartmoney.com, 313
Stocks.about.com, 313

streaming media. *See* webcasting

students
High School Journalism, 473
North Gate: Berkeley's Graduate School of Journalism, 474
Poynter.org, 474

substance abuse. *See* addictions/recovery

Sudoku (puzzles), 341

suicide prevention
American Association of Suicidology, 837
American Foundation for Suicide Prevention (AFSP), 837
Befriends International, 837
Community Lifelines, 837
Covenant House, 837
National Strategy for Suicide Prevention, 837
National Suicide Prevention Lifeline, 837
SAVE: Suicide Help, 838
SFSP: Suicide Prevention, 838
Suicide Facts, 838
Suicide Prevention Advocacy Network, 838
Yellow Ribbon Suicide Prevention Program, 838

summer camps
American Camping Association, 142
Camp Channel, 142
Christian Camping International, 142
Kids Camps, 142
Summer Camps, 142

surfing
Board Building, 927
Closely Guarded Secrets of the UK Surfing World, 927
Coastal British Columbia, 927
International Surfing Museum, 927
SG Magazine, 927
Surf World Museum-Torquay, 927
Surfer Magazine, 730
Surfermag.com, 927
Surfing in South Africa, 928
Surfing Magazine, 927
Surfline, 928
Surfrider Foundation USA, 273, 928
WSP Sports, 928

Sweden, 573

swimming
Australia Swimming, 928
CDC: Health Swimming, 928
D&J Sports, 928
FINA, 929
International Swimming Hall of Fame, 929
NCAA Men's Swimming and Diving, 929
NCAA Women's Swimming and Diving, 929
STORMFAX Safe Ocean Swimming Guide, 929
Swimmers Guide Online, 929
Swimming Science Journal, 929
Swimming Teachers' Association, 929
Swimming World Magazine, 930
SwimNews Online, 930
United States Masters Swimming, 930
USA Swimming, 930
WebSwim, 930

T

table tennis
- Butterfly Online, 839
- Classic Hardbat Table Tennis, 839
- Denis' Table Tennis World, 839
- International Paralympic Table Tennis Committee, 839
- International Table Tennis Federation, 839
- Megaspin.net, 839
- National Collegiate Table Tennis, 839
- North America Table Tennis, Inc., 840
- Ping-Pong.com, 840
- Sport of Table Tennis, The, 840
- Table Tennis, 840
- Total Table Tennis, 840
- USA Table Tennis, 840
- World Table Tennis News, 840

Tae Kwon Do
- General Tae Kwon Do Info, 527
- Unofficial Tae Kwon Do Hyung Resource Page, 528
- World Taekwondo Federation, The, 528

Tai Chi
- International Taoist Tai Chi Society, 528
- Taoism and the Philosophy of Tai Chi Chuan, 528
- Wudang.com, 528

Taiwan. *See* Asia, history

tattoos/body art
- Altered Body, 841
- Body Art Studios, 841
- Body Jewelry, 841
- Earth Henna Kits, 841
- everytattoo.com, 841
- Kingpin Tattoo Supply, 841
- Tattoo Fun, 841
- Tattoodles, 842

taxes
- 1040.com, 843
- Ameriprise, 780
- Bankrate.com, 843
- Citizens for Tax Justice, 843
- eSmartforms, 843
- Essential Links to Taxes, 843
- Forbes: Taxes, 843
- H&R Block, 843
- income, 201
- IRS News, 844
- IRS.gov, 843
- Kiplinger Online, 844
- MoneyCentral on Taxes, 844
- SmartMoney.com Tax Center, 844
- SmartPros Accounting, 844
- State and Local Taxes, 844
- State Sales Tax Rates, 844
- Tax Analysts, 844
- Tax Glossary, 845
- Tax Guide for Investors, 845
- Tax Prophet, The, 845
- Tax Resources on the Web, 845
- Tax Sites, 845
- TaxFoundation.org, 845
- TaxHelp Online.com, 845
- TurboTax, 845
- United States Tax Code Online, 845
- Yahoo! Finance Tax Center, 845

teaching. *See also* education
- Activity Search, 846
- American Federation of Teachers, 846
- ArtsEdge, 846
- Classroom CONNECT, 846
- DiscoverySchool.com, 846
- Edheads, 846
- Education Index, 847
- Education Place, 847
- Education Week on the Web, 847
- Education World, 847
- Education.com, 846
- Educational Resources, 847
- Educator's Reference Desk, 847
- Federal Resources for Educational Excellence (FREE), 847
- Global SchoolHouse, 848
- goENC.com, 848
- Harcourt School Publishing, 848
- Intel Education Initiative, 848
- Kathy Schrock's Guide for Educators, 848
- Lesson Plans Page, 848
- McGraw-Hill School Division, 848
- National Education Association, 848
- New York Times Learning Network, 849
- PBS Teacher's Source, 849
- Puffin House, The, 849
- Scholastic.com, 849
- Teachers.net, 849
- Technical Education Research Centers (TERC), 849
- U.S. Department of Education-Funding Opportunities, 849
- USA Today Education, 850
- Virtual Reference Desk, 850

teas. *See* coffee and teas

technology
- BYTE Magazine, 725
- Computerworld Online, 725
- CyberJournalist.net, 628
- Discover Magazine, 726
- Electric Auto Association, The, 58
- Engadget, 865
- Feedroom, The, 628
- firebox.com, 865
- Forbes Online, 124
- Gizmodo, 866
- HotWired, 727
- Internetweek Online, 727
- Longhorn Blogs, 105
- MacWorld, 727
- MakeZine.com, 728
- museums, 574-575
- networking, 616-621
- Pearson Technology Group, 118
- PM Zone, 729
- Popular Science, 626, 729
- Questacon: The National Science and Technology Center, 252
- Science Magazine Home, 729
- ScienceDaily Magazine-Your Link to the Latest Research News, 729

Scientific American, 730
SciTech Daily Review, 730
SeniorNet, 801
SlashNOT, 332
Slate, 634
Tech Soup, 637
techbargains.com, 78
Third Age, 782
Webopedia.com, 756
Windows IT Pro, 731
Wired Seniors, 801
Wired.com, 243
Yahoo! News, 627
ZDNet, 732
ZDNet-PC Magazine, 627

teens. *See also* adolescents; children
About Parenting Teens, 661
ADOL: Adolescence Directory On-Line, 661
alcohol and drug abuse/prevention, 4-8
Awesome Library for Teens, 757
Bolt, 851
Campaign for Our Children, 661
Canadian Parents Online, 659
CanTeen, 146
Cool Nurse, 643
Cool Spot, The, 5
CyberTeens, 851
Dear Lucie, 662
Drinking: A Student's Guide, 5
Drug Testing, 662
Facts for Families, 659
Family Development Program: Parenting Teens Publications, 662
Family Education Network: A Parenting and Education Resource, 659
Family Resource Center, 659
FamilyTime, 659
Favorite Teenage Angst Books, 851
Girls Life Magazine, 851
Girl Power! Campaign, 659
GirlSite, 851
homework help, 255-256, 262
iParenting.com, 660
IPL Teen Division, 851
John Rosemond, 660
KidsHealth.org: For Teens, 662
KidSource, 660
Kiwibox, 851
Kotex.com, 662
LIQUIDGENERATION.com, 852
Listen Up!, 852
Mothering Magazine, 660
MyFuture, 852
National Campaign to Prevent Teen Pregnancy, 711
National Families in Action, 662
National Parenting Center, The, 660
NCF-National Center for Fathering, 660
Next Step Magazine, 852
ParenTalk Newsletter: Adolescence, 662
Parenthood.com, 660
Parenting.com, 661
Parenting.org, 661
Parents-Talk.com, 661
Planned Parenthood Federation of America, Inc., 714
Positive Parenting, 661
Raising Successful Teenagers, 662
SmartGirl, 852
Talking with Kids About Tough Issues, 662
TechnoTeen, 852
Teen Advice Online, 17, 852
Teen Challenge World Wide Network, 663
Teen Depression, 551
Teen Help, 663
Teen Ink, 852
Teen Sexuality, 809
Teenager Driving Contract, 852
Teenager E-Books, 853
Teenagers Today, 853
TeenLink, 853
Teenmag.com, 853
TeenPeople.com, 853
Teenwire, 714
WholeFamily Center, The, 661
WireTap, 853
Working Mother, 661
Xenith.net, 853
Youth Outlook, 853
Youth Radio, 606

telephone directories. *See also* phone books
411 Locate, 441
411.com, 441
AT&T AnyWho Info, 441
Infobel World, 441
Internet Address Finder, 441
Switchboard.com, 441
WorldPages, 441
YellowPages.com, 441

telephony (Internet). *See also* chats and social groups (Internet); phone books
Net2Phone, 440
PalTalk, 440
REBOL Internet Operating System, 440
Skype, 440

television. *See also* webcasting
A&E, 854
A&E Traveler, 877
ABC, 854
ABC Family, 854
abcNEWS.com, 631
AMC, 854
American Experience, The, 452
American Journalism Review, 473, 627
Animal Planet, 854
Antiques Roadshow, 42
Ariel's Simpsons Trivia Quiz, 342
Arthur on PBS, 477
Assocaited Press, 627
BBCi, 854
BET, 854
Big Cartoon Database, 420
Biography, 101, 854
BookNotes, 514
Bravo, 854
C-SPAN, 706, 854
Captain Planet, 478
Cartoon Network.com, 185, 420, 854

cartoons, 185, 420-421, 478
CBC.ca News, 624
CBS, 854
CBS News, 631
Channel One, 478
Cinemax, 854
CMT.com, 591, 854
CNBC, 854
CNN, 854
CNN Interactive, 631
CNN/Money Magazine Retirement, 780
College Sports TV, 325
Comedy Central, 331, 418, 854
CourtTV, 507, 854
Dark Shadows, 789
Daystrom Institute Technical Library, 790
Diet Channel, The, 940
Discovery Channel, 854
Discovery Channel School, 250
Discovery Channel: Discovery Kids, 479
Discovery Channel: When Dinosaurs Roamed America, 233
Disney Channel, 854
Disney.com-The Website for Families, 36
DIY Network, 854
Dr. Phil, 558
drDrew, 16
E! Online, 562, 854
E.W. Scripps, 726
educational television (K-12)
Bill Nye the Science Guy's Nye Labs Online, 253
Biography, 253
Cable in the Classroom, 253
ChannelOne.com, 253
Children's Television Workshop, 253
Discovery Channel, The, 254
KET: Kentucky Educational Television, 254
Merrow Report, 254
MyETV: South Carolina Educational TV and Radio, 254
Noggin, 254
PBS Teacher Source, 254
Stephen Hawking's Universe, 254
Street Cents Online, 255
Encore, 854
Encyclopedia of Fantastic Film and Television, 790
ESPN, 854
ESPN Fantasy Baseball, 83
ESPN Hockey Site, 395
ESPN Soccer, 829
ESPN's College Football Page, 325
ESPN's IndyCar Page, 56
ESPN's Men's College Basketball Site, 86
ESPN.com Boxing, 121
ESPN.com, 631
EXPN Extreme Sports, 292
Extreme Sports Channel, 292
Face of Russia, The, 387
Federal Communication Commission, 629
FIT TV, 854
Flip That House, 749
Flip This House, 749
Food Network, 204, 854
Fooling with Words with Bill Moyers, 698
FOX, 854
Fox Sports NASCAR Site, 57
FoxNews.com, 632, 854
FX, 854
G4 Media Network, 335
GAC TV: Great American Country TV, 591
Gameshow Network, 854
Global Episode Opinion Survey, 790
Golf Channel, 854
Hallmark Channel, 854
Harvest Online, 772
HBO (Home Box Office), 854
HBO Boxing, 122
HGTV, 855
History Channel, 375, 855
History Channel: The History of Mexico, 385
History of Hanukkah, 397
History of the World Timeline, 389
Home and Garden Television: Electrical, 405
Home Shopping Network, 810
Hometime.com, 401, 409
horror, 412
i (independent TV), 855
In The Life TV.org, 348
Indie Film Channel, 855
iQVC, 810
JAZZ, 594
Jerry Beck's Cartoon Research, 421
Junkyard Wars, 475
Kids WB!, 482
Life of Birds, 104
Lifetime Online, 855, 951
Listen Up!, 852
Mark Kistler's Imagination Station, 483
Masterpiece Theatre & MYSTERY!, 607
Mr. Rogers' Neighborhood, 483
MSNBC, 632, 855
MTV, 855
mtvU, 180
MuchMusic, 581
MyOAN, 424
Mystery Net, 607
Nancy's Notions (PBS), 803
NASA Television, 70
National Cartoon Museum, 421
National Museum of Photography, Film, and Television, 574
NBC, 855
New Inventors, 453
New York Times: Television, 855
NewsLink, 629
Nick Jr., 483
Nickelodeon, 855
Noggin, 483
Nova Online: Lost on Everest, 784
Oprah's Picks, 113
Outdoor Life, 855
Oxygen.com, 855, 952
PBS, 855
PBS Kids Games, 488

PBS Kids, 484
PBS Nature: Horses, 416
PBS Teacher's Source, 849
PBS: Online NewsHour, 630
Pentagon Channel, 855
Reading Rainbow, 484
Rock on TV, 581
Satellite News, 791
Sci-Fi, 855
Sci-Fi Site, The, 792
Science Fiction and Fantasy World, 792
Science Fiction Crowsnest, 791
Science Fiction Museum Hall of Fame, 792
Science Fiction Weekly, 725, 792
SciFi Source, 793
SCIFI.COM, 792
Secret Garden, 345
Sesame Workshop, 73, 484
SF-Lovers, 793
Showtime, 855
Showtime Championship Boxing, 122
Simpsons, The, 187
SITCOM, 863
So You Think You Can Dance, 210
South Park, 187
SpeedTV, 855
Spongebob Squarepants, 187
Star Trek, 793
STARZ!, 855
TBS Superstation, 855
TCM, 855
Television Without Pity, 855
This Old House, 410
Thomas the Tank Engine Page, 486
Titan TV, 855
TiVo, 855
TLC, 855
TNT, 855
Travel Channel Online, 855, 879
TV Guide Online, 855
TV History: The First 75 Years, 856
TV Land, 855-856
TV Magic Guide.com, 518
TV Party, 856
TV Sci-Fi and Fantasy Database, The, 793
U.S. Mexican War, 386
Ultimate TV, 856
UPN, 855
USA, 855
Variety.com, 856
VH1.COM, 582, 855
Walter Cronkite School of Journalism & Mass Communication, 474
WB, 855
WE: Women's Entertainment, 855, 953
Weather, 855
Wedding Channel, The, 934, 939
WGN, 855
World of Poetry, 700
wrestling, 958-959
Yahoo! TV, 856
Zap2it, 856
ZOOM, 491

Tennessee
Memphis Zoo Home Page, 970
Nashville Scene, 889
St. Jude's Children's Research Hospital, 368

tennis
American Tennis Professionals, 857
CBS Sportsline: Tennis, 857
Davis Cup, 857
GoTennis, 857
International Tennis Federation Online, 857
table tennis, 839-840
Tennis Canada, 857
Tennis Magazine, 730
Tennis Online, 857
Tennis Server, 858
Tennis Warehouse, 858
Tennis Welcome Center, 858
Tennis: A Research Guide, 858
TennisOne, 857
U.S. Open, 858
United States Professional Tennis Association (USPTA), 858
United States Tennis Association, 858
USA Today: Tennis, 858
Wimbledon, 858
WTA Tour, 859
Yahoo! Tennis News, 859

terrorism
America's War Against Terrorism, 917
BBC News War on Terror, 917
Center for Defense Information, 895
CNN: War Against Terror, 917
Defend America, 901
DefenseLINK, 895
Department of Homeland Security, 896
United States of America: National Security, 918
Washington Post: War on Terror, 918

Texas
AIDS Outreach Center, 365
Central Texas Bluegrass Association, 586
Dallas Zoo, The, 969
Fort Worth Zoo, 969
Galveston Island Offical Tourism site, 884
Museum of Fine Arts, Houston, 570
San Antonio Zoo, The, 971
Texas State Parks, 676

Thailand government information/services, 361. *See also* Asia, history

theater and musical
Albany, New York Theatre and the Arts, 860
American Ballet Theatre, 210
American Conservatory Theater, 860
American Repertory Theatre, 860
American Theater Web, 860
American Variety Stage, 860
Backstage, 860
Broadway Online, 860
Broadway Play Publishing, Inc., 861
Broadway.com, 860
Children's Theatre, The, 861

ChildrensTheatrePlays, 861
Current Theatre, 861
Educational Theatre Association, 861
English Actors at the Turn of the Century, 861
Grand Theatre, 861
League of American Theatres and Producers, 861
Live Design, 861
London Theatre Guide Online, 862
Musicals.net, 862
Now Casting, 862
Playbill Online, 862
Public Theater, The, 862
Put on a Play, 862
Roundabout Theatre Company, 862
Screen Actor's Guild, 862
Shakespeare Theatre, 863
Shakespeare: Subject to Change, 862
SITCOM, 863
TheaterMania.com, 863
Tony Awards Online, 863
WWW Virtual Library Theatre and Drama, 863

theaters (movies/film). *See* movies/films, theaters

theme parks. *See* amusement and theme parks

thesauri. *See* dictionaries and thesauri

timeshares

2nd Market Timeshare Resales, 752
Hotel Timeshare Resales, 752
RCI vacationNET, 752
Sell My Timeshare Now!, 752
Stroman, 753
TimeLinx, 753
Timeshare Beat, The, 753
Timeshare User's Group, 753
TimeSharing Today, 753
Vacation Timeshare Rentals, 753

toddlers. *See* babies and toddlers

Tourette's syndrome

The Facts About Tourette Syndrome, 556
Tourette's Syndrome Association, Inc., 556
Tourette's Syndrome Information Support Site, 556
Tourette's Syndrome Plus, 556

toys and games

Archie McPhee, 864
AreYouGame.com, 864
Barbie.com, 175
Boardgames.com, 864
BRIO, 864
CatToys.com, 155
Cool LEGO Site of the Week, 479
Copernicus, The, 864
Creativity for Kids, 864
CurrentCodes.com, 77
Discovery Toys, 864
Disney Online Store, 865
Engadget, 865
Etch-a-Sketch, 865
eToys, 663, 865
EXTEX Toys, 865
FAO SCHWARZ, 865
firebox.com, 865
Fisher-Price, 865
Gallery of Monster Toys, The, 865
Genius Babies.com, 866
Gizmodo, 866
Hasbro World, 866
Hot Wheels/Matchbox Cars, 175-176
Into The Wind, 866
KBKids, 866
Latoys.com, 866
Learning Curve International, 866
LEGO Company, The, 482
Lego World, 866
Little Tikes, 866
Mastermind Educational Toys, 867
Mattel, 867
Nintendo, 867
Rokenbok, 867
Schylling, 867
Sega, 867
Toys for Tots, 867
Toys R Us, 867

track and field

Armory Track & Field Center, 868
Athletics Canada, 868
Cool Running, 868
Everything Track and Field, 868
High Jump, 868
International Association of Athletics Federations, 868
Kelly's Running Warehouse, 868
Road Runner Sports Shoe Store, 869
Runner's Web, 869
Runner's World Online, 869
Running and Track & Field, 869
Running Network, 869
Running4.com, 869
Shot Put, 869
Sports Coach, 869
Track and Field News, 870
Training for 400m/800m: An Alternative Plan, 870
USA Track and Field, 870
USA Triathalon, 870

trains. *See* railroads

transgender issues. *See* gay/lesbian/bisexual/transgender issues

trash removal, 475

travel and vacation

Adoption Travel, 10
adventure travel/ecotourism
Adventure Center, 13
Adventure Travel Tips, 13
Alpine Ascents International, 13
Backroads, 13
EarthRiver Expeditions, 13
GORPtravel.com, 13
Great Pacific Adventures, 13
iExplore, 13-14
Mountain Travel Sobek, 14
Outside Online, 14
Recreation.gov, 14
Rod and Gun, 14
Silver Lining Tours, 14
Smithsonian Journeys, 14

A B C D E F G H I J K L M N O P Q R S T U V W X Y Z

Storm Chasing Adventure Tours, 14
Walking Adventures International, 14

air travel
Aer Lingus, 22
Air Canada, 122, 43
Air Traffic Control System, 871
Air Travel Health Tips, 871
Airfare.com, 77
Airlines of the Web, 871
AirSafe.com, 68, 871
Alaska Airlines, 22
Aloha Airlines, 22
American Airlines, 22
ATA, 22
Austrian Airlines, 22
British Airways, 22
Cathay Pacific, 22
China Airlines, 22
Continental, 22
Delta, 22
Flight Arrivals, 871
Flyer Talk, 871
Frontier, 22
Hawaiian Airlines, 22
JetBlue Airways, 22
Lufthansa, 22
Malaysia Airlines, 23
Mexicana Airlines, 23
Midwest Airlines, 23
New England Airlines, 23
Northwest, 23
Qantas Airlines, 23
Seat Guru, 871
Singapore Airlines, 23
SkyWest Airlines, 23
Southwest, 23
Spirit Airlines, 23
Transportation Security Administration, 871
Turkish Airlines, 23
United, 23
US Airways, 23

amusement and theme parks
Adventure City, 36
Anheuser-Busch Theme Parks, 36
Canobie Lake Park, 36
Cedar Point, 36
Disney.com-The Website for Families, 36
Great Escape and Splashwater Kingdom, 36
Hershey Park, 37
LEGOLAND California, 37
Paramount Canada's Wonderland, 143
Paramount's Great America, 37
Paramount's Kings Island, 37
Sea World, 37
Six Flags Theme Parks, 37
Theme Park Review, 37
Universal Studios, 37
Walt Disney World, 38

Artista Creative Safaris for Women, 46

Austria Ski Vacation Packages, 824

BargainTravel.com, 872

bicycle tours
Adventure Cycling Association, 92
Big Island Mountain Biking Trail Guide, 95
Mountain Bike Trailsource, 96
Mountain Workshop Dirt Camp, 96
Trails.com, 96
Trails from Rails, 94
VBT, 94
Western Spirit Cycling, 96

birding tours
Birder, 102
Birding in British Columbia, 103
Field Guides, 103
Hot Spots for Birders, 103

budget travel
11th Hour Vacations, 872
Backpack Europe on a Budget, 872
Bargain Travel Cruises-Cheap Cruises, 875
BestFares.com, 872
budget hotels, 872
Busabout Europe, 872
Cheap Weekend Getaways, 891
Council Travel, 872
Cruise Value Center, 875
DiscountAirfares.com, 872
Economy Travel, 872
Expedia, 873
Hostels.com, 873
Hotels.com, 873
Hotwire.com, 873
LastMinuteTravel.com, 873
Lowestfare.com, 873
Moment's Notice, 873
Orbitz, 873
Priceline.com, 873
SkyAuction.com, 874
Travelocity, 874

business travel, 123

Canada, 143-144

car travel
Advantage Rent-A-Car, 151
Alamo Rent A Car, 151
ASIRT: Association for Safe International Road Travel, 874
Auto Europe Car Rentals, 874
Avis, 151
BreezeNet's Rental Car Guide and Reservations, 874
Budget Rent a Car, 151
Dollar Rent A Car, 151
Drive Europe, 874
Economy Car Rental Aruba, 151
Enterprise Rent-A-Car, 151
Europcar, 151
Fox Rent A Car, 151
Fun Roads, 874
Hertz, 151
MomsMinivan, 874
National Car, 151
Payless Car Rental, 151
Pet Car Travel Tips, 874
Rent-A-Wreck, 151
Road Trips, 874

Route 66, 875
Scenic Byways and Other Recreational Drives, 875
traveling in the USA, 875
Center for Disease Control: Travel Health, 374
ConsumerWorld Bargains, 77
cruises
Bargain Travel Cruises-Cheap Cruises, 875
Carnival Cruises, 875
Cruise Value Center, 875
Cruise.com, 875
CruiseGuide, 875
CruiseStar.com, 875
Crystal Cruises, 876
Freighter World Cruises, 876
Holland America Line, 876
i-cruise.com, 876
Norwegian Cruise Line, 876
Orient-Express Trains & Cruises, 887
Princess Cruises, 876
Royal Caribbean, 876
Schooner Mary Day, 876
Delta SkyLinks Home Page, 69
Department of Transportation (U.S.), 897
Dick Ritger Bowling Camps, 120
Elderhostel, 798
Fear of Flying, 69
gay/lesbian/bisexual/transgender issues, 350
Flight Safety, 69
Gimponthego.com, 374
Gulf Coast Angler's Association, 315
Horizons Unlimited, 560
information/travel tips
100% Pure New Zealand, 876
A&E Traveler, 877
Abercrombie & Kent, 877
Away.com, 877
Citysearch, 877
Ecotourism Explorer, 877
FamilyTravelForum, 877
Fodor's Travel Online, 877
Frommer's, 877
IgoUgo, 877
Journeywoman, 878
Let's Go, 878
Lonely Planet Online, 878
Luxury Link Travel Services, 878
North American Virtual Tourist, The, 878
One Bag, 878
Pets Welcome, 878
Premier Golf Classics Destinations, 878
Rough Guides, 879
Specialty Travel Guide, 879
timeout.com, 879
Travel Channel Online, 879
Travel Medicine, 879
Travel.com, 879
Travelite FAQ, The, 879
Travellerspoint Travel Community, 879
TravelSource, 879
TripAdvisor, 880
Virtual Tourist, 880
World Hum, 880
International Ecotourism Society, 275
international travel
AFRICANET, 880
Airhitch, 880
CDC (Centers for Disease Control and Prevention), 880
Czech Info Center, 880
European Visits, 881
Eurotrip.com, 881
Eurotrotter, 881
FranceEscape, 881
Grand Circle Travel, 881
Help for World Travelers, 881
Hobo Traveler, 881
Inn26, 881
International Travel and Health, 881
International Travel Guide for Mallorca and the Balearic Islands, 882
International Travel Maps and Books, 882
International Travel News, 882
Kintetsu International Travel, 882
Mexico Travel Guide, 882
Monaco Online, 882
Orient-Express Trains & Cruises, 887
Planeta, 882
Rick Steves' Europe Through the Back Door, 882
Salzburg, Austria, 882
Sri Lanka Internet Services, 882
TravelAdvice.net, 883
United States State Department Travel Warnings and Consular Info Sheets, 883
Universal Currency Converter, 883
Vancouver, British Columbia, 883
island travel
All-Inclusives Resort and Cruise Vacation Source, 883
America's Caribbena Paradise, 883
Club Med, 883
Elite Island Resorts, 883
Fiji Islands Travel Guide, 884
Galveston Island Official Tourism Site, 884
Hideaway Holidays: Travel Specialists to the Pacific Islands, 884
Islands.com, 884
Isles of Scilly, 884
Maui Travel & Tourism, 884
NetWeb Bermuda, 884
Virgin Islands, 884
World Beaches, 884
lodging
1st Traveler's Choice, 884
Alaskan Cabin, Cottage, and Lodge Catalog, 885
all-hotels.com, 885

Big Bear Mountain Resorts, 824
Boston Mills-Brandywine Ski Resort, 824
Choice Hotels, 885
Colorado Vacation Guide, 885
Cool Works' Ski Resorts and Ski/Snowboard Country Jobs, 824
Cyber Rentals, 885
Glenmore Lodge, 288
GoSki.com, 824
Hotelguide.com, 885
InnSite, 885
International Bed and Breakfast Guide, 885
Lake Tahoe's West Shore Lodging, 885
Lodging Guide World Wide, 885
LodgingGuide, 886
Lodgings International, 886
National Lodging Directory, The, 886
Professional Association of Innkeepers International, 886
Stowe Mountain Resort, 826
Travel Web, 886
Vacation Direct, 886
West Virginia Lodging Guide, 886
MDTravelHealth, 374
Mexexperience, 386
MexOnline, 557
National Parks and Monuments, 383
News Directory, 625
Priceline.com, 78
RoomSaver.com, 79
Skiing in Jackson Hole, 825
SnoCountry Mountain Reports, 826
TouristFlorida.com, 79
train travel
Amtrak, 886
European and British Rail Passes, 886
Grand Canyon Railway, 887
Orient-Express Trains & Cruises, 887
Train Traveling, 887
VIA Rail Canada, 887
TravelASSIST Magazine, 731
Travel Health Online, 374
TravelChinaGuide: History, 380
U.S. travel
Alabama Wonder Full, 887
Alaskan Travel Guide, 887
Arizona Guide, The, 887
Arkansas: The Natural State, 887
Atlanta Travel Guide, 888
Blue Ridge Country, 888
California Travel Guide, 888
Cambridge, Massachusetts, 888
Cincinnati Vacation Gateways, 888
Colorado.com, 888
George Washington's Mount Vernon Estate, 888
Idaho, 889
Iowa Tourism Office, 889
Las Vegas, 889
Louisiana Travel Guide, 889
Michigan: Travel Michigan, 889
Minneapolis, 889
Nashville Scene, 889
Nebraska Travel and Tourism, 889
New Jersey and You, 889
New Mexico: America's Land of Enchantment, 890
New York State, 890
NH.com: New Hampshire, 890
Oregon: Travel Information, 890
Santa Fe, New Mexico, Travel Information, 890
Seattle.com, 890
South Dakota World Wide Website, 890
TheGrandCanyon.com, 888
Utah! Travel and Adventure Online, 890
Virginia Is for Lovers, 890
Washington, D.C., 891
WorldWeb.com, 891
Yankee, Traveler, The, 891
weekend getaways
Cheap Weekend Getaways, 891
Concierge Travel, 891
EscapeMaker Weekend Getaway Ideas, 891
Lovetripper, 891
Romantic Weekend Getaways, 891
Sandals Resorts, 892
site59.com, 892
TotalEscape, 892
Trip Spot, 892
VacationIdea.com, 892
Washington Post Weekend Getaways Guide, 892
World Traveler Luggage and Travel Goods, 816
Yahoo! News, 627
Zagat.com, 880
trigonometry, 533
trivia games
Ariel's Simpsons Trivia Quiz, 342
Daily, 100, The, 342
FunTrivia.com, 342
Trivia Company's Trivia Wars, 342
Turkey, government information/services, 361

U

U.S. Virgin Islands
America's Caribbean Paradise, 883
Virgin Islands, 884
UFOs
U UFO Database, 894
Burning Man, 331
Coast to Coast AM with George Noory, 893
CSETI-The Center for the Study of Extraterrestrial Intelligence, 893
CSICOP, 893

A B C D E F G H I J K L M N O P Q R S T U V W X Y Z

Fortean Times, 332
International UFO Museum and Research Center, 893
J. Allen Hynek Center for UFO Studies, The, 893
Kidnapped by UFOs?, 893
MUFON, 894
National UFO Reporting Center, 894
Obiwan's UFO-Free Paranormal Page, 413
Rense.com, 894
UFO Info, 894
UFO Roundup, 894
UFO Seek, 894

United Kingdom
Abercrombie & Kent, 877
American-British British-American Dictionary, The, 500
Architecture.com, 44
ballet.co, 210
BBC News, 629
BBCi, 854
Bleep, 576
British Airways, 22
British North America Philatelic Society Stamp Collecting for Kids, 177
British Prime Ministers, 718
British Timeline, 384
BSAC Snorkeling, 926
Cats Protection League, 154
Children's Express UK, 478
Closely Guarded Secrets of the UK Surfing World, 927
Economist, The, 633
Energize For Life Detox and Cleanse Guide, 29
England Landmarks and Historical Sites, 382
English Actors at the Turn of the Century, 861
English Nature, 611
European and British Rail Passes, 886
FanGrok, 790
Focal an Lae: The Word of the Day in Irish, 504
Gaelic Languages Info, 504
Glenmore Lodge, 288
government information/services, 361
Guinness, 90
History On-Line, 376
ifyouski.com, 824
Imperial War Museum, 913
Isles of Scilly Travel Centre, 884
Jesus Army, 772
London Theatre Guide Online, 862
Music in Scotland, 593
Natural History Museum in the United Kingdom, 573
NHBS Environmental Bookstore, 115
Nursing Standard, 645
Origins.net, 352
Philatelic Collections, 177
Politics and Current Affairs Forum, 382
Portico: The British Library, 759
Rowing Service, The, 923
Royal Opera House, 597
Sub-Aqua Association, 926
Temple Records, 593
Welsh Course, A, 505

United States
Flight Arrivals, 871
Fourth of July, The, 397
government information/services
Administration on Aging (AOA), 797
American Presidents: Life Portraits, 718
Ben's Guide to U.S. Government for Kids, 489
BISNIS, 130
CDC (Centers for Disease Control and Prevention), 880
CDC's Tobacco Info-Quit Site, 7
Center for Defense Information, 895
Center for Disease Control: Travel Health, 374
Centers for Disease Control and Prevention: HIV, 366
Centers for Medicare and Medicaid Services, 798
Central Intelligence Agency, 895
Child Welfare Information Gateway, 11
CIA History for Kids, 388
Citizenship and Immigration Services, 895
Civil Rights Division (of the Department of Justice), 167
Congressional Budget Office, 895
Defense Almanac, 762
DefenseLINK, 895
Department of Commerce, 896
Department of Education, 896
Department of Energy, 896
Department of Health and Human Services, 896
Department of Homeland Security, 896
Department of Justice, 896
Department of Labor, 896
Department of State, 897
Department of the Interior, 896
Department of the Treasury, 897
Department of Transportation, 897
Department of Veterans Affairs, 897
Disability.gov, 369
Environmental Protection Agency's Office of Water, 276
Environmental Protection Agency, 276
Environmental Protection Agency, 897
Export-Import Bank of the United States, 130
FAA, 69
FDA: Food and Drug Administration, 536
Federal Bureau of Investigation, 507, 897
Federal Citizen Information Center, 897

A B C D E F G H I J K L M N O P Q R S T U V W X Y Z

Federal Communications Commission, 629
Federal Railroad Administration, 740
Federal Trade Commission's E-Commerce Publications, 242
Federal Trade Commission, 897
Federal Trade Commission: Franchises and Business Opportunities, 127
FedStats, 898
FedWorld Information Network, 898
FedWorld.gov, 762
FEMA: Federal Emergency Management Agency, 269
FirstGov for Consumers, 201
FirstGov for Seniors, 799
FirstGov, 898
FREE: Federal Resources for Education Excellence, 261
House Committee on Agriculture, 20
HUD for Senior Citizens, 799
HUD Housing FHA Home Page, 747
HUD: U.S. Department of Housing and Urban Development, 743
IRS.gov, 843
IRS: Charities, 636
Law Research: The United States Department of Justice, 168
Library of Congress, The, 758
MarineLINK, 898
Medicare.gov, 800
NASA Home Page, 70
NASA Television, 70
National Archives and Records Administration, 759
National Institutes of Health, 364
Office for Civil Rights: U.S. Department of Education, 168
Office of Personnel Development, 467
OSHA (Occupational Safety and Health Administration), 373
Peace Corps, 898
POTUS: Presidents of the United States, 718
President's Council on Physical Fitness and Exercise, 281
Presidents of the United States, The, 719
Railroad Retirement Board, 781
Recreation.gov, 14
Small Business Administration, 135
Social Security Administration: Disability Benefits, 369
Social Security Online, 801
Social Security Retirement Planner, 782
Transportation Security Administration, 871
U.S. Army, 898
U.S. Bureau of Justice Statistics, 456
U.S. Census Bureau, 764
U.S. Consumer Product Safety Commission, 202
U.S. Department of Education, 244, 760
U.S. Department of Education-Funding Opportunities, 849
U.S. Department of Health and Human Services, 539, 834
U.S. Department of Labor, 471
U.S. Department of Labor: Social Workers, 834
U.S. Department of State: Russian History, 388
U.S. Department of Treasury Auctions, 54
U.S. Fish and Wildlife Service, 425
U.S. Fish and Wildlife Service-National Wetlands Inventory, 275
U.S. International Trade Commission, 132
U.S. Navy, 898
U.S. Patent and Trademark Office, 454
United States Fish and Wildlife Service, 316
United States House of Representatives, 898
United States Postal Service, 135
United States Senate, 899
United States State Department Travel Warnings and Consular Info Sheets, 883
United States Trade Representative, 132
USDA (United States Department of Agriculture), 21
USGS Learning Web, 354
Vital Records Information: United States, 764
Welcome to the White House, 899
White House for Kids, The, 486

history
American Memory, 388
Ancestors in the Americas, 377
Chronology of U.S. Historical Documents, A, 382
CIA History for Kids, 388
Cultures & History of the Americas, 377
Eyes of Glory, 388
George Washington's Mount Vernon, 382
Henry Ford Estate: Fair Lane, 383
Hispanic History in the Americas, 377
History of the Americas, 377
Mount Rushmore, 383
National Civil Rights Museum, 383
National Parks and Monuments, 383
National Security Archive, 388
National Trust for Historic Preservation, 389

Our Documents, 383
Outline of U.S. History, 388
Smithsonian National Museum of American History, 389
Statue of Liberty-Ellis Island Foundation, 384
Susan B. Anthony House Museum and National Landmark, 384
TheHistoryNet, 388
USHistory.org, 389

travel
Alabama Wonder Full, 887
Alaskan Travel Guide, 887
Arizona Guide, The, 887
Arkansas: The Natural State, 887
Atlanta Travel Guide, 888
Blue Ridge Country, 888
California Travel Guide, 888
Cambridge, Massachusetts, 888
Cincinnati Vacation Gateways, 888
Colorado.com, 888
George Washington's Mount Vernon Estate, 888
Idaho, 889
Iowa Tourism Office, 889
Las Vegas, 889
Louisiana Travel Guide, 889
Michigan: Travel Michigan, 889
Minneapolis, 889
Nashville Scene, 889
Nebraska Travel and Tourism, 889
New Jersey and You, 889
New Mexico: American's Land of Enchantment, 890
New York State, 890
NH.com: New Hampshire, 890
North American Virtual Tourist, The, 878
Oregon: Travel Information, 890
Santa Fe, new Mexico, Travel Information, 890
Seattle.com, 890
South Dakota World Wide Website, 890
TheGrandCanyon.com, 888
Traveling in the USA, 875
Utah! Travel and Adventure Online, 890
Virginia Is for Lovers, 890
Washington, D.C., 891
WorldWeb.com, 891
Yankee Traveler, The, 891

universities. *See* colleges and universities

Utah
Cannes Film Festival, 563
Canyonlands, 673
Utah! Travel and Adventure Online, 890

V

vacations. *See* travel and vacation

vampires
Anne Rice, Official Site, 414
Bram Stoker's Dracula, 414
Federal Vampire and Zombie Agency, 414
Temple of the Vampire, 414
Vampire Church, 414
Vampire Rave, 414

vegetables. *See* gardening; landscaping

Vermont, 826

veteran and military organizations
Air Force Association, 900
American Battle Monuments Commission, 900
American Legion, The, 900
American War Library, The, 757
AMVETS, 900
Army and Air Force Exchange Service, 900
Defend America, 901
Department of Veterans Affairs, 897, 901
Department of Veteran Affairs Debt Management, 223
Disabled American Veterans, 901
Gulf War Veteran Resource Pages, 901
Korean War 50th Anniversary, 901
Military USA, 901
Military.com, 901
MOAA, 902
National Coalition for Homeless Veterans, 902
Paralyzed Veterans of America, 369, 902
Soldier City, 902
U.S. Department of Housing and Urban Development Veteran Resource Center (HUDVET), 902
Veterans News and Information Service, 634, 902
Vets4Hire.com, 471
VFW: Veterans of Foreign Wars, 902
Vietnam Veterans of America, 903

veterinary medicine
AAHA HealthyPet.com, 904
American Animal Hospital Association (AAHA), 681
American College of Veterinary Surgeons, 904
American Veterinary Medical Association, 904
Animal Health Information, 682
AVA Online, 904
AVMA (American Veterinary Medical Association) Network, The, 682
Center for Veterinary Medicine, 904
CyberPet, 682
Department of Animal Science: Oklahoma State University, 904
DoctorDog.com: Cat and Dog Supplies and Pet Health Care, 682
Exotic Pet Vet, 681
International Veterinary Information Service, 905

Kentucky Equine Research, 905
Merck Veterinary Manual, 905
Murdoch University: Division of Veterinary and Biomedical Sciences, 905
NOAH: Network of Animal Health, 905
OncoLink: Veterinary Oncology, 905
Pet Columns from University of Illinois College of Veterinary Medicine (CVM), 683
PetPlace.com, 683
Pets Need Dental Care, Too, 683
PetSage-Pet Care Products, 683
ThePetCenter.com, 682
Veterinary Oncology, 684
Veterinary Pet Insurance, 905
VeterinaryPartner.com, 684
Washington State University College of Veterinary Medicine, 905

video and multimedia. *See also* electronics
Amazon.com, 907
Blockbuster, 908
Break.com, 418
Buy.com, 908
DVDs, 906-907
Film Festival Today, 906
Hollywood Video, 908
Martial Arts Books and Videos, 525
movies/films
CinemaNow!, 562
E! Online, 562
festivals, 562
festivals, 563
Film Affinity, 562
Film Bug: Guide to the Movie Stars, 562
independent film, 563
independent film, 564
Internet Movie Database, 562
Movies.com, 562
reviews, 564
studios, 564-565
theaters, 565-566
museums, 573-574
Oddcast, 906
Outpost, 908
Reel.com, 908
search engines, 907
Suncoast Video, 908
Things from Another World, 908
Time Life, 118
Video In Production, 938
Without a Box, 906
ZED, 906

video games. *See also* games and puzzles
cheat codes (games), 336, 339-340
Chumbo.com, 188
MacGamer.com, 191
Nintendo, 867
Sega, 867

Vietnam War. *See also* Asia, history
Vets with a Mission, 916
Vietnam Online, 917
Vietnam Veterans Memorial, 917
Vietnam Veterans of America, 903
Vietnam War Pictorial, The, 917
Wars for Viet Nam:, 1945-1975, The, 917

vineyards. *See* wine

Virgin Islands. *See* U.S. Virgin Islands

Virginia
Electronic Text Center at the University of Virginia, The, 515
George Washington's Mount Vernon Estate, 888
Richmond Moving Image Co-Op, 563
Virginia Is for Lovers, 890

viruses (computers). *See* antivirus software/resources

vitamins and supplements
eNutrition.com, 909
Medline Plus, 909
MotherNature.com, 909
Nature Made, 909
Pharmaton, 909
Puritan's Pride, 909
vitacost.com, 910
VitaminShoppe.com, 910

volleyball
American Volleyball Coaches Association, 911
American Wallyball Association, 911
FIVB WWW Home Page, 911
NCAA Men's and Women's Volleyball, 911
USA Volleyball, 911
Volleyball Hall of Fame, 912
Volleyball Magazine, 912
Volleyball.com, 911

volunteering
20 Ways for Teenagers to Help Other People by Volunteering, 641
Advice for Volunteers, 641
Corporation for National and Community Service, 641
Energize, 641
Global Volunteers, 641
Idealist, 641
Peace Corps, 641
Points of Light Foundation, 642
SERVEnet, 642
VISTA-Volunteers in Service to America, 642
Volunteer Today, 642
Volunteerism in Canada, 642
VolunteerMatch, 642
Volunteers of America, 642
Wilderness Volunteers, 642

W

Wales. *See* United Kingdom

walking
American Volkssport Association, 284
Hiking and Walking Home Page, 284
Kids Walk to School, 284
Pedestrian and Bicycle Information Center, 284
Racewalk.com, 284
Walking Connection, The, 284
Walking Site, The, 284

warfare
America's Wars, 913
American Battle Monuments, 900
American Civil War, 115, 914-915
American War Library, The, 757
AntiWar.com, 913
Cold War, 915-916
Cost of War, 913
DEBKAfile, 913
DefendAmerica, 913
Defense Almanac, 762
GlobalSecurity.org, 913
Gulf War, 901
Imperial War Museum, 913
Institute for War and Peace Reporting, 914
Jane's Defence Weekly, 633
Jane's Information Group, 914
Korean War, 901, 916
Strategy Page, 914
Stratfor Security Consulting Intelligence Agency, 914
terrorism, 895-896, 901, 917-918
Vietnam War, 903, 916-917
World War I, 383, 918-919
World War II, 572, 919

Washington (state)
Children's Hospital and Regional Medical Center, Seattle, 368
KAOS: Welcome to KAOS!, 604
Mesa Verde National Park, 675
Northwest Trek, 675
Olympic National Park, 675
Redhook Ale Brewery, 91
Seattle Opera, 597
Seattle.com, 890
Washington State University College of Veterinary Medicine, 905
Washington Trails Association, 141
Woodland Park Zoo (Seattle, WA), 971

Washington, D.C.
Charitable Choices, 638
Gallaudet University, Washington, D.C., 218
National Gallery of Art, 570
National Museum of the American Indian, 567
National Zoo, 970
Shakespeare Theatre, 863
Smithsonian Institution, The, 571
Smithsonian National Air and Space Museum, 70
Smithsonian National Museum of American History, 389
Smithsonian National Museum of Natural History, 573
Smithsonian Natural History Museum, 376
Washington Post, 633
Washington Post Weekend Getaways Guide, 892
Washington, D.C., 891

watches. *See also* jewelry
Fossil, 920
RGM Watch Repair and Restoration, 463
Rolex, 920
Swatch.com, 920
Tag Heuer, 920
Timex, 920
ToolsGS, 463
Watch Repair FAQ, 920
Watches Planet, 920

water sports. *See also* boats and sailing
canoeing/kayaking, 150
diving, 924-926, 929
jetskis, 459-460
rafting, 921-922
rowing, 922-924
snorkeling, 926
surfing, 927-928
swimming, 928-930
water-skiing, 930-931

weather and meteorology
AccuWeather.com, 932
Atlantic Tropical Weather Center, 932
CNN Weather, 932
Defense Meteorological Satellite Program, 932
El Nino, 932
Florida Weather Monitor, 932
Intellicast, 932
My-Cast Weather, 933
National Hurricane Center Tropical Prediction Center, 933
National Oceanic and Atmospheric Administration, 272, 647
National Severe Storms Laboratory, 933
National Weather Center: Interactive Weather Center, 933
National Weather Service, 933
Ocean Weather, 933
Old Farmer's Almanac, 763
Silver Lining Tours, 14
Storm Chasing Adventure Tours, 14
UM Weather, 933
Weather Channel, 934
Weather Underground, The, 934
Weather World, 934
WeatherBug, 934
WeatherOnline!, 934
Yahoo! Weather, 934

web page development
1-2-3 ASPX, 447
AJAX, 447
ASP Resource Index, 447
ASP Today, 447
ASPWire, 447
Bare Bones Guide to HTML, 447
Brainjar, 447
Builder.com, 447
CGI Resource Index, 448
CoffeeCup Software, 450
CoolPage, 450
Database Journal, 448
Developers Network, 450
developerWorks: Java Technology, 448
DevX, 448
Dreamweaver, 448
FreeScripts, 448
FrontPage, 450
HTML Goodies, 450
HTML Writers Guild, 448
Jars.com, 448
Java.sun.com, 448

Macromedia, 450
Matt's Script Archive, 448
.NET, 449
PageResource.com, 449
Pagetutor.com, 451
Perl.com, 449
PHP, 449
Python.org, 449
Sausage Software, 451
ScriptSearch, 449
SiteExperts.com, 449
SitePal, 451
Slashdot, 451
SQL Server Magazine, 449
W3 Schools, 449
Web Developer's Virtual Library, 449
WebDeveloper.com, 450
Webmonkey for Kids, 450
Webmonkey.com, 450
XMetal, 451

webcasting. *See also* television
Digital Webcast, 935
Discovery Education: United Streaming, 935
International Webcasting Association, 935
QuickTime for Developers, 935
Real Networks, 935
Streaming Media World, 935
StreamingMedia.com, 936
WebCasting.com, 936
Windows Media Developer Center, 936
you-niversity.com, 936

weblogs. *See* blogs and blogging

webstorefronts (small businesses), support for
aplus.net, 136
Bigstep.com, 136
EarthLink Business, 136
HostMySite.com, 136
PayPal, 136
ProStores, 136
TopHosts.com, 136
ValueWeb, 136

webzines
Asia Pacific News, 633
Drudge Report, 633
Economist, The, 633
Emerging Markets, 633
Jane's Defence Weekly, 633
Jane's Foreign Report, 633
Salon.com, 633
Slate, 634
Smoking Gun, The, 634
Veterans News and Information Service, 634
WEBZINE, 634

wedding planning
Ask Ginka, 937
Best Man, The, 937
Bliss! Weddings, 937
Bridal Bargains, 77
Bridalink Store, 937
Brides and Grooms, 938
Brides.com, 937
Great Bridal Expo, 938
Grooms Online, 938
Knot: Weddings for the Real World, The, 938
Lovetripper, 891
Romantic Weekend Getaways, 891
Today's Bride Online Magazine, 938
Ultimate Internet Wedding Guide, 938
USA Bride, 938
Video In Production, 938
Wedding Bells, 939
Wedding Channel, The, 939
Wedding Photography-Advice for the Bride and Groom, 939
WeddingSolutions.com, 939
WedNet, 939

weekend getaways. *See also* travel and vacations
Cheap Weekend Getaways, 891
Concierge Travel, 891
EscapeMaker Weekend Getaway Ideas, 891
Lovetripper, 891
Romantic Weekend Getaways, 891
Sandals Resorts, 892
Site59, 892
TotalEscape, 892
Trip Spot, 892
VacationIdea.com, 892
Washington Post Weekend Getaways Guide, 892

weight loss. *See also* diet and nutrition
American Dietetic Association, 940
Ask Dr. Weil, 940
Best of Weight Loss, 940
CyberDiet, 940
Diet Channel, The, 940
Doctor's Guide to Obesity, 940
eDiets.com, 941
Fast Food Facts, 941
HealthCentral, 942
Jenny Craig, 941
L A Weight Loss Centers, 941
Natural Nutrition, 941
Nutrisystem, 941
Prevention.com-Weight Loss and Fitness, 941-942
Shape Up America, 942
Weight Watchers, 942

weightlifting and bodybuilding
Fitness Online, 281
Gold's Gym, 284
International Powerlifting Federation, 285
International Weightlifting Federation, 285
USA Weightlifting, 285
Weight Training & Weightlifting Exercises, 285
Weights.net, 285

Welsh (languages/lingustics), 505

West Virginia, 886

whitewater rafting. *See* rafting

wines
Ambrosia, 943
Bordeaux, 943
Buyers and Cellars Wine Education, 943
Edgerton's Wine Price File, 943
Fetzer Vineyards, 943
Food & Wine Magazine, 943
Food and Wine Access, 943
Geerlings & Wade, 943
Global Wine Club, 944
Gruppo Italiano Vini, 944

Internet Guide to Wine and Frequently Asked Questions, 944
Into Wine, 944
K&L Wine Merchants, 944
Kahn's Fine Wines, 944
Kendall Jackson Wineries, 944
Marilyn Merlot, 944
Merryvale Vineyards, 944
Napa Valley Virtual Visit, 945
Ronn Wiegand, Master of Wine, 945
Spanish Wines, 945
Sutter Home, 945
Vampire Vineyards, 945
Wine Access, 945
Wine and Dine E-Zine, 725
Wine Broker, The, 945
Wine Enthusiast, 945
Wine Institute, 946
Wine Lover's Page, 946
Wine Messenger, 946
Wine on the Web: The Talking Wine Magazine, 946
Wine Spectator, 946
Wine-Searcher, 946
Wine.com, 947
Wine: UC Davis Department of Viticulture and Enology, 946
WineBusiness.com, 946
Wines on the Internet, 947
Zachys Online, 947

Wisconsin

General Research Resources, 762
Leinenkugel's Leinie Lodge, 90
Pabst Brewing Company, 90

women

AFL-CIO: Working Women Working Together, 948
Amelia Earhart, 68
American Association of University Women (AAUW), 948
American Women's History, 948
Amnesty International USA Women's Human Rights, 948
Artemis Search for Women's Studies Programs, 948
Artista Creative Safaris for Women, 46
Association for Women's Rights in Development, 948
AWARE, 949
Biographies of Women Mathematicians, 532
BizWomen, 949
Bizy Moms, 128
Bizy Moms: A Complete Resource for Work-at-Home Moms, 670
Business Women's Network Interactive, The, 949
cancer, 145-147
CatalystWomen.org, 949
Celebration of Women Writers, A, 949
Center for Reproductive Law and Policy, 949
Chistell Publishing, 949
ClubMom, 665
Cosmopolitan, 726
Daremore Quotes, 736
Diotima: Women and Gender in the Ancient World, 949
Expect the Best from a Girl, 950
Femina, 16
Feminist Arts-Music, 950
Feminist Majority Foundation Online, 950
Feminist Science Fiction, Fantasy, and Utopia, 790
Feminist.com, 950
Girl Dating Tips, 215
Girl Incorporated, 950
Girl Power!, 950
Girl Power! Bodywise, 552
Glamour, 727
Global Fund for Women, 950
health, 956
HerRoom.com, 812
Home-Based Working Moms, 670
Human Rights Watch, 950
International Female Boxers Association, 122
Journeywoman, 878
Kotex.com, 662
La Leche League International, 678
Lane Bryant, 812
Lifetime Online, 951
Loganberry Books, 115
LPGA.com, 359
Machon Chana, 951
Main Street Mom, 671
Melpomene, 281
Miserly Moms: Stay-At-Home Mom (SAHM) Links, 671
Monday Morning Moms, 163
MOST-Mothers of Supertwins, 665
Mothering Magazine, 660
Mothers Without Custody, 666
Ms. Magazine, 728
National Association for Female Executives, 951
National Museum of Women in the Arts, 951
National Organization for Women (NOW), The, 951
National Organization of Mothers of Twins Clubs, 664
National Partnership for Women & Families (NPWF), 951
National Women's Hall of Fame, 951
National Women's Health Association, 552
National Women's History Project, 376, 951
NCAA Women's Softball, 835
NCAA Women's Swimming and Diving, 929
NEWoman, 952
NWSA-National Women's Studies Associations, 952
Office of International Women's Issues, 952
Office of Women's Business Ownership, 952
Office on Violence Against Women, 239
OWBO Online Women's Business Center, 952
Oxygen.com, 952
pregnancy and birth, 710-717
Safe Place, A, 239
Shescape Online, 952
Society of Women Engineers, 953
Spinsters Ink, 953

sports
- *basketball, 85-88*
- *NCAA Women's Rowing, 922*
- *Sports Illustrated for Women, 953*
- *Women's Pro Rodeo Association, 787*

Susan B. Anthony House Museum and National Landmark, 384
TASC: The American Surrogacy Center, Inc., 953
United Nations and the Status of Women, The, 953
Victorian Women Writers, 516
Vogue, 731
WAHM (Work at Home Moms), 671
WE: Women's Entertainment, 953
Web by Women, foir Women, 953
WISE (Women's Initiative for Self Empowerment), 953
Woman Spirit, 809
Woman's Work, 472
WomanOwned.com-Business Information for Women Entrepreneurs, 953
Women and Politics Institute, The, 954
Women and Social Movements in the United States: 1600-2000, 954
Women in Aviation History: The Ninety Nines, 954
Women In Music, 603
Women in the Arts, 348
Women of Country, 591
WomenRunners.com, 283
Women's Auto Help Center, 59
Women's Human Rights Net, 954
Women's Human Rights Resources, 954
Women's Network, The, 950
Women's Professional Billiard Association, 98
Women's Quotes, 738
Women's Work, 129
WomensNet, 954
WomenWatch, 954
Working Moms Refuge, 954
Working Mother, 661
WWWomen!, 955
Yale Journal of Law and Feminism, 955

woodworking
- Popular WoodNet, 957
- Popular Woodworking, 957
- Wood Online, 731
- WoodWeb, 957
- Woodworker's Central, 957
- Woodworking.com, 957

world history
- Encyclopedia of World History, 389
- History of the World Timeline, 389
- HistoryWorld, 389
- HyperHistory, 390
- World History Archives, 390

World War I, 383
- Encyclopedia of the First World War, 918
- FIRST WORLD WAR.COM, 918
- Great War, The, 918
- War Times Journal: The Great War, 918
- World War I Document Archives, 918
- World War I: Trenches on the Web, 918
- World War One, 919

World War II, 572
- Axis History Factbook, 919
- Second World War Encyclopedia, 919
- U.S. National World War II Memorial, 919
- War Times Journal: World War II, 919
- World War 2 Timeline, 919
- World War Two, 919

wrestling
- Pro Wrestling Daily, 958
- Professional Wrestling Online Museum, 958
- ProWrestling.com, 958
- SLAM!, 958
- TheMat.com, 958
- Total Nonstop Wrestling on Spike TV, 958
- World Wrestling Entertainment, 959
- WrestleZone, 959
- Wrestling Planet, 959
- Wrestling USA Magazine, 959

writing. *See also* authors; literature; reference
- 11 Rules of Writing, 960
- A+ Research and Writing, 960
- About.com-Freelance Writers, 960
- AuthorLink!, 960
- Bartleby.com, 960
- Business Writing Tips, 960
- Celebration of Women Writers, A, 949
- Children's Writing Resource Center, 961
- Chistell Publishing, 949
- Diary Project, 479
- Feminist Science Fiction, Fantasy, and Utopia, 790
- Grammar and Style Notes, 500
- IAAY Expository Writing Tutorial, 961
- Indispensible Writing Resources, 961
- Isle of Lesbos, The, 348
- Kidz Cafe, 491
- Look What I Found in My Brain!, 791
- poetry, 180, 698-700
- Proposal Writing, 961
- Purdue Online Writing Lab (OWL), 961
- RoseDog.com, 961
- Sci-Fi Site, The, 792
- Science Fiction and Fantasy World, 792
- Science Fiction and Fantasy Writers of America (SFWA), 792
- Science Fiction Museum Hall of Fame, 792
- Screenwriters Online, 961
- SFF Net, 793
- Spinsters Ink, 953
- Stories from the Web, 485
- Teen Ink, 852
- World Science Fiction Society, 794
- Write News, The, 961

Writers on the Net, 961
Writers Write, 962
Writing Den, 962
Writing for Dollars, 962
Writing for the Web, 962
Writing-World.com, 962
Xenith.net, 853
Xlibris, 962
Yound Authors Workshop, 962
Wyoming
Skiing in Jackson Hole, 825
Yellowstone Net, 676

X - Y

yoga
A2ZYoga, 963
ABC of Yoga, 963
Ayurveda Yoga Ultra-Nutrition, 26
Body Trends, 963
Kundalini Support Center, 963
Sahaja Yoga Meditation, 963
Santosha.com, 963
Siddha Yoga Meditation, 964
Sivananda Yoga "Om" Page, 964
Step-by-Step Yoga Postures, 964
World of Yoga, A, 964
Yoga Alliance, 964
Yoga Directory, The, 965
Yoga Journal, 965
Yoga Site, 965
Yoga Synergy, 965
Yoga.com, 964
Yogabasics.com, 964
youth organizations
America's Promise, 966
B'nai B'rith Youth Organization, 966
Boy Scouts of America, 966
Boys and Girls Clubs of America, 966
CYO: Catholic Youth Organization, 966
Girl Scounts, 966
National 4-H Council, 966
National Association of Peer Programs, 967
National Mentoring Center, 967
Operation Fit Kids, 967
YMCA, 967
Young People's Ministries, 967
YouthLink, 967

Z

Zimbabwe, 592
zoos
Albuquerque Aquarium, The, 968
American Zoo and Aquarium Association, 968
Audabon Nature Institute, 611
Birmingham Zoo, 968
Bronx Zoo, The, 968
Brookfield Zoo, 968
Cincinnati Zoo and Botanical Garden, 968
Cleveland Metroparks Zoo, 968
Dallas Zoo, The, 969
Denver Zoo, 969
Fort Worth Zoo, 969
Indianapolis Zoo, The, 969
Kids World 2000: Animals, Zoos and Aquariums, 969
Lincoln Park Zoo, 969
Los Angeles Zoo, The, 969
Memphis Zoo Home Page, 970
National Zoo, 970
North Carolina Zoological Park, The, 970
Oakland Zoo, 970
Oregon Zoo, 970
Philadelphia Zoo Online, 970
Phoenix Zoo, The, 970
Pittsburgh Zoo and Aquarium, 971
San Antonio Zoo, The, 971
San Diego Zoo, 971
San Francisco Zoo, 971
St. Louis Zoo, The, 971
Wildlife Conservation Society/Bronx Zoo, 273
Woodland Park Zoo (Seattle, WA), 971
ZooWeb, 971

THIS BOOK IS SAFARI ENABLED

INCLUDES FREE 45-DAY ACCESS TO THE ONLINE EDITION

The Safari® Enabled icon on the cover of your favorite technology book means the book is available through Safari Bookshelf. When you buy this book, you get free access to the online edition for 45 days.

Safari Bookshelf is an electronic reference library that lets you easily search thousands of technical books, find code samples, download chapters, and access technical information whenever and wherever you need it.

TO GAIN 45-DAY SAFARI ENABLED ACCESS TO THIS BOOK:

- Go to **http://www.quepublishing.com/safarienabled**
- Complete the brief registration form
- Enter the coupon code found in the front of this book on the "Copyright" page

If you have difficulty registering on Safari Bookshelf or accessing the online edition, please e-mail customer-service@safaribooksonline.com.